The International
Encyclopedia of Quotations

The
International
Encyclopedia
of
Quotations

An encyclopedia of quotations
from every age
for every occasion

compiled by

John P. Bradley, Leo F. Daniels, Thomas C. Jones

Published by J. G. Ferguson Publishing Company *Chicago*

ACKNOWLEDGMENTS

For permission to use quotations from the copyrighted material listed below, the publisher wishes to thank the following:

Abelard-Schuman, *Charles Chaplin* by T. Huff; quotes by Sir William Osler; both reprinted with permission of Abelard-Schuman. Abingdon Press, *In Quest of the Kingdom* by Dr. Leslie Weatherhead; reprinted by permission of Abingdon Press, Hodder & Stoughton, Ltd. and the author. *Toward the Great Awakening* by Sidney W. Powell, reprinted by permission of Abingdon Press; *Religion and Leisure in America,* edited by Robert Lee; *The Story of Methodism,* edited by Robert W. Goodloe. American Academy of Political and Social Science, May, 1966 issue; "The Returning Volunteer"; "The Future of the Peace Corps." Association Press, *To Be A Man* by Robert Warren Spike, 1961. Atheneum Publishers, *Confessions of an Advertising Man* by David Ogilvy, © 1963 by David Ogilvy Trustee; *John F. Kennedy, President* by Hugh Sidey, © 1963, 1964 by Hugh Sidey; both reprinted by permission of Atheneum. Estate of Albert Einstein, *Einstein on Peace* by Albert Einstein, reprinted by permission of the Estate of Albert Einstein.

Joseph Barth, quote from the *Ladies' Home Journal,* April, 1961, reprinted by permission of Joseph Barth. Jacques Barzun, quote from *The Saturday Evening Post,* May 3, 1958, reprinted by permission of Jacques Barzun. Beacon Press, *The Vanishing Adolescent,* copyright © 1959, 1964 by Edgar Z. Friedenberg. The Bruce Publishing Company, *Personality Development Adjustment in Adolescence* by Alexander A. Schneiders. Scott Buchanan, *Poetry and Mathematics,* reprinted by permission of Scott Buchanan. H. S. M. Burns, former President, Shell Oil Company, quote from *Men at the Top* by Osborn Elliot, reprinted by permission of H. S. M. Burns. Margaret Freeman Cabell, *Jurgen* by James Branch Cabell, reprinted by permission of Margaret Freeman Cabell. *Chicago Daily News,* Sydney J. Harris' column, March 27, 1958, reprinted by permission of the *Chicago Daily News.* The Christian Century Foundation, quote from *Guideposts* by Dr. Albert Schweitzer, copyright 1955 Christian Century Foundation, reprinted by permission from September 7, 1955 issue of *The Christian Century.* The Christian Science Monitor; Fairfax Cone, as quoted in *The Christian Science Monitor,* March 20, 1963; David Ormsby-Gore, as quoted in *The Christian Science Monitor,* October 25, 1960; Willem Adolf Visser't Hooft, as quoted in *The Christian Science Monitor,* December 5, 1963; Dr. Karl Menninger, as quoted in *The Christian Science Monitor,* August 4, 1959; and Roscoe Pound, as quoted in *The Christian Science Monitor,* April 24, 1963. Columbia University Press, *The Mentally Ill in America,* edited by André Deutsch. Cowles Communications, Inc., "Age of Payola" by William Attwood, *Look Magazine,* March 29, 1960. Thomas Y. Crowell Company, quotes from Max Beerbohm, Dwight D. Eisenhower, William Faulkner, Billy Graham, Judge Learned Hand, Aldous Huxley, John XXIII, Martin Luther King, Sinclair Lewis, Henry Cabot Lodge, Jr., Russell Lynes, Somerset Maugham, Jawaharlal Nehru, Paul VI, Brigadier-General David Sarnoff, Ralph W. Sockman, as found in *Best Quotes of '55, '56, '57,* by James B. Simpson, copyright © 1957 by James B. Simpson; and for extracts from addresses by John F. Kennedy as found in *Memorable Quotations of John F. Kennedy,* by Maxwell Meyersohn, copyright © 1965 by Maxwell Meyersohn. Crown Publishers, from *Men at War* by Ernest Hemingway, © 1942 by Crown Publishers, Inc., used by permission of Crown Publishers, Inc. Curtis Brown Ltd., *Water in the Wine* by April Oursler Armstrong, reprinted by permission of Curtis Brown Ltd. The Curtis Publishing Company, quote from Heloise Cruse in an article by Maxine Cheshire in *The Saturday Evening Post*, March 2, 1963, © 1963 The Curtis Publishing Company, reprinted by permission of *The Saturday Evening Post*; quote from Christian Dior, reprinted by permission of *The Saturday Evening Post*, © 1956 by The Curtis Publishing Company.

The Dial Press, *The Fire Next Time* by James Baldwin, copyright © 1963, 1962 by James Baldwin, reprinted by permission of the publisher, The Dial Press, Inc. Dodd, Mead & Company, Inc., *Zuleika Dobson* by Max Beerbohm, reprinted by permission of Dodd, Mead & Company, Inc. and William Heinemann Ltd., publishers of the British edition. Dover Publications, Inc., *Modern Quotations for Ready Reference* by Arthur Richmond, reprinted by permission of the publisher. The Dreiser Trust, *Sister Carrie* by Theodore Dreiser, reprinted by permission of The Dreiser Trust. E. P. Dutton & Co. Inc., *Samuel Butler's Notebooks* edited by Geoffrey Keynes and Brian Hill, reprinted by permission of E. P. Dutton Inc., The Executors of The Samuel Butler Estate, and Jonathan Cape Ltd.

Norma Millay Ellis, "Dirge Without Music," copyright 1928, 1955 by Edna St. Vincent Millay and Norma Millay Ellis, "Renascence," copyright 1912, 1940 by Edna St. Vincent Millay, "Love is not All," from Sonnet XXX of "Fatal Interview," copyright 1931, 1958 by Edna St. Vincent Millay and Norma Millay Ellis; all from *Collected Poems*, published by Harper & Row, Publishers, reprinted by permission of Norma Millay Ellis. *Ebony* Magazine, "Outgrowing the Ghetto Mind," August 1963. Esquire Incorporated, *Great Men and Moments in Sport in Esquire*, January 1962.

Farrar, Straus & Giroux, Inc., *The Elder Statesman* by T. S. Eliot, copyright © 1959 by Thomas Stearns Eliot, reprinted by permission of Farrar, Straus & Giroux, Inc. and Faber and Faber Ltd.; *What the Jews Believe* by Philip Bernstein. Fearon Publishers, *And May God Have Mercy: The Case Against Capital Punishment* by Eugene B. Block.

Grossman Publishers, Inc., *Bitter Greetings* by J. Carper. Rudolf F. Flesch, Editor, *Book of Unusual Quotations*, published by Harper & Row, Publishers, Inc., copyright © 1957 by the Editor, reprinted by permission of the Editor. Guideposts Associates, Inc., quote from "Letter to a Troubled Friend" by Sidney Fields, copyright *Guideposts Magazine*; quote of Pope Pius XII, reprinted from September 1955 issue of *Guideposts Magazine*; both reprinted by permission of Guideposts Associates, Inc., Carmel, New York.

Harcourt, Brace & World, Inc., *The Cocktail Party* by T. S. Eliot, copyright, 1950, by T. S. Eliot, *The Confidential Clerk* by T. S. Eliot, copyright 1954 by T. S. Eliot. *Murder in the Cathedral* by T. S. Eliot, copyright 1935 by Harcourt, Brace & World, Inc., copyright 1963 by T. S. Eliot; all reprinted by permission of the publisher, and Faber & Faber Ltd.; *Land Without Justice* by Milovan Djilas, © 1958 by Harcourt, Brace & World, Inc., reprinted by permission of Harcourt, Brace & World, Inc. and Methuen & Company, Ltd.; *The Modern Temper* by Joseph Wood Krutch, copyright 1929 by Harcourt, Brace & World, Inc., copyright 1957 by Joseph Wood Krutch, reprinted by permission of the publisher; *London Perceived* by V. S. Pritchett, © 1962 by V. S. Pritchett, reprinted by permission of Harcourt, Brace & World, Inc. and Chatto and Windus Ltd.; *The Human Comedy* by William Saroyan, copyright 1943 by William Saroyan, reprinted by permission of Harcourt, Brace & World, Inc. and Laurence Pollinger Limited; *Anne Frank: A Portrait in Courage* by Ernest Schnabel, copyright © 1958 by Fischer Bucherei KG, reprinted by permission of Harcourt, Brace & World, Inc. and Fischer Bucherei KG. Harper & Row, Publishers, *Fables in Slang* by George Ade; "Sofia Trenton" (Stanza 28) by Leonard Bacon; quote of Robert Benchley; *The Conquest of Civilization* by James Henry Breasted; *The Drive Toward Reason* by Lyman Bryson, Harper & Row, 1954; quotes from Samuel Langhorne Clemens; *Except the Lord* by Joyce Carey; *Through these Men* by John Mason Brown; *The Colby Essays* by Frank Moore Colby; quotes of Cyril Connolly; *Under Western Eyes* by Joseph Conrad; *Christian Perfection* by François de Fenelon, Harper & Row, 1947; *Riverside Sermons* by Harry Emerson Fosdick, Harper & Row, 1958; *Behind the Curtain* by John Gunther, Harper & Row, 1949; *Excellence* by John W. Gardner; *Promise at Dawn* by Romain Gary, Harper & Row, 1961; *The Passionate State of Mind* by Eric Hoffer, Harper & Row, 1955; *The Conflict in Education* by Robert Maynard Hutchins, Harper & Row, 1963; quotes of Aldous Huxley; *American Heroes and Hero-Worship* by Gerald W. Johnson; quotes of Arthur Koestler; *Profiles in Courage* by John F. Kennedy, Harper & Row, 1955; *The Art of Accepting* by Russell Lynes, Harper & Row, 1954; quotes of André Maurois; quotes of Eleanor Roosevelt; *On Active Service in Peace and War* by Henry L. Stimson; *The Hundredth Archbishop of Canterbury* by Arthur Michael Ramsey; *The Mind in the Making* by James Harvey Robinson; *Men and Events* by H. R. Trevor-Roper, Harper & Row, 1958; all reprinted by permission of Harper & Row, Publishers. *The Second Tree from the Corner* by E. B. White, Harper & Row, 1954, reprinted by permission of the publisher and Hamish Hamilton; *The Web and the Rock* by Thomas Wolfe, reprinted by permission of Harper & Row, Publishers. Harvard University Press, *General Education in a Free Society* by James Bryant Conant; *Holmes-Laski Letters* edited by Mark DeWolfe Howe, copyright 1953 by the

President and Fellows of Harvard College; both reprinted by permission of Harvard University Press; *Science and Government* by C. P. Snow. Quote of Ernest O. Hauser in *The Saturday Evening Post*, Dec. 7, 1962, reprinted by permission of the author. Quote of Ernest Havemann in *Life* Magazine, Sept. 29, 1961, reprinted by permission of the author. Hawthorn Books, Inc., *Law and Morals* by Norman St. John-Stevas, Hill & Wang Incorporated, "Wit" and "Soul and Circumstance" by Mark Van Doren, from *Collected and New Poems: 1924–1963* by Mark Van Doren, copyright © 1963 by Mark Van Doren, reprinted by permission of Hill and Wang, Inc. and Nannine Joseph. Estate of Alice Hilton, *Time and Time Again* by James Hilton, reprinted by permission of the Estate of Alice Hilton. Holt, Rinehart and Winston, Inc., *The Woman Who Would Be Queen* by Geoffrey Bocca, copyright 1954 by Geoffrey Bocca, reprinted by permission of Holt, Rinehart and Winston, Inc. and Littauer and Wilkinson; *Escape from Freedom* by Erich Fromm, copyright 1941 by Erich Fromm, reprinted by permission of Holt, Rinehart and Winston, Inc. and Laurence Pollinger Limited; "Revelation," "Precaution," "The Lesson for Today," all from *Complete Poems of Robert Frost*, copyright 1934 by Holt, Rinehart and Winston, Inc., copyright 1936, 1942, © 1962 by Robert Frost, reprinted by permission of Holt, Rinehart and Winston, Inc.; quote of Robert Frost from *Contemporary Quotations* compiled by James B. Simpson, published by Holt, Rinehart and Winston, Inc., reprinted by permission of the Estate of Robert Frost and Holt, Rinehart and Winston, Inc.; *The Fine Art of Literary Mayhem* by Myrick Land, copyright © 1962, 1963 by Myrick Land, reprinted by permission of Holt, Rinehart and Winston, Inc. and Nannine Joseph; *Must You Conform?* by Robert Lindner, copyright © 1956 by Robert Lindner, reprinted by permission of Holt, Rinehart and Winston, Inc. and Harold Ober Associates; *Next Generation* by David Pryce-Jones; *Common Sense Coronary Care . . . And Prevention* by Dr. Peter J. Steincrohn; reprinted by permission of Holt, Rinehart & Winston, Inc. Houghton Mifflin Company, *Silent Spring* by Rachel Carson; *Triumph and Tragedy* by Winston Churchill; *Parkinson's Second Law* by C. Northcote Parkinson. W. W. Howells for *Hither and Thither in Germany*; reprinted by permission of the author. Humanities Press Inc., *Patria Mia* by Ezra Pound, New York: Humanities Press Inc. 1950, published in England by Peter Owen, reprinted by permission of the publishers. Bishop Gerald Kennedy, *A Reader's Notebook* by Bishop Gerald Kennedy, published by Harper & Row, Publishers, reprinted by permission of the author.

The John Day Company, Inc., *The Importance of Living* by Lin Yutang; *Young People and Smoking* by Arthur H. Cain; copyright © 1964 by Arthur H. Cain.

Alfred A. Knopf, Inc., *The Spoor of Spooks and Other Nonsense* by Bergen Evans; copyright 1946, 1954 by Bergen Evans.

Life Magazine, quote of Pope Paul VI, issue of July 5, 1963; quote of James Thurber, issue of March 14, 1960; quote of Alan Watts, issue of April 21, 1961; all reprinted by permission of *Life* Magazine. J. B. Lippincott Company, *Your English Words* by John Moore, copyright © 1961 by John Moore, published in the United States by J. B. Lippincott Company, reprinted by permission of J. B. Lippincott Company and Harold Matson Company, Inc.; "To a Child" from *Poems* by Christopher Morley, published by J. B. Lippincott Company, reprinted by permission of J. B. Lippincott Company and the Estate of Christopher Morley. Little, Brown and Company, *The Complete Poems of Emily Dickinson*, edited by Thomas H. Johnson, published by Little, Brown and Company, copyright 1929, ©1957 by Mary L. Hampson, reprinted by permission of the publishers; *Dialogues of Alfred N. Whitehead*, published by Little, Brown and Company, copyright 1954 by Lucien Price, reprinted by permission of the publishers. Max Lerner, column in the *New York Post*, November 24, 1963, reprinted by permission of the author.

The Macmillan Company, *Silas Crockett* by Mary Ellen Chase, published by The Macmillan Company; *Dialogue with Death* by Arthur Koestler, published by The Macmillan Company; both reprinted by permission of the publishers. Ellen C. Masters, "Lucinda Matlock," "Seth Compton," "The Village Atheist," all from *The Spoon River Anthology* by Edgar Lee Masters, The Macmillan Company, 1914, 1942, reprinted by permission of Ellen C. Masters. McGraw-Hill Book Company, *Quentin Reynolds* by Quentin Reynolds, published by McGraw-Hill Book Company, 1963; *My First Fifty Years in Politics* by Joseph W. Martin, Jr., published by McGraw-Hill Book Company, 1960; *Green Grows Ivy* by Ivy Baker Priest, published by McGraw-Hill Book Company, 1958; *Making Good in Management* by Clarence B. Randell, published by McGraw-Hill Book Company, 1964; *The World of Carmel Snow* by Carmel Snow, published by McGraw-Hill Book Company, 1962; all reprinted by permission of the publishers. Frederick Muller Ltd., *The Boy with a Cart* by Christopher Fry, published by Frederick Muller Ltd., London, reprinted by permission of the publishers.

The Estate of George Jean Nathan, *The House of Satan* by George Jean Nathan, published by permission of the Trustees of the Estate of George Jean Nathan and Julie Haydon Nathan. New Book Society of India, *Wit and Wisdom of India* edited by N. B. Sen, © 1961 by New Book Society of India, reprinted by permission of the editor. New Directions Publishing Corporation, *Seeds of Contemplation* by Thomas Merton, copyright 1949 by Our Lady of Gethsemani Monastery, reprinted by permission of New Directions Publishing Corporation. *New Republic* for "The Hippie Business" by David Sanford; © 1967 by Harrison-Blaine of New Jersey, Inc. *New York Post,* quote from Jean Cocteau in Leonard Lyons column, *New York Post,* June 27, 1956, reprinted by permission of *New York Post* © 1956, New York Post Corporation. *The New York Times,* quotes from various issues of *The New York Times,* © 1937, 1945, 1956, 1957, 1958, 1959, 1960, 1961, 1962, 1963, 1964, 1966, 1967 by The New York Times Company, reprinted by permission. *The New Yorker* for quote from "Talk of the Town," February 20, 1960. Newsweek, Inc., quotes from various issues of *Newsweek,* copyright, Newsweek, Inc., October, 1955; December, 1955; March, 1961; August, 1955; December, 1960; May, 1955; October, 1962; November, 1959; June 1958; June, 1955; August, 1963; December, 1963; August, 1960; May, 1961; July, 1956; May, 1960; May, 1956; March, 1958; February, 1957; August, 1958, reprinted by permission. W. W. Norton & Company, Inc., *Letters of Rainer Maria Rilke,* Vols. I and II, translated by Jane Bannard Greene and M. D. Herter Norton, Vol. I copyright 1945, Vol. II copyright 1947, 1948, both by W. W. Norton & Company, Inc., reprinted by permission of W. W. Norton & Company, Inc. and Insel-Verlag, Wiesbaden, Germany; W. W. Norton & Company, Inc. for *The Psychology of Personal Constructs* by George H. Kelly; copyright 1955 by George A. Kelly.

The Observer, quote of Prime Minister of Belgium, London, February 3, 1963, reprinted by permission of *The Observer.* Oxford University Press, "Pied Beauty" by Gerard Manley Hopkins and "All Lovely Things" by Conrad Aiken, both from *Magill's Quotations in Context* edited by Frank N. Magill, published by Harper & Row, Publishers, copyright © 1965 by the editor, reprinted by permission of Oxford University Press.

Joseph Palmeri, *French Wit and Wisdom* edited and translated by Joseph Palmeri, reprinted by permission of the Editor. *Parade* Magazine, interview in December, 1963 issue, reprinted by permission of *Parade.* Drew Pearson, quote from his article in *The Saturday Evening Post,* November 3, 1956, reprinted by permission of the author. Penguin Books Ltd., *Penguin Dictionary of Quotations* compiled by John Michael, © 1960 by the compiler, reprinted by permission of Penguin Books Ltd. Philosophical Library, Inc., *Dictionary of American Maxims* edited by David Kin, © 1955 by Philosophical Library, Inc., reprinted by permission of the publishers. Prentice-Hall, Inc. for *The Methodist Way of Life* by Gerald Hamilton Kennedy; *The Baptist Way of Life* by Brooks Hays and John E. Steely; *How I Multiplied My Income and Happiness in Selling* by Frank Bettger. Putnam's & Coward-McCann, quote of Simon Weil, reprinted by permission of Putnam's & Coward-McCann and Routledge & Kegan Paul Ltd.

The Reader's Digest, quotes from the issues of April, 1955; December, 1954; July, 1958, reprinted by permission of *The Reader's Digest.* Henry Regnery Company, quote of Sydney Harris, reprinted by permission of Henry Regnery Company.

Leah Salisbury, Inc., article "On Keeping the Sense of Wonder" by Christopher Fry, copyright © 1955 by Condé Nast Publications, Inc., reprinted by permission of Leah Salisbury, Inc. *Saturday Review,* article "So You Want to Write a Book" by Paul Reynolds, issue of July 13, 1963; "Schools are for Learning" by John H. Fischer, issue of Sept. 17, 1960; Staff Editorial, issue of March 23, 1963; "The Books are on the Wing" by Lon Tinkle, issue of April 12, 1958; "First Lady, First Person" by Barbara Ward, issue of Sept. 30, 1961; "The Future of the City" by Frank Lloyd Wright, issue of May 21, 1955; all reprinted by permission of *Saturday Review.* Charles Scribner's Sons, *Death in the Afternoon* by Ernest Hemingway, reprinted by permission of Charles Scribner's Sons and Jonathan Cape, Ltd.; "Notes on the Next War" from *By-Line: Ernest Hemingway* edited by William White; reprinted by permission of Charles Scribner's Sons and William Collins & Sons, Co., Ltd.; *Reason in Art, Reason in Science, Reason in Common Sense, Winds of Doctrine, Persons and Places, Reason in Society,* and "O World" from *Poems* by George Santayana, reprinted by permission of Charles Scribner's Sons and Constable & Co. Ltd. Sheed & Ward Inc., *Tremendous Trifles* and *What's Wrong with the World* both by G. K. Chesterton, reprinted by permission of Sheed & Ward Inc., A. P. Watt & Son, and Miss Dorothy Collins. Simon and Schuster, *How to Read a Book* by Mortimer Adler, copyright © 1957 by Simon and Schuster; *A Commonplace Book* by Charles P. Curtis, copyright © 1957 by Simon and Schuster; *The Age of Reason* by Will and Ariel Durant, Vol. 11 of *The Story of Civilization,* copyright © 1961 by Will and Ariel Durant; *A Child of the Century* by Ben Hecht, all reprinted by permission of Simon and Schuster. *Bertrand Russell: The Passionate Sceptic* by Alan Wood, copyright © 1957 by George Allen & Unwin Ltd., reprinted by permission of Simon and Schuster and George Allen & Unwin Ltd. *Human Society in Ethics and Politics* by Bertrand Russell, copyright © 1952, 1954, 1955 by Bertrand Russell, reprinted by permission of Simon and Schuster and George Allen & Unwin Ltd. *The American Way of Death* by Jessica Mitford, copyright © 1963 by Jessica Mitford, reprinted by permission of Simon and Schuster and Hutchinson Publishing Group Ltd. *The Age of Faith* by Will Durant, reprinted by permission of Simon and Schuster. Adlai Stevenson III, for quotes of Adlai Stevenson, reprinted by permission of Adlai Stevenson III. *The Sunday Times,* London, quotes from the issues of February 27, 1957; February 4 and February 28, 1962, reprinted by permission of *The Sunday*

Times. Horace Sutton, "You Can't Live in New York," *The Saturday Evening Post*, March 11, 1961, reprinted by permission of the author.

This Week magazine, "You Can do the Impossible" by Maxwell Maltz, *This Week*, July 24, 1955; "Hope in your Heart" by John La Farge, *This Week*, Oct. 9, 1960; "How to be a Winner" by Vernon Law, *This Week*, August 14, 1960; all three copyright by William I. Nichols, reprinted by permission of *This Week*. *The Jewish Festivals*, renewal copyright © 1966 by Tillie Schauss; reprinted by permission of the Union of American Hebrew Congregations.

Vanguard Press, Inc., *Puritanism and Democracy* by Ralph Barton, copyright 1944 by Ralph Barton Perry, reprinted by permission of Vanguard Press, Inc. The Viking Press Inc., *The Death of a Salesman* by Arthur Miller, reprinted by permission of The Viking Press Inc. and Ashley Famous Agency Inc.; *The Grapes of Wrath* and *East of Eden* by John Steinbeck, reprinted by permission of The Viking Press, Inc. and McIntosh & Otis, Inc.; *A Portrait of the Artist as a Young Man* by James Joyce, reprinted by permission of The Viking Press Inc. and The Society of Authors; *Women in Love* by D. H. Lawrence, reprinted by permission of The Viking Press Inc. and

Laurence Pollinger Ltd.; quotes of Graham Greene, reprinted by permission of The Viking Press Inc. and Laurence Pollinger Ltd.; *The Loyalty of Free Men* by Alan Barth, copyright 1951 by Alan Barth; Rev. Charles L. Wallis, quote of Samuel Butler in *Speaker's Resources from Contemporary Literature* edited by Charles L. Wallis, reprinted by permission of Harper & Row, Publishers.

John Wiley & Sons for *Cybernetics* by Norbert Wiener. The World Publishing Company, *The Rape of the Mind* by Dr. Joost A. M. Meerloo; *The Cultured Man* by Ashley Montagu; *Second Thoughts* by François Mauriac; *Supressed Books: A History of the Conception of Literary Obscenity* by Alec Craig; all reprinted by permission of the publishers. John David Wright, quote in *Fortune* Magazine, September 1955, reprinted by permission of the author.

Yale University Press, *War, Essays, The Forgotten Man*, all by William Graham Sumner, reprinted by permission of the publishers. Mary Yost Associates, "Truth" from *The Sign of the Four* by Sir Arthur Conan Doyle, reprinted by permission of the Estate of Sir Arthur Conan Doyle.

Introduction

There are a number of excellent quotation books on the market that have, over the years, won wide acceptance. By and large, these works place an emphasis on familiar quotations, fully referenced and drawn from the great works of literature. *The International Encyclopedia of Quotations* is a different kind of quotation book—it attempts to meet a different need. Today, when so many people find themselves, often at short notice, with a speech to give, a discussion to lead, an assignment to write, there is a need for a book of quotations, familiar and unfamiliar, from whatever source, that are useful for this purpose. This is the need that *The International Encyclopedia of Quotations* hopes to meet, and thus earn for itself its own special appeal.

TWO GENERAL AIMS

In setting out to meet this particular need of our times the compilers had two general aims in mind: (1) to provide the reader with an abundance of quotations, international in flavor and ranging from earliest times to the present day; (2) to arrange this large and varied collection for the most convenient use possible. In other words, *The International Encyclopedia of Quotations* with some twenty thousand quotations, its alphabetic arrangement of topic-headings, cross references, and indexes is for everyone who wants to put a quotation book to work.

This emphasis, however, on its more practical features should not obscure another aspect of the book. Drawing its material from ancient, medieval, modern, and contemporary sources, it provides the reader with a cross section of the wisdom, inspiration, and humor of thousands of the world's greatest minds. This collection of quotations can, then, be a delightful and instructive companion for anyone who has nothing more practical in mind than simply browsing through its contents.

ARRANGEMENT AND DESIGN

The quotations are organized in three sections. First, there is an extensive general section comprising quotations from all historical periods, with their diversity of authors. Secondly, there is a section containing quotations from the Bible. Thirdly, there is a section comprised of quotations from the works of Shakespeare. Since the Bible and Shakespeare's works have always been accorded a particular importance it was decided that quotations from these two sources should be arranged in their own special sections.

The convenience of the reader determined the design of the book. Throughout all three sections, therefore, the quotations have been organized alphabetically by topic. Within each section quotations are again organized under each topic-heading: in the general section, alphabetically by author; in the Bible section, as the Books are found in the Old and New Testaments; in the Shakespeare section, alphabetically by individual work.

Further features that help the reader to make maximum use of this work are: cross references after the last quotation of each topic; Author Index; Index of Other Sources; Bible Reference Index; Shakespeare Reference Index; and Subject Index.

INDEXES

The Author Index, besides listing the names of all authors quoted in the book and the page numbers on which their quotations appear, also supplies such helpful information as: birth and death dates, alternative spellings of names, pseudonyms, nationality, and profession. While this information can be helpful to a reader who is interested in knowing something of the background of the authors quoted in the book, the Author Index does not, of course, pretend to be a substitute for a biographical dictionary.

The Index of Other Sources lists such sources as periodicals, associations, and newspapers. A brief description of these sources, together with the page numbers on which their quotations are found, is given in this index.

References for all biblical passages quoted are listed in the Bible Reference Index. Similarly, the Shakespeare Reference Index gives references for all quotations from the works of Shakespeare.

The fifth and final index in the book is the Subject Index. Before describing this index a few preliminary observations are in order. In a work such as this, where quotations are arranged by topics, the organization of the material involves at times a certain arbitrariness. For instance, some quotations contain more than one important idea and could be placed under any one of a number of topic-headings. The decision as to which topic-heading is most suitable has to be made by the compiler.

Let's take one of Somerset Maugham's quotations as an example: "Pain and suffering do not ennoble the human spirit. Pain and suffering breed meanness, bitterness, cruelty. It is only happiness that ennobles." Under which topic-heading should this quotation be placed? Pain? Suffering? Happiness? If the compiler places it under Happiness it becomes, for all practical purposes, lost to the reader looking for a quotation or idea on pain or suffering. Furthermore, what about the reader who is looking for ideas on meanness, or bitterness, or cruelty?

The International Encyclopedia of Quotations answers this problem with a comprehensive Subject Index which lists and gives the location of all the significant ideas throughout the book. Thus, to return to our example, the reader who is looking for ideas on pain and suffering will find in the Subject Index a number of references to quotations touching on these ideas, among them the quotation by Maugham. Likewise, the Subject Index will lead the reader who is looking for ideas on meanness, bitterness, or cruelty to the pertinent quotations in the book.

The Subject Index, then, gives the reader a bird's-eye view of the contents of the book. Besides listing (in bold-faced type) all topic-headings, this index cuts across all topical groupings in all three sections of the book, and organizes for ready reference all the thoughts in the entire work that the compilers judged to be significant and likely to be of particular interest to the reader.

HOW TO USE THE BOOK

The International Encyclopedia of Quotations is designed to be used as a dictionary, the topic headings serving as entries. If, for example, the reader wants to find a quotation on "government," or if he wants to trigger some thoughts on this subject, he simply turns to the topic-heading GOVERNMENT and reads the quotations that appear, alphabetical-ly arranged by author, under this topic-heading. If he does not find there anything to his liking, the cross references at the end of this topic will lead him to the following related topic-headings: AUTHORITY, DE-MOCRACY, DEMOCRATIC PARTY, LAW, PARTY, POLITICS, PRESIDENT, REPUBLIC, REPUBLICAN PARTY, STATESMANSHIP.

The reader may follow any of these related paths, or, if he wants to pursue the idea "government" further, he can turn to the Subject Index where, as the following sample shows, he will find references to other pages in the book where quotations on this subject appear:

> **government,** 28, 201, 335–339,
> **905**
> banks, a power greater than,
> 67
> Bill of Rights and, 638
> business and, 103
> choice of nation, 306
> corruption in, 172
> democracy, demanding form
> of, 202
> dependent on arms, 50
> and dissension, 886
> dissent, necessary for, 200

As has been mentioned previously, there are, throughout the book, thousands of significant thoughts that are not listed as topic-headings: these thoughts can be located by consulting the Subject Index. For instance, the reader will not find a topic-heading for "manhood," but in the Subject Index he will discover under the entry "manhood" a number of references to quotations about this subject:

> manhood, 24
>> at adolescence, 10
>> conspiracy against, 164
>> disappointment of, 200
>> and oath, 945
>> and responsibility, 627
>> sacrifice of, 35–36
>> and vows, 759
>> and youth, 200
>> (*See also* adult, men)

The Subject Index is also helpful to the reader who happens to know something about a quotation, but not enough to determine under which topic-heading it would fall. To locate this quotation he need only know one of its important thoughts and find this thought among the entries in the Subject Index. If, for example, the reader remembers that the late Martin Luther King, Jr. made a moving statement about "having a dream," but can recall nothing more, he can locate the quotation he wants by looking under "dream" in the Subject Index.

A COOPERATIVE EFFORT

The International Encyclopedia of Quotations, which is based on *The New Dictionary of Thoughts* originally compiled by Tryon Edwards and most recently revised by Ralph Emerson Browns, owes its completion to many people. It is not possible to mention here everyone who shared in the considerable labor that is inevitably involved in producing this kind of book. Particular mention must be made, however, of a few whose constant and competent cooperation was indispensable. Mr. and Mrs. William D. Rowe, Jr. gave invaluable assistance in research, and Miss Dorothy McKittrick, our permissions editor, performed what even a brief glance at the list of acknowledgements shows to be a gigantic task. To them and to all others who helped in preparing this book the compilers express their gratitude.

J.P.B.
L.F.D.
T.C.J.

Contents

Thoughts from Ancient, Medieval, Modern and Contemporary Times

A

ABILITY

There may be luck in getting a good job—but there's no luck in keeping it.
Jonathan Ogden Armour

The question "Who ought to be boss?" is like asking "Who ought to be the tenor in the quartet?" Obviously, the man who can sing tenor.
Henry Ford

The winds and the waves are always on the side of the ablest navigators.
Edward Gibbon

Faith in the ability of a leader is of slight service unless it be united with faith in his justice.
George Washington Goethals

Surely we can more shrewdly judge a youth's character and ability by what he sets himself to do and carries out, under proper guidance, on his own initiative, than by his fulfillment, however brilliant, of a standardized task.
Robert Silliman Hillyer

There is something that is much more scarce, something finer far, something rarer than ability. It is the ability to recognize ability.
Elbert Green Hubbard

What we do upon some great occasion will probably depend on what we already are; and what we are will be the result of previous years of self-discipline.
Henry Parry Liddon

A few highly endowed men will rescue the world for centuries to come.
John Henry Newman

Ability hits the mark where presumption overshoots and diffidence falls short.
Nicholas of Cusa

We should be on our guard against the temptation to argue directly from skill to capacity, and to assume when a man displays skill in some feat, his capacity is therefore considerable.
Tom Hatherley Pear

Without the assistance of natural capacity, rules and precepts are of no efficacy.
Quintilian

The ability to deal with people is as purchasable a commodity as sugar or coffee. And I pay more for that ability than for any other under the sun.
John Davison Rockefeller

A dwarf is small, even if he stands on a mountain; a colossus keeps his height, even if he stands in a well.
Seneca

As long as a man imagines that he cannot do a certain thing, so long . . . is it impossible for him to do it.
Baruch (Benedict) Spinoza

Men are often capable of greater things than they perform. They are sent into the world with bills of credit, and seldom draw to their full extent.
Horace Walpole

A man likes his wife to be just clever enough to comprehend his cleverness, and just stupid enough to admire it.
Israel Zangwill

See also: ACTION, CHARACTER, GENIUS, POWER, STRENGTH, TALENT.

ABORTION

A woman who intentionally destroys a fetus is guilty of murder. And we do not even talk about the fine distinction as to its being completely formed or unformed.
Basil the Great

1

It is a capital crime to destroy an embryo in the womb.

Ishmael

Countries with legalized abortion have sanctioned unchangeable social custom. Countries with liberal abortion laws have legitimatized current medical practice. Countries with stringent abortion laws have buried their heads in the sands of time.

Robert E. Hall

Mature women, as mature human beings with all the respect and dignity to be accorded mature human beings, should have the right to decide whether or not they carry a specific pregnancy to term.

Harold Rosen

See also: BIRTH CONTROL, MOTHER, POPULATION, STERILIZATION.

ABSENCE

Absence makes the heart grow fonder:
Isle of Beauty, fare thee well!

Thomas Haynes Bayly

Wives in their husbands' absences grow subtler, and daughters sometimes run off with the butler.

George Gordon Byron (Lord Byron)

The absent are never without fault. nor the present without excuse.

Benjamin Franklin

When a man is out of sight, it is not too long before he is out of mind.

Thomas à Kempis

Absence lessens weak and increases violent passions, as wind extinguishes tapers and lights up a fire.

Duc François de La Rochefoucauld

The absent are like children, helpless to defend themselves.

Charles Reade

The joy of meeting pays the pangs of absence; else who could bear it?

Nicholas Rowe

See also: FAREWELL, LONELINESS, MEETING, MEMORY, PARTING.

ABSOLUTION.

The sunshine dreaming upon Salmon's height
Is not so sweet and white

As the most heretofore sin-spotted Soul
That darts to its delight
Straight from the absolution of a faithful fight.

Coventry Kersey Dighton Patmore

He's half absolv'd who has confess'd.

Matthew Prior

Absolve the sins of your people, we beseech you, O Lord, and may we be delivered by your goodness from the bonds of our sins which, in our weakness, we have committed.

Roman Missal

See also: CLEMENCY, FORGIVENESS.

ABSTINENCE

Complete abstinence is easier than perfect moderation.

Augustine of Hippo

It is continued temperance which sustains the body for the longest period of time, and which most surely preserves it free from sickness.

Wilhelm von Humboldt

To set the mind above the appetites is the end of abstinence, which if not a virtue, is the groundwork of a virtue.

Samuel Johnson

Always rise from the table with an appetite, and you will never sit down without one.

William Penn

See also: ASCETICISM, FASTING, MODERATION, TEMPERANCE.

ABSURDITY

There is nothing so absurd or ridiculous that has not at some time been said by some philosopher. Fontenelle says he would undertake to persuade the whole republic of readers to believe that the sun was neither the cause of light or heat, if he could only get six philosophers on his side.

Oliver Goldsmith

The privilege of absurdity; to which no living creature is subject but man only.

Thomas Hobbes

There are people whose whole merit consists in speaking and acting absurdly, though with good results, and who would spoil all if they changed their conduct.

Duc François de La Rochefoucauld

To pardon those absurdities in ourselves which we condemn in others, is neither better nor worse than to be more willing to be fools ourselves than to have others so.

Alexander Pope

See also: NONSENSE, RIDICULE, SARCASM.

ABUSE

It is the wit and policy of sin to hate those we have abused.

Sir William Davenant

Abuse of any one generally shows that he has marked traits of character. The stupid and indifferent are passed by in silence.

Tryon Edwards

It is not he who gives abuse that affronts, but the view that we take of it as insulting; so that when one provokes you it is your own opinion which is provoking.

Epictetus

The difference between coarse and refined abuse is the difference between being bruised by a club and wounded by a poisoned arrow.

Samuel Johnson

I never yet heard man or woman much abused that I was not inclined to think the better of them, and to transfer the suspicion or dislike to the one who found pleasure in pointing out the defects of another.

Jane Porter

Almost nobody is worth the hurt one causes oneself when one wounds him.

Jean Rostand

There are none more abusive to others than they that lie most open to it themselves; but the humor goes round, and he that laughs at me today will have somebody to laugh at him tomorrow.

Seneca

See also: CALUMNY, CRUELTY, DETRACTION, INJURY, INSULT, SLANDER.

ACCENT

I once knew a fellow who spoke a dialect with an accent.

Irvin Shrewsbury Cobb

The twentieth century is only the nineteenth speaking with a slightly American accent.

Philip Guedalla

Accent is the soul of language; it gives to it both feeling and truth.

Jean Jacques Rousseau

See also: LANGUAGE, SPEECH, TALKING.

ACCEPTANCE

And truly he who here
Hath run his bright career,
And served men nobly, and acceptance found,
And borne to light and right his witness high,
What could he better wish than then to die,
And wait the issue sleeping underground?

Matthew Arnold

She who ne'er answers till a husband cools,
Or, if she rules him never shows she rules;
Charms by accepting, by submitting, sways,
Yet has her humour most, when she obeys.

Alexander Pope

It is fraud to accept what you cannot repay.

Pubilius Syrus

See also: DESIRE, ESTEEM, HOSPITALITY, LOVE, WELCOME.

ACCIDENT

Accident counts for much in companionship as in marriage.

Henry Brooks Adams

What men call accident is the doing of God's providence.

Gamaliel Bailey

As on the ground, so also in the air, planes collide with disquieting consequences for those within when the public provision for air traffic control fails to keep pace with private use of the airways.

John Kenneth Galbraith

No accidents are so unlucky but that the wise may draw some advantage from them; nor are there any so lucky but that the foolish may turn them to their own prejudice.

Duc François de La Rochefoucauld

At first laying down, as a fact fundamental, That nothing with God can be accidental.

Henry Wadsworth Longfellow

Nothing is or can be accidental with God.

Henry Wadsworth Longfellow

More than half of all airline accidents occur on takeoffs, approaches, or landings, at or around airports. More air crashes, therefore, must and can be made survivable.

Almer Stillwell (Mike) Monroney

What reason, like the careful ant, draws laboriously together, the wind of accident sometimes collects in a moment.

Johann Christoph Friedrich von Schiller

See also: AUTOMOBILE, AVIATION, CHANCE, FATE, FORTUNE, LUCK, MISFORTUNE.

ACCURACY

Happy is the one possessing
The superior holy blessing
Of a judgment and a taste
Accurate, refined and chaste.

Aristophanes

Accuracy of statement is one of the first elements of truth; inaccuracy is a near kin to falsehood.

Tryon Edwards

Insanity is often the logic of an accurate mind overtaxed.

Oliver Wendell Holmes

In all pointed sentences, some degree of accuracy must be sacrificed to conciseness.

Samuel Johnson

Accuracy is the twin brother of honesty; inaccuracy, of dishonesty.

Charles Simmons

See also: FACT, REALISM, SCIENCE.

ACHIEVEMENT

Every man who is high up loves to think that he has done it all himself; and the wife smiles, and lets it go at that.

Sir James Matthew Barrie

Death comes to all
But great achievements build a monument
Which shall endure until the sun grows cold.

Georg Fabricius

Mere longevity is a good thing for those who watch Life from the side lines. For those who play the game, an hour may be a year, a single day's work an achievement for eternity.

Gabriel Heatter

The mode by which the inevitable comes to pass is effort.

Oliver Wendell Holmes

About all some men accomplish in life is to send a son to Harvard.

Edgar Watson Howe

If your determination is fixed, I do not counsel you to despair. Few things are impossible to diligence and skill. . . . Great works are performed, not by strength, but perseverance.

Samuel Johnson

Nothing will ever be attempted if all possible objections must be first overcome.

Samuel Johnson

I feel that the greatest reward for doing is the opportunity to do more.

Jonas Edward Salk

Half a man's life is devoted to what he calls improvements, yet the original had some quality which is lost in the process.

Elwyn Brooks White

See also: AIM, AMBITION, DECISION, LABOR, PURPOSE, SUCCESS, WORK.

ACQUAINTANCE

It is good discretion not to make too much of any man at the first; because one cannot hold out that proportion.

Francis Bacon

I love the acquaintance of young people, because, in the first place, I don't like to think myself growing old. In the next place, young acquaintances must last longest, if they do last; and then young men have more virtue than old men; they have more generous sentiments in every respect.

Samuel Johnson

If a man does not make new acquaintances as he advances through life, he will soon find himself left alone; one should keep his friendships in constant repair.

Samuel Johnson

Never say you know a man till you have divided an inheritance with him.

Johann Kaspar Lavater

The wisest man I have ever known once said to me: "Nine out of every ten people improve on acquaintance"; and I have found his words true.

Frank Arthur Swinnerton

See also: ASSOCIATE, COMPANIONSHIP, FAMILIARITY, FRIENDSHIP.

ACQUIREMENT

Calm's not life's crown, though calm is well.
'Tis all perhaps which man acquires,
But 'tis not what our youth desires.
Matthew Arnold

It sounds like stories from the land of spirits
If any man obtain that which he merits
Or any merit that which he obtains.
Samuel Taylor Coleridge

That which we acquire with most difficulty
we retain the longest; as those who have
earned a fortune are commonly more careful
of it than those by whom it may have been
inherited.
Charles Caleb Colton

Every noble acquisition is attended with its
risks; he who fears to encounter the one must
not expect to obtain the other.
Metastasio

See also: GAIN, POSSESSIONS, PROPERTY, RICH
AND POOR, WEALTH.

ACTION

Good thoughts, though God accept them, yet
toward men are little better than good dreams
except they be put in action.
Francis Bacon

What man knows should find expression in
what he does. The chief value of superior
knowledge is that it leads to a performing
manhood.
Christian Nestell Bovee

The margin between that which men naturally do, and that which they can do, is
so great that a system which urges men on
to action and develops individual enterprise
and initiative is preferable, in spite of the
wastes that necessarily attend that process.
Louis Dembitz Brandeis

A good action is never lost; it is a treasure
laid up and guarded for the doer's need.
Pedro Calderón de la Barca

The end of man is action, and not thought,
though it be of the noblest.
Thomas Carlyle

Nothing ever happens but once in this world.
What I do now I do once for all. It is over
and gone, with all its eternity of solemn
meaning.
Thomas Carlyle

Our grand business is not to see what lies
dimly at a distance, but to do what lies
clearly at hand.
Thomas Carlyle

Every action of our lives touches on some
chord that will vibrate in eternity.
Edwin Hubbel Chapin

We should not be so taken up in the search
for truth, as to neglect the needful duties of
active life; for it is only action that gives a
true value and commendation to virtue.
Cicero

Deliberate with caution, but act with decision; and yield with graciousness, or oppose
with firmness.
Charles Caleb Colton

We may believe that our words—which we
assume to express our principles—represent
us more truly even than our actions, but to
outsiders it is the actions that are more eloquent than the words.
Henry Steele Commager

Action may not always bring happiness; but
there is no happiness without action.
Benjamin Disraeli

Nobody has any right to find life uninteresting or unrewarding who sees within the
sphere of his own activity a wrong he can
help to remedy or within himself an evil he
can hope to overcome.
Charles William Eliot

Every noble activity makes room for itself.
Ralph Waldo Emerson

Not alone to know, but to act according to
your knowledge, is your destination proclaims
the voice of your soul. Not for indolent contemplation and study of yourself, nor for
brooding over emotions of piety—no, for action was existence given you; your actions,
and your actions alone, determine your worth.
Immanuel Hermann von Fichte

It is by acts and not by ideas that people live.
Anatole France

Our actions are not altogether our own; they
depend less upon us than upon chance. They
are given to us from every hand; we do not
always deserve them.
Anatole France

Actions are ours; their consequences belong to heaven.

Sir Philip Francis

In the divine account-books only our actions are noted, not what we have read or what we have spoken.
Mohandas Karamchand (Mahatma) Gandhi

It is my firm conviction that all good action is bound to bear fruit in the end.
Mohandas Karamchand (Mahatma) Gandhi

Manliness consists not in bluff, bravado or lordliness. It consists in daring to do the right and facing consequences, whether it is in matters social, political or other. It consists in deeds, not in words.
Mohandas Karamchand (Mahatma) Gandhi

Indolence is a delightful but distressing state; we must be doing something to be happy. Action is no less necessary than thought to the instinctive tendencies of the human frame.
William Hazlitt

Mark this well, you proud men of action! you are, after all, nothing but unconscious instruments of the men of thought.
Heinrich Heine

Act well at the moment, and you have performed a good action for all eternity.
Johann Kaspar Lavater

A society will bear down most heavily upon those actions towards which its members are most vividly drawn, but which some ghostly superstition causes them to fear.
Ludwig Lewisohn

The actions of men are the best interpreters of their thoughts.
John Locke

Activity is God's medicine; the highest genius is willingness and ability to do hard work. Any other conception of genius makes it a doubtful, if not a dangerous possession.
Robert Stuart MacArthur

Existence was given us for action. Our worth is determined by the good deeds we do, rather than by the fine emotions we feel.
Elias Lyman Magoon

I have never heard anything about the resolutions of the apostles, but a great deal about their acts.
Horace Mann

I don't act, I react.
Gamal Abdel Nasser

Action to be effective must be directed to clearly conceived ends.
Jawaharlal Nehru

Every action has to be judged from its possible consequences.
Jawaharlal Nehru

Healthy people and healthy countries act in the present and look to the future.
Jawaharlal Nehru

It is not what you say that matters, but what you do. Think, therefore, of the vast opportunities that the world offers to those who are keen of mind, strong of character and fleet of foot.
Jawaharlal Nehru

The more action and thought are allied and integrated, the more effective they become and the happier you grow. There will then be no inner conflict between a wish to do something and inability to act or between thinking one way and acting in another. The happiest man is he whose thinking and action are co-ordinated.
Jawaharlal Nehru

Our chief defect is that we are more given to talking about things than to doing them.
Jawaharlal Nehru

Success often comes to those who dare and act; it seldom goes to the timid who are ever afraid of the consequences.
Jawaharlal Nehru

There is only one thing that remains to us, that cannot be taken away: to act with courage and dignity and to stick to the ideals that have given meaning to life.
Jawaharlal Nehru

When I cannot act effectively, I try at any rate to preserve a certain integrity of mind, and I wait for the time when I can act more effectively.
Jawaharlal Nehru

The acts of this life are the destiny of the next.
Oriental Proverb

To do an evil act is base. To do a good one without incurring danger, is common enough.

But it is the part of a good man to do great
and noble deeds though he risks everything
in doing them.

Plutarch

I once covered the state of Iowa in deputa-
tion work. We traveled by automobile. One
morning in the road ahead of our car there
appeared a little gopher. He had enough time
to get away if he had made a run for it, but
instead he sat up to make a survey. That was
the mistake. After we had passed there was
no gopher. There are times that demand action rather than deliberation. Such is our
time. "The day of march has come."

Sidney Waterbury Powell

Doing is the great thing. For if, resolutely,
people do what is right, in time they come
to like doing it.

John Ruskin

If you have no friends to share or rejoice in
your success in life—if you cannot look back
to those to whom you owe gratitude, or forward to those to whom you ought to afford
protection, still it is no less incumbent on you
to move steadily in the path of duty: for your
active exertions are due not only to society;
but in humble gratitude to the Being who
made you a member of it, with powers to
serve yourself and others.

Sir Walter Scott

Only the actions of the just smell sweet and
blossom in the dust.

James Shirley

Heaven never helps the man who will not act.

Sophocles

To will and not to do when there is opportunity, is in reality not to will; and to love what
is good and not to do it, when it is possible,
is in reality not to love it.

Emanuel Swedenborg

The actions of men are like the index of a
book; they point out what is most remarkable
in them.

David Thomas

Happiness is in action, and every power is
intended for action; human happiness, therefore, can only be complete as all the powers
have their full and legitimate play.

David Thomas

Unselfish and noble actions are the most radiant pages in the biography of souls.

David Thomas

Some time ago a boy was carrying a basket of
eggs in the street. He tripped on the curb-
stone, dropped the basket, and smashed the
eggs. People gathered round, as people do.
One said, "What a pity!" Another said, "Poor
little chap! I hope he won't get the sack."
Another said, "I am sorry he is crying. Let's
comfort him." Then one man stepped out of
the crowd, put his hand in his pocket and
said, "I care half-a-crown." Turning to the
man next to him, he said, "How much do
you care?" He said, "I care a shilling." In a
little time they translated feeling into action.

Leslie Dixon Weatherhead

Essentially, culture should be for action, and
its effect should be to divest labor from the
associations of aimless toil.

Alfred North Whitehead

Periods of tranquility are seldom prolific of
creative achievement. Mankind has to be
stirred up.

Alfred North Whitehead

We cannot think first and act afterwards.
From the moment of birth we are immersed
in action, and can only fitfully guide it by
taking thought.

Alfred North Whitehead

Out of the strain of the doing,
Into the peace of the done.

Julia Louise Matilda Woodruff

Thought and theory must precede all salutary
action; yet action is nobler in itself than
either thought or theory.

William Wordsworth

See also: DEED, LABOR, WELL-DOING, WORK.

ACTOR AND ACTRESS

The most difficult character in comedy is that
of the fool, and he must be no simpleton that
plays that part.

Miguel de Cervantes Saavedra

Have patience with the jealousies and petu-
lances of actors, for their hour is their eternity.

Richard Garnett

An actor should take lessons from the painter
and the sculptor. Not only should he make
attitude his study, but he should highly develop his mind by an assiduous study of the
best writers, ancient and modern, which will
enable him not only to understand his parts,
but to communicate a nobler coloring to his
manners and mien.

Johann Wolfgang von Goethe

On the stage he was natural, simple, affect-
ing;
'Twas only when he was off he was acting.
Oliver Goldsmith

Actors are the only honest hypocrites. Their
life is a voluntary dream; and the height of
their ambition is to be beside themselves.
They wear the livery of other men's fortunes:
their very thoughts are not their own.
William Hazlitt

It is with some violence to the imagination
that we conceive of an actor belonging to the
relations of private life, so closely do we
identify these persons in our mind with the
characters they assume upon the stage.
Charles Lamb

The profession of the player, like that of the
painter, is one of the imitative arts, whose
means are pleasure, and whose end should
be virtue.
William Shenstone

See also: MOTION PICTURE, TELEVISION, THE-
ATER, TRAGEDY.

ADAM AND EVE

Whilst Adam slept, Eve from his side arose:
Strange his first sleep should be his last re-
pose.
Anonymous

When Eve saw her reflection in a pool, she
sought Adam and accused him of infidelity.
Ambrose Gwinnett Bierce

"The serpent tempted me and I did eat."
So much of paradisal nature, Eve's!
Her daughters ever since prefer to urge
"Adam so starved me I was fain accept
The apple any serpent pushed my way."
Robert Browning

When Eve upon the first of Men
That apple press'd with specious cant
Oh! what a thousand pities then
That Adam was not Adamant!
Thomas Hood

Adam, the goodliest man of men since born
His sons, the fairest of her daughters Eve.
John Milton

In Adam's fall
We sinned all.
The New England Primer

The woman was not taken
From Adam's head, you know,
So she must not command him,
'Tis evidently so;
The woman was not taken
From Adam's feet, you see,
So he must not abuse her—
The meaning seems to be.
The woman she was taken
From under Adam's arm,
Which shows he must protect her
From injury and harm.
Scottish Nuptial Song

See also: CREATION, MAN, MARRIAGE, WOMAN.

ADAPTABILITY

If you are at Rome live in the Roman style;
if you are elsewhere live as they live elsewhere.
Ambrose of Milan

One learns to itch where one can scratch.
Ernest Bramah (Smith)

Adaptability is not imitation. It means power
of resistance and assimilation.
Mohandas Karamchand (Mahatma) Gandhi

The weather-cock on the church-spire, though
made of iron, would soon be broken by the
storm-wind if it . . . did not understand the
noble art of turning to every wind.
Heinrich Heine

We seldom find things just to our taste in this
world. We have to accommodate ourselves to
what we can get, and put up with that as
human beings.
Sir Rabindranath Tagore

See also: ADJUSTMENT, CUSTOM, DOCILITY.

ADJUSTMENT

Every new adjustment is a crisis in self-
esteem.
Eric Hoffer

You must adjust. . . . This is the legend
imprinted in every schoolbook, the invisible
message on every blackboard. Our schools
have become vast factories for the manufacture of robots.
Robert Lindner

Adjustment as an educational goal is a pricked
balloon. To adjust to the twentieth century
is to come to terms with madness. What is

needed is the adjustment of our environment to ourselves, or rather to what we would like ourselves to be.

Max Rafferty

See also: ADAPTABILITY, CONFORMITY, HAR-
MONY, MENTAL HEALTH.

ADMINISTRATION

It has been said that England invented the phrase, 'Her Majesty's Opposition'; that it was the first government which made a criticism of administration as much a part of the polity as administration itself. This critical opposition is the consequence of cabinet government.

Walter Bagehot

Administration not only has to be good but has also to be felt to be good by the people affected.

Jawaharlal Nehru

The administrator, whether he is low down or high up in the scale, must give the impression, even if that impression is not one hundred per cent correct, that he is working through the public will and carrying it out. Of course, this cannot always be done; the administrator cannot carry out everybody's will; but he must give the broad impression that he is functioning in accordance with the public will, always thinking of public grievances, trying to remedy them, and consulting the people.

Jawaharlal Nehru

Any government, if it has to function adequately, must have the support of the country.

Jawaharlal Nehru

There are only three rules of sound administration, pick good men, tell them not to cut corners, and back them to the limit; and picking good men is the most important.

Adlai Ewing Stevenson

See also: BUSINESS, EXECUTIVE, GOVERNMENT,
PARTY, POLITICS, STATESMANSHIP.

ADMIRATION

Admiration is a very short-lived passion that decays on growing familiar with its object unless it be still fed with fresh discoveries and kept alive by perpetual miracles rising up to its view.

Joseph Addison

There is a wide difference between admiration and love. The sublime, which is the cause of the former, always dwells on great objects and terrible; the latter on small ones and pleasing; we submit to what we admire, but we love what submits to us: in one case we are forced, in the other we are flattered, into compliance.

Edmund Burke

No nobler feeling than this, of admiration for one higher than himself, dwells in the breast of man. It is to this hour, and at all hours, the vivifying influence in man's life.

Thomas Carlyle

Admiration is the daughter of ignorance.

Benjamin Franklin

We have an innate propensity to get ourselves noticed, and noticed favorably, by our kind. No more fiendish punishment could be devised, were such a thing physically possible, than that one should be turned loose in society and remain absolutely unnoticed by all the members thereof.

William James

We always love those who admire us; we do not always love those whom we admire.

Duc François de La Rochefoucauld

The only things one can admire at length are those one admires without knowing why.

Jean Rostand

To cultivate sympathy you must be among living beings and thinking about them; to cultivate admiration, among beautiful things and looking at them.

John Ruskin

See also: APPLAUSE, APPRECIATION, ESTEEM,
REVERENCE.

ADOLESCENCE

Despite our exaggerated concern for and almost prurient interest in the "teen-ager," we have no neutral term for persons between the ages of, say, fourteen and twenty-one. "Adolescent" has overtones at once pedantic and erotic, suggestive of primitive fertility rites and of the orgies of classical antiquity. "Young person" meets the requirements of British jurisprudence in referring precisely to a portion of this age range, but it is too poor in connotations to be a useful phrase in ordinary speech. "Teen-ager" remains the choice for popular usage. It is patronizing, and sounds rather uneasy and embarrassed; but these qualities may add to its appeal, for many of us do indeed respond to adolescence with forced joviality.

Edgar Z. Friedenberg

Adolescence is a kind of emotional seasickness. Both are funny, but only in retrospect.

Arthur Koestler

Adolescence is certainly far from a uniformly pleasant period. Early manhood might be the most glorious time of all were it not that the sheer excess of life and vigor gets a fellow into continual scrapes.

Donald Robert Perry (Don) Marquis

In this world of human affairs there is no worse nuisance than a boy at the age of fourteen. He is neither ornamental nor useful. It is impossible to shower affection on him as on a little boy; and he is always getting in the way. If he talks with a childish lisp he is called a baby, and if he answers in a grown-up way he is called impertinent. In fact any talk at all from him is resented. Then he is at the unattractive, growing age. He grows out of his clothes with indecent haste; his voice grows hoarse and breaks and quavers; his face grows suddenly angular and unsightly. It is easy to excuse the short-comings of early childhood, but it is hard to tolerate even unavoidable lapses in a boy of fourteen. The lad himself becomes painfully self-conscious. When he talks with elderly people he is either unduly forward, or else so unduly shy that he appears ashamed of his very existence.

Sir Rabindranath Tagore

See also: AGE, AGE AND YOUTH, AGES OF MAN, HIPPIE, YOUTH.

ADORATION

In wonder all philosophy began: in wonder it ends. . . . But the first wonder is the offspring of ignorance: the last is the parent of adoration.

Samuel Taylor Coleridge

Blind adoration, in the age of action, is perfectly valueless, is often embarrassing and equally often painful.

Mohandas Karamchand (Mahatma) Gandhi

Our God and soldiers we alike adore
Ev'n at the brink of danger; not before:
After deliverance, both alike requited,

Our God's forgotten, and our soldiers
   slighted.

Francis Quarles

See also: GOD, HONOR, REVERENCE, WORSHIP.

ADULT

Grow up as soon as you can. It pays. The only time you really live fully is from thirty to sixty. . . . The young are slaves to dreams; the old servants of regrets. Only the middle-aged have all their five senses in keeping of their wits.

(William) Hervey Allen

An adult is one who has ceased to grow vertically but not horizontally.

Anonymous

Leaving aside physical maturity, adulthood can be thought of as dependent on the following factors: (1) emotional and economic independence, (2) willing acceptance of personal and social responsibility, (3) self-identity and self-control, and (4) goal-directedness and a realistic attitude regarding the future.

Alexander Aloysius Schneiders

See also: AGE; AGE, MIDDLE; AGE, OLD; AGES OF MAN.

ADULTERY

What men call gallantry, and gods adultery,
Is much more common where the climate's
   sultry.

George Gordon Byron (Lord Byron)

When a man says, "Get out of my home! What do you want my wife for?"—there is no need for an answer.

Miguel de Cervantes Saavedra

The marriage system created a new sport—adultery.

Holbrook Jackson

Even to imagine the physical pleasures of adultery will cause us to feel its guilt.

Lactantius

See also: DIVORCE, HUSBAND AND WIFE, MARRIAGE, SEX.

ADVANCEMENT

I have found some of the best reasons I ever had for remaining at the bottom simply by looking at the men at the top.

Frank Moore Colby

In the world there are only two ways of raising one's self, either by one's own industry or by the weakness of others.

Jean de La Bruyère

The man who makes an appearance in the business world, the man who creates personal interest, is the man who gets ahead. Be liked and you will never want.

Arthur Miller

Speak softly and carry a big stick; you will go far.

Theodore Roosevelt

See also: AMBITION, IMPROVEMENT, PROGRESS, REFORM, SUCCESS, WORK.

ADVENTURE

The adventurer is within us, and he contests for our favour with the social man we are obliged to be. These two sorts of life are incompatibilities; one we hanker after, the other we are obliged to. There is no other conflict so deep and bitter as this.

William Bolitho

Adventure is not outside a man; it is within.

David Grayson (Ray Stannard Baker)

We live in a wonderful world that is full of beauty, and charm and adventure. There is no end to the adventures that we can have if only we seek them with our eyes open. So many people seem to go about their life's business with their eyes shut. Indeed, they object to other people keeping their eyes open. Unable to play themselves, they dislike the play of others.

Jawaharlal Nehru

Plunge into the deep without fear, with the gladness of April in your heart.

Sir Rabindranath Tagore

You can't cross the sea merely by standing and staring at the water. Don't let yourself indulge in vain wishes.

Sir Rabindranath Tagore

Without adventure civilization is in full decay.

Alfred North Whitehead

See also: ASTRONAUT, DISCOVERY, INVENTION, ROMANCE, SPACE, TRAVEL.

ADVERSARY

Three fourths of the miseries and misunderstandings in the world will disappear if we step into the shoes of our adversaries and understand their standpoint. We will then agree with our adversaries or think of them charitably.

Mohandas Karamchand (Mahatma) Gandhi

I cannot praise a fugitive and cloistered virtue unexercised and unbreathed, that never sallies out and seeks her adversary, but slinks out of the race where that immortal garland is to be run for, not without heat and dust.

John Milton

It is always more difficult to fight one's own failings than the power of an adversary.

Jawaharlal Nehru

See also: COLD WAR, CONTROVERSY, QUARREL, RIVALRY.

ADVERSITY

No man is more unhappy than the one who is never in adversity; the greatest affliction of life is never to be afflicted.

Anonymous

Prosperity is the blessing of the Old Testament; adversity of the New, which carrieth the greater benediction and the clearer revelation of God's favor. Prosperity is not without many fears and distastes; adversity not without many comforts and hopes.

Francis Bacon

Heaven often smites in mercy, even when the blow is severest.

Joanna Baillie

Adversity is a severe instructor, set over us by one who knows us better than we do ourselves, as he loves us better too. He that wrestles with us strengthens our nerves and sharpens our skill. Our antagonist is our helper. This conflict with difficulty makes us acquainted with our object, and compels us to consider it in all its relations. It will not suffer us to be superficial.

Edmund Burke

Adversity is the first path to truth.

George Gordon Byron (Lord Byron)

Friendship, of itself a holy tie,
Is made more sacred by adversity.

John Dryden

Adversity is the trial of principle. Without it a man hardly knows whether he is honest or not.

Henry Fielding

He that can heroically endure adversity will bear prosperity with equal greatness of soul; for the mind that cannot be dejected by the former is not likely to be transported with the latter.

Henry Fielding

Prosperity is a great teacher; adversity is a greater. Possession pampers the mind; privation trains and strengthens it.

William Hazlitt

Adversity has the effect of eliciting talents which in prosperous circumstances would have lain dormant.

Horace

Adversity has ever been considered the state in which a man most easily becomes acquainted with himself, then especially, being free from flatterers.

Samuel Johnson

Prosperity is too apt to prevent us from examining our conduct; but adversity leads us to think properly of our state, and so is most beneficial to us.

Samuel Johnson

The flower that follows the sun does so even in cloudy days.

Robert Leighton

Look at a man in the midst of doubt and danger, and you will learn in his hour of adversity what he really is. It is then that true utterances are wrung from the recesses of his breasts. The mask is torn off; the reality remains.

Lucretius

Who hath not known ill fortune, never knew himself, or his own virtue.

David Mallet

Prosperity is no just scale; adversity is the only balance to weigh friends.

Plutarch

I never met with a single instance of adversity which I have not in the end seen was for my good. I have never heard of a Christian on his deathbed complaining of his afflictions.

Alexander Moncrief Proudfit

Genuine morality is preserved only in the school of adversity; a state of continuous prosperity may easily prove a quicksand to virtue.

Johann Christoph Friedrich von Schiller

Adversity is like the period of the former and of the latter rain,—cold, comfortless, unfriendly to man and to animal; yet from that season have their birth the flower and the fruit, the date, the rose, and the pomegranate.

Sir Walter Scott

The good things of prosperity are to be wished; but the good things that belong to adversity are to be admired.

Seneca

It's a different song when everything's wrong, when you're feeling infernally mortal; when it's ten against one, and hope there is none, buck up, little soldier, and chortle!

Robert William Service

Stars may be seen from the bottom of a deep well, when they cannot be discerned from the top of a mountain. So are many things learned in adversity which the prosperous man dreams not of.

Charles Haddon Spurgeon

See also: AFFLICTION, CALAMITY, DEPRESSION, DIFFICULTY, DISAPPOINTMENT, DISGRACE, FAILURE, HARDSHIP, ILLS, MISERY, MISFORTUNE, SICKNESS, SORROW, SUFFERING, TRIALS, TROUBLE.

ADVERTISING

Advertising is the principal reason why the business man has come to inherit the earth.

James Randolph Adams

Great designers seldom make great advertising men, because they get overcome by the beauty of the picture—and forget that merchandise must be sold.

James Randolph Adams

If advertising had a little more respect for the public, the public would have a lot more respect for advertising.

James Randolph Adams

Millions of dollars' worth of advertising shows such little respect for the reader's intelligence that it amounts almost to outright insult.

James Randolph Adams

The most common trouble with advertising is that it tries too hard to impress people.

James Randolph Adams

Pride is a great urge to action; but remember, you who advertise, that the pride must be on the part of the buyer. On the part of the seller, it is vanity.

James Randolph Adams

The great art in writing advertisements is the finding out of a proper method to catch the reader's eye; without which, a good thing may pass over unobserved, or lost among commissions of bankrupt.

Joseph Addison

Advertising did not invent the products or services which called forth jobs, nor inspire the pioneering courage that built factories and machinery to produce them. What advertising did was to stimulate ambition and desire—the craving to possess, which is the strongest incentive to produce. To satisfy this craving the little factory was impelled to turn itself into a growing factory; and then, by the pressure of mass demand, into many factories. Mass production made possible mass economies, reflected in declining prices, until the product that began as the luxury of the rich became the possession of every family that was willing to work.

Bruce Barton

As a profession advertising is young; as a force it is as old as the world. The first four words ever uttered, "Let there be light," constitute its charter. All nature is vibrant with its impulse.

Bruce Barton

The faults of advertising are only those common to all human institutions. If advertising speaks to a thousand in order to influence one, so does the church. And if it encourages people to live beyond their means, so does matrimony. Good times, bad times, there will always be advertising. In good times, people want to advertise; in bad times, they have to.

Bruce Barton

Packaging in America is an art with liabilities. The people are prone to be charmed with package and disregard the contents.

Hans Bendix

In advertising there is a saying that if you can keep your head while all those around you are losing theirs—then you just don't understand the problem.

Hugh Malcolm Beville

Doing business without advertising is like winking at a girl in the dark. You know what you are doing, but nobody else does.

Steuart Henderson Britt

The business that considers itself immune to the necessity for advertising sooner or later finds itself immune to business.

Derby Brown

Advertising promotes that divine discontent which makes people strive to improve their economic status.

Ralph Starr Butler

Sanely applied advertising could remake the world.

Stuart Chase

When I had looked at the lights of Broadway by night, I said to my American friends: "What a glorious garden of wonders this would be, to any one who was lucky enough to be unable to read."

Gilbert Keith Chesterton

Advertising nourishes the consuming power of men. It sets up before a man the goal of a better home, better clothing, better food for himself and his family. It spurs individual exertion and greater production.

Sir Winston Leonard Spencer Churchill

Advertising is the life of trade.

(John) Calvin Coolidge

Advertising ministers to the spiritual side of trade.

(John) Calvin Coolidge

[Advertising] is often vulgar, strident and offensive. And it induces a definite cynicism and corruption in both practitioners and audience owing to the constant intermingling of truth and lies.

Charles Anthony Raven Crosland

Advertising is the essence of public contact.

Cyrus Herman Kotzschmar Curtis

You can tell the ideals of a nation by its advertisements.

Norman Douglas

The advertising man is a liaison between the products of business and the mind of the nation. He must know both before he can serve either.

Glenn Frank

Why shouldn't the housewife know that there are x number of hours' service in her washing machine? The manufacturer knows and the marketer knows. Shouldn't the consumer also know?

Betty Furness

Honesty in advertising and selling will do the job, and this will be found to be the best policy when science has replaced guesswork in gauging consumer demands.

Elizabeth Hawes

Advertising . . . brings savings in its wake. On the distribution side it speeds up the turnover of stock and thus makes lower retail margins possible, without reducing the shopkeeper's income. On the manufacturing side it is one of the factors that make large scale production possible and who would deny that large scale production leads to lower costs?

Geoffrey Heyworth (Lord Heyworth)

Advertising is a guarantee of quality. A firm which has spent a substantial sum advocating the merits of a product and accustoming the consumer to expect a standard that is both high and uniform, dare not later reduce the quality of its goods. Sometimes the public is gullible, but not to the extent of continuing to buy a patently inferior article.

Sir Frederic Hooper

It used to be that a fellow went on the police force after everything else failed, but today he goes in the advertising game.

Frank McKinney (Kin) Hubbard

The advertisement is one of the most interesting and difficult of modern literary forms.

Aldous Leonard Huxley

If a fellow wants to be a nobody in the business world, let him neglect sending the mail man to somebody on his behalf.

Charles Franklin Kettering

Advertising is the key to world prosperity; without it to-day modern business would be paralyzed.

Julius Klein

Advertising may be described as the science of arresting the human intelligence long enough to get money from it.

Stephen Butler Leacock

Half the money I spend on advertising is wasted, and the trouble is I don't know which half.

William Hesketh Lever (Lord Leverhulme)

In the advertising industry to be successful you must, of necessity, accumulate a group of creative people. This probably means a fairly high percentage of high strung, brilliant, eccentric nonconformists.

William Claire Menninger

The task of our Soviet advertising is to give people exact information about the goods that are on sale, to help to create new demands, to cultivate new tastes and requirements, to promote the sale of new kinds of goods and to explain their uses to the consumer. The primary task of Soviet advertising is to give a truthful, exact, apt and striking description of the nature, quality and properties of the goods advertised.

Anastas Ivanovich Mikoyan

I would rather pay ten million dollars for trademark-goodwill without property than one million dollars for property without trademark-goodwill.

George Keenan Morrow

The average family is now exposed to more than 1500 advertisements a day. No wonder they have acquired a talent for skipping the advertisements in newspapers and magazines, and going to the bathroom during television commercials.

David Mackenzie Ogilvy

Competition for the consumer's attention is becoming more ferocious every year. She is being bombarded by a billion dollars' worth of advertising a month. Thirty thousand brand names are competing for a place in her memory. If you want your voice to be heard above this earsplitting barrage, your voice must be unique. It is our business to make our clients' voices heard above the crowd.

David Mackenzie Ogilvy

I always use my clients' products. This is not toadyism, but elementary good manners.

David Mackenzie Ogilvy

I know of a brewer who sells more of his beer to the people who never see his advertising than to the people who see it every week. Bad advertising can unsell a product.

David Mackenzie Ogilvy

It is the professional duty of the advertising agent to conceal his artifice. When Aeschines spoke, they said "How well he speaks." But when Demosthenes spoke, they said, "Let us march against Philip." I'm for Demosthenes.

David Mackenzie Ogilvy

The late Aneurin Bevan thought that advertising was "an evil service." Arnold Toynbee (of Winchester and Balliol) "cannot think of any circumstances in which advertising would not be an evil." Professor Galbraith (Harvard) holds that advertising tempts people to squander money on "unneeded" possessions when they ought to be spending it on public works.

David Mackenzie Ogilvy

Much of the messy advertising you see on television today is the product of committees. Committees can criticize advertisements, but they should never be allowed to create them.

David Mackenzie Ogilvy

Some manufacturers illustrate their advertisements with abstract paintings. I would only do this if I wished to conceal from the reader what I was advertising.

David Mackenzie Ogilvy

Publicity has been developed into a fine art, being able, for instance, to make you think you've longed all your life for something you never even heard of before.

Ohio State Journal

Advertisers, too, boast a tremendous passion for the truth and look upon themselves as teachers, teaching people what they want or should want.

Houston Peterson

Living in an age of advertisement, we are perpetually disillusioned.

John Boynton Priestly

The full-blown caress of publicity, perfected and refined by masters of the art of ballyhoo.

Henry Morton Robinson

If I were starting life over again, I am inclined to think that I would go into the advertising business in preference to almost any other . . . The general raising of the standards of modern civilization among all people during the past half century would have been impossible without the spreading of the knowledge of higher standards by means of advertising.

Franklin Delano Roosevelt

Advertising is the foot on the accelerator, the hand on the throttle, the spur on the flank that keeps our economy surging forward.

Robert W. Sarnoff

Advertising is the genie which is transforming America into a place of comfort, luxury and ease for millions.

William Allen White

See also: BUSINESS, COMMERCIALS, PUBLICITY, TELEVISION.

ADVICE

When a man has been guilty of any vice of folly, the best atonement he can make for it is to warn others not to fall into the like.

Joseph Addison

It is easy when we are in prosperity to give advice to the afflicted.

Aeschylus

We give advice by the bucket, but take it by the grain.

William Rounseville Alger

Never give advice in a crowd.

Arabian Proverb

He that gives good advice, builds with one hand; he that gives good counsel and example, builds with both; but he that gives good admonition and bad example, builds with one hand and pulls down with the other.

Francis Bacon

The worst men often give the best advice.

Philip James Bailey

He who calls in the aid of an equal understanding doubles his own; and he who profits by a superior understanding raises his powers to a level with the heights of the superior understanding he unites with.

Edmund Burke

Let no man value at a little price a virtuous woman's counsel.

George Chapman

Advice is like snow; the softer it falls the longer it dwells upon, and the deeper it sinks into the mind.

Samuel Taylor Coleridge

To profit from good advice requires more wisdom than to give it.
John Churton Collins

Giving advice is sometimes only showing our wisdom at the expense of another.
Anthony Ashley Cooper (Lord Shaftesbury)

An empty stomach is not a good political adviser.
Albert Einstein

They that will not be counselled, cannot be helped. If you do not hear reason she will rap you on the knuckles.
Benjamin Franklin

Good counsels observed are chains of grace.
Thomas Fuller

To accept good advice is but to increase one's own ability.
Johann Wolfgang von Goethe

Unasked advice is a trespass on sacred privacy.
Henry Stanley Haskins

A good scare is worth more to a man than good advice.
Edgar Watson (Ed) Howe

A bad cold wouldn't be so annoying if it weren't for the advice of our friends.
Frank McKinney (Kin) Hubbard

Advice is seldom welcome. Those who need it most, like it least.
Samuel Johnson

No man is so foolish but he may sometimes give another good counsel, and no man so wise that he may not easily err if he takes no other counsel than his own. He that is taught only by himself has a fool for a master.
Ben (Benjamin) Jonson

It takes nearly as much ability to know how to profit by good advice as to know how to act for one's self.
Duc François de La Rochefoucauld

Men give away nothing so liberally as their advice.
Duc François de La Rochefoucauld

Nothing is less sincere than our mode of asking and giving advice. He who asks seems to have deference for the opinion of his friend, while he only aims to get approval of his own and make his friend responsible for his action. And he who gives repays the confidence supposed to be placed in him by a seemingly disinterested zeal, while he seldom means anything by his advice but his own interest or reputation.
Duc François de La Rochefoucauld

I realize that advice is worth what it costs—that is nothing.
Douglas MacArthur

A man shows lack of nerve when he asks for advice and still more when he takes the advice that is given.
Peter McArthur

All of us are too apt to advise others—and I am an equal sinner with them—and do not, in our turn, learn from others. Psychology means a good deal and, however right we may think ourselves to be, a great deal depends on how others are feeling about the course of events.
Jawaharlal Nehru

It is only too easy to make suggestions and later try to escape the consequences of what we say.
Jawaharlal Nehru

Take it from me, do not advise too much: do the job yourself. That is the only advice you can give to others. Do it and others will follow.
Jawaharlal Nehru

Every man, however wise, needs the advice of some sagacious friend in the affairs of life.
Plautus

Advice is like castor oil, easy enough to give but dreadful uneasy to take.
Henry Wheeler Shaw (Josh Billings)

When a man seeks your advice he generally wants your praise.
Philip Dormer Stanhope (Lord Chesterfield)

How is it possible to expect mankind to take advice when they will not so much as take warning?
Jonathan Swift

Do not have the conceit to offer your advice to people who are far greater than you in every respect.
Sir Rabindranath Tagore

There are plenty of men to say good things, but very few to listen. That requires strength of mind.

Sir Rabindranath Tagore

Do not give to your friends the most agreeable counsels, but the most advantageous.

Henry Theodore Tuckerman

The only thing to do with good advice is to pass it on. It is never of any use to oneself.

Oscar Wilde

See also: COUNSEL, GUIDANCE, INSTRUCTION.

AFFECTATION

The hardest tumble a man can make is to fall over his own bluff.

Ambrose Gwinnett Bierce

Affectation is certain deformity. By forming themselves on fantastic models the young begin with being ridiculous, and often end in being vicious.

Hugh Blair

Great vices are the proper objects of our detestation, and smaller faults of our pity, but affectation appears to be the only true source of the ridiculous.

Henry Fielding

Affectation naturally counterfeits those excellencies which are farthest from our attainment, because knowing our defects we eagerly endeavor to supply them with artificial excellence.

Samuel Johnson

Affectation in gesture, speaking, and manner is often a result of inertness or indifference; and it seems as if devotion to an object or serious business made men natural.

Jean de La Bruyère

We are never so ridiculous by the qualities we have, as by those we affect to have.

Duc François de La Rochefoucauld

Affectation lights a candle to our defects, and though it may gratify ourselves, it disgusts all others.

Johann Kaspar Lavater

Affectation in any part of our carriage is but the lighting up of a candle to show our de-

fects, and never fails to make us taken notice of, either as wanting in sense or sincerity.

John Locke

Don't laugh at a youth for his affectations; he is only trying on one face after another to find his own.

Logan Pearsall Smith

Affectation goes a longer way than open boasting.

Sir Rabindranath Tagore

See also: CANT, HYPOCRISY, INSINCERITY, OSTENTATION, PRETENSION.

AFFECTION

Of all earthly music that which reaches farthest into heaven is the beating of a truly loving heart.

Henry Ward Beecher

Our affections are our life. We live by them; they supply our warmth.

William Ellery Channing

Mature affection, homage, devotion, does not easily express itself. Its voice is low. It is modest and retiring, it lays in ambush and waits. Such is the mature fruit. Sometimes a life glides away, and finds it still ripening in the shade. The light inclinations of very young people are as dust compared to rocks.

Charles John Huffam Dickens

Affection, like melancholy, magnifies trifles; but the magnifying of the one is like looking through a telescope at heavenly objects; that of the other, like enlarging monsters with a microscope.

(James Henry) Leigh Hunt

The affections are like lightning: you cannot tell where they will strike till they have fallen.

Jean Baptiste Henri Lacordaire

When a sick child does not want to take its medicine, the mother, though quite well, drinks some herself to console the child with the idea that both are in the same plight. That is not a question of medical treatment, but of personal love, and if that love is lacking, however reasonable the mother's actions may be, the relation of mother and child is hurt, and with it is lost the desired effect.

Sir Rabindranath Tagore

See also: ADMIRATION, COURTSHIP, DEVOTION, ESTEEM, FRIENDSHIP, KISS, LOVE, TENDERNESS.

AFFLICTION

Come then, affliction, if my Father wills, and be my frowning friend. A friend that frowns is better than a smiling enemy.

Anonymous

Paradoxical as it may seem, God means not only to make us good, but to make us also happy, by sickness, disaster and disappointment.

Cyrus Augustus Bartol

Affliction comes to us all not to make us sad, but sober, not to make us sorry, but wise; not to make us despondent, but by its darkness to refresh us, as the night refreshes the day; not to impoverish, but to enrich us, as the plough enriches the field; to multiply our joy, as the seed, by planting, is multiplied a thousand-fold.

Henry Ward Beecher

No Christian but has his Gethsemane; but every praying Christian will find there is no Gethsemane without its angel.

Thomas Binney

There is such a difference between coming out of sorrow merely thankful for belief, and coming out of sorrow full of sympathy with, and trust in, Him who has released us.

Phillips Brooks

As threshing separates the wheat from the chaff, so does affliction purify virtue.

Richard Eugene Burton

I have learned more of experimental religion since my little boy died than in all my life before.

Horace Bushnell

Never was there a man of deep piety, who has not been brought into extremities—who has not been put into fire—who has not been taught to say, "Though he slay me, yet will I trust in him."

Richard Cecil

It is a great thing, when the cup of bitterness is pressed to our lips, to feel that it is not fate or necessity, but divine love working upon us for good ends.

Edwin Hubbel Chapin

The gem cannot be polished without friction, nor man perfected without trials.

Chinese Proverb

It is not until we have passed through the furnace that we are made to know how much dross there is in our composition.

Charles Caleb Colton

As in nature, as in art, so in grace; it is rough treatment that gives souls, as well as stones, their lustre. The more the diamond is cut the brighter it sparkles; and in what seems hard dealing, there God has no end in view but to perfect his people.

Thomas Guthrie

The most generous vine, if not pruned, runs out into many superfluous stems and grows at last weak and fruitless: so doth the best man if he be not cut short in his desires, and pruned with afflictions.

Joseph Hall

Strength is born in the deep silence of long-suffering hearts; not amid joy.

Felicia Dorothea Browne Hemans

Extraordinary afflictions are not always the punishment of extraordinary sins, but sometimes the trial of extraordinary graces. Sanctified afflictions are spiritual promotions.

Matthew Henry

I thank God for my handicaps, for through them, I have found myself, my work and my God.

Helen Adams Keller

Ah! if you only knew the peace there is in an accepted sorrow.

Jeanne de la Motte-Guyon (Madame Guyon)

It may serve as a comfort to us, in all our calamities and afflictions, that he that loses anything and gets wisdom by it is a gainer by the loss.

Sir Roger L'Estrange

It is from the remembrance of joys we have lost that the arrows of affliction are pointed.

Henry Mackenzie

By afflictions God is spoiling us of what otherwise might have spoiled us. When he makes the world too hot for us to hold, we let it go.

Sir John Powell

That which thou dost not understand when thou readest, thou shalt understand in the day of thy visitation; for many secrets of religion are not perceived till they be felt, and are not felt but in the day of calamity.

Jeremy Taylor

Though all afflictions are evils in themselves, yet they are good for us, because they discover to us our disease and tend to our cure.

John Tillotson

Affliction is a divine diet which though it be not pleasing to mankind, yet Almighty God hath often imposed it as a good, though bitter, physic, to those children whose souls are dearest to him.

Izaak Walton

Amid my list of blessings infinite, stands this the foremost, "that my heart has bled."

Edward Young

See also: ADVERSITY, CALAMITY, DISEASE, MISFORTUNE, SICKNESS, SUFFERING, TRIALS, TROUBLE.

AFRICA

The drums of Africa still beat in my heart. They will not let me rest while there is a single Negro boy or girl without a chance to prove his worth.

Mary McLeod Bethune

We carry within us the wonders we seek without us:
There is all Africa and her prodigies in us.

Sir Thomas Browne

"Here and here did England help me: how can I help England?"—say,
Whoso turns as I, this evening, turn to God to praise and pray,
While Jove's planet rises yonder, silent over Africa.

Robert Browning

The wind of change is blowing through the continent [Africa].

Harold Macmillan

Africa for Africans means Africa for the Africans and not Africa as a hunting ground for alien ambitions.

Adlai Ewing Stevenson

See also: BLACK POWER, NEGRO, RACE.

AGE

Age acquires no value save through thought and discipline.

James Truslow Adams

He who would pass his declining years with honor and comfort, should, when young, consider that he may one day become old, and remember when he is old, that he has once been young.

Joseph Addison

One's age should be tranquil, as childhood should be playful. Hard work at either extremity of life seems out of place. At mid-day the sun may burn, and men labor under it; but the morning and evening should be alike calm and cheerful.

Matthew Arnold

Age—that period of life in which we compound for the vices that we still cherish by reviling those that we no longer have the enterprise to commit.

Ambrose Gwinnett Bierce

Eclipses of the sun and moon happen far too often to suit me.

Edward Bluestone

Old age has deformities enough of its own. It should never add to them the deformity of vice.

Cato the Younger

Age does not depend upon years, but upon temperament and health. Some men are born old, and some never grow so.

Tryon Edwards

I don't believe one grows older. I think that what happens early on in life is that at a certain age one stands still and stagnates.

Thomas Stearns Eliot

Age that lessens the enjoyment of life, increases our desire of living.

Oliver Goldsmith

The Grecian ladies counted their age from their marriage, not from their birth.

Homer

Age is rarely despised but when it is contemptible.

Samuel Johnson

Cautious age suspects the flattering form, and only credits what experience tells.

Samuel Johnson

At sixty a man has passed most of the reefs and whirlpools. Excepting only death, he has no enemies left to meet. . . . That man has awakened to a new youth. . . . Ergo, he is young.

George Benjamin Luks

When a woman tells you her age, it's all right to look surprised, but don't scowl.

Wilson Mizner

It is curious how age seems to have the same effect on a people or a race as it has on an individual—it makes them slow of movement, inelastic in mind and body, conservative and afraid of change.

Jawaharlal Nehru

A graceful and honorable old age is the childhood of immortality.

Pindar

I always thought when you got older, you got wiser. Well, it doesn't help. You know what it's all about, but don't let anybody tell you that lessens the pain.

Samson Raphaelson

A man is not old as long as he is seeking something.

Jean Rostand

As one grows into one's middle sixties death seems more reasonable than it does in childhood and youth.

William Allen White

Growing old gracefully should begin with youth.

Walter Béran Wolfe

See also: ADOLESCENCE; AGE AND YOUTH; AGE, MIDDLE; AGE, OLD; AGES OF MAN; HIPPIE; YOUTH.

AGE, THE

The age of the centuries is the youth of the world.

Francis Bacon

The spirit of the age is the very thing a great man changes.

Benjamin Disraeli

When a career is all finished and left safely behind in the past, a woman can be as sentimental as she will about her own day and age, giving scorn and damnation to the present.

Grace Moore

See also: ANXIETY, SPACE, TECHNOLOGY, TIME.

AGE AND YOUTH

As I approve of a youth that has something of the old man in him, so I am no less pleased with an old man that has something of the youth. He that follows this rule, may be old in body, but can never be so in mind.

Cicero

In youth we learn; in age we understand.

Marie von Ebner-Eschenbach

Forty is the old age of youth; fifty is the youth of old age.

French Proverb

She had lost in youth what she had won in weight.

Heinrich Heine

Youth is fair, a graceful stag,
    Leaping, playing in the park.
Age is gray, a toothless hag,
    Stumbling in the dark.

Isaac Loeb Peretz

Denunciation of the young is a necessary part of the hygiene of older people and greatly assists in the circulation of their blood.

Logan Pearsall Smith

Though every old man has been young, and every young one hopes to be old, there seems to be a most unnatural misunderstanding between those two stages of life. This unhappy want of commerce arises from arrogance or exultation in youth, and irrational despondence or self-pity in age.

Sir Richard Steele

All sorts of allowances are made for the illusions of youth; and none, or almost none, for the disenchantments of age.

Robert Louis Stevenson

And alas, youth is inexperienced and wilful, therefore it is but meet that the old should take charge of the household, and the young take to the seclusion of forest shades and the severe discipline of courting.

Sir Rabindranath Tagore

What a man does in youth darkens his face in old age.

Talmud

A young tree bends, an old tree breaks.

Yiddish Proverb

See also: AGE, HIPPIE, YOUTH.

AGE, MIDDLE

Probably the happiest period in life most frequently is in middle age, when the eager passions of youth are cooled, and the infirmities of age not yet begun; as we see that the shadows, which are at morning and evening so large, almost entirely disappear at mid-day.

Thomas Arnold

If a man's curve of efficiency is ascending at 45, and keeps on ascending just after that period, it may well move upward for his whole life; but if there is a turn downward at 45, he will never recover.

Nicholas Murray Butler

One of the many things nobody ever tells you about middle age is that it's such a nice change from being young.

Dorothy Canfield Fisher

Of middle age the best that can be said is that a middle-aged person has likely learned to have a little fun in spite of his troubles.

Donald Robert Perry (Don) Marquis

You who are crossing forty may not know it, but you are the luckiest generation ever. Every day brings forth some new thing that adds to the joy of life after forty. Work becomes easy and brief. Play grows richer and longer. Leisure lengthens. Life's afternoon is brighter, warmer, fuller of song; and long before the shadows stretch, every fruit grows ripe.

Walter Boughton Pitkin

See also: ADULT, AGE, AGES OF MAN.

AGE, OLD

When one becomes indifferent to women, to children, and to young people, he may know that he is superannuated, and has withdrawn from what is sweetest and purest in human existence.

Amos Bronson Alcott

While one finds company in himself and his pursuits, he cannot feel old, no matter what his years may be.

Amos Bronson Alcott

Life is precious to the old person. He is not interested merely in thoughts of yesterday's good life and tomorrow's path to the grave. He does not want his later years to be a sentence of solitary confinement in society. Nor does he want to be a death watch.

David Bacharach Allman

There are no diseases of the aged, but simply diseases among the aged.

American Medical Association, 1960

To know how to grow old is the master-work of wisdom, and one of the most difficult chapters in the great art of living.

Henri Frédéric Amiel

Men of age object too much, consult too long, adventure too little, repent too soon, and seldom drive business home to the full period, but content themselves with a mediocrity of success.

Francis Bacon

A man is not old until regrets take the place of dreams.

John Barrymore

To me, old age is always fifteen years older than I am.

Bernard Mannes Baruch

We grow neither better nor worse as we get old, but more like ourselves.

May Lamberton Becker

To resist the frigidity of old age one must combine the body, the mind, and the heart. And to keep these in parallel vigor one must exercise, study, and love.

Charles Victor de Bonstetten

All of us, as the years slip by, face increasingly the problem of living with the abiding subtractions of death. These create gaps which cannot be filled and leave us suddenly lonely in the midst of crowds.

John Mason Brown

Old age is wise for itself, but not for the community. It is wise in declining new enterprises, for it has not the power or the time to execute them; wise in shrinking from difficulty, for it has not the strength to overcome it; wise in avoiding danger, for it lacks the faculty of ready and swift action by which dangers are parried and converted into advantages. But this is not wisdom for mankind at large, by whom new enterprises must be undertaken, dangers met, and difficulties surmounted.

William Cullen Bryant

It is when a man begins to live in the past, the good old days, that the boat begins to drift downstream, eventually coming to rest in stagnant waters.

Frank Case

Old age isn't so bad when you consider the alternative.

Maurice Chevalier

Old age has been charged with being insensible to pleasure and to the enjoyments arising from the gratification of the senses—a most blessed and heavenly effect, truly, if it eases us of what in youth was the sorest plague of life.

Cicero

That which is called dotage, is not the weak point of all old men, but only of such as are distinguished by their levity and weakness.

Cicero

In old age life's shadows are meeting eternity's day.

McDonald Clarke

There are three classes into which all the women past seventy years of age I have ever known, were divided: that dear old soul; that old woman; that old witch.

Samuel Taylor Coleridge

Some men are born old, and some never seem so. If we keep well and cheerful we are always young, and at last die in youth, even when years would count us old.

Tryon Edwards

Old men's eyes are like old men's memories; they are strongest for things a long way off.

George Eliot (Mary Ann Evans)

I grow old . . . I grow old . . .
I shall wear the bottoms of my trousers rolled.

Thomas Stearns Eliot

You take all the experience and judgment of men over fifty out of the world and there wouldn't be enough left to run it.

Henry Ford

I am in the prime of senility.

Benjamin Franklin

If wrinkles must be written upon our brows, let them not be written upon the heart. The spirit should not grow old.

James Abram Garfield

As a preventative to mental old age a daily mile trot with your imagination cannot be equalled!

Ray Giles

Age does not make us childish, as some say; it finds us true children.

Johann Wolfgang von Goethe

It is only necessary to grow old to become more charitable and even indulgent. I see no fault committed by others that I have not committed myself.

Johann Wolfgang von Goethe

So long as you are learning, you are not growing old. It's when a man stops learning that he begins to grow old.

Joseph Hergesheimer

A person is always startled when he hears himself seriously called old for the first time.

Oliver Wendell Holmes

If reverence is due from others to the old, they ought also to respect themselves; and by grave, prudent, and holy actions, put a crown of glory upon their own gray heads.

Ezekiel Hopkins

How beautiful can time with goodness make an old man look.

Douglas William Jerrold

We dread old age, which we are not sure of reaching.

Jean de La Bruyère

We hope to grow old, yet we fear old age; that is, we are willing to live, and afraid to die.

Jean de La Bruyère

The blemishes of the mind, like those of the face, grow worse as we grow old.

Duc François de La Rochefoucauld

In growing old we become both more foolish and more wise.

Duc François de La Rochefoucauld

Old age is a tyrant who forbids, at the penalty of life, all the pleasures of youth.

Duc François de La Rochefoucauld

It is not by the gray of the hair that one knows the age of the heart.

Edward G. Bulwer-Lytton (Baron Lytton)

When we are out of sympathy with the young, then I think our work in this world is over.

George Macdonald

An old man who has lived in the exercise of virtue, looking back without a blush on his past days, and pointing to that better state where alone he can be perfectly rewarded, is a figure the most venerable that can well be imagined.

Henry Mackenzie

The older I grow the more I distrust the familiar doctrine that age brings wisdom.

Henry Louis Mencken

It is because the old have forgotten life that they preach wisdom.

Philip Moeller

Age imprints more wrinkles on the mind than it does on the face, and souls are never or very rarely seen that, in growing old, do not smell sour and musty.

Michel Eyquem de Montaigne

Without fullness of experience, length of days is nothing. When fullness of life has been achieved, shortness of days is nothing. That is perhaps why the young, . . . have usually so little fear of death; they live by intensities that the elderly have forgotten.

Lewis Mumford

I am getting old and the sign of old-age is that I begin to philosophize and ponder over problems which should not be my concern at all.

Jawaharal Nehru

A comfortable old age is the reward of a well-spent youth; instead of its introducing dismal and melancholy prospects of decay, it should give us hopes of eternal youth in a better world.

Ray Palmer

Old age adds to the respect due to virtue, but it takes nothing from the contempt inspired by vice; it whitens only the hair.

John Petit-Senn

Our youth and manhood are due to our country, but our declining years are due to ourselves.

Pliny the Elder

When we are young, we are slavishly employed in procuring something whereby we may live comfortably when we grow old; and when we are old, we perceive it is too late to live as we proposed.

Alexander Pope

She even had still that borrowed glory, with which she used to paint and adorn her countenance, to restore the irreparable injury done to her by years.

Jean Baptiste Racine

As winter strips the leaves from around us, so that we may see the distant regions they formerly concealed, so old age takes away our enjoyments only to enlarge the prospect of the coming eternity.

Jean Paul Richter

Like a morning dream, life becomes more and more bright the longer we live, and the reason of everything appears more clear. What has puzzled us before seems less mysterious, and the crooked paths look straighter as we approach the end.

Jean Paul Richter

I won't be old till my feet hurt, and they only hurt when I don't let 'em dance enough, so I'll keep right on dancing.

Bill (Bojangles) Robinson

Age is no cause for veneration. An old crocodile is still a menace and an old crow sings not like a nightingale.

Dagobert David Runes

Nothing is more disgraceful than that an old man should have nothing to show to prove that he has lived long, except his years.

Seneca

That old man dies prematurely whose memory records no benefits conferred. They only have lived long who have lived virtuously.

Richard Brinsley Sheridan

The vices of old age have the stiffness of it too; and as it is the unfittest time to learn in, so the unfitness of it to unlearn will be found much greater.

Robert South

When a noble life has prepared old age, it is not decline that it reveals, but the first days of immortality.

Madame de Staël

How many fancy they have experience simply because they have grown old.

Stanislas I (Leszczyński)

A healthy old fellow, who is not a fool is the happiest creature living.

Sir Richard Steele

Years do not make sages; they only make old men.

Anne Sophie Swetchine

Every one desires to live long, but no one would be old.

Jonathan Swift

No wise man ever wished to be younger.

Jonathan Swift

When men grow virtuous only in old age, they are merely making a sacrifice to God of the devil's leavings.

Jonathan Swift

There cannot live a more unhappy creature than an ill-natured old man, who is neither capable of receiving pleasures, nor sensible of conferring them on others.

Sir William Temple

There is not a more repulsive spectacle than an old man who will not forsake the world, which has already forsaken him.

Friedrich Gotttren August Tholuck

Woe to the man who becomes old without becoming wise; woe to him if this world shuts its door without the future having opened its doors to him.

Friedrich Gotttren August Tholuck

Since I must be old and have the gout, I have long turned those disadvantages to my own account, and plead them to the utmost when they will save me from doing anything I dislike.

Horace Walpole

I fear vastly more a futile, incompetent old age than I do any form of death.

William Allen White

See also: AGE, AGE AND YOUTH, ANTIQUITY.

AGES OF MAN

Youth is a blunder, Manhood a struggle, Old Age a regret.

Benjamin Disraeli

At twenty, the will reigns; at thirty, the wit; at forty, the judgment; afterward, proportion of character.

Henry Grattan

See also: ADOLESCENCE; ADULT; AGE, MIDDLE; AGE, OLD; BABY; CHILDHOOD; CHILDREN; INFANCY.

AGGRESSION

The truth is often a terrible weapon of aggression. It is possible to lie, and even to murder, with the truth.

Alfred Adler

It is the habit of every aggressor nation to claim that it is acting on the defensive.

Jawaharlal Nehru

See also: ANGER, COMMUNISM, ENEMY, NAZISM, WAR.

AGITATION

We believe in excitement when the theme is great; in agitation when huge evils are to be reformed. It is thus that a state or nation clears itself of great moral wrongs, and effects important changes. Still waters gather to themselves poisonous ingredients, and scatter epidemics and death. The noisy, tumbling brook, and the rolling and roaring ocean, are pure and healthful.

Philip Pendleton Cooke

The purely agitational attitude is not good enough for a detailed consideration of a subject.

Jawaharlal Nehru

Agitation is the marshalling of the conscience of a nation to mould its laws.

Sir Robert Peel

Agitation is the method that plants the school by the side of the ballot-box.

Wendell Phillips

Agitation prevents rebellion, keeps the peace, and secures progress. Every step she gains is gained forever. Muskets are the weapons of animals. Agitation is the atmosphere of the brains.

Wendell Phillips

See also: ARGUMENT, DISCUSSION, PUBLICITY, REFORM.

AGNOSTICISM

Agnosticism is the philosophical, ethical, and religious dry-rot of the modern world.

Francis Ellingwood Abbot

There is only one greater folly than that of the fool who says in his heart there is no God, and that is the folly of the people that says with its head that it does not know whether there is a God or not.

Otto Eduard Leopold von Bismark

I do not consider it an insult, but rather a compliment to be called an agnostic. I do not pretend to know where many ignorant men are sure—that is all that agnosticism means.

Clarence Seward Darrow

The mystery of the beginning of all things is insoluble by us; and I for one must be content to remain an agnostic.

Charles Robert Darwin

Agnosticism simply means that a man shall not say he knows or believes that for which he has no grounds for professing to believe.

Thomas Henry Huxley

It is wrong for a man to say that he is certain of the objective truth of any proposition unless he can produce evidence which logically justifies that certainty. This is what agnosticism asserts.

Thomas Henry Huxley

I do not see much difference between avowing that there is no God, and implying that nothing definite can for certain be known about Him.

John Henry Newman

See also: ATHEISM, GOD, UNBELIEF.

AGREEMENT

I do not want people to be very agreeable, as it saves me the trouble of liking them a great deal.

Jane Austen

He that complies against his will
Is of his own opinion still.

Samuel Butler

"My idea of an agreeable person," said Hugo Bohun, "is a person who agrees with me."

Benjamin Disraeli

We hardly find any persons of good sense save those who agree with us.

Duc François de La Rochefoucauld

When people agree with me I always feel that I must be wrong.

Oscar Wilde

See also: HARMONY, TREATY, UNITY.

AGRICULTURE

A study of depressions since the Civil War brings out the conclusion that if a decline in the agricultural purchasing power did not actually *start* the general economic collapse it added almost immediately its immense weight to the general collapse with a vast and devastating impetus.

Louis Bromfield

When agricultural land and its productivity falls below a certain standard in relation to population, meat, poultry and dairy products become either prohibitively high in price or altogether unobtainable and a direct cereal diet becomes the necessity of the bulk of any population.

Louis Bromfield

Of the fifty percent of the globe's soil which can be cultivated, only ten percent is being used.

Josue de Castro

The first three men in the world were a gardener, a ploughman, and a grazier; and if any object that the second of these was a murderer, I desire him to consider that as soon as he was so, he quitted our profession, and turned builder.

Abraham Cowley

The farther we get away from the land, the greater our insecurity.

Henry Ford

There seem to be but three ways for a nation to acquire wealth: the first is by war, as the Romans did, in plundering their conquered neighbors—this is robbery; the second by commerce, which is generally cheating; the third by agriculture, the only honest way, wherein man receives a real increase of the seed thrown into the ground, in a kind of continual miracle, wrought by the hand of God in his favor, as a reward for his innocent life and his virtuous industry.

Benjamin Franklin

Family farm agriculture has withstood the test of time and competition. It has made this country the envy of the world and American farm production the greatest production miracle in the history of mankind.

Orville L. Freeman

Agriculture is the foundation of manufactures, since the productions of nature are the materials of art.

Edward Gibbon

Let the farmer forevermore be honored in his calling, for they who labor in the earth are the chosen people of God.

Thomas Jefferson

Agriculture not only gives riches to a nation, but the only riches she can call her own.

Samuel Johnson

Trade increases the wealth and glory of a country; but its real strength and stamina are to be looked for among the cultivators of the land.

William Pitt (Lord Chatham)

In a moral point of view, the life of the agriculturist is the most pure and holy of any class of men; pure, because it is the most healthful, and vice can hardly find time to contaminate it; and holy, because it brings the Deity perpetually before his view, giving him thereby the most exalted notions of supreme power, and the most endearing view of the divine benignity.

Lord John Russell

Whoever makes two ears of corn, or two blades of grass to grow where only one grew before, deserves better of mankind, and does more essential service to his country than the whole race of politicians put together.

Jonathan Swift

Command large fields, but cultivate small ones.

Virgil

The farmers are the founders of civilization and prosperity.

Daniel Webster

Agriculture for an honorable and high-minded man, is the best of all occupations or arts by which men procure the means of living.

Xenophon

See also: COUNTRY, GARDEN, INDUSTRY.

AIM

Have a purpose in life, and having it, throw into your work such strength of mind and muscle as God has given you.

Thomas Carlyle

Resolve to live with all my might while I do live, and as I shall wish I had done ten thousand ages hence.

Jonathan Edwards

High aims form high characters, and great objects bring out great minds.

Tryon Edwards

Aim at the sun, and you may not reach it; but your arrow will fly far higher than if aimed at an object on a level with yourself.

Joel Hawes

What are the aims which at the same time duties?—they are the perfecting of ourselves, and the happiness of others.

Immanuel Kant

In great attempts it is glorious even to fail.

Dionysius Cassius Longinus

Not failure, but low aim, is crime.

James Russell Lowell

The man who seeks one, and but one, thing in life may hope to achieve it; but he who seeks all things, wherever he goes, only reaps, from the hopes which he sows, a harvest of barren regrets.

Edward G. Bulwer-Lytton (Baron Lytton)

Providence has nothing good or high in store for one who does not resolutely aim at something high or good. A purpose is the eternal condition of success.

Theodore Thornton Munger

Aim at perfection in everything, though in most things it is unattainable; however, they who aim at it, and persevere, will come much nearer to it, than those whose laziness and despondency make them give it up as unattainable.

Philip Dormer Stanhope (Lord Chesterfield)

See also: ASPIRATION, DESIRE, IDEAL, INTENTION, OBJECTIVE, PURPOSE.

AIRPLANE: see AVIATION.

AIR POLLUTION

The Air Quality Act of 1967 gives the country, for the first time, a comprehensive plan for setting and enforcing standards for clean air.

Hervey Gilbert Machen

President Johnson has declared that the American people have a "right to air that they and their children can breathe without fear."

Hervey Gilbert Machen

Technology already exists that can be adapted to the internal-combustion engine to meet the air-pollution standards proposed for it.

Stewart Lee Udall

See also: AUTOMOBILE, HEALTH, TECHNOLOGY.

ALCOHOL

Always remember, that I have taken more out of alcohol than alcohol has taken out of me.

Sir Winston Leonard Spencer Churchill

No other national health problem has been so seriously neglected as alcoholism. Many doctors decline to accept alcoholics as patients. Most hospitals refuse to admit alcoholics. Available methods of treatment have not been widely applied. Research on alcoholism and excessive drinking has received virtually no significant support.

John W. Gardner

Alcoholism is tragically high on the list of our nation's health problems. Five million Americans are alcoholics. They bring incalculable grief to millions of families. They cost their families, their employers and society billions of dollars.

Lyndon Baines Johnson

A man takes a drink, the drink takes another, and the drink takes the man.

Sinclair Lewis

Much of what is popularly believed about alcohol and alcoholism simply is not supported by modern knowledge. The public must know that there are treatment methods now available which can be effective. The public must know that how much a man drinks may be less important than when he drinks, how he drinks, and why he drinks.

John Emerson Moss

We are recognizing that alcoholism is a disease—no more moral or immoral than tuberculosis or pneumonia—and that we have not dealt with it adequately.

John Emerson Moss

Two great European narcotics, alcohol and Christianity.

Friedrich Wilhelm Nietzsche

Extensive interviews show that not one alcoholic has ever actually seen a pink elephant.

Yale University,
Center of Alcohol Studies

See also: DISEASE, DRINK, DRUNKENNESS,

ALCOHOLISM: *see* ALCOHOL.

ALIMONY

Alimony is like buying oats for a dead horse.

Arthur (Bugs) Baer

You never realize how short a month is until you pay alimony.

John Barrymore

Alimony was never intended to assure a perpetual state of secured indolence.

Samuel H. Hofstadter

She is as implacable an adversary as a wife suing for alimony.

William Wycherley

See also: DIVORCE, HUSBAND AND WIFE, MARRIAGE, WIFE.

ALLEGORY

Allegories, when well chosen, are like so many tracks of light in a discourse, that make everything about them clear and beautiful.

Joseph Addison

A man conversing in earnest, if he watch his intellectual process, will find that a material image, more or less luminous, arises in his mind with every thought which furnishes the vestment of the thought. Hence good writing and brilliant discourse are perpetual allegories.

Ralph Waldo Emerson

A man's life of any worth is a continual allegory.

John Keats

Allegories are fine ornaments and good illustrations, but not proof.

Martin Luther

The allegory of a sophist is always screwed; it crouches and bows like a snake, which is never straight, whether she go, creep, or lie still; only when she is dead, she is straight enough.

Martin Luther

See also: FABLE, LITERATURE, MYTH.

ALLIANCE

Equal and exact justice to all men, of whatever state or persuasion, religious or political; peace, commerce, and honest friendship with all nations,—entangling alliances with none; the support of the State governments in all their rights, as the most competent administrations for our domestic concerns, and the surest bulwarks against anti-republican tendencies; the preservation of the general government in its whole constitutional vigour, as the sheet anchor at home and safety abroad; . . . freedom of religion; freedom of the press; freedom of person under the protection of the habeas corpus; and trial by juries impartially selected,—these principles form the bright constellation which has gone before us, and guided our steps through an age of revolution and reformation.

Thomas Jefferson

[Utopians] never enter into any alliance with any other state. They think leagues are useless things, and reckon that if the common ties of human nature do not knit men together the faith of promises will have no great effect on them.

Sir Thomas More

It is our true policy to steer clear of permanent alliances with any portion of the foreign world.

George Washington

See also: AGREEMENT, TREATY, UNION, UNITY.

AMBASSADOR

Ambassadors are the eyes and ears of states.
Francesco Guicciardini

Foreign affairs are utterly realistic today. A false step, a false phrase, makes all the difference. The first thing that an ambassador of ours has to learn is to shut his mouth and give up public or even private speaking. It is not a habit which we have developed in our past careers—that of being completely silent. Yet this habit has to be developed, and in private one has to be silent lest what one says injures the cause of the nation or creates international ill-will.

Jawaharlal Nehru

An ambassador is an honest man sent to lie and intrigue abroad for the benefit of his country.

Sir Henry Wotton

See also: DIPLOMACY, POLITICIAN.

AMBIGUITY

Clearly spoken, Mr. Fogg; you explain English by Greek.

Benjamin Franklin

I fear explanations explanatory of things explained.

Abraham Lincoln

That must be wonderful; I have no idea of what it means.

Molière (Jean Baptiste Poquelin)

See also: ACCURACY, CERTAINTY, OBSCURITY.

AMBITION

A noble man compares and estimates himself by an idea which is higher than himself; and a mean man, by one lower than himself. The one produces aspiration; the other ambition, which is the way in which a vulgar man aspires.

Henry Ward Beecher

As love is a universal element of biography, so, in almost equal measure, is ambition, the desire for success and glory, to do something notable in the world that men will cherish and remember.

Gamaliel Bradford

He who surpasses or subdues mankind, must look down on the hate of those below.
George Gordon Byron (Lord Byron)

The noblest spirit is most strongly attracted by the love of glory.

Cicero

It is attempting to reach the top at a single leap, that so much misery is caused in the world.

William Cobbett

Ambition is the avarice of power; and happiness herself is soon sacrificed to that very lust of dominion which was first encouraged only as the best means of obtaining it.

Charles Caleb Colton

Ambition makes the same mistake concerning power, that avarice makes as to wealth. She begins by accumulating it as a means to happiness, and finishes by continuing to accumulate it as an end.

Charles Caleb Colton

All ambitions are lawful except those which climb upward on the miseries or credulities of mankind.

Joseph Conrad

Ambition is like love, impatient both of delays and rivals.

Sir John Denham

Ambition is the germ from which all growth of nobleness proceeds.
Thomas Dunn English

A strategy that uses up its strength in the defensive, gradually paralyzes a people's initiative and activity.
Joseph Paul Goebbels

Ambition is not a weakness unless it be disproportioned to the capacity. To have more ambition than ability is to be at once weak and unhappy.
George Stillman Hillard

Nothing is too high for the daring of mortals: we storm heaven itself in our folly.
Horace

Some folks can look so busy doing nothin' that they seem indispensable.
Frank McKinney (Kin) Hubbard

Where ambition can cover its enterprises, even to the person himself, under the appearance of principle, it is the most incurable and inflexible of passions.
David Hume

The slave has but one master, the ambitious man has as many as there are persons whose aid may contribute to the advancement of his fortunes.
Jean de La Bruyère

Ambition has one heel nailed in well, though she stretch her fingers to touch the heavens.
William Lilly

Most people would succeed in small things if they were not troubled by great ambitions.
Henry Wadsworth Longfellow

Ambition is but the evil shadow of aspiration.
George Macdonald

Ambition is so powerful a passion in the human breast, that however high we reach we are never satisfied.
Niccolò Machiavelli

Ambition is the spur that makes man struggle with destiny. It is heaven's own incentive to make purpose great and achievement greater.
Donald Grant Mitchell

Ambition is not a vice of little people.
Michel Eyquem de Montaigne

A life spent in constant labor is a life wasted, save a man be such a fool as to regard a fulsome obituary notice as ample reward.
George Jean Nathan

I am not using the words pride and ambition in a small personal sense. I do not mean the pride of getting money, which is the silliest of all types of pride. Pride should consist in doing your job in the best possible manner. If you are a scientist, think of becoming an Einstein, not merely a reader in your university. If you are a medical man, think of some discovery which will bring healing to the human race. If you are an engineer, aim at some new invention. The mere act of aiming at something big makes you big.
Jawaharlal Nehru

People who Do Things exceed my endurance; God, for a man that solicits insurance!
Dorothy Parker

The tallest trees are most in the power of the winds, and ambitious men of the blasts of fortune.
William Penn

Great souls, by nature half divine, soar to the stars, and hold a near acquaintance with the gods.
Nicholas Rowe

It is the constant fault and inseparable evil quality of ambition, that it never looks behind it.
Seneca

To be ambitious of true honor and of the real glory and perfection of our nature is the very principle and incentive of virtue; but to be ambitious of titles, place, ceremonial respects, and civil pageantry, is as vain and little as the things are which we court.
Sir Philip Sidney

Ambition is an idol on whose wings great minds are carried to extremes, to be sublimely great, or to be nothing.
Thomas Southerne

Ambition often puts men upon doing the meanest offices: so climbing is performed in the same posture as creeping.
Jonathan Swift

How like a mounting devil in the heart rules the unreined ambition.
Nathaniel Parker Willis

Ambition has but one reward for all:
A little power, a little transient fame,
A grave to rest in, and a fading name!

William Winter

Too low they build who build below the skies.

Edward Young

I'm a self-made man, but I think if I had it to do over again, I'd call in someone else.

Roland Young

See also: AIM, ASPIRATION, DESIRE, ENTER-
PRISE, IDEAL, INTENTION, PURPOSE,
SUCCESS, WORK.

AMERICA

If there is anything this nation has to give the world beyond its technological and organizational skill, it is surely that sense of expectancy which has possessed us and which, up to this time, we have never completely lost.

James Donald Adams

We can prate as we like about the idealism of America, but it is only money success which really counts.

James Truslow Adams

America, thou half-brother of the world;
With something good and bad of every land.

Philip James Bailey

America is the country where you buy a lifetime supply of aspirin for one dollar and use it up in two weeks.

John Barrymore

America has never forgotten and will never forget—the nobler things that brought her into being and that light her path—the path that was entered upon only one hundred and fifty years ago. . . . How young she is! It will be centuries before she will adopt that maturity of custom—the clothing of the grave —that some people believe she is already fitted for.

Bernard Mannes Baruch

America has been the intellectual battle-ground of the nations.

Randolph Silliman Bourne

America has believed that in differentiation, not in uniformity, lies the path of progress. It acted on this belief; it has advanced human happiness, and it has prospered.

Louis Dembitz Brandeis

Half the misunderstandings between Britain and America are due to the fact that neither will regard the other as what it is—in an important sense of the word—a foreign country. Each thinks of the other as a part of itself which has somehow gone off the lines. . . . What would have been pardonable and even commendable in a foreigner is blame-worthy in a cousin.

Sir John Buchan

Let America realize that self-scrutiny is not treason, self-examination is not disloyalty.

Richard James Cushing

This Administration believes that we must not and need not tolerate a boom-and-bust America. We believe that America's prosperity does not and need not depend upon war or the preparation for war.

Dwight David Eisenhower

America is another name for opportunity. Our whole history appears like a last effort of divine Providence in behalf of the human race.

Ralph Waldo Emerson

America is showing some signs of that fatal presumption, that overextension of power and mission, which brought ruin to ancient Athens, to Napoleonic France and to Nazi Germany.

James William Fulbright

Having done so much and succeeded so well, America is now at that historical point at which a great nation is in danger of losing its perspective on what is within the realm of its power and what is beyond it.

James William Fulbright

The source of a nation's strength is its domestic life, and if America has a service to perform in the world it is in large part the service of its own example.

James William Fulbright

If all Europe were to become a prison, America would still present a loop-hole of escape; and, God be praised! that loop-hole is larger than the dungeon itself.

Heinrich Heine

America—a place where the people have the right to complain about the lack of freedom.

Louis Hirsch

The American system of rugged individualism.

Herbert Clark Hoover

A great social and economic experiment, noble in motive and far-reaching in purpose.
Herbert Clark Hoover

Let America be America again,
Let it be the dream it used to be.
(James) Langston Hughes

I am certain that, however great the hardships and the trials which loom ahead, our America will endure and the cause of human freedom will triumph.
Cordell Hull

America has meant to the world a land in which the common man who means well and is willing to do his part has access to all the necessary means of a good life.
Alvin Saunders Johnson

If there is one word that describes our form of society in America, it may be the word— voluntary.
Lyndon Baines Johnson

Judge America not by the extremists, but by the great majority of Americans—of all races— who live in peace with their fellow man. Judge America by the typical family, for you will not see it anywhere else on earth. Judge America by her accomplishments and by her potential which is even greater.
Lyndon Baines Johnson

Robert Kennedy affirmed this country, affirmed the essential decency of its people, their longing for peace, their desire to improve conditions of life for all. During his life, he knew far more than his share of personal tragedy. Yet he never abandoned his faith in America.
Lyndon Baines Johnson

This nation has never left the field of battle in abject surrender of a cause for which it has fought. We shall not do so now [Vietnamese War].
Lyndon Baines Johnson

We will serve all of the nation, not one section or one sector, or one group, but all Americans. These are the *United* States—a united people with a united purpose.
Lyndon Baines Johnson

I believe in an America where religious intolerance will someday end—where all men and all churches are treated as equal—where every man has the same right to attend or not to attend the church of his choice—where

there is no Catholic vote, no anti-Catholic vote . . . and where Catholics, Protestants, and Jews . . . will refrain from those attitudes of disdain and division which have so often marred their works in the past, and promote instead the American ideal of brotherhood.
John Fitzgerald Kennedy

We in this country, in this generation, are— by destiny rather than choice—the watchmen on the walls of world freedom. We ask, therefore, that we may be worthy of our power and responsibility—that we may exercise our strength with wisdom and restraint —and that we may achieve in our time and for all time the ancient vision of peace on earth, goodwill toward men. That must always be our goal—and the righteousness of our cause must always underlie our strength. For as was written long ago: "Except the Lord keep the city, the watchman waketh but in vain."
John Fitzgerald Kennedy

All the sparrows on the roof-top are crying about the fact that the most imperialist nation that is supporting the colonial regime in the colonies is the United States of America and (the US representative) is indignant over that. What innocence, may I ask, is being played here when it is known that this virtuous damsel has already got a dozen illegitimate children?
Nikita Sergeevich Khruschev

America is a tune. It must be sung together.
Gerald Stanley Lee

Intellectually I know that America is no better than any other country; emotionally I know she is better than every country.
Sinclair Lewis

In general, we have been too generous in the gift of office and power . . . to men who do not understand the genius of America and who have little awareness of the backgrounds of the American way of life. . . . Most of us will agree that it makes little difference where or when a man was born if he had this vivid sense of American history, if he has learned to put Country above Party, . . . if freedom means more than personal security and if he refuses to tolerate appeasement of tyranny as the price of peace.
McIlyar Hamilton Lichliter

The genius of America is in its ability to make adjustments. That was the condition of conquering a virgin continent. . . . We are adaptable, and because we are adaptable, we are strong.

David Eli Lilienthal

Our society in America is founded . . . upon a faith in man as an end in itself.

David Eli Lilienthal

Unearned security during a long century had the effect upon our national habits of mind which the lazy enjoyment of unearned income so often has upon the descendants of a hard-working grandfather. It caused us to forget that man has to earn his security and his liberty as he has to earn his living.

Walter Lippmann

I would rather see the United States respected than loved by other nations.

Henry Cabot Lodge

It is worth saying once again that no nation has ever come into the possession of such powers for good or ill, for freedom or tyranny, for friendship or enmity among the peoples of the world, and that no nation in history has used those powers, by and large, with greater vision, restraint, responsibility and courage.

London Times

It was in making education not only common to all, but in some sense compulsory on all, that the destiny of the free republics of America was practically settled.

James Russell Lowell

If there is a country in the world where concord, according to common calculation, would be least expected, it is America. Made up, as it is, of people from different nations, accustomed to different form and habits of government, speaking different languages, and more different in their modes of worship, it would appear that the union of such a people was impracticable. But by the simple operation of constructing government on the principles of society and the rights of man, every difficulty retires, and the parts are brought into cordial unison.

Thomas Paine

This is what I call the American idea, a government of the people, by the people, and for the people—a government of the principles of eternal justice, the unchanging law of God.

Theodore Parker

The child of two continents, America can be explained in its significant traits by neither alone.

Vernon Louis Parrington

The educated American is profoundly skeptical about machines, inclined to regard every invention as obsolescent as soon as it has been made, but naïvely trustful about political platitudes or philosophical half-truths.

Eustace Percy

The American may not be a materialist but he has certainly hallowed commercialism, and made of it both a romantic and a moral adventure.

Agnes Repplier

I believe the major threats to our country come from within, not from without. These threats are a decline in religious conviction, decline in moral character, decline in the quality of family life and in our understanding of the principle of personal responsibility.

George Romney

I pledge you—I pledge myself—to a new deal for the American people.

Franklin Delano Roosevelt

An ordering of society which relegates religion, democracy and good faith among nations to the background can find no place within it for the ideals of the Prince of Peace. The United States rejects such an ordering, and retains its ancient faith.

Franklin Delano Roosevelt

Our country, right or wrong. When right, to be kept right; when wrong, to be put right.

Carl Schurz

There is a New America every morning when we wake up. It is upon us whether we will it or not. The New America is the sum of many small changes—a new subdivision here, a new school there, a new industry where there had been swampland—changes that add up to a broad transformation of our lives. Our task is to guide these changes. For, though change is inevitable, change for the better is a full-time job.

Adlai Ewing Stevenson

We in this country are committed to narrowing the gap between promise and performance, between equality in law and equality in fact, between opportunity for the well-to-do and opportunity for the poor, between education for the successful and education for the whole people.

Adlai Ewing Stevenson

With the supermarket as our temple and the singing commercial as our litany, are we likely to fire the world with an irresistible vision of America's exalted purposes and inspiring way of life?

Adlai Ewing Stevenson

The reason American cities are prosperous is that there is no place to sit down.

Alfred Joseph Talley

To us Americans much has been given; of us much is required. With all our faults and mistakes, it is our strength in support of the freedom our forefathers loved which has saved mankind from subjection to totalitarian power.

Norman Mattoon Thomas

We are proud still to call ours a young nation. Hence we forget what we should remember: Our nation under the present Constitution has had a longer life unchallenged and unchanged by violent rebellion than any great nation on earth except Great Britain.

Norman Matton Thomas

America is a large, friendly dog in a very small room. Every time it wags its tail, it knocks over a chair.

Arnold Joseph Toynbee

America has proved that it is practicable to elevate the mass of mankind—the laboring or lower class—to raise them to self-respect, to make them competent to act a part in the great right and the great duty of self-government; and she has proved that this may be done by education and the diffusion of knowledge. She holds out an example a thousand times more encouraging than ever was presented before to those nine-tenths of the human race who are born without hereditary fortune or hereditary rank.

Daniel Webster

We have now at last grasped the hardest of all the truths this nation has had to learn; however remote the aggression, however distant the social or economic disasters that afflict other peoples, sooner or later we ourselves will feel their impact.

Sumner Welles

In America you must live life with a smile, even before your toothbrush has had time to reach your mouth.

William (Vilhelm), Prince of Sweden

If the American dream is for Americans only, it will remain our dream and never be our destiny.

René de Visme Williamson

America is not a mere body of traders; it is a body of free men. Our greatness is built upon our freedom—is moral, not material. We have a great ardor for gain; but we have a deep passion for the rights of man.

(Thomas) Woodrow Wilson

America lives in the heart of every man everywhere who wishes to find a region where he will be free to work out his destiny as he chooses.

(Thomas) Woodrow Wilson

Joy is a fruit that Americans eat green.

Armando Zegri Cespedes

See also: AMERICANA, AMERICANISM, AMERICANS, NATION, PRESIDENT.

AMERICANA

Symphonies in bars and cabs, classical drama on television any day of the week, highbrow paperbacks in mountainous profusion (easier to buy than to read), "art seminars in the home," capsule operas . . . this cornucopia thrust at the inexperienced and pouring out its contents over us all deadens attention and keeps taste still-born, like any form of gross feeding.

Jacques Martin Barzun

And this is good old Boston,
The home of the bean and the cod,
Where the Lowells talk to the Cabots,
And the Cabots talk only to God.

John Collins Bossidy

The Middle West is the apotheosis of American civilization.

Randolph Silliman Bourne

The American imagination releases itself very easily in the short story—and has done so since the beginning of our national history. We have been a country of tall-tale tellers, and swappers of anecdotes, certainly since the frontier began to move westward.

Henry Seidel Canby

This four-year tragedy [the Civil War] . . . is the Hamlet and King Lear of the American past . . . and the strange thing is that it does not leave us depressed, disheartened, or discouraged. It is precisely through the great tragedies that we get our most significant and uplifting experience.

(Charles) Bruce Catton

There is and has long been . . . a special bond between New York and me. . . . How often, at difficult moments, I looked to New York, I listened to New York, to find out what you were thinking and feeling here, and always I found a comforting echo.

Charles André Joseph Marie de Gaulle

A good many of us today are content to be fat, dumb and happy. With a polyunsaturated diet of the coming 35-hour week, the fly-now-pay-later vacation, and fringe benefits, many of us live in a chromium-plated world where the major enemy we face is crab-grass.

John Herschel Glenn

You must learn the American language, if you want to understand the American people.

Thomas Chandler Haliburton

Science and time and necessity have propelled us, the United States, to be the general store for the world, dealers in everything. Most of all, merchants for a better way of life.

Claudia Alta (Lady Bird) Johnson

The exercise of power in this century has meant for all of us in the United States not arrogance but agony. We have used our power not willingly and recklessly ever, but always reluctantly and with restraint.

Lyndon Baines Johnson

We get our economic services in the way that at the time seems to work best. . . . We do not start with all the economic or political answers. We make up the answers as we go along. . . . The fact is that we have hardly an ounce of economic dogmatism in us.

David Eli Lilienthal

A great variety of collective activities provided substitute pageantry to a society which had eschewed kings, nobility and courts. What Americans called "togetherness" was part of their mystique. Rooted in vehement and intransigent individualism, they became more than any other Western people, a collectivity.

Malcolm Muggeridge

It was, they told themselves, the American century. And so it was, in the sense that what they had all mankind wanted. Along the wide turnpike roads their cars endlessly processed; the appurtenances of affluence poured in a quenchless stream from industry's bountiful conveyor-belt. Madison Avenue experts easily persuaded them to want more, and to consume more. Television screens held up to them the image of their own well-being. Their way of life was the blueprint on which all other ways of life, including the Communists, were based. They were rich, and if wealth was power, then they were powerful indeed. But was it?

Malcolm Muggeridge

Our national flower is the concrete cloverleaf.

Lewis Mumford

Poets have celebrated the wit and sonority of the names of American towns, but to our way of thinking they are not a patch on the telephone exchanges of New York. We linger over the rippling liquefaction of "SUsquehanna," the sturdiness of "MOnument," the liveliness of "SPring." We dote on forthright "CAnal" and sing of sweet "LOrraine." These are names to dial and conjure with. And what of our rich legacy from an OLder CIvilization —stirring names like "TRafalgar," "OXford," "WHitehall," "CHelsea," and "REgent"? Is this great tradition to be curtailed on behalf of intercity dialing?

New Yorker

Our American keynote . . . a certain generosity; a certain carelessness, or looseness, if you will; a hatred of the sordid; an ability to forget the part for the sake of the whole; a desire for largeness; a willingness to stand exposed.

Ezra Loomis Pound

Always the path of American destiny has been into the unknown. Always there arose enough of reserves of strength, balances of sanity, portions of wisdom to carry the nation through to a fresh start with ever-renewing vitality.

Carl Sandburg

The pneumatic noisemaker is becoming the emblematic Sound of New York, the way the bells of Big Ben are the Sound of London.

Horace Ashley Sutton

Air-conditioning has bequeathed America a new—some say even better—reading season.

People with brains spend the summer in their non-sweat, air-conditioned cars, offices, and homes, reaching for a good book instead of a hot beer, leaving the delights of ant-ridden picnics . . . to those who would rather burn their skins than illuminate their minds.

Lon Tinkle

We want the spirit of America to be efficient; we want American character to be efficient; we want American character to display itself in what I may, perhaps, be allowed to call spiritual efficiency—clear disinterested thinking and fearless action along the right lines of thought.

(Thomas) Woodrow Wilson

See also: AMERICA, AMERICANISM, AMERICANS, BOSTON, NEW YORK.

AMERICANISM

Every effort to confine Americanism to a single pattern, to constrain it to a single formula, is disloyalty to everything that is valid to Americanism.

Henry Steele Commager

Of "Americanism" of the right sort we cannot have too much. Mere vaporing and boasting become a nation as little as a man. But honest, outspoken pride and faith in our country are infinitely better and more to be respected than the cultivated reserve which sets it down as ill-bred and in bad taste ever to refer to our country except by way of deprecation, criticism, or general negation.

Henry Cabot Lodge

When an Office Holder, or one that has been found out, can't think of anything to deliver a speech on, he always falls back on the good old subject, Americanism.

Will (William Penn Adair) Rogers

See also: AMERICA, AMERICANA, AMERICANS.

AMERICANS

The greatest—and, too often, overlooked—resources this country has at its command today are the compassion, concern, and commonsense of our citizens.

Gordon Llewellyn Allott

If Americans could only believe in America.

Raymond Clapper

The actual God of many Americans, perhaps of most, is simply the current of American life, which is large and hopeful enough to employ all the idealism they have.

Charles Horton Cooley

The general belief still is that Americans are not destined to renounce, but to enjoy.

Herbert Croly

Americans want a good standard of living—not simply to accumulate possessions, but to fulfill a legitimate aspiration for an environment in which their families may live meaningful and happy lives. Our people are committed, therefore, to the creation and preservation of opportunity for every citizen, opportunity to lead a more rewarding life. They are equally committed to our alleviation of unavoidable misfortune and distress among their fellow citizens.

Dwight David Eisenhower

An American is one who loves justice and believes in the dignity of man.

Harold Le Claire Ickes

An American is one who will fight for his freedom and that of his neighbor.

Harold Le Claire Ickes

An American is one who will sacrifice property, ease and security in order that he and his children may retain the rights of free men.

Harold Le Claire Ickes

Americans are prosperous as men have never been in recorded history. Yet, there is in the land a certain restlessness, a questioning.

Lyndon Baines Johnson

The American people have a genius for splendid and unselfish action, and into the hands of America God has placed the destinies of afflicted humanity.

Pius XII (Eugenio Pacelli)

The American people never carry an umbrella. They prepare to walk in eternal sunshine.

Alfred Emanuel Smith

See also: AMERICA, AMERICANA, AMERICANISM, CITIZENSHIP, LOYALTY.

AMIABILITY

When the righteous man turneth away from his righteousness that he hath committed and doeth that which is neither quite lawful nor quite right, he will generally be found to have gained in amiability what he has lost in holiness.

Samuel Butler

To be amiable is most certainly a duty, but it is not to be exercised at the expense of any virtue. He who seeks to do the amiable always, can at times be successful only by the sacrifice of his manhood.

William Gilmore Simms

How easy to be amiable in the midst of happiness and success.

Anne Sophie Swetchine

See also: CHEERFULNESS, GOOD HUMOR, GOOD NATURE.

AMUSEMENT

If those who are the enemies of innocent amusements had the direction of the world, they would take away the spring and youth, the former from the year, the latter from human life.

Honoré de Balzac

Amusement to an observing mind is study.

Benjamin Disraeli

Dwell not too long upon sports; for as they refresh a man that is weary, so they weary a man that is refreshed.

Thomas Fuller

Christian discipleship does not involve the abandonment of any innocent enjoyment. Any diversion or amusement which we can use so as to receive pleasure and enjoyment to ourselves, and do no harm to others, we are perfectly free to use; and any that we cannot use without injury to ourselves or harm to others, we have no right to use, whether we are Christians or not.

(Solomon) Washington Gladden

I am a great friend to public amusements, for they keep people from vice.

Samuel Johnson

Amusement that is excessive and followed only for its own sake, allures and deceives us, and leads us down imperceptibly in thoughtlessness to the grave.

Blaise Pascal

The mind ought sometimes to be diverted, that it may return the better to thinking.

Phaedrus

All amusements to which virtuous women are not admitted, are, rely upon it, deleterious in their nature.

William Makepeace Thackeray

See also: CARDS, DANCE, DIVERSION, PLEASURE, RECREATION, THEATER.

ANALOGY

Though analogy is often misleading, it is the least misleading thing we have.

Samuel Butler

Analogy, although it is not infallible, is yet that telescope of the mind by which it is marvelously assisted in the discovery of both physical and moral truth.

Charles Caleb Colton

Those who reason only by analogies, rarely reason by logic, and are generally slaves to imagination.

Charles Simmons

Analogy is milk for babes, but abstract truths are strong meat.

Martin Farquhar Tupper

See also: COMPARISON, SIMILARITY.

ANARCHY

Anarchy is the choking, sweltering, deadly, and killing rule of no rule; the consecration of cupidity and braying of folly and dim stupidity and baseness, in most of the affairs of men. Slop-shirts attainable three half-pence cheaper by the ruin of living bodies and immortal souls.

Thomas Carlyle

Anarchy is hatred of human authority; atheism of divine authority—two sides of the same whole.

James Macpherson

When the rich assemble to concern themselves with the business of the poor it is called charity. When the poor assemble to concern themselves with the business of the rich it is called anarchy.

Paul Richard

There lives no greater fiend than Anarchy;
She ruins states, turns houses out of doors,
Breaks up in rout the embattled soldiery.

Sophocles

See also: COMMUNISM, CRIME, FREEDOM, REVOLUTION, RIOT, TERROR, VIOLENCE.

ANCESTRY

Honorable descent is, in all nations, greatly esteemed. It is to be expected that the children of men of worth will be like the progenitors; for nobility is the virtue of a family.

Aristotle

Some decent, regulated pre-eminence, some preference given to birth, is neither unnatural nor unjust nor impolitic.

Edmund Burke

We inherit nothing truly, but what our actions make us worthy of.

George Chapman

It is a shame for a man to desire honor only because of his noble progenitors, and not to deserve it by his own virtue.

John Chrysostom

It is with antiquity as with ancestry, nations are proud of the one, and individuals of the other; but if they are nothing in themselves, that which is their pride ought to be their humiliation.

Charles Caleb Colton

Nobility of birth does not always insure a corresponding nobility of mind; if it did, it would always act as a stimulus to noble actions; but it sometimes acts as a clog rather than a spur.

Charles Caleb Colton

It is of no consequence of what parents a man is born, so he be a man of merit.

Horace

It is the highest of earthly honors to be descended from the great and good. They alone cry out against a noble ancestry who have none of their own.

Ben (Benjamin) Jonson

He that can only boast of a distinguished lineage, boast of that which does not belong to himself; but he that lives worthily of it is always held in the highest honor.

Junius

It is fortunate to come of distinguished ancestry. It is not less so to be such that people do not care to inquire whether you are of high descent or not.

Jean de La Bruyère

Some men by ancestry are only the shadow of a mighty name.

Lucan

It would be more honorable to our distinguished ancestors to praise them in words less, but in deeds to imitate them more.

Horace Mann

Blood will tell but often it tells too much.

Donald Robert Perry (Don) Marquis

Birth is nothing where virtue is not.

Molière (Jean Baptiste Poquelin)

Everyone has ancestors and it is only a question of going back far enough to find a good one.

Howard Kenneth Nixon

The man who has nothing to boast of but his illustrious ancestry, is like the potato—the best part under ground.

Sir Thomas Overbury

Nothing is more disgraceful than for a man who is nothing, to hold himself honored on account of his forefathers; and yet hereditary honors are a noble and splendid treasure to descendants.

Plato

Remember, remember always, that all of us, and you and I especially, are descended from immigrants and revolutionists.

Franklin Delano Roosevelt

Consider whether we ought not to be more in the habit of seeking honor from our descendants than from our ancestors; thinking it better to be nobly remembered than nobly born; and striving so to live, that our sons, and our sons' sons, for ages to come, might still lead their children reverently to the doors out of which we had been carried to the grave, saying, "Look, this was his house, this was his chamber."

John Ruskin

The glory of ancestors sheds a light around posterity; it allows neither their good or bad qualities to remain in obscurity.

Sallust

The environment fosters and selects; the seed must contain the potentiality and direction of the life to be selected.

George Santayana

What can we see in the longest kingly line in Europe, save that it runs back to a successful soldier?

Sir Walter Scott

The origin of all mankind was the same: it is only a clear and good conscience that makes a man noble, for that is derived from heaven itself.

Seneca

How poor are all hereditary honors, those poor possessions from another's deeds, unless our own just virtues form our title, and give a sanction to our fond assumption.

James Shirley

Mere family never made a man great. Thought and deed, not pedigree, are the passports to enduring fame.

Mikhail Dmitrievich Skobelev

The happiest lot for a man, as far as birth is concerned, is that it should be such as to give him but little occasion to think much about it.

Richard Whately

Pride in boasting of family antiquity, makes duration stand for merit.

Johann Georg von Zimmerman

See also: BIRTH, NOBILITY, PARENTS, SNOB.

ANECDOTE

Some people exclaim, "Give me no anecdotes of an author, but give me his works"; and yet I have often found that the anecdotes are more interesting than the works.

Benjamin Disraeli

That when a man fell into his anecdotage, it was a sign for him to retire.

Benjamin Disraeli

Anecdotes are sometimes the best vehicles of truth, and if striking and appropriate are often more impressive and powerful than argument.

Tryon Edwards

Occasionally a single anecdote opens a character; biography has its comparative anatomy, and a saying or a sentiment enables the skillful hand to construct the skeleton.

Robert Eldridge Aris Willmott

See also: BIOGRAPHY, STORYTELLING.

ANGEL

The angels may have wider spheres of action and nobler forms of duty than ourselves, but truth and right to them and to us are one and the same thing.

Edwin Hubbel Chapin

We are never like angels till our passion dies.

Thomas Dekker

Millions of spiritual creatures walk the earth unseen, both when we sleep and when we wake.

John Milton

The guardian angels of life sometimes fly so high as to be beyond our sight, but they are always looking down upon us.

Jean Paul Richter

See also: DEVIL, GOD, HEAVEN, SPIRIT.

ANGER

Men often make up in wrath what they want in reason.

William Rounseville Alger

A hundred years before there was any scientific psychiatry, there was a famous doctor in England by the name of John Hunter. Dr. Hunter had a heart attack which nearly killed him. Being a good physician, he knew even in those days the importance of the emotions in affecting the heart. When he recovered, he said: "My life is in the hands of any rascal who chooses to annoy and tease me!" He was unable to keep his temper, however, and one day he became angry and dropped dead. Though his death was caused by his emotions, it was not imaginary. His temper brought on a very real blood clot in the wall of his heart.

Eric Berne

I was angry with my friend;
I told my wrath, my wrath did end.
I was angry with my foe;
I told it not, my wrath did grow.

William Blake

Violence in the voice is often only the death rattle of reason in the throat.

John Frederick Boyes

Life appears to me too short to be spent in nursing animosity or registering wrong.

Charlotte Brontë

An angry man opens his mouth and closes his eyes.

Cato the Elder

The fire you kindle for your enemy often burns yourself more than him.

Chinese Proverb

The intoxication of anger, like that of the grape, shows us to others, but hides us from ourselves. We injure our own cause in the opinion of the world when we too passionately defend it.

Charles Caleb Colton

When anger rises, think of the consequences.

Confucius

Beware of the fury of a patient man.

John Dryden

Moslem Spain had seventy libraries; rich men displayed their Morocco bindings, and bibliophiles collected rare or beautifully illuminated books. The scholar al-Hadram, at an auction in Cordova, found himself persistently outbid for a book he desired, until the price offered far exceeded the value of the volume. The successful bidder explained that there was a vacant place in his library, into which this book would precisely fit. "I was so vexed," adds al-Hadram, "that I could not help saying to him, 'He gets the nut who has no teeth' (Maqqari, II, 3)."

Will (William James) Durant

To rule one's anger is well; to prevent it is still better.

Tryon Edwards

Anger and intolerance are the twin enemies of correct understanding.

Mohandas Karamchand (Mahatma) Gandhi

Anger is a sort of madness and the noblest causes have been damaged by advocates affected with temporary lunacy.

Mohandas Karamchand (Mahatma) Gandhi

I do sometimes become extremely angry with myself but I also pray to be delivered from that devil and God has given me power to suppress my anger.

Mohandas Karamchand (Mahatma) Gandhi

It is not that I do not get angry. I do not give vent to anger. I cultivate the quality of patience as angerlessness, and generally speaking, succeed. But I only control my anger when it comes.

Mohandas Karamchand (Mahatma) Gandhi

Anger, even when it punishes the faults of delinquents, ought not to precede reason as its mistress, but attend as a handmaid at the back of reason, to come to the front when bidden. For once it begins to take control of the mind, it calls just what it does cruelly.

Gregory I (Gregory the Great)

Anger may be kindled in the noblest breasts; but in these the slow droppings of an unforgiving temper never take the shape and consistency of enduring hatred.

George Stillman Hillard

When angry, count ten before you speak; if very angry, count a hundred.

Thomas Jefferson

The flame of anger, bright and brief, sharpens the barb of love.

Walter Savage Landor

Anger ventilated often hurries towards forgiveness; anger concealed often hardens into revenge.

Edward G. Bulwer-Lytton (Baron Lytton)

Anger is as a stone cast into a wasp's nest.

Malabar Proverb

Consider how much more you often suffer from your anger and grief, than from those very things for which you are angry and grieved.

Marcus Aurelius

The worst tempered people I've ever met were people who knew they were wrong.

Wilson Mizner

All anger is not sinful, because some degree of it, and on some occasions, is inevitable. But it becomes sinful and contradicts the rule of Scripture when it is conceived upon slight and inadequate provocation, and when it continues long.

William Paley

Temperate anger well becomes the wise.

Philemon

He best keeps from anger who remembers that God is always looking upon him.

Plato

Frequent fits of anger produce in the soul a propensity to be angry; which ofttimes ends in choler, bitterness, and morosity, when the mind becomes ulcerated, peevish, and querulous, and is wounded by the least occurrence.

Plutarch

To be angry is to revenge the faults of others on ourselves.

Alexander Pope

An angry man is again angry with himself when he returns to reason.

Pubilius Syrus

Anger begins in folly, and ends in repentance.

Pythagoras

Beware of him that is slow to anger; for when it is long coming, it is the stronger when it comes, and the longer kept. Abused patience turns to fury.

Francis Quarles

Keep cool and you command everybody.

Louis Antoine Léon de Saint-Just

Anger raises invention, but it overheats the oven.

George Savile (Marquis of Halifax)

He that would be angry and sin not, must not be angry with anything but sin.

Thomas Secker

Anger, if not restrained, is frequently more hurtful to us than the injury that provokes it.

Seneca

The greatest remedy for anger is delay.

Seneca

Queen Elizabeth, who knew something about hot temper, once said to a courtier who had lost his head, "Ah, Sir Philip, anger often makes men witty but it always keeps them poor."

Ralph Washington Sockman

It's far better to make people angry than to make them ashamed.

Sir Rabindranath Tagore

You can meet an opinion by another opinion, or one argument by another, but in matters in which the understanding is concerned it is barbarous to try and use anger as a punishment.

Sir Rabindranath Tagore

Anger is a noble infirmity; the generous failing of the just; the one degree that riseth above zeal, asserting the prerogative of virtue.

Martin Farquhar Tupper

See also: AGGRESSION, DISSENT, PASSION, QUARREL, RAGE, RESENTMENT.

ANGLICANISM

The true Church of England, at this moment, lies in the Editors of its newspapers. These preach to the people daily, weekly.

Thomas Carlyle

I die a Christian, according to the Profession of the Church of England, as I found it left me by my Father.

Charles I of Great Britain

Sir Richard Steele has observed that there is this difference between the Church of Rome and the Church of England: the one professes to be infallible—the other to be never in the wrong.

Charles Caleb Colton

The Church of England is not a mere depositary of doctrine.

Benjamin Disraeli

I was brought up in the Church of England and in the High Church party which is much the best religion I have ever come across. But Lemprière's "Classical Dictionary," read when I was eight, made me prefer paganism to Christianity; I abandoned Christianity at thirteen, and became an atheist at twenty-one.

Alfred Edward Housman

The Archbishop of Canterbury has encouraged Anglicans to work for the time when they will merge their uniqueness in the restoration of the visible unity of the church; this goal they are to strive for by rigorously maintaining their links with both their Protestant and their Catholic ancestry.

David Jenkins

The hope is that Anglicanism will continue to be a historically produced unique amalgam of a Catholic and Reformed understanding of authority, continuity, and freedom.

David Jenkins

And so I recognize in the Anglican Church a time-honored institution of noble historical memories, a monument of ancient wisdom, a momentous arm of political strength, a great national organ, a source of vast popular advantage, and, to a certain point, a witness and teacher of religious truth. . . . But that it is something sacred, that it is an oracle of revealed doctrine, that it can claim a share in St. Ignatius or St. Cyprian, that it can take the rank, contest the teaching, and stop the path of the Church of St. Peter, that it can call itself "the bride of the Lamb," this is the view of it which simply disappeared from my mind on my conversion, and which it would be almost a miracle to reproduce.

John Henry Newman

When an Anglican is asked, "Where was your Church before the Reformation?" his best answer is to put the counter-question, "Where was your face before you washed it?"

Arthur Michael Ramsey

"The Church of England," I said, seeing that Mr. Inglesant paused, "is no doubt a compromise."

Joseph Henry Shorthouse

"Place before your eyes two precepts, and two only. One is Preach the Gospel; and the other is—*Put down enthusiasm*" [From Archbishop Manners Sutton's valedictory speech on Bishop Heber's consecration to the See of Calcutta] . . . The Church of England in a nutshell.

Mary Augusta Ward (Mrs. Humphrey Ward)

See also: CHRISTIANITY, CHURCH, ENGLAND.

ANIMAL

Physiological experiment on animals is justifiable for real investigation, but not for mere damnable and detestable curiosity.

Charles Robert Darwin

There is no fundamental difference between man and the higher animals in their mental faculties.

Charles Robert Darwin

They say that the first inclination which an animal has is to protect itself.

Diogenes Laertius

All animals are equal, but some animals are more equal than others.

George Orwell (Eric Blair)

Nothing can be more obvious than that all animals were created solely and exclusively for the use of man.

Thomas Love Peacock

Caesar once, seeing some wealthy strangers at Rome, carrying up and down with them in their arms and bosoms young puppy-dogs and monkeys, embracing and making much of them, took occasion not unnaturally to ask whether the women in their country were not used to bear children.

Plutarch

Let dogs delight to bark and bite,
For God hath made them so;
Let bears and lions growl and fight,
For 'tis their nature too.

Isaac Watts

See also: APE, ASS, BEE, CAT, COW, DOG, ELEPHANT, HORSE, LAMB, LION, MOUSE, OX, PIG, SHEEP, SNAKE.

ANNOYANCE

Speak roughly to your little boy,
    And beat him when he sneezes;
He only does it to annoy,
    Because he knows it teases.

Lewis Carroll (Charles Lutwidge Dodgson)

Petty vexations may at times be petty, but still they are vexations. The smallest and most inconsiderable annoyances are the most piercing. As small letters weary the eyes most, so also the smallest affairs disturb us most.

Michel Eyquem de Montaigne

Petty repeated annoyances, arising from unpleasantness or incongruity of character, have been the occasion of such estrangement as to make it impossible for man and wife to live together with any content.

Plutarch

See also: ANGER, RESENTMENT.

ANSWER

What is truth? said jesting Pilate; and would not stay for an answer.

Francis Bacon

Examinations are formidable even to the best prepared, for the greatest fool may ask more than the wisest man can answer.

Charles Caleb Colton

Ah, what a dusty answer gets the soul
When hot for certainties in this our life!

George Meredith

She who ne'er answers till a husband cools,
Or if she rules him, never shows she rules.

Alexander Pope

An answer is invariably the parent of a great family of new questions.

John Ernst Steinbeck

See also: ARGUMENT, KNOWLEDGE, QUESTION.

ANTAGONISM

He that wrestles with us strengthens our nerves, and sharpens our skill. Our antagonist is our helper.

Edmund Burke

In a world which exists by the balance of Antagonism, the respective merit of the Conservator or the Innovator must ever remain debatable.

Thomas Carlyle

In proportion as the antagonism between classes within the nation vanishes, the hostility of one nation to another will come to an end.

Karl Marx

See also: AGGRESSION, ANGER, CONTROVERSY, DIFFERENCE, OPPOSITION.

ANTICIPATION

Draw your Salary before Spending it.
George Ade

Sorrow itself is not so hard to bear as the thought of sorrow coming. Airy ghosts that work no harm do terrify us more than men in steel with bloody purposes.
Thomas Bailey Aldrich

Nothing is so good as it seems beforehand.
George Eliot (Mary Ann Evans)

All earthly delights are sweeter in expectation than in enjoyment; but all spiritual pleasures more in fruition than in expectation.
Owen Felltham

Among so many sad realities we can but ill endure to rob anticipation of its pleasant visions.
Henry Giles

To tremble before anticipated evils, is to bemoan what thou hast never lost.
Johann Wolfgang von Goethe

The hours we pass with happy prospects in view are more pleasant than those crowned with fruition. In the first case we cook the dish to our own appetite; in the last it is cooked for us.
Oliver Goldsmith

We part more easily with what we possess than with our expectations of what we hope for: expectation always goes beyond enjoyment.
Henry Home (Lord Kames)

Few enterprises of great labor or hazard would be undertaken if we had not the power of magnifying the advantages we expect from them.
Samuel Johnson

It is worse to apprehend than to suffer.
Jean de La Bruyère

Our desires always disappoint us; for though we meet with something that gives us satisfaction, yet it never thoroughly answers our expectation.
Duc François de La Rochefoucauld

It has been well said that no man ever sank under the burden of the day. It is when to-morrow's burden is added to the burden of to-day that the weight is more than a man can bear.
George Macdonald

Why need a man forestall his date of grief, and run to meet that he would most avoid?
John Milton

He who foresees calamities, suffers them twice over.
Beilby Porteus

Suffering itself does less afflict the senses than the anticipation of suffering.
Quintilian

We often tremble at an empty terror, yet the false fancy brings a real misery.
Johann Christoph Friedrich von Schiller

Nothing is so wretched or foolish as to anticipate misfortunes. What madness is it to be expecting evil before it comes.
Seneca

It is expectation makes blessings dear. Heaven were not heaven if we knew what it were.
Sir John Suckling

See also: EXPECTATION, FORETHOUGHT, HOPE, PURSUIT.

ANTIQUITY

When ancient opinions and rules of life are taken away, the loss cannot possibly be estimated. From that moment we have no compass to govern us, nor can we know distinctly to what port to steer.
Edmund Burke

Those old ages are like the landscape that shows best in the purple distance, all verdant and smooth, and bathed in mellow light.
Edwin Hubbel Chapin

Antiquity is enjoyed not by the ancients who lived in the infancy of things, but by us who live in their maturity.
Charles Caleb Colton

Those we call the ancients were really new in everything.

Blaise Pascal

Time consecrates and what is gray with age becomes religion.

Johann Christoph Friedrich von Schiller

All things now held to be old were once new. What to-day we hold up by example, will rank hereafter as precedent.

Tacitus

See also: AGE; AGE, OLD; HISTORY; MYTHOLOGY; PAST; RUINS; TIME; TRADITION.

ANTI-SEMITISM

Thus Anne Frank's voice was preserved out of the millions that were silenced. No louder than a child's whisper, it speaks for those millions and has outlasted the raucous shouts of the murderers, soaring above the clamorous voices of passing time.

Ernst Georg Schnabel

There is not the slightest ground for anti-Semitism among us.

William Howard Taft

They are not Jews in America; they are American citizens.

(Thomas) Woodrow Wilson

See also: BIGOTRY, ISRAEL, JEWS, JUDAISM, NAZISM, PREJUDICE.

ANXIETY

Never trouble trouble till trouble troubles you.

Anonymous

Anxiety is the poison of human life; the parent of many sins and of more miseries. In a world where everything is doubtful, and where we may be disappointed, and be blessed in disappointment, why this restless stir and commotion of mind? Can it alter the cause, or unravel the mystery of human events?

Hugh Blair

Where everything is bad it must be good to know the worst.

Francis Herbert Bradley

Better be despised for too anxious apprehensions, than ruined by too confident security.

Edmund Burke

Anxiety is a word of unbelief or unreasoning dread. We have no right to allow it. Full faith in God puts it to rest.

Horace Bushnell

We have a lot of anxieties, and one cancels out another very often.

Sir Winston Leonard Spencer Churchill

Sufficient to each day are the duties to be done and the trials to be endured. God never built a Christian strong enough to carry to-day's duties and to-morrow's anxieties piled on the top of them.

Theodore Ledyard Cuyler

Anxiety is the rust of life, destroying its brightness and weakening its power. A childlike and abiding trust in Providence is its best preventive and remedy.

Tryon Edwards

Do not anticipate trouble, or worry about what may never happen. Keep in the sunlight.

Benjamin Franklin

An undivided heart which worships God alone, and trusts him as it should, is raised above anxiety for earthly wants.

John Cunningham Geikie

If pleasures are greatest in anticipation, just remember that this is also true of trouble.

Elbert Green Hubbard

One of the most useless of all things is to take a deal of trouble in providing against dangers that never come. How many toil to lay up riches which they never enjoy; to provide for exigencies that never happen; to prevent troubles that never come; sacrificing present comfort and enjoyment in guarding against the wants of a period they may never live to see.

William Jay

How much have cost us the evils that never happened!

Thomas Jefferson

Borrow trouble for yourself, if that's your nature, but don't lend it to your neighbors.

Rudyard Kipling

Let us be of good cheer, remembering that the misfortunes hardest to bear are those which never come.

James Russell Lowell

Never meet trouble half-way.

John Ray

See *also*: CARE, FEAR, IMAGINATION, NEUROSIS, UNCERTAINTY, WORRY.

APATHY

Philosophy should always know that indifference is a militant thing. It batters down the walls of cities and murders the women and children amid the flames and the purloining of altar vessels. When it goes away it leaves smoking ruins, where lie citizens bayonetted through the throat. It is not a children's pastime like mere highway robbery.

Stephen Crane

The tyranny of a prince in an oligarchy is not as dangerous to the common good as the apathy of the citizens in a democracy.

Charles de Secondat (Baron de Montesquieu)

The long mechanic pacings to and fro,
The set gray life, the apathetic end.

Alfred, Lord Tennyson

See *also*: INDIFFERENCE, INSENSIBILITY.

APE

How like a hateful ape,
Detected, grinning, 'midst his pilfered hoard,
A cunning man appears, whose secert frauds
Are opened to the day!

Joanna Baillie

There was an Ape in the days that were earlier;
Centuries passed, and his hair became curlier;
Centuries more gave a thumb to his wrist—
Then he was Man—and a Positivist.

Mortimer Collins

An ape is an ape even though it wear golden ornaments.

Latin Proverb

See *also*: ANIMAL, EVOLUTION.

APHORISM

Aphorisms are portable wisdom, the quintessential extracts of thought and feeling.

William Rounseville Alger

Exclusively of the abstract sciences the largest and worthiest portion of our knowledge consists of aphorisms, and the greatest and best of men is but an aphorism.

Samuel Taylor Coleridge

The excellence of aphorisms consists not so much in the expression of some rare or abstruse sentiment, as in the comprehension of some useful truth in few words.

Samuel Johnson

The aphorism should be a light vessel holding a heavy load.

Jacob Klatzkin

See *also*: APOTHEGM, EPIGRAM, MAXIM, PROVERB, TRUISM.

APOLOGY

Apologies only account for the evil which they cannot alter.

Benjamin Disraeli

No sensible person ever made an apology.

Ralph Waldo Emerson

Apology is only egotism wrong side out. Nine times out of ten the first thing a man's companion knows of his short-comings, is from his apology.

Oliver Wendell Holmes

I do not trouble my spirit to vindicate itself . . . , I see the elementary laws never apologize.

Walt (Walter) Whitman

See *also*: BASHFULNESS, DEFERENCE, EXCUSE, HUMILITY, MEEKNESS, MODESTY, REGRET, REMORSE, REPENTANCE.

APOTHEGM

Nor do apothegms only serve for ornament and delight, but also for action and civil use, as being the edge tools of speech, which cut and penetrate the knots of business and affairs.

Francis Bacon

There are but few proverbial sayings that are not true, for they are all drawn from experience itself, which is the mother of all sciences.

Miguel de Cervantes Saavedra

He is a benefactor of mankind who contracts the great rules of life into short sentences, that may be easily impressed on the memory, and so recur habitually to the mind.

Samuel Johnson

Few of the many wise apothegms which have been uttered from the time of the seven sages of Greece to that of poor Richard, have prevented a single foolish action.

Thomas Babington Macauley

Nothing hits harder, or sticks longer in the memory, than an apothegm.

Sir James Augustus Henry Murray

Under the veil of these curious sentences are hid those germs of morals which the masters of philosophy have afterwards developed into so many volumes.

Plutarch

Apothegms to thinking minds are the seeds from which spring vast fields of new thought, that may be further cultivated, beautified, and enlarged.

Andrew Michael Ramsay

Sensible men show their sense by saying much in few words. If noble actions are the substance of life, good sayings are its ornament and guide.

Charles Simmons

See also: APHORISM, EPIGRAM, EPITAPH, MAXIM, PROVERB, QUOTATION, TRUISM, WORD.

APPAREL

Beauty when most unclothed is clothed best.

Phineas Fletcher

It sounds rather silly to attach so much importance to a head-dress. What is much more important is what is inside the head, not what is on top of it. But little things sometimes become symbols of big things.

Jawaharlal Nehru

No man is esteemed for gay garments but by fools and women.

Sir Walter Raleigh

She wears her clothes as if they were thrown on her with a pitchfork.

Jonathan Swift

The naked is without a credential, it's the made-up clothes that define us.

Sir Rabindranath Tagore

Let it be observed, that slovenliness is no part of religion; that neither this, nor any text of Scripture, condemns neatness of apparel. Certainly this is a duty, not a sin. "Cleanliness is, indeed, next to godliness."

John Wesley

See also: APPEARANCE, DRESS, FASHION.

APPEARANCE

Half the work that is done in this world is to make things appear what they are not.

Elias Root Beadle

Foolish men mistake transitory semblances for eternal fact, and go astray more and more.

Thomas Carlyle

The bosom can ache beneath diamond brooches; and many a blithe heart dances under coarse wool.

Edwin Hubbel Chapin

A graceful presence bespeaks acceptance.

John Collier

You are only what you are when no one is looking.

Robert Chambers (Bob) Edwards

An intelligent look in men is what regularity of features is in women: it is the kind of beauty to which the most vain may aspire.

Jean de La Bruyère

A man of the world must seem to be what he wishes to be thought.

Jean de La Bruyère

Beware, so long as you live, of judging men by their outward appearance.

Jean de La Fontaine

He who observes the speaker more than the sound of his words, will seldom meet with disappointments.

Johann Kaspar Lavater

The distinguishing characters of the face, and the lineaments of the body, grow more plain and visible with time and age; but the peculiar physiognomy of the mind is most discernible in children.

John Locke

With different persons, we may be quite different individuals. We cling, however, to the illusion that we remain identical for all persons and every situation.

Luigi Pirandello

You may turn into an archangel, a fool, or a criminal—no one will see it. But when a button is missing—everyone sees that.

Erich Maria Remarque

Your first appearance, he said to me, is the gauge by which you will be measured; try to manage that you may go beyond yourself in after times, but beware of ever doing less.

Jean Jacques Rousseau

There are no greater wretches in the world than many of those whom people in general take to be happy.

Seneca

The shortest and surest way to live with honor in the world, is to be in reality what we would appear to be.

Socrates

How little do they see what is, who frame their hasty judgments upon that which seems.

Robert Southey

There are fools who judge men by their outside.

Sir Rabindranath Tagore

You may judge a flower or a butterfly by its looks, but not a human being.

Sir Rabindranath Tagore

The world is governed more by appearances than by realities, so that it is fully as necessary to seem to know something as to know it.

Daniel Webster

See also: AFFECTATION, DRESS, FACE, FASHION, LOOKS.

APPETITE

Good cheer is no hindrance to a good life.

Aristippus

Animals feed; man eats. Only the man of intellect and judgment knows how to eat.

Anthelme Brillat-Savarin

Reason should direct and appetite obey.

Cicero

Temperance and labor are the two best physicians of man; labor sharpens the appetite, and temperance prevents from indulging to excess.

Jean Jacques Rousseau

A well-governed appetite is a great part of liberty.

Seneca

See also: BREAD, COOKING, DESIRE, DIET, DINNER, DRINK, EATING.

APPLAUSE

Man's first care should be to avoid the reproaches of his own heart, and next to escape the censures of the world. If the last interfere with the first it should be entirely neglected. But if not, there cannot be a greater satisfaction to an honest mind than to see its own approbation seconded by the applauses of the public.

Joseph Addison

Praise from the common people is generally false, and rather follows the vain than the virtuous.

Francis Bacon

Applause is the spur of noble minds; the end and aim of weak ones.

Charles Caleb Colton

Great minds had rather deserve contemporaneous applause without obtaining it, than obtain without deserving it. If it follow them it is well, but they will not deviate to follow it.

Charles Caleb Colton

When the million applaud you, seriously ask what harm you have done; when they censure you, what good!

Charles Caleb Colton

A slowness to applaud betrays a cold temper or an envious spirit.

Hannah More

Neither human applause nor human censure is to be taken as the test of truth; but either should set us upon testing ourselves.

Richard Whately

See also: APPRECIATION, COMPLIMENT, FAME, FLATTERY, PRAISE.

APPRECIATION

One of the Godlike things of this world is the veneration done to human worth by the hearts of men.

Thomas Carlyle

Contemporaries appreciate the man rather than the merit; but posterity will regard the merit rather than the man.

Charles Caleb Colton

We must never undervalue any person. The workman loves not to have his work despised in his presence. Now God is present everywhere, and every person is his work.

Francis of Sales

Next to invention is the power of interpreting invention; next to beauty the power of appreciating beauty.

Margaret Fuller (Marchioness Ossoli)

We are very much what others think of us. The reception our observations meet with gives us courage to proceed, or damps our efforts.

William Hazlitt

You will find poetry nowhere unless you bring some with you.

Joseph Joubert

It is with certain good qualities as with the senses; those who have them not can neither appreciate nor comprehend them in others.

Duc François de La Rochefoucauld

He is incapable of a truly good action who finds not a pleasure in contemplating the good actions of others.

Johann Kaspar Lavater

In proportion as our own mind is enlarged we discover a greater number of men of originality. Commonplace people see no difference between one man and another.

Blaise Pascal

Next to excellence is the appreciation of it.

William Makepeace Thackeray

See also: ADMIRATION, APPLAUSE, DISCERNMENT, ESTIMATION, GRATITUDE, SENSIBILITY, TASTE.

APPROACH

Gentle in manner, strong in performance.

Claudio Aquaviva

It is a fundamental rule of human life that, if the approach is good, the response is good.

Jawaharlal Nehru

A scientific approach is essential in whatever domain of life you are functioning. If you do not have the approach, you lose yourself, flounder and cannot make any progress at all.

Jawaharlal Nehru

See also: METHOD, POINT OF VIEW.

APRIL

Oh, to be in England
Now that April's there

Robert Browning

Whan that Aprille with his shoures sote
The droghte of Marche hath perced to the rote,
And bathed every veyne in swich liquor
Of which vertu engendered is the flour.

Geoffrey Chaucer

Oh, the lovely fickleness of an April day!

William Hamilton Gibson

Again the blackbirds sing; the streams
Wake, laughing, from their winter dreams,
And tremble in the April showers
The tassels of the maple flowers.

John Greenleaf Whittier

See also: FLOWER, SPRING.

ARCHITECTURE

Houses are built to live in, more than to look on; therefore let use be preferred before uniformity, except where both may be had.

Francis Bacon

Architecture is a mirror, though not a passive one, reflecting the forces and ideas of a time.

Richard Marsh Bennett

A Gothic church is a petrified religion.

Samuel Taylor Coleridge

Greek architecture is the flowering of geometry.

Ralph Waldo Emerson

Architecture is the printing press of all ages, and gives a history of the state of society in which the structure was erected, from the cromlachs of the Druids to the toyshops of bad taste. The Tower and Westminster Abbey are glorious pages in the history of time, and tell the story of an iron despotism, and of the cowardice of an unlimited power.

Sydney Owenson Morgan (Lady Morgan)

The [New York] skyscrapers began to rise again, frailly massive, elegantly utilitarian, images in their grace, audacity and inconclusiveness, of the whole character of the people who produced them.

Malcolm Muggeridge

Architecture is the art which so disposes and adorns the edifices raised by man, that the sight of them may contribute to his mental health, power, and pleasure.

John Ruskin

The architecture of a nation is great only when it is as universal and established as its language, and when provincial differences are nothing more than so many dialects.

John Ruskin

Architecture is a handmaid of devotion. A beautiful church is a sermon in stone, and its spire a finger pointing to heaven.

Philip Schaff

Architecture is frozen music.

Madame de Staël

More sensible is a row of stone that bounds an honest man's field than a hundred-gated Thebes that has wandered far from the true end of life. Most of the stone a nation hammers goes towards its tomb only. . . . As for the religion and love of art of the builders, it is much the same the world over, whether the building be an Egyptian temple or the U.S. Bank. It costs more than it comes to. The mainspring is vanity, assisted by the love of garlic and bread and butter. . . . Many are concerned about the monuments of the West and East, to know who built them. For my part, I should like to know who in those days did not build them—who were above such trifling.

Henry David Thoreau

Last summer I made my fourth visit to the Cathedral of Chartres and nearby bought a small stereoscope with exquisitely detailed pictures of that incomparable structure. Before giving this fascinating toy to the young girl for whom it was intended, I showed the pictures to one of the men in my family, who remarked with something like an exalted sigh: "Here everything goes upward." It struck me then that this simple, heart-felt exclamation epitomized the spirit of Gothic as truly, if not as richly, as volumes might do.

Jean Starr Untermeyer

Architecture presents man, literature tells you about him, painting will picture him to you. You can listen and hear him, but if you want to realize him and experience him go into his buildings, and that's where you'll find him as he is. He can't hide there from you and he can't hide from himself.

Frank Lloyd Wright

Early in life I had to choose between honest arrogance and hypocritical humility. I chose honest arrogance and have seen no occasion to change.

Frank Lloyd Wright

Novelty is mistaken for Progress. Of steel and glass we have aplenty; but what of the imaginative and creative powers which makes of these glittering materials structures responsible to the needs of the Human Individual? What of Real Sun, Real Air, Real Leisure?

Frank Lloyd Wright

See also: ART, BUILDING, CITY.

ARGUMENT

Wise men argue causes; fools decide them.

Anacharsis

Testimony is like an arrow shot from a long-bow; its force depends on the strength of the hand that draws it. But argument is like an arrow from a cross-bow, which has equal force if drawn by a child or a man.

Robert Boyle

Behind every argument is someone's ignorance.

Louis Dembitz Brandeis

The greatest danger in any argument is that real issues are often clouded by superficial ones, that momentary passions may obscure permanent realities.

Mary Ellen Chase

People generally quarrel because they cannot argue.

Gilbert Keith Chesterton

The first duty of a wise advocate is to convince his opponents that he understands their arguments, and sympathises with their just feelings.

Samuel Taylor Coleridge

Never give 'em more than one barr'l to start with. But if they are foolish enough to ask for more, then give 'em the other barr'l right between the eyes.

John Wesley Dafoe

Prejudices are rarely overcome by argument; not being founded in reason they cannot be destroyed by logic.

Tryon Edwards

To bung up a man's eyes ain't the way to enlighten him.
Thomas Chandler Haliburton (Sam Slick)

Be calm in arguing; for fierceness makes error a fault, and truth discourtesy.
George Herbert

The best way I know of to win an argument is to start by being in the right.
Quintin McGarel Hogg (Lord Hailsham)

Heat and animosity, contest and conflict, may sharpen the wits, although they rarely do; they never strengthen the understanding, clear the perspicacity, guide the judgment, or improve the heart.
Walter Savage Landor

An ill argument introduced with deference will procure more credit than the profoundest science with a rough, insolent, and noisy management.
John Locke

Debate is the death of conversation.
Emil Ludwig

In order to carry on an argument you must descend to the other man's level.
Peter McArthur

When a man argues for victory and not for truth, he is sure of just one ally, that is the devil. Not the defeat of the intellect, but the acceptance of the heart is the only true object in fighting with the sword of the spirit.
George Macdonald

He who establishes his argument by noise and command shows that his reason is weak.
Michel Eyquem de Montaigne

Nothing is more certain than that much of the force as well as grace of arguments, as well as of instructions, depends on their conciseness.
Alexander Pope

In argument similes are like songs in love; they describe much, but prove nothing.
Matthew (Matt) Prior

Clear statement is argument.
William Greenough Thayer Shedd

Argument, as usually managed, is the worst sort of conversation, as in books it is generally the worst sort of reading.
Jonathan Swift

See also: AGITATION, ANSWER, CONTENTION, CONTRADICTION, CONTROVERSY, DIFFERENCE, DISCUSSION, OPPOSITION, ORATORY, QUARREL, RHETORIC.

ARISTOCRACY

Aristocracy has three successive ages: the age of superiorities, that of privileges, and that of vanities. Having passed out of the first, it degenerates in the second, and dies away in the third.
Vicomte François René de Chateaubriand

A social life that worships money or makes social distinction its aim, is, in spirit, an attempted aristocracy.
Ralph Waldo Emerson

Some will always be above others. Destroy the inequality to-day, and it will appear again to-morrow.
Ralph Waldo Emerson

Among the masses, even in revolution, aristocracy must ever exist. Destroy it in the nobility, and it becomes centered in the rich and powerful Houses of Commons. Pull them down, and it still survives in the master and foreman in the workshop.
François Pierre Guillaume Guizot

I never could believe that Providence had sent a few men into the world, ready booted and spurred to ride, and millions ready saddled and bridled to be ridden.
Richard Rumbold

See also: NOBILITY, PLACE, POSITION, RANK, STATION, TITLE.

ARMAMENT

No amount of treaties can be relied on to prevent war, so long as the nations continue to have and exercise the unrestricted right of arming themselves against each other.
(Edgar Algernon) Robert Cecil

Nations are quite capable of starving every other side of life—education, sanitation, housing, public health, everything that contributes to life, physical, intellectual, moral, and spiritual, in order to maintain their armaments.
Goldsworthy Lowes Dickinson

It is immoral for developed and rich nations of the world to give or sell armaments to developing countries. The United States is not alone in giving and selling weapons to countries that can hardly afford them and thereby increasing the probability of war. France, Britain, the U.S.S.R., Czechoslovakia are also guilty. I believe some treaty is necessary to put a stop to this.

Linus Pauling

See also: ARMS, NUCLEAR ENERGY, NUCLEAR WARFARE, WAR.

ARMS

Physical possession of arms is the last necessity of the brave.

Mohandas Karamchand (Mahatma) Gandhi

Possession of arms implies an element of fear, if not of cowardice.

Mohandas Karamchand (Mahatma) Gandhi

The force of arms only reveals man's weakness.

Sir Rabindranath Tagore

See also: ARMAMENT, GUN, WAR.

ARMY

The best armor is to keep out of gunshot.

Francis Bacon

The army is a school where obedience is taught, and discipline is enforced; where bravery becomes a habit and morals too often are neglected; where chivalry is exalted, and religion undervalued; where virtue is rather understood in the classic sense of fortitude and courage, than in the modern and Christian sense of true moral excellence.

William Ladd

There should be no distance between the people generally and the armed services; they are all one, because recruitment to the armed forces is made from the masses.

Jawaharlal Nehru

No government and no people can do without, let us say, armed force for defence, for protection, for security, and the rest of it. Nevertheless, I do believe fundamentally that armed force does not solve any problems. It is the spirit of man that triumphs—even over death.

Jawaharlal Nehru

The army is a good book in which to study human life. One learns there to put his hand to everything. The most delicate and rich are forced to see poverty and live with it; to understand distress; and to know how rapid and great are the revolutions and changes of life.

Alfred Victor de Vigny

See also: DRAFT, NAVY, SOLDIER, WAR.

ARROGANCE

The arrogance of age must submit to be taught by youth.

Edmund Burke

When men are most sure and arrogant they are commonly most mistaken, giving views to passion without that proper deliberation which alone can secure them from the grossest absurdities.

David Hume

He despises me, I suppose, because I live in an alley: tell him his soul lives in an alley.

Ben (Benjamin) Jonson

See also: BLUSTER, BOAST, BOLDNESS, CONCEIT, INSULT, INTOLERANCE, PRIDE, SNOB.

ART

Never judge a work of art by its defects.

Washington Allston

Real art is illumination. . . . It adds stature to life.

(Justin) Brooks Atkinson

The arts—those activities whereby man would clamber from the beasts to fly among the gods.

Bernard Iddings Bell

Art is concerned not with botany but with flowers, not with root causes but with ultimate values, not with sex but with love, not with human nature but with human beings.

Gerald Bullett

Art and revolt will die only with the last man.

Albert Camus

A product of the untalented, sold by the unprincipled to the utterly bewildered.

Al Capp (Alfred Gerald Caplin)

Art, like morality, consists in drawing the line somewhere.

Gilbert Keith Chesterton

Art produces ugly things which frequently become beautiful with time. Fashion, on the other hand, produces beautiful things which always become ugly with time.

Jean Cocteau

A work that aspires, however humbly, to the condition of art should carry its justification in every line.

Joseph Conrad

Art, as far as it has the ability, follows nature, as a pupil imitates his master, so that art must be, as it were, a descendant of God.

Dante Alighieri

The object of art is to crystallize emotion into thought, and then fix it in form.

François Alexandre Nicolas Chéri Delsarte

As long as art is the beauty parlor of civilization, neither art nor civilization is secure.

John Dewey

Art is the stored honey of the human soul, gathered on wings of misery and travail.

Theodore Dreiser

In sculpture did any one ever call the Apollo a fancy piece; or say of the Laocoön how it might be made different? A masterpiece of art has, to the mind, a fixed place in the chain of being, as much as a plant or a crystal.

Ralph Waldo Emerson

Nothing that is not an art is of any lasting importance at all, the meanest novel being humanly more valuable than the most formidable of material achievements or the most carefully thought out of legal codes.

Ford Madox Ford

Who can deny that much that passes for science and art today destroys the soul instead of uplifting it and instead of evoking the best in us, panders to our basest passions?

Mohandas Karamchand (Mahatma) Gandhi

Art is a collaboration between God and the artist, and the less the artist does the better.

André Gide

The highest problem of any art is to cause by appearance the illusion of a higher reality.

Johann Wolfang von Goethe

The artist is the child in the popular fable, every one of whose tears was a pearl. Ah!

the world, that cruel stepmother, beats the poor child the harder to make him shed more pearls.

Heinrich Heine

Artists are nearest God. Into their souls he breathes his life, and from their hands it comes in fair, articulate forms to bless the world.

Josiah Gilbert Holland

Art has been caught in the vicious circle which chains the artist to publicity and through it to fashion, both of which are again dependent on commercial interests.

Johan Huizinga

The mission of art is to represent nature; not to imitate her.

William Morris Hunt

Sincerity in art is not an affair of will, of a moral choice between honesty and dishonesty. It is mainly an affair of talent.

Aldous Leonard Huxley

Art does not lie in copying nature. Nature furnishes the material by means of which to express a beauty still unexpressed in nature. The artist beholds in nature more than she herself is conscious of.

Henry James

In the briefest time, in a foreign land with which we have great differences, you lifted the eyes of men beyond the things which make us adversaries to the things which make us brothers; to the hunger of all men for beauty; the respect of all men for excellence; the delight of all men in art.

Lyndon Baines Johnson

The ordinary true, or purely real, cannot be the object of the arts. Illusion on a ground of truth, that is the secret of the fine arts.

Joseph Joubert

Those who love art and are truly susceptible to its spell, do die young in the sense that they remain young to their dying day.

Otto Herman Kahn

Arts and letters, like science, spontaneously orchestrate to one another so that no sooner does a land mature a variant in its culture than it is imported by other lands, for the most part without passport and without tariff.

Horace Meyer Kallen

To suppress the liberty of art is like Herod's slaughter of the innocents—an attempt to kill off the alteration of the ideas, ideals, and ways and works of men at the source.

Horace Meyer Kallen

It's clever, but is it art?

Rudyard Kipling

Right now, anyone who finds a way to make a lamp out of a Coca-Cola bottle gets more protection than a man who creates a work of art.

Christopher La Farge

Would that we could at once paint with the eyes! In the long way from the eye through the arm to the pencil, how much is lost!

Gotthold Ephraim Lessing

Art does not imitate nature, but founds itself on the study of nature—takes from nature the selections which best accord with its own intention, and then bestows on them that which nature does not possess, viz.: the mind and soul of man.

Edward G. Bulwer-Lytton (Baron Lytton)

All art is a revolt against man's fate.

André Malraux

Art is a creative effort of which the well-springs lie in the spirit, and which brings us at once the most intimate self of the artist and the secret concurrences which he has perceived in things by means of a vision or intuition all his own, and not to be expressed in ideas and in words-expressible only in the work of art.

Jacques Maritain

It is necessary that the object that the artist is shaping, whether it be a vase of clay or a fishing boat, be significant of something other than itself. This object must be a sign as well as an object; a meaning must animate it, and make it say more than it is.

Jacques Maritain

Art is an effort to create, beside the real world, a more human world.

André Maurois

The true work of art is but a shadow of the divine perfection.

Michelangelo (Buonarroti)

Art is a faithful mirror of the life and civilization of a period. When Indian civilization was full of life, it created things of beauty and the arts flourished, and its echoes reached distant countries.

Jawaharlal Nehru

The art of a people is a true mirror of their minds.

Jawaharlal Nehru

Creative arts must be allowed and encouraged to grow with as little interference as possible. It is only when they manifestly become a social menace or a social danger that government must move, and move with a firm trend.

Jawaharlal Nehru

How can any art flourish widely when the people of the country are hampered and restricted and suppressed at every turn and live in an atmosphere of fear?

Jawaharlal Nehru

If my husband would ever meet a woman on the street who looked like the women in his paintings, he would fall over in a dead faint.

Mrs. Pablo Picasso

The learned understand the reason of art; the unlearned feel the pleasure.

Quintilian

The perfection of art is to conceal art.

Quintilian

Half of art is knowing when to stop.

Arthur William Radford

Art is the economy of feeling; it is emotion cultivating good form.

Sir Herbert Read

A work of art always surprises us; it has worked its effect before we have become conscious of its presence.

Sir Herbert Read

Art must be a true falsehood, and not a false truth.

Jean Rostand

All great art is the expression of man's delight in God's work, not his own.

John Ruskin

All that is good in art is the expression of one soul talking to another, and is precious according to the greatness of the soul that utters it.

John Ruskin

Always design a thing by considering it in its next larger context—a chair in a room, a room in a house, a house in an environment, environment in a city plan.

Eero Saarinen

The arts may die of triviality, as they were born of enthusiasm.

George Santayana

Nothing is so poor and melancholy as art that is interested in itself and not in its subject.

George Santayana

There is no more potent antidote to low sensuality than admiration of the beautiful. All the higher arts of design are essentially chaste, without respect to the object. They purify the thoughts, as tragedy purifies the passions. Their accidental effects are not worth consideration; for there are souls to whom even a vestal is not holy.

August Wilhelm von Schlegel

The mother of the useful art, is necessity; that of the fine arts, is luxury. The former have intellect for their father; the latter, genius, which itself is a kind of luxury.

Arthur Schopenhauer

There is no such thing as modern art. There is art—and there is advertising.

Albert Sterner

Music and art must have their prominent seats of honour, and not merely a tolerant nod of recognition.

Sir Rabindranath Tagore

More important than the fact that a nation is judged by its art is the fact that a nation lives by its art, and the things men live by are more important than the things they live on.

Allen Tucker

The measure of the creator is the amount of life he puts into his work.

Carl Van Doren

Why is it that our modern world insists upon drawing such a very sharp line of demarcation between the arts and the crafts? In the days when the arts were really an integral part of people's daily lives, that line of demarcation did not exist. . . . But today the artist lives on one side of the street and the craftsman lives on the other side and the two hardly speak to each other.

Hendrik Willem van Loon

Whoever understands the art of a country is at least partially equipped to understand the people of that country.

Forbes Watson

It is only an auctioneer who can equally and impartially admire all schools of art.

Oscar Wilde

The most immoral and disgraceful and dangerous thing that anybody can do in the arts is knowingly to feed back to the public its own ignorance and cheap tastes.

Edmund Wilson

Supreme art is a traditional statement of certain heroic and religious truth, passed on from age to age, modified by individual genius, but never abandoned.

William Butler Yeats

Art is life, not something to be placed in a shrine and substituted for life.

Phillip Newell Youtz

See also: ARCHITECTURE, BEAUTY, DANCE, LITERATURE, MUSIC, ORNAMENT, PAINTING, THEATER.

ARTIST

An artist cannot speak about his art any more than a plant can discuss horticulture.

Jean Cocteau

I am bored to death by the artist who, in front of his work when showing it, starts groaning out his explanation of what he has attempted to achieve. One look at the work is enough.

Sir Jacob Epstein

There are infinite modes of expression in the world of art, and to insist that only by one road can the artist attain his ends is to limit him.

Sir Jacob Epstein

An artist has more than two eyes, that's a fact.

Thomas Chandler Haliburton

An artist creates form from out of what he needs; the function compels the form.

Alfred Kazin

In free society art is not a weapon and it does not belong to the sphere of polemics and ideology. Artists are not engineers of the soul. It may be different elsewhere. But democratic society—in it—the highest duty of the writer, the composer, the artist is to remain true to himself and to let the chips fall where they may.

John Fitzgerald Kennedy

However skillful an artist may be, and however perfect his technique, if he unhappily has nothing to tell us, his work is valueless.

Jacques Maritain

The only artist who does not deserve respect is the one who works to please the public, for commercial success or for official success.

Jacques Maritain

The artist is the only man who knows what to do with beauty.

Jean Rostand

An artist must try, scrupulously, to render truth, but have the luck of not being able to do so.

Jean Rostand

A marvelous spectacle to behold in art: supreme skill disinterestedly employed.

Jean Rostand

An artist is a dreamer consenting to dream of the actual world.

George Santayana

The pride of the artisan in his art and its uses is pride in himself. . . . It is in his skill and ability to make things as he wishes them to be that he rejoices.

George Santayana

The artist is the lover of Nature; therefore he is her slave and her master.

Sir Rabindranath Tagore

An artist pays for every genuine discovery with a decrease in the importance of his ego. A person loses something of himself for everything beautiful he has created.

Paul Ambroise Valéry

Every true artist, so far as his art went, has always got out of himself—has forgotten his personal interests and become Man thinking for the whole race.

Herbert George Wells

See also: ART.

ASCETICISM

Personally I dislike the praise of poverty and suffering. I do not think they are at all de-

sirable, and they ought to be abolished. Nor do I appreciate the ascetic life as a social ideal, though it may suit individuals. I understand and appreciate simplicity, equality, self-control, but not the mortification of the flesh. Just as an athlete requires to train his body, I believe that the mind and habits have also to be trained and brought under control.

Jawaharlal Nehru

I recommend no sour ascetic life. I believe not only in the thorns on the rosebush, but in the roses which the thorns defend. Asceticism is the child of sensuality and superstition. She is the secret mother of many a secret sin. God, when he made man's body, did not give us a fibre too much, nor a passion too many.

Theodore Parker

Three forms of asceticism have existed in this weak world. Religious asceticism, being the refusal of pleasure and knowledge for the sake, as supposed, of religion; seen chiefly in the middle ages. Military asceticism, being the refusal of pleasure and knowledge for the sake of power; seen chiefly in the early days of Sparta and Rome. And monetary asceticism, consisting in the refusal of pleasure and knowledge for the sake of money seen in the present days of London and Manchester.

John Ruskin

Asceticism is something forced, and therefore insecure, unless it be a refuge and happy relief from indulgences that are insatiable, always fretful, always oppressive and remorseful.

George Santayana

See also: ABSTINENCE, CELIBACY, CHASTITY, SELF-CONTROL, SELF-DENIAL.

ASIA

Applying historical experience, it seems to me that the crisis in Southeast Asia can only be resolved on a lasting basis by the neutralization of the entire region as between the United States and China.

James William Fulbright

Lack of interest in Asia today is isolation in its most reckless form.

Paul Hasluck

Forgetting that what we are *for* has been the source of our strength more than what we are *against*, we made anticommunism the guiding principle of our policy in Asia.

George S. McGovern

Asia is a huge continent and the peoples of Asia are all different from one another, as they were reared in different cultures and traditions. In spite of all this, I think it is still true to say that there is such a thing as Asian sentiment.

Jawaharlal Nehru

Asia, the mother of continents and the cradle of history's major civilizations is renascent today. The dawn of its newly acquired freedom is turbulent because during these past two centuries its growth was arrested, frustration was widespread and new forces appeared.

Jawaharlal Nehru

In Asia we have been kept down and are now trying to catch up with others who are ahead of us. We have been engrossed in things of the past and time has passed us by. We have not been able to keep pace with it and so we must run now. We cannot afford to walk but then when we run we also stumble and fall and try to get up again. We realize that speed, especially in an age-old continent like Asia, involves risks and dangers but we have no choice in the matter.

Jawaharlal Nehru

In this atomic age, Asia will have to function effectively in the maintenance of peace. Indeed, there can be no peace unless Asia plays her part.

Jawaharlal Nehru

Owing to false and incomplete history many of us have been led to think that Europe has always dominated over the rest of the world, and Asia has always let the legions of the West thunder past and has plunged in thought again. We have forgotten that for millennia the legions of Asia overran Europe, and modern Europe itself largely consists of the descendants of these invaders from Asia. We have forgotten that it was India that finally broke the military power of Alexander. Thought has undoubtedly been the glory of Asia and specially of India, but in the field of action the record of Asia has been equally great.

Jawaharlal Nehru

There is a strange unity between India and eastern and south-eastern Asia. The unity has been given by the thread of the Buddha legend which has bound these people together and woven many a common motive in art and literature and music and song.

Jawaharlal Nehru

This dynamic Asia from which great streams of culture flowed in all directions gradually became static and unchanging. Other peoples and other continents come to the fore and with their new dynamism spread out and took possession of great parts of the world. This mighty continent became just a field for the rival imperialisms of Europe, and Europe became the centre of history and progress in human affairs.

Jawaharlal Nehru

We are great countries of the world, who live in freedom without dictation. If there is anything that Asia wants to tell the world, it is that there is going to be no dictation in the future. There will be no yes-men in Asia nor in Africa, I hope. We had enough of that in the past. We value the friendship of the great countries, but we can only sit with them as brothers.

Jawaharlal Nehru

The whole spirit and outlook of Asia are peaceful and the emergence of Asia in world affairs will be a powerful influence for world peace.

Jawaharlal Nehru

Asia, as I see it, is likely to be the area of our most difficult foreign policy decisions, not only in the immediate future but for many decades to come. This is not surprising, because even that restricted part of Asia which stretches from Pakistan and India eastward to China and Japan contains over half the population of the world; most of the people in this area live in underdeveloped and therefore relatively unstable countries: and our knowledge of these lands, both within the Government and in the public at large, is probably less adequate than in the case of any other major part of the world.

Edwin Oldfather Reischauer

Monolithic conspiracy has little future in the soil of Asia's diversity. But rapid change, even upheaval, will continue to be a part of the scene, as Asian countries seek to close the gap between themselves and the advanced nations.

Edwin Oldfather Reischauer

We forget that in Asia great kingdoms were founded, philosophy, science, arts and literatures flourished, and all the great religions of the world had their cradles. Therefore, it cannot be said that there is anything inherent in the soil and climate of Asia to produce mental inactivity and to atrophy the faculties which impel men to go forward. For centuries we did hold torches of civilization in the East when the West slumbered in darkness, and that could never be the sign of sluggish mind or narrowness of vision.

Sir Rabindranath Tagore

See also: CHINA, INDIA, ISRAEL, VIETNAM.

ASPIRATION

No bird soars too high if he soars with his own wings.

William Blake

'Tis not what man does which exalts him, but what man would do!

Robert Browning

It seems to me we can never give up longing and wishing while we are thoroughly alive. There are certain things we feel to be beautiful and good, and we must hunger after them.

George Eliot (Mary Ann Evans)

There is no sorrow I have thought more about than that—to love what is great, and try to reach it, and yet to fail.

George Eliot (Mary Ann Evans)

What we truly and earnestly aspire to be, that in some sense we are. The mere aspiration, by changing the frame of the mind, for the moment realizes itself.

Anna Brownell Murphy Jameson

It is for us to pray not for tasks equal to our powers, but for powers equal to our tasks, to go forward with a great desire forever beating at the door of our hearts as we travel towards our distant goal.

Helen Adams Keller

Be always displeased with what thou art if thou desire to attain to what thou art not, for where thou hast pleased thyself, there thou abidest.

Francis Quarles

The heart is a small thing, but desireth great matters. It is not sufficient for a kite's dinner, yet the whole world is not sufficient for it.

Francis Quarles

Man ought always to have something that he prefers to life; otherwise life itself will seem to to him tiresome and void.

Johann Gottfried Seume

Man can climb to the highest summits but he cannot dwell there long.

George Bernard Shaw

It is not for man to rest in absolute contentment. He is born to hopes and aspirations as the sparks fly upward, unless he has brutified his nature and quenched the spirit of immortality which is his portion.

Robert Southey

There are glimpses of heaven to us in every act, or thought, or word, that raises us above ourselves.

Arthur Penrhyn Stanley

God has never ceased to be the one true aim of all right human aspirations.

Alexandre Vinet

They build too low who build beneath the skies.

Edward Young

See also: AMBITION, DESIRE, EFFORT, IDEAL, PURPOSE.

ASS

The world is a bundle of hay,
　Mankind are the asses that pull,
Each tugs in a different way,—
　And the greatest of all is John Bull!

George Gordon Byron (Lord Byron)

There is no glory in outstripping donkeys.

Martial

Obstinacy and heat of opinion are the surest proof of stupidity. Is there anything so assured, resolved, disdainful, contemplative, solemn, and serious as the ass?

Michel Eyquem de Montaigne

Every man who has declared that some other man is an ass or a scoundrel, gets angry when the other man conclusively demonstrates that the assertion was erroneous.

Wilhelm Friedrich Nietzsche

See also: ANIMAL.

ASSASSINATION

An intelligent Russian once remarked to us, "Every country has its own constitution; ours is absolutism moderated by assassination."

Anonymous

Assassination has never changed the history of the world.

Benjamin Disraeli

Almost from the moment the horror occurred, television changed. It was no longer a small box containing entertainment, news, and sports; suddenly, it was a window opening onto violently unpredictable life in Washington and in Dallas, where a President [John F. Kennedy] had been assassinated.

Newsweek

War is the statesman's game, the priest's delight,
The layer's jest, the hired assassin's trade.

Percy Bysshe Shelley

See also: MURDER, PRESIDENT.

ASSERTION

Assertion, unsupported by fact, is nugatory. Surmise and general abuse, in however elegant language, ought not to pass for truth.

Junius

It is an impudent kind of sorcery to attempt to blind us with the smoke, without convincing us that the fire has existed.

Junius

Weigh not so much what men assert, as what they prove. Truth is simple and naked, and needs not invention to apparel her comeliness.

Sir Philip Sidney

Never assert anything without first being certain of it.

Theresa of Jesus

See also: CONTROVERSY, CONVERSATION, TALK, THEORY, WORD.

ASSOCIATE

When we live habitually with the wicked, we become necessarily their victims or their disciples; on the contrary, when we associate with the virtuous we form ourselves in imitation of their virtues, or at least lose, every day, something of our faults.

Agapetus I

In all societies it is advisable to associate if possible with the highest; not that they are always the best, but because, if disgusted there, we can always descend; but if we begin with the lowest to ascend is impossible.

Charles Caleb Colton

No company is far preferable to bad, because we are more apt to catch the vices of others than their virtues, as disease is more contagious than health.

Charles Caleb Colton

A man should live with his superiors as he does with his fire: not too near, lest he burn; nor too far off, lest he freeze.

Diogenes

When a dove begins to associate with crows its feathers remain white but its heart grows black.

German Proverb

It is only when men associate with the wicked with the desire and purpose of doing them good, that they can rely upon the protection of God to preserve them from contamination.

Charles Hodge

Those unacquainted with the world take pleasure in intimacy with great men; those who are wiser fear the consequences.

Horace

If you wish to be held in esteem, you must associate only with those who are estimable.

Jean de La Bruyère

We gain nothing by being with such as ourselves: we encourage each other in mediocrity. I am always longing to be with men more excellent than myself.

Charles Lamb

If you always live with those who are lame, you will yourself learn to limp.

Latin Proverb

You may depend upon it that he is a good man whose intimate friends are all good, and whose enemies are decidedly bad.

Johann Kaspar Lavater

Evil communications corrupt good manners.

Menander of Athens

Be very circumspect in the choice of thy company. In the society of thine equals thou shalt enjoy more pleasure; in the society of thy superiors thou shalt find more profit. To be the best in the company is the way to grow worse; the best means to grow better is to be the worst there.

Francis Quarles

See also: ACQUAINTANCE, CAMARADERIE, COMPANIONSHIP, FRIENDSHIP, SOCIETY.

ASSOCIATION

There is no man who has not some interesting associations with particular scenes, or airs, or books, and who does not feel their beauty or sublimity enhanced to him by such connections.

Archibald Alison

What we most love and revere generally is determined by early associations.
Oliver Wendell Holmes, Jr.

He whose heart is not excited on the spot which a martyr has sanctified by his sufferings, or at the grave of one who has greatly benefited mankind, must be more inferior to the multitude in his moral, than he possibly can be above them in his intellectual nature.
Robert Southey

See also: DREAM, MEMORY, REVERIE.

ASTROLOGY

Ye stars! which are the poety of Heaven,
If in your bright leaves we would read the fate
Of men and empires,—'tis to be forgiven,
That in our aspirations to be great,
Our destinies o'erleap their mortal state,
And claim a kindred with you.
George Gordon Byron (Lord Byron)

There is a weakness in our country— a tendency to look to the sky and stars for guidance and to try to foresee the future by astrology. Blessed be those who are so interested. But our work lies in visualizing the future of our country not by looking to the stars and basing our calculations on their movements but by assessing our strength, resources and means and knowing how best to use them.
Jawaharlal Nehru

When princes meet, astrologers may mark it
An ominous conjunction, full of boding,
Like that of Mars with Saturn.
Sir Walter Scott

See also: FUTURE, STAR.

ASTRONAUT

Father, we thank you, especially for letting me fly this flight . . . for the privilege of being able to be in this position, to be in this wondrous place, seeing all these many startling, wonderful things that You have created.
Leroy Gordon Cooper

I could see the daytime side of the earth very well. The shores of the continents, islands, important rivers, great water surfaces, ridges and cities were clearly distinguishable. From a spaceship visibility is, of course, not so good as from a plane, but it is still good and even very good.
Yuri Alekseyevich Gagarin

It's hard to beat a day in which you are permitted the luxury of four sunsets.
John Herschel Glenn

It is not a question of mooning him but of demooning him. Our national emblem is already on the moon, but we don't want to place a coffin beside it.
Nikita Sergeevich Khrushchev

America's first spaceman had performed flawlessly. The costly one-ton capsule had functioned with near perfection, as it rose to a maximum height of one hundred fifteen miles, then reached at a top speed of fifty-one hundred miles per hour to its impact point three hundred two miles downrange. Each of the thousands of Americans who had been involved had done his job splendidly. America had a new hero, a new chapter in history, and a new claim on the limitless frontier of space.
William Roy Shelton

See also: SCIENCE, SPACE, TECHNOLOGY.

ASTRONOMY

Mankind explores his physical environment in many ways; but no science produces such exaltation—and humbling—of the human spirit as astronomy.
Bruce Bliven

The contemplation of celestial things will make a man both speak and think more sublimely and magnificently when he comes down to human affairs.
Cicero

No one can contemplate the great facts of astronomy without feeling his own littleness and the wonderful sweep of the power and providence of God.
Tryon Edwards

An undevout astronomer is mad.
Edward Young

See also: MOON, SCIENCE, STAR, SUN.

ATHEISM

To be an atheist requires an infinitely greater measure of faith than to receive all the great truths which atheism would deny.

Joseph Addison

Atheism is rather in the life than in the heart of man.

Francis Bacon

A little philosophy inclineth men's minds to atheism; but depth in philosophy bringeth men's minds to religion; for while the mind of man looketh upon second causes scattered, it may sometimes rest in them, and go no further. But when it beholdeth the chain of them, confederate and linked together it must needs fly to Providence and Deity.

Francis Bacon

There was never miracle wrought by God to convert an atheist, because the light of nature might have led him to confess a God.

Francis Bacon

A traveller amid the scenery of the Alps, surrounded by the sublimest demonstrations of God's power, had the hardihood to write against his name, in an album kept for visitors, "An atheist." Another who followed, shocked and indignant at the inscription, wrote beneath it, "If an atheist, a fool; if not, a liar!"

George Barrell Cheever

The three great apostles of practical atheism that make converts without persecuting, and retain them without preaching, are health, wealth, and power.

Charles Caleb Colton

Virtue in distress, and vice in triumph, make atheists of mankind.

John Dryden

Atheism is never the error of society, in any stage or circumstance whatever. In the belief of a Deity savage and sage have alike agreed.

Henry Fergus

The atheist is one of the most daring beings in creation—a contemner of God who explodes his laws by denying his existence.

John Foster

Whoever considers the study of anatomy can never be an atheist.

Edward Herbert

There are no atheists in the foxholes of Bataan.

Douglas MacArthur

There are pseudo-atheists who believe that they do not believe in God and who in reality unconsciously believe in Him, because the God whose existence they deny is not God but something else.

There are practical atheists who believe that they believe in God (and who perhaps believe in Him in their brains) but who in reality deny his existence by each one of their deeds.

There are absolute atheists . . . Absolute atheism is in no way a mere absence of belief in God. It is rather a refusal of God, a fight against God, a challenge to God.

Jacques Maritain

Atheism is a disease of the soul, before it becomes an error of the understanding.

Plato

Few men are so obstinate in their atheism, that a pressing danger will not compel them to the acknowledgment of a divine power.

Plato

Atheists put on a false courage in the midst of their darkness and misapprehensions, like children who when they fear to go in the dark, will sing or whistle to keep up their courage.

Alexander Pope

An atheist is a man who has no invisible means of support.

Fulton John Sheen

What can be more foolish than to think that all this rare fabric of heaven and earth could come by chance, when all the skill of art is not able to make an oyster? To see rare effects, and no cause; a motion, without a mover; a circle, without a centre; a time, without an eternity; a second, without a first: these are things so against philosophy and natural reason, that he must be a beast in understanding who can believe in them. The thing formed, says that nothing formed it; and that which is made, is, while that which made it is not! This folly is infinite.

Jeremy Taylor

See also: AGNOSTICISM, COMMUNISM, DOUBT, GOD, SKEPTICISM, UNBELIEF.

ATOM: *see* NUCLEAR ENERGY.

ATOMIC BOMB:
see NUCLEAR WARFARE.

ATTENTION

Consideration is the soil in which wisdom may be expected to grow, and strength be given to every upspringing plant of duty.
Ralph Waldo Emerson

Few things are impracticable in themselves: and it is for want of application, rather than of means, that men fail of success.
Duc François de La Rochefoucauld

If I have made any improvement in the sciences, it is owing more to patient attention than to anything beside.
Sir Isaac Newton

The power of applying attention, steady and undissipated, to a single object, is the sure mark of a superior genius.
Philip Dormer Stanhope (Lord Chesterfield)

Attention makes the genius; all learning, fancy, science, and skill depend upon it. Newton traced his great discoveries to it. It builds bridges, opens new worlds, heals diseases, carries on the business of the world. Without it taste is useless, and the beauties of literature unobserved.
Robert Eldridge Aris Willmott

See also: DILIGENCE, INDUSTRY, OBSERVATION, PERCEPTION, THOUGHT, VIGILANCE, WATCHFULNESS.

AUDIENCE

The Puritan hated bear-baiting not because it gave pain to the bear but because it gave pleasure to the spectators.
Thomas Babington Macaulay

I never failed to convince an audience that the best thing they could do was to go away.
Thomas Love Peacock

The audience strummed their catarrhs.
Alexander Woollcott

See also: APPLAUSE, MOTION PICTURES, SHOWMANSHIP, THEATER.

AUSTRALIA

Australia is so kind that, just tickle her with a hoe, and she laughs with a harvest.
Douglas William Jerrold

Australia . . . is the Cinderella of continents: the youngest in settlement by Europeans, the most isolated by geography, the most reluctant to yield natural resources, the smallest in population.
Douglas Pike

From early years the "typical Australian" was thought to be the nomadic bushman. In different decades he was shepherd, stockman, shearer and drover, but always an independent wage-earner with no permanent place of his own. . .
Douglas Pike

Over all that vast area of Australia not broken up by the plough the ground is an open book for those who can read. The history of the wild is written there. Reptiles and animals cannot live without making and leaving their mark. Even birds must alight sometimes and register themselves by their tracks.
Arthur William Upfield

See also: AMERICA, CANADA, ENGLAND, IRELAND, NATION.

AUTHORITY

Nothing is more gratifying to the mind of man than power or dominion.
Joseph Addison

Every great advance in natural knowledge has involved the absolute rejection of authority.
Thomas Henry Huxley

All authority belongs to the people.
Thomas Jefferson

The highest duty is to respect authority.
Leo XIII (Gioacchino Vincenzo Pecci)

He who is firmly seated in authority soon learns to think security, and not progress, the highest lesson of statecraft.
James Russell Lowell

See also: COMMANDER, DISSENT, GOVERNMENT, KING, OBEDIENCE, OFFICE, POWER, PRECEDENT.

AUTHORSHIP

Writers seldom choose as friends those self-contained characters who are never in trouble, never unhappy or ill, never make mistakes, and always count their change when it is handed to them.
Catherine Drinker Bowen

Being a writer in a library is rather like being a eunuch in a harem.

John Braine

To write well is to think well, to feel well, and to render well; it is to possess at once intellect, soul, and taste.

Georges Louis Leclerc de Buffon

No fathers or mothers think their own children ugly; and this self-deceit is yet stronger with respect to the offspring of the mind.

Miguel de Cervantes Saavedra

Writing a book is an adventure; to begin with it is a toy and an amusement, then it becomes a master, and then it becomes a tyrant; and the last phase is just as you are about to be reconciled to your servitude—you kill the monster and fling it . . . to the public.

Sir Winston Leonard Spencer Churchill

There are three difficulties in authorship:—to write anything worth publishing—to find honest men to publish it—and to get sensible men to read it.

Charles Caleb Colton

In America only the successful writer is important, in France all writers are important, in England no writer is important, and in Australia you have to explain what a writer is.

Geoffrey Cotterell

If there is a special Hell for writers it would be in the forced contemplation of their own works, with all the misconceptions, the omissions, the failures that any finished work of art implies. . . . Naturally you do find passages that seem to come through. Invention isn't all failure: I suppose in Hell the successful passages would fade away just as you were starting to read them.

John Roderigo Dos Passos

He who purposes to be an author, should first be a student.

John Dryden

Talent alone cannot make a writer; there must be a man behind the book.

Ralph Waldo Emerson

No author is so poor that he cannot be of some service, if only as a witness of his time.

Claude Fauchet

Modern poets talk against business, poor things, but all of us write for money. Beginners are subjected to trial by market, poor things.

Robert Lee Frost

Every author in some degree portrays himself in his works, even if it be against his will.

Johann Wolfgang von Goethe

The most original authors are not so because they advance what is new, but because they put what they have to say as if it had never been said before.

Johann Wolfgang von Goethe

Authorship is a royal priesthood; but woe to him who rashly lays unhallowed hands on the ark or altar, professing a zeal for the welfare of the race, only to secure his own selfish ends.

Horace Greeley

What it all adds up to is that I write novels about what interests me and I can't write about anything else. And one of the things which interests me most is discovering the humanity in the apparently inhuman character.

Graham Greene

The two most engaging powers of an author, are, to make new things familiar, and familiar things new.

Samuel Johnson

Literature plays an important role in our country, helping the Party to educate the people correctly, to instill in them advanced, progressive ideas by which our Party is guided. And it is not without reason that writers in our country are called engineers of the human soul.

Nikita Sergeevich Khrushchev

A good author, and one that writes carefully, often discovers that the expression of which he has been long in search without being able to discover it, and which he has at last found, is that which was the most simple, the most natural, and which seems as if it ought to have presented itself at once, and without effort, to the mind.

Jean de La Bruyère

It is quite as much of a trade to make a book, as to make a clock. It requires more than mere genius to be an author.

Jean de La Bruyère

The whole genius of an author consists in describing well, and delineating character well. Homer, Plato, Virgil, Horace, only excel other writers by their expressions and images: we must indicate what is true if we mean to write naturally, forcibly, and delicately.

Jean de La Bruyère

Clear writers, like clear fountains, do not seem so deep as they are; the turbid seem the most profound.

Walter Savage Landor

A great writer is the friend and benefactor of his readers.

Thomas Babington Macaulay

The real reason for the universal applause that comforts the declining years of the author who exceeds the common span of man is that intelligent people, after the age of thirty, read nothing at all. As they grow older, the books they read in their youth are lit with its glamour, and with every year that passes they ascribe greater merit to the author that wrote them.

(William) Somerset Maugham

Writing is a difficult trade which must be learned slowly by reading great authors; by trying at the outset to imitate them; by daring them to be original; by destroying one's first productions; by comparing subsequent works to recognized masterpieces and, once more, by destroying them; by crossing out whole passages; by weeping from despair; by being more severe with oneself than even the critics will be. After ten years of such arduous activity, if one has talent, one may begin to write in an acceptable manner.

André Maurois

Some of our best writers are Europeans. They are well educated, they work hard, they are less conventional, and they are more objective in their approach to the American consumer.

David Mackenzie Ogilvy

The writer is the Faust of modern society, the only surviving individualist in a mass age. To his orthodox contemporaries he seems a semi-madman.

Boris Leonidovich Pasternak

The chief glory of a country, says Johnson, arises from its authors. But this is only when they are oracles of wisdom. Unless they teach virtue they are more worthy of a halter than of the laurel.

Jane Porter

Never write on a subject without first having read yourself full on it; and never read on a subject till you have thought yourself hungry on it.

Jean Paul Richter

Authorship, according to the spirit in which it is pursued, is an infancy, a pastime, a labor, handicraft, an art, a science, or a virtue.

August Wilhelm von Schlegel

The devoted writer of humor must continue to try to come as close to the truth as he can, even if he gets burned in the process, but I don't think he will get too badly burned. His faith in the good will, the soundness, and the sense of humor of his countrymen will always serve as his asbestos curtain.

James Grover Thurber

Satire lies about men of letters during their lives, and eulogy after their death.

Voltaire (François Marie Arouet)

See also: BOOK, INK, JOURNALISM, LITERATURE, NEWSPAPER, NOVELIST, NOVELS, POET, POETRY, PRESS, STYLE, WRITING.

AUTOBIOGRAPHY

No British autobiography has ever been frank, and consequently no British autobiography has ever been good. Of all forms of literature it is the one least adapted to the national genius. You could not imagine a British Rousseau, still less a British Benvenuto Cellini.

Sir Arthur Conan Doyle

All biography diminishes in interest when the subject has won celebrity—or some reputation that hardly comes up to a celebrity. But autobiography at least saves a man or woman that the world is curious about from the publication of a string of mistakes called "Memoirs."

George Eliot (Mary Ann Evans)

Autobiography is now as common as adultery, and hardly less reprehensible.

Edward Grigg (Lord Altrincham)

Autobiography is an unrivalled vehicle for telling the truth about other people.

Philip Guedalla

See also: BIOGRAPHY.

AUTOMATION

The Christian notion of the possibility of redemption is incomprehensible to the computer.

Vance Oakley Packard

We live at a time when automation is ushering in a second industrial revolution.

Adlai Ewing Stevenson

Automation was a new extension of the Industrial Revolution in which machines began to be used to replace the work of men. With automation, machines now began to be used to control other machines.

David Charles Whitney

If it keeps up, man will atrophy all his limbs but the push-button finger.

Frank Lloyd Wright

See also: COMPUTER, CYBERNETICS, LEISURE, SCIENCE, TECHNOLOGY, WORK.

AUTOMOBILE

The automobile has not merely taken over the street, it has dissolved the living tissue of the city. Its appetite for space is absolutely insatiable; moving and parked, it devours urban land, leaving the buildings as mere islands of habitable space in a sea of dangerous and ugly traffic. . . . Gas-filled, noisy and hazardous, our streets have become the most inhumane landscape in the world.

James Marston Fitch

What a lucky thing the wheel was invented before the automobile; otherwise, can you imagine the awful screeching?

Samuel Hoffenstein

It seems to make an auto driver mad if he misses you.

Frank McKinney (Kin) Hubbard

There seems to be an excess of everything except parking space and religion.

Frank McKinney (Kin) Hubbard

Carriages without horses shall go,
And accidents fill the world with woe
[16th century].

Martha (Mother) Shipton

See also: ACCIDENT, AIR POLLUTION, TRANSPORTATION, TRAVEL.

AUTOMOBILE RACING

Race cars have always been driven on the ragged edge, or just beyond it, and, although the speed at which the ragged edge is encountered moves up or down with road conditions and engineering developments in the car, the fact of the ragged edge and of death lurking just beyond it does not change at all. Drivers have always moved as close as they could get and still get back alive; some moved too close and did not get back.

Robert Daley

There are those who would dispute that racing automobiles is a sport at all, would contend it is a form of insanity. But if sport can be defined at all, we would venture our definition in which it most certainly must be included. Sport is a contest, a microcosm of life in which is condensed all of the risks, challenges, skills, thrills, disappointments and exultations of man's course along the road which ends inevitably in death. Behind the wheel of a racing car, life is so compressed that it may well end around the next hairpin turn.

Esquire

When a man has taken something, some material and, with his own two hands, transformed it into something else, he has made not a machine out of it, but a soul, a living, breathing soul. Well, then, he goes to a race and he hears this soul which he has created, hears it being mistreated, hears that it is not going right—" . . . "It makes a man suffer, here. A man cannot bear such things. And so I do not go to races because I suffer too much there."

Enzo Ferrari

See also: AUTOMOBILE, SPORTS.

AUTUMN

The melancholy days are come, the saddest of the year.

William Cullen Bryant

A moral character is attached to autumnal scenes. The flowers fading like our hopes, the leaves falling like our years, the clouds fleeting like our illusions, the light diminishing like our intelligence, the sun growing colder like our affections, the rivers becoming frozen like our lives—all bear secret relations to our destinies.

Vicomte François René de Chateaubriand

The leaves in autumn do not change color from the blighting touch of frost, but from the process of natural decay. They fall when the fruit is ripened, and their work is done. And their splendid coloring is but their graceful and beautiful surrender of life when they have finished their summer offering of service to God and man. And one of the great lessons the fall of the leaf teaches, is this: Do your work well and then be ready to depart when God shall call.

Tryon Edwards

Season of mist and mellow fruitfulness.

John Keats

The Sabbath of the year.

John Logan

I have come hither to enjoy the fine weather, and bid farewell to the leaves. They are still on the trees, they have only changed colour: instead of being green, they are the colour of the dawn, and such a variety of colours that it composes a brocade of gold, rich and magnificent, which we would find more beautiful than green, were it not the signal for a change of seasons.

Marquise de Sévigné

See also: SPRING, SUMMER, WINTER.

AVARICE

Avarice is the vice of declining years.

George Bancroft

Avarice, in old age, is foolish; for what can be more absurd than to increase our provisions for the road the nearer we approach to our journey's end?

Cicero

Poverty wants some things, luxury many, avarice all things.

Abraham Cowley

All the good things of the world are no further good to us than as they are of use; and of all we may heap up we enjoy only as much as we can use, and no more.

Daniel Defoe

The lust of gold, unfeeling and remorseless, the last corruption of degenerate man.

Samuel Johnson

Avarice increases with the increasing pile of gold.

Juvenal

The lust of avarice has so totally seized upon mankind that their wealth seems rather to possess them, than they to possess their wealth.

Pliny the Elder

Avarice is the besetting vice of a propertied society but that avarice is in fact a vice is nowhere questioned.

Max Radin

Avarice, ambition, lust, etc. are species of madness.

Baruch (Benedict) Spinoza

The avaricious man is like the barren sandy ground of the desert which sucks in all the rain and dew with greediness, but yields no fruitful herbs or plants for the benefit of others.

Zeno

See also: COVETOUSNESS, GAIN, GOLD, MISER, MONEY, POSSESSIONS, RICHES, SELF-ISHNESS, USERER, WEALTH.

AVERAGE

The plain man is the basic clod
From which we grow the demigod;
And in the average man is curled
The hero stuff that rules the world.

Sam Walter Foss

Give me a man that is capable of a devotion to anything, rather than a cold, calculating average of all the virtues!

Francis Bret Harte

I am only an average man but, by George, I work harder at it than the average man.

Theodore Roosevelt

A jury is a group of twelve people of average ignorance.

Herbert Spencer

See also: COMMON MAN, CONFORMITY, MAJORITY, MEDIOCRITY.

AVIATION

Armies do not protect against the aerial way.

Alexander Graham Bell

Never in the field of human conflict was so much owed by so many to so few [Tribute to the Royal Air Force].

Sir Winston Leonard Spencer Churchill

In aeronautics one finds new things only by looking for them.

Juan de la Cierva

Soon shall thy arm, unconquer'd steam! afar
Drag the slow barge, or drive the rapid car;
Or on wide-waving wings expanded bear
The flying chariot through the field of air.

Erasmus Darwin

All except very short distance, high class, passenger travel will be by air in the days to come.

Anthony Herman Gerard Fokker

Bombardment from the air is legitimate only when directed at a military objective, the destruction or injury of which would constitute a distinct military disadvantage to the belligerent.

The Hague Convention

Congestion over and at major airports has become intolerable.

Jacob K. Javits

In the development of no other branch of engineering has scientific work been so intensive or so rapid.

Alexander Klemin

Now at the first half-century of engine-driven flight, we are confronted with the stark fact that the historical significance of aircraft has been primarily military and destructive.

Charles Augustus Lindbergh

More people travel by air today than by any other means of commercial transportation. It is time to give them the type of protection that modern technology is capable of providing.

Almer Stillwell (Mike) Monroney

Lindbergh Flies Alone. Alone? Is he alone at whose right side rides Courage, with Skill within the cockpit and Faith upon his left? Does solitude surround the brave when Adventure leads the way and Ambition reads the dials? Is there no company with him for whom the air is cleft by Daring and the darkness is made light by Emprise? True, the fragile bodies of his weaker fellows do not weigh down his plane; true, the fretful minds of weaker men are lacking from his crowded cabin; but as his airship keeps her course he holds communion with those rarer spirits that inspire to intrepidity and by their sustaining potency give strength to arm, resource to mind, content to soul. Alone? With what other companions would that man fly to whom the choice is given?

The New York Sun

For I dipt into the future far as human eye can see,
Saw the vision of the world, and all the wonder that would be;
Saw the heavens filled with commerce, argosies of magic sails,
Pilots of the purple twilight, dropping down with costly bales;
Heard the heavens filled with shouting, and there rained a ghastly dew
From the nations' airy navies, grappling in the central blue.

Alfred, Lord Tennyson

In a few years the young man and even the young woman who has not learned to fly will be regarded as natural phenomena as to-day are those who cannot drive automobiles.

Frank Aloysius Tichenor

A bird is an instrument working according to mathematical law, which instrument it is within the capacity of man to reproduce with all its movements.

Leonardo da Vinci

See also: ASTRONAUT, SPACE, SPEED, TRANSPORTATION, TRAVEL.

AWKWARDNESS

God may forgive sins, he said, but awkwardness has no forgiveness in heaven or earth.

Ralph Waldo Emerson

Men lose more conquests by their own awkwardness than by any virtue in the woman.

Ninon de Lenclos (Anne Lenclos)

Awkwardness is a more real disadvantage than it is generally thought to be: it often occasions ridicule, and always lessens dignity.

Philip Dormer Stanhope (Lord Chesterfield)

See also: BASHFULNESS, MANNERS.

B

BABBLE

They always talk who never think.
Matthew (Matt) Prior

The arts babblative and scribblative.
Robert Southey

Fire and sword are but slow engines of destruction in comparison with the babbler.
Sir Richard Steele

See also: BORE, GOSSIP, RUMOR, TALKING.

BABY

A rose with all its sweetest leaves yet folded.
George Gordon Byron (Lord Byron)

There is no finer investment for any community than putting milk into babies.
Sir Winston Leonard Spencer Churchill

Could we understand half what mothers say
and do to us when infants, we should be filled
with such conceit of our own importance as
would make us insupportable through life.
Happy the child whose mother is tired of
talking nonsense to him before he is old
enough to know the sense of it.
Augustus and Julius Hare

The coarsest father gains a new impulse to
labor from the moment of his baby's birth.
Every stroke he strikes is for his child. New
social aims, and new moral motives come
vaguely up to him.
Thomas Wentworth Storrow Higginson

Some wonder that children should be given
to young mothers. But what instruction does
the babe bring to the mother! She learns patience, self-control, endurance; her very arm
grows strong so that she holds the dear burden
longer than the father can.
Thomas Wentworth Storrow Higginson

A sweet new blossom of humanity, fresh fallen
from God's own home, to flower on earth.
Gerald Massey

Man, a dunce uncouth, errs in age and youth:
babies know the truth.
Algernon Charles Swinburne

A babe in the house is a well-spring of pleasure, a messenger of peace and love, a resting
place for innocence on earth, a link between
angels and men.
Martin Farquhar Tupper

See also: AGES OF MAN, BIRTH, BIRTH CON-
TROL, CHILDHOOD, CHILDREN, FAM-
ILY, INFANCY.

BACHELOR

I have no wife or children, good or bad, to
provide for; a mere spectator of other men's
fortunes and adventures, and how they play
their parts; which, methinks, are diversely
presented unto me, as from a common theatre
or scene.
Richard Eugene Burton

A single man has not nearly the value he
would have in a state of union. He is an incomplete animal. He resembles the odd half
of a pair of scissors.
Benjamin Franklin

A man unattached and without wife, if he
have any genius at all, may raise himself
above his original position, may mingle with
the world of fashion, and hold himself on a
level with the highest; this is less easy for him
who is engaged: it seems as if marriage put
the whole world in their proper rank.
Jean de La Bruyère

Bachelors know more about women than
married men; if they didn't, they'd be married
too.
Henry Louis Mencken

It is impossible to believe that the same God who permitted His own son to die a bachelor regards celibacy as an actual sin.

Henry Louis Mencken

By persistently remaining single a man converts himself into a permanent public temptation.

Oscar Wilde

See also: CHASTITY, FREEDOM, INDEPENDENCE, LIBERTY.

BACKBITING

He who backbites an absent friend, who does not defend him when others find fault; who loves to raise men's laughter, and to get the name of a witty fellow; who can pretend what he never saw; who cannot keep secrets entrusted to him; this man is a dangerous individual. Beware of him, Roman.

Horace

Were there no hearers, there would be no backbiters.

Horace

We far more often backbite our neighbour from vanity than from malice.

Duc François de La Rochefoucald

Face-flatterer and backbiter are the same.

Alfred, Lord Tennyson

See also: CALUMNY, DETRACTION, REPUTATION, SCANDAL, SLANDER.

BADNESS

Oh the gladness of her gladness when she's glad,
And the sadness of her sadness when she's sad,
But the gladness of her gladness
And the sadness of her sadness
Are as nothing, Charles
To the badness of her badness when she's bad.

Sir James Matthew Barrie

Often even an entire city has reaped the evil of a bad man.

Hesiod

I hate mankind, for I think myself one of the best of them, and I know how bad I am.

Samuel Johnson

See also: CRIME, EVIL, SIN, WRONG.

BALDNESS

His head was bald and shone as any glass,
So did his face, as if it had been greased.

Geoffrey Chaucer

He had no wool on the top of his head
In the place where the wool ought to grow.

Stephen Collins Foster

There's one thing about baldness: it's neat.

Don Herold

With locks of gold to-day;
To-morrow silver-gray;
Then blosson-bald. Behold!
O man, thy fortune told!
[The Dandelion]

John Banister Tabb

See also: BEARD, HAIR.

BALLAD

Let me write the ballads of a nation, and I care not who may make its laws.

Andrew Fletcher of Saltoun

Ballads are the vocal portraits of the national mind.

Charles Lamb

A well composed song or ballad strikes the mind, and softens the feelings, and produces a greater effect than a moral work, which convinces our reason but does not warm our feelings or effect the slightest alteration of our habits.

Napoleon I (Bonaparte)

See also: LITERATURE, MUSIC, POETRY, SONG, WRITING.

BANK

A power has risen up in the government greater than the people themselves, consisting of many and various and powerful interests, combined into one mass, and held together by the cohesive power of the vast surplus in the banks.

John Caldwell Calhoun

A bank is a place where they lend you an umbrella in fair weather and ask for it back again when it begins to rain.

Robert Lee Frost

Banking establishments are more dangerous than standing armies.

Thomas Jefferson

He couldn't design a cathedral without it looking like the First Supernatural Bank!

Eugene Gladstone O'Neill

See also: AVARICE, GAIN, GOLD, MISER, POSSESSIONS, PROSPERITY, RICHES, WEALTH.

BAPTISTS

Well, my husband and I would have enjoyed being Southern Baptists but we decided we just weren't physically equal to it.

Anonymous

The first Baptist churches arose out of a situation in which consciences were subjected to official control, and the establishment of a single religious belief and its corresponding institution was accepted as the normal, right, and orderly course of governmental action.

Brooks Hays and John E. Steely

The most casual student of Baptists and their way of life will be impressed by the great diversity existing within this family called by a common name.

Brooks Hays and John E. Steely

Since Baptists stress personal religious experience as essential for Christian discipleship, and as prerequisite for church membership, evangelism is sometimes called the life-blood of our churches.

Brooks Hays and John E. Steely

Among the Baptists there exists a wide latitude of belief and practice. Increasing numbers and the impact of cultural pluralism inevitably developed a diversity of views. Lack of a strong juridical authority and a magisterium has favored the proliferation of ideas and attitudes.

Norman H. Maring

Baptists constitute the largest Protestant denomination in the United States, comprising over twenty-three million members.

Norman H. Maring

In more recent times, Martin Luther King and William Hamilton (exponent of the death-of-God theology) have been numbered among the Baptists. Much more representative, however, is Billy Graham, the most renowned revivalist of our times. His moderate conservatism in theology and social matters more nearly typifies the great mass of Baptists.

Norman H. Maring

Numerous Baptists have been actively engaged in promoting closer relationships and removing artificial barriers to fellowship between Protestants and Roman Catholics.

Norman H. Maring

See also: CHRISTIAN, CHRISTIANITY, CHURCH, PROTESTANTISM, RELIGION, WORSHIP.

BARGAIN

Sometimes one pays most for the things one gets for nothing.

Alfred Einstein

There are very honest people who do not think that they have had a bargain unless they have cheated a merchant.

Anatole France

One of the difficult tasks in this world is to convince a woman that even a bargain costs money.

Edgar Watson (Ed) Howe

Sacrifice is a form of bargaining.

Holbrook Jackson

There are many things in which one gains and the other loses; but if it is essential to any transaction that only one side shall gain, the thing is not of God.

George Macdonald

See also: ADVERTISING, COMMERCE, ECONOMY, FRUGALITY, GAIN, THRIFT, SELLING.

BASEBALL

He was thrown out trying to steal second; his head was full of larceny but his feet were honest.

Arthur (Bugs) Baer

It [baseball] frequently escapes from the pattern of sport and assumes the form of a virile ballet. It is purer than any dance because the actions of the players are not governed by music or crowded into a formula by a director. The movement is natural and unrehearsed and controlled only by the unexpected flight of the ball.

James J. (Jimmy) Cannon

A ball player's got to be kept hungry to become a big-leaguer. That's why no boy from a rich family ever made the big leagues.

Joseph Paul (Joe) DiMaggio

Good ballplayer,
long striding, lean and supple,
at ease, mutely remote from greatness
until a single swing, the home run plucked
from children's dreams,
stopped time.

After that, still the good ballplayer,
still youthful,
he found each swing, each game,
each wild, reverberating cheer
was anticlimax.

Esquire

Perhaps no sport demands more of a man over
a sustained period of time than baseball. Day
in and day out, season after season, nearly
every move a player makes is recorded. The
sum total of all these moves is his accomplishment.

Esquire

Any ballplayer that don't sign autographs for
little kids ain't an American. He's a Communist.

Rogers Hornsby

Speed without control has ruined many a
good pitcher.

New York Herald-Tribune

The game still has plenty of problems but
there is a genuine love for it in the U.S.
Perhaps the ranks of young men who would
play for $150 a month and ride busses in the
minors have thinned, but there'll always be
the one who will play for nothing, just for
the feeling that comes with bending a third
strike past some frustrated batter, or for the
elation that follows a ball's arc over a distant
fence. That's the young man whose name will
probably make headlines five, ten or fifteen
years hence.

Harold Rosenthal

Baseball has the great advantage over cricket
of being sooner ended.

George Bernard Shaw

The baseball mind is a jewel in the strict
sense—that is to say, a stone of special value,
rare beauty, and extreme hardness. Cut, polished and fixed in the Tiffany setting of a
club owner's skull, it resists change as a diamond resists erosion.

Walter Wellesley (Red) Smith

See also: HERO, SPORTS.

BASENESS

Baseness of character or conduct not only
sears the conscience, but deranges the intellect. Right conduct is connected with right
views of truth.

Charles Caleb Colton

There is a law of forces which hinders bodies
from sinking beyond a certain depth in the
sea; but in the ocean of baseness the deeper
we get the easier the sinking.

James Russell Lowell

Every base occupation makes one sharp in its
practice and dull in every other.

Sir Philip Sidney

See also: CORRUPTION, CRIME, DEPRAVITY, DIS-
    HONESTY, FRAUD, MEANNESS, MIS-
    CHIEF, RIGHT AND WRONG, TREASON,
    VICE, WICKEDNESS.

BASHFULNESS

Bashfulness is an ornament to youth, but a
reproach to old age.

Aristotle

Bashfulness is a great hindrance to a man,
both in uttering his sentiments and in understanding what is proposed to him; it is therefore good to press forward with discretion,
both in discourse and company of the better
sort.

Francis Bacon

Bashfulness may sometimes exclude pleasure,
but seldom opens any avenue to sorrow or
remorse.

Samuel Johnson

We must prune it with care, so as only to
remove the redundant branches, and not injure the stem, which has its root in a generous
sensitiveness to shame.

Plutarch

See also: BLUSH, DIFFIDENCE, FEAR, HUMILITY,
    MEEKNESS, MODESTY, RESERVE, SEN-
    SITIVENESS.

BASKETBALL

It is very natural . . . for basketball coaches,
like other insane people, to think they are
somebody else.

Henry Clifford (Doc) Carlson

Basketball's sustained tempo and the hairline
judgment of what is legal body contact
make it the toughest sport to officiate. No

other game brings players, officials, coaches, substitutes, writers and spectators into such close juxtaposition. None breeds more noise, controversy and general madness.

Tim Cohane

It [basketball] is played and watched by more people than any other sport, it is economical, and when properly played it is unmatched for sustained action. Not even hockey or football demands more speed, stamina and maneuverability.

Tim Cohane

Great players . . . have the poise and grace of outstanding ballet dancers. The game is one that requires balance, co-ordination, speedy reactions. It tempts every normal young boy because it does not require great physical strength, but mental stability and courage. The player must be in superb physical shape to have the endurance the game demands. It also demands unselfish co-operation; it provides valuable training, mental and physical.

Ward Lambert

The premium on height and shooting ability remains pretty much fixed. The six footer has to be a wizard to get a second look from pro scouts. The fellow who can't pop them in from every angle and every distance—consistently—doesn't last too long in the pros.

Harold Rosenthal

Pro basketball is a child of the space generation. It was played long before; in fact there were players who got around to playing for a couple of dollars on their day off shortly after Dr. Naismith hung the peachbaskets on either end of that Springfield YMCA gym back in the 90's. It was strictly dance-hall stuff and local-crowd rowdyism, however, until the arena owners in the Eastern half of the U.S. got together right after World War II and set up the BAA.

Harold Rosenthal

See also: SPORTS.

BASTARD

Almost in every kingdom the most ancient families have been at first princes' bastards; their worthiest captains, best wits, greatest scholars, bravest spirits in all our annals, have been base born.

Robert Burton

She named the infant "Pearl," being of great price,—purchased with all she had.

Nathaniel Hawthorne

How convenient it would be to many of our great men and great families of doubtful origin, could they have the privilege of the heroes of yore, who, whenever their origin was involved in obscurity, modestly announced themselves descended from a god.

Washington Irving

See also: ANCESTRY, BIRTH, PARENT.

BATTLE

News of battle!—news of battle!
Hark! 'tis ringing down the street;
And the archways and the pavement
Bear the clang of hurrying feet.

William Edmonstoune Aytoun

He had fought like a pagan who defends his religion.

Stephen Crane

Waterloo was a battle of the first rank won by a captain of the second.

Victor Marie Hugo

I am not a bit anxious about my battles. If I am anxious I don't fight them. I wait until I am ready.

Sir Bernard Law Montgomery

See also: ARMY, CONTENTION, COURAGE, COWARDICE, REBELLION, REVOLUTION, SOLDIER, VIOLENCE, WAR.

BEARD

Beard was never the true standard of brains.

Thomas Fuller

"Let the man that woos to win
Woo with an unhairy chin;"
Thus she said, and as she bid
Each devoted Vizier did.

Richard Garnett

There was an Old Man with a beard,
Who said: "It is just as I feared!
  Two Owls and a Hen,
  Four Larks and a Wren
Have all built their nests in my Beard."

Edward Lear

See also: BALDNESS, HAIR.

BEAST

Man, biologically considered, and whatever else he may be into the bargain, is the most formidable of all beasts of prey, and, indeed, the only one that preys systematically on his own species.

William James

For without money, George,
  A man is but a beast:
But bringing money, thou shalt be
  Always my welcome guest.

Thomas Percy

The people are a many-headed beast.

Alexander Pope

A man that doth not use his Reason, is a tame
Beast; Man that abuses it, is a wild one.

George Savile (Marquis of Halifax)

See also: ANIMAL, APE, ASS, ELEPHANT, LION,
OX, SNAKE.

BEAUTY

Beauty is the gift of God.

Aristotle

Beauty is as summer fruits which are easy to
corrupt and cannot last; and for the most part
it makes a dissolute youth, and an age a little
out of countenance; but if it light well, it
makes virtues shine and vice blush.

Francis Bacon

The best part of beauty is that which no
picture can express.

Francis Bacon

Beauty is but the sensible image of the Infinite. Like truth and justice it lives within us;
like virtue and the moral law it is a companion of the soul.

George Bancroft

It's a sort of bloom on a woman. If you have
it you don't need to have anything else; and
if you don't have it, it doesn't much matter
what else you have.

Sir James Matthew Barrie

To cultivate the sense of the beautiful, is one
of the most effectual ways of cultivating an
appreciation of the divine goodness.

Christian Nestell Bovee

The need for beauty is as positive a natural
impulsion as the need for food.

Luther Burbank

An appearance of delicacy, and even of fragility, is almost essential to beauty.

Edmund Burke

Beauteous, even where beauties most abound.

George Gordon Byron (Lord Byron)

Every year of my life I grow more convinced
that it is wisest and best to fix our attention
on the beautiful and the good, and dwell as
little as possible on the evil and the false.

Richard Cecil

All beauty does not inspire love; some
beauties please the sign without captivating
the affections.

Miguel de Cervantes Saavedra

Beauty in a modest woman is like fire at a
distance, or a sharp sword beyond reach. The
one does not burn, or the other wound those
that come not too near them.

Miguel de Cervantes Saavedra

No man receives the full culture of a man in
whom the sensibility to the beautiful is not
cherished; and there is no condition of life
from which it should be excluded. Of all
luxuries this is the cheapest, and the most
at hand, and most important to those conditions where coarse labor tends to give grossness to the mind.

William Ellery Channing

The most natural beauty in the world is
honesty and moral truth. For all beauty is
truth. True features make the beauty of the
face; true proportions, the beauty of architecture; true measures, the beauty of harmony
and music.

Anthony Ashley Cooper (Lord Shaftesbury)

Beauty is not caused. It is.

Emily Elizabeth Dickinson

Zest is the secret of all beauty. There is no
beauty that is attractive without zest.

Christian Dior

Nothing but beauty and wisdom deserve
immortality.

Will (William James) Durant

If you tell a woman she is beautiful, whisper
it softly; for if the devil hears it he'll echo it
many times.

Francis Alexander Durivage

Beauty is the mark God sets on virtue. Every
natural action is graceful; every heroic act is
also decent, and causes the place and the
bystanders to shine.

Ralph Waldo Emerson

Never lose an opportunity of seeing anything
that is beautiful; for beauty is God's hand-
writing—a wayside sacrament. Welcome it in
every fair face, in every fair sky, in every fair
flower, and thank God for it as a cup of
blessing.

Ralph Waldo Emerson

It would surprise any of us if we realized how
much store we unconsciously set by beauty,
and how little savor there would be left in
life if it were withdrawn.

John Galsworthy

True beauty consists in purity of heart.
Mohandas Karamchand (Mahatma) Gandhi

Beauty is an outward gift which is seldom
despised, except by those to whom it has been
refused.

Edward Gibbon

The criterion of true beauty is, that it increases on examination; if false, that it lessens.
There is therefore, something in true beauty
that corresponds with right reason, and is not
the mere creation of fancy.

Fulke Greville (First Baron Brooke)

After all, it is the divinity within that makes
the divinity without; and I have been more
fascinated by a woman of talent and intelligence, though deficient in personal charms,
than I have been by the most regular beauty.

Washington Irving

Beauty is truth, truth beauty.

John Keats

A thing of beauty is a joy forever.

John Keats

The common foible of women who have been
handsome is to forget that they are no longer
so.

Duc François de La Rochefoucauld

That which is striking and beautiful is not
always good; but that which is good is always
beautiful.

Ninon de Lenclos (Anne Lenclos)

If beauty delights the mind, it is because
beauty is essentially a certain excellence of
perfection in the proportion of things to the
mind.

Jacques Maritain

Beauty is the first present nature gives to
women and the first it takes away.

George Brossin Méré

In every man's heart there is a secret nerve
that answers to the vibrations of beauty.

Christopher Darlington Morley

If the nose of Cleopatra had been a little
shorter, it would have changed the history of
the world.

Blaise Pascal

There should be as little merit in loving a
woman for her beauty, as a man for his prosperity, both being equally subject to change.

Alexander Pope

Beauty at once so strange and so brotherly—
kin of the eye that takes it in and the mind
that marvels at it.

Jean Rostand

Beauty in art is often nothing but ugliness
subdued.

Jean Rostand

Every trait of beauty may be referred to some
virtue, as to innocence, candor, generosity,
modesty, or heroism.

Jacques Henri Bernardin de Saint Pierre

I pray thee, O God, that I may be beautiful
within.

Socrates

To give pain is the tyranny; to make happy,
the true empire of beauty.

Sir Richard Steele

Beauty is momentary in the mind—
The fitful tracing of a portal;
But in the flesh it is immortal.

Wallace Stevens

You can take no credit for beauty at sixteen.
But if you are beautiful at sixty, it will be
your own soul's doing.

Marie Carmichael Stopes

In all ranks of life the human heart yearns
for the beautiful; and the beautiful things
that God makes are his gift to all alike.

Harriet Elizabeth Beecher Stowe

Beauty and her twin brother Truth require
leisure and self-control for their growth. But
the greed of gain has no time or limit to its
capaciousness. Its one object is to produce
and consume. It has pity neither for beautiful
nature nor for living human beings. It is
ruthlessly ready without a moment's hesitation to crush beauty and life out of them,
moulding them into money.

Sir Rabindranath Tagore

Loveliness needs not the aid of foreign ornament, but is, when unadorned, adorned the
most.

Thomas Thomson

The thing that we speak of as beauty does not
have to be sought in distant lands, it need
not be looked for even so far as around the
corner. It is here close about us or it is nowhere.

Allen Tucker

Even virtue is more fair when it appears in a
beautiful person.

Virgil

Beauty comes and passes, is lost the moment
that we touch it, can no more be stayed or
held than one can stay the flowing of a river.

Thomas Clayton Wolfe

See also: ART, CHARM, COUNTENANCE, FACE,
GRACEFULNESS, LOOKS, ORNAMENT.

BED

In bed we laugh; in bed we cry;
In bed are born; in bed we die;
The near approach the bed doth show,
Of human bliss to human woe.

Isaac de Benserade

The bed is a bundle of paradoxes: we go to
it with reluctance, yet we quit it with regret;
we make up our minds every night to leave
it early, but we make up our bodies every
morning to keep it late.

Charles Caleb Colton

Early to bed, and early to rise, makes a man
healthy, wealthy, and wise.

Benjamin Franklin

What a delightful thing rest is! The bed has
become a place of luxury to me. I would not
exchange it for all the thrones in the world.

Napoleon I (Bonaparte)

See also: NIGHT, REPOSE, REST, SLEEP.

BEE

The bee is held in more honor than other
animals, not because she labors, but because
she labors for others.

John Chrysostom

Bees work for man, and yet they never bruise
  Their Master's flower, but leave it having
    done.
As fair as ever and as fit to use,
  So both the flower doth stay and honey run.

George Herbert

The bee that hath honey in her mouth hath
a sting in her tail.

John Lyly

How doth the little busy bee
  Improve each shining hour,
And gather honey all the day
  From every opening flower.

Isaac Watts

See also: ANIMAL.

BEGGING

Borrowing is not much better than begging.

Gotthold Ephraim Lessing

He who begs timidly courts a refusal.

Seneca

Common people do not pray; they only beg.

George Bernard Shaw

A court is an assembly of noble and distinguished beggers.

Charles Maurice de Talleyrand-Périgord

See also: ADVERSITY, DEPRESSION, POVERTY.

BEGINNING

Begin; to begin is half the work. Let half
still remain; again begin this, and thou wilt
have finished.

Ausonius

Let us watch well our beginnings, and results
will manage themselves.

Alexander Clark

It is the beginning of the end.

Charles Maurice de Talleyrand-Périgord

The first step, my son, which one makes in
the world, is the one on which depends the
rest of our days.

Voltaire (François Marie Arouet)

See also: BIRTH, DISCOVERY, END, INNOVATION,
INVENTION, ORIGINALITY, PAST.

BEHAVIOR

Behavior is a mirror in which every one
displays his image.

Johann Wolfgang von Goethe

Be nice to people on your way up because
you'll meet them on your way down.

Wilson Mizner

The behavior of women in our culture has largely been in response to the behavior of males toward them. Men have placed a high premium upon sexual attractiveness; . . . and women, therefore, concentrate on making themselves sexually attractive.

Ashley Montagu

Levity of behavior is the bane of all that is good and virtuous.

Seneca

If animals had reason, they would act just as ridiculous as we menfolks do.

Henry Wheeler Shaw (Josh Billings)

I don't say we all ought to misbehave, but we ought to look as if we could.

Orson Welles

He doesn't act on the stage—he behaves.

Oscar Wilde

See also: ACTION, CONDUCT, ETIQUETTE, GOOD BREEDING, MANNERS, MORALITY.

BELIEF

It is a singular fact that many men of action incline to the theory of fatalism, while the greater part of men of thought believe in a divine providence.

Honoré de Balzac

He who doubts from what he sees
Will ne'er believe, do what you please.
If the Sun and Moon should doubt,
They'd immediately go out.

William Blake

Without a belief a man is helpless against the dragons.

(Matthew) Heywood Campbell Broun

Modern man has tried the suspense of believing nothing and because suspense is soon unbearable, he has ended by believing almost anything.

George Arthur Buttrick

No iron chain, or outward force of any kind, could ever compel the soul of man to believe or to disbelieve: it is his own indefeasible light, that judgment of his; he will reign and believe there by the grace of God alone!

Thomas Carlyle

There is no unbelief;
Whoever plants a seed beneath the sod
And waits to see it push away the clod,
  He trusts in God.

Elizabeth York Case

He that will believe only what he can fully comprehend, must have a very long head or a very short creed.

Charles Caleb Colton

Few men realize that their life, the very essence of their character, their capabilities and their audacities, are only the expression of their belief in the safety of their surroundings.

Joseph Conrad

We easily believe that which we wish.

Pierre Corneille

Believe only half of what you see and nothing that you hear.

Dinah Maria Mulock Craik

It hurts more to have a belief pulled than to have a tooth pulled, and no intellectual novocain is available.

Elmer Holmes Davis

Nothing is so easy as to deceive one's self; for what we wish, that we readily believe.

Demosthenes

The conclusion of belief is not so much a conclusion as a resolution.

Lotan Harold DeWolf

A man must not swallow more beliefs than he can digest.

(Henry) Havelock Ellis

Belief consists in accepting the affirmations of the soul; unbelief, in denying them.

Ralph Waldo Emerson

The practical effect of a belief is the real test of its soundness.

James Anthony Froude

Whenever I visit a country and ask about the leading political personality and talk to him, I try to focus on two questions: What are the real sources of power behind this man? What does he believe in most?

John Gunther

He who expects men to be always as good as their beliefs, indulges a groundless hope; and he who expects men to be always as bad as their beliefs, vexes himself with a needless fear.

Jean Daniel Kieffer

In belief lies the secret of all valuable exertion.

Edward G. Bulwer-Lytton (Baron Lytton)

A well-bred man keeps his beliefs out of his conversation.

André Maurois

One person with a belief is equal to a force of ninety-nine who have only interests.

John Stuart Mill

A man may be a heretic in the truth; and if he believes things, only on the authority of others without other reason, then, though his belief be true, yet the very truth he holds becomes heresy.

John Milton

Nothing is so firmly believed as what we least know.

Michel Eyquem de Montaigne

Paul was the first of the followers of Christ to point out that in order to be Christians they had to stop being Jews. By insisting that the Messiah's message was supernational as well as supernatural, he helped to prevent the young Christian religion from becoming a captive sect of Judaism.

Newsweek

We are slow to believe that which if believed would hurt our feelings.

Ovid

I am inclined to judge a belief quite differently, according to whether it asks the right to be one or insists on being the only one.

Jean Rostand

I am not afraid of those tender and scrupulous consciences who are ever cautious of professing and believing too much; if they are sincerely wrong, I forgive their errors and respect their integrity. The men I am afraid of are those who believe everything, subscribe to everything, and vote for everything.

William Davies Shipley

Our generation is remarkable, or seems remarkable to those who have known no other, for the number of persons who must believe something, but do not know what.

Evelyn Underhill

See also: CONVICTION, CREDULITY, CREED, DOCTRINE, FAITH, HOPE, OPINION, PREJUDICE, RELIGION, SECT, THEORY, TRUST.

BELL

How soft the music of those village bells,
Falling at intervals upon the ear
In cadence sweet; now dying all away,
Now pealing loud again, and louder still,
Clear and sonorous, as the gale comes on!

John Donne

The bells themselves are the best of preachers;
Their brazen lips are learned teachers,
From their pulpits of stone in the upper air,
Sounding aloft, without crack or flaw,
Shriller than trumpets under the Law,
Now a sermon, and now a prayer.
The clangorous hammer is the tongue,
This way, that way, beaten and swung,
That from mouth of brass, as from mouth of gold
May be taught the Testaments, New and Old.

Henry Wadsworth Longfellow

Hear the sledges with the bells,
    Silver bells!
What a world of merriment their melody foretells!
How they tinkle, tinkle, tinkle,
    In the icy air of night,
While the stars that over-sprinkle
All the Heavens seem to twinkle
    With a crystalline delight:
Keeping time, time, time,
In a sort of Runic rhyme
To the tintinnabulation that so musically wells
    From the bells, bells, bells, bells,
        Bells, bells, bells-
From the jingling and the tinkling of the bells.

Edgar Allan Poe

Ring out the old, ring in the new,
Ring, happy bells, across the snow.

Alfred, Lord Tennyson

See also: CHURCH, MUSIC, NOISE, SOUND.

BENEFICENCE

Men resemble the gods in nothing so much as in doing good to their fellow creatures.

Cicero

I never knew a child of God being bankrupted by his benevolence. What we keep we may lose, but what we give to Christ we are sure to keep.

Theodore Ledyard Cuyler

We enjoy thoroughly only the pleasure that we give.

Alexandre Dumas (père)

Rich people should consider that they are
only trustees for what they possess, and
should show their wealth to be more in doing good than merely in having it. They
should not reserve their benevolence for purposes after they are dead, for those who give
not of their property till they die show that
they would not then if they could keep it
any longer.

Joseph Hall

Money spent on ourselves may be a millstone
about the neck; spent on others it may give
us wings like eagles.

Roswell Dwight Hitchcock

Beneficence is a duty; and he who frequently
practises it, and sees his benevolent intentions
realized comes, at length, really to love him
to whom he has done good.

Immanuel Kant

The greatest pleasure I know is to do a good
action by stealth, and to have it found out by
accident.

Charles Lamb

Of all the virtues necessary to the completion of the perfect man, there is none to be
more delicately implied and less ostentatiously
vaunted than that of exquisite feeling or universal benevolence.

Edward G. Bulwer-Lytton (Baron Lytton)

Time, which gnaws and diminishes all things
else, augments and increaseth benefits; because a noble action of liberality doth grow
continually by our generously thinking of it
and remembering it.

François Rabelais

He that does good to another, does good also
to himself, not only in the consequences, but
in the very act; for the consciousness of well
doing is, in itself, ample reward.

Seneca

It is another's fault if he be ungrateful; but it
is mine if I do not give. To find one thankful
man, I will oblige a great many that are not
so. I had rather never receive a kindness than
never bestow one. Not to return a benefit is
a great sin; but not to confer one is a greater.

Seneca

We should give as we would receive cheerfully, quickly, and without hesitation; for
there is no grace in a benefit that sticks to
the fingers.

Seneca

We can't do for another without at the same
time doing for ourselves.

Ralph Waldo Trine

See also: BENEVOLENCE, CHARITY, GENEROSITY,
    GIFT, GOODNESS, HELP, KINDNESS,
    MAGNANIMITY, PHILANTHROPY.

BENEVOLENCE

In this world it is not what we take up, but
what we give up, that makes us rich.

Henry Ward Beecher

It is good for us to think that no grace or
blessing is truly ours till we are aware that
God has blessed some one else with it through
us.

Phillips Brooks

Rare benevolence! the minister of God.

Thomas Carlyle

He who wishes to secure the good of others,
has already secured his own.

Confucius

Never did any soul do good, but it came
readier to do the same again, with more enjoyment. Never was love, or gratitude, or
bounty practised, but with increasing joy,
which made the practiser still more in love
with the fair act.

Anthony Ashley Cooper (Lord Shaftesbury)

There cannot be a more glorious object in
creation than a human being replete with benevolence, meditating in what manner he may
render himself most acceptable to the Creator
by doing good to his creatures.

Henry Fielding

It is the glory of the true religion that it in-
culcates and inspires a spirit of benevolence.
It is a religion of charity, which none other
ever was. Christ went about doing good; he
set the example to his disciples, and they
abounded in it.

Thomas Fuller

He only does not live in vain, who employs
his wealth, his thought, his speech to advance
the good of others.

Hindu Maxim

The disposition to give a cup of cold water to
a disciple, is a far nobler property than the
finest intellect.

William Dean Howells

It is good to think well; it is divine to act well.
Horace Mann

Genuine benevolence is not stationary, but peripatetic; it goes about doing good.
William Nevins

It is no great part of a good man's lot to enjoy himself. To be good and to do good are his ends, and the glory is to be revealed hereafter.
Samuel Irenaeus Prime

Do not wait for extraordinary circumstances to do good actions: try to use ordinary situations.
Jean Paul Richter

The one who will be found in trial capable of great acts of love is ever the one who is always doing considerate small ones.
Frederick William Robertson

I truly enjoy no more of the world's good things than what I willingly distribute to the needy.
Seneca

This is the law of benefits between men; the one ought to forget at once what he has given, and the other ought never to forget what he has received.
Seneca

To feel much for others, and little for ourselves; to restrain our selfish, and exercise our benevolent affections, constitutes the perfection of human nature.
Adam Smith

Benevolent feeling ennobles the most trifling actions.
William Makepeace Thackeray

See also: BENEFICENCE, WELLDOING.

BERLIN

All free men, wherever they may live, are citizens of Berlin. And therefore, as a free man, I take pride in the words *"Ich bin ein Berliner"* [I am a Berliner].
John Fitzgerald Kennedy

The freedom of the city is not negotiable. We cannot negotiate with those who say, "What's mine is mine and what's yours is negotiable."
John Fitzgerald Kennedy

I hear it said that West Berlin is militarily untenable—and so was Bastogne, and so, in

fact, was Stalingrad. Any danger spot is tenable if men—brave men—will make it so.
John Fitzgerald Kennedy

You live in a defended island of freedom, but your life is part of the main. So let me ask you . . . to lift your eyes beyond the dangers of today to the hopes of tomorrow, beyond the freedom merely of this city of Berlin and all your country of Germany to the advance of freedom everywhere, beyond the wall to the day of peace with justice, beyond yourselves and ourselves to all mankind.
John Fitzgerald Kennedy

I consider Berlin as a test case, as a sort of litmus paper that will show the direction of Western intentions.
Nikita Sergeevich Khrushchev

See also: AMERICA, COMMUNISM, DEMOCRACY, GERMANY, RUSSIA.

BEST

The best you get is an even break.
Franklin Pierce Adams

Only a mediocre person is always at his best.
(William) Somerset Maugham

One of the rarest things that a man ever does is to do the best he can.
Henry Wheeler Shaw (Josh Billings)

Everything is for the best in this best of possible worlds.
Voltaire (François Marie Arouet)

I am as bad as the worst but, thank God, I am as good as the best.
Walt (Walter) Whitman

See also: EXCELLENCE, GOODNESS, PURITY, RECTITUDE, VIRTUE, WORTH.

BIBLE

The Bible is the bedrock of Christianity.
Walter Matthew Abbott

I speak as a man of the world to men of the world; and I say to you, Search the Scriptures! The Bible is the book of all others, to be read at all ages, and in all conditions of human life; not to be read once or twice or thrice through, and then laid aside, but to be read in small portions of one or two chapters every day, and never to be intermitted, unless by some overruling necessity.
John Quincy Adams

In what light soever we regard the Bible, whether with reference to revelation, to history, or to morality, it is an invaluable and inexhaustable mine of knowledge and virtue.

John Quincy Adams

So great is my veneration for the Bible, that the earlier my children begin to read it the more confident will be my hopes that they will prove useful citizens to their country and respectable members of society.

John Quincy Adams

The Bible is to us what the star was to the wise men; but if we spend all our time in gazing upon it, observing its motions, and admiring its splendor, without being led to Christ by it, the use of it will be lost to us.

Thomas Adams

They who are not induced to believe and live as they ought by those discoveries which God hath made in Scripture, would stand out against any evidence whatever; even that of a messenger sent express from the other world.

Francis Atterbury

There never was found, in any age of the world, either religion or law that did so highly exalt the public good as the Bible.

Francis Bacon

The Holy Bible is not only great but high explosive literature. It works in strange ways and no living man can tell or know how that book in its journeyings through the world has started an individual soul 10,000 different places into a new life, a new belief, a new conception and a new faith.

Stanley Baldwin

The Bible rose to the place it now occupies because it deserved to rise to that place, and not because God sent anybody with a box of tricks to prove its divine authority.

Bruce Barton

Voltaire spoke of the Bible as a short-lived book. He said that within a hundred years it would pass from common use. Not many people read Voltaire to-day, but his house has been packed with Bibles as a depot of a Bible society.

Bruce Barton

Sink the Bible to the bottom of the ocean, and still man's obligations to God would be unchanged. He would have the same path to tread, only his lamp and his guide would be gone; the same voyage to make, but his chart and compass would be overboard.

Henry Ward Beecher

So far as I have observed God's dealings with my soul, the flights of preachers sometimes entertained me, but it was Scripture expressions which did penetrate my heart, and in a way peculiar to themselves.

John (of Haddington) Brown

The Bible is the only cement of nations, and the only cement that can bind religious hearts together.

Christian Karl Josias von Bunsen

Read Demosthenes or Cicero; read Plato, Aristotle, or any others of that class; I grant you that you will be attracted, delighted, moved, enraptured by them in a surprising manner; but if, after reading them, you turn to the perusal of the sacred volume, whether you are willing or unwilling, it will affect you so powerfully, it will so penetrate your heart, and impress itself so strangely on your mind that, compared with its energetic influence, the beauties of rhetoricians and philosophers will almost entirely disappear; so that it is easy to perceive something divine in the sacred Scriptures, which far surpasses the highest attainments and ornaments of human industry.

John Calvin

A noble book! All men's book! It is our first, oldest statement of the never-ending problem —man's destiny, and God's ways with him here on earth; and all in such free-flowing outlines,—grand in its sincerity; in its simplicity and its epic melody.

Thomas Carlyle

The incongruity of the Bible with the age of its birth; its freedom from earthly mixtures; its original, unborrowed, solitary greatness; the suddenness with which it broke forth amidst the general gloom; these, to me, are strong indications of its Divine descent: I cannot reconcile them with a human origin.

William Ellery Channing

No lawyer can afford to be ignorant of the Bible.

Rufus Choate

I know the Bible is inspired because it finds me at greater depths of my being than any other book.

Samuel Taylor Coleridge

Scholars may quote Plato in their studies, but the hearts of millions will quote the Bible at their daily toil, and draw strength from its inspiration, as the meadows draw it from the brook.

Moncure Daniel Conway

Do you know a book that you are willing to put under your head for a pillow when you lie dying? That is the book you want to study while you are living. There is but one such book in the world.

Joseph Cook

The grand old Book of God still stands, and this old earth, the more its leaves are turned over and pondered, the more it will sustain and illustrate the sacred Word.

James Dwight Dana

The Bible is a window in this prison of hope, through which we look into eternity.

John Sullivan Dwight

All the distinctive features and superiority of our republican institutions are derived from the teachings of Scripture.

Edward Everett

Sometimes Preachers preposterously quote the Scripture only for the sake of Decency of Ornament: and it is not then regarded as the Word of God; but as the Invention of Man.

François de Salignac de La Mothe-Fénelon

A Bible and a newspaper in every house, a good school in every district—all studied and appreciated as they merit—are the principal support of virtue, morality, and civil liberty.

Benjamin Franklin

The Bible, thoroughly known, is literature in itself—the rarest and richest in all departments of thought and imagination which exists.

James Anthony Froude

It is a belief in the Bible, the fruit of deep meditation, which has served me as the guide of my moral and literary life.—I have found it a capital safely invested, and richly productive of interest.

Johann Wolfgang von Goethe

It has been truly said that any translation of the masterpiece (the Bible) must be a failure.

Edgar Johnson Goodspeed

Hold fast to the Bible as the sheet-anchor of your liberties; write its precepts in your hearts, and practice them in your lives. To the influence of this book we are indebted for all the progress made in true civilization, and to this we must look as our guide in the future. "Righteousness exalteth a nation; but sin is a reproach to any people."

Ulysses Simpson Grant

It is impossible to mentally or socially enslave a Bible-reading people. The principles of the Bible are the groundwork of human freedom.

Horace Greeley

Holy Scripture is a stream of running water, where alike the elephant may swim, and the lamb walk without losing its feet.

Gregory I (Gregory the Great)

The highest earthly enjoyments are but a shadow of the joy I find in reading God's word.

Lady Jane Grey

The word of God will stand a thousand readings; and he who has gone over it most frequently is the surest of finding new wonders there.

James Hamilton

I have always believed in the inspiration of the Holy Scriptures, whereby they have become the expression to man of the Word and Will of God.

Warren Gamaliel Harding

There is a Book worth all other books which were ever printed.

Patrick Henry

All human discoveries seem to be made only for the purpose of confirming more and more strongly the truths that come from on high and are contained in the sacred writings.

Sir John Frederick William Herschel

Give to the people who toil and suffer, for whom this world is hard and bad, the belief that there is a better made for them. Scatter Gospels among the villages, a Bible for every cottage.

Victor Marie Hugo

I have always said, I always will say, that the studious perusal of the sacred volume will make better citizens, better fathers, and better husbands.

Thomas Jefferson

Cities fall, empires come to nothing, kingdoms fade away as smoke. Where is Numa, Minos, Lycurgus? Where are their books? and what has become of their laws? But that this book no tyrant should have been able to consume, no tradition to choke, no heretic maliciously to corrupt; that it should stand unto this day, amid the wreck of all that was human, without the alteration of one sentence so as to change the doctrine taught therein, —surely there is a very singular providence, claiming our attention in a most remarkable manner.

John Jewel

The Bible remained for me a book of books, still divine—but divine in the sense that all great books are divine which teach men how to live righteously.

Sir Arthur Keith

Just as all things upon earth represent and image forth all the realities of another world, so the Bible is one mighty representative of the whole spiritual life of humanity.

Helen Adams Keller

The general diffusion of the Bible is the most effectual way to civilize and humanize mankind; to purify and exalt the general system of public morals; to give efficacy to the just precepts of international and municipal law; to enforce the observance of prudence, temperance, justice and fortitude; and to improve all the relations of social and domestic life.

James Kent

To say nothing of its holiness or authority, the Bible contains more specimens of genius and taste than any other volume in existence.

Walter Savage Landor

All that I am I owe to Jesus Christ, revealed to me in His divine Book.

David Livingstone

The Bible is one of the greatest blessings bestowed by God on the children of men. It has God for its author; salvation for its end, and truth without any mixture for its matter. It is all pure, all sincere; nothing too much; nothing wanting.

John Locke

In my investigation of natural science, I have always found that, whenever I can meet with anything in the Bible on my subjects, it al-ways affords me a firm platform on which to stand.

Matthew Fontaine Maury

There are no songs comparable to the songs of Zion; no orations equal to those of the prophets; and no politics like those which the Scriptures teach.

John Milton

The Bible furnishes the only fitting vehicle to express the thoughts that overwhelm us when contemplating the stellar universe.

Ormsby MacKnight Mitchel

The Gospel is not merely a book—it is a living power—a book surpassing all others. I never omit to read it, and every day with the same pleasure. Nowhere is to be found such a series of beautiful ideas, and admirable moral maxims, which pass before us like the battalions of a celestial army . . . The soul can never go astray with this book for its guide.

Napoleon I (Bonaparte)

We account the Scriptures of God to be the most sublime philosophy. I find more sure marks of authenticity in the Bible than in any profane history whatever.

Sir Isaac Newton

Men cannot be well educated without the Bible.

Eliphalet Nott

After reading the doctrines of Plato, Socrates, or Aristotle, we feel that the specific difference between their words and Christ's is the difference between an inquiry and a revelation.

Joseph Parker

If there is any one fact or doctrine, or command, or promise in the Bible which has produced no practical effect on your temper, or heart, or conduct, be assured you do not truly believe it.

Edward Payson

I believe a knowledge of the Bible without a college course is more valuable than a college course without a Bible.

William Lyon Phelps

The longer you read the Bible, the more you will like it; it will grow sweeter and sweeter; and the more you get into the spirit of it, the more you will get into the spirit of Christ.

William Romaine

Peruse the works of our philosophers; with all their pomp of diction, how mean, how contemptible, are they, compared with the Scriptures! Is it possible that a book at once so simple and sublime should be merely the work of man? The Jewish authors were incapable of the diction, and strangers to the morality contained in the Gospel, the marks of whose truths are so striking and inimitable that the inventor would be a more astonishing character than the hero.

Jean Jacques Rousseau

To my early knowledge of the Bible I owe the best part of my taste in literature, and the most precious, and on the whole, the one essential part of my education.

John Ruskin

The most learned, acute, and diligent student cannot, in the longest life, obtain an entire knowledge of this one volume. The more deeply he works the mine, the richer and more abundant he finds the ore; new light continually beams from this source of heavenly knowledge, to direct the conduct, and illustrate the work of God and the ways of men; and he will at last leave the world confessing, that the more he studied the Scriptures, the fuller conviction he had of his own ignorance, and of their inestimable value.

Sir Walter Scott

There is no book on which we can rest in a dying moment but the Bible.

John Selden

The whole hope of human progress is suspended on the ever-growing influence of the Bible.

William Henry Seward

Nobody ever outgrows Scripture; the book widens and deepens with our years.

Charles Haddon Spurgeon

You never get to the end of Christ's words. There is something in them always behind. They pass into proverbs, into laws, into doctrines, into consolations; but they never pass away, and after all the use that is made of them they are still not exhausted.

Arthur Penrhyn Stanley

The Biblical record is far more concerned with events than it is with ideas. Ideas there are, but they are subordinated to events. The conviction, usually unstated, is that God re-

veals Himself much more fully in history than in nature or in any other way. . . . The men who wrote the words of the Bible were contented, for the most part, with telling a story.

David Elton Trueblood

A loving trust in the Author of the Bible is the best preparation for a wise and profitable study of the Bible itself.

Henry Clay Trumbull

After all, the Bible must be its own argument and defence. The power of it can never be proved unless it is felt. The authority of it can never be supported unless it is manifest. The light of it can never be demonstrated unless it shines.

Henry Jackson Van Dyke

I cannot too greatly emphasize the importance and value of Bible study—more important than ever before in these days of uncertainties, when men and women are apt to decide questions from the standpoint of expediency rather than on the eternal principles laid down by God, Himself.

John Wanamaker

That the truths of the Bible have the power of awakening an intense moral feeling in every human being; that they make bad men good, and send a pulse of healthful feeling through all the domestic, civil, and social relations; that they teach men to love right, and hate wrong, and seek each other's welfare as children of a common parent; that they control the baleful passions of the heart, and thus make men proficient in self-government; and finally that they teach man to aspire after conformity to a being of infinite holiness, and fill him with hopes more purifying, exalted, and suited to his nature than any other book the world has ever known—these are facts as incontrovertible as the laws of philosophy, or the demonstrations of mathematics.

Francis Wayland

I believe that the Bible is to be understood and received in the plain and obvious meaning of its passages; for I cannot persuade myself that a book intended for the instruction and conversion of the whole world should cover its true meaning in any such mystery and doubt that none but critics and philosophers can discover it.

Daniel Webster

I have read the Bible through many times, and now make it a practice to read it through once every year. It is a book of all others for lawyers, as well as divines; and I pity the man who cannot find in it a rich supply of thought and of rules for conduct.

Daniel Webster

Philosophical argument, especially that drawn from the vastness of the universe, in comparison with the apparent insignificance of this globe, has sometimes shaken my reason for the faith that is in me; but my heart has always assured and reassured me that the gospel of Jesus Christ must be a divine reality.

Daniel Webster

The Scriptures principally teach what man is to believe concerning God, and what duty God requires of man.

Westminster Shorter Catechism

When you have read the Bible, you will know it is the word of God, because you will have found it the key to your own heart, your own happiness and your own duty.

(Thomas) Woodrow Wilson

See also: CHRISTIAN, CHRISTIANITY, GOSPEL, JUDAISM, THEOLOGY.

BIGNESS

And so I penned
It down, until at last it came to be,
For length and breadth, the bigness which
    you see.
[Apology for his book *Pilgrim's Progress*]

John Bunyan

The mountain and the squirrel
Had a quarrel;
And the former called the latter "Little Prig."
Bun replied,
"You are doubtless very big;
But all sorts of things and weather
Must be taken in together,
To make up a year
And a sphere."

Ralph Waldo Emerson

Our spiritual peril is the new idolatry—the worship of the God of Bigness and the God of Speed.

McIlyar Hamilton Lichliter

Bigness is bigness in spite of a hundred mistakes.

Jawaharlal Nehru

See also: BUSINESS, DISTINCTION, GOVERNMENT, GREATNESS, SIZE.

BIGOTRY

A man must be both stupid and uncharitable who believes there is no virtue or truth but on his own side.

Joseph Addison

In totalitarian governments the bigots rule.

Lyman Lloyd Bryson

The bigot for the most part clings to opinions adopted without investigation, and defended without argument, while he is intolerant of the opinions of others.

Charles Buck

There is no tariff so injurious as that with which sectarian bigotry guards its commodities. It dwarfs the soul by shutting out truths from other continents of thought, and checks the circulation of its own.

Edwin Hubbel Chapin

Bigotry murders religion to frighten fools with her ghost.

Charles Caleb Colton

The bigot sees religion, not as a sphere, but a line; and it is the line in which he is moving. He is like an African buffalo—sees right forward, but nothing on the right or the left. He would not perceive a legion of angels or devils at the distance of ten yards, on the one side or the other.

John Foster

There is no bigotry like that of "free thought" run to seed.

Horace Greeley

The mind of the bigot is like the pupil of the eye; the more light you pour upon it, the more it will contract.

Oliver Wendell Holmes

When once a man is determined to believe, the very absurdity of the doctrine does but confirm him in his faith.

Junius

Bigotry has no head, and cannot think; no heart, and cannot feel. When she moves, it is in wrath; when she pauses it is amidst ruin; her prayers are curses—her God is a demon—her communion is death.

Daniel O'Connell

How it infuriates a bigot, when he is forced
to drag into the light his dark convictions.
Logan Pearsall Smith

See also: ENTHUSIASM, DOGMATISM, INTOLER-
ANCE, PERSECUTION, PREJUDICE, RAC-
ISM, ZEAL.

BILLS

Dreading that climax of all human ills,
The inflammation of his weekly bills.
George Gordon Byron (Lord Byron)

Wilt thou seal up the avenues of ill?
Pay every debt, as if God wrote the bill.
Ralph Waldo Emerson

It is only by not paying one's bills that one
can hope to live in the memory of the commercial classes.
Oscar Wilde

See also: BORROWING, CREDIT, DEBT.

BIOGRAPHY

The art of Biography
Is different from Geography.
Geography is about maps,
But Biography is about chaps.
Edmund Clerihew Bentley

Biography is the most universally pleasant
and profitable of all reading.
Thomas Carlyle

No great man lives in vain. The history of the
world is but the biography of great men.
Thomas Carlyle

Rich as we are in biography, a well-written
life is almost as rare as a well-spent one; and
there are certainly many more men whose
history deserves to be recorded than persons
able and willing to furnish the record.
Thomas Carlyle

Most biographies are of little worth. They
are panegyrics, not lives. The object is, not to
let down the hero; and consequently what is
most human, most genuine, most characteristic in his history, is excluded. No department
of literature is so false as biography.
William Ellery Channing

One anecdote of a man is worth a volume of
biography.
William Ellery Channing

There is properly no history, only biography.
Ralph Waldo Emerson

The best teachers of humanity are the lives of
great men.
Orson Squire Fowler

The remains of great and good men, like
Elijah's mantle, ought to be gathered up and
preserved by their survivors; that as their
works follow them in the reward of them,
they may stay behind in their benefit.
Matthew Henry

The poor dear dead have been laid out in
vain; turned into cash, they are laid out again.
Thomas Hood

History can be formed from permanent monuments and records; but lives can only be written from personal knowledge, which is growing every day less, and in a short time is lost
forever.
Samuel Johnson

Those only who live with a man can write
his life with any genuine exactness and discrimination, and few people who have lived
with a man know what to remark about him.
Samuel Johnson

Of all studies, the most delightful and useful
is biography. The seeds of great events lie
near the surface; historians delve too deep
for them. No history was ever true; but lives
which I have read, if they were not, had the
appearance, the interest, the utility of truth.
Walter Savage Landor

A life that is worth writing at all, is worth
writing minutely and truthfully.
Henry Wadsworth Longfellow

Biography, especially of the great and good,
who have risen by their own exertions to
eminence and usefulness, is an inspiring and
ennobling study. Its direct tendency is to reproduce the excellence it records.
Horace Mann

The most poignantly personal autobiography
of a biographer is the biography he has written of another man.
George Jean Nathan

To be ignorant of the lives of the most celebrated men of antiquity is to continue in a
state of childhood all our days.
Plutarch

Biographies of great, but especially of good men, are most instructive and useful as helps, guides, and incentives to others. Some of the best are almost equivalent to gospels—teaching high living, high thinking, and energetic actions for their own and the world's good.

Samuel Smiles

My advice is, to consult the lives of other men as we would a looking-glass, and from thence fetch examples for our own imitation.

Terence

Research is the opium of the biographers; when the fit is on them, any fact no matter how small, must be included just because it is available.

Time

Every great man nowadays has his disciples, and it is always Judas who writes the biography.

Oscar Wilde

Biography is the personal and home aspect of history.

Robert Eldridge Aris Willmott

See also: AUTHORSHIP, AUTOBIOGRAPHY, BOOK, HISTORY, LETTER, LIFE, WRITING.

BIRD

Sweet bird! thy bower is ever green,
  Thy sky is ever clear;
Thou hast no sorrow in thy song,
  No winter in thy year!
Michael Bruce (or John Logan)

Vainly the fowler's eye
  Might mark thy distant flight to do thee wrong,
As, darkly painted on the crimson sky,
  Thy figure floats alone.
William Cullen Bryant

Even when the bird walks we see that it has wings.

Antoine-Marin Lemierre

The swallow is come!
The swallow is come!
  O, fair are the seasons, and light
Are the days that she brings,
With her dusky wings,
  And her bosom snowy white!
Henry Wadsworth Longfellow

Hear how the birds, on ev'ry
  blooming spray,

With joyous musick wake the
  dawning day!
Alexander Pope

A sparrow fluttering about the church is an antagonist which the most profound theologian in Europe is wholly unable to overcome.

Sydney Smith

Art thou the bird whom Man loves best,
The pious bird with the scarlet breast,
  Our little English Robin;
The bird that comes about our doors
When autumn winds are sobbing?
William Wordsworth

See also: ANIMAL.

BIRTH

Born on Monday, fair in the face;
Born on Tuesday, full of God's grace;
Born on Wednesday, sour and sad;
Born on Thursday, merry and glad;
Born on Friday, worthily given;
Born on Saturday, work hard for your living:
Born on Sunday, you will never know want.
Anonymous

Of all vanities and fopperies, the vanity of high birth is the greatest. True nobility is derived from virtue, not from birth. Titles, indeed, may be purchased; but virtue is the only coin that makes the bargain valid.

Richard Eugene Burton

Those who have nothing else to recommend them to the respect of others but only their blood, cry it up at a great rate, and have their mouths perpetually full of it. By this mark they commonly distinguish themselves; but you may depend upon it there is no good bottom, nothing of the true worth of their own when they insist so much and set their credit on that of others.

Pierre Charron

Features alone do not run in the blood; vices and virtues, genius and folly, are transmitted through the same sure but unseen channel.

William Hazlitt

About the only thing we have left that actually discriminates in favor of the plain people is the stork.

Frank McKinney (Kin) Hubbard

High birth is a gift of fortune which should never challenge esteem toward those who receive it, since it costs them neither study nor labor.

Jean de La Bruyère

The fate of nations is intimately bound up with their powers of reproduction. All nations and all empires first felt decadence gnawing at them when their birth rate fell off.

Benito Mussolini

If children were brought into the world by an act of pure reason alone, would the human race continue to exist?

Arthur Schopenhauer

What is birth to a man if it be a stain to his dead ancestors to have left such an offspring?

Sir Philip Sidney

Our birth is nothing but our death begun,
As tapers waste the moment they take fire.

Edward Young

See also: ANCESTRY, BABY, BIRTH CONTROL, CHILDREN, DEATH, FAMILY, FATHER, INFANCY, MOTHER, PARENT.

BIRTH CONTROL

Intercourse with even a legitimate wife is unlawful and wicked if the conception of offspring is prevented.

Augustine of Hippo

Whenever I hear people discussing birth control, I always remember that I was the fifth.

Clarence Seward Darrow

Artificial methods are like putting a premium upon vice. They make a man and woman reckless. And respectability that is being given to the methods must hasten the dissolution of the restraints that public opinion puts upon one. Adoption of artificial methods must result in imbecility and nervous prostration. The remedy will be found to be worse than the disease. It is wrong and immoral to seek to escape the consequences of one's acts. It is good for a person who over-eats to have an ache and a fast. It is bad for him to indulge his appetite and then escape the consequence by taking tonics or other medicine. It is still worse for a person to indulge in his animal passions and escape the consequences of his acts. Nature is relentless and will have full revenge for any such violation of her laws.

Mohandas Karamchand (Mahatma) Gandhi

There can be no two opinions about the necessity of birth control. But the only method handed down from ages past is self-control or Brahmacharya. It is an infallible sovereign remedy doing good to those who practise it. And medical men will earn the gratitude of mankind, if, instead of devising artificial means of birth control, they will find out the means of self-control. The union is meant not for pleasure but for bringing forth progeny. And union is a crime when the desire for progeny is absent.

Mohandas Karamchand (Mahatma) Gandhi

I believe that a statute making it a criminal offence for married couples to use contraceptives is an intolerable and unjustifiable invasion of privacy in the conduct of the most intimate concerns of an individual's personal life.

John Marshall Harlan

Everyone should remember that the union of the two sexes is meant solely for the purpose of procreation.

Lactantius

Where there is a clearly felt moral obligation to limit or avoid parenthood, the method must be decided on Christian principles. The primary and obvious method is complete abstinence from intercourse (as far as may be necessary) in a life of discipline and self-control lived in the power of the Holy Spirit. Nevertheless in those cases where there is such a clearly-felt moral obligation to limit or avoid parenthood, and where there is a morally sound reason for avoiding complete abstinence, the conference agrees that other methods may be used, provided that this is done in the light of the same Christian principles. The Conference records its strong condemnation of the use of any methods of conception control from motives of selfishness, luxury, or mere convenience.

The Lambeth Conference, 1930

Family planning is a necessary complement to the war on poverty effort; it is a program which provides the individual with information necessary for her to make a choice as to whether she wishes to have more children and when she wishes to have them.

Walter F. Mondale

There is an old saying here that a man must do three things during life: plant trees, write books and have sons. I wish they would plant more trees and write more books.

Luis Muñoz Marín

Any use whatsoever of matrimony exercised in such a way that the act is deliberately frustrated in its natural power to generate life is an offence against the law of God and of nature, and those who indulge in such are branded with the guilt of grave sin.

Pius XI (Achille Ambrogio Damiano Ratti)

I can still see them, those poor, weak, wasted, frail women, pregnant year after year like so many automatic breeding machines. . . . Realizing that there was no one, no man on the scene, no doctor, no nurse, no social worker who would help them, I resolved that women should have some knowledge of their own bodies, some knowledge of contraception, that they should be rescued from their sex servitude. You ask me how I could face all the persecution, the martyrdom, the opposition. I'll tell you how. I knew I was right. It was as simple as that. *I knew I was right.*

Margaret Higgins Sanger

No woman can call herself free who does not own and control her body. No woman can call herself free until she can choose consciously whether she will or will not be a mother.

Margaret Higgins Sanger

We have been God-like in our planned breeding of our domesticated plants and animals, but we have been rabbit-like in our unplanned breeding of ourselves.

Arnold Joseph Toynbee

See also: ABORTION, BIRTH, POPULATION, SEX.

BIRTHDAY

JANUARY
By her who in this month is born,
No gems save *Garnets* should be worn;
They will insure her constancy,
True friendship and fidelity.

FEBRUARY
The February born will find
Sincerity and peace of mind;
Freedom from passion and from care,
If they the *Pearl* (also *green amethyst*)
    will wear.

MARCH
Who in this world of ours their eyes
In March first open shall be wise;
In days of peril firm and brave,
And wear a *Bloodstone* to their grave.

APRIL
She who from April dates her years,
Diamonds should wear, lest bitter tears
For vain repentance flow; this stone,
Emblem of innocence is known.

MAY
Who first beholds the light of day
In spring's sweet flowery month of May
And wears an *Emerald* all her life,
Shall be a loved and happy wife.

JUNE
Who comes with Summer to the earth
And owes to June her day of birth,
With ring of *Agate* on her hand,
Can health, wealth, and long life command.

JULY
The glowing *Ruby* should adorn
Those who in warm July are born,
Then will they be exempt and free
From love's doubt and anxiety.

AUGUST
Wear a *Sardonyx* or for thee
No conjugal felicity.
The August-born without this stone
'Tis said must live unloved and lone.

SEPTEMBER
A maiden born when Autumn leaves
Are rustling in September's breeze,
A *Sapphire* on her brow should bind,
'Twill cure diseases of the mind.

OCTOBER
October's child is born for woe,
And life's vicissitudes must know;
But lay an *Opal* on her breast,
And hope will lull those woes to rest.

NOVEMBER
Who first comes to this world below
With drear November's fog and snow
Should prize the *Topaz'* amber hue-
Emblem of friends and lovers true.

DECEMBER
If cold December gave you birth,
The month of snow and ice and mirth,
Place on your hand a *Turquoise* blue,
Success will bless what'er you do.

Anonymous

A diplomat is a man who always remembers a woman's birthday but never remembers her age.

Robert Lee Frost

New Year's Day is every man's birthday.

Charles Lamb

Believing, hear what you deserve to hear;
Your birthday as my own to me is dear.
Blest and distinguish'd days! which we should
    prize
The first, the kindest bounty of the skies.
But yours gives most; for mine did only lend
Me to the world; yours gave to me a friend.

Martial

My birthday !—what a different sound
　　That word had in my youthful years;
And how each time the day comes round,
　　Less and less white its mark appears.
Thomas Moore

See also: BABY, BIRTH, CELEBRATION.

BITTERNESS

The soreness which may not pass the lips is
felt the more keenly within.
Sir Rabindranath Tagore

The fairest things have fleetest end,
　　Their scent survives their close:
But the rose's scent is bitterness
　　To him that loved the rose.
Francis Thompson

But hushed be every thought that springs
From out the bitterness of things.
William Wordsworth

See also: ANGER, DISSENT, FORGIVENESS, HATE,
　　RAGE, RESENTMENT.

BLACK POWER

This is the significance of black power. For
once, black people are going to use the words
they want to use—not just the words whites
want to hear. And they will do this no matter
how often the press tries to stop the use of
the slogan by equating it with racism or
separatism.
Stokely Carmichael

The new black man wants to live, and to live
means that we must not become static or
merely believe in self-defense. We must boldly go out and attack the white Western world
at its power centers.
James Forman

Black Power—I don't know what that is. But
I know what American power is. Our wing
isn't a black wing, or a white wing or a green
wing—it's technicolor all-American.
David James, Jr.

The Black Power advocates of today consciously feel that they are the most militant
group in the Negro protest movement. Yet
they have retreated from a direct confrontation with American society on the issue of
integration and, by preaching separatism, unconsciously function as an accommodation to
white racism. Much of their economic program, as well as their interest in Negro history, self-help, racial solidarity and separation, is reminiscent of Booker T. Washington.

The rhetoric is different, but the programs
are remarkably similar.
Commission on Civil Disorder, 1968

The frustrations of powerlessness have led
some Negroes to the conviction that there is
no effective alternative to violence as a means
of achieving redress of grievances, and of
"moving the system." These frustrations are
reflected in alienation and hostility toward
the institutions of law and government and
the white society which controls them, and
in the reach toward racial consciousness and
solidarity reflected in the slogan "Black
Power."
Commission on Civil Disorder, 1968

See also: AFRICA, NEGRO, RACE, RACISM.

BLAME

When the million applaud, you ask yourself
what harm you have done; when they censure
you, what good.
Charles Caleb Colton

We blame in others only the faults by which
we do not profit.
Alexander Dumas (père)

All of us are prone to put the blame for our
inefficiency and failure upon society, environment, early training—any place but on our
own precious selves.
Howard Kenneth Nixon

Do not blame your food because you have no
appetite.
Sir Rabindranath Tagore

Let not the sword-blade mock its handle for
being blunt.
Sir Rabindranath Tagore

See also: ABUSE, CENSURE, CONTROVERSY, CRIT-
　　ICISM, GUILT.

BLESSEDNESS

Blessedness consists in the accomplishment of
our desires, and in our having only regular
desires.
Augustine of Hippo

Condition, circumstance, is not the thing;
Bliss is the same in subject or in king.
Alexander Pope

The beloved of the Almighty are the rich who
have the humility of the poor, and the poor
who have the magnanimity of the rich.
Saadi (Muslih-ud-Din)

True blessedness consisteth in a good life and a happy death.

Solon

See also: DELIGHT, GLORY, HAPPINESS, HOLI-
NESS, JOY, MISERY, PERFECTION.

BLESSING

Blessings ever wait on virtuous deeds, and though a late, a sure reward succeeds.

William Congreve

Reflect upon your present blessings, of which every man has many: not on your past mis-fortunes, of which all men have some.

Charles John Huffam Dickens

The good things of life are not to be had singly, but come to us with a mixture; like a schoolboy's holiday, with a task affixed to the tail of it.

Charles Lamb

There are three requisites to the proper en-joyment of earthly blessings: a thankful re-flection, on the goodness of the giver; a deep sense of our own unworthiness; and a recol-lection of the uncertainty of our long possess-ing them. The first will make us grateful; the second, humble; and the third, moderate.

Hannah More

Health, beauty, vigor, riches, and all the other things called goods, operate equally as evils to the vicious and unjust, as they do as bene-fits to the just.

Plato

With blessing everything is possible.

Sir Rabindranath Tagore

It is generally true that all that is required to make men unmindful of what they owe to God for any blessing, is, that they should receive that blessing often and regularly.

Richard Whately

See also: BENEFICENCE, GIFT, HAPPINESS.

BLINDNESS

What a blind person needs is not a teacher but another self.

Helen Adams Keller

O loss of sight, of thee I most complain!
Blind among enemies, O worse than chains,
Dungeon, or beggary, or decrepit age!

John Milton

There's none so blind as they that won't see.

Jonathan Swift

Back to the primal gloom
    Where life began,
As to my mother's womb
    Must I a man
        Return:
Not to be born again,
    But to remain;
And in the school of darkness learn
    What mean
    "The things unseen."

John Banister Tabb

See also: EYE, IGNORANCE.

BLOCKHEAD

A blockhead cannot come in, nor go away, nor sit, nor rise, nor stand, like a man of sense.

Jean de La Bruyère

There never was any party, faction, sect, or cabal whatsoever, in which the most ignorant were not the most violent; for a bee is not a busier animal than a blockhead.

Alexander Pope

Heaven and earth fight in vain against a dunce.

Johann Christoph Friedrich von Schiller

See also: DULNESS, FOOL, IGNORANCE.

BLOOD

I have nothing to offer but blood, toil, tears and sweat.

Sir Winston Leonard Spencer Churchill

If French and German blood is now to be spilled, as it was twenty-five years ago . . . then each of the two peoples will fight confi-dent of its own victory. But surely Destruc-tion and Barbarism will be the real victors [Letter to Adolf Hitler].

Edouard Daladier

The blood of the martyrs is the seed of the church.

Tertullian

The old blood is bold blood, the wide world round.

Byron Webber

See also: ANCESTRY, BATTLE, BIRTH, PARENT,
REVOLUTION, WAR.

BLUNDER

Great blunders are often made, like large ropes, of a multitude of fibers.
Victor Marie Hugo

Blessed are the forgetful: for they get the better even of their blunders.
Friedrich Wilhelm Nietzsche

A blunder at the right moment is better than cleverness at the wrong time.
Carolyn Wells

We usually call our blunders mistakes, and our friends style our mistakes blunders.
Henry Benjamin Wheatley

See also: ERROR, MISTAKE, WRONG.

BLUSH

Blushing is the livery of virtue, though it may sometimes proceed from guilt.
Francis Bacon

The ambiguous livery worn alike by modesty and shame.
Francis Maitland Balfour

Better a blush on the face than a blot on the heart.
Miguel de Cervantes Saavedra

It is better for a young man to blush, than to turn pale.
Cicero

Man is the only animal that blushes. Or needs to.
Samuel Langhorne Clemens (Mark Twain)

A blush is the color of virtue.
Diogenes

The blush is nature's alarm at the approach of sin, and her testimony to the dignity of virtue.
Thomas Fuller

The blush is beautiful, but it is sometimes inconvenient.
Carlo Goldoni

When a girl ceases to blush, she has lost the most powerful charm of her beauty.
Gregory I (Gregory the Great)

Men blush less for their crimes, than for their weaknesses and vanity.
Jean de La Bruyère

Whoever blushes seems to be good.
Menander of Athens

Playful blushes, that seem but luminous escapes of thought.
Thomas Moore

Whoever blushes, is already guilty; true innocence is ashamed of nothing.
Jean Jacques Rousseau

The troubled blood through his pale face was seen to come and go with tidings from his heart, as it a running messenger had been.
Edmund Spenser

See also: ANXIETY, BASHFULNESS, DIFFIDENCE, FEAR, MEEKNESS.

BLUSTERING

They that are loudest in their threats are the weakest in the execution of them. It is probable that he who is killed by lightning hears no noise; but the thunder-clap which follows, and which most alarms the ignorant, is the surest proof of their safety.
Charles Caleb Colton

It is with narrow souled people as with narrow necked bottles; the less they have in them, the more noise they make in pouring it out.
Alexander Pope

Commonly they whose tongue is their weapon, use their feet for defense.
Sir Philip Sidney

See also: ARROGANCE, BOASTING, EQUANIMITY, SNOB, THREAT.

BOASTING

Men of real merit, whose noble and glorious deeds we are ready to acknowledge are not yet to be endured when they vaunt their own actions.
Aeschines

But it is intolerable that a silly fool, with nothing but empty birth to boast of, should in his isolence array himself in the merits of others, and vaunt an honour which does not belong to him.
Nicolas Boileau-Despréaux

Friendship should be a private pleasure, not a public boast. I loathe those braggarts who are forever trying to invest themselves with importance by calling important people by their first names in or out of print. . . . Such first-naming for effect makes me cringe.

John Mason Brown

Self-laudation abounds among the unpolished, but nothing can stamp a man more sharply as ill-bred.

Charles Buxton

There is this benefit in brag, that the speaker is unconsciously expressing his own ideal. Humor him by all means; draw it all out, and hold him to it.

Ralph Waldo Emerson

With all his tumid boasts, he's like the swordfish, who only wears his weapon in his mouth.

Samuel Madden

Those who boast are seldom the great.

Jawaharlal Nehru

Usually the greatest boasters are the smallest workers. The deep rivers pay a larger tribute to the sea than shallow brooks, and yet empty themselves with less noise.

William Secker

Where boasting ends, there dignity begins.

Edward Young

See also: ARROGANCE, BLUSTERING, CONCEIT, EGOTISM, SELF-PRAISE, VANITY.

BODY

God made the human body, and it is the most exquisite and wonderful organization which has come to us from the divine hand. It is a study for one's whole life. If an undevout astronomer is mad, an undevout physiologist is madder.

Henry Ward Beecher

Our bodies are apt to be our autobiographies.

Frank Gelett Burgess

Our body is a well-set clock, which keeps good time, but if it be too much or indiscreetly tampered with, the alarm runs out before the hour.

Joseph Hall

It is shameful for a man to rest in ignorance of the structure of his own body, especially when the knowledge of it mainly conduces to his welfare, and directs his application of his own powers.

Melanchthon (Philip Schwarzert)

A human being is an ingenious assembly of portable plumbing.

Christopher Darlington Morley

Can any honor exceed that which has been conferred on the human body? Can any powers exceed the powers—any glory exceed the glory with which it is invested?—No wonder the apostle should beseech men to present their bodies a living sacrifice to God.

John Pulsford

Our bodies are but dust, but they can bring praise to him that formed them. Dull and tuneless in themselves, they can become glorious harps on which the music of piety may be struck to heaven.

William Morley Punshon

If there be anything common to us by nature, it is the members of our corporeal frame; yet the apostle taught that these, guided by the spirit as its instruments, and obeying a holy will, become transfigured, so that, in his language, the body becomes a temple of the Holy Ghost, and the meanest faculties, the lowest appetites, the humblest organs are ennobled by the spirit mind which guides them.

Frederick William Robertson

See also: DOCTOR, HEALTH, MORTALITY, SOUL.

BOLDNESS

Boldness is ever blind, for it sees not dangers and inconveniences; whence it is bad in council though good in execution.

Francis Bacon

Fortune befriends the bold.

John Dryden

Carried away by the irresistible influence which is always exercised over men's minds by a bold resolution in critical circumstances.

François Pierre Guillaume Guizot

Fools rush in where angels fear to tread.

Alexander Pope

It is wonderful what strength of purpose and boldness and energy of will are roused by the assurance that we are doing our duty.

Sir Walter Scott

Who bravely dares must sometimes risk a fall.

Tobias George Smollett

See also: BRAVERY, CONFIDENCE, COURAGE, COWARDICE, HEROISM, IMPUDENCE, RASHNESS, RECKLESSNESS, VALOR.

BOOK

Books are the legacies that genius leaves to mankind, to be delivered down from generation to generation, as presents to those that are yet unborn.

Joseph Addison

All books will become light in proportion as you find light in them.

Mortimer Jerome Adler

That is a good book which is opened with expectation, and closed with delight and profit.

Amos Bronson Alcott

Some books are to be tasted; others swallowed; and some few to be chewed and digested.

Francis Bacon

Without books, God is silent, justice dormant, natural science at a stand, philosophy lame, letters dumb, and all things involved in darkness.

Albert Bartholin

Books are the metempsychosis; the symbol and presage of immortality. The dead are scattered, and none shall find them; but behold they are here.

Henry Ward Beecher

Books are not men and yet they are alive.

Stephen Vincent Benét

Books are embalmed minds.

Christian Nestell Bovee

In books, it is the chief of all perfections to be plain and brief.

Joseph Butler

There is a kind of physiognomy in the titles of books no less than in the faces of men, by which a skillful observer will know as well what to expect from the one as the other.

Joseph Butler

After all manner of professors have done their best for us, the place we are to get knowledge is in books. The true university of these days is a collection of books.

Thomas Carlyle

If a book come from the heart it will contrive to reach other hearts. All art and authorcraft are of small account to that.

Thomas Carlyle

Books are standing counselors and preachers, always at hand, and always disinterested; having this advantage over oral instructors, that they are ready to repeat their lesson as often as we please.

Talbot Wilson Chambers

A good book, in the language of the booksellers, is a salable one; in that of the curious, a scarce one; in that of men of sense, a useful and instructive one.

Talbot Wilson Chambers

The best books for a man are not always those which the wise recommend, but often those which meet the peculiar wants, the natural thirst of his mind, and therefore awaken interest and rivet thought.

William Ellery Channing

Books are the true levellers. They give to all who faithfully use them, the society, the spiritual presence of the greatest and best of our race.

William Ellery Channing

Every man is a volume if you know how to read him.

William Ellery Channing

God be thanked for books; they are the voices of the distant and the dead, and make us heirs of the spiritual life of past ages.

William Ellery Channing

The man who does not read good books has no advantage over the man who can't read them.

Samuel Langhorne Clemens (Mark Twain)

The society of dead authors has this advantage over that of the living: they never flatter us to our faces, nor slander us behind our backs, nor intrude upon our privacy, nor quit their shelves until we take them down.

Charles Caleb Colton

The book salesman should be honored because he brings to our attention, as a rule, the very books we need most and neglect most.

Frank Crane

A good book is the very essence of a good man. His virtues survive in it, while the foibles and faults of his actual life are forgotten. All the goodly company of the excellent and great sit around my table, or look down on me from yonder shelves, waiting patiently to answer my questions and enrich me with their wisdom. A precious book is a foretaste of immortality.

Theodore Ledyard Cuyler

The world of books is the most remarkable creation of man. Nothing else that he builds ever lasts. Monuments fall. Nations perish. Civilizations grow old and die out. And after an era of darkness new races build others. But in the world of books are volumes that have seen this happen again and again, and yet live on, still young, still as fresh as the day they were written, still telling men's hearts of the hearts of men centuries dead.

Clarence Shepard Day, Jr.

Choose an author as you choose a friend.

Wentworth Dillon (Earl of Roscommon)

Books are the best of things if well used; if abused, among the worst. They are good for nothing but to inspire. I had better never see a book than be warped by its attraction clean out of my own orbit, and made a satellite instead of a system.

Ralph Waldo Emerson

The colleges, while they provide us with libraries, furnish no professors of books; and I think no chair is so much needed.

Ralph Waldo Emerson

Never read any book that is not a year old.

Ralph Waldo Emerson

When I get a little money, I buy books; and if any is left, I buy food and clothes.

Erasmus

We are as liable to be corrupted by books, as by companions.

Henry Fielding

Few are sufficiently sensible of the importance of that economy in reading which selects, almost exclusively, the very first order of books. Why, except for some special reason, read an inferior book, at the very time you might be reading one of the highest order?

John Watson Foster

Thou mayst as well expect to grow stronger by always eating as wiser by always reading. Too much overcharges Nature, and turns more into disease than nourishment. 'Tis thought and digestion which makes books serviceable, and give health and vigor to the mind.

Thomas Fuller

Books are those faithful mirrors that reflect to our mind the minds of sages and heroes.

Edward Gibbon

The silent influence of books, is a mighty power in the world; and there is a joy in reading them known only to those who read them with desire and enthusiasm. Silent, passive, and noiseless though they be, they yet set in action countless multitudes, and change the order of nations.

Henry Giles

In good books is one of the best safeguards from evil. Life's first danger has been said to be an empty mind which, like an unoccupied room, is open for base spirits to enter. The taste for reading provides a pleasant and elevating preoccupation.

Henry Whittemore Grout

Of all men perhaps the book-lover needs most to be reminded that man's business here is to know for the sake of living, not to live for the sake of knowing.

Frederic Harrison

The best of a book is not the thought which it contains, but the thought which it suggests; just as the charm of music dwells not in the tones but in the echoes of our hearts.

Oliver Wendell Holmes

The most foolish kind of a book is a kind of leaky boat on the sea of wisdom; some of the wisdom will get in anyhow.

Oliver Wendell Holmes

Be as careful of the books you read, as of the company you keep; for your habits and character will be as much influenced by the former as by the latter.

Edwin Paxton Hood

My books kept me from the ring, the dog-pit, the tavern, and the saloon. The associate of Pope and Addison, the mind accustomed to the noble though silent discourse of Shakespeare and Milton, will hardly seek or put up with low or evil company and slaves.

Thomas Hood

I do not believe that by the study of books one can obtain the equivalent of contact with men. As I observe the profusion of educational opportunities in the multitude of books and periodicals. I realize what is needed is not more information, but better judgment.
Charles Evans Hughes

It is books that teach us to refine our pleasures when young, and to recall them with satisfaction when we are old.
(James Henry) Leigh Hunt

He that loves not books before he comes to thirty years of age, will hardly love them enough afterward to understand them.
Edward Hyde (Earl of Clarendon)

There is no worse robber than a bad book.
Italian Proverb

Books [says Bacon] can never teach the use of books; the student must learn by commerce with mankind to reduce his speculations to practice. No man should think so highly of himself as to suppose he can receive but little light from books, nor so meanly as to believe he can discover nothing but what is to be learned from them.
Samuel Johnson

Books that you may carry to the fireside, and hold readily in your hand, are the most useful after all.
Samuel Johnson

Books to judicious compilers, are useful; to particular arts and professions, they are absolutely necessary; to men of real science, they are tools: but more are tools to them.
Samuel Johnson

Dead counsellors are the most instructive, because they are heard with patience and reverence.
Samuel Johnson

There is no book so poor that it would not be a prodigy if wholly wrought out by a single mind, without the aid of prior investigators.
Samuel Johnson

Tradition is but a meteor, which, if it once falls, cannot be rekindled. Memory, once interrupted, is not to be recalled. But written learning is a fixed luminary, which, after the cloud that had hidden it has passed away, is again bright in its proper station. So books

are faithful repositories, which may be awhile neglected or forgotten, but when opened again, will again impart instruction.
Samuel Johnson

Truly each new book is as a ship that bears us away from the fixity of our limitations into the movement and splendor of life's infinite ocean.
Helen Adams Keller

A bad book is the worse that it cannot repent. It has not been the devil's policy to keep the masses of mankind in ignorance; but finding that they will read, he is doing all in his power to poison their books.
Edward Norris Kirk

When a book raises your spirit, and inspires you with noble and manly thoughts, seek for no other test of its excellence. It is good, and made by a good workman.
Jean de La Bruyère

I love to lose myself in other men's minds. When I am not walking, I am reading. I cannot sit and think; books think for me.
Charles Lamb

The wise man reads both books and life itself.
Lin Yutang

Books are but waste paper unless we spend in action the wisdom we get from thought.
Edward G. Bulwer-Lytton (Baron Lytton)

Master books, but do not let them master you. Read to live, not live to read.
Edward G. Bulwer-Lytton (Baron Lytton)

The past but lives in written words: a thousand ages were blank if books had not evoked their ghosts, and kept the pale unbodied shades to warn us from fleshless lips.
Edward G. Bulwer-Lytton (Baron Lytton)

A house without books is like a room without windows. No man has a right to bring up his children without surrounding them with books, if he has the means to buy them. It is a wrong to his family. Children learn to read by being in the presence of books. The love of knowledge comes with reading and grows upon it. And the love of knowledge, in a young mind, is almost a warrant against the inferior excitement of passions and vices.
Horace Mann

The book to read is not the one which thinks for you, but the one which makes you think. No book in the world equals the Bible for that.

James McCosh

From the moment I picked your book up until I laid it down I was convulsed with laughter. Some day I intend reading it.

Groucho (Julius Henry) Marx

To produce a mighty book, you must choose a mighty theme. No great and enduring volume can ever be written on the flea, though many there be that have tried it.

Herman Melville

A person who publishes a book willfully appears before the populace with his pants down . . . If it is a good book nothing can hurt him. If it is a bad book, nothing can help him.

Edna St. Vincent Millay

Deep versed in books, but shallow in himself.

John Milton

A good book is the precious life-blood of a master-spirit, embalmed and treasured up on purpose for a life beyond.

John Milton

The one invincible thing is a good book; neither malice nor stupidity can crush it.

George Moore

The constant habit of perusing devout books is so indispensable, that it has been termed the oil of the lamp of prayer. Too much reading, however, and too little meditation, may produce the effect of a lamp inverted; which is extinguished by the very excess of that aliment, whose property is to feed it.

Hannah More

A dose of poison can do its work only once, but a bad book can go on poisoning people's minds for any length of time.

Sir John Murray

The buying of more books than one can peradventure read is nothing less than the soul reaching towards infinity, and this passion is the only thing that raises us above the beasts that perish.

Alfred Edward Newton

Divide your attention equally between men and books.

Sir William Osler

The books that help you most, are those which make you think the most. The hardest way of learning is that of easy reading; but a great book that comes from a great thinker is a ship of thought, deep freighted with truth and beauty.

Theodore Parker

The last thing that we discover in writing a book, is to know what to put at the beginning.

Blaise Pascal

Books are immortal sons deifying their sires.

Plato

There is no book so bad but something valuable may be derived from it.

Pliny the Elder

To buy books only because they were published by an eminent printer, is much as if a man should buy clothes that did not fit him, only because made by some famous tailor.

Alexander Pope

Upon books the collective education of the race depends; they are the sole instruments of registering, perpetuating, and transmitting thought.

Henry Rogers

When a new book comes out I read an old one.

Henry Rogers

We all know that books burn—yet we have the greater knowledge that books cannot be killed by fire. People die, but books never die. No man and no force can abolish memory.

Franklin Delano Roosevelt

The great books are those that grow with man.

Jean Rostand

For certain books, survival is due punishment.

Jean Rostand

No book can be so good as to be profitable when negligently read.

Seneca

A best-seller is the gilded tomb of a mediocre talent.

Logan Pearsall Smith

A book is somehow sacred. A dictator can kill and maim people, can sink to any kind of tyranny and only be hated, but when books are burned the ultimate in tyranny has happened.

John Ernst Steinbeck

Books, like proverbs, receive their chief value from the stamp and esteem of the ages through which they have passed.

Sir William Temple

If a secret history of books could be written, and the author's private thoughts and meanings noted down alongside of his story, how many insipid volumes would become interesting, and dull tales excite the reader!

William Makepeace Thackeray

Upon the voyage of life there are few books of which we may hope to make life-long companions; and, as in the other relations of life, it behooves us, if we hope to avoid calamity on our voyage, to choose our mates with discretion.

Chauncey Brewster Tinker

A good book is the best of friends, the same to-day and forever.

Martin Farquhar Tupper

A book may be genuinely great without being in the least popular, or may be immensely popular without having any important element of greatness. This distinction has not been often enough observed.

Carl Van Doren

The books of Nature and of Revelation equally elevate our conceptions and invite our piety; they are both written by the finger of the one eternal, incomprehensible God.

Thomas Watson

If religious books are not widely circulated amoung the masses in this country, and the people do not become religious, I do not know what is to become of us as a nation. And the thought is one to cause solemn reflection on the part of every patriot and Christian. If truth be not diffused, error will be.

Daniel Webster

Reading Christians are growing Christians. When Christians cease to read, they cease to grow.

John Wesley

Reading is the work of the alert mind, is demanding, and under ideal conditions produces finally a sort of ecstasy. This gives the experience of reading a sublimity and power unequaled by any other form of communication.

Elwyn Brooks White

Books are to be called for and supplied on the assumption that the process of reading is not a half-sleep, but in the highest sense an exercise, a gymnastic struggle—that the reader is to do something for himself.

Walt (Walter) Whitman

There is no such thing as a moral or an immoral book. Books are well written or badly written. That is all.

Oscar Wilde

See also: ALLEGORY, AUTHORSHIP, BALLAD, BIOGRAPHY, FABLE, FICTION, HISTORY, INDEX, INK, LEARNING, LETTER, LIBRARY, LITERATURE, NOVEL, PEN, POETRY, PREFACE, READING, RHETORIC, ROMANCE, STUDY, STYLE, TRAGEDY, WORD, WRITING.

BORE

He's the kind of a bore who's here today and here tomorrow.

Binnie Barnes

Any subject can be made interesting, and therefore any subject can be made boring.

Hilaire (Joseph Hilary Pierre) Belloc

There are some kinds of men who cannot pass their time alone; they are the flails of occupied people.

Vicomte Louis Gabriel Ambroise de Bonald

It is hoped that, with all modern improvements, a way will be discovered of getting rid of bores; for it is too bad that a poor wretch can be punished for stealing your handkerchief or gloves, and that no punishment can be inflicted on those who steal your time, and with it your temper and patience, as well as the bright thoughts that might have entered your mind, if they had not been frightened away by the bore.

George Gordon Byron (Lord Byron)

Society is now one polish'd horde,
Form'd of two mighty tribes, the *Bores* and *Bored*.

George Gordon Byron (Lord Byron)

Few men are more to be shunned than those who have time, but know not how to improve it, and so spend it in wasting the time of their neighbors, talking forever though they have nothing to say.

Tryon Edwards

No society seems ever to have succumbed to boredom. Man had developed an obvious capacity for surviving the pompous reiteration of the commonplace.
John Kenneth Galbraith

When people are bored, it is primarily with their own selves that they are bored.
Eric Hoffer

We are almost always wearied in the company of persons with whom we are not permitted to be weary.
Duc François de La Rochefoucauld

There are few wild beasts more to be dreaded than a talking man having nothing to say.
Jonathan Swift

The secret of making one's self tiresome, is, not to know when to stop.
Voltaire (François Marie Arouet)

See also: BABBLE, BLOCKHEAD, DULLNESS, LOQUACITY, MONOTONY, OBSCURITY.

BORROWING

The borrower runs in his own debt.
Ralph Waldo Emerson

The shoulders of a borrower are always a little straighter than those of a beggar.
Morris Leopold Ernst

Getting into debt, is getting into a tanglesome net.
Benjamin Franklin

If you would know the value of money, go and try to borrow some. He that goes a-borrowing goes a-sorrowing.
Benjamin Franklin

Borrowing is not much better than begging.
Gotthold Ephraim Lessing

Never call a man a fool; borrow from him.
Addison Mizner

It is folly to borrow when there is no prospect of or ability to pay back.
Jawaharlal Nehru

Live within your income, even if you have to borrow money to do so.
Henry Wheeler Shaw (Josh Billings)

See also: BANK, CREDIT, DEBT, LENDING, PLAGIARISM.

BOSTON

If you hear an owl hoot: "To whom" instead of "To who," you can make up your mind he was born and educated in Boston.
Anonymous

And this is good old Boston,
The home of the bean and the cod,
Where the Lowells talk to the Cabots,
And the Cabots talk only to God.
John Collins Bossidy

Boston runs to brains as well as to beans and brown bread. But she is cursed with an army of cranks whom nothing short of a straightjacket or a swamp-elm club will ever control.
William Cowper Brann

See also: AMERICANA, CITY, NEW YORK.

BOXING

The code of fair play which rules most games is not apparent in the boxing racket. The bribing of referees and judges happens as often as a certain type of manager can get to them. It is not considered wrong to scream for justice and accuse honest officials of being crooks when your man has lost on the square. The reputations of honest officials are often damaged by managers even when they give a true verdict against a fighter. Most managers who do not holler consider themselves to be slackers and the shrieking of lies is supposed to signify love of your fighter.
James J. (Jimmy) Cannon

They all have exceptional hand speed; hand speed and heart are what boxing is all about.
Tim Cohane

Boxing journalists are apt to write with pained surprise about the poor showing made in some particular fight by a hitherto stout-hearted pugilist. If only they would learn a few elementary facts about the anatomy and physiology of the brain, the explanation would readily emerge. Better still, let them attend a few post-mortem examinations upon those who succumb to boxing, so that they can see what havoc may be wrought upon the lobes of a repeatedly hammered brain.
James Hamilton Doggart

The longest fight never lasted a day. The greatest champion never held his title twenty years. The memory of the crowd survives the strength, courage, stamina and reflexes of the greatest of champions. A new "tiger" always waits to take the belt from any man, because he is a man and his body is perishable.

Esquire

Boxing, since its first recorded fervid beginnings (Cain vs. Abel) has managed to turn up strange personalities in stranger situations. The space generation has enjoyed its full measure of these, with perhaps an occasional bonus. To begin, it started with perhaps the best of the heavyweight champions, Joe Louis, and toward the end offered perhaps the most controversial, Muhammed Ali, born Cassius Clay.

Harold Rosenthal

In the 60's came that TV producers' dream, intercontinental live sports, bringing with it additional money for promoter and athlete alike. Who would ever have thought a generation earlier that the European rights to a heavyweight championship fight held in Lewiston, Maine would have been worth as much as was taken in at the gate in live money?

Harold Rosenthal

Today, a youth who doesn't know one end of a wrench from another can make more money in some unionized trade just standing and holding that wrench than he would by standing in a dusty ring permitting someone to boff away at his beak. Even the caveman was smart enough not to expose his features to the opposition a second time, unless forced to by a gnawing emptiness in his belly.

Harold Rosenthal

See also: SPORTS.

BOY

The fact that boys are allowed to exist at all is evidence of a remarkable Christian forbearance among men.

Ambrose Gwinnett Bierce

It used to be a good hotel, but that proves nothing—I used to be a good boy.

Samuel Langhorne Clemens (Mark Twain)

Boys will be boys, and so will a lot of middle-aged men.

Frank McKinney (Kin) Hubbard

A boy's will is the wind's will.

Henry Wadsworth Longfellow

Just at the age 'twixt boy and youth,
When thought is speech, and speech is truth.

Sir Walter Scott

You save an old man and you save a unit; but save a boy, and you save a multiplication table.

Gipsy Rodney Smith

Who feels injustice; who shrinks before a slight; who has a sense of wrong so acute, and so glowing a gratitude for kindness, as a generous boy?

William Makepeace Thackeray

Blessings on thee, little man,
Barefoot boy, with cheek of tan!
With thy turned-up pantaloons,
And thy merry whistled tunes;
With thy red lip, redder still
Kissed by Strawberries on the hill;
With the sunshine on thy face,
Through thy torn brim's jaunty grace;
From my heart I give thee joy,—
I was once a barefoot boy!

John Greenleaf Whittier

See also: ADOLESCENCE, AGE, AGE AND YOUTH, CHILDHOOD, CHILDREN, GIRL.

BRAINS

The brain is a wonderful organ; it starts working the moment you get up in the morning, and does not stop until you get into the office.

Robert Lee Frost

Brains well prepared are the monuments where human knowledge is more surely engraved.

Jean Jacques Rousseau

When God endowed human beings with brains, He did not intend to guarantee them.

Charles de Secondat (Baron de Montesquieu)

See also: ABILITY, CHARACTER, INTELLIGENCE, GENIUS, MIND.

BRAVERY

The brave man is not he who feels no fear, for that were stupid and irrational; but he whose noble soul subdues its fear, and bravely dares the danger nature shrinks from.

Joanna Baillie

At the bottom of not a little of the bravery that appears in the world, there lurks a miserable cowardice. Men will face powder and steel because they have not the courage to face public opinion.

Edwin Hubbel Chapin

No man can be brave who considers pain the greatest evil of life; or temperate, who regards pleasure as the highest good.

Cicero

Nature often enshrines gallant and noble hearts in weak bosoms; oftenest, God bless her, in woman's breast.

Charles John Huffam Dickens

All brave men love; for he only is brave who has affections to fight for, whether in the daily battle of life, or in physical contests.

Nathanial Hawthorne

Let us act in the spirit of Thucydides that "the bravest are surely those who have the clearest vision of what is before them, glory and danger alike, and yet notwithstanding go out to meet it."

Henry Alfred Kissinger

True bravery is shown by performing without witnesses what one might be capable of doing before all the world.

Duc François de La Rochefoucauld

Physical bravery is an animal instinct; moral bravery is a much higher and truer courage.

Wendell Phillips

Some one praising a man for his foolhardy bravery, Cato, the elder said, "There is a wide difference between true courage and a mere contempt of life."

Plutarch

The best hearts are ever the bravest.

Laurence Sterne

Bravery ceases to be bravery at a certain point, and becomes mere foolhardiness.

Sir Rabindranath Tagore

See also: COURAGE, HERO, VALOR.

BREAD

Back of the loaf is the snowy flour,
  And back of the flour the mill,
And back of the mill is the wheat and the
    shower,
  And the sun and the Father's will.

Maltbie Davenport Babcock

If from his home the lad that day
  His five small loaves had failed to take,
Would Christ have wrought—can any say—
  This miracle beside the lake?

Margaret Junkin Preston

Honesty is the rarest wealth anyone can possess, and yet all the honesty in the world ain't lawful tender for a loaf of bread.

Henry Wheeler Shaw (Josh Billings)

See also: DIET, DINNER, EATING.

BREAKFAST

The giraffe must get up at six in the morning if it wants to have its breakfast in its stomach by nine.

Samuel Butler

Never work before breakfast; if you have to work before breakfast, get your breakfast first.

Henry Wheeler Shaw (Josh Billings)

I think breakfast so pleasant because no one is conceited before one o'clock.

Sydney Smith

See also: DIET, DINNER, EATING.

BREVITY

Brevity is the best recommendation of speech, whether in a senator or an orator.

Cicero

Have something to say; say it, and stop when you've done.

Tryon Edwards

Never be so brief as to become obscure.

Tryon Edwards

The one prudence of life is concentration.

Ralph Waldo Emerson

Genuine good taste consists in saying much in few words, in choosing among our thoughts, in having order and arrangement in what we say, and in speaking with composure.

François de Salignac de La Mothe-Fénelon

One rare, strange virtue in speeches, and the secret of their mastery, is, that they are short.

Fitz-Greene Halleck

When you introduce a moral lesson let it be brief.

Horace

I saw one excellency within my reach—it was brevity, and I determined to obtain it.

William Jay

The fewer the words, the better the prayer.

Martin Luther

Talk to the point, and stop when you have reached it. Be comprehensive in all you say or write. To fill a volume about nothing is a credit to nobody.

John Neal

Words are like leaves, and where they most abound, much fruit of sense beneath is rarely found.

Alexander Pope

Say all you have to say in the fewest possible words, or your reader will be sure to skip them; and in the plainest possible words, or he will certainly misunderstand them.

John Ruskin

Brevity to writing is what charity is to all other virtues; righteousness is nothing without the one, nor authorship without the other.

Sydney Smith

If you would be pungent, be brief; for it is with words as with sunbeams—the more they are condensed, the deeper they burn.

Robert Southey

See also: SIMPLICITY, VERBOSITY.

BRIBERY

An honest politician is one who when he is bought will stay bought.

Simon Cameron

The universe is not rich enough to buy the vote of an honest man.

Gregory I (Gregory the Great)

The distinction between a campaign contribution and a bribe is almost a hairline difference.

Russell B. Long

Judges and senators have been bought with gold.

Alexander Pope

Every man has his price.

Sir Robert Walpole

See also: CONSPIRACY, CORRUPTION, DISHONESTY, MORALITY, TREASON.

BROADMINDEDNESS:
see OPENMINDEDNESS.

BROTHERHOOD

The brotherhood of man is an integral part of Christianity no less than the Fatherhood of God; and to deny the one is no less infidel than to deny the other.

Lyman Abbott

Grant us brotherhood, not only for this day but for all our years—a brotherhood not of words but of acts and needs.

Stephen Vincent Benét

For any church, country, nation, or other group to believe that it is the only people in whom God is interested, or that it has special merit because of color, race, or belief, that they are inherently superior and loved by God, without regard to the lives they live, is not only a great and dangerous fallacy, but is a continuing barrier to peace.

Hugh B. Brown

Our doctrine of equality and liberty and humanity comes from our belief in the brotherhood of man, through the fatherhood of God.

(John) Calvin Coolidge

Many times I realize how much my own outer and inner life is built upon the labors of my fellow-men, both living and dead, and how earnestly I must exert myself in order to give in return as much as I have received.

Albert Einstein

The universe is but one great city, full of beloved ones, divine and human, by nature endeared to each other.

Epictetus

There is no brotherhood of man without the fatherhood of God.

Henry Martyn Field

We are all tarred with the same brush, and are children of one and the same Creator, and as such the divine powers within us are infinite. To slight a single human being is to slight those divine powers, and thus to harm not only that being but with him the whole world.

Mohandas Karamchand (Mahatma) Gandhi

Jesus throws down the dividing prejudices of nationality, and teaches universal love, without distinction of race, merit, or rank. A man's neighbor is every one that needs help.

John Cunningham Geikie

Help thy brother's boat across, and lo! thine own has reached the shore.

Hindu Proverb

If God is thy father, man is thy brother.

Alphonse Marie Louis de Prat de Lamartine

The crest and crowning of all good, life's final star, is Brotherhood.

(Charles) Edwin Markham

To live is not to live for one's self alone; let us help one another.

Menander of Athens

If civilization is to survive, we must cultivate the science of human relationships—the ability of all peoples, of all kinds, to live together, in the same world at peace.

Franklin Delano Roosevelt

Humanity cannot go forward, civilization cannot advance, except as the philosophy of force is replaced by that of human brotherhood.

Francis Bowes Sayre

The race of mankind would perish did they cease to aid each other. We cannot exist without mutual help. All therefore that need aid have a right to ask it from their fellowmen; and no one who has the power of granting can refuse it without guilt.

Sir Walter Scott

However degraded or wretched a fellow mortal may be, he is still a member of our common species.

Seneca

We are members of one great body, planted by nature in a mutual love, and fitted for a social life. We must consider that we were born for the good of the whole.

Seneca

Brotherhood . . . is, in essence, a hope on the road—the long road—to fulfillment. To claim it to be already a full-grown fact is to be guilty of hypocrisy. To admit it to be always a fiction is to be guilty of cynicism. Let us avoid both.

Thomas Vernor Smith

However dark the prospects, however intractable the opposition, however devious and mendacious the diplomacy of our opponents, we ourselves have to carry so clear and intense a picture of our common humanity that we see the brother beneath the enemy and snatch at every opportunity to break through to his reason and his conscience, and, indeed, his enlightened self-interest.

Adlai Ewing Stevenson

It is clear that for Pope John the human race is not a cold abstraction, but a single precious family whose life, interests, responsibilities and well-being are a constant and loving preoccupation.

Adlai Ewing Stevenson

On this shrunken globe, men can no longer live as strangers.

Adlai Ewing Stevenson

Our prayer is that men everywhere will learn finally, to live as brothers, to respect each other's differences, to heal each other's wounds, to promote each other's progress, and to benefit from each other's knowledge. If the evangelical virtue of charity can be translated into political terms, aren't these our goals?

Adlai Ewing Stevenson

We cannot hope to command brotherhood abroad unless we practice it at home.

Harry S Truman

We do not want the men of another color for our brothers-in-law, but we do want them for our brothers.

Booker Taliaferro Washington

See also: CHRIST, CHRISTIANITY, COMMUNISM, COMPANIONSHIP, ECUMENISM, EQUALITY, FRIENDSHIP, HUMANITY, MAN, SELFISHNESS, SOCIETY, UNITED NATIONS.

BUDDHISM

Buddha has always had a great appeal for me. It is difficult for me to analyse this appeal but it is not a religious appeal, and I am not interested in the dogmas that have grown up round Buddhism. It is the personality that has drawn me. So also the personality of Christ has attracted me greatly.

Jawaharlal Nehru

Buddha's way was the Middle Path, between the extremes of self-indulgence and self-mortification.

Jawaharlal Nehru

I believe that it is essentially through the message of the Buddha that we can look at our problems in the right perspective, and draw back from conflict, and from competing with one another in the realm of conflict, violence and hatred. Every action has certain consequences. A good action has certain good consequences. An evil action has evil consequences. That I believe is as good a law of nature as any physical or chemical law. If that is so, hatred, which is evil, must have evil consequences and, indeed, leads to the growth of violence.

Jawaharlal Nehru

See also: BELIEF, CHURCH, RELIGION

BUILDING

Never build after you are five-and-forty; have five years' income in hand before you lay a brick; and always calculate the expense at double the estimate.

Henry Kett

Something men have that half-gods never know, the power to sensitize cold, lifeless things; to make stones breathe, and out of metal grow escarpments that deny the need of wings.

Virginia Taylor McCormick

He that is fond of building will soon ruin himself without the help of enemies.

Plutarch

See also: ARCHITECTURE, ART, CITY, HOUSE.

BUSINESS

Business without profit is not business any more than a pickle is candy.

Charles Frederick Abbott

To manage a business successfully requires as much courage as that possessed by the soldier who goes to war. Business courage is the more natural because all the benefits which the public has in material wealth come from it.

Charles Frederick Abbott

There is nothing more requisite in business than dispatch.

Joseph Addison

In civil business; what first? boldness; what second and third? boldness: and yet boldness is a child of ignorance and baseness.

Francis Bacon

We should keep in mind that the humanities come before the dollars. Our first duty runs to man before business, but we must not forget that sometimes the two are interchangeable.

Bernard Mannes Baruch

That I should make him that steals my coat a present of my cloak—what would become of business?

Katharine Lee Bates

The gambling known as business looks with austere disfavor upon the business known as gambling.

Ambrose Gwinnett Bierce

The heart of economics . . . is the satisfaction of wants. So it's just good business to create a want that only your factory can satisfy. But nature doesn't have factories, so it's obvious that the creation of such a demand is probably unnatural . . . wrong. And when you encourage people to do the wrong things, you're really creating a pattern of life—a way of living—that you shouldn't.

Ralph Borsodi

In the field of modern business, so rich in opportunity for the exercise of man's finest and most varied mental faculties and moral qualities, mere money-making cannot be regarded as the legitimate end . . . since with the conduct of business human happiness or misery is inextricably interwoven.

Louis Dembitz Brandeis

It is in the interest of the community that a man in a free business, in a competitive business, shall have the incentive to make as much money as he can.

Louis Dembitz Brandeis

The goals of business are inseparable from the goals of the whole community. Every attempt to sever the organic unity of business and the community inflicts equal hardship on both.

Earl Bunting

The best mental effort in the game of business is concentrated on the major problem of securing the consumer's dollar before the other fellow gets it.

Stuart Chase

There are two times in a man's life when he should not speculate; when he can't afford it and when he can.

Samuel Langhorne Clemens (Mark Twain)

The business of America is business.

(John) Calvin Coolidge

After all, what the worker does is buy back from those who finance him the goods that he himself produces. Pay him a wage that enables him to buy, and you fill your market with ready consumers.

James John Davis

I do not believe government can run any business as efficiently as private enterprise, and the victim of every such experiment is the public.

Thomas Edmund Dewey

The man who is above his business may one day find his business above him.

Samuel Drew

All business proceeds on beliefs, or judgments of probabilities, and not on certainties.

Charles William Eliot

Business is never so healthy as when, like a chicken, it must do a certain amount of scratching for what it gets.

Henry Ford

Business needs more of the professional spirit. The professional spirit seeks professional integrity, from pride, not from compulsion. The professional spirit detects its own violations and penalizes them.

Henry Ford

Some day the ethics of business will be universally recognized, and in that day Business will be seen to be the oldest and most useful of all the professions.

Henry Ford

I am impatient with the slavish and stereotyped thinking which has led some businessmen to consider security a bad word and to brand all concern for human and social progress as Communism or creeping socialism. I'm all for chasing the sacred cows out of business.

Henry Ford II

The widespread suspicion and even hostility of businessmen to government, even when, as in the case of the Eisenhower Administra-

tion, it was presumptively sympathetic to business, is one of the great constants in our political life.

John Kenneth Galbraith

The "tired business man" is one whose business is usually not a successful one.

Joseph Ridgeway Grundy

Punctuality is the soul of business.

Thomas Chandler Haliburton

Anybody can cut prices, but it takes brains to make a better article.

Alice Hubbard

The art of winning in business is in working hard—not taking things too seriously.

Elbert Green Hubbard

A man's success in business today turns upon his power of getting people to believe he has something that they want.

Gerald Stanley Lee

Wealthy owners and all masters of labor should be mindful of this—that to exercise pressure upon the indigent and the destitute for the sake of gain, and to gather one's profit out of the need of another, is condemned by all laws, human and divine.

Leo XIII (Gioacchino Vincenzo Pecci)

Big Business is basic to the very life of this country; and yet many—perhaps most—Americans have a deep-seated fear and an emotional repugnance to it. Here is a monumental contradiction.

David Eli Lilienthal

Big business is a superior economic tool by which to provide those *things* that constitute the physical basis of living . . . [Also] in Bigness we have the material foundation of a society which can further the highest values known to men, values we describe as "spiritual."

David Eli Lilienthal

The problem is not whether business will survive in competition with business, but whether any business will survive at all in the face of social change.

Laurence Joseph McGinley

Business is a combination of war and sport.

André Maurois

Never do something you do not approve of
in order more quickly to accomplish something you do approve of, for there are no safe
shortcuts in piloting a business.

John Pierpont Morgan

The phenomenon I refer to . . . is the tidal
wave of craving for convenience that is
sweeping over America. Today convenience
is the success factor of just about every type
of produce and service that is showing steady
growth.

Charles G. Mortimer

In the modern world of business, it is useless
to be a creative, original thinker unless you
can also sell what you create. Management
cannot be expected to recognize a good idea
unless it is presented to them by a good salesman.

David Mackenzie Ogilvy

Our business needs massive transfusions of
talent. And talent, I believe, is most likely to
be found among nonconformists, dissenters,
and rebels.

David Mackenzie Ogilvy

Free competition, . . . though within certain
limits just and productive of good results,
cannot be the ruling principle of the economic world.

Pius XI (Achille Ambrogio Damiano Ratti)

In our days not alone is wealth accumulated,
but immense power and despotic economic
domination is concentrated in the hands of
a few, and that those few are for the most
part not the owners, but only the trustees and
directors of invested funds, who administer
them at their good pleasure . . . so that no
one dare breathe against their will.

Pius XI (Achille Ambrogio Damiano Ratti)

Executive ability is deciding quickly and
getting somebody else to do the work.

John Garland Pollard

An excellent monument might be erected to
the Unknown Stockholder. It might take the
form of a solid stone ark of faith apparently
floating in a pool of water.

Felix Riesenberg

No business is above Government; and
Government must be empowered to deal
adequately with any business that tries to
rise above Government.

Franklin Delano Roosevelt

No business which depends for existence on
paying less than living wages to its workers
has any right to continue in this country.

Franklin Delano Roosevelt

We demand that big business give people a
square deal; in return we must insist that
when anyone engaged in big business honestly endeavours to do right, he shall himself
be given a square deal.

Theodore Roosevelt

If the Golden Rule is to be preached at all
in these modern days, when so much of our
life is devoted to business, it must be
preached specially in its application to the
conduct of business.

Ferdinand Schureman Schenck

In spite of the Lincolns and the Theodore
Roosevelts, the American business community
has not had an inspiring record in politics.
Business fought Jackson; it fought Lincoln;
it fought Theodore Roosevelt and Wilson and
Franklin D. Roosevelt; and, on virtually all
the issues of controversy, Americans now believe the business community to have been
wrong.

Arthur Meier Schlesinger

A criminal is a person with predatory instincts
who has not sufficient capital to form a
corporation.

Howard Scott

Success or failure in business is caused more
by the mental attitude even than by mental
capacities.

Walter Dill Scott

A business consultant is a person who knows
much less about your business than you do
yourself, but who is prepared to advise you
how to run it, for a fee which your business
could not possibly afford to pay even if it was
run properly instead of according to his
advice.

Sir John Roughton Simpson

Nobody ever pries into another man's concerns, but with a design to do, or to be able
to do him a mischief.

Robert South

Men of great parts are often unfortunate in
the management of public business, because
they are apt to go out of the common road
by the quickness of their imagination.

Jonathan Swift

Not because of any extraordinary talents did
he succeed, but because he had a capacity on
a level for business and not above it.

Tacitus

Did you ever expect a Corporation to have
a conscience, when it has no soul to be
damned, and no body to be kicked?

Edward Thurlow (Lord Thurlow)

Private capital and private management are
entitled to adequate reward for efficiency,
but business must recognize that its reward
results from the employment of the resources
of the nation. Business is a public trust and
must adhere to national standards in the
conduct of its affairs.

Harry S Truman

The lawyer and the doctor and other professional men have often a touch of civilization.
The banker and the merchant seldom.

Jim Tully

Business men boast of their skill and cunning
but in philosophy they are like little children.
Bragging to each other of successful depreda-
tions they neglect to consider the ultimate
fate of the body.

Arthur David Waley

When it comes to selling the business system,
we get as drab as a crutch, as unexciting as a
chorus girl in a flannel nightgown.

Walter Berthau Weisenburger

The way to stop financial "joy-riding" is to
arrest the chauffeur, not the automobile.

(Thomas) Woodrow Wilson

Business is like riding a bicycle. Either you
keep moving or you fall down.

John David Wright

Markets as well as mobs respond to human
emotions; markets as well as mobs can be
inflamed to their own destruction.

Owen D. Young

See also: ADVERTISING, ADMINISTRATION, COM-
MERCE, EMPLOYMENT, EXECUTIVES,
FINANCE, FREE ENTERPRISE, INDUS-
TRY, OCCUPATION, SPECULATION,
TRADE, UNEMPLOYMENT.

BUSY

Occupation is a necessity to the young. They
love to be busy about something, however
trifling; and if not directed to some useful
employment will soon engage in something
that is evil, thus verifying the old proverb,
"That idleness is the mother of mischief."

Henry Ward Beecher

The busy have no time for tears.

George Gordon Byron (Lord Byron)

I have lived to know that the great secret of
human happiness is this: never suffer your
energies to stagnate. The old adage of "too
many irons in the fire," conveys an abominable lie. You cannot have too many—poker,
tongs, and all—keep them all going.

Adam Clarke

Occupation is the necessary basis of all enjoyment.

(James Henry) Leigh Hunt

No thoroughly occupied man was ever yet
very miserable.

Letitia Elizabeth Landon

You see men of the most delicate frames
engaged in active and professional pursuits
who really have no time for idleness. Let
them become idle,—let them take care of
themselves, let them think of their health,—
and they die! The rust rots the steel which
use preserves.

Edward G. Bulwer-Lytton (Baron Lytton)

Occupation is the scythe of time.

Napoleon I (Bonaparte)

Let a man choose what condition he will, and
let him accumulate around him all the goods
and gratifications seemingly calculated to
make him happy in it; if that man is left at
any time without occupation or amusement,
and reflects on what he is, the meagre,
languid felicity of his present lot will not bear
him up. He will turn necessarily to gloomy
anticipations of the future; and unless his
occupation calls him out of himself, he is
inevitably wretched.

Blaise Pascal

The want of occupation is no less the plague
of society, than of solitude.

Jean Jacques Rousseau

The great happiness of life, I find, after all, to consist in the regular discharge of some mechanical duty.

  Johann Christoph Friedrich von Schiller

See also: BUSINESS, DILIGENCE, PERSEVERENCE, WORK.

BUT

The meanest, most contemptible kind of praise is that which first speaks well of a man, and then qualifies it with a "but."

  Henry Ward Beecher

Oh, now comes that bitter word—but, which makes all nothing that was said before, that smooths and wounds, that strikes and dashes more than a flat denial, or a plain disgrace.

  Samuel Daniel

"But" is a word that cools many a warm impulse, stifles many a kindly thought, puts a dead stop to many a brotherly deed. No one would ever love his neighbor as himself if he listened to all the "buts" that could be said.

  Edward G. Bulwer-Lytton (Baron Lytton)

I know of no manner of speaking so offensive as that of giving praise, and closing it with an exception.

  Sir Richard Steele

See also: COMPARISON, CONTRADICTION, CONTRAST, EXCEPTION.

BUTTERFLY

I'd be a butterfly born in a bower,
Where roses and lilies and violets meet.

  Thomas Haynes Bayly

The caterpillar on the leaf
Repeats to thee thy mother's grief.
Kill not the moth nor butterfly,
For the Last Judgement draweth nigh.

  William Blake

Bees sip honey from flowers and hum their thanks when they leave. The gaudy butterfly is sure that the flowers owe thanks to him.

  Sir Rabindranath Tagore

See also: ANIMAL, BEE.

C

CALAMITY

Calamity is man's true touchstone.
Francis Beaumont and John Fletcher

Calamity is the perfect glass wherein we truly see and know ourselves.
Sir William Davenant

When any calamity has been suffered, the first thing to be remembered, is, how much has been escaped.
Samuel Johnson

A trouble is a trouble, and the general idea, in the country, is to treat it as such, rather than to snatch the knotted cords from the hand of God and deal out murderous blows.
William McFee

It is only from the belief of the goodness and wisdom of a supreme being, that our calamities can be borne in the manner which becomes a man.
Henry Mackenzie

He who foresees calamities, suffers them twice over.
Beilby Porteus

See also: ADVERSITY, CRISIS, PANIC, WAR.

CALENDAR

Events are sometimes the best calendar.
Benjamin Disraeli

It fell in the ancient periods
  Which the brooding Soul surveys,
Or ever the wild Time coined itself
  Into calendar month and days.
Ralph Waldo Emerson

Thirty days hath September,
April, June, and November,
February has twenty-eight alone,
All the rest have thirty-one;

Excepting leap-year,—that's the time
When February's days are twenty-nine.
The Return from Parnassus (London, 1606)

Most modern calendars mar the sweet simplicity of our lives by reminding us that each day that passes is the anniversary of some perfectly uninteresting event.
Oscar Wilde

Though it would be dangerous to make calendars the basis of Culture, we should all be much improved if we began each day with a fine passage of English poetry.
Oscar Wilde

See also: AGE, THE; FUTURE; PAST; PRESENT; TIME.

CALUMNY

Caluminate enough, something of the calumny always sticks.
Pierre Augustin Caron de Beaumarchais

To seem disturbed at calumny, is the way to make it believed, and stabbing your defamer, will not prove you innocent. Live an exemplary life, and then your good character will overcome and refute the calumny.
Hugh Blair

We cannot control the evil tongues of others, but a good life enables us to despise them.
Cato the Elder

Calumny is like the wasp that worries you, which it is not best to try to get rid of unless you are sure of slaying it; for otherwise it returns to the charge more furious than ever.
Sébastien Roch Nicolas Chamfort

The upright man, if he suffer calumny to move him, fears the tongue of man more than the eye of God.
Charles Caleb Colton

Opposition and calumny are often the brightest tribute that vice and folly can pay to virtue and wisdom.

Rutherford Birchard Hayes

The calumniator inflicts wrong by slandering the absent; and he who gives credit to the calumny before he knows it is true, is equally guilty. The person traduced is doubly injured; by him who propagates, and by him who credits the slander.

Herodotus

False praise can please, and calumny affright, none but the vicious and the hypocrite.

Horace

I am beholden to calumny, that she hath so endeavored to belie me. It shall make me set a surer guard on myself, and keep a better watch upon my actions.

Ben (Benjamin) Jonson

The opposite of what is said about people and things is often the truth.

Jean de La Bruyère

He that lends an easy and credulous ear to calumny, is either a man of very ill morals, or he has no more sense and understanding than a child.

Menander of Athens

Never chase a lie; if you let it alone, it will soon run itself to death. You can work out a good character faster than calumny can destroy it.

Eliphalet Nott

Believe nothing against another but on good authority; and never report what may hurt another, unless it be a greater hurt to some other to conceal it.

William Penn

At every word, a reputation dies.

Alexander Pope

Close thine ear against him that opens his mouth against another. If thou receive not his words, they fly back and wound him. If thou receive them, they flee forward and wound thee.

Francis Quarles

I never listen to calumnies; because if they are untrue, I run the risk of being deceived; and if they are true, of hating persons not worth thinking about.

Charles de Secondat (Baron de Montesquieu)

Those who ought to be most secure against calumny, are generally those who least escape it.

Stanislas I (Leszczyński)

Neglected calumny soon expires; show that you are hurt, and you give it the appearance of truth.

Tacitus

To persevere in one's duty and be silent, is the best answer to calumny.

George Washington

See also: ABUSE, BABBLE, LYING, SLANDER.

CALVINISM

The Pope put his foot on the neck of kings, but Calvin and his cohorts crushed the whole human race under their heels in the name of the Lord of Hosts.

Oliver Wendell Holmes

The doctrines of Jesus are simple, and tend all to the happiness of man. . . . But compared with these the demoralizing dogmas of Calvin.
1. That there are three Gods.
2. That good works, or the love of our neighbor, is nothing.
3. That faith is every thing, and the more incomprehensible the proposition, the more merit the faith.
4. That reason in religion is of unlawful use.
5. That God, from the beginning, elected certain individuals to be saved, and certain others to be damned; and that no crimes of the former can damn them; no virtues of the latter save them.

Thomas Jefferson

The basis of Calvin's theology is the belief that through the Bible alone can God be known in His wholeness as the Creator, Redeemer and Lord of the world. He is not so discernible in any other place—in the creation, or in man's conscience, or in the course of history and experience. And since, if we are to know of God, we must go to the place where He is to be found, it is to the Scriptures that we must go, and there we shall find Him as He is. . . . The Scriptures are not Man's guesses about the mystery of God, nor are they the conclusions that men have drawn from certain data at their disposal. On the contrary, they are the unveiling of the mystery of God by God Himself; God's gracious revelation of Himself to ignorant and sinful men. Far from being a stage, even the last stage, of man's quest for the well at the world's end, the Bible is the place where God comes from above and beyond the world to show Himself to His people.

Thomas Henry Louis Parker

Among the English Puritans, who on the questions of ecclesiastical polity and infant baptism split into various groups . . . Calvinism was the common doctrinal ground that united them.

Ivor B. Thomas

Calvin, far more than Luther, thought that Scripture provides a rule of conduct for the Christian life. His descendants have often been so preoccupied with carrying out that rule that they have fallen into the trap of thinking that thereby they earn their own salvation—the very notion that Calvin sought to destroy.

Ivor B. Thomas

Calvin taught that the State was divinely instituted and that all citizens ought to be obedient to those whom God has placed over them. Only when the State infringes upon the honor of God may the citizen take up arms to overthrow its tyranny.

Ivor B. Thomas

Calvin was preeminently a biblical theologian, one who saw the whole task of theology as being a commentary on Scripture. God speaks to man through Scripture and it is the responsibility of man to listen.

Ivor B. Thomas

One of the characteristic features of Calvinism has been its concern with the day to day behavior of Christian man.

Ivor B. Thomas

Beginning with the absolute perfection of God and the absolute dependence of all His creatures on His will, John Calvin builds up a system of theology with the divine decree as its center. Predestination, election, total depravity, irresistible grace and everlasting perseverance of the elect, follow as necessary corollaries.

Andrew Constantinides Zenos

See also: CHRISTIANITY, PROTESTANTISM, SECT.

CAMARADERIE

The company of just and righteous men is better than wealth and a rich estate.

Euripides

Forsooth, brethren, fellowship is heaven and lack of fellowship is hell; fellowship is life and lack of fellowship is death; and the deeds that ye do upon the earth, it is for fellowship's sake that ye do them.

William Morris

To disbelieve in marriage is easy; to love a married woman is easy; but to betray a comrade, to be disloyal to a host, to break the covenant of bread and salt, is impossible.

George Bernard Shaw

See also: COMPANIONSHIP, FRIENDSHIP.

CANADA

Long live free Quebec!

Charles André Joseph Marie de Gaulle

One's first impression when the plane loses height over Newfoundland is of an unfinished struggle. The Atlantic is reluctant to relinquish its sway, undisputed for so many hundreds of miles, and the countless lakes seem locked in a struggle for supremacy with the land. This feeling of the unfinished grows stronger as the journey proceeds across this continent so vast that the sixteen million inhabitants concentrated in a relatively thin strip north of the United States border still seem like pioneers on a bridgehead.

Economist

The real meaning of the Canadian experience has been that nation's efforts to create a meaningful and separate identity in the northern half of the North American Continent.

Dante B. Fascell

Americans as a nation do not know a great deal about Canada. This is our misfortune.

Walter Gordon

Our other sense of Canada is that of a vacation land. It *is* a vacation land and I think if you were to poll the ordinary citizen in the United States, he would suggest to you that his concept of Canada is either that of a place where a verry, verry British group is trying to hang on to British accents and British designs, or of the picturesque French-Canadian rural country side.

Harlan Henthorne Hatcher

See also: AMERICA, ENGLAND.

CANCER

Vast resources must indeed be mustered in the search for cancer's Achilles heel. Each advance has been hard fought, yet scientists are more hopeful than ever before. They are confident that they will come up with the answers. At stake is triumph in a human adventure of the highest drama. And with this triumph will come the prize of a lessening of human suffering and of premature death throughout the world.

Orlando A. Battista

Every blast of cancer propaganda makes millions of people worry.

George Washington Crile, Jr.

It is possible that today cancer phobia causes more suffering than cancer itself.

George Washington Crile, Jr.

Surely the medical profession can teach the people who have incurable cancer to live with their cancers in equanimity. When faith is strong there comes a time of peace.

George Washington Crile, Jr.

See also: DISEASE, SICKNESS.

CANDOR

Examine what is said, not him who speaks.

Arabian Proverb

Give me the avowed, the erect, the manly foe, bold I can meet,—perhaps may turn his blow! But of all plagues, good Heavens, thy wrath can send, save, save, oh save me from the *candid friend!*

George Canning

Candor is the brightest gem of criticism.

Benjamin Disraeli

There is no wisdom like frankness.

Benjamin Disraeli

The diligent fostering of a candid habit of mind, even in trifles, is a matter of high moment both to character and opinions.

John Saul Howson

Friends, if we be honest with ourselves, we shall be honest with each other.

George Macdonald

Innocence in genius, and candor in power, are both noble qualities.

Madame de Staël

Making my breast transparent as pure crystal, that the world, jealous of me, may see the foulest thought my heart doth hold.

George Villiers (2d Duke of Buckingham)

It is great and manly to disdain disguise; it shows our spirit, and proves our strength.

Edward Young

See also: FRANKNESS, SINCERITY, TRUTH.

CANT

Cant is itself properly a double-distilled lie, the materia prima of the devil, from which all falsehoods, imbecilities, and abominations body themselves, and from which no true thing can come.

Thomas Carlyle

Cant is good to provoke common sense.

Ralph Waldo Emerson

Cant is the voluntary overcharging or prolongation of a real sentiment; hypocrisy is the setting up pretence to a feeling you never had, and have no wish for.

William Hazlitt

Of all the cants in this canting world, though the cant of hypocrites may be the worst, the cant of criticism is the most tormenting.

Laurence Sterne

See also: AFFECTATION, HYPOCRISY, INSINCERITY, PRETENSION, SELF-RIGHTEOUSNESS, SOPHISTRY.

CAPITAL AND LABOR

By bourgeoisie is meant the class of modern capitalists, owners of the means of social production and employers of wage-labor. By proletariat, the class of modern wage-laborers who, having no means of production of their own, are reduced to selling their labor-power in order to live.

Friedrich Engels

Capital is a result of labor, and is used by labor to assist it in further production. Labor is the active and initial force, and labor is therefore the employer of capital.

Henry George

Each needs the other: capital cannot do without labor, nor labor without capital.

Leo XIII (Gioacchino Vincenzo Pecci)

Labor is prior to, and independent of, capital. Capital is only the fruit of labor, and could never have existed if labor had not first existed. Labor is the superior of capital, and deserves much the higher consideration.

Abraham Lincoln

Capital is dead labor that, vampirelike, lives only by sucking living labor, and lives the more, the more labor is suck.

Karl Marx

We are coming to see that there should be no stifling of Labor by Capital, or of Capital by Labor; and also that there should be no stifling of Labor by Labor, or of Capital by Capital.

John Davison Rockefeller, Jr.

Labor in this country is independent and proud. It has not to ask the patronage of capital, but capital solicits the aid of labor.

Daniel Webster

It is time for both labor and management to grow up, to recognize each other as essential factors in the same basic enterprise—United States industry—and to settle their affairs among themselves without recourse to government.

Wendell Lewis Willkie

See also: BUSINESS, CAPITALISM, COMMERCE, COMMUNISM, EMPLOYMENT, FINANCE, INDUSTRY, LABOR, TRADE UNIONS, TRADES, TRADING, UNEMPLOYMENT, WORK.

CAPITAL PUNISHMENT

Capital punishment has become an increasingly controversial practice, and the movement to abolish it has become a matter of great social significance in the United States and in many other countries.

Eugene B. Block

The question of capital punishment has been the subject of endless discussion and will probably never be settled so long as men believe in punishment.

Clarence Seward Darrow

The long and distressing controversy over capital punishment is very unfair to anyone meditating murder.

Geoffrey Francis Fisher

No one knows how many innocent men, erroneously convicted of murder, have been put to death by American governments. For, once a convicted man is dead, all interest in vindicating him generally evaporates.

Jerome New Frank

I shall ask for the abolition of the punishment of death until I have the infallibility of human judgement demonstrated to me.

Thomas Jefferson

If we are to abolish the death penalty, I should like to see the first step taken by my friends the murderers.

Alphonse Karr

The worst use you can put a man to is to kill him.

Alphonso David Rockwell

Criminals do not die by the hands of the law; they die by the hands of other men.

George Bernard Shaw

See also: CRIME, DEATH, PUNISHMENT.

CAPITALISM

In arguing that capitalism as such is not the cause of war, I must not be taken as arguing that capitalists do not often believe in war, believe that they and their country benefit from it.

Sir Norman Angell

The organization of society on the principle of private profit . . . is leading both to the deformation of humanity by unregulated industrialism, and to the exhaustion of natural resources.

Thomas Stearns Eliot

The dynamo of our economic system is self-interest which may range from mere petty greed to admirable types of self-expression.

Felix Frankfurter

The American people will find it hard, as I do, to accept a situation in which a tiny handful of steel executives whose pursuit of private power and profit exceeds their sense of public responsibility, can show such utter contempt for the interest of 185 million Americans.

John Fitzgerald Kennedy

Capitalism is at its ebb . . . This does not mean that it is already lying down with its legs stretched out; much work has yet to be done to bring it to such a state. But this is inevitable, just as death inevitably comes to a living organism or plant after a specific stage of development.

Nikita Sergeevich Khrushchev

Capitalism is congenitally unable to allow black men to be free.

Julius Lester

The rich people today are those who have plenty of surplus, the poor have none at all.

It is not so much because one person works more than another, but nowadays a person who does not work at all gets the surplus, while the hard worker often gets no part of it. This seems a very silly arrangement. Many people think that it is because of this stupid arrangement that there are so many poor people in the world.

Jawaharlal Nehru

The fundamental idea of modern capitalism is not the right of the individual to possess and enjoy what he has earned, but the thesis that the exercise of this right redounds to the general good.

Ralph Barton Perry

What we mean when we say we are for or against capitalism is that we like or dislike a certain civilization or scheme of life.

Joseph Alois Schumpeter

It would be wrong to think that the Second World War was a casual occurrence or the result of mistakes of any particular statesmen, though mistakes undoubtedly were made. Actually the war was the inevitable result of the development of world economic and political forces on the basis of modern monopoly capitalism. Marxists have declared more than once that the capitalist system of world economy harbors elements of general crises and armed conflicts and that, hence, the development of world capitalism in our time proceeds not in the form of smooth and even progress but through crises and military catastrophes.

Joseph Stalin

See also: BUSINESS, CAPITAL AND LABOR, EXECUTIVE, FINANCE, INDUSTRY, MONEY.

CARDS

It is very wonderful to see persons of the best sense passing hours together in shuffling and dividing a pack of cards with no conversation but what is made up of a few game-phrases, and no other ideas but those of black or red spots ranged together in different figures. Would not a man laugh to hear any one of his species complaining that life is short?

Joseph Addison

With spots quadrangular of diamond form, Ensanguined hearts, clubs typical of strife, And spades, the emblems of untimely graves.

William Cowper

The bizarre world of cards . . . a world of pure power politics where rewards and punishments were meted out immediately. A deck of cards was built like the purest of hierarchies, with every card a master to those below it, a lackey to those above it. And there were the "masses"—long suits—which always asserted themselves in the end, triumphing over the kings and aces.

Ely Culbertson

Cards were at first for benefits designed, Sent to amuse, not to enslave the mind.

David Garrick

See also: AMUSEMENT, CHANCE, DICE, DIVERSION, FORTUNE, GAMBLING, LUCK, RECREATION, WAGER.

CARE

"Many of our cares," says Scott, "are but a morbid way of looking at our privileges." We let our blessings get mouldy, and then call them curses.

Henry Ward Beecher

Care admitted as a guest, quickly turns to be master.

Christian Nestell Bovee

This world has cares enough to plague us; but he who meditates on others' woe, shall, in that meditation, lose his own.

Richard Cumberland

The every-day cares and duties, which men call drudgery, are the weights and counterpoises of the clock of time, giving its pendulum a true vibration, and its hands a regular motion; and when they cease to hang upon the wheels, the pendulum no longer swings, the hands no longer move, and the clock stands still.

Henry Wadsworth Longfellow

We can easily manage, if we will only take, each day, the burden appointed for it. But the load will be too heavy for us if we carry yesterday's burden over again to-day, and then add the burden of the morrow to the weight before we are required to bear it.

John Newton

Cares are often more difficult to throw off than sorrows; the latter die with time; the former grow upon it.

Jean Paul Richter

Providence has given us hope and sleep as a compensation for the many cares of life.

Voltaire (François Marie Arouet)

See also: ANXIETY, ATTENTION, CAUTION, INDIFFERENCE, RESPONSIBILITY, WATCHFULNESS, WORRY.

CAREER

People don't choose their careers: they are engulfed by them.

John Roderigo Dos Passos

In a free market, in an age of endemic inflation, it is unquestionably more rewarding, in purely pecuniary terms, to be a speculator or a prostitute than a teacher, preacher, or policeman.

John Kenneth Galbraith

Analyzing what you haven't got as well as what you have is a necessary ingredient of a career.

Grace Moore

To find a career to which you are adapted by nature, and then to work hard at it, is about as near to a formula for success and happiness as the world provides.

Mark Sullivan

See also: AMBITION, EMPLOYMENT, GUIDANCE, OCCUPATION, OPPORTUNITY, TRADE, VOCATION, WORK.

CARICATURE

Take my advice, and never draw caricature. By the long practice of it I have lost the enjoyment of beauty. I never see a face but distorted, and never have the satisfaction to behold the human face divine.

William Hogarth

Parodies and caricatures are the most penetrating of criticisms.

Aldous Leonard Huxley

Nothing conveys a more inaccurate idea of a whole truth than a part of a truth so prominently brought forth as to throw the other parts into shadow. This is the art of caricature, by the happy use of which you might caricature the Apollo Belvidere.

Edward G. Bulwer-Lytton (Baron Lytton)

See also: EXAGGERATION, RIDICULE, SATIRE.

CAT

It has been the providence of nature to give this creature nine lives instead of one.

Bidpai

Ignorant people think it's the noise which fighting cats make that is so aggravating, but it ain't so; it's the sickening grammar they use.

Samuel Langhorne Clemens (Mark Twain)

A cat in Gloves catches no Mice.

Benjamin Franklin

Cat: a pygmy lion who loves mice, hates dogs, and patronizes human beings.

Oliver Herford

See also: ANIMAL, DOG.

CATHOLICISM

If the Christian religion, as I understand it, or as you understand it, should maintain its ground, as I believe it will, yet Platonic, Pythagoric, Hindoo, and cabalistic Christianity, which is Catholic Christianity, and which has prevailed for 1500 years, has received a mortal wound, of which the monster must finally die. Yet so strong is his constitution, that he may endure for centuries before he expires.

John Quincy Adams

Wherever a Catholic sun doth shine, there is lots of laughter and good red wine; At least I've always found it so, Benedicamus Domino!

Hilaire Belloc

Catholic theology has nothing to do with democracy, for or against, in the sense of a machinery of voting or a criticism of particular privileges. It is not committed to support what Whitman said for democracy, or even what Jefferson or Lincoln said for democracy.

Gilbert Keith Chesterton

The Catholic Church, that imperishable handiwork of our all-merciful God, has for her immediate and natural purpose the saving of souls and securing our happiness in heaven. Yet in regard to things temporal, she is the source of benefits as manifold and great as if the chief end of her existence were to ensure the prospering of our earthly life. And indeed, wherever the Church has set her foot, she has straightway changed the face of things, and has attempered the moral tone of the people with a new civilization and with virtues before unknown. All nations which have yielded to her sway have become eminent by their gentleness, their sense of justice, and the glory of their high deeds.

Leo XIII (Gioacchino Vincenzo Pecci)

The Roman Church is filled with men who are led into it merely by ambition, who, though they might have been useful and respectable as laymen, are hypocritical and immoral.

Thomas Babington Macaulay

In the present day there are 20 well-known gowns and 70 veils of the Virgin Mary, each pronounced to be the real one; 12 heads of St. John the Baptist, in tolerably perfect condition, besides numerous large fragments of his skull and seven extra jaws, each of great note, and held in much reverence in different parts of Europe. St. Julienne has 20 bodies and 26 separate heads, whilst St. George and St. Pancras each possess 30 heads, and St. Peter has 16; St. Peter the Dominican only possesses 2 bodies, but he makes up for the deficiency in the number of his fingers 56 of which are scattered throughout Europe.

Eveline Bertha Mitford

O that thy creed were sound!
For thou dost soothe the heart, thou Church
   of Rome,
   By thy unwearied watch and varied round
Of service, in thy Saviour's holy home.
   I cannot walk the city's sultry streets,
   But the wide porch invites to still retreats
Where passion's thirst is calm'd, and care's
   unthankful gloom.

John Henry Newman

The Roman Catholic Church was then, as it is now, a great democracy. There was no peasant so humble but that he might not become a priest, and no priest so obscure that he might not become Pope of Christendom; and every chancellery in Europe, every court in Europe, was ruled by these learned, trained and accomplished men—the priesthood of that great and dominant body. What kept government alive in the Middle Ages was this constant rise of the sap from the bottom, from the rank and file of the great body of the people through the open channels of the priesthood.

(Thomas) Woodrow Wilson

See also: CHRISTIANITY, CHURCH, PROTESTANTISM, SECT.

CAUSE

We are tired of great causes.

Francis Scott Key Fitzgerald

The cause is everything. Those even who are dearest to us must be shunted for the sake of the cause.

Mohandas Karamchand (Mahatma) Gandhi

Great causes and little men go ill together.

Jawaharlal Nehru

When a person is prepared to die for a cause, and indeed to glory in such a death, it is impossible to suppress him or the cause he represents.

Jawaharlal Nehru

No cause can command the deepest loyalties and the greatest sacrifices of men till it is presented under a moral aspect.

Arthur Meier Schlesinger

God is the free cause of all things.

Baruch (Benedict) Spinoza

See also: BEGINNING, RESULT.

CAUTION

It is better to be safe than sorry.

American Proverb

I don't like these cold, precise, perfect people, who, in order not to speak wrong, never speak at all, and in order not to do wrong, never do anything.

Henry Ward Beecher

Whenever our neighbor's house is on fire, it cannot be amiss for the engines to play a little on our own. Better to be despised for too anxious apprehensions, that ruined by too confident security.

Edmund Burke

All is to be feared where all is to be lost.

George Gordon Byron (Lord Byron)

None pities him that's in the snare, who warned before, would not beware.

Robert Herrick

It is well to learn caution by the misfortunes of others.

Publilius Syrus

Take warning by the misfortunes of others, that others may not take example from you.
Saadi (Muslih-ud-Din)

He that is over-cautious will accomplish but very little.
Johann Christoph Friedrich von Schiller

Caution in crediting, and reserve in speaking, and in revealing one's self to but very few, are the best securities both of a good understanding with the world, and of the inward peace of our own minds.
Thomas à Kempis

More firm and sure the hand of courage strikes, when it obeys the watchful eye of caution.
James Thomson

See also: CONSERVATISM, COWARDICE, DISCRETION, PRUDENCE, RASHNESS, REFLECTION, VIGILANCE, WATCHFULNESS.

CELEBRATION

On such an occasion as this,
 All time and nonsense scorning,
Nothing shall come amiss,
 And we won't go home till morning.
John Baldwin Buckstone

One should only celebrate a happy ending; celebrations at the beginning exhaust the joy and energy needed to urge us onward and sustain us in the long struggle. And of all the celebrations a wedding is the worst; no day should be kept more quietly and humbly.
Johann Wolfgang von Goethe

If an earthquake were to engulf England tomorrow, the English would manage to meet and dine somewhere among the rubbish, just to celebrate the event.
Douglas Jerrold

See also: HOLIDAY.

CELIBACY

If a mistaken marriage can be purgatory, mistaken celibacy is hell.
Robert Hugh Benson

I would be married, but I'd have no wife,
I would be married to a single life.
Richard Crashaw

Marriage has many pains, but celibacy has no pleasures.
Samuel Johnson

See also: BACHELOR, CHASTITY.

CENSORSHIP

Only the suppressed word is dangerous.
Ludwig Börne

So many new ideas are at first strange and horrible though ultimately valuable that a very heavy responsibility rests upon those who would prevent their dissemination.
John Burdon Sanderson Haldane

There really is a very poor market in Denmark for erotic literature, now that it is no longer forbidden fruit.
Hans Reitzel

I am opposed to censorship. Censors are pretty sure to be fools. I have no confidence in the suppression of every-day facts.
James Harvey Robinson

Four to six months before the [censorship] law was changed [in Denmark] you would distribute 20,000 to 25,000 copies of a new pornographic title. Now [1968] only about half of that number are printed, and a third of them come back.
Jørgen Rothenborg

All censorship exists to prevent anyone from challenging conceptions and existing institutions. All progress is initiated by challenging current conceptions and executed by supplanting existing institutions. Consequently the first condition of progress is the removal of censorship. There is the whole case against censorship in a nutshell.
George Bernard Shaw

Censorship reflects a society's lack of confidence in itself. It is a hallmark of an authoritarian regime.
Potter Stewart

See also: BOOKS, FREEDOM, MOTION PICTURES, OBSCENITY, PORNOGRAPHY, PRESS, THEATER.

CENSURE

There is no defense against reproach but obscurity; it is a kind of concomitant to greatness, as satires and invectives were an essential part of a Roman triumph.
Joseph Addison

It is impossible to indulge in habitual severity of opinion upon our fellow-men without injuring the tenderness and delicacy of our own feelings.

Henry Ward Beecher

The readiest and surest way to get rid of censure, is to correct ourselves.

Demosthenes

Most of our censure of others is only oblique praise of self, uttered to show the wisdom and superiority of the speaker. It has all the invidiousness of self-praise, and all the ill-desert of falsehood.

Tryon Edwards

We hand folks over to God's mercy, and show none ourselves.

George Eliot (Mary Ann Evans)

If any one speak ill of thee, consider whether he hath truth on his side; and if so, reform thyself, that his censures may not affect thee.

Epictetus

Few persons have sufficient wisdom to prefer censure, which is useful, to praise which deceives them.

Duc François de La Rochefoucauld

He is always the severest censor on the merits of others who has the least worth of his own.

Elias Lyman Magoon

The villain's censure is extorted praise.

Alexander Pope

The most censorious are generally the least judicious, or deserving, who, having nothing to recommend themselves, will be finding fault with others. No man envies the merit of another who has enough of his own.

Rule of Life

The censure of those who are opposed to us, is the highest commendation that can be given us.

Seigneur de Saint-Evremond

Censure is the tax a man pays to the public for being eminent.

Jonathan Swift

There are but three ways for a man to revenge himself for the censure of the world: to despise it; to return the like; or to live so as to avoid it. The first of these is usually pre-

tended; the last is almost impossible; the universal practice is for the second.

Jonathan Swift

He that well and rightly considereth his own works will find little cause to judge hardly of another.

Thomas à Kempis

Horace appears in good humor while he censures, and therefore his censure has the more weight, as supposed to proceed from judgment and not from passion.

Edward Young

See also: ABUSE, CRITICISM, REPROOF.

CEREMONY

The ceremonies you have seen today are ancient and some of their origins are veiled in the mists of the past, but their spirit and their meaning shine through the ages, never, perhaps, more brightly than now.

Elizabeth II

Ceremonies differ in every country; they are only artificial helps which ignorance assumes to imitate politeness, which is the result of good sense and good nature.

Oliver Goldsmith

Ceremony resembles that base coin which circulates through a country by royal mandate; it serves every purpose of real money at home, but is entirely useless if carried abroad. A person who should attempt to circulate his native trash in another country would be thought either ridiculous or culpable.

Oliver Goldsmith

To divest either politics or religion of ceremony, is the most certain method of bringing either into contempt. The weak must have their inducements to admiration as well as the wise; and it is the business of a sensible government to impress all ranks with a sense of subordination, whether this be effected by a diamond buckle, a virtuous edict, a sumptuary law, or a glass necklace.

Oliver Goldsmith

If we use no ceremony toward others, we shall be treated without any. People are soon tired of paying trifling attentions to those who receive them with coldness, and return them with neglect.

William Hazlitt

To dispense with ceremony is the most delicate mode of conferring a compliment.
Edward G. Bulwer-Lytton (Baron Lytton)

To repose our confidence in forms and ceremonies, is superstition; but not to submit to them is pride or self-conceit.
Blaise Pascal

Ceremonies are no aid to blessedness.
Baruch (Benedict) Spinoza

All ceremonies are, in themselves, very silly things; but yet a man of the world should know them. They are the outworks of manners and decency, which would too often be broken in upon, if it were not for that defence which keeps the enemy at a proper distance.
Philip Dormer Stanhope (Lord Chesterfield)

Ceremony is the invention of wise men to keep fools at a distance; as good breeding is an expedient to make fools and wise men equals.
Sir Richard Steele

See also: ETIQUETTE, FORMALISM, OSTENTATION, SIMPLICITY.

CERTAINTY

Years make men restless—they needs must spy
Some certainty, some sort of end assured,
Some sparkle, though from topmost beacon-tip,
That warrants life a harbor through the haze.
Robert Browning

Certainty generally is illusion, and repose is not the destiny of man.
Oliver Wendell Holmes, Jr.

Certitude is not the test of certainty. We have been cocksure of many things that were not so.
Oliver Wendell Holmes, Jr.

He is no wise man that will quit a certainty for an uncertainty.
Samuel Johnson

In these matters the only certainty is that there is nothing certain.
Pliny the Elder

Ah, what a dusty answer gets the soul
When hot for certainties in this our life!
George Meredith

See also: DOUBT, FACT, KNOWLEDGE, QUESTION, SUCCESS, TRUTH.

CHALLENGE

If we face our tasks with the resolution to solve them, who shall say that anything is impossible.
Sir Wilfred Thomason Grenfell

The new frontier of which I speak is not a set of promises—it is a set of challenges. It sums up not what I intend to offer the American people, but what I intend to ask of them. It appeals to their pride, not their pocketbook —it holds out the promise of more sacrifice instead of more security.
John Fitzgerald Kennedy

My greatest inspiration is a challenge to attempt the impossible.
Albert Abraham Michelson

It does not cost much courage to challenge.
Sir Rabindranath Tagore

See also: CONQUEST, CONTENTION.

CHANCE

Chance never writ a legible book; never built a fair house; never drew a neat picture; never did any of these things, nor ever will; nor can it, without absurdity, be supposed to do them, which are yet works very gross and rude, and very easy and feasible, as it were, in comparison to the production of a flower or a tree.
Isaac Barrow

Chance and the moment, what we call the breaks, so often influence our lives that they cannot be ignored.
Frank Case

Chance is a nickname of Providence.
Sébastien Roch Nicolas Chamfort

There is no such thing as chance or accident, the words merely signify our ignorance of some real and immediate cause.
Adam Clarke

Great things spring from casualities.
Benjamin Disraeli

Many shining actions owe their success to chance, though the general or statesmen runs away with the applause.
Henry Home (Lord Kames)

Chance generally favors the prudent.
Joseph Joubert

Though men pride themselves on their great deeds, they are often not the result of design, but of chance.

Duc François de La Rochefoucald

Chance is always powerful. Let your hook be always cast; in the pool where you least expect it, there will be a fish.

Ovid

There is no such thing as chance; and what seems to us the merest accident springs from the deepest source of destiny.

Johann Christoph Friedrich von Schiller

The doctrine of chances is the bible of the fool.

William Gilmore Simms

What can be more foolish than to think that all this rare fabric of heaven and earth could come by chance, when all the skill of art is not able to make an oyster!

Jeremy Taylor

How often events, by chance, and unexpectedly, come to pass, which you had not dared even to hope for!

Terence

Chance is a word void of sense; nothing can exist without a cause.

Voltaire (François Marie Arouet)

See also: ACCIDENT, LUCK, MISFORTUNE.

CHANGE

He that will not apply new remedies must expect new evils.

Francis Bacon

Action and reaction, ebb and flow, trial and error, change—this is the rhythm of living. Out of our over-confidence, fear; out of our fear, clearer vision, fresh hope. And out of hope—progress.

Bruce Barton

We are restless because of incessant change, but we would be frightened if change were stopped.

Lyman Lloyd Bryson

Encourage as much change as is possible in your environment.

Frank Gelett Burgess

If a great change is to be made in human affairs, the minds of men will be fitted to it;

the general opinions and feelings will draw that way. Every fear and hope will forward it; and they who persist in opposing this mighty current will appear rather to resist the decrees of Providence itself, than the mere designs of men. They will not be so much resolute and firm as perverse and obstinate.

Edmund Burke

To-day is not yesterday. We ourselves change. How then, can our works and thoughts, if they are always to be the fittest, continue always the same. Change, indeed, is painful, yet ever needful; and if memory have its force and worth, so also has hope.

Thomas Carlyle

The world is a scene of changes; to be constant in nature were inconstancy.

Abraham Cowley

Change is an easy panacea. It takes character to stay in one place and be happy there.

Elizabeth Clarke Dunn

Perfection is immutable, but for things imperfect, to change is the way to perfect them. Constancy without knowledge cannot be always good; and in things ill, it is not virtue but an absolute vice.

Owen Felltham

Most of the change we think we see in life is due to truths being in and out of favor.

Robert Lee Frost

All change is not growth, as all movement is not forward.

Ellen Anderson Gholson Glasgow

To blind oneself to change is not therefore to halt it.

Isaac Goldberg

Such are the vicissitudes of the world, through all its parts, that day and night, labor and rest, hurry and retirement, endear each other. Such are the changes that keep the mind in action; we desire, we pursue, we obtain, we are satiated; we desire something else, and begin a new pursuit.

Samuel Johnson

Changing conditions demand changing methods, and to hold to outgrown methods because of a loyalty to an irrelevancy destroys our integrity and encourages the lie.

Gerald Hamilton Kennedy

The world hates change, yet it is the only thing that has brought progress.

Charles Franklin Kettering

Change of heart is no more redemption than hunger is dinner. We must have honesty, love, justice in the heart of the business world, but for these we must also have the (institutional) forms which will fit them.

Henry Demarest Lloyd

It isn't so much that hard times are coming; the change observed is mostly soft times going.

Groucho (Julius Henry) Marx

Our age was destined to experience a decisive change . . . the revival of religious wars in the form of warfare between political ideologies, with concomitant torture, punishment, and extermination of the dissenters.

Hans Joachim Morgenthau

We need courage to throw away old garments which have had their day and no longer fit the requirements of the new generations . . .

Fridtjof Nansen

Everything changes continually. What is history, indeed, but a record of change. And if there had been very few changes in the past, there would have been little of history to write.

Jawaharlal Nehru

Nothing in the world that is alive remains unchanging. All Nature changes from day to day and minute to minute, only the dead stop growing and are quiescent. Fresh water runs on, and if you stop it, it becomes stagnant. So also is it with the life of man and the life of a nation.

Jawaharlal Nehru

The wheel of change moves on, and those who were down go up and those who were up go down.

Jawaharlal Nehru

The circumstances of the world are so variable, that an irrevocable purpose or opinion is almost synonymous with a foolish one.

William Henry Seward

In this world of change naught which comes stays, and naught which goes is lost.

Anne Sophie Swetchine

Change is our ally, and we face squarely those who fight change because the status quo has been good to them. The divine right of the successful is as false a notion as the divine right of Kings.

Willard Wirtz

See also: FICKLENESS, IMPROVEMENT, INCONSTANCY, INNOVATION, INSTABILITY, MUTABILITY, NOVELTY, PROGRESS, REFORM, REVOLUTION, VARIETY.

CHANUKKOH: *see* HANUKKAH.

CHARACTER

He who acts wickedly in private life, can never be expected to show himself noble in public conduct. He that is base at home, will not acquit himself with honor abroad; for it is not the man, but only the place that is changed.

Aeschines

A man may be outwardly successful all his life long, and die hollow and worthless as a puff-ball; and he may be externally defeated all his life long, and die in the royalty of a kingdom established within him. A man's true estate of power and riches, is to be in himself; not in his dwelling, or position, or external relations, but in his own essential character. That is the realm in which he is to live, if he is to live as a Christian man.

Henry Ward Beecher

A man's character is the reality of himself. His reputation is the opinion others have formed of him. Character is in him;—reputation is from other people—that is the substance, this is the shadow.

Henry Ward Beecher

Nothing can work me damage, except myself. The harm that I sustain I carry about me, and never am a real sufferer but by my own fault.

Bernard of Clairvaux

In each human heart are a tiger, a pig, an ass, and a nightingale; diversity of character is due to their unequal activity.

Ambrose Gwinnett Bierce

Let us not say, Every man is the architect of his own fortune; but let us say, Every man is the architect of his own character.

George Dana Boardman

No amount of ability is of the slightest avail without honor.

Andrew Carnegie

The miracle, or the power, that elevates the few is to be found in their industry, application, and perseverance under the promptings of a brave, determined spirit.

Samuel Langhorne Clemens (Mark Twain)

There is no single royal road to character—a variety of routes will always need to be used. The development of right character in youth is too important to risk disregarding any promising line of attack.

Frank Cody

As there is much beast and some devil in man, so is there some angel and some God in him. The beast and the devil may be conquered, but in this life never destroyed.

Samuel Taylor Coleridge

Truthfulness is a corner-stone in character, and if it be not firmly laid in youth, there will ever after be a weak spot in the foundation.

Jefferson Davis

The best characters are made by vigorous and persistent resistance to evil tendencies; whose amiability has been built upon the ruins of ill-temper, and whose generosity springs from an over-mastered and transformed selfishness. Such a character, built up in the presence of enemies, has far more attraction than one which is natively pleasing.

Henry Martyn Dexter

Characters do not change. Opinions alter, but characters are only developed.

Benjamin Disraeli

Do what you know and perception is converted into character.

Ralph Waldo Emerson

Taste and habits change progressively. In the old days the lady with a past repented and died; to-day she repents and lives happily ever after.

Daniel Frohman

You cannot dream yourself into a character; you must hammer and forge one for yourself.

James Anthony Froude

All your scholarship, all your study of Shakespeare and Wordsworth would be in vain, if at the same time you do not build your character, and attain mastery over your thoughts and actions. When you have attained self-mastery and learnt to control your passions, you will not utter notes of despair.

You cannot give your hearts and profess poverty of action. To give one's heart is to give all. You must, to start with, have hearts to give. And this you can do if you will cultivate them.

Mohandas Karamchand (Mahatma) Gandhi

A chivalrous boy would always keep his mind pure, his eyes straight, and his hands unpolluted. You do not need to go to any school to learn these fundamental maxims of life, and if you will have this triple character with you, you will build on a solid foundation.

Mohandas Karamchand (Mahatma) Gandhi

A man of character will make himself worthy of any position he is given.

Mohandas Karamchand (Mahatma) Gandhi

There are no two opinions about the fact that intellect rather than riches will lead. It might equally be admitted that the heart rather than the intellect will eventually lead. Character, not brain, will count at the crucial moment.

Mohandas Karamchand (Mahatma) Gandhi

Our character is but the stamp on our souls of the free choices of good and evil we have made through life.

John Cunningham Geikie

If you would create something, you must be something.

Johann Wolfgang von Goethe

Talents are best nurtured in solitude; character is best formed in the stormy billows of the world.

Johann Wolfgang von Goethe

A tree will not only lie as it falls but it will fall as it leans.

Joseph John Gurney

Character is perfectly educated will.

Baron Friedrich von Hardenberg (Novalis)

Many people have character who have nothing else.

Don Herold

Character must stand behind and back up everything—the sermon, the poem, the picture, the play. None of them is worth a straw without it.

Josiah Gilbert Holland

There is a broad distinction between character and reputation, for one may be destroyed by slander, while the other can never be harmed save by its possessor. Reputation is in no man's keeping. You and I cannot determine what other men shall think and say about us. We can only determine what they *ought* to think of us and say about us.

Josiah Gilbert Holland

The great thing in this world is not so much where we are, but in what direction we are moving.

Oliver Wendell Holmes

Character is the result of two things: Mental attitude and the way we spend our time.

Elbert Green Hubbard

What others say of me matters little, what I myself say and do matters much.

Elbert Green Hubbard

Only what we have wrought into our character during life can we take away with us.

Baron Alexander von Humboldt

If you can talk with crowds and keep your virtue, or walk with kings—nor lose the common touch, if neither foes nor loving friends can hurt you, if all men count with you, but none too much: if you can fill the unforgiving minute with sixty seconds' worth of distance run, yours is the earth and everything that's in it, and—which is more—you'll be a man, my son.

Rudyard Kipling

It is when a man has lost his position in the world, or great wealth, that the silliness of his character, which was overlaid, is made apparent, and which was there though no one perceived it.

Jean de La Bruyère

There is no act in a man's conduct, however simple and inconsiderable, in which there does not appear some slight peculiarities that reveal his secret character. A fool does not enter a room, nor leave it, nor sit down, nor rise up, nor is he silent, nor does he stand on his legs, like a man of sense and understanding.

Jean de La Bruyère

Weakness of character is the only defect which cannot be amended.

Duc François de La Rochefoucauld

Men are not to be judged by their looks, habits, and appearances; but by the character of their lives and conversations, and by their works. 'Tis better that a man's own works than that another man's words should praise him.

Sir Roger L'Estrange

Character is built out of circumstances. From exactly the same materials one man builds palaces, while another builds hovels.

George Henry Lewes

There is nothing so fatal to character as half-finished tasks.

David Lloyd George

I would like to see a state of society in which every man and woman preferred the old Scottish Sunday to the modern French one. We should then find solid and eternal foundations of character and self-command.

James Ramsay MacDonald

There is not a man or woman, however poor they may be, but have it in their power, by the grace of God, to leave behind them the grandest thing on earth, character; and their children might rise up after them and thank God that their mother was a pious woman, or their father a pious man.

Norman Macleod

Should one tell you that a mountain had changed its place, you are at liberty to doubt it; but if any one tells you that a man has changed his character, do not believe it.

Mahomet (Mohammed)

If I take care of my character, my reputation will take care of itself.

Dwight Lyman Moody

Character is doubtless of far more importance than mere intellectual opinion.

John Morley

The harder you throw down a football and a good character, the higher they rebound; but a thrown reputation is like an egg.

Austin O'Malley

In the destiny of every moral being there is an object more worthy of God than happiness. It is character. And the grand aim of man's creation is the development of a grand character—and grand character is, by its very nature, the product of probationary discipline.

Austin Phelps

No more fatal error can be cherished than that any character can be complete without the religious element. The essential factors in character building are religion, morality, and knowledge.

Josiah Little Pickard

Never does a man portray his own character more vividly, than in his manner of portraying another.

Jean Paul Richter

Make but few explanations. The character that cannot defend itself is not worth vindicating.

Frederick William Robertson

The most important thing for a young man is to establish a credit—a reputation, character.

John Davison Rockefeller

Character building begins in our infancy and continues until death.

Anna Eleanor Roosevelt

A sound body is a first-class thing; a sound mind is an even better thing; but the thing that counts for most in the individual as in the nation, is character, the sum of those qualities which make a man a good man and a woman a good woman.

Theodore Roosevelt

Character is the basis of happiness and happiness the sanction of character.

George Santayana

Men best show their character in trifles, where they are not on their guard. It is in insignificant matters, and in the simplest habits, that we often see the boundless egotism which pays no regard to the feelings of others, and denies nothing to itself.

Arthur Schopenhauer

We shall never wander from Christ while we make character the end and aim of all our intellectual discipline; and we shall never misconceive character while we hold fast to Christ, and keep him first in our motto and our hearts.

Sylvester Scovel

The most tragic thing in the world is a man of genius who is not also a man of honor.

George Bernard Shaw

Good character is human nature in its best form. It is moral order embodied in the individual. Men of character are not only the

conscience of society, but in every well governed state they are its best motive power; for it is moral qualities which, in the main, rule the world.

Samuel Smiles

To be worth anything, character must be capable of standing firm upon its feet in the world of daily work, temptation, and trial; and able to bear the wear and tear of actual life. Cloistered virtues do not count for much.

Samuel Smiles

The shortest and surest way to live with honor in the world, is to be in reality what we would appear to be; all human virtues increase and strengthen themselves by the practice and experience of them.

Socrates

Not education, but character, is man's greatest need and man's greatest safeguard.

Herbert Spencer

Give us a character on which we can thoroughly depend, which we know to be based on principle and on the fear of God, and it is wonderful how many brilliant and popular and splendid qualities we can safely and gladly dispense with.

Arthur Penrhyn Stanley

Grave was the man in years, in looks, in word,
    His locks were grey, yet was his courage green,
Of worth and might the noble badge he bore,
Old scars of grievous wounds received of yore.

Torquato Tasso

Every man, as to character, is the creature of the age in which he lives. Very few are able to raise themselves above the ideas of their times.

Voltaire (François Marie Arouet)

Character and personal force are the only investments that are worth anything.

Walt (Walter) Whitman

Most people are other people. Their thoughts are someone else's opinions, their lives a mimicry, their passions a quotation.

Oscar Wilde

If you will think of what you ought to do for other people, your character will take care of itself. Character is a by-product, and any man who devotes himself to its cultivation in his own case will become a selfish prig.

(Thomas) Woodrow Wilson

Character is made by what you stand for; reputation by what you fall for.

Alexander Woollcott

It is not money, nor is it mere intellect, that governs the world; it is moral character, and intellect associated with moral excellence.

Theodore Dwight Woolsey

See also: DISPOSITION, DISTINCTION, INDIVIDUALITY, INTEGRITY, LOOKS, NATURE, PRINCIPLES, TEMPER.

CHARITY

A man should fear when he enjoys only the good he does publicly. Is it not publicity rather than charity, which he loves? Is it not vanity, rather than benevolence, that gives such charities?

Henry Ward Beecher

The spirit of the world has four kinds of spirits diametrically opposed to charity, resentment, aversion, jealously, and indifferences.

Jacques Bénigne Bossuet

Posthumous charities are the very essence of selfishness when bequeathed by those who, even alive, would part with nothing.

Charles Caleb Colton

It is an old saying, that charity begins at home; but this is no reason that it should not go abroad: a man should live with the world as a citizen of the world; he may have a preference for the particular quarter or square, or even alley in which he lives, but he should have a generous feeling for the welfare of the whole.

Richard Cumberland

First daughter to the love of God, is charity to man.

William Drennan

One must be poor to know the luxury of giving.

George Eliot (Mary Ann Evans)

Not he who has much is rich, but he who gives much.

Erich Fromm

The more charity, the more peace.

Hillel

The truly generous is truly wise, and he who loves not others, lives unblest.

Henry Home (Lord Kames)

The charity that hastens to proclaim its good deeds, ceases to be charity, and is only pride and ostentation.

William Hutton

Be charitable and indulgent to every one but thyself.

Joseph Joubert

Beneficence is a duty; and he who frequently practices it and sees his benevolent intentions realized, at length comes to love him to whom he has done good.

Immanuel Kant

Prayer carries us half-way to God, fasting brings us to the door of his palace, and, alms-giving procures us admission.

Koran

A bone to the dog is not charity. Charity is the bone shared with the dog, when you are just as hungry as the dog.

Jack London

Charity is infinitely divisable. He who has a little can always give a little.

Peter McArthur

Every good act is charity. Your smiling in your brother's face, is charity; an exhortation of your fellow-man to virtuous deeds, is equal to alms-giving; your putting a wanderer in the right road, is charity; your assisting the blind, is charity; your removing stones, and thorns, and other obstructions from the road, is charity; your giving water to the thirsty, is charity. A man's true wealth hereafter, is the good he does in this world to his fellow-man. When he dies, people will say, "What property has he left behind him?" but the angels will ask, "What good deeds has he sent before him."

Mahomet (Mohammed)

I would have none of that rigid and circumspect charity which is never exercised without scrutiny, and which always mistrusts the reality of the necessities laid open to it.

Jean Baptiste Massillon

Charity is never lost: it may meet with ingratitude, or be of no service to those on whom it was bestowed, yet it ever does a work of beauty and grace upon the heart of the giver.

Conyers Middleton

Nothing truly can be termed my own, but what I make my own by using well; those deeds of charity which we have done, shall stay forever with us; and that wealth which we have so bestowed, we only keep; the other is not ours.

Conyers Middleton

When faith and hope fail, as they do sometimes, we must try charity, which is love in action. We must speculate no more on our duty, but simply do it. When we have done it, however blindly, perhaps Heaven will show us why.

Dinah Maria Mulock

In giving of thine alms inquire not so much into the person, as his necessity. God looks not so much on the merits of him that requires, as to the manner of him that relieves. If the man deserve not, thou has given to humanity.

Francis Quarles

The last, best fruit that comes late to perfection, even in the kindliest soul, is tenderness toward the hard, forbearance toward the unforbearing, warmth of heart toward the cold, and philanthropy toward the misanthropic.

Jean Paul Richter

Great minds, like heaven, are pleased in doing good, though the ungrateful subjects of their favors are barren in return.

Nicholas Rowe

How often it is difficult to be wisely charitable—to do good without multiplying the sources of evil. To give alms is nothing unless you give thought also. It is written, not "blessed is he that feedeth the poor," but "blessed is he that considereth the poor." A little thought and a little kindness are often worth more than a great deal of money.

John Ruskin

Let him who neglects to raise the fallen, fear lest, when he falls, no one will stretch out his hand to lift him up.

Saadi (Muslih-ud-Din)

Every genuinely benevolent person loathes almsgiving and mendicity.

George Bernard Shaw

Our true acquisitions lie only in our charities, we gain only as we give.

William Gilmore Simms

While actions are always to be judged by the immutable standard of right and wrong, the judgment we pass upon men must be qualified by considerations of age, country, situation, and other incidental circumstances; and it will then be found, that he who is most charitable in his judgment, is generally the least unjust.

Robert Southey

Care of the poor is incumbent on society as a whole.

Baruch (Benedict) Spinoza

We are rich only through what we give; and poor only through what we refuse and keep.

Anne Sophie Swetchine

Loving kindness is greater than laws; and the charities of life are more than all ceremonies.

Talmud

Pity, forbearance, long-sufferance, fair interpretation, excusing our brother, and taking in the best sense, and passing the gentlest sentence, are certainly our duty; and he that does not so is an unjust person.

Jeremy Taylor

It is not the shilling I give you that counts, but the warmth that it carries with it from my hand.

Miguel de Unamuno y Jugo

In my youth I thought of writing a satire on mankind, but now in my age I think I should write an apology for them.

Horace Walpole

The charities that soothe, and heal, and bless, Lie scattered at the feet of men like flowers.

William Wordsworth

See also: BENEFICENCE, BENEVOLENCE, GENEROSITY, GOODNESS, HELP, KINDNESS, LIBERALITY, MAGNANIMITY, PHILANTHROPY, SELFISHNESS, WELL-DOING.

CHARM

If you have charm, you don't need to have anything else; and if you don't have it, it doesn't matter what else you have.

Sir James Matthew Barrie

Charm is almost as poor a butter for parsnips as good intentions.

(Matthew) Heywood Campbell Broun

Charm is more than beauty.

Yiddish Proverb

See also: BEAUTY, GRACEFULNESSS.

CHASTITY

A man defines his standing at the court of chastity, by his views of women. He cannot be any man's friend, nor his own, if not hers.
Amos Bronson Alcott

That chastity of honor, which feels a stain like a wound.
Edmund Burke

Chastity enables the soul to breathe a pure air in the foulest places. Continence makes her strong, no matter in what condition the body may be. Her sway over the senses makes her queenly: her light and peace render her beautiful.
Joseph Joubert

There needs not strength to be added to inviolate chastity; the excellency of the mind makes the body impregnable.
Sir Philip Sidney

Chastity is a wealth that comes from abundance of love.
Sir Rabindranath Tagore

See also: ASCETICISM, CELIBACY, INNOCENCE, LICENTIOUSNESS, MAIDENHOOD.

CHEERFULNESS

A cheerful temper joined with innocence will make beauty attractive, knowledge delightful, and wit good-natured. It will lighten sickness, poverty, and affliction; convert ignorance into an amiable simplicity, and render deformity itself agreeable.
Joseph Addison

I have always preferred cheerfulness to mirth. The former is an act, the latter a habit of the mind. Mirth is short and transient; cheerfulness, fixed and permanent. Mirth is like a flash of lightning, that breaks through a gloom of clouds, and glitters for a moment. Cheerfulness keeps up a kind of daylight in the mind, filling it with a steady and perpetual serenity.
Joseph Addison

To be free-minded and cheerfully disposed at hours of meals, and of sleep, and of exercise, is one of the best precepts of long-lasting.
Francis Bacon

The cheerful live longest in years, and afterwards in our regards. Cheerfulness is the offshoot of goodness.
Christian Nestell Bovee

Oh, give us the man who sings at his work.
Thomas Carlyle

Wondrous is the strength of cheerfulness, and its power of endurance—the cheerful man will do more in the same time, will do it better, will persevere in it longer, than the sad or sullen.
Thomas Carlyle

You find yourself refreshed by the presence of cheerful people. Why not make earnest effort to confer that pleasure on others? Half the battle is gained if you never allow yourself to say anything gloomy.
Lydia Maria Francis Child

To make knowledge valuable, you must have the cheerfulness of wisdom. Goodness smiles to the last.
Ralph Waldo Emerson

An ounce of cheerfulness is worth a pound of sadness to serve God with.
Thomas Fuller

The true source of cheerfulness is benevolence. The soul that perpetually overflows with kindness and sympathy will always be cheerful.
Parke Godwin

If the soul be happily disposed everything becomes capable of affording entertainment, and distress will almost want a name.
Oliver Goldsmith

The mind that is cheerful at present will have no solicitude for the future, and will meet the bitter occurrences of life with a smile.
Horace

To be happy, the temperament must be cheerful and gay, not gloomy and melancholy. A propensity to hope and joy, is real riches; one to fear and sorrow, is real poverty.
David Hume

Honest good humor is the oil and wine of a merry meeting, and there is no jovial companionship equal to that where the jokes are rather small and the laughter abundant.
Washington Irving

Cheer up, the worst is yet to come.
Philander Chase Johnson

The habit of looking on the best side of every event is worth more than a thousand pounds a year.

Samuel Johnson

Keep your face to the sunshine and you cannot see the shadow.

Helen Adams Keller

Every one must have felt that a cheerful friend is like a sunny day, which sheds its brightness on all around; and most of us can, as we choose, make of this world either a palace or a prison.

Sir John Lubbock

The highest wisdom is continual cheerfulness; such a state, like the region above the moon, is always clear and serene.

Michel Eyquem de Montaigne

Burdens become light when cheerfully borne.

Ovid

Cheerfulness is as natural to the heart of a man in strong health, as color to his cheek; and wherever there is habitual gloom, there must be either bad air, unwholesome food, improperly severe labor, or erring habits of life.

John Ruskin

If good people would but make their goodness agreeable, and smile instead of frowning in their virtue, how many would they win to the good cause.

James Ussher

God is glorified, not by our groans but by our thanksgivings; and all good thought and good action claim a natural alliance with good cheer.

Edwin Percy Whipple

See also: AMIABILITY, GAIETY, GOOD HUMOR, HAPPINESS, SMILE, VIVACITY.

CHILDHOOD

I think I can say I had as unhappy a childhood as the next braggart.

Peter De Vries

Childhood has no forebodings; but then it is soothed by no memories of outlived sorrow.

George Eliot (Mary Ann Evans)

In the man whose childhood has known caresses and kindness, there is always a fibre of memory that can be touched to gentle issues.

George Eliot (Mary Ann Evans)

Childhood sometimes does pay a second visit to a man; youth never.

Anna Brownell Murphy Jameson

The interests of childhood and youth are the interests of mankind.

Edmund Storer Janes

Childhood and genius have the same master-organ in common—inquisitiveness. Let childhood have its way, and as it began where genius begins, it may find what genius finds.

Edward G. Bulwer-Lytton (Baron Lytton)

Childhood shows the man, as morning shows the day.

John Milton

Childhood is the sleep of reason.

Jean Jacques Rousseau

See also: AGE, AGES OF MAN, BABY, CHILDREN, YOUTH.

CHILDREN

If a child annoys you, quiet him by brushing his hair. If this doesn't work, use the other side of the brush on the other end of the child.

Anonymous

Children sweeten labors, but they make misfortunes more bitter. They increase the cares of life, but they mitigate the remembrance of death.

Francis Bacon

You cannot teach a child to take care of himself unless you will let him try to take care of himself. He will make mistakes; and out of these mistakes will come his wisdom.

Henry Ward Beecher

Many children, many cares; no children, no felicity.

Christian Nestell Bovee

The child's heart curseth deeper in the silence than the strong man in his wrath.

Elizabeth Barrett Browning

The first duty to children is to make them happy. If you have not made them so, you have wronged them. No other good they may get can make up for that.

Charles Buxton

Bachelors' wives and old maids' children are always perfect.

Sébastien Roch Nicolas Chamfort

What gift has Providence bestowed on man that is so dear to him as his children?

Cicero

I have often thought what a melancholy world this would be without children; and what an inhuman world, without the aged.

Samuel Taylor Coleridge

Children do not know how their parents love them, and they never will till the grave closes over those parents, or till they have children of their own.

Philip Pendleton Cooke

In the long course of my legal profession, I have met with several sons who had, in circumstance of difficulty, abandoned their fathers; but never did I meet with a father that would not cheerfully part with his last shilling to save or bless his son.

David Daggett

What the best and wisest parent wants for his own child that must the community want for all its children.

John Dewey

I love these little people; and it is not a slight thing, when they, who are so fresh from God, love us.

Charles John Huffam Dickens

It always grieves me to contemplate the initiation of children into the ways of life when they are scarcely more than infants. It checks their confidence and simplicity, two of the best qualities that heaven gives them, and demands that they share our sorrows before they are capable of entering into our enjoyments.

Charles John Huffam Dickens

When children sound silly, you will always find that it is in imitation of their elders.

Ernest Dimnet

Let all children remember, if ever they are weary of laboring for their parents, that Christ labored for his; if impatient of their commands, that Christ cheerfully obeyed; if reluctant to provide for their parents, that Christ forgot himself and provided for his mother amid the agonies of the crucifixion. The affectionate language of this divine example to every child is, "Go thou and do likewise."

John Sullivan Dwight

Of nineteen out of twenty things in children, take no special notice; but if, as to the twentieth, you give a direction or command, see that you are obeyed.

Tryon Edwards

Beware of fatiguing them by ill-judged exactness. If virtue offers itself to the child under a melancholy and constrained aspect, while liberty and license present themselves under an agreeable form, all is lost, and your labor is in vain.

François de Salignac de La Mothe-Fénelon

It is dangerous to confuse children with angels.

David Patrick Maxwell Fyfe

In praising or loving a child, we love and praise not that which is, but that which we hope for.

Johann Wolfgang von Goethe

Where children are, there is the golden age.

Baron Friedrich von Hardenberg (Novalis)

The tasks set to children should be moderate. Over-exertion is hurtful both physically and intellectually, and even morally. But it is of the utmost importance that they should be made to fulfil all their tasks correctly and punctually. This will train them for an exact and conscientious discharge of their duties in after life.

Augustus and Julius Hare

We are weakest
When we are caught contending with our children!

Charles Heavysege

Feel the dignity of a child. Do not feel superior to him, for you are not.

Robert Henri

An infallible way to make your child miserable, is to satisfy all his demands. Passion swells by gratification; and the impossibility of satisfying every one of his wishes will oblige you to stop short at last after he has become headstrong.

Henry Home (Lord Kames)

God sends children for another purpose than merely to keep up the race—to enlarge our hearts; and to make us unselfish and full of kindly sympathies and affections; to give our souls higher aims; to call out all our faculties to extended enterprise and exertion; and to

bring round our firesides bright faces, happy smiles, and loving, tender hearts. My soul blesses the great Father, every day, that he has gladdened the earth with little children.
Mary Botham Howitt

Whether it be for good or evil, the education of the child is principally derived from its own observation of the actions, words, voice, and looks of those with whom it lives. The friends of the young, then, cannot be too circumspect in their presence to avoid every and the least appearance of evil.
John Jebb

Children have more need of models than of critics.
Joseph Joubert

In bringing up a child, think of its old age.
Joseph Joubert

Children have neither past nor future; and what scarcely ever happens to us, they enjoy the present.
Jean de La Bruyère

As very rough weather destroys the buds of spring, so does too early an experience of life's hard toil blight the young promise of a child's faculties, and render any true education impossible.
Leo XIII (Gioacchino Vincenzo Pecci)

Children generally hate to be idle. All the care then should be, that their busy humor should be constantly employed in something that is of use to them.
John Locke

A torn jacket is soon mended, but hard words bruise the heart of a child.
Henry Wadsworth Longfellow

Children are God's apostles, sent forth, day by day, to preach of love, and hope and peace.
James Russell Lowell

Infancy isn't what it is cracked up to be. Children, not knowing that they are having an easy time, have a good many hard times. Growing and learning and obeying the rules of their elders, or fighting against them, are not easy things to do.
Donald Robert Perry (Don) Marquis

Many a man spanks his children for things his own father should have spanked out of him.
Donald Robert Perry (Don) Marquis

Lord, give to men who are old and rougher the things that little children suffer, and let keep bright and undefiled the young years of the little child.
John Masefield

Genuine appreciation of other people's children is one of the rarer virtues.
Harlan Miller

By the time the youngest children have learned to keep the place tidy, the oldest grandchildren are on hand to tear it to pieces again.
Christopher Darlington Morley

The vast army of children all over the world, outwardly different in many ways, speaking different languages, wearing different kinds of clothes and yet so very like one another. If you bring them together, they play or quarrel but even their quarrelling is some kind of play. They do not think of differences amongst themselves, differences of class or caste or colour or status. They are wiser than their fathers and mothers. As they grow up, unfortunately, their natural wisdom is often eclipsed by the teaching and behaviour of their elders. At school they learn many things which are no doubt useful but they gradually forget that the essential thing is to be human and kind and playful and to make life richer for ourselves and others.
Jawaharlal Nehru

The plays of natural lively children are the infancy of art. Children live in a world of imagination and feeling. They invest the most insignificant object with any form they please, and see in it whatever they wish to see.
Adam Gottlob Oehlenschläger

Before you beat a child, be sure you yourself are not the cause of the offense.
Austin O'Malley

As the vexations men receive from their children hasten the approach of age, and double the force of years, so the comforts they reap from them are balm to all their sorrows, and disappoint the injuries of time. Parents repeat their lives in their offspring; and their esteem for them is so great, that they feel their sufferings and taste their enjoyments as much as if they were their own.
Ray Palmer

Just as the twig is bent, the tree is inclined.
Alexander Pope

At eleven, one does not often ask why things happen, because nothing seems strange enough to provoke the question.

Agnes Repplier

All the gestures of children are graceful; the reign of distortion and unnatural attitudes commences with the introduction of the dancing master.

Sir Joshua Reynolds

The smallest children are nearest to God, as the smallest planets are nearest the sun.

Jean Paul Richter

Experience teaches us that a greater number of children delicately brought up die than others. Provided that we do not make them work beyond their strength, we risk less by employing than by sparing them.

Jean Jacques Rousseau

The training of children is a profession, where we must know how to lose time in order to gain it.

Jean Jacques Rousseau

There is no possible method of compelling a child to feel sympathy or affection.

Bertrand Arthur William Russell

There should be no enforced respect for grown-ups. We cannot prevent children from thinking us fools by merely forbidding them to utter their thoughts; in fact, they are more likely to think ill of us if they dare not say so.

Bertrand Arthur William Russell

Nature kindly warps our judgment about our children, especially when they are young, when it would be a fatal thing for them if we did not love them.

George Santayana

With children we must mix gentleness with firmness. They must not always have their own way, but they must not always be thwarted. If we never have headaches through rebuking them, we shall have plenty of heartaches when they grow up. Be obeyed at all costs; for if you yield up your authority once, you will hardly get it again.

Charles Haddon Spurgeon

Children share with geniuses an open, inquiring, uninhibited quality of mind.

Chauncey Guy Suits

Every child comes with the message that God is not yet discouraged of man.

Sir Rabindranath Tagore

Children have one great advantage. Eventually they will grow up and sometime even they will learn better.

Hendrik Willem van Loon

Every child born into the world is a new thought of God, an ever-fresh and radiant possibility.

Kate Douglas Smith Wiggin

The potential possibilities of any child are the most intriguing and stimulating in all creation.

Ray Lyman Wilbur

The best way to make children good is to make them happy.

Oscar Wilde

Before I got married I had six theories about bringing up children. Now I have six children, and no theories.

John Wilmot (Earl of Rochester)

The sweetest roamer is a boy's young heart.

George Edward Woodberry

The child is father of the man.

William Wordsworth

Each child carries his own blessing into the world.

Yiddish Proverb

A small child is a pig, a big child is a wolf.

Yiddish Proverb

Small children disturb your sleep, big children your life.

Yiddish Proverb

Small children, small joys; big children, big annoys.

Yiddish Proverb

See also: ADOLESCENCE, AGES OF MAN, BABY, CHILDHOOD, DAUGHTER, FAMILY, INFANCY, SCHOOL, YOUTH.

CHINA

I think the world is heading for a gigantic disaster; I think we are on a collision course with China. I hope and pray that some reason will come, that some group will rise in China and bring reason to these people.

William Franklin (Billy) Graham

Who knows what will happen in a few decades? Intellectuals are against Marxism. Neither our agricultural nor our industrial problems have been solved.

Mao Tse-tung

China is not only the largest country in the world; for many centuries it was the most advanced, and the Chinese are certainly, and not entirely without reason, the proudest people in the world. But they have been subjected to a century and more of national humiliation at the hands of technologically superior powers. We must be especially careful to understand this historic legacy under which the Chinese labor in their relations with the outside world.

Edwin Oldfather Reischauer

We should not concentrate so exclusively on the problem of containing Chinese aggressiveness but instead should place more emphasis on finding ways to bring the Chinese into meaningful contact with us and other nations, so that they will learn more about the realities of the outside world and will thus in time come to realize that they must accommodate themselves to these realities.

Edwin Oldfather Reischauer

But to a large extent China's failures seem linked to the traditional Chinese view of the outside world. Never in their history have the Chinese worked within a framework of allies and alliances. Traditionally they have known only one basic diplomatic link: that of a single vassal state which pledged allegiance to Peking. They are accustomed to dealing with individual nations one at a time.

Charles Taylor

See also: ASIA, COMMUNISM, VIETNAM.

CHIVALRY

The age of chivalry has gone, and one of calculators and economists has succeeded.

Edmund Burke

Chivalry is the most delicate form of contempt.

Albert Léon Guérard

The age of chivalry is never past, so long as there is a wrong left unredressed on earth.

Charles Kingsley

Collision is as necessary to produce virtue in men, as it is to elicit fire in inanimate matter; and so chivalry is of the essence of virtue.

Bertrand Arthur William Russell

See also: COURAGE, COURTESY, GOOD BREEDING, REVERENCE, ROMANCE.

CHOICE

Be ignorance thy choice where knowledge leads to woe.

James Beattie

Life often presents us with a choice of evils rather than of good.

Charles Caleb Colton

Between two evils, choose neither; between two goods, choose both.

Tryon Edwards

God offers to every mind its choice between truth and repose.

Ralph Waldo Emerson

The measure of choosing well, is, whether a man likes and finds good in what he has chosen.

Charles Lamb

Choose always the way that seems the best, however rough it may be; custom will soon render it easy and agreeable.

Pythagoras

See also: DECISION, FREEDOM, LIBERTY, NECESSITY, RESOLUTION, WILL, WISH.

CHRIST

Take, then, your paltry Christ,
    Your gentleman God.
We want the carpenter's son,
    With his saw and hod.

Francis Adams

As the print of the seal on the wax is the express image of the seal itself, so Christ is the express image—the perfect representation of God.

Ambrose of Milan

Jesus Christ, the condescension of divinity, and the exaltation of humanity.

Phillips Brooks

Jesus to the Negro is no simple religious saviour, worshipped on Sundays and forgotten during the week. He is the incarnation of the suffering soul of a race.

Victor Francis Calverton

Every step toward Christ kills a doubt. Every thought, word, and deed for Him carries you away from discouragement.

Theodore Ledyard Cuyler

An era in human history is the life of Jesus, and its immense influence for good leaves all the perversion and superstition that has accrued almost harmless.

Ralph Waldo Emerson

This is part of the glory of Christ as compared with the chiefest of His servants that He alone stands at the absolute center of humanity, the one completely harmonious man, unfolding all which was in humanity, equally and fully on all sides, the only one in whom the real and ideal met and were absolutely one. He is the absolute and perfect truth, the highest that humanity can reach; at once its perfect image and supreme Lord.

Alice French

The dual substance of Christ—the yearning, so human, so superhuman, of man to attain to God or, more exactly, to return to God and identify himself with him—has always been a deep inscrutable mystery to me. This nostalgia for God, at once so mysterious and so real, has opened in me large wounds and also large flowing springs.

Nikos Kazantzakis

In his life, Christ is an example, showing us how to live; in his death, he is a sacrifice, satisfying for our sins; in his resurrection, a conqueror; in his ascension, a king; in his intercession, a high priest.

Martin Luther

God never gave a man a thing to do, concerning which it were irreverent to ponder how the Son of God would have done it.

George Macdonald

The nature of Christ's existence is mysterious, I admit; but this mystery meets the wants of man. Reject it and the world is an inexplicable riddle; believe it, and the history of our race is satisfactorily explained.

Napoleon I (Bonaparte)

Jesus Christ is a God to whom we can approach without pride, and before whom we may abase ourselves without despair.

Blaise Pascal

He who was foretold and foreshadowed by the holy religion of Judea, which was designed to free the universal aspiration of mankind from every impure element, he has come to instruct, to obey, to love, to die, and by dying to save mankind.

Edmond Dehaut de Pressensé

All history is incomprehensible without Christ.

Joseph Ernest Renan

Day by day we should weigh what we have granted to the spirit of the world against what we have denied to the spirit of Jesus, in thought and especially in deed.

Albert Schweitzer

As little as humanity will ever be without religion, as little will it be without Christ.

David Friedrich Strauss

See also: ATHEISM, CHRISTIAN, CHRISTIANITY, CRUCIFIXION, ECUMENISM, GOD, RESURRECTION.

CHRISTIAN

A Christian is nothing but a sinful man who has put himself to school to Christ for the honest purpose of becoming better.

Henry Ward Beecher

Christians and camels receive their burdens kneeling.

Ambrose Gwinnett Bierce

The only way to realize that we are God's children is to let Christ lead us to our Father.

Phillips Brooks

The Christian needs a reminder every hour; some defeat, surprise, adversity, peril; to be agitated, mortified, beaten out of his course, so that all remains of self will be sifted out.

Horace Bushnell

The Christian has greatly the advantage of the unbeliever, having everything to gain and nothing to lose.

George Gordon Byron (Lord Byron)

Christians have burned each other, quite persuaded that all the Apostles would have done as they did.

George Gordon Byron (Lord Byron)

We appease our consciences by telling ourselves that we are charged with saving souls, that the Christian Easter is a liberation from sin . . . Yet we are pastors of human beings, charged also with their bodies. Never has any one of us met a disembodied soul.

Helder Pessoa Camara

A man can no more be a Christian without facing evil and conquering it, than he can be a soldier without going to battle, facing the cannon's mouth, and encountering the enemy in the field.

Edwin Hubbel Chapin

The best advertisement of a workshop is first-class work. The strongest attraction to Christianity is a well-made Christian character.

Theodore Ledyard Cuyler

One truly Christian life will do more to prove the divine origin of Christianity than many lectures. It is of much greater importance to develop Christian character, than to exhibit Christian evidences.

John Monro Gibson

It is more to the honor of a Christian by faith to overcome the world, than by monastical vows to retreat from it; more for the honor of Christ to serve him in the city, than to serve him in the cell.

Matthew Henry

He is no good Christian who thinks he can be safe without God, or not safe with him.

John Prentis Kewley Henshaw

Faith makes, life proves, trials confirm, and death crowns the Christian.

Johann Georg Christian Hopfner

Every occupation, plan, and work of man, to be truly successful, must be done under the direction of Christ, in union with his will, from love to him, and in dependence on his power

Friedrich Max Müller

Let it not be imagined that the life of a good Christian must be a life of melancholy and gloominess; for he only resigns some pleasures to enjoy others infinitely better.

Blaise Pascal

No man is so happy as the real Christian; none so rational, so virtuous, so amiable. How little vanity does he feel, though he believes himself united to God! How far is he from abjectness, though he ranks himself with the worms of the earth.

Blaise Pascal

The Christian life is not merely knowing or hearing, but doing the will of Christ.

Frederick William Robertson

That there should be a Christ, and that I should be Christless; that there should be a cleansing, and that I should remain foul; that there should be a Father's love, and I should be an alien; that there should be a heaven, and I should be cast into hell, is grief embittered, sorrow aggravated.

Charles Haddon Spurgeon

Not long ago I was reading the Sermon on the Mount with a rabbi. At nearly each verse he showed me very similar passages in the Hebrew Bible and Talmud. When we reached the words, "Resist not evil," he did not say, "This too is in the Talmud," but asked, with a smile, "Do the Christians obey this command?" I had nothing to say in reply, especially as at that particular time, Christians, far from turning the other cheek, were smiting the Jews on both cheeks.

Count Lev (Leo) Nikolaevich Tolstoi

It is a truth that stands out with startling distinctness on the pages of the New Testament, that God has no sons who are not servants.

Herbert Dickinson Ward

The Christian faith reposes in a person rather than a creed. Christ is the personal, living center of theology, around which the whole Christian system is ensphered. Christ is the personal source of the individual Christian life; the personal head of the whole Christian church; the personal sovereign of the kingdom of grace.

Ronald Burton Welch

See also: CHRIST, CHRISTIANITY.

CHRISTIANITY

The distinction between Christianity and all other systems of religion consists largely in this, that in these others men are found seeking after God, while Christianity is God seeking after men.

Thomas Arnold

There never was found in any age of the world, either philosophy, or sect, or religion, or law, or discipline, which did so highly exalt the good of the community, and increase private and particular good as the holy Christian faith. Hence, it clearly appears that it was one and the same God that gave the Christian law to men, who gave the laws of nature to the creatures.

Francis Bacon

There was never law, or sect, or opinion did so much magnify goodness, as the Christian religion doth.

Francis Bacon

It matters little whether or no Christianity makes men richer. But it does make them truer, purer, nobler. It is not more wealth that the world wants, a thousandth part as much as it is more character; not more investments, but more integrity; not money, but manhood; not regal palaces, but regal souls.

Edward Griffin Beckwith

There's not much practical Christianity in the man who lives on better terms with angels and seraphs, than with his children, servants, and neighbors.

Henry Ward Beecher

We cannot utter a dozen words without some turn, some touch, some reference which goes back to Christian myth, Christian liturgy, or Christian doctrine. . . . It holds true of Soviet Slavs and Nazi Teutons despite their bitter hatred of Christianity, and of European Jews whether they have left the synagogue or still cling to it.

Bernhard Berenson

Jesus was sitting in Moses' chair.
They brought the trembling woman there.
Moses commands she be ston'd to death.
What was the sound of Jesus' breath?
He laid His hand on Moses' law;
The ancient Heavens, in silent awe,
Writ with curses from pole to pole,
All away began to roll.

William Blake

The blood shed on the Cross for the redemption of mankind, as well as that which is shed invisibly every day in the Chalice of the Sacrament of the Altar, is naturally and supernaturally Jewish blood.

Léon Bloy

We show too passive a vision of Christianity. In a certain way we have made Marx right by offering the oppressed of both the poor and the rich countries an opiate for the people.

Helder Pessoa Camara

Christianity has not been tried and found wanting; it has been found difficult and not tried.

Gilbert Keith Chesterton

Christianity is not a theory or speculation, but a life; not a philosophy of life, but a life and a living process.

Samuel Taylor Coleridge

Christianity, rightly understood, is identical with the highest philosophy; the essential doctrines of Christianity are necessary and eternal truths of reason.

Samuel Taylor Coleridge

Let any of those who renounce Christianity, write fairly down in a book all the absurdities they believe instead of it, and they will find it requires more faith to reject Christianity than to embrace it.

Charles Caleb Colton

Christianity is not a religion of transcendental abstraction, or brilliant speculation; its children are neither monks, mystics, epicureans, nor stoics. It is the religion of loving, speaking, and doing, as well as believing. It is a life as well as a creed. It has a rest for the heart, a word for the tongue, a way for the feet, and a work for the hand. The same Lord who is the foundation of our hopes, the object of our faith, and the subject of our love, is also the model of our conduct, for "He went about doing good, leaving us an example that we should follow his steps."

John Cumming

Christianity is Judaism for the multitude.

Benjamin Disraeli

"Learn of me," says the philosopher, "and ye shall find restlessness." "Learn of me," says Christ, "and ye shall find rest."

William Henry Drummond

Christianity is the record of a pure and holy soul, humble, absolutely disinterested, a truth-speaker, and bent on serving, teaching, and uplifting men. It teaches that to love the All-perfect is happiness.

Ralph Waldo Emerson

There is not a single spot between Christianity and atheism on which a man can firmly fix his foot.

Nathaniel Emmons

We not only can be, but we must be Christians; only, however, if we recognize that Christianity is progressive historical development still in the making.

Rudolf Christoph Eucken

The steady discipline of intimate friendship with Jesus results in men becoming like him.
Harry Emerson Fosdick

As to Jesus of Nazareth, my opinion of whom you particularly desire, I think the system of morals and his religion, as he left them to us, is the best the world ever saw, or is likely to see.
Benjamin Franklin

Give Christianity a common law trial; submit the evidence pro and con to an impartial jury under the direction of a competent court, and the verdict will assuredly be in its favor.
John Bannister Gibson

To preach pie in the sky and to do nothing about the knife in a man's back is hardly Christianity.
Ugo Groppi

He [Christ], though a born Dauphin of Heaven, is democratically minded . . . he is not a God of shaven and shorn bookish pedants and laced men-at-arms . . . he is a modest God of the People, a citizen God, *un bon dieu citoyen.*
Heinrich Heine

Christianity is characteristically a religion of invasion; and yet it is no less a religion of pervasion also. It is a religion which has always done its best work by silent and unobserved penetration, by a process of spreading yeastlike suggestion.
Franklin Simpson Hickman

There is a feeling among us that no kind of Christianity is psychologically suited to our time and our civilization, that we need less faith in the supernatural and more in the courage and intelligence of human beings.
Frank Snowden Hopkins

Christendom is accounted for only by Christianity; and Christianity burst too suddenly into the world to be of the world.
Frederic Dan Huntington

Christianity always suits us well enough so long as we suit it. A mere mental difficulty is not hard to deal with. With most of us it is not reason that makes faith hard, but life.
Jean Ingelow

Had the doctrines of Jesus been preached always as pure as they came from his lips, the whole civilized world would now have been Christians.
Thomas Jefferson

The time is past when Christians in America can take a long spoon and hand the gospel to the black man out the back door.
Mordecai Wyatt Johnson

Too often an institution serves to bless the majority opinion. Today when too many move to the rhythmic beat of the status quo, whoever would be a Christian must be a nonconformist.
Martin Luther King, Jr.

Christianity everywhere gives dignity to labor, sanctity to marriage, and brotherhood to man. Where it may not convince, it enlightens; where it does not convert it restrains; where it does not renew, it refines; where it does not sanctify, it subdues and elevates. It is profitable alike for this world, and for the world that is to come.
Sir George St. Patrick Lawrence

It was not the outer grandeur of the Roman but the inner simplicity of the Christian that lived on through the ages.
Charles Augustus Lindbergh

Heathenism was the seeking religion; Judaism, the hoping religion; Christianity is the reality of what heathenism sought and Judaism hoped for.
Christoph Ernest Luthardt

The real security of Christianity is to be found in its benevolent morality; in its exquisite adaption to the human heart; in the facility with which it accommodates itself to the capacity of every human intellect; in the consolation which it bears to every house of mourning; and in the light with which it brightens the great mystery of the grave.
Thomas Babington Macaulay

There is one single fact which we may oppose to all the wit and argument of infidelity, namely, that no man ever repented of being a Christian on his death-bed.
Hannah More

With Christianity came a new civilization, and a new order of ideas. Tastes were cultivated, manners refined, views broadened, and natures spiritualized.
Patrick Francis Mullany (Father Azarias)

Christianity is a missionary religion, converting, advancing, aggressive, encompassing the world; a non-missionary church is in the bands of death.
Friedrich Max Müller

Christianity ruined emperors, but saved peoples. It opened the palaces of Constantinople to the barbarians, but it opened the doors of cottages to the consoling angels of Christ.

Louis Charles Alfred de Musset

Christianity came to India long before it went to England or Western Europe, and when even in Rome it was a despised and proscribed sect. Within 100 years or so of the death of Jesus, Christian missionaries came to South India by sea. They were received courteously and permitted to preach their new faith. They converted a large number of people, and their descendants have lived there, with varying fortunes, to this day.

Jawaharlal Nehru

Christianity is politically the dominant religion today, because it is the religion of the dominant peoples of Europe. But it is strange to think of the rebel Jesus preaching nonviolence and ahimsa and a revolt against the social order, and then to compare him with his loud-voiced followers of today, with their imperialism and armaments and wars and worship of wealth. The Sermon on the Mount and modern European and American Christianity-how amazingly dissimilar they are!

Jawaharlal Nehru

After reading the doctrines of Plato, Socrates, or Aristotle, we feel that the specific difference between their words and Christ's is the difference between an inquiry and a revelation.

Joseph Parker

Christianity as an idea begins with thinking of God in the same way that a true son thinks of his father; Christianity as a life, begins with feeling and acting toward God as a true son feels and acts toward his father.

Charles Henry Parkhurst

Through its whole history the Christian religion has developed supreme affinities for best things. For the noblest culture, for purest morals, for magnificent literatures, for most finished civilizations, for most energetic national temperaments, for most enterprising races, for the most virile and progressive stock of mind, it has manifested irresistible sympathies. Judging its future by its past, no other system of human thought has so splendid a destiny. It is the only system which possesses undying youth.

Austin Phelps

Whatever men may think of religion, the historic fact is, that in proportion as the institutions of Christianity lose their hold upon the multitudes, the fabric of society is in peril.

Arthur Tappan Pierson

Christianity is more than history. It is also a system of truths. Every event which its history records, either is a truth, or suggests or expresses a truth, which man needs assent to or to put into practice.

Noah Porter

The first founder of Christianity was Isaiah. By introducing into the Jewish world the concept of ethical religion, of justice, and of the relative unimportance of sacrifices, he antedated Jesus by more than seven centuries.

Joseph Ernest Renan

It is through Christianity that Judaism has really conquered the world. Christianity is the masterpiece of Judaism, its glory and the fulness of its evolution.

Joseph Ernest Renan

The true Christian is the true citizen, lofty of purpose, resolute in endeavor, ready for a hero's deeds, but never looking down on his task because it is cast in the day of small things; scornful of baseness, awake to his own duties as well as to his rights, following the higher law with reverence, and in this world doing all that in his power lies, so that when death comes he may feel that mankind is in some degree better because he lived.

Theodore Roosevelt

The true social reformer is the faithful preacher of Christianity; and the only organization truly potent for the perfection of Society, is the Christian Church. I know of nothing which, as a thought, is more superficial, or which, as a feeling, is better entitled to be called hatred of men, than that which disregards the influence of the gospel in its efforts for social good, or attempts to break its hold on mankind by destroying their faith in its living power.

Julius Hawley Seelye

Christianity is the basis of republican government, its bond of cohesion, and its life-giving law. More than the Magna Charta itself the Gospels are the roots of English liberty. That Magna Charta, and the Petition of Right, with our completing Declaration, was possible only because the Gospels had been before them.

Richard Salter Storrs

Christianity has its best exponents in the lives of the saints. It is only when our creeds pass into the iron of the blood that they become vital and organic. Faith if not transmuted into character, has lost its power.

Charles Lemuel Thompson

Where science speaks of improvement, Christianity speaks of renovation; where science speaks of development, Christianity speaks of sanctification; where science speaks of progress, Christianity speaks of perfection.

Joseph Parrish Thompson

Christianity is the companion of liberty in all its conflicts—the cradle of its infancy, and the divine source of its claims.

Alexis de Tocqueville

The sum of the whole matter is this, that our civilization cannot survive materially unless it be redeemed spiritually. It can be saved only by becoming permeated with the spirit of Christ and being made free and happy by the practices which spring out of that spirit.

(Thomas) Woodrow Wilson

See also: BROTHERHOOD, CHRISTIAN, CHURCH, CREED, CROSS, ECUMENISM, FAITH, GOSPEL, RELIGION, SECT, WORSHIP.

CHRISTMAS

Once in royal David's city
  Stood a lowly cattle shed,
Where a Mother laid her Baby
  In a manger for his bed:
Mary was that Mother mild.
Jesus Christ her little Child.

Cecil Frances Humphreys Alexander

Whosoever shall be found observing any such day as Christmas or the like, either by forbearing labor, feasting, or any other way, as a festival, shall be fined five shillings.

Massachusetts Bay Colony General Court

This is the month, and this the happy morn,
Wherein the Son of Heaven's eternal King,
Of Wedded Maid and Virgin Mother born,
Our great redemption from above did bring;
For so the holy sages once did sing,
That He our deadly forfeit should release,
And with His Father work us a perpetual
  peace.

John Milton

And after him came next the chill December:
Yet he, through merry feasting which he
  made

And great bonfires, did not the cold remember;
His Saviour's birth his mind so much did glad.

Edmund Spenser

See also: CELEBRATION, CHRIST, CHRISTIANITY.

CHURCH

Business checks up on itself frequently to be sure that it still is headed for its original goals. Is there not need for a similar check-up on the part of the church?

Bruce Barton

The only way the church can defend her own territory is by fighting not for it but for the salvation of the world. Otherwise the church becomes a "religious society" which fights in its own interests and thereby ceases to be the church of God and of the world.

Dietrich Bonhoeffer

Surely the church is a place where one day's truce ought to be allowed to the dissensions and animosities of mankind.

Edmund Burke

The Church of Christ is the world's only social hope and the sole promise of Peace.

Douglas Haig

The way to preserve the peace of the church is to preserve its purity.

Matthew Henry

Mahatma Gandhi tells of his contact with a Christian family in South Africa who gave him a standing invitation to dinner every Sunday, and afterwards they all attended the Wesleyan Church. He describes it: "The service did not make a favorable impression on me. The sermons seemed to be uninspiring. The congregation did not strike me as being particularly religious. They were not an assembly of devout souls; they appeared rather to be worldly-minded people going to Church for recreation and in conformity to custom. Here, at times, I would involuntarily doze. I was ashamed, but some of my neighbors, who were in no better case, lightened the shame. I could not go on long like this, and soon gave up attending the service."

Eli Stanley Jones

It is of no avail to talk of the church in general, the church in the abstract, unless the concrete particular local church which the people attend can become a center of light and leading, of inspiration and guidance, for its specific community.

Rufus Matthew Jones

If the church refrains from an all-out effort to liberate our fellow man from the root causes of enslavement, she will deservedly bear the stigma of the Levite who left the wounded helpless by the wayside and escaped to his own "sacramental" functions.

Stephan Cardinal Kim

Every manifestation in the Church of lack of freedom, however harmless, however much under cover, whatever religious trimmings it may have, contributes toward making the Church less believable in the eyes of the world and of men in general; and that is a miserable disaster.

Hans Küng

The United Nations Secretariat is more catholic than the Roman Curia of the Catholic Church.

Hans Küng

It takes *men,* not a creed, to make a church.

Cleland Boyd McAfee

If the growth of modern science has taught anything to religion and to the modern world, it is that the method of progress is the method of evolution, not the method of revolution. Let every man reflect well on these things before he assists in stabbing to death, or in allowing to starve to death, organized religion in the United States.

Robert Andrews Millikan

Everything that touches man concerns the Church, and the Church is interested closely in every generous effort that tends to advance humanity, not only in its way to heaven, but also in its search for well being, justice, peace, and happiness on earth.

Paul VI (Giovanni Battista Montini)

Let the world know this: the Church looks at the world with profound understanding, with sincere admiration and with the sincere intention not of conquering it but of serving it, not of despising it but of appreciating it, not of condemning it but of strengthening it.

Paul VI (Giovanni Battista Montini)

We open our arms to all those who glory in the name of Christ. We call them with the sweet name of brothers, and let them know they will find in us constant comprehension

and benevolence, that they will find in Rome the paternal house.

Paul VI (Giovanni Battista Montini)

[Young people] recognize the paradox of the joyless herald of the Good News and are repelled by it.

Archbishop John Quinn

When an Anglican is asked, "Where was your Church before the Reformation?" his best answer is to put the counter-question, "Where was your face before you washed it?"

Arthur Michael Ramsey

Going to church will not make you a saint, any more than going to school will make you a scholar.

Charles Haddon Spurgeon

I never weary of great churches. It is my favorite kind of mountain scenery. Mankind was never so happily inspired as when it made a cathedral.

Robert Louis Balfour Stevenson

Going to church doesn't make you a Christian any more than going to a garage makes you an automobile.

William Ashley (Billy) Sunday

No church or other association truly thrives unless struggles and differences are alive within it.

George Macaulay Trevelyan

The churches were urged by Paul in his letter to the Corinthians to give and take correction from each other. They are all responsible for each other. They must not be polite to each other but speak openly and frankly. There is no danger of self-righteousness from this, because correction is also a reminder to ourselves.

Willem Adolf Visser t'Hooft

See also: CHRISTIANITY, RELIGION, WORSHIP.

CHURCH AND STATE

No religion can long continue to maintain its purity when the church becomes the subservient vassal of the state.

Felix Adler

Politics and the pulpit are terms that have little agreement. No sound ought to be heard in the church but the healing voice of Christian charity. . . . Surely the church is a place where one day's truce ought to be allowed to the dissensions and animosities of mankind.

Edmund Burke

In the relationship between man and religion, the state is firmly committed to a position of neutrality.

Thomas Campbell (Tom) Clark

American Catholics rejoice in our separation of Church and State; and I can conceive no combination of circumstances likely to arise which should make a union desirable either to Church or State.

James Gibbons

Religion cannot sink lower than when somehow it is raised to a state religion . . . it becomes then an avowed mistress.

Heinrich Heine

I believe in an America where the separation of church and state is absolute—where no Catholic prelate would tell the President, should he be a Catholic, how to act, and no Protestant minister would tell his parishioners for whom to vote—where no church or church school is granted any public funds or political preference—and where no man is denied public office merely because his religion differs from the President who might appoint him or the people who might elect him.

John Fitzgerald Kennedy

We remain atheist, and we do everything we can to liberate a certain part of the people from the opium attraction of religion which still exists. But every person can practice the religion that pleases him, and care is taken never to annoy priests. Now that Soviet power has become so great, most priests have stopped their opposition to the Soviet Government.

Nikita Sergeevich Khrushchev

See also: CHRISTIANITY, CHURCH, SECT, STATE.

CINEMA: see MOTION PICTURE.

CIRCUMSTANCE

Men are the sport of circumstances, when the circumstances seem the sport of men.

George Gordon Byron (Lord Byron)

Man is not the creature of circumstances, circumstances are the creatures of men.

Nelson Glueck

He is happy whose circumstances suit his temper; but he is more excellent who can suit his temper to any circumstances.

David Hume

Circumstances form the character; but like petrifying waters they harden while they form.

Letitia Elizabeth Landon

Circumstances are the rulers of the weak; they are but the instruments of the wise.

Samuel Lover

Circumstances! I make circumstances!

Napoleon I (Bonaparte)

It is not the situation which makes the man, but the man who makes the situation. The slave may be a freeman. The monarch may be a slave. Situations are noble or ignoble, as we make them.

Frederick William Robertson

Men are not altered by their circumstances, but as they give them opportunities of exerting what they are in themselves; and a powerful clown is a tyrant in the most ugly form in which he can possibly appear.

Sir Richard Steele

Occasions do not make a man either strong or weak, but they show what he is.

Thomas à Kempis

Wait not, my soul, on circumstance;
It does not wait for you.
It nibbles at you now, and will
Devour you; I say true.

Mark Van Doren

See also: ACCIDENT, CHANGE, ENVIRONMENT, FACT, OPPORTUNITY, PLACE.

CITIZENSHIP

The most important office, . . . that of private citizen.

Louis Dembitz Brandeis

Too many, I suspect, think of serving America only in terms of romantic martyrdom. They are willing to die for their country, but they do not know how to go about living for it.

Albert Carr

Finally, whether you are citizens of America or citizens of the world, ask of us here the same high standards of strength and sacrifice which we ask of you. With a good conscience our only sure reward, with history the final judge of our deeds, let us go forth to lead the land we love, asking His blessing and His help, but knowing that here on earth God's work must truly be our own.

John Fitzgerald Kennedy

Now the trumpet summons us again—not as a call to bear arms, though arms we need—not as a call to battle, though embattled we are—but a call to bear the burden of a long twilight struggle year in and year out, "rejoicing in hope, patient in tribulation"—a struggle against the common enemies of man: tyranny, poverty, disease and war itself.

John Fitzgerald Kennedy

Neither democracy nor effective representation is possible until each participant in the group—and this is true equally of a household or a nation—devotes a measurable part of his life to furthering its existence.

Lewis Mumford

Citizenship consists in the service of the country.

Jawaharlal Nehru

Voting is the least arduous of a citizen's duties. He has the prior and harder duty of making up his mind.

Ralph Barton Perry

See also: AMERICA, BENEFICENCE, DUTY, HERO, PATRIOTISM, RIGHTS, SOLDIER.

CITY

There is no solitude more dreadful for a stranger, an isolated man, than a great city. So many thousands of men, and not one friend.

Pierre Claude Victoire Boiste

The city is an epitome of the social world. All the belts of civilization intersect along its avenues. It contains the products of every moral zone and is cosmopolitan, not only in a national, but in a moral and spiritual sense.

Edwin Hubbel Chapin

Suburbanites come into the city every day, make their living, then go back to a couple acres of land, drink a couple of martinis and chuckle over urban problems.

John Collins

The twelve largest central cities now contain over two-thirds of the Negro population outside the South, and one-third of the Negro total in the United States.

Commission on Civil Disorder, 1968

God the first garden made, and Cain the first city.

Abraham Cowley

Cities force growth, and make men talkative and entertaining, but they make them artificial.

Ralph Waldo Emerson

I have found by experience, that they who have spent all their lives in cities, contract not only an effeminacy of habit, but of thinking.

Oliver Goldsmith

In the decade between 1950 and 1960, 11 million Americans moved from rural areas and small towns to the cities, and that movement is still going on at the rate of 500,000 to 600,000 per year. Since 1950, 5,300,000 poor, largely Southern Negroes have moved from rural areas and small towns to the large cities, and this fact is a part of the present problems we face, of a very deep crisis nature, in most of the cities of America.

Fred R. Harris

There is hardly one in three of us who live in the cities who is not sick with unused self.

Ben Hecht

There is nothing I know of that we need more urgently in the cities of this country than health care and housing for the elderly—unless it's for the young.

Lyndon Baines Johnson

If you suppress the exorbitant love of pleasure and money, idle curiosity, iniquitous purpose, and wanton mirth, what a stillness would there be in the greatest cities.

Jean de La Bruyère

The circuited city of the future will not be the huge hunk of concentrated real estate created by the railway. It will take on a totally new meaning under conditions of very rapid movement. It will be an information megalopolis. What remains of the configuration of former "cities" will be very much like World's Fairs—places in which to show off new technology, not places of work or residence. They will be preserved, museumlike, as living monuments to the railway era. If we were to dispose of the city now, future societies would reconstruct them, like so many Williamsburgs.

(Herbert) Marshall McLuhan

The city has always been the decisive battle ground of civilization and religion. It intensifies all the natural tendencies of man. From its fomented energies, as well as from its greater weight of numbers, the city controls. Ancient civilizations rose and fell with their leading cities. In modern times, it is hardly too much to say, "as goes the city so goes the world."

Simon John McPherson

The present economic scheme of the big city depends upon the expectation of a stable income from an investment, public and private, that becomes ever more speculative, unstable, and insecure. The growth of such a city means an increase of insecurity.

Lewis Mumford

The problem of the cities is perhaps the most critical domestic issue with which this country has been confronted since the Civil War, if not since the founding of the Republic.

Edmund S. Muskie

The union of men in large masses is indispensible to the development and rapid growth of their higher faculties. Cities have always been the fireplaces of civilization, whence light and heat radiated out into the dark, cold world.

Theodore Parker

Towns are the sink of the human race. At the end of some generations races perish or degenerate; it is necessary to renew them, and it is always the country which furnishes this renewal.

Jean Jacques Rousseau

Without exception our cities are hopelessly bound by tradition, outmoded building codes, restrictive legislation, and the abortions of their historical development.

Athelstan Frederick Spilhaus

See also: BOSTON, COUNTRY, CRIME, CRISIS, LONDON, NEW YORK, RIOT, ROME, SLUM.

CIVIL RIGHTS: see RIGHTS.

CIVILIZATION

In civilization no man can live wholly to or for himself, and whoever would achieve power, influence, or success must cater to the tastes and whims of those who have the granting of these things in their hands.

James Truslow Adams

Civilization is a constant quest for nonviolent means of solving conflicts; it is a common quest for peace.

Max Ascoli

Civilization is the upward struggle of mankind, in which millions are trampled to death that thousands may mount on their bodies.

Francis Maitland Balfour

No civilization other than that which is Christian, is worth seeking or possessing.

Otto Eduard Leopold von Bismarck

Human wants are continually shaped and reshaped by civilization, its technical and social standards and its progress.

Karl Brandt

The fact that man possessed the capacity to rise from bestial savagery to civilization, at a time when it had *never before been done,* is the greatest fact in the history of the universe as known to us. For this amazing new capability, transcending merely physical development and the evolution of more efficient organs, disclosed a kind of buoyancy of the *human spirit,* never before displayed in the history of life on our planet.

James Henry Breasted

Civilizations are never made up of wholly consistent parts.

Lyman Lloyd Bryson

You think that a wall as solid as the earth separates civilization from barbarism. I tell you the division is a thread, a sheet of glass. A touch here, a push there, and you bring back the reign of Saturn.

Sir John Buchan

The test of a civilization is in the way that it cares for its helpless members.

Pearl Sydenstricker Buck

The three great elements of modern civilization, Gunpowder, Printing, and the Protestant Religion.

Thomas Carlyle

Can you tell me, in a world that is flagrant with the failures of civilisations, what there is particularly immortal about yours?

Gilbert Keith Chesterton

Civilization will not last, freedom will not survive, peace will not be kept, unless a very large majority of mankind unite together to defend them and show themselves possessed of a constabulary power before which barbaric and atavistic forces will stand in awe.

Sir Winston Leonard Spencer Churchill

The ease, the luxury, and the abundance of the highest state of civilization, are as productive of selfishness as the difficulties, the privations, and the sterilities of the lowest.
Charles Caleb Colton

Each of us, thinking of his own nation, is inclined to believe that the peculiar kind of ideas that form its culture would be beneficial to the rest of the world if they were universally adopted.
Raoul De Sales

We are never allowed to forget that we are not merely individuals, but part of a vast conglomeration of other individuals to whom we are bound by some very material common interests, and also by a series of taboos, symbols, more or less verified legends, and a considerable quantity of sacred falsehoods.
Raoul De Sales

The measure of civilization is the degree in which the method of cooperative intelligence replaces the method of brute conflict.
John Dewey

Increased means and leisure are the two civilizers of man.
Benjamin Disraeli

Like human behavior, civilization is made and not born. Like life itself, it must be nourished day by day, ceaselessly, with new energy and new materials, or it sickens and dies.
Charles H. Dorsey

Civilization begins with order, grows with liberty and dies with chaos.
Will (William James) Durant

A civilization is not destroyed by barbarian invasion from without; it is destroyed by barbarian multiplication within.
Will (William James) Durant

The greatest problem of Western civilization is that it is breeding from the bottom and dying from the top.
Will (William James) Durant

So I should say that civilizations begin with religion and stoicism; they end with skepticism and unbelief, and the undisciplined pursuit of individual pleasure. A civilization is born stoic and dies epicurean.
Will (William James) Durant

Tired civilizations, like senile souls, are apt to be deterministic; unable to overcome the forces of death, they dignify their fatigue as fatality, and their defeat as destiny.
Will (William James) Durant

The post office, with its educating energy, augmented by cheapness, and guarded by a certain religious sentiment in mankind, so that the power of a wafer, or a drop of wax guards a letter as it flies over sea and land, and bears it to its address as if a battalion of artillery had brought it, I look upon as a first measure of civilization.
Ralph Waldo Emerson

A sufficient and sure method of civilization is the influence of good women.
Ralph Waldo Emerson

The true test of civilization is, not the census, nor the size of cities, nor the crops, but the kind of man that the country turns out.
Ralph Waldo Emerson

The greatest danger to a civilized nation is the man who has no stake in it, and nothing to lose by rejecting all that civilization stands for.
Henry Ford II

Civilization, in the real sense of the term, consists not in the multiplication, but in the deliberate and voluntary reduction of wants. This alone promotes real happiness and contentment, and increases the capacity for service.
Mohandas Karamchand (Mahatma) Gandhi

The distinguishing characteristic of modern civilization is an indefinite multiplicity of human wants. The Characteristic of ancient civilization is an imperative restriction upon, and a strict regulating of, these wants.
Mohandas Karamchand (Mahatma) Gandhi

Do the people of the world not yet realize that by fighting on until the bitter end I am not only performing my sacred duty to my people, but standing guard in the last citadel of collective security? Are they too blind to see that I have my responsibilities to the whole of humanity to face? I must still hold on until my tardy allies appear. And if they never come, then I say prophetically and without bitterness: The West will perish.
Haile Selassie (Ras Taffari)

Christianity has carried civilization along with it, whithersoever it has gone. And as if to show that the latter does not depend on physical causes, some of the countries, the most civilized in the days of Augustus, are now in a state of hopeless barbarism.

Augustus and Julius Hare

It is only an uncivilized world which would worship civilization.

Henry Stanley Haskins

Civilization is the process of reducing the infinite to the finite.

Oliver Wendell Holmes

The path of civilization is paved with tin cans.

Elbert Green Hubbard

Our culture is essentially periodical: we believe that all that is deserves to perish and to have something else put in its place.

Randall Jarrell

The quality of a civilization depends on a balance of body, mind and spirit in its people, measured on a scale less human than divine. . . . To survive, we must keep this balance. To progress, we must improve it. Science is upsetting it with an overemphasis of mind and a neglect of spirit and body.

Charles Augustus Lindbergh

The degree of a nation's civilization is marked by its disregard for the necessities of existence.

(William) Somerset Maugham

Nations, like individuals, live or die, but civilization cannot perish.

Giuseppe Mazzini

Human beings . . . should become civilized, that is, so related to each other that their thinking is a concerted attempt to reach common answers to common problems. They should practice a friendliness of the mind. Violence . . . is savagery. Civilization is reasonableness.

Alexander Meiklejohn

Civilizations, like empires, fall, not so much because of the strength of the enemy outside, as through the weakness and decay within.

Jawaharlal Nehru

Fine buildings, fine pictures and books and everything that is beautiful are certainly signs of civilization. But an even better sign is a fine man who is unselfish and works with others for the good of all. To work together is better than to work singly, and to work together for the common good is the best of all.

Jawaharlal Nehru

If the world suffers from mental deterioration or from moral degradation, then something goes wrong at the very root of civilization or culture. Even though that civilization may drag out for a considerable period, it grows less and less vital and ultimately tumbles down.

Jawaharlal Nehru

Sometimes civilized people themselves act barbarously, and if this happens, civilization may destroy itself.

Jawaharlal Nehru

The civilization of a country consists in the quality of life that is lived there, and this equality shows plainest in the things that people choose to talk about when they talk together, and in the way they choose to talk about them.

Albert Jay Nock

Ours is a paradoxical world. . . . The nations with the highest standard of living, the greatest capacity to take care of their people economically, the broadest education, and the most enlightened morality and religion exhibit the least capacity to avoid mutual destruction in war. It would seem that the more civilized we become the more incapable of maintaining civilization we are.

Filmer Stuart Cuckow Northrop

The old Hindoo saw, in his dream, the human race led out to its various fortunes. First, men were in chains, that went back to an iron hand—then he saw them led by threads from the brain, which went upward to an unseen hand. The first was despotism, iron, and ruling by force. The last was civilization, ruling by ideas.

Wendell Phillips

The great fact to remember is that the trend of civilization itself is forever upward.

Franklin Delano Roosevelt

The military superiority of Europe to Asia is not an eternal law of nature, as we are tempted to think, and our superiority in civilization is a mere delusion.

Bertrand Arthur Russell

Unless man has the wit and the grit to build his civilization on something better than material power, it is surely idle to talk plans for a stable peace.

Francis Bowes Sayre

You are dying. I see in you all the characteristic stigma of decay. I can prove to you that your great wealth and your great poverty, your capitalism and your socialism, your wars and your revolutions, your atheism and your pessimism and your cynicism, your immorality, your broken-down marriages, your birth control, that is bleeding you from the bottom and killing you off at the top in the brains—I can prove to you that those were the characteristic marks of the dying ages of ancient States—Alexandria and Greece and neurotic Rome.

Oswald Spengler

In order to civilize a people, it is necessary first to fix it, and this cannot be done without inducing it to cultivate the soil.

Alexis de Tocqueville

Though sixteen civilizations may have perished already to our knowledge, and nine others may be now at the point of death, we—the twenty-sixth—are not compelled to submit the riddle of our fate to the blind arbitrament of statistics. The divine spark of creative power is still alive in us, and, if we have the grace to kindle it into flame, then the stars in their courses cannot defeat our efforts to attain the goal of human endeavor.

Arnold Joseph Toynbee

All that is best in the civilization of to-day, is the fruit of Christ's appearance among men.

Daniel Webster

Human civilization is an outgrowth of language, and language is the product of advancing civilization.

Alfred North Whitehead

A living civilization requires learning, but it lies beyond it.

Alfred North Whitehead

Anyone can be a barbarian; it requires a terrible effort to be or remain a civilized man.

Leonard Sidney Woolf

Human beings can no more remain civilized during a revolution than they can during a war.

Leonard Sidney Woolf

Civilization: Art and religion are soul of our civilization. Go to them for there love exists.

Frank Lloyd Wright

See also: CULTIVATION, CULTURE, IMPROVEMENT, PROGRESS, REFINEMENT.

CLASS

There may be said to be two classes of people in the world: those who constantly divide the people of the world into two classes, and those who do not.

Robert Charles Benchley

As property has its duties as well as its rights, rank has its bores as well as its pleasures.

Benjamin Disraeli

The middle class, that prisoner of the barbarian 20th century.

Sinclair Lewis

There was one point by which it [Israel] was distinguished from the other nations of antiquity, namely, its comparative absence of caste, its equality of religious relations.

Arthur Penrhyn Stanley

There is nothing to which men cling more tenaciously than the privileges of class.

Leonard Sidney Woolf

See also: ARISTOCRACY, NOBILITY, RANK, STATION, TITLE.

CLEANLINESS

Beauty commonly produces love, but cleanliness preserves it. Age itself is not unamiable while it is preserved clean and unsullied—like a piece of metal constantly kept smooth and bright, which we look on with more pleasure than on a new vessel cankered with rust.

Joseph Addison

Cleanliness may be recommended as a mark of politeness, as it produces affection, and as it bears analogy to purity of mind. As it renders us agreeable to others, so it makes us easy to ourselves. It is an excellent preservative of health; and several vices, destructive both to body and mind, are inconsistent with the habit of it.

Joseph Addison

Cleanliness of body was ever esteemed to proceed from a due reverence to God.

Francis Bacon

So great is the effect of cleanliness upon man, that it extends even to his moral character. Virtue never dwelt long with filth; nor do I believe there ever was a person scrupulously attentive to cleanliness who was a consummate villain.

Benjamin Thompson (Count Rumford)

A soldier must admire the singular attention that was paid (in Israel) to the rules of cleanliness.

George Washington

Certainly, this is a duty—not a sin. Cleanliness is, indeed, next to Godliness.

John Wesley

See also: DIRT, PURITY.

CLEMENCY

Clemency, which we make a virtue of, proceeds sometimes from vanity, sometimes from indolence, often from fear, and almost always from a mixture of all three.

Duc François de La Rochefoucauld

It is not right to show promiscuous and general clemency; and to forgive everyone is as much cruelty as to forgive no one.

Seneca

If you preserve me uninjured, I shall be a lasting example of your clemency.

Tacitus

See also: COMPASSION, CRUELTY, FORGIVENESS, GENTLENESS, LENIENCY, MERCY, PATIENCE, PITY, SYMPATHY.

CLERGY

Not so much what a man says in the pulpit, but what he does out of the pulpit, gives power to his ministry.

Henry Berkowitz

A Catholic priest walks as if heaven belonged to him; a Protestant clergyman . . . as if he had taken a lease on it.

Heinrich Heine

In the eyes of the young those qualities [of Jesus] that are most important—joy, love and kindness, patience and tolerance, an open mind and a willingness to listen, a spirit of compassion and concern, simplicity and directness—are often missing in the ministers.

Archbishop John Quinn

Popular religion may be summed up as respect for ecclesiastics.

Baruch (Benedict) Spinoza

See also: CHRISTIANITY, CHURCH, MINISTER.

CLEVERNESS

Clever men are good, but they are not the best.

Thomas Carlyle

The doctrine of human equality reposes on this: that there is no man really clever who has not found that he is stupid.

Gilbert Keith Chesterton

It takes a clever man to turn cynic, and a wise man to be clever enough not to.

Fannie Hurst

Be good, sweet maid, and let who can be clever;
   Do lovely things, not dream them all day long;
And so make Life, Death, and that vast Forever
   One grand sweet song.

Charles Kingsley

It is great cleverness to know how to conceal our cleverness.

Duc François de La Rochefoucauld

The worst part of an eminent man's conversation is, nine times out of ten, to be found in that part which he means to be clever.

Edward G. Bulwer-Lytton (Baron Lytton)

See also: ABILITY, INTELLIGENCE, SKILL.

CLIMATE

Coal is a portable climate.

Ralph Waldo Emerson

They change their climate, not their disposition, who run beyond the sea.

Horace

You will find in northern climates people who have few vices, many virtues, much sincerity and frankness. Approach southern countries, you will think that you are removed altogether from morality; strong passions will multiply crimes; every one will try to take over others all the advantages which may favour their passions. In temperate regions you will see people changeable in their manners, even in their vices and virtues; the climate has not a quality firm enough to fix even these.

Charles de Secondat (Baron de Montesquieu)

See also: CLOUD, RAIN, SUN, WEATHER.

CLOCK

When Charles V retired in weariness from the greatest throne in the world to the solitude of the monastery at Yuste, he occupied his leisure for some weeks in trying to regulate two clocks. It proved very difficult. One day, it is recorded, he turned to his assistant and said: "To think that I attempted to force the reason and conscience of thousands of men into one mould, and I cannot make two clocks agree!"

(Henry) Havelock Ellis

Some men are like a clock on a roof; they are useful only to the neighbors.

Austin O'Malley

The clock indicates the moment—but what does eternity indicate?

Walt (Walter) Whitman

See also: TIME.

CLOUD

Come watch with me the azure turn to rose
In yonder West: the changing pageantry,
The fading Alps and archipelagoes,
And spectral cities of the sunset-sea.

Thomas Bailey Aldrich

That looked as though an angel, in his upward flight, had left his mantle floating in mid-air.

Joanna Baillie

I am the daughter of earth and water,
    And the nursling of the sky:
I pass through the pores of the ocean and
        shores;
    I change, but cannot die.

Percy Bysshe Shelley

I bring fresh showers for the thirsting flowers,
    From the seas and the streams;
I bear light shade for the leaves when laid
    In their noon-day dreams.

Percy Bysshe Shelley

Those playful fancies of the mighty sky.

Albert Richard Smith

See also: RAIN, SUN, WEATHER.

CO-EXISTENCE

We are firmly convinced that cooperation in the interests of peace and international security is also possible with those Western governments and political figures who look soberly on the international situation, and who are ready to follow in practice the principles of peaceful coexistence with different social systems.

Leonid Il'ich Brezhnev

Let the competition between America and Russia descend from outer space and extend to the more crucial area of the peaceful resolution of all international differences here on earth.

Israel R. Margolies

Once you recognize, as I believe it is recognized the world over, that war is no solution, and that the two major protagonists are too powerful to be dismissed one by the other, then you have to co-exist, you have to understand, you have to be restrained and you have to deal with each other. If you reject coexistence the alternative is war and mutual destruction.

Jawaharlal Nehru

Co-existence is not a form of passive acceptance of things as they are. It is waging the contest between freedom and tyranny by peaceful means. It will involve negotiations and adjustment—compromise but not appeasement—and I will never shrink from these if they would advance the world toward a secure peace.

Adlai Ewing Stevenson

See also: AMERICA, PEACE, RUSSIA, WAR.

COLD, COMMON

The threat of a neglected cold is for doctors what the threat of purgatory is for priests—a gold mine.

Sébastien Roch Nicolas Chamfort

A bad cold wouldn't be so annoying if it weren't for the advice of our friends.

Frank McKinney (Kin) Hubbard

A cold is both positive and negative; sometimes the Eyes have it and sometimes the Nose.

William Lyon Phelps

A cold in the head causes less suffering than an idea.

Jules Renard

See also: DISEASE, SICKNESS.

COLD WAR

We are in the midst of a cold war.

Bernard Mannes Baruch

Real, total war has become information war. It is being fought by subtle electric informational media—under cold conditions, and constantly. The cold war is the real war front—a surround—involving everybody—all the time —everywhere.

(Herbert) Marshall McLuhan

See also: COMMUNISM, DEMOCRACY, WAR.

COLONIALISM

To campaign against colonialism is like barking up a tree that has already been cut down.

Sir Andrew Benjamin Cohen

All the sparrows on the roof-tops are crying about the fact that the most imperialist nation that is supporting the colonial regime in the colonies is the United States and the [U. S. representative] is indignant over that. What innocence, may I ask, is being played here when it is known that this virtuous damsel has already got a dozen illegitimate children?

Nikita Sergeevich Khrushchev

It is very unfair—to be accused of being Communist on the basis of anti-colonialism. I think anti-colonialism was invented by the United States of America.

Kwame Nkrumah

See also: CAPITALISM, CHANGE, FOREIGN AID, FOREIGN POLICY, REVOLUTION.

COMFORT

Giving comfort under affliction requires that penetration into the human mind, joined to that experience which knows how to soothe, how to reason, and how to ridicule, taking the utmost care not to apply those arts improperly.

Henry Fielding

I have enjoyed many of the comforts of life, none of which I wish to esteem lightly; yet I confess I know not any joy that is so dear to me, that so fully satisfies the inmost desires of my mind, that so enlivens, refines, and elevates my whole nature, as that which I derive from religion—from faith in God. May this God be thy God, thy refuge, thy comfort, as he has been mine.

Johann Kaspar Lavater

The comforts we enjoy here below, are not like the anchor in the bottom of the sea, that holds fast in a storm, but like the flag upon the top of the mast, that turns with every wind.

Christopher Love

Of all created comforts, God is the leader; you are the borrower, not the owner.

Samuel Rutherford

It is a little thing to speak a phrase of common comfort, which by daily use has almost lost its sense; and yet, on the ear of him who thought to die unmourned, it will fall like the choicest music.

Sir Thomas Noon Talfourd

Most of our comforts grow up between our crosses.

Edward Young

See also: COMPASSION, CONSOLATION, ENCOURAGEMENT, PITY, SYMPATHY.

COMMANDER

A man must require just and reasonable things if he would see the scales of obedience properly trimmed. From orders which are improper, springs resistance which is not easily overcome.

Basil the Great

It is better to have a lion at the head of an army of sheep, than a sheep at the head of an army of lions.

Daniel Defoe

He who rules must humor full as much as he commands.

George Eliot (Mary Ann Evans)

A brave captain is as a root, out of which, as branches, the courage of his soldiers doth spring.

Sir Philip Sidney

The right of commanding is no longer an advantage transmitted by nature; like an inheritance, it is the fruit of labors, the price of courage.

Voltaire (François Marie Arouet)

See also: ARMY, AUTHORITY, SOLDIER.

COMMERCE

I am wonderfully delighted to see a body of men thriving in their own fortunes, and at the same time promoting the public stock; or, in other words, raising estates for their own families by bringing into their country whatever is wanting, and carrying out of it whatever is superfluous.

Joseph Addison

The only type of economic structure in which government is free and in which the human spirit is free is one in which commerce is free.

Thurman Wesley Arnold

It may almost be held that the hope of commercial gain has done nearly as much for the cause of truth, as even the love of truth itself.

Christian Nestell Bovee

The old idea of a good bargain was a transaction in which one man got the better of another. The new idea of a good contract is a transaction which is good for both parties to it.

Louis Dembitz Brandeis

Every dollar spent for missions has added hundreds to the commerce of the world.

Nathan George Clark

Commerce may well be termed the younger sister, for, in all emergencies, she looks to agriculture both for defence and for supply.

Charles Caleb Colton

Commerce is no missionary to carry more or better than you have at home. But what you have at home, be it gospel, or be it drunkenness, commerce carries the world over.

Edward Everett Hale

Merchants throughout the world have the same religion.

Heinrich Heine

Perfect freedom is as necessary to the health and vigor of commerce, as it is to the health and vigor of citizenship.

Patrick Henry

Commerce tends to wear off those prejudices which maintain destruction and animosity between nations. It softens and polishes the manners of men. It unites them by one of the strongest of all ties—the desire of supplying their mutual wants. It disposes them to peace by establishing in every state an order of citizens bound by their interest to be the guardians of public tranquility.

Frederick William Robertson

See also: BUSINESS, INDUSTRY, SELLING.

COMMERCIALS

[A soap commercial:] It gets the dirt off. It doesn't make you twenty years younger, it won't win you a husband (or wife), it won't patch up a busted romance, but it gets the dirt off.

John Crosby

But today there are more and more raucous pitchmen who come into our living rooms (which we have graciously permitted them to use temporarily as stores) and make our evenings hideous with their repeated blasts about bad breath, irregularity, upset stomach, B. O., sinus pains, and headaches that hammer the hell out of us.

Don Herold

Many advertising men themselves believe today that commercials are ruining television.

Don Herold

I do know that people get pretty mad when they have three commercials thrown at them between television programs—as well as confess their inability to remember so much exposed to them in so short a time.

Walter Weir

See also: ADVERTISING, RADIO, TELEVISION.

COMMITMENT

To approve is more difficult than to admire.

Hugo Von Hofmannsthal

From compromise and things half done,
  Keep me with stern and stubborn pride;
And when at last the fight is won,
  God, keep me still unsatisfied.

Louis Untermeyer

See also: DEVOTION, FAITH, PATRIOTISM.

COMMITTEE

A committee is a group that keeps minutes and loses hours.

Milton Berle

When it comes to facing up to serious problems, each candidate will pledge to appoint a committee. And what is a committee? A group of the unwilling, picked from the unfit, to do the unnecessary. But it all sounds great in a campaign speech.

Richard Long Harkness

If you want to kill any idea in the world today, get a committee working on it.

Charles Franklin Kettering

See also: ORGANIZATION.

COMMON COLD: *see* COLD, COMMON

COMMON MAN

The greatest service we can do the Common Man is to abolish him.

Sir Norman Angell

When wilt Thou save the people?
O God of mercy, when?
Not kings and lords, but nations!
Not thrones and crowns, but men!
Flowers of Thy heart, O God are they;
Let them not pass, like weeds, away—
God save the people!

Ebenezer Elliott

Rob the average man of his life-illusion, and you rob him of his happiness at the same stroke.

Henrik Ibsen

One night he dreamed that he was in a crowd, when someone recognized him as the President, and exclaimed in surprise, "He is a very common-looking man." Whereupon he answered, "Friend, the Lord prefers common-looking people. That is the reason he makes so many of them."

Abraham Lincoln

The century on which we are entering can be and must be the century of the common man.

Henry Agard Wallace

And God, who studies each commonplace
    soul,
Out of commonplace things makes His beautiful whole.

Sarah Chauncey Woolsey (Susan Coolidge)

See also: MAN, MOB, POPULACE, PUBLIC, SOCIETY, STATE.

COMMON SENSE

If you haven't grace, the Lord can give it to you. If you haven't learning, I'll help you to get it. But if you haven't common sense, neither I, nor the Lord can give it to you.

John Brown (of Haddington)

If common sense has not the brilliancy of the sun, it has the fixity of the stars.

Fernan Caballero

Common sense is, of all kinds, the most uncommon. It implies good judgment, sound discretion, and true and practical wisdom applied to common life.

Tryon Edwards

No man is quite sane. Each has a vein of folly in his composition—a slight determination of blood to the head, to make sure of holding him hard to some one point which he has taken to heart.

Ralph Waldo Emerson

"Knowledge, without common sense," says Lee, is "folly; without method, it is waste; without kindness, it is fanaticism; without religion, it is death." But with common sense, it is wisdom; with method, it is power; with charity, it is beneficence; with religion, it is virtue, and life, and peace.

Frederic William Farrar

There is nobody so irritating as somebody with less intelligence and more sense than we have.

Don Herold

The figure which a man makes in life, the reception which he meets with in company, the esteem paid him by his acquaintance—all these depend as much upon his good sense and judgment, as upon any other part of his character. A man of the best intentions, and farthest removed from all injustice and violence, would never be able to make himself much regarded, without a moderate share of parts and understanding.

David Hume

He was one of those men who possess almost every gift, except the gift of the power to use them.

Charles Kingsley

Common sense is only a modification of talent. Genius is an exaltation of it. The difference is, therefore, in degree, not nature.

Edward G. Bulwer-Lytton (Baron Lytton)

The crown of all faculties is common sense. It is not enough to do the right thing, it must be done at the right time and place. Talent knows what to do; tact knows when and how to do it.

William Matthews

One pound of learning requires ten pounds of common sense to apply it.

Persian Proverb

Fine sense, and exalted sense, are not half as useful as common sense. There are forty men of wit to one man of sense. He that will carry nothing about him but gold, will be every day at a loss for readier change.

Alexander Pope

Freedom of the press and freedom of the radio are the common means by which the common man gets his common information on which must depend his common sense.

Samuel Moor (Sam) Shoemaker

Common sense is the knack of seeing things as they are, and doing things as they ought to be done.

Calvin Ellis Stowe

To act with common sense according to the moment, is the best wisdom I know; and the best philosophy is to do one's duties, take the world as it comes, submit respectfully to one's lot; bless the goodness that has given us so much happiness with it, whatever it is; and despise affectation.

Horace Walpole

Common sense is genius in homespun.

Alfred North Whitehead

See also: INTELLIGENCE, PRUDENCE.

COMMUNICATIONS MEDIA

The chief reasons that demagogues thrive is that the newspapers—and the radio—pretend to take them seriously.

Raymond Clapper

I think everybody in the television and radio professions has a right to think of himself as a man bearing a great responsibility as a crusader, and help to do this job of education, of ourselves and others about us, and to bring home here an understanding of what goes on in the rest of the world.

Dwight David Eisenhower

It is a medium of entertainment which permits millions of people to listen to the same joke at the same time, and yet remain lonesome.

Thomas Stearns Eliot

A world community can exist only with world communication, which means something more than extensive shortwave facilities scattered about the globe. It means common understanding, a common tradition, common ideas, and common ideals.

Robert Maynard Hutchins

At the high speeds of electric communication, purely visual means of apprehending the world are no longer possible; they are just too slow to be relevant or effective.

(Herbert) Marshall McLuhan

Electric circuitry profoundly involves men with one another. Information pours upon us, instantaneously and continuously. As soon as information is acquired, it is very rapidly replaced by still newer information. Our electrically-configured world has forced us to move from the habit of data classification to the mode of pattern recognition. We can no longer build serially, block-by-block, step-by-step, because instant communication insures that all factors of the environment and of experience co-exist in a state of active interplay.

(Herbert) Marshall McLuhan

In an electric information environment, minority groups can no longer be contained—ignored. Too many people know too much about each other. Our new environment compels commitment and participation. We have become irrevocably involved with, and responsible for, each other.

(Herbert) Marshall McLuhan

Media, by altering the environment, evoke in us unique ratios of sense perceptions. The extension of any one sense alters the way we think and act—the way we perceive the world.

(Herbert) Marshall McLuhan

We shall never be able to remove suspicion and fear as potential causes of war until communication is permitted to flow, free and open, across international boundaries.

Harry S Truman

The modern world is not given to uncritical admiration. It expects its idols to have feet of clay, and can be reasonably sure that press and camera will report their exact dimensions.

Barbara Ward (Lady Jackson)

The fantastic advances in the field of electronic communication constitute a greater danger to the privacy of the individual.

Earl Warren

See also: TECHNOLOGY, TELEVISION, SPACE.

COMMUNISM

One of the great errors of the ordinary citizen is his assumption that anarchy and Communism are related and similar political philosophies; it is impossible to conceive two philosophies more antipathetic and this antipathy reveals itself immediately in violent clashes wherever the doctrines of anarchy and Communism encounter each other.

Louis Bromfield

An iron curtain has descended across the Continent.

Sir Winston Leonard Spencer Churchill

The typical ex-communist American intellectual in fact has experienced two conversions. . . . But, in his new enlightenment, what has he found out? Why? that freedom must not be given up, that treason is evil, that murder and terrorism must not be condoned, that communism is not democratic, that democracy is precious. That is his harvest from two dark nights of the soul. . . . See it as pitiful waste or see it as the innocence of a saint, but what is it as intelligence? . . . Where was he when they were distributing minds?

Bernard Augustine De Voto

From reading many records in cases involving Communists, I gather that many who joined may not have had subversion as a purpose. Some seemed to be sheer sentimentalists; others seemed utterly confused. Yet there has been a readiness to identify all who joined the party at any period of its existence with all of the aims espoused by it. That is guilt by association—a concept which is foreign to our history.

William Orville Douglas

The Soviet Communist program is too rigid to be readily exportable. Conformity is demanded to an absurd degree . . . even in the realm of art, science and literature. Such compulsory conformity is bound to lead to widespread unrest, discontent, and even revolt in peoples with distinctive loyalties to church and state and their own traditions.

John Foster Dulles

We cannot successfully combat Soviet Communism in the world and frustrate its methods of fraud, terrorism, and violence unless we have a faith with spiritual appeal that translates itself into practices which, in our modern complex society, get rid of the sordid, degrading conditions of life in which the spirit cannot grow.

John Foster Dulles

Communism is, in deepest sense, a gigantic failure. Even in the countries it dominates, hundreds of millions who dwell there still cling to their religious faith; still are moved by aspirations for justice and freedom that cannot be answered merely by more steel or by bigger bombers; still seek a reward that is beyond money or place or power;

still dream of the day that they may walk fearlessly in the fullness of human freedom. The destiny of man is freedom and justice under his Creator. Any ideology that denies this universal faith will ultimately perish or be recast. This is the first great truth that must underlie all our thinking, all our striving in this struggling world.

Dwight David Eisenhower

What is a communist?—One who has yearnings for equal division of unequal earnings. Idler or bungler, he is willing to fork out his penny and pocket your shilling.

Ebenezer Elliott

The evil of communism is not its doctrinal content, which at worst is utopian, but its fanatical certainty of itself, its messianic zeal and its brutal intolerance of dissent.

James William Fulbright

The Communist is a Socialist in a violent hurry.

George Woolley Gough

Communism possesses a language which every people can understand. Its elements are hunger, envy, and death.

Heinrich Heine

Communism, though it be at present but little discussed, and now yearns away its life in forgotten garrets on wretched straw-pallets, is still the gloomy hero to whom a great if transitory part is assigned in the modern tragedy, and which only waits its cue to enter on the stage. We should never lose sight of this.

Heinrich Heine

It is with dread and horror that I think of the time when these gloomy iconoclasts will attain power; when their heavy hands will break without pity all the marble statues of beauty which are so dear to my heart. They will . . . fell my groves of laurel and plant potatoes in their place, . . . and ah! my book of songs will be used by the grocers to make paper cornets in which to put coffee or snuff for the cold women of the future.

Heinrich Heine

The closer one gets to the communists, the less obscurity there is about their aim to take over the governments of Asia by force. Here in Southeast Asia, the free governments see a clear, concerted plan. They are not talking about nuances, they are talking about survival.

Hubert Horatio Humphrey

Communism is a nonassimilable political ideology. . . . A true progressive movement has no chance of success unless it rigidly excludes Communists.

Harold Le Claire Ickes

Your levelers wish to level down as far as themselves. But they cannot bear leveling up to themselves. They would all have some people under them. Why not then have some people above them?

Samuel Johnson

There are many people in the world who really don't understand—or say they don't—what is the great issue between the free world and the Communist world . . . There are some who say that Communism is the wave of the future . . . And there are some who say in Europe and elsewhere "we can work with the Communists." . . . And there are even a few who say that it's true that Communism is an evil system but it permits us to make economic progress. Let them come to Berlin!

John Fitzgerald Kennedy

If we allow ourselves to become allied with those to whom the cry of 'Communism' is only an excuse for the perpetuation of privilege, if we assist with military materials and other aid governments which use that aid to prevent reform for the people, then we will give the communists a strength which they cannot attain by anything they might do.

Robert Francis Kennedy

The Communist must act like a surgeon who takes a sharp knife and operates on a man's body to cut out malignant growths and thus makes possible the further development and strengthening of the organism. This is our approach to the life of our society and to our work.

Nikita Sergeevich Khrushchev

Each year humanity takes a step towards Communism. Maybe not you, but at all events your grandson will surely be a Communist.

Nikita Sergeevich Khrushchev

No one is born a Communist. I know it from experience. In the Soviet Union farmers keep on looking in the barn for "their horses" even after they have given them to the collective.

Nikita Sergeevich Khrushchev

All the experiences of the Chinese people, accumulated in the course of successive decades, tell us to carry out a people's democratic dictatorship.

Mao Tse-tung

Communism has nothing to do with love. Communism is an excellent hammer which we use to destroy our enemy.

Mao Tse-tung

Let the ruling classes tremble at a Communist revolution. The proletarians have nothing to lose but their chains. They have a world to win. Workers of all countries, unite!

Karl Marx

The theory of Communism may be summed up in one sentence: Abolish all private property.

Karl Marx

All this business of Communism conquering the world. No doubt you can quote from their texts . . . [But] read the old tracts of any religion—they all wanted to conquer the world. Nevertheless they settled down after the first burst of enthusiasm . . . When there are enough things to go around, it is far better to produce them than to break each other's heads.

Jawaharlal Nehru

Communism is admittedly framed to keep all power in the hands of the workers, and to give no quarter to capitalism or to those who want to bring back capitalism.

Jawaharlal Nehru

The conviction of the Communist that he represents the interests of the future of humanity can only be compared with the faith and zeal of a religious enthusiast.

Jawaharlal Nehru

There is no basis for the Marxist hope that an "economy of abundance" will guarantee social peace; for men may fight as desperately for "power and glory" as for bread.

Reinhold Niebuhr

I am against interpreting everything in terms of the great international Communist conspiracy and seeing Communists as supermen. They're not supermen. Their feet of clay extend up almost to their brains.

Edwin Oldfather Reischauer

I do not know of a single person really qualified as an authority on Communism who does not agree that the best weapon against the Communists is exposure—revealing the truth about them, revealing what they are, letting the public know the kind of activities they are engaged in. Communists and other conspirators cannot stand to have the searchlight of truth beamed at them. It hurts them, discredits them, it undermines, to a large degree, their subversive activities.

Richard L. Roudebush

And to the Soviet Union I would say: There are laws of history more profound, more inescapable than the laws dreamed up by Marx and Lenin—laws which belong not to class relationships or stages of economic development, but to the nature and destiny of man himself.

Adlai Ewing Stevenson

We know how irrevocable a communist takeover can be. Yet we know, too, how easy it is to mistake genuine local revolt for communist subversion.

Adlai Ewing Stevenson

Communists are running rampant through the land. They are fomenting strife and discord and are inciting racial and religious rancor and hatred, resulting in riots, bloodshed, death, and destruction. They are undertaking to demean and denigrate the good people of America and our Government by spitting on, stamping, and burning our national banner, the American flag.

William Munford Tuck

See also: ARISTOCRACY, CAPITALISM, CHINA, CO-EXISTENCE, DEMOCRACY, EQUALITY, LEVELER, REVOLUTION, RUSSIA.

COMPANIONSHIP

It is good discretion not to make too much of any man at the first, because one cannot hold out in that proportion.

Francis Bacon

Be cautious with whom you associate, and never give your company or your confidence to those of whose good principles you are not sure.

William Hart Coleridge

Be kind to your companions, but be firm.

Benjamin Disraeli

What is companionship where nothing that improves the intellect is communicated, and where the larger heart contracts itself to the model and dimension of the smaller.

Walter Savage Landor

The most agreeable of all companions is a simple, frank man, without any high pretensions to an oppressive greatness; one who loves life, and understands the use of it; obliging, alike at all hours; above all, of a golden temper, and steadfast as an anchor. For such an one we gladly exchange the greatest genius, the most brilliant wit, the profoundest thinker.

Gotthold Ephraim Lessing

It has not always been easy for youth . . . to face death in all its hideous forms in the far corners of the world. But what, perhaps more than anything else, nerved them for the difficult task which their country asked of them, was the realization that *God went with them all the way.*

John Anthony O'Brien

We forget that there is no hope of joy except in human relations. If I summon up those memories that have left me with an enduring savor, if I draw up the balance sheet of the hours in my life that have truly counted, surely I find only those that no wealth could have procured me. True riches cannot be bought.

Antoine de Saint-Exupéry

No man can possibly improve in any company for which he has not respect enough to be under some degree of restraint.

Philip Dormer Stanhope (Lord Chesterfield)

Take rather than give the tone of the company you are in. If you have parts, you will show them, more or less, upon every subject; and if you have not, you had better talk sillily upon a subject of other people's choosing than of your own.

Philip Dormer Stanhope (Lord Chesterfield)

No man can be provident of his time, who is not prudent in the choice of his company.

Jeremy Taylor

Good company, and good discourse are the very sinews of virtue.

Izaak Walton

See also: CAMARADERIE, FRIENDSHIP.

COMPARISON

The superiority of some men is merely local. They are great because their associates are little.·

Samuel Johnson

If we rightly estimate what we call good and evil, we shall find it lies much in comparison.

John Locke

See also: ANALOGY, CONTRAST, SIMILARITY.

COMPASSION

It is the crown of justice and the glory, where it may kill with right, to save with pity.

Francis Beaumont and John Fletcher

Far from being a handicap to command, compassion is the measure of it. For unless one values the lives of his soldiers and is tormented by their ordeal, he is unfit to command.

Omar Nelson Bradley

The dew of compassion is a tear.

George Gordon Byron (Lord Byron)

Man may dismiss compassion from his heart, but God will never.

William Cowper

The mind is no match with the heart in persuasion; constitutionality is no match with compassion.

Everett McKinley Dirksen

Compassion to an offender who has grossly violated the laws, is, in effect, a cruelty to the peaceable subject who has observed them.

Junius

See also: CLEMENCY, MERCY, PITY.

COMPENSATION

If the poor man cannot always get meat, the rich man cannot always digest it.

Henry Giles

All advantages are attended with disadvantages. A universal compensation prevails in all conditions of being and existence.

David Hume

Whatever difference may appear in the fortunes of mankind, there is, nevertheless, a certain compensation of good and evil which makes them equal.

Duc François de La Rochefoucauld

When you are disposed to be vain of your mental acquirements, look up to those who are more accomplished than yourself, that you may be fired with emulation; but when you feel dissatisfied with your circumstances, look down on those beneath you, that you may learn contentment.

Hannah More

No evil is without its compensation. The less money, the less trouble. The less favor, the less envy. Even in those cases which put us out of wits, it is not the loss itself, but the estimate of the loss that troubles us.

Seneca

When fate has allowed to any man more than one great gift, accident or necessity seems usually to contrive that one shall encumber and impede the other.

Algernon Charles Swinburne

See also: JUSTICE, LOSS, RECOMPENSE, RETRIBUTION, REWARD.

COMPETITION

To vie is not to rival.

Benjamin Disraeli

Today we are competing for men's hearts, and minds, and trust all over the world. In such a competition, what we are at home and what we do at home is even more important than what we say abroad.

Dwight David Eisenhower

Competition is the very life of science.

Horace Meyer Kallen

See also: CONTENTION, OPPOSITION, RIVALRY.

COMPLAINT

It is a general popular error to imagine the loudest complainers for the public to be the most anxious for its welfare.

Edmund Burke

I have always despised the whining yelp of complaint, and the cowardly feeble resolve.

Robert Burns

Murmur at nothing: if our ills are irreparable, it is ungrateful; if remediless, it is vain.

Charles Caleb Colton

We do not wisely when we vent complaint and censure. We cry out for a little pain, when we do but smile for a great deal of contentment.

Owen Felltham

Had we not faults of our own, we should take less pleasure in complaining of others.

François de Salignac de La Mothe-Fénelon

I will not be as those who spend the day in complaining of headache, and the night in drinking the wine that gives it.

Johann Wolfgang von Goethe

Every one must see daily instances of people who complain from a mere habit of complaining; and make their friends uneasy, and strangers merry, by murmuring at evils that do not exist, and repining at grievances which they do not really feel.

Richard Graves

The man who is fond of complaining, likes to remain amid the objects of his vexation. It is at the moment that he declares them insupportable that he will most strongly revolt against every means proposed for his deliverance. This is what suits him. He asks nothing better than to sigh over his position and to remain in it.

François Pierre Guillaume Guizot

Grumblers are commonly an idle set. Having no disposition to work themselves, they spend their time in whining and complaining both about their own affairs and those of their neighbors.

Matthew Henry

The usual fortune of complaint is to excite contempt more than pity.

Samuel Johnson

Just as you are pleased at finding faults, you are displeased at finding perfections.

Johann Kaspar Lavater

We have no more right to put our discordant states of mind into the lives of those around us and rob them of their sunshine and brightness than we have to enter their houses and steal their silverware.

Julia Moss Seton

I pity the man who can travel from Dan to Beersheba, and cry it is all barren.

Laurence Sterne

There is a very large and very knowing class of misanthropes who rejoice in the name of grumblers, persons who are so sure that the world is going to ruin that they resent every attempt to comfort them as an insult to their sagacity, and accordingly seek their chief consolation in being inconsolable, and their chief pleasure in being displeased.

Edwin Percy Whipple

See also: DISCONTENTMENT.

COMPLIMENT

The compliments which please us most are those which mark our differences—however slight and even silly—from the rest of the human race.

Katherine Brush

Soft soap is always a sign that there's dirty water about.

John Dickson Carr

Compliments are pleasant but tend towards complacency and laziness, while complaints stir you to new and necessary effort.

Frank Case

A deserved and discriminating compliment is often one of the strongest encouragements and incentives to the diffident and self-distrustful.

Tryon Edwards

Compliments which we think are deserved, we accept only as debts, with indifference; but those which conscience informs us we do no merit, we receive with the same gratitude that we do favors given away.

Oliver Goldsmith

Some people pay a compliment as if they expected a receipt.

Frank McKinney (Kin) Hubbard

Compliments of congratulation are always kindly taken, and cost nothing but pen, ink, and paper. I consider them as draughts upon good breeding, where the exchange is always greatly in favor of the drawer.

Philip Dormer Stanhope (Lord Chesterfield)

See also: APPLAUSE, FLATTERY, PRAISE.

COMPROMISE

An appeaser is one who feeds a crocodile—hoping it will eat him last.

Sir Winston Leonard Spencer Churchill

The essence of all successful international negotiation is compromise.

Anthony Robert Eden

Compromise is but the sacrifice of one right or good in the hope of retaining another, too often ending in the loss of both.

Tryon Edwards

My candle burns at both ends;
It will not last the night;
But, ah, my foes, and oh, my friends—
It gives a lovely light.

Edna St. Vincent Millay

Even when one compromises, one should never compromise in regard to the basic truth. One may limit the application of it, remembering always the basic way, the basic objective and where the aim lies. If we always remember the basic objective, and always aim that way, it may be permissible, as a next step, to say something much less than that which people understand. But if we forget the basic objective, then the small step may lead us astray.

Jawaharlal Nehru

Life is always forcing us to compromise.

Jawaharlal Nehru

Better bend than break.

Scottish Proverb

From the beginning of our history the country has been afflicted with compromise. It is by compromise that human rights have been adandoned. I insist that this shall cease. The country needs repose after all its trials; it deserves repose. And repose can only be found in everlasting principles.

Charles Sumner

From compromise and things half done,
    Keep me with stern and stubborn pride;
And when at last the fight is won,
    God, keep me still unsatisfied.

Louis Untermeyer

See also: EXPEDIENCY, FIRMNESS, HARMONY.

COMPUTER

The evolution of computers is a significant part of human evolution, and an appreciation of their importance may provide fresh insights into our place as the most rapidly evolving species on earth.

John Edward Pfeiffer

If it ever comes to actual warfare, computers will have to be mobilized by the tens of thousands. The air over a battlefield is buzzing with information as well as more tangible flying things. . . . Only computers can coordinate on-the-spot battle activities, and they would be important targets for the enemy. If one of them were destroyed, the result might be a chaotic informational traffic jam.

John Edward Pfeiffer

One of the most significant developments in science is the rise of general-purpose electronic computers during the second half of the twentieth century.

John Edward Pfeiffer

Our kind of evolution depends on cultural changes, on what we learn, on the things we build. In a basic sense, human evolution *is* the evolution of machines, and of these, computers are the most significant. Perhaps more than anything else, the design of artificial—intelligence systems will determine our future as a species.

John Edward Pfeiffer

Within its brief lifetime the computer has become indispensable in many areas.

John Edward Pfeiffer

As the use of computers expanded, new professions were created of personnel especially trained to work with these sophisticated machines. The most important of these new jobs was that of a computer programmer—a person who could work out the complicated mathematical programs needed to tell the computers what to do.

David Charles Whitney

See also: CYBERNETICS, SCIENCE, TECHNOLOGY.

CONCEALMENT

"Thou shalt not get found out" is not one of God's commandments; and no man can be saved by trying to keep it.

Leonard Bacon

To conceal anything from those to whom I am attached, is not in my nature. I can never close my lips where I have opened my heart.

Charles John Huffam Dickens

It is great cleverness to know how to conceal our cleverness.

Duc François de La Rochefoucauld

He who can conceal his joys, is greater than he who can hide his griefs.

Johann Kaspar Lavater

See also: CANDOR, CONSPIRACY, DISGUISE, DISSIMULATION, EVASION, RESERVE, SECRECY, SPYING.

CONCEIT

Conceit is God's gift to little men.

Bruce Barton

It is easier to put an ox into an eggcup than for a man full of conceit to receive wisdom.

Ernest Bramah (Smith)

If its colors were but fast colors, self-conceit would be a most comfortable quality. But life is so humbling, mortifying, disappointing to vanity, that a great man's idea of himself gets washed out of him by the time he is forty.

Charles Buxton

Self-conceit is a weighty quality, and will sometimes bring down the scale when there is nothing else in it. It magnifies a fault beyond proportion, and swells every omission into an outrage.

Jeremy Collier

I've never any pity for conceited people, because I think they carry their comfort about with them.

George Eliot (Mary Ann Evans)

The less a man thinks or knows about his virtues the better we like him.

Ralph Waldo Emerson

The weakest spot in every man is where he thinks himself to be the wisest.

Nathaniel Emmons

No man was ever so much deceived by another, as by himself.

Fulke Greville (First Baron Brooke)

Conceit is the most contemptible, and one of the most odious qualities in the world. It is vanity driven from all other shifts, and forced to appeal to itself for admiration.

William Hazlitt

One of the surprising things of this world is the respect a worthless man has for himself.

Edgar Watson Howe

He who is always his own counsellor will often have a fool for his client.

John Hunter

In one thing men of all ages are alike: they have believed obstinately in themselves.

Friedrich Heinrich Jacobi

There are few people who are more often in the wrong than those who cannot endure to be thought so.

Duc François de La Rochefoucauld

He who gives himself airs of importance, exhibits the credentials of impotence.

Johann Kaspar Lavater

If he could only see how small a vacancy his death would leave, the proud man would think less of the place he occupies in his lifetime.

Gabriel Legouvé

Whenever nature leaves a hole in a person's mind, she generally plasters it over with a thick coat of self-conceit.

Henry Wadsworth Longfellow

All men who know not where to look for truth save in the narrow well of self, will find their own image at the bottom and mistake it for what they are seeking.

James Russell Lowell

He that fancies himself very enlightened, because he sees the deficiencies of others, may be very ignorant, because he has not studied his own.

Edward G. Bulwer-Lytton (Baron Lytton)

I look upon the too good opinion that man has of himself, as the nursing mother of all false opinions, both public and private.

Michel Eyquem de Montaigne

We are very apt to be full of ourselves, instead of Him that made what we so much value, and but for whom we have no reason to value ourselves. For we have nothing that we can call our own, no, not ourselves; for we are all but tenants, and at will too, of the great Lord of ourselves, and of this great farm, the world that we live upon.

William Penn

It is the admirer of himself, and not the admirer of virtue, that thinks himself superior to others.

Plutarch

Conceit is to nature, what paint is to beauty; it is not only needless, but it impairs what it would improve.

Alexander Pope

Conceit may puff a man up, but can never prop him up.

John Ruskin

Wind puffs up empty bladders; opinion, fools.

Socrates

The best of lessons, for a good many people, would be, to listen at a key-hole.—It is a pity for such that the practice is dishonorable.

Anne Sophie Swetchine

When Providence wishes to destroy the small, it does so by putting big words into their little mouths.

Sir Rabindranath Tagore

They say that every one of us believes in his heart, or would like to have others believe, that he is something which he is not.

William Makepeace Thackeray

People wrapped up in themselves never unfold.

Puzant Kevork Thomajan

Conceit and confidence are both of them cheats. The first always imposes on itself; the second frequently deceives others.

Johann Georg von Zimmerman

See also: ARROGANCE, BOASTING, PRIDE, SNOB, VANITY.

CONCENTRATION

Depend upon it, Sir, when a man knows he is to be hanged in a fortnight, it concentrates his mind wonderfully.

Samuel Johnson

I wish you could invent some means to make me at all happy without you. Every hour I am more and more concentrated in you; every thing else tastes like chaff in my mouth.

John Keats

To concentrate too long on any one subject will cause the loss of perspective and a commonsense viewpoint.

Jules Ormont

See also: ATTENTION, OBSERVATION.

CONDEMNATION

Men might be better if we better deemed
Of them. The worst way to improve the world
Is to condemn it.

Philip James Bailey

When we condemn other people we generally mean indirectly to flatter ourselves.

John Stuart Blackie

Minds of moderate caliber ordinarily condemn everything which is beyond their range.

Duc François de La Rochefoucauld

See also: CENSURE, CRITICISM.

CONDUCT

When we are asked further, what is conduct? —let us answer: Three-fourths of life.

Matthew Arnold

The force that rules the world is conduct, whether it be moral or immoral.

Nicholas Murray Butler

In all the affairs of life let it be your great care, not to hurt your mind, or offend your judgment. And this rule, if observed carefully in all your deportment, will be a mighty security to you in your undertakings.

Epictetus

Every one of us, whatever our speculative opinions, knows better than he practices, and recognizes a better law than he obeys.

James Anthony Froude

It is not enough that you form, and even follow the most excellent rules for conducting yourself in the world; you must, also, know when to deviate from them, and where lies the exception.

Fulke Greville (First Baron Brooke)

Fools measure actions, after they are done, by the event; wise men beforehand, by the rules of reason and right. The former look to the end, to judge of the act. Let me look to the act, and leave the end with God.

Joseph Hall

Conduct is the great profession. Behavior is the perpetual revealing of us. What a man does, tells us what he is.

Frederick Dan Huntington

The ultimate test for us of what a truth means is the conduct it dictates or inspires.

William James

The integrity of men is to be measured by their conduct, not by their professions.

Junius

After all, what counts is not creed but conduct.

Sir Sarvepalli Radhakrishnan

Everybody lives and acts partly according to his own, partly according to other people's ideas.

Count Lev (Leo) Nikolaevich Tolstoi

See also: BEHAVIOR, COURTESY, GOOD BREEDING, MANNERS, MORALITY.

CONFESSION

Confession of sin comes from the offer of mercy. Mercy displayed causes confession to flow, and confession flowing opens the way for mercy. If I have not a contrite heart, God's mercy will never be mine; but if God had not manifested his mercy in Christ, I could never have had a contrite heart.

Neil Arnott

The confession of evil works is the first beginning of good works.

Augustine of Hippo

Confession is good for the soul only in the sense that a tweed coat is good for dandruff —it is a palliative rather than a remedy.

Peter De Vries

All the good writers of confessions, from Augustine onwards, are men who are still a little in love with their sins.

Anatole France

A clean confession combined with a promise never to commit the sin again, when offered before one who has the right to receive it, is the purest type of repentance.

Mohandas Karamchand (Mahatma) Gandhi

There could not be a cleansing without a clean confession.

Mohandas Karamchand (Mahatma) Gandhi

A man should never be ashamed to own he has been in the wrong, which is but saying, in other words, that he is wiser to-day than he was yesterday.

Alexander Pope

It is not our wrong actions which it requires courage to confess, so much as those which are ridiculous and foolish.

Jean Jacques Rousseau

Be not ashamed to confess that you have been in the wrong. It is but owning what you need not be ashamed of—that you now have more sense than you had before, to see your error; more humility to acknowledge it, more grace to correct it.

Jeremiah Seed

Why does no man confess his vices? because he is yet in them. It is for a waking man to tell his dream.

Seneca

Depression comes, not from having faults, but from the refusal to face them. There are tens of thousands of persons today suffering from fears which in reality are nothing but the effects of hidden sins.

Fulton John Sheen

No person is ever made better by having someone else tell him how rotten he is; but many are made better by avowing the guilt themselves.

Fulton John Sheen

See also: CONSCIENCE, GUILT, MORALITY, SIN, TRUTH.

CONFIDENCE

All confidence which is not absolute and entire, is dangerous. There are few occasions but where a man ought either to say all, or conceal all; for, how little soever you have revealed of your secret to a friend, you have already said too much if you think it not safe to make him privy to all particulars.

Francis Beaumont

Let us have a care not to disclose our hearts to those who shut up theirs against us.

Francis Beaumont

There are cases in which a man would be ashamed not to have been imposed upon. There is a confidence necessary to human intercourse, and without which men are often more injured by their own suspicions, than they could be by the perfidy of others.

Edmund Burke

When young, we trust ourselves too much; and we trust others too little when old. Rashness is the error of youth; timid caution of age.

Charles Caleb Colton

They can conquer who believe they can.

John Dryden

The human heart, at whatever age, opens only to the heart that opens in return.
Maria Edgeworth

Self-trust is the essence of heroism.
Ralph Waldo Emerson

Trust men and they will be true to you; treat them greatly and they will show themselves great.
Ralph Waldo Emerson

That man who has inspired confidence in another has never lost anything in this world.
Mohandas Karamchand (Mahatma) Gandhi

Never put much confidence in such as put no confidence in others. A man prone to suspect evil is mostly looking in his neighbor for what he sees in himself. As to the pure all things are pure, even so to the impure all things are impure.
Augustus and Julius Hare

Confidence is a plant of slow growth; especially in an aged bosom.
Samuel Johnson

Confidence always gives pleasure to the man in whom it is placed. It is a tribute which we pay to his merit; it is a treasure which we entrust to his honour; it is a pledge which gives him a right over us, and a kind of dependence to which we subject ourselves voluntarily.
Duc François de La Rochefoucauld

Confidence, in conversation, has a greater share than wit.
Duc François de La Rochefoucauld

Trust him little who praises all; him less who censures all; and him least who is indifferent to all.
Johann Kaspar Lavater

If we are truly prudent we shall cherish those noblest and happiest of our tendencies—to love and to confide.
Edward G. Bulwer-Lytton (Baron Lytton)

Confidence imparts a wondrous inspiration to its possessor. It bears him on in security, either to meet no danger, or to find matter of glorious trial.
John Milton

Confidence in another man's virtue, is no slight evidence of one's own.
Michel Eyquem de Montaigne

To confide, even though to be betrayed, is much better than to learn only to conceal. In the one case your neighbor wrongs you; —but in the other you are perpetually doing injustice to yourself.
William Gilmore Simms

Society is built upon trust, and trust upon confidence in one another's integrity.
Robert South

I think I have learned, in some degree at least, to disregard the old maxim "Do not get others to do what you can do yourself." My motto on the other hand is, "do not do that which others can do as well."
Booker Taliaferro Washington

See also: BOLDNESS, DOUBT, FAITH, SELF-CONFIDENCE, TRUST.

CONFLICT: *see* CONTENTION.

CONFORMITY

These are the days when men of all social disciplines and all political faiths seek the comfortable and the accepted; when the man of controversy is looked upon as a disturbing influence; when originality is taken to be a mark of instability; and when, in minor modification of the scriptural parable, the bland lead the bland.
John Kenneth Galbraith

I was part of that strange race of people aptly described as spending their lives doing things they detest to make money they don't want to buy things they don't need to impress people they dislike.
Emile Henry Gauvreau

If we conform too much, we become conventional nobodies, and lose our individuality; on the other hand, if we rebel too much, we are on the "outs" with the rest of our fellowmen, and get nowhere.
Joseph Jastrow

You must adjust . . . This is the legend imprinted in every schoolbook, the invisible message on every blackboard. Our schools have become vast factories for the manufacture of robots.
Robert Linder

Fair fame is won as a rule by all who cheerfully take things as they find them and interfere with no established custom.
Philo

See also: CUSTOM, PRECEDENT, TRADITION.

CONGRESS

Representing local interests as it does, the House furnishes a sort of recurrent plebiscite on the foreign policy of the United States.

Paul Findley

Think of what would happen to us in America if there were no humorists; life would be one long Congressional Record.

Tom Masson

There are two periods when Congress does no business: one is before the holidays, and the other after.

George Denison Prentice

With Congress, every time they make a joke it's a law; and every time they make a law it's a joke.

Will (William Penn Adair) Rogers

I think that when the Constitution provides that Congress should be a coequal branch with the executive, it means just that. That is the only way that we will have a democratic government. If the Congress does not make itself a coequal branch, it will end up as an appendage dangling from the executive.

Ralph Webster Yarborough

See also: GOVERNMENT.

CONQUEST

One must not conquer too much if one wants to have tribute too.

Arthur Feiler

This abominable nation [Jews] has succeeded in spreading its customs throughout all lands; the conquered have given their laws to the conquerors.

Seneca

Minds are not conquered by force, but by love and highmindedness.

Baruch (Benedict) Spinoza

See also: REVOLUTION, WAR.

CONSCIENCE

A tender conscience is an inestimable blessing; that is, a conscience not only quick to discern what is evil, but instantly to shun it, as the eyelid closes itself against the mote.

Nehemiah Adams

A good conscience is to the soul what health is to the body; it preserves constant ease and serenity within us, and more than countervails all the calamities and afflictions which can befall us without.

Joseph Addison

Blind is he who sees not his own conscience; lame is he who wanders from the right way.

Anthony of Padua

A good conscience is the palace of Christ; the temple of the Holy Ghost; the paradise of delight; the standing Sabbath of the saints.

Augustine of Hippo

What we call conscience, is, in many instances, only a wholesome fear of the constable.

Christian Nestell Bovee

Conscience is God's vicegerent on earth, and, within the limited jurisdiction given to it, it partakes of his infinite wisdom and speaks in his tone of absolute command. It is a revelation of the being of a God, a divine voice in the human soul, making known the presence of its rightful sovereign, the author of the law of holiness and truth.

Francis Bowen

Conscience is a great ledger book in which all our offences are written and registered, and which time reveals to the sense and feeling of the offender.

Richard Eugene Burton

That conscience approves of any given course of action, is, of itself, an obligation.

Joseph Butler

It is astonishing how soon the whole conscience begins to unravel if a single stitch drops. One single sin indulged in makes a hole you could put your head through.

Charles Buxton

Man's conscience is the oracle of God.

George Gordon Byron (Lord Byron)

There is no future pang can deal that justice on the self-condemned, he deals on his own soul.

George Gordon Byron (Lord Byron)

The torture of a bad conscience is the hell of a living soul.

John Calvin

Tenderness of conscience is always to be distinguished from scrupulousness. The conscience cannot be kept too sensitive and tender; but scrupulousness arises from bodily or mental infirmity, and discovers itself in a multitude of ridiculous, superstitious, and painful feelings.

Richard Cecil

O faithful conscience, delicately clear, how doth a little failing wound thee sore!

Dante Alighieri

A good digestion depends upon a good conscience.

Benjamin Disraeli

Conscience is merely our own judgment of the right or wrong of our actions, and so can never be a safe guide unless enlightened by the word of God.

Tryon Edwards

We never do evil so thoroughly and heartily as when led to it by an honest but perverted, because mistaken, conscience.

Tryon Edwards

I've very seldom heard people mention their consciences
Except to observe that their consciences were clear.

Thomas Stearns Eliot

Conscience, which ought to confront us with our real sins, is commonly used to distract our attention from them and to center it on less important matters.

Harry Emerson Fosdick

I simply want to please my own conscience, which is God.

Mohandas Karamchand (Mahatma) Gandhi

In matters of conscience, the law of the majority has no place.

Mohandas Karamchand (Mahatma) Gandhi

The only tyrant I accept in this world is the still voice within.

Mohandas Karamchand (Mahatma) Gandhi

There is a higher court than courts of justice and that is the court of conscience. It supersedes all other courts.

Mohandas Karamchand (Mahatma) Gandhi

The men who succeed best in public life are those who take the risk of standing by their own convictions.

James Abram Garfield

Conscience, true as the needle to the pole points steadily to the pole-star of God's eternal justice, reminding the soul of the fearful realities of the life to come.

Ezra Hall Gillett

Conscience—that vicegerent of God in the human heart, whose still, small voice the loudest revelry cannot drown.

William Henry Harrison

What other dungeon is so dark as one's own heart! What jailer so inexorable as one's self!

Nathaniel Hawthorne

The surest way to work up a crusade in favor of some good cause is to promise people that they will have a chance of maltreating someone. . . . To be able to destroy with good conscience, to be able to behave badly and call your bad behavior "righteous indignation"— this is the height of psychological luxury, the most delicious of moral treats.

Aldous Leonard Huxley

Conscience, though ever so small a worm while we live, grows suddenly into a serpent on our deathbed.

Douglas William Jerrold

One man alone with his conscience—whether in the laboratory, or the classroom, or on the street corner—is to be jealously guarded from the thousand who, believing him wrong, would deny his right to search and his right to speak the truth. On that fact we have built a free and great and diverse country.

Lyndon Baines Johnson

The relation is very close between our capacity to act at all and our conviction that the action we are taking is right. . . . Without that belief, most men will not have the energy and will to persevere in the action.

Walter Lippman

I am more afraid of my own heart, than of the Pope and all his cardinals. I have within me the great Pope, self.

Martin Luther

The Anglo-Saxon conscience does not prevent the Anglo-Saxon from sinning; it merely prevents him from enjoying his sin.

Salvador de Madariaga y Rojo

He that is conscious of crime, however bold by nature, becomes a coward.

Menander of Athens

Conscience is the inner voice that warns us somebody may be looking.

Henry Louis Mencken

Conscience is justice's best minister. It threatens, promises, rewards, and punishes, and keeps all under its control. The busy must attend to its remonstrances; the most powerful submit to its reproof, and the angry endure its upbraidings. While conscience is our friend, all is peace; but if once offended, farewell to the tranquil mind.

Lady Mary Wortley Montagu

My dominion ends where that of conscience begins.

Napoleon I (Bonaparte)

Conscience is the true vicar of Christ in the soul; a prophet in its information; a monarch in its peremptoriness; a priest in its blessings or anathemas, according as we obey or disobey it.

John Henry Newman

A disciplined conscience is a man's best friend. It may not be his most amiable, but it is his most faithful monitor.

Austin Phelps

Cowardice asks, Is it safe? Expediency asks, Is it politic? Vanity asks, Is it popular? but Conscience asks, Is it right?

William Morley Punshon

In artistic work one needs nothing so much as conscience: it is the sole standard.

Rainer Maria Rilke

Conscience is the voice of the soul, as the passions are the voice of the body. No wonder they often contradict each other.

Jean Jacques Rousseau

Man's conscience is the supreme judge of what is true or false, good or evil. A person who lives professing a belief he does not hold has lost the only true, the only immutable thing—his conscience.

Dagobert David Runes

The foundation of true joy is in the conscience.

Seneca

A good conscience fears no witness, but a guilty conscience is solicitous even in solitude. If we do nothing but what is honest,

let all the world know it. But if otherwise, what does it signify to have nobody else know it, so long as I know it myself? Miserable is he who slights that witness.

Seneca

We cannot live better than in seeking to become better, nor more agreeably than in having a clear conscience.

Socrates

There is no witness so terrible—no accuser so powerful as conscience which dwells within us.

Sophocles

The voice of conscience is so delicate that it is easy to stifle it; but it is also so clear that it is impossible to mistake it.

Madame de Staël

Conscience warns us as a friend before it punishes as a judge.

Stanislas I (Leszczyński)

Conscience, honor, and credit, are all in our interest; and without the concurrence of the former, the latter are but impositions upon ourselves and others.

Sir Richard Steele

Trust that man in nothing who has not a conscience in everything.

Laurence Sterne

He will easily be content and at peace, whose conscience is pure.

Thomas à Kempis

Conscience tells us that we ought to do right, but it does not tell us what right is—that we are taught by God's word.

Henry Clay Trumbull

If a man has made up his mind that a certain wrong course is the right one, the more he follows his conscience the more hopeless he is as a wrongdoer. One is pretty far gone in an evil way when he serves the devil conscientiously.

Henry Clay Trumbull

A clean and sensitive conscience, a steadfast and scrupulous integrity in small things as well as great, is the most valuable of all possessions, to a nation as to an individual.

Henry Jackson Van Dyke

Labor to keep alive in your heart that little spark of celestial fire called conscience.

George Washington

Preserve your conscience always soft and sensitive. If but one sin force its way into that tender part of the soul and is suffered to dwell there, the road is paved for a thousand iniquities.

Isaac Watts

Conscience is the reason, employed about questions of right and wrong, and accompanied with the sentiments of approbation or condemnation.

William Whewell

See also: CONSCIENTIOUS OBJECTION, DEPRAVITY, HONOR, INTEGRITY, MORALITY, PRINCIPLE, RIGHTS, VIRTUE.

CONSCIENTIOUS OBJECTION

People have not been horrified by war to a sufficient extent. . . . War will exist until that distant day when the conscientious objector enjoys the same reputation and prestige as the warrior does today.

John Fitzgerald Kennedy

Contemplating this melancholy state of humanity, the Council wishes to recall first of all the permanent binding force of universal natural law and its all-embracing principles. Man's conscience itself gives ever more emphatic voice to these principles. Therefore, actions which deliberately conflict with these same principles, as well as orders commanding such actions, are criminal. Blind obedience cannot excuse those who yield to them. Among such must first be counted those actions designed for the methodical extermination of an entire people, nation, or ethnic minority. These actions must be vehemently condemned as horrendous crimes. The courage of those who openly and fearlessly resist men who issue such commands merits supreme commendation.

Vatican II

See also: CONSCIENCE, DISSENT, MORALITY.

CONSCRIPTION: *see* DRAFT.

CONSEQUENCE

Logical consequences are the scarecrows of fools and the beacons of wise men.

Thomas Henry Huxley

No action, whether foul or fair,
Is ever done, but it leaves somewhere
A record, written by fingers ghostly,
As a blessing or a curse.

Henry Wadsworth Longfellow

A hen can't be slaughtered without blood being shed.

Yiddish Proverb

If you chop wood, chips will fall.

Yiddish Proverb

See also: RESULT.

CONSERVATION

As soils are depleted, human health, vitality and intelligence go with them.

Louis Bromfield

The conservation of natural resources is, and has been for a half a century, the paramount domestic issue before the American people.

Henry Steele Commager

Fundamental experiments in the economic realm have not been popular. Both American business and American labor have been suspicious of fundamental experiments, and suspicious, too, of ideas and philosophies.

Henry Steele Commager

Conservation is ethically sound. It is rooted in our love of the land, our respect for the rights of others, our devotion to the rule of law.

Lyndon Baines Johnson

To sustain an environment suitable for man we must fight on a thousand battlegrounds. Despite all of our wealth and knowledge, we cannot create a redwood forest, or a wild river, or a gleaming seashore. But we can keep those we have.

Lyndon Baines Johnson

There is no sin punished more implacably by nature than the sin of resistance to change.

Anne Spencer Morrow Lindbergh

See also: AIR POLLUTION, FORETHOUGHT, FRUGALITY, WATER POLLUTION.

CONSERVATISM

There are men so conservative they believe nothing should be done for the first time.

Anonymous

The conservative may clamor against reform, but he might as well clamor against the centrifugal force. He sighs for "the good old times." He might as well wish the oak back into the acorn.

Edwin Hubbel Chapin

A conservative Government is an organized hypocrisy.

Benjamin Disraeli

We are reformers in spring and summer. In autumn and winter we stand by the old. Reformers in the morning; conservatives at night. Reform is affirmative; conservatism, negative. Conservatism goes for comfort; reform for truth.

Ralph Waldo Emerson

A conservative is a man who is too cowardly to fight and too fat to run.

Elbert Green Hubbard

A conservative is a man who will not look at the new moon, out of respect for that "ancient institution," the old one.

Douglas William Jerrold

Men can know more than their ancestors did if they start with a knowledge of what their ancestors had already learned. . . . That is why a society can be progressive only if it conserves its traditions.

Walter Lippmann

Religion is the source of both radicalism and conservatism.

Reinhold Niebuhr

A Conservative is a man with two perfectly good legs who, however, has never learned to walk.

Franklin Delano Roosevelt

To defend every abuse, to defend every self-interest, every encrusted position of privilege in the name of country—when in fact it is only love of the status quo—that, indeed is the lie in the soul to which any conservative society is prone.

Adlai Ewing Stevenson

We are in one sense a very conservative people—for no nation in history has had so much to conserve.

Adlai Ewing Stevenson

Generally young men are regarded as radicals. This is a popular misconception. The most

conservative persons I ever met are college undergraduates.

(Thomas) Woodrow Wilson

See also: CAUTION, EXTREMES, LIBERAL, MODERATION, PRUDENCE.

CONSIDERATION: see ATTENTION.

CONSISTENCY

With consistency a great soul has simply nothing to do. He may as well concern himself with his shadow on the wall.

Ralph Waldo Emerson

Change is a condition of progress. An honest man cannot afford to observe mechanical consistency when the mind revolts against anything as an error.

Mohandas Karamchand (Mahatma) Gandhi

Constant development is the law of life, and a man who always tries to maintain his dogmas in order to appear consistent drives himself into a false position.

Mohandas Karamchand (Mahatma) Gandhi

Those who honestly mean to be true contradict themselves more rarely than those who try to be consistent.

Oliver Wendell Holmes

Without consistency there is no moral strength.

John Jason Owen

Intellectual consistency is far from being the first want of our nature, and is seldom a primary want in minds of great persuasive, as distinguished from convincing power.

William Strahan

Do I contradict myself? Very well then I contradict myself. (I am large, I contain multitudes.)

Walt (Walter) Whitman

See also: CONSTANCY, FIDELITY, FIRMNESS.

CONSOLATION

Quiet and sincere sympathy is often the most welcome and efficient consolation to the afflicted. Said a wise man to one in deep sorrow, "I did not come to comfort you; God only can do that; but I did come to say how deeply and tenderly I feel for you in your affliction."

Tryon Edwards

For every bad there might be a worse; and when one breaks his leg let him be thankful it was not his neck.

Joseph Hall

God has commanded time to console the unhappy.

Joseph Joubert

The powers of Time as a comforter can hardly be overstated; but the agency by which he works is exhaustion.

Letitia Elizabeth Landon

Consolation, indiscreetly pressed upon us when we are suffering under affliction, only serves to increase our pain and to render our grief more poignant.

Jean Jacques Rousseau

Before an affliction is digested, consolation comes too soon; and after it is digested, it comes too late; but there is a mark between these two, as fine almost as a hair, for a comforter to take aim at.

Laurence Sterne

See also: COMFORT, ENCOURAGEMENT, INSENSIBILITY, SYMPATHY.

CONSPIRACY

Conspiracies no sooner should be formed than executed.

Joseph Addison

Society everywhere is in conspiracy against the manhood of every one of its members.

Ralph Waldo Emerson

Combinations of wickedness would overwhelm the world by the advantage which licentious principles afford, did not those who have long practiced perfidy grow faithless to each other.

Samuel Johnson

See also: CONCEALMENT, CORRUPTION, REVOLUTION, SECRECY, SPYING, TREASON, WIRETAPPING.

CONSTANCY

Without constancy there is neither love, friendship, nor virtue in the world.

Joseph Addison

A good man it is not mine to see. Could I see a man possessed of constancy, that would satisfy me.

Confucius

The secret of success is constancy of purpose.

Benjamin Disraeli

It is often constancy to change the mind.

John Hoole

Constancy is the complement of all other human virtues.

Giuseppe Mazzini

Constancy, far from being a virtue, seems often to be the besetting sin of the human race, daughter of laziness and self-sufficiency, sister of sleep, the cause of most wars and practically all persecutions.

Freya Madeleine Stark

See also: DEVOTION, FAITH, FIDELITY, FIRMNESS, INCONSTANCY.

CONSTITUTION

The Constitution was essentially an economic document based upon the concept that the fundamental rights of private property are anterior to government and morally beyond the reach of popular majorities.

Charles Austin Beard

A Constitution is not intended to embody a particular economic theory, whether of paternalism and the organic relation of the citizen to the state or laissez faire.

Oliver Wendell Holmes, Jr.

We are under a Constitution, but the Constitution is what the judges say it is.

Charles Evans Hughes

A Constitution if it is out of touch with the people's life, aims and aspirations, becomes rather empty; if it falls below those aims, it drags the people down. It should be something higher to keep people's eyes and minds up to a certain high mark.

Jawaharlal Nehru

Not the Constitution but free land, and an abundance of natural resources open to a fit people, made the democratic type of society in America for three centuries.

Frederick Jackson Turner

See also: GOVERNMENT, LAW.

CONTEMPLATION

Contemplation may be defined as the soul's true unerring intuition, or as the unhesitating apprehension of truth. Consideration, however, is thought which is earnestly directed toward research, or the application of the mind to the search for truth. In practice both contemplation and consideration are used interchangeably.

Bernard of Clairvaux

In order to improve the mind, we ought less to learn, than to contemplate.

René Descartes

Contemplation is nothing else but a secret, peaceful, and loving infusion of God, which, if yielded to, will set the soul on fire with the Spirit of love.

John of the Cross

And Wisdom's self
Oft seeks to sweet retired solitude,
Where, with her best nurse Contemplation,
She plumes her feathers, and lets grow her
    wings.

John Milton

See also: MEDITATION, PRAYER, THOUGHT.

CONTEMPT

Despise not any man, and do not spurn anything; for there is no man that hath not his hour, nor is there anything that hath not its place.

Simon Ben Azzai

Speak with contempt of no man. Every one hath a tender sense of reputation. And every man hath a string, which he may, if provoked too far, dart out at one time or another.

Richard Eugene Burton

Christ saw much in this world to weep over, and much to pray over; but he saw nothing in it to look upon with contempt.

Edwin Hubbel Chapin

The basest and meanest of all human beings are generally the most forward to despise others. So that the most contemptible are generally the most contemptuous.

Henry Fielding

Contempt is the only way to triumph over calumny.

Marquise de Maintenon

Contempt is commonly taken by the young for an evidence of understanding; but it is neither difficult to acquire, nor meritorious when acquired. To discover the imperfec-

tions of others is penetration; to hate them for their faults is contempt. We may be clear-sighted without being malevolent, and make use of the errors we discover, to learn caution, not to gratify satire.

Sydney Smith

See also: ARROGANCE, DISGRACE, ESTEEM, INSULT, MALICE, MALEVOLENCE, RIDICULE, SNOB, WRONG.

CONTENTION

Tranquility will roof a house, but discord can wear away the foundations of a city.

Ernest Bramah (Smith)

Never contend with one that is foolish, proud, positive, testy, or with a superior, or a clown, in matter of argument.

Thomas Fuller

I have always found that to strive with a superior, is injurious; with an equal, doubtful; with an inferior, sordid and base; with any, full of unquietness.

Joseph Hall

Where two "supremes" meet there is bound to be trouble.

Jawaharlal Nehru

Where two discourse, if the anger of one rises, he is the wise man who lets the contest fall.

Plutarch

Weakness on both sides, is, as we know, the trait of all quarrels.

Voltaire (François Marie Arouet)

See also: ARGUMENT, CONTRADICTION, CONTROVERSY, DIFFERENCE, FACTION, OPPOSITION, QUARREL, RIVALRY, WAR.

CONTENTMENT

A contented mind is the greatest blessing a man can enjoy in this world; and if, in the present life, his happiness arises from the subduing of his desires, it will arise in the next from the gratification of them.

Joseph Addison

A wise man will always be contented with his condition, and will live rather according to the precepts of virtue, than according to the customs of his country.

Antisthenes

There is a sense in which a man looking at the present in the light of the future, and taking his whole being into account, may be contented with his lot: that is Christian contentment. But if a man has come to that point where he is so content that he says, "I do not want to know any more, or do any more, or be any more," he is in a state in which he ought to be changed into a mummy! Of all hideous things a mummy is the most hideous; and of mummies, the most hideous are those that are running about the streets and talking.

Henry Ward Beecher

One who is contented with what he has done will never become famous for what he will do. He has lain down to die, and the grass is already growing over him.

Christian Nestell Bovee

True contentment depends not upon what we have; a tub was large enough for Diogenes, but a world was too little for Alexander.

Charles Caleb Colton

Whether happiness may come or not, one should try and prepare one's self to do without it.

George Eliot (Mary Ann Evans)

I am always content with what happens; for I know that what God chooses is better than what I choose.

Epictetus

To be content with even the best people, we must be contented with little and bear a great deal. Those who are most perfect have many inperfections, and we have great faults; between the two, mutual toleration becomes very difficult.

François de Salignac de La Mothe-Fénelon

You traverse the world in search of happiness, which is within the reach of every man; a contented mind confers it all.

Horace

If we fasten our attention on what we have, rather than on what we lack, a very little wealth is sufficient.

Francis Johnson

The fountain of content must spring up in the mind; and he who has so little knowledge of human nature as to see happiness by changing anything but his own disposition, will waste his life in fruitless efforts, and multiply the griefs which he proposes to remove.

Samuel Johnson

A man who finds no satisfaction in himself, seeks for it in vain elsewhere.

Duc François de La Rochefoucauld

The secret of contentment is knowing how to enjoy what you have, and to be able to lose all desire for things beyond your reach.

Lin Yutang

It is right to be contented with what we have, never with what we are.

Sir James Mackintosh

They that deserve nothing should be content with anything. Bless God for what you have, and trust God for what you want. If we cannot bring our condition to our mind, we must bring our mind to our condition; if a man is not content in the state he is in, he will not be content in the state he would be in.

Erskine Mason

If two angels were sent down from heaven, one to conduct an empire, and the other to sweep a street, they would feel no inclination to change employments.

John Newton

One should be either sad or joyful. Contentment is a warm sty for eaters and sleepers.

Eugene Gladstone O'Neill

If you are but content you have enough to live upon with comfort.

Plautus

Contentment is natural wealth, luxury is artificial poverty.

Socrates

Since we cannot get what we like, let us like what we can get.

Spanish Proverb

The noblest mind the best contentment has.

Edmund Spenser

When loss and gain are alike to one that is real gain.

Sir Rabindranath Tagore

The wise man is content with half a loaf, or any fraction for that matter, rather than no bread.

Sir Rabindranath Tagore

Contentment with the divine will is the best remedy we can apply to misfortunes.

Sir William Temple

Want of desire is the greatest riches.
Louis Jean Baptiste Etienne Vigée

See also: AMUSEMENT, COMFORT, ENJOYMENT, HAPPINESS, PEACE, PLEASURE.

CONTRADICTION

We must not contradict, but instruct him that contradicts us; for a madman is not cured by another running mad also.
Antisthenes

Assertion is not argument; to contradict the statement of an opponent is not proof that you are correct.
Samuel Johnson

If a man never contradicts himself, it is because he never says anything.
Miguel de Unamuno y Jugo

See also: CONTENTION, OPPOSITION.

CONTRAST

Where there is much light, the shadow is deep.
Johann Wolfgang von Goethe

The lustre of diamonds is invigorated by the interposition of darker bodies; the lights of a picture are created by the shades; the highest pleasure which nature has indulged to sensitive perception is that of rest after fatigue.
Samuel Johnson

If there be light, then there is darkness; if cold, then heat; if height, depth also; if solid, then fluid; hardness and softness; roughness and smoothness; calm and tempest; prosperity and adversity; life and death.
Pythagoras

The rose and the thorn, and sorrow and gladness are linked together.
Saadi (Muslih-ud-Din)

It is a very poor, though common pretence to merit, to make it appear by the faults of other men; a mean wit or beauty may pass in a room where the rest of the company are allowed to have none; it is something to sparkle among diamonds; but to shine among pebbles is neither credit nor value worth the pretending.
Sir William Temple

Joy and grief are never far apart. In the same street the shutters of one house are closed, while the curtains of the next are brushed by the shadows of the dance. A wedding party returns from the church; and a funeral winds to its door. The smiles and sadness of life are the tragi-comedy of Shakespeare. Gladness and sighs brighten and dim the mirror he beholds.
Robert Eldridge Aris Willmott

See also: BUT, COMPARISON, CONTRADICTION.

CONTROVERSY

Most controversies would soon be ended, if those engaged in them would first accurately define their terms, and then adhere to their definitions.
Tryon Edwards

There is no learned man but will confess he hath much profited by reading controversies; his senses awakened, his judgment sharpened, and the truth which he holds more firmly established. In logic they teach that contraries laid together more evidently appear; and controversy being permitted, falsehood will appear more false, and truth more true.
John Milton

All important questions are controversial, if by "controversial" is meant that there are at least two sides that can conceivably be taken. If two sides are not already taken, the attempt to suppress a question on the ground that it is controversial will make it controversial.
Ralph Barton Perry

What Cicero says of war may be applied to disputing,—it should always be so managed as to remember that the only true end of it is peace. But generally, disputants are like sportsmen—their whole delight is in the pursuit; and a disputant no more cares for the truth, than the sportsman for the hare.
Alexander Pope

Disagreement is refreshing when two men lovingly desire to compare their views to find out truth. Controversy is wretched when it is only an attempt to prove another wrong. Religious controversy does only harm. It destroys humble inquiry after truth, and throws all the energies into an attempt to prove ourselves right—a spirit in which no man gets at truth.
Frederick William Robertson

See also: ARGUMENT, CONTENTION, DISCUSSION.

CONVALESCENCE: *see* ILLNESS.

CONVERSATION

In private conversation between intimate friends the wisest men very often talk like the weakest; for, indeed, the talking with a friend is nothing else but thinking aloud.

Joseph Addison

One would think that the larger the company is, the greater variety of thoughts and subjects would be started in discourse; but instead of this, we find that conversation is never so much straitened and confined as in large assemblies.

Joseph Addison

For good or ill, your conversation is your advertisement. Every time you open your mouth you let men look into your mind. Do they see it well clothed, neat, businesslike?

Bruce Barton

Generally speaking, poverty of speech is the outward evidence of poverty of mind.

Bruce Barton

Drawing on my fine command of language, I said nothing.

Robert Charles Benchley

The world of conversationalists, in my experience, is divided into two classes, those who listen to what the other person has to say, and those who use the interval to plan their next remark.

Bruce Bliven

Good talk is like good scenery—continuous, yet constantly varying, and full of the charm of novelty and surprise.

Randolph Silliman Bourne

There's lots of people—this town wouldn't hold them; who don't know much excepting what's told them.

William Carleton

I don't like to talk much with people who always agree with me. It is amusing to coquette with an echo for a little while, but one soon tires of it.

Thomas Carlyle

In company it is a very great fault to be more forward in setting off one's self, and talking to show one's parts, than to learn the worth, and be truly acquainted with the abilities of men. He that makes it his business not to know, but to be known, is like a foolish tradesman, who makes all the haste he can to sell off his old stock, but takes no thought of laying in any new.

Pierre Charron

A single conversation across the table with a wise man is worth a month's study of books.

Chinese Proverb

When in the company of sensible men, we ought to be doubly cautious of talking too much, lest we lose two good things—their good opinion and our own improvement; for what we have to say we know, but what they have to say we know not.

Charles Caleb Colton

The heart and the strength of the democratic way of living are the processes of effective give-and-take communication, of conference, of consultation, of exchange and pooling of experiences,—of free conversation if you will.

John Dewey

Americans cannot realize how many chances for mental improvement they lose by their inveterate habit of keeping up six conversations when there are twelve in the room.

Ernest Dimnet

Conversation is an art in which a man has all mankind for competitors.

Ralph Waldo Emerson

Conversation is the laboratory and workshop of the student.

Ralph Waldo Emerson

Conversation warms the mind, enlivens the imagination, and is continually starting fresh game that is immediately pursued and taken, which would never have occurred in the duller intercourse of epistolary correspondence.

Benjamin Franklin

We sometimes disputed, and very fond we were of argument, and very desirous of confuting one another, which is apt to become a very bad habit. I had caught it by reading my father's books of dispute about religion. Persons of good sense, I have since observed, seldom fall into it, except lawyers, university men, and men of all sorts that have been bred at Edinburgh.

Benjamin Franklin

Silence is one great art of conversation.

William Hazlitt

We never converse willingly when talking is our profession.

Heinrich Heine

He kept up with the current literature, and distilled from it a polite essence, with which he knew how to perfume his conversation.

William Dean Howells

Patrick Henry was more impressed by Washington's quiet conversation than by the fervid oratory of others. When asked whom he considered the greatest man in Congress, he answered: "Rutledge, if you speak of eloquence, is by far the greatest orator, but Colonel Washington, who has no pretensions to eloquence, is a man of more solid judgment and information than any man on that floor."

Rupert Hughes

Among well-bred people, a mutual deference is affected; contempt of others disguised; authority concealed; attention given to each in his turn; and an easy stream of conversation is maintained, without vehemence, without interruption, without eagerness for victory, and without any airs of superiority.

David Hume

A gossip is one who talks to you about others; a bore is one who talks to you about himself; and a brilliant conversationalist is one who talks to you about yourself.

Lisa Kirk

As it is the characteristic of great wits to say much in few words, so it is of small wits to talk much, and say nothing.

Duc François de La Rochefoucauld

One reason why we find so few people rational and agreeable in conversation is, that there is scarcely any one not rather thinking on what he is intending to say, than on answering exactly the question put to him. The cleverest and the most complaisant are satisfied if they only seem attentive, though we can discover in their eyes and distraction that they are wandering from what is addressed to them, and are impatient to return to what they were saying; whereas they should recollect that if they wish to please or convince others, they must not be overanxious to please themselves, and that to listen attentively, and to answer precisely, is the greatest perfection of conversation.

Duc François de La Rochefoucauld

He who sedulously attends, pointedly asks, calmly speaks, coolly answers, and ceases when he has no more to say, is in possession of some of the best requisites of conversation.

Johann Kasper Lavater

There cannot be a greater rudeness than to interrupt another in the current of his discourse.

John Locke

Most remarks that are worth making are commonplace remarks. The thing that makes them worth saying is that we really mean them.

Robert Staughton Lynd

Conversation opens our views, and gives our faculties a more vigorous play; it puts us upon turning our notions on every side, and holds them up to a light that discovers those latent flaws which would probably have lain concealed in the gloom of unagitated abstraction.

William Melmoth (Sir Thomas Fitzoborne)

It is good to rub and polish our brain against that of others.

Michel Eyquem de Montaigne

It were endless to dispute upon everything that is disputable.

William Penn

All bitter feelings are avoided, or at least greatly reduced by prompt face-to-face discussion.

Walter Boughton Pitkin

Know how to listen, and you will profit even from those who talk badly.

Plutarch

Inject a few raisins of conversation into the tasteless dough of existence.

William Sydney Porter (O. Henry)

The tone of good conversation is flowing and natural; it is neither heavy nor frivolous; it is learned without pedantry, lively without noise, polished without equivocation. It is made up neither of lectures nor epigrams. Those who really converse, reason without arguing, joke without punning, are skillful to unite wit and reason, maxims and sallies, ingenious raillery and severe morality. They speak of everything that every one may have something to say; they do not investigate too closely, for fear of wearying; questions are introduced as if by the by, and are treated with rapidity; precision leads to elegance; each one gives his opinion and supports it with few words: no one attacks with heat another's opinion, no one supports his own obstinately. They discuss in order to enlighten themselves, and leave off discussing where dispute would begin; every one gains information; everyone amuses himself, and every one goes away satisfied; nay, the sage himself may carry away from what he has heard matter worthy of silent meditation.

Jean Jacques Rousseau

Not only to say the right thing in the right place, but far more difficult, to leave unsaid the wrong thing at the tempting moment.

George Augustus Henry Sala

The pith of conversation does not consist in exhibiting your own superior knowledge on matters of small importance, but in enlarging, improving, and correcting the information you possess, by the authority of others.

Sir Walter Scott

Be sincere. Be simple in words, manners and gestures. Amuse as well as instruct. If you can make a man laugh, you can make him think and make him like and believe you.

Alfred Emanuel Smith

Never hold any one by the button, or the hand, in order to be heard out; for if people are unwilling to hear you, you had better hold your tongue than them.

Philip Dormer Stanhope (Lord Chesterfield)

It is wonderful that so many shall entertain those with whom they converse by giving them the history of their pains and aches; and imagine such narrations their quota of the conversation. This is, of all other, the meanest help to discourse, and a man must not think at all, or think himself very insignificant when he finds an account of his headache answered by another's asking what is the news in the last mail.

Sir Richard Steele

Take as many half minutes as you can get, but never talk more than half a minute without pausing and giving others an opportunity to strike in.

Jonathan Swift

The first ingredient in conversation is truth; the next, good sense; the third, good humor; and the fourth, wit.

Sir William Temple

The conversation exchanged at a dinner or tea may instruct and mature a man more rapidly than the reading of a hundred volumes.

Paul Ambroise Valéry

See also: DISCUSSION, REPARTEE, TALKING.

CONVERSION

Conversion is a deep work—a heart-work. It goes throughout the man, throughout the mind, throughout the members, throughout the entire life.

Joseph Alleine

Conversion is no repairing of the old building; but it takes all down and erects a new structure. The sincere Christian is quite a new fabric, from the foundation to the top-stone all new.

Joseph Alleine

Where there is a sound conversion, then a man is wholly given unto God, body, soul, and spirit. He regards not sin in his heart, but hath a respect to all God's commandments.

Robert Bolton

In what way, or by what manner of working God changes a soul from evil to good—how he impregnates the barren rock with priceless gems and gold—is, to the human mind, an impenetrable mystery.

Samuel Taylor Coleridge

Conversion is but the first step in the divine life. As long as we live we should more and more be turning from all that is evil, and to all that is good.

Tryon Edwards

Cases of real honest conversion are quite possible. If some people, for their inward satisfaction and growth, change their religion, let them do so. I am, then, not against conversion. But I am against the modern methods of it. Conversion, now-adays, has become a matter of business, like any other.

Mohandas Karamchand (Mahatma) Gandhi

Conversion in self-purification, self-realization, is the crying need of the times.

Mohandas Karamchand (Mahatma) Gandhi

Conversion, without conviction, is a mere change and not conversion which is a revolution in one's life.

Mohandas Karamchand (Mahatma) Gandhi

Surely conversion is a matter between man and his Maker who alone knows His creature's hearts.

Mohandas Karamchand (Mahatma) Gandhi

As to the value of conversions, God only can judge. He alone can know how wide are the steps which the soul has to take before it can approach to a community with him, to the dwelling of the perfect, or to the intercourse and friendship of higher natures.

Johann Wolfgang von Goethe

Conversion is not implanting eyes, for they exist already; but giving them a right direction, which they have not.

Plato

See also: CHANGE, IMPROVEMENT, PROGRESS, REFORM, RELIGION.

CONVICTION

There are only two kinds of people in the modern world who know what they are after. One, quite frankly, is the Communist. The other, equally frankly, is the convinced Christian. . . . The rest of the world are amiable nonentities.

Geoffrey Francis Fisher

One needs to be slow to form convictions, but once formed they must be defended against the heaviest odds.

Mohandas Karamchand (Mahatma) Gandhi

We can be staunch in our own convictions, but we have no control over those of others.

Sir Rabindranath Tagore

The best lack conviction, while the worst are full of passionate intensity.

William Butler Yeats

See also: BELIEF, OPINION, PRINCIPLE.

COOKING

Cookery is become an art, a noble science; cooks are gentlemen.

Robert Burton

The intention of every other piece of prose may be discussed and even mistrusted; but the purpose of a cookery book is one and unmistakable. Its object can conceivably be no other than to increase the happiness of mankind.

Joseph Conrad

Too many cooks spoil the broth.

English Proverb

We may live without poetry, music, and art;
We may live without conscience, and live without heart;
We may live without friends; we may live without books;
But civilized man cannot live without cooks.
He may live without books,—what is knowledge but grieving?
He may live without hope,—what is hope but deceiving?
He may live without love,—what is passion but pining?
But where is the man that can live without dining?

Edward R. Bulwer Lytton (Owen Meredith)

See also: BREAKFAST, DIET, DINNER, EATING.

COOPERATION

The fact that in Greater New York eight million people have developed ways of working together in peace and dignity is more important than all of New York's skyscrapers, world famous though they are.

David Eli Lilienthal

There could be no adequate civilization, no Christianity, until cooperation had displaced competition, and men were become equal in economic rights as they were in franchise rights.

Vernon Louis Parrington

In the present state of human society . . . we deem it advisable that the wage contract should, when possible, be modified somewhat by a contract of partnership, as is already being tried in various ways to the no small gain both of the wage-earners and of the employers. In this way wage-earners are made sharers in some sort in the ownership, or the management, or the profits.

Pius XI (Achille Ambrogio Damiano Ratti)

Universal experience teaches us that no nation has ever yet risen from want and poverty to a better and loftier station without the unremitting toil of all its citizens, both employers and employed. . . . Unless brains, capital and labor combine together for common effort, men's toil cannot produce due fruit.

Pius XI (Achille Ambrogio Damiano Ratti)

See also: FRIENDSHIP, HELP, UNITY.

COQUETTE

There is one antidote only for coquetry, and that is true love.

Madame Dorothée Deluzy

The characteristic of coquettes is affectation governed by whim. Their life is one constant lie; and the only rule by which you can form any judgment of them is, that they are never what they seem.

Henry Fielding

An accomplished coquette excites the passions of others, in proportion as she feels none herself.

William Hazlitt

God created the coquette as soon as he had made the fool.

Victor Marie Hugo

A coquette is like a recruiting sergeant, always on the lookout for fresh victims.

Douglas William Jerrold

The most effective coquetry is innocence.

Alphonse de Lamartine

A coquette is a young lady of more beauty than sense, more accomplishments than learning, more charms of person than graces of mind, more admirers than friends, more fools than wise men for attendants.

Henry Wadsworth Longfellow

See also: FICKLENESS, FLATTERY, GALLANTRY, INCONSTANCY.

CORPORATION

Today it is generally recognized that all corporations possess an element of public interest. A corporation director must think not only of the stockholder but also of the laborer, the supplier, the purchaser, and the ultimate consumer. Our economy is but a chain which can be no stronger than any one of its links. We all stand together or fall together in our highly industrialized society of today.

William Orville Douglas

History proves that, owing to a change in social conditions, functions that were at one time performed by small bodies can be performed today only by large corporations. Nevertheless, just as it is wrong to take from the individual and commit to the community functions that private enterprise and industry can perform, so it is an injustice, a serious evil and a violation of right order for a large organization to arrogate to itself functions which could be performed efficiently by smaller ones.

Pius XI (Achille Ambrogio Damiano Ratti)

It is truly enough said that a corporation has no conscience; but a corporation of conscientious men is a corporation with a conscience. Law never made men a whit more just; and, by means of their respect for it, even the well-disposed are daily made the agents of injustice. A common and natural result of an undue respect for law is, that you may see a file of soldiers, colonels, captains, corporals, privates, powdermonkeys, and all, marching in admirable order over hill and dale to the wars, against their wills, ay, against their common sense and conscience, which makes it very steep marching indeed, and produces a palpitation of the heart.

Henry David Thoreau

Did you ever expect a corporation to have a conscience, when it has no soul to be damned, and no body to be kicked?

Edward Thurlow (First Baron Thurlow)

There was a time when corporations played a minor part in our business affairs, but now they play the chief part, and most men are the servants of corporations.

(Thomas) Woodrow Wilson

See also: BUSINESS, COMMERCE, INDUSTRY.

CORRUPTION

Corrupt influence is itself the perennial spring of all prodigality, and of all disorder; it loads us more than millions of debt; takes away vigor from our arms, wisdom from our councils, and every shadow of authority and credit from the most venerable parts of our constitution.

Edmund Burke

A little corruption in government is too much corruption.

David Louis Cohn

The corruptions of the country are closely allied to those of the town, with no difference but what is made by another mode of thought and living.

Jonathan Swift

See also: BRIBERY, CONSPIRACY, DISHONESTY, FRAUD, HONESTY, TREASON.

COUNSEL

In counsel it is good to see dangers; but in execution, not to see them unless they be very great.

Francis Bacon

There is as much difference between the counsel that a friend giveth, and that a man giveth himself, as there is between the counsel of a friend and a flatterer.

Francis Bacon

Whoever is wise is apt to suspect and be diffident of himself, and upon that account is willing to hearken unto counsel; whereas the foolish man, being, in proportion to his folly, full of himself, and swallowed up in conceit, will seldom take any counsel but his own, and for the very reason that it is his own.

John Balguy

Good counsels observed, are chains to grace, which, neglected, prove halters to strange, undutiful children.

Thomas Fuller

Counsel and conversation are a second education, which improve all the virtue, and correct all the vice of the first, and of nature itself.

Edward Hyde (Earl of Clarendon)

Consult your friend on all things, especially on those which respect yourself. His counsel may then be useful where your own self-love might impair your judgment.

Seneca

See also: EDUCATION, GUIDANCE, INSTRUCTION, LAWYER, TEACHING.

COUNTENANCE: see FACE.

COUNTRY

I consider it the best part of an education to have been born and brought up in the country.

Amos Bronson Alcott

You can take a boy out of the country but you can't take the country out of a boy.

Arthur (Bugs) Baer

Men are taught virtue and a love of independence, by living in the country.

Menander of Athens

The country is both the philosopher's garden and his library, in which he reads and contemplates the power, wisdom, and goodness of God.

William Penn

If country life be healthful to the body, it is no less so to the mind.

Giovanni Ruffini

See also: AGRICULTURE, CITY, CONSERVATION, NATION, NATURE, STATE.

COURAGE

Courage that grows from constitution, often forsakes a man when he has occasion for it; courage which arises from a sense of duty, acts in a uniform manner.

Joseph Addison

Courage is rightly esteemed the first of human qualities because it is the quality which guarantees all others.

Sir Winston Leonard Spencer Churchill

This is no time for ease and comfort. It is the time to dare and endure.

Sir Winston Leonard Spencer Churchill

Conscience is the root of all true courage; if a man would be brave let him obey his conscience.

James Freeman Clarke

Physical courage which despises all danger, will make a man brave in one way; and moral courage, which despises all opinion, will make a man brave in another. The former would seem most necessary for the camp; the latter for the council; but to constitute a great man both are necessary.

Charles Caleb Colton

To see what is right and not to do it, is want of courage.

Confucius

True courage is cool and calm. The bravest of men have the least of a brutal, bullying insolence, and in the very time of danger are found the most serene and free.

Anthony Ashley Cooper (Lord Shaftesbury)

Courage from hearts and not from numbers grows.

John Dryden

Those nervous persons who may be terrified by imaginary dangers are often courageous in the face of real danger.

Henry Havelock Ellis

Courage can be a very difficult neurosis.

Graham Greene

The bravest thing you can do when you are not brave is to profess courage and act accordingly.

Corra May White Harris

The truest courage is always mixed with circumspection this being the quality which distinguishes the courage of the wise from the hardiness of the rash and foolish.

William Jones of Nayland

The courage of life is often a less dramatic spectacle than the courage of a final moment; but it is no less than a magnificent mixture of triumph and tragedy. A man does what he must—in spite of personal consequences, in spite of obstacles and dangers and pressures—and that is the basis of all human morality.

John Fitzgerald Kennedy

One must have the courage to say "no," even at the risk of displeasing others.

Fritz Künkel

We can never be certain of our courage till we have faced danger.

Duc François de La Rochefoucauld

It is an error to suppose that courage means courage in everything. Most people are brave only in the dangers to which they accustom themselves, either in imagination or practice.

Edward G. Bulwer-Lytton (Baron Lytton)

A coward flees backward, away from new things. A man of courage flees forward, in the midst of new things.

Jacques Maritain

If we survive danger it steels our courage more than anything else.

Barthold Georg Niebuhr

Courage in danger is half the battle.

Plautus

Courage consists not in hazarding without fear, but being resolutely minded in a just cause.

Plutarch

Courage consists, not in blindly overlooking danger, but in seeing and conquering it.

Jean Paul Richter

We lack the courage to be where we are:—
We live too much to travel in old roads,
To triumph in old fields.

Edwin Arlington Robinson

Far better it is to dare mighty things, to win glorious triumphs, even though checkered by failure, than to take rank with those poor spirits who neither enjoy much nor suffer much, because they live in the gray twilight that knows neither victory nor defeat.

Theodore Roosevelt

Courageous behavior is easier for a man who fails to apprehend dangers.

Bertrand Arthur William Russell

Courage ought to be guided by skill, and skill armed by courage. Hardiness should not darken wit, nor wit cool hardiness. Be valiant as men despising death, but confident as unwonted to be overcome.

Sir Philip Sidney

A great deal of talent is lost in this world for the want of a little courage.

Sydney Smith

Those in this world who have the courage to try and solve in their own lives new problems of life are the ones who raise society to greatness! Those who merely live according to rule do not advance society, they only carry it along.

Sir Rabindranath Tagore

True courage is not the brutal force of vulgar heroes, but the firm resolve of virtue and reason.

Alfred North Whitehead

The curse of our deification of physical courage is that a display of it, in the individual or in a nation, can disguise a total bankruptcy in the essential virtues.

Ida Alexa Ross Wylie

See also: BOLDNESS, BRAVERY, CONFIDENCE, COWARDICE, FIRMNESS, FORTITUDE, HERO, RASHNESS, VALOR.

COURT

I believe it is a matter of common knowledge that a number of Supreme Court decisions have effectively whittled down on the entire structure of our internal security laws.

John Milan Ashbrook

The place of justice is a hallowed place.

Francis Bacon

No matter whether the Constitution follows the flag or not, the Supreme Court follows the election returns.

Finley Peter Dunne

The authority of the Supreme Court must not . . . be permitted to control the Congress, or the Executive, when acting in their legislative capacities.

Andrew Jackson

Some Supreme Court decisions have caused great frustration and confusion and produced much disarray in law enforcement and criminal justice procedures. They placed strained if not distorted constructions on the Constitution, overruled long-established judicial precedents, shackled law enforcement officials; and, by dubiously invoking specious procedural technicalities and grossly exaggerating the legitimate virtues of civil liberties, many guilt-confessed and confirmed criminals have been released on society.

John L. McClellan

When we find that the highest court in the land feels free to exercise the license or privilege to overrule the law of the land, not by statute, not by amendment to the Constitution, but simply by court edict, to overrule what has been the law of the land for more than 100 years, simply to satisfy their whim with respect to what they think the law should be, then it is no wonder that civil rights leaders and extremists today say, "We have a right, a moral right, not to obey any law that we disagree with."

John L. McClellan

The penalty for laughing in a courtroom is six months in jail; if it were not for this penalty, the jury would never hear the evidence.

Henry Louis Mencken

In my opinion, the recent decisions of the Supreme Court have done more than any other single thing to contribute to a general atmosphere to cause crime to increase in this country. When criminals know that they can commit crimes and may not be apprehended, but if apprehended stand a good chance of being allowed to get off on a mere technicality, it only encourages more crime.

James Strom Thurmond

See also: CRIME, JUSTICE, LAWYER, RIGHTS.

COURTESY

The small courtesies sweeten life; the greater, ennoble it.

Christian Nestell Bovee

The courtesies of a small and trivial character are the ones which strike deepest to the grateful and appreciating heart. It is the picayune compliments which are the most appreciated; far more than the double ones we sometimes pay.

Henry Clay

Life is not so short but that there is always time for courtesy.

Ralph Waldo Emerson

We should be as courteous to a man as we are to a picture, which we are willing to give the advantage of the best light.

Ralph Waldo Emerson

The whole of heraldry and chivalry is in courtesy. A man of fine manners shall pronounce your name with all the ornament that titles of nobility could add.

Ralph Waldo Emerson

There is no outward sign of true courtesy that does not rest on a deep moral foundation.

Johann Wolfgang von Goethe

Small kindnesses, small courtesies, small considerations, habitually practised in our social intercourse, give a greater charm to the character than the display of great talents and accomplishments.

Mary Ann Kelty

When saluted with a salutation, salute the person with a better salutation, or at least return the same, for God taketh account of all things.

Koran

Courtesy is a science of the highest importance. It is, like grace and beauty in the body, which charm at first sight, and lead on to further intimacy and friendship, opening a door that we may derive instruction from the example of others, and at the same time enabling us to benefit them by our example, if there be anything in our character worthy of imitation.

Michel Eyquem de Montaigne

Approved valor is made precious by natural courtesy.

Sir Philip Sidney

A churlish courtesy rarely comes but either for gain or falsehood.

Sir Philip Sidney

The disadvantage of politeness is that it is not intelligible to all classes of people.

Sir Rabindranath Tagore

How beautiful is humble courtesy!

Sir Rabindranath Tagore

See also: CHARM, GOOD BREEDING, MANNERS, POLITENESS, REFINEMENT.

COURTSHIP

The pleasantest part of a man's life is generally that which passes in courtship, provided his passion be sincere, and the party beloved, kind, with discretion. Love, desire, hope, all the pleasing motions of the soul, rise in the pursuit.

Joseph Addison

With women worth being won, the softest lover ever best succeeds.

Aaron Hill

I profess not to know how women's hearts are wooed and won. To me they have always been matters of riddle and admiration.

Washington Irving

She half consents, who silently denies.

Ovid

Let a woman once give you a task and you are hers, heart and soul; all your care and trouble lend new charms to her for whose sake they are taken. To rescue, to revenge, to instruct, or to protect a woman, is all the same as to love her.

Jean Paul Richter

Courtship consists in a number of quiet attentions, not so pointed as to alarm, nor so vague as not to be understood.

Laurence Sterne

See also: AFFECTION, FLATTERY, GALLANTRY, HUSBAND AND WIFE, KISS, LOVE, RO- MANCE, WIFE.

COVETOUSNESS

The covetous man pines in plenty, like Tantalus up to the chin in water, and yet thirsty.

Thomas Adams

If money be not thy servant, it will be thy master. The covetous man cannot so properly be said to possess wealth, as that may be said to possess him.

Francis Bacon

After hypocrites, the greatest dupes the devil has are those who exhaust an anxious existence in the disappointments and vexations of business, and live miserably and meanly only to die magnificently and rich. They serve the devil without receiving his wages, and for the empty foolery of dying rich, pay down their health, happiness, and integrity.

Charles Caleb Colton

When all sins are old in us and go upon crutches, covetousness does but then lie in her cradle.

Thomas Dekker

The only gratification a covetous man gives his neighbors, is, to let them see that he himself is as little better for what he has, as they are.

William Penn

Refrain from covetousness, and thy estate shall prosper.

Plato

Covetousness is both the beginning and end of the devil's alphabet—the first vice in corrupt nature that moves, and the last which dies.

Robert South

Covetousness, by a greediness of getting more, deprives itself of the true end of getting; it loses the enjoyment of what it had got.

Thomas Sprat

Covetousness swells the principal to no purpose, and lessens the use to all purposes.

Jeremy Taylor

The covetous man heaps up riches, not to enjoy, but to have them; he starves himself in the midst of plenty; cheats and robs himself of that which is his own, and makes a hard shift to be as poor and miserable with a great estate as any man can be without it.

John Tillotson

See also: AVARICE, SELFISHNESS.

COW

I never saw a Purple Cow,
  I never hope to see one;
But I can tell you, anyhow
  I'd rather see than be one.

Frank Gelett Burgess

The cow is an object of worship and veneration to millions in India. I count myself among them.

Mohandas Karamchand (Mahatma) Gandhi

Cow-protection is the gift of Hinduism to the world.

Mohandas Karamchand (Mahatma) Gandhi

A cow is a very good animal in the field; but we turn her out of a garden.

Samuel Johnson

A cow goes on giving milk all her life even though what appears to be her self-interest urges her to give gin.

Henry Lewis Mencken

See also: ANIMAL, FARM.

COWARDICE

Bullies are always to be found where there are cowards.

Mohandas Karamchand (Mahatma) Gandhi

Cowards can never be moral.

Mohandas Karamchand (Mahatma) Gandhi

Fear has its use but cowardice has none.

Mohandas Karamchand (Mahatma) Gandhi

Cowardice is not synonymous with prudence. —It often happens that the better part of discretion is valor.

William Hazlitt

Cowardice . . . is almost always simply a lack of ability to suspend the functioning of the imagination.

Ernest Hemingway

It is the coward who fawns upon those above him. It is the coward who is insolent whenever he dares be so.

Junius

See also: BRAVERY, FEAR, PANIC.

CREATION

All things bright and beautiful,
   All creatures great and small,
All things wise and wonderful,
   The Lord God made them all.

Cecil Frances Humphreys Alexander

God has put something noble and good into every heart which His hand created.

Samuel Langhorne Clemens (Mark Twain)

I can see, and that is why I can be so happy, in what you call the dark, but which to me is golden. I can see a God-made world, not a man-made world.

Helen Adams Keller

See also: CREATIVITY, EVOLUTION, GOD.

CREATIVITY

Creative people are especially observant, and they value accurate observation (telling themselves the truth) more than other people do . . . They are by constitution more vigorous, and have available to them an exceptional fund of psychic and physical energy.

Frank X. Barron

Creation is a drug I can't do without.

Cecil Blount De Mille

Man is made to create, from the poet to the potter.

Benjamin Disraeli

The creative process requires more than reason. Most original thinking isn't even verbal. It requires "a groping experimentation with ideas, governed by intuitive hunches and inspired by the unconscious." The majority of business men are incapable of original thinking, because they are unable to escape from the tyranny of reason. Their imaginations are blocked.

David Mackenzie Ogilvy

Few of the great creators have bland personalities. They are cantankerous egotists, the kind of men who are unwelcome in the modern corporation.

David Mackenzie Ogilvy

See also: ARCHITECTURE, ART, ARTIST, LITERATURE, THEATER.

CREDIT

Nothing so cements and holds together all the parts of a society as faith or credit, which can never be kept up unless men are under some force or necessity of honestly paying what they owe to one another.

Cicero

The most trifling actions that affect a man's credit are to be regarded. The sound of your hammer at five in the morning, or nine at night, heard by a creditor, makes him easier six months longer; but if he sees you at a billiard table, or hears your voice at a tavern when you should be at work, he sends for his money the next day.

Benjamin Franklin

No man's credit is as good as his money.

Edgar Watson Howe

Credit is like a looking-glass, which, when once sullied by a breath, may be wiped clear again; but if once cracked can never be repaired.

Sir Walter Scott

See also: BANK, BORROWING, CREDITOR, DEBT, LENDING, MONEY, TRUST, USURER.

CREDITOR

It takes a man to make a devil; and the fittest man for such a purpose is a snarling, waspish, red-hot, fiery, creditor.

Henry Ward Beecher

Creditors have better memories than debtors; they are a superstitious sect, great observers of set days and times.

Benjamin Franklin

The creditor whose appearance gladdens the heart of a debtor may hold his head in sunbeams, and his foot on storms.

Johann Kaspar Lavater

See also: CREDIT, DEBT.

CREDULITY

There's a sucker born every minute.

Phineas Taylor Barnum

The more gross the fraud, the more glibly will it go down and the more greedily will it be swallowed, since folly will always find faith wherever impostors will find impudence.

Christian Nestell Bovee

Your noblest natures are most credulous.

George Chapman

Beyond all credulity is the credulousness of atheists, who believe that chance could make the world, when it cannot build a house.

McDonald Clarke

When people are bewildered they tend to become credulous.

(John) Calvin Coolidge

Generous souls are still most subject to credulity.

Sir William Davenant

We believe at once in evil, we only believe in good upon reflection. Is not this sad?

Madame Dorothée Deluzy

Credulity is belief on slight evidence, with no evidence, or against evidence. In this sense it is the infidel, not the believer, who is credulous. "The simple," says Solomon, "believeth every word."

Tryon Edwards

I cannot spare the luxury of believing that all things beautiful are what they seem.

Fitz-Greene Halleck

O credulity, thou hast as many ears as fame has tongues, open to every sound of truth, as falsehood.

William Havard

The great masses of the people . . . will more easily fall victims to a great lie than to a small one.

Adolf Hitler

Credulity is the common failing of inexperienced virtue; and he who is spontaneously suspicious may justly be charged with radical corruption.

Samuel Johnson

The most positive men are the most credulous, since they most believe themselves, and advise most with their falsest flatterer and worst enemy,—their own self-love.

Alexander Pope

To take for granted as truth all that is alleged against the fame of others, is a species of credulity that men would blush at on any other subject.

Jane Porter

The only disadvantage of an honest heart is credulity.

Sir Philip Sidney

You believe easily that which you hope for earnestly.

Terence

Some people have the peculiar ability to divide their minds into watertight compartments, being critical and rational in matters of science but credulous as children when it comes to religion.

Alan Watts

See also: BELIEF, DOUBT, FAITH, IGNORANCE, INNOCENCE, LYING, SIMPLICITY.

CREED

If you have a Bible creed, it is well; but is it filled out and inspired by Christian love?
James Fairbairn Brodie

In politics, as in religion, we have less charity for those who believe the half of our creed, than for those who deny the whole of it.
Charles Caleb Colton

A good creed is a gate to the city that hath foundations; a misleading creed may be a road to destruction, or if both misleading and alluring it may become what Shakespeare calls a primrose path to the eternal bonfire.
Joseph Cook

When anything assumes the strength of a creed, it becomes self-sustained and derives the needed support from within.
Mohandas Karamchand (Mahatma) Gandhi

Attempt to adhere rigidly to an outworn creed may take us off at a tangent from this curve of life and lead us to disaster.
Jawaharlal Nehru

Creeds and rites have no value in themselves; that human welfare is the one object towards which religious enthusiasm has to be directed.
Sir Rabindranath Tagore

Though I do not like creeds in religious matters, I verily believe that creeds had something to do with our Revolution. In their religious controversies the people of New England had always been accustomed to stand on points; and when Lord North undertook to tax them, then they stood on points also. It so happened, fortunately, that their opposition to Lord North was a point on which they were all united.
Daniel Webster

See also: BELIEF, FAITH, RELIGION, TRUST.

CRIME

"Payola" is the year's new word. It doesn't sound as ugly as "bribe," but it means the same thing. It was first coined to describe the money that disc jockeys took to plug certain records. Now the word is being applied to almost any shady deal involving a payoff.
William Attwood

Crimes lead into one another. They who are capable of being forgers, are capable of being incendiaries.
Edmund Burke

The real significance of crime is in its being a breach of faith with the community of mankind.
Joseph Conrad

A transgression, a crime, entering a man's existence, eats it up like a malignant growth, consumes it like a fever.
Joseph Conrad

Physical deformity calls forth our charity. But the infinite misfortunate of moral deformity calls forth nothing but hatred and vengeance.
Clarence Seward Darrow

One crime is everything; two nothing.
Madame Dorothée Deluzy

There is no den in the wide world to hide a rogue. Commit a crime and the earth is made of glass. Commit a crime, and it seems as if a coat of snow fell on the ground, such as reveals in the woods the track of every partridge, and fox, and squirrel.
Ralph Waldo Emerson

Set a thief to catch a thief.
English Proverb

Crime will last as long as old and gloomy humanity. But the number of criminals has lessened with the number of the wretched. The slums of the great cities are the feeding-grounds of crime.
Anatole France

Whoever profits by the crime is guilty of it.
French Proverb

Crime is not punished as an offence against God, but as prejudicial to society.
James Anthony Froude

All crime is a kind of disease and should be treated as such.
Mohandas Karamchand (Mahatma) Gandhi

Crimes sometimes shock us too much; vices almost always too little.
Augustus and Julius Hare

We are a fact-gathering organization only. We don't clear anybody. We don't condemn anybody. Just the minute the F.B.I. begins making recommendations on what should be done with its information, it becomes a Gestapo.
John Edgar Hoover

The idea that a State, any more than a corporation, commits crimes is a fiction. Crimes always are committed only by persons.

Robert Houghwout Jackson

The apprehension and conviction of a criminal is doomed to ultimate futility if we do not deal effectively with him while he is in the hands of the law. Today the nation's correctional system is undermanned and underequipped. We must make it a strong arm in our total effort to protect the public from crime.

Lyndon Baines Johnson

Organized crime constitutes nothing less than a guerilla war against society.

Lyndon Baines Johnson

Revolvers and nightsticks are clearly inadequate for the many different crises faced by the police. New weapons and chemicals—effective but causing no permanent injury—have been and are being developed.

Lyndon Baines Johnson

Under the direction of the organized crime and racketeering section of the Department of Justice, a "strike force" program has recently been initiated. Experienced investigators and attorneys from several Federal departments and agencies work together in a campaign concentrated on a single, organized criminal syndicate in a particular geographic area.

Lyndon Baines Johnson

We at every level of Government know that the American people have had enough of rising crime and lawlessness. . . . There is no more urgent business before this Congress than to pass the safe streets act.

Lyndon Baines Johnson

We must bring modern crime detection and protective equipment into our banks. Robberies of financial institutions have increased continuously in the past decade.

Lyndon Baines Johnson

A criminal becomes a popular figure because he unburdens in no small degree the consciences of his fellow man, for now they know once more where evil is to be found.

Carl Gustav Jung

If I hear that another woman has been raped, I just know that within 30 minutes I'm going to get a call from the White House: "I

thought I told you to clean up that crime situation."

Nicholas de Belleville Katzenbach

If poverty is the mother of crimes, want of sense is the father of them.

Jean de La Bruyère

Men blush less for their crimes than for their weaknesses and vanity.

Jean de La Bruyère

We easily forget crimes that are known only to ourselves.

Duc François de La Rochefoucauld

We'll whack away at crime with every damn thing we've got.

John Vliet Lindsay

Whenever man commits a crime heaven finds a witness.

Edward G. Bulwer-Lytton (Baron Lytton)

The idea of having a lawyer present before you can ask a man a question about whether he has committed a crime is taking absurdity to the extreme.

John L. McClellan

No matter how much money is spent for upgrading police departments, for modern equipment, for research and other purposes, crime will not be successfully abated, nor respect for law and order restored so long as criminals who have voluntarily confessed their crimes go unpunished. The traditional right of the people to have their prosecuting attorneys place in evidence before juries the voluntary confessions and incriminating statements made by defendants should be restored.

John L. McClellan

Organized crime is spreading and becoming more subtle and entrenched. Its multibillion dollar annual take from our economy through the illegitimate enterprises and rackets which it controls grows continuously and enormously, and its suffering victims increase and multiply proportionately.

John L. McClellan

(There is) the persistent failure of the law to distinguish between crime as an accident, incidental explosive event, crime as a behavior pattern expressive of chronic unutterable rage and frustration, crime as a business or elected way of life.

Karl Augustus Menninger

The contagion of crime is like that of the plague. Criminals collected together corrupt each other. They are worse than ever when, at the termination of their punishment, they return to society.

Napoleon I (Bonaparte)

No program of crime prevention will be effective without a massive overhaul of the lower criminal courts.

National Crime Commission, 1967

If people starve, what are they to do? Judges and magistrates wax eloquent about the increase of crime; but are blind to the obvious economic causes of it.

Jawaharlal Nehru

Ignorant people imagine that if the punishment is not severe enough crimes will increase. As a matter of fact, the exact reverse is the truth.

Jawaharlal Nehru

Small crimes always precede great ones. Never have we seen timid innocence pass suddenly to extreme licentiousness.

Jean Baptiste Racine

A man may be disconcerted because of unconscious wants. For instance, Americans need rest, but do not know it. I believe this to be a large part of the explanation of the crime wave in the United States.

Bertrand Arthur William Russell

In 1967, nearly two out of every 100 Americans will be the victim of a serious crime, a statistic I find the most shocking of all. A society founded on law and order simply cannot tolerate threat so severe and so widespread as this.

Richard Schultz Schweiker

And who are the greater criminals—those who sell the instruments of death, or those who buy them and use them?

Robert Emmet Sherwood

Fear follows crime, and is its punishment.

Voltaire (François Marie Arouet)

See also: CORRUPTION, DISHONESTY, FRAUD, GUILT, MURDER, OFFENSE, POLICE, RIOT, SIN, VICE, WICKEDNESS, WRONG.

CRISIS

Crises and deadlocks when they occur have at least this advantage, that they force us to think.

Jawaharlal Nehru

Every little thing counts in a crisis.

Jawaharlal Nehru

These are the times that try men's souls.

Thomas Paine

The turning points of lives are not the great moments. The real crises are often concealed in occurrences so trivial in appearance that they pass unobserved.

William E. Woodward

See also: CIRCUMSTANCE, EVENT.

CRITICISM

It is ridiculous for any man to criticize the works of another if he has not distinguished himself by his own performances.

Joseph Addison

I am bound by my own definition of criticism: a disinterested endeavour to learn and propagate the best that is known and thought in the world.

Matthew Arnold

My ambition is to be a critic-at-large of things-as-they-are. I want to find out everything there is to know about the intimate structure of things. I want to reduce the whole system to absurdity. I want to laugh the powers-that-be out of existence in a great winnowing gale of laughter.

Samuel Nathaniel Behrman

It is a maxim with me, that no man was ever written out of a reputation but by himself.

Richard Bentley

The legitimate aim of criticism is to direct attention to the excellent. The bad will dig its own grave, and the imperfect may safely be left to that final neglect from which no amount of present undeserved popularity can rescue it.

Christian Nestell Bovee

Is it in destroying and pulling down that skill is displayed? The shallowest understanding, the rudest hand, is more than equal to that task.

Edmund Burke

The rule in carving holds good as to criticism; never cut with a knife what you can cut with a spoon.

Charles Buxton

Silence is sometimes the severest criticism.
Charles Buxton

Criticism is dangerous, because it wounds a man's precious pride, hurts his sense of importance, and arouses his resentment.
Dale Carnegie

I have adhered to my rule of never criticizing any measure of war or policy after the event unless I had before expressed publically or formally my opinion or warning about it. Indeed in the after-light I have softened many of the severities of contemporary controversy.
Sir Winston Leonard Spencer Churchill

It is easy to criticise an author, but difficult to appreciate him.
Luc de Clapiers (Marquis de Vauvenargues)

Listen carefully to first criticisms made of your work. Note just what it is about your work that the critics don't like—then cultivate it. That's the only part of your work that's individual and worth keeping.
Jean Cocteau

It is much easier to be critical than to be correct.
Benjamin Disraeli

The most noble criticism is that in which the critic is not the antagonist so much as the rival of the author.
Benjamin Disraeli

Honest criticism and sensitive appreciation are directed not upon the poet but upon the poetry.
Thomas Stearns Eliot

Criticism is the adventure of the soul among masterpieces.
Anatole France

Criticism of public men is a welcome sign of public awakening. It keeps workers on the alert.
Mohandas Karamchand (Mahatma) Gandhi

Healthy, well-informed, balanced criticism is the ozone of public life. A most democratic minister is likely to go wrong without ceaseless watch from the public.
Mohandas Karamchand (Mahatma) Gandhi

It is good to see ourselves as others see us. Try as we may, we are never able to know ourselves fully as we are, especially the evil side of us. This we can do only if we are not angry with our critics; but, will take, in good heart, whatever they might have to say.
Mohandas Karamchand (Mahatma) Gandhi

Throughout my life I have gained more from my critic friends than from my admirers, especially when the criticism was made in courteous and friendly language.
Mohandas Karamchand (Mahatma) Gandhi

The artist, without respect to medium, is interested in criticism because it is a form of public opinion. Also, because it *creates* public opinion.
John Gassner

It is a barren kind of criticism which tells you what a thing is not.
Rufus Wilmot Griswold

Criticism, as it was first instituted by Aristotle, was meant as a standard of judging well.
Samuel Johnson

The pleasure of criticism takes from us that of being deeply moved by very beautiful things.
Jean de La Bruyère

The proper function of a critic is to save the tale from the artist who created it.
David Herbert Lawrence

The strength of criticism lies only in the weakness of being criticised.
Henry Wadsworth Longfellow

The opinion of the great body of the reading public, is very materially influenced even by the unsupported assertions of those who assume a right to criticise.
Thomas Babington Macaulay

Criticism in a free man's country is made on certain assumptions, one of which is the assumption that the government belongs to the people and is at all times subject to the people's correction and criticism.
Archibald MacLeish

I have never found, in a long experience of politics, that criticism is ever inhibited by ignorance.
Harold Macmillan

People ask you for criticism, but they only want praise.
(William) Somerset Maugham

There are some literary critics . . . who remind me of a gong at a grade crossing clanging loudly and vainly as the train roars by.
Christopher Darlington Morley

Criticism is the art wherewith a critic tries to guess himself into a share of the author's fame.
George Jean Nathan

I think it is right that we should encourage honest criticism, and have as much public discussion of our problems as possible.
Jawaharlal Nehru

No one, however great he may be, should be above criticism. But when criticism becomes a mere refuge for inaction there is something wrong with it.
Jawaharlal Nehru

Get your enemies to read your works in order to mend them; for your friend is so much your second self that he will judge too much like you.
Alexander Pope

Ten censure wrong, for one that writes amiss.
Alexander Pope

No work of the mind exists—book, theory, hypothesis—which may not be criticized either from above or below. And often is; both ways simultaneously.
Jean Rostand

Criticism surprises the soul in the arms of convention.
George Santayana

Neither praise nor blame is the object of true criticism. Justly to discriminate, firmly to establish, wisely to prescribe, and honestly to award—these are the true aims and duties of criticism.
William Gilmore Simms

Half of the secular unrest and dismal, profane sadness of modern society comes from the vain idea that every man is bound to be a critic of life.
Henry van Dyke

Criticism is the child and handmaid of reflection.—It works by censure, and censure implies a standard.
Richard Grant White

See also: CALUMNY, CENSURE, CRITIC, DETRACTION, DISSENT, ESTIMATION, PRAISE, REPROOF.

CRITICS

He, whose first emotion on the view of an excellent production is to undervalue it, will never have one of his own to show.
John Aikin

Even the lion has to defend himself against flies.
German Proverb

Only God can form and paint a flower, but any foolish child can pull it to pieces.
John Monro Gibson

The severest critics are always those who have either never attempted, or who have failed in original composition.
William Hazlitt

Critics are a kind of freebooters in the republic of letters, who, like deer, goats, and diverse other graminivorous animals, gain subsistence by gorging upon buds and leaves of the young shrubs of the forest, thereby robbing them of their verdure and retarding their progress to maturity.
Washington Irving

Critics are sentinels in the grand army of letters, stationed at the corners of newspapers and reviews, to challenge every new author.
Henry Wadsworth Longfellow

Some critics are like chimney-sweepers; they put out the fire below, and frighten the swallows from their nests above; they scrape a long time in the chimney, cover themselves with soot, and bring nothing away but a bag of cinders, and then sing out from the top of the house, as if they had built it.
Henry Wadsworth Longfellow

There is scarcely a good critic of books born in our age, and yet every fool thinks himself justified in criticising persons.
Edward G. Bulwer-Lytton (Baron Lytton)

There are some critics who change everything that comes under their hands to gold; but to this privilege of Midas they join sometimes his ears.
John Petit-Senn

A critic is a legless man who teaches running.
Channing Pollock

The actual definition of reviewmanship is now, I think, stabilized. In its shortest form it is 'How to be one up on the author without actually tampering with the text.' In other words, how, as a critic, to show that it is really you yourself who should have written the book, if you had had the time, and since you hadn't, you are glad that someone else has, although obviously it might have been done better.

Stephen Potter

Critics who find purpose in the smallest details of masterpieces make one think of those naturalists who assign a role to every least hair of living organisms.

Jean Rostand

Take heed of critics even when they are not fair; resist them even when they are.

Jean Rostand

A drama critic is a man who leaves no turn unstoned.

George Bernard Shaw

Critics in New York are made by their dislikes, not by their enthusiasms.

Irwin Shaw

Pay no attention to what the critics say; there has never been set up a statue in honor of a critic.

Jean Sibelius

See also: CRITICISM, DISSENT.

CROSS

The cross is the only ladder high enough to touch Heaven's threshold.

George Dana Boardman

The greatest of all crosses is self. If we die in part every day, we shall have but little to do on the last. These little daily deaths will destroy the power of the final dying.

François de Salignac de La Mothe-Fénelon

The cross of Christ, on which he was extended, points, in the length of it, to heaven and earth, reconciling them together; and in the breadth of it, to former and following ages, as being equally salvation to both.

Samuel Rutherford

Carry the cross patiently, and with perfect submission; and in the end it shall carry you.

Thomas à Kempis

See also: CHRISTIANITY, CRUCIFIXION, EASTER.

CROWD

Every crowd has a silver lining.

Phineas Taylor Barnum

All one has to do to gather a large crowd in New York is to stand on the curb a few moments and gaze intently at the sky.

George Jean Nathan

Sea of upturned faces.

Sir Walter Scott

The thing which in the subway is called congestion is highly esteemed in the night spots as intimacy.

Simeon Strunsky

Man goes into the noisy crowd to drown his own clamour of silence.

Sir Rabindranath Tagore

See also: COMMON MAN, MOB, POPULACE.

CRUCIFIXION

How strange! The very people who had given the world a God, and whose whole life was inspired by devotion to God, were stigmatized as deicides!

Heinrich Heine

If the Jews did commit an inexplicable crime nearly two thousand years ago, we have had no authority given to us—even if we could determine who were the descendants of the persons guilty of that crime—to visit the sins of the fathers upon the children . . . unto the three hundredth or four hundredth generation. That awful power is not ours.

Sir Robert Peel

Crowns of roses fade—crowns of thorns endure. Calvaries and crucifixions take deepest hold of humanity—the triumphs of might are transient—they pass and are forgotten—the sufferings of right are graven deepest on the chronicle of nations.

Abram Joseph Ryan

In the heart is the prey for gods,
Who crucify hearts, not hands.

Algernon Charles Swinburne

See also: CHRISTIANITY, CROSS.

CRUELTY

Cruelty and fear shake hands together.

Honoré de Balzac

Man's inhumanity to man, makes countless thousands mourn.

Robert Burns

One of the ill effects of cruelty is that it makes the by-standers cruel.

Sir Thomas Fowell Buxton

Detested sport, that owes its pleasures to another's pain.

William Cowper

I would not enter on my list of friends the man who needlessly sets foot upon a worm.

William Cowper

Cruelty is the child of ignorance.

Clarence Seward Darrow

Cruelty, like every other vice, requires no motive outside of itself; it only requires opportunity.

George Eliot (Mary Ann Evans)

Cruelty to dumb animals is one of the distinguishing vices of the lowest and basest of the people. Wherever it is found, it is a certain mark of ignorance and meanness.

William Jones of Nayland

Where does discipline end? Where does cruelty begin? Somewhere between these, thousands of children inhabit a voiceless hell.

François Mauriac

Brutality degrades everybody. It degrades the sufferer; it degrades also the person who makes others suffer.

Jawaharlal Nehru

All cruelty springs from hard-heartedness and weakness.

Seneca

See also: ABUSE, MEANNESS, NAZISM, PERSECUTION, PUNISHMENT, VIOLENCE, WAR.

CUBA

Eventually millions of men will take responsibility for public problems of all kinds. In my personal experience, I see how much easier everything is done in Cuba today on account of the numbers of men who have acquired experience, who have broadened their intelligence in coping with problems. And it will increase more and more.

Fidel Castro

In Cuba, people had been talking so long about revolution and revolutionary programs that the ruling classes paid no attention. They believed that ours was simply one more program, that all revolutionaries change and become conservatives with the passage of time. As a matter of fact, the opposite has happened to me. With the passing of time my thought has become more and more radical.

Fidel Castro

There are some people who have some illusions about the Cuban Revolution because tens of thousands of people have chosen not to live under socialism. What they forget is that millions of our citizens will never leave their country or change their way of life. The idea of going to the United States has always been a big attraction for a certain number of people because it is the wealthiest nation in the world. However, in spite of the fact that we are still poor and underdeveloped, the overwhelming majority of our men and women will never abandon their country.

Fidel Castro

Although serious problems remain, the crisis is over in Cuba, and it is now apparent that Fidel Castro and his Revolution are likely to remain a part of our world for some time to come.

Lee Lockwood

It is time for us to accept the Cuban Revolution as a *fait accompli* and to begin to deal with it in a way which does us more credit as a democratic people.

Lee Lockwood

Literally everybody and everything Cuban has changed, including, certainly, Castro himself. It is now clear that the real Cuban Revolution began *after* January 1959 and is still going on. And like any true revolution, it has brought with it violent controversy and division.

Lee Lockwood

See also: COMMUNISM, DEMOCRACY, DICTATOR.

CULTIVATION

That is true cultivation which gives us sympathy with every form of human life, and enables us to work most successfully for its advancement. Refinement that carries us away from our fellow-men is not God's refinement.

Henry Ward Beecher

Partial culture runs to the ornate; extreme culture to simplicity.

Christian Nestell Bovee

Whatever expands the affections, or enlarges the sphere of our sympathies—whatever makes us feel our relation to the universe and all that it inherits in time and in eternity, and to the great and beneficent cause of all, must unquestionably refine our nature, and elevate us in the scale of being.

William Ellery Channing

Cultivation to the mind, is as necessary as food to the body.

Cicero

It matters little whether a man be mathematically, or philologically, or artistically cultivated, so he be but cultivated.

Johann Wolfgang von Goethe

The highest purpose of intellectual cultivation is, to give a man a perfect knowledge and mastery of his own inner self.

Baron Friedrich von Hardenberg (Novalis)

To be cultivated, one must read slowly and with a lingering appreciation the comparatively few books which have been written by men who lived, thought, and felt with style.

Aldous Leonard Huxley

It is very rare to find ground which produces nothing. If it is not covered with flowers, fruit trees, and grains, it produces briars and pines. It is the same with man; if he is not virtuous, he becomes vicious.

Jean de La Bruyère

Virtue and talents, though allowed their due consideration, yet are not enough to procure a man a welcome wherever he comes. Nobody contents himself with rough diamonds, or wears them so. When polished and set, then they give a lustre.

John Locke

As the soil, however rich it may be, cannot be productive without culture, so the mind, without cultivation, can never produce good fruit.

Seneca

See also: EDUCATION, ELEGANCE, GOOD BREEDING, REFINEMENT.

CULTURE

The great aim of culture [is] the aim of setting ourselves to ascertain what perfection is and how to make it prevail.

Matthew Arnold

Culture of the mind must be subservient to the heart.

Mohandas Karamchand (Mahatma) Gandhi

A nation's culture resides in the hearts and in the soul of its people.

Mohandas Karamchand (Mahatma) Gandhi

No culture can live, if it attempts to be exclusive.

Mohandas Karamchand (Mahatma) Gandhi

Culture exists the moment man discovers that the hand armed with the flint is capable of things which without it would have been beyond his reach.

Johan Huizinga

Culture and civilization are difficult to define, and I shall not try to define them. But among the many things that culture includes are certainly restraint over oneself and consideration for others. If a person has not got this self-restraint and has no consideration for others, one can certainly say that he is uncultured.

Jawaharlal Nehru

Culture cannot be copied suddenly; it has to take root. A backward nation merely aping advanced nations changes the gold and silver of real culture into tinsel.

Jawaharlal Nehru

Culture is the widening of the mind and of the spirit.

Jawaharlal Nehru

See also: ARCHITECTURE, ART, CULTIVATION, LITERATURE, MANNERS, THEATER.

CUNNING

Cunning is only the mimic of discretion, and may pass upon weak men, as vivacity is often mistaken for wit, and gravity for wisdom.

Joseph Addison

We take cunning for a sinister or crooked wisdom, and certainly there is a great difference between a cunning man and a wise man, not only in point of honesty, but in point of ability.

Francis Bacon

A cunning man overreaches no one half as much as himself.

Henry Ward Beecher

Cleverness and cunning are incompatible. I never saw them united. The latter is the resource of the weak, and is only natural to them. Children and fools are always cunning, but clever people never.

George Gordon Byron (Lord Byron)

The certain way to be cheated is to fancy one's self more cunning than others.

Pierre Charron

A cunning man is never a firm man; but an honest man is; a double-minded man is always unstable; a man of faith is firm as a rock. There is a sacred connection between honesty and faith; honesty is faith applied to worldly things, and faith is honesty quickened by the Spirit to the use of heavenly things.

Edward Irving

Cunning has effect from the credulity of others. It requires no extraordinary talents to lie and deceive.

Samuel Johnson

In a great business there is nothing so fatal as cunning management.

Junius

Discretion is the perfection of reason, and a guide to us in the duties of life; cunning is a kind of instinct, that only looks out after our immediate interests and welfare. Discretion is only found in men of strong sense and good understanding; cunning is often to be met with in brutes themselves, and in persons who are but the fewest removes from them.

Jean de La Bruyère

The greatest of all cunning is to seem blind to the snares which we know are laid for us; men are never so easily deceived as while they are endeavoring to deceive others.

Duc François de La Rochefoucauld

The most sure way of subjecting yourself to be deceived, is to consider yourself more cunning than others.

Duc François de La Rochefoucauld

Cunning is the ape of wisdom.

John Locke

Cunning signifies, especially, a habit or gift of overreaching, accompanied with enjoyment and a sense of superiority. It is associated with small and dull conceit, and with an absolute want of sympathy or affection. It is the intensest rendering of vulgarity, absolute and utter.

John Ruskin

Cunning pays no regard to virtue, and is but the low mimic of wisdom.

Henry St. John (Lord Bolingbroke)

See also: DECEIT, SUBTLETY.

CURIOSITY

The first and simplest emotion which we discover in the human mind, is curiosity.

Edmund Burke

Every man ought to be inquisitive through every hour of his great adventure down to the day when he shall no longer cast a shadow in the sun. For if he dies without a question in his heart, what excuse is there for his continuance?

Frank Moore Colby

The curiosity of an honorable mind willingly rests where the love of truth does not urge it further onward and the love of its neighbor bids it stop. In other words, it willingly stops at the point where the interests of truth do not beckon it onward, and charity cries "Halt."

Samuel Taylor Coleridge

Curiosity is one of the permanent and certain characteristics of a vigorous intellect. Every advance into knowledge opens new prospects and produces new incitements to further progress.

Samuel Johnson

The gratification of curiosity rather frees us from uneasiness, than confers pleasure. We are more pained by ignorance, than delighted by instruction. Curiosity is the thirst of the soul.

Samuel Johnson

There are different kinds of curiosity: one the offspring of interested motives, leading us to the desire of learning what may be useful to us; and the other arising from feelings of pride, which makes us desire to know what others are ignorant of.

Duc François de La Rochefoucauld

Avoid him who, for mere curiosity, asks three questions running about a thing that cannot interest him.

Johann Kaspar Lavater

Curiosity in children is but an appetite for knowledge. One great reason why children abandon themselves wholly to silly pursuits and trifle away their time insipidly is, because they find their curiosity balked, and their inquiries neglected.

John Locke

The over curious are not over wise.

Philip Massinger

Is there a keener sense in a woman than her sense of curiosity?

Guy de Maupassant

A person who is too nice an observer of the business of the crowd, like one who is too curious in observing the labor of bees, will often be stung for his curiosity.

Alexander Pope

Men are more inclined to ask curious questions, than to obtain necessary instruction.

Pasquier Quesnel

The Semitic peoples lack almost entirely a sense of curiosity and the faculty of laughter.

Joseph Ernest Renan

How many a noble art, now widely known, owes its young impulse to this power alone.

Charles Sprague

Inquisitive people are the funnels of conversation; they do not take anything for their own use, but merely to pass it on to others.

Sir Richard Steele

Curiosity is looking over other people's affairs, and overlooking our own.

Heman Lincoln Wayland

Curiosity is as much the parent of attention, as attention is of memory.

Richard Whately

Sieze the moment of excited curiosity on any subject, to solve your doubts; for if you let it pass, the desire may never return, and you may remain in ignorance.

William Wirt

See also: INDIFFERENCE, INQUIRY, INQUISITIVE-
        NESS, QUESTION, SCIENCE, SPECULA-
        TION, WONDER.

CURSE

There's a great text in Galatians,
    Once you trip on it, entails
Twenty-nine distinct damnations,
    One sure, if another fails.
If I trip him just a-dying
    Sure of Heaven as sure can be,
Spin him round and send him flying
    Off to Hell, a Manichee?

Robert Browning

Curses are like young chickens, and still come home to roost.

Edward G. Bulwer-Lytton (Baron Lytton)

Dinna curse him, sir; I have heard it said that a curse was like a stone flung up to the heavens, and most likely to return on the head of him that sent it.

Sir Walter Scott

The foolish and wicked practice of profane cursing and swearing is a vice so mean and low that every person of sense and character detests and despises it.

George Washington

See also: ABUSE, OATH, PROFANITY, THREAT.

CUSTOM

Men commonly think according to their inclinations, speak according to their learning and imbibed opinions, but generally act according to custom.

Francis Bacon

There is no tyrant like custom, and no freedom where its edicts are not resisted.

Christian Nestell Bovee

There are not unfrequently substantial reasons underneath for customs that appear to us absurd.

Charlotte Brontë

Custom reconciles us to everything.

Edmund Burke

Custom doth make dotards of us all.

Thomas Carlyle

Custom is often only the antiquity of error.

Cyprian of Carthage

Customs may not be as wise as laws, but they are always more popular.

Benjamin Disraeli

The custom and fashion of to-day will be the awkwardness and outrage of tomorrow—so arbitrary are these transient laws.
Alexandre Dumas (père)

In this great society wide lying around us, a critical analysis would find very few spontaneous actions. It is almost all custom and gross sense.
Ralph Waldo Emerson

Custom may lead a man into many errors, but it justifies none.
Henry Fielding

We must gladly give up custom that is against reason, justice, and religion of the heart. We must not ignorantly cling to bad custom and part with it when we must, like a miser parting with his ill-gotten hoard out of pressure and expediency.
Mohandas Karamchand (Mahatma) Gandhi

The despotism of custom is on the wane. We are not content to know that things are; we ask whether they ought to be.
John Stuart Mill

The way of the world is to make laws, but follow customs.
Michel Eyquem de Montaigne

Choose always the way that seems best, however rough it may be, and custom will soon render it easy and agreeable.
Pythagoras

Men are never more offended than when we depreciate their ceremonies and usages. Seek to oppress them, and it is sometimes a proof of the esteem with which you regard them; depreciate their customs, it is always a mark of contempt.
Charles de Secondat (Baron de Montesquieu)

As the world leads, we follow.
Seneca

The custom that comes through all ages is not the King's own. Like heaven's air, it belongs to all men.
Sir Rabindranath Tagore

Custom is the law of fools.
Sir John Vanbrugh

Custom is the universal sovereign.
John Wolcot (Peter Pindar)

Be not so bigoted to any custom as to worship it at the expense of truth.
Johann Georg von Zimmermann

See also: CONFORMITY, FASHION, HABIT, PRECEDENT, TRADITION.

CYBERNETICS

To me, there is something superbly symbolic in the fact that an astronaut, sent up as assistant to a series of computers, found that he worked more accurately and more intelligently than they. Inside the capsule, *man* is still in charge.
Adlai Ewing Stevenson

We have decided to call the entire field of control and communication theory, whether in the machine or in the animal, by the name of *Cybernetics*.
Norbert Wiener

See also: COMPUTER, SCIENCE, TECHNOLOGY.

CYNIC

The cynic is one who never sees a good quality in a man, and never fails to see a bad one. He is the human owl, vigilant in darkness and blind to light, mousing for vermin, and never seeing noble game.
Henry Ward Beecher

To admire nothing is the motto which men of the world always affect. They think it vulgar to wonder or be enthusiastic. They have so much corruption and charlatanism, that they think the credit of all high qualities must be delusive.
Sir Samuel Egerton Brydges

A cynic is just a man who found out when he was about ten that there wasn't any Santa Claus, and he's still upset.
James Gould Cozzens

It will generally be found that those who sneer habitually at human nature, and affect to despise it, are among its worst and least pleasant samples.
Charles John Huffam Dickens

Don't be a cynic, and bewail and bemoan. Omit the negative propositions. Don't waste yourself in rejection, nor bark against the bad, but chant the beauty of the good.—Set down nothing that will help somebody.
Ralph Waldo Emerson

It takes a clever man to turn cynic, and a wise man to be clever enough not to.

Fannie Hurst

Never, never, never be a cynic, even a gentle one. Never help out a sneer, even at the devil.

(Nicholas) Vachel Lindsay

A cynic is a man who knows the price of everything, and the value of nothing.

Oscar Wilde

See also: CYNICISM, DOUBT, PREJUDICE, SATIRE, SKEPTICISM, SNEER.

CYNICISM

Watch what people are cynical about, and one can often discover what they lack, and subconsciously, beneath their touchy condescension, deeply wish they had.

Harry Emerson Fosdick

Still the mind smiles at its own rebellions.

(John) Robinson Jeffers

Cynicism is the intellectual cripple's substitute for intelligence. It is the dishonest businessman's substitute for conscience. It is the communicator's substitute, whether he is advertising man or editor or writer, for self-respect.

(Joseph) Russell Lynes

The only deadly sin I know is cynicism.

Henry Lewis Stimson

See also: CYNIC, HATE, PESSIMISM, SKEPTICISM.

D

DANCE

A good education is usually harmful to a dancer. A good calf is better than a good head.

Agnes George DeMille

Without dancing you can never attain a perfectly graceful carriage, which is of the highest importance in life.

Benjamin Disraeli

Yes, the dance throughout all ages
Was a pious act of faith.

Heinrich Heine

The chief benefit of dancing is to learn one how to sit still.

Samuel Johnson

See also: AMUSEMENT, JAZZ, MUSIC.

DANGER

Danger levels man and brute, and all are fellows in their need.

George Gordon Byron (Lord Byron)

We should never so entirely avoid danger as to appear irresolute and cowardly; but, at the same time, we should avoid unnecessarily exposing ourselves to danger, than which nothing can be more foolish.

Cicero

External danger can only be faced effectively when there is internal peace and order and an organised nation.

Jawaharlal Nehru

The person who runs away exposes himself to that very danger more than a person who sits quietly.

Jawaharlal Nehru

Let the fear of a danger be a spur to prevent it; he that fears not, gives advantage to the danger.

Francis Quarles

A timid person is frightened before a danger; a coward during the time; and a courageous person afterward.

Jean Paul Richter

There is nobody who is not dangerous for some one.

Marquise de Sévigné

The atomic bomb in the hands of a Francis of Assisi would be less harmful than a pistol in the hand of a thug; what makes the bomb dangerous is not the energy it contains, but the man who uses it.

Fulton John Sheen

The effect of undefined danger, that is, danger whose magnitude is not known, is frequently out of proportion to its actual import.

Hans Speier

We are confronted by a first danger, the destructiveness of applied atomic energy. And then we are confronted by a second danger, that we do not enough appreciate the first danger.

Raymond Gram Swing

See also: ADVENTURE, BRAVERY, CARE, COURAGE, FEAR.

DAUGHTER

To a father waxing old nothing is dearer than a daughter. Sons have spirits of higher pitch, but less inclined to sweet, endearing fondness.

Euripides

My son is my son till he have got him a wife,
But my daughter's my daughter all the days
of her life.

Thomas Fuller

A daughter is an embarrassing and ticklish possession.

Menander of Athens

See also: CHILDREN, FATHER, MOTHER.

DAY

Every day is a little life, and our whole life is but a day repeated. Therefore live every day as if it would be the last. Those that dare lose a day, are dangerously prodigal; those that dare misspend it are desperate.

Joseph Hall

Count that day lost, whose low descending sun views from thy hand no worthy action done.

Charles Stanford

Enjoy the blessings of the day if God sends them: and the evils bear patiently and sweetly; for this day only is ours: we are dead to yesterday, and not born to to-morrow.

Jeremy Taylor

See also: LIGHT, MORNING, NIGHT, SUN.

DEATH

Every minute dies a man, and one and one-sixteenth is born.

Anonymous

It is as natural to man to die, as to be born; and to a little infant, perhaps the one is as painful as the other.

Francis Bacon

As long as we are living, God will give us living grace, and he won't give us dying grace till it's time to die. What's the use of trying to feel like dying when you ain't dying, nor anywhere near it?

Henry Ward Beecher

How shocking must thy summons be O death, to him that is at ease in his possessions! who, counting on long years of pleasure here, is quite unfurnished for the world to come.

Hugh Blair

A few more years shall roll,
  A few more seasons come,
And we shall be with those that rest,
  Asleep within the tomb.

Horatius Bonar

O death! We thank thee for the light that thou wilt shed upon our ignorance.

Jacques Bénigne Bossuet

Certainly there is no happiness within this circle of flesh, nor is it in the optics of these eyes to behold felicity; the first day of our Jubilee is death.

Sir Thomas Browne

Let dissolution come when it will, it can do the Christian no harm, for it will be but a passage out of a prison into a palace; out of a sea of troubles into a haven of rest; out of a crowd of enemies, to an innumerable company of true, loving, and faithful friends; out of shame, reproach, and contempt, into exceeding great and eternal glory.

John Bunyan

Tom's no more—and so no more of Tom.

George Gordon Byron (Lord Byron)

Death, to a good man, is but passing through a dark entry, out of one little dusky room of his father's house, into another that is fair and large, lightsome and glorious, and divinely entertaining.

McDonald Clarke

Each person is born to one possession which outvalues all the others—his last breath.

Samuel Langhorne Clemens (Mark Twain)

Whoever has lived long enough to find out what life is, knows how deep a debt of gratitude we owe to Adam, the first great benefactor of our race. He brought death into the world.

Samuel Langhorne Clemens (Mark Twain)

Time is a system of folds which only death can unfold.

Jean Cocteau

Death is the liberator of him whom freedom cannot release; the physician of him whom medicine cannot cure; the comforter of him whom time cannot console.

Charles Caleb Colton

Death has nothing terrible which life has not made so. A faithful Christian life in this world is the best preparation for the next.

Tryon Edwards

And I have seen the eternal Footman hold my
  coat, and snicker,
And in short, I was afraid.

Thomas Stearns Eliot

Let death be daily before your eyes, and you will never entertain any abject thought, nor too eagerly covet anything.

Epictetus

Death destroys a man, but the idea of death saves him—that is the best account of it that has yet been given.

Edward Morgan Forster

There is no better armor against the shafts of death than to be busied in God's service.

Thomas Fuller

Fear of death makes us devoid both of valour and religion. For, want of valour is want of religious faith.

Mohandas Karamchand (Mahatma) Gandhi

It is because we fear death so much for ourselves that we shed tears over the death of others.

Mohandas Karamchand (Mahatma) Gandhi

Our scriptures tell us that childhood, old age and death are incidents only, to this perishable body of ours and that man's spirit is eternal and immortal. That being so, why should we fear death? And where there is no fear of death there can be no sorrow over it, either.

Mohandas Karamchand (Mahatma) Gandhi

To be afraid of death is like being afraid of discarding an old worn-out garment.

Mohandas Karamchand (Mahatma) Gandhi

The bad man's death is horror; but the just does but ascend to glory from the dust.

William Habington

A wise and due consideration of our latter end, is neither to render us sad, melancholy, disconsolate, or unfit for the business and offices of life; but to make us more watchful, vigilant, industrious, sober, cheerful, and thankful to that God who hath been pleased thus to make us serviceable to him, comfortable to ourselves, and profitable to others; and after all this, to take away the bitterness and sting of death, through Jesus Christ our Lord.

Sir Matthew Hale

Death did not first strike Adam, the first sinful man, nor Cain, the first hypocrite, but Abel, the innocent and righteous. The first soul that met death overcame death; the first soul parted from earth went to heaven. Death argues not displeasure, because he whom God loved best dies first, and the murderer is punished with living.

Joseph Hall

I never think he is quite ready for another world who is altogether weary of this.

Hugh Hamilton

Death, the fusty pendant, spares the rose as little as the thistle; he forgets not a lonely blade of grass in the remotest wilderness; he thoroughly and incessantly destroys.

Heinrich Heine

Leaves have their time to fall, and flowers to wither at the North-wind's breath, and stars to set—but all, thou hast all seasons for thine own, O death!

Felicia Dorothea Browne Hemans

Death is as the foreshadowing of life. We die that we may die no more.

Herman Hooker

Whom the gods love die young no matter how long they live.

Elbert Green Hubbard

A dislike of death is no proof of the want of religion. The instincts of nature shrink from it, for no creature can like its own dissolution. But though death is not desired, the result of it may be, for dying to the Christian is the way to life eternal.

William Jay

What is certain in death is somewhat softened by what is uncertain: it is an indefiniteness in the time, which holds a certain relation to the infinite, and to what is called eternity.

Jean de La Bruyère

Death is not a foe, but an inevitable adventure.

Sir Oliver Joseph Lodge

There is no death! What seems so is transition; this life of mortal breath is but a suburb of the life elysian, whose portal we call death.

Henry Wadsworth Longfellow

The gods conceal from men the happiness of death, that they may endure life.

Lucan

We picture death as coming to destroy; let us rather picture Christ as coming to save. We think of death as ending; let us rather think of life as beginning, and that more abundantly. We think of losing; let us think of gaining. We think of parting, let us think of meeting. We think of going away; let us think of arriving. And as the voice of death whispers "You must go from earth," let us hear the voice of Christ saying, "You are but coming to Me!"

Norman Macleod

Even death may prove unreal at the last, and stoics be astounded into heaven.

Herman Melville

He whom the gods love, dies young.

Menander of Athens

Death and love are the two wings that bear the good man to heaven.

Michelangelo (Buonarroti)

Down, down, down into the darkness of the grave
Gently they go, the beautiful, the tender, the kind;
Quietly they go, the intelligent, the witty, the brave.
I know. But I do not approve. And I am not resigned.

Edna St. Vincent Millay

Death is the golden key that opens the palace of eternity.

John Milton

O death where is thy sting? O grave, where is thy victory? Where, indeed? Many a badly stung survivor, faced with the aftermath of some relative's funeral, has ruefully conceded that the victory has been won hands down by a funeral establishment—in disastrously unequal battle.

Jessica Mitford

Men fear death, as if unquestionably the greatest evil, and yet no man knows that it may not be the greatest good.

William Mitford

He who should teach men to die, would, at the same time, teach them to live.

Michel Eyquem de Montaigne

It is not death, it is dying that alarms me.

Michel Eyquem de Montaigne

Where death awaits us is uncertain: we ought to expect it everywhere. The premeditation of death is the premeditation of liberty: he who has learnt to die has unlearnt to serve. There is no evil in life to the man who is thoroughly convinced that to be deprived of life is no evil; to be ready to die frees us from bondage and thraldom.

Michel Eyquem de Montaigne

I know of but one remedy against the fear of death that is effectual and that will stand the test either of a sick-bed, or of a sound mind— that is, a good life, a clear conscience, an honest heart, and a well-ordered conversation; to carry the thoughts of dying men about us, and so to live before we die as we shall wish we had when we come to it.

John Norris

As a rule, man dies as he had lived, uninfluenced by the thought of a future life.

Sir William Osler

There are so many little dyings that it doesn't matter which of them is death.

Kenneth Patchen

Not by lamentations and mournful chants ought we to celebrate the funeral of a good man, but by hymns, for in ceasing to be numbered with mortals he enters upon the heritage of a diviner life.

Plutarch

On death and judgment, heaven and hell, who oft doth think, must needs die well.

Sir Walter Raleigh

The darkness of death is like the evening twilight; it makes all objects appear more lovely to the dying.

Jean Paul Richter

If Socrates died like a philosopher, Jesus Christ died like a God.

Jean Jacques Rousseau

Man does not die. Man imagines that it is death he fears; but what he fears is the unforeseen, the explosion. What man fears is himself, not death. There is no death when you meet death.

Antoine de Saint-Exupéry

Is death the last sleep? No, it is the last and final awakening.

Sir Walter Scott

We call it death to leave this world, but were we once out of it, and enstated into the happiness of the next, we should think it were dying indeed to come back to it again.

Thomas Sherlock

Be of good cheer about death, and know this of a truth, that no evil can happen to a good man, either in life or after death.

Socrates

A free man thinks of death least of all things; and his wisdom is a meditation not of death but of life.

Baruch (Benedict) Spinoza

We understand death for the first time when he puts his hand upon one whom we love.

Madame de Staël

Death: where the changing mist of doubts will vanish at a breath, and the mountain peaks of eternal truth will appear.

Sir Rabindranath Tagore

If it is necessary to die in order to live like men, what harm in dying?

Sir Rabindranath Tagore

Sometimes the imminence of death provokes so desperate a reaction in the body that the life is saved.

Sir Rabindranath Tagore

Every minute dies a man, every minute one is born.

Alfred, Lord Tennyson

Some people are so afraid to die that they never begin to live.

Henry Jackson Van Dyke

We need have no quarrel with death. Death has its uses. It plays a positive part in the economy of life. It is not that it defeats life. If anything does that, it is perhaps meaninglessness.

George Wald

One may live as a conqueror, a king, or a magistrate; but he must die a man. The bed of death brings every human being to his pure individuality, to the intense contemplation of that deepest and most solemn of all relations —the relation between the creature and his Creator.

Daniel Webster

Death is the crown of life. Were death denied, poor man would live in vain; to live would not be life; even fools would wish to die.

Edward Young

Men may live fools, but fools they cannot die.

Edward Young

Better a noble death than a wretched life.

Yiddish Proverb

Death does not knock on the door.

Yiddish Proverb

There's no bad mother, and no good death.

Yiddish Proverb

See also: EPITAPH, FUNERAL, GRAVE, IMMORTALITY, LIFE, MORTALITY.

DEBT

"Out of debt, out of danger," is, like many other proverbs, full of wisdom; but the word danger does not sufficiently express all that the warning demands. For a state of debt and embarrassment is a state of positive misery, and the sufferer is as one haunted by an evil spirit, and his heart can know neither rest nor peace till it is cast out.

Charles Bridges

Paying of debts is, next to the grace of God, the best means of delivering you from a thousand temptations to vanity and sin. Pay your debts, and you will not have wherewithal to buy costly toys or pernicious pleasures. Pay your debts, and you will not have what to lose to a gamester. Pay your debts, and you will of necessity abstain from many indulgences that war against the spirit and bring you into captivity to sin, and cannot fail to end in your utter destruction, both of soul and body.

Patrick Bernard Delany

Debt is a prolific mother of folly and of crime.

Benjamin Disraeli

Think what you do when you run in debt; you give to another power over your liberty. If you cannot pay at the time, you will be ashamed to see your creditor; will be in fear when you speak to him; will make poor, pitiful, sneaking excuses, and by degrees come to lose your veracity, and sink into base, downright lying; for the second vice is lying, the first is running in debt. A freeborn man ought not to be ashamed nor afraid to see or speak to any man living, but poverty often deprives a man of all spirit and virtue. It is hard for an empty bag to stand upright.

Benjamin Franklin

Run not into debt, either for wares sold, or money borrowed; be content to want things that are not of absolute necessity, rather than to run up the score: such a man pays, at the latter end, a third part more than the principal, and is in perpetual servitude to his creditors; lives uncomfortably; is necessitated to increase his debts to stop his creditors' mouths; and many times falls into desperate courses.

Sir Matthew Hale

Do not accustom yourself to consider debt only as an inconvenience; you will find it a calamity.

Samuel Johnson

Youth is in danger until it learns to look upon debts as furies.

Edward G. Bulwer-Lytton (Baron Lytton)

Debt is the secret foe of thrift, as vice and idleness are its open foes. The debt-habit is the twin brother of poverty.

Theodore Thornton Munger

A small debt produces a debtor; a large one, an enemy.

Publilius Syrus

I have discovered the philosopher's stone, that turns everything into gold: it is, "Pay as you go."

John Randolph

Poverty is hard, but debt is horrible. A man might as well have a smoky house and a scolding wife, which are said to be the two worst evils of our life.

Charles Haddon Spurgeon

A man who owes a little can clear it off in a little time, and, if he is prudent, he will: whereas a man, who, by long negligence, owes a great deal, despairs of ever being able to pay, and therefore never looks into his accounts at all.

Philip Dormer Stanhope (Lord Chesterfield)

See also: BORROWING, CREDIT, LENDING.

DECEIT

The first and worst of all frauds is to cheat one's self. All sin is easy after that.

Gamaliel Bailey

Many an honest man practices on himself an amount of deceit, sufficient, if practiced on another, and in a little different way, to send him to the State prison.

Christian Nestell Bovee

He that has no real esteem for any of the virtues, can best assume the appearance of them all.

Charles Caleb Colton

Idiots only may be cozened twice.

John Dryden

Of all the evil spirits abroad in the world, insincerity is the most dangerous.

James Anthony Froude

Have I not told you times without number that ultimately a deceiver only deceives himself?

Mohandas Karamchand (Mahatma) Gandhi

No one more easily deceives others than he who is accustomed and has the reputation never to deceive.

Francesco Guicciardini

No man, for any considerable period, can wear one face to himself and another to the multitude, without finally getting bewildered as to which may be true.

Nathaniel Hawthorne

It is double pleasure to deceive the deceiver.

Jean de La Fontaine

The silly when deceived exclaims loudly, the fool complains; the man of integrity walks away and is silent.

François de La Noue

It is as easy to deceive one's self without perceiving it, as it is difficult to deceive others without their finding it out.

Duc François de La Rochefoucauld

The resolution never to deceive exposes us to be often deceived.

Duc François de La Rochefoucauld

The sure way to be cheated is to think one's-self more cunning than others.

Duc François de La Rochefoucauld

The surest way of making a dupe is to let your victim suppose you are his.

Edward G. Bulwer-Lytton (Baron Lytton)

One is easily fooled by that which one loves.

Molière (Jean Baptiste Poquelin)

Who dares think one thing and another tell, my heart detests him as the gates of hell.

Alexander Pope

O, what a tangled web we weave, when first we practice to deceive.

Sir Walter Scott

All deception in the course of life is indeed nothing else but a lie reduced to practice, and falsehood passing from words into things.

Robert South

We must make a difference between speaking to deceive and being silent to be impenetrable.

Voltaire (François Marie Arouet)

There are three persons you should never deceive: your physician, your confessor, and your lawyer.

Horace Walpole

See also: CANT, DISGUISE, DISHONESTY, EQUIVOCATION, FALSEHOOD, FRAUD, HYPOCRISY, LYING, SELF-DECEPTION.

DECENCY

Virtue and decency are so nearly related that it is difficult to separate them from each other but in our imagination.

Cicero

Want of decency is want of sense.

Wentworth Dillon (Earl of Roscommon)

Decency is the least of all laws, but yet it is the law which is most strictly observed.

Duc François de La Rochefoucauld

See also: CENSORSHIP, MODESTY, OBSCENITY, PORNOGRAPHY, REFINEMENT.

DECEPTION: *see* DECEIT.

DECISION

The block of granite which was an obstacle in the pathway of the weak becomes a stepping-stone in the pathway of the strong.

Thomas Carlyle

It is a poor and disgraceful thing not to be able to reply, with some degree of certainty, to the simple questions, "What will you be? What will you do?"

John Watson Foster

Perhaps no mightier conflict of mind occurs ever again in a life-time than that first decision to unseat one's own tooth.

Gene Fowler

The best way out is always through.

Robert Lee Frost

All human acts involve more chance than decision.

André Gide

I hate to see things done by halves. If it be right, do it boldly,—if it be wrong leave it undone.

Bernard Gilpin

He that cannot decidedly say "No," when tempted to evil, is on the highway to ruin. He loses the respect even of those who would tempt him, and becomes but the pliant tool and victim of their evil designs.

Joel Hawes

There is nothing more to be esteemed than a manly firmness and decision of character. I like a person who knows his own mind and sticks to it; who sees at once what, in given circumstances, is to be done, and does it.

William Hazlitt

When desperate ills demand a speedy cure, distrust is cowardice, and prudence folly.

Samuel Johnson

Here I stand; I can do no otherwise. God help me. *Amen.*

Martin Luther

The man who has not learned to say "No" will be a weak if not a wretched man as long as he lives.

Alexander Maclaren

Men must be decided on what they will not do, and then they are able to act with vigor in what they ought to do.

Mencius

A decision is the action an executive must take when he has information so incomplete that the answer does not suggest itself.

Arthur William Radford

When we can say "no," not only to things that are wrong and sinful, but also to things pleasant, profitable, and good which would hinder and clog our grand duties and our chief work, we shall understand more fully what life is worth, and how to make the most of it.

Charles Augustus Stoddard

See also: EXECUTIVE, FIRMNESS, INDECISION, POSITIVENESS, RESOLUTION.

DEED

Good actions ennoble us, and we are the sons of our own deeds.

Miguel de Cervantes Saavedra

It is our own past which has made us what we are. We are the children of our own deeds. Conduct has created character; acts have grown into habits, each year has pressed into us a deeper moral print; the lives we have led have left us such as we are to-day.

John Bacchus Dykes

A noble deed is a step toward God.

Josiah Gilbert Holland

We are our own fates. Our deeds are our own doomsmen. Man's life was made not for creeds, but actions.

Edward R. Bulwer Lytton (Owen Meredith)

Look on little deeds as great, on account of Christ, who dwells in us, and watches our life; look on great deeds as easy, on account of His great power.

Blaise Pascal

Good deeds ring clear through heaven like a bell.

Jean Paul Richter

We should believe only in deeds; words go for nothing everywhere.

Fernando de Rojas

A life spent worthily should be measured by deeds, not years.

Richard Brinsley Sheridan

We can judge a man faithful or unfaithful only by his works.

Baruch (Benedict) Spinoza

See also: ACTION, WELL-DOING.

DEFEAT

Defeat is a school in which truth always grows strong.

Henry Ward Beecher

It is defeat that turns bone to flint, and gristle to muscle, and makes men invincible, and formed those heroic natures that are now in ascendency in the world. Do not then be afraid of defeat. You are never so near to victory as when defeated in a good cause.

Henry Ward Beecher

Defeat never comes to any man until he admits it.

Josephus Daniels

Heroes are made in the hour of defeat. Success is, therefore, well described as a series of glorious defeats.

Mohandas Karamchand (Mahatma) Gandhi

No man is defeated without some resentment, which will be continued with obstinacy while he believes himself in the right, and asserted with bitterness, if even to his own conscience he is detected in the wrong.

Samuel Johnson

Those who are prepared to die for any cause are seldom defeated.

Jawaharlal Nehru

What is defeat? Nothing but education; nothing but the first step to something better.

Wendell Phillips

Give me the heart to fight and lose.

Louis Untermeyer

See also: FAILURE, VICTORY.

DEFENSE

Local defense must be reinforced by the further deterrent of massive retaliatory power.

John Foster Dulles

There is only one defense—a defense compounded of eternal vigilance, sound policies, and high courage.

John Foster Dulles

Why when a man is struck does he defend himself? Because he has life. A stone can bear all sorts of blows quietly.

Sir Rabindranath Tagore

See also: ARMAMENT, ARMS, ARMY, NAVY, SELF-DEFENSE, SOLDIER, WAR.

DEFERENCE

Deference is the instinctive respect which we pay to the great and good. The unconscious acknowledgement of the superiority or excellence of others.

Tryon Edwards

Deference is the most delicate, the most indirect, and the most elegant of all compliments, and before company is the genteelest kind of flattery.

William Shenstone

Deference often shrinks and withers as much upon the approach of intimacy, as the sensitive plant does upon the touch of one's finger.

William Shenstone

See also: ADMIRATION, HUMILITY, MEEKNESS.

DEFINITION

A large part of the discussions of disputants come from the want of accurate definition. Let one define his terms and then stick to the definition, and half the differences in philosophy and theology would come to an end, and be seen to have no real foundation.

Tryon Edwards

Just definitions either prevent or put an end to disputes.

Nathaniel Emmons

I am apt to think that men find their simple ideas agree, though in discourse they confound one another with different names.

John Locke

All arts acknowledge that then only we know certainly, when we can define; for definition is that which refines the pure essence of things from the circumstance.

John Milton

See also: ACCURACY, OBSCURITY, THOUGHT.

DEFORMITY

Deformity is daring; it is its essence to overtake mankind by heart and soul and make itself the equal, aye, the superior of others.

George Gordon Byron (Lord Byron)

Deformity of heart I call the worst deformity of all; for what is form, or face, but the soul's index, or its case?

Charles Caleb Colton

Do you suppose we owe nothing to Pope's deformity? He said to himself, "If my person be crooked, my verses shall be straight."

William Hazlitt

See also: BEAUTY, DISEASE, UGLINESS.

DELAY

Some one speaks admirably of the well-ripened fruit of sage delay.

Honoré de Balzac

It is one of the illusions, that the present hour is not the critical, decisive hour. Write it on your heart that every day is the best day in the year. No man has learned anything rightly until he knows and feels that every day is doomsday.

Thomas Carlyle

The wisest are the most annoyed to lose time.

Dante Alighieri

The surest method of arriving at a knowledge of God's eternal purposes about us is to be found in the right use of the present moment. Each hour comes with some little fagot of God's will fastened upon its back.

Frederick William Faber

Delay has always been injurious to those who are prepared.

Lucan

To-morrow I will live, the fool does say: to-day itself's too late; the wise lived yesterday.

Martial

A good thing perpetually postponed is only a negation. Universal happiness, or the welfare of mankind, includes the present as well as the future.

Ralph Barton Perry

Every delay is hateful, but it gives wisdom.

Publilius Syrus

God keep you from "It is too late." When the fool has made up his mind the market has gone by.

Spanish Proverb

See also: FUTURE, HASTE, PAST, PROCRASTINATION, TIME, WASTE.

DELICACY

An appearance of delicacy, and even of fragility, is almost essential to beauty.

Edmund Burke

Delicacy is to the affections what grace is to beauty.

Baron Joseph Marie de Gérando

Weak men, often, from the very principle of their weakness, derive a certain susceptibility, delicacy, and taste, which render them, in these particulars, much superior to men of stronger and more consistent minds, who laugh at them.

Fulke Greville (First Baron Brooke)

True delicacy, that most beautiful heart-leaf of humanity, exhibits itself most significantly in little things.

Mary Botham Howitt

If you destroy delicacy and a sense of shame in a young girl you deprave her very fast.

Harriet Elizabeth Beecher Stowe

The finest qualities of our nature, like the bloom on fruits, can be preserved only by the most delicate handling.

Henry David Thoreau

See also: CULTIVATION, REFINEMENT, SENSIBILITY, SENSITIVENESS, TACT, TASTE.

DELIGHT

I am convinced that we have a degree of delight, and that no small one, in the real misfortunes and pains of others.

Edmund Burke

Sensual delights soon end in loathing, quickly bring a glutting surfeit, and degenerate into torments when they are continued and unintermitted.

John Howe

What more felicity can fall to man than to enjoy delight with liberty?

Edmund Spenser

As high as we have mounted in delight, in our dejection do we sing as low.

William Wordsworth

See also: DIVERSION, ENJOYMENT, HAPPINESS, JOY, RECREATION.

DELUSION

No man is happy without a delusion of some kind. Delusions are as necessary to our happiness as realities.

Christian Nestell Bovee

The worst deluded are the self-deluded.

Christian Nestell Bovee

The disappointment of manhood succeeds the delusion of youth.

Benjamin Disraeli

You think a man to be your dupe. If he pretends to be so, who is the greatest dupe—he or you?

Jean de La Bruyère

Were we perfectly acquainted with the object, we should never passionately desire it.

Duc François de La Rochefoucauld

When our vices quit us, we flatter ourselves with the belief that it is we who quit them.

Duc François de La Rochefoucauld

See also: ERROR, MISTAKE, SELF-DECEPTION.

DEMOCRACY

There can be no democracy unless it is a dynamic democracy. When our people cease to participate—to have a place in the sun—then all of us will wither in the darkness of decadence. All of us will become mute, demoralized, lost souls.

Saul David Alinsky

Democracy is a culture—that is, the deliberate cultivation of an intellectual passion in people with intellects and feelings. Like most passions it is at times vague, heedless, even unpractical, but always as real as the affinity of dog and bone.

Jacques Martin Barzun

The real democratic American idea is, not that every man shall be on a level with every other, but that every one shall have liberty, without hindrance, to be what God made him.

Henry Ward Beecher

We are committed primarily to democracy. The essential justice for which we are striving is an incident of our democracy, not the main end.

Louis Dembitz Brandeis

False democracy shouts Every man down to the level of the average. True democracy cries All men up to the height of their fullest capacity for service and achievement.

Nicholas Murray Butler

The devil was the first democrat.

George Gordon Byron (Lord Byron)

Democracy will itself accomplish the salutary universal change from the delusive to the real, and make a new blessed world of us bye and bye.

Thomas Carlyle

The democratic faith is this: that the most terribly important things must be left to ordinary men themselves—the mating of the sexes, the rearing of the young, the laws of the state.

Gilbert Keith Chesterton

The first of all democratic doctrines is that all men are interesting.

Gilbert Keith Chesterton

If our democracy is to flourish, it must have criticism; if our government is to function it must have dissent.

Henry Steele Commager

We have discovered, to our dismay, that those who subscribe to the principles that Jefferson called "self-evident" are in the minority among the peoples of the globe, and that we are now required to vindicate those principles as never before in our past.

Henry Steele Commager

Today we all realize that democracy is not a self-perpetuating virus adapted to any body politic—that was the assumption of a previous generation. Democracy we now know to be a special type of organism requiring specific nutriment materials—some economic, some social and cultural.

James Bryant Conant

The country still has faith in the rule of the people it's going to elect next.

Proctor Fyffe (Ted) Cook

It would be folly to argue that the people cannot make political mistakes. They can and do make grave mistakes. They know it, they pay the penalty, but compared with the mistakes which have been made by every kind of autocracy they are unimportant.

(John) Calvin Coolidge

In a democracy, the individual enjoys not only the ultimate power but carries the ultimate responsibility.

Norman Cousins

Sure the people are stupid; the human race is stupid. Sure Congress is an inefficient instrument of government. But the people are not stupid enough to abandon representative government for any other kind, including government by the guy who knows.

Bernard Augustine De Voto

A democracy is more than a form of government; it is primarily a mode of associated living, of conjoint communicated experience.

John Dewey

Democracy is on trial in the world, on a more colossal scale than ever before.

Charles Fletcher Dole

The sound direction of the counter movement to communism in the democracies . . . is the creation of the human welfare state—the great political invention of the twentieth century.

William Orville Douglas

There can be no perfect democracy curtailed by color, race or poverty. But with all we accomplish all, even peace.

William Edward Burghardt Du Bois

Human dignity, economic freedom, individual responsibility, these are the characteristics that distinguish democracy from all other forms devised by man.

Dwight David Eisenhower

Parliamentary institutions, with their free speech and respects for the rights of minorities, and the inspiration of a broad tolerance in thought and its expression—all this we conceive to be a precious part of our way of life and outlook. . . . I ask you now to cherish them and to practice them, too.

Elizabeth II

Democracy is based upon the conviction that there are extraordinary possibilities in ordinary people.

Harry Emerson Fosdick

Democracy is always a beckoning goal, not a safe harbor. For freedom is an unremitting endeavor, never a final achievement.

Felix Frankfurter

Nature herself vindicates democracy. For nature plants gifts and graces where least expected, and under circumstances that defy all the little artifices of man.

Felix Frankfurter

The measure of a democracy is the measure of the freedom of its humblest citizens.

John Galsworthy

While democracy must have its organization and controls, its vital breath is individual liberty.

Charles Evans Hughes

Democracy has not failed; the intelligence of the race has failed before the problems the race has raised.

Robert Maynard Hutchins

As I see it, democracy encourages the nimble charlatan at the expense of the thinker, and prefers the plausible wizard with quack remedies to the true statesman.

Sir James Hopwood Jeans

Democracy is ever eager for rapid progress, and the only progress which can be rapid is progress down hill.

Sir James Hopwood Jeans

A democracy is the most difficult kind of government to operate. It represents the last flowering, really, of the human experience.
John Fitzgerald Kennedy

We hold the view that the people come first, not the government.
John Fitzgerald Kennedy

Men have always found it easy to be governed. What is hard is for them to govern themselves.
Max Lerner

Of the many things we have done to democracy in the past, the worst has been the indignity of taking it for granted.
Max Lerner

We are threatened with the loss of the people's confidence, the very foundation of democratic government.
David Eli Lilienthal

A world of science and great machines is still a world of men; our modern task is more difficult, but the opportunity for democratic methods can be even greater than in the days of the ax and the hand loom.
David Eli Lilienthal

It is the most beautiful truth in morals that we have no such thing as a distinct or divided interest from our race. In their welfare is ours; and by choosing the broadest paths to effect their happiness, we choose the surest and shortest to our own.
Edward G. Bulwer-Lytton (Baron Lytton)

Democracy is the most demanding of all forms of government in terms of the energy, imagination and public spirit required of the individual.
George Catlett Marshall

The thing of capital importance for democracy is publicity—no underhand dealing but candor and integrity toward friend and foe alike.
Jan Garrigue Masaryk

You don't have a democracy. It's a photocracy.
Sir Robert Gordon Menzies

Democracy is a kingless regime infested by many kings who are sometimes more exclusive, tyrannical, and destructive than one, if he be a tyrant.
Benito Mussolini

Democracy does not simply mean shouting loudly and persistently, though that might occasionally have some value. Freedom and democracy require responsibility and certain standards of behaviour and self-discipline.
Jawaharlal Nehru

Democracy has many virtues, but one of its concomitants is wastage of time and energy.
Jawaharlal Nehru

Democracy, if it means anything, means equality; not merely the equality of possessing a vote, but economic and social equality.
Jawaharlal Nehru

Democracy is good. I say this because other systems are worse.
Jawaharlal Nehru

Parliamentary democracy demands many virtues. It demands, of course, ability. It demands a certain devotion to work. But it demands also a large measure of co-operation, of self-discipline, of restraint.
Jawaharlal Nehru

With all my admiration and love for democracy, I am not prepared to accept the statement that the largest number of people are always right.
Jawaharlal Nehru

You may define democracy in a hundred ways but surely one of its definitions is self-discipline of the community. The less the imposed discipline and the more the self-discipline, the higher is the development of democracy.
Jawaharlal Nehru

A Christian view of human nature is more adequate for the development of a democratic society than either the optimism with which democracy has become historically associated or the moral cynicism which inclines human communities to tyrannical political strategies.
Reinhold Niebuhr

Democracy . . . [is] a system of self-determination. It's the right to make the wrong choice.
John Patrick

Democracy is both the best and the most difficult form of political organization—the most difficult because it is the best.
Ralph Barton Perry

Lycurgus being asked why he, who in other respects appeared to be so zealous for the rights of men, did not make his government democratic rather than an oligarchy, replied, "Go you and try a democracy in your own house."

Plutarch

We will have to do anything, no matter what it takes to get democracy to work in one state before it can work in the rest of the country.

Eugene Clifton Reed

Democracy, the practice of self-government, is a covenant among free men to respect the rights and liberties of their fellows.

Franklin Delano Roosevelt

We must be the great arsenal of democracy.

Franklin Delano Roosevelt

If there were a people consisting of gods, they would be governed democratically. So perfect a government is not suitable to men.

Jean Jacques Rousseau

Envy is the basis of democracy.

Bertrand Arthur William Russell

In a democracy both deep reverence and a sense of the comic are requisite.

Carl Sandburg

Democracy has two excesses to avoid: the spirit of inequality, which leads it to aristocracy, or to the government of a single individual; and the spirit of extreme equality, which conducts it to despotism, as the despotism of a single individual finishes by conquest.

Charles de Secondat (Baron de Montesquieu)

It was a very fine sight, last century, to see the impotent efforts of the English to establish among them a democracy. As those who took part in public affairs had no principle, as their ambition was irritated by the success of Cromwell, who had been the most daring, as the spirit of one faction was only put down by the spirit of another, the government was in a constant state of change; the astonished people sought for democracy, and found it nowhere. After much violence, many shocks and storms, they found it necessary to fall back on the very government which they had proscribed.

Charles de Secondat (Baron de Montesquieu)

The love of the republic in a democracy is that of democracy; the love of democracy is that of equality. The love of democracy is also the love of frugality. Every one being obliged in it to have the same happiness, and the same advantages, ought to taste the same pleasures, and to form the same hopes; a thing which one can only expect from general frugality.

Charles de Secondat (Baron de Montesquieu)

The principle of democracy degenerates, not only when it loses the spirit of equality, but also when it takes to itself the spirit of extreme equality, and when every one wishes to be equal to those whom it has chosen to rule. For then, the people not being able to submit to the authority which it has conferred, wishes to do everything by its own hands, to deliberate for the senate, to execute for the magistrates, and to assume the power of the judges.

Charles de Secondat (Baron de Montesquieu)

Knowledge and goodness—these make degrees in heaven, and they must be the graduating scale of a true democracy.

Catharine Maria Sedgwick

All the ills of democracy can be cured by more democracy.

Alfred Emanuel Smith

I believe democracy to be of all forms of government the most natural, and the most consonant with individual liberty. In it no one transfers his natural right so absolutely that he has no further voice in affairs, he only hands it over to the majority of a society, whereof he is a unit. Thus all men remain, as they were in the state of nature, equals.

Baruch (Benedict) Spinoza

"It is a great blessing," says Pascal "to be born a man of quality, since it brings a man as far forward at eighteen or twenty as another would be at fifty, which is a clear gain of thirty years." These thirty years are commonly wanting to the ambitious characters of democracies. The principle of equality, which allows every man to arrive at everything, prevents all men from rapid advancement.

Alexis de Tocqueville

The progress of democracy seems irresistible, because it is the most uniform, the most ancient, and the most permanent tendency which is to be found in history.

Alexis de Tocqueville

In this critical time in the affairs of the world, it is vital that the democratic nations show their concern for the well-being of men everywhere and their desire for a better life for mankind.

Harry S Truman

The world must be made safe for democracy.

(Thomas) Woodrow Wilson

In art, democracy means that some thought of your own, some feeling you have about the thing yourself, should enter into everything you have to do, so that everything you have may be your own and everything you do be sincerely yourself.

Frank Lloyd Wright

The distinction between democracy and dictatorship tends to disappear during a war.

Frieda Wunderlich

The essential problem is how to govern a large-scale world with small-scale minds.

Sir Alfred Zimmern

See also: AMERICA, EQUALITY, LEVELER, LIBERTY, REPUBLIC.

DEMOCRATIC PARTY

The Democratic Party ain't on speaking terms with itself.

Finley Peter Dunne

I never said all Democrats were saloonkeepers; what I said was all saloonkeepers were Democrats.

Horace Greeley

They are troubadours of trouble and crooners of catastrophe.

Clare Boothe Luce

I don't buy the idea, and there is nothing in the record to sustain the idea that labor needs the Democratic Party. I am sure it is the other way around.

George Meany

I am here tonight as a delegate to this convention [Democratic National Convention, August, 15, 1956] because without prefix, without suffix and without apology, I am a Democrat.

Sam Rayburn

See also: PARTY, POLITICIAN, POLITICS, PRESIDENT, REPUBLICAN PARTY.

DEPENDENCE

In an arch, each single stone, which, if severed from the rest, would be perhaps defenceless, is sufficiently secured by the solidity and entireness of the whole fabric of which it is a part.

Robert Boyle

God has made no one absolute. The rich depend on the poor, as well as the poor on the rich. The world is but a magnificent building; all the stones are gradually cemented together. No one subsists by himself alone.

Owen Felltham

No degree of knowledge attainable by man is able to set him above the want of hourly assistance.

Samuel Johnson

Depend on no man, on no friend but him who can depend on himself. He only who acts conscientiously toward himself, will act so toward others.

Johann Kaspar Lavater

Those who lean too much on others tend to become weak and helpless themselves.

Jawaharlal Nehru

The more the individual ostensibly emerges from the community to establish his own independence and uniqueness, the more he becomes dependent upon a wider system of mutual services. Men have never been individually self-sufficient.

Reinhold Niebuhr

How beautifully is it ordered, that as many thousands work for one, so must every individual bring his labor to make the whole. The highest is not to despise the lowest, nor the lowest to envy the highest; each must live in all and by all. So God has ordered, that men, being in need of each other, should learn to love each other, and to bear each other's burdens.

George Augustus Henry Sala

There is none so great but he may both need the help and service, and stand in fear of the power and unkindness, even of the meanest of mortals.

Seneca

The beautiful must ever rest in the arms of the sublime. The gentle need the strong to sustain it, as much as the rock-flowers need rocks to grow on, or the ivy the rugged wall which it embraces.

Harriet Elizabeth Beecher Stowe

The acknowledgment of weakness which we make in imploring to be relieved from hunger and from temptation, is surely wisely put in our prayer. Think of it, you who are rich, and take heed how you turn a beggar away.

William Makepeace Thackeray

Dependence is a perpetual call upon humanity, and a greater incitement to tenderness and pity than any other motive whatever.

William Makepeace Thackeray

Heaven's eternal wisdom has decreed, that man should ever stand in need of man.

Theocritus

See also: FREEDOM, INDEPENDENCE, POVERTY, SERVANT, SLAVERY.

DEPRAVITY

It is not occasionally that the human soul is under the influence of depravity; but this is its habit and state till the soul is renewed by grace.

Thomas Dick

Men sometimes affect to deny the depravity of our race; but it is as clearly taught in the lawyers' office and in courts of justice, as in the Bible itself. Every prison, and fetter, and scaffold, and bolt, and bar, and chain is evidence that man believes in the depravity of man.

Tryon Edwards

Every man has his devilish moments.

Johann Kaspar Lavater

Original sin is in us, like the beard. We are shaved to-day and look clean, and have a smooth chin; to-morrow our beard has grown again, nor does it cease growing while we remain on earth. In like manner original sin cannot be extirpated from us; it springs up in us as long as we live. Nevertheless we are bound to resist it to our utmost strength, and to cut it down unceasingly.

Martin Luther

We are all sinful; and whatever one of us blames in another each one will find in his

Seneca

See also: BASENESS, MEANESS, MORALITY, VICE.

DEPRESSION

The times are not so bad as they seem; they couldn't be.

John Franklin Carter

Depressions may bring people closer to the church—but so do funerals.

Clarence Seward Darrow

A too exclusive concern with the ideas of little men has brought statesmanship virtually to a standstill. A too exclusive concern with the interests of big men has stalled the economic machine.

Glenn Frank

See also: ADVERSITY, DESPAIR, MELANCHOLY, NEUROSIS, PANIC, POVERTY, SUICIDE.

DESIRE

It should be an indispensable rule in life to contract our desires to our present condition, and whatever may be our expectations to live within the compass of what we actually possess. It will be time enough to enjoy an estate when it comes into our hands; but if we anticipate our good fortune we shall lose the pleasure of it when it arrives, and may possibly never possess what we have so foolishly counted on.

Joseph Addison

When a man's desires are boundless, his labors are endless. They will set him a task he can never go through, and cut him out work he can never finish. The satisfaction he seeks is always absent, and the happiness he aims at is ever at a distance.

John Balguy

We trifle when we assign limits to our desires, since nature hath set none.

Christian Nestell Bovee

Nothing is far and nothing is dear, if one desires. The world is little, human life is little. There is only one big thing—desire. And before it, when it is big, all is little.

Willa Sibert Cather

The thirst of desire is never filled, nor fully satisfied.

Cicero

There is nothing capricious in nature; and the implanting of a desire indicates that its gratification is in the constitution of the creature that feels it.

Ralph Waldo Emerson

Everyone would have something, such perhaps as we are ashamed to utter. The proud man would have honor; the covetous man, wealth and abundance; the malicious, revenge on his enemies; the epicure, pleasure and long life; the barren, children; the wanton, beauty; each would be humored in his own desire, though in opposition both to God's will, and his own good.

Joseph Hall

In moderating, not in satisfying desires, lies peace.

Reginald Heber

By annihilating the desires, you annihilate the mind. Every man without passions has within him no principle of action, nor motive to act.

Claude Adrien Helvetius

Our nature is inseparable from desires, and the very word desire—the craving for something not possessed—implies that our present felicity is not complete.

Thomas Hobbes

However rich or elevated we may be, a nameless something is always wanting to our imperfect fortune.

Horace

Every desire bears its death in its very gratification. Curiosity languishes under repeated stimulants, and novelties cease to excite surprise, until at length we do not wonder even at a miracle.

Washington Irving

Some desire is necessary to keep life in motion; he whose real wants are supplied, must admit those of fancy.

Samuel Johnson

Where necessity ends, desire and curiosity begin; no sooner are we supplied with everything nature can demand, than we sit down to contrive artificial appetites.

Samuel Johnson

The soul of man is infinite in what it covets.

Ben (Benjamin) Jonson

What man knows is everywhere at war with what he wants.

Joseph Wood Krutch

He who can wait for what he desires takes the course not to be exceedingly grieved if

he fails of it; he on the contrary who labors after a thing too impatiently thinks the success when it comes is not a recompense equal to all the pains he has been at about it.

Jean de La Bruyére

Before we passionately desire anything which another enjoys, we should examine as to the happiness of its possessor.

Duc François de La Rochefoucauld

It is much easier to suppress a first desire than to satisfy those that follow.

Duc François de La Rochefoucauld

Desires are the pulses of the soul; as physicians judge by the appetite, so may you by desires.

Thomas Manton

There are two tragedies in life. One is not to get your heart's desire. The other is to get it.

George Bernard Shaw

Desire is the essence of a man.

Baruch (Benedict) Spinoza

The stoical schemes of supplying our wants by lopping off our desires, is like cutting off our feet when we want shoes.

Jonathan Swift

Sometimes the Devil proposes to us great desires, so that we shall not put our hand to what we have to do, and serve our Lord in possible things, but stay content with having desired impossible ones.

Theresa of Jesus (Teresa de Avila)

What you can't acquire, don't desire.

Yiddish Proverb

See also: AMBITION, APPETITE, COVETOUSNESS, INCLINATION, LOVE, LUST, WISH.

DESOLATION

What is the worst of woes that wait on age? What stamps the wrinkle deeper on the brow? To view each loved one blotted from life's page, and be alone on earth.

George Gordon Byron (Lord Byron)

No soul is desolate as long as there is a human being for whom it can feel trust and reverence.

George Eliot (Mary Ann Evans)

No one is so utterly desolate, but some heart, though unknown, responds unto his own.
Henry Wadsworth Longfellow

Unhappy he, who from the first of joys—society—cut off, is left alone, amid this world of death!
James Thomson

See also: EMPTINESS, MISERY, POVERTY, RUINS.

DESPAIR

Now Giant Despair had a wife, and her name was Diffidence.
John Bunyan

Despair is like forward children, who, when you take away one of their playthings, throw the rest into the fire for madness. It grows angry with itself, turns its own executioner, and revenges its misfortunes on its own head.
Pierre Charron

Despair gives courage to the weak. Resolved to die, he fears no more, but rushes on his foes, and deals his deaths around.
Jeremy Collier

Beware of desperate steps. The darkest day, live till to-morrow, will have passed away.
William Cowper

Despair is the conclusion of fools.
Benjamin Disraeli

Despair is the damp of hell, as joy is the serenity of heaven.
John Donne

It is possible, even probable, that hopelessness among a people can be a far more potent cause of war than greed. War—in such case—is a symptom, not the disease.
Dwight David Eisenhower

What we call despair is often only the painful eagerness of unfed hope.
George Eliot (Mary Ann Evans)

He that despairs degrades the Deity, and seems to intimate that He is insufficient, or not just to his word; in vain hath he read the Scriptures, the world, and man.
Owen Felltham

Considering the unforeseen events of this world, we should be taught that no human condition should inspire men with absolute despair.
Henry Fielding

Religion converts despair, which destroys, into resignation, which submits.
Marguerite Gardiner (Lady Blessington)

Despair gives the shocking ease to the mind that mortification gives to the body.
Fulke Greville (First Baron Brooke)

The worst poison: to despair of one's own power!
Heinrich Heine

A drowning man will catch at any rope.
Maimonides

Despair is the absolute extreme of self-love. It is reached when a man deliberately turns his back on all help from anyone else in order to taste the rotten luxury of knowing himself to be lost.
Thomas Merton

He who despairs wants love and faith, for faith, hope, and love are three torches which blend their light together, nor does the one shine without the other.
Metastasio

If after all that we have lived and thought,
All come to Nought—
If there be nothing after Now,
And we be nothing anyhow,
And we know that—why live?
'Twere sure but weaklings' vain distress
To suffer dungeons where so many doors
Will open on the cold eternal shores
That look sheer down
To the dark tideless floods of Nothingness
Where all who know may drown.
Edwin Arlington Robinson

He that despairs measures Providence by his own little contracted model and limits infinite power to finite apprehensions.
Robert South

The fact that God has prohibited despair gives misfortune the right to hope all things, and leaves hope free to dare all things.
Anne Sophie Swetchine

It is impossible for that man to despair who remembers that his Helper is omnipotent.
Jeremy Taylor

See also: DEPRESSION, DESPONDENCE, DISAPPOINTMENT, GHETTO, HOPE, MELANCHOLY, POVERTY, SADNESS, SORROW, SUICIDE.

DESPONDENCY

Despondency is ingratitude; hope is God's worship.

Henry Ward Beecher

To believe a business impossible is the way to make it so. How many feasible projects have miscarried through despondency, and been strangled in their birth by a cowardly imagination.

Jeremy Collier

Despondency is not a state of humility. On the contrary, it is the vexation and despair of a cowardly pride; nothing is worse. Whether we stumble, or whether we fall, we must only think of rising again and going on in our course.

François de Salignac de La Mothe-Fénelon

Some persons depress their own minds, despond at the first difficulty, and conclude that making any progress in knowledge, further than serves their ordinary business, is above their capacity.

John Locke

Life is a warfare; and he who easily desponds deserts a double duty—he betrays the noblest property of man, which is dauntless resolution; and he rejects the providence of that all-gracious Being who guides and rules the universe.

Jane Porter

To despond is to be ungrateful beforehand. Be not looking for evil. Often thou drainest the gall of fear while evil is passing by thy dwelling.

Martin Farquhar Tupper

See also: DESPAIR

DESPOTISM

It is odd to consider the connection between despotism and barbarity, and how the making one person more than man makes the rest less.

Joseph Addison

All despotisms, under whatever name they masquerade, are efforts to freeze history, to stop change, to solidify the human spirit.

Charles Austin Beard

There is only one way by which a despotism can be altered, that is by revolution, by the kind of violence employed in its establishment.

Charles Austin Beard

Despots govern by terror. They know that he who fears God fears nothing else, and therefore they eradicate from the mind, through their Voltaire and Helvetius, and the rest of that infamous gang, that only sort of fear which generates true courage.

Edmund Burke

Despotism can no more exist in a nation until the liberty of the press be destroyed, than the night can happen before the sun is set.

Charles Caleb Colton

The arguments for the limitation and decentralization of power remain valid, even when that power is concentrated in the hands of an oligarchy of socialists. . . . It is just benevolent despotism; and there is nothing in the record of history to justify us in the belief that any benevolent despotism will for long retain its benevolence.

Aldous Leonard Huxley

All depotism is bad; but the worst is that which works with the machinery of freedom.

Junius

In times of anarchy one may seem a despot in order to be a savior.

Honoré Riqueti (Comte de Mirabeau)

As virtue is necessary in a republic, and honor in a monarchy, fear is what is required in a despotism. As for virtue, it is not at all necessary, and honor would be dangerous there.

Charles de Secondat (Baron de Montesquieu)

When the savages wish to have fruit they cut down the tree and gather it. That is exactly a despotic government.

Charles de Secondat (Baron de Montesquieu)

I will believe in the right of one man to govern a nation despotically when I find a man born into the world with boots and spurs, and a nation born with saddles on their backs.

Algernon Sidney

There is something among men more capable of shaking despotic power than lightning, whirlwind, or earthquake; that is the threatened indignation of the whole civilized world.

Daniel Webster

See also: DICTATOR, DISSENT, NAZISM, OPPRESSION, SLAVERY, TYRANNY.

DESTINY

Destiny is the scapegoat which we make responsible for all our crimes and follies; a

necessity which we set down for invincible when we have no wish to strive against it.
Arthur James Balfour

Destiny is not a matter of chance, it is a matter of choice; it is not a thing to be waited for, it is a thing to be achieved.
William Jennings Bryan

Death and life have their determined appointments; riches and honors depend upon heaven.
Confucius

I do not mean to expose my ideas to ingenious ridicule by maintaining that everything happens to every man for the best; but I will contend, that he who makes the best use of it, fulfills the part of a wise and good man.
Richard Cumberland

We make our fortunes, and we call them fate.
Benjamin Disraeli

Thoughts lead on to purposes; purposes go forth in action; actions form habits; habits decide character; and character fixes our destiny.
Tryon Edwards

Destiny waits in the hand of God, shaping the still unshapen . . .
Destiny waits in the hand of God, not in the hands of statesmen
Who do, some well, some ill, planning and guessing,
Having their aims which turn in their hands in the patter of time.
Thomas Stearns Eliot

Men heap together the mistakes of their lives, and create a monster they call Destiny.
John Oliver Hobbes

No man of woman born, coward or brave, can shun his destiny.
Homer

Lots of folks confuse bad management with destiny.
Frank McKinney (Kin) Hubbard

Our future may lie beyond our vision, but it is not completely beyond our control. It is the shaping impulse of America that neither faith nor nature nor the irresistible tides of history but the work of our own hands matched to reason and principle will determine our destiny.
Robert Francis Kennedy

That which God writes on thy forehead, thou wilt come to it.
Koran

Destiny is but a phrase of the weak human heart—the dark apology for every error. The strong and virtuous admit no destiny. On earth conscience guides; in heaven God watches. And destiny is but the phantom we invoke to silence the one and dethrone the other.
Edward G. Bulwer-Lytton (Baron Lytton)

There is a destiny that makes us brothers—none goes his way alone.
(Charles) Edwin Markham

The acts of this life are the destiny of the next.
Oriental Proverb

Things do not happen because God foresees them in the distant future; but because they will happen, God knows them before they happen.
Origen

The clew of our destiny, wander where we will, lies at the cradle foot.
Jean Paul Richter

That which is not allotted the hand cannot reach; and what is allotted you will find wherever you may be.
Saadi (Muslih-ud-Din)

Nothing comes to pass but what God appoints. Our fate is decreed, and things do not happen by chance, but every man's portion of joy or sorrow is predetermined.
Seneca

Destiny is an invention of the cowardly and the resigned.
Ignazio Silone

Man proposes, but God disposes.
Thomas à Kempis

Philosophers never stood in need of Homer or the Pharisees to be convinced that everything is done by immutable laws; that everything is settled; that everything is the necessary effect of some previous cause.
Voltaire (François Marie Arouet)

If a man is destined to drown, he will drown even in a spoonful of water.
Yiddish Proverb

See also: ASTROLOGY, CHANCE, FATE, FORTUNE, GOD.

DESTRUCTION

All destruction has by no means been followed by rejuvenation, and the great destroyers of life remain an enigma to us.

Jakob Burckhardt

A man may devote himself to death and destruction to save a nation; but no nation will devote itself to death and destruction to save mankind.

Samuel Taylor Coleridge

It is possible to make a garden into a wilderness quickly; but it is not easy to re-convert the wilderness into a garden.

Jawaharlal Nehru

When man, that master of destruction, of self-destruction, wounds himself, it is the wound itself that forces him to live.

Friedrich Wilhelm Nietzsche

See also: AGGRESSION, CONTENTION, NUCLEAR WARFARE, RUINS, WAR, WIND.

DETERMINATION

One never can achieve anything lasting in this world by being irresolute.

Mohandas Karamchand (Mahatma) Gandhi

What faith can you place in a general or a soldier who lacks resolution and determination, and who says, "I shall keep guard as long as I can"?

Mohandas Karamchand (Mahatma) Gandhi

There is no road too long to the man who advances deliberately and without undue haste; there are no honours too distant to the man who prepares himself for them with patience.

Jean de La Bruyère

See also: DECISION, DIFFICULTY, RESOLUTION, SUCCESS, WILL.

DETERMINISM

I do not believe we can have any freedom at all in the philosophical sense, for we act not only under external compulsion but also by inner necessity.

Albert Einstein

Ultimately a man sets the measure of his own freedom and his own bondage by the level at which he chooses to establish his convictions. The man who orders his life in terms of many special and unflexible convictions about temporary matters makes himself the victim of circumstances. Each little prior conviction that is not open to review is a hostage he gives to fortune; it determines whether the events of tomorrow will bring happiness or misery. The man whose prior convictions encompass a broad perspective, and are cast in terms of principles rather than rules, has a much better chance of discovering those alternatives which will lead eventually to his emancipation.

George A. Kelly

In our own nature there are more singular points—where prediction, except from absolutely perfect data and guided by the omniscience of contingency, becomes impossible—than there are in any lower organisation. But singular points are by their very nature isolated, and from no appreciable fraction of the continuous course of our existence. Hence predictions of human conduct may be made in many cases. First, with respect to those who have no character at all, especially when considered in crowds, after the statistical method. Second, with respect to individuals of confirmed character, with respect to actions of the kind for which their character is confirmed.

James Clerk Maxwell

See also: FREEDOM, WILL.

DETRACTION

Whoever feels pain in hearing a good character of his neighbor, will feel pleasure in the reverse; and those who despair to rise to distinction by their virtues are happy if others can be depressed to a level with themselves.

John Marshall Barker

To make beads of the faults of others, and tell them over every day, is infernal. If you want to know how devils feel, you do know if you are such an one.

Henry Ward Beecher

If we considered detraction to be bred of envy, and nested only in deficient minds, we should find that the applauding of virtue would win us far more honor than seeking to disparage it. That would show we loved what we commended, while this tells the world we grudge at what we want ourselves.

Owen Felltham

In some dispositions there is such an envious kind of pride that they cannot endure that any but themselves should be set forth for excellent; so that when they hear one justly praised, they will either seek to dismount his virtues, or if they be like a clear light, they will stab him with a "but" of detraction.

Owen Felltham

Unjustifiable detraction always proves the weakness as well as meanness of the one who employs it. To be constantly carping at, and exaggerating petty blemishes in the characters of others putting an unfavorable construction on their language, or "damning with faint praise" their deeds, betrays, on the part of the detractor, a conscious inability to maintain a reputable standing on legitimate and honorable ground.

Elias Lyman Magoon

We are likely to believe the worst about another because the capacity for evil is so pronounced in ourselves.

Louis Nizer

I take it as a matter not to be disputed, that if all knew what each said of the other, there would not be four friends in the world. This seems proved by the quarrels and disputes caused by the disclosures which are occasionally made.

Blaise Pascal

The world is full of wooden people who are always doing their best to whittle others down.

Puzant Kevork Thomajan

There is no readier way for a man to bring his own worth into question, than by endeavoring to detract from the worth of other men.

John Tillotson

The man that makes a character, makes foes.

Edward Young.

See also: BABBLE, CALUMNY, GOSSIP, SLANDER.

DEVIATION

Ah! to what gulfs a single deviation from the track of human duties leads!

George Gordon Byron (Lord Byron)

Deviation from either truth or duty is a downward path, and none can say where the descent will end.—"He that despiseth small things shall fall by little and little."

Tryon Edwards

When people once begin to deviate, they do not know where to stop.

George III

See also: COMPROMISE, INCONSTANCY, INSTABILITY, NONCONFORMITY.

DEVIL

The devil is no idle spirit, but a vagrant, runagate walker, that never rests in one place. The motive, cause, and main intention of his walking is to ruin man.

Thomas Adams

Talk of devils being confined to hell, or hidden by invisibility! We have them by shoals in the crowded towns and cities of the world. Talk of raising the devil! What need for that, when he is constantly walking to and fro in our streets, seeking whom he may devour.

Anonymous

The devil knoweth his own, and is a particular bad paymaster.

Francis Marion Crawford

I think that if the devil doesn't exist, but man has created him, he has created him in his own image and likeness.

Fëdor Mikhailovich Dostoevski

The devil has at least one good quality, that he will flee if we resist him. Though cowardly in him, it is safety for us.

Tryon Edwards

No sooner is a temple built to God, but the devil builds a chapel hard by.

George Herbert

The Devil and me, we don't agree;
I hate him; and he hates me.

Salvation Army Hymn

He who would fight the devil with his own weapons, must not wonder if he finds him an overmatch.

Robert South

As no good is done, or spoken, or thought by any man without the assistance of God, working in and with those that believe in him, so there is no evil done, or spoken, or thought without the assistance of the devil, who worketh with strong though secret power in the children of unbelief. All the works of our evil nature are the work of the devil.

John Wesley

See also: ANGEL, GOD, HELL.

DEVOTION

It is of the utmost importance to season the passions of the young with devotion, which seldom dies in the mind that has received an early tincture of it. Though it may seem extinguished for a while by the cares of the world, the heats of youth, or the allurements of vice, it generally breaks out and discovers itself again as soon as discretion, consideration, age, or misfortunes have brought the man to himself. The fire may be covered and overlaid but cannot be entirely quenched and smothered.

Joseph Addison

The inward sighs of humble penitence rise to the ear of heaven, when pealed hymns are scattered to the common air.

Joanna Baillie

The best and sweetest flowers in paradise, God gives to his people when they are on their knees in the closet. Prayer, if not the very gate of heaven, is the key to let us into its holiness and joys.

Thomas Brooks

Solid devotions resemble the rivers which run under the earth—they steal from the eyes of the world to seek the eyes of God; and it often happens that those of whom we speak least on earth, are best known in heaven.

Nicolas Caussin

All the duties of religion are eminently solemn and venerable in the eyes of children. But none will so strongly prove the sincerity of the parent; none so powerfully awaken the reverence of the child; none so happily recommend the instruction he receives, as family devotions, particularly those in which petitions for the children occupy a distinguished place.

John Sullivan Dwight

Satan rocks the cradle when we sleep at our devotions.

Joseph Hall

All is holy where devotion kneels.

Oliver Wendell Holmes

The most illiterate man who is touched with devotion, and uses frequent exercises of it, contracts a certain greatness of mind, mingled with a noble simplicity, that raises him above others of the same condition. By this, a man in the lowest condition will not appear mean, or in the most splendid fortune insolent.

Samuel Johnson

The secret heart is devotion's temple; there the saint lights the flame of purest sacrifice, which burns unseen but not unaccepted.

Hannah More

The private devotions and secret offices of religion are like the refreshing of a garden with the distilling and petty drops of a water-pot; but addressed from the temple, they are like rain from heaven.

Jeremy Taylor

See also: AFFECTION, FIDELITY, HATE, LOVE, PIETY, WORSHIP.

DEW

Dew-drops—nature's tears, which she sheds on her own breast for the fair which die. The sun insists on gladness; but at night, when he is gone, poor nature loves to weep.

Gamaliel Bailey

Earth's liquid jewelry, wrought of the air.

Gamaliel Bailey

Dew-drops are the gems of morning, but the tears of mournful eye.

Samuel Taylor Coleridge

Stars of the morning—dew drops—which the sun impearls on every leaf and flower.

John Milton

The dews of evening—those tears of the sky for the loss of the sun.

Philip Dormer Stanhope (Lord Chesterfield)

See also: MORNING, NIGHT, RAIN.

DICE

I look upon every man as a suicide from the moment he takes the dice-box desperately in his hand; all that follows in his career from that fatal time is only sharpening the dagger before he strikes it to his heart.

Richard Cumberland

I never hear the rattling of dice that it does not sound to me like the funeral bell of the whole family.

Douglas William Jerrold

The best throw with the dice, is to throw them away.

Proverb

See also: CARDS, CHANCE, FORTUNE, GAMBLING, LUCK, WAGER.

DICTATOR

Photographers are the only dictators in America.

Mahmut Celâl Bayar

Dictators ride to and fro upon tigers which they dare not dismount. And the tigers are getting hungry.

Sir Winston Leonard Spencer Churchill

Dictators are born when a nation's people are desperate, when self-government breaks down. They are avoided when government meets its responsibilities efficiently.

Raymond Clapper

Dictatorships usually present a formidable exterior. They seem, on the outside, to be hard, glittering, and irresistible. Within, they are full of rottenness.

John Foster Dulles

The appetite for power of a dictator always grows with its use: it is never satisfied; it cannot brook any opposition.

Jawaharlal Nehru

A dictator can be very thorough, especially if he happens to be popular.

Jawaharlal Nehru

No dictator in history has ever dared to run the gauntlet of a really free election.

Franklin Delano Roosevelt

In your dread of dictators you established a state of society in which every ward boss is a dictator, every financier a dictator, every private employer a dictator, all with the livelihood of the workers at their mercy, and no public responsibility.

George Bernard Shaw

See also: DEMOCRACY, DESPOTISM, OPPRESSION, TYRANNY.

DIET

One meal a day is enough for a lion, and it ought to be for a man.

George Fordyce

In general, mankind, since the improvement of cookery, eat twice as much as nature requires.

Benjamin Franklin

Vegetarianism is harmless enough, although it is apt to fill a man with wind and self-righteousness.

Sir Robert Hutchison

Simple diet is best; for many dishes bring many diseases; and rich sauces are worse than even heaping several meats upon each other.

Pliny the Elder

If thou wouldst preserve a sound body, use fasting and walking; if a healthful soul, fasting and praying. Walking exercises the body; praying exercises the soul; fasting cleanses both.

Francis Quarles

A fig for your bill of fare; show me your bill of company.

Jonathan Swift

Regimen is better than physic. Every one should be his own physician. We should assist, not force nature. Eat with moderation what you know by experience agrees with your constitution. Nothing is good for the body but what we can digest. What can procure digestion? Exercise. What will recruit strength? Sleep. What will alleviate incurable evils? Patience.

Voltaire (François Marie Arouet)

See also: BREAKFAST, COOKING, DINNER, EATING, FEASTING, VEGETARIANISM.

DIFFERENCE

If men would consider not so much wherein they differ, as wherein they agree, there would be far less of uncharitableness and angry feeling in the world.

Joseph Addison

Diversity in the Creed, Unanimity in the Deed.

Felix Adler

The difference is no less real because it is of degree.

Benjamin Nathan Cardozo

Oh, it's strange, isn't it,
That as one gets to know a person better
One finds them in some ways very like oneself
In unexpected ways. And then you begin
To discover differences inside the likeness.

Thomas Stearns Eliot

Even differences prove helpful, where there are tolerance, charity and truth.

Mohandas Karamchand (Mahatma) Gandhi

Honest differences are often a healthy sign of progress.

Mohandas Karamchand (Mahatma) Gandhi

It is not our differences that really matter.
It is the meanness behind, that is ugly.
Mohandas Karamchand (Mahatma) Gandhi

Our besetting sin is not difference, but our littleness.
Mohandas Karamchand (Mahatma) Gandhi

That among all the differences which exist, the only ones which interest us strongly are those we do not take for granted.
William James

It is only those who have no culture and no belief in culture who resent differences among men and the exploration of the human imagination.
Alfred Kazin

In all differences consider that both you and your opponent or enemy are mortal, and that ere long your very memories will be extinguished.
Aurélie de Faucamberge (Aurel) Mortier

See also: ARGUMENT, CONTROVERSY, FACTION, OPPOSITION, QUARREL.

DIFFICULTY

The best way out of a difficulty is through it.
Anonymous

Difficulties are God's errands; and when we are sent upon them we should esteem it a proof of God's confidence—as a compliment from him.
Henry Ward Beecher

Difficulty is a severe instructor, set over us by the Supreme guardian and legislator, who knows us better than we know ourselves, and loves us better too. He that wrestles with us strengthens our nerves and sharpens our skill. Our antagonist is our helper.
Edmund Burke

Difficulties show men what they are. In case of any difficulty God has pitted you against a rough antagonist that you may be a conqueror, and this cannot be without toil.
Epictetus

The greatest difficulties lie where we are not looking for them.
Johann Wolfgang von Goethe

Our energy is in proportion to the resistance it meets. We attempt nothing great but from

a sense of difficulties we have to encounter; we persevere in nothing great but from a pride in overcoming them.
William Hazlitt

It cannot be too often repeated that it is not helps, but obstacles, not facilities, but difficulties that make men.
William Mathews

The greater the obstacle, the more glory we have in overcoming it; the difficulties with which we are met are the maids of honor which set off virtue.
Moliére (Jean Baptiste Poquelin)

Life would be dull and colourless but for the obstacles that we have to overcome and the fights that we have to win.
Jawaharlal Nehru

There are difficulties in your path. Be thankful for them. They will test your capabilities of resistance; you will be impelled to persevere from the very energy of the opposition. But what of him that fails? What does he gain? Strength for life. The real merit is not in the success but in the endeavor; and win or lose, he will be honored and crowned.
William Morley Punshon

What is required of us is that we *love the difficult* and learn to deal with it. In the difficult are the friendly forces, the hands that work on us.
Rainer Maria Rilke

Difficulties strengthen the mind, as labor does the body.
Seneca

No man who is occupied in doing a very difficult thing, and doing it very well, ever loses his self-respect.
George Bernard Shaw

What is difficulty? Only a word indicating the degree of strength requisite for accomplishing particular objects; a mere notice of the necessity for exertion; a bugbear to children and fools; only a stimulus to men.
Samuel Warren

See also: ADVERSITY, DETERMINATION, HARDSHIP, SIMPLICITY, TROUBLE.

DIFFIDENCE

Diffidence may check resolution, and obstruct performance, but it compensates its embarrassments by more important advantages. It conciliates the proud, and softens the severe; averts envy from excellence, and censure from miscarriage.

Samuel Johnson

Nothing sinks a young man into low company, both of men and women, so surely as timidity and diffidence of himself. If he thinks he shall not please, he may depend upon it that he will not. But with proper endeavors to please, and a degree of persuasion that he shall, it is almost certain that he will.

Philip Dormer Stanhope (Lord Chesterfield)

We are as often duped by diffidence as by confidence.

Philip Dormer Stanhope (Lord Chesterfield)

See also: BASHFULNESS, BLUSH, MEEKNESS.

DIGNITY

When nothing is permitted to retain dignity, nothing retains for long the allegiance of man.

Herbert Sebastian Agar

Dignity consists not in possessing honors, but in the consciousness that we deserve them.

Aristotle

Dignity of position adds to dignity of character, as well as to dignity of carriage. Give us a proud position, and we are impelled to act up to it.

Christian Nestell Bovee

Dignity is like a top hat. Neither is very much use when you are standing on it.

Christopher Hollis

True dignity is never gained by place, and never lost when honors are withdrawn.

Philip Massinger

Dignity and love do not blend well, nor do they continue long together.

Ovid

Most of the men of dignity, who awe or bore their more genial brethren, are simply men who possess the art of passing off their insensibility for wisdom, their dullness for depth, and of concealing imbecility of intellect under haughtiness of manner.

Edwin Percy Whipple

See also: HONOR, PRIDE, RIGHTS, WORK.

DILIGENCE

The expectations of life depend upon diligence; the mechanic that would perfect his work must first sharpen his tools.

Confucius

Diligence is the mother of good luck, and God gives all things to industry. Work while it is called to-day, for you know not how much you may be hindered to-morrow. One to-day is worth two to-morrows; never leave that till to-morrow which you can do to-day.

Benjamin Franklin

What we hope ever to do with ease, we must learn first to do with diligence.

Samuel Johnson

Who makes quick use of the moment, is a genius of prudence.

Johann Kaspar Lavater

He who labors diligently need never despair; for all things are accomplished by diligence and labor.

Menander of Athens

See also: EFFORT, INDUSTRY, LABOR, PERSEVERANCE, WORK.

DINNER

A good dinner sharpens wit, while it softens the heart.

John Doran

Before dinner, men meet with great inequality of understanding, and those who are conscious of their inferiority have the modesty not to talk: when they have drunk wine, every man feels himself happy, and loses that modesty, and grows impudent and vociferous; but he is not improved; he is only not sensible of his defects.

Samuel Johnson

A dinner lubricates business.

William Scott (Baron Stowell)

See also: BREAKFAST, DIET, EATING.

DIPLOMACY

When a diplomat says yes he means perhaps; when he says perhaps he means no; when he says no he is no diplomat.

Anonymous

I have discovered the art of deceiving diplomats. I speak the truth, and they never believe me.

Conte Camillo Benso di Cavour

I never refuse. I never contradict. I sometimes forget.

Benjamin Disraeli

When the world thermometer registers, "not war, not peace," it is hard to decide whether to follow military judgments or political judgments.

John Foster Dulles

Modern diplomats approach every problem with an open mouth.

Arthur J. Goldberg

Governments are quite familiar with the process of sending inaccurate messages to each other.

David Dean Rusk

High in the art of living comes the wisdom of never letting anyone do anything for you until he so longs to do it that you know he is doing it with real joy.

David Seabury

See also: DISCRETION, GOVERNMENT, POLITICS, JUDGMENT, TACT.

DIRT

"Ignorance," says Ajax, "is a painless evil." So, I should think, is dirt, considering the merry faces that go along with it.

George Eliot (Mary Ann Evans)

If dirt was trumps, what hands you would hold!

Charles Lamb

Dirt is not dirt, but only something in the wrong place.

Henry John Temple (Viscount Palmerston)

See also: AIR POLLUTION, DISEASE, IMPURITY, SCANDAL, WATER POLLUTION.

DISAPPOINTMENT

We mount to heaven mostly on the ruins of our cherished schemes, finding our failures were successes.

Amos Bronson Alcott

The best enjoyment is half disappointment to what we intend or would have in this world.

Gamaliel Bailey

It is sometimes of God's mercy that men in the eager pursuit of worldy aggrandizement are baffled; for they are very like a train going down an inclined plane—putting on the brake

is not pleasant, but it keeps the car on the track and from ruin.

Henry Ward Beecher

The disappointment of manhood succeeds to the delusion of youth.

Benjamin Disraeli

In the light of eternity we shall see that what we desired would have been fatal to us, and that what we would have avoided was essential to our well-being.

François de Salignac de La Mothe-Fénelon

An old man once said, "When I was young, I was poor; when old, I became rich; but in each condition I found disappointment. When I had the faculties for enjoyment, I had not the means; when the means came, the faculties were gone."

Comtesse de Gasparin

He who expects much will be often disappointed; yet disappointment seldom cures us of expectation, or has any other effect than that of producing a moral sentence or peevish exclamation.

Samuel Johnson

How disappointment tracks the steps of hope.

Letitia Elizabeth Landon

Man must be disappointed with the lesser things of life before he can comprehend the full value of the greater.

Edward G. Bulwer-Lytton (Baron Lytton)

There is many a thing which the world calls disappointment, but there is no such a word in the dictionary of faith. What to others are disappointments are to believers intimations of the way of God.

John Newton

Means spirits under disappointment, like small beer in a thunder-storm, always turn sour.

John Randolph

See also: DEFEAT, DESPONDENCY, FAILURE.

DISARMAMENT

There is no more dangerous misconception than this which misconstrues the arms race as the cause rather than a symptom of the tensions and divisions which threaten nuclear war. If the history of the past fifty years teaches us anything, it is that peace does not follow disarmament—disarmament follows peace.

Bernard Mannes Baruch

We have the duty to slow down the arms race between us, in both conventional and nuclear weapons and defenses. Any additional race would impose on our peoples, and on all mankind, an additional waste of resources with no gain in security to either side.

Lyndon Baines Johnson

Moral disarmament is to safe-guard the future; material disarmament is to save the present, that there may be a future to safeguard.

Elihu Root

See also: NUCLEAR WARFARE, PEACE, TREATY.

DISCERNMENT

Perspicuity is the framework of profound thoughts.

Luc de Clapiers (Marquis de Vauvenargues)

The idiot, the Indian, the child, and the unschooled farmer's boy stand nearer to the light by which nature is to be read, than the dissector or the antiquary.

Ralph Waldo Emerson

After a spirit of discernment, the next rarest things in the world are diamonds and pearls.

Jean de La Bruyère

Penetration or discernment has an air of divination; it pleases our vanity more than any other quality of the mind.

Duc François de La Rochefoucauld

To succeed in the world, it is much more necessary to possess the penetration to discern who is a fool, than to discover who is a clever man.

Alexandre de Talleyrand-Périgord

See also: COMMON SENSE, DISCRETION, INTELLIGENCE, UNDERSTANDING, WISDOM.

DISCIPLINE

In the order named, these are the hardest to control: Wine, Women and Song.

Franklin Pierce Adams

A man in old age is like a sword in a shop window. Men that look upon the perfect blade do not imagine the process by which it was completed. Man is a sword; daily life is the workshop; and God is the artificer; and

those cares which beat upon the anvil, and file the edge, and eat in, acid-like, the inscription on the hilt—those are the very things that fashion the man.

Henry Ward Beecher

The discipline which corrects the baseness of worldy passions, fortifies the heart with virtuous principles, enlightens the mind with useful knowledge, and furnishes it with enjoyment from within itself, is of more consequence to real felicity, than all the provisions we can make of the goods of fortune.

Hugh Blair

Of course it is essential that the authority of officers in the military service be preserved. That's the reason they have set rules for the method of communication between privates and higher officers. For, believe me, if there were too much rubbing of elbows between officers and men it would soon be discovered that there were many captains who should be in shirt sleeves and many men in shirt sleeves who should be captains.

Charles Gates Dawes

Discipline is learnt in the school of adversity.

Mohandas Karamchand (Mahatma) Gandhi

A disciplined army of a few hundred picked men has, time without number, routed countless undisciplined hordes.

Mohandas Karamchand (Mahatma) Gandhi

If boys and girls do not learn discipline in their schooldays, money and time spent on their education is so much national loss.

Mohandas Karamchand (Mahatma) Gandhi

There will have to be rigid and iron discipline before we achieve anything great and enduring, and that discipline will not come by mere academic argument and appeal to reason and logic.

Mohandas Karamchand (Mahatma) Gandhi

I am myself a believer in discipline. And yet I suppose there can be too much of discipline.

Jawaharlal Nehru

To be in good moral condition requires at least as much training as to be in good physical condition.

Jawaharlal Nehru

No pain, no palm; no thorns, no throne; no gall, no glory; no cross, no crown.

William Penn

A stern discipline pervades all nature, which is a little cruel that it may be very kind.

Edmund Spenser

See also: AUTHORITY, EDUCATION, ORDER, PARENTS, PUNISHMENT, SELF-IMPROVEMENT, STUDY.

DISCONTENTMENT

One thing only has been lent to youth and age in common—discontent.

Matthew Arnold

All the discontented people I know are trying sedulously to be something they are not, to do something they cannot do.

Ray Stannard Baker (David Grayson)

The weakest people are often the most rebellious, finding in universal discontent their excuse for no positive and resolute agreement with anything.

Pearl Sydenstricker Buck

A perverse and fretful disposition makes any state of life unhappy.

Cicero

The root of all discontent is self-love.

James Freeman Clarke

Restlessness is discontent—and discontent is the first necessity of progress. Show me a thoroughly satisfied man—and I will show you a failure.

Thomas Alva Edison

Discontent is the want of self-reliance; it is infirmity of will.

Ralph Waldo Emerson

Discontents are sometimes the better part of our life. I know not which is the most useful. Joy I may choose for pleasure; but adversities are the best for profit; and sometimes these do so far help me, that I should, without them, want much of the joy I have.

Owen Felltham

Discontent is like ink poured into water, which fills the whole fountain full of blackness. It casts a cloud over the mind, and renders it more occupied about the evil which disquiets than about the means of removing it.

Owen Felltham

All human situations have their inconveniences. We feel those of the present, but neither see nor feel those of the future; and hence we often make troublesome changes without amendment, and frequently for the worse.

Benjamin Franklin

There are two kinds of discontent in this world: the discontent that works, and the discontent that wrings its hands. The first gets what it wants, and the second loses what it had. There is no cure for the first but success, and there is no cure at all for the second.

Gordon Graham

Noble discontent is the path to heaven.

Thomas Wentworth Storrow Higginson

Our discontent is from comparison: were better states unseen, each man would like his own.

John Norris

Save me from impious discontent at aught thy wisdom has denied or thy goodness has lent.

Alexander Pope

A good man and a wise man may, at times, be angry with the world, and at times grieved for it; but no man was ever discontented with the world if he did his duty in it.

Robert Southey

We love in others what we lack ourselves, and would be everything but what we are.

Charles Augustus Stoddard

That which makes people dissatisfied with their condition, is the chimerical idea they form of the happiness of others.

James Thomson

The splendid discontent of God with Chaos, made the world; and from the discontent of man the world's best progress springs.

Ella Wheeler Wilcox

Discontent is the first step in the progress of a man or a nation.

Oscar Wilde

Poor in abundance, famished at a feast.

Edward Young

See also: COMPLAINT, CONTENTMENT, DISSENT, FRETFULNESS, GRUMBLING, MOROSENESS, REBELLION, RESTLESSNESS, TROUBLE.

DISCOVERY

Through every rift of discovery some seeming anomaly drops out of the darkness, and falls, as a golden link, into the great chain of order.

Edwin Hubbel Chapin

A new principle is an inexhaustible source of new views.

Luc de Clapiers (Marquis de Vauvenargues)

It is a mortifying truth, and ought to teach the wisest of us humility, that many of the most valuable discoveries have been the result of chance rather than of contemplation, and of accident rather than of design.

Charles Caleb Colton

If I have ever made any valuable discoveries, it has been owing more to patient attention, than to any other talent.

Sir Isaac Newton

All great discoveries are made by men whose feelings run ahead of their thinking.

Charles Henry Parkhurst

It is the modest, not the presumptuous inquirer, who makes a real and safe progress in the discovery of divine truths. He follows God in his works and in his word.

Henry St. John (Lord Bolingbroke)

See also: INNOVATION, INVENTION, NOVELTY, ORIGINALITY, RESEARCH.

DISCRETION

There are many shining qualities in the mind of man; but none so useful as discretion. It is this which gives a value to all the rest, and sets them at work in their proper places, and turns them to the advantage of their possessor. Without it, learning is pedantry; wit, impertinence; virtue itself looks like weakness; and the best parts only qualify a man to be more sprightly in errors, and active to his own prejudice. Though a man has all other perfections and wants discretion, he will be of no great consequence in the world; but if he has this single talent in perfection, and but a common share of others, he may do what he pleases in his station of life.

Joseph Addison

Discretion in speech, is more than eloquence.

Francis Bacon

Discretion is the salt, and fancy the sugar of life; the one preserves, the other sweetens it.

Christian Nestell Bovee

A sound discretion is not so much indicated by never making a mistake, as by never repeating it.

Christian Nestell Bovee

I have never been hurt by anything I didn't say.

(John) Calvin Coolidge

If thou art a master, be sometimes blind, if a servant, sometimes deaf.

Thomas Fuller

The greatest parts, without discretion, may be fatal to their owner. Polyphemus, deprived of his eye, was only the more exposed on account of his enormous strength and stature.

David Hume

Discretion is the perfection of reason, and a guide to us in all the duties of life. It is only found in men of sound sense and good understanding.

Jean de La Bruyère

It is a profound mistake to think that everything has been discovered; as well think the horizon the boundary of the world.

Antoine-Marin Lemierre

Be discreet in all things, and so render it unnecessary to be mysterious about any.

Arthur Wellesley (First Duke Wellington)

Open your mouth and purse cautiously, and your stock of wealth and reputation shall, at least in repute, be great.

Johann Georg von Zimmerman

See also: COMMON SENSE, INTELLIGENCE, PRUDENCE, REFLECTION, SENSE.

DISCUSSION

It is not the facts which guide the conduct of men, but their opinions about facts; which may be entirely wrong. We can only make them right by discussion.

Sir Norman Angell

Discussion should be one of the most important things in the world, for it is almost our only arena of thinking . . . Without discussion intellectual experience is only an exercise in a private gymnasium.

Randolph Silliman Bourne

A good discussion increases the dimensions of everyone who takes part.

Randolph Silliman Bourne

A good discussion . . . is fundamentally a co-operation. It progresses towards some common understanding.

Randolph Silliman Bourne

Public discussions are useful because they disturb complacency and lead to the restless uncertainty about one's self that has long been known as the beginning of wisdom.

Lyman Lloyd Bryson

Free and fair discussion will ever be found the firmest friend to truth.

George Campbell

Discussion, even if stormy, often winnows truth from error—a good never to be expected in an uninquiring age.

William Ellery Channing

In debate, rather pull to pieces the argument of thine antagonist, than offer him any of thine own; for thus thou will fight him in his own country.

Henry Fielding

The pain of dispute exceeds, by much, its utility. All disputation makes the mind deaf, and when people are deaf I am dumb.

Joseph Joubert

Gratuitous violence in argument betrays a conscious weakness of the cause, and is usually a signal of despair.

Junius

Men are never so likely to settle a question rightly, as when they discuss it freely.

Thomas Babington Macaulay

He who knows only his own side of the case, knows little of that.

John Stuart Mill

I have always thought that the best way to find out what is right and what is not right, what should be done and what should not be done, is not to give a sermon, but to talk and discuss, and out of the discussion sometimes a little bit of the truth comes out.

Jawaharlal Nehru

Do not use thyself to dispute against thine own judgment to show thy wit, lest it prepare thee to be indifferent about what is right; nor against another man to vex him, or for mere trial of skill, since to inform or be informed ought to be the end of all conferences.

William Penn

It is in disputes, as in armies, where the weaker side sets up false lights, and makes a great noise to make the enemy believe them more numerous and strong than they really are.

Jonathan Swift

Whosoever is afraid of submitting any question, civil or religious, to the test of free discussion, is more in love with his own opinion than with truth.

Thomas Watson

He that is not open to conviction, is not qualified for discussion.

Richard Whately

See also: ARGUMENT, CONTROVERSY, CONVERSATION, SILENCE.

DISEASE

Sickness and disease are in weak minds the sources of melancholy; but that which is painful to the body, may be profitable to the soul. Sickness puts us in mind of our mortality, and, while we drive on heedlessly in the full career of worldly pomp and jollity, kindly pulls us by the ear, and brings us to a proper sense of our duty.

Richard Eugene Burton

It is with disease of the mind, as with those of the body; we are half dead before we understand our disorder, and half cured when we do.

Charles Caleb Colton

There are no better grounds on which we can meet other nations and demonstrate our own concern for peace and the betterment of mankind than in a common battle against disease.

John William Gardner

If I had my way I'd make health catching instead of disease.

Robert Green Ingersoll

The disease and its medicine are like two factions in a besieged town; they tear one another to pieces, but both unite against their common enemy Nature.

Francis Jeffrey

We live longer than our forefathers; but we suffer more, from a thousand artificial anxieties and cares. They fatigued only the muscles; we exhaust the finer strength of the nerves.

Edward G. Bulwer-Lytton (Baron Lytton)

When the Czar has a cold all Russia coughs.
Russian Proverb

See also: CANCER, DEATH, DOCTOR, HEALTH, HEART DISEASE, MEDICINE, MENTAL HEALTH, PAIN.

DISGRACE

Disgrace does not consist in the punishment, but in the crime.
Conte Vittorio Alfieri

Do not talk about disgrace from a thing being known, when the disgrace is, that the thing should exist.
William Falconer

No one can disgrace us but ourselves.
Josiah Gilbert Holland

Whatever disgrace we may have deserved or incurred, it is almost always in our power to re-establish our character.
Duc François de La Rochefoucauld

See also: DEFEAT, HONOR, INFAMY, SHAME.

DISGUISE

Mankind is pure and simple only at a masque ball, where the waxen mask covers the usual mask of flesh.
Heinrich Heine

Men would not live long in society, were they not the mutual dupes of each other.
Duc François de La Rochefoucauld

Were we to take as much pains to be what we ought to be, as we do to disguise what we really are, we might appear like ourselves without being at the trouble of any disguise whatever.
Duc François de La Rochefoucauld

We are so used to disguising ourselves for others, that in the end we don't know who we are.
Duc François de La Rochefoucauld

Disguise yourself as you may to your fellow-men, if you are honest with yourself conscience will make known your real character, and the heart-searching one always knows it.
Edward Payson

See also: CONCEALMENT, DECEIT, DISSIMULATION, HYPROCRISY.

DISHONESTY

So grasping is dishonesty, that it is no respecter of persons; it will cheat friends as well as foes; and were it possible, would cheat even God himself.
George Bancroft

If you attempt to beat a man down and so get his goods for less than a fair price, you are attempting to commit burglary as much as though you broke into his shop to take the things without paying for them. There is cheating on both sides of the counter, and generally less behind it than before.
Henry Ward Beecher

I have known a vast quantity of nonsense talked about bad men not looking you in the face. Don't trust that idea. Dishonesty will stare honesty out of countenance any day in the week, if there is anything to be got by it.
Charles John Huffam Dickens

Every man takes care that his neighbor shall not cheat him. But a day comes when he begins to care that he do not cheat his neighbor. Then all goes well. He has changed his market-cart into a chariot of the sun.
Ralph Waldo Emerson

He who purposely cheats his friend, would cheat his God.
Johann Kaspar Lavater

I could never draw the line between meanness and dishonesty. What is mean, so far as I can see, slides by indistinguishable gradations into what is dishonest.
George Macdonald

See also: BRIBERY, CORRUPTION, CRIME, DECEIT, FALSEHOOD, FRAUD, HYPOCRISY, INJUSTICE, LYING.

DISILLUSIONMENT

Wisdom comes by disillusionment.
George Santayana

There is nothing more demoralizing than sudden, overwhelming disillusionment.
Dorothy Thompson

See also: CYNICISM, DELUSION, KNOWLEDGE.

DISOBEDIENCE

Rogues differ little. Each begun first as a disobedient son.
Chinese Proverb

Wherever there is authority, there is a natural inclination to disobedience.
Thomas Chandler Haliburton

That men so universally disobey God bespeaks alienation and enmity of mind, for as obedience proceeds from love so disobedience proceeds from enmity.

John Howe

Those people who know precisely the right time to disobey orders are a big help to humanity, but they're mighty scarce.

Robert Alexander Wason

See also: AUTHORITY, CONSCIENCE, DISCIPLINE, DISSENT, OBSTINACY, PERVERSENESS, REBELLION, REVOLUTION.

DISPATCH

Measure not dispatch by the times of sitting, but by the advancement of business.

Francis Bacon

To choose time is to save time. There be three parts of business—the preparation, the debate or examination, and the perfection; whereof if you look for dispatch let the middle only be the work of many and the first and last the work of few.

Francis Bacon

True dispatch is a rich thing, for time is the measure of business, as money is of wares; and business is bought at a dear hand where there is small dispatch.

Francis Bacon

Use dispatch. Remember that the world only took six days for its creation. Ask me for whatever you please except time; that is the only thing which is beyond my power.

Napoleon I (Bonaparte)

Dispatch is the soul of business.

Philip Dormer Stanhope (Lord Chesterfield)

See also: DELAY, HASTE, PROMPTNESS, PUNCTUALITY, TIME.

DISPOSITION

A good disposition is more valuable than gold; for the latter is the gift of fortune, but the former is the dower of nature.

Joseph Addison

A tender-hearted, compassionate disposition, which inclines men to pity and to feel the misfortunes of others, and which is incapable of involving any man in ruin and misery, is, of all tempers of mind, the most amiable; and though it seldom receives much honor, is worthy of the highest.

Henry Fielding

Envy's memory is nothing but a row of hooks to hang up grudges on. Some people's sensibility is a mere bundle of aversions; and you hear them display and parade it, not in recounting the things they are attached to, but in telling you how many things and persons "they cannot bear."

John Watson Foster

The most phlegmatic dispositions ofter contain the most inflammable spirits, as fire is struck from the hardest flints.

William Hazlitt

See also: CHARACTER, INCLINATION, PERSONALITY, TEMPER.

DISSENT

If one or two have the boldness to use any liberty of judgment, they must undertake the task all by themselves; they can have no advantage from the company of others. And if they can endure this also, they will find their industry and largeness of mind no slight hindrance to their fortune. For the studies of men in these places are confined and as it were imprisoned in the writings of certain authors, from whom if any man dissent he is straightway arraigned as a turbulent person and an innovator.

Francis Bacon

[Sergeant O'Malley's courage] far outweighs the reluctance of men who exercise so well the right of dissent but let others fight to protect them from those whose very philosophy is to do away with the right of dissent.

Lyndon Baines Johnson

Massive strikes, sit-in demonstrations, civil disobedience, and turbulent disorder are advocated and engaged in as a means for achieving redress for alleged grievances. Thus, violence begets violence, due process of law is subverted, and the rights of others are contemptuously violated and abused. Many of these demonstrations seem to have taken on aspects of blackmail and extortion.

John L. McClellan

When we find that the highest court in the land feels free to exercise the license or privilege to overrule the law of the land, not by statute, not by amendment to the Constitution, but simply by court edict, to overrule what has been the law of the land for more than 100 years, simply to satisfy their whim with respect to what they think the law should be, then it is no wonder that civil rights leaders and extremists today say, "We have a right, a moral right, not to obey any law that we disagree with."

John L. McClellan

If all mankind minus one were of one opinion, and only one person were of the contrary opinion, mankind would be no more justified in silencing that one person, than he, if he had the power, would be justified in silencing mankind.

John Stuart Mill

Protection . . . against the tyranny of the magistrate is not enough: there needs protection also against the tyranny of the prevailing opinion and feeling; against the tendency of society to impose, by other means than civil penalties, its own ideas and practices as rules of conduct on those who dissent from them.

John Stuart Mill

The United States can . . . be proud that it has institutions and a structure that permit its citizens to express honest dissent, even though those who do so may be maligned by the highest official in the land.

New York Times

Dissent does not include the freedom to destroy the system of law which guarantees freedom to speak, assemble and march in protest. Dissent is not anarchy.

Seymour F. Simon

Who is there to say what is good dissent and what is bad dissent. Who can frame fair and meaningful standards to measure what is creative, constructive or responsible in disagreement and what is destructive. Are these decisions which can safely be left to a local police chief or a municipal administrator or the majority or to public opinion or perhaps to those good people who simply want to remain comfortable and uninvolved?

Seymour F. Simon

The right to dissent is basic to a free democracy. The right to dissent and the right of the people to peaceably assemble are guaranteed by the Constitution. The motive behind the dissent or protest, even where opposed by the majority, has no relevance. Under our Constitution and under our laws the majority must respect the right to lawful dissent as the exercise of free speech. The majority may one day require the right to dissent to defend itself.

Herbert Tenzer

Mere unorthodoxy or dissent from the prevailing mores is not to be condemned. The absence of such voices would be a symptom of grave illness in our society.

Earl Warren

See also: ARGUMENT, CONTROVERSY, DIFFERENCE, NONCONFORMITY, OPPOSITION.

DISSIMULATION

Dissimulation in youth is the forerunner of perfidy in old age. It degrades parts and learning, obscures the luster of every accomplishment, and sinks us into contempt. The path of falsehood is a perplexing maze. One artifice leads on to another, till, as the intricacy of the labyrinth increases, we are left entangled in our own snare.

Hugh Blair

Dissimulation is ever productive of embarrassment; whether the design is evil or not, artifice is always dangerous and almost inevitably disgraceful.

Jean de La Bruyère

Dissimulation is often humble, often polished, grave, smooth, decorous; but it is rarely gay and jovial, a hearty laughter, or a merry, cordial, boon companion.

Edward G. Bulwer-Lytton (Baron Lytton)

See also: DISGUISE, HYPOCRISY.

DISTANCE

Distance lends enchantment to the view.

Thomas Campbell

Distance sometimes endears friendship, and absence sweeteneth it—for separation from those we love shows us, by the loss, their real value and dearness to us.

Jeremiah Brown Howell

Distance in truth produces in idea the same effect as in real perspective. Objects are softened, rounded, and rendered doubly graceful. The harsher and more ordinary points of character are melted down, and those by which it is remembered are the more striking outlines that mark sublimity, grace, or beauty. There are mists, too, as in the natural horizon, to conceal what is less pleasing in distant objects; and there are happy lights, to stream in full glory upon those points which can profit by brilliant illumination.

Sir Walter Scott

The thing which seems so glorious when viewed from the heights of the country's cause, looks so muddy when seen from the bottom. One begins by getting angry, and then feels disgusted.

Sir Rabindranath Tagore

Sweetest melodies are those that are by distance made more sweet.

William Wordsworth

See also: ABSENCE, FAMILIARITY, LONELINESS, RESERVE, TRANSPORTATION, TRAVEL.

DISTINCTION

You may fail to shine in the opinion of others both in your conversation and actions, from being superior, as well as inferior to them.

Fulke Greville (First Baron Brooke)

Talent and worth are the only eternal grounds of distinction. To these the Almighty has affixed his everlasting patent of nobility, and these it is which make the bright immortal names to which our children, as well as others, may aspire.

Catharine Maria Sedgwick

How men long for celebrity! Some would willingly sacrifice their lives for fame, and not a few would rather be known by their crimes than not known at all.

Sir John Sinclair

All our distinctions are accidental. Beauty and deformity, though personal qualities, are neither entitled to praise or censure; yet it so happens that they color our opinion of those qualities to which mankind have attached importance.

Johann Georg von Zimmermann

See also: EMINENCE, FAME, GLORY.

DISTRUST

The disease of mutual distrust among nations is widely spread and is the bane of modern civilization.

Franz Boas

Self-distrust is the cause of most of our failures. In the assurance of strength, there is strength, and they are the weakest, however strong, who have no faith in themselves or their own powers.

Christian Nestell Bovee

Excessive distrust is not less hurtful than its opposite. Most men become useless to him who is unwilling to risk being deceived.

Luc de Clapiers (Marquis de Vauvenargues)

What loneliness is more lonely than distrust?

George Eliot (Mary Ann Evans)

To think and feel we are able, is often to be so.

Joel Hawes

However much we may distrust men's sincerity, we always believe that they speak to us more sincerely than to others.

Duc François de La Rochefoucauld

Our want of trust justifies the deceit of others.

Duc François de La Rochefoucauld

A certain amount of distrust is wholesome, but not so much of others as of ourselves. Neither vanity nor conceit can exist in the same atmosphere with it.

Albertine Adrienne Necker de Saussure

As health lies in labor, and there is no royal road to it but through toil, so there is no republican road to safety but in constant distrust.

Wendell Phillips

The feeling of distrust is always the last which a great mind acquires.

Jean Baptiste Racine

Nothing is more certain of destroying any good feelings that may be cherished toward us than to show distrust. On the contrary confidence leads us naturally to act kindly; we are affected by the good opinion others entertain of us, and are not easily induced to lose it.

Marquise de Sévigné

See also: DOUBT, SUSPICION, TRUST.

DIVERSION

Of all the diversions of life, there is none so proper to fill up its empty spaces as the reading of useful and entertaining authors.

Joseph Addison

Let the world have whatever sports and recreations please them best, provided they be followed with discretion.

Richard Eugene Burton

Diversions are most properly applied to ease and relieve those who are oppressed by being too much employed. Those that are idle have no need of them, and yet they, above all others, give themselves up to them. To unbend our thoughts when they are too much stretched by our cares is not more natural than it is necessary; but to turn our whole life into a holiday is not only ridiculous, but destroys pleasure instead of increasing it.

John Faucit Saville

See also: AMUSEMENT, HAPPINESS, PLEASURE, RECREATION.

DIVORCE

Paper napkins never return from a laundry, nor love from a trip to the law courts.

John Barrymore

The ancient Romans are said to have shrunk with horror from the first examples of divorce, but before long all sense of decency was blunted in their soul; the meager restraint of passion died out, and the marriage vow was so often broken that what some writers have affirmed would seem to be true—namely, women used to count years not by the change of consuls, but by their husbands.

Leo XIII (Gioacchino Vincenzo Pecci)

Divorce by mutual consent, subject to time, subject to reconciliation, subject to all such approaches, so that nothing may be done in a hurry, is right and proper. It will produce a happier adjustment and a better relationship between the parties than would be produced if one party thinks that he can misbehave as much as he likes and nothing will happen.

Jawaharlal Nehru

Many people seem to imagine that by bringing in divorce you break up the system of marriage. I am absolutely convinced that by bringing in divorce you make for happier marriages, normally.

Jawaharlal Nehru

Divorce is like matrimony: a fellow has got to go through it three or four times before he knows how.

Edgar Saltus

See also: HUSBAND AND WIFE, MARRIAGE.

DOCILITY

Willingness to be taught what we do not know, is the sure pledge of growth both in knowledge and wisdom.

Hugh Blair

A docile disposition will, with application, surmount every difficulty.

Manilius

It is the docile who achieve the most impossible things in this world.

Sir Rabindranath Tagore

See also: DEFERENCE, HUMILITY, MEEKNESS, OBEDIENCE, OBSTINACY, SUBMISSION.

DOCTOR

Nor bring, to see me cease to live,
Some doctor full of phrase and fame,
To shake his sapient head and give
The ill he cannot cure a name.

Matthew Arnold

When one's all right, he's prone to spite
    The doctor's peaceful mission;
But when he's sick, it's loud and quick
    He bawls for a physician.

Eugene Field

There's another advantage of being poor—a doctor will cure you faster.

Frank McKinney (Kin) Hubbard

There are only two sorts of doctors: those who practice with their brains, and those who practice with their tongues.

Sir William Osler

See also: DISEASE, HEALTH, MEDICINE, PAIN.

DOCTRINE

Doctrine is the necessary foundation of duty; if the theory is not correct, the practice cannot be right. Tell me what a man believes, and I will tell you what he will do.

Tryon Edwards

Pure doctrine always bears fruit in pure benefits.

Ralph Waldo Emerson

The question is not whether a doctrine is beautiful but whether it is true. When we wish to go to a place, we do not ask whether the road leads through a pretty country, but whether it is the right road.

Augustus and Julius Hare

Say what men may, it is doctrine that moves the world. He who takes no position will not sway the human intellect.

William Greenough Thayer Shedd

If you want war, nourish a doctrine. Doctrines are the most frightful tyrants to which

men are ever subject, because doctrines get inside of a man's reason and betray him against himself. Civilized men have done their fiercest fighting for doctrines.
William Graham Sumner

The doctrine that rectifies the conscience, purifies the heart, and produces love to God and man, is necessarily true, whether men can comprehend all its depths and relations or not.
James Barr Walker

A clash of doctrines is not a disaster—it is an opportunity.
Alfred North Whitehead

See also: BELIEF, CREED, FAITH, THEORY.

DOG

Who loves me will also love my dog.
Bernard of Clairvaux

The cowardly dog barks more violently than it bites.
Quintus Curtius Rufus

And in that town a dog was found,
  As many dogs there be,
Both mongrel, puppy, whelp and hound,
  And curs of low degree.
Oliver Goldsmith

Brothers and sisters I bid you beware
Of giving your heart to a dog to tear.
Rudyard Kipling

I am his Highness' dog at Kew;
Pray tell me, sir, whose dog are You?
Alexander Pope

Gentlemen of the Jury: The one, absolute, unselfish friend that man can have in this selfish world, the one that never deserts him, the one that never proves ungrateful or treacherous, is his dog.
George Graham Vest

See also: ANIMAL, CAT.

DOGMATISM

Those who refuse the long drudgery of thought, and think with the heart rather than the head, are ever most fiercely dogmatic.
Peter Bayne

It is always safe to be dogmatic about tomorrow.
(Matthew) Heywood Campbell Broun

Man's faith, instead of always remaining the great creative factor, sometimes betrays him into the impasse of stubborn, sterile dogmatism.
Michael John Demiashkevich

Any stigma will do to beat a dogma.
Philip Guedalla

Nothing can be more unphilosophical than to be positive or dogmatical on any subject. When men are the most sure and arrogant, they are commonly the most mistaken and have there given reins to passion without that proper deliberation and suspense which alone can secure them from the grossest absurdities.
David Hume

Those who differ most from the opinions of their fellow-men are the most confident of the truth of their own.
Sir James Mackintosh

A dogmatical spirit inclines a man to be censorious of his neighbors. Every one of his opinions appears to him written as with sunbeams, and he grows angry that his neighbors do not see it in the same light. He is tempted to disdain his correspondents as men of low and dark understanding because they do not believe what he does.
Isaac Watts

See also: BIGOTRY, FANATICISM, OPENMINDEDNESS, PEDANTRY, ZEAL.

DOMESTIC

Our notion of the perfect society embraces the family as its center and ornament. Nor is there a paradise planted until the children appear in the foreground to animate and complete the picture.
Amos Bronson Alcott

Domestic happiness—thou only bliss of paradise that has survived the fall.
William Cowper

Frankly, I do not myself feel at all like my great Tudor forebear who was blessed with neither husband nor children, who ruled as a despot and was never able to leave her native shores.
Elizabeth II

No money is better spent than what is laid out for domestic satisfaction. A man is pleased that his wife is dressed as well as other people, and the wife is pleased that she is so dressed.

Samuel Johnson

See also: FAMILY, HOME, TRAVEL.

DOUBT

In contemplation, if a man begins with certainties he shall end in doubts; but if he be content to begin with doubts, he shall end in certainties.

Francis Bacon

Who never doubted, never half believed. Where doubt is, there truth is—it is her shadow.

Gamaliel Bailey

A bitter and perplexed, "What shall I do?" is worse to man than worse necessity.

Samuel Taylor Coleridge

The doubter's dissatisfaction with his doubt is as great and widespread as the doubt itself.

Jan De Witt

Doubt, indulged and cherished, is in danger of becoming denial; but if honest, and bent on thorough investigation, it may soon lead to full establishment in the truth.

Tryon Edwards

Doubt is a pain too lonely to know that faith is his twin brother.

Kahlil Gibran

Give me the benefit of your convictions, if you have any, but keep your doubts to yourself, for I have enough of my own.

Johann Wolfgang von Goethe

We know accurately only when we know little, with knowledge doubt increases.

Johann Wolfgang von Goethe

Human knowledge is the parent of doubt.

Fulke Greville (First Baron Brooke)

The worst of worms: the dagger thoughts of doubt.

Heinrich Heine

To have doubted one's own first principles, is the mark of a civilized man.

Oliver Wendell Holmes

Doubt comes in at the window when inquiry is denied at the door.

Benjamin Jowett

"If you are in doubt," says Talleyrand, "whether to write a letter or not—don't!" And the advice applies to many doubts in life besides that of letter writing.

Edward R. Bulwer Lytton (Owen Meredith)

I respect faith, but doubt is what gets you an education.

Wilson Mizner

Doubt is almost a natural phase of life; but as certainly as it is natural, it is also temporary, unless it is unwisely wrought into conduct.

Theodore Thornton Munger

Doubt is brother devil to despair.

John Boyle O'Reilly

The heart-breaking hesitation of Lincoln, the troublesome doubts and perplexed questionings, reveal as nothing else could the simple integrity of his nature.

Vernon Louis Parrington

The end of doubt is the beginning of repose.

Petrarch

Never do anything concerning the rectitude of which you have a doubt.

Pliny the Elder

Beware of doubt—faith is the subtle chain that binds us to the infinite.

Elizabeth Oakes Smith

Doubt is the disease of this inquisitive, restless age. It is the price we pay for our advanced intelligence and civilization—the dim night of our resplendent day. But as the most beautiful light is born of darkness, so the faith that springs from conflict is often the strongest and best.

Robert James Turnbull

Misgive, that you may not mistake.

Richard Whately

When you doubt, abstain.

Zoroaster

See also: AGNOSTICISM,   CYNICISM,   DISTRUST,   INCREDULITY, SKEPTICISM.

DRAFT

Today, protests against the draft have once again erupted with vehemence. But this time they are bloodless, confined to sit-ins, picketing, draft card burning and verbal onslaughts. Our citizenry is not likely to set upon draft

officials with clubs; we have grown accustomed to the draft's power to compel a
man to military service.

Jean Elinor Carper

It is perhaps ominous that so many of our
most intelligent youths refuse to consider
military service one of the obligations of
citizenship, but see in it only an interference
in their private lives. These young men are
prepared to ask us to provide them with fel-
lowships, scholarships, and grants in aid to
enter graduate schools, not because they wish
to contribute to the sum of human knowledge,
but simply to dodge the draft.

John (Cresswell) Keats

A young man who does not have what it
takes to perform military service is not likely
to have what it takes to make a living.

John Fitzgerald Kennedy

If the Selective Service System did not exist,
it would be impossible to invent it.

Daniel Patrick Moynihan

Implicit in draft deferment tests is the theory
of a race of Aryan supermen and the belief
that rare great minds alone are fit to direct
the destinies of a nation and to dispose of
the lives of the untutored masses. Instead of
a social democracy where equality is encouraged to flourish, these draft deferment
tests lay the foundation for a racial aristocracy. These tests are reminiscent of Hitler's
twin system of eugenics and education—weed
out the intellectually deprived or socially un-
desirables by conscripting them for cannon
fodder.

Adam Clayton Powell

Peacetime conscription is the greatest step
toward regimentation and militarism ever undertaken by the Congress of the United
States.

Burton Kendall Wheeler

See also: ARMY, CONSCIENCE, NAVY, SOLDIER,
WAR.

DRAMA: see THEATER.

DREAM

Dreams full oft are found of real events the
forms and shadows.

Joanna Baillie

As dreams are the fancies of those that sleep,
so fancies are but the dreams of those awake.

Sir Thomas Pope Blount

Children of the night, of indigestion bred.

Charles Churchill

Nothing so much convinces me of the bound-
lessness of the human mind as its operations
in dreaming.

William Benton Clulow

A lost but happy dream may shed its light
upon our waking hours, and the whole day
may be infected with the gloom of a dreary
or sorrowful one; yet of neither may we be
able to recover a trace.

Walter John de la Mare

Dreaming permits each and every one of us
to be quietly and safely insane every night of
our lives.

William Charles Dement

Existence would be intolerable if we were
never to dream.

Anatole France

I am a dreamer. I am, indeed, a practical
dreamer. My dreams are not airy nothings.
I want to convert my dreams into realities,
as far as possible.

Mohandas Karamchand (Mahatma) Gandhi

Sir, do not mock our dreamers. . . . Their
words become the seeds of freedom.

Heinrich Heine

A world of the dead in the hues of life.

Felicia Dorothea Browne Hemans

Men never cling to their dreams with such
tenacity as at the moment when they are
losing faith in them, and know it, but do not
dare to confess it to themselves.

William Graham Sumner

If you have built castles in the air, your work
need not be lost; there is where they should
be. Now put foundations under them.

Henry David Thoreau

See also: FANCY, IMAGINATION, REVERIE.

DRESS

A fine coat is but a livery when the person
who wears it discovers no higher sense than
that of a footman.

Joseph Addison

Had Cicero himself pronounced one of his
orations with a blanket about his shoulders,

more people would have laughed at his dress than admired his eloquence.

Joseph Addison

The body is the shell of the soul, and dress the husk of that shell; but the husk often tells what the kernel is.

Anonymous

Two things in my apparel I will chiefly aim at —commodiousness and decency; more than these is not commendable; yet I hate an effeminate spruceness, as much as a fantastic disorder. A neglected comeliness is the best ornament.

Anonymous

If honor be your clothing, the suit will last a lifetime; but if clothing be your honor, it will soon be worn threadbare.

William Arnot

Dress has a moral effect upon the conduct of mankind. Let any gentleman find himself with dirty boots, old surtout, soiled neckcloth, and a general negligence of dress, and he will, in all probability, find a corresponding disposition in negligence of address.

John Shute Barrington

The perfection of dress is in the union of three requisites—in its being comfortable, cheap, and tasteful.

Christian Nestell Bovee

Eat to please thyself, but dress to please others.

Benjamin Franklin

An emperor in his night-cap would not meet with half the respect of an emperor with a crown.

Oliver Goldsmith

The vanity of loving fine clothes and new fashions, and valuing ourselves by them, is one of the most childish pieces of folly.

Sir Matthew Hale

In civilized society external advantages make us more respected. A man with a good coat on his back meets with a better reception than he who has a bad one. You may analyze this and say, what is there in it? But that will avail you nothing, for it is a part of a general system.

Samuel Johnson

In clothes clean and fresh there is a kind of youth with which age should surround itself.

Joseph Joubert

In the indications of female poverty there can be no disguise. No woman dresses below herself from caprice.

Charles Lamb

I hate to see men overdressed; a man ought to look like he's put together by accident, not added up on purpose.

Christopher Darlington Morley

Those who think that in order to dress well it is necessary to dress extravagantly or grandly, make a great mistake. Nothing so well becomes true feminine beauty as simplicity.

George Denison Prentice

No man is esteemed for gay garments, but by fools and women.

Sir Walter Raleigh

The only medicine which does women more good than harm, is dress.

Jean Paul Richter

A loose and easy dress contributes much to give to both sexes those fine proportions of body that are observable in the Grecian statues, and which serve as models to our present artists.

Jean Jacques Rousseau

The plainer the dress with greater luster does beauty appear. Virtue is the greatest ornament, and good sense the best equipage.

George Savile (Marquis of Halifax)

Persons are often misled in regard to their choice of dress by attending to the beauty of colors, rather than selecting such colors as may increase their own beauty.

William Shenstone

Dress yourself fine, where others are fine, and plain, where others are plain; but take care always that your clothes are well made and fit you, for otherwise they will give you a very awkward air.

Philip Dormer Stanhope (Lord Chesterfield)

Next to clothes being fine, they should be well made, and worn easily: for a man is only the less genteel for a fine coat, if, in wearing it, he shows a regard for it, and is not as easy in it as if it were a plain one.

Philip Dormer Stanhope (Lord Chesterfield)

Clothes don't make the man, but good clothes have got many a man a good job.

Herbert Harold Vreeland

As to matters of dress, I would recommend one never to be first in the fashion nor the last out of it.

John Wesley

There is new strength, repose of mind, and inspiration in fresh apparel.

Ella Wheeler Wilcox

See also: FASHION, LOOKS, STYLE, TASTE.

DRINK

The first draught serveth for health, the second for pleasure, the third for shame, and the fourth for madness.

Anacharsis

I feel no pain dear mother now
But oh, I am so dry!
O take me to a brewery
And leave me there to die.

Anonymous

Strong drink is not only the devil's way into a man, but man's way to the devil.

Adam Clarke

Drink is more a disease than a vice. I know scores of men who would gladly leave off drink if they could. Diseased persons have got to be helped against themselves. The drink curse has desolated many a labourer's home.

Mohandas Karamchand (Mahatma) Gandhi

Nothing but ruin stares a nation in the face that is prey to the drink habit.

Mohandas Karamchand (Mahatma) Gandhi

Only those women who have drunkards as their husbands know what havoc the drink devil works in homes that once were orderly and peace-loving.

Mohandas Karamchand (Mahatma) Gandhi

Every moderate drinker could abandon the intoxicating cup, if he would; every inebriate would if he could.

John Bartholomew Gough

Whisky is a good thing in its place. There is nothing like it for preserving a man when he is dead. If you want to keep a dead man, put him in whisky; if you want to kill a live man put whisky in him.

Thomas Guthrie

The maxim, "in vino veritas—that a man who is well warmed with wine will speak truth,"

may be an argument for drinking, if you suppose men in general to be liars; but sir, I would not keep company with a fellow, who lies as long as he is sober, and whom you must make drunk before you can get a word of truth out of him.

Samuel Johnson

I drink to make other people interesting.

George Jean Nathan

Frustrate a Frenchman, he will drink himself to death; an Irishman, he will die of angry hypertension; a Dane, he will shoot himself; an American, he will get drunk, shoot you, then establish a million dollar aid program for your relatives. Then he will die of an ulcer.

Stanley Arthur Rudin

See also: ABSTINENCE, ALCOHOL, DRUNKENNESS, ENJOYMENT, INTEMPERANCE, WINE.

DRUGS

So many people are taking drugs, it's no wonder they are prepared to believe that the Martians are coming.

Tatomir Anzelic

Some press reports allege that I see no difference between smoking marijuana and having a cocktail. This is false . . . smoking marijuana and drinking both present dangers to the individual.

James Lee Goddard

Whether or not marijuana is a more dangerous drug than alcohol is debatable—I don't happen to think it is.

James Lee Goddard

Heroin addiction is largely an urban problem, focused in slum areas. But hallucinogens, such as marijuana and LSD (lysergic acid diethylamide) have spread to suburban and rural regions, and are taken by far too many American youths. The improper use of dangerous drugs—barbiturates, pep pills, speed, other amphetamines—cuts across all segments of the population.

Lyndon Baines Johnson

The illegal sale of LSD, a powerful hallucinogen, is only a misdemeanor punishable by a maximum prison term of one year for the first offence. There is no penalty at present for possession of LSD for personal use.

Lyndon Baines Johnson

In no area of law enforcement is there a greater need for a concentrated drive than in dealing with the growing problem of narcotics and dangerous drugs.

Lyndon Baines Johnson

The time has come to stop the sale of slavery to the young.

Lyndon Baines Johnson

See also: ALCOHOL, CRIME, DRUNKENNESS.

DRUNKENNESS

Drunkenness is a flattering devil, a sweet poison, a pleasant sin, which whosoever hath, hath not himself, which whosoever doth commit, doth not commit sin, but he himself is wholly sin.

Augustine of Hippo

All the armies on earth do not destroy so many of the human race, nor alienate so much property, as drunkenness.

Francis Bacon

There is scarcely a crime before me that is not, directly or indirectly, caused by strong drink.

Sir John Duke Coleridge

Some of the domestic evils of drunkenness are houses without windows, gardens without fences, fields without tillage, barns without roofs, children without clothing, principles, morals, or manners.

Benjamin Franklin

Intoxicating drinks have produced evils more deadly, because more continuous, than all those caused to mankind by the great historic scourges of war, famine, and pestilence combined.

William Gladstone

Habitual intoxication is the epitome of every crime.

Douglas William Jerrold

Let there be an entire abstinence from intoxicating drinks throughout this country during the period of a single generation, and a mob would be as impossible as combustion without oxygen.

Horace Mann

A drunkard is like a whisky bottle, all neck and belly and no head.

Austin O'Malley

All excess is ill; but drunkenness is of the worst sort. It spoils health, dismounts the mind, and unmans men. It reveals secrets, is quarrelsome, lascivious, impudent, dangerous, and mad. He that is drunk is not a man, because he is void of reason that distinguishes a man from a beast.

William Penn

Beware of drunkenness, lest all good men beware of thee. Where drunkenness reigns, there reason is an exile, virtue a stranger, and God an enemy; blasphemy is wit, oaths are rhetoric, and secrets are proclamations.

Francis Quarles

Of all vices take heed of drunkenness. Other vices are but the fruits of disordered affections; this disorders, nay banishes reason. Other vices but impair the soul; this demolishes her two chief faculties; the understanding and the will. Other vices make their own way; this makes way for all vices. He that is a drunkard is qualified for all vice.

Francis Quarles

It were better for a man to be subject to any vice, than to drunkenness; for all other vanities and sins are recovered, but a drunkard will never shake off the delight of beastliness; for the longer it possesseth a man, the more he will delight in it, and the older he groweth the more he shall be subject to it; for it dulleth the spirits, and destroyeth the body as ivy doth the old tree; or as the worm that engendereth in the kernel of the nut.

Sir Walter Raleigh

The sight of a drunkard is a better sermon against that vice than the best that was ever preached on the subject.

John Faucit Saville

Drunkenness is nothing else but a voluntary madness.

Seneca

Drunkenness places man as much below the level of the brutes, as reason elevates him above them.

Sir John Sinclair

Troops of furies march in the drunkard's triumph.

Johann Georg von Zimmerman

See also: ALCOHOL, DRINK, DRUGS.

DUEL

Duelling makes a virtue of pride and revenge;
and, in defiance of the laws, both of God
and man, assumes itself the right of avenging
its own wrongs and even exults in the blood
of its murdered victim.

Joel Hawes

A duelist is only a Cain in high life.

Douglas William Jerrold

Duelling, as a punishment, is absurd, because
it is an equal chance whether the punishment
falls upon the offender, or the person offended. Nor is it much better as a reparation,
it being difficult to explain in what the satisfaction consists, or how it tends to undo an
injury, or to afford a compensation for the
damage already sustained.

William Paley

See also: MURDER, VIOLENCE.

DULNESS

What a comfort a dull but kindly man is, to
be sure, at times! A ground glass shade over
a gas-light does not bring more solace to our
dazzled eyes than such an one to our minds.

Oliver Wendell Holmes

A dull man is so near a dead man that he is
hardly to be ranked in the list of the living;
and as he is not be buried whilst half alive,
so he is as little to be employed whilst he is
half dead.

John Faucit Saville

Early to rise and early to bed makes a male
healthy and wealthy and dead.

James Grover Thurber

See also: BLOCKHEAD, BORE, LOQUACITY, MO-
NOTONY, VERBOSITY.

DUMBNESS

Silence in love bewrays more woe
  Then words, through ne'er so witty:
A beggar that is dumb, you know,
  May challenge double pity.

Sir Walter Raleigh

If she lacked speech, she did not lack a pair
of large dark eyes, shaded with long lashes;
and her lips trembled like a leaf in response to
any thought that rose in her mind.

Sir Rabindranath Tagore

They who from birth have had no other
speech than the trembling of their lips learn

a language of the eyes, endless in expression,
deep as the sea, clear as the heavens, wherein
play dawn and sunset, light and shadow. The
dumb have a lonely grandeur like Nature's
own.

Sir Rabindranath Tagore

See also: SILENCE.

DUTY

When the soul resolves to perform every duty,
immediately it is conscious of the presence of
God.

Francis Bacon

Duty must be accepted as the dominant conception in life.

Louis Dembitz Brandeis

Duty by habit is to pleasure turned.

Sir Samuel Egerton Brydges

To what gulfs a single deviation from the
path of human duties leads!

George Gordon Byron (Lord Byron)

Men do less than they ought, unless they do
all that they can.

Thomas Carlyle

Our grand business is not to see what lies
dimly in the distance, but to do what lies
clearly at hand.

Thomas Carlyle

Duties are ours, events are God's. This removes an infinite burden from the shoulders
of a miserable, tempted, dying creature. On
this consideration only can he securely lay
down his head and close his eyes.

Richard Cecil

No human being, man or woman, can act up
to a sublime standard without giving offence.

William Ellery Channing

There is no mean work, save that which is
sordidly selfish; no irreligious work, save that
which is morally wrong; in every sphere of
life the post of honor is the post of duty.

Edwin Hubbel Chapin

There is not a moment without some duty.

Cicero

This span of life was lent for lofty duties, not
for selfishness, not to be whiled away in aimless dreams, but to improve ourselves and
serve mankind.

Aubrey Thomas de Vere

Duty scorns prudence.

Benjamin Disraeli

Think ever that you are born to perform great duties.

Benjamin Disraeli

Duty performed gives clearness and firmness to faith, and faith thus strengthened through duty becomes the more assured and satisfying to the soul.

Tryon Edwards

Can any man or woman choose duties? No more than they can choose their birthplace, or their father and mother.

George Eliot (Mary Ann Evans)

The reward of one duty done is the power to fulfill another.

George Eliot (Mary Ann Evans)

So nigh is grandeur to our dust, so near is God to man, when duty whispers low, "Thou must," the youth replies, "I can."

Ralph Waldo Emerson

Be not diverted from your duty by any idle reflections the silly world may make upon you, for their censures are not in your power and should not be at all your concern.

Epictetus

We do not choose our own parts in life, and have nothing to do with selecting those parts. Our simple duty is confined to playing them well.

Epictetus

Exactness in little duties is a wonderful source of cheerfulness.

Frederick William Faber

I believe that we are conforming to the divine order and the will of Providence when we are doing even indifferent things that belong to our condition.

François de Salignac de La Mothe-Fénelon

It is wonderful what strength and boldness of purpose and energy will come from the feeling that we are in the way of duty.

John Watson Foster

Reverence the highest; have patience with the lowest; let this day's performance of the meanest duty be thy religion.

Sarah Margaret Fuller

Duty will be merit when debt becomes a donation.

Mohandas Karamchand (Mahatma) Gandhi

The never-ending cycle of duty and right goes ceaselessly on.

Mohandas Karamchand (Mahatma) Gandhi

Performance of one's duty should be independent of public opinion. I have all along held that one is bound to act according to what to one appears to be right even though it may appear wrong to others. And experience has shown that that is the only correct course. I admit that there is always a possibility of one's mistaking right for wrong and vice versa but often one learns to recognise wrong only through unconscious error. On the other hand, if a man fails to follow the light within for fear of public opinion or any other similar reason, he would never be able to know right from wrong and in the end lose all sense of distinction between the two.

Mohandas Karamchand (Mahatma) Gandhi

The true source of rights is duty. If we all discharge our duties, rights will not be far to seek.

Mohandas Karamchand (Mahatma) Gandhi

Duty is a power that rises with us in the morning, and goes to rest with us at night. It is co-extensive with the action of our intelligence. It is the shadow that cleaves to us, go where we will.

William Gladstone

Do the duty that lies nearest to thee.

Johann Wolfgang von Goethe

Duty is carrying on promptly and faithfully the affairs now before you. It is to fulfill the claims of to-day.

Johann Wolfgang von Goethe

Man is not born to solve the problem of the universe, but to find out what he has to do; and to restrain himself within the limits of his comprehension.

Johann Wolfgang von Goethe

Every duty that is bidden to wait comes back with seven fresh duties at its back.

Charles Kingsley

This is the feeling that gives a man true courage—the feeling that he has a work to do at all costs; the sense of duty.

Charles Kingsley

Duty is the grandest of ideas, because it implies the idea of God, of the soul, of liberty, of responsibility, of immortality.

Jean Baptiste Henri Lacordaire

The brave man wants no charms to encourage him to duty, and the good man scorns all warnings that would deter him from doing it.

Edward G. Bulwer-Lytton (Baron Lytton)

The best preparation for the future is the present well seen to, the last duty well done.

George Macdonald

Do the truth ye know, and you shall learn the truth you need to know.

George Macdonald

I find the doing of the will of God leaves me no time for disputing about His plans.

George Macdonald

It is surprising how practical duty enriches the fancy and the heart, and action clears and deepens the affections.

James Martineau

Duty has nothing to do with what somebody else conceives to be for the common good—that is, with morality in the derivative sense of the mores of a people.

Robert Andrews Millikan

Know thyself and do thine own work, says Plato; and each includes the other and covers the whole duty of man.

Michel Eyquem de Montaigne

Perish discretion when it interferes with duty.

Hannah More

We are apt to mistake our vocation by looking out of the way for occasions to exercise great and rare virtues, and by stepping over the ordinary ones that lie directly in the road before us.

Hannah More

Those who seek rights must share in the obligations also. Indeed, if the duties and obligations are accepted, then rights flow of themselves.

Jawaharlal Nehru

We talk of the rights of individuals and nations, but it must be remembered that every right carries an obligation with it. There has been far too much emphasis on rights and far too little on obligations; if obligations were undertaken, rights would naturally flow from them.

Jawaharlal Nehru

It is one of the worst of errors to suppose that there is any path of safety except that of duty.

William Nevins

The duty of man is plain and simple, and consists but of two points; his duty to God, which every man must feel; and his duty to his neighbor, to do, as he would be done by.

Thomas Paine

By doing our duty, we learn to do it.

Edward Bouverie Pusey

Try to put well in practice what you already know; and in so doing, you will, in good time, discover the hidden things which you now inquire about. Practice what you know, and it will help to make clear what now you do not know.

Rembrandt

Every duty which we omit, obscures some truth which we should have known.

John Ruskin

Duty is an abstraction rather than a catalogue of things to do.

James Thomson Shotwell

The consideration that human happiness and moral duty are inseparably connected, will always continue to prompt me to promote the former by inclucating the practice of the latter.

George Washington

See also: OBLIGATION, RESPONSIBILITY, RIGHTS, TRUST.

E

EARNESTNESS

Without earnestness no man is ever great or does really great things. He may be the cleverest of men; he may be brilliant, entertaining, popular; but he will want weight.

Peter Bayne

There are important cases in which the difference between half a heart and a whole heart makes just the difference between signal defeat and a splendid victory.

Andrew Kennedy Boyd

A man in earnest finds means, or if he cannot find, creates them.

William Ellery Channing

The superior man is slow in his words and earnest in his conduct.

Confucius

There is no substitute for thoroughgoing, ardent, and sincere earnestness.

Charles John Huffam Dickens

Earnestness commands the respect of mankind. A wavering, vacillating, dead-and-alive Christian does not get the respect of the Church or of the world.

John Hall

Earnestness is enthusiasm tempered by reason.

Blaise Pascal

Do you wish to become rich? You may become so if you desire it in no half-way, but thoroughly. Do you wish to master any science or accomplishment? Give yourself to it and it lies beneath your feet. This world is given as the prize for the men in earnest; and that which is true of this world, is truer still of the world to come.

Frederick William Robertson

See also: EFFORT, ENTHUSIASM, SINCERITY.

EARTH

Earth, with her thousand voices, praises God.

Samuel Taylor Coleridge

No man created the earth or its natural resources. And no man or government has a moral title to the earth's ownership. If it is to be used, and we have to use it in order to live, then it has to be treated as a trust. We have to hold the earth in trust.

Ralph Borsodi

The earth's a stage which God and nature do with actors fill.

Thomas Heywood

The pagans do not know God, and love only the earth. The Jews know the true God, and love only the earth. The Christians know the true God, and do not love the earth.

Blaise Pascal

The waters deluge man with rain, oppress him with hail, and drown him with inundations; the air rushes in storms, prepares the tempest, or lights up the volcano; but the earth, gentle and indulgent, ever subservient to the wants of man, spreads his walks with flowers, and his table with plenty; returns, with interest, every good committed to her care; and though she produces the poison, she still supplies the antidote; though constantly teased more to furnish the luxuries of man than his necessities, yet even to the last she continues her kind indulgence, and, when life is over, she piously covers his remains in her bosom.

Pliny the Elder

How far must suffering and misery go before we see that even in the day of vast cities and powerful machines, the good earth is our mother and that if we destroy her, we destroy ourselves?

Paul Bigelow Sears

The Earth, it seems to me, may well be the Siberia, the Perth Amboy, of the inhabited planets of the Universe.

James Grover Thurber

Earth, thou great footstool of our God, who reigns on high; thou fruitful source of all our raiment, life, and food; our house, our parent, and our nurse.

Isaac Watts

Until 1957 most scientists believed that the earth was about 3,350 million years old. But in that year American scientists, using radiocarbon dating, found that meteorites are about 4.5 billion years old. They added almost a billion years to the earth's age by a new hypothesis that the earth, too, must be 4.5 billion years old, because it must have been formed at the same time as the meteorites.

David C. Whitney

See also: AGRICULTURE, NATURE, WORLD.

EAST AND WEST

I would heartily welcome the Union of East and West provided it is not based on brute-force.

Mohandas Karamchand (Mahatma) Gandhi

Oh, East is East, and West is West, and never
    the twain shall meet,
Till Earth and Sky stand presently at God's
    great Judgment Seat.

Rudyard Kipling

I have always resisted this idea of dividing the world into the Orient and the Occident. I do not believe in such divisions. There have, of course, been differences in racial and national outlook and in ideals but to talk of the East and the West as such has little meaning.

Jawaharlal Nehru

See also: AMERICA, CHINA, COLD WAR, COLO-
    NIALISM, ENGLAND, FRANCE, GER-
    MANY, INDIA, NATION, RUSSIA.

EASTER

The great Easter truth is not that we are to live newly after death—that is not the great thing—but that we are to be here and now by the power of the resurrection; not so much that we are to live forever as that we are to, and may, live nobly now because we are to live forever.

Phillips Brooks

'Tis the day of resurrection:
    Earth! tell it out abroad!
The Passover of gladness!
    The Passover of God!
From death to life eternal,
    From this world to the Sky,

Our Christ hath brought us over,
    With hymns of victory.

John Chrysostom

Rise, Heir of fresh eternity,
    From Thy virgin tomb:
Rise mighty Man of wonders, and Thy world
    with Thee
Thy tomb, the universal east,
    Nature's new womb,
Thy tomb, fair immortality's perfumed nest.

Richard Crashaw

Break the box and shed the nard;
Stop not now to count the cost;
Hither bring pearl, opal, sard;
Reck not what the poor have lost;
Upon Christ throw all away:
Know ye, this Easter Day.

Gerard Manley Hopkins

See also: CELEBRATION, CHRISTMAS, PASSOVER,
    RESURRECTION, SPRING.

EATING

Part of the secret of success in life is to eat what you like and let the food fight it out inside.

Samuel Langhorne Clemens (Mark Twain)

One should eat to live, not live to eat.

Benjamin Franklin

Go to your banquet, then, but use delight,
So as to rise still with an appetite.

Robert Herrick

By eating what is sufficient man is enabled to work; he is hindered from working and becomes heavy, idle, and stupid if he takes too much. As to bodily distempers occasioned by excess, there is no end of them.

Thomas Rymer Jones

The difference between a rich man and a poor man, is this—the former eats when he pleases, and the latter when he can get it.

Sir Walter Raleigh

For the sake of health medicines are taken by weight and measure; so ought food to be, or by some similar rule.

Philip Skelton

The turnpike road to most people's hearts, I find, lies through their mouths, or I mistake mankind.

John Wolcot (Peter Pindar)

See also: BREAKFAST, COOKING, DIET, DINNER,
    FEAST, GLUTTONY, INDIGESTION.

ECCENTRICITY

Even beauty cannot palliate eccentricity.

Honoré de Balzac

Eccentricity has always abounded when and where strength of character has abounded. And the amount of eccentricity in a society has been proportional to the amount of genius, mental vigor, and moral courage it contained.

John Stuart Mill

Oddities and singularities of behavior may attend genius, but when they do, they are its misfortunes and blemishes. The man of true genius will be ashamed of them, or, at least, will never affect to be distinguished by them.

Sir William Temple

See also: NONCONFORMITY, SINGULARITY.

ECHO

Where we find echoes we generally find emptiness and hollowness; it is the contrary with the echoes of the heart.

John Frederick Boyes

That tuneful nymph, the babbling echo, who has not learned to conceal what is told her, nor yet is able to speak till another speaks.

Ovid

The shadow of a sound; a voice without a mouth, and words without a tongue.

Horatio Smith

See also: NOISE, SOUND.

ECONOMICS

When the ground rules get bent so far out of shape that the speculators have a better chance of making money than the people doing the real work, watch out! The system is falling apart.

Paul Ehrlich

There is always present the two twin dangers of deflation and inflation. And the function of government so far as it affects this matter at all is to be watchful, to be vigilant and alert, and to take measures from time to time that tend to move in one direction if the signs are we are moving in another.

Dwight David Eisenhower

We believe profoundly that constant and unnecessary governmental meddling in our economy leads to a standardized, weakened and tasteless society that encourages dull mediocrity, whereas private enterprise, dependent upon the vigor of healthful competition, leads to individual responsibility, pride of accomplishment and, above all, national strength.

Dwight David Eisenhower

We cannot forever be an Atlas . . . supporting the rest of the world.

Dwight David Eisenhower

A stable American economy cannot be sustained if the world's economy is in chaos. International cooperation is absolutely essential and vital.

Gerald Rudolph Ford

Like theology, and unlike mathematics, economics deals with matters which men consider very close to their lives.

John Kenneth Galbraith

The most impressive increases in output in the history of both the United States and other western countries have occurred since men began to concern themselves with reducing the risks of the competitive system.

John Kenneth Galbraith

One of the greatest pieces of economic wisdom is to know what you do not know.

John Kenneth Galbraith

I must confess that I do not draw a sharp or any distinction between economics and ethics. Economics that hurt the moral well-being of an individual or a nation are immoral and thereafter sinful. Thus the economics that permit one country to prey upon another are immoral. It is sinful to eat American wheat and let my neighbour, the grain dealer, starve for want of custom.

Mohandas Karamchand (Mahatma) Gandhi

If a religion cuts at the very fundamentals of economics it is not a true religion but only a delusion.

Mohandas Karamchand (Mahatma) Gandhi

In the old days we used to say that when the United States economy sneezed the rest of the world went to bed with pneumonia. Now when the United States economy sneezes the other countries say "Gesundheit."

Walter E. Heller

Economists have not yet earned the right to be listened to attentively.

John Maynard Keynes

We talk of freedom, but today political freedom does not take us far unless there is economic freedom. Indeed, there is no such thing as freedom for a man who is starving or for a country which is poor. The poor whether they are nations or individuals have little place in this world.

Jawaharlal Nehru

If each nation seeks selfishly to look out for its own interests without remembering the needs of its neighbors, we can create an economic crisis of hurricane proportions which will make us all beggars.

John Scali

The face which we present to the world . . . is the face of the individual or the family as a high consumption unit with minimal social links or responsibilities—father happily drinking his beer, mother dreamily fondling soft garments newly rinsed in a wonderful new detergent, the children gaily calling from the new barbecue pit for a famous sauce for their steak.

Adlai Ewing Stevenson

The life and spirit of the American economy is progress and expansion.

Harry S Truman

See also: BUSINESS, CAPITALISM, COMMUNISM, ECONOMY, GOVERNMENT.

ECONOMY

The man who will live above his present circumstances, is in great danger of soon living much beneath them; or as the Italian proverb says, "The man that lives by hope, will die by despair."

Joseph Addison

A man's ordinary expenses ought to be but to the half of his receipts, and if he thinks to wax rich, but to the third part.

Francis Bacon

The world abhors closeness, and all but admires extravagance; yet a slack hand shows weakness, and a tight hand strength.

Sir Thomas Fowell Buxton

There are but two ways of paying a debt; increase of industry in raising income, or increase of thrift in laying out.

Thomas Carlyle

Not to be covetous, is money; not to be a purchaser, is a revenue.

Cicero

Ere you consult fancy, consult your purse.

Benjamin Franklin

If you know how to spend less than you get, you have the philosopher's stone.

Benjamin Franklin

Let honesty and industry be thy constant companions, and spend one penny less than thy clear gains; then shall thy pocket begin to thrive; creditors will not insult, nor want oppress, nor hunger bite, nor nakedness freeze thee.

Benjamin Franklin

A man may, if he knows not how to save as he gets, keep his nose all his life to the grindstone and die not worth a groat after all.

Benjamin Franklin

Take care of the pence, and the pounds will take care of themselves.

Benjamin Franklin

No man is rich whose expenditures exceed his means; and no one is poor whose incomings exceed his outgoings.

Thomas Chandler Haliburton

It is of no small commendation to manage a little well. To live well in abundance is the praise of the estate, not of the person. I will study more how to give a good account of my little, than how to make it more.

Joseph Hall

The back door robs the house.

George Herbert

Without economy none can be rich, and with it few will be poor.

Samuel Johnson

A sound economy is a sound understanding brought into action. It is calculation realized; it is the doctrine of proportion reduced to practice; it is foreseeing contingencies and providing against them; it is expecting contingencies and being prepared for them.

Hannah More

Large enterprises make the few rich, but the majority prosper only through the careful-

ness and detail of thrift. He is already poverty-stricken whose habits are not thrifty.
Theodore Thornton Munger

He who is taught to live upon little owes more to his father's wisdom than he that has a great deal left him does to his father's care.
William Penn

Nothing is cheap which is superfluous, for what one does not need, is dear at a penny.
Plutarch

There is no gain so certain as that which arises from sparing what you have.
Publilius Syrus

Economy, whether public or private, means the wise management of labor, mainly in three senses; applying labor rationally, preserving its produce carefully, and distributing its produce seasonally.
John Ruskin

Economy is in itself a source of great revenue.
Seneca

Economy is half the battle of life; it is not so hard to earn money, as to spend it well.
Charles Haddon Spurgeon

The art of living easily as to money is to pitch your scale of living one degree below your means.
Sir Henry Taylor

See also: BUSINESS, ECONOMICS, MONEY.

ECSTASY

Jupiter, now assuredly is the time when I could readily consent to be slain, lest life should sully this ecstasy with some disaster.
Terence

Rapture, for the most part, is irresistible. It comes, generally, as a shock, quick and sharp, before you can collect your thoughts, or help yourself in any way, and you see and feel it as a cloud, or a strong eagle rising upwards, and carrying you away on its wings.
Theresa of Jesus

Ecstasy is so far superior to all other experiences possible to man that we have neither words nor means for the description of it.
Petr Dem'ianovich Uspenskii

See also: DRUGS, HAPPINESS, JOY.

ECUMENISM

We can be united in a unity of love by joining in dialogue, not debate, and by becoming more familiar with our respective beliefs. We will soon find that we can agree more than disagree.
Richard James Cushing

I hope that by going to visit the Pope I have enabled everybody to see that the words Catholic and Protestant, as ordinarily used, are completely out of date. They are almost always used now purely for propaganda purposes. That is why so much trouble is caused by them.
Geoffrey Francis Fisher

I say to you Baptists, "Go on being good Baptists, thinking that you are more right than anybody else." Unless you think it I have no use for you at all. The Church of England does precisely the same itself.
Geoffrey Francis Fisher

It is true, as has been said, that in one sense what may pass between the Pope and myself may be trivialities. In another sense, the fact of talking trivialities is itself a portent of great significance. But the pleasantries which we exchange may, as one church leader said, be pleasantries about profundities.
Geoffrey Francis Fisher

Religion has so often been made the breeding ground of the vice of intolerance, that promotion of mutual understanding by scholarly study among those of different faiths and opinions is in itself a high educational service to the community.
Raymond Collyer Knox

We speak now to the representatives of the Christian denominations separated from the Catholic Church, who have nevertheless been invited to take part as observers in this solemn assembly. . . . If we are in any way to blame for that separation, we humbly beg God's forgiveness and ask pardon, too, of our brethren who feel themselves to have been injured by us.
Paul VI (Giovanni Battista Montini)

Helping refugees is a true part of Christian unity because it is binding up human lives.
Arthur Michael Ramsey

See also: BELIEF, CHRISTIANITY, CHURCH, JUDAISM, MOHAMMEDANISM, RELIGION.

EDITOR

The composing room has an unlimited supply of periods available to terminate short, simple sentences.

Turner Catledge

One creative line is worth all the creative editing in this ably edited world.

William De Witt Hyde

Every editor of newspapers pays tribute to the devil.

Jean de La Fontaine

A good many young writers make the mistake of enclosing a stamped self-addressed envelope, big enough for the manuscript to come back in. This is too much of a temptation for the editor.

Ringgold (Ring) Wilmer Lardner

There are just two people entitled to refer to themselves as "we"; one is the editor and the other is the fellow with a tapeworm.

Edgar Wilson (Bill) Nye

See also: BOOK, COMMUNICATIONS MEDIA, INDEX, JOURNALISM, NEWSPAPER, PEN, PRESS, TELEVISION.

EDUCATION

Nothing in education is so astonishing as the amount of ignorance it accumulates in the form of inert facts.

Henry Brooks Adams

There are obviously two educations. One should teach us how to make a living and the other how to live.

James Truslow Adams

What sculpture is to a block of marble, education is to the human soul. The philosopher, the saint, the hero, the wise, and the good, or the great, very often lie hid and concealed in a plebeian, which a proper education might have disinterred and brought to light.

Joseph Addison

There can be but a single goal of education, and that—education to courage.

Alfred Adler

Observation more than books, experience rather than persons, are the prime educators.

Amos Bronson Alcott

The whole object of education is, or should be, to develop mind. The mind should be a thing that works. It should be able to pass judgment on events as they arise, make decisions.

Sherwood Anderson

Education does not commence with the alphabet; it begins with a mother's look, with a father's nod of approbation or a sign of reproof; with a sister's gentle pressure of the hand, or a brother's noble act of forbearance; with handfuls of flowers in green dells, on hills, and daisy meadows; with birds' nests admired, but not touched; with creeping ants, and almost imperceptable emmets; with humming-bees and glass beehives; with pleasant walks in shady lanes, and with thoughts directed in sweet and kindly tones and words to nature, to beauty, to acts of benevolence, to deeds of virtue, and to the source of all good—to God Himself!

Anonymous

What is fatal to the humanities is that they have been professionalized as if their end and purpose were the same as that of the sciences.

William Arrowsmith

Unless an individual is free to obtain the fullest education with which his society can provide him, he is being injured by society.

Wystan Hugh Auden

The test and the use of man's education is that he finds pleasure in the exercise of his mind.

Jacques Martin Barzun

It is a sufficient miracle if a college education, made up of many parts and many contracts with divergent minds, removes a little ignorance. Values (so called) are not taught; they are breathed in or imitated.

Jocques Barzun

For thirty years we have inverted the sensible order of things. We have tried instruction to instill virtue, and experience to remove ignorance. I contend that ignorance is best removed by instruction and that virtue is best instilled by experience.

Jacques Barzun

The aim of education should be to teach us rather how to think, than what to think—rather to improve our minds, so as to enable us to think for ourselves, than to load the memory with the thoughts of other men.

James Beattie

Education is the knowledge of how to use the whole of oneself. Many men use but one or two faculties out of the score with which they are endowed. A man is educated who knows how to make a tool of every faculty —how to open it, how to keep it sharp, and how to apply it to all practical purposes.

Henry Ward Beecher

We now have an even more persuasive educational institution than the schools and churches ramming the goods that factories produce down the throats of our people . . . and that educational institution is called advertising.

Ralph Borsodi

Education is the only cure for certain diseases the modern world has engendered, but if you don't find the disease, the remedy is superfluous.

Sir John Buchan

The academic community has in it the biggest concentration of alarmists, cranks and extremists this side of the giggle house.

William Frank Buckley, Jr.

Education is the cheap defense of nations.

Edmund Burke

He has seen but little of life who does not discern everywhere the effect of early education on men's opinions and habits of thinking. Children bring out of the nursery that which displays itself throughout their lives.

Richard Cecil

There is a moral as well as an intellectual objection to the custom, frequent in these times, of making education consist in a mere smattering of twenty different things, instead of in the mastery of five or six.

Sir Edwin Chadwick

He is to be educated not because he is to make shoes, nails, and pins, but because he is a man.

William Ellery Channing

Today toys are recognized by educators and welfare workers as a vital part of child de-velopment comparable with the need for nourishing food and instruction in the three Rs.

Paul Terry Cherington

I have never let my schooling interfere with my education.

Samuel Langhorne Clemens (Mark Twain)

Soap and education are not as sudden as a massacre, but they are more deadly in the long run.

Samuel Langhorne Clemens (Mark Twain)

Education in a democratic society must equip children to develop their potential and to participate fully in American life. For the community at large, the schools have discharged this responsibility well. But for many minorities, and particularly for the children of the ghetto, the schools have failed to provide the educational experience which could overcome the effects of discrimination and deprivation.

Commission on Civil Disorder, 1968

Neither piety, virtue, nor liberty can long flourish in a community where the education of youth is neglected.

Peter Cooper

It makes little difference what the trade, business, or branch of learning, in mechanical labor, or intellectual effort, the educated man is always superior to the common laborer. One who is in the habit of applying his powers in the right way will carry system into any occupation, and it will help him as much to handle a rope as to write a poem.

Francis Marion Crawford

The sure foundations of the State are laid in knowledge, not in ignorance; and every sneer at education, at culture, and at book-learning which is the recorded wisdom of the experience of mankind, is the demagogue's sneer at intelligent liberty, inviting national degeneracy and ruin.

George William Curtis

After centuries of education we still have plenty of primitives—some of them white-collar or even top-hat primitives . . . people who seem actuated only by hatred and fear and envy.

Elmer Holmes Davis

The aim of education should be to teach the child to think, not what to think.

John Dewey

We learn to do by doing.

John Dewey

The focus of that total experience which we call "going to college" is the day-to-day relationship between the undergraduates as a person and the college as an institutional embodiment of other people's purposes.

John Sloan Dickey

"Reeling and writhing, of course to begin with," Mock Turtle replied, "and the different branches of arithmetic—ambition, distraction, uglification and derision."

Charles Lutwidge Dodgson (Lewis Carroll)

If we are to receive full service from government, the universities must give us trained men. That means a constant reorientation of university instruction and research not for the mere purpose of increasing technical proficiency but for the purpose of keeping abreast with social and economic change. . . . Government is no better than its men.

William Orville Douglas

It is essential that the student acquire an understanding of and a lively feeling for values. He must acquire a vivid sense of the beautiful and of the morally good. Otherwise he—with his specialized knowledge—more closely resembles a well-trained dog than a harmoniously developed person.

Albert Einstein

The school should always have as its aim that the young man leave it as a harmonious personality, not as a specialist. This in my opinion is true in a certain sense even for technical schools. . . . The development of general ability for independent thinking and judgment should always be placed foremost, not the acquisition of special knowledge.

Albert Einstein

Unless education continues to be free—free in its response to local community needs, from any suggestion of political domination, and free from impediments to the pursuits of knowledge by teachers and students—it will cease to serve the purposes of free men.

Dwight David Eisenhower

We know that education, centrally controlled, finally would lead to a kind of control in other fields which we don't want and will never have. So we are dedicated to the proposition that the responsibility for educating our young is primarily local.

Dwight David Eisenhower

In some small field each child should . . . attain, within the limited range of its experience and observation, the power to draw a justly limited inference from observed facts.

Charles William Eliot

Liberal education develops a sense of right, duty and honor; and more and more in the modern world, large business rests on rectitude and honor as well as on good judgment.

Charles William Eliot

In the degree in which I have been privileged to know the intimate secrets of hearts, I ever more realize how great a part is played in the lives of men and women by some little concealed germ of abnormality. For the most part they are occupied in the task of stifling and crushing those germs, treating them like weeds in their gardens. There is another and better way, even though more difficult and more perilous. Instead of trying to suppress the weeds that can never be killed, they may be cultivated into useful or beautiful flowers. For it is impossible to conceive any impulse in a human heart which cannot be transformed into Truth or into Beauty or into Love.

(Henry) Havelock Ellis

The secret of education lies in respecting the pupil.

Ralph Waldo Emerson

That which we are we are all the while teaching, not voluntary, but involuntarily.

Ralph Waldo Emerson

We have in America the largest public school system on earth, the most expensive college buildings, the most extensive curriculum, but nowhere else is education so blind to its objectives, so indifferent to any specific outcome as in America. One trouble has been its negative character. It has aimed at the repression of faults rather than the creation of virtues.

William Herbert Perry Faunce

I wish every immigrant could know that Lincoln spent only one year in school under the tutelage of five different teachers, and that the man still could be the author of the Gettysburg address.

John Huston Finley

Nations . . . borrow billions for war; no nation has ever borrowed largely for education. Probably no nation is rich enough to pay for both war and civilization. We must make our choice; we cannot have both.

Abraham Flexner

If a man empties his purse into his head, no man can take it away from him. An investment in knowledge always pays the best interest.

Benjamin Franklin

States should spend money and effort on this great all-underlying matter of spiritual education as they have hitherto spent them on beating and destroying each other.

John Galsworthy

It is gross superstitution to suppose that knowledge can be obtained only by going to schools and colleges. The world produced brilliant students before schools and colleges came into being. There is nothing so ennobling or lasting as self-study. Schools and colleges make most of us mere receptacles for holding the superfluities of knowledge. Wheat is left out and mere husk is taken in.

Mohandas Karamchand (Mahatma) Gandhi

Literary education is intended only to quicken our service.

Mohandas Karamchand (Mahatma) Gandhi

Rest assured that literary education is no good without character.

Mohandas Karamchand (Mahatma) Gandhi

There is no school equal to a decent home and no teachers equal to honest virtuous parents.

Mohandas Karamchand (Mahatma) Gandhi

We labour under a sort of superstition that the child has nothing to learn during the first five years of its life. On the contrary, the fact is that the child never learns in after-life what it does in its first five years. The education of the child begins with conception.

Mohandas Karamchand (Mahatma) Gandhi

We can advance and develop democracy but little faster than we can advance and develop the average level of intelligence and knowledge within the democracy. That is the problem that confronts modern educators.

Samuel Gompers

Every citizen of this country, whether he pounds nails, raises corn, designs rockets or writes poetry, should be taught to know and love his American heritage; to use the lan-

guage well; to understand the physical universe, and to enjoy the arts. The dollars he gains in the absence of enlightenment like this will be earned in drudgery and spent in ignorance.

Calvin Edward Gross

Very few can be trusted with an education.

Louise Imogen Guiney

Science teaching (for children) should begin, not with the mythical body in rest or uniform motion, but with the human body.

John Burdon Sanderson Haldane

There is nothing like education for bringing to light, and assessing, the essential inequality between one mind and another.

Gordon Hewart

Education in its widest sense includes everything that exerts a formative influence, and causes a young person to be, at a given point, what he is.

Mark Hopkins

The first thing education teaches you is to walk alone.

Alfred Aloysius (Trader) Horn

I care not what subject is taught if only it be taught well.

Thomas Henry Huxley

Dull boys are more likely than others to get into difficulties, largely because they want, and need, more work with their hands and less intellectual work, but do not get it.

Edgar Hutchinson Johnson

We have entered an age in which education is not just a luxury permitting some men an advantage over others. It has become a necessity without which a person is defenceless in this complex, industrialized society . . . We have truly entered the century of the educated man.

Lyndon Baines Johnson

A child miseducated is a child lost.

John Fitzgerald Kennedy

The human mind is our fundamental resource.

John Fitzgerald Kennedy

I want to emphasize in the great concentration which we now place upon scientists and engineers how much we still need the men and women educated in the liberal tradition, willing to take the long look, undisturbed by prejudices and slogans of the moment, who attempt to make an honest judgment on difficult events.

John Fitzgerald Kennedy

It might be said now that I have the best of both worlds. A Harvard education and a Yale degree.

John Fitzgerald Kennedy

Our progress as a nation can be no swifter than our progress in education.

John Fitzgerald Kennedy

We must educate people today for a future in which the choices to be faced cannot be anticipated by even the wisest now among us.

John Fitzgerald Kennedy

Give vocational training to the manually minded, and the children's courts of the future will have less to do.

Lewis E. Lawes

If I were founding a university I would found first a smoking room; then when I had a little more money in hand I would found a dormitory; then after that, or more probably with it, a decent reading room and a library. After that, if I still had more money that I couldn't use, I would hire a professor and get some textbooks.

Stephen Butler Leacock

In [earlier] days a boy on the classical side officially did almost nothing but classics. I think this was wise; the greatest service we can do to education today is to teach fewer subjects. No one has time to do more than a very few things well before he is twenty, and when we force a boy to be a mediocrity in a dozen subjects we destroy his standards, perhaps his life.

Clive Staples (C. S.) Lewis

He that has found a way to keep a child's spirit easy, active, and free, and yet at the same time to restrain him from many things he has a mind to, and to draw him to things that are uneasy to him, has, in my opinion, got the true secret of education.

John Locke

Too much attention has been paid to making education attractive by smoothing the path as compared with inducing strenuous voluntary effort.

Abbott Lawrence Lowell

When you educate a man you educate an individual; when you educate a woman you educate a whole family.

Robert Morrison MacIver

The dropout represents a rejection of nineteenth-century technology as manifested in our educational establishments.

(Herbert) Marshall McLuhan

It is a matter of the greatest urgency that our educational institutions realize that we now have civil war among these environments created by media other than the printed word. The classroom is now in a vital struggle for survival with the immensely persuasive "outside" world created by new informational media. Education must shift from instruction, from imposing of stencils, to discovery—to probing and exploration and to the recognition of the language of forms.

(Herbert) Marshall McLuhan

Learning, the educational process, has long been associated only with the glum. We speak of the "serious" student. Our time presents a unique opportunity for learning by means of humor—a perceptive or incisive joke can be more meaningful than platitudes lying between two covers.

(Herbert) Marshall McLuhan

The teach-in represents an attempt to shift education from instruction to discovery, from brainwashing students to brainwashing instructors. It is a big, dramatic reversal.

(Herbert) Marshall McLuhan

Education is our only political safety. Outside of this ark all is deluge.

Horace Mann

A human being is not, in any proper sense, a human being till he is educated.

Horace Mann

The man who strives to educate himself—and no one else can educate him—must win a certain victory over his own nature. He must learn to smile at his dear idols, analyze his every prejudice, scrap if necessary his fondest and most consoling belief, question his presuppositions, and take his chances with the truth.

Everett Dean Martin

The aim of education should be to convert the mind into a living fountain, and not a reservoir. That which is filled by merely pumping in, will be emptied by pumping out.

John Mitchell Mason

Intelligence plus experience creates ideas, and experimentation with that form of chemistry —the contact of ideas with events—is the field of adult education.

Felix Muskett Morley

All the world over there is a realisation that only through right education can a better order of society be built up.

Jawaharlal Nehru

Education is not something in the air, cut off from the daily life of the student or from his future work as a citizen. Real education, it is felt, must be based on the actual environment and experiences of the child, and it must fit him for the work he will have to do in after-life.

Jawaharlal Nehru

Education should be a conscious, methodical application of the best means in the wisdom of the ages to the end that youth may know how to live completely.

Austin O'Malley

Character development is the great, if not the sole, aim of education.

William James O'Shea

I may safely predict that the education of the future will be inventive-minded. It will believe so profoundly in the high value of the inventive or creative spirit that it will set itself to develop that spirit by all means within its power.

Harry Allen Overstreet

Education is a debt due from the present to future generations.

George Peabody

The best education in the world is that got by struggling to get a living.

Wendell Phillips

Educational institutions will become, more and more purely, institutions for educating people; and, as they become this, they will cease to be seats of scientific inquiry save on the very lowest level.

Walter Boughton Pitkin

A degree is not an education, and the confusion on this point is perhaps the gravest

weakness in American thinking about education.

Prospect for America

Russia's real threat to us will come through their educational and not through their military processes. Military systems and techniques are transitory—they now change every few years. An intelligent and well educated body of citizens is something you will have forever.

Hyman George Rickover

Instruction ends in the schoolroom, but education ends only with life. A child is given to the universe to be educated.

Frederick William Robertson

Education equips us with ephemeral knowledge and tenacious dislikes.

Jean Rostand

Education comes to us from nature, men, or things. The inward development of our faculties and organs is the education of nature; the use which we are taught to make of this development is the education of men; and what we gain from our own experience of the objects around us is the education of things.

Jean Jacques Rousseau

The more purely intellectual aim of education should be the endeavor to make us see and imagine the world in an objective manner as far as possible as it really is in itself, and not merely through the distorting medium of personal desires.

Bertrand Arthur William Russell

Education is the established church of the United States. It is one of the religions that Americans believe in. It has its own orthodoxy, its pontiffs and its noble buildings.

Sir Michael Ernest Sadler

The great difficulty in education is to get experience out of ideas.

George Santayana

Only a long and still unfinished education has taught men to separate emotions from things and ideas from their objects.

George Santayana

To know the laws of God in nature and revelation, and then to fashion the affections and will into harmony with those laws—this is education.

Sylvester Scovel

The best school of discipline is home—family life is God's own method of training the young; and homes are very much what women make them.

Samuel Smiles

Education is a weapon, whose effects depend on who holds it in his hands and at whom it is aimed.

Joseph Stalin

The worst education that teaches self-denial is better than the best that teaches everything else and not that.

John Sterling

The problem of education is twofold: first to know, and then to utter. Everyone who lives any semblance of an inner life thinks more nobly and profoundly than he speaks.

Robert Louis Balfour Stevenson

Although in recent years not more than one boy in one hundred has been educated in the private schools of the United States, those schools have . . . educated approximately as many leaders as all the public schools combined.

Arthur Edwin Traxler

Education . . . has produced a vast population able to read but unable to distinguish what is worth reading.

George Macaulay Trevelyan

Education with inert ideas is not only useless; it is, above all things, harmful.

Alfred North Whitehead

Education is the apprenticeship of life.

Robert Eldridge Aris Willmott

See also: DISCIPLINE, INSTRUCTION, LEARNING, READING, SCHOOL, STUDY, TEACHING, TRUTH, UNIVERSITY.

EFFICIENCY

A sense of the value of time—that is, of the best way to divide one's time into one's various activities—is an essential preliminary to efficient work; it is the only method of avoiding hurry.

(Enoch) Arnold Bennett

Loyal and efficient work in a great cause, even though it may not be immediately recognized, ultimately bears fruit.

Jawaharlal Nehru

Obviously, the highest type of efficiency is that which can utilize existing material to the best advantage.

Jawaharlal Nehru

It is more than probable that the average man could, with no injury to his health, increase his efficiency fifty percent.

Walter Dill Scott

See also: ABILITY, COMPUTER, CYBERNETICS, DILIGENCE, GENIUS, INDUSTRY, METHOD, ORDER, TALENT, TECHNOLOGY.

EFFORT

Remember that the faith that removes mountains always carries a pick.

Anonymous

The fact is, nothing comes; at least, nothing good. All has to be fetched.

Charles Buxton

The strong man meets his crisis with the most practical tools at hand. They may not be the best tools but they are available, which is all-important. He would rather use them, such as they are, than do nothing.

Raymond Clapper

If you would relish food, labor for it before you take it; if enjoy clothing, pay for it before you wear it; if you would sleep soundly, take a clear conscience to bed with you.

Benjamin Franklin

Glory lies in the attempt to reach one's goal and not in reaching it.

Mohandas Karamchand (Mahatma) Gandhi

It is for us to make the effort. The result is always in God's hands.

Mohandas Karamchand (Mahatma) Gandhi

Providence has its appointed hour for everything. We cannot command results; we can only strive.

Mohandas Karamchand (Mahatma) Gandhi

Things don't turn up in this world until somebody turns them up.

James Abram Garfield

It is common sense to take a method and try it. If this fails, admit it frankly and try another. But above all, try something.

Franklin Delano Roosevelt

It is hard to fail, but it is worse never to have tried to succeed. In this life we get nothing save by effort.

Theodore Roosevelt

See also: ACTION, DILIGENCE, ENERGY, ENTER-
PRISE, EXERTION, INDUSTRY, LABOR,
PERSEVERANCE, WORK.

EGOTISM

Self-interest is but the survival of the animal in us. Humanity only begins for man with self-surrender.

Henri Frédéric Amiel

Egotism is the tongue of vanity.

Sébastien Roch Nicolas Chamfort

To speak ill of others is a dishonest way of praising ourselves; let us be above such transparent egotism. . . . If you can't say good and encouraging things, say nothing. Nothing is often a good thing to say, and always a clever thing to say.

Will (William James) Durant

What hypocrites we seem to be whenever we talk of ourselves! Our words sound so humble while our hearts are so proud.

Augustus and Julius Hare

It is a false principle, that because we are entirely occupied with ourselves, we must equally occupy the thoughts of others.—The contrary inference is the fair one.

William Hazlitt

Some people, when they hear an echo, think they originated the sound.

Ernest Hemingway

An egotist will always speak of himself, either in praise or censure; but a modest man ever shuns making himself the subject of his conversation.

Jean de La Bruyère

We often boast that we are never bored; but we are so conceited that we do not perceive how often we bore others.

Duc François de La Rochefoucauld

Egotism is the anesthetic that dulls the pain of stupidity.

Frank William Leahy

When all is summed up, a man never speaks of himself without loss; his accusations of himself are always believed; his praises never.

Michel Eyquem de Montaigne

Do you wish men to speak well of you? Then never speak well of yourself.

Blaise Pascal

The more you speak of yourself, the more you are likely to lie.

Johann Georg von Zimmermann

See also: ARROGANCE, BOASTING, SELFISHNESS,
SELF-PRAISE, VANITY.

EGYPT

I don't know if Nasser is right or wrong, but I do know that he is inevitable.

Anonymous

It [Nile] flows through old hushed Egypt and its sands,
Like some great mighty thought threading a dream,
And times and things, as in that vision, seem
Keeping along it their eternal stands.

(James Henry) Leigh Hunt

Sound the loud timbrel o're Egypt's dark sea!
Jehovah has triumph'd—his people are free.

Thomas Moore

We're a sentimental people. We like a few kind words better than millions of dollars given in a humiliating way.

Gamal Abdel Nasser

Within the Arab circle there is a role wandering aimlessly in search of a hero. For some reason it seems to me that this role is beckoning to us—to move, to take up its lines, put on its costumes and give it life. Indeed, we are the only ones who can play it. The role is to spark the tremendous latent strengths in the region surrounding us to create a great power, which will then rise up to a level of dignity and undertake a positive part in building the future of mankind.

Gamal Abdel Nasser

As one approaches Cairo, the great pyramids of Giza vividly remind one of Egypt's ancient history. Then the landscape suddenly becomes filled with hundreds of minarets and skyscrapers, bringing sharply to mind the juxtaposition of the medieval and the modern.

Georgiana Gerlinger Stevens

The desert in which the Egyptians live has always had a profound effect on them. For six thousand years they have struggled to alter this desert by expanding their oases—and they are still struggling with this task today. . . . The very narrowness of the cultivated strip along the entire length of the Nile River indicates how precious watered land is, and what struggles have been required to conquer the Egyptian desert.

Georgiana Gerlinger Stevens

Egypt has been historically hospitable to minorities, including Jews and Christians, and even to many thousands who refused to take Egyptian citizenship so as to escape taxation.

Georgiana Gerlinger Stevens

Aziz Ezzet, a gentleman of importance in Egypt, says his name can be pronounced by opening a soda bottle slowly.

Harry V. Wade

Many of the comforts and refinements that made Egypt so pleasant for the foreigners have passed away. But just because life is not so good for foreigners does not mean it is worse for the masses of Egyptians. For most of them, they have real opportunities for the first time in their lives. At last, Egyptians are in control of Egypt. They may do things badly, but they are doing it themselves. And that is the way they like it.

Wilton Wynn

See also: EAST AND WEST, MOHAMMEDANISM, ISRAEL, NATION, RUINS.

ELECTRONICS: *see* TECHNOLOGY.

ELEGANCE

Taste and elegance, though they are reckoned only among the smaller and secondary morals, are of no mean importance in the regulations of life. A moral taste is not of force to turn vice into virtue; but it recommends virtue with something like the blandishments of pleasure, and it infinitely abates the evils of vice.

Edmund Burke

Elegance is something more than ease—more than a freedom from awkwardness and restraint. It implies a precision, a polish, and a sparkling which is spirited, yet delicate.

William Hazlitt

When the mind loses its feeling for elegance, it grows corrupt and grovelling, and seeks in the crowd what ought to be found at home.

Walter Savage Landor

Elegance is good taste *plus* a dash of daring.

Carmel Snow

See also: CULTIVATION, FASHION, REFINEMENT, TASTE.

ELEPHANT

When you have got an elephant by the hind legs and he is trying to run away, it's best to let him run.

Abraham Lincoln

It is the little bits of things that fret and worry us: we can dodge an elephant, but we can't a fly.

Henry Wheeler Shaw (Josh Billings)

I love to look on these overgrown beasts, with their vast bodies, their immense strength, their ungainly proportions, their docile harmlessness. Their very size and clumsiness make me fell a kind of tenderness for them—their unwieldy bulk has something infantile about it. Moreover, they have large hearts. When they get wild and are furious, but when they calm down they are peace itself.

Sir Rabindranath Tagore

See also: ANIMAL.

ELOQUENCE

No man ever did, or ever will become most truly eloquent without being a constant reader of the Bible, and an admirer of the purity and sublimity of its language.

Fisher Ames

Eloquence is logic on fire.

Lyman Beecher

Eloquence is vehement simplicity.

Richard Cecil

Those who would make us feel, must feel themselves.

Charles Churchill

Brevity is a great charm of eloquence.

Cicero

The pleasure of eloquence is, in greatest part, owing often to the stimulus of the occasion which produces it—to the magic of sympathy which exalts the feeling of each, by radiating on him the feeling of all.

Ralph Waldo Emerson

There is no eloquence without a man behind it.

Ralph Waldo Emerson

Eloquence is the transference of thought and emotion from one heart to another, no matter how it is done.

John Bartholomew Gough

Honesty is one part of eloquence. We persuade others by being in earnest ourselves.

William Hazlitt

Talking and eloquence are not the same. To speak and to speak well are two things. A fool may talk, but a wise man speaks.

Ben (Benjamin) Jonson

There is not less eloquence displayed in the tone of voice, the eyes, and the gesture, than in the choice of words.

Duc François de La Rochefoucauld

True eloquence consists in saying all that is proper, and nothing more.

Duc François de La Rochefoucauld

The truest eloquence is that which holds us too mute for applause.

Edward G. Bulwer-Lytton (Baron Lytton)

Eloquence is in the assembly, not merely in the speaker.

William Pitt (Lord Chatham)

It is but a poor eloquence which only shows that the orator can talk.

Sir Joshua Reynolds

Speech is the body; thought, the soul, and suitable action the life of eloquence.

Charles Simmons

It is of eloquence as of a flame; it requires matter to feed it, and motion to excite it; and it brightens as it burns.

Tacitus

Eloquence is relative. One can no more pronounce on the eloquence of any composition, than on the wholesomeness of a medicine without knowing for whom it is intended.

Richard Whately

See also: DISCUSSION, ORATORY, RHETORIC.

EMINENCE

It is folly for an eminent man to think of escaping censure, and a weakness for him to be affected by it. All the illustrious persons of antiquity, and indeed of every age in the world, have passed through this fiery persecution.

Joseph Addison

The road to eminence and power from obscure condition ought not to be made too easy, nor a thing too much of course. If rare merit be the rarest of all rare things, it ought to pass through some sort of probation. The temple of honor ought to be seated on an eminence. If it be open through virtue, let it be remembered, too, that virtue is never tried but by some difficulty and some struggle.

Edmund Burke

Every man ought to aim at eminence, not by pulling others down, but by raising himself; and enjoy the pleasures of his own superiority, whether imaginary or real, without interrupting others in the same felicity.

Samuel Johnson

See also: DISTINCTION, FAME, GLORY.

EMOTION

By starving emotions we become humorless, rigid and stereotyped; by repressing them we become literal, reformatory and holier-than-thou; encouraged, they perfume life; discouraged, they poison it.

Joseph Collins

The stress of passion often discloses an aspect of the personality completely ignored till then by its closest intimates.

Joseph Conrad

Emotion is not something shameful, subordinate, second-rate; it is a supremely valid phase of humanity at its noblest and most mature.

Joshua Loth Liebman

All loving emotions, like plants, shoot up most rapidly in the tempestuous atmosphere of life.

Jean Paul Richter

The reason why writers fail when they attempt to evoke horror is that horror is something invented after the fact, when one is recreating the experience over again in the memory. Horror does not manifest itself in the world of reality.

Antoine de Saint-Exupéry

The taste for emotion may become a dangerous taste; we should be very cautious how we attempt to squeeze out of human life more ecstasy and paroxysm than it can well afford.

Sydney Smith

Emotion turning back on itself, and not leading on to thought or action, is the element of madness.

John Sterling

Intellect is to emotion as our clothes are to our bodies: we could not very well have civilized life without clothes, but we would be in a poor way if we had only clothes without bodies.

Alfred North Whitehead

See also: DESOLATION, FEELINGS, HEART, PASSION, SENSIBILITY.

EMPIRE

It is not for their long reigns, nor their frequent changes which occasion the fall of empires, but their abuse of power.

George Crabbe

Extended empire, like expanded gold, exchanges solid strength for feeble splendor.

Samuel Johnson

As a general truth, nothing is more opposed to the well-being and freedom of men, than vast empires.

Alexis de Tocqueville

See also: COLONIALISM, DESPOTISM, KING, NATION, POWER, STATE, TYRANNY.

EMPLOYMENT

Every man's task is his life-preserver.

George Barrell Emerson

Employment is nature's physician, and is essential to human happiness.

Galen

The employer generally gets the employees he deserves.

Sir Walter Gilbey

Cheerfulness is the daughter of employment; and I have known a man come home, in high spirits, from a funeral, merely because he has had the management of it.

George Horne

Be always employed about some rational thing, that the devil find thee not idle.

Jerome (Eusebius Hieronymus)

He that does not bring up his son to some honest calling and employment brings him up to be a thief.

Jewish Proverb

The safe and general antidote against sorrow, is employment. It is commonly observed, that among soldiers and seamen, though there is much kindness, there is little grief; they see their friend fall without that lamentation which is indulged in security and idleness, because they have no leisure to spare from the care of themselves; and whoever shall keep his thoughts equally busy, will find himself equally unaffected by irretrievable losses.

Samuel Johnson

Not to enjoy life, but to employ life, ought to be our aim and inspiration.

John Ross Macduff

The devil never tempted a man whom he found judiciously employed.

Charles Haddon Spurgeon

Employment gives health, sobriety, and morals. Constant employment and well-paid labor produce, in a country like ours, general prosperity, content, and cheerfulness.

Daniel Webster

See also: BUSINESS, BUSY, DILIGENCE, EFFORT, INDUSTRY, LABOR, OCCUPATION, POVERTY, WORK.

EMPTINESS

Leave the sick hearts that honour could not move,
And half-men, and their dirty songs and dreary,
And all the little emptiness of love.

Rupert Brooke

Four things are grievously empty: a head without brains, a wit without judgment, a heart without honesty, and a purse without money.

John Earle

So well-bred spaniels civilly delight
In mumbling of the game they dare not bite.
Eternal smiles his emptiness betray,
As shallow streams run dimpling all the way.

Alexander Pope

See also: DESOLATION, DESPONDENCY, MISERY, POVERTY.

EMULATION

Emulation admires and strives to imitate great actions; envy is only moved to malice.

Honoré de Balzac

Emulation is a noble passion. It is enterprising, but just withal. It keeps within the terms of honor, and makes the contest for glory just and generous; striving to excel, not by depressing others, but by raising itself.

Francis Beaumont

Without emulation we sink into meanness, or mediocrity, for nothing great or excellent can be done without it.

Francis Beaumont

Emulation has been termed a spur to virtue, and assumes to be a spur of gold. But it is a spur composed of baser materials, and if tried in the furnace will be found wanting.

Charles Caleb Colton

Emulation looks out for merits, that she may exalt herself by a victory; envy spies out blemishes, that she may have another by a defeat.

Charles Caleb Colton

Emulation, in the sense of a laudable ambition, is founded on humility, for it implies that we have a low opinion of our present, and think it necessary to advance and make improvement.

Joseph Hall

Emulation is the devil-shadow of aspiration. To excite it is worthy only of the commonplace vulgar schoolmaster, whose ambition is to show what fine scholars he can turn out, that he may get the more pupils.

George Macdonald

There is a long and wearisome step between admiration and imitation.

Jean Paul Richter

The desire . . . of those who are naturally different to become socially alike makes for moral suicide, as if cows wished to behave like bulls, or bulls like cows.

George Santayana

See also: EXAMPLE, IMITATION, RIVALRY.

ENCOURAGEMENT

Correction does much, but encouragement does more. Encouragement after censure is as the sun after a shower.

Johann Wolfgang von Goethe

We ought not to raise expectations which it is not in our power to satisfy. It is more pleasing to see smoke brightening into flame, than flame sinking into smoke.

Samuel Johnson

I believe that any man's life will be filled with constant and unexpected encouragement, if he makes up his mind to do his level best each day, and as nearly as possible reaching the high-water mark of pure and useful living.

Booker Taliaferro Washington

All may do what has by man been done.

Edward Young

See also: COMFORT, GUIDANCE, HELP, INSPIRATION, PRAISE, SYMPATHY.

END

If well thou hast begun, go on; it is the end that crowns us, not the fight.

Robert Herrick

In everything we ought to look to the end.

Jean de La Fontaine

The end must justify the means.

Matthew Prior

It is the beginning of the end.

Charles Maurice de Talleyrand-Périgord

See also: AIM, BEGINNING, DEATH, PURPOSE.

ENDURANCE

Not in the achievement, but in the endurance of the human soul, does it show its divine grandeur, and its alliance with the infinite God.

Edwin Hubbel Chapin

The greater the difficulty, the more glory in surmounting it. Skilful pilots gain their reputation from storms and tempests.

Epicurus

The palm-tree grows best beneath a ponderous weight, and even so the character of man. The petty pangs of small daily cares have often bent the character of men, but great misfortunes seldom.

Lajos Kossuth

He conquers who endures.

Persius

By bravely enduring, an evil which cannot be avoided is overcome.

Proverb

To endure is the first thing that a child ought to learn, and that which he will have most need to know.

Jean Jacques Rousseau

Happy the man who can endure the highest and lowest fortune. He who has endured such vicissitudes with equanimity has deprived misfortune of its power.

Seneca

There is nothing in the world so much admired as a man who knows how to bear unhappiness with courage.

Seneca

A man can bear more than ten oxen can pull.

Yiddish Proverb

See also: FORTITUDE, STRENGTH, WILL, ZEAL.

ENEMY

Plutarch has written an essay on the benefits which a man may receive from his enemies; and among the good fruits of enmity, mentions this in particular, that by the reproaches which it casts upon us we see the worst side of ourselves.

Joseph Addison

Though all things do to harm him what they can, no greater enemy to himself than man.

William Alexander (Earl of Stirling)

The fine and noble way to destroy a foe, is not to kill him; with kindness you may so change him that he shall cease to be so; then he's slain.

Charles Aleyn

Observe your enemies, for they first find out your faults.

Antisthenes

Men of sense often learn from their enemies. It is from their foes, not their friends, that cities learn the lesson of building high walls and ships of war; and this lesson saves their children, their homes, and their properties.

Aristophanes

I wish my deadly foe, no worse
Than want of friends, and empty purse.

Nicholas Breton

Some men are more beholden to their bitterest enemies than to friends who appear to be sweetness itself. The former frequently tell the truth, but the latter never.

Cato the Elder

If you want enemies, excel others; if friends, let others excel you.

Charles Caleb Colton

Make no enemies.—He is insignificant indeed who can do thee no harm.

Charles Caleb Colton

It is much safer to reconcile an enemy than to conquer him; victory may deprive him of his poison, but reconciliation of his will.

Owen Felltham

There are always people whom it is a privilege to dislike—a privilege one would miss by not knowing them.

Willis Fisher

There is no little enemy.

Benjamin Franklin

There is no enemy can hurt us but by our own hands. Satan could not hurt us, if our own corruption betrayed us not. Afflictions cannot hurt us without our own impatience. Temptations cannot hurt us, without our own yieldance. Death could not hurt us, without the sting of our owns sins. Sins could not hurt us, without our own impenitence.

Joseph Hall

Instead of loving your enemies, treat your friends a little better.

Edgar Watson Howe

Have you fifty friends?—it is not enough. Have you one enemy?—it is too much.

Italian Proverb

Our enemies come nearer the truth in the opinions they form of us than we do in our opinion of ourselves.

Duc François de La Rochefoucauld

Be assured those will be thy worst enemies, not to whom thou hast done evil, but who have done evil to thee. And those will be thy best friends, not to whom thou hast done good, but who have done good to thee.

Johann Kaspar Lavater

If we could read the secret history of our enemies, we should find in each man's life sorrow and suffering enough to disarm all hostility.

Henry Wadsworth Longfellow

Whatever the number of a man's friends, there will be times in his life when he has one too few; but if he has only one enemy, he is lucky indeed if he has not one too many.

Edward G. Bulwer-Lytton (Baron Lytton)

However rich or powerful a man may be it is the height of folly to make personal enemies; for one unguarded moment may yield you to the revenge of the most despicable of mankind.

George Lyttleton

Enemy advances, we retreat: enemy halts, we harass; enemy tires, we attack; enemy retreats, we pursue.

Mao Tse-tung

I am persuaded that he who is capable of being a bitter enemy can never possess the necessary virtues that constitute a true friend.

William Melmoth

We should never make enemies, if for no other reason, because it is so hard to behave toward them as we ought.

Ray Palmer

Let us carefully observe those good qualities wherein our enemies excel us, and endeavor to excel them by avoiding what is faulty, and imitating what is excellent in them.

Plutarch

It is the enemy whom we do not suspect who is the most dangerous.

Fernando de Rojas

O wise man, wash your hands of that friend who associates with your enemies.

Saadi (Muslih-ud-Din)

A merely fallen enemy may rise again, but the reconciled one is truly vanquished.

Johann Christoph Frederich von Schiller

A man cannot be too careful in the choice of his enemies.

Oscar Wilde

See also: CONTENTION, FRIENDSHIP, QUARREL, VIOLENCE, WAR.

ENERGY

The reward of a thing well done, is to have done it.

Ralph Waldo Emerson

This world belongs to the energetic.

Ralph Waldo Emerson

Energy will do anything that can be done in the world; and no talents, no circumstances, no opportunities will make a two-legged animal a man without it.

Johann Wolfgang von Goethe

He alone has energy who cannot be deprived of it.

Johann Kaspar Lavater

There is no genius in life like the genius of energy and activity.

Donald Grant Mitchell (Ik Marvel)

The truest wisdom, in general, is a resolute determination.

Napoleon I (Bonaparte)

See also: EFFORT, INDUSTRY, NUCLEAR ENERGY, POWER, WORK.

ENGLAND

We have in England a particular bashfulness in every thing that regards religion.

Joseph Addison

One has often wondered whether upon the whole earth there is anything so unintelligent, so unapt to perceive how the world is really going, as an ordinary young Englishman of our upper class.

Matthew Arnold

England is the mother of Parliaments.

John Bright

Our principal exports all labelled and packed,
At the ends of the earth are delivered intact;
Our soap and our salmon can travel in tins,
Between the two poles and as like as two pins.
So that Lancashire merchants whenever they
like
Can water the beer of a man in Klondike,
Or poison the meat of a man in Bombay,
And that is the meaning of Empire Day.

Gilbert Keith Chesterton

It was the nation and the race dwelling all 'round the globe that had the lion's heart. I had the luck to be called upon to give the lion's roar. I also hope that I sometimes suggested to the lion the right place to use his claws.

Sir Winston Leonard Spencer Churchill

We are indeed a nation of shopkeepers.

Benjamin Disraeli

In the end it may well be that Britain will be honored by the historians more for the way she disposed of an empire than for the way in which she acquired it.

(William) David Ormsby-Gore Harlech

The most repulsive race which God in His wrath ever created.

Heinrich Heine

Silence—a conversation with an Englishman.

Heinrich Heine

Their superiority consists in that they have no imagination.

Heinrich Heine

The British are an insular race, and long success and prosperity has made them look down on almost all others.

Jawaharlal Nehru

The English are a sensitive people and yet, when they go to foreign countries, there is a strange lack of awareness about them. In India, where the relation of ruler and ruled makes mutual understanding difficult, this lack of awareness is peculiarly evident. Almost, one would think that it is deliberate, so that they may see only what they want to see and be blind to all else. But facts do not vanish because they are ignored, and when they compel attention, there is feeling of displeasure and resentment at the unexpected happening, as of some trick having been played.

Jawaharlal Nehru

As an industrial nation, once the most powerful of all, we are passing through a period of self-denigration of such intensity that some might think a death wish behind it.

John Partridge

Although Londoners are, more than any other city people, wary of foreigners, although London landladies are Britannias armed with helmet, shield, trident, and have faces with the word "No" stamped like a coat of arms on them, the place is sentimental and tolerant. The attitude to foreigners is like the attitude to dogs: Dogs are neither human nor British, but so long as you keep them under control, give them their exercise, feed them, pat them, you will find their wild emotions are amusing, and their characters interesting.

Victor Sawdon Pritchett

The English are proud; the French are vain.

Jean Jacques Rousseau

It is a fact that great eaters of flesh are in general more cruel and ferocious than other men; this observation holds good in all places and times; the barbarism of the English is well known.

Jean Jacques Rousseau

The English are a busy people: they have not time to become elegant and refined.

Charles de Secondat (Baron de Montesquieu)

If I were asked with what the English are peculiarly led away, in truth I could not very well tell, neither war, nor high birth, nor dignities, nor gallantry, nor mania for ministerial favour. They wish that men should be men; the only two things they set a value on are riches and merit.

Charles de Secondat (Baron de Montesquieu)

I have a deep love and great respect for the British race as human beings. It has produced great-hearted men, thinkers of great thoughts, doers of great deeds. It has given rise to a great literature. I know that these people love justice and freedom, and hate lies. They are clean in their minds, frank in their manners, true in their friendship; in their behaviour they are honest and reliable. The personal experience which I have had of their literary men has roused my admiration not merely for their power of thought or expression but for their chivalrous humanity. We have felt the greatness of this people as we feel the sun; but as for the Nation, it is for us a thick mist of a stifling nature covering the sun itself.

Sir Rabindranath Tagore

I was impressed by the evidence of liberal humanity in the character of the English and thus I was led to set them on the pedestal of my highest respect. This generosity in their national character had not yet been vitiated by imperialist pride.

Sir Rabindranath Tagore

The typical Englishman is a strong being who takes a cold bath in the morning and talks about it for the rest of the day.

Ellen Cicely Wilkinson

In every country in the world in which there has been a devaluation of currency or rank inflation it is those people who are living on fixed incomes—the retired people of those countries—that are hurt the worst. They are being pauperized. That is true in Britain today. Those who are living in retirement or on fixed incomes in Britain today are those who will be hurt the most because of the devaluation of the pound.

John J. Williams

See also: AMERICA, AUSTRALIA, CANADA, COLONIALISM, FRANCE, NATION.

ENGLISHMEN: *see* ENGLAND.

ENJOYMENT

Only mediocrity of enjoyment is allowed to man.

Hugh Blair

Those who would enjoyment gain must find it in the purpose they pursue.

Sarah Josepha Buell Hale

Let all seen enjoyments lead to the unseen fountain from whence they flow.

Thomas Chandler Haliburton

Restraint is the golden rule of enjoyment.

Letitia Elizabeth Landon

The less you can enjoy, the poorer and scantier yourself; the more you can enjoy, the richer and more vigorous.

Johann Kaspar Lavater

I have always said and felt that true enjoyment cannot be expressed in words.

Jean Jacques Rousseau

All solitary enjoyments quickly pall, or become painful.

James Sharp

No enjoyment, however inconsiderable, is confined to the present moment. A man is the happier for life from having made once an agreeable tour, or lived for any length of time with pleasant people, or enjoyed any considerable interval of innocent pleasure.

Sidney Smith

I have told you of the Spaniard who always put on his spectacles when about to eat cherries, that they might look bigger and more tempting. In like manner I make the most of my enjoyments; and though I do not cast my cares away, I pack them in as little compass as I can, and carry them as conveniently as I can for myself, and never let them annoy others.

Robert Southey

See also: AMUSEMENT, DELIGHT, JOY, LEISURE, PLEASURE, RECREATION.

ENNUI

Ambition itself is not so reckless of human life as ennui. Clemency is a favorite attribute of the former, but ennui has the taste of a cannibal.

George Bancroft

Ennui is the desire of activity without the fit means of gratifying the desire.

George Bancroft

Ennui is a word which the French invented, though of all nations in Europe they know the least of it.

George Bancroft

I do pity unlearned gentlemen on a rainy day.

Lucius Cary (2d Viscount Falkland)

Ennui has, perhaps, made more gamblers than avarice; more drunkards than thirst; and perhaps as many suicides as despair.

Charles Caleb Colton

The victims of ennui paralyze all the grosser feelings by excess, and torpify all the finer by disuse and inactivity. Disgusted with this world and indifferent about another, they at last lay violent hands upon themselves, and assume no small credit for the sangfroid with which they meet death. But alas! such beings can scarcely be said to die, for they have never truly lived.

Charles Caleb Colton

I have measured out my life with coffee spoons.

Thomas Stearns Eliot

Ennui was born one day of uniformity.

Lamotte-Houdar

There is nothing so insupportable to man as to be in entire repose, without passion, occupation, amusement, or application. Then it is that he feels his own nothingness, isolation, insignificance, dependent nature, powerlessness, emptiness. Immediately there issue from his soul *ennui*, sadness, chagrin, vexation, despair.

Blaise Pascal

That which renders life burdensome to us, generally arises from the abuse of it.

Jean Jacques Rousseau

See also: BORE, IDLENESS, INDIFFERENCE.

ENTERPRISE

The method of the enterprising is to plan with audacity, and execute with vigor; to sketch out a map of possibilities, and then to treat them as probabilities.

Christian Nestell Bovee

The margin between that which men naturally do, and that which they can do, is so great that a system which urges men on to action and develops individual enterprise and initiative is preferable, in spite of the wastes that necessarily attend their process.

Louis Dembitz Brandeis

Attempt the end, and never stand to doubt; nothing so hard but search will find it out.

Robert Herrick

Kites rise against, not with the wind. No man ever worked his passage anywhere in a dead calm.

John Neal

To do anything in this world worth doing, we must not stand back shivering and thinking of the cold and danger, but jump in, and scramble through as well as we can.

Sydney Smith

See also: CAPITALISM, COURAGE, EFFORT, FREE ENTERPRISE, IMAGINATION.

ENTHUSIASM

Great designs are not accomplished without enthusiasm of some sort. It is the inspiration of everything great. Without it no man is to be feared, and with it none despised.

Christian Nestell Bovee

No wild enthusiast ever yet could rest,
Till half mankind were, like himself possest.

William Cowper

Every production of genius must be the production of enthusiasm.

Benjamin Disraeli

Truth is never to be expected from authors whose understandings are warped with enthusiasm; for they judge all actions and their causes by their own perverse principles, and a crooked line can never be the measure of a straight one.

John Dryden

Enthusiasm begets heroism.

Semen Markovich Dubnov

Every great and commanding movement in the annals of the world is the triumph of enthusiasm. Nothing great was ever achieved without it.

Ralph Waldo Emerson

Enthusiasts soon understand each other.

Washington Irving

We act as though comfort and luxury were the chief requirements of life, when all that we need to make us really happy is something to be enthusiastic about.

Charles Kingsley

The world belongs to the Enthusiast who keeps cool.

William McFee

How much easier it was to do great and venturesome deeds in moments of enthusiasm and excitement than to carry on from day to day when the glow was past.

Jawaharlal Nehru

The enthusiasm of old men is singularly like that of infancy.

Gérard de Nerval

Each generation produces its squad of "moderns" with peashooters to attack Gibraltar.

Channing Pollock

Enthusiasm is the best protection in any situation. Wholeheartedness is contagious. Give yourself, if you wish to get others.

David Seabury

No virtue is safe that is not enthusiastic.

Sir John Robert Seeley

The sense of this word among the Greeks affords the noblest definition of it; enthusiasm signifies "God in us."

Madame de Staël

An excess of excitement, and a deficiency of enthusiasm, may easily characterize the same person or period. Enthusiasm is grave, inward, self-controlled; mere excitement is outward, fantastic, hysterical, and passing in a moment from tears to laughter; from one aim to its very opposite.

John Sterling

Enthusiasm always exaggerates the importance of important things and overlooks their deficiencies.

Hugh Stevenson Tigner

Let us recognize the beauty and power of true enthusiasm; and whatever we may do to enlighten ourselves or others, guard against checking or chilling a single earnest sentiment.

Henry Theodore Tuckerman

See also: DEVOTION, EARNESTNESS, ZEAL.

ENVIRONMENT

Heredity is nothing but stored environment.

Luther Burbank

Complete adaptation to environment means death. The essential point in all response is the desire to control environment.

John Dewey

Civilizations come to birth in environments that are unusually difficult and not unusually easy.

Arnold Joseph Toynbee

See also: CIRCUMSTANCE, CRIME, GHETTO, OPPORTUNITY, POVERTY.

ENVY

A man that hath no virtue in himself ever envieth virtue in others; for men's minds will either feed upon their own good, or upon others' evil; and who wanteth the one will prey upon the other; and whoso is out of hope to attain to another's virtue, will seek to come at even hand by depressing another's fortune.

Francis Bacon

Men of noble birth are noted to be envious toward new men when they rise; for the distance is altered; it is like a deceit of the eye, that when others come on they think themselves go back.

Francis Bacon

There is no surer mark of the absence of the highest moral and intellectual qualities than a cold reception of excellence.

Gamaliel Bailey

Envy, like the worm, never runs but to the fairest fruit; like a cunning bloodhound, it singles out the fattest deer in the flock. Abraham's riches were the Philistines' envy, and Jacob's blessings had Esau's hatred.

Francis Beaumont

Every other sin hath some pleasure annexed to it, or will admit of some excuse, but envy wants both. We should strive against it, for

if indulged in it will be to us a foretaste of hell upon earth.

Richard Eugene Burton

Envy is like a fly that passes all a body's sounder parts, and dwells upon the sores.

George Chapman

As a moth gnaws a garment, so doth envy consume a man.

John Chrysostom

No crime is so great to envy as daring to excel.

Charles Churchill

The benevolent have the advantage of the envious, even in this present life; for the envious man is tormented not only by all the ill that befalls himself, but by all the good that happens to another; whereas the benevolent man is the better prepared to bear his own calamities unruffled, from the complacency and serenity he has secured from contemplating the prosperity of all around him.

Charles Caleb Colton

The envious praise only that which they can surpass; that which surpasses them they censure.

Charles Caleb Colton

Envy's memory is nothing but a row of hooks to hang up grudges on.

John Watson Foster

Whoever feels pain in hearing a good character of his neighbor, will feel a pleasure in the reverse. And those who despair to rise in distinction by their virtues, are happy if others can be depressed to a level with themselves.

Benjamin Franklin

Fools may our scorn, not envy raise, for envy is a kind of praise.

John Gay

The envious man grows lean at the success of his neighbor.

Horace

If envy, like anger, did not burn itself in its own fire, and consume and destroy those persons it possesses before it can destroy those it wishes worst to, it would set the whole world on fire, and leave the most excellent persons the most miserable.

Edward Hyde (Earl of Clarendon)

All envy is proportionate to desire; we are uneasy at the attainments of another, according as we think our own happiness would be advanced by the addition of that which be withheld from us; and therefore whatever depresses immoderate wishes, will, at the same time, set the heart free from the corrosion of envy, and exempt us from that vice which is, above most others, tormenting to ourselves, hateful to the world, and productive of mean artifices and sordid projects.

Samuel Johnson

I am told so much evil of that man, and I see so little of it in him, that I begin to suspect that he possesses some inconvenient merit which extinguishes that of others.

Jean de La Bruyère

Envy is more irreconcilable than hatred.

Duc François de La Rochefoucauld

The truest mark of being born with great qualities, is being born without envy.

Duc François de La Rochefoucauld

We are often vain of even the most criminal of our passions; but envy is so shameful a passion that we never dare to acknowledge it.

Duc François de La Rochefoucauld

Envy has no other quality but that of detracting from virtue.

Livy

Other passions have objects to flatter them, and which seem to content and satisfy them for a while. There is power in ambition, pleasure in luxury, and pelf in covetousness; but envy can gain nothing but vexation.

Michel Eyquem de Montaigne

Envy always implies conscious inferiority wherever it resides.

Pliny the Elder

Envy will merit, as its shade, pursue
But, like a shadow, proves the substance true.

Alexander Pope

Wherever I find envy, I take a pleasure in provoking it; I always praise before an envious man those who make him grow pale.

Charles de Secondat (Baron de Montesquieu)

Base envy withers at another's joy, and hates the excellence it cannot reach.

James Thomson

Envy makes us see what will serve to accuse others, and not perceive what may justify them.

Daniel Wilson

If we did but know how little some enjoy of the great things that they possess, there would not be much envy in the world.

Edward Young

See also: AVARICE, COVETOUSNESS, EMULATION, JEALOUSY, RIVALRY.

EPIGRAM

The feathered arrow of an epigram has sometimes been wet with the heart's blood of its victim.

Isaac D'Israeli

An epigram is a gag that's played Carnegie Hall.

Oscar Levant

An epigram is a half-truth so stated as to irritate the person who believes the other half.

Shailer Mathews

See also: APHORISM, APOTHEGM, LANGUAGE, MAXIM, PROVERB, QUOTATION, SLOGAN, TRUISM.

EPITAPH

And were an epitaph to be my story
I'd have a short one ready for my own.
I would have written of me on my stone:
I had a lover's quarrel with the world.

Robert Lee Frost

Some persons make their own epitaphs, and bespeak the reader's goodwill. It were, indeed, to be wished, that every man would early learn in this manner to make his own, and that he would draw it up in terms as flattering as possible, and that he would make it the employment of his life to deserve it.

Oliver Goldsmith

Here lies a nuisance dedicated to sanity.

David Low

See also: DEATH, EPIGRAM.

EQUALITY

All service ranks the same with God—
With God, whose puppets, best and worst,
Are we; there is no last nor first.

Robert Browning

We believe, as asserted in the Declaration of Independence, that all men are created equal; but that does not mean that all men are or can be equal in possessions, in ability, or in merit; it simply means that all shall stand equal before the law.

William Jennings Bryan

Whatever difference there may appear to be in men's fortunes, there is still a certain compensation of good and ill in all, that makes them equal.

Pierre Charron

The doctrine of human equality reposes on this: that there is no man really clever who has not found that he is stupid.

Gilbert Keith Chesterton

There are many humorous things in the world: among them the white man's notion that he is less savage than the other savages.

Samuel Langhorne Clemens (Mark Twain)

Kings and their subjects, masters and slaves, find a common level in two places—at the foot of the cross and in the grave.

Charles Caleb Colton

When the principle of equality before God is applied to the present society, it has explosive consequences for the secular polity.

Harvey Gallagher Cox

The idea of bringing all men on an equality with each other has always been a pleasant dream: the law cannot equalize men in spite of nature.

Luc de Clapiers (Marquis de Vauvenargues)

It is not true that equality is a law of nature. Nature has no equality. Its sovereign law is subordination and dependence.

Luc de Clapiers (Marquis de Vauvenargues)

Those who might themselves be subject to equalization have rarely been enthusiastic about equality as a subject of social comment.

John Kenneth Galbraith

Classless society is the ideal not merely to be aimed at but to be worked for.

Mohandas Karamchand (Mahatma) Gandhi

Had He made any distinctions of high and low between man and man, they would have been visible as are the distinctions between, say, an elephant and an ant. But He has endowed all human beings impartially with the same shape and the same natural wants.

Mohandas Karamchand (Mahatma) Gandhi

In the eyes of God, who is the creator of all, His creatures are all equal.

Mohandas Karamchand (Mahatma) Gandhi

It can never be an act of merit to look down upon any human being as inferior to us.

Mohandas Karamchand (Mahatma) Gandhi

It is wrong, it is sinful, to consider some people lower than ourselves.

Mohandas Karamchand (Mahatma) Gandhi

There will never be real equality so long as one feels inferior or superior to the other.

Mohandas Karamchand (Mahatma) Gandhi

We are all His creatures; and just as in the eyes of parents all their children are absolutely equal, so also in God's eyes all His creatures must be equal.

Mohandas Karamchand (Mahatma) Gandhi

Freedom and equality! They are not to be found on earth below or in heaven above. The stars on high are not alike, . . . and all obey an iron-like law.

Heinrich Heine

I have no respect for the passion for equality, which seems to me merely idealizing envy.

Oliver Wendell Holmes

So far is it from being true that men are naturally equal, that no two people can be half an hour together but one shall acquire an evident superiority over the other.

Samuel Johnson

Even though we face the difficulties of today and tomorrow, I still have a dream. I have a dream that one day this nation will rise up and live out the true meaning of its creed: "We hold these truths to be self-evident, that all men are created equal."

Martin Luther King, Jr.

Equality is the share of every one at their advent upon earth; and equality is also theirs when placed beneath it.

Ninon de Lenclos (Anne Lenclos)

By the law of God, given by him to humanity, all men are free, are brothers, and are equals.

Guiseppe Mazzini

Not merely from moral and humanitarian grounds but also from the point of view of political common sense has it become essential to raise the standard of the common man and to give him full opportunity of progress. A social structure which denies him this opportunity stands self-condemned and must be changed.

Jawaharlal Nehru

Political freedom or political equality is the very basis on which you build up other equalities. At the same time political equality may cease to have meaning if there is gross economic inequality.

Jawaharlal Nehru

All men are by nature equal, made, all, of the same earth by the same Creator, and however we deceive ourselves, as dear to God is the poor peasant as the mighty prince.

Plato

The desire for social equality is not unmixed with a certain eagerness to be rid of the bother of pity.

Jean Rostand

Everyone shares the gross stuff of his being with others; all men are essentially consubstantial.

Jean Rostand

In the state of nature, there is an equality *de facto* real and indestructible, because it is impossible in that state that the simple difference between man and man should be so great as to render one dependent on the other. There is in the social state an equality *de jure* chimerical and vain, because the means destined to maintain it serves to destroy it; and because the public force employed by the strong to oppress the feeble breaks the kind of equilibrium which nature had placed between them.

Jean Jacques Rousseau

We must recover the element of quality in our traditional pursuit of equality. We must not, in opening our schools to everyone, confuse the idea that all should have equal chance with the notion that all have equal endowments.

Adlai Ewing Stevenson

In the gates of eternity the black hand and the white hold each other with an equal clasp.

Harriet Elizabeth Beecher Stowe

The equality of conditions is more complete in the Christian countries of the present day, than it has been at any time, or in any part of the world. Its gradual development is a providential fact, and it possesses all the characteristics of a divine decree; it is universal, it is durable, and it constantly eludes all human interference; and all events, as well as all men, contribute to its progress.

Alexis de Tocqueville

When the political power of the clergy was founded and began to exert itself, and they opened their ranks to all classes, to the poor and the rich, the villain and the lord, equality penetrated into the government through the church; and the being who as a serf must have vegetated in perpetual bondage, took his place, as a priest, in the midst of nobles, and not unfrequently above the head of kings.

Alexis de Tocqueville

We conclude that in the field of public education the doctrine of "separate but equal" has no place. Separate educational facilities are inherently unequal [Brown vs. Board of Education of Topeka, May 17, 1954].

United States Supreme Court

Men are equal; it not birth but virtue that makes the difference.

Voltaire (François Marie Arouet)

They who say all men are equal speak an undoubted truth, if they mean that all have an equal right to liberty, to their property, and to their protection of the laws. But they are mistaken if they think men are equal in their station and employments, since they are not so by their talents.

Voltaire (François Marie Arouet)

There can be no equality, nor any approach to equality, except among men economically independent and economically comparable.

Walter Edward Weyl

The Constitution does not provide for first and second class citizens.

Wendell Lewis Wilkie

It is not tolerance that one is entitled to in America. It is the right of every citizen in America to be treated by other citizens as an equal.

Wendell Lewis Wilkie

At the baths, all are equal.

Yiddish Proverb

See also: DEMOCRACY, EQUITY, JUSTICE, LEV-
ELER, RIGHTS.

EQUANIMITY

The excellence of equanimity is beyond all
praise. One of this disposition is not dejected
in adversity, nor elated in prosperity: he is
affable to others, and contented in himself.

Charles Buck

I have three personal ideals. One, to do the
day's work well and not to bother about to-
morrow. . . . The second ideal has been to act
the Golden Rule, as far as in me lay, toward
my professional brethren and toward the patients committed to my care. And the third
has been to cultivate such a measure of
equanimity as would enable me to bear success with humility, the affection of my friends
without pride, and to be ready when the day
of sorrow and grief came to meet it with the
courage befitting a man.

Sir William Osler

In this thing one man is superior to another,
that he is better able to bear prosperity or
adversity.

Philemon

See also: PEACE, RESIGNATION, SELF-CONTROL.

EQUITY

Equity is that exact rule of righteousness or
justice which is to be observed between man
and man. It is beautifully and comprehen-
sively expressed in the words of the Saviour,
"All things whatsoever ye would that men
should do to you, do ye even so to them, for
this is the law and the prophets."

Charles Buck

I am no leveller; I look upon an artificial
equality as equally pernicious with a facti-
tious aristocracy; both depressing the energies
and checking the enterprise of a nation.

Benjamin Disraeli

The dream of equity will win.

Carl Sandburg

Equity in law is the same that the spirit is
in religion, what every one pleases to make
it: sometimes they go according to conscience, sometimes according to law, sometimes according to the rule of court.

John Selden

See also: EQUALITY, INJUSTICE, JUSTICE, LAW,
RECOMPENSE.

EQUIVOCATION

There is no possible excuse for a guarded
lie. Enthusiastic and impulsive people will
sometimes falsify thoughtlessly, but equivocation is malice prepense.

Hosea Ballou

He who is guilty of equivocation, may well
be suspected of hypocrisy.

Samuel Maunder

A sudden lie may sometimes be only man-
slaughter upon truth; but by a carefully con-
structed equivocation truth is always, with
malice aforethought, deliberately murdered.

George Morley

When thou art obliged to speak, be sure to
speak the truth; for equivocation is half way
to lying, and lying is the whole way to hell.

William Penn

See also: CONCEALMENT, DECEIT, DISHONESTY,
DISSIMULATION, FALSEHOOD, HYPOC-
RISY, LYING, SOPHISTRY.

ERROR

An error doesn't become a mistake until you
refuse to correct it.

Orlando A. Battista

There are errors which no wise man will
treat with rudeness, while there is a probability that they may be the refraction of some
great truth still below the horizon.

Samuel Taylor Coleridge

Error ceases to be error when it is corrected.

Mohandas Karamchand (Mahatma) Gandhi

Realization of an error, which amounts to
a fixed resolve never to repeat it, is enough
penance.

Mohandas Karamchand (Mahatma) Gandhi

There is no defeat in the confession of one's
error. The confession itself is victory.

Mohandas Karamchand (Mahatma) Gandhi

No tempting form of error is without some
latent charm derived from truth.

Alexander Keith

Find earth where grows no weed, and you
may find a heart wherein no error grows.

Thomas Knowles

We live in terror of doing the wrong thing
instead of in hope of finding the right.

Harold Joseph Laski

Our understandings are always liable to error. Nature and certainty are very hard to come at, and infallibility is mere vanity and pretence.

Marcus Aurelius

Errors that last the shortest time are always the best.

Molière (Jean Baptiste Poquelin)

My principal method for defeating error and heresy, is, by establishing the truth. One purposes to fill a bushel with tares; but if I can fill it first with wheat, I may defy his attempts.

John Newton

Error commonly has some truth in what it affirms, is wrong generally in what it denies.

Francis Landey Patton

Error will slip through a crack, while truth will stick in a doorway.

Henry Wheeler Shaw (Josh Billings)

Few practical errors in the world are embraced on conviction, but on inclination; for though the judgment may err on account of weakness, yet, where one error enters at this door, ten are let into it through the will; that, for the most part, being set upon those things which truth is a direct obstacle to the enjoyment of; and where both cannot be had, a man will be sure to buy his enjoyment, though he pays down truth for the purchase.

Robert South

Men are apt to prefer a prosperous error to an afflicted truth.

Jeremy Taylor

In all science error precedes the truth, and it is better it should go first than last.

Horace Walpole

Half the truth will very often amount to absolute falsehood.

Richard Whately

See also: CRIME, DELUSION, FALSEHOOD, FORGIVENESS, MISTAKE, SIN, UNDERSTANDING, VICE, WICKEDNESS, WRONG.

ESPIONAGE: *see* SPYING.

ESTEEM

The chief ingredients in the composition of those qualities that gain esteem and praise, are good nature, truth, good sense, and good breeding.

Joseph Addison

The esteem of wise and good men is the greatest of all temporal encouragements to virtue; and it is a mark of an abandoned spirit to have no regard to it.

Edmund Burke

It is difficult to esteem a man as highly as he would wish.

Luc de Clapiers (Marquis de Vauvenargues)

Esteem cannot be where there is no confidence; and there can be no confidence where there is no respect.

Henry Giles

Esteem has more engaging charms than friendship and even love. It captivates hearts better, and never makes ingrates.

Duc François de La Rochefoucauld

All true love is founded on esteem.

George Villiers (2d Duke of Buckingham)

See also: ADMIRATION, LOVE, RESPECT.

ETERNITY

Eternity is in love with the productions of time.

William Blake

Eternity is not an everlasting flux of time, but time is a short parenthesis in a long period.

John Donne

Eternity has no gray hairs! The flowers fade, the heart withers, man grows old and dies, the world lies down in the sepulchre of ages, but time writes no wrinkles on the brow of eternity.

Reginald Heber

This is eternal life; a life of everlasting love, showing itself in everlasting good works; and whosoever lives that life, he lives the life of God, and hath eternal life.

Charles Kingsley

The thought of eternity consoles for the shortness of life.

Chrétien Malesherbes

The speck of life in time's great wilderness
This narrow isthmus 'twixt two boundless seas,
The past, the future, two eternities!

Thomas Moore

I saw Eternity the other night
Like a great ring of pure and endless light,
   All calm, as it was bright.

                   Henry Vaughan

Try as we may, we cannot capture a present moment, for it eludes us like gossamer. Once captured, it is in the past. . . . The present moment exists but cannot be "timed" and so is itself timeless. The timeless now is the eternal moment where all living happens, and thus eternal life is here and now and nowhere else.

                   Barry Wood

See also: FUTURE, GOD, HEAVEN, HELL, IMMORTALITY, TIME.

ETHICS

My belief is that no human being or society composed of human beings ever did or ever will come to much unless their conduct was governed and guided by the love of some ethical idea.

             Thomas Henry Huxley

A lively and lasting sense of filial duty is more effectually impressed on the mind of a son or daughter by reading King Lear, than by all the dry volumes of ethics, and divinity, that ever were written.

                Thomas Jefferson

From the poetry of Lord Byron they drew a system of ethics, compounded of misanthropy and voluptuousness, a system in which the two great commandments were, to hate your neighbour, and to love your neighbour's wife.

         Thomas Babington Macauley

Somewhat allied to the philosophy of religion is the science of ethics. It is equally useless. . . . [It] is as useless a science as can be conceived. . . . As long as ethics is recognized as not being a matter of vital importance or in any way touching the student's conscience, it is, to a normal and healthy mind, a civilizing and valuable study—somewhat more so than the theory of whist, much more so than the question of landing of Columbus, which things are insignificant not at all because they are useless, nor even because they are little in themselves, but simply and solely because they are detached from the great continuum of ideas.

            Charles Sanders Peirce

See also: CONDUCT, CONSCIENCE, MORALITY.

ETIQUETTE

The propriety of some persons seems to consist in having improper thoughts about their neighbors.

           Francis Herbert Bradley

Good taste rejects excessive nicety; it treats little things as little things, and is not hurt by them.

   François Salignac de La Mothe-Fénelon

We must conform, to a certain extent, to the conventionalities of society, for they are the ripened results of a varied and long experience.

            Archibald Alexander Hodge

Who needs a book of etiquette? Everyone does . . . for we must all learn the socially acceptable ways of living. . . . Even in primitive societies there are rules, some . . . as complex and inexplicable as many of our own. Their original *raison d'être* or purpose is lost, but their acceptance is still unquestioned.

               Amy Vanderbilt

See also: CUSTOM, GOOD BREEDING, MANNERS.

EUGENICS

Adolescence lengthens now with every generation; parental care increases as blind fertility disappears.

         Will (William James) Durant

Eugenics is supported by politically-minded scientists and scientifically-minded politicians as an antidote to democracy.

        Bertrand Arthur William Russell

It is in this direction, of bringing out the uniqueness of every person, that human genetics has been making its greatest strides and can yet make its greatest contributions.

             Amram Scheinfeld

A sensible eugenics program, therefore, would seek to replace the reckless or haphazard direction of human evolution with intelligent and carefully planned guidance.

             Amram Scheinfeld

The only fundamental and possible Socialism is the socialization of the selective breeding of Man: in other terms, of human evolution. We must eliminate the Yahoo, or his vote will wreck the commonwealth.

            George Bernard Shaw

See also: ABORTION, ANCESTRY, BIRTH, LIFE, PARENT.

EULOGY

Eulogy—praise of a person who has either the advantages of wealth and power, or the consideration to be dead.

           Ambrose Gwinnett Bierce

I would rather have a plain coffin without a flower, a funeral without a eulogy, than a life without the sweetness of love and sympathy. Let us learn to anoint our friends beforehand for their burial. Post-mortem kindness does not cheer the burdened spirit. Flowers on the coffin cast no fragrance backward over the weary way.

George William Childs

My brother [Robert F. Kennedy] need not be idealized or enlarged in death beyond what he was in life. He should be remembered simply as a good and decent man who saw wrong and tried to right it, saw suffering and tried to heal it, saw war and tried to stop it.

Edward Moore Kennedy

What worth is eulogy's blandest breath,
When whispered in ears that are hushed in
death?

Margaret Preston

See also: DEATH, EPITAPH, FUNERAL, PRAISE, RHETORIC.

EUROPE

Consider the American continent! How simple it is! How broad! How large! How grand in design! A strip of coast, a range of mountains, a plain, a second range, a second strip of coast! That is all! Contrast the complexity of Europe, its lack of symmetry, its variety, irregularity, disorder and caprice! The geography of the two continents already foreshadows the differences in their civilizations.

Goldsworthy Lowes Dickinson

We are part of the community of Europe, and we must do our duty as such.

William Ewart Gladstone

In Western Europe there are now only small countries—those that know it, and those that do not know it yet.

Théotiste Lefèvre

Some day, taking its pattern from the United States, there will be founded a United States of Europe.

George Washington

See also: ENGLAND, FRANCE, GERMANY, IRELAND, ITALY, NETHERLANDS, RUSSIA.

EUTHANASIA

To me disease is evil, old age, decrepitude, with incurable disease the final evil. . . .

Thanks be to those, scientists or others, who have invented or discovered these poisons . . . perhaps for an almost quiet exit, the door somewhat softly opened. An end to my being a nuisance to others.

Sherwood Anderson

A last duty. Human life consists in mutual service. No grief, pain, misfortune or broken heart is excuse for cutting off one's life while any power of service remains. But when all usefullness is over, when one is assured of an imminent and unavoidable death, it is the simplest of human rights to choose a quick and easy death in place of a slow and horrible one.

Charlotte Perkins Gilman

Since the experience of Nazi Germany during the war the whole euthanasia movement has fallen into disrepute. Under these circumstances Christians are fully justified in opposing any attempt to introduce legalized euthanasia and can be reasonable confident that their efforts will be successful.

Norman Antony Francis St. John-Stevas

The basis of Christian opposition to euthanasia is not that in the Christian view life has absolute value, but that the disposal of life is in God's hands. Man has no absolute control over his life but holds it as a trust. He has the use of it but may not destroy it at will. Furthermore, Christians recognize the principle of the sanctity of life. The only occasion when a Christian may take the life of a human being is when he is an unjust aggressor against an individual or the common good.

Norman Antony Francis St. John-Stevas

If a patient in agony begs to die, another may not touch him.

Sefer Hasidim

Doctors are only human beings, with few if any supermen among them. They make honest mistakes, like other men, because of the limitations of the human mind. They might conceivably agree on legal euthanasia in a certain case, only to find on autopsy, that they had made a wrong diagnosis. I mention these matters because of the difficulty involved in the decision as to incurability, though it must be admitted that errors in that direction are exceedingly rare.

Abraham Leo Wolbarst

See also: ABORTION, DEATH, MERCY, MURDER.

EVENING

It is the hour when from the boughs
   The nightingale's high note is heard;
It is the hour when lovers' vows
   Seem sweet in every whispered word;
And gentle winds, and waters near,
Make music to the lonely ear.
Each flower the dews have lightly wet,
And in the sky the stars are met,
And on the wave is deeper blue,
And on the leaf a browner hue,
And in the heaven that clear obscure,
So softly dark, and darkly pure.
Which follows the decline of day,
As Twilight melts beneath the moon away.
     George Gordon Byron (Lord Byron)

The curfew tolls the knell of parting day,
   The lowing herd winds slowly o'er the
      lea,
The ploughman homeward plods his weary
     way.
   And leaves the world to darkness and to
   me.
     Thomas Gray

Day hath put on his jacket,
  and around
His burning bosom buttoned
  it with stars.
     Oliver Wendell Holmes

The holy time is quiet as a Nun
Breathless with adoration.
     William Wordsworth

See also: MORNING, NIGHT, SUNSET, TWILIGHT.

EVENT

Coming events cast their shadows before.
     Thomas Campbell

There is little peace or comfort in life if we
are always anxious as to future events. He
that worries himself with the dread of possible
contingencies will never be at rest.
     Samuel Johnson

Events of great consequence often spring
from trifling circumstances.
     Livy

See also: ACCIDENT, CHANGE, CIRCUMSTANCE.

EVIDENCE

Hear one side and you will be in the dark;
hear both sides, and all will be clear.
     Thomas Chandler Haliburton

A wise man proportions his belief to the
evidence.
     David Hume

Upon any given point, contradictory evidence
seldom puzzles the man who has mastered the
laws of evidence, but he knows little of the
laws of evidence who has not studied the unwritten law of the human heart; and without
this last knowledge a man of action will not
attain to the practical, nor will a poet achieve
the ideal.
   Edward G. Bulwer-Lytton (Baron Lytton)

Some circumstantial evidence is very strong,
as when you find a trout in the milk.
     Henry David Thoreau

See also: EQUITY, FACT, LAW, LAWYER.

EVIL

He who is good is free, even if he is a slave;
he who is evil is a slave, even if he is a king.
     Augustine of Hippo

The caterpillar on the leaf
Repeats to thee thy mother's grief.
Kill not the moth nor butterfly,
For the Last Judgement draweth nigh.
     William Blake

A dog starv'd at his master's gate
Predicts the ruin of the State,
A horse misus'd upon the road
Calls to Heaven for human blood.
Each outcry of the hunted hare
A fibre from the brain does tear,
A skylark wounded in the wing,
A cherubim does cease to sing.
     William Blake

He who shall hurt the little wren
Shall never be belov'd by men.
He who the ox to wrath has mov'd
Shall never be by woman lov'd
     William Blake

The only thing necessary for the triumph of
evil is for good men to do nothing.
     Edmund Burke

All evils are equal when they are extreme.
     Pierre Corneille

Often even an entire city has reaped the evil
fruit of a bad man.
     Hesiod

Here lies one whose name was writ in water.
John Keats

A person may cause evil to others not only by his actions but by his inaction, and in either case he is justly accountable to them for the injury.
John Stuart Mill

All good to me is lost;
Evil, be thou my good.
John Milton

The oldest and best known evil was ever more supportable than the one that was new and untried.
Michel Eyquem de Montaigne

A bad thing has only to continue for long for the world to get used to it.
Jawaharlal Nehru

Evil unchecked grows, evil tolerated poisons the whole system.
Jawaharlal Nehru

People who always seek evil in others find it. This applies to nations as well as individuals.
Jawaharlal Nehru

We can take it that all of us have something angelic in us, something divine in us, but also that we have a good deal of the Satan in us. Whether we are a country or an individual, we should try out the good in ourselves and take the good from others and thereby suppress the evil aspects.
Jawaharlal Nehru

You cannot fight evil with evil; you cannot fight barbarism with barbarism.
Jawaharlal Nehru

What is evil?—Whatever springs from weakness.
Friedrich Wilhelm Nietzsche

As men are unable to find a remedy for death, misery, and ignorance, they have bethought themselves, as the next best thing, if they are to have happiness, not to think of them.
Blaise Pascal

Men never do evil so completely and cheerfully as when they do it from religious convictions.
Blaise Pascal

Bear the ills you have, lest worse befall you.
Phaedrus

When to mischief mortals bend their will,
How soon they find fit instruments of ill!
Alexander Pope

The war against physical evil, like every other war, must not be conducted with such fury as to render men incapable of the arts of peace.
Bertrand Arthur William Russell

Not only does magisterial power exist because of evil, but it exists by evil. Violence is employed to maintain it; and all violence involves criminality. Soldiers, policemen, and jailers; swords, batons, and fetters,—are instruments for inflicting pain; and all infliction of pain is, in the abstract, wrong. The state employs evil weapons to subjugate evil, and is alike contaminated by the objects with which it deals and the means by which it works.
Herbert Spencer

Whatever hinders man's perfecting of his reason and capability to enjoy the rational life, is alone called evil.
Baruch (Benedict) Spinoza

There are a thousand hacking at the branches of evil to one who is striking at the root.
Henry David Thoreau

See also: ADVERSITY, CRIME, ILLS, INJUSTICE, PUNISHMENT, SIN, WRONG.

EVOLUTION

The expression often used by Mr. Herbert Spencer of the Survival of the Fittest is more accurate, and is sometimes equally convenient.
Charles Robert Darwin

I have called this principle, by which each slight variation, if useful, is preserved, by the term of Natural Selection.
Charles Robert Darwin

Every form of consciousness is a reaction to a way of life that existed before, and an adaptation to new realities.
Charles Alan Reich

Civilization is a progress from an indefinite, incoherent homogeneity toward a definite, coherent heterogeneity.
Herbert Spencer

This survival of the fittest, which I have here sought to express in mechanical terms is that which Mr. Darwin has called "natural selection, or the preservation of favoured races in the struggle for life."

Herbert Spencer

See also: CHANGE, IMPROVEMENT, SCIENCE.

EXAGGERATION

The speaking in a perpetual hyperbole is comely in nothing but in love.

Francis Bacon

Some so speak in exaggerations and superlatives that we need to make a large discount from their statements before we can come at their real meaning.

Tryon Edwards

We always weaken whatever we exaggerate.

Jean François de Laharpe

We are not helped in fighting evil by exaggerating its extent. In rejecting or refuting the exaggeration, men often make the truth a victim.

Norman Mattoon Thomas

See also: DECEIT, DISHONESTY, LYING.

EXAMPLE

Example is the school of mankind; they will learn at no other.

Edmund Burke

Not the cry, but the flight of the wild duck, leads the flock to fly and follow.

Chinese Proverb

Few things are harder to put up with than the annoyance of a good example.

Samuel Langhorne Clemens (Mark Twain)

I am absolutely convinced that no wealth in the world can help humanity forward, even in the hands of the most devoted worker in this cause. The example of great and pure individuals is the only thing that can lead us to noble thoughts and deeds. Money only appeals to selfishness and irresistibly invites abuse. Can anyone imagine Moses, Jesus, or Gandhi armed with the moneybags of Carnegie?

Albert Einstein

I am only coming to Princeton to do research, not to teach. There is too much education altogether, especially in American schools. The only rational way of educating is to be an example—if one can't help it, a warning example.

Albert Einstein

How easily we ignore the fact that those who admire us
Will imitate our vices as well as our virtues—
Or whatever the qualities for which they did admire us!
And that again may nourish the faults that they were born with.

Thomas Stearns Eliot

People seldom improve when they have no model but themselves to copy after.

Oliver Goldsmith

I am satisfied that we are less convinced by what we hear than by what we see.

Herodotus

So act that your principle of action might safely be made a law for the whole world.

Immanuel Kant

Example is not the main thing in life—it is the only thing.

Albert Schweitzer

Men trust rather to their eyes than to their ears. The effect of precepts is, therefore, slow and tedious, while that of examples is summary and effectual.

Seneca

Noble examples stir us up to noble actions, and the very history of large and public souls inspires a man with generous thoughts.

Seneca

Live with wolves, and you will learn to howl.

Spanish Proverb

See also: EMULATION, INFLUENCE, PRECEDENT.

EXCELLENCE

Nothing is such an obstacle to the production of excellence as the power of producing what is good with ease and rapidity.

John Aikin

There are three marks of a superior man: being virtuous, he is free from anxiety; being wise, he is free from perplexity; being brave, he is free from fear.

Confucius

It is a wretched taste to be gratified with mediocrity when the excellent lies before us.

Isaac D'Israeli

One that desires to excel should endeavor it in those things that are in themselves most excellent.

Epictetus

Those who attain to any excellence commonly spend life in some one single pursuit, for excellence is not often gained upon easier terms.

Samuel Johnson

The pursuit of excellence is less profitable than the pursuit of bigness, but it can be more satisfying.

David Mackenzie Ogilvy

All things excellent are as difficult as they are rare.

Baruch (Benedict) Spinoza

See also: EMINENCE, GREATNESS, MERIT, PERFECTION, WORTH.

EXCEPTION

No rule is so general, which admits not some exception.

Robert Burton

How glorious it is—and also how painful—to be an exception.

(Louis Charles) Alfred de Musset

Every system should allow loopholes and exceptions, for if it does not it will in the end crush all that is best in man.

Bertrand Arthur William Russell

See also: BUT, DISSENT, NONCONFORMITY.

EXCESS

The best principles, if pushed to excess, degenerate into fatal vices. Generosity is nearly allied to extravagance; charity itself may lead to ruin; and the sternness of justice is but one step removed from the severity of oppression.

Archibald Alison

There can be no excess to love, to knowledge, to beauty, when these attributes are considered in the purest sense.

Ralph Waldo Emerson

The body oppressed by excesses, bears down the mind, and depresses to the earth any portion of the divine Spirit we had been endowed with.

Horace

There seems to be an excess of everything except parking space and religion.

Frank McKinney (Kin) Hubbard

Our senses can grasp nothing that is in extreme. Too much noise deafens us; too much light blinds us; too great a distance or too much proximity equally prevents us from being able to see; too long and too short a discourse obscures our knowledge of a subject; too much of truth stuns us.

Blaise Pascal

Excess generally causes reaction and produces a change in the opposite direction, whether it be in the seasons, or in individuals, or in government.

Plato

He who indulges his sense in any excesses, renders himself obnoxious to his own reason; and to gratify the brute in him, displeases the man, and sets his two natures at variance.

Sir Walter Scott

Pliability and liberality, when not restrained within due bounds, must ever turn to the ruin of their possessor.

Tacitus

See also: DISSIPATION, EXTREMES, GLUTTONY, INTEMPERANCE, MODERATION, SELF-CONTROL.

EXCUSE

He that is good for making excuses, is seldom good for anything else.

Benjamin Franklin

Don't make excuses—make good.

Frank McKinney (Kin) Hubbard

Uncalled for excuses are practical confessions.

Charles Simmons

See also: APOLOGY, REGRET.

EXECUTIVE

A good manager is a man who isn't worried about his own career but rather the careers of those who work for him. My advice: Don't worry about yourself. Take care of those who work for you and you'll float to greatness on their achievements.

Hendry Stuart Mackenzie Burns

In the United States no business executive has arrived until, on one sunny summer morning, he walks in procession with the right combination of solemnity and relaxed amiability and receives a reputable honorary degree.

John Kenneth Galbraith

The typical successful American businessman was born in the country where he worked like hell so he could live in the city where he worked like hell so he could live in the country.

Donald Robert Perry (Don) Marquis

Many minor executives prefer a generous expense account to a raise in salary which would be heavily taxed and more soberly spent. It is they who support the so-called "expense account restaurants," places of exotic decor where patrons lunch in a darkness which is all but complete. They cannot see to read the prices on the menu, but these, in the special circumstances, are irrelevant.

Cyril Northcote Parkinson

See also: BUSINESS, PRESIDENT.

EXERCISE

Whenever I feel like exercise, I lie down until the feeling passes.

Robert Maynard Hutchins

Games played with the ball, and others of that nature are too violent for the body and stamp no character on the mind.

Thomas Jefferson

Such is the constitution of man, that labor may be styled its own reward. Nor will any external incitements be requisite if it be considered how much happiness is gained, and how much misery escaped, by frequent and violent agitation of the body.

Samuel Johnson

One man in a thousand can play tennis through his fifties—witness William Randolph Hearst. But the rest of us must drop it early, or it will drop us with a bang.

Walter Boughton Pitkin

See also: EXERTION, HEALTH, SPORTS, WORK.

EXERTION

Life is certainly only worth-while as it represents struggle for worthy causes. There is no struggle in perfect security. I am quite certain that the human being could not continue to exist if he had perfect security.

Dwight David Eisenhower

Every man's task is his life-preserver.

Ralph Waldo Emerson

It is only the constant exertion and working of our sensitive, intellectual, moral, and physical machinery that keeps us from rusting, and so becoming useless.

Charles Simmons

See also: EFFORT, EXERCISE.

EXISTENCE

I think, therefore I am.

René Descartes

In joy and in sorrow, in work and in rest, in life and in death, in victory and in defeat, in this world and in the next, all hail to the "I exist."

Sir Rabindranath Tagore

Merely to exist is not enough.

Sir Rabindranath Tagore

Zen does not confuse spirituality with thinking about God while one is peeling potatoes. Zen spirituality is just to peel the potatoes. . . . Zen is a way of liberation, concerned not with discovering what is good or bad or advantageous but what is.

Alan Wilson Watts

See also: EXISTENTIALISM, LIFE, PHILOSOPHY.

EXISTENTIALISM

Existentialism is nothing but an attempt to draw all consequences from a consistent atheistic position.

Jean-Paul Sartre

I am responsible for myself and everybody else. I am creating a certain image of man of my own choosing. . . . This helps us in understanding what the content is of such rather grandiloquent words as anguish, forlornness, despair.

Jean-Paul Sartre

All the contemporary existentialists are phenomenologists; that is to say, they try to render explicit, *by means of description*, what is implicit in the realities which we live in our daily lives, but which we live without being sufficiently aware of them.

Roger Troisfontaines

Existentialism is not to be identified with the eccentric attitude of young men and women with uncombed hair, who dance the latest gyrations and who, when they remember to do so, declare that the world is absurd: a fact which permits them to take all the liberty they like with even the most elementary moral obligations. This eccentric attitude has nothing to do with existential philosophy.

Roger Troisfontaines

Sartre is not the whole of existentialism; nor is he the first French existentialist. Gabriel Marcel had developed the broad lines of existential philosophy long before Sartre had published anything at all.

Roger Troisfontaines

See also: EXISTENCE, LIFE, PHILOSOPHY.

EXPECTATION

What we anticipate seldom occurs; what we least expect generally happens.

Benjamin Disraeli

Nothing is so good as it seems beforehand.

George Eliot (Mary Ann Evans)

We love to expect, and when expectation is either disappointed or gratified, we want to be again expecting.

Samuel Johnson

It is folly to expect men to do all that they may reasonably be expected to do.

Richard Whately

Blessed are those that nought expect, For they shall not be disappointed.

John Wolcot (Peter Pindar)

See also: ANTICIPATION, HOPE, PURSUIT.

EXPEDIENCY

Expediency may tip the scales when arguments are nicely balanced.

Benjamin Nathan Cardozo

When private virtue is hazarded on the perilous cast of expediency, the pillars of the republic, however apparent their stability, are infected with decay at the very centre.

Edwin Hubbel Chapin

No man is justified in doing evil on the ground of expediency.

Theodore Roosevelt

See also: COMPROMISE, INTEREST, MEANS, OPPORTUNITY, PRINCIPLE.

EXPENSE

Riches are for spending, and spending for honor and good actions; therefore extraordinary expense must be limited by the worth of the occasion.

Francis Bacon

Gain may be temporary and uncertain; but ever while you live, expense is constant and certain: and it is easier to build two chimneys than to keep one in fuel.

Benjamin Franklin

Never buy a thing you don't want merely because it is dear.

Oscar Wilde

See also: BARGAIN, EXTRAVAGANCE, MONEY.

EXPERIENCE

All experience is an arch to build upon.

Henry Brooks Adams

Experience is one thing you can't get for nothing.

Anonymous

By experience we find out a shorter way by a long wandering. Learning teacheth more in one year than experience in twenty.

Roger Ascham

Experience is a revelation in the light of which we renounce our errors of youth for those of age.

Ambrose Gwinnett Bierce

Youth thinks intelligence a good substitute for experience, and his elders think experience a substitute for intelligence.

Lyman Lloyd Bryson

When I was a boy of fourteen, my father was so ignorant I could hardly stand to have the old man around. But when I got to be twenty-one, I was astonished at how much the old man had learned in seven years.

Samuel Langhorne Clemens (Mark Twain)

A sadder and a wiser man,
He rose the morrow morn.

Samuel Taylor Coleridge

Theory may mislead us; experience must be our guide.

Henry Steele Commager

Experience cannot deliver to us necessary truths; truths completely demonstrated by reason. Its conclusions are particular, not universal.

John Dewey

Experience keeps a dear school; but fools will learn in no other, and scarce in that; for it is true, we may give advice, but we cannot give conduct.

Benjamin Franklin

Experience is no more transferable in morals than in art.

James Anthony Froude

Experience is a good school, but the fees are high.

Heinrich Heine

Some people have had nothing else but experience.

Don Herold

Experience is remolding us every moment, and our mental reaction on any given thing is really a resultant of our experience of the whole world up to that date.

William James

Experience is a hard teacher because she gives the test first, the lesson afterwards.

Vernon Sanders Law

One thorn of experience is worth a whole wilderness of warning.

James Russell Lowell

The value of experience is not in seeing much, but in seeing wisely.

Sir William Osler

We are constantly misled by the ease with which our minds fall into the ruts of one or two experiences.

Sir William Osler

Nothing is a waste of time if you use the experience wisely.

François Auguste René Rodin

Men are wise in proportion, not to their experience, but to their capacity for experience.

George Bernard Shaw

You can't put the facts of experience in order while you are getting them, especially if you are getting them in the neck.

(Joseph) Lincoln Steffens

No man was ever so completely skilled in the conduct of life, as not to receive new information from age and experience.

Terence

When I was young I was sure of everything; in a few years, having been mistaken a thousand times, I was not half so sure of most things as I was before; at present, I am hardly sure of anything but what God has revealed to me.

John Wesley

See also: AGE, OLD; DISILLUSIONMENT; OBSERVATION; SUFFERING; WISDOM.

EXPERIMENT

We cannot advance without new experiments in living, but no wise man tries every day what he has proved wrong the day before.

James Truslow Adams

There must be power in the states and the nation to remould, through experimentation, our economic practices and institutions to meet changing social and economic needs.

Louis Dembitz Brandeis

It is common sense to take a method and try it. If it fails, admit it frankly and try another. But above all, try something.

Franklin Delano Roosevelt

See also: INVENTION, OBSERVATION, SCIENCE.

EXPERT

An expert is one who knows more and more about less and less.

Nicholas Murray Butler

The public do not know enough to be experts, yet know enough to decide between them.

Samuel Butler

Even when the experts all agree, they may well be mistaken.

Bertrand Arthur William Russell

See also: EDUCATION, EXPERIENCE, KNOWLEDGE, SCIENCE, WISDOM.

EXTRAVAGANCE

The passion of acquiring riches in order to support a vain expense, corrupts the purest souls.

François de Salignac de La Mothe-Fénelon

The covetous man never has money; the prodigal will have none shortly.

Ben (Benjamin) Jonson

Waste of time is the most extravagant and costly of all expenses.

Theophrastus

That is suitable to a man, in point of ornamental expense, not which he can afford to have, but which he can afford to lose.

Richard Whately

See also: EXPENSE, PRODIGALITY, WASTE.

EXTREMES

All extremes are error. The reverse of error is not truth, but error still. Truth lies between these extremes.

Richard Cecil

Extremes, though contrary, have the like effects. Extreme heat kills, and so extreme cold: extreme love breeds satiety, and so extreme hatred; and too violent rigor tempts chastity, as does too much license.

George Chapman

Neither great poverty, nor great riches will hear reason.

Henry Fielding

We must not overlook the important role that extremists play. They are the gadflies that keep society from being too complacent or self-satisfied; they are, if sound, the spearhead of progress.

Abraham Flexner

I never dared be radical when young
For fear it would make me conservative when old.

Robert Lee Frost

There is perhaps in all misfits a powerful secret craving to turn the whole of humanity into misfits. Hence partly their passionate advocacy of a drastically new social order. For we are all misfits when we have to adjust ourselves to the wholly new.

Eric Hoffer

There is a mean in everything. Even virtue itself hath its stated limits, which, not being strictly observed, it ceases to be virtue.

Horace

The man who can be nothing but serious, or nothing but merry, is but half a man.

(James Henry) Leigh Hunt

Mistrust the man who finds everything good; the man who finds everything evil; and still more the man who is indifferent to everything.

Johann Kaspar Lavater

Both in individuals, and in masses, violent excitement is always followed by remission, and often by reaction. We are all inclined to depreciate what we have over-praised, and, on the other hand, to show undue indulgence where we have shown undue rigor.

Thomas Babington Macaulay

Too austere a philosophy makes few wise men; to rigorous politics, few good subjects; too hard a religion, few persons whose devotion is of long continuance.

Seigneur de Saint-Evremond

The greatest flood has soonest ebb; the sorest tempest, the most sudden calm; the hottest love, the coldest end; and from the deepest desire often ensues the deadliest hate.

Socrates

Extreme views are never just; something always turns up which disturbs the calculations founded on their data.

Tancred

The eye speaks with an eloquence and truthfulness surpassing speech. It is the window out of which the winged thoughts often fly unwittingly. It is the tiny magic mirror on whose crystal surface the moods of feeling fitfully play, like the sunlight and shadow on a quiet stream.

Henry Theodore Tuckerman

See also: EXCESS, INTEMPERANCE.

EYE

The eye is the pulse of the soul; as physicians judge the heart by the pulse, so we by the eye.

Thomas Adams

A beautiful eye makes silence eloquent; a kind eye makes contradiction an assent; an enraged eye makes beauty deformed. This little member gives life to every other part about us.

Joseph Addison

The intelligence of affection is carried on by the eye only. Good breeding has made the tongue falsify the heart and act a part of continued restraint, while Nature has preserved the eyes to herself, that she may not be disguised or misrepresented.

Joseph Addison

That fine part of our constitution, the eye, seems as much the receptacle and seat of our passions, appetites, and inclinations, as the mind itself; at least it is the outward portal to introduce them to the house within, or rather the common thoroughfare to let our affections pass in and out. Love, anger, pride, and avarice, all visibly move in those little orbs.

Joseph Addison

A wanton eye is the messenger of an unchaste heart.

Augustine of Hippo

Men are born with two eyes, but only one tongue, in order that they should see twice as much as they say.

Charles Caleb Colton

Sweet, Silent rhetoric of persuading eyes.

Sir William Davenant

An eye can threaten like a loaded and levelled pistol, or can insult, like hissing or kicking; or in its altered mood, can, by beams of kindness, make the heart dance with joy. Some eyes have no more expression than blueberries, while others are as deep as a well which you can fall into.

Ralph Waldo Emerson

Eyes are bold as lions, roving, running, leaping, here and there, far and near.—They speak all languages; wait for no introduction; ask no leave of age or rank; respect neither poverty nor riches, neither learning nor power, nor vitrue, nor sex, but intrude, and come again, and go through and through you in a moment of time. What inundation of life and thought is discharged from one soul into another through them!

Ralph Waldo Emerson

One of the most wonderful things in nature is a glance of the eye; it transcends speech; it is the bodily symbol of identity.

Ralph Waldo Emerson

The eye of the master will do more work than both his hands.

Benjamin Franklin

It is the eyes of other people that ruin us. If all but myself were blind I should neither want a fine house nor fine furniture.

Benjamin Franklin

Our eyes, when gazing on sinful objects, are out of their calling, and out of God's keeping.

Thomas Fuller

Eyes raised toward heaven are always beautiful, whatever they may be.

Joseph Joubert

Who has a daring eye, tells downright truths and downright lies.

Johann Kaspar Lavater

Lovers are angry, reconciled, entreat, thank, appoint, and finally speak all things by their eyes.

Michel Eyquem de Montaigne

Eyes will not see when the heart wishes them to be blind. Desire conceals truth, as darkness does the earth.

Seneca

The dearest things in the world are our neighbor's eyes; they cost everybody more than anything else in housekeeping.

Sydney Smith

Her eyes are homes of silent prayer.

Alfred, Lord Tennyson

See also: COUNTENANCE, FACE, LOOKS, VISION.

F

FABLE

Fables take off from the severity of instruction, and enforce at the same time that they conceal it.
Joseph Addison

The virtue which we gather from a fable or an allegory, is like the health we get by hunting, as we are engaged in an agreeable pursuit that draws us on with pleasure, and makes us insensible of the fatigues that accompany it.
Joseph Addison

Fables, like parables, are more ancient than formal arguments and are often the most effective means of presenting and impressing both truth and duty.
Tryon Edwards

See *also*: ALLEGORY, FANCY, LITERATURE, MYTHOLOGY, RELIGION.

FACE

When I see a man with a sour, shriveled face, I cannot forbear pitying his wife; and when I meet with an open ingenuous countenance, I think on the happiness of his friends, his family, and his relations.
Joseph Addison

A beautiful face is a silent commendation.
Francis Bacon

I more and more see this, that we judge men's abilities less from what they say or do, than from what they look. 'Tis the man's face that gives him weight. His doings help, but not more than his brow.
Charles Buxton

He had a face like a benediction.
Miguel de Cervantes Saavedra

It matters more what's in a woman's face than what's on it.
Claudette Colbert

There is in every human countenance, either a history or a prophecy, which must sadden, or at least soften, every reflecting observer.
Samuel Taylor Coleridge

As the language of the face is universal, so it is very comprehensive. It is the shorthand of the mind, and crowds a great deal in a little room. A man may look a sentence as soon as speak a word.
Jeremy Collier

A cheerful face is nearly as good for an invalid as healthy weather.
Benjamin Franklin

The countenance is the title-page which heralds the contents of the human volume, but like other title-pages it sometimes puzzles, often misleads, and often says nothing to the purpose.
William Matthews

The features come insensibly to be formed and assume their shape from the frequent and habitual expression of certain affections of the soul. These affections are marked on the countenance; nothing is more certain than this; and when they turn into habits, they must leave on it durable impressions.
Jean Jacques Rousseau

Faces are as legible as books, with this in their favor, that they may be perused in much less time, and are less liable to be misunderstood.
Frederick Saunders

The faces which have charmed us the most escape us the soonest.
Sir Walter Scott

If we could but read it, every human being carries his life in his face, and is good-looking, or the reverse, as that life has been good or evil. On our features the fine chisels of thought and emotion are eternally at work.

Alexander Smith

Truth makes the face of that person shine who speaks and owns it.

Robert South

A cheerful, easy, open countenance will make fools think you a good-natured man, and make designing men think you an undesigning one.

Philip Dormer Stanhope (Lord Chesterfield)

Look in the face of the person to whom you are speaking if you wish to know his real sentiments, for he can command his words more easily than his countenance.

Philip Dormer Stanhope (Lord Chesterfield)

We are all sculptors and painters, and our material is our own flesh and blood and bones. Any nobleness begins, at once, to refine a man's features; any meanness or sensuality to imbrute them.

Henry David Thoreau

Trust not too much to an enchanting face.

Virgil

He had the sort of face that, once seen, is never remembered.

Oscar Wilde

See also: APPEARANCE, EYE, LOOKS, NOSE.

FACTION

A feeble government produces more factions than an oppressive one.

Fisher Ames

Faction is the excess and abuse of party. It begins when the first idea of private interest, preferred to public good, gets footing in the heart. It is always dangerous, yet always contemptible.

Richard Chenevix

Faction is the demon of discord armed with power to do endless mischief, and intent only on destroying whatever opposes its progress. Woe to that state in which it has found an entrance.

George Crabbe

Seldom is faction's ire in haughty minds extinguished but by death; it oft, like flame suppressed, breaks forth again, and blazes higher.

Sir Thomas Erskine May

See also: CONTENTION, CREED, PARTY, SECT.

FACTS

Facts are to the mind, what food is to the body. On the due digestion of the former depend the strength and wisdom of the one, just as vigor and health depend on the other. The wisest in council, the ablest in debate, and the most agreeable companion in the commerce of human life, is that man who has assimilated to his understanding the greatest number of facts.

Edmund Burke

Facts are God's arguments; we should be careful never to misunderstand or pervert them.

Tryon Edwards

Any fact is better established by two or three good testimonies than by a thousand arguments.

Nathaniel Emmons

From principles is derived probability, but truth or certainty is obtained only from facts. Every day of my life makes me feel more and more how seldom a fact is accurately stated; how almost invariably when a story has passed through the mind of a third person it becomes, so far as regards the impression it makes in further repetitions, little better than a falsehood; and this, too, though the narrator be the most truth-seeking person in existence.

Nathaniel Hawthorne

Facts, as such, never settled anything. They are working tools only. It is the implications that can be drawn from facts that count, and to evaluate these requires wisdom and judgment that are unrelated to the computer approach to life.

Clarence Belden Randall

See also: CREDULITY, FICTION, SCIENCE, STATISTICS, TRUTH.

FAILING

Careless their merits or their faults to scan,
His pity gave ere charity began.
Thus to relieve the wretched was his pride,
And even his failings lean'd to Virtue's side.

Oliver Goldsmith

If we had no failings ourselves we should not take so much pleasure in finding out those of others.

Duc François de La Rochefoucauld

Such is the force of envy and ill-nature, that the failings of good men are more published to the world than their good deeds; and one fault of a well-deserving man shall meet with more reproaches than all his virtues will with praise.

Nathaniel Parker Willis

See also: ERROR, FAULT, IMPERFECTION, SIN, WEAKNESS.

FAILURE

We are all of us failures—at least, the best of us are.

Sir James Matthew Barrie

A failure establishes only this, that our determination to succeed was not strong enough.

Christian Nestell Bovee

They never fail who die in a great cause.

George Gordon Byron (Lord Byron)

The only people who never fail are those who never try.

Ilka Chase

Failure is instructive. The person who really thinks learns quite as much from his failures as from his successes.

John Dewey

Failure, when sublime, is not without its purpose.

Benjamin Disraeli

Sometimes a noble failure serves the world as faithfully as a distinguished success.

Edward Dowden

One of the worst stings of defeat is the sympathy that goes with it.

Robert Chambers (Bob) Edwards

The things that come to the man who waits are seldom the things he waited for.

Robert Chambers (Bob) Edwards

There is only one real failure in life that is possible, and that is, not to be true to the best one knows.

Frederic William Farrar

I never blame failure—there are too many complicated situations in life—but I am absolutely merciless towards lack of effort.

Francis Scott Key Fitzgerald

One who fears failure limits his activities. Failure is only the opportunity to more intelligently begin again.

Henry Ford

Failure is often God's own tool for carving some of the finest outlines in the character of his children; and, even in this life, bitter and crushing failures have often in them the germs of new and quite unimagined happiness.

Thomas Hodgkin

Failure is, in a sense, the highway to success, inasmuch as every discovery of what is false leads us to seek earnestly after what is true, and every fresh experience points out some form of error which we shall afterward carefully avoid.

John Keats

We have forty million reasons for failure, but not a single excuse.

Rudyard Kipling

Never give a man up until he has failed at something he likes.

Lewis E. Lawes

It is always too late, or too little, or both. And that is the road to disaster.

David Lloyd George

Failure comes only when we forget our ideals and objectives and principles and begin to wander away from the road which leads to their realization.

Jawaharlal Nehru

If you have made mistakes, even serious mistakes, there is always another chance for you. And supposing you have tried and failed again and again, you may have a fresh start any moment you choose, for this thing that we call "failure" is not the falling down, but the staying down.

Mary Pickford

No one can run downhill as fast as a thoroughbred.

Ashton Stevens

It is an awful condemnation for a man to be brought by God's providence face to face with

a great possibility of service and of blessing, and then to show himself such that God has to put him aside, and look for other instruments.

John Watson (Ian Maclaren)

He only is exempt from failures who makes no efforts.

Richard Whately

See also: DEFEAT, DESPAIR, SUCCESS.

FAITH

Living our faith in a world of men who consider sex apart from the Christian mystery, in a world convinced of the *virtue* of birth prevention, can be true heroic unsung martyrdom.

(Grace) April Oursler Armstrong

Faith is to believe, on the word of God, what we do not see, and its reward is to see and enjoy what we believe.

Augustine of Hippo

There never was found in any age of the world, either philosopher or sect, or law, or discipline which did so highly exalt the public good as the Christian faith.

Francis Bacon

There is one sure criterion of judgment as to religious faith in doctrinal matters; can you reduce it to practice? If not, have none of it.

Hosea Ballou

Faith without works is like a bird without wings; though she may hop about on earth, she will never fly to heaven. But when both are joined together, then doth the soul mount up to her eternal rest.

Francis Beaumont

Christian faith is nothing else but the soul's venture. It ventures to Christ, in opposition to all legal terrors. It ventures on Christ in opposition to our guiltiness. It ventures for Christ, in opposition to all difficulties and discouragements.

William Bridges

Man is not naturally a cynic; he wants pitifully to believe, in himself, in his future, in his community and in the nation in which he is a part.

Louis Bromfield

No coward soul is mine,
No trembler in the world's storm-troubled sphere:
I see Heaven's glories shine,
And faith shines equal, arming me from fear.

Emily Brontë

To believe only possibilities, is not faith, but mere Philosophy.

Sir Thomas Browne

Never yet did there exist a full faith in the divine word which did not expand the intellect while it purified the heart; which did not multiply the aims and objects of the understanding, while it fixed and simplified those of the desires and passions.

Samuel Taylor Coleridge

Faith and works are as necessary to our spiritual life as Christians, as soul and body are to our life as men; for faith is the soul of religion, and works, the body.

Charles Caleb Colton

You may be deceived if you trust too much, but you will live in torment if you do not trust enough.

Frank Crane

Faith was once almost universally thought to be acceptance of a definite body of intellectual propositions, acceptance being based upon authority—preferably that of revelation from on high. . . . Of late there has developed another conception of faith. This is suggested by the words of an American thinker: "Faith is tendency toward action." According to such a view, faith is the matrix of formulated creeds and the inspiration of endeavor. . . . Faith in itself is the sole ultimate authority.

John Dewey

We are establishing an all-time world record in the production of material things. What we lack is a righteous and dynamic faith. Without it, all else avails us little. The lack cannot be compensated for by politicians, however able; or by diplomats, however astute; or by scientists, however inventive; or by bombs, however powerful.

John Foster Dulles

Science has sometimes been said to be opposed to faith, and inconsistent with it. But all science, in fact, rests on a basis of faith, for it assumes the permanence and uniformity of natural laws—a thing which can never be demonstrated.

Tryon Edwards

All I have seen teaches me to trust the Creator for all I have not seen.
Ralph Waldo Emerson

It is faith among men that holds the moral elements of society together, as it is faith in God that binds the world to his throne.
William Maxwell Evarts

Faith is the function of the heart. It must be enforced by reason. The two are not antagonistic as some think. The more intense one's faith is, the more it whets one's reason. When faith becomes blind it dies.
Mohandas Karamchand (Mahatma) Gandhi

Faith knows no disappointment.
Mohandas Karamchand (Mahatma) Gandhi

Indeed one's faith in one's plans and methods is truly tested when the horizon before one in the blackest.
Mohandas Karamchand (Mahatma) Gandhi

It is a poor faith that needs fair weather for standing firm. That alone is true faith that stands the foulest weather.
Mohandas Karamchand (Mahatma) Gandhi

One's faith has got to be bright and intelligent before it can enkindle faith in others.
Mohandas Karamchand (Mahatma) Gandhi

There is no cause for despondency for a man who has faith and resolution.
Mohandas Karamchand (Mahatma) Gandhi

Epochs of faith, are epochs of fruitfulness; but epochs of unbelief, however glittering are barren of all permanent good.
Johann Wolfgang von Goethe

Faith in order, which is the basis of science, cannot reasonably be separated from faith in an ordainer, which is the basis of religion.
Asa Gray

Christian faith is a grand cathedral, with divinely pictured windows. Standing without, you can see no glory, nor can imagine any, but standing within every ray of light reveals a harmony of unspeakable splendors.
Nathaniel Hawthorne

Much knowledge of divine things is lost to us through want of faith.
Heraclitus

Faith must have adequate evidence, else it is mere superstition.
Archibald Alexander Hodge

When men cease to be faithful to their God, he who expects to find them so to each other will be much disappointed.
George Horne

There is no great future for any people whose faith has burned out or congealed. History records the ominous fact that national degeneration takes place where faith or vision fail or wane as surely as it does when economic assets shrink or when there is a dearth of sound money currency.
Rufus Matthew Jones

There is a limit where the intellect fails and breaks down, and this limit is where the questions concerning God, and freewill, and immortality arise.
Immanuel Kant

Strike from mankind the principle of faith, and men would have no more history than a flock of sheep.
Edward G. Bulwer-Lytton (Baron Lytton)

The Calvinistic people of Scotland, Switzerland, Holland, and New England, have been more moral than the same classes among other nations. Those who preached faith, or in other words a pure mind, have always produced more popular virtue than those who preached good acts, or the mere regulation of outward works.
Sir James Mackintosh

Faith is courage; it is creative while despair is always destructive.
David Saville Muzzey

All the scholastic scaffolding falls, as a ruined edifice, before one single word—faith.
Napoleon I (Bonaparte)

I sometimes wonder at the faith of people in a beneficent Providence: how it survives shock after shock, and how disaster itself and disproof of beneficence are considered but tests of the soundness of that faith.
Jawaharlal Nehru

It is strange how much people with simple faith will put up with. It is because of this that religion has become one of the biggest and most paying businesses in many countries.
Jawaharlal Nehru

Faith [is] . . . the result of the act of the will, following upon a conviction that to believe is a duty.

John Henry Newman

Faith affirms many things respecting which the senses are silent, but nothing which they deny. It is superior to their testimony, but never opposed to it.

Blaise Pascal

Whatever is the subject of faith should not be submitted to reason, and much less should bend to it.

Blaise Pascal

Ignorance as to unrevealed mysteries is the mother of a saving faith; and understanding in revealed truths is the mother of a sacred knowledge. Understand not therefore that thou mayest believe, but believe that thou mayest understand. Understanding is the wages of a lively faith, and faith is the reward of an humble ignorance.

Francis Quarles

The errors of faith are better than the best thoughts of unbelief.

Thomas Russell

The only known cure for fear is faith.

Lena Kellogg Sadler

O world, thou choosest not the better part!
It is not wisdom to be only wise,
And on the inward vision close the eyes,
But it is wisdom to believe the heart.
Columbus found a world and had no chart,
Save one that faith deciphered in the skies;
To trust the soul's invincible surmise
Was all his science and his only art.
Our knowledge is a torch of smoky pine
That lights the pathway but one step ahead
Across a void of mystery and dread.
Bid, then, the tender light of faith to shine
By which alone the mortal heart is led
Unto the thinking of the thought divine.

George Santayana

Faith is like love: it cannot be forced. As trying to force love begets hatred, so trying to compel religious belief leads to unbelief.

Arthur Schopenhauer

The saddest thing that can befall a soul is when it loses faith in God and woman.

Alexander Smith

Faith does nothing alone—nothing of itself, but everything under God, by God, through God.

John Stoughton

Faith is the root of all blessings. Believe, and you shall be saved; believe, and you must needs be satisfied; believe, and you cannot but be comforted and happy.

Jeremy Taylor

Living faith is a rock with roots.

Puzant Kevork Thomajan

Despotism may govern without faith, but Liberty cannot.

Alexis de Tocqueville

What I admire in Columbus is not his having discovered a world, but his having gone to search for it on the faith of an opinion.

Anne Robert Jacques Turgot

Faith in an all-seeing and personal God, elevates the soul, purifies the emotions, sustains human dignity, and lends poetry, nobility, and holiness to the commonest state, condition, and manner of life.

Juan Valera y Alcalá Galiano

Under the influence of the blessed spirit, faith produces holiness, and holiness strengthens faith. Faith, like a fruitful parent, is plenteous in all good works; and good works, like dutiful children, confirm and add to the support of faith.

Juan Valera y Alcalá Galiano

Belief is holding to a rock; faith is learning how to swim—and this whole universe swims in boundless space.

Alan Watts

The steps of faith fall on the seeming void, but find the rock beneath.

John Greenleaf Whittier

Faith is the root of all good works; a root that produces nothing is dead.

Daniel Wilson

Faith is not only a means of obeying, but a principal act of obedience; not only an altar on which to sacrifice, but a sacrifice itself, and perhaps, of all, the greatest. It is a submission of our understandings; an oblation of our idolized reason to God, which he requires so indispensably, that our whole will and

affections, though seemingly a larger sacrifice, will not, without it, be received at his hands.
Edward Young

Some wish they did, but no man disbelieves.
Edward Young

See also: BELIEF, CREED, RELIGION.

FALL: *see* AUTUMN.

FALSEHOOD

Falsehood and fraud grow up in every soil, the product of all climes.
Joseph Addison

All that one gains by falsehood is, not to be believed when he speaks the truth.
Aristotle

Not the least misfortune in a prominent falsehood is the fact that tradition is apt to repeat it for truth.
Hosea Ballou

Falsehood often lurks upon the tongue of him, who, by self-praise, seeks to enhance his value in the eyes of others.
James Gordon Bennett

Falsehood is so easy, truth so difficult! Examine your words well and you will find that even when you have no motive to be false it is very hard to say the exact truth, even about your own immediate feelings—much harder than to say something fine about them which is not the exact truth.
George Eliot (Mary Ann Evans)

Dishonor waits on perfidy. A man should blush to think a falsehood; it is the crime of cowards.
Charles Johnson

It is more from carelessness about the truth, than from intention of lying that there is so much falsehood in the world.
Samuel Johnson

Half a fact is a whole falsehood. He who gives the truth a false coloring by his false manner of telling it, is the worst of liars.
Elias Lyman Magoon

If falsehood had, like truth, but one face only, we should be upon better terms; for we should then take the contrary to what the liar says for certain truth; but the reverse of truth hath a hundred figures, and is a field indefinite without bound or limit.
Michel Eyquem de Montaigne

Falsehood has an infinity of combinations, but truth has only one mode of being.
Jean Jacques Rousseau

The telling of a falsehood is like the cut of a sabre; for though the wound may heal, the scar of it will remain.
Saadi (Muslih-ud-Din)

Falsehoods not only disagree with truths, but they usually quarrel among themselves.
Daniel Webster

See also: DECEIT, DISHONESTY, LYING.

FAME

Our admiration of a famous man lessens upon our nearer acquaintance with him; and we seldom hear of a celebrated person without a catalogue of some of his weaknesses and infirmities.
Joseph Addison

Fame—a few words upon a tombstone, and the truth of those not to be depended on.
Christian Nestell Bovee

Fame is no sure test of merit, but only a probability of such, it is an accident, not a property of man.
Thomas Carlyle

It often happens that those of whom we speak least on earth are best known in heaven.
Nicolas Caussin

It is the penalty of fame that a man must ever keep rising. "Get a reputation, and then go to bed," is the absurdest of all maxims. "Keep up a reputation or go to bed," would be nearer the truth.
Edwin Hubbel Chapin

Worldly fame is nothing but a breath of wind that blows now this way, now that, and changes name as it changes sides.
Dante Alighieri

Your fame is as the grass, whose hue comes and goes, and His might withers it, by whose power it sprang from the lap of the earth.
Dante Alighieri

Fame, like the river, is narrowest where it is bred, and broadest afar off.

Sir William Davenant

Fame is a fickle food
Upon a shifting plate.

Emily Elizabeth Dickinson

Men think highly of those who rise rapidly in the world, whereas nothing rises quicker than dust, straw, and feathers.

Augustus and Julius Hare

Few people make much noise after their deaths who did not do so while living.

William Hazlitt

The temple of fame stands upon the grave; the flame upon its altars is kindled from the ashes of the dead.

William Hazlitt

He that pursues fame with just claims, trusts his happiness to the winds; but he that endeavors after it by false merit, has to fear, not only the violence of the storm, but the leaks of his vessel.

Samuel Johnson

To get a name can happen but to few: it is one of the few things that cannot be bought. It is the free gift of mankind, which must be deserved before it will be granted, and is at last unwillingly bestowed.

Samuel Johnson

That fame is the universal passion is by nothing more discovered than by epitaphs. The generality of mankind are not content to sink ingloriously into the grave, but wish to be paid that tribute after their deaths, which in many cases may not be due to the virtues of their lives.

Henry Kett

There is not in the world so toilsome a trade as the pursuit of fame: life concludes before you have so much as sketched your work.

Jean de La Bruyère

Time has a doomsday book, on whose pages he is continually recording illustrious names. But as often as a new name is written there, an old one disappears. Only a few stand in illuminated characters never to be effaced.

Henry Wadsworth Longfellow

I courted fame but as a spur to brave and honest deeds; who despises fame will soon renounce the virtues that deserve it.

David Mallet

If fame is only to come after death, I am in no hurry for it.

Martial

Do you wish that people think well of you? Then don't speak well of yourself.

Blaise Pascal

We speak of fame as the reward of genius, whereas in truth genius, the imaginative dominion of experience, is its own reward, and fame is but a foolish image by which its worth is symbolized.

George Santayana

Of all the possessions of this life fame is the noblest: when the body has sunk into the dust the great name still lives.

Johann Christoph Friedrich von Schiller

Let us satisfy our own consciences, and trouble not ourselves by looking for fame. If we deserve it, we shall attain it: if we deserve it not we cannot force it. The praise bad actions obtain dies soon away; if good deeds are at first unworthily received, they are afterward more properly appreciated.

Seneca

Only the actions of the just smell sweet and blossom in the dust.

James Shirley

Fame is the perfume of heroic deeds.

Socrates

Fame has also this great drawback, that if we pursue it, we must direct our lives so as to please the fancy of men.

Baruch (Benedict) Spinoza

What is fame? The advantage of being known by people of whom you yourself know nothing, and for whom you care as little.

Stanislas I (Leszczyński)

The way to fame is like the way to heaven, through much tribulation.

Laurence Sterne

No true and permanent fame can be founded except in labors which promote the happiness of mankind.

Charles Sumner

Even the best things are not equal to their fame.

Henry David Thoreau

What a heavy burden is a name that has too soon become famous.

Voltaire (François Marie Arouet)

Much of reputation depends on the period in which it rises. In dark periods, when talents appear, they shine like the sun through a small hole in the window-shutter, and the strong beam dazzles amid the surrounding gloom. Open the shutter, and the general diffusion of light attracts no notice.

Sir Robert Walpole

See also: ESTEEM, GLORY, HONOR.

FAMILIARITY

When a man becomes familiar with his goddess, she quickly sinks into a woman.

Joseph Addison

A good neighbor is a fellow who smiles at you over the back fence but doesn't climb over it.

Arthur (Bugs) Baer

Familiarity breeds contempt—and children.

Samuel Langhorne Clemens (Mark Twain)

All objects lose by too familiar a view.

John Dryden

The confidant of my vices is my master, though he were my valet.

Johann Wolfgang von Goethe

Though familiarity may not breed contempt, it takes off the edge of admiration.

William Hazlitt

Familiarities are the aphides that imperceptibly suck out the juices intended for the germ of love.

Walter Savage Landor

Vice is a monster of such frightful mien
As to be hated, needs but to be seen;
But seen too oft, familiar with her face,
We first endure, then pity, then embrace.

Alexander Pope

The thicker one gets with some people, the thinner they become.

Puzant Kevork Thomajan

See also: ACQUAINTANCE, FRIENDSHIP.

FAMILY

The family is the miniature commonwealth upon whose integrity the safety of the larger commonwealth depends.

Felix Adler

Civilization varies with the family, and the family with civilization. Its highest and most complete realization is found where enlightened Christianity prevails; where woman is exalted to her true and lofty place as equal with the man; where husband and wife are one in honor, influence, and affection, and where children are a common bond of care and love. This is the idea of a perfect family.

William Aikman

A happy family is but an earlier heaven.

Sir John Bowring

A house without a roof would scarcely be a more different home, than a family unsheltered by God's friendship, and the sense of being always rested in His providential care and guidance.

Horace Bushnell

The ties of family and of country were never intended to circumscribe the soul. If allowed to become exclusive, engrossing, clannish, so as to shut out the general claims of the human race, the highest end of Providence is frustrated, and home, instead of being the nursery, becomes the grave of the heart.

William Ellery Channing

The greatest thing in family life is to take a hint when a hint is intended—and not to take a hint when a hint isn't intended.

Robert Lee Frost

In my judgment, one of the basic reasons we have had crime, lawlessness, and disorder in the United States has been the breakdown of the family unit.

Robert Francis Kennedy

The family is a society limited in numbers, but nevertheless a true society, anterior to every state or nation, with rights and duties of its own, wholly independent of the commonwealth.

Leo XIII (Gioacchino Vincenzo Pecci)

Where can a man better be than with his family?

Jean François Marmontel

As are families, so is society. If well ordered, well instructed, and well governed, they are the springs from which go forth the streams of national greatness and prosperity—of civil order and public happiness.

William Makepeace Thayer

See also: BIRTH, CHILDREN, FATHER, MOTHER, PARENT.

FANATICISM

Of all things wisdom is the most terrified with epidemical fanaticism, because, of all enemies, it is that against which she is the least able to furnish any kind of resource.

Edmund Burke

The downright fanatic is nearer to the heart of things than the cool and slippery disputant.

Edwin Hubbel Chapin

A fanatic is one who can't change his mind and won't change the subject.

Sir Winston Leonard Spencer Churchill

Fanaticism, the false fire of an overheated mind.

William Cowper

The blind fanaticism of one foolish honest man may cause more evil than the united efforts of twenty rogues.

Baron Friedrich Melchior von Grimm

We often excuse our own want of philanthropy by giving the name of fanaticism to the more ardent zeal of others.

Henry Wadsworth Longfellow

Fanatic faith, once wedded fast to some dear falsehood, hugs it to the last.

Thomas Moore

Without fanaticism one cannot accomplish anything.

María Eva (Duarte) Perón

What is fanaticism to-day is the fashionable creed to-morrow, and trite as the multiplication table a week after.

Wendell Phillips

Fanaticism consists in redoubling your effort when you have forgotten your aim.

George Santayana

Fanaticism harkens only to its own counsel, which it believes to be inspired.

Francis Wilson

See also: INTOLERANCE, TOTALITARIANISM.

FANCY

Most marvellous and enviable is that fecundity of fancy which can adorn whatever it touches, which can invest naked fact and dry reasoning with unlooked for beauty, make flowers bloom even on the brow of the precipice, and turn even the rock itself into moss and lichens. This faculty is most important for the vivid and attractive exhibition of truth to the minds of men.

Thomas Fuller

Fancy rules over two thirds of the universe, the past and future, while reality is confined to the present.

Jean Paul Richter

Every fancy that we would substitute for a reality, is, if we saw aright, and saw the whole, not only false, but every way less beautiful and excellent, than that which we sacrifice to it.

John Sterling

See also: CREATIVITY, DREAM, IMAGINATION, REVERIE, SPECULATION, WONDER.

FAREWELL

Like some low and mournful spell, we whisper that sad word, "farewell."

Park Benjamin

In that fatal word—howe'er we promise, hope, believe, there breathes despair.

George Gordon Byron (Lord Byron)

That bitter word, which closed all earthly friendships, and finished every feast of love —farewell!

Robert Pollok

See also: DEATH, PARTING, WELCOME.

FARMING: see AGRICULTURE.

FASCISM

Unhappy events abroad have retaught us two simple truths about the liberty of a democratic people. The first truth is that the liberty of a democracy is not safe if the people tolerate the growth of private power to a point where it becomes stronger than their democratic State itself. That, in its essence, is fascism—ownership of government by an individual, by a group, or by any other controlling private power.

Franklin Delano Roosevelt

We shall not be able to claim that we have gained total victory in this war if any vestige of Fascism in any of its malignant forms is permitted to survive anywhere in the world.

Franklin Delano Roosevelt

Fascism is a political, social and economic form of society wherein by virtue of a merger which has been accomplished between certain powerful financial interests and a military machine, the entire nation is under the dictatorship of this oligarchy. Individuality and freedom are suppressed "in the interests of the state" which happens to be none other than the dictating oligarchy. Since so radical a change in a form of government is not very easily accomplished, the transition to Fascism is, at first, made easier by demagogic political agitation of the kind which is described as "We are all things to all men." To gain the backing of powerful industrialists . . . a form of society is offered which will protect their objective; disunity is created by playing political groups against each other, social and economic groups against each other. A confused and disunited people can offer no effective resistance to the seizure of power by this newly-merged oligarchy ["Classes in Citizenship and War"].

United States Army

See also: NAZISM, DESPOTISM, TYRANNY.

FASHION

Change of fashions is the tax which industry imposes on the vanity of the rich.

Sébastien Roch Nicolas Chamfort

Fashion is the science of appearances, and it inspires one with the desire to seem rather than to be.

Edwin Hubbel Chapin

Fashion can be bought. Style one must possess. I have seen a Texas cowboy swing himself into his saddle with more real elegance, more style, than many gentlemen on the hunting field.

Edna Woolman Chase

Custom is the law of one description of fools, and fashion of another; but the two parties often clash, for precedent is the legislator of the first, and novelty of the last!

Charles Caleb Colton

The customs and fashions of men change like leaves on the bough, some of which go, and others come.

Dante Alighieri

Thus grows up fashion, an equivocal semblance; the most puissant, the most fantastic and frivolous, the most feared and followed, and which morals and violence assault in vain.

Ralph Waldo Emerson

Fashion is the great governor of the world. It presides not only in matters of dress and amusement, but in law, physic, politics, religion, and all other things of the gravest kind. Indeed, the wisest men would be puzzled to give any better reason why particular forms in all these have been at certain times universally received, and at other times universally rejected, than that they were in, or out of fashion.

Henry Fielding

Fashion is only the attempt to realize art in living forms and social intercourse.

Oliver Wendell Holmes

Be not too early in the fashion, nor too long out of it; nor at any time in the extremes of it.

Johann Kaspar Lavater

A fop of fashion is the mercer's friend, the tailor's fool, and his own foe.

Johann Kaspar Lavater

Poor Englishwomen! . . . When it comes to their clothes—well, the French reaction is a shrug, the Italian reaction a spreading of the hands and a lifting of the eyes and the American reaction simply one of amused contempt.

James Laver

Fashion is, for the most part, nothing but the ostentation of riches.

John Locke

Fashion must be forever new, or she becomes insipid.

James Russell Lowell

It is absurd to suppose that everything fashionable is bad, as it would be to suppose that everything unfashionable is good.

Alfred William Momerie

Fashion is a tyrant from which nothing frees us. We must suit ourselves to its fantastic tastes. But being compelled to live under its foolish laws, the wise man is never the first to follow nor the last to keep it.
Etienne Pavillon

Fashion too often makes a monstrous noise,
Bids us, a fickle jad, like fools adore
The poorest trash, the meanest toys.
Peter Pindar (John Wolcot)

Except when it comes to bravery, we are a nation of mice. We dress and behave with timid circumspection. Good taste is the worst vice ever invented.
Dame Edith Sitwell

Every generation laughs at the old fashions, but follows religiously the new.
Henry David Thoreau

Fashion seldom interferes with nature without diminishing her grace and efficiency.
Henry Theodore Tuckerman

Fashion is a form of ugliness so intolerable that we have to alter it every six months.
Oscar Wilde

Fashion is what one wears oneself. What is unfashionable is what other people wear.
Oscar Wilde

See also: APPEARANCE, DRESS, STYLE.

FASTIDIOUSNESS

Fastidiousness is the envelope of indelicacy.
Thomas Chandler Haliburton

Like other spurious things, fastidiousness is often inconsistent with itself, the coarsest things are done, and the cruelest things said by the most fastidious people.
Caroline Matilda Stansbury Kirkland

Fastidiousness is only another form of egotism; and all men who know not where to look for truth, save in the narrow well of self, will find their own image at the bottom, and mistake it for what they are seeking.
James Russell Lowell

See also: CLEANLINESS, DRESS, TASTE.

FASTING

Subdue your flesh by fasting and abstinence from meat and drink, as far as health allows.
Augustine of Hippo

Fasting is medicine.
John Chrysostom

Fasting is useful, when mind co-operates with starving body, that is to say, when it cultivates a distaste for the objects that are denied to the body.
Mohandas Karamchand (Mahatma) Gandhi

More caution and perhaps more restraint are necessary in breaking a fast than in keeping it.
Mohandas Karamchand (Mahatma) Gandhi

Of what use is it to force the flesh merely if the spirit refuses to co-operate? You may starve even unto death but if at the same time the mind continues to hanker after objects of the sense, your fast is a sham and a delusion.
Mohandas Karamchand (Mahatma) Gandhi

Any one who has been fasting for a month will look spiritual and gentle.
Jawaharlal Nehru

See also: ABSTINENCE, MODERATION, SELF-DE-NIAL, TEMPERANCE.

FAT: *see* FATNESS.

FATALISM

Fatalism is the refuge of a conscience-stricken mind, maddened at the sight of evils which it has brought upon itself, and cannot remove.
John Henry Newman

Fatalism, whether pious or pessimistic, stands flatly discredited. It serves as an excuse for practical inaction or mental indolence. To believe that the future is predestined by non-human causes saves men from the trouble of doing; to believe that conscious will is merely a mask for irrational impulses saves men from the trouble of thinking.
Ralph Barton Perry

See also: DESTINY, END, FATE, PESSIMISM.

FATE

Fate is the friend of the good, the guide of the wise, the tyrant of the foolish, the enemy of the bad.

William Rounseville Alger

'Tis Fate that flings the dice,
    And as she flings
Of kings makes peasants,
    And of peasants kings.

John Dryden

All things are ordered by God, but his providence takes in our free agency, as well as his own sovereignty.

Tryon Edwards

A strict belief in fate is the worst kind of slavery; on the other hand there is comfort in the thought that God will be moved by our prayers.

Epicurus

All is created and goes according to order, yet o'er our lifetime rules an uncertain fate.

Johann Wolfgang von Goethe

Fate is not the ruler, but the servant of Providence.

Edward G. Bulwer-Lytton (Baron Lytton)

Fate! there is no fate. Between the thought and the success God is the only agent.

Edward G. Bulwer-Lytton (Baron Lytton)

God overrules all mutinous accidents, brings them under his laws of fate, and makes them all serviceable to his purpose.

Marcus Aurelius

Whatever may happen to thee, it was prepared for thee from all eternity; and the implication of causes was, from eternity, spinning the thread of thy being, and of that which is incident to it.

Marcus Aurelius

In two senses we are precisely what we worship. Ourselves are Fate.

Herman Melville

The Moving Finger writes; and having writ,
Moves on; nor all your Piety nor Wit
Shall lure it back to cancel half a Line,
Nor all your Tears wash out a Word of it.

Omar Khayyám

What must be shall be; and that which is a necessity to him that struggles, is little more than choice to him that is willing.

Seneca

Man has the capacity of almost complete control of fate. If he fails it will be by the ignorance or folly of men.

Edward Lee Thorndike

See also: DESTINY, FATALISM, FORTUNE.

FATHER

My son is 7 years old. I am 54. It has taken me a great many years to reach that age. I am more respected in the community, I am stronger, I am more intelligent, and I think I am better than he is. I don't want to be a pal, I want to be a father.

Clifton Fadiman

By profession I am a soldier and take pride in that fact. But I am prouder—infinitely prouder—to be a father. A soldier destroys in order to build; the father only builds, never destroys. The one has the potentiality of death; the other embodies creation and life. And while the hordes of death are mighty, the battalions of life are mightier still. It is my hope that my son, when I am gone, will remember me not from the battle but in the home repeating with him our simple daily prayer.

Douglas MacArthur

The fundamental defect of fathers is that they want their children to be a credit to them.

Bertrand Arthur William Russell

There was a time when father amounted to something in the United States. He was held with some esteem in the community; he had some authority in his own household; his views were sometimes taken seriously by his children; and even his wife paid heed to him from time to time.

Adlai Ewing Stevenson

See also: CHILDREN, MOTHER, PARENT.

FATHERLAND

He who abandons his fatherland, stands in mid-air, with no ground to sustain him.

Berthold Auerbach

When the fatherland faded from my eyes I found it again in my heart.

Heinrich Heine

I fancy the proper means for increasing the love we bear to our native country, is, to reside some time in a foreign one.
William Shenstone

How dear is fatherland to all noble hearts.
Voltaire (François Marie Arouet)

Our country is that spot to which our heart is attached.
Voltaire (François Marie Arouet)

Our country, however bounded or described —still our country, to be cherished in all our hearts—to be defended by all our hands.
Robert Charles Winthrop

See also: CITIZENSHIP, LOYALTY, NATION.

FATNESS

The size of a woman's stomach depends largely on her surroundings.
Eugene Field

The more waist, the less speed.
Oliver Herford

She had a lot of fat that did not fit.
Herbert George Wells

See also: BIGNESS, DIET, FASTING, SIZE.

FAULT

There is so much good in the worst of us,
And so much bad in the best of us,
That it ill behooves any of us
To find fault with the rest of us.
Anonymous

To reprove small faults with undue vehemence, is as absurd as if a man should take a great hammer to kill a fly on his friend's forehead.
Anonymous

Observe your enemies for they first find out your faults.
Antisthenes

When I feel like finding fault I always begin with myself and then I never get any further.
Ray Stannard Baker (David Grayson)

We should correct our own faults by seeing how uncomely they appear in others.
Francis Beaumont

The greatest of faults is to be conscious of none.
Thomas Carlyle

Think of your own faults the first part of the night when you are awake, and of the faults of others the latter part of the night when you are asleep.
Chinese Proverb

Faults of the head are punished in this world, those of the heart in another; but as most of our vices are compound, so also is their punishment.
Charles Caleb Colton

To acknowledge our faults when we are blamed, is modesty; to discover them to one's friends, in ingenuousness, is confidence; but to proclaim them to the world, if one does not take care, is pride.
Confucius

Every one is eagle-eyed to see another's faults and deformity.
John Dryden

If we were faultless we should not be so much annoyed by the defects of those with whom we associate.
François de Salignac de La Mothe-Fénelon

He will be immortal who liveth till he be stoned by one without fault.
Thomas Fuller

There is no one without faults, not even men of God. They are men of God not because they are faultless, but because they know their own faults, they strive against them, they do not hide them and are ever ready to correct themselves.
Mohandas Karamchand (Mahatma) Gandhi

If the best man's faults were written on his forehead, he would draw his hat over his eyes.
Thomas Gray

Bad men excuse their faults; good men will leave them.
Ben (Benjamin) Jonson

He who exhibits no faults is a fool or a hypocrite whom we should distrust.
Joseph Joubert

If we didn't have any faults, we wouldn't take such delight in noticing them in others.
Duc François de La Rochefoucauld

Only great men have great faults.
Duc François de La Rochefoucauld

We confess small faults, in order to insinuate that we have no great ones.
Duc François de La Rochefoucauld

We easily forget our faults when they are only known to ourselves.
Duc François de La Rochefoucauld

If you are pleased at finding faults, you are displeased at finding perfections.
Johann Kaspar Lavater

If thou wouldst bear thy neighbor's faults, cast thine eyes upon thine own.
Miguel de Molinos

It is far better to know our own weaknesses and failings than to point out those of others.
Jawaharlal Nehru

We learn by trial and error. And if we have the capacity to learn by trial and error, then, on the whole, it is well with us. It is only those who refuse to learn that get into great difficulties.
Jawaharlal Nehru

To find fault is easy; to do better may be difficult.
Plutarch

You will find it less easy to uproot faults, than to choke them by gaining virtues.
John Ruskin

The lowest people are generally the first to find fault with show or equipage; especially that of a person lately emerged from his obscurity. They never once consider that he is breaking the ice for themselves.
William Shenstone

Men are almost always cruel on their neighbors' faults, and make the overthrow of others the badge of their own ill-masked virtue.
Sir Philip Sidney

Endeavor to be always patient of the faults and imperfections of others; for thou hast many faults and imperfections of thine own that require forbearance. If thou art not able to make thyself that which thou wishest, how canst thou expect to mold another in conformity to thy will?
Thomas à Kempis

Ten thousand of the greatest faults in our neighbors are of less consequence to us than one of the smallest in ourselves.
Richard Whately

See also: FAILING, IMPERFECTION.

FEAR

No one loves the man whom he fears.
Aristotle

God planted fear in the soul as truly as he planted hope or courage. It is a kind of bell or gong which rings the mind into quick life and avoidance on the approach of danger. It is the soul's signal for rallying.
Henry Ward Beecher

Often the fear of one evil leads us into a worse.
Nicolas Boileau-Despréaux

The most dangerous person is the fearful; he is the most to be feared.
Ludwig Börne

Early and provident fear is the mother of safety.
Edmund Burke

No passion so effectually robs the mind of all its powers of acting and reasoning as fear.
Edmund Burke

The most drastic and usually the most effective remedy for fear is direct action.
William Burnham

Nothing in life is to be feared. It is only to be understood.
Marie Curie

If a man harbors any sort of fear, it percolates through all his thinking, damages his personality, makes him landlord to a ghost.
Lloyd Cassel Douglas

Fear is a basic emotion, part of our native equipment, and like all normal emotions has a positive function to perform. Comforting formulas for getting rid of anxiety may be just the wrong thing. Books about "peace of mind" can be bad medicine. To be afraid when one should be afraid is good sense.
Dorothy Fosdick

One of the strange phenomena of the last century is the spectacle of religion dropping the appeal to fear while other human interests have picked it up.
Harry Emerson Fosdick

Fear has its use, but cowardice has none. I may not put my finger into the jaws of a snake, but the very sight of the snake need not strike terror into me. The trouble is that we often die many times before death overtakes us.

Mohandas Karamchand (Mahatma) Gandhi

There are very few monsters who warrant the fear we have of them.

André Gide

Fear on guilt attends, and deeds of darkness; the virtuous breast ne'er knows it.

William Havard

'Tis fools who never fear.

Heinrich Heine

The fear of becoming a "has been" keeps some people from becoming anything.

Eric Hoffer

All fear is painful, and when it conduces not to safety, is painful without use. Every consideration, therefore, by which groundless terrors may be removed, adds something to human happiness.

Samuel Johnson

Fear is implanted in us as a preservative from evil; but its duty, like that of other passions, is not to overbear reason, but to assist it. It should not be suffered to tyrannize in the imagination, to raise phantoms of horror, or to beset life with supernumerary distresses.

Samuel Johnson

We must face what we fear; that is the case of the core of the restoration of health.

Max Lerner

Fear is nature's warning signal to get busy.

Henry Charles Link

He who fears being conquered is sure of defeat.

Napoleon I (Bonaparte)

As fear is close companion to falsehood, so truth follows fearlessness.

Jawaharlal Nehru

Fear blinds and makes desperate.

Jawaharlal Nehru

Fear often produces cruelty and frightfulness.

Jawaharlal Nehru

Logic and cold reason are poor weapons to fight fear and distrust. Only faith and generosity can overcome them.

Jawaharlal Nehru

A man who is afraid will do anything.

Jawaharlal Nehru

When fear comes our vision is clouded, and it becomes difficult to distinguish between the guilty and innocent.

Jawaharlal Nehru

There is a virtuous fear which is the effect of faith, and a vicious fear which is the product of doubt and distrust. The former leads to hope as relying on God, in whom we believe; the latter inclines to despair, as not relying upon God, in whom we do not believe. Persons of the one character fear to lose God; those of the other character fear to find him.

Blaise Pascal

The only thing we have to fear is fear itself.

Franklin Delano Roosevelt

The experience of overcoming fear is extraordinarily delightful.

Bertrand Arthur William Russell

Our instinctive emotions are those that we have inherited from a much more dangerous world, and contain, therefore, a larger portion of fear than they should.

Bertrand Arthur William Russell

Worry is a form of fear, and all forms of fear produce fatigue. A man who has learned not to feel fear will find the fatigue of daily life enormously diminished.

Bertrand Arthur William Russell

Fear of self is the greatest of all terrors, the deepest of all dread, the commonest of all mistakes. From it grows failure. Because of it, life is a mockery. Out of it comes despair.

David Seabury

Fear is the tax that conscience pays to guilt.

George Sewell

Fear is two-fold; a fear of solicitous anxiety, such as makes us let go our confidence in God's providence, and a fear of prudential caution, whereby, from a due estimate of approaching evil, we endeavor our own security. The former is wrong and forbidden; the latter not only lawful, but laudable.

Robert South

There is no hope unmingled with fear, and no fear unmingled with hope.

Baruch (Benedict) Spinoza

Fear is the mother of foresight.

Sir Henry Taylor

There is nothing to fear except the persistent refusal to try to find out the truth, the persistent refusal to analyze the causes of happenings. Fear grows in darkness, if you think there's a bogeyman around, turn on the light.

Dorothy Thompson

Desponding fear, of feeble fancies full, weak and unmanly, loosens every power.

James Thomson

Fear follows crime, and is its punishment.

Voltaire (François Marie Arouet)

It is only the fear of God that can deliver us from the fear of man.

John Witherspoon

See also: ANXIETY, CARE, COWARDICE, NEUROSIS, PANIC, SUPERSTITION.

FEASTING

When I behold a fashionable table set out in all its magnificence, I fancy that I see gouts and dropsies, fevers and lethargies, with other innumerable distempers, lying in ambuscade among the dishes. Nature delights in the most plain and simple diet. Every animal, but man, keeps to one dish. Herbs are the food of this species, fish of that, and flesh of a third. Man falls upon everything that comes in his way; not the smallest fruit or excrescence of the earth, scarce a berry or a mushroom can escape him.

Joseph Addison

It is not the quantity of the meat, but the cheerfulness of the guests, which makes the feast.

Edward Hyde (Earl of Clarendon)

He that feasts every day, feasts no day.

Charles Simmons

See also: DIET, EATING, GLUTTONY.

FEELINGS

Is it not marvellous how full people are—all people—of humor, tragedy, passionate human longings, hopes, fears—if only you can unloosen the floodgates!

Ray Stannard Baker (David Grayson)

Feeling does not become stronger in the religious life by waiting, but by using it.

Henry Ward Beecher

Feeling in the young precedes philosophy, and often acts with a better and more certain aim.

William Carleton

Every human feeling is greater and larger than its exciting cause—a proof, I think, that man is designed for a higher state of existence.

Samuel Taylor Coleridge

Half our mistakes in life arise from feeling where we ought to think, and thinking where we ought to feel.

John Churton Collins

Human affairs inspire in noble hearts only two feelings—admiration or pity.

Anatole France

The heart has often been compared to the needle of the compass for its constancy; has it ever been so for its variations? Yet were any man to keep minutes of his feelings from youth to age, what a table of variations would they present—how numerous, how diverse, how strange!

Augustus and Julius Hare

Only feeling understands feeling.

Heinrich Heine

The heart that is soonest awake to the flowers is always the first to be touched by the thorns.

Thomas Moore

It is difficult for an appeal to the mind and to the intellect to go far. Most people unfortunately do not think. They feel and act according to their feelings.

Jawaharlal Nehru

Emotions . . . become more violent when expression is stifled.

Philo

Our higher feelings move our animal nature; and our animal nature, irritated, may call back a semblance of those emotions; but the whole difference between nobleness and baseness lies in the question, whether the feeling begins from below or above.

Frederick William Robertson

Our feelings were given us to excite to action, and when they end in themselves, they are cherished to no good purpose.

Daniel Keyte Sandford

When a man is prey to his emotions, he is not his master.

Baruch (Benedict) Spinoza

See also: EMOTION, HEART, SENSIBILITY, SEN-SITIVENESS, SENTIMENT.

FICKLENESS

Everything by starts, and nothing long.

John Dryden

Fickleness has its rise in our experience of the fallaciousness of present pleasure, and in our ignorance of the vanity of that which is absent.

Blaise Pascal

They are the weakest-minded and the hardest-hearted men that most love change.

John Ruskin

A fickle memory is bad; a fickle course of conduct is worse; but a fickle heart and purposes, worst of all.

Charles Simmons

See also: CHANGE, INCONSTANCY, INDECISION, INSTABILITY, IRRESOLUTION.

FICTION

The best part of the fiction in many novels is the notice that the characters are all purely imaginary.

Franklin Pierce Adams

Fiction is no longer a mere amusement; but transcendent genius accommodating itself to the character of the age, has seized upon this province of literature, and turned fiction from a toy into a mighty engine.

William Ellery Channing

Fiction—if it at all aspires to be art—must appeal to temperament. And in truth it must be, like painting, like music, like all art, the appeal of one temperament to all the other innumerable temperaments whose subtle and resistless power endows passing events with their true meaning, and creates the moral, the emotional atmosphere of the place and time. Such an appeal to be effective must be an impression conveyed through the senses; and, in fact, it cannot be made in any other way, because temperament whether individual or collective, is not amenable to persuasion.

Joseph Conrad

Fiction is not falsehood, as some seem to think. It is rather the fanciful and dramatic grouping of real traits around imaginary scenes or characters. It may give false views of men or things, or it may, in the hands of a master, more truthfully portray life than sober history itself.

Tryon Edwards

I have often maintained that fiction may be much more instructive than real history.

John Watson Foster

Man is a poetical animal and delights in fiction.

William Hazlitt

The best histories may sometimes be those in which a little of the exaggeration of fictitious narrative is judiciously employed. Something is lost in accuracy, but much is gained in effect. The fainter lines are neglected, but the great characteristic features are imprinted on the mind forever.

Thomas Babington Macaulay

Every fiction that has ever laid strong hold on human belief is the mistaken image of some great truth.

James Martineau

The reason that fiction is more interesting than any other form of literature to those of us who really like to study people, is that in fiction the author can really tell the truth without hurting anyone and without humiliating himself too much.

Anna Eleanor Roosevelt

The most influential books and the truest in their influence, are works of fiction. They repeat, rearrange, and clarify the lessons of life, disengage us from ourselves, constrain us to the acquaintance of others, and show us the web of experience, but with a single change. That monstrous, consuming *ego* of ours struck out.

Robert Louis Balfour Stevenson

Those who delight in the study of human nature, may improve in the knowledge of it, and in the profitable application of it by the perusal of the best selected fictions.

Richard Whately

See also: ALLEGORY, BOOK, FABLE, ROMANCE.

FIDELITY

Nothing is more noble, nothing more venerable than fidelity. Faithfulness and truth are the most sacred excellences and endowments of the human mind.

Cicero

Trust reposed in noble natures obliges them the more.

John Dryden

Fidelity is the sister of justice.

Horace

Full allegiance to the community can be given only by a man's second nature, ruling over his first and primitive nature, and treating it as not finally himself. Then the disciplines and the necessities and the constraints of a civilized life have ceased to be alien to him, and imposed from without. They have become his own inner imperatives.

Walter Lippmann

Faithful found among the faithless, his loyalty he kept, his love, his zeal, nor number, nor example with him wrought to swerve from truth, or change his constant mind.

John Milton

Fidelity is seven-tenths of business success.

James Parton

It goes far toward making a man faithful to let him understand that you think him so; and he that does but suspect I will deceive him gives me a sort of right to do it.

Seneca

Another of our highly prized virtues is fidelity. We are immensely pleased with ourselves when we are faithful.

Ida Alexa Ross Wylie

See also: CONSTANCY, DEVOTION, FAITH.

FIGHT

I will not cease from Mental Fight,
Nor shall my Sword sleep in my hand
Till we have built Jerusalem,
In England's green and pleasant Land.

William Blake

We shall go on to the end, we shall fight in France, we shall fight on the seas and oceans, we shall fight with growing confidence and growing strength in the air, we shall defend our island, whatever the cost may be, we shall fight on the beaches, we shall fight on the landing grounds, we shall fight in the fields and in the streets, we shall fight in the hills; we shall never surrender, and even if, which I do not for a moment believe, this island or a large part of it were subjugated and starving, then our Empire beyond the seas, armed and guarded by the British fleet, would carry on the struggle, until in God's good time, the New World, with all its power and might steps forth to the rescue and liberation of the old.

Sir Winston Leonard Spencer Churchill

We fight to great disadvantage when we fight with those who have nothing to lose.

Francesco Guicciardini

I repeat it, sir, we must fight! And appeal to arms and to the God of Hosts is all that is left us.

Patrick Henry

See also: ARGUMENT, CONTENTION, VIOLENCE.

FINANCE

There is no such thing as an innocent purchaser of stocks.

Louis Dembitz Brandeis

A financier is a pawn-broker with imagination.

Sir Arthur Wing Pinero

A holding company is a thing where you hand an accomplice the goods while the policeman searches you.

Will (William Penn Adair) Rogers

See also: BANK, BUSINESS, ECONOMICS, GAIN, MONEY, SPECULATION.

FIRE

The fire which seems extinguished often slumbers under the ashes; he who dares to stir it may find himself suddenly startled.

Pierre Corneille

From little spark may burst a mighty flame.

Dante Alighieri

Some heart once pregnant with celestial fire.

Thomas Gray

A crooked log makes a straight fire.

George Herbert

The most tangible of all visible mysteries—fire.

(James Henry) Leigh Hunt

See also: COOKING, DANGER, LIGHT.

FIREARM: *see* GUN.

FIRMNESS

Firmness, both in suffering and exertion, is a character which I would wish to possess. I have always despised the whining yelp of complaint, and the cowardly feeble resolve.

Robert Burns

That profound firmness which enables a man to regard difficulties but as evils to be surmounted, no matter what shape they may assume.

Henry Cockton

It is only persons of firmness that can have real gentleness. Those who appear gentle are, in general, only a weak character, which easily changes into asperity.

Duc François de La Rochefoucauld

The firm, without pliancy, and the pliant, without firmness, resemble vessels without water, and water without vessels.

Johann Kaspar Lavater

The greatest firmness is the greatest mercy.

Henry Wadsworth Longfellow

When firmness is sufficient, rashness is unnecessary.

Napoleon I (Bonaparte)

Firmness of purpose is one of the most necessary sinews of character, and one of the best instruments of success. Without it genius wastes its efforts in a maze of inconsistencies.

Philip Dormer Stanhope (Lord Chesterfield)

I know no real worth but that tranquil firmness which meets dangers by duty, and braves them without rashness.

Stanislas I (Leszczyński)

Your salvation is in your own hands; in the stubborness of your minds, the tenacity of your hearts, and such blessings as God, sorely tried by His children, shall give us. Nature is indifferent to the survival of the human species, including Americans.

Adlai Ewing Stevenson

The purpose firm is equal to the deed.

Edward Young

See also: CONSTANCY, DECISION, POSITIVENESS, PURPOSE, RESOLUTION.

FISHING

When the wind is in the East,
Then the fishes bite the least;
When the wind is in the West,
Then the fishes bite the best;
When the wind is in the North,
Then the fishes do come forth;
When the wind is in the South,
It blows the bait in the fish's mouth.

Anonymous

There is no use in your walking five miles to fish when you can depend on being just as unsuccessful near home.

Samuel Langhorne Clemens (Mark Twain)

I would rather fish than eat, particularly eat fish.

Corey Ford

You must lose a fly to catch a trout.

George Herbert

A fishing-rod is a stick with a hook at one end and a fool at the other.

Samuel Johnson

When one is catching fish, a silent companion is best of all.

Sir Rabindranath Tagore

Angling may be said to be so like the mathematics that it can never be fully learnt.

Izaak Walton

As no man is born an artist, so no man is born an angler.

Izaak Walton

See also: FOOD, RIVER, SEA, SPORTS, WATER POLLUTION.

FLAG

A flag is a necessity for all nations. Millions have died for it.

Mohandas Karamchand (Mahatma) Gandhi

It is no doubt a kind of idolatry which it would be a sin to destroy. For a flag represents an ideal. The unfurling of the Union Jack evokes in the English breast sentiments whose strength it is difficult to measure. The Stars and Stripes mean a world to the Americans. The Star and the Crescent will call forth the best bravery in Islam.

Mohandas Karamchand (Mahatma) Gandhi

With a flag you can lead people wherever you want.

Theodor Herzl

See also: CITIZENSHIP, LOYALTY, NATION, PATRIOTISM, SOLDIER.

FLATTERY

The most skilful flattery is to let a person talk on, and be a listener.

Joseph Addison

It is better to fall among crows than flatterers; for those devour only the dead—these the living.

Antisthenes

It has well been said that the archflatterer, with whom all petty flatterers have intelligence, is a man's self.

Francis Bacon

Flattery corrupts both the receiver and the giver; and adulation is not of more service to the people than to kings.

Edmund Burke

Flattery is from the teeth out. Sincere appreciation is from the heart out.

Dale Carnegie

Some there are who profess to despise all flattery, but even these are, nevertheless, to be flattered, by being told that they do despise it.

Charles Caleb Colton

Imitation is the sincerest flattery.

Nathaniel Cotton

The lie that flatters I abhor the most.

William Cowper

Flattery is the destruction of all good fellowship: it is like qualmish liqueur in the midst of a bottle of wine.

Benjamin Disraeli

We love flattery, even when we see through it, and are not deceived by it, for it shows that we are of importance enough to be courted.

Ralph Waldo Emerson

Flattery is never so agreeable as to our blind side; commend a fool for his wit, or a knave for his honesty, and they will receive you into their bosom.

Henry Fielding

There is no flattery so adroit or effectual as that of implicit assent.

William Hazlitt

He that is much flattered soon learns to flatter himself. We are commonly taught our duty by fear or shame, but how can they act upon a man who hears nothing but his own praises?

Samuel Johnson

To be flattered is grateful, even when we know that our praises are not believed by those who pronounce them; for they prove at least our power, and show that our favor is valued, since it is purchased by the meanness of falsehood.

Samuel Johnson

Of all wild beasts preserve me from a tryant; and of all tame, from a flatterer.

Ben (Benjamin) Jonson

Flattery is a kind of bad money, to which our vanity gives currency.

Duc François de La Rochefoucauld

If we did not flatter ourselves, the flattery of others would not injure us.

Duc François de La Rochefoucauld

Self-love is the greatest of flatterers.

Duc François de La Rochefoucauld

We sometimes think we hate flattery, when we only hate the manner in which we have been flattered.

Duc François de La Rochefoucauld

A death-bed flattery is the worst of treacheries. Ceremonies of mode and compliment are mightily out of season when life and salvation come to be at stake.

Sir Roger L'Estrange

There is no tongue that flatters like a lover's; and yet in the exaggeration of his feelings, flattery seems to him commonplace.

Edward G. Bulwer-Lytton (Baron Lytton)

The art of flatterers is to take advantage of the foibles of the great, to foster their errors, and never to give advice which may annoy.

Molière (Jean Baptiste Poquelin)

The most subtle flattery a woman can receive is that conveyed by actions, not by words.

Albertine Adrienne Necker de Saussure

There is an oblique way of reproof, which takes off the sharpness of it, and an address in flattery, which makes it agreeable, though never so gross; but of all flatterers, the most skilful is he who can do what you like, without saying anything which argues he does it for your sake.

Alexander Pope

Flatterers are the worst kind of traitors for they will strengthen thy imperfections, encourage thee in all evils, correct thee in nothing, but so shadow and paint all thy vices and follies as thou shalt never, by their will, discern good from evil, or vice from virtue.

Sir Walter Raleigh

Men find it more easy to flatter than to praise.

Jean Paul Richter

None are more taken in by flattery than the proud, who wish to be the first and are not.

Baruch (Benedict) Spinoza

Allow no man to be so free with you as to praise you to your face. Your vanity, by this means, will want its food, but at the same time your passion for esteem will be more fully gratified; men will praise you in their actions; where you now receive one compliment, you will then receive twenty civilities.

Sir Richard Steele

Flattery is okay if you handle it right. It's like smoking cigarettes. Quite all right, as long as you don't inhale.

Adlai Ewing Stevenson

Nothing is so great an instance of ill-manners as flattery. If you flatter all the company, you please none; if you flatter only one or two, you affront the rest.

Jonathan Swift

The only benefit of flattery is that by hearing what we are not, we may be instructed what we ought to be.

Jonathan Swift

Tis an old maxim in the schools, that flattery is the food of fools. Yet now and then your men of wit will condescend to take a bit.

Jonathan Swift

Flatterers are the worst kind of enemies.

Tacitus

Know thyself, thine evil as well as thy good, and flattery shall not harm thee; her speech shall be a warning, a humbling, and a guide; for wherein thou lackest most, there chiefly will thy sycophant commend thee.

Martin Farquhar Tupper

To flatter is to steal.

Yiddish Proverb

See also: APPLAUSE, COMPLIMENT, PRAISE.

FLIRTATION

A worthless woman! mere cold clay
　As all false things are! but so fair,
She takes the breath of men away
　Who gaze upon her unaware:
I would not play her larcenous tricks
　To have her looks!

Elizabeth Barrett Browning

　Merely innocent flirtation,
Not quite adultery, but adulteration.

George Gordon Byron (Lord Byron)

God has given you women a plentiful supply of coquetry to start with, and on the top of that you have the milliner and the jeweller to help you.

Sir Rabindranath Tagore

See also: COQUETTE, COURTSHIP, ROMANCE.

FLOWER

Flowers are the sweetest things that God ever made and forgot to put a soul into.

Henry Ward Beecher

Flowers are Love's truest language; they
　betray,
　Like the divining rods of Magi old,
　Where precious wealth lies buried, not
　　of gold,
But love—strong love, that never can decay!

Park Benjamin

How the universal heart of man blesses flowers! They are wreathed round the cradle, the marriage altar, and the tomb. They should deck the brow of the youthful bride, for they are in themselves a lovely type of marriage. They should twine round the tomb, for their perpetually renewed beauty is a symbol of the resurrection. They should festoon the altar, for their fragrance and beauty ascend in perpetual worship before the most high.

Lydia Maria Francis Child

　Flowers are words
Which even a babe may understand.

Arthur Cleveland Coxe

The flowers are nature's jewels, with whose wealth she decks her summer beauty.

George Croly

The rose is fragrant, but it fades in time:
The violet sweet, but quickly past the prime:
White lilies hang their heads and soon decay,
And white snow in minutes melts away.

John Dryden

It is with flowers as with moral qualities; the bright are sometimes poisonous, but I believe never the sweet.

Augustus and Julius Hare

The instinctive and universal taste of mankind selects flowers for the expression of its finest sympathies, their beauty and fleetingness serving to make them the most fitting symbols of those delicate sentiments for which language seems almost too gross a medium.

George Stillman Hillard

Every rose is an autograph from the hand of God on his world about us. He has inscribed his thoughts in these marvellous hieroglyphics which sense and science have, these many thousand years, been seeking to understand.

Theodore Parker

In eastern lands they talk in flowers, and tell in a garland their loves and cares.

James Gates Percival

Your voiceless lips, O, flowers, are living preachers—each cup a pulpit, and each leaf a book.

Horatio Smith

There is not the least flower but seems to hold up its head and to look pleasantly, in the secret sense of the goodness of its heavenly Maker.

Robert South

To analyze the charms of flowers is like dissecting music; it is one of those things which it is far better to enjoy, than to attempt fully to understand.

Henry Theodore Tuckerman

To me the meanest flower that blows can give thoughts that do often lie too deep for tears.

William Wordsworth

See also: AGRICULTURE, BEAUTY, CLOUD, GARDEN, LOVE, NATURE, SPRING.

FOLLY

A good folly is worth whatever you pay for it.

George Ade

There is a foolish corner even in the brain of the sage.

Aristotle

We spend half our lives unlearning the follies transmitted to us by our parents, and the other half transmitting our own follies to our offspring.

Isaac Goldberg

He who lives without folly is not so wise as he imagines.

Duc François de La Rochefoucauld

Folly consists in drawing of false conclusions from just principles, by which it is distinguished from madness, which draws just conclusions from false principles.

John Locke

See also: FOOL, INDISCRETION, RASHNESS.

FOOL

A fool may be known by six things: anger, without cause; speech, without profit; change, without progress; inquiry, without object; putting trust in a stranger, and mistaking foes for friends.

Arabian Proverb

Every single forward step in history has been taken over the bodies of empty-headed fools who giggled and snickered.

Bruce Barton

There is no greater fool than he that says, "There is no God," unless it be the one who says he does not know whether there is one or not.

Otto Eduard Leopold von Bismarck

The world is full of fools; and he who would not wish to see one, must not only shut himself up alone, but must also break his looking-glass.

Nicolas Boileau-Despréaux

A fool always finds some greater fool to admire him.

Nicolas Boileau-Despréaux

It is all too often forgotten that the ancient symbol for prenascence of the world is a fool, and that foolishness, being a divine state, is not a condition to be either proud or ashamed of.

George Spencer Brown

Nothing is more intolerable than a prosperous fool; and hence we see men who, at one time, were affable and agreeable, completely changed by prosperity, despising old friends and clinging to new.

Cicero

Let us be thankful for the fools; but for them the rest of us could not succeed.

Samuel Langhorne Clemens (Mark Twain)

Nobody can describe a fool to the life, without much patient self-inspection.

Frank Moore Colby

To pursue trifles is the lot of humanity; and whether we bustle in a pantomime, or strut at a coronation, or shout at a bonfire, or harangue in a senate-house; whatever object we follow, it will at last conduct us to futility and disappointment. The wise bustle and laugh as they walk in the pageant, but fools bustle and are important; and this probably, is all the difference between them.

Oliver Goldsmith

None but a fool is always right.

Augustus and Julius Hare

I am always afraid of a fool; one cannot be sure me is not a knave.

William Hazlitt

No fools are so troublesome as those who have some wit.

Duc François de La Rochefoucauld

We sometimes see a fool possessed of talent, but never of judgment.

Duc François de La Rochefoucauld

There are many more fools in the world than there are knaves, otherwise the knaves could not exist.

Edward G. Bulwer-Lytton (Baron Lytton)

There is hope for the man who can occasionally make a spontaneous and irrevocable ass of himself.

Peter McArthur

He who has been once very foolish will never be very wise.

Michel Eyquem de Montaigne

To be a man's own fool is bad enough; but the vain man is everybody's.

William Penn

If any young man expects without faith, without thought, without study, without patient, persevering labor, in the midst of and in spite of discouragement, to attain anything in this world that is worth attaining, he will simply wake up, by-and-by, and find that he has been playing the part of a fool.

Minot Judson Savage

What the fool does in the end, the wise man does in the beginning.

Spanish Proverb

A fool can no more see his own folly than he can see his ears.

William Makepeace Thackeray

A man never knows what a fool he is until he hears himself imitated by one.

Sir Herbert Beerbohm Tree

O Heaven! he who thinks himself wise is a great fool.

Voltaire (François Marie Arouet)

A fool at forty is a fool indeed.

Edward Young

Fools with bookish knowledge, are children with edged weapons, they hurt themselves, and put others in pain. The half-learned is more dangerous than the simpleton.

Johann Georg von Zimmermann

See also: ASS, BLOCKHEAD, BORE, DULNESS, FOLLY, IGNORANCE, RECKLESSNESS.

FOOTBALL

To the spectator no sport has more spectacle than football. To the man on the field, no sport offers greater glory—or greater pain. He must be a man, for he spends much of his time literally on the field (with a number of other men on top of him). But when he breaks loose—ah! what can compare with that great moment?

Esquire

In literature, the theater and moving pictures, the escape has a powerful hold upon the imagination of the average man. The story of dangers avoided and obstacles surmounted is one of which we never tire. The American game of football is such a story constantly enacted before our eyes. Its great protagonists are not easily forgotten.

Paul Gallico

Styles and tastes change in football. Now, the forward passer has become the hero because of the large slices of enemy territory that can be vanquished by the accuracy of his heaves. But there is still no thrill comparable to the one furnished by a fast, shifty, elusive runner who tucks that windjammed pig rind under his arm and swivel-hips his way through a broken field to climax his effort by crossing the goal line standing up.

Paul Gallico

Football today is far too much a sport for the few who can play it well; the rest of us, and too many of our children, get our exercise from climbing up the seats in stadiums, or from walking across the room to turn on our television sets. And this is true for one sport after another, all across the board.

John Fitzgerald Kennedy

Pro football's explosive growth in every direction, territorially, financially, and in fan interest, has been by far the biggest story in sports of the past several decades.

Harold Rosenthal

Remember those hippy buttons with the strange legends? One read, "God is Alive and Living in Green Bay."

Harold Rosenthal

See also: SPORTS.

FORBEARANCE

If thou would'st be borne with, then bear with others.

Thomas Fuller

We should meet abuse by forbearance. Human nature is so constituted that if we take absolutely no notice of anger or abuse, the person indulging in it will soon weary of it and stop.

Mohandas Karamchand (Mahatma) Gandhi

It is a noble and great thing to cover the blemishes and excuse the failings of a friend; to draw a curtain before his stains, and to display his perfection; to bury his weaknesses in silence, but to proclaim his virtues on the house-top.

Robert South

Cultivate forbearance till your heart yields a fine crop of it. Pray for a short memory as to all unkindnesses.

Charles Haddon Spurgeon

See also: GENTLENESS, PATIENCE, TOLERANCE.

FORCE

Force is not a remedy.

John Bright

We should all feel relief if methods of mass destruction were abolished. But that would not mean "peace." It might mean that we should die a little later rather than a little sooner; it might mean that we should die slowly rather than quickly; but it would not have much bearing on whether or not our world was to be one where myriads of human beings were degraded to the status of broken-spirited pack animals.

John Foster Dulles

In this age of the rule of brute force, it is almost impossible for any one to believe that any one else could possibly reject the law of the final supremacy of brute force.

Mohandas Karamchand (Mahatma) Gandhi

The wielder of brute force does not scruple about the means to be used.

Mohandas Karamchand (Mahatma) Gandhi

Who overcomes by force, hath overcome but half his foe.

John Milton

Force rules the world, and not opinion; but opinion is that which makes use of force.

Blaise Pascal

When force is necessary, there it must be applied boldly, decisively and completely. But one must know the limitations of force; one must know when to blend force with a maneuver, the blow with an agreement.

Leon Trotsky

See also: ENERGY, OPPRESSION, PERSECUTION, POWER, REVOLUTION, STRENGTH, VIOLENCE, WAR.

FOREIGN AID

Our nation's foreign aid efforts are, in my opinion, still necessary, they are an integral part of America's ceaseless striving to build a just and peaceful world.

Dwight David Eisenhower

If someone has a substitute for foreign aid, I'd like to hear about it. The investment we make in foreign aid . . . is certainly less than that necessary to treat the symptoms of massive economic crises and disorder and war.

Hubert Horatio Humphrey

Although we recognize the shortsightedness of isolation, we do not embrace the equally futile prospect of total and endless dependence. The United States can never do more than supplement the efforts of the developing countries themselves.

Lyndon Baines Johnson

See also: AMERICA, FOREIGN POLICY, HELP, POVERTY, RICHES.

FOREIGN POLICY

A basic prerequisite to a people's foreign policy is . . . a well-informed public . . . The world is still suffering a hangover from the era when international agreements were secret and private arrangements between rulers.

James Francis Byrnes

Neither wealth nor might will determine the outcome of the struggles in Asia. They will turn on emotional factors too subtle to measure. Political alliances of an enduring nature will be built not on the power of guns or dollars, but on affection.

William Orville Douglas

A nation's security in war and peace demands participation in the community of nations.

Dwight David Eisenhower

We must never forget that international friendship is achieved through rumors ignored, propaganda challenged and exposed; through patient loyalty to those who have proved themselves worthy of it; through help freely given, where help is needed and merited . . . Peace is more product of our day-to-day living than of a spectacular program, intermittently executed.

Dwight David Eisenhower

What we call foreign affairs is no longer foreign affairs. It's a local affair. Whatever happens in Indonesia is important to Indiana. Whatever happens in any corner of the world has some effect on the farmer in Dickinson County, Kansas, or on a worker in a factory.

Dwight David Eisenhower

The foreign policy of the United States is rooted in its life at home. We will not permit human rights to be restricted in our own country. And we will not support policies abroad which are based on the rule of mi-

norities or the discredited notion that men are unequal before the law.

Lyndon Baines Johnson

A foreign policy consists in bringing into balance, with a comfortable surplus of power in reserve, the nation's commitments and the nation's power.

Walter Lippmann

The United States has no mandate from on high to police the world, and no inclination to do so. There have been classic cases in which our deliberate non-action was the wisest action of all.

Robert Strange McNamara

The time has passed when foreign affairs and domestic affairs could be regarded as separate and distinct. The borderline between the two has practically ceased to exist.

Walter Bedell Smith

We must thread our way between imperialism and isolationism, between the disavowal of the responsibilities of our power and the assertion of our power beyond our resources.

Adlai Ewing Stevenson

The fact is that our foreign policy is now and will be for generations the paramount, the absorbing question before us. *And upon its wise solution will depend* the domestic welfare of the American people.

Wendell Lewis Willkie

See also: FOREIGN AID, GOVERNMENT, UNITED NATIONS, WAR.

FORESIGHT: *see* FORETHOUGHT.

FORETHOUGHT

In life, as in chess, forethought wins.

Sir Thomas Fowell Buxton

To have too much forethought is the part of a wretch; to have too little is the part of a fool.

Richard Cecil

As a man without forethought searcely deserves the name of man, so forethought without reflection is but a phrase for the instinct of the beast.

Samuel Taylor Coleridge

Human foresight often leaves its proudest possessor only a choice of evils.

Charles Caleb Colton

If a man take no thought about what is distant, he will find sorrow near at hand.

Confucius

Happy those who knowing they are subject to uncertain changes, are prepared and armed for either fortune; a rare principle, and with much labor learned in wisdom's school.

Philip Massinger

The pace of events is moving so fast that unless we can find some way to keep our sights on tomorrow, we cannot expect to be in touch with today.

(David) Dean Rusk

Whoever fails to turn aside the ills of life by prudent forethought, must submit to the course of destiny.

Johann Christoph Friedrich von Schiller

It is only the surprise and newness of the thing which makes terrible that misfortune, which by premeditation might be made easy to us; for what some people make light by sufferance, others do by foresight.

Seneca

Few things are brought to a successful issue by impetuous desire, but most by calm and prudent forethought.

Thucydides

Whatever is foretold by God will be done by man; but nothing will be done by man because it is foretold by God.

William Wordsworth

See also: CAUTION, PROVIDENCE, PRUDENCE.

FORGETFULNESS

And we forget because we must
And not because we will.

Matthew Arnold

It is the lot of man to suffer, it is also his fortune to forget.

Benjamin Disraeli

Though the past haunt me as a spirit, I do not ask to forget.

Felicia Dorothea Browne Hemans

There is a noble forgetfulness—that which does not remember injuries.

Charles Simmons

When out of sight, quickly also out of mind.

Thomas à Kempis

See also: NEGLECT, OBLIVION, PAST.

FORGIVENESS

Forgive many things in others; nothing in yourself.

Ausonius

They who forgive most, shall be most forgiven.

Gamaliel Bailey

"I can forgive, but I cannot forget," is only another way of saying, "I will not forgive." Forgiveness ought to be like a cancelled note—torn in two, and burned up, so that it never can be shown against one.

Henry Ward Beecher

Mutual Forgiveness of each vice,
Such are the Gates of Paradise.

William Blake

Nothing in this lost and ruined world bears the meek impress of the Son of God so surely as forgiveness.

Alice Cary

He who is ready to forgive only invites offences.

Pierre Corneille

It is easier to forgive an enemy than a friend.

Madame Dorothée Deluzy

May I tell you why it seems to me a good thing for us to remember wrong that has been done us? That we may forgive it.

Charles John Huffam Dickens

His heart was as great as the world, but there was no room in it to hold the memory of a wrong.

Ralph Waldo Emerson

To err is human and it must be held to be equally human to forgive if we, though being fallible, would like rather to be forgiven than punished and reminded of our deeds.

Mohandas Karamchand (Mahatma) Gandhi

To forgive is not to forget. The merit lies in loving in spite of the vivid knowledge that the one that must be loved is not a friend. There is no merit in loving an enemy when you forget him for a friend.

Mohandas Karamchand (Mahatma) Gandhi

The weak can never forgive. Forgiveness is the attribute of the strong.

Mohandas Karamchand (Mahatma) Gandhi

Forgiveness is the most necessary and proper work of every man; for, though, when I do not a just thing, or a charitable, or a wise, another man may do it for me, yet no man can forgive my enemy but myself.

Edward Herbert

He that cannot forgive others, breaks the bridge over which he himself must pass if he would ever reach heaven; for every one has need to be forgiven.

George Herbert

It is in vain for you to expect, it is impudent for you to ask of God forgiveness for yourself if you refuse to exercise this forgiving temper as to others.

Benjamin Hoadly

It is hard for a haughty man ever to forgive one that has caught him in a fault, and whom he knows has reason to complain of him: his resentment never subsides till he has regained the advantage he has lost, and found means to make the other do him equal wrong.

Jean de La Bruyère

He who has not forgiven an enemy has never yet tasted one of the most sublime enjoyments of life.

Johann Kaspar Lavater

Forgive thyself little, and others much.

Robert Leighton

A Christian will find it cheaper to pardon than to resent. Forgiveness saves the expense of anger, the cost of hatred, the waste of spirits.

Hannah More

A brave man thinks no one his superior who does him an injury; for he has it then in his power to make himself superior to the other by forgiving it.

Alexander Pope

To err is human; to forgive, divine.

Alexander Pope

A wise man will make haste to forgive, because he knows the full value of time and will not suffer it to pass away in unnecessary pain.

Rambler

Humanity is never so beautiful as when praying for forgiveness, or else forgiving another.

Jean Paul Richter

When thou forgivest, the man who has pierced thy heart stands to thee in the relation of the sea-worm, that perforates the shell of the mussel, which straightway closes the wound with a pearl.

Jean Paul Richter

The narrow soul knows not the godlike glory of forgiving.

Nicholas Rowe

It has been a maxim with me to admit of easy reconciliation with a person whose offence proceeded from no depravity of heart; but where I was convinced it did so, to forego, for my own sake, all opportunities of revenge. I have derived no small share of happiness from this principle.

William Shenstone

The more we know, the better we forgive. Whoe'er feels deeply, feels for all that live.

Madame de Staël

Little, vicious minds abound with anger and revenge, and are incapable of feeling the pleasure of forgiving their enemies.

Philip Dormer Stanhope (Lord Chesterfield)

Only the brave know how to forgive; it is the most refined and generous pitch of virtue human nature can arrive at.

Laurence Sterne

A more glorious victory cannot be gained over another man, than this, that when the injury began on his part, the kindness should begin on ours.

John Tillotson

To be able to bear provocation is an argument of great reason, and to forgive it of a great mind.

John Tillotson

It is very easy to forgive others their mistakes; it takes more grit and gumption to forgive them for having witnessed your own.

Jessamyn West

See also: CLEMENCY, MERCY, PARDON, PITY.

FORM

Everything owes its being to form.

Boethius

Forms are necessary as vehicles and expressions of the spirit, as well as a means of fortifying it.

Abraham Geiger

Of what use are forms, seeing at times they are empty? Of the same use as barrels, which, at times, are empty too.

Augustus and Julius Hare

Get used to thinking that there is nothing Nature loves so well as to change existing forms and to make new ones like them.

Marcus Aurelius

See also: APPEARANCE, CUSTOM, FORMALISM, LOOKS, TRADITION.

FORMALISM

The house of the formalist is as empty of religion as the white of an egg is of savor.

John Bunyan

Formalism is the hall-mark of the national culture.

Henry Louis Mencken

It is the tendency, if not the essence of formalism to set the outward institutions of religion above its inward truths; to be punctilious in the round of ceremonial observances, while neglectful of those spiritual sacrifices with which God is well pleased; to substitute means in the room of ends, and to rest in the type and symbol without rising to the glorious reality.

John Pearson

See also: CEREMONY, ETIQUETTE, FORM.

FORTITUDE

True fortitude is seen in great exploits that justice warrants and that wisdom guides.

Joseph Addison

The fortitude of the Christian consists in patience, not in enterprises which the poets call heroic and which are commonly the effects of interest, pride, and wordly honor.

John Dryden

Fortitude I take to be the quiet possession of a man's self, and an undisturbed doing his duty whatever evils beset, or dangers lie in the way. In itself an essential virtue, it is a guard to every other virtue.

John Locke

There is a strength of quiet endurance as significant of courage as the most daring feats of prowess.

Henry Theodore Tuckerman

See also: COURAGE, ENDURANCE, RESOLUTION, STRENGTH, WILL.

FORTUNE

Fortune is like the market, where many times if you stay a little the price will fall; and, again, it is sometimes like a Sibyl's offer, which at first offereth the commodity at full, then consumeth part and part, and still holdeth up the price.

Francis Bacon

It cannot be denied that outward accidents conduce much to fortune; favor, opportunity, death of others, occasion fitting virtue: but chiefly, the mold of a man's fortune is in his own hands.

Francis Bacon

The way of fortune is like the milky-way in the sky; which is a number of small stars, not seen asunder, but giving light together: so it is a number of little and scarce discerned virtues, or rather faculties and customs, that make men fortunate.

Francis Bacon

Misfortune is the ballast which maintains our equilibrium on the sea of life, when we no longer have fortunes to carry.

Ludwig Börne

Fortune knocks at every man's door once in a life, but in a good many cases the man is in a neighboring saloon and does not hear her.

Samuel Langhorne Clemens (Mark Twain)

The wheel of fortune turns round incessantly, and who can say to himself, "I shall to-day be uppermost."

Confucius

It is a madness to make fortune the mistress of events, because in herself she is nothing, but is ruled by prudence.

John Dryden

To be thrown upon one's own resources, is to be cast into the very lap of fortune; for our faculties then undergo a development and display an energy of which they were previously unsusceptible.

Benjamin Franklin

The fortunate circumstances of our lives are generally found, at last, to be of our own producing.

Oliver Goldsmith

Fortune is ever seen accompanying industry.

Oliver Goldsmith

Human life is more governed by fortune than by reason.

David Hume

Ill fortune never crushed that man whom good fortune deceived not.

Ben (Benjamin) Jonson

There is nothing keeps longer than a middling fortune, and nothing melts away sooner than a great one. Poverty treads upon the heels of great and unexpected riches.

Jean de La Bruyère

It requires greater virtues to support good than bad fortune.

Duc François de La Rochefoucauld

We should manage our fortunes as we do our health—enjoy it when good, be patient when it is bad, and never apply violent remedies except in an extreme necessity.

Duc François de La Rochefoucauld

Fortune is the rod of the weak, and the staff of the brave.

James Russell Lowell

Fortune gives too much to many, but to none enough.

Martial

Fortune, to show us her power, and abate our presumption, seeing she could not make fools wise, has made them fortunate.

Michel Eyquem de Montaigne

Depend not on fortune, but on conduct.

Publilius Syrus

Fortune does not change men; it only unmasks them.

Marie Jean Riccoboni

The bad fortune of the good turns their faces up to heaven; the good fortune of the bad bows their heads down to the earth.

Saadi (Muslih-ud-Din)

There is no one, says another, whom fortune does not visit once in his life; but when she does not find him ready to receive her, she walks in at the door, and flies out at the window.

Charles de Secondat (Baron de Montesquieu)

We are sure to get the better of fortune if we do but grapple with her.

Seneca

Fortune is always on the side of the largest battalions.

Marquise de Sévigné

The power of fortune is confessed only by the miserable, for the happy impute all their success to prudence or merit.

Jonathan Swift

Fortune is a great deceiver. She sells very dear the things she seems to give us.

Vincent Voiture

From fortune to misfortune is just a span, but from misfortune to fortune is quite a distance.

Yiddish Proverb

Many have been ruined by their fortunes, and many have escaped ruin by the want of fortune. To obtain it the great have become little, and the little great.

Johann Georg von Zimmerman

See also: ACCIDENT, CHANCE, DESTINY, FATE, LUCK, WEALTH.

FRANCE

France, fam'd in all great arts, in none supreme.

Matthew Arnold

France was long a despotism tempered by epigrams.

Thomas Carlyle

Everything that is French on the ground, in the air and on the seas, and every foreign element stationed in France must be under the sole control of French authorities.

Charles André Joseph Marie de Gaulle

I was France. I was the state, the government. I spoke in the name of France. I was the independence and sovereignty of France.

Charles André Joseph Marie de Gaulle

The whole world recognizes that order and progress have once again got a chance in our country. What to do with it? Ah, to do a great deal. For we have to transform our old France into a new country and marry it to its time. France must find prosperity in this way. This must be our great national ambition.

Charles André Joseph Marie de Gaulle

It is high time that Americans forgo spending tourist dollars in France for a while, and it is a good time for our Government to demand that De Gaulle, instead of attempting to undercut international confidence in the dollar, devote himself to the payment of the $7 billion debt which France owes this country.

O. Clark Fisher

The French resemble monkeys who go climbing up a tree, from branch to branch, and never stop till they have reached the highest branch, and show their hinder parts when they get there.

Francis I

France is sacred territory,
Blessed fatherland of freedom.

Heinrich Heine

Honor to the French! they have taken good care of the two greatest human needs—good eating and civic equality.

Heinrich Heine

The nature of the French requires that their sovereign should be grave and earnest.

Jean de La Bruyère

I had been afraid in the course of my ten years' absence from France that the French might have lost their charming inefficiency, so inconsistent, so inherent in every last one of them and their institutions, as full of reports and surprises as a rocket.

Elliot Harold Paul

Of course, the relatively friendly French newspapers seldom get anything about America or Americans straight, and unintentionally, sometimes, cause as much damage or confusion in the Paris public mind as the sworn enemies of the United States. Of whatever shade of public opinion, Paris newspapers have an utter disregard of people's names and plain facts.

Elliot Harold Paul

Paris is a bill poster's town. Its walls and kiosks display a continually changing variety of sheets and placards advertising theatrical shows, plays, concerts, recitals, circuses, political or scientific meetings, lectures, soirées, fairs and all kinds of exhibitions, from the historical to the ultra-modern.

Elliot Harold Paul

There is no unemployment in France. The French are energetic and industrious. They are brave. They try hard, and keep going, in the face of no matter what discouragements. At their worst they can be as arrogant as Hindus, as stubborn as Basques, as taciturn as Finns, but they have guts.

Elliot Harold Paul

We must, however, do justice to the French; their promises are not mere words; the offers they make are almost always sincere; but they have an appearance of being interested in yours affairs that is more apt to deceive than words. None but fools can be imposed upon by the hypocritical offers of the Swiss. The French have a more winning manner, inasmuch as it is more natural: one would imagine that they do not express all that they mean, in order that you may be more agreeably surprised. I must say even more than this; they are not insincere in their feelings towards you; they are naturally obliging, tender-hearted, kind, and even, in spite of all that is said against them, more thoroughly true than any other nation; but they are giddy and volatile. No doubt they feel all that they express, but the feeling goes as it came. In speaking to you they are fully occupied with you and your affairs, but out of sight they forget altogether your existence. Nothing is engraved on their heart; everything is the mere impress of the moment.

Jean Jacques Rousseau

See also: ENGLAND, EUROPE, GERMANY, UNITED NATIONS.

FRANKNESS

A "No" uttered from deepest conviction is better and greater than a "Yes" merely uttered to please, or what is worse, to avoid trouble.

Mohandas Karamchand (Mahatma) Gandhi

Behind the political problems, there are psychological problems, and these are always more difficult to handle. The only way to do so is perfect frankness with each other.

Jawaharlal Nehru

Frankness hurts often enough, but it is almost always desirable, especially between those who have to work together. It helps one to see oneself in proper perspective from another's and a more critical viewpoint.

Jawaharlal Nehru

See also: CANDOR, SINCERITY, TRUTH.

FRAUD

The first and worst of all frauds is to cheat oneself.

Gamaliel Bailey

The more gross the fraud the more glibly will it go down, and the more greedily be swallowed, since folly will always find faith where imposters will find impudence.

Charles Caleb Colton

Though fraud in all other actions be odious, yet in matters of war it is laudable and glorious, and he who overcomes his enemies by stratagem is as much to be praised as he who overcomes them by force.

Niccolò Machiavelli

For the most part fraud in the end secures for its companions repentance and shame.

Charles Simmons

All frauds, like the wall daubed with untempered mortar, with which men think to buttress up an edifice, always tend to the decay of what they are devised to support.

Richard Whately

See also: DECEIT, DISHONESTY, FALSEHOOD.

FREE ENTERPRISE

Free competition and still more economic domination must be kept within just and definite limits, and must be brought under the effective control of the public authority, in matters appertaining to this latter's competence.

Pius XI (Achille Ambrogio Damiano Ratti)

Private enterprise is ceasing to be free enterprise.

Franklin Delano Roosevelt

Of course I believe in free enterprise but in my system of free enterprise, the democratic principle is that there never was, never has been, never will be, room for the ruthless exploitation of the many for the benefit of the few.

Harry S Truman

I see two alternatives before us. We can write morals into law, and enforce those morals harshly, or we can return to a true Free Enterprise System, which has the sink-or-swim justice of Caesar Augustus built into it. I emphatically favor the latter alternative. We must be hard, for we must become again a nation of swimmers, with the sinkers quietly disposing of themselves.

Kurt Vonnegut, Jr.

See also: BUSINESS, EFFORT, ENTERPRISE.

FREE WILL

We do not what we ought;
What we ought not, we do;
And lean upon the thought
That chance will bring us through;
But our own acts, for good or ill, are mightier
powers.

Matthew Arnold

From the use of the word *free-will*, no liberty can be inferred of the will, desire, or inclination, but the liberty of the man; which consisteth in this, that he finds no stop, in doing what he has the will, desire, or inclination to do.

Thomas Hobbes

Though the law of causality, of cause and effect, functions, yet there is a measure of freedom to the individual to shape his own destiny.

Jawaharlal Nehru

There is no such thing as free will. The mind is induced to wish this or that by some cause, and that cause is determined by another cause, and so on back to infinity.

Baruch (Benedict) Spinoza

See also: DETERMINISM, FREEDOM, WILL.

FREEDOM

What is life? It is not to stalk about, and draw fresh air, or gaze upon the sun; it is to be free.

Joseph Addison

As long as there are in the world countries where the citizens exert an influence on their political future by choosing between different programs, the dictators cannot feel secure.

Max Ascoli

Freedom is power, a concentrated, skilful capacity to act.

Max Ascoli

The hard experience of our times proves that when the citizens of a nation voluntarily or involuntarily give up their political freedom they endanger the citizens of all the other nations.

Max Ascoli

The organization of freedom is increasingly complex; yet its final results, its achievements and failures, are to be seen and felt by everybody.

Max Ascoli

Free society is a fine thing but one does not spend much time thinking of liberty when his only freedom is to die of want, while others squander.

Fulgencio Batista y Zaldivar

If our brothers are oppressed, then we are oppressed. If they hunger, we hunger. If their freedom is taken away, our freedom is not secure.

Stephen Vincent Benét

The last freedom—freedom to flee.

Berliner Illustrirte

There is no legitimacy on earth but in a government which is the choice of the nation.

Joseph Bonaparte

Experience teaches us to be most on our guard to protect liberty when the government's purposes are beneficent.

Louis Dembitz Brandeis

Men born to freedom are naturally alert to repel invasion of their liberty to evil-minded rulers. The greatest dangers to liberty lurk in insidious encroachment by men of zeal, well-meaning but without understanding.

Louis Dembitz Brandeis

If any ask me what a free government is, I answer, that for any practical purpose, it is what the people think so.

Edmund Burke

The only freedom worth possessing is that which gives enlargement to a people's energy, intellect, and virtues. The savage makes his boast of freedom. But what is its worth? He is, indeed, free from what he calls the yoke of civil institutions. But other and worse chains bind him. The very privation of civil government is in effect a chain; for, by withholding protection from property it virtually shackles the arm of industry, and forbids exertion for the melioration of his lot. Progress, the growth of intelligence and power, is the end and boon of liberty; and, without this, a people may have the name, but want the substance and spirit of freedom.

William Ellery Channing

It is by the goodness of God that we have in our country three unspeakably precious things: freedom of speech, freedom of conscience, and the prudence never to practise either.

Samuel Langhorne Clemens (Mark Twain)

He is the freeman whom the truth makes free, and all are slaves beside.

William Cowper

A free life is the only life worthy of a human being. That which is not free is not responsible, and that which is not responsible is not moral. In other words, freedom is the condition of morality.

Thomas Davidson

The discipline that is identical with trained power is also identical with freedom . . . Genuine freedom, in short, is intellectual; it rests in the trained power of thought.

John Dewey

No Christian and no church is altogether impervious to betraying to the worldly powers the freedom granted us by Christ.

East and West German Protestant Leaders

All our freedoms are a single bundle, all must be secure if any is to be preserved.

Dwight David Eisenhower

The pact of Munich was a more fell blow to humanity than the atom bomb at Hiroshima. Suffocation of human freedom among a once free people, however quietly and peacefully accomplished, is more far-reaching in its implications and its effects on their future than the destruction of their homes, industrial centers and transportation facilities. Out of rubble heaps, willing hands can rebuild a better city; but out of freedom lost can stem only generations of hate and bitter struggle and brutal oppression.

Dwight David Eisenhower

No man is free who is not master of himself.

Epictetus

A bird or butterfly sitting with wings closed —a human form sitting with arms and legs chained or with ears and mouth shut—is but a worm in a womb. To open these gates is to free the spiritual body, to greet the sunrise, the rainbow, the universe. To hesitate, to doubt, is to become the stone you dread.

David V. Erdman

Freedom is always won by a few brave, self-sacrificing souls who will stake everything for the sake of honour.

Mohandas Karamchand (Mahatma) Gandhi

Freedom is not worth having if it does not connote freedom to err.

Mohandas Karamchand (Mahatma) Gandhi

Freedom's battles are not fought without paying heavy prices. Just as man would not cherish the thought of living in a body other than his own, so nations do not like to live under other nations, however noble and great the latter may be.

Mohandas Karamchand (Mahatma) Gandhi

If the individual ceases to count, what is left of society? Individual freedom alone can make a man voluntarily surrender himself completely to the service of society. If it is wrested from him he becomes an automaton and society is ruined. No society can possibly be built on a denial of individual freedom. It is contrary to the very nature of man. Just as a man will not grow horns or a tail, so he will not exist as man if he has no mind of his own. In reality even those who do not believe in the liberty of the individual believe in their nature.

Mohandas Karamchand (Mahatma) Gandhi

None are more hopelessly enslaved than those who falsely believe they are free.

Johann Wolfgang von Goethe

Giving others the freedom to be stupid is one of the most important and hardest steps to take in spiritual progress. Conveniently the opportunity to take that step is all around us every day.

Thaddeus Golos

It is impossible to enslave, mentally or socially, a Bible-reading people. The principles of the Bible are the groundwork of human freedom.

Horace Greeley

The greatest glory of a free-born people is to transmit that freedom to their children.

William Havard

Freedom presupposes order, and order presupposes rules and the ability to enforce them.

Roger William Heyns

The basic test of freedom is perhaps less in what we are free to do than in what we are free not to do.

Eric Hoffer

Martin Luther King stands with out other American martyrs in the cause of freedom and justice. His death is a terrible tragedy and a sorrow to his family, to our nation, to our conscience. The criminal act that took his life brings shame to our country.

The apostle of nonviolence has been the victim of violence. The cause for which he marched and worked I am sure will find a new strength.

The plight of discrimination, poverty and neglect must be erased from America, and an America of full freedom, full and equal opportunity, is the living memorial he deserves, and it shall be his living memorial.

Hubert Horatio Humphrey

Freedom of religion, freedom of the press, and freedom of person under the protection of the habeas corpus, these are principles that have guided our steps through an age of revolution and reformation.

Thomas Jefferson

Until every American, whatever his color or wherever his home, enjoys and uses his franchise, the work which Lincoln began will remain unfinished.

Lyndon Baines Johnson

Education is the first resort as well as the last, for a world-wide solution of the problem of freedom.

Horace Meyer Kallen

Where the artists keep free no other sort or condition of man long remains bound.

Horace Meyer Kallen

All free men, wherever they may live, are citizens of Berlin. And therefore, as a free man, I take pride in the words *"Ich bin ein Berliner"* [I am a Berliner].

John Fitzgerald Kennedy

Freedom is not merely a word or an abstract theory, but the most effective instrument for advancing the welfare of man.

John Fitzgerald Kennedy

If men and women are in chains, anywhere in the world, then freedom is endangered everywhere.

John Fitzgerald Kennedy

In the long history of the world, only a few generations have been granted the role of defending freedom in its hour of maximum danger. I do not shrink from this responsibility—I welcome it. I do not believe that any of us would exchange places with any other people or any other generation. The energy, the faith, the devotion which we bring to this endeavour will light our country and all who serve it—and the glow from that fire can truly light the world.

John Fitzgerald Kennedy

No one can doubt that the wave of the future is not the conquest of the world by a single dogmatic creed but the liberation of the diverse energies of free nations and free men.

John Fitzgerald Kennedy

The unity of freedom has never relied on uniformity of opinion.

John Fitzgerald Kennedy

We must present to the world a concept of freedom which has not been diluted by the evils of prejudice and discrimination.

John Fitzgerald Kennedy

There are two freedoms, the false where one is free to do what he likes, and the true where he is free to do what he ought.

Charles Kingsley

The cause of freedom is identified with the destinies of humanity, and in whatever part of the world it gains ground, by and by it will be a common gain to all who desire it.

Lajos Kossuth

We hear them cry "Freedom, freedom," yet they demonstrate little awareness that with freedom goes responsibility.

Eduard Kuhn

Void of freedom, what would virtue be?

Alphonse de Lamartine

Real freedom comes from the mastery, through knowledge, of historic conditions and race character which makes possible a free and intelligent use of experience for the purpose of progress.

Hamilton Wright Mabie

Many politicians lay it down as a self-evident proposition, that no people ought to be free till they are fit to use their freedom. The maxim is worthy of the fool in the old story, who resolved not to go into the water till he had learned to swim.

Thomas Babington Macaulay

It is under the driving power of competition, of freedom of choice that it is possible for each individual to exercise to the fullest his God-given right of liberty, and to reap the just rewards of proper human behavior.

Hughston Maynard McBain

Free will is not the liberty to do whatever one likes, but the power of doing whatever one sees ought to be done, even in the very face of otherwise overwhelming impulse. There lies freedom indeed.

George Macdonald

He is free who knows how to keep in his own hands the power to decide, at each step, the course of his life, and who lives in a society which does not block the exercise of that power.

Salvador de Madariaga y Rojo

The only freedom which deserves the name is that of pursuing our own good, in our own way, so long as we do not attempt to deprive others of theirs, or impede their efforts to obtain it.

John Stuart Mill

Freedom is a goddess hard to win; she demands, as of old, human sacrifice from her votaries.

Jawaharlal Nehru

Freedom, like everything else, indeed, more than everything else, carries certain responsibilities and obligations and a certain discipline with it. If a sense of responsibility, obligation and discipline is lacking, then it is not freedom but the absence of freedom.

Jawaharlal Nehru

Man requires freedom in his social organization because he is "essentially" free, which is to say, that he has the capacity for indeterminate transcendence over the processes and limitations of nature.

Reinhold Niebuhr

This is what I call the American idea of freedom—a government of all the people, by all the people, for all the people; of course, a government of the principles of eternal justice—the unchanging law of God.

Theodore Parker

The truly free man is he who knows how to decline a dinner invitation without giving an excuse.

Jules Renard

We look forward to a world founded upon four essential human freedoms. The first is freedom of speech and expression—everywhere in the world. The second is freedom of every person to worship God in his own way —everywhere in the world. The third is freedom from want . . . everywhere in the world. The fourth is freedom from fear . . . anywhere in the world.

Franklin Delano Roosevelt

We will accept only a world consecrated to freedom of speech and expression—freedom of every person to worship God in his own way—freedom from want—and freedom from terrorism.

Franklin Delano Roosevelt

The man truly free only wishes what he is able to accomplish and does what pleases him.

Jean Jacques Rousseau

A man may not always eat and drink what is good for him; but it is better for him and less ignominious to die of the gout freely than to have a censor officially appointed over his diet, who after all could not render him immortal.

George Santayana

The fundamental principle freedom is magnanimity. It cannot build the structure of its desire if the eye of the architect is distorted by hatred and envy.

James Thomson Shotwell

Easier were it to hurl the rooted mountain from its base, than force the yoke of slavery upon men determined to be free.

Robert Southey

This I believe: that the free, exploring mind of the individual human is the most valuable thing in the world. And this I would fight for: the freedom of the mind to take any direction it wishes, undirected. And this I must fight against: any idea, religion, or government which limits or destroys the individual. This is what I am and what I am about. I can understand why a system built on a pattern must try to destroy the free mind, for this is one thing which can by inspection destroy such a system. Surely I can understand this, and I hate it and I will fight against it to preserve the one thing that separates us from the uncreative beasts.

John Ernst Steinbeck

Freedom rings wherever opinions clash.

Adlai Ewing Stevenson

A hungry man is not a free man.

Adlai Ewing Stevenson

My definition of a free society is a society where it is safe to be unpopular.

Adlai Ewing Stevenson

We have confused the free with the free and easy.

Adlai Ewing Stevenson

We shall lead in that degree to which we build a vital and healthy society. As we solve our own problems, economic, social, and above all, moral, we shall help other peoples solve theirs. By demonstrating the limitless powers of a free society which knows how to liberate the full creative energy of man, we shall fulfill the destiny that history has assigned us.

Adlai Ewing Stevenson

I would rather sit on a pumpkin, and have it all to myself, than to be crowded on a velvet cushion.

Henry David Thoreau

True freedom consists with the observance of law. Adam was as free in paradise as in the wilds to which he was banished for his transgression.

Bonnell Thornton

He who is free by nature can become a slave by destiny.

Paul Tillich

Men and women cannot be really free until they have plenty to eat, and time and ability to read and think and talk things over.

Henry Agard Wallace

Freedom is risky and includes the risk that anyone may go to hell in his own way.

Alan Watts

The essence of freedom is the practicability of purpose.

Alfred North Whitehead

Freedom of the press is the staff of life for any vital democracy.

Wendell Lewis Willkie

The highest and best form of efficiency is the spontaneous cooperation of a free people.

(Thomas) Woodrow Wilson

Only free peoples can hold their purpose and their honor steady to a common end, and prefer the interests of mankind to any narrow interest of their own.

(Thomas) Woodrow Wilson

Something deeper than politics or race is at stake, and that is a human right, the right of a man to think and feel honestly.

Richard Wright

See also: DISSENT, EQUALITY, FREEDOM OF THE PRESS, FREEDOM OF SPEECH, INDE-PENDENCE, LIBERTY.

FREEDOM OF THE PRESS

The function of the press is very high. It is almost holy. It ought to serve as a forum for the people, through which the people may know freely what is going on. To misstate or suppress the news is a breach of trust.

Louis Dembitz Brandeis

The press is not only free, it is powerful. That power is ours. It is the proudest that man can enjoy. It was not granted by monarchs; it was not gained for us by aristocracies; but it sprang from the people, and, with an immortal instinct, it has always worked for the people.

Benjamin Disraeli

If by the liberty of the press, we understand merely the liberty of discussing the propriety of public measures and political opinions, let us have as much of it as you please; but, if it means the liberty of affronting, calumniating, and defaming one another, I own myself willing to part with my share of it whenever our legislators shall please to alter the law; and shall cheerfully consent to exchange my liberty of abusing others for the privilege of not being abused myself.

Benjamin Franklin

The people have a right to insist that freedom of the press should mean freedom from any deleterious influence, whether imposed by interests too strong for the publisher to resist, or self-imposed for benefits received or hoped for.

Harold Le Claire Ickes

The liberty of the press is a blessing when we are inclined to write against others, and a calamity when we find ourselves overborne by the multitude of our assailants.

Samuel Johnson

Let it be impressed upon your minds, let it be instilled into your children, that the liberty of the press is the palladium of all the civil, political, and religious rights.

Junius

It merely expresses one of the elements of our times, the indifference to personal privacy, the assumption that a free press means a licensed press and the fact that today there is too much privilege on the part of the reporter to invade the privacy, the decency, the self-respect of the individual who is being interviewed.

Hans von Kaltenborn

The preservation of a free press is utterly dependent on a free economy. When its major financial support comes from advertising, the press must sell its space impartially in a system of competitive business enterprise. The greater the competition, the more ample will be the field of sales.

Raymond Moley

The free press is the mother of all our liberties and of our progress under liberty.

Adlai Ewing Stevenson

See also: FREEDOM, JOURNALISM, NEWSPAPER, PRESS, RESPONSIBILITY.

FREEDOM OF SPEECH

Freedom of speech does not travel exclusively on a one-way street marked "search for Truth." It often enough travels on a one-way street marked "Private Profit," or on another marked "Anything to Win the Election."

Carl Lotus Becker

My view is, without deviation, without exception, without any ifs, buts, or whereases, that freedom of speech means that you shall not do something to people either for the views they have, or the views they express, or the words they speak or write.

Hugo La Fayette Black

Democracy needs more free speech, for even the speech of foolish people is valuable if it serves to guarantee the right of the wise to talk.

David Cushman Coyle

I realize that there are certain limitations placed upon the right of free speech. I may not be able to say all I think, but I am not going to say anything I do not think.

Eugene Victor Debs

Just as erroneous statements must be protected to give freedom of expression the breathing space it needs to survive, so statements criticizing public policy and the implementation of it must be similarly protected.
Earl Warren

This nation will survive, this state will prosper, the orderly business of life will go forward if only men can speak in whatever way given them to utter what their hearts hold—by voice, by posted card, by letter or by press.
William Allen White

I have always been among those who believed that the greatest freedom of speech was the greatest safety, because if a man is a fool the best thing to do is to encourage him to advertise the fact by speaking.
(Thomas) Woodrow Wilson

See also: DISSENT, FREEDOM, FREEDOM OF THE PRESS, LIBERTY.

FRIENDSHIP

A friend in power is a friend lost.
Henry Brooks Adams

Friendship improves happiness, and abates misery, by doubling our joy, and dividing our grief.
Joseph Addison

The friendships of the world are oft confederacies in vice, or leagues of pleasure.
Joseph Addison

In poverty and other misfortunes of life, true friends are a sure refuge. The young they keep out of mischief; to the old they are a comfort and aid in their weakness, and those in the prime of life they incite to noble deeds.
Aristotle

Those friends are weak and worthless, that will not use the privilege of friendship in admonishing their friends with freedom and confidence, as well of their errors as of their danger.
Francis Bacon

Friendship is neither a formality nor a mode: it is rather a life.
Ray Stannard Baker (David Grayson)

I made courtiers; I never pretended to make friends, said Napoleon. . . . On a rocky little island he fretted away the last years of his life—alone.
Bruce Barton

Better are the blows of a friend than the false kisses of an enemy.
Thomas à Becket

It is one of the severest tests of friendship to tell your friend his faults. So to love a man that you cannot bear to see a stain upon him, and to speak painful truth through loving words, that is friendship.
Henry Ward Beecher

A man must get friends as he would get food and drink for nourishment and sustenance.
Randolph Silliman Bourne

False friends are like our shadow, keeping close to us while we walk in the sunshine, but leaving us the instant we cross into the shade.
Christian Nestell Bovee

Kindred weaknesses induce friendships as often as kindred virtues.
Christian Nestell Bovee

False friendship, like the ivy, decays and ruins the walls it embraces; but true friendship gives new life and animation to the object it supports.
Richard Eugene Burton

Friendship without self-interest is one of the rare and beautiful things of life.
James Francis Byrnes

Friendship is Love without his wings!
George Gordon Byron (Lord Byron)

Do you want to make friends? Be friendly. Forget yourself.
Dale Carnegie

You can make more friends in two months by becoming interested in other people than you can in two years by trying to get other people interested in you.
Dale Carnegie

Friends should not be chosen to flatter. The quality we prize is that rectitude which will shrink from no truth. Intimacies which increase vanity destroy friendship.
William Ellery Channing

He is our friend who loves more than admires us, and would aid us in our great work.
William Ellery Channing

Be more prompt to go to a friend in adversity than in prosperity.

Chilon

They seem to take the sun out of the world that take friendship out of life.

Cicero

The friends of today are like melons; we must try fifty before we find a good one.

Claude-Mermet

The firmest friendships have been formed in mutual adversity; as iron is most strongly united by the fiercest flame.

Charles Caleb Colton

Never contract friendship with a man that·is not better than thyself.

Confucius

There are three friendships which are advantageous: friendship with the upright, with the sincere, and with the man of much observation. Friendship with the man of specious airs with the insinuatingly soft, and with the glib-tongued, these are injurious.

Confucius

All men have their frailties; and whoever looks for a friend without imperfections, will never find what he seeks. We love ourselves notwithstanding our faults, and we ought to love our friends in like manner.

Cyrus

The only way to have a friend is to be one.

Ralph Waldo Emerson

We take care of our health, we lay up money, we make our roof tight and our clothing sufficient, but who provides wisely that he shall not be wanting in the best property of all—friends?

Ralph Waldo Emerson

Life has no blessing like a prudent friend.

Euripides

No man can expect to find a friend without faults, nor can he propose himself to be so to another. Every man will have something to do for his friend, and something to bear with in him. Only the sober man can do the first; and for the latter, patience is requisite. It is better for a man to depend on himself than to be annoyed with either a madman or a fool.

Owen Felltham

The most powerful and the most lasting friendships are usually those of the early season of our lives, when we are most susceptible of warm and affectionate impressions. The connections into which we enter in any after-period decrease in strength as our passions abate in heat; and there is not, I believe, a single instance of a vigorous friendship that ever struck root in a bosom chilled by years.

Sir Thomas Fitzosborne (William Melmoth)

Let me live in a house by the side of the road and be a friend to man.

Sam Walter Foss

It is best to live as friends with those in time with whom we would be to all eternity.

Thomas Fuller

Purchase not friends by gifts; when thou ceasest to give, such will cease to love.

Thomas Fuller

The test of friendship is assistance in adversity, and that, too, unconditional assistance. Co-operation which needs consideration is a commercial contract and not friendship. Conditional co-operation is like adulterated cement which does not bind.

Mohandas Karamchand (Mahatma) Gandhi

True friendship is an identity of souls rarely to be found in this world. Only between like natures can friendship be altogether worthy and enduring. Friends react on one another. Hence in friendship there is very little scope for reform. I am of opinion that all exclusive intimacies are to be avoided, for man takes in vice far more readily than virtue. And he who would be friend with God must remain alone, or make the whole world his friend.

Mohandas Karamchand (Mahatma) Gandhi

Friendship is always a sweet responsibility, never an opportunity.

Kahlil Gibran

What an argument in favor of social connections is the observation that by communicating our grief we have less, and by communicating our pleasure we have more.

Fulke Greville (First Baron Brooke)

It is great to have friends when one is young, but indeed it is still more so when you are getting old. When we are young, friends are, like everything else, a matter of course. In the old days we know what it means to have them.

Edvard Grieg

Men must make ever new relationships until finally they achieve universal humanity.

Joseph Kinmont Hart

The difficulty is not so great to die for a friend, as to find a friend worth dying for.

Henry Home

If a man does not make new acquaintances as he passes through life, he will soon find himself left alone. A man should keep his friendships in constant repair.

Samuel Johnson

Two persons cannot long be friends if they cannot forgive each other's little failings.

Jean de La Bruyère

Friendship is the shadow of the evening, which strengthens with the setting sun of life.

Jean de La Fontaine

Nothing more dangerous than a friend without discretion; even a prudent enemy is preferable.

Jean de La Fontaine

However rare true love may be, it is still less so than genuine friendship.

Duc François de La Rochefoucauld

A true friend is the greatest of blessings, and that which we think least about acquiring.

Duc François de La Rochefoucauld

If you want to make a dangerous man your friend, let him do you a favor.

Lewis E. Lawes

One of the surest evidences of friendship that one can display to another, is telling him gently of a fault. If any other can excel it, it is listening to such a disclosure with gratitude, and amending the error.

Edward G. Bulwer-Lytton (Baron Lytton)

Friendship is one mind in two bodies.

Mencius

He alone has lost the art to live who cannot win new friends.

Silas Weir Mitchell

The best way to keep your friends is not to give them away.

Wilson Mizner

A home-made friend wears longer than one you buy in the market.

Austin O'Malley

A friend that you have to buy won't be worth what you pay for him, no matter what that may be.

George Denison Prentice

That friendship will not continue to the end which is begun for an end.

Francis Quarles

Thou mayest be sure that he that will in private tell thee of thy faults, is thy friend, for he adventures thy dislike, and doth hazard thy hatred; there are few men that can endure it, every man for the most part delighting in self-praise, which is one of the most universal follies that bewitcheth mankind.

Sir Walter Raleigh

We learn our virtues from the friends who love us; our faults from the enemy who hates us. We cannot easily discover our real character from a friend. He is a mirror, on which the warmth of our breath impedes the clearness of the reflection.

Jean Paul Richter

Now, nothing makes so much impression on the heart of man as the voice of friendship when it is really known to be such; for we are aware that it never speaks to us except for our advantage. We can suppose that a friend is deceived, but not that he wishes to deceive us. Sometimes we run counter to his advice, but we never despise it.

Jean Jacques Rousseau

Friendship is almost always the union of a part of one mind with a part of another; people are friends in spots.

George Santayana

That is a choice friend who conceals our faults from the view of others, and discovers them to our own.

William Secker

Old friends are best. King James used to call for his old shoes; they were the easiest for his feet.

John Selden

Be careful to make friendship the child and not the father of virtue, for many are rather good friends than good men; so, although they do not like the evil their friend does, yet they like him who does the evil; and though no counselors of the offence, they yet protect the offender.

Sir Philip Sidney

There is nothing so great that I fear to do it for my friend; nothing so small that I will disdain to do it for him.

Sir Philip Sidney

Life is to be fortified by many friendships. To love and to be loved is the greatest happiness of existence.

Sydney Smith

Be slow to fall into friendship; but when thou art in, continue firm and constant.

Socrates

Get not your friends by bare compliments, but by giving them sensible tokens of your love. It is well worth while to learn how to win the heart of a man the right way. Force is of no use to make or preserve a friend, who is an animal that is never caught nor tamed but by kindness and pleasure. Excite them by your civilities, and show them that you desire nothing more than their satisfaction; oblige with all your soul that friend who has made you a present of his own.

Socrates

A true friend is the gift of God, and he only who made hearts can untie them.

Robert South

Real friendship is a slow grower, and never thrives unless engrafted upon a stock of known and reciprocal merit.

Philip Dormer Stanhope (Lord Chesterfield)

Depth of friendship does not depend upon length of acquaintance.

Sir Rabindranath Tagore

He that doth a base thing in zeal for his friend burns the golden thread that ties their hearts together.

Jeremy Taylor

God save me from my friends, I can protect myself from my enemies.

Duc Claude Louis Hector de Villars

Friendship is a plant of slow growth, and must undergo and withstand the shocks of adversity before it is entitled to the appellation.

George Washington

Friendship is the only cement that will ever hold the world together.

(Thomas) Woodrow Wilson

Heaven gives us friends, to bless the present scene; resumes them to prepare us for the next.

Edward Young

See also: ACQUAINTANCE, ASSOCIATE, BROTHER-HOOD, COMPANIONSHIP, ENEMY, LOVE.

FRUGALITY

Frugality is founded on the principle that all riches have limits.

Edmund Burke

Eat it up, make it do, wear it out.

(John) Calvin Coolidge

The way to wealth is as plain as the way to market. It depends chiefly on two words, industry and frugality; that is, waste neither time nor money, but make the best use of both. Without industry and frugality nothing will do; with them, everything.

Benjamin Franklin

If frugality were established in the state, if our expenses were laid out rather in the necessaries than the superfluities of life, there might be fewer wants, and even fewer pleasures, but infinitely more happiness.

Oliver Goldsmith

There'll be no pockets in your shroud.

James Jerome Hill

Frugality may be termed the daughter of prudence, the sister of temperance, and the parent of liberty. He that is extravagant will quickly become poor, and poverty will enforce dependence and invite corruption.

Samuel Johnson

He seldom lives frugally who lives by chance. Hope is always liberal, and they that trust her promises make little scruple of revelling to-day on the profits of to-morrow.

Samuel Johnson

He that spareth in everything is an inexcusable niggard. He that spareth in nothing is an inexcusable madman. The mean is to spare in what is least necessary, and to lay out more liberally in what is most required.

Charles Montagu (Baron Halifax)

Frugality is good if liberality be joined with it. The first is leaving off superfluous expenses; the last is bestowing them for the benefit of those who need. The first, without the last, begets covetousness; the last without the first begets prodigality.

William Penn

With parsimony a little is sufficient; without it nothing is sufficient; but frugality makes a poor man rich.

Seneca

Nature is avariciously frugal. In matter it allows no atom to elude its grasp; in mind, no thought or feeling to perish. It gathers up the fragments that nothing be lost.

David Thomas

The doctrine of thrift for the poor is dumb and cruel, like advising them to try and lift themselves by their bootstraps.

Norman Mattoon Thomas

See also: ECONOMY, MISER, SELF-DENIAL.

FUN

The mirth and fun grew fast and furious.

Robert Burns

Fun is like life insurance: the older you get, the more it costs.

Frank McKinney (Kin) Hubbard

I live in the crowds of jollity, not so much to enjoy company as to shun myself.

Samuel Johnson

See also: AMUSEMENT, CARDS, DANCE, DIVERSION, RECREATION.

FUNERAL

Spare me the whispering crowded room,
  The friends who come and gape and go,
The ceremonious air of gloom—
  All, which makes death a hideous show.

Matthew Arnold

Caskets!—a vile modern phrase, which compels a person of sense and good taste to shrink more disgustfully than ever before from the idea of being buried at all.

Nathaniel Hawthorne

The pomp that is attendant on funerals feeds rather the vanity of the living than does honour to the dead.

Duc François de La Rouchefoucauld

Chop-fallen funeral processions, with their dignity curtailed by present-day traffic conditions.

Thomas Mann

See also: DEATH, EULOGY, EPITAPH.

FUTURE

God will not suffer man to have a knowledge of things to come; for if he had prescience of his prosperity, he would be careless; and if understanding of his adversity, he would be despairing and senseless.

Augustine of Hippo

We should live for the future, and yet should find our life in the fidelities of the present; the last is the only method of the first.

Henry Ward Beecher

When all else is lost, the future still remains.

Christian Nestell Bovee

The golden age is not in the past, but in the future; not in the origin of human experience, but in its consummate flower; not opening in Eden, but out from Gethsemane.

Edwin Hubbel Chapin

What is already passed is not more fixed than the certainty that what is future will grow out of what has already passed, or is now passing.

George Barrell Cheever

I never think of the future. It comes soon enough.

Albert Einstein

We do not know very much of the future
Except that from generation to generation
The same things happen again and again.
Men learn little from others' experience.
But in the life of one man, never
The same time returns.

Thomas Stearns Eliot

Age and sorrow have the gift of reading the future by the past.

Frederic William Farrar

We are always looking to the future; the present does not satisfy us. Our ideal, whatever it may be, lies further on.

Ezra Hall Gillett

My interest is in the future because I am going to spend the rest of my life there.

Charles Franklin Kettering

Everything that looks to the future elevates human nature; for life is never so low or so little as when occupied with the present.

Letitia Elizabeth Landon

The veil which covers the face of futurity is woven by the hand of mercy.
Edward G. Bulwer-Lytton (Baron Lytton)

The best preparation for the future, is the present well seen to, and the last duty done.
George Macdonald

The future has to be lived before it can be written about.
Jawaharlal Nehru

Let us have done with the past and its bickering and face the future.
Jawaharlal Nehru

What will be, is.
Austin O'Malley

The present is never our goal: the past and the present are our means: the future alone is our goal. Thus we are never living, but we hope to live; and looking forward always to be happy, it is inevitable that we should never be so.
Blaise Pascal

Too many people are afraid of Tomorrow— their happiness is poisoned by a phantom.
William Lyon Phelps

I believe the future is only the past again, entered through another gate.
Sir Arthur Pinero

My faith! that man is a fool who shall trust the future. He who laughs on Friday will weep on Sunday.
Jean Baptist Racine

It is horrible to see everything one detested in the past coming back again under the banners of the future.
Jean Rostand

The future is not important any more.
Gertrude Stein

See also: AGE, EXISTENCE, PAST, PRESENT.

FUTURE STATE

It is the divinity that stirs within us. 'Tis heaven itself that points out an hereafter, and intimates eternity to man.
Joseph Addison

Why will any man be so impertinently officious as to tell me all prospect of a future state is only fancy and delusion? Is there any merit in being the messenger of ill news? If it is a dream, let me enjoy it, since it makes me both the happier and better man.
Joseph Addison

I feel my immortality o'ersweep all pains, all tears, all time, all fears, and like the eternal thunders of the deep, peal to my ears this truth—"Thou livest forever."
George Gordon Byron (Lord Byron)

There is, I know not how, in the minds of men, a certain presage, as it were, of a future existence, and this takes the deepest root, and is most discoverable, in the greatest geniuses and most exalted souls.
Cicero

There's none but fears a future state; and when the most obdurate swear they do not, their trembling hearts belie their boasting tongues.
John Dryden

The grand difficulty is to feel the reality of both worlds, so as to give each its due place in our thoughts and feelings: to keep our mind's eye and our heart's eye ever fixed on the land of promise, without looking away from the road along which we are to travel toward it.
Augustus and Julius Hare

Belief in a future life is the appetite of reason.
Walter Savage Landor

If there were no future life, our souls would not thirst for it.
Jean Paul Richter

What a world were this; how unendurable its weight, if they whom death had sundered did not meet again?
Robert Southey

Divine wisdom, intending to detain us some time on earth, has done well to cover with a veil the prospect of the life to come; for if our sight could clearly distinguish the opposite bank, who would remain on this tempestuous coast of time?
Madame de Staël

See also: ETERNITY, FUTURE, HEAVEN, HELL, IMMORTALITY.

G

GAIN

The true way to gain much, is never to desire to gain too much. He is not rich that possesses much, but he that covets no more; and he is not poor that enjoys little, but he that wants too much.

Francis Beaumont

Every joy is gain
And gain is gain, however small.

Robert Browning

Sometimes the best gain is to lose.

George Herbert

See also: AVARICE, POSSESSIONS, PROPERTY.

GALLANTRY

Gallantry to women—the sure road to their favor—is nothing but the appearance af extreme devotion to all their wants and wishes, a delight in their satisfaction, and a confidence in yourself as being able to contribute toward it.

William Hazlitt

Gallantry, though a fashionable crime, is a very detestable one.

Hugh Kelly

Gallantry consists in saying the most empty things in an agreeable manner.

Duc François de La Rochefoucauld

Conscience has no more to do with gallantry, than it has with politics.

Richard Brinsley Sheridan

See also: COMPLIMENT, COURTSHIP, FLATTERY, GOOD BREEDING, KISS, MANNERS, VOW.

GAMBLING

Gambling is a kind of tacit confession that those engaged therein do, in general, exceed the bounds of their respective fortunes; and therefore they cast lots to determine on whom the ruin shall at present fall, that the rest may be saved a little longer.

Sir William Blackstone

The urge to gamble is so universal and its practice so pleasurable that I assume it must be evil.

(Matthew) Heywood Campbell Broun

Gambling is an ancient and universal form of play.

Stuart Chase

Gambling is a revolt against boredom.

Stuart Chase

There are two times in a man's life when he should not speculate: when he can't afford it, and when he can.

Samuel Langhorne Clemens (Mark Twain)

Gambling is the child of avarice, but the parent of prodigality.

Charles Caleb Colton

Keep flax from fire, and youth from gaming.

Benjamin Franklin

In a way it is worse than the plague or the quake. For it destroys the soul within. A person without the soul is a burden upon the earth. No doubt war against gambling is not so simple as war against plague or earthquake distress. In the latter there is more or less co-operation from the sufferers. In the former the sufferers invite and hug their sufferings. To wean the gambler from his vice is like weaning the drunkard from the drink habit. This war against gambling is therefore an uphill task.

Mohandas Karamchand (Mahatma) Gandhi

Some play for gain; to pass time others play; both play the fool; who gets by play is loser in the end.

James Heath

317

Play not for gain, but sport; who plays for more than he can lose with pleasure stakes his heart.

George Herbert

Curst is the wretch enslaved to such a vice, who ventures life and soul upon the dice.

Horace

It may be that the race is not always to the swift, nor the battle to the strong—but that's the way to bet.

(Alfred) Damon Runyon

Gambling, betting on horses, among other things, is a way of life. The manner in which a man chooses to gamble indicates his character or his lack of it.

William Saroyan

There is nothing that wears out a fine face like the vigils of the card-table, and those cutting passions which naturally attend them. Hollow eyes, haggard looks, and pale complexions are the natural indications of a female gamester. Her morning sleeps are not able to repay her midnight watchings.

Sir Richard Steele

Gambling is the child of avarice, the brother of iniquity, and the father of mischief.

George Washington

All gaming, since it implies a desire to profit at the expense of others, involves a breach of the tenth commandment.

Richard Whately

The first winner is the last loser.

Yiddish Proverb

See also: CARDS, CHANCE, DICE, LUCK, WAGER.

GARDEN

To cultivate a garden is to walk with God.

Christian Nestell Bovee

My garden is a lovesome thing—God wot!
Rose plot,
Fringed pool,
Fern grot—
The veriest school
Of peace; and yet the fool
Contends that God is not.—
Not God in gardens! When the sun is cool!
Nay, but I have a sign!
'Tis very sure God walks in mine.

Thomas Edward Brown

Who loves a garden loves a greenhouse too.

William Cowper

His gardens next your admiration call,
On every side you look, behold the wall!
No pleasing intricacies intervene,
No artful wildness to perplex the scene;
Grove nods at grove, each alley has a brother,
And half the platform just reflects the other,
The suffering eye inverted nature sees,
Trees cut to statues, statues thick as trees;
With here a fountain never to be play'd,
And there a summer-house that knows no shade.

Alexander Pope

See also: AGRICULTURE, FLOWER, NATURE.

GENEROSITY

A man there was, tho' some did count him mad,
The more he cast away, the more he had.

John Bunyan

Men of the noblest dispositions think themselves happiest when others share their happiness with them.

William Duncan

Humanitarianism is a link that binds together all Americans . . . Whenever tragedy or disaster has struck in any corner of the world, the American people has promptly and generously extended its hand of mercy and help. Generosity has never impoverished the giver; it has enriched the lives of those who have practiced it. . . . And the bread we have cast upon the waters has been returned in blessings a hundredfold.

Dwight David Eisenhower

True generosity is a duty as indispensably necessary as those imposed on us by law. It is a rule imposed by reason, which should be the sovereign law of a rational being.

Oliver Goldsmith

One great reason why men practise generosity so little in the world is, their finding so little there: generosity is catching; and if so many men escape it, it is in a great degree from the same reason that countrymen escape the smallpox,—because they meet with no one to give it them.

Fulke Greville (First Baron Brooke)

The truly generous is the truly wise, and he who loves not others, lives unblest.

Henry Home (Lord Kames)

How much easier it is to be generous than just! Men are sometimes bountiful who are not honest.

Junius

What seems to be generosity is often no more than disguised ambition, which overlooks a small interest in order to secure a great one.

Duc François de La Rochefoucauld

Generosity during life is a very different thing from generosity in the hour of death; one proceeds from genuine liberality and benevolence, the other from pride or fear.

Horace Mann

Generosity is not only good morals but is often good politics and sound expediency.

Jawaharlal Nehru

Not that it is bad to be generous. On the contrary generosity pays in the end provided you are not generous at somebody's expense or at the expense of your own country.

Jawaharlal Nehru

What I gave, I have; what I spent, I had; what I kept, I lost.

Old Epitaph

I would have a man generous to his country, his neighbors, his kindred, his friends, and most of all his poor friends. Not like some who are most lavish with those who are able to give most to them.

Pliny the Elder

He that gives all, though but little gives much; because God looks not to the quantity of the gift, but to the quality of the givers.

Francis Quarles

If there be any truer measure of a man than by what he does, it must be by what he gives.

Robert South

There is wisdom in generosity, as in everything else. A friend to everybody is often a friend to nobody; or else, in his simplicity, he robs his family to help strangers, and so becomes brother to a beggar.

Charles Haddon Spurgeon

He who gives what he would as readily throw away, gives without generosity; for the essence of generosity is in self-sacrifice.

Sir Henry Taylor

See also: BENEFICENCE, BENEVOLENCE, CHARITY, GOODNESS, HELP, KINDNESS.

GENETICS: *see* HEREDITY.

GENIUS

Genius is a superior aptitude to patience.

Comte Georges Louis Buffon

Genius . . . has been defined as a supreme capacity for taking trouble. . . . It might be more fitly described as a supreme capacity for getting its possessors into trouble of all kinds and keeping them therein so long as the genius remains.

Samuel Butler

Cleverness is a sort of genius for instrumentality. It is the brain of the hand. In literature, cleverness is more frequently accompanied by wit, genius, and sense, than by humor.

Samuel Taylor Coleridge

Talent, lying in the understanding, is often inherited; genius, being the action of reason and imagination, rarely or never.

Samuel Taylor Coleridge

When human power becomes so great and original that we can account for it only as a kind of divine inspiration, we call it genius.

William Crashaw

Genius is entitled to respect, only when it promotes the peace and improves the happiness of mankind.

Robert Devereux (Lord Essex)

Fortune has rarely condescended to be the companion of genius.

Isaac D'Israeli

Genius must be born; it never can be taught.

John Dryden

Genius is one per cent inspiration and ninety-nine per cent perspiration.

Thomas Alva Edison

Great geniuses have the shortest biographies.

Ralph Waldo Emerson

Genius is the ability to put into effect what is in your mind, there's no other definition of it.

Francis Scott Key Fitzgerald

Genius is commonly developed in men by some deficiency that stabs them wide awake

and becomes a major incentive. Obstacles can be immensely arousing and kindling.
Harry Emerson Fosdick

One of the strongest characteristics of genius is the power of lighting its own fire.
John Watson Foster

Genius is the gold in the mine; talent is the miner who works and brings it out.
Marguerite Gardiner (Lady Blessington)

The first and last thing required of genius is the love of truth.
Johann Wolfgang von Goethe

A great genius forms itself on another great genius less by assimilation than by friction. One diamond grinds another.
Heinrich Heine

Genius is nothing but continued attention.
Claude Adrien Helvetius

Genius may have its limitations, but stupidity is not thus handicapped.
Elbert Green Hubbard

Genius is a promontory jutting out into the infinite.
Victor Marie Hugo

The richest genius, like the most fertile soil, when uncultivated, shoots up into the rankest weeds; and instead of vines and olives for the pleasure and use of man, produces to its slothful owner the most abundant crop of poisons.
David Hume

Genius, as an explosive power, beats gunpowder hollow.
Thomas Henry Huxley

Genius is but a mind of large general powers accidentally determined in a particular direction.
Samuel Johnson

To encounter genius always makes us afraid, even when we perceive it in ourselves.
Fritz Künkel

Between genius and talent there is the proportion of the whole to its part.
Jean de La Bruyère

Genius always gives its best at first; prudence, at last.
Johann Kaspar Lavater

All the means of action—the shapeless masses—the materials—lie everywhere about us. What we need is the celestial fire to change the flint into the transparent crystal, bright and clear. That fire is genius.
Henry Wadsworth Longfellow

Genius is infinite painstaking.
Henry Wadsworth Longfellow

There is no work of genius which has not been the delight of mankind; no word of genius to which the human heart and soul have not, sooner or later, responded.
James Russell Lowell

Genius is, as a rule, a response to apparently hostile limitations.
Robert Lynd

Genius does what it must, and talent what it can.
Edward R. Bulwer Lytton (Owen Meredith)

It is wonderful what a personal interest the average man takes in discussions as to what constitutes genius.
Peter McArthur

If we are to have genius we must put up with the inconvenience of genius, a thing the world will never do; it wants geniuses, but would like them just like other people.
George Moore

Genius, without religion, is only a lamp on the outer gate of a palace; it may serve to cast a gleam of light on those that are without, while the inhabitant is in darkness.
Hannah More

Genius is supposed to be a power of producing excellencies which are out of the reach of the rules of art; a power which no precepts can teach, and which no industry can acquire.
Sir Joshua Reynolds

Genius has catalytic powers: it allows the realization in cold blood of certain spiritual acts which under ordinary circumstances require the high temperatures of passion.
Jean Rostand

Great inequalities in the terrain of the mind create the disequilibrium propitious to genius.
Jean Rostand

Genius is only a superior power of seeing.
John Ruskin

The lamp of genius burns quicker than the lamp of life.

Johann Christoph Friedrich von Schiller

There never appear more than five or six men of genius in an age, and if they were united the world could not stand before them.

Jonathan Swift

When a true genius appears in the world, you may know him by this sign, that the dunces are all in confederacy against him.

Jonathan Swift

True genius sees with the eye of a child and thinks with the brain of a genii.

Puzant Kevork Thomajan

The world can never nail down genius but it can crucify it.

Puzant Kevork Thomajan

The function of genius is not to give new answers, but to pose new questions which time and mediocrity can resolve.

Hugh Redwald Trevor-Roper

Genius finds its own road, and carries its own lamp.

Robert Eldridge Aris Willmott

Genius is no snob. It does not run after titles or seek by preference the high circles of society.

(Thomas) Woodrow Wilson

Genius is inconsiderate, self-relying, and, like unconscious beauty, without any intention to please.

Isaac Mayer Wise

See also: ABILITY, ART, CREATIVITY, INSPIRA-TION, TALENT.

GENOCIDE

In Maidanek, Poland, there was only one place where the children were treated kindly; at the entrance to the gas chambers each one was handed a sweet.

Gideon Maks Hausner

No one can demand that you be neutral toward the crime of genocide. If . . . there is a judge in the whole world who can be neutral toward this crime that judge is not fit to sit in judgment.

Gideon Maks Hausner

I personally arranged on orders received from Himmler in May 1941 the gassing of two million persons between June/July 1941 and the end of 1943 during which·time I was commandant of Auschwitz.

Rudolf Hess

At the United Nations, and in its various specialized agencies, there were painstakingly hammered out legally binding conventions aimed at erecting a sturdy edifice to the dignity of man. Acts committed with an intent to destroy in whole or in part an ethnic, racial, or religious group were branded an international crime—the crime of genocide.

William Proxmire

The third Reich is dead. But can any of us be sure that genocide is gone, never again to appear? I doubt it. Genocide has survived for too long in human history in too many places, under too many guises.

William Proxmire

Among private persons, we punish murderers and massacres. What do we do respecting wars, and the glorious crime of murdering whole nations? The love of conquest is a murderess. Conquerors are scourges not less harmful to humanity than floods and earth-quakes.

Seneca

See also: MURDER, NAZISM, RACISM.

GENTILE

Where the preamble declares, that coercion is a departure from the plan of the holy author of our religion, an amendment was proposed by inserting the words, "Jesus Christ," so that it should read, "A departure from the plan of Jesus Christ, the holy author of our religion;" the insertion was rejected by a great majority, in proof that they meant to comprehend, within the mantle of its protection, the Jew and the Gentile, the Christian and Mohammedan, the Hindoo and Infidel of every denomination.

Thomas Jefferson

The Church . . . cannot forget that she received the revelation of the Old Testament through the people with whom God in his inexpressible mercy deigned to establish the Ancient Covenant. Nor can she forget that she draws sustenance from the root of that good olive tree onto which have been grafted the wild olive branches of the Gentiles. Indeed, the Church believes that by His cross Christ, our Peace, reconciled Jew and Gentile, making them both one in Himself.

Vatican Council II

See also: CHRISTIAN, JEWS, JUDAISM.

GENTLEMAN

A gentleman is any man who wouldn't hit a woman with his hat on.

Fred Allen

The gentleman is a Christian product.

George Henry Calvert

You may depend upon it, religion is, in its essence, the most gentlemanly thing in the world. It will, alone, gentilize, if unmixed with cant; and I know nothing else, which, alone, will.

Samuel Taylor Coleridge

He that can enjoy the intimacy of the great, and on no occasion disgust them by familiarity, or disgrace himself by servility, proves that he is as perfect a gentleman by nature, as his companions are by rank.

Charles Caleb Colton

I like him. He is every other inch a gentleman.

Noel Pierce Coward

The flowering of civilization is the finished man—the man of sense, of grace, of accomplishment, of social power—the gentleman.

Ralph Waldo Emerson

Repose and cheerfulness are the badge of the gentleman—repose in energy.

Ralph Waldo Emerson

We sometimes meet an original gentleman, who, if manners had not existed, would have invented them.

Ralph Waldo Emerson

Thoughtfulness for others, generosity, modesty, and self-respect are the qualities which make a real gentleman or lady, as distinguished from the veneered article which commonly goes by that name.

Thomas Henry Huxley

Education begins the gentleman, but reading, good company, and reflection must finish him.

John Locke

It is a grand old name, that of gentleman, and has been recognized as a rank and power in all stages of society. To possess this character is a dignity of itself, commanding the instinctive homage of every generous mind, and those who will not bow to titular rank will yet do homage to the gentleman. His qualities depend not upon fashion or manners, but upon moral worth; not on personal possessions, but on personal qualities.

Samuel Smiles

Men of courage, men of sense, and men of letters are frequent: but a true gentleman is what one seldom sees.

Sir Richard Steele

Perhaps a gentleman is a rarer man than some of us think for. Which of us can point out many such in his circle; men whose aims are generous, whose truth is not only constant in its kind, but elevated in its degree; whose want of meanness makes them simple, who can look the world honestly in the face with an equal manly sympathy for the great and the small.

William Makepeace Thackeray

To be a gentleman is to be honest, to be gentle, to be generous, to be brave, to be wise, and possessing all those qualities to exercise them in the most graceful outward manner.

William Makepeace Thackeray

The true gentleman is subtly poised between an inner tact and an outer deference.

Puzant Kevork Thomajan

A gentleman? . . . Individual conscience will rule his social acts. By love of quality as against quantity he will choose his way through life. He will learn to know the difference between the curious and the beautiful. Truth will be a divinity to him. As his gentlehood cannot be conferred, so it may not be inherited. This gentleman of democracy will be found in any honest occupation at any level of fortune, loving beauty, doing his best and being kind.

Frank Lloyd Wright

See also: COURTESY, GOOD BREEDING, MANNERS, POLITENESS.

GENTLENESS

True gentleness is founded on a sense of what we owe to him who made us, and to the common nature which we all share. It arises from reflection on our own failings and wants, and from just views of the condition and duty of men. It is native feeling heightened and improved by principle.

Hugh Blair

Nothing is so strong as gentleness; nothing so gentle as real strength.

Francis of Sales

True gentleness is love in society, holding intercourse with those around it. It is considerateness; it is tenderness of feeling; it is promptitude of sympathy; it is love in all its depths, and in all its delicacy. It is everything included in that matchless grace, "the gentleness of Christ."

James Hamilton

The only rank which elevates a woman is that which a gentle spirit bestows upon her.
Sir Arthur Wing Pinero

Bear in mind that true wisdom is always joined with mildness, that malice never converts.

Gabriel Riesser

We are indebted to Christianity for gentleness, especially toward women.

Charles Simmons

See also: COMPASSION, GENTLEMAN, HUMAN NATURE, KINDNESS, MERCY.

GERMANY

The danger of German militarism has disappeared. It is not there any more.

Konrad Adenauer

There is only one place for us in the world. That is at the side of the free peoples. Our goal is: A free and united Germany in a free and united Europe.

Konrad Adenauer

Let us put Germany, so to speak, in the saddle! you will see that she can ride.
Otto Eduard Leopold von Bismarck

We do not live in the Bavarian forests. We do not live on the west bank of the Rhine. We live behind the Communist guns in this encircled city. That is a geographical fact. But we belong to the West and we will continue belonging to the West.

Willy Brandt

Christianity . . . has somewhat softened the brutal Germanic lust for battle, but could not

destroy it; and when the cross, that restraining talisman, falls to pieces, then will break forth again the ferocity of the old fighters, the insane Berserker rage whereof northern poets have sung . . . and at last Thor with his giant hammer will leap aloft and shatter the gothic cathedrals.

Heinrich Heine

The German is like a slave who obeys the mere nod or word of his master, and needs neither ships nor chains. Servility is inherent in him—it is in his soul.

Heinrich Heine

Germans need neither freedom nor equality. They are a speculative race, . . . dreamers who live only in the past and future, and have no present.

Heinrich Heine

We Germans will never produce another Goethe, but we may produce another Caesar.
Oswald Spengler

The East Germans are obsessed with reunification. It is the most important problem here, a political as well as a human problem. Everybody talks about it all the time—students and workers, Communists and non-Communists, old and young people.

Joseph Wechsberg

To me Goethe was always synonymous with Weimar, the German Athens, the shrine of German classicism.

Joseph Wechsberg

See also: ENGLAND, EUROPE, FRANCE, NAZISM, UNITED NATIONS.

GHETTO

Ghetto thinking, the result of years of ghetto living, is the avoidance of action or degrading oneself to be permitted to survive.

Bruno Bettelheim

The abrasive relationship between the police and the ghetto community has been a major—and explosive—source of grievance, tension and disorder. The blame must be shared by the total society.

Commission on Civil Disorder, 1968

Discrimination prevents access to many non-slum areas, particularly the suburbs, where good housing exists. In addition, by creating a "back pressure" in the racial ghettos, it makes it possible for landlords to break up apartments for denser occupancy, and keeps prices and rents of deteriorated ghetto housing higher than they would be in a truly free market.

Commission on Civil Disorder, 1968

In the black ghettos segregation and poverty converge on the young to destroy opportunity and enforce failure. Crime, drug addiction, dependency on welfare, and bitterness and resentment against society in general and white society in particular are the result.

Commission on Civil Disorder, 1968

It is time now to end the destruction and the violence, not only in the streets of the ghetto but in the lives of people.

Commission on Civil Disorder, 1968

What white Americans have never fully understood—but what the Negro can never forget—is that white society is deeply implicated in the ghetto. White institutions created it, white institutions maintain it, and white society condones it.

Commission on Civil Disorder, 1968

The ghetto uprisings can be traced to two principal factors—housing and jobs. Education and job training are relatively longer term tasks, but it is inexcusable to continue to deny decent housing to Negro families who can afford it now.

Congressional Report on Housing, 1967

With the shedding of the ghetto mentality and upper-class complacency, the Negro is through with wearing the mask of ambivalence; he is done with survivor's double talk, for he is beginning to think like a man and act like a man and what is most important, to be treated as one.

Ebony

Looking upon their host countries as profane soil and their fellow citizens as children of error and superstition, Jews grouped themselves in a quarter of the city all their own. The "ghetto" was a voluntary reality hundreds of years before the term was coined or legislation regarding it enacted.

Edward Hugh Flannery

Patterns varied, but usually the ghetto was located in a poorer region of the city and enclosed by high walls, its gates guarded by Christian gatekeepers, paid by the confined. Some of the most famous ghettos were those in Prague, Venice, Frankfurt-on-the-Main,

and Rome. Most were unbelievably overcrowded, often comprising a single street of abnormally tall houses, crammed with people who lived ever in dread of plagues and fires that frequently struck.

Edward Hugh Flannery

Thus the ghetto, so carefully designed to cut off the Jew from all Christian contact, began to crumble well before the political edicts of the late eighteenth and nineteenth centuries abolished it altogether.

Edward Hugh Flannery

See also: CITY, CRIME, NEGRO, POVERTY, RICH AND POOR, RIOT, SLUM.

GIFT

The best thing to give to your enemy is forgiveness; to an opponent, tolerance; to a friend, your heart; to your child, a good example; to a father, deference; to your mother, conduct that will make her proud of you; to yourself, respect; to all men, charity.

Francis Maitland Balfour

Examples are few of men ruined by giving. Men are heroes in spending—cravens in what they give.

Christian Nestell Bovee

The secret of giving affectionately is great and rare; it requires address to do it well; otherwise we lose instead of deriving benefit from it.

Pierre Corneille

One must be poor to know the luxury of giving.

George Eliot (Mary Ann Evans)

Give according to your means, or God will make your means according to your giving.

John Hall

There is a gift that is almost a blow, and there is a kind word that is munificence; so much is there in the way of doing things.

Sir Arthur Helps

When a friend asks, there is no tomorrow.

George Herbert

A gift, its kind, its value, and appearance; the silence or the pomp that attends it; the style in which it reaches you, may decide the dignity or vulgarity of the giver.

Johann Kaspar Lavater

The manner of giving shows the character of the giver, more than the gift itself.

Johann Kaspar Lavater

Who gives a trifle meanly is meaner than the trifle.

Johann Kaspar Lavater

What we get out of life is in direct proportion to what we put into it.

Herbert Henry Lehman

It is the will, and not the gift that makes the giver.

Gotthold Ephraim Lessing

Presents which our love for the donor has rendered precious are ever the most acceptable.

Ovid

Every gift, though it be small, is in reality great if given with affection.

Pindar

Independence is of more value than any gifts; and to receive gifts is to lose it. Men most commonly seek to oblige thee only that they may engage thee to serve them.

Saadi (Muslih-ud-Din)

That which is given with pride and ostentation is rather an ambition than a bounty.

Seneca

We should give as we would receive, cheerfully, quickly, and without hesitation; for there is no grace in a benefit that sticks to the fingers.

Seneca

He who loves with purity considers not the gift of the lover, but the love of the giver.

Thomas à Kempis

See also: BENEFICENCE, GENEROSITY, PHILANTHROPY, WELL-DOING.

GIRL

Maidens, like moths, are ever caught by glare,
And Mammon wins his way where Seraphs might despair.

George Gordon Byron (Lord Byron)

'Tis true, your budding Miss is very charming,
But shy and awkward at first coming out,
So much alarmed, that she is quite alarming,
All Giggle, Blush; half Pertness and half Pout;

And glancing at *Mamma,* for fear there's harm in
What you, she, it, or they may be about.
The nursery still lisps out in all they utter,—
Besides, they always smell of bread and butter.

George Gordon Byron (Lord Byron)

It is a common phenomenon that just the prettiest girls find it so difficult to get a man. That was already the case in antiquity . . . all the three Graces have remained single.

Heinrich Heine

A homely girl hates mirrors.

Proverb

See also: BOY, DAUGHTER, WOMAN.

GIVING: see GIFT.

GLORY

As to be perfectly just is an attribute of the divine nature, to be so to the utmost of our abilities is the glory of man.

Joseph Addison

Let us not disdain glory too much; nothing is finer, except virtue. The height of happiness would be to unite both in this life.

Vicomte François René de Chateaubriand

True glory takes root, and even spreads; all false pretences, like flowers, fall to the ground; nor can any counterfeit last long.

Cicero

Glory, built on selfish principles, is shame and guilt.

William Cowper

By skillful conduct and artificial means a person may make a sort of name for himself; but if the inner jewel be wanting, all is vanity, and will not last.

Johann Wolfgang von Goethe

Our greatest glory consists not in never falling, but in rising every time we fall.

Oliver Goldsmith

The glory of a people, and of an age, is always the work of a small number of great men, and disappears with them.

Baron Friedrich Melchior von Grimm

The shortest way to glory is to be guided by conscience.

Henry Home (Lord Kames)

No flowery road leads to glory.
Jean de La Fontaine

Glory is never where virtue is not.
Jean Lefranc (Marquis de Pompignan)

He that first likened glory to a shadow, did better than he was aware of; they are both vain. Glory, also, like the shadow, goes sometimes before the body, and sometimes in length infinitely exceeds it.
Michel Eyquem de Montaigne

The delights of glory are so great, that to whatever it is attached, even to death, we love it.
Blaise Pascal

True glory consists in doing what deserves to be written; in writing what deserves to be read; and in so living as to make the world happier and better for our living in it.
Pliny the Elder

Real glory springs from the silent conquest of ourselves. Without that, the conqueror is nought but the foist slave.
Joseph Parrish Thompson

See also: DISTINCTION, EMINENCE, FAME, HONOR, PRAISE.

GLUTTONY

Their kitchen is their shrine, the cook their priest, the table their altar, and their belly their god.
Charles Buck

As houses well stored with provisions are likely to be full of mice, so the bodies of those who eat much are full of diseases.
Diogenes

I saw few die of hunger—of eating, a hundred thousand.
Benjamin Franklin

They whose sole bliss is eating, can give but that one brutish reason why they live.
Juvenal

Swinish gluttony ne'er looks to heaven amid his gorgeous feast, but with besotted, base ingratitude, crams and blasphemes his feeder.
John Milton

He who is a slave to his belly seldom worships God.
Saadi (Muslih-ud-Din)

The pleasures of the palate deal with us like the Egyptian thieves, who strangle those whom they embrace.
Seneca

See also: ABSTINENCE, DIET, EATING, EXCESS, FATNESS, FEASTING, INTEMPERANCE.

GOD

The nature of God is a circle of which the centre is everywhere and the circumference is nowhere.
Anonymous

Reason in man is rather like God in the world.
Thomas Aquinas

For science, God is simply *the stream of tendency by which all things seek to fulfil the law of their being.*
Matthew Arnold

They that deny God, destroy man's nobility; for clearly man is of kin to the beasts by his body, and if he be not of kin to God by his spirit, he is a base and ignoble creature.
Francis Bacon

We cannot too often think, that there is a never sleeping eye that reads the heart, and registers our thoughts.
Francis Bacon

There is nothing on earth worth being known but God and our own souls.
Gamaliel Bailey

An old mystic says somewhere, "God is an unutterable sigh in the innermost depths of the soul." With still greater justice, we may reverse the proposition, and say the soul is a never ending sigh after God.
Theodore Christlieb

There is something in the nature of things which the mind of man, which reason, which human power cannot effect, and certainly that which produces this must be better than man. What can this be but God?
Cicero

There is a God in science, a God in history, and a God in conscience, and these three are one.
Joseph Cook

In all the vast and the minute, we see the unambiguous footsteps of the God, who gives its luster to the insect's wing, and wheels his throne upon the rolling worlds.

William Cowper

You can believe in God without believing in immortality, but it is hard to see how anybody can believe in immortality and not believe in God.

Ernest Dimnet

Nature is too thin a screen; the glory of the omnipresent God bursts through everywhere.

Ralph Waldo Emerson

God rules the world not from the outside, not by gravity and chemical affinity, but in the hearts of men: as your soul is, so is the fate of the world you live in and move in. Nothing is outside.

Egon Friedell

If one wishes to work in the fear of God, one should be indifferent about popular praise or blame.

Mohandas Karamchand (Mahatma) Gandhi

Mankind is notoriously too dense to read the signs that God sends from time to time. We require drums to be beaten into our ears, before we should wake from our trance and hear the warning and see that to lose oneself in all is the only way to find oneself.

Mohandas Karamchand (Mahatma) Gandhi

Man's ultimate aim is the realisation of God, and all his activities—social, political, religious have to be guided by the ultimate aim of the vision of God. The immediate service of all human beings becomes a necessary part of the endeavour simply because the only way to find God is to see Him in His creation and be one with it.

Mohandas Karamchand (Mahatma) Gandhi

He who waits for God fails to understand that he possesses Him. Believe that God and happiness are one, and put all your happiness in the present moment.

André Gide

The best way to know God is to love many things.

Vincent van Gogh

I just want to lobby for God.

William Franklin (Billy) Graham

A man who writes of himself without speaking of God is like one who identifies himself without giving his address.

Ben Hecht

The name of God is Truth.

Hindu Proverb

Glory be to God for dappled things—
  For skies of couple-colour as a brinded cow;
  For rose-miles all in stipple upon trout that swim;
Fresh-firecoal chestnut-falls; finches' wings;
  Landscape plotted and pieced—fold, fallow, and plough;
  And all trades, their gear and tackle and trim.

Gerard Manley Hopkins

Performing miracles in a crisis—so much easier than loving God selflessly every moment of the day! Which is why most crises arise—because people find it so hard to behave properly at ordinary times.

Aldous Leonard Huxley

We know God easily, if we do not constrain ourselves to define him.

Joseph Joubert

I should like to see a man sober in his habits, moderate, chaste, just in his dealings, assert that there is no God; he would speak at least without interested motives: but such a man is not to be found.

Jean de La Bruyère

It is one of my favorite thoughts, that God manifests himself to mankind in all wise, good, humble, generous, great and magnanimous men.

Johann Kaspar Lavater

Let the chain of second causes be ever so long, the first link is always in God's hand.

George Lavington

I propose that God should be openly and audibly invoked at the United Nations in accordance with any one of the religious faiths which are represented here. I do so in the conviction that we cannot make the United Nations into a successful instrument of God's peace without God's help—and that with His help we cannot fail.

Henry Cabot Lodge

Live near to God, and so all things will appear to you little in comparison with eternal realities.

Robert Murray McCheyne

How often we look upon God as our last and feeblest resource! We go to him because we have nowhere else to go. And then we learn that the storms of life have driven us, not upon the rocks, but into the desired haven.
George Macdonald

Anyone who is looking around for a simulated icon of the deity in Newtonian guise might well be disappointed. The phrase "God is dead" applies aptly, correctly, validly to the Newtonian universe which is dead. The groundrule of that universe, upon which so much of our Western world is built, has dissolved.
(Herbert) Marshall McLuhan

God should be the object of all our desires, the end of all our actions, the principle of all our affections, and the governing power of our whole souls.
Jean Baptiste Massillon

A deity without personality, and hence without consciousness, is no more capable of awakening the sense of religion in the heart of man than is the all-pervading air of the universal force of gravitation.
John Anthony O'Brien

We do not base our argument for God's existence upon the untenable assumption that conscience is a mystical faculty in the mind, independent of reason, . . . nor upon the equally untenable assumption that every pronouncement of conscience is an infallible echoing of the voice of God. We base it upon the fact that there is a moral order in the universe, mirrored in the stern commands of conscience to do what is right and to avoid what is wrong.
John Anthony O'Brien

Belief in a cruel God makes a cruel man.
Thomas Paine

Two men please God—who serves Him with all his heart because he knows Him; who seeks Him with all his heart because he knows Him not.
Count Nikita Ivanovich Panin

To escape from evil we must be made, as far as possible, like God; and this resemblance consists in becoming just, and holy, and wise.
Plato

In all thine actions think that God sees thee, and in all his actions labor to see him. That will make thee fear him, and this will move thee to love him. The fear of God is the beginning of knowledge, and the knowledge of God is the perfection of love.
Francis Quarles

Belief in and dependence on God is absolutely essential. It will be an integral part of our public life as long as I am Governor.
Ronald Reagan

I don't say what God is, but it's a name
That somehow answers us when we are driven
To feel and think how little we have to do
With what we are.
Edwin Arlington Robinson

God is, by definition, ultimate reality. And one cannot argue whether ultimate reality exists. One can only ask what ultimate reality is like.
John Arthur Thomas Robinson

Being good is not the hard thing; what is, is being so under the conditions life imposes.
Jean Rostand

I fear God, and next to God I chiefly fear him who fears him not.
Saadi (Muslih-ud-Din)

Only through love can we attain to communion with God.
Albert Schweitzer

Our love for God is tested by the question of whether we seek Him or His gifts.
Ralph Washington Sockman

If God were not a necessary being of himself, he might almost seem to be made for the use and benefit of men.
John Tillotson

There is a beauty in the name appropriated by the Saxon nations to the Deity, unequalled except by his most venerated Hebrew appellation. They called him "GOD," which is literally "THE GOOD." The same word thus signifying the Deity and His most endearing quality.
Charles Tennyson Turner

If God did not exist it would be necessary to invent him.
Voltaire (François Marie Arouet)

It is impossible to govern the world without God. He must be worse than an infidel that lacks faith, and more than wicked that has not gratitude enough to acknowledge his obligation.

George Washington

He (God) is the poet of the world, with tender patience leading it by his vision of truth, beauty, and goodness.

Alfred North Whitehead

I firmly believe in Divine Providence. Without belief in Providence I think I should go crazy. Without God the world would be a maze without a clue.

(Thomas) Woodrow Wilson

A foe to God was never a true friend to man.

Edward Young

See also: AGNOSTICISM, ATHEISM, FAITH, OMNIPOTENCE, OMNIPRENCE.

GOLD

If they ask us why it is that we say more on the money question than we say upon the tariff question, I reply that, if protection has slain its thousands, the gold standard has slain its tens of thousands.

William Jennings Bryan

You shall not press down upon the brow of labor this crown of thorns—you shall not crucify mankind upon a cross of gold!

William Jennings Bryan

A mask of gold hides all deformities.

Thomas Dekker

It is much better to have your gold in the hand than in the heart.

Thomas Fuller

It is observed of gold, in an old epigram, that to have it is to be in fear, and to want it is to be in sorrow.

Samuel Johnson

The lust of gold, unfeeling and remorseless; the last corruption of degenerate man.

Samuel Johnson

Gold, like the sun, which melts wax, but hardens clay, expands great souls and contracts bad hearts.

Antoine Rivarol

There is no place so high that an ass laden with gold cannot reach it.

Fernando de Rojas

How few, like Daniel, have God and gold together.

Henry Montague Villiers

Gold's father is dirt, yet it regards itself as noble.

Yiddish Proverb

See also: AVARICE, ECONOMICS, MONEY, RICHES, WEALTH.

GOLDEN RULE

Do to every man as you would have him do to you; and do not unto another what you would not have him do to you.

Confucius

For the laws of nature, as justice, equity, modesty, mercy, and, in sum, *doing to others as we would be done to,* of themselves, without the terror of some power to cause them to be observed, are contrary to our natural passions, that carry us to partiality, pride, revenge, and the like. And covenants, without the sword, are but words, and of no strength to secure a man at all.

Thomas Hobbes

This is the sum of all true righteousness: deal with others as thou wouldst thyself be dealt by. Do nothing to thy neighbor which thou wouldst not have him do to thee hereafter.

Mahabharata

Do not do unto others as you would that they should do unto you. Their tastes may not be the same.

George Bernard Shaw

Do not do to your fellowmen what is hateful to you.

Talmud

See also: CHARITY, CHRIST, KINDNESS, LOVE.

GOLF

Golf is a game which is entirely different from any other sport, because the ball is at rest. You can take as long as you like to hit it—or practically as long as you like—and fellows who only watch the experts play can't understand why these little shots should be so difficult—because they are made to look so easy. They never stop to realize that one stroke thrown away, one little false movement, one moment's lack of concentration, one disconcerting move on the part of the gallery, is enough to ruin a man's entire score. The quiet adds to the tension. The game calls for perfect nerve and muscular control and complete co-ordination.

Thomas D. (Tommy) Armour

In other games you get another chance. In baseball you get three cracks at it; in tennis you lose only one point. But in golf the loss of one shot has been responsible for the loss of heart.

Thomas D. (Tommy) Armour

No doubt the public knows less about the inside intricacies of first-class golf than of any other sport. It seems to be their particular delight to watch a famous golfer miss a shot and then hold him up to ridicule.

Thomas D. (Tommy) Armour

Golf is the only sport in which man competes strictly with himself. There are of course, terrain, wind, water and luck to contend with, but these opponents, as well as those human obstacles between the tee and the cup—the loving cup that is—are incidental. The other golfers have all these hazards in common too, including themselves.

Esquire

See also: SPORTS.

GOOD BREEDING

Good-breeding shows itself most, where to an ordinary eye it appears the least.

Joseph Addison

One may know a man that never conversed in the world, by his excess of good-breeding.

Joseph Addison

Good-breeding is the art of showing men, by external signs, the internal regard we have for them. It arises from good sense, improved by conversing with good company.

Cato the Elder

The summary of good-breeding may be reduced to this rule: "Behave to all others as you would they should behave to you."

Henry Fielding

Among well-bred people, a mutual deference is affected; contempt of others disguised; authority concealed; attention given to each in his turn; and an easy stream of conversation maintained, without vehemence, without interruption, without eagerness for victory, and without any airs of superiority.

David Hume

I had sooner play cards against a man who was quite skeptical about ethics, but bred to believe that "a gentleman does not cheat," than against an irreproachable moral philosopher who had been brought up among sharpers. In battle it is not syllogisms that will keep the reluctant nerves to their post in the third hour of the bombardment.

Clive Staples (C. S.) Lewis

Good qualities are the substantial riches of the mind; but it is good-breeding that sets them off to advantage.

John Locke

Virtue itself often offends, when coupled with bad manners.

Thomas Middleton

Good-breeding is benevolence in trifles, or the preference of others to ourselves in the daily occurrences of life.

William Pitt (Lord Chatham)

Good-breeding is the result of much good sense, some good nature, and a little self-denial for the sake of others, and with a view to obtain the same indulgence from them.

Philip Dormer Stanhope (Lord Chesterfield)

A man's own good-breeding is the best security against other people's ill-manners. It carries along with it a dignity that is respected by the most petulant. Ill-breeding invites and authorizes the familiarity of the most timid. No man ever said a pert thing to the Duke of Marlborough. No man ever said a civil one to Sir Robert Walpole.

Philip Dormer Stanhope (Lord Chesterfield)

The scholar, without good-breeding, is a pedant; the philosopher, a cynic; the soldier, a brute; and every man disagreeable.

Philip Dormer Stanhope (Lord Chesterfield)

The highest point of good-breeding is to show a very nice regard to your own dignity, and with that in your own heart, to express your value for the man above you.

Sir Richard Steele

Wisdom, valor, justice, and learning, cannot keep a man in countenance that is possessed with these excellencies, if he wants that inferior art of life and behaviour, called good breeding.

Sir Richard Steele

See also: COURTESY, ETIQUETTE, MANNERS, PO-LITENESS, REFINEMENT.

GOOD HUMOR

Honest good humor is the oil and wine of a merry meeting, and there is no jovial companionship equal to that where the jokes are rather small, and the laughter abundant.

Washington Irving

Some people are commended for a giddy kind of good humor, which is no more a virtue than drunkenness.

Alexander Pope

Without the ability to be gay and to treat serious things lightly after the serious thinking is done and the decisions reached, I doubt whether any man could long carry the job of being President of the United States.

Anna Eleanor Roosevelt

See also: AMIABILITY, CHEERFULNESS, HAPPINESS, JOY, SMILE.

GOOD NATURE

Good nature is more agreeable in conversation than wit, and gives a certain air to the countenance which is more amiable than beauty. It shows virtue in the fairest light; takes off, in some measure, from the deformity of vice; and makes even folly and impertinence supportable.

Joseph Addison

Good nature is one of the richest fruits of true Christianity.

Henry Ward Beecher

Good sense and good nature are never separated; and good nature is the product of right reason. It makes allowance for the failings of others by considering that there is nothing perfect in mankind; and by distinguishing that which comes nearest to excellence, though not absolutely free from faults, will certainly produce candor in judging.

John Dryden

A shrewd observer once said, that in walking the streets of a slippery morning, one might see where the good natured people lived, by the ashes thrown on the ice before the doors.

Benjamin Franklin

Good nature is the very air of a good mind; the sign of a large and generous soul, and the peculiar soil in which virtue prospers.

Godfrey Goodman

Good nature is the beauty of the mind, and like personal beauty, wins almost without

anything else—sometimes, indeed, in spite of positive deficiencies.

Jonas Hanway

An inexhaustible good nature is one of the most precious gifts of heaven, spreading itself like oil over the troubled sea of thought, and keeping the mind smooth and equable in the roughest weather.

Washington Irving

See also: BENEVOLENCE, EQUANIMITY.

GOOD WILL

Good Will is the mightiest practical force in the world.

Charles Fletcher Dole

I am quite convinced that in the treatment of nations to one another, as in the case of individuals, only out of goodwill will you get goodwill and no amount of intrigues and cleverness will get you good results out of evil ways.

Jawaharlal Nehru

We attach more importance to a decision arrived at through goodwill, than to the merely logical decision, for logic is a very feeble and unworthy substitute for goodwill. I would rather have goodwill and co-operation than logic.

Jawaharlal Nehru

Good will is the best charity.

Yiddish Proverb

See also: BENEVOLENCE, GOOD NATURE, KINDNESS, PATIENCE.

GOODNESS

To an honest mind, the best prerequisites of a place are the advantages it gives for doing good.

Joseph Addison

Goodness is easier to recognize than to define.

Wystan Hugh Auden

We may be as good as we please, if we please to be good.

Isaac Barrow

A good deed is never lost. He who sows courtesy, reaps friendship; he who plants kindness, gathers love; pleasure bestowed upon a grateful mind was never sterile, but generally gratitude begets reward.

Basil the Great

Your actions, in passing, pass not away, for every good work is a grain of seed for eternal life.

Bernard of Clairvaux

All the fame which ever cheated humanity into higher notions of its own importance would never weigh in my mind against the pure and pious interest which a virtuous being may be pleased to take in my welfare.

George Gordon Byron (Lord Byron)

Goodness consists not in the outward things we do, but in the inward thing we are. To be good is the great thing.

Edwin Hubbel Chapin

There are two perfectly good men; one dead, and the other unborn.

Chinese Proverb

In nothing do men approach so nearly to the gods as in doing good to men.

Cicero

Never did any soul do good, but it came readier to do the same again, with more enjoyment. Never was love, or gratitude, or bounty practised but with increasing joy, which made the practiser still more in love with the fair act.

Anthony Ashley Cooper (Lord Shaftesbury)

To love the public, to study universal good, and to promote the interest of the whole world, as far as it lies in our power, is the height of goodness, and makes that temper which we call divine.

Anthony Ashley Cooper (Lord Shaftesbury)

The Good is that which satisfies want, craving, which fulfills or makes complete the need which stirs to action.

John Dewey

A good man who goes wrong is just a bad man who has been found out.

Robert Chambers (Bob) Edwards

By desiring what is perfectly good, even when we do not quite know what it is, and cannot do what we would, we are part of the divine power against evil, widening the skirts of light and making the struggle with darkness narrower.

George Eliot (Mary Ann Evans)

He who loves goodness harbors angels, reveres reverence, and lives with God.

Ralph Waldo Emerson

Those who want to be good are not in a hurry. They know that to impregnate people with good takes a long time.

Mohandas Karamchand (Mahatma) Gandhi

Whatever mitigates the woes, or increases the happiness of others, is a just criterion of goodness; and whatever injures society at large, or any individual in it, is a criterion of iniquity.

Oliver Goldsmith

Goodness is love in action, love with its hand to the plow, love with the burden on its back, love following his footsteps who went about continually doing good.

James Hamilton

Nothing can make a man truly great but being truly good and partaking of God's holiness.

Matthew Henry

In the heraldry of heaven goodness precedes greatness, and so on earth it is more powerful. The lowly and lovely may often do more good in their limited sphere than the gifted.

George Horne

Good is that which makes for unity; evil is that which makes for separateness.

Aldous Leonard Huxley

There may be a certain pleasure in vice, but there is a higher in purity and virtue. The most commanding of all delights is the delight in goodness. The beauty of holiness is but one beauty, but it the highest. It is the loss of the sense of sin and shame that destroys both men and states.

Independent

Goodness, if it is to be really goodness and not merely conventional behavior, must be freely acquired; it cannot be imposed from without by discipline, and cannot be achieved by merely keeping the rules.

Cyril Edwin Mitchinson Joad

As I know more of mankind I expect less of them, and am ready to call a man a good man upon easier terms than I was formerly.

Samuel Johnson

He is good that does good to others. If he suffers for the good he does, he is better still; and if he suffers from them to whom he did good, he has arrived to that height of goodness that nothing but an increase of his sufferings can add to it; if it proves his death, his virtue is at its summit; it is heroism complete.

Jean de La Bruyère

Nothing is more rarely to be found than real goodness; those even who think that they possess it are generally only good-natured or weak.

Duc François de La Rochefoucauld

We must first be made good, before we can do good; we must first be made just, before our works can please God—for when we are justified by faith in Christ, then come good works.

Hugh Latimer

You are not very good if you are not better than your best friends imagine you to be.

Johann Kaspar Lavater

A good man doubles the length of his existence; to have lived so as to look back with pleasure on our past life is to live twice.

Martial

Choose your own good and call it good.
For I could never make you see
That no one knows what is good
Who knows not what is evil;
And no one knows what is true
Who knows not what is false.

Edgar Lee Masters

Goodness thinks no ill where no ill seems.

John Milton

The good life is not only good for one's conscience; it is good for art, good for knowledge, good for health, good for fellowship.

Lewis Mumford

I search in vain in history to find the similar to Jesus Christ, or anything which can approach the gospel. Neither history, nor humanity, nor the ages, nor nature, offer me anything with which I am able to compare or explain it. There is nothing there which is not beyond the march of events and above the human mind. What happiness it gives to those who believe it! What marvels there which those admire who reflect upon it!

Napoleon I (Bonaparte)

The good are heaven's peculiar care.

Ovid

Let no man delude himself by the belief that the good things of life will endure through the sheer quality of their goodness. In a Heaven of Platonic essences, yes—but not in the realm of existence. . . . Even imperishable truth . . . invulnerable to argument, may nevertheless cease to exist, if truth-loving men are exterminated or if their love of truth is corrupted.

Ralph Barton Perry

Suppression and coercion cannot be avoided in this imperfect world, but let us clearly and once for all realise that good-will cannot be achieved but by good-will.

Chakravarti Rajagopalacharia

It is a law of our humanity, that man must know good through evil. No great principle ever triumphed but through much evil. No man ever progressed to greatness and goodness but through great mistakes.

Frederick William Robertson

Anyone who proposes to do good must not expect people to roll stones out of his way, but must accept his lot calmly if they roll a few more upon it.

Albert Schweitzer

A good man is influenced by God himself, and has a kind of divinity within him; so it may be a question whether he goes to heaven, or heaven comes to him.

Seneca

He that does good to another, does also good to himself; not only in the consequence, but in the very act of doing it; for the consciousness of well-doing is an ample reward.

Seneca

Let a man be never so ungrateful or inhuman, he shall never destroy the satisfaction of my having done a good office.

Seneca

To be doing good is man's most glorious task.

Sophocles

He that is a good man, is three quarters of his way toward the being a good Christian, wheresoever he lives, or whatsoever he is called.

Robert South

I have known some men possessed of good qualities which were very serviceable to others, but useless to themselves; like a sundial on the front of a house, to inform and benefit the neighbors and passengers, but not the owner within.

Jonathan Swift

It seems to me it is only noble to be good. Kind hearts are more than coronets.

Alfred, Lord Tennyson

Be not merely good; be good for something.

Henry David Thoreau

Real goodness does not attach itself merely to this life—it points to another world. Political or professional reputation cannot last forever, but a conscience void of offence before God and man is an inheritance for eternity.

Daniel Webster

Do all the good you can, in all the ways you can, to all the souls you can, in every place you can, at all the times you can, with all the zeal you can, as long as ever you can.

John Wesley

His daily prayer, far better understood in acts than in words, was simply doing good.

John Greenleaf Whittier

The best portion of a good man's life is his little, nameless, unremembered acts of kindness and of love.

William Wordsworth

Better good than pious.

Yiddish Proverb

See also: CHARITY, INTEGRITY, MORALITY.

GOSPEL

There is not a book on earth so favorable to all the kind and to all the sublime affections, or so unfriendly to hatred, persecution, tyranny, injustice, and every sort of malevolence as the gospel. It breathes, throughout, only mercy, benevolence, and peace.

James Beattie

The gospel in all its doctrines and duties appears infinitely superior to any human composition. It has no mark of human ignorance, imperfection, or sinfulness, but bears the signature of divine wisdom, authority, and importance, and is most worthy of the supreme attention and regard of all intelligent creatures.

Nathaniel Emmons

God writes the gospel not in the Bible alone, but on trees, and flowers, and clouds, and stars.

Martin Luther

The gospel is the fulfillment of all hopes, the perfection of all philosophy, the interpreter of all revelations, and a key to all the seeming contradictions of truth in the physical and moral world.

Hugh Miller

It is a strange and sickly world into which the gospel leads us—a world apparently out of a Russian novel.

Friederich Wilhelm Nietzsche

We can learn nothing of the gospel except by feeling its truths. There are some sciences that may be learned by the head, but the science of Christ crucified can only be learned by the heart.

Charles Haddon Spurgeon

Did you ever notice that while the gospel sets before us a higher and more blessed heaven than any other religion, its hell is also deeper and darker than any other?

Samuel Warren

See also: BIBLE, CHRIST, CHRISTIAN, CHRISTIANITY, PREACHING.

GOSSIP

Truth is not exciting enough to those who depend on the characters and lives of their neighbors for all their amusement.

George Bancroft

In private life I never knew any one interfere with other people's disputes but that he heartily repented of it.

Thomas Carlyle

Gossip is the henchman of rumor and scandal.

Octave Feuillet

To report what has been told in confidence and to add a few embellishments is a common human frailty and it is not new. . . . Perhaps the politician's "No Comment" is not enlightening, but it is often safe and sane.

McIlyar Hamilton Lichliter

I hold it to be a fact, that if all persons knew what each said of the other, there would not be four friends in the world.

Blaise Pascal

Let the greatest part of the news thou hearest be the least part of what thou believest, lest the greatest part of what thou believest be the least part of what is true. Where lies are easily admitted, the father of lies will not easily be kept out.

Francis Quarles

Tale bearers are just as bad as tale makers.

Richard Brinsley Sheridan

There is a set of malicious, prating, prudent gossips, both male and female, who murder characters to kill time; and will rob a young fellow of his good name before he has years to know the value of it.

Richard Brinsley Sheridan

Gossip is the art of saying nothing in a way that leaves practically nothing unsaid.

Walter Winchell

News-hunters have great leisure, with little thought; much petty ambition to be thought intelligent, without any other pretension than being able to communicate what they have just learned.

Johann Georg von Zimmermann

See also: CALUMNY, DETRACTION, TONGUE.

GOVERNMENT

Few consider how much we are indebted to government, because few can represent how wretched mankind would be without it.

Joseph Addison

It is better for a city to be governed by a good man than even by good laws.

Aristotle

Ideally, government is the means by which all the individual wills are assured complete freedom of moral choice and at the same time prevented from ever clashing.

Wystan Hugh Auden

When any of the four pillars of government, religion, justice, counsel, and treasure, are mainly shaken or weakened, men had need to pray for fair weather.

Francis Bacon

Accountancy—that is government.

Louis Dembitz Brandeis

Government is not an exact science.

Louis Dembitz Brandeis

Government is a contrivance of human wisdom to provide for human *wants*. Men have a right that these wants should be provided for by this wisdom.

Edmund Burke

No government ought to exist for the purpose of checking the prosperity of its people or to allow such a principle in its policy.

Edmund Burke

Society cannot exist unless a controlling power upon will and appetite be placed somewhere; and the less of it there is within, the more there must be without. It is ordained in the eternal constitution of things, that men of intemperate minds cannot be free. Their passions forge their fetters.

Edmund Burke

Government alone cannot meet and master the great social problems of our day. It will take public-interest partnerships of a scope we cannot yet perceive.

Joseph Anthony Califano, Jr.

Though the people support the government, the government should not support the people.

(Stephen) Grover Cleveland

Governments are necessarily continuing concerns. They have to keep going in good times and in bad. They therefore need a wide margin of safety. If taxes and debt are made all the people can bear when times are good, there will be certain disaster when times are bad.

(John) Calvin Coolidge

A government of statesmen or of clerks? Of Humbug or of Humdrum?

Benjamin Disraeli

The greatest of all evils is a weak government.

Benjamin Disraeli

Administrative government is here to stay. It is democracy's way of dealing with the over-complicated social and economic problems of today. . . . It is already clear that if these administrative powers are to be exercised sparingly, enlightened business need only take the lead. And if these powers are to be exercised wisely, enlightened business must work at the round table rather than in the courts. . . . The responsibilities of administrative agencies and of business demand statesmanship on both sides.

William Orville Douglas

We instinctively have greater faith in the counterbalancing effect of many social, philosophic and economic forces than in arbitrary law. We will not accord to the central government unlimited authority, any more than we will bow our necks to the dictates of the uninhibited seekers after personal power in finance, labor or any other field.

Dwight David Eisenhower

The less government we have the better—the fewer laws and the less confided power. The antidote to this abuse of formal government is the influence of private character, the growth of the individual.

Ralph Waldo Emerson

It is a perversion to call that a state of freedom where one class rules to the disadvantage of another. A benevolent despotism may be more tolerable than an intolerant class democracy.

Ralph Tyler Flewelling

We settle things by a majority vote, and the psychological effect of doing that is to create the impression that the majority is probably right. Of course, on any fine issue the majority is sure to be wrong. Think of taking a majority vote on the best music. Jazz would win over Chopin. Or on the best novel. Many cheap scribblers would win over Tolstoy. And any day a prizefight will get a bigger crowd, larger gate receipts and wider newspaper publicity than any new revelation of goodness, truth or beauty could hope to achieve in a century.

Harry Emerson Fosdick

Good government is no substitute for self-government.

Mohandas Karamchand (Mahatma) Gandhi

A government is an instrument of service only in so far as it is based upon the will and consent of the people. It is an instrument of oppression when it enforces submission at the point of the bayonet. Oppression therefore ceases when people cease to fear the bayonet.

Mohandas Karamchand (Mahatma) Gandhi

We get the Government we deserve. When we improve, the Government is also bound to improve.

Mohandas Karamchand (Mahatma) Gandhi

The proper function of a government is to make it easy for the people to do good and difficult for them to do evil.

William Gladstone

The best of all governments is that which teaches us to govern ourselves.

Johann Wolfgang von Goethe

The doctrine of separation of powers, which developed over a period of two millenia, is firmly embedded in the warp and woof of our Constitution.

George L. Hart, Jr.

The partnership between the Federal Government and the states and localities is a partnership which requires that all partners are adequately equipped to fully participate in their responsibilities.

Hubert Horatio Humphrey

The actual achievement of democracy is that it gives a tolerably good time to the underdog. Or, at least, it tries; and it is, I think, for this reason that most of us accept it as our political creed.

Sir James Hopwood Jeans

The Government of this nation can never be any better than the people who work for it, the tools they have, and the people whom they serve.

Lyndon Baines Johnson

Government is an art and a precious obligation; and when it has a job to do, I believe it should do it. And this requires not only great ends but that we propose concrete means of achieving them.

John Fitzgerald Kennedy

You can't run a government solely on a business basis. . . . Government should be human. It should have a heart.

Herbert Henry Lehman

This nation, under God, shall have a new birth of freedom, that government of the people, by the people, for the people, shall not perish from the earth.

Abraham Lincoln

If . . . the people find that they must choose whether they will be represented in an assembly which is incompetent to govern, or whether they will be governed without being represented, . . . they will choose authority, which promises to be paternal, in preference to freedom which threatens to be fratricidal. For large communities cannot do without being governed.

Walter Lippmann

All free governments, whatever their name, are in reality governments by public opinion; and it is on the quality of this public opinion that their prosperity depends.

James Russell Lowell

The principal foundation of all states is in good laws and good arms.

Niccolò Machiavelli

Self-interest is not only a legitimate, but a fundamental cause for national policy: one which needs no cloak of hypocrisy . . . It is vain to expect governments to act continuously on any other ground than national interest.

Alfred Thayer Mahan

The bees got their governmental system settled millions of years ago but the human race is still groping.

Donald Robert Perry (Don) Marquis

He that would govern others, first should be the master of himself, richly endued with depth of understanding and height of knowledge.

Philip Massinger

The creation of constitutional government is a most significant mark of the distrust of human beings in human nature. It signalizes a profound conviction, born of experience, that human beings vested with authority must be restrained by something more potent than their own discretion.

Raymond Moley

We should free the state from the past. Weed it out. Fumigate it. Put it back on the job of serving the present.

Raymond Moley

As rationalism sees it, the world is governed by laws which are accessible to human reason.

Hans Joachim Morgenthau

Before we can have a sound village government, we must have a world government. Families cannot be permanently united with any prospect of a good life together until mankind is united.

Lewis Mumford

The form of government is after all a means to an end; even freedom itself is a means, the end being human well-being, human growth, the ending of poverty and disease and suffering, and the opportunity for every one to live the "good life," physically and mentally.

Jawaharlal Nehru

A government in a democratic society is a reflection of the will of the people and it should continue to be a reflection of this all the time.

Jawaharlal Nehru

Any government has in the last analysis to be justified by the quality of the life which it promotes.

Ralph Barton Perry

Government is only a necessary evil, like other go-carts and crutches. Our need of it shows exactly how far we are still children. All overmuch governing kills the self-help and energy of the governed.

Wendell Phillips

The punishment suffered by the wise who refuse to take part in the government, is to live under the government of bad men.

Plato

For forms of government let fools contest. That which is best administered is best.

Alexander Pope

A king may be a tool, a thing of straw; but if he serves to frighten our enemies, and secure our property, it is well enough; a scarecrow is a thing of straw, but it protects the corn.

Alexander Pope

Men well governed should seek after no other liberty, for there can be no greater liberty than a good government.

Sir Walter Raleigh

In national affairs a million is only a drop in the budget.

Arthur Burton Rascoe

Government owes its birth to the necessity of preventing and repressing the injuries which associated individuals have to fear from one another. It is the sentinel who watches, in order that the common laborer be not disturbed.

Guillaume Thomas François Raynal

The path we will chart is not an easy one. It demands much of those chosen to govern, but also from those who did the choosing, and let there be no mistake about this: we have come to a cross-roads—a time of decision—and the path we follow turns away from any idea that the government and those who serve it are omnipotent. It is a path impossible to follow unless we have faith in the collective wisdom and genius of the people. Along this path government will lead but not rule, listen but not lecture. It is the path of the creative society.

Ronald Reagan

Better the occasional faults of a government that lives in a spirit of charity than the consistent omissions of a government in the ice of its own indifference.

Franklin Delano Roosevelt

A Government can be no better than the public opinion which sustains it.

Franklin Delano Roosevelt

Underlying all the constitutional relationships we talk about is the necessity for standards of honesty, truth and integrity. Our own system of free government cannot operate if those standards are not honored.

Paul Spyros Sarbanes

The culminating point of administration is to know well how much power, great or small, we ought to use in all circumstances.

Charles de Secondat (Baron de Montesquieu)

The deterioration of every government begins almost always by the decay of the principles on which it was founded.

Charles de Secondat (Baron de Montesquieu)

In the course of a long government there is a deterioration by insensible degrees, and it is not possible to retrace one's steps except by an effort.

Charles de Secondat (Baron de Montesquieu)

That is the most perfect government under which a wrong to the humblest is an affront to all.

Solon

The vigorous and growing opposition of organized labor to all schemes of government ownership in industry in one of the most hopeful and encouraging facts in American political life.

John Spargo

The ultimate aim of government is . . . to free every man from fear, that he may live in all possible security. . . . In fact, the true aim of government is liberty.

Baruch (Benedict) Spinoza

I think government should be as small in scope and as local as possible.

Adlai Ewing Stevenson

If I were asked what the greatest danger is today in the conduct of democracy's affairs I suppose I would think first of war—but second, and immediately, of a very different kind of thing—of what seems to me the possibility that we in America are becoming so big, so organized, so institutionalized, so governmentalized—yes, and so standardized—that there is increasing danger that the individual and his precious diversity will be squeezed out completely.

Adlai Ewing Stevenson

It seems to me that government is like a pump, and what it pumps up is just what we are, a fair sample of the intellect, the ethics and the morals of the people, no better, no worse.

Adlai Ewing Stevenson

No matter what theory of the origin of government you adopt, if you follow it out to its legitimate conclusions it will bring you face to face with the moral law.

Henry van Dyke

Government is not mere advice; it is authority, with power to enforce its laws.

George Washington

The very idea of the power and right of the people to establish government presupposes the duty of every individual to obey the established government.

George Washington

While just government protects all in their religious rites, true religion affords government its surest support.

George Washington

It is to self-government, the great principle of popular representation and administration, the system that lets in all to participate in its counsels, that we owe what we are, and what we hope to be.

Daniel Webster

Nothing will ruin the country if the people themselves will undertake its safety; and nothing can save it if they leave that safety in any hands but their own.

Daniel Webster

The acts of governments are transitory while relations between peoples are lasting.

Sumner Welles

The true strength of rulers and empires lies not in armies or emotions, but in the belief of men that they are inflexibly open and truthful and legal. As soon as a government departs from that standard it ceases to be anything more than "the gang in possession," and its days are numbered.

Herbert George Wells

One gauge of the increasing size of the government was the amount of money it spent. From 1947 to 1967 the annual expenses of the government almost quadrupled—from $40 billion in 1947 to about $145 billion in 1967. This meant that, while in 1947 the government spent an average of $280 per year for every man, woman, and child in the United States, in 1967 the government was spending about $725 per year—or over twice as much—for every person in the population.

David Charles Whitney

Only free people can hold their purpose and their honor steady to a common end, and prefer the interest of mankind to any narrow interest of their own.

(Thomas) Woodrow Wilson

See also: AUTHORITY, DEMOCRACY, DEMOCRATIC PARTY, LAW, PARTY, POLITICS, PRESIDENT, REPUBLIC, REPUBLICAN PARTY, STATESMANSHIP.

GRACE

Grace comes into the soul, as the morning sun into the world; first a dawning; then a light; and at last the sun in his full and excellent brightness.

Thomas Adams

"What is grace?" was asked of an old colored man, who, for over forty years, had been a slave. "Grace," he replied, "is what I should call giving something for nothing."

Anonymous

The Christian graces are like perfumes, the more they are pressed, the sweeter they smell; like stars that shine brightest in the dark; like trees which, the more they are shaken, the deeper root they take, and the more fruit they bear.

Francis Beaumont

God appoints our graces to be nurses to other men's weaknesses.

Henry Ward Beecher

You pray for the graces of faith and hope and love; but prayer alone will not bring them. They must be wrought in you through labor and patience and suffering.

Henry Ward Beecher

There is no such way to attain to greater measure of grace as for a man to live up to the little grace he has.

Phillips Brooks

As heat is opposed to cold, and light to darkness, so grace is opposed to sin. Fire and water may as well agree in the same vessel, as grace and sin in the same heart.

Thomas Brooks

As grace is first from God, so it is continually from him, as much as light is all day long from the sun, as well as at first dawn or at sun-rising.

Jonathan Edwards

Grace is but glory begun, and glory is but grace perfected.

Jonathan Edwards

The being of grace must go before the increase of it; for there is no growth without life, and no building without a foundation.

George Lavington

The growth of grace is like the polishing of metals. There is first an opaque surface; by and by you see a spark darting out, then a strong light; till at length it sends back a perfect image of the sun that shines upon it.

Edward Payson

See also: BLESSEDNESS, CHRIST, GOD, GOODNESS.

GRACEFULNESS

A graceful and pleasing figure is a perpetual letter of recommendation.

Francis Bacon

It is graceful in a man to think and speak with propriety, to act with deliberation, and in every occurrence of life to find out and persevere in the truth.

Cicero

How inimitably graceful children are before they learn to dance.

Samuel Taylor Coleridge

All the actions and attitudes of children are graceful because they are the offspring of the moment, without affectation, and free from all pretense.

Henry Fuseli

Gracefulness has been defined to be the outward expression of the inward harmony of the soul.

William Hazlitt

Grace is to the body, what good sense is to the mind.

Duc François de La Rochefoucauld

See also: BEAUTY, CHARM, DELICACY, FASHION, STYLE.

GRAMMAR

Everything bows to success, even grammar.

Victor Marie Hugo

The rights of nations and of kings sink into questions of grammar if grammarians discuss them.

Samuel Johnson

George Moore wrote brilliant English until he discovered grammar.

Oscar Wilde

See also: AUTHORSHIP, BOOK, WRITING.

GRATITUDE

If gratitude is due from children to their earthly parent, how much more is the gratitude of the great family of men due to our father in heaven.

Hosea Ballou

He who remembers the benefits of his parents is too much occupied with his recollections to remember their faults.

Pierre Jean de Béranger

A grateful thought toward heaven is of itself a prayer.

Rudolph Block (Bruno Lessing)

He who receives a benefit should never forget it; he who bestows should never remember it.

Pierre Charron

No metaphysician ever felt the deficiency of language so much as the grateful.

Charles Caleb Colton

Gratitude is a virtue most deified and yet most deserted; it is the ornament of rhetoric and the libel of practical life.

John Wien Forney

Gratitude is one of the least articulate of the emotions, especially when it is deep.

Felix Frankfurter

To the generous mind the heaviest debt is that of gratitude, when it is not in our power to repay it.

Benjamin Franklin

When I find a great deal of gratitude in a poor man, I take it for granted there would be as much generosity if he were rich.

Alexander Pope

Two kinds of gratitude: the sudden kind
We feel for what we take, the larger kind
We feel for what we give.

Edwin Arlington Robinson

Gratitude to God makes even a temporal blessing a taste of heaven.

William Romaine

He enjoys much who is thankful for little; a grateful mind is both a great and a happy mind.

Thomas Secker

Epicurus says, "gratitude is a virtue that has commonly profit annexed to it." And where is the virtue that has not? But still the virtue is to be valued for itself, and not for the profit that attends it.

Seneca

He that urges gratitude pleads the cause both of God and men, for without it we can neither be sociable nor religious.

Seneca

If I only have the will to be grateful, I am so.

Seneca

It is another's fault if he be ungrateful, but it is mine if I do not give. To find one thankful man, I will oblige a great many that are not so.

Seneca

There is as much greatness of mind in acknowledging a good turn, as in doing it.

Seneca

We can be thankful to a friend for a few acres or a little money; and yet for the freedom and command of the whole earth, and for the great benefits of our being, our life, health, and reason, we look upon ourselves as under no obligation.

Seneca

Gratitude to God should be as habitual as the reception of mercies is constant, as ardent as the number of them is great, as devout as the riches of divine grace and goodness is incomprehensible.

Charles Simmons

Our thanks should be as fervent for mercies received, as our petitions for mercies sought.

Charles Simmons

Those who make us happy are always thankful to us for being so; their gratitude is the reward of their benefits.

Anne Sophie Swetchine

From David learn to give thanks for everything. Every furrow in the Book of Psalms is sown with the seeds of thanksgiving.

Jeremy Taylor

The gratitude of place-expectants is a lively sense of future favors.

Horace Walpole

Gratitude is not only the memory but the homage of the heart—rendered to God for his goodness.

Nathaniel Parker Willis

See also: APPRECIATION, THANKFULNESS.

GRAVE

When I look upon the tombs of the great, every motion of envy dies within me; when I read the epitaphs of the beautiful, every inordinate desire goes out.

Joseph Addison

The churchyard is the market-place where all things are rated at their true value, and those who are approaching it talk of the world and its vanities with a wisdom unknown before.

Richard Baxter

We weep over the graves of infants and the little ones taken from us by death; but an early grave may be the shortest way to heaven.

Tryon Edwards

A grave, wherever found, preaches a short and pithy sermon to the soul.

Nathaniel Hawthorne

The grave buries every error, covers every defect, extinguishes every resentment. From its peaceful bosom spring none but fond regrets and tender recollections. Who can look down upon the grave of an enemy, and not feel a compunctious throb that he should have warred with the poor handful of dust that lies moldering before him.

Washington Irving

O how small a portion of earth will hold us when we are dead, who ambitiously seek after the whole world while we are living.

Philip II of Macedonia

Of all the pulpits from which the human voice is ever sent forth, there is none from which it reaches so far as from the grave.

John Ruskin

Only the actions of the just smell sweet and blossom in the dust.

James Shirley

An angel's arm can't snatch me from the grave; legions of angels can't confine me there.

Edward Young

See also: DEATH, END, EPITAPH, FUNERAL.

GRAVITY

Gravity is only the bark of wisdom; but it preserves it.

Confucius

Gravity is the very essence of imposture; it not only mistakes other things, but is apt perpetually to mistake itself.

Anthony Ashley Cooper (Lord Shaftesbury)

Those wanting wit affect gravity, and go by the name of solid men.

John Dryden

There is a gravity which is not austere nor captious, which belongs not to melancholy nor dwells in contraction of heart, but arises from tenderness and hangs on reflection.

Walter Savage Landor

Gravity is a mysterious carriage of the body, invented to cover the defects of the mind.

Duc François de La Rochefoucauld

Too much gravity argues a shallow mind.

Johann Kaspar Lavater

As in a man's life, so in his studies, it is the most beautiful and humane thing in the world so to mingle gravity with pleasure, that the one may not sink into melancholy, nor the other rise up into wantonness.

Pliny the Elder

How can we manage to take those things really seriously whose seriousness depends entirely upon ourselves?

Jean Rostand

There is a care for trifles which proceeds from love and conscience, and which is most holy; and there is a care for trifles which comes of idleness and frivolity, and is most base. And so, also, there is a gravity proceeding from thought, which is most noble, and a gravity proceeding from dullness and mere incapability for enjoyment, which is most base.

John Ruskin

There is a false gravity that is a very ill symptom; and as rivers which run very slowly have always most mud at the bottom, so a solid stiffness in the constant course of a man's life, is the sign of a thick bed of mud at the bottom of his brain.

John Faucit Saville

The very essence of assumed gravity is design, and consequently deceit; a taught trick to gain credit with the world for more sense and knowledge than a man is worth.

Laurence Sterne

Gravity—the body's wisdom to conceal the mind.

Edward Young

See also: EARNESTNESS, SADNESS.

GREAT BRITAIN: *see* ENGLAND.

GREATNESS

A contemplation of God's works, a generous concern for the good of mankind, and the unfeigned exercise of humility—these only, denominate men great and glorious.

Joseph Addison

Men in great place are thrice servants; servants of the sovereign or state, servants of fame, and servants of business; so that they have no freedom, neither in their persons, in their actions, nor in their times. It is a strange desire to seek power over others, and to lose power over a man's self.

Francis Bacon

Greatness lies not in being strong, but in the right using of strength.

Henry Ward Beecher

A really great man is known by three signs—generosity in the design, humanity in the execution, moderation in success.

Otto Eduard Leopold von Bismarck

No man has come to true greatness who has not felt in some degree that his life belongs to his race, and that what God gives him he gives him for mankind.

Phillips Brooks

Those who have in their minds the pattern of greatness recognize this pattern wherever they find it. They belong to the freemasonry of the enlightened, whatever their condition may be or wherever they live.

Van Wyck Brooks

The true test of a great man—that, at least, which must secure his place among the highest order of great men—is, his having been in advance of his age.

Henry Peter Brougham (Lord Brougham)

He is greatest who is most often in men's good thoughts.

Samuel Butler

What millions died that Caesar might be great.

Thomas Campbell

Great men are the commissioned guides of mankind, who rule their fellows.

Thomas Carlyle

The greatest man is he who chooses the right with invincible resolution; who resists the sorest temptations from within and without; who bears the heaviest burdens cheerfully; who is calmest in storms, and most fearless under menace and frowns; and whose reliance on truth, on virtue, and on God, is most unfaltering.

William Ellery Channing

The price of greatness is responsibility.
Sir Winston Leonard Spencer Churchill

Great men undertake great things because they are great; fools, because they think them easy.
Luc de Clapiers (Marquis de Vauvenargues)

Keep away from people who try to belittle your ambitions. Small people always do that, but the really great make you feel that you, too, can become great.

Samuel Langhorne Clemens (Mark Twain)

Great minds must be ready not only to take opportunities, but to make them.

Charles Caleb Colton

Speaking generally, no man appears great to his contemporaries, for the same reason that no man is great to his servants—both know too much of him.

Charles Caleb Colton

Subtract from the great man all that he owes to opportunity, all that he owes to chance, and all that he has gained by the wisdom of his friends and the folly of his enemies, and the giant will often be seen to be a pigmy.

Charles Caleb Colton

Times of general calamity and confusion have ever been productive of the greatest minds. The purest ore is produced from the hottest furnace, and the brightest thunderbolt is elicited from the darkest storms.

Charles Caleb Colton

The truly great consider first, how they may gain the approbation of God; and secondly, that of their own conscience; having done this, they would then willingly conciliate the good opinion of their fellowmen.

Charles Caleb Colton

The man who does his work, any work, conscientiously, must always be in one sense a great man.

Dinah Maria Mulock Craik

A great man may be the personification and type of the epoch for which God destines him, but he is never its creator.

Jean Henri Merle d'Aubigné

Everything great is not always good, but all good things are great.

Demosthenes

It is easy in the world to live after the world's opinion—it is easy in solitude to live after your own; but the great man is he who, in the midst of the world, keeps with perfect sweetness the independence of solitude.

Ralph Waldo Emerson

There never was yet a truly great man that was not at the same time truly virtuous.

Benjamin Franklin

The truly great man is he who would master no one, and one who would be mastered by none.

Kahlil Gibran

The world cannot do without great men, but great men are very troublesome to the world.

Johann Wolfgang von Goethe

Greatness is so often a courteous synonym for great success.

Philip Guedalla

He is great enough that is his own master.

Joseph Hall

Nothing can make a man truly great but being truly good, and partaking of God's holiness.

Matthew Henry

The really great man is endowed with a higher degree of sensitiveness, so that seeing a little sooner and farther than his fellows the coming situations, he can size them up in advance.

Lewis Blaine Hershey

He is great who can do what he wishes; he is wise who wishes to do what he can.

August Wilhelm Iffland

Nothing can be truly great which is not right.

Samuel Johnson

The superiority of some men is merely local. They are great because their associates are little.

Samuel Johnson

Great men lose somewhat of their greatness by being near us; ordinary men gain much.

Walter Savage Landor

Great souls are not those which have less passion and more virtue than common souls, but only those which have greater designs.

Duc François de La Rochefoucauld

However brilliant an action may be, it ought not to pass for great when it is not the result of a great design.

Duc François de La Rochefoucauld

He only is great who has the habits of greatness; who, after performing what none in ten thousand could accomplish, passes on like Samson, and "tells neither father nor mother of it."

Johann Kaspar Lavater

The difference between one man and another is by no means so great as the superstitious crowd supposes. But the same feelings which in ancient Rome produced the apotheosis of a popular emperor, and in modern times the canonization of a devout prelate, lead men to cherish an illusion which furnishes them with something to adore.

Thomas Babington Macaulay

If any man seeks for greatness, let him forget greatness and ask for truth, and he will find both.

Horace Mann

Only the mediocrities of life hide behind the alibi "in conference." The great of this earth are not only simple but accessible.

Isaac Frederick Marcosson

The great men of the earth are but marking stones on the road of humanity; they are the priests of its religion.

Giuseppe Mazzini

Human beings like to make gods of their great men.

Jawaharlal Nehru

No country and no people can rise to greatness unless they have something of the stuff of greatness in them.

Jawaharlal Nehru

Those who are truly great have a message that cannot be confined within a particular country but is for all the world.

Jawaharlal Nehru

Not a day passes over the earth but men and women of no note do great deeds, speak great words, and suffer noble sorrows. Of these obscure heroes, philosophers, and martyrs the greater part will never be known till that hour when many that were great shall be small, and the small great.

Charles Reade

Great men never make bad use of their superiority; they see it, and feel it, and are not less modest. The more they have, the more they know their own deficiencies.

Jean Jacques Rousseau

Great minds, like heaven, are pleased in doing good, though the ungrateful subjects of their favors are barren in return.

Nicholas Rowe

He who comes up to his own idea of greatness, must always have had a very low standard of it in his mind.

John Ruskin

Great is he who enjoys his earthenware as if it were plate, and not less great is the man to whom all his plate is no more than earthenware.

Seneca

He who is great when he falls is great in his prostration, and is no more an object of contempt than when men tread on the ruins of sacred buildings, which men of piety venerate no less than if they stood.

Seneca

In the truly great, virtue governs with a scepter of knowledge and wisdom.

Sir Philip Sidney

There never was any heart truly great and gracious, that was not also tender and compassionate.

Robert South

It is the nature of man to rise to greatness if greatness is expected of him.

John Ernst Steinbeck

The elements of greatness and of popularity have been confused for the reason, most of all, that they are very frequently seen together.

Carl Van Doren

It is to be lamented that great characters are seldom without a blot.

George Washington

A solemn and religious regard to spiritual and eternal things is an indispensable element of all true greatness.

Daniel Webster

High stations tumult, not bliss create. None think the great unhappy, but the great.

Edward Young

See also: DISTINCTION, EMINENCE, FAME, GLORY, HONOR, REPUTATION.

GREECE

Fair Greece! sad relic of departed worth!
Immortal, though no more; though fallen, great!

George Gordon Byron (Lord Byron)

The isles of Greece, the isles of Greece!
    Where burning Sappho loved and sung,
Where grew the arts of war and peace,
    Where Delos rose, and Phoebus sprung!
Eternal summer gilds them yet,
But all, except their sun, is set.

George Gordon Byron (Lord Byron)

When the sceptre shall have passed away from England; when, perhaps, travellers from distant regions shall in vain labor to decipher on some mouldering pedestal the name of our proudest chief; shall hear savage hymns chanted to some misshapen idol, over the ruined dome of our proudest temple; and shall see a single naked fisherman wash his nets in the river of the ten thousand masts; her [Athens'] influence and her glory will still survive, fresh in eternal youth.

Thomas Babington Macaulay

See also: ANTIQUITY, ART, DEMOCRACY, EAST AND WEST, EUROPE, HEBRAISM AND HELLENISM, HISTORY, LITERATURE, NATION, PAST, UNITED, NATIONS.

GREED: see AVARICE.

GRIEF

No grief is so acute but that time ameliorates it.

Cicero

There is no greater grief than to remember days of joy when misery is at hand.

Dante Alighieri

Grief is the agony of an instant; the indulgence of grief the blunder of a life.

Benjamin Disraeli

Great grief makes sacred those upon whom its hand is laid. Joy may elevate, ambition glorify, but only sorrow can consecrate.

Horace Greeley

While grief is fresh, every attempt to divert only irritates. You must wait till it be digested, and then amusement will dissipate the remains of it.

Samuel Johnson

Grief knits two hearts in closer bonds than happiness ever can; common sufferings are far stronger links than common joys.

Alphonse de Lamartine

Well has it been said that there is no grief like the grief which does not speak.

Henry Wadsworth Longfellow

If the internal griefs of every man could be read, written on his forehead, how many who now excite envy, would appear to be objects of pity?

Metastasio

Never does a man know the force that is in him till some mighty affection or grief has humanized the soul.

Frederick William Robertson

Why destroy present happiness by a distant misery which may never come at all, or you may never live to see it? Every substantial grief has twenty shadows, and most of them shadows of your own making.

Sydney Smith

Sorrow's crown of sorrow is remembering happier things.

Alfred, Lord Tennyson

Excess of grief for the dead is madness; for it is an injury to the living, and the dead know it not.

Xenophon

Who fails to grieve when just occasion calls, or grieves too much, deserves not to be blest: inhuman, or effeminate, his heart.

Edward Young

See also: SADNESS, SORROW, TEARS.

GUESS

Guess, if you can, and choose, if you dare.

Pierre Corneille

A woman's guess is much more accurate than a man's certainty.

Rudyard Kipling

The most useful part of wisdom is for a man to give a good guess, what others think of him. It is a dangerous thing to guess partially, and a melancholy thing to guess right.

George Savile (Marquis of Halifax)

Some minds are as little logical or argumentative as nature; they can offer no reason or "guess," but they exhibit the solemn and incontrovertible fact. If a historical question arises, they cause the tombs to be opened.

Henry David Thoreau

See also: SPECULATION, THEORY, WONDER.

GUEST

Every guest hates the others, and the host hates them all.

Albanian Proverb

To what happy accident is it that we owe so unexpected a visit?

Oliver Goldsmith

The first day, a guest; the second, a burden; the third, a pest.

Edouard René Laboulaye

True friendship's laws are by this rule expressed:
Welcome the coming, speed the parting guest.

Alexander Pope

See also: HOSPITALITY, VISITOR.

GUIDANCE

The divine guidance often comes when the horizon is the blackest.

Mohandas Karamchand (Mahatma) Gandhi

He that takes truth for his guide, and duty for his end, may safely trust to God's providence to lead him aright.

Blaise Pascal

That man may safely venture on his way,
Who is so guided that he cannot stray.

Sir Walter Scott

See also: ADVICE, COUNSEL, EDUCATION.

GUILT

The guilty is he who meditates a crime; the punishment is his who lays the plot.

Conte Vittorio Alfieri

Adversity, how blunt are all the arrows of thy quiver in comparison with those of guilt.

Hugh Blair

God hath yoked to guilt, her pale tormentor, misery.

William Cullen Bryant

Guilt is the very nerve of sorrow.

Horace Bushnell

Oh, that pang, where more than madness lies,
The worm that will not sleep, and never dies.

George Gordon Byron (Lord Byron)

To what deep gulfs a single deviation from the track of human duties leads.

George Gordon Byron (Lord Byron)

The greatest incitement to guilt is the hope of sinning with impunity.

Cicero

Fraud and falsehood are his weak and treacherous allies, and he lurks trembling in the dark, dreading every ray of light, lest it should discover him, and give him up to shame and punishment.

Henry Fielding

The guilty mind debases the great image that it wears, and levels us with brutes.

William Havard

Oh, what a state is guilt! how wild, how wretched, when apprehension can form nought but fears, and we distrust security itself.

William Havard

Guilt once harbored in the conscious breast, intimidates the brave, degrades the great.

Samuel Johnson

The consequences of our crimes long survive their commission, and, like the ghosts of the murdered, forever haunt the steps of the malefactor.

Sir Walter Scott

Let wickedness escape, as it may at the bar, it never fails of doing justice upon itself; for every guilty person is his own hangman.

Seneca

Guilt upon the conscience, like rust upon iron, both defiles and consumes it, gnawing and creeping into it, as that does which at last eats out the very heart and substance of the metal.

Robert South

From the body of one guilty deed a thousand ghostly fears and haunting thoughts proceed.

William Wordsworth

Let no man trust the first false step of guilt: it hangs upon a precipice, whose steep descent in lost perdition ends.

Edward Young

See also: CONSCIENCE, CRIME, NEUROSIS, REMORSE, REPENTANCE, SIN.

GUN

Because it appears that we have reached a point in this community where a person is not safe in or out of his home we recommend that consideration be given to the possibility that every person have a firearm, or firearms, in his home.

County Grand Jury, Nashville, Tenn.

Guns will make us powerful; butter will only make us fat.

Hermann Göring

Newspapers and radios proclaim each day the tragic toll of death and injury caused by firearms. An estimated 750,000 Americans have died by this means since 1900—far more than have died at the hands of all our enemies in all the wars we have fought.

Lyndon Baines Johnson

We are long past the point where we can allow an enemy of society to buy and use a weapon of death and disorder—when existing state laws would not even allow the same person to drive a car or vote.

Lyndon Baines Johnson

We cannot control crime without controlling the random and wanton distribution of guns.

Lyndon Baines Johnson

See also: ARMAMENT, ARMS, DEATH, INJURY, VIOLENCE, WAR.

H

HABIT

Habit, if not resisted, soon becomes necessity.

Augustine of Hippo

Habit, if wisely and skillfully formed, becomes truly a second nature; but unskillfully and unmethodically directed, it will be as it were the ape of nature, which imitates nothing to the life, but only clumsily and awkwardly.

Francis Bacon

What a curious phenomenon it is that you can get men to die for the liberty of the world who will not make the little sacrifice that is needed to free themselves from their own individual bondage.

Bruce Barton

Sow an act, and you reap a habit; sow a habit, and you reap a character; sow a character, and you reap a destiny.

George Dana Boardman

If an idiot were to tell you the same story every day for a year, you would end by believing him.

Edmund Burke

Habit is the deepest law of human nature.

Thomas Carlyle

Habit is habit and not to be flung out of the window by any man, but coaxed downstairs a step at a time.

Samuel Langhorne Clemens (Mark Twain)

Man's destined purpose is to conquer old habits, to overcome the evil in him and to restore good to its rightful place.

Mohandas Karamchand (Mahatma) Gandhi

We cannot, in a moment, get rid of habits of a lifetime.

Mohandas Karamchand (Mahatma) Gandhi

The phrases that men hear or repeat continually, end by becoming convictions and ossify the organs of intelligence.

Johann Wolfgang von Goethe

Habit converts luxurious enjoyments into dull and daily necessities.

Aldous Leonard Huxley

The chains of habit are generally too small to be felt until they are too strong to be broken.

Samuel Johnson

Habits work more constantly and with greater force than reason, which, when we have most need of it, is seldom fairly consulted, and more rarely obeyed.

John Locke

Habit is a cable. We weave a thread of it every day, and at last we cannot break it.

Horace Mann

Habits are at first cobwebs, then cables.

Spanish Proverb

Habit is ten times nature.

Arthur Wellesley (First Duke Wellington)

When a man boasts of his bad habits, you may rest assured they are the best he has.

(Thomas) Woodrow Wilson

See also: CUSTOM, FASHION, TRADITION.

HAIR

By common consent gray hairs are a crown of glory; the only object of respect that can never excite envy.

George Bancroft

Hair, 'tis the robe which curious nature weaves to hang upon the head, and to adorn our bodies. When we are born, God doth bestow that garment. When we die, then like a soft and silken canopy it still is over us. In spite of death, our hair grows in the grave, and that alone looks fresh, when all our other beauty is gone.

Thomas Dekker

Beware of her fair locks, for when she winds them round a young man's neck, she will not set him free again.

Johann Wolfgang von Goethe

The hair is the richest ornament of women. Of old, virgins used to wear it loose, except when they were in mourning.

Martin Luther

Soft hair, on which light drops a diadem.

Gerald Massey

Fair tresses man's imperial race ensnare,
And beauty draws us with a single hair.

Alexander Pope

The hairs of age are messengers which bid us to repent and pray. Of death they are the harbingers that do prepare the way.

William Sandys Wright Vaux

The first gray hair is a summons from the Angel of Death.

Yiddish Proverb

See also: BALDNESS, BEARD, FASHION, HIPPIE.

HAND

For through the South the custom still commands
The gentleman to kiss the lady's hands.

George Gordon Byron (Lord Byron)

God looks at pure, not full, hands.

Publilius Syrus

Other parts of the body assist the speaker but the hands speak themselves. By them we ask, promise, invoke, dismiss, threaten, entreat, deprecate. By them we express fear, joy, grief, our doubts, assent, or penitence; we show moderation or profusion, and mark number and time.

Quintilian

The hand is the mind's only perfect vassal; and when, through age or illness, the connection between them is interrupted, there are few more affecting tokens of human decay.

Henry Theodore Tuckerman

See also: HELP, ORATORY, RHETORIC, WOMAN.

HANUKKAH

The Chanukkoh lights originated in an old nature festival, that was observed in winter by certain Jewish groups, in the season when the days begin to lengthen. In time the lights were eventually tied up with Chanukkoh.

Hayyim Schauss

Chanukkoh, today, stands for two ideals: first, for the achievement of religious liberty and, secondly, in the minds of large masses of Jewry, for a revival of a sentiment for the national development of the Jewish people.

Hayyim Schauss

The outstanding Chanukkoh night is that on which the fifth candle is lit, especially for the children. As this is the evening when families gather and the children are given Chanukkoh-money. Special food is served, either pancakes or pudding. The children eat pancakes and count their coins, and consider themselves fortunate.

Hayyim Schauss

See also: PASSOVER, YOM KIPPUR.

HAPPINESS

I have now reigned above fifty years in victory or peace, beloved by my subjects, dreaded by my enemies, and respected by my allies. Riches and honors, power and pleasure, have waited on my call, nor does any earthly blessing appear to have been wanting to my felicity. In this situation, I have diligently numbered the days of pure and genuine happiness which have fallen to my lot; they amount to fourteen. O man, place not thy confidence in this present world!

Abd-er-Rahman III

The true happiness is of a retired nature, and an enemy to pomp and noise; it arises, in the first place, from the enjoyment of one's self; and in the next, from the friendship and conversation of a few select companions; it loves shade and solitude, and naturally haunts groves and fountains, fields and meadows; in short, it feels everything it wants within itself, and receives no addition from multitudes of witnesses and spectators. On the contrary, false happiness loves to be in a crowd, and to draw the eyes of the world upon her. She does not receive satisfaction from the applauses which she gives herself, but from the admiration which she raises in others. She flourishes in courts and palaces, theatres and assemblies, and has no existence but when she is looked upon.

Joseph Addison

Purpose and happiness are not embodied in the mechanism of institutions, but in free men.

Max Ascoli

Happiness consists in the attainment of our desires, and in our having only right desires.

Augustine of Hippo

Happiness sneaks in through a door you didn't know you left open.

John Barrymore

Happiness is not the end of life; character is.

Henry Ward Beecher

Health is the greatest of all possessions; a pale cobbler is better than a sick king.

Isaac Bickerstaffe

Happy the man who, unknown to the world, lives content with himself in some retired nook! whom the love of this nothing called Fame has never intoxicated with its vain smoke: who makes all his pleasure dependent on his liberty action, and gives an account of his leisure to no one but himself.

Nicolas Boileau-Despréaux

The Greeks said grandly in their tragic phrase, "Let no one be called happy till his death"; to which I would add, "Let no one, till his death, be called unhappy."

Elizabeth Barrett Browning

Philosophical happiness is to want little; civil or vulgar happiness is to want much and enjoy much.

Edmund Burke

All who would win joy, must share it; happiness was born a twin.

George Gordon Byron (Lord Byron)

The secret of happiness is renunciation.

Andrew Carnegie

Service to a just cause rewards the worker with more real happiness and satisfaction than any other venture of life.

Carrie Chapman Catt

Happiness is like a sunbeam, which the least shadow intercepts, while adversity is often as the rain of spring.

Chinese Proverb

Happiness can be built only on virtue, and must of necessity have truth for its foundation.

Samuel Taylor Coleridge

Happiness lies, first of all, in health.

George William Curtis

Search for a single, inclusive good is doomed to failure. Such happiness as life is capable of comes from the full participation of all our powers in the endeavor to wrest from each changing situation of experience its own full and unique meaning.

John Dewey

To find out what one is fitted to do and to secure an opportunity to do it is the key to happiness.

John Dewey

The happiest women, like the happiest nations, have no history.

George Eliot (Mary Ann Evans)

There is but one way to tranquillity of mind and happiness; let this, therefore, be always ready at hand with thee, both when thou wakest early in the morning, and all the day long, and when thou goest late to sleep, to account no external things thine own, but commit all these to God.

Epictetus

To be happy is not the purpose of our being, but to deserve happiness.

Immanuel Hermann von Fichte

Happiness makes up in height for what it lacks in length.

Robert Lee Frost

If I may speak of myself, my happy hours have far exceeded, and far exceed, the scanty numbers of the Caliph of Spain; and I shall not scruple to add, that many of them are due to the pleasing labor of composing my history.

Edward Gibbon

Assuredly, all nature informs us that man is born for happiness.

André Gide

He only is happy as well as great who needs neither to obey nor command in order to be something.

Johann Wolfgang von Goethe

We take greater pains to persuade others that we are happy, than in endeavoring to be so ourselves.

Oliver Goldsmith

It is not the possession of good things which brings happiness—it is the ability to enjoy what comes. Happiness is an aptitude.

Bernard Grasset

The happiest life is that which constantly exercises and educates what is best in us.

Philip Gilbert Hamerton

Call no man happy till you know the end of his life. Till then, at most, he can only be counted fortunate.

Herodotus

I am more and more convinced that our happiness or unhappiness depends far more on the way we meet the events of life, than on the nature of those events themselves.

Baron Alexander von Humboldt

Human happiness seems to consist in three ingredients; action, pleasure, and indolence. And though these ingredients ought to be mixed in different proportions, according to the disposition of the person, yet no one ingredient can be entirely wanting without destroying in some measure the relish of the whole composition.

David Hume

Happiness, like every other emotional state, has blindness and insensibility to opposing facts given it as its instinctive weapon for self-protection against disturbance.

William James

That all who are happy, are equally happy, is not true. A peasant and a philosopher may be equally *satisfied*, but not equally *happy*. Happiness consists in the multiplicity of agreeable consciousness. A peasant has not capacity for having equal happiness with a philosopher.

Samuel Johnson

There are as many nights as days, and the one is just as long as the other in the year's course. Even a happy life cannot be without a measure of darkness, and the word "happy" would lose its meaning if it were not balanced by sadness. It is far better to take things as they come along with patience and equanimity.

Carl Gustav Jung

As we are now living in an eternity, the time to be happy is today.

Grenville Kleiser

Seek not happiness too greedily, and be not fearful of unhappiness.

Lao-tzu

Few things are needful to make the wise man happy, but nothing satisfies the fool;—and this is the reason why so many of mankind are miserable.

Duc François de La Rochefoucauld

There is one way of attaining what we may term, if not utter, at least mortal happiness; it is by a sincere and unrelaxing activity for the happiness of others.

Edward G. Bulwer-Lytton (Baron Lytton)

In vain do they talk of happiness who never subdued an impulse in obedience to a principle. He who never sacrificed a present to a future good, or a personal to a general one, can speak of happiness only as the blind do of colors.

Horace Mann

No man is happy who does not think himself so.

Marcus Aurelius

Best trust the happy moments. What they gave makes man less fearful of the certain grave and gives his work compassion and new eyes, the days that make us happy make us wise.

John Masefield

Pain and suffering do not ennoble the human spirit. Pain and suffering breed meanness, bitterness, cruelty. It is only happiness that ennobles.

(William) Somerset Maugham

There is no record in history of a happy philosopher: they exist only in romantic legends.

Henry Louis Mencken

Happiness, after all, is an inner state of mind. It is little dependent on outside environment. Happiness has very little to do, for instance, with whether you are rich or not rich. Some of the most miserable persons I have come across in my life are the rich people. It is true that poverty makes one miserable in a very acute way. But my point is that it is not wealth but co-ordination of one's thought and action which removes inner conflicts. It is in that way that integration of personality is achieved.

Jawaharlal Nehru

Happiness is the harvest of a quiet eye.

Austin O'Malley

The foolish man seeks happiness in the distance, the wise grows it under his feet.

James Oppenheim

Happiness is neither within us only, or without us; it is the union of ourselves with God.

Blaise Pascal

Real happiness is not dependent on external things. The pond is fed from within. The kind of happiness that stays with you is the happiness that springs from inward thoughts and emotions. You must cultivate your mind if you wish to achieve enduring happiness. You must furnish your mind with interesting thoughts and ideas. For an empty mind seeks pleasure as a substitute for happiness.

William Lyon Phelps

Do not speak of your happiness to one less fortunate than yourself.

Plutarch

Reason's whole pleasure, all the joys of sense, lie in three words, health, peace, and competence.

Alexander Pope

A man thinks himself happy when he thinks he has set his course toward what he thinks he loves.

Jean Rostand

I accept life unconditionally. . . . Most people ask for happiness on condition. Happiness can only be felt if you don't set any condition.

Artur Rubinstein

Happiness is not a station you arrive at, but a manner of traveling.

Margaret Lee Runbeck

Contempt for happiness is usually contempt for other people's happiness, and is an elegant disguise for hatred of the human race.

Bertrand Arthur William Russell

If there were in the world today any large number of people who desired their own happiness more than they desired the unhappiness of others, we could have a paradise in a few years.

Bertrand Arthur William Russell

The secret of happiness is this: let your interests be as wide as possible, and let your reactions to the things and persons that interest you be as far as possible friendly rather than hostile.

Bertrand Arthur William Russell

Happiness is the only sanction of life; where happiness fails, existence remains a mad and lamentable experiment.

George Santayana

The greatest happiness you can have is knowing that you do not necessarily require happiness.

William Saroyan

True happiness renders men kind and sensible; and that happiness is always shared with others.

Charles de Secondat (Baron de Montesquieu)

The true felicity of life is to be free from anxieties and perturbations; to understand and do our duties to God and man, and to enjoy the present without any serious dependence on the future.

Seneca

This is the true joy of life—the being used for a purpose recognized by yourself as a mighty one, the being thoroughly worn out before you are thrown to the scrap-heap; the being a force of nature instead of a feverish, selfish clod of ailments and grievances.

George Bernard Shaw

Happiness is essentially a state of going somewhere, wholeheartedly, one-directionally, without regret or reservation.

William Herbert Sheldon

Happiness is a wine of the rarest vintage, and seems insipid to a vulgar taste.

Logan Pearsall Smith

The haunts of happiness are varied, but I have more often found her among little children, home firesides, and country houses than anywhere else.

Sydney Smith

Objects we ardently pursue bring little happiness when gained; most of our pleasures come from unexpected sources.

Herbert Spencer

Bliss *is* virtue, not its reward.
Baruch (Benedict) Spinoza

The habit of being happy enables one to be freed, or largely freed, from the domination of outward conditions.
Robert Louis Balfour Stevenson

Happiness is possible even in pain and suffering. But pleasure alone can never create happiness.
Paul Tillich

You never see the stock called Happiness quoted on the exchange.
Henry van Dyke

Happiness is no laughing matter.
Richard Whately

What is happiness, anyhow? Is this one of its hours—so impalpable—a mere breath, an evanescent tinge? I am not sure—so let me give myself the benefit of the doubt. Hast Thou, pellucid, in Thy azure depths, medicine for case like mine?
Walt (Walter) Whitman

See also: CONTENTMENT, ENJOYMENT, JOY.

HARDSHIP

He who has battled with poverty and hard toil will be found stronger and more expert than he who could stay at home from the battle, concealed among the provision wagons, or unwatchfully abiding by the stuff.
Thomas Carlyle

It is not helps, but obstacles, not facilities but difficulties, that make men.
William Mathews

Kites rise against, not with the wind. No man ever worked his passage anywhere in a dead calm.
John Neal

Ability and necessity dwell near each other.
Pythagoras

See also: ADVERSITY, DIFFICULTY, LOSS, MISERY, POVERTY, TRIALS, TROUBLE.

HARLOT

The Harlot's cry from Street to Street
Shall weave Old England's winding Sheet.
William Blake

The harlot does not know how to love; she knows only how to ensnare. Her kiss is poisonous and her mouth is a pernicious drug.
John Chrysostom

She weaves the winding-sheet of souls, and lays them in the urn of everlasting death.
Robert Pollok

Phryne had talents for mankind;
Open she was and unconfin'd,
    Like some free port of trade.
Alexander Pope

See also: LICENTIOUSNESS, SENSUALITY, VICE.

HARMONY

There shall never be one lost good!
    What was, shall live as before;
    The evil is null, is nought, is silence implying sound;
What was good shall be good, with for evil so much good more;
    On the earth the broken arcs; in the heaven, a perfect round.
Robert Browning

From harmony, from heavenly harmony,
    This universal frame began:
    From harmony to harmony
Through all the compass of the notes it ran,
The diapason closing full in Man.
John Dryden

Untwisting all the chains that tie
The hidden soul of harmony.
John Milton

A strong wind arising somewhere creates a cyclone in one place and an anti-cyclone in another. So if harmony is to be achieved by the individual, it has to be supported by same kind of social harmony throughout the world.
Jawaharlal Nehru

Here earth and water seem to strive again;
Not chaos-like together crush'd and bruised,
But, as the world, harmoniously confused;
Where order in variety we see,
And where, though all things differ, all agree.
Alexander Pope

See also: CONSISTENCY, MUSIC, ORDER.

HASTE

The more haste ever the worse speed.
Charles Churchill

No two things differ more than hurry and despatch. Hurry is the mark of a weak mind; despatch of a strong one.

Charles Caleb Colton

No man who is in a hurry is quite civilized.

Will (William James) Durant

Manners require time, and nothing is more vulgar than haste.

Ralph Waldo Emerson

Fraud and deceit are ever in a hurry. Take time for all things. Great haste makes great waste.

Benjamin Franklin

There's absolutely no reason for being rushed along with the rush. Everybody should be free to go very slow. . . . What you want, what you're hanging around in the world waiting for, is for something to occur to you.

Robert Lee Frost

Haste is of the devil.

Koran

Unreasonable haste is the direct road to error.

Molière (Jean Baptiste Poquelin)

Whoever is in a hurry shows that the thing he is about is too big for him. Haste and hurry are very different things.

Philip Dormer Stanhope (Lord Chesterfield)

Rapidity does not always mean progress, and hurry is akin to waste. The old fable of the hare and the tortoise is just as good now, and just as true, as when it was first written.

Charles Augustus Stoddard

Though I am always in haste, I am never in a hurry.

John Wesley

Quickly got, quickly lost.

Yiddish Proverb

See also: DISPATCH, PROMPTNESS.

HATE

Hatred is the vice of narrow souls; they feed it with all their littlenesses, and make it the pretext of base tyrannies.

Honoré de Balzac

Certainly the nationalism of which hatred and vanity are the governing traits has become in the twentieth century a planetary nuisance.

Van Wyck Brooks

Hatred does not cease by hatred, but only by love; this is the eternal rule.

Buddha

Hatred is the madness of the heart.

George Gordon Byron (Lord Byron)

Heaven has no rage like love to hatred turned.

William Congreve

Let us then live happily, not hating those who hate us. In the midst of those who hate us, let us dwell free from hatred.

Dhammapada

There are glances of hatred that stab, and raise no cry of murder.

George Eliot (Mary Ann Evans)

Hating people is like burning down your own house to get rid of a rat.

Harry Emerson Fosdick

Hatred is active, and envy passive dislike; there is but one step from envy to hate.

Johann Wolfgang von Goethe

The passion of hatred is so durable and so inveterate, that the surest prognostic of death in a sick man is a wish for reconciliation.

Jean de La Bruyère

We are grown used to seeing the gate-twisted faces of young persons and adults in news pictures and on television, crying out the most violent threats and expressing a virulence of venom against their country and its authority. All this is a piece of the mosaic of hate that has poisoned this country.

Ralph Emerson McGill

A man who lives, not by what he loves but what he hates, is a sick man.

Archibald MacLeish

It is dangerous and harmful to be guided in our life's course by hatreds and aversions, for they are wasteful of energy and limit and twist the mind and prevent it from perceiving the truth.

Jawaharlal Nehru

Dislike what deserves it, but never hate, for that is of the nature of malice, which is applied to persons, not to things.

William Penn

If you hate your enemies, you will contract such a vicious habit of mind as by degrees will break out upon those who are your friends, or those who are indifferent to you.

Plutarch

I will tell you what to hate. Hate hypocrisy; hate cant; hate intolerance, oppression, injustice, Pharisaism; hate them as Christ hated them—with a deep, abiding, God-like hatred.

Frederick William Robertson

When our hatred is violent, it sinks us even beneath those we hate.

Duc François de La Rochefoucauld

To hate fatigues.

Jean Rostand

A man's hatred of his own condition no more helps to improve it than hatred of other people tends to improve them.

George Santayana

We must stop preaching hatred, stop bringing up new generations to preserve and carry out the lethal fantasies of the old generation, stop believing that the gun or the bomb can solve anything, or that a revolution is any use if it closes doors and limits choices instead of opening both as wide as possible.

Adlai Ewing Stevenson

It is human nature to hate him whom you have injured.

Tacitus

I shall never permit myself to stoop so low as to hate any man.

Booker Taliaferro Washington

See also: ENEMY, JEALOUSY, MALEVOLENCE, MALICE, RESENTMENT, REVENGE.

HEAD

The dome of Thought, the palace of the Soul.

George Gordon Byron (Lord Byron)

A woman's head is always influenced by heart; but a man's heart by his head.

Marguerite Gardiner (Lady Blessington)

The head, truly enlightened, will have a wonderful influence in purifying the heart; and the heart really affected with goodness will much conduce to the directing of the head.

Thomas Sprat

See also: HEART, MIND, THOUGHT.

HEALTH

He who has health, has hope; and he who has hope, has everything.

Arabian Proverb

If you want to know if your brain is flabby feel of your legs.

Bruce Barton

Many a man who would not dream of putting too much pressure in his automobile tires lays a constant overstrain on his heart and arteries.

Bruce Barton

Half the spiritual difficulties that men and women suffer arise from a morbid state of health.

Henry Ward Beecher

To become a thoroughly good man is the best prescription for keeping a sound mind in a sound body.

Francis Bowen

With stupidity and sound digestion man may fret much; but what in these dull unimaginative days are the terrors of conscience to the diseases of the liver.

Thomas Carlyle

Science has shown that health is not a matter of chance, and that, to a large extent, health must come from the kitchen if it comes at all. For this reason, each housewife is personally responsible for the degree of well-being her family enjoys.

Adelle Davis

What a searching preacher of self-command is the varying phenomenon of health.

Ralph Waldo Emerson

Some people think that doctors and nurses can put scrambled eggs back into the shell.

Dorothy Canfield Fisher

Be sober and temperate, and you will be healthy.

Benjamin Franklin

It is health which is real wealth and not pieces of gold and silver.

Mohandas Karamchand (Mahatma) Gandhi

Take care of your health; you have no right to neglect it, and thus become a burden to yourself, and perhaps to others.

William Hall

Health is certainly more valuable than money, because it is by health that money is procured; but thousands and millions are of small avail to alleviate the tortures of the gout, to repair the broken organs of sense, or resuscitate the powers of digestion. Poverty is, indeed, an evil from which we naturally fly; but let us not run from one enemy to another, nor take shelter in the arms of sickness.

Samuel Johnson

To preserve health is a moral and religious duty, for health is the basis of all social virtues. We can no longer be useful when not well.

Samuel Johnson

It is a wearisome disease to preserve health by too strict a regimen.

Duc François de La Rochefouauld

If the mind, that rules the body, ever so far forgets itself as to trample on its slave, the slave is never generous enough to forgive the injury, but will rise and smite the oppressor.

Henry Wadsworth Longfellow

Life is not to live, but to be well.

Martial

Health lies in labor, and there is no royal road to it but through toil.

Wendell Phillips

Health, beauty, vigor, riches, and all the other things called good, operate equally as evils to the vicious and unjust, as they do as benefits to the just.

Plato

Without health life is not life; it is not living life. Without health life is only a state of languor and an image of death.

François Rabelais

The ingredients of health and long life, are great temperance, open air, easy labor, and little care.

Sir Philip Sidney

Regimen is better than physic. Every one should be his own physician. We ought to assist, and not to force nature. Eat with moderation what agrees with your constitution. Nothing is good for the body but what we can digest. What medicine can procure digestion? Exercise. What will recruit strength? Sleep. What will alleviate incurable evils? Patience.

Voltaire (François Marie Arouet)

Look to your health; and if you have it, praise God and value it next to a good conscience; for health is the second blessing that we mortals are capable of—a blessing that money cannot buy; therefore value it, and be thankful for it.

Izaak Walton

Gold that buys health can never be ill spent;
Nor hours laid out in harmless merriment.

Jean Webster

It is the superstition of medicine that is responsible for all the health cults of modern times. You have elevated the desire for health, youth and longevity to the position of a religion.

Stephen Samuel Wise

See also: DISEASE, DOCTOR, MENTAL HEALTH.

HEALTH, MENTAL:
                    see MENTAL HEALTH.

HEART

All our actions take their hue from the complexion of the heart, as landscapes their variety from light.

Francis Bacon

The heart has reasons that reason does not understand.

Jacques Bénigne Bossuet

There is no instinct like that of the heart.

George Gordon Byron (Lord Byron)

The heart seldom feels what the mouth expresses.

Jean Galbert de Campistron

The heart of a wise man should resemble a mirror, which reflects every object without being sullied by any.

Confucius

A loving heart is the truest wisdom.

Charles John Huffam Dickens

The nice, calm, cold thought, which in women shapes itself so rapidly that they hardly know it as thought, should always travel to the lips by way of the heart. It does so in those women whom all love and admire.

Oliver Wendell Holmes

A kind heart is a fountain of gladness, making everything in its vicinity to freshen into smiles.

Washington Irving

It is better to break one's heart than to do nothing with it.

Margaret Kennedy

All who know their own minds, do not know their own hearts.

Duc François de La Rochefoucauld

The human heart is like the millstone in a mill; when you put wheat under it, it turns and grinds the wheat into flour. If you put no wheat in, it still grinds on, but then it is itself it grinds and slowly wears away.

Martin Luther

When the heart speaks, glory itself is an illusion.

Napoleon I (Bonaparte)

The heart of a good man is the sanctuary of God in this world.

Albertine Adrienne Necker de Saussure

The heart is the best logician.

Wendell Phillips

It's impossible to break the heart of a young, beautiful and healthy woman.

Samson Raphaelson

Nothing is less in our power than the heart, and far from commanding we are forced to obey it.

Jean Jacques Rousseau

When the heart is won, the understanding is easily convinced.

Charles Simmons

Men, as well as women, are oftener led by their hearts than their understandings. The way to the heart is through the senses; please the eyes and ears, and the work is half done.

Philip Dormer Stanhope (Lord Chesterfield)

The ways of the heart, like the ways of providence, are mysterious.

Henry Ware

What I am concerned about in this fast-moving world in a time of crises, both in foreign and domestic affairs, is not so much a program as a spirit of approach, not so much a mind as a heart. A program lives today and dies tomorrow. A mind, if it be open, may change with each new day, but the spirit and the heart are as unchanging as the tides.

Owen D. Young

See also: EMOTION, FEELINGS, HEART DISEASE, LOVE, SENSIBILITY, SOUL.

HEART DISEASE

Angina pectoris is a halfhearted disease. People who have it aren't sick enough to go to bed, yet they aren't well either.

Peter Joseph Steincrohn

A good appetite is often bad medicine for the coronary patient.

Peter Joseph Steincrohn

There are no dramatic short cuts for the coronary patient, but the long road of medical research has led to some hopeful accomplishments.

Peter Joseph Steincrohn

While heart disease is far from being understood by medical men, and while it continues to be a leading cause of death, especially in the United States, much progress is being made and there is great hope for the future.

Peter Joseph Steincrohn

See also: DISEASE, HEALTH, SMOKING.

HEAVEN

It is heaven upon earth to have a man's mind move in charity, rest in providence, and turn upon the poles of truth.

Francis Bacon

To appreciate heaven well 'tis good for a man to have some fifteen minutes of hell.

William Carleton

What a man misses mostly in heaven is company.

Samuel Langhorne Clemens (Mark Twain)

Great Spirit, give to me a heaven not so large as yours but large enough for me.

Emily Elizabeth Dickinson

"Do you think we shall know each other in heaven?" said one friend to another. "Yes," was the answer. "Do you think we shall be greater fools there than here?"

Augusta Jane Evans

I would not give one moment of heaven for all the joy and riches of the world, even if it lasted for thousands and thousands of year.

Martin Luther

Heaven to me's a fair blue stretch of sky, earth's just a dusty road.

John Masefield

Earth has no sorrow that heaven cannot heal.

Thomas Moore

If I ever reach heaven I expect to find three wonders there: first, to meet some I had not thought to see there; second, to miss some I had expected to see there; and third, the greatest wonder of all, to find myself there.

John Newton

Heav'n is but the vision of fullfill'd desire. And hell the shadow from a soul on fire.

Omar Khayyám

Heaven must be in me before I can be in heaven.

Charles Stanford

Better limp all the way to heaven than not get there at all.

William Ashley (Billy) Sunday

No man will go to heaven when he dies who has not sent his heart thither while he lives. Our greatest security is to be derived from duty, and our only confidence from the mercy of God through Jesus Christ.

Daniel Wilson

See also: FUTURE STATE, HELL, PARADISE.

HEBRAISM AND HELLENISM

The wisdom of the Greeks, when compared to that of the Jews, is absolutely bestial; for apart from God there can be no wisdom, nor any understanding and insight.

Martin Luther

When Socrates and Plato began to speak of truth and justice, they were no longer Greeks, but Jews.

Friedrich Wilhelm Nietzsche

The Greek grasped the present moment, and was the artist; the Jew worshipped the timeless spirit, and was the prophet.

Isaac Mayer Wise

See also: GREECE, HEBREW, JEW, JUDAISM.

HEBREW

The Hebrews have done more to civilize men than any other nation. If I were an atheist, and believed in blind eternal fate, I should still believe that fate had ordained the Jews to be the most essential instrument for civilizing the nations.

John Adams

Hebrew idioms run into the English tongue with a particular grace and beauty. . . . They give a force and energy to our expressions, warm and animate our language, and convey our thoughts in most ardent and intense phrases than any that are to be met with in our own tongue.

Joseph Addison

How came they here? What burst of Christian hate,
  What persecution, merciless and blind,
Drove o'er the sea—that desert desolate—
  These Ishmaels and Hagars of mankind?

Henry Wadsworth Longfellow

The words of the Hebrew tongue have a peculiar energy. It is impossible to convey so much so briefly in any other language.

Martin Luther

See also: HEBRAISM AND HELLENISM, JEW.

HELL

Hell is truth seen too late—duty neglected in its season.

Tryon Edwards

What is hell? Hell is oneself,
Hell is alone, the other figures in it
Merely projections. There is nothing to escape
  from
And nothing to escape to. One is always
  alone.

Thomas Stearns Eliot

Hell is full of good meanings and wishings.

George Herbert

Men might go to heaven with half the labor they put forth to go to hell, if they would but venture their industry in the right way.

Ben (Benjamin) Jonson

When the world dissolves, all places will be hell that are not heaven.

Christopher Marlowe

The mind is its own place, and in itself can make a heaven of hell, a hell of heaven.

John Milton

Hell is as ubiquitous as condemning conscience.

Frederick William Robertson

One path leads to paradise, but a thousand to hell.

Yiddish Proverb

See also: DEVIL, HEAVEN, PUNISHMENT, SIN.

HELP

Help thyself and God will help thee.

George Herbert

Light is the task where many share the toil.

Homer

When a person is down in the world, an ounce of help is better than a pound of preaching.

Edward G. Bulwer-Lytton (Baron Lytton)

Nothing makes one feel so strong as a call for help.

George MacDonald

God helps them that help themselves.

Proverb

See also: BENEFICENCE, CHARITY, GENEROSITY, PHILANTHROPY, WELL-DOING.

HEREDITY

Heredity is an omnibus in which all our ancestors ride, and every now and then one of them puts his head out and embarrasses us.

Oliver Wendell Holmes

It is not only what we have inherited from our fathers that exists again in us, but all sorts of old dead ideas and all kinds of old dead beliefs. . . . They are not actually alive in us; but there they are dormant, all the same, and we can never be rid of them. Whenever I take up a newspaper and read

it, I fancy I see ghosts creeping between the lines. There must be ghosts all over the world.

Henrik Ibsen

Several matters of profound importance have already become clear: bacteria or fruit fly, mouse or man, the chemical nature of the hereditary material is universally the same; the main pattern of hereditary transmission of traits is the same for all forms of life reproducing sexually; and the nature of the effects of high-energy radiations upon the genetic material is likewise universally the same in principle [Genetics Committee].

National Academy of Science

See also: BIRTH, ENVIRONMENT, PARENT.

HERO

Unbounded courage and compassion joined proclaim him good and great, and make the hero and the man complete.

Joseph Addison

The world's battlefields have been in the heart chiefly; more heroism has been displayed in the household and the closet, than on the most memorable battlefields of history.

Henry Ward Beecher

Let us so bear ourselves that if the British Commonwealth lasts for a thousand years, men will still say, "This was their finest hour."

Sir Winston Leonard Spencer Churchill

Heroes in history seem to us poetic because they are there. But if we should tell the simple truth of some of our neighbors, it would sound like poetry.

George William Curtis

To believe in the heroic makes heroes.

Benjamin Disraeli

Mankind is not disposed to look narrowly into the conduct of great victors when their victory is on the right side.

George Eliot (Mary Ann Evans)

Self-trust is the essence of heroism.

Ralph Waldo Emerson

Nobody, they say, is a hero to his valet. Of course not; for one must be a hero to understand a hero. The valet, I dare say, has great respect for some person of his own stamp.

Johann Wolfgang von Goethe

The greatest obstacle to being heroic is the doubt whether one may not be going to prove one's self a fool. The truest heroism is to resist the doubt; and the profoundest wisdom to know when it ought to be resisted and when obeyed.

Nathaniel Hawthorne

When the will defies fear, when duty throws the gauntlet down to fate, when honor scorns to compromise with death—this is heroism.

Robert Green Ingersoll

There is only one gift sufficient to honor [heroes] . . ., namely the assurance to every man in uniform "that their cause is a good cause."

Lyndon Baines Johnson

The heroes of literary history have been no less remarkable for what they have suffered, than for what they have achieved.

Samuel Johnson

The impartiality of history is not that of the mirror, which merely reflects objects but of the judge who sees, listens, and decides.

Alphonse de Lamartine

There are heroes in evil as well as in good.

Duc François de La Rochefoucauld

The hero is a man who has fought impressively for a cause of which we approve.

Dumas Malone

Worship your heroes from afar; contact withers them.

Albertine Adrienne Necker de Saussure

Ordinary men and women are not usually heroic. They think of their daily bread and butter, of their children, of their household worries and the like. But a time comes when a whole people become full of faith for a great cause, and then even simple, ordinary men and women become heroes, and history becomes stirring and epoch-making. Great leaders have something in them which inspires a whole people and makes them do great deeds.

Jawaharlal Nehru

Heroes are not known by the loftiness of their carriage; the greatest braggarts are generally the merest cowards.

Jean Jacques Rousseau

Take away ambition and vanity, and where will be your heroes and patriots?

Seneca

A light supper, a good night's sleep, and a fine morning have sometimes made a hero of the same man who, by an indigestion, a restless night, and rainy morning would have proved a coward.

Philip Dormer Stanhope (Lord Chesterfield)

See also: BRAVERY, COURAGE, FORTITUDE.

HINDUISM

Hinduism believes in the oneness not of merely all human life, but in the oneness of all that lives.

Mohandas Karamchand (Mahatma) Gandhi

Hinduism is the most tolerant of all religions.

Mohandas Karamchand (Mahatma) Gandhi

Hinduism, as a faith, is vague, amorphous, many-sided, all things to all men. It is hardly possible to define it, or indeed to say definitely whether it is a religion or not, in the usual sense of the word. In its present form, and even in the past, it embraces many beliefs and practices, from the highest to the lowest, often opposed to or contradicting each other. Its essential spirit seems to be to live and let live.

Jawaharlal Nehru

The word "Hindu" does not occur at all in our ancient literature. The first reference to it in an Indian book is, I am told, in a Tantrik work of the eighth century A.C., where "Hindu" means a people and not the followers of a particular religion.

Jawaharlal Nehru

See also: BELIEF, FAITH, INDIA, RELIGION.

HIPPIE

This alliance between hippies and political radicals is bound to break up. There's just too big a jump from the slogan of "Flower Power" to the deadly realm of politics.

Steve Decanio

There is, of course, a low as well as a high side to the hippie phenomenon. . . . seriously disturbed people and teen-age runaways make up a sizable fringe of the Movement. Equally unsettling is the incipient anti-intellectualism of the hippies—to say nothing of the dangers of drug-taking. The hippie's euphoria is too often bought at the price of his intellectual and critical faculties. Indeed, the hippie's life is so lacking in competitive tension and tangible goals that it risks an overpowering boredom.

Newsweek

They smile and call themselves a new race. They want to change the United States from within—by means of a vague regimen of all-embracing love. They are nonviolent, mystical, bizarre. Psychedelic drugs are their Nirvana, a euphoric disdain for anything "square" is their most common bond. Like the beatniks of the '50s, they are in the long tradition of Bohemia: seeking a vision of the totally free life. They are, of course, the hippies.

Newsweek

These days we are all asking ourselves what has gotten into our young people. The answer to that depends on whether you are an optimist or a pessimist. I do not have any figures on the total population of hippies in the United States, but I do believe that their presence is more than offset by the good work that our 12,000 Peace Corps volunteers are doing abroad.

Benjamin S. Rosenthal

Society seems fascinated by the hippies, but isn't quite sure it approves of all the things they do, like blowing grass, and making love, and thumbing their noses at society. Hippie artifacts that have been appropriated often have to be cleaned up a bit for mass consumption.

David Sanford

The flourishing hippy scene is a matter of desperate concern to the political activists. They see a whole generation of rebels drifting off to a drugged limbo, ready to accept almost anything as long as it comes with enough "soma."

Hunter S. Thompson

The word "hip" translates roughly as "wise" or "tuned-in." A hippy is somebody who "knows" what's really happening, and who adjusts or grooves with it.

Hunter S. Thompson

See also: ADOLESCENCE, AGE AND YOUTH, DISSENT, DRUGS, HAIR.

HISTORY

Neither history nor economics can be intelligently studied without a constant reference to the geographical surroundings which have affected different nations.

Henry Brooks Adams

There is nothing that solidifies and strengthens a nation like reading the nation's history, whether that history is recorded in books, or embodied in customs, institutions, and monuments.

Joseph Anderson

It often happens that only from the words of a good story-teller do we realize what we have done and what we have missed, and what we should have done and what we shouldn't have. It is perhaps in these stories, oral and written, that the true history of mankind can be found and that through them one can perhaps sense if not fully know the meaning of that history.

Ivo Andrić

Out of monuments, names, words, proverbs, traditions, private records and evidences, fragments of stories, passages of books, and the like, we do save and recover somewhat from the deluge of time.

Francis Bacon

The history of America is just one gigantic land exploitation . . . and very few people realize that this creates exactly the conditions which make individuals—in desperation—turn to socialism and communism.

Ralph Borsodi

An age is a chaos while one is living in it, and the past would be a chaos also if it were not interpreted for us. . . . To generalize about the present is therefore a hazardous undertaking although we are compelled to undertake it.

Van Wyck Brooks

History gives us a kind of chart, and we dare not surrender even a small rushlight in the darkness. The hasty reformer who does not remember the past will find himself condemned to repeat it.

Sir John Buchan

History is the essence of innumerable biographies.

Thomas Carlyle

Grecian history is a poem; Latin history, a picture; modern history a chronicle.

Vicomte François René de Chateaubriand

Not to know what has been transacted in former times is to be always a child. If no use is made of the labors of past ages, the world must remain always in the infancy of knowledge.

Cicero

If men could learn from history, what lessons it might teach us! But passion and party blind our eyes, and the light which experience gives is a lantern on the stern which shines only on the waves behind us.

Samuel Taylor Coleridge

The more we know of history, the less shall we esteem the subjects of it; and to despise our species is the price we must too often pay for our knowledge of it.

Charles Caleb Colton

What are all histories but God manifesting himself, shaking down and trampling under foot whatsoever he hath not planted.

Oliver Cromwell

We find but few historians who have been diligent enough in their search for truth. It is their common method to take on trust what they distribute to the public; by which means, a falsehood, once received from a famed writer, becomes traditional to posterity.

John Dryden

Truth is very liable to be left-handed in history.

Alexandre Dumas (père)

History has for its object the singular results arising from the passions and caprices of men, and exhibits a succession of such strange events that in ancient times they imagined a blind and crazed divinity had the direction of the affairs of the world.

Bernard Le Bovier de Fontenelle

In history, what we consider causes are really consequences—consequences of causes that lie beyond history. The true course of history does not consist of events.

Egon Friedell

History is a voice forever sounding across the centuries the laws of right and wrong. Opinions alter, manners change, creeds rise and fall, but the moral law is written on the tablets of eternity.

James Anthony Froude

History is little more than the register of the crimes, follies, and misfortunes of mankind.

Edward Gibbon

The best thing which we derive from history is the enthusiasm that it raises in us.

Johann Wolfgang von Goethe

History is fine, but a country should not live in its past or off its past glories.

Edward Heath

History is the glass through which we may behold, with ancestral eyes, not only the various deeds of past ages and the old accidents that attend them, but also discern the different humors of men.

Jeremiah Brown Howell

History is but a kind of Newgate calendar, a register of the crimes and miseries that man has inflicted on his fellow-man.

Washington Irving

The present state of things is the consequence of the past; and it is natural to inquire as to the sources of the good we enjoy or the evils we suffer. If we act only for ourselves, to neglect the study of history is not prudent; if intrusted with the care of others, it is not just.

Samuel Johnson

We must consider how very little history there is; I mean real, authentic history. That certain kings reigned, and certain battles were fought, we can depend on as true; but all the coloring, all the philosophy of history is conjecture.

Samuel Johnson

We live in a moment of history where change is so speeded up that we begin to see the present only when it is disappearing.

Ronald David Laing

History is neither more nor less than biography on a large scale.

Alphonse de Lamartine

History may be read as the story of the magnificent rearguard action fought during several thousand years by dogma against curiosity.

Robert Lynd

He alone reads history aright, who, observing how powerfully circumstances influence the feelings and opinions of men, how often vices pass into virtues, and paradoxes into axioms, learns to distinguish what is accidental and transitory in human nature from what is essential and immutable.

Thomas Babington Macaulay

History has its foreground and its background, and it is principally in the management of its perspective that one artist differs from another. Some events must be represented on a large scale, others diminished; the great majority will be lost in the dimness of the horizon, and a general idea of their joint effect will be given by a few slight touches.

Thomas Babington Macaulay

Our heritage is composed of all the voices that can answer our questions.

André Malraux

The history of mankind is one of continuous development from the realm of necessity to the realm of freedom. This process is never-ending.

Mao Tse-tung

The men who make history, have not time to write it.

Prince Klemens von Metternich

What is history but a fable agreed upon?

Napoleon I (Bonaparte)

Whoever wants to see a brick must look at its pores, and must keep his eye close to it. But whoever wants to see a cathedral cannot see it as he sees a brick. This demands a respect for distance.

José Ortega y Gasset

[Jewish] history encloses the length of all our histories.

Blaise Pascal

We read history through our prejudices.

Wendell Phillips

The Jewish thinkers were the first who sought for a general theory of the progress of our species . . . The Jew, thanks to a kind of prophetic sense which renders the Semite at times marvelously apt to see the great lines of the future, has made history enter into religion.

Joseph Ernest Renan

History must speak for itself. A historian is content if he has been able to shed some light.

William Lawrence Shirer

History makes us some amends for the shortness of life.

Philip Skelton

This I hold to be the chief office of history, to rescue virtuous actions from the oblivion to which a want of records would consign them, and that men should feel a dread of being considered infamous in the opinions of posterity, from their depraved expressions and base actions.

Tacitus

The science of history, the object of which is the self-knowledge of nations and of humanity.

Count Lev (Leo) Nikolaevich Tolstoi

Historians generally illustrate rather than correct the ideas of the communities within which they live and work.

Arnold Joseph Toynbee

"History repeats itself" and "History never repeats itself" are about equally true . . . We never know enough about the infinitely complex circumstances of any past event to prophesy the future by analogy.

George Macaulay Trevelyan

Many historians take pleasure in putting into the mouths of princes what they have neither said nor ought to have said.

Voltaire (François Marie Arouet)

Human history becomes more and more a race between education and catastrophe.

Herbert George Wells

It is a great pity that every human being does not, at an early stage of his life, have to write a historical work. He would then realize that the human race is in quite a jam about truth.

Dame Rebecca West

History can only be understood by seeing it as the theatre of diverse groups of idealists respectively urging ideals incompatible for conjoint realization.

Alfred North Whitehead

History presents the pleasantest features of poetry and fiction—the majesty of the epic, the moving accidents of the drama, and the surprises and moral of the romance.

Robert Eldridge Aris Willmott

See also: ANTIQUITY, BIOGRAPHY, PAST, RUINS.

HOLIDAY

That vague kind of penitence which holidays awaken next morning.
Charles John Huffam Dickens

He took his first holiday in forty years yesterday, and picked out a cemetery plot.
Frank McKinney (Kin) Hubbard

Who first invented work, and bound the free and holiday-rejoicing spirit down?
Charles Lamb

See also: CELEBRATION, FEASTING, LEISURE.

HOLINESS

Holiness is the symmetry of the soul.
Philip Henry

Even the merest gesture is holy if it is filled with faith.
Franz Kafka

A holy life is a voice; it speaks when the tongue is silent, and is either a constant attraction or a perpetual reproof.
Robert Leighton

The essence of true holiness consists in conformity to the nature and will of God.
Samuel Lucas

Holiness consisteth not in a cowl or in a garment of gray. When God purifies the heart by faith, the market is sacred as well as the sanctuary; neither remaineth there any work or place which is profane.
Martin Luther

Not all the pomp and pageantry of worlds reflect such glory on the eye supreme, as the meek virtues of the holy man.
Robert Montgomery

The serene, silent beauty of a holy life is the most powerful influence in the world, next to the might of the Spirit of God.
Blaise Pascal

Holiness is what is loved by all the gods. It is loved because it is holy, and not holy because it is loved.
Plato

See also: GRACE, PIETY, PURITY, REVERENCE.

HOLLAND: *see* NETHERLANDS.

HOME

America's future will be determined by the home and the school. The child becomes largely what it is taught, hence we must watch what we teach it, and how we live before it.
Jane Addams

Eighty per cent of our criminals come from unsympathetic homes.
Hans Christian Andersen

Many a man who pays rent all his life owns his own home; and many a family has successfully saved for a home only to find itself at last with nothing but a house.
Bruce Barton

Without hearts there is no home.
George Gordon Byron (Lord Byron)

A hundred men may make an encampment, but it takes a woman to make a home.
Chinese Proverb

We have comforts that kings might consider luxuries, yet it is real punishment for us to stay at home; we have wealth and occupation, but little of that peace of mind surpassing wealth which the sage finds in meditation.
Joseph Collins

Only the home can found a state.
Joseph Cook

The family circle is the supreme conductor of Christianity.
Henry Drummond

To most men their early home is no more than a memory of their early years. The image is never marred. There's no disappointment in memory, and one's exaggerations are always on the good side.
George Eliot (Mary Ann Evans)

Home is the place where, when you have to go there, they have to take you in.
Robert Lee Frost

Hard indeed, in a world which has come to feel that it is more important to have an automobile to get away from home with, than to have a home which you might like to stay in.
Katharine Fullerton Gerould

He is the happiest, be he king or peasant, who finds peace in his home.

Johann Wolfgang von Goethe

To Adam paradise was home. To the good among his decendants, home is paradise.

Augustus and Julius Hare

A man is always nearest to his good when at home and farthest from it when away.

Josiah Gilbert Holland

It was the policy of the good old gentleman to make his children feel that home was the happiest place in the world; and I value this delicious home-feeling as one of the choicest gifts a parent can bestow.

Washington Irving

To be happy at home is the ultimate aim of all ambition; the end to which every enterprise and labor tends, and of which every desire prompts the prosecution.

Samuel Johnson

Men are free when they are in a living homeland, not when they are straying and breaking away.

David Herbert Lawrence

Home, the spot of earth supremely blest,
A dearer, sweeter spot than all the rest.

Robert Montgomery

A man travels the world over in search of what he needs and returns home to find it.

George Moore

If this world affords true happiness, it is to be found in a home where love and confidence increase with the years, where the necessities of life come without severe strain, where luxuries enter only after their cost has been carefully considered.

Alfred Edward Newton

Be it ever so humble, there's no place like home.

John Howard Payne

Just a wee cot—the cricket's chirr—
Love and the smiling face of her.

James Whitcomb Riley

What is home? A roof to keep out the rain. Four walls to keep out the wind. Floors to keep out the cold. Yes, but home is more than that. It is the laugh of a baby, the song of a mother, the strength of a father.

Warmth of living hearts, light from happy eyes, kindness, loyalty, comradeship. Home is first school and first church for young ones, where they learn what is right, what is good and what is kind. Where they go for comfort when they are hurt or sick. Where joy is shared and sorrow eased. Where fathers and mothers are respected and loved. Where children are wanted. Where the simplest food is good enough for kings because it is earned. Where money is not so important as loving-kindness. Where even the teakettle sings from happiness. That is home. God bless it.

Ernestine Schumann-Heink

There is a magic in that little word, home; it is a mystic circle that surrounds comforts and virtues never known beyond its hallowed limits.

Robert Southey

A dining room table with children's eager, hungry faces around it, ceases to be a mere dining room table, and becomes an altar.

Simeon Strunsky

Every house where love abides and friendship is a guest, is surely home, and home, sweet home; for there the heart can rest.

Henry van Dyke

See also: DOMESTIC, FAMILY, FATHER, HOUSE, MOTHER.

HOMELAND: *see* FATHERLAND.

HONESTY

I had rather starve and rot and keep the privilege of speaking the truth as I see it, than of holding all the offices that capital has to give from the presidency downward.

Henry Brooks Adams

Be so true to thyself as thou be not false to others.

Francis Bacon

He who says there is no such thing as an honest man, is himself a knave.

George Berkeley

Refined policy has ever been the parent of confusion, and ever will be so, as long as the world endures. Plain good intention, which is as easily discovered at the first view as fraud is surely detected at last, is of no mean force in the government of mankind.

Genuine simplicity of heart is a healing and cementing principle.

Edmund Burke

Make yourself an honest man, and then you may be sure there is one rascal less in the world.

Thomas Carlyle

Hope of ill gain is the beginning of loss.

Democritus

Don't place too much confidence in a man who boasts of being as honest as the day is long. Wait until you meet him at night.

Robert Chambers (Bob) Edwards

Honesty is the best policy.

Benjamin Franklin

If he does really think that there is no distinction between virtue and vice, when he leaves our houses let us count our spoons.

Samuel Johnson

Men are able to trust one another, knowing the exact degree of dishonesty they are entitled to expect.

Stephen Butler Leacock

Put it out of the power of truth to give you an ill character. If anybody reports you not to be an honest man let your practice give him the lie.

Marcus Aurelius

A culture which prizes honesty because "honesty is the best policy" is not honest. It is shrewd. And shrewdness is violence become crafty.

Alexander Meiklejohn

All other knowledge is hurtful to him who has not honesty and good-nature.

Michel Eyquem de Montaigne

An honest man's the noblest work of God.

Alexander Pope

It would be an unspeakable advantage, both to the public and private, if men would consider that great truth, that no man is wise or safe, but he that is honest.

Sir Walter Raleigh

If honesty did not exist, we ought to invent it as the best means of getting rich.

Honoré Riqueti (Comte de Mirabeau)

The best standard by which to judge the honesty of nations as well as men is whether they keep their word.

Lewis Baxter Schwellenbach

The shortest and surest way to live with honor in the world, is to be in reality what we would appear to be; and if we observe, we shall find, that all human virtues increase and strengthen themselves by the practice and experience of them.

Socrates

I hope I shall always possess firmness and virtue enough to maintain what I consider the most enviable of all titles, the character of an honest man.

George Washington

"Honesty is the best policy"; but he who acts only on that principle is not an honest man. No one is habitually guided by it in practice. An honest man is always before it, and a knave is generally behind it.

Richard Whately

See also: CANDOR, INTEGRITY, JUSTICE, SINCERITY, TRUTH.

HONOR

Better to die ten thousand deaths than wound my honor.

Joseph Addison

Honor is like the eye, which cannot suffer the least impurity without damage. It is a precious stone, the price of which is lessened by a single flaw.

Jacques Bénigne Bossuet

Our own heart, and not other men's opinion, forms our true honor.

Samuel Taylor Coleridge

Here honor binds me, and I wish to satisfy it.

Pierre Corneille

Woman's honor is nice as ermine; it will not bear a soil.

John Dryden

I would prefer total destruction of myself and my all to purchasing safety at the cost of my manhood.

Mohandas Karamchand (Mahatma) Gandhi

It is any day better to stand erect with a broken and bandaged head than to crawl on one's belly, in order to be able to save one's head.

Mohandas Karamchand (Mahatma) Gandhi

No cost is too heavy for the preservation of one's honour, especially religious honour.

Mohandas Karamchand (Mahatma) Gandhi

Purity is the feminine, truth the masculine of honor.

Augustus and Julius Hare

Hope and faith, however dim they be,
Can turn the grave beneath to paradise.

Micah Joseph Lebensohn

The difference between a moral man and a man of honor is that the latter regrets a discreditable act even when it has worked.

Henry Louis Mencken

No man is ever too old to enjoy fancy regalia, a secret password and a salute.

Louis Nizer

Hereditary honors are a noble and splendid treasure to descendants.

Plato

Let honor be to us as strong an obligation as necessity is to others.

Pliny the Elder

The giving of riches and honors to a wicked man is like giving strong wine to him that hath a fever.

Plutarch

Honor and shame from no condition rise;
Act well your part, there all the honor lies.

Alexander Pope

That nation is worthless that will not, with pleasure, venture all for its honor.

Johann Christoph Friedrich von Schiller

Those who cry out the loudest against the misuse of honor and the vanity of the world, are those who most greedily covet it.

Baruch (Benedict) Spinoza

See also: DISTINCTION, ESTEEM, FAME, GLORY, HONESTY, INTEGRITY.

HOPE

Hope calculates its schemes for a long and durable life; presses forward to imaginary points of bliss; and grasps at impossibilities;

and consequently very often ensnares men into beggary, ruin, and dishonor.

Joseph Addison

Hope is the most beneficial of all the affections, and doth much to the prolongation of life, if it be not too often frustrated; but entertaineth the fancy with an expectation of good.

Francis Bacon

Before you give up hope, turn back and read the attacks that were made upon Lincoln.

Bruce Barton

I live on hope, and that I think do all who come into this world.

Robert Seymour Bridges

Man is, properly speaking, based upon hope; he has no other possession but hope; this world of his is emphatically the place of hope.

Thomas Carlyle

Hope animates the wise, lures the presumptuous and indolent, who rely inconsiderately on its promises.

Luc de Clapiers (Marquis de Vauvenargues)

Hope writes the poetry of the boy, but memory that of the man. Man looks forward with smiles, but backward with sighs. Such is the wise providence of God. The cup of life is sweetness at the brim—the flavor is impaired as we drink deeper, and the dregs are made bitter that we may not struggle when it is taken from our lips.

Ralph Waldo Emerson

He that lives on hopes will die fasting.

Benjamin Franklin

When every hope is gone, "when helpers fail and comforts flee," I find that help arrives somehow, from I know not where. Supplication, worship, prayer are no superstitions; they are acts more real than the acts of eating, drinking, sitting or walking. It is no exaggeration to say that they alone are real, all else is unreal.

Mohandas Karamchand (Mahatma) Gandhi

In all things it is better to hope than to despair.

Johann Wolfgang von Goethe

My country owes me nothing. It gave me, as it gives every boy and girl, a chance. It gave me schooling, independence of action, opportunity for service and honor. In no other land could a boy from a country village, without inheritance or influential friends, look forward with unbounded hope.
Herbert Clark Hoover

Hope is a delusion; no hand can grasp a wave or a shadow.
Victor Marie Hugo

A propensity to hope and joy is real riches; one to fear and sorrow, real poverty.
David Hume

Unfortunately many Americans live on the outskirts of hope—some because of their poverty, some because of their color, and all too many because of both. Our task is to help replace their despair with opportunity.
Lyndon Baines Johnson

It is necessary to hope, though hope should be always deluded; for hope itself is happiness, and its frustrations, however frequent, are yet less dreadful than its extinction.
Samuel Johnson

Whatever enlarges hope will also exalt courage.
Samuel Johnson

Where there is no hope, there can be no endeavor.
Samuel Johnson

You cannot put a great hope into a small soul.
Jenkin Lloyd Jones

Each time a man stands for an ideal, or acts to improve the lot of others, or strikes out against injustice, he sends forth a tiny ripple of hope.
Robert Francis Kennedy

The prophet of despair gains a shouting audience. But one who speaks from hope will be heard long after the noise dies down.
John La Farge

We speak of hope; but is not hope only a more gentle name for fear.
Letitia Elizabeth Landon

Hope and fear are inseparable.
Duc François de La Rochefoucauld

Hope, however deceitful, serves at least to lead us to the end of life by an agreeable path.
Duc François de La Rochefoucauld

One must have something to dream of.
Nikolai Lenin

Hope is a necessity for normal life, and the major weapon against the suicide impulse. Hope is not identical with optimism. Optimism is distant from reality; like pessimism, it emphasizes the importance of "I". Hope is modest, humble, selfless; it implies progress; it is an adventure, a going forward—a confident search for a rewarding life.
Karl Augustus Menninger

The worldly hope men set their hearts upon turns ashes—or it prospers; and anon, like snow upon the desert's dusty face, lighting a little hour or two—is gone.
Omar Khayyám

Hope springs eternal in the human breast; Man never is, but always to be blest.
Alexander Pope

Hope is but the dream of those that wake.
Matthew Prior

Hope is brightest when it dawns from fears.
Sir Walter Scott

We do not raise our hands to the void for things beyond hope.
Sir Rabindranath Tagore

The mighty hopes that make us men.
Alfred, Lord Tennyson

Hope is the only good that is common to all men; those who have nothing else possess hope still.
Thales

See also: ANTICIPATION, CONFIDENCE, EXPECTATION, FAITH, TRUST.

HOSPITALITY

If a man be gracious to strangers, it shows that he is a citizen of the world, and his heart is no island, cut off from other islands, but a continent that joins them.
Francis Bacon

It is a true saying that we must eat many measures of salt together to be able to discharge the functions of friendship.
Cicero

Come in the evening, or come in the morning;
Come when you're looked for, or come without warning.

Thomas Osborne Davis

True friendship's laws are by this rule exprest,—
Welcome the coming, speed the parting guest.

Homer

See also: GUEST, KINDNESS, VISITOR, WELCOME.

HOUSE

The house was more covered with mortgages than with paint.

George Ade

Houses are built to live in, more than to look at; therefore let use be preferred before uniformity, except where both may be had.

Francis Bacon

My precept to all who build, is, that the owner should be an ornament to the house, and not the house to the owner.

Cicero

My dwelling was small, and I could hardly entertain an echo in it.

Henry David Thoreau

See also: BUILDING, HOME.

HOUSEKEEPING

I never saw an athletic girl that thought she was strong enough to do indoor work.

Frank McKinney (Kin) Hubbard

Housework displays feminine beauty in its most varied and alluring forms.

Sir Rabindranath Tagore

The ideal voice for radio may be defined as having no substance, no sex, no owner, and a message of importance to every housewife.

Harry Vincent Wade

See also: FAMILY, HOME, HOUSE, WIFE, WORK.

HUMAN NATURE

A man's nature is best perceived in privateness, for there is no affectation; in passion, for that putteth a man out of his precepts; and in a new case or experiment, for there custom leaveth him.

Francis Bacon

When someone asked a [Dublin] judge what remained in his mind, what had most deeply impressed him, during his fifty years in the criminal courts, his answer was, "The goodness of human nature."

Van Wyck Brooks

We have provided for the survival of man against all enemies except his fellow man.

Lyman Lloyd Bryson

Humanity cannot be degraded by humiliation. It is its very character to submit to such things. There is a consanguinity between benevolence and humility. They are virtues of the same stock.

Edmund Burke

It will be very generally found that those who sneer habitually at human nature, and affect to despise it, are among its worst and least pleasant samples.

Charles John Huffam Dickens

However exquisitely human nature may have been described by writers, the true practical system can be learned only in the world.

Henry Fielding

If the beasts had intelligent speech at their command, they would state a case against man that would stagger humanity.

Mohandas Karamchand (Mahatma) Gandhi

A man must arrange his physical and cultural circumstances so that they do not hinder him in his service of humanity, on which all his energies should be concentrated.

Mohandas Karamchand (Mahatma) Gandhi

The great religions have spoken ill of original human nature; but they have never despaired of its possibilities.

William Ernest Hocking

Christianity is the highest perfection of humanity.

Samuel Johnson

A rational nature admits of nothing which is not serviceable to the rest of mankind.

Marcus Aurelius

One must either take interest in the human situation or else parade before the void.

Jean Rostand

I hate Spiders I dislike all kinds of Insects. Their cold intelligence, their empty, stereotyped, unremitted industry repel me. And I am not altogether happy about the future of the Human Race; when I think of the slow refrigeration of the Earth, the Sun's waning, and the ultimate, inevitable collapse of the Solar System, I have grave misgivings.

Logan Pearsall Smith

Human nature is not so much depraved as to hinder us from respecting goodness in others, though we ourselves want it. We love truth too well to resist the charms of sincerity.

Sir Richard Steele

I am a man, and whatever concerns humanity is of interest to me.

Terence

See also: BROTHERHOOD, LIFE, MAN, SOCIETY.

HUMAN RIGHTS: *see* RIGHTS.

HUMILITY

It was pride that changed angels into devils; it is humility that makes men as angels.

Augustine of Hippo

Should you ask me, What is the first thing in religion? I should reply, The first, second, and third thing therein—nay, all—is humility.

Augustine of Hippo

It is no great thing to be humble when you are brought low; but to be humble when you are praised is a great and rare attainment.

Bernard of Clairvaux

Without humility there can be no humanity.

Sir John Buchan

Humility is not a weak and timid quality; it must be carefully distinguished from a groveling spirit. There is such a thing as an honest pride and self-respect. Though we may be servants of all, we should be servile to none.

Edwin Hubbel Chapin

Humility is the root, mother, nurse, foundation, and bond of all virtue.

John Chrysostom

Humility is the solid foundation of all the virtues.

Confucius

True humility is not an abject, groveling, self-despising spirit; it is but a right estimate of ourselves as God sees us.

Tryon Edwards

There are plenty of the well-endowed, thank God. . . . It strikes me as unfair, and even in bad taste, to select a few of them for boundless admiration, attributing superhuman powers of mind and character to them. This has been my fate, and the contrast between the popular estimate of my powers and achievements and the reality is simply grotesque.

Albert Einstein

The street is full of humiliations to the proud.

Ralph Waldo Emerson

After crosses and losses men grow humbler and wiser.

Benjamin Franklin

A humble person is not himself conscious of his humility. Truth and the like perhaps admit of measurement, but not humility. Inborn humility can never remain hidden, and yet the possessor is unaware of its existence.

Mohandas Karamchand (Mahatma) Gandhi

Humility should make the possessor realise that he is as nothing. Directly one imagines oneself to be something, there is egotism. If a man who keeps observances, who is proud of keeping them, will lose much if not all of their value. And a man who is proud of his virtue often becomes a curse to society. Society will not appreciate it, and he himself will fail to reap any benefit from it. Only a little thought will suffice to convince us that all creatures are nothing more than a mere atom in this universe. Our existence as embodied beings is purely momentary; what are a hundred years in eternity? But if we shatter the chains of egotism, and melt into the ocean of humanity, we share its dignity. To feel that we are something is to set up a barrier between God and ourselves; to cease feeling that we are something is to become one with God. A drop in the ocean partakes of the greatness of its parent, although it is unconscious of it, but it is dried up as soon as it enters upon an existence independent of the ocean. We do not exaggerate when we say that life on earth is a mere bubble.

Mohandas Karamchand (Mahatma) Gandhi

Much misconstruction and bitterness are spared to him who thinks naturally upon what he owes to others, rather than on what he ought to expect from them.

Elizabeth de Meulan Guizot

The doctrines of grace humble man without degrading, and exalt without inflating him.

Charles Hodge

Humility is not renunciation of pride but the substitution of one pride for another.

Eric Hoffer

Humility is a state of mind appropriate to perception of the truth of things. A soul that has not attained humility is not prepared to grasp the truth of the world in its fullness.

Jacob Klatzkin

Humility is the altar on which God wishes us to offer sacrifices to Him.

Duc François de La Rochefoucauld

No end of people wish to be pious; but nobody wishes to be humble.

Duc François de La Rochefoucauld

Humility and love are the essence of true religion; the humble formed to adore; the loving to associate with eternal love.

Johann Kaspar Lavater

If thou wouldst find much favor and peace with God and man, be very low in thine own eyes. Forgive thyself little and others much.

Robert Leighton

True humility makes way for Christ, and throws the soul at his feet.

John Mitchell Mason

A humble man can do great things with an uncommon perfection because he is no longer concerned about accidentals, like his own interests and his own reputation, and therefore he no longer needs to waste his efforts in defending them.

Thomas Merton

To be humble to superiors, is duty; to equals, is courtesy; to inferiors, is nobleness; and to all, safety; it being a virtue that, for all its lowliness, commandeth those it stoops to.

Thomas Moore

Let us be a little humble; let us think that the truth may not perhaps be entirely with us. Let us co-operate with others; let us, even when we do not appreciate what others say, respect their views and their ways of life.

Jawaharlal Nehru

Acquire the art of detachment, the virtue of method, and the quality of thoroughness, but above all the grace of humility.

Sir William Osler

Sense shines with a double lustre when set in humility.

William Penn

Epaminondas, finding himself lifted up in the day of his public triumph, the next day went drooping and hanging down his head; and being asked what was the reason of his so great dejection, made answer: "Yesterday I felt myself transported with vainglory, therefore I chastise myself for it to-day."

Plutarch

I believe the first test of a truly great man is his humility.

John Ruskin

The beloved of the Almighty are the rich who have the humility of the poor, and the poor who have the magnanimity of the rich.

Saadi (Muslih-ud-Din)

God walks with the humble; he reveals himself to the lowly; he gives understanding to the little ones; he discloses his meaning to pure minds, but hides his grace from the curious and the proud.

Thomas à Kempis

Humility, like darkness, reveals the heavenly lights.

Henry David Thoreau

True dignity abides with him only, who, in the silent hour of inward thought, can still suspect, and still revere himself, in lowliness of heart.

William Wordsworth

Humility is the first lesson we learn from reflection, and self-distrust the first proof we give of having obtained a knowledge of ourselves.

Johann Georg von Zimmermann

See also: DOCILITY, MEEKNESS, MODESTY, RESIGNATION.

HUMOR

These poor gentlemen endeavor to gain themselves the reputation of wits and humorists by such monstrous conceits as almost qualify them for bedlam; not considering that humor should always lie under the check of reason, and that it requires the direction of the nicest judgment, by so much the more as it indulges itself in the most boundless freedoms.

Joseph Addison

Belief in the general humorousness of the human race is more deep-rooted for that every man is certain that he himself is not without sense of humor.

Sir Max Beerbohm

Humor is falling downstairs if you do it while in the act of warning your wife not to.

Kenneth Bird

True humor springs not more from the head than from the heart. It is not contempt; its essence is love. It issues not in laughter, but in still smiles, which lie far deeper.

Thomas Carlyle

For health and the constant enjoyment of life, give me a keen and ever present sense of humor; it is the next best thing to an abiding faith in providence.

George Barrell Cheever

We love a joke that hands us a pat on the back while it kicks the other fellow down stairs.

Charles Leroy Edson

If I had no sense of humour, I would long ago have committed suicide.

Mohandas Karamchand (Mahatma) Gandhi

Humor is an affirmation of dignity, a declaration of man's superiority to all that befalls him.

Romain Gary

Wit may be a thing of pure imagination, but humor involves sentiment and character. Humor is of a genial quality; dwells in the same character with pathos, and is always mingled with sensibility.

Henry Giles

There is certainly no defence against adverse fortune which is, on the whole, so effectual as an habitual sense of humor.

Thomas Wentworth Storrow Higginson

A man isn't poor if he can still laugh.

Raymond Hitchcock

With the fearful strain that is on me night and day, if I did not laugh I should die.

Abraham Lincoln

Good-humor is goodness and wisdom combined.

Edward R. Bulwer Lytton (Owen Meredith)

You may know many things about humour; you may use it with deadly or uproarious effect; you may enjoy it or earn your bread with it; you may classify it and discover penetrating truths about it. But you still do not know what it is.

George Mikes

The longer I live the more I think of humor as in truth the saving sense.

Jacob August Riis

The world is a perpetual caricature of itself; at every moment it is the mockery and the contradiction of what it is pretending to be. But as it nevertheless intends all the time to be something different and highly dignified, at the next moment it corrects and checks and tries to cover up the absurd thing it was; so that a conventional world, a world of masks, is superimposed on the reality, and passes in every sphere of human interest for the reality itself. Humor is the perception of this illusion, whilst the convention continues to be maintained, as if we had not observed its absurdity.

George Santayana

Good humor isn't a trait of character, it is an art which requires practice.

David Seabury

I live in a constant endeavor to fence against the infirmities of ill-health, and other evils of life, by mirth. I am persuaded that every time a man smiles—but much more so when he laughs—it adds something to this fragment of life.

Laurence Sterne

Good humor is one of the best articles of dress one can wear in society.

William Makepeace Thackeray

Humor is the other side of tragedy. Humor is a serious thing. I like to think of it as one of our greatest and earliest national resources which must be preserved at all costs.

It came over on the Mayflower and we should have it, all of it.

James Grover Thurber

See also: JESTING, LEVITY, RIDICULE, SATIRE, WIT.

HUNGER

Even today, after some hundreds of thousands of years of striving, two thirds of the world's population live in a permanent state of hunger. . . . There is not a single county in South America in which the population is free of hunger.

Josue de Castro

Hunger is the most degrading of adversities; it demonstrates the inability of existing culture to satisfy the most fundamental human necessities, and it always implies society's guilt.

Josue de Castro

Overpopulation does not cause starvation . . . starvation is the cause of overpopulation. . . . Consider that the three countries of the world that are held to be absolutely overpopulated are China, India and Japan; and it appears that the more these places are assailed by starvation the more the number of their inhabitants grows.

Josue de Castro

Our own conception of democracy, no matter how earnestly venerated by ourselves, is of little importance to men whose immediate concern is the preservation of physical life. With famine and starvation the lot of half the world, food is of far more current importance to them than are political ideas. The degree of our sacrifice in feeding the hungry is the degree of our understanding of the world today.

Dwight David Eisenhower

God Himself dare not appear to a hungry man except in the form of bread.

Mohandas Karamchand (Mahatma) Gandhi

Hunger-strike has positively become a plague. On the slightest pretext some people want to resort to hunger-strike.

Mohandas Karamchand (Mahatma) Gandhi

There should be no hunger-strike on any account. Though there are circumstances conceivable in which a hunger-strike may be justified, hunger-strike in order to secure release or redress of grievances is wrong.

Mohandas Karamchand (Mahatma) Gandhi

More than half the people of the world are living in conditions approaching misery. . . . For the first time in history humanity possesses the knowledge and the skill to relieve the suffering of these people.

Harry S Truman

Hunger used to be the silent enemy of man. Starvation used to be the silent way of death. Not any more. Instead of silence, it can mean a resounding roar of violence.

Herbert J. Waters

Hunger does not breed reform; it breeds madness, and all the ugly distempers that make an ordered life impossible.

(Thomas) Woodrow Wilson

See also: APPETITE, DIET, FASTING, POPULATION, POVERTY, TEMPERANCE.

HUSBAND

All husbands are alike, but they have different faces so you can tell them apart.

Anonymous

An archaeologist is the best husband any woman can have: the older she gets, the more interested he is in her.

Agatha Mary Clarissa Christie

A husband's patience atones for all crimes.

Heinrich Heine

With thee goes
Thy husband, him to follow thou art bound;
Where he abides, think there thy native soil.

John Milton

See also: FAMILY, HUSBAND AND WIFE, MARRIAGE, WIFE.

HUSBAND AND WIFE

I must declare with all the power I can command that sensual attraction even between husband and wife in unnatural. Marriage is meant to cleanse the hearts of the couple of sordid passions and take them nearer to God. Lustless love between husband and wife is not possible. Man is not a brute.

Mohandas Karamchand (Mahatma) Gandhi

It is more necessary for a husband to draw closer to his wife when she is about to fall.

Mohandas Karamchand (Mahatma) Gandhi

Practically all problems in the realm of judgment, in the realm of operating a business involving men and women, in the realm of government, whether executive, legislative or judicial, can be handled more efficiently by a man and wife, in our estimation. The American people, in our judgment, if they had sense, would elect a man president and a wife as vice-president.

Bruce Gould

There are only about twenty murders a year in London and not all are serious—some are just husbands killing their wives.

George Horace Hatherill

There is a peculiar beauty about godly old age—the beauty of holiness. Husband and wife who have fought the world side by side, who have made common stock of joy or sorrow, and become aged together, are not unfrequently found curiously alike in personal appearance, in pitch and tone of voice, just as twin pebbles on the beach, exposed to the same tidal influences, are each other's *alter ego.*

Alexander Smith

See also: FAMILY, HUSBAND, MARRIAGE, WIFE.

HYDROGEN BOMB:
            see NUCLEAR WARFARE.

HYPOCRISY

A bad man is worse when he pretends to be a saint.

Francis Bacon

The worst sort of hypocrite and liar is the man who lies to himself in order to feel at ease.

Hilaire Belloc

A man who hides behind the hypocrite is smaller than the hypocrite.

William Edward Biederwolf

Saint abroad and devil at home.

John Bunyan

Hypocrisy is folly. It is much easier, safer, and pleasanter to be the thing which a man aims to appear, than to keep up the appearance of what he is not.

Richard Cecil

If the devil ever laughs, it must be at hypocrites; they are the greatest dupes he has; they serve him better than any others, but receive no wages; nay, what is still more extraordinary, they submit to greater mortifica-

tions to go to hell, than the sincerest Christian to go to heaven.

Charles Caleb Colton

Behavior which appears superficially correct but is intrinsically corrupt always irritates those who see below the surface.

James Bryant Conant

Beware of him those days when he receives communion.

Jacques Du Lorens

No man can, for any considerable time, wear one face to himself, and another to the multitude, without finally getting bewildered as to which is the true one.

Nathaniel Hawthorne

There is some virtue in almost every vice except hypocrisy; and even that, while it is a mockery of virtue, is, at the same time, a compliment to it.

William Hazlitt

We are companions in hypocrisy.

William Dean Howells

The hypocrite shows the excellence of virtue by the necessity he thinks himself under of seeming to be virtuous.

Samuel Johnson

No man is a hypocrite in his pleasures.

Samuel Johnson

Hypocrisy is the homage that vice pays to virtue.

Duc François de La Rochefoucauld

Satan was the first that practised falsehood under saintly show.

John Milton

He who is only good that the world may know it, and because he will be more esteemed in proportion as his goodness is known; he, who will only do good on condition that his virtuous conduct may come under the eyes of men, is one from whom not much advantage can be expected.

Michel Eyquem de Montaigne

An atheist is but a mad ridiculous derider of piety; but a hypocrite makes a sober jest of God and religion; he finds it easier to be upon his knees than to rise to a good action; like an impudent debtor, who goes every day to talk familiarly to his creditor, without ever paying what he owes.

Alexander Pope

In modern society everyone faces in some degree the problem of making his public face the same as his private face.

Adlai Ewing Stevenson

Hypocrisy is much more eligible than open infidelity and vice, it wears the livery of religion, and is cautious of giving scandal.

Jonathan Swift

I hope you have not been leading a double life, pretending to be wicked and being really good all the time. That would be hypocrisy.

Oscar Wilde

See also: AFFECTATION, DECEIT, LYING.

I

IDEA

Ideas in the mind are the transcript of the world; words are the transcript of ideas; and writing and printing are the transcript of words.

Joseph Addison

Our land is not more the recipient of the men of all countries than of their ideas.

George Bancroft

When young men are beginning life, the most important period, it is often said, is that in which their habits are formed. That is a very important period. But the period in which the ideas of the young are formed and adopted is more important still. For the ideal with which you go forth to measure things determines the nature, so far as you are concerned, of everything you meet.

Henry Ward Beecher

Bred to think as well as speak by rote, we furnish our minds, as we furnish our houses, with the fancies of others, and according to the mode and age of our country. We pick up our ideas and notions in common conversation, as in schools.

Henry St. John (Lord Bolingbroke)

A new idea is delicate. It can be killed by a sneer or a yawn; it can be stabbed to death by a quip and worried to death by a frown on the right man's brow.

Charles D. Brower

If you want to get across an idea, wrap it up in a person.

Ralph Bunche

I would swap a whole cartload of precedents any time for one brand new idea.

Luther Burbank

The ideas I stand for are not mine. I borrowed them from Socrates. I swiped them from Chesterfield. I stole them from Jesus. And I put them in a book. If you don't like their rules, whose would you use?

Dale Carnegie

Events are only the shells of ideas; and often it is the fluent thought of ages that is crystallized in a moment by the stroke of a pen or the point of a bayonet.

Edwin Hubbel Chapin

Hang ideas. They are tramps, vagabonds, knocking at the back door of your mind, each taking a little of your substance, each carrying away some crumb of that belief in a few simple notions you must cling to if you want to live decently and would like to die easy.

Joseph Conrad

An idea, like a ghost, according to the common notion of ghosts, must be spoken to a little before it will explain itself.

Charles John Huffam Dickens

Ideas are the roots of creation.

Ernest Dimnet

Man's fear of ideas is probably the greatest dike holding back human knowledge and happiness.

Morris Leopold Ernst

Ideas control the world.

James Abram Garfield

Books won't stay banned. They won't burn. Ideas won't go to jail. In the long run of history, the censor and the inquisitor have always lost. The only sure weapon against bad ideas is better ideas.

Alfred Whitney Griswold

In these days we fight our ideas, and newspapers are our fortresses.

Heinrich Heine

Many ideas grow better when transplanted into another mind than in the one where they sprung up. That which was a weed in one becomes a flower in the other, and a flower again dwindles down to a mere weed by the same change. Healthy growths may become poisonous by falling upon the wrong mental soil, and what seemed a nightshade in one mind unfolds as a morning-glory in the other.

Oliver Wendell Holmes

An idea that is not dangerous is unworthy of being called an idea at all.

Elbert Green Hubbard

No army can withstand the strength of an idea whose time has come.

Victor Marie Hugo

A healthful hunger for a great idea is the beauty and blessedness of life.

Jean Ingelow

An idea, to be suggestive, must come to the individual with the force of a revelation.

William James

Except under the pressure of some enormous event, general ideas filter only slowly into the mind and conscience of democratic societies.

Russell Amos Kirk

An idea isn't responsible for the people who believe in it.

Donald Robert Perry (Don) Marquis

A soul occupied with great ideas best performs small duties.

Harriet Martineau

To die for an idea; it is unquestionably noble. But how much nobler it would be if men died for ideas that were true!

Henry Louis Mencken

Ideas make their way in silence like the waters that, filtering behind the rocks of the Alps, loosen them from the mountains on which they rest.

Jean Henri Merle d'Aubigné

New ideas can be good or bad, just the same as old ones.

Franklin Delano Roosevelt

What we call the contagious force of an idea is the force of the people who have embraced it.

George Santayana

By what strange law of mind is it, that an idea long overlooked, and trodden under foot as a useless stone, suddenly sparkles out in new light as a discovered diamond?

Harriet Elizabeth Beecher Stowe

Ideas, though vivid and real, are often indefinite, and are shy of the close furniture of words.

Martin Farquhar Tupper

Ideas are the factors that lift civilization. They create revolutions. There is more dynamite in an idea than in many bombs.

John Heyl Vincent

Ideas are like beards; men do not have them until they grow up.

Voltaire (François Marie Arouet)

See also: CONTEMPLATION, SPECULATION, THEORY, THOUGHT.

IDEAL

The attainment of an ideal is often the beginning of a disillusion.

Stanley Baldwin

Idealists give invaluable service, they give the distant view, which makes progress, as it makes a walk, exhilarating.

Samuel Augustus Barnett

The life of the young man is his visions, hope of the future, plans of achievement and success for himself.

Arthur Brisbane

Absolute idealism [is] the last, boldest and most grandiose systematic defense of God, immortality and eternal values.

May Brodbeck

The "liberal" of our times has become all too often little more than a sentimentalist "with both feet planted firmly in mid-air."

Louis Bromfield

No ideal is as good as a fact.

Richard Clarke Cabot

Ideals were not archaic things, beautiful and impotent; they were the real sources of power among men.

Willa Sibert Cather

No folly is more costly than the folly of intolerant idealism.

> Sir Winston Leonard Spencer Churchill

It is a welcome symptom in an age which is
commonly denounced as materialistic, that it
makes heroes of men whose goals lie wholly
in the intellectual and moral sphere. This
proves that knowledge and justice are ranked
above wealth and power by a large section
of the human race. . . . This idealistic outlook is particularly prevalent in America,
which is decried as a singularly materialistic
country.

> Albert Einstein

Idealism increases in direct proportion to
one's distance from the problem.

> John Galsworthy

For ideals, too, are roads, not goals; they are
stepping-stones. In their death we live; over
their corpses we climb to dizzier heights.

> Isaac Goldberg

Ideals are the world's masters.

> Josiah Gilbert Holland

Words without actions are the assassins of
idealism.

> Herbert Clark Hoover

Idealism is the noble toga that political gentlemen drape over their will to power.

> Aldous Leonard Huxley

Naturalism seeks to interpret the world by
investigation of origins; idealism by investigation of ends. . . . The one explains the
higher by the lower; the other the lower by
the higher.

> William Ralph Inge

As he [Robert F. Kennedy] said many times,
in many parts of this nation, to those he
touched and who sought to touch him: "Some
men see things as they are and say why. I
dream things that never were and say, why
not?"

> Edward Moore Kennedy

Ideality is only the avant-courier of the
mind, and where that, in a healthy and normal state goes, I hold it to be a prophecy
that realization can follow.

> Horace Mann

Ideals are like the stars: we never reach
them, but like the mariners of the sea, we
chart our course by them.

> Carl Schurz

We build statues of snow, and weep to see
them melt.

> Sir Walter Scott

Ideal beauty is a fugitive which is never located.

> Marquise de Sévigné

See also: AIM, ASPIRATION, CHARACTER, DE-
SIRE, MORALITY.

IDEALISM: see IDEAL.

IDLENESS

Prolonged idleness paralyzes initiative.

> Anonymous

Lost time is never found again.

> John Hill Aughey

If you are idle you are on the way to ruin,
and there are few stopping places upon it. It
is rather a precipice than a road.

> Henry Ward Beecher

Idleness is the enemy of the soul.

> Benedict of Nursia

Idleness is the bane of body and mind, the
nurse of naughtiness, the chief author of all
mischief, one of the seven deadly sins, the
cushion upon which the devil chiefly reposes,
and a great cause not only of melancholy,
but of many other diseases; for the mind is
naturally active; and if it be not occupied
about some honest business, it rushes into
mischief or sinks into melancholy.

> Richard Eugene Burton

In idleness there is perpetual despair.

> Thomas Carlyle

Idleness is an inlet to disorder, and makes
way for licentiousness. People who have
nothing to do are quickly tired of their own
company.

> Jeremy Collier

From its very inaction, idleness ultimately
becomes the most active cause of evil; as a
palsy is more to be dreaded than a fever.
The Turks have a proverb, which says, that
the devil tempts all other men, but that idle
men tempt the devil.

> Charles Caleb Colton

The first external revelations of the dry-rot in men is a tendency to lurk and lounge; to be at street corners without intelligible reason; to be going anywhere when met; to be about many places rather than any; to do nothing tangible but to have an intention of performing a number of tangible duties tomorrow or the day after.

Charles John Huffam Dickens

An idle brain is the devil's workshop.

English Proverb

Troubles spring from idleness, and grievous toils from needless ease: many without labor would live by their own wits only, but they break for want of stock.

Benjamin Franklin

Purity of mind and idleness are incompatible.

Mohandas Karamchand (Mahatma) Gandhi

Laziness grows on people; it begins in cobwebs and ends in iron chains. The more business a man has to do the more he is able to accomplish, for he learns to economize his time.

Sir Matthew Hale

The way to be nothing is to do nothing.

Nathaniel Howe

It is impossible to enjoy idling thoroughly unless one has plenty of work to do.

Jerome Klapka Jerome

To be idle and to be poor have always been reproaches; and therefore every man endeavors with his utmost care to hide his poverty from others, and his idleness from himself.

Samuel Johnson

It is a mistake to imagine, that the violent passions only, such as ambition and love, can triumph over the rest. Idleness, languid as it is, often masters them all; she influences all our designs and actions, and insensibly consumes and destroys both passions and virtues.

Duc François de La Rochefoucauld

In my opinion the want of occupation is no less the plague of society than of solitude. Nothing is so apt to narrow the mind; nothing produces more trifling, silly stories, mischief-making, lies, than being eternally shut up in a room with one another, reduced as the only alternative to be constantly twaddling. When everybody is occupied, we only speak when we have something to say; but when we are doing nothing, we are compelled to be always talking; and of all torments that is the most annoying and the most dangerous.

Jean Jacques Rousseau

Not only is he idle who is doing nothing, but he that might be better employed.

Socrates

It is an undoubted truth that the less one has to do the less time one finds to do it in. One yawns, one procrastinates, one can do it when one will, and, therefore, one seldom does it at all; whereas, those who have a great deal of business must buckle to it; and then they always find time enough to do it.

Philip Dormer Stanhope (Lord Chesterfield)

Satan finds some mischief still for idle hands to do.

Isaac Watts

Many are discontented with the name of idler, who are nevertheless content to do worse than nothing.

Johann Georg von Zimmermann

See also: INDOLENCE, LEISURE, SLOTH.

IDOLATRY

There are four classes of idols which beset men's minds. To these for distinction's sake I have assigned names,—calling the first class *Idols of the Tribe;* the second, *Idols of the Cave;* the third, *Idols of the Market-place;* the fourth, *Idols of the Theater.*

Francis Bacon

We boast our emancipation from many superstitions; but if we have broken any idols, it is through a transfer of idolatry.

Ralph Waldo Emerson

Whatever a man seeks, honours, or exalts more than God, that is the god of his idolatry.

William Bernard Ullathorne

To think that now our life is only drest
For show; mean handy-work of craftsman, cook,
Or groom!—We must run glittering like a brook
In the open sunshine, or we are unblest;

The wealthiest man among us is the best;
No grandeur now in nature or in book
Delights us. Rapine, avarice, expense,
This is idolatry; and these we adore;
Plain living and high thinking are no more.
William Wordsworth

See also: DEVIL, GOD, WORSHIP.

IGNORANCE

To be ignorant of one's ignorance is the malady of ignorance.
Amos Bronson Alcott

Politicians, largely common men themselves, have never learned that it is impossible to underestimate the intelligence of the common man.
Anonymous

It is better to be a beggar than ignorant; for a beggar only wants money, but an ignorant person wants humanity.
Aristippus

The full area of ignorance is not mapped: we are at present only exploring its fringes.
John Desmond Bernal

We must abandon the prevalent belief in the superior wisdom of the ignorant.
Daniel Boorstin

Ignorance is a prolonged infancy, only deprived of its charm.
Marquis Catherine Stanislas de Boufflers

As if anything were so common as ignorance! The multitude of fools is a protection to the wise.
Cicero

Ignorance is the night of the mind, but a night without moon or star.
Confucius

The narrower the mind, the broader the statement.
Proctor Fyffe (Ted) Cook

Genuine ignorance is . . . profitable because it is likely to be accompanied by humility, curiosity, and open-mindedness; whereas ability to repeat catch-phrases, cant terms, familiar propositions, gives the conceit of learning and coats the mind with varnish waterproof to new ideas.
John Dewey

Ignorance of communism, fascism, or any other police-state philosphy is far more dangerous than ignorance of the most virulent disease.
Dwight David Eisenhower

Ignorance is not so damnable as humbug, but when it prescribes pills it may happen to do more harm.
George Eliot (Mary Ann Evans)

Where ignorance is bliss 'tis folly to be wise.
Thomas Gray

A man is never astonished or ashamed that he does not know what another does; but he is surprised at the gross ignorance of the other in not knowing what he knows.
Thomas Chandler Haliburton

Ignorance gives a sort of eternity to prejudice and perpetuity to error.
Robert Hall

The highest reach of human science is the scientific recognition of human ignorance.
Sir William Hamilton

Most ignorance is vincible ignorance. We don't know because we don't want to know.
Aldous Leonard Huxley

In the natural world ignorance is visited as sharply as willful disobedience; incapacity meets the same punishment as crime. Nature's discipline is not even a word and a blow and the blow first, but the blow without the word. It is left for the sufferer to find out why the blow was given.
Thomas Henry Huxley

Ignorance, when voluntary, is criminal, and a man may be properly charged with that evil which he neglected or refused to learn how to prevent.
Samuel Johnson

Ignorance, which in behavior mitigates a fault, is, in literature, a capital offence.
Joseph Joubert

There is a modern delusion, cultivated by the lazy and the arty, that originality is the prerogative of ignorance.
Horace Meyer Kallen

Gross ignorance produces a dogmatic spirit. He who knows nothing, thinks that he can teach others what he has himself just been learning: he who knows much, scarcely believes that what he is saying can be unknown to others, and consequently speaks with more hesitation.

Jean de La Bruyère

Nothing is so dangerous as an ignorant friend; a wise enemy is worth much more.

Jean de La Fontaine

Ignorance is a voluntary misfortune.

Nicholas Ling

The ignorant man always adores what he cannot understand.

Cesare Lombroso

If thou art wise thou knowest thine own ignorance; and thou art ignorant if thou knowest not thyself.

Martin Luther

It is not wisdom but ignorance that teaches men presumption. Genius may sometimes be arrogant, but nothing is so diffident as knowledge.

Edward G. Bulwer-Lytton (Baron Lytton)

The ignorance that knows itself, and judges and condemns itself, is not an absolute ignorance; which to be, it must be ignorant of itself.

Michel Eyquem de Montaigne

Ignorance deprives men of freedom because they do not know what alternatives there are. It is impossible to choose to do what one has never "heard of."

Ralph Barton Perry

It was a man, and not an ostrich, who invented the dictum that "what you don't know won't hurt you." The truth is the precise opposite. Most of what exists is invisible, and the greatest dangers are those which, . . . surprise their victims disarmed as well as ignorant.

Ralph Barton Perry

Do not take the yardstick of your ignorance to measure what the ancients knew and call everything which you do not know lies.

Wendell Phillips

Better be unborn than untaught, for ignorance is the root of misfortune.

Plato

There never was any party, faction, sect, or cabal whatsoever, in which the most ignorant were not the most violent; for a bee is not a busier animal than a blockhead. However, such instruments are, perhaps, necessary; for it may be with states as with clocks, which must have some dead weight hanging at them, to help and regulate the motion of the finer and more useful parts.

Alexander Pope

Everybody is ignorant, only on different subjects.

Will (William Penn Adair) Rogers

A wise man in the company of those who are ignorant, has been compared to a beautiful girl in the company of blind men.

Saadi (Muslih-ud-Din)

Have the courage to be ignorant of a great number of things, in order to avoid the calamity of being ignorant of everything.

Sydney Smith

Any frontal attack on ignorance is bound to fail because the masses are always ready to defend their most precious possession—their ignorance.

Hendrik Willem van Loon

So long as thou art ignorant be not ashamed to learn. Ignorance is the greatest of all infirmities, and, when justified, the chiefest of all follies.

Izaak Walton

It is not the crook in modern business that we fear, but the honest man who doesn't know what he is doing.

Owen D. Young

See also: BLOCKHEAD, DULNESS, FOOL.

ILLNESS: *see* SICKNESS.

ILLS

Think of the ills from which you are exempt, and it will aid you to bear patiently those which now you may suffer.

Richard Cecil

It is better to try to bear the ills we have, than to anticipate those which may never come.

Duc François de La Rochefoucauld

We satisfied ourselves, the other day, that there was no real ill in life except severe

bodily pain; everything else is the child of the imagination, and depends on our thoughts. All other ills find a remedy either from time, or moderation, or strength of mind.
Marquise de Sévigné

We trust, that somehow, good will be the final goal of ill.
Alfred, Lord Tennyson

See also: ADVERSITY, AFFLICTION, CALAMITY, POVERTY, TRIALS, WAR.

ILLUSION

A pleasant illusion is better than a harsh reality.
Christian Nestell Bovee

Nothing is more sad than the death of an illusion.
Arthur Koestler

The loss of our illusions is the only loss from which we never recover.
Marie Louise de la Ramée (Ouida)

In youth we feel richer for every new illusion; in maturer years, for every one we lose.
Anne Sophie Swetchine

See also: DELUSION, FANCY, IMAGINATION.

IMAGINATION

Lack of imagination causes cruelty.
Louis Dembitz Brandeis

We are all of us imaginative in some form or other, for images are the brood of desire.
George Eliot (Mary Ann Evans)

The first of our senses which we should take care never to let rust through disuse is that sixth sense, the imagination . . . I mean the wide-open eye which leads us always to see truth more vividly, to apprehend more broadly, to concern ourselves more deeply, to be, all our life long, sensitive and awake to the powers and responsibilities given to us as human beings.
Christopher Fry

The imagination can be happy in places where the whole man is not.
Katharine Fullerton Gerould

Imagined woes pain none the less.
Heinrich Heine

It is the divine attribute of the imagination, that when the real world is shut out it can create a world for itself, and with a necromantic power can conjure up glorious shapes and forms, and brilliant visions to make solitude populous, and irradiate the gloom of a dungeon.
Washington Irving

No man will be found in whose mind airy notions do not sometimes tyrannize, and force him to hope or fear beyond the limits of sober probability.
Samuel Johnson

Whatever makes the past or future predominate over the present, exalts us in the scale of thinking beings.
Samuel Johnson

He who has imagination without learning has wings and no feet.
Joseph Joubert

Artists treat facts as stimuli for imagination, whereas scientists use imagination to coordinate facts.
Arthur Koestler

Imagination, where it is truly creative, is a faculty, not a quality; its seat is in the higher reason, and it is efficient only as the servant of the will. Imagination, as too often understood, is mere fantasy—the image-making power, common to all who have the gift of dreams.
James Russell Lowell

Solitude is as needful to the imagination as society is wholesome for the character.
James Russell Lowell

Imagination rules the world.
Napoleon I (Bonaparte)

If your imagination is fired by an idea or a problem, then the work that you do will be vital whether you do it as a chief engineer or a small engineer, a mechanic or even as an unskilled labourer. It is sad that imagination counts for so little today and we work in grooves. I suppose too much imagination would lead us astray and we do have to keep our feet on the gound. Nevertheless, too little of it is also a handicap.
Jawaharlal Nehru

Imagination disposes of everything; it creates beauty, justice, and happiness, which are everything in this world.

Blaise Pascal

Often it is just lack of imagination that keeps a man from suffering very much.

Marcel Proust

Imagination ennobles appetites which in themselves are low, and spirtualizes acts which, else, are only animal. But the pleasures which begin in the senses only sensualize.

Frederick William Robertson

The world of reality has its limits; the world of imagination is boundless. Not being able to enlarge the one, let us contract the other; for it is from their difference that all the evils arise which render us unhappy.

Jean Jacques Rousseau

I have often noticed that the suffering which is most difficult, if not impossible, to forgive is unreal, imagined suffering. . . . The worst, most obstinate grievances are imagined ones.

Laurens Van der Post

Of all the mean and feeble things that ever crawled on its belly in the mud, the human imagination is the meanest and feeblest!

Herbert George Wells

The human race built most nobly when limitations were greatest and, therefore, when most was required of imagination in order to build at all. Limitations seem to have always been the best friends of architecture.

Frank Lloyd Wright

See also: CREATIVITY, DREAM, FANCY.

IMITATION

Was Christ a man like us?—Ah! let us try
If we then, too, can be such men as he!

Matthew Arnold

Imitation belittles.

Christian Nestell Bovee

To escape from provinciality is good, provided we make distinctions; but, besides provinciality of place, there is also "time-provinciality," as Professor Whitehead calls it. This is the illusion that to be modern is worth all the other virtues; . . . as if to keep up with the mode were more important than any of the great realities of life and death.

Van Wyck Brooks

It is by imitation, far more than by precept, that we learn everything; and what we learn thus, we acquire not only more effectually, but more pleasantly. This forms our manners, our opinions, our lives.

Edmund Burke

Insist on yourself; never imitate. Your own gift you can present every moment with the cumulative force of a whole life's cultivation; but of the adopted talent of another, you have only an extemporaneous half-possession. That which each can do best none but his Maker can teach him.

Ralph Waldo Emerson

Imitators are a servile race.

Charles Fontaine

Imitation is the sincerest flattery.

Mohandas Karamchand (Mahatma) Gandhi

Men are so constituted that every one undertakes what he sees another successful in, whether he has aptitude for it or not.

Johann Wolfgang von Goethe

I hardly know so true a mark of a little mind as the servile imitation of others.

Fulke Greville (First Baron Brooke)

He who imitates evil always goes beyond the example that is set; he who imitates what is good always falls short.

Francesco Guicciardini

When people are free to do as they please, they usually imitate each other.

Eric Hoffer

Mimicry, though it be imitation, is not flattery, rather ridicule; because the mimic can reproduce the airs of his models and parody their seriousness and self-importance without being pledged to any of their physical or moral commitments.

George Santayana

Man is an imitative creature, and whoever is foremost leads the herd.

Johann Christoph Friedrich von Schiller

See also: CONFORMITY, EMULATION, EXAMPLE.

IMMIGRANT

Not the absorption capacity of the land, but the creative ability of a people, is the true yardstick with which we can measure the immigration potentialities of the land.

David Ben-Gurion

Today, whites tend to exaggerate how well and quickly they escaped from poverty. The fact is that immigrants who came from rural backgrounds, as many Negroes do, are only now, after three generations, finally beginning to move into the middle class.

Commission on Civil Disorder, 1968

When the European immigrants arrived, they gained an economic foothold by providing the unskilled labor needed by industry. Unlike the immigrant, the Negro migrant found little opportunity in the city. The economy, by then matured, had little use for the unskilled labor he had to offer.

Commission on Civil Disorder, 1968

See also: FATHERLAND, HOME, NATION.

IMMORTALITY

'Tis the divinity that stirs within us; 'tis heaven itself that points out an hereafter and intimates eternity to man.

Joseph Addison

Whatsoever that be within us that feels, thinks, desires, and animates, is something celestial, divine, and, consequently, imperishable.

Aristotle

Probably nobody completely repudiates a faith in immortality. A man may doubt it in his mind, but he still believes it in his faith.

George Arthur Buttrick

When I consider the wonderful activity of the mind, so great a memory of what is past, and such a capacity of penetrating into the future; when I behold such a number of arts and sciences, and such a multitude of discoveries thence arising, I believe and am firmly persuaded that a nature which contains so many things within itself cannot but be immortal.

Cicero

The old, old fashion—death! Oh, thank God, all who see it, for that older fashion yet—of immortality!

Charles John Huffam Dickens

One short sleep past, we wake eternally, and death shall be no more.

John Donne

We are much better believers in immortality than we can give grounds for. The real evidence is too subtle, or is higher than we can write down in propositions.

Ralph Waldo Emerson

I decline to accept the end of man. It is easy enough to say that man is immortal simply because he will endure: that when the last ding-dong of doom has clanged and faded from the last worthless rock hanging tideless in the last red and dying evening, that even then there will still be one more sound: that of his puny inexhaustible voice, still talking. I refuse to accept this. I believe that man will not merely endure: he will prevail. He is immortal, not because he alone among creatures has an inexhaustible voice, but because he has a soul, a spirit capable of compassion and sacrifice and endurance.

William Faulkner

The average man, who does not know what to do with this life, wants another one which shall last forever.

Anatole France

Those who hope for no other life are dead even for this.

Johann Wolfgang von Goethe

I believe in my survival after death. Like many others before me, I have experienced "intimations of immortality." I can no more explain these than the brown seed can explain the flowering tree. Deep in the soil in time's midwinter, my very stirring and unease seem a kind of growing pain toward June.

Robert Silliman Hillyer

Nothing short of an eternity could enable men to imagine, think, and feel, and to express all they have imagined, thought and felt. Immortality, which is the spiritual desire, is the intellectual necessity.

Edward G. Bulwer-Lytton (Baron Lytton)

The seed dies into a new life, and so does man.

George Macdonald

What springs from earth dissolves to earth again, and heaven-born things fly to their native seat.

Marcus Aurelius

We do not believe in immortality because we have proved it, but, we forever try to prove it because we believe it.

James Martineau

The belief of a future state is a troublesome check on human passions, and one can never make libertines tranquil and resolute without having first made them unbelievers.

Jean Baptiste Massillon

Immortality is not a gift,
Immortality is an achievement;
And only those who strive mightily
Shall possess it.

Edgar Lee Masters

Without a belief in personal immortality religion is like an arch resting on one pillar, or like a bridge ending in an abyss.

Friedrich Max Müller

Every natural longing has its natural satisfaction. If we thirst, God has created liquids to gratify thirst. If we are susceptible of attachment, there are beings to gratify our love. If we thirst for life and love eternal, it is likely that there are an eternal life and an eternal love to satisfy that craving.

Frederick William Robertson

Immortality is the genius to move others long after you yourself have stopped moving.

Frank Rooney

The majority of the elements of which we are made are potentially immortal. Death is a collective phenomenon.

Jean Rostand

Not all the subtleties of metaphysics can make me doubt a moment of the immortality of the soul, and of a beneficent providence. I feel it, I believe it, I desire it I hope it, and will defend it to my last breath.

Jean Jacques Rousseau

Nothing can be meaner than the anxiety to live on, to live on anyhow and in any shape; a spirit with any honor is not willing to live except in its own way, and a spirit with any wisdom is not overeager to live at all.

George Santayana

Immortality is the greatness of our being; the scene for attaining the fullness and perfection of our existence.

Charles Simmons

All men's souls are immortal, but the souls of the righteous are both immortal and divine.

Socrates

Faith in the hereafter is as necessary for the intellectual, as for the moral character; and to the man of letters, as well as the Christian, the present forms but the slightest portion of his existence.

Robert Southey

We feel and know that we are eternal.

Baruch (Benedict) Spinoza

The date of human life is too short to recompense the cares which attend the most private conditions; therefore it is that our souls are made, as it were, too big for it, and extend themselves in the prospect of a longer existence.

Sir Richard Steele

Nature does not know extinction; all it knows is transformation. Everything science has taught, and continues to teach me, strenghens the belief in the continuity of our spiritual existence after death.

Wernher vonBraun

The monuments of the nations are all protests against nothingness after death; so are statutes and inscriptions; so is history.

Lewis (Lew) Wallace

I think that Man is immortal, but not men.

Herbert George Wells

Seems it strange that thou shouldst live forever? Is it less strange that thou shouldst live at all? This is a miracle; and that no more.

Edward Young

See also: ETERNITY, MORTALITY, SOUL.

IMPATIENCE

I have not so great a struggle with my vices, great and numerous as they are, as I have with my impatience. My efforts are not absolutely useless; yet I have never been able to conquer this ferocious wild beast.

John Calvin

In all evils which admit a remedy, impatience should be avoided, because it wastes that time and attention in complaints which, if properly applied, might remove the cause.

Samuel Johnson

Such is our impatience, our hatred of procrastination in everything but the amendment of our practices and the adornment of our nature, one would imagine we were dragging time along by force, and not he us.

Walter Savage Landor

He who fumes at his quandaries becomes their victim.

David Seabury

See also: HASTE, IMPULSE, PATIENCE.

IMPERFECTION

What an absurd thing it is to pass over all the valuable parts of a man, and fix our attention on his infirmities.

Joseph Addison

He censures God who quarrels with the imperfections of men.

Edmund Burke

It is only imperfection that complains of what is imperfect. The more perfect we are, the more gentle and quiet we become toward the defects of others.

François de Salignac de La Mothe-Fénelon

I am too conscious of mine own imperfections to rake into and dilate upon the failings of other men; and though I carry always some ill-nature about me, yet it is, I hope, no more than is in this world necessary for a preservative.

Andrew Marvell

The finer the nature, the more flaws will show through the clearness of it; and it is a law of this universe that the best things shall be seldomest seen in their best forms.

John Ruskin

See also: FAILING, FAULT, WEAKNESS.

IMPERTINENCE

He is guilty of impertinence who considers not the circumstances of time, or engrosses the conversation, or makes himself the subject of his discourse, or pays no regard to the company he is in.

Cicero

A man has no more right to say an uncivil thing than to act one; no more right to say a rude thing to another than to knock him down.

Samuel Johnson

Receive no satisfaction for premeditated impertinence; forget it, and forgive it, but keep inexorably at a distance him who offered it.

Johann Kaspar Lavater

See also: ARROGANCE, BOLDNESS, IMPUDENCE, INSULT.

IMPOSSIBILITY

Most of the things worth doing in the world had been declared impossible before they were done.

Louis Dembitz Brandeis

It is not a lucky word, this same "impossible"; no good comes of those who have it so often in their mouth.

Thomas Carlyle

One great difference between a wise man and a fool is, the former only wishes for what he may possibly obtain; the latter desires impossibilities.

Democritus

Nothing is impossible; there are ways that lead to everything, and if we had sufficient will we should always have sufficient means. It is often merely for an excuse that we say things are impossible.

Duc François de La Rochefoucauld

"Impossible!" That is not good French.

Napoleon I (Bonaparte)

"Impossible"—never let me hear that foolish word again.

Honoré Riqueti (Comte de Mirabeau)

Three incredible things among incredible things: pure mechanism of the brute creation, passive obedience, and the infallibility of the Pope.

Charles de Secondat (Baron de Montesquieu)

See also: ABSURDITY, PERFECTION, REALIST.

IMPRESSION

If you would stand well with a great mind, leave him with a favorable impression of yourself; if with a little mind, leave him with a favorable opinion of himself.

Samuel Taylor Coleridge

The least and most imperceptible impressions received in our infancy have consequences very important and of long duration. It is with these first impressions as with a river, whose waters we can easily turn at its source; with the same facility we may turn the minds of children to what direction we please.

John Locke

The mind unlearns with difficulty what has long been impressed on it.

Seneca

See also: APPEARANCE, BELIEF, FEELING.

IMPROVEMENT

Judge of thine improvement, not by what thou speakest or writest, but by the firmness of thy mind, and the government of thy passions and affections.

Thomas Fuller

People seldom improve when they have no other model but themselves to copy after.

Oliver Goldsmith

If a better system is thine, impart it; if not, make use of mine.

Horace

Slumber not in the tents of your fathers. The world is advancing. Advance with it.

Giuseppe Mazzini

The law of worthy life is fundamentally the law of strife; it is only through labor and painful effort, by grim energy and resolute courage that we move into better things.

Theodore Roosevelt

All of us, who are worth anything, spend our manhood in unlearning the follies, or expiating the mistakes of our youth.

Percy Bysshe Shelley

Much of the wisdom of one age, is the folly of the next.

Charles Simmons

See also: PROGRESS, SELF-IMPROVEMENT.

IMPROVIDENCE

How full or how empty our lives, depends, we say, on Providence. Suppose we say, more or less on improvidence.

Christian Nestell Bovee

Waste not, want not; willful waste makes woeful want.

Benjamin Franklin

What maintains one vice, would bring up two children.

Benjamin Franklin

See also: EXTRAVAGANCE, PRODIGALITY, WASTE.

IMPUDENCE

The way to avoid the imputation of impudence is, not to be ashamed of what we do, but never to do what we ought to be ashamed of.

Cicero

The man who cannot blush, and who has no feelings of fear, has reached the acme of impudence.

Menander of Athens

He that knows the world will not be bashful; he who knows himself will not be impudent.

Charles Simmons

A true and genuine impudence is ever the effect of ignorance, without the least sense of it.

Sir Richard Steele

See also: BOLDNESS, IMPERTINENCE, INSULT.

IMPULSE

A true history of human events would show that a far larger proportion of our acts are the results of sudden impulses and accident, than of that reason of which we so much boast.

Peter Cooper

Since the generality of persons act from impulse much more than from principle, men are neither so good nor so bad as we are apt to think them.

Augustus and Julius Hare

Our first impulses are good, generous heroical; reflection weakens and kills them.

Louis Aimé Martin

What persons are by starts, they are by nature—you see them at such times off their guard. Habit may restrain vice, and virtue may be obscured by passion, but intervals best discover man.

Laurence Sterne

See also: INCLINATION, INSTINCT.

INACTIVITY

Learning teaches how to carry things in suspense without prejudice till you resolve.

Francis Bacon

The keenest pangs the wretched find are rapture to the dreary void,—the leafless desert of the mind—the waste of feelings unemployed.

George Gordon Byron (Lord Byron)

In the meantime, our policy is a masterly inactivity.

John Caldwell Calhoun

Doing nothing with a deal of skill.

William Cowper

Nature knows no pause in her progress and development, and attaches her curse on all inaction.

Johann Wolfgang von Goethe

If he had sat still, the enemy's army would have mouldered to nothing.

Edward Hyde (Earl of Clarendon)

Thoughtful, disciplined, intended inaction.

John Randolph

See also: IDLENESS, INDOLENCE, SLOTH.

INCLINATION

All men that are ruined are ruined on the side of their natural propensities.

Edmund Burke

Almost everyone has a predominant inclination, to which his other desires and actions submit, and which governs him, though perhaps with some intervals, through the whole course of his life.

David Hume

A good inclination is but the first rude draught of virtue; but the finishing strokes are from the will; which, if well disposed, will, by degrees perfect; if ill disposed, will, by the superinduction of ill habits, quickly deface it.

Robert South

See also: DESIRE, IMPULSE, INSTINCT, WISH.

INCONSISTENCY

Mutability of temper and inconsistency with ourselves is the greatest weakness of human nature.

Joseph Addison

How often in this world are the actions that we condemn the result of sentiments that we love, and opinions that we admire.

Anna Brownell Murphy Jameson

No author ever drew a character consistent to human nature, but he was forced to ascribe to it many inconsistencies.

Edward G. Bulwer-Lytton (Baron Lytton)

Some persons do first, think afterward, and then repent forever.

Thomas Secker

We are always complaining that our days are few, and acting as though there would be no end of them.

Seneca

A conscience enlightened, and yet a heart erratic, make mankind a bundle of marvelous incongruities and inconsistencies.

Charles Simmons

See also: CHANGE, FICKLENESS, INCONSTANCY, INSTABILITY, MUTABILITY.

INCONSTANCY

Nothing that is not a real crime makes a man appear so contemptible and little in the eyes of the world as inconstancy, especially when it regards religion or party. In either of these cases, though a man perhaps does but his duty in changing his side, he not only makes himself hated by those he left, but is seldom heartily esteemed by those he comes over to.

Joseph Addison

Clocks will go as they are set; but man, irregular man, is never constant, never certain.

Thomas Otway

Inconstancy is but a name to fright poor lovers from a better choice.

Joseph Rutter

See also: CHANGE, FICKLENESS, MUTABILITY.

INCREDULITY

Nothing is so contemptible as that affectation of wisdom which some display by universal incredulity.

Oliver Goldsmith

Incredulity robs us of many pleasures, and gives us nothing in return.

James Russell Lowell

It is always well to accept your own shortcomings with candor but to regard those of your friends with polite incredulity.

(Joseph) Russell Lynes

The incredulous are of all men the most credulous; they believe the miracles of Vespasian, in order not to believe those of Moses.

Blaise Pascal

Some men will believe nothing but what they can comprehend; and there are but few things that such are able to comprehend.

Seigneur de Saint-Evremond

The amplest knowledge has the largest faith. Ignorance is always incredulous.

Robert Eldridge Aris Willmott

See also: AGNOSTICISM, CYNICISM, UNBELIEF.

INDECISION

The wavering mind is but a base possession.

Euripides

There is nothing in the world more pitiable than an irresolute man, oscillating between two feelings, who would willingly unite the two, and who does not perceive that nothing can unite them.

Johann Wolfgang von Goethe

There is no more miserable human being than one in whom nothing is habitual but indecision.

William James

When a man has not a good reason for doing a thing, he has one good reason for letting it alone.

Thomas Scott

See also: IRRESOLUTION, WEAKNESS.

INDEPENDENCE

Without moral and intellectual independence, there is no anchor for national independence.

David Ben-Gurion

The word independence is united to the ideas of dignity and virtue; the word dependence, to the ideas of inferiority and corruption.

Jeremy Bentham

No one can build his security upon the nobleness of another person.

Willa Sibert Cather

Happy the man to whom heaven has given a morsel of bread without laying him under

the obligation of thanking any other for it than heaven itself.

Miguel de Cervantes Saavedra

It is not the greatness of a man's means that makes him independent, so much as the smallness of his wants.

William Cobbett

Let all your views in life be directed to a solid, however moderate, independence; without it no man can be happy, nor even honest.

Junius

The moral progression of a people can scarcely begin till they are independent.

James Martineau

Go to New England, and visit the domestic firesides, if you would see the secret of American Independence. Religion has made them what they are.

Tomás Cipriano de Mosquera

See also: FREEDOM, LIBERTY, SELF-RELIANCE.

INDEX

I have come to regard a good book as curtailed of half its value if it has not a pretty full index. It is almost impossible without such a guide to reproduce on demand the most striking thoughts or facts the book contains, whether for citation or further consideration.

Horace Binney

An index is a necessary implement, without which a large author is but a labyrinth without a clue to direct the readers within.

Thomas Fuller

Those authors who are voluminous would do well, if they would be remembered as long as possible, not to omit a duty which authors in general, and especially modern authors neglect, that of appending to their works a good index.

Henry Rogers

Get thorough insight into the index, by which the whole book is governed.

Jonathan Swift

See also: BOOK, LIBRARY, STUDY.

INDIA

Everything in India attracts me. It has everything that a human being with the highest possible aspirations can want.
  Mohandas Karamchand (Mahatma) Gandhi

India has an uncanny way of bringing out extremes in people, I suppose because we have been afflicted and enriched by centuries of migrations, moved like a pawn between this ruler and that. Our capacity for a single allegiance has been dulled. Instead we have developed an ability to be compassionate and cruel, sensitive and callous, deep and fickle.
  Ved Parkash Mehta

There is a terrible lack of urgency in India. Most of the books I have read about India miss the mark. Either they are too optimistic or too pessimistic about her future, and I think optimism is the more dangerous. If everyone keeps on talking about India with sympathetic optimism, we may be deluded long enough to permit democracy to slip away from us. We may soft-pedal ourselves into disaster.
  Ved Parkash Mehta

Since that early dawn of history innumerable peoples, conquerors and settlers, pilgrims and students have trekked into the Indian plains from the highlands of Asia and have influenced Indian life and culture and art; but always they have been absorbed and assimilated. India was changed by these contacts and yet she remained essentially her own old self. Like the ocean she received the tribute of a thousand rivers, and though she was disturbed often enough, and storms raged over the surface of her waters, the sea continued to be the sea.
  Jawaharlal Nehru

The whole history of India for thousands of years past shows her essential unity and the vitality and adaptability of her culture. This vitality took her message in art and thought and religion to the Far East; it took the shape of great colonizing expeditions to Malaysia, to Java and Sumatra and the Philippines and Borneo, as the remains of great monuments there, a thousand years old, bear testimony.
  Jawaharlal Nehru

Whatever her actual strength may or may not be, India is potentially a very powerful country and possesses the qualities and factors that go a long way to make a country grow strong, healthy and prosperous.
  Jawaharlal Nehru

See also: ASIA, BUDDHISM.

INDIFFERENCE

Most people are *on* the world, not in it—having no conscious sympathy or relationship to anything about them—undiffused, separate, and rigidly alone like marbles of polished stone, touching but separate.
  John Muir

Nothing for preserving the body like having no heart.
  John Petit-Senn

Indifference is the invincible giant of the world.
  Marie Louise de la Ramée (Ouida)

The worst sin towards our fellow creatures is not to hate them, but to be indifferent to them; that's the essence of inhumanity.
  George Bernard Shaw

See also: INSENSIBILITY, INTEREST, NEGLECT, SELF-INTEREST.

INDIGESTION

Indigestion is charged by God with enforcing morality on the stomach.
  Victor Marie Hugo

Dyspepsia is the remorse of a guilty stomach.
  Alexander Kerr

Old friendships are destroyed by toasted cheese, and hard salted meat has led to suicide. Unpleasant feelings of the body produce correspondent sensations of the mind, and a great scene of wretchedness is sketched out by a morsel of indigestible and misguided food.
  Sydney Smith

See also: EATING, FEASTING, GLUTTONY.

INDISCRETION

An indiscreet man is more hurtful than an ill-natured one; for the latter will only attack his enemies, and those he wishes ill to; the other injures indifferently both friends and foes.
  Joseph Addison

Three things too much, and three too little
are pernicious to man; to speak much, and
know little; to spend much, and have little;
to presume much, and be worth little.

Miguel de Cervantes Saavedra

For good and evil in our actions meet;
Wicked is not much worse than indiscreet.

John Donne

See also: FOLLY, MISTAKE, RASHNESS.

INDIVIDUALISM: see INDIVIDUALITY.

INDIVIDUALITY

Have the courage to be different without
being contrary—without flaunting your independence. The quality that makes us interesting, that makes us outstanding personalities, is the courage to be ourselves.

Anonymous

The protagonist of freedom is the individual,
but its production is always a social venture.

Max Ascoli

In the balancing process between individual
and society . . . the greater weight is to be
given to society, except only when this would
erode the fundamental worth of the individual. Hence, the precise amount of liberty
allowable in every given situation is to be
determined by the question, is it necessary
to preserve essential human dignity?

Brendan Francis Brown

Not armies, not nations, have advanced the
race; but here and there, in the course of
ages, an individual has stood up and cast his
shadow over the world.

Edwin Hubbel Chapin

Individuality is either the mark of genius or
the reverse. Mediocrity finds safety in standardization.

Frederick Evan Crane

Everything without tells the individual that
he is nothing; everything within persuades
him that he is everything.

Ximénès Doudan

The individual must be free, able to develop to the utmost of his ability, employing all
opportunities that confront him for his own
and his family's welfare; otherwise he is
merely a cog in a machine. The society must
be stable, assured against violent upheaval
and revolution; otherwise it is nothing but a

temporary truce with chaos. But freedom for
the individual must never degenerate into
the brutish struggle for survival that we call
barbarism. Neither must the stability of society ever degenerate into the enchained servitude of the masses that we call statism.

Dwight David Eisenhower

Modern life has become so highly integrated, so inextricably socialized, so definitely
organic, that the very concept of the individual is becoming obsolete.

Henry Pratt Fairchild

The common phrase, "building a personality" is a misnomer. Personality is not so much
like a structure as like a river it continuously
flows, and to be a person is to be engaged
in a perpetual process of becoming.

Harry Emerson Fosdick

The ancient dichotomy of the individual and
society will sooner or later be dissolved as
we understand that society is in each individual and what we call "social adjustment"
is essentially the individual's relation to himself.

Laurence Kelso Frank

In every culture the individual is of necessity
cribbed, cabined and confined within the
limitations of what his culture tells him to
see, to believe, to do and to feel.

Laurence Kelso Frank

Human faculties are common, but that
which converges these faculties into my
identity, separates me from every other
man. That other man cannot think my
thoughts, speak my words, do my works. He
cannot have my sins, and I cannot have his
virtues.

Henry Giles

The American system of rugged individualism.

Herbert Clark Hoover

It was perhaps ordained by Providence, to
hinder us from tyrannizing over one another,
that no individual should be of so much importance as to cause, by his retirement or
death, any chasm in the world.

Samuel Johnson

The epoch of individuality is concluded, and
it is the duty of reformers to initiate the

epoch of association. Collective man is omnipotent upon the earth he treads.

Giuseppe Mazzini

Delight is to him—a far, far upward, and inward delight—who against the proud gods and commodores of this earth, ever stands forth his own inexorable self.

Herman Melville

The worth of a state, in the long run, is the worth of the individuals composing it.

John Stuart Mill

Individuality is everywhere to be spared and respected as the root of everything good.

Jean Paul Richter

You are tried alone; alone you pass into the desert; alone you are sifted by the world.

Frederick William Robertson

We require individualism which does not wall man off from community; we require community which sustains but does not suffocate the individual.

Arthur Meier Schlesinger

It is said that if Noah's ark had had to be built by a company, they would not have laid the keel yet; and it may be so. What is many men's business is nobody's business. The greatest things are accomplished by individual men.

Charles Haddon Spurgeon

See also: CHARACTER, ECCENTRICITY.

INDOLENCE

I look upon indolence as a sort of suicide; for the man is efficiently destroyed, though the appetite of the brute may survive.

Cicero

Indolence is the sleep of the mind.

Luc de Clapiers (Marquis de Vauvenargues)

The darkest hour in the history of any young man is when he sits down to study how to get money without honestly earning it.

Horace Greeley

Nothing ages like laziness.

Edward G. Bulwer-Lytton (Baron Lytton)

By nature's laws, immutable and just, enjoyment stops where indolence begins.

Robert Pollok

I look upon indolence as a sort of suicide; for the man is effectually destroyed, though the appetite of the brute may survive.

Philip Dormer Stanhope (Lord Chesterfield)

Indolence, methinks, is an intermediate state between pleasure and pain, and very much unbecoming any part of our life after we are out of the nurse's arms.

Sir Richard Steele

See also: IDLENESS, SLOTH.

INDULGENCE

Those who love dainties are likely soon to be beggars.

Benjamin Franklin

Live only for to-day, and you ruin tomorrow.

Charles Simmons

This body has one fault, that the more people pamper it, the more its wants are made known.

Teresa of Avila (Theresa of Jesus)

See also: ABSTINENCE, DRINK, DRUNKENNESS, EATING, LICENTIOUSNESS.

INDUSTRIOUSNESS

It is better to wear out than to rust out.

Richard Cumberland

Industry need not wish, and he that lives upon hopes will die fasting. There are no gains without pains. He that hath a trade hath an estate, and he that hath a calling hath an office of profit and honor; but then the trade must be worked at, and the calling followed, or neither the estate nor the office will enable us to pay our taxes. If we are industrious, we shall never starve; for, at the workingman's house hunger looks in, but dares not enter. Nor will the bailiff or the constable enter, for industry pays debts, while idleness and neglect increase them.

Benjamin Franklin

Like the bee, we should make our industry our amusement.

Oliver Goldsmith

If you have great talents, industry will improve them; if moderate abilities, industry will supply their deficiencies. Nothing is denied to well-directed labor; nothing is ever to be attained without it.

Sir Joshua Reynolds

One loses all the time which he might employ to better purpose.

Jean Jacques Rousseau

Industry keeps the body healthy, the mind clear, the heart whole, and the purse full.

Charles Simmons

If you have great talents, industry will improve them; if but moderate abilities, industry will supply their deficiencies.

Samuel Smiles

A man who gives his children habits of industry provides for them better than by giving them a fortune.

Richard Whately

See also: WORK, LABOR.

INDUSTRY

The problem in British industry is outdated, outmoded factories, and outdated, outmoded and ill equipped management.

James Conway

Absentee management, no matter how honest and able, cannot equal local management. . . . And it certainly does not sit well with labor, investors, consumers, and the communities back home. It is their industry and they should be in on it.

William Orville Douglas

Despite our demonstrated capacity for cooperative teamwork, some among us seem to accept the shibboleth of an unbridgeable gap between those who hire and those who are employed . . . that for one side to profit, the other must be depressed. Such distorted doctrine is false and foreign to the American scene.

Dwight David Eisenhower

The next war criminals will come from the chemical and electronics industries.

Alfred Krupp

See also: BUSINESS, CAPITALISM, COMMERCE.

INEQUALITY

No amount of artificial reinforcement can offset the natural inequalities of human individuals.

Henry Pratt Fairchild

There is always inequity in life. Some men are killed in a war, and some men are wounded, and some men are stationed in the Antarctic and some are stationed in San Francisco. It's very hard in military or personal life to assure complete equality. Life is unfair.

John Fitzgerald Kennedy

It is impossible to reduce civil society to one dead level. Socialists may in that intent do their utmost, but all striving against nature is in vain. . . . People differ in capacity, skill, health, strength; and unequal fortune is a necessary result of unequal condition. Such inequality is far from being disadvantageous either to individuals or to the community.

Leo XIII (Gioacchino Vincenzo Pecci)

Some must follow, and some command, though all are made of clay.

Henry Wadsworth Longfellow

In the human species there seem to be two kinds of inequality: the one which I call natural or physical, because it is established by nature, and which consists in the difference of ages, health, strength of body, qualities of mind or soul; the other, which may be called moral or political inequality, because it depends on a kind of mutual agreement, and is established, or at least authorized, by the consent of men. This latter consists in the different privileges which some enjoy to the prejudice of others, as by being more rich, honored, powerful than they are, or by making themselves be obeyed.

Jean Jacques Rousseau

See also: EQUALITY, EQUITY, INJUSTICE, NEGRO, SEGREGATION.

INFAMY

The most infamous are found of fame; and those who fear not guilt, yet start at shame.

Charles Churchill

What grief can there be that time doth not make less? But infamy, time never can suppress.

Michael Drayton

Infamy is where it is received. If thou art a mud wall, it will stick; if marble, it will rebound. If thou storm, it is thine; if thou contemn it, it is his.

Francis Quarles

See also: BASENESS, DEPRAVITY, DISGRACE.

INFANCY

They who have lost an infant are never, as it were, without an infant child. Their other children grow up to manhood and womanhood, and suffer all the changes of mortality; but this one is rendered an immortal child, for death has arrested it with his kindly harshness, and blessed it into an eternal image of youth and innocence.

(James Henry) Leigh Hunt

Of all the joys that brighten suffering earth, what joy is welcomed like a newborn child?

Caroline Elizabeth Sarah Norton

Heaven lies about us in our infancy.

William Wordsworth

See also: BABY, CHILDHOOD, CHILDREN.

INFERIORITY

No man likes to have his intelligence or good faith questioned, especially if he has doubts about it himself.

Henry Brooks Adams

To be a human being means to possess a feeling of inferiority which constantly presses towards its own conquest. The paths to victory are as different in a thousand ways as the chosen goals of perfection. The greater the feeling of inferiority that has been experienced, the more powerful is the urge to conquest and the more violent the emotional agitation.

Alfred Adler

We must interpret a bad temper as a sign of inferiority.

Alfred Adler

No one can make you feel inferior without your consent.

Anna Eleanor Roosevelt

See also: IGNORANCE, MEDIOCRITY, WEAKNESS.

INFIDELITY

Infidelity, indeed, is the root of all sin; for did man heartily believe the promises to obedience, and the threats to disobedience, they could hardly be so unreasonable as to forfeit the one or incur the other.

Isaac Barrow

The nurse of infidelity is sensuality.

Richard Cecil

Man may doubt here and there, but mankind does not doubt. The universal conscience is larger than the individual conscience, and that constantly comes in to correct and check our infidelity.

Hugh Reginald Haweis

Faith in God hallows and confirms the union between parents and children, and subjects and rulers. Infidelity relaxes every band, and nullifies every blessing.

Johann Heinrich Pestalozzi

It is always safe to follow the religious belief that our mother taught us; there never was a mother yet who taught her child to be an infidel.

Henry Wheeler Shaw (Josh Billings)

Men always grow vicious before they become unbelievers; but if you would once convince profligates by topics drawn from the view of their own quiet, reputation, and health, their infidelity would soon drop off.

Jonathan Swift

See also: ADULTERY, INSINCERITY, UNBELIEF.

INFLUENCE

No man should think himself a zero, and think he can do nothing about the state of the world.

Bernard Mannes Baruch

There are nine chances in ten that every man who goes with me will lose his life in the undertaking. But there are times when dead men are worth more than living ones.

John Brown (of Haddington)

Virtue will catch, as well as vice, by contact; and the public stock of honest manly principle will daily accumulate.

Edmund Burke

If you had the seeds of pestilence in your body you would not have a more active contagion than you have in your tempers, tastes, and principles. Simply to be in this world, whatever you are, is to exert an influence—an influence too, compared with which mere language and persuasion are feeble.

Horace Bushnell

Not one false man but does unaccountable mischief.

Thomas Carlyle

Men are won, not so much by being blamed, as by being encompassed with love.
William Ellery Channing

Blessed is the influence of one true, loving human soul on another.
George Eliot (Mary Ann Evans)

Every thought which genius and piety throw into the world alters the world.
Ralph Waldo Emerson

When men do anything for God, the very least thing, they never know where it will end, nor what amount of work it will do for Him. Love's secret, therefore, is to be always doing things for God, and not to mind because they are such very little ones.
Frederick William Faber

Those who fear influences and avoid them make a tacit avowal of the poverty of their souls.
André Gide

He who wishes to exert a useful influence must be careful to insult nothing. Let him not be troubled by what seems absurd, but consecrate his energies to the creation of what is good. He must not demolish, but build. He must raise temples where mankind may come and partake of the purest pleasures.
Johann Wolfgang von Goethe

The world has been shaken, but there is very little evidence that it has been moved.
John Burdon Sanderson Haldane

It doesn't matter that thirty-four other American cities are windier than Chicago. People look for wind when they come here—and they find what they look for. There's a lesson in this for all of us.
Sydney Harris

"Pharisaically, I used to think [Sebastian Barnack wrote] I was without responsibility for what was happening in the world. But the habit of sensuality and pure aestheticism is a process of God-proofing. To indulge in it is to become a spiritual mackintosh, shielding the little corner of time, of which one is the centre, from the least drop of eternal reality. But the only hope for the world of time lies in being constantly drenched by that which lies beyond time. Guaranteed God-proof, we exclude from our surroundings the only influence that is able to neutralize the destructive energies of ambition, covetousness and the love of power."
Aldous Leonard Huxley

Always so act that the immediate motive of thy will may become a universal rule for all intelligent beings.
Immanuel Kant

A good man does good merely by living.
Edward G. Bulwer-Lytton (Baron Lytton)

It is the age that forms the man, not the man that forms the age. Great minds do indeed react on the society which has made them what they are, but they only pay with interest what they have received.
Thomas Babington Macaulay

Race and temperament go for much in influencing opinion.
Sydney Owenson Morgan (Lady Morgan)

Each person is a temporary focus of forces, vitalities, and values that carry back into an immemorial past and that reach forward into an inthinkable future.
Lewis Mumford

Each and every one of us has one obligation, during the bewildered days of our pilgrimage here: the saving of his own soul, and secondarily and incidentally thereby affecting for good such other souls as come under our influence.
Kathleen Norris

The least movement is of importance to all nature. The entire ocean is affected by a pebble.
Blaise Pascal

A word or a nod from the good, has more weight than the eloquent speeches of others.
Plutarch

The words that a father speaks to his children in the privacy of home are not heard by the world, but, as in whispering galleries, they are clearly heard at the end, and by posterity.
Jean Paul Richter

Let him that would move the world, first move himself.
Socrates

Though her (Lady Elizabeth Hastings) mien carries much more invitation than command, to behold her is an immediate check to loose behavior; to love her was a liberal education.

Sir Richard Steele

Iron sharpens iron; scholar, the scholar.

Talmud

The life of a faithful Christian man is a guide to paradise.

Thomas à Kempis

Planets do not govern the soul, or guide the destinies of men, but trifles, lighter than straws, are levers in the building up of character.

Martin Farquhar Tupper

I really believe that more harm is done by old men who cling to their influence than by young men who anticipate it.

Owen D. Young

See also: EXAMPLE, GUIDANCE, POWER.

INFORMATION

Knowledge is of two kinds: we know a subject ourselves, or we know where we can find information upon it.

Samuel Johnson

All my life, as down an abyss without a bottom, I have been pouring vanloads of information into that vacancy of oblivion I call my mind.

Logan Pearsall Smith

One has information only to the extent to which one has tended to communicate one's experience.

Harry Stack Sullivan

See also: COMMUNICATIONS MEDIA, NEWS.

INGRATITUDE

Nothing more detestable does the earth produce than an ungrateful man.

Ausonius

He that forgets his friend is ungrateful to him; but he that forgets his Saviour is unmerciful to himself.

John Bunyan

If you pick up a starving dog and make him prosperous, he will not bite you. That is the principal difference between a dog and a man.

Samuel Langhorne Clemens (Mark Twain)

When we would, with utmost detestation, single some monster from the traitor herd, 'tis but to say ingratitude is his crime.

James Anthony Froude

We often fancy we suffer from ingratitude, while in reality we suffer from self-love.

Walter Savage Landor

We seldom find people ungrateful so long as it is thought we can serve them.

Duc François de La Rochefoucauld

He that doth public good for multitudes, finds few are truly grateful.

Philip Massinger

One great cause of our insensibility to the goodness of our Creator is the very extensiveness of his bounty.

William Paley

One ungrateful man does an injury to all who stand in need of aid.

Publilius Syrus

A grateful dog is better than an ungrateful man.

Saadi (Muslih-ud-Din)

We can be thankful to a friend for a few acres, or a little money; and yet for the freedom and command of the whole earth, and for the great benefits of our being, our life, health, and reason, we look upon ourselves as under no obligation.

Seneca

What unthankfulness is to forget our consolations, and to look upon matters of grievance; to think so much upon two or three crosses as to forget an hundred blessings.

Richard Sibbes

There neither is, or ever was, any person remarkably ungrateful, who was not also insufferably proud; nor any one proud, who was not equally ungrateful.

Robert South

He that calls a man ungrateful, sums up all the evil of which one can be guilty.

Jonathan Swift

Ingratitude is treason to mankind.

James Thomson

He that is ungrateful has no guilt but one;
all other crimes may pass for virtues in him.
Edward Young

See also: GRATITUDE, SELFISHNESS.

INHERITANCE

Children inherit the qualities of the parents
no less than their physical features. Environment does play an important part, but the
original capital on which a child starts in life
is inherited from its ancestors. I have also
seen children successfully surmounting the
effects of an evil inheritance. That is due to
purity being an inherent attribute of the
soul.
Mohandas Karamchand (Mahatma) Gandhi

Enjoy what thou hast inherited from thy
sires if thou wouldst really possess it. What
we employ and use is never an oppressive
burden; what the moment brings forth, that
only can it profit by.
Johann Wolfgang von Goethe

What madness is it for a man to starve himself to enrich his heir, and so turn a friend
into an enemy! For his joy at your death will
be proportioned to what you leave him.
Seneca

They who provide much wealth for their
children but neglect to improve them in virtue, do like those who feed their horses
high, but never train them to be useful.
Socrates

Who comes for the inheritance is often
made to pay for the funeral.
Yiddish Proverb

See also: DEATH, EUGENICS, WILLS.

INJURY

If men wound you with injuries, meet them
with patience: hasty words rankle the
wound, soft language dresses it, forgiveness
cures it, and oblivion takes away the scar. It
is more noble by silence to avoid an injury
than by argument to overcome it.
Francis Beaumont

Nothing can work me damage except myself. The harm that I sustain I carry about
with me, and am never a real sufferer but
by my own fault.
Bernard of Clairvaux

No man is hurt but by himself.
Diogenes

Christianity commands us to pass by injuries;
policy, to let them pass by us.
Benjamin Franklin

Slight small injuries, and they will become
none at all.
Thomas Fuller

If the other person injures you, you may
forget the injury; but if you injure him you
will always remember.
Kahlil Gibran

No man ever did a designed injury to another, but at the same time he did a greater to
himself.
Henry Home (Lord Kames)

The purpose of an injury is to vex and trouble me. Now, nothing can do that to him
that is truly valiant.
Samuel Johnson

The injuries of life, if rightly improved, will
be to us as the strokes of the statuary on his
marble, forming us to a more beautiful
shape, and making us fitter to adorn the
heavenly temple.
Cotton Mather

He who has injured thee was either stronger
or weaker than thee. If weaker, spare him; if
stronger, spare thyself.
Seneca

The injuries we do, and those we suffer, are
seldom weighed in the same balance.
Charles Simmons

See also: ABUSE, CRUELTY, ILLS, SLANDER.

INJUSTICE

No one will dare maintain that it is better to
do injustice than to bear it.
Aristotle

Why the injustice and the cruelty go on—
year after year—century after century—without change—because—as they grow older—
people become—tolerant!
Samuel Nathaniel Behrman

If thou suffer injustice, console thyself; the
true unhappiness is in doing it.
Democritus

The man who wears injustice by his side,
though powerful millions followed him to

war, combats against the odds—against high heaven.

William Havard

Surely they who devour the possessions of orphans unjustly shall swallow down nothing but fire into their bellies, and shall broil in raging flames.

Koran

Any one entrusted with power will abuse it if not also animated with the love of truth and virtue, no matter whether he be a prince, or one of the people.

Jean de La Fontaine

Injustice arises either from precipitation, or indolence, or from a mixture of both. The rapid and slow are seldom just; the unjust wait either not at all, or wait too long.

Johann Kaspar Lavater

Of all injustice, that is the greatest which goes under the name of law; and of all sorts of tyranny the forcing of the letter of the law against the equity, is the most insupportable.

Sir Roger L'Estrange

Did the mass of men know the actual selfishness and injustice of their rulers, not a government would stand a year. The world would foment with revolution.

Theodore Parker

He who commits injustice is ever made more wretched than he who suffers it.

Plato

See also: INEQUALITY, JUSTICE, PERSECUTION, RACISM, TYRANNY.

INK

That colored slave that waits for your thought, and sends that thought, without a voice, to the ends of the earth.

Anonymous

A drop of ink may make a million think.

George Gordon Byron (Lord Byron)

My ways are as broad as the king's high road, and my means lie in an inkstand.

Robert Southey

See also: AUTHORSHIP, PEN, WRITING.

INNOCENCE

Innocence, most often, is a good fortune and not a virtue.

Anatole France

Vulgar innocence and ignorance are mortal, they have pretty faces, but wholly without expression, and of a transient beauty; the noble sisters are immortal, their lofty forms are unchangeable, and their countenances are still radiant with the light of paradise. They dwell in heaven, and visit only the noblest and most severely tried of mankind.

Baron Friedrich von Hardenberg (Novalis)

He is armed without who is innocent within, be this thy screen, and this thy wall of brass.

Horace

Against the head which innocence secures, insidious malice aims her darts in vain; turned backward by the powerful breath of heaven.

Samuel Johnson

They that know no evil will suspect none.

Ben (Benjamin) Jonson

Innocence is but a poor substitute for experience.

Edward G. Bulwer Lytton (Baron Lytton)

Innocence is never accustomed to blush.

Molière (Jean Baptiste Poquelin)

There is no man so good, who, were he to submit all his thoughts and actions to the law, would not deserve hanging ten times in his life.

Michel Eyquem de Montaigne

Innocence and mystery never dwell long together.

Albertine Adrienne Necker de Saussure

Innocence is a desirable thing, a dainty thing, an appealing thing, in its place; but carried too far, it is merely ridiculous.

Dorothy Parker

To be innocent is to be not guilty; but to be virtuous is to overcome our evil inclinations.

William Penn

But innocence has nothing to dread.

Jean Baptiste Racine

Innocence is like polished armor; it adorns and defends.

> *Robert South*

There is no courage but in innocence; no constancy but in an honest cause.

> *Thomas Southerne*

The innocence that feels no risk and is taught no caution, is more vulnerable than guilt, and oftener assailed.

> *Nathaniel Parker Willis*

See also: GUILT, IGNORANCE, JUSTICE, PURITY, VIRTUE.

INNOVATION

To innovate is not to reform.

> *Edmund Burke*

The ridiculous rage for innovation, which only increases the weight of the chains it cannot break, shall never fire my blood!

> *Johann Christoph Friedrich von Schiller*

It will always do to change for the better.

> *James Thomson*

See also: CHANGE, DISCOVERY, IMAGINATION, INVENTION, NOVELTY, ORIGINALITY.

INQUIRY

All calm inquiry conducted among those who have their main principles of judgment in common, leads, if not to an approximation of views, yet, at least, to an increase of sympathy.

> *Thomas Arnold*

It is a shameful thing to be weary of inquiry when what we search for is excellent.

> *Cicero*

Free inquiry, if restrained within due bounds, and applied to proper subjects, is a most important privilege of the human mind; and if well conducted, is one of the greatest friends to truth. But when reason knows neither its office nor its limits, and when employed on subjects foreign to its jurisdiction, it then becomes a privilege dangerous to be exercised.

> *Jean Henri Merle d'Aubigné*

It is error only, and not truth, that shrinks from inquiry.

> *Thomas Paine*

Let not the freedom of inquiry be shackled. If it multiplies contentions among the wise and virtuous, it exercises the charity of those who contend. If it shakes for a time the belief that is rested only on prejudice, it finally settles it on the broader and more solid basis of conviction.

> *Henry Kirke White*

See also: CURIOSITY, QUESTION, SCIENCE.

INQUISITIVENESS

The man who is inquisitive into the secrets of your affairs, with which he has no concern, should be an object of your caution. Men no more desire another's secrets to conceal them, than they would another's purse for the pleasure only of carrying it.

> *Henry Fielding*

Shun the inquisitive, for you will be sure to find him leaky. Open ears do not keep conscientiously what has been intrusted to them, and a word once spoken flies, never to be recalled.

> *Horace*

In ancient days the most celebrated precept was, "know thyself"; in modern times it has been supplanted by the more fashionable maxim, "Know thy neighbor and everything about him."

> *Samuel Johnson*

An inquisitive man is a creature naturally very vacant of thought itself, and therefore forced to apply to foreign assistance.

> *Sir Richard Steele*

See also: BABBLE, GOSSIP, RUMOR.

INSANITY

Every sense hath been o'erstrung, and each frail fibre of the brain sent forth her thoughts all wild and wide.

> *George Gordon Byron (Lord Byron)*

Great wits are sure to madness near allied, And thin partitions do their bounds divide.

> *John Dryden*

Insanity destroys reason, but not wit.

> *Nathaniel Emmons*

Insane people easily detect the nonsense of other people.

> *John Hallam*

Insanity is often the logic of an accurate mind overtaxed.

Oliver Wendell Holmes

All power of fancy over reason is a degree of insanity.

Samuel Johnson

This wretched brain gave way, and I became a wreck, at random driven, without one glimpse of reason, or of heaven.

Thomas Moore

There is no insanity so devastating in man's life as utter sanity.

William Allen White

See also: DELUSION, MADNESS.

INSENSIBILITY

There is a calm, viscous insensibility which will baffle even the gods, and calmly say, Try all your lightnings here, and see whether I cannot quench them.

Thomas Carlyle

A thorough and mature insensibility is rarely to be acquired but by a steady perseverance in infamy.

Junius

Who can all sense of others' ills escape, is but a brute, at best, in human shape.

Juvenal

See also: DULNESS, INDIFFERENCE, SENSIBILITY.

INSIGHT: *see* DISCERNMENT.

INSINCERITY

Nothing is more disgraceful than insincerity.

Cicero

Of all the evil spirits abroad at this hour in the world, insincerity is the most dangerous.

James Anthony Froude

Insincerity in a man's own heart must make all his enjoyments—all that concerns him, unreal; so that his whole life must seem like a merely dramatic representation.

Nathaniel Hawthorne

It is a shameful and unseemly thing to think one thing and speak another, but how odious to write one thing and think another.

Seneca

See also: DECEIT, DISHONESTY, DISSIMULATION, HYPOCRISY, PRETENSION, TREACHERY.

INSPIRATION

I know the Bible is inspired, because it finds me at greater depths of my being than any other book.

Samuel Taylor Coleridge

When the minstrel sees two beautiful eyes, Then songs from his inmost bosom arise.

Heinrich Heine

The best evidence that the Bible is the inspired world of God is to be found within its covers. It proves itself.

Charles Hodge

Inspiration springs more readily from knowledge than from ignorance.

Horace Meyer Kallen

There is a deity within us who breathes that divine fire by which we are animated.

Ovid

Poets are the hierophants of an unapprehended inspiration; the mirrors of the gigantic shadows which futurity casts upon the present.

Percy Bysshe Shelley

See also: CREATIVITY, GENIUS, GOD.

INSTABILITY

Everything by starts, and nothing long.

John Dryden

Some have at first for wits, then poets passed; Turned critics next, and proved plain fools at last.

Alexander Pope

A rolling stone can gather no moss.

Publilius Syrus

It will be found that they are the weakest-minded and the hardest-hearted men, that most love change.

John Ruskin

He who begins many things finishes nothing.

Charles Simmons

See also: CHANGE, FICKLENESS, INCONSTANCY, INDECISION, IRRESOLUTION.

INSTINCT

There is not, in my opinion, anything more mysterious in nature than this instinct in animals, which thus rise above reason, and yet fall infinitely short of it.

Joseph Addison

Who taught the parrot his "Welcome"? Who taught the raven in a drought to throw pebbles into a hollow tree where she espied water, that the water might rise so as she might come to it? Who taught the bee to sail through such a vast sea of air, and to find the way from a flower in a field to her hive? Who taught the ant to bite every grain of corn that she burieth in her hill, lest it should take root and grow?

Francis Bacon

Improvable reason is the distinction between man and the animal.

Thomas Binney

Though reason is progressive, instinct is stationary. Five thousand years have added no improvement to the hive of the bee, or the house of the beaver.

Charles Caleb Colton

A goose flies by a chart which the Royal Geographical Society could not mend.

Oliver Wendell Holmes

The instinctive feeling of a great people is often wiser than its wisest men.

Lajos Kossuth

We only listen to those instincts which are our own, and only give credit to the evil when it has befallen us.

Jean de La Fontaine

The active part of man consists of powerful instincts, some of which are gentle and continuous; others violent and short; some baser, some nobler, and all necessary.

Francis William Newman

The instinct of brutes and insects can be the effect of nothing else than the wisdom and skill of a powerful everliving agent.

John Newton

Beasts, birds, and insects, even to the minutest and meanest of their kind, act with the unerring providence of instinct; man, the while, who possesses a higher faculty, abuses it, and therefore goes blundering on. They, by their unconscious and unhesitating obedience to the laws of nature, fulfill the end of their existence; he, in willful neglect of the laws of God, loses sight of the end of his.

Robert Southey

See also: COMMON SENSE, IMPULSE, INCLINATION, MOTIVE.

INSTRUCTION

The wise are instructed by reason; ordinary minds, by experience; the stupid, by necessity; and brutes by instinct.

Cicero

In moral lessons the understanding must be addressed before the conscience, and the conscience before the heart, if we would make the deepest impressions.

Nathaniel Emmons

A good newspaper and Bible in every house, a good schoolhouse in every district, and a church in every neighborhood, all appreciated as they deserve, are the chief support of virtue, morality, civil liberty, and religion.

Benjamin Franklin

See also: EDUCATION, GUIDANCE, TEACHING.

INSULT

I once met a man who had forgiven an injury. I hope some day to meet the man who has forgiven an insult.

Sir Thomas Fowell Buxton

There is an insolence which none but those who themselves deserve contempt can bestow, and those only who deserve no contempt can bear.

Henry Fielding

Whatever be the motive of an insult it is always best to overlook it; for folly scarcely can deserve resentment, and malice is punished by neglect.

Samuel Johnson

Oppression is more easily borne than insult.

Junius

The slight that can be conveyed in a glance, in a gracious smile, in a wave of the hand, is often the ne plus ultra of art. What insult is so keen or so keenly felt, as the polite insult which it is impossible to resent?

Julia Kavanagh

There are two insults which no human will endure: the assertion that he hasn't a sense of humor, and the doubly impertinent assertion that he has never known trouble.

Sinclair Lewis

The only graceful way to accept an insult is to ignore it; if you can't ignore it, top it; if you can't top it, laugh at it; if you can't laugh at it, it's probably deserved.

(Joseph) Russell Lynes

The greater part of mankind are more sensitive to contemptuous language, than to unjust acts; they can less easily bear insult than wrong.

Plutarch

He who puts up with insult invites injury.

Proverb

It is often better not to see an insult than to avenge it.

Seneca

See also: IMPERTINENCE, OFFENSE.

INTEGRITY

Nothing more completely baffles one who is full of trick and duplicity, than straightforward and simple integrity in another.

Charles Caleb Colton

A man of integrity will never listen to any plea against conscience.

Henry Home

Undoubtedly, there is little integration or integrity in most men's characters; there is only habit and a plodding limitation in life and mind; and if social pressure were not added to lack of opportunity disorderly lives would be more common than they are.

George Santayana

See also: HONESTY, HONOR, RECTITUDE.

INTELLECT

God has placed no limits to the exercise of the intellect he has given us, on this side of the grave.

Francis Bacon

Culture of intellect without religion in the heart, is only civilized barbarism, and disguised animalism.

Baron Christian Karl Josias von Bunsen

The education of the intellect is a great business; but an unconsecrated intellect is the saddest sight on which the sun looks down.

Sir Edwin Chadwick

Intellect alone is a dry and rattling thing.

Ilka Chase

If a man's eye is on the Eternal, his intellect will grow.

Ralph Waldo Emerson

Don't despair of a student if he has one clear idea.

Nathaniel Emmons

The men of action are, after all, only the unconscious instruments of the men of thought.

Heinrich Heine

The more we know of any one ground of knowledge, the further we see into the general domains of intellect.

(James Henry) Leigh Hunt

The intellect has only one failing, which, to be sure, is a very considerable one. It has no conscience. Napoleon is the readiest instance of this. If his heart had borne any proportion to his brain, he had been one of the greatest men in all history.

James Russell Lowell

Brains well prepared are the monuments where human knowledge is most surely engraved.

Jean Jacques Rousseau

Intellect is brain force.

Johann Christoph Friedrich von Schiller

See also: MIND, REASON, UNDERSTANDING.

INTELLECTUALS

A nation that cannot trust its intellectuals cannot trust itself.

Alfred Whitney Griswold

Intellectuals . . . regard over-simplification as the original sin of the mind and have no use for the slogans, the unqualified assertions and sweeping generalizations which are the propagandist's stock in trade.

Aldous Leonard Huxley

The responsible intellectual who moves between his campus and Washington knows above all that his task is, in the language of the current generation, 'to cool it', to bring what my generation called, 'not heat but light' to public affairs.

Lyndon Baines Johnson

It's among the intelligentsia, and especially among those who like to play with thoughts and concepts without really taking part in the cultural endeavors of their epoch, that

we often find the glib compulsion to explain everything and to understand nothing.
Joost Abraham Maurits Meerloo

If the intellectual has any function in society it is to preserve a cool and unbiased judgment in the face of all solicitations to passion.
Bertrand Arthur William Russell

See also: INTELLECT, INTELLIGENCE, WISDOM.

INTELLIGENCE

It is impossible to underrate human intelligence—beginning with one's own.
Henry Brooks Adams

A Negro cook told her children, "When you don't have an education, you've got to use your brains."
Anonymous

Intelligence increases mere physical ability one half. The use of the head abridges the labor of the hands.
Henry Ward Beecher

They who have read about everything are thought to understand everything, too, but it is not always so; reading furnishes the mind only with materials of knowledge; it is thinking that makes what we read ours. We are of the ruminating kind, and it is not enough to cram ourselves with a great load of collections—we must chew them over again.
William Ellery Channing

Though the influence on government of the American intellectual has fluctuated, there has never been a time when it was not considerable.
Bernard Augustine De Voto

I think America is richer in intelligence than any other country in the world; and that its intelligence is more scattered than in any country of the world.
Will (William James) Durant

The test of a first-rate intelligence is the ability to hold two opposed ideas in the mind, at the same time, and still retain the ability to function.
Francis Scott Key Fitzgerald

If we allow that ugliness is always within us, then we are free to create beauty. If we know that stupidity is always within us, then we are free to emphasize . . . intelligence.
Thaddeus Golas

The use of intelligence is the highest privilege and the deadliest menace of humanity.
Joseph Jastrow

The difference between intelligence and an education is this—that intelligence will make you a good living.
Charles Franklin Kettering

We must despise no sort of talents; they all have their separate uses and duties; all have the happiness of man for their object; they all improve, exalt, and gladden life.
Sydney Smith

It is no proof of a man's understanding to be able to confirm whatever he pleases; but to be able to discern that what is true is true, and that what is false is false; this is the mark and character of intelligence.
Emanuel Swedenborg

See also: COMMON SENSE, DISCERNMENT, DISCRETION, JUDGEMENT, KNOWLEDGE, PERCEPTION, PRUDENCE, SENSE.

INTELLIGENTSIA:
see INTELLECTUALS.

INTEMPERANCE

If we could sweep intemperance out of the country, there would be hardly poverty enough left to give healthy exercise to the charitable impulses.
Phillips Brooks

Wise men mingle mirth with their cares, as a help either to forget or overcome them; but to resort to intoxication for the ease of one's mind, is to cure melancholy by madness.
Pierre Charron

Intemperance is a dangerous companion. It throws people off their guard, betrays them to a great many indecencies, to ruinous passions, to disadvantages in fortune; makes them discover secrets, drive foolish bargains, engage in gambling, and often stagger from the tavern to the stews.
Charles Caleb Colton

Bacchus has drowned more men than Neptune.
Giuseppe Garibaldi

The body, overcharged with the excess of yesterday, weighs down the mind together with itself, and fixes to the earth that particle of the divine spirit.

Horace

The habit of intemperance by men in office has occasioned more injury to the public, and more trouble to me, than all other causes; and, were I to commence my administration again, the first question I would ask respecting a candidate for office, would be, "Does he use ardent spirits?"

Thomas Jefferson

Greatness of any kind has no greater foe than the habit of drinking.

Sir Walter Scott

I never drink. I cannot do it on equal terms with others. It costs them only one day; but it costs me three; the first in sinning, the second in suffering, and the third in repenting.

Laurence Sterne

One drinking saloon in a community means rags and misery for some of its people, and sixty thousand saloons in the nation mean rags and misery multiplied sixty thousand times. Universal happiness and prosperity cannot exist in the same land with the saloon any more than peace and safety can exist in a sheep-fold when the wolf has entered it.

Charles Augustus Stoddard

He that tempts me to drink beyond my measure, civilly invites me to a fever.

Jeremy Taylor

In our world death deputes intemperance to do the work of age.

Edward Young

See also: DISSIPATION, DRINK, INDULGENCE.

INTENTION

God takes men's hearty desires and will, instead of the deed, where they have not power to fulfill it; but he never took the bare deed instead of the will.

Richard Baxter

In the works of man as in those of nature, it is the intention which is chiefly worth studying.

Johann Wolfgang von Goethe

Many good purposes and intentions lie in the churchyard.

Philip Henry

It is easy to say what one intends: the difficult thing, sometimes, is to have an intention.

Jean Rostand

See also: AIM, MOTIVE, PURPOSE.

INTEREST

Interest makes some people blind, and others quick-sighted.

Francis Beaumont

There are no uninteresting things, there are only uninterested people.

Gilbert Keith Chesterton

It is more than possible, that those who have neither character nor honor, may be wounded in a very tender part, their interest.

Junius

Interest speaks all languages, and acts all parts, even that of disinterestedness itself.

Duc François de La Rochefoucauld

The virtues and vices are all put in motion by interest.

Duc François de La Rochefoucauld

The behavior of nations over a long period of time is the most reliable, though not the only, index of their national interest.

Walter Lippmann

Interest has the security, though not the virtue of a principle. As the world goes, it is the surest side; for men daily leave both relations and religion to follow it.

William Penn

I take it to be a principal rule of life, not to be too much addicted to any one thing.

Terence

How difficult it is to persuade a man to reason against his interest, though he is convinced that equity is against him.

John Trusler

See also: ATTENTION, LENDING.

INTERNATIONALISM

But let me say we hold firmly to a vital paradox and to a fixed purpose: We maintain strength only in order some day to yield it— in league with all other nations.

Dwight David Eisenhower

My nationalism is intense internationalism. I am sick of the strife between nations or religions.

Mohandas Karamchand (Mahatma) Gandhi

We are in the midst of a great transition from narrow nationalism to internationalism.

Lyndon Baines Johnson

See also: UNITED NATIONS.

INTOLERANCE

Nothing dies so hard, or rallies so often as intolerance.

Henry Ward Beecher

Racial and religious intolerance in the United States is dynamite—guaranteed, if it explodes, to blow up everyone.

Henry Seidel Canby

Intolerance has been the curse of every age and state.

Samuel Davies

In the blood of the Martyrs to intolerance are the seeds of unbelief.

Walter Lippmann

The devil loves nothing better than the intolerance of reformers, and dreads nothing so much as their charity and patience.

James Russell Lowell

It were better to be of no church than to be bitter for any.

William Penn

The intolerant man is the real pedant.

Jean Paul Richter

See also: BIGOTRY, DOGMATISM, FANATICISM, PERSECUTION, TYRANNY, ZEAL.

INTOXICATION: see DRUNKENNESS.

INTUITION: see PERCEPTION.

INVENTION

He that invents a machine augments the power of a man and the well-being of mankind.

Henry Ward Beecher

Where we cannot invent, we may at least improve; we may give somewhat of novelty to that which was old, condensation to that which was diffuse, perspicuity to that which was obscure, and currency to that which was recondite.

Charles Caleb Colton

It is frivolous to fix pedantically the date of particular inventions. They have all been invented over and over fifty times. Man is the arch machine, of which all these shifts drawn from himself are toy models. He helps himself on each emergency by copying or duplicating his own structure, just so far as the need is.

Ralph Waldo Emerson

We human beings who can invent and produce such incredible machines of war can become and must become no less ingenious in social engineering to eliminate the economic fears in the hearts of men and women.

Joshua Loth Liebman

All our inventions have endowed material forces with intellectual life, and degraded human life into a material force.

Karl Marx

Invention, strictly speaking, is little more than a new combination of those images which have been previously gathered and deposited in the memory. Nothing can be made of nothing; he who has laid up no materials can produce no combinations.

Sir Joshua Reynolds

Invention is the talent of youth, as judgment is of age.

Jonathan Swift

See also: CREATIVITY, DISCOVERY.

INVESTIGATION: see INQUIRY.

IRELAND

Ireland is moving in the mainstream of current world events . . . Your future is as promising as your past is proud and your destiny lies not as a peaceful island in a sea of trouble but as a maker and a shaper of world peace.

John Fitzgerald Kennedy

Ireland is a country in which the probable never happens and the impossible always does.

Sir John Pentland Mahaffy

I have lived for twenty years in Ireland and for seventy-two in England; but the twenty came first; and in Britain I am still a foreigner and shall die one.

George Bernard Shaw

See also: CANADA, ENGLAND, UNITED NATIONS.

IRONY

Irony is the gaiety of reflection and the joy of wisdom.

Anatole France

Clap an extinguisher upon your irony if you are unhappily blessed with a vein of it.

Charles Lamb

Irony is to the high-bred what billingsgate is to the vulgar; and when one gentleman thinks another gentleman an ass, he does not say it point-blank; he implies it in the politest terms he can invent.

Edward G. Bulwer-Lytton (Baron Lytton)

A taste for irony has kept more hearts from breaking than a sense of humor—for it takes irony to appreciate the joke which is on oneself.

Jessamyn West

See also: HUMOR, SARCASM, SATIRE, WIT.

IRRESOLUTION

Irresolution on the schemes of life which offer themselves to our choice, and inconstancy in pursuing them, are the greatest causes of all our unhappiness.

Joseph Addison

Irresolution is a worse vice than rashness. He that shoots best may sometimes miss the mark; but he that shoots not at all can never hit it. Irresolution loosens all the joints of a state; like an ague, it shakes not this nor that limb, but all the body is at once in a fit. The irressolute man is lifted from one place to another; so hatcheth nothing, but addles all his actions.

Owen Felltham

Irresolution frames a thousand horrors, embodying each.

John Martyn

See also: INDECISION, INSTABILITY, WEAKNESS.

ISLAM: see MOHAMMEDANISM.

ISRAEL

His Majesty's Government views with favor the establishment in Palestine of a national home for the Jewish people, and will use their best endeavors to facilitate the achievement of this object, it being clearly understood that nothing shall be done which shall prejudice the civil and religious rights of existing non-Jewish communities in Palestine, or the rights and political status enjoyed by the Jews in any other country.

Arthur James Balfour

Israel's economic and cultural progress is due to three things: the pioneering spirit that inspires the best of our immigrant and Israeli youth, who respond to the challenge of our desolate areas and the ingathering of the exiles; the feeling of Diaspora Jewry that they are partners in the enterprise of Israel's resurgence in the ancient homeland of the Jewish people; and the power of science, and technology which Israel unceasingly—and not without success—tries to enhance.

David Ben-Gurion

Jerusalem at midday in midsummer is a city of stone in a land of iron with a sky of brass.

Benjamin Disraeli

We will reject any form of armistice and we reject all kinds of euphemisms designed to provide our neighbors with an escape route from the necessity of formal interstate relations.

Abba Solomon Eban

One possible solution to this explosive issue might be the neutralization of the sacred soil of Israel, sanctified by the traditions of three great faiths, as a kind of spiritual Switzerland. Throughout history, this tiny land, whose passionate prophets transformed mankind, has stood on the strategic crossroads of three continents and was crushed repeatedly in the collision of extending empires. Now at last, out of reverence for its priceless religious legacy, let the world set Israel aside from the common market place of power and politics, and establish it as a holy land eternally remote from the machinations of military men.

Israel R. Margolies

For a little while longer there will be the sense of living under the shadow of God's wings; then the modern age will take over and the light of the patriarchs will go out. It is a somber thought, and the Israelis are well aware of its implications. They answer that risks must be taken whenever a desert is reclaimed, and the greater the risks, the more honor there is in the endeavor.

Pierre Stephen Robert Payne

Israel is very largely the work of Ben-Gurion. He mapped out the strategy which brought it into being, organized its defenses, stamped it with his own character and inspired it with his beliefs. . . . Wherever you travel in Israel, you find evidence of his ideas, his theories, his implacable desire to give the Jews a place in the sun. It is not only that he is more responsible than any other man for the creation of the state, but the state is almost unthinkable without his guiding presence. So much springs from him that you sometimes find yourself wondering where Ben-Gurion ends and Israel begins.

Pierre Stephen Robert Payne

One can wander through the streets and alleyways of Jerusalem and out into the Judean hills with almost no sense of the passing of time. Morning comes, and then afternoon, and all that has happened is that the light has shifted a little on the golden stone. Time vanishes, and becomes space, becomes stone and air. There is almost no sense that great events are taking place, for they have already taken place.

Pierre Stephen Robert Payne

When you leave the coast and go up to Jerusalem, you are in splendid company. For thousands upon thousands of years men and women have made the same journey and seen the same familiar landmarks. . . . The ghosts linger and throw their shadows on the road which winds across the plain and climbs the steep Judean mountains. It is a wild road, which seems to have cut loose from the ordinary life of mankind, so pounded by prayers and blood and legends that it resembles nothing so much as a shadowed highway of the imagination: not real, only to be guessed at, having its existence in the furthest reaches of the human spirit and in the wilderness of the human heart.

Pierre Stephen Robert Payne

The unique fusion of people and place is turning the Jew into the Israeli, however intricate and emotional and indispensable the remaining links with the Diaspora may be. A social artificiality has hardened into a way of life, aided—indeed inspired—by Arab hostility which has paradoxically not been without benefit to Israel, quickening the Israeli self-awareness and defensiveness, forging the new identity under a sense of danger, enabling it to find a coherent expression.

David Pryce-Jones

Whatever its detractors say, or hope, Israel is here to stay, unless there is a holocaust of such disaster that it becomes irrelevant which countries have been eliminated. A new personality is evolving as a new generation grows up, which has less intimate memories of past tragedies but a more acute perception of Middle East realities.

David Pryce-Jones

See also: JEW, JUDAISM.

ISOLATIONISM

Both in war and in peace, it has been my conviction that no man can isolate himself from the men and women he is attempting to serve and really sense what is in their hearts and minds.

Dwight David Eisenhower

There can be no such thing as Fortress America. If ever we were reduced to the isolation implied by that term we would occupy a prison, not a fortress.

Dwight David Eisenhower

If we lose touch with the river of change and enter a backwater, become self-centered and self-satisfied, and ostrichlike ignore what happens elsewhere, we do so at our peril.

Jawaharlal Nehru

It is a dangerous thing to isolate oneself; dangerous both for an individual and for a nation.

Jawaharlal Nehru

See also: FOREIGN AID.

ITALY

Open my heart and you will see
Graved inside of it, "Italy."
Robert Browning

That soft bastard Latin,
Which melts like kisses from a female mouth.
George Gordon Byron (Lord Byron)

Have you ever seen a lamb become a wolf?
The Italian race is a race of sheep. Eighteen years are not enough to change them. It takes a hundred and eighty, and maybe a hundred and eighty centuries.
Benito Mussolini

You may have the universe if I may have Italy.
Giuseppe Verdi

See also: NATION, UNITED NATIONS.

J

JAPAN

The best in Japanese culture today is the unself-conscious ability of the lowliest individual to appreciate beauty.

Lucy Herndon Crockett

Before Pearl Harbor the average American . . . imagined Japan in terms of Fujiyama, Madame Butterfly, cherry blossoms, and that decorative, slightly hush-hush figure, the geisha girl.

Lucy Herndon Crockett

Yesterday, December 7, 1941—a date which will live in infamy—the United States of America was suddenly and deliberately attacked by naval and air forces of the Empire of Japan.

Franklin Delano Roosevelt

See also: ASIA, EAST AND WEST, NATION, NUCLEAR WARFARE, UNITED NATIONS.

JAZZ

The chief trouble with jazz is that there is not enough of it; some of it we have to listen to twice.

Don Herold

Jazz will endure as long as people hear it through their feet instead of their brains.

John Philip Sousa

See also: DANCE, MUSIC, NOISE, SOUND.

JEALOUSY

Jealousy is . . . a tiger that tears not only its prey but also its own raging heart.

Michael Beer

Jealousy is the sister of love, as the devil is the brother of angels.

Catherine Stanislas Jean de Boufflers

Jealousy sees things always with magnifying glasses which make little things large, of dwarfs giants, of suspicions truths.

Miguel de Cervantes Saavedra

. . . jealous rather in the manner of a miser who underpays his servant and therefore suspects his honesty.

John Collier

All jealousy must be strangled in its birth, or time will soon make it strong enough to overcome the truth.

Sir William Davenant

What frenzy dictates, jealousy believes.

John Gay

To doubt is an injury; to suspect a friend is a breach of friendship; jealousy is a seed sown but in vicious minds; prone to distrust, because apt to deceive.

George Grenville (Baron Lansdowne)

In jealousy there is more of self-love, than of love to another.

Duc François de La Rochefoucauld

Jealousy is the greatest of misfortunes, and the least pitied by those who cause it.

Duc François de La Rochefoucauld

Jealousy lives upon doubts. It becomes madness or ceases entirely as soon as we pass from doubt to certainty.

Duc François de La Rochefoucauld

Women detest a jealous man whom they do not love, but it angers them when a man they do love is not jealous.

Ninon de Lenclos (Anne Lenclos)

Jealousy is the injured lover's hell.

John Milton

He who is next heir to supreme power, is always suspected and hated by him who actually wields it.

Tacitus

See also: COVETOUSNESS, ENVY, RIVALRY.

JERUSALEM: *see* ISRAEL.

JESTING

Men ought to find the difference between saltness and bitterness. Certainly, he that hath a satirical vein, as he maketh others afraid of his wit, so he had need be afraid of others' memory.

Francis Bacon

The Arabians have a saying, that it is not good to jest with God, death, or the devil; for the first neither can nor will be mocked; the second mocks all men one time or another; and the third puts an eternal sarcasm on those that are too familiar with him.

Francis Beaumont

Many a true word is spoken in jest.

English Proverb

Laughter should dimple the cheek, not furrow the brow. A jest should be such that all shall be able to join in the laugh which it occasions; but if it bears hard upon one of the company, like the crack of a string, it makes a stop in the music.

Owen Felltham

He that will lose his friend for a jest deserves to die a beggar by the bargain. Such let thy jests be, that they may not grind the credit of thy friend; and make not jests so long that thou becomest one.

Thomas Fuller

Be not affronted at a jest; if one throw ever so much salt at thee thou wilt receive no harm unless thou art raw and ulcerous.

Junius

Judge of a jest when you have done laughing.

William Lloyd

The jest loses its point when he who makes it is the first to laugh.

Johann Christoph Friedrich von Schiller

A joker is near akin to a buffoon; and neither of them is the least related to wit.

Philip Dormer Stanhope (Lord Chesterfield)

See also: HUMOR, LEVITY, REPARTEE, WIT.

JESUS CHRIST: *see* CHRIST.

JEWEL: *see* BIRTHDAY.

JEWS

Jews are a distinct nationality.

Louis Dembitz Brandeis

No individual should be subjected anywhere, by reason of the fact that he is a Jew, to a denial of any common right or opportunity enjoyed by non-Jews.

Louis Dembitz Brandeis

The great wrong that Shakespeare did the Jewish people was . . . that by emphasizing at every evil point Shylock's race and religion, he made him as a type of his people. . . . Shakespeare painted many other villains . . . yet never did he associate their religious creed with them. . . . The villainies they executed were individual, the villainy of Shylock was made to be Jewish.

Edward N. Calisch

If the statistics are right, the Jews constitute but one per cent of the human race. It suggests a nebulous dim puff of star dust lost in the blaze of the Milky Way. Properly the Jew ought hardly to be heard of; but he is heard of, has always been heard of. . . . He has made a marvelous fight in this world, in all the ages; and he has done it with his hands tied behind him.

Samuel Langhorne Clemens (Mark Twain)

When with true American enthusiasm we recall the story of our war for independence and rejoice in the indomitable courage and fortitude of our revolutionary heroes, we should not fail to remember how well the Jews of America performed their part in the struggle.

(Stephen) Grover Cleveland

The Jew is the pilgrim of commerce, trading with every nation and blending with none.

John Conybeare

If I am right the Germans will say I was a German, and the French will say I was a Jew; if I am wrong the Germans will say I was a Jew and the French will say I was a German.

Albert Einstein

No race has ever surpassed the Jewish descriptions of either the beauties or the terrors of the nature which environs man.

Charles William Eliot

The Jews are among the aristocracy of every land. If a literature is called rich in the possession of a few classic tragedies, what shall we say to a national tragedy, lasting for fifteen hundred years, in which the poets and actors were also the heroes?

George Eliot (Mary Ann Evans)

The character of a people, like the character of a person, should not be measured by its worst, but rather by its best; and, reckoned by that rule and by that standard, Israel's rank is high.

David H. Greer

The Jews, the Swiss Guard of deism.

Heinrich Heine

The Jews are with us as a perpetual lesson to teach us modesty and civility.

Oliver Wendell Holmes

They are a piece of stubborn antiquity, compared with which Stonehenge is in its nonage. They date beyond the Pyramids.

Charles Lamb

Though we boast of rank, we must admit that we are but of pagan stock while the Jews are of the blood of Christ. . . . The Glory came from them, not from us.

Martin Luther

In time of distress, Jews least of all . . . try to escape by recourse to drink or suicide.

Friedrich Wilhelm Nietzsche

The Jews are beyond all doubt the strongest, toughest, and purest race at present living in Europe.

Friedrich Wilhelm Nietzsche

While the Jews of the United States have remained loyal to their faith, and their race traditions, they have become indissolubly incorporated in the great army of American Citizenship.

Theodore Roosevelt

It takes ten Jews to make a Greek, and ten Greeks to make an Armenian.

Turkish Proverb

May the children of the Stock of Abraham, who dwell in this land, continue to merit and enjoy the good will of the other inhabitants, while everyone shall sit in safety under his own vine and fig-tree, and there shall be none to make them afraid.

George Washington

The Church repudiates all persecutions against any man. Moreover, mindful of her common patrimony with the Jews . . . she deplores the hatred, persecutions, and dis-plays of anti-Semitism directed against the Jews at any time and from any source.

Vatican Council II.

See also: GENOCIDE, ISRAEL, JUDAISM, NAZISM, PREJUDICE, YIDDISH.

JOB: *see* WORK.

JOURNALISM

I would sooner call myself a journalist than an author, for a journalist is a journeyman.

Gilbert Keith Chesterton

Get your facts first, and then you can distort 'em as you please.

Samuel Langhorne Clemens (Mark Twain)

The sole aim of journalism should be service. The press is a great power, but just as an unchained torrent of water submerges the whole country-side and devastates crops, even so an uncontrolled pen serves but to destroy. If the control is from without, it proves more poisonous than want of control. It can be profitable only when exercised from within. If this line of reasoning is correct, how many of the journals in the world would stand the test? But who would stop those that are useless? And who should be the judge? The useful and the useless must, like good and evil generally, go on together, and man must make his choice.

Mohandas Karamchand (Mahatma) Gandhi

I am insatiably curious about the state of our world. I revel in the recitation of the daily and weekly grist of journalism. . . . So let us drudge on about our inescapably impossible task of providing every week a first rough draft of a history that will never be completed about a world we can never understand.

Philip Graham

A journalist is a grumbler, a censurer, a giver of advice, a regent of sovereigns, a tutor of nations. Four hostile newspapers are more to be feared than a thousand bayonets.

Napoleon I (Bonaparte)

The fault I find with journalism is that it forces us to take an interest in some fresh triviality or other every day, whereas only three or four books in a lifetime gives us anything that is of real importance.

Marcel Proust

A news sense is really a sense of what is important, what is vital, what has color and life what people are interested in. That's journalism.

Arthur Burton Rascoe

All journalists are, by virtue of their handicraft, alarmists; this is their way of making themselves interesting.

George Allardice Riddell

The journalist holds up an umbrella, protecting society from the fiery hail of conscience.

George William Russell

See also: INFORMATION, NEWSPAPER, PRESS.

JOY

Man is the merriest, the most joyous of all the species of creation. Above and below him all are serious.

Joseph Addison

Joy is more divine than sorrow, for joy is bread and sorrow is medicine.

Henry Ward Beecher

Tranquil pleasures last the longest; we are not fitted to bear long the burden of great joys.

Christian Nestell Bovee

Grief can take care of itself, but to get full value of a joy you must have somebody to divide it with.

Samuel Langhorne Clemens (Mark Twain)

Here below is not the land of happiness; it is only the land of toil; and every joy which comes to us only to strengthen us for some greater labor that is to succeed.

Immanuel Hermann von Fichte

Great joy, especially after a sudden change of circumstances, is apt to be silent, and dwells rather in the heart than on the tongue.

Henry Fielding

He who can conceal his joys is greater than he who can hide his griefs.

Johann Kaspar Lavater

We lose the peace of years when we hunt after the rapture of moments.

Edward G. Bulwer-Lytton (Baron Lytton)

The most profound joy has more of gravity than of gaiety in it.

Michel Eyquem de Montaigne

There are some people who have the quality of richness and joy in them and they communicate it to everything they touch. It is first of all a physical quality; then it is a quality of the spirit.

Thomas Clayton Wolfe

See also: ENJOYMENT, HAPPINESS, SMILE.

JUDAISM

Judaism lives not in an abstract creed, but in its institutions.

Jacob Auerbach

Jesus was so much filled with the last and deepest thoughts of his people that he appears to us as the incarnation of the genius of Judaism.

Kurt Breysig

The religion of the Jews is, indeed, a light; but it is as the light of the glow-worm, which gives no heat, and illumines nothing but itself.

Samuel Taylor Coleridge

The history of the Jewish religion was the profoundest and richest that any nation had, and indeed was . . . the religious history of the human race.

Adolf von Harnack

Jesus was not a Christian, he was a Jew. He did not proclaim a new faith, but taught men to do the will of God. According to Jesus, as to the Jews generally, this will of God is to be found in the Law and the other canonical Scriptures.

Julius Wellhausen

See also: ISRAEL, JEW, RELIGION.

JUDGE

Judges ought to be more learned than witty, more reverent than plausible, and more advised than confident. Above all things, integrity is their portion and proper virtue.

Francis Bacon

Judges are apt to be naïve, simple-minded men.

Oliver Wendell Holmes, Jr.

Judges must be in number, for few will always do the will of few.

Niccolò Machiavelli

No one expects the judge to embrace every offender and invite him to dinner, but a human element in a trial and sentence would certainly improve matters. The judges are too impersonal, distant, and too little aware of the consequences of the sentences they award. If their awareness could be increased, as well as a sense of fellow-feeling with the prisoner, it would be a great gain. This can only come when the two belong to more or less the same class.

Jawaharlal Nehru

The hungry judges soon the sentence sign,
And wretches hang that jurymen may dine.

Alexander Pope

Four things belong to a judge: to hear courteously, to answer wisely, to consider soberly, and to decide impartially.

Socrates

See also: COURT, JUSTICE, LAW, LAWYER.

JUDGMENT

The wise determine from the gravity of the case; the irritable, from sensibility to oppression; the high-minded, from disdain and indignation at abusive power in unworthy hands.

Edmund Burke

To judge by the event, is an error all abuse and all commit; for in every instance, courage, if crowned with success, is heroism; if clouded by defeat, temerity.

Charles Caleb Colton

You shall judge of a man by his foes as well as by his friends.

Joseph Conrad

As the touchstone which tries gold, but is not itself tried by gold, such is he who has the true standard of judgment.

Epictetus

The contemporary mind may in rare cases be taken by storm; but posterity never. The tribunal of the present is accessible to influence; that of the future is incorrupt.

William Gladstone

A flippant, frivolous man may ridicule others, may controvert them, scorn them; but he who has any respect for himself seems to have renounced the right of thinking meanly of others.

Johann Wolfgang von Goethe

The seat of knowledge is in the head; of wisdom, in the heart. We are sure to judge wrong if we do not feel right.

William Hazlitt

Judgment is forced upon us by experience.

Samuel Johnson

The rule of Descartes, who is unwilling that we should come to a decision on the most insignificant matters before we have got a clear and distinct knowledge of them, is so seemly and so fair that it ought to be extended to the judgment we pass on men.

Jean de La Bruyère

We must not form our opinion of men as of a picture or a piece of sculpture, by one and a first view; there is an inward depth and a heart, which we must fathom: the veil of modesty hangs over merit, and the mask of hypocrisy conceals malignity. There are only a small number of judges able to distinguish what is real, and who have a right to give an opinion. It is only little by little, and when laid bare by times and opportunities, that perfect virtue and consummate vice at last show themselves in their true colours.

Jean de La Bruyère

Lynx-eyed to our neighbors, and moles to ourselves.

Jean de La Fontaine

Everyone complains of the badness of his memory, but nobody of his judgment.

Duc François de La Rochefoucauld

The greater part of people judge of men either by the company with whom they live, or by their fortune.

Duc François de La Rochefoucauld

Think wrongly, if you please; but in all cases think for yourself.

Gotthold Ephraim Lessing

We judge ourselves by what we feel capable of doing; others judge us by what we have done.

Henry Wadsworth Longfellow

Judge thyself with the judgment of sincerity, and thou wilt judge others with the judgment of charity.

John Mitchell Mason

It is with our judgments as with our watches: no two go just alike, yet each believes his own.

Alexander Pope

How little do they see what really is, who frame their hasty judgment upon that which seems.

Robert Southey

The most necessary talent in a man of conversation, which is what we ordinarily intend by a gentleman, is a good judgment. He that has this in perfection is master of his companion, without letting him see it; and has the same advantage over men of other qualifications, as one that can see would have over a blind man of ten times his strength.

Sir Richard Steele

Never be a judge between thy friends in any matter where both set their hearts upon the victory. If strangers or enemies be litigants, whatever side thou favorest, thou gettest a friend; but when friends are the parties thou losest one.

Jeremy Taylor

I mistrust the judgment of every man in a case in which his own wishes are concerned.

Arthur Wellesley (Duke of Wellington)

In our judgment of human transactions, the law of optics is reversed; we see the most indistinctly the objects which are close around us.

Richard Whately

One cool judgment is worth a thousand hasty councils. The thing to do is to supply light and not heat.

(Thomas) Woodrow Wilson

See also: DECISION, DISCERNMENT, JUDGE, PRUDENCE, UNDERSTANDING, WISDOM.

JURY

The point most liable to objection in the jury system, is the power which any one or more of the twelve have to starve the rest into compliance with their opinion; so that the verdict may possibly be given by strength of constitution, not by conviction of conscience: and "wretches hang that jurymen may dine."

Roger Boyle (Lord Orrery)

The institution of the jury, if confined to criminal cases, is always in danger; but when once it is introduced into civil proceedings, it defies the aggressions of time and of man.

Alexis de Tocqueville

Whenever a jury, through whimsical or ill-founded scruples, suffer the guilty to escape, they become responsible for the augmented danger of the innocent.

Daniel Webster

You stand here convicted of seeking to corrupt the administration of justice. You stand here convicted of having tampered, really, with the very soul of this nation. You stand here convicted of having struck at the very foundation upon which everything else in this nation depends, the very basis of civilization, and that is the administration of justice, because without a fair, proper, and lawful administration of justice nothing else would be possible in this country.

Frank Wiley Wilson

See also: COURT, JUDGE, LAW, LAWYER.

JUSTICE

Justice discards party, friendship, and kindred, and is therefore represented as blind.

Joseph Addison

To be perfectly just is an attribute of the divine nature; to be so to the utmost of our abilities, is the glory of man.

Joseph Addison

Justice is to give to every man his own.

Aristotle

He who goes no futher than bare justice, stops at the beginning of virtue.

Hugh Blair

Justice is only possible when to every man belongs the power to resist and claim redress for wrongs.

Robert Stephen Briffault

Justice is itself the great standing policy of civil society; and any departure from it, under any circumstance, lies under the suspicion of being no policy at all.

Edmund Burke

Whenever a separation is made between liberty and justice, neither, in my opinion, is safe.

Edmund Burke

He who is only just is cruel. Who on earth could live were all judged justly?

George Gordon Byron (Lord Byron)

Justice, though due to the accused, is due to the accuser also. The concept of fairness must not be strained till it is narrowed to a filament. We are to keep the balance true.

Benjamin Nathan Cardozo

Justice is the bread of the nation; it is always hungry for it.

Vicomte François René de Chateaubriand

Justice consists in doing no injury to men; decency in giving them no offense.

Cicero

Justice advances with such languid steps that crime often escapes from its slowness. Its tardy and doubtful course causes many tears to be shed.

Pierre Corneille

All are not just because they do no wrong; but he who will not wrong me when he may, he is truly just.

Richard Cumberland

Justice is the first virtue of those who command, and stops the complaints of those who obey.

Denis Diderot

Though force can protect in emergency, only justice, fairness, consideration and co-operation can finally lead men to the dawn of eternal peace.

Dwight David Eisenhower

Justice is as strictly due between neighbor nations, as between neighbor citizens. A highwayman is as much a robber when he plunders in a gang, as when single; and a nation that makes an unjust war is only a great gang of robbers.

Benjamin Franklin

Justice without wisdom is impossible.

James Anthony Froude

Justice delayed, is justice denied.

William Ewart Gladstone

One man's word is no man's word; we should quietly hear both sides.

Johann Wolfgang von Goethe

To embarrass justice by a multiplicity of laws, or hazard it by a confidence in our judges, are, I grant, the opposite rocks on which legislative wisdom has ever split; in one case the client resembles that emperor

who is said to have been suffocated with the bedclothes, which were only designed to keep him warm; in the other, that town which let the enemy take possession of its walls, in order to show the world how little they depended upon aught but courage for safety.

Oliver Goldsmith

Justice is the tolerable accommodation of the conflicting interests of society.

Learned Hand

God's mill grinds slow but sure.

George Herbert

Mankind are always found prodigal both of blood and treasure in the maintenance of public justice.

David Hume

Justice is the constant desire and effort to render to every man his due.

Justinian I

The achievement of justice is an endless process.

John Fitzgerald Kennedy

The love of justice in most men is only the fear of themselves suffering by injustice.

Duc François de La Rochefoucauld

Man is unjust, but God is just; and finally justice triumphs.

Henry Wadsworth Longfellow

There are no living communities which do not have some notions of justice, beyond their historic laws, by which they seek to gauge the justice of their legislative enactments.

Reinhold Niebuhr

Justice and power must be brought together, so that whatever is just may be powerful, and whatever is powerful may be just.

Blaise Pascal

Justice is the insurance we have on our lives and property, and obedience is the premium we pay for it.

William Penn

If thou desire rest unto thy soul, be just. He that doth no injury, fears not to suffer injury; the unjust mind is always in labor; it either practises the evil it hath projected, or projects to avoid the evil it hath deserved.

Francis Quarles

An honest man nearly always thinks justly.
Jean Jacques Rousseau

What is in conformity with justice should also be in conformity to the laws.
Socrates

Strike if you will, but hear me.
Themistocles

Expediency and justice frequently are not even on speaking terms.
Arthur Hendrick Vandenberg

The sentiment of justice is so natural, and so universally acquired by all mankind, that it seems to be independent of all law, all party, all religion.
Voltaire (François Marie Arouet)

Justice is the great interest of man on earth. It is the ligament which holds civilized beings and civilized nations together. Wherever her temple stands, and so long as it is duly honored, there is a foundation for social security, general happiness, and the improvement and progress of our race. And whoever labors on this edifice with usefulness and distinction, whoever clears its foundations, strengthens its pillars, adorns its entablatures, or contributes to raise its august dome still higher in the skies, connects himself, in name, and fame, and character, with that which is and must be as durable as the frame of human society.
Daniel Webster

Rather suffer an injustice than commit one.
Yiddish Proverb

See also: EQUALITY, EQUITY, LAW, RIGHTS.

K

KINDNESS

Half the misery of human life might be extinguished if men would alleviate the general curse they lie under by mutual offices of compassion, benevolence, and humanity.

Joseph Addison

The true and noble way to kill a foe, is not to kill him; you, with kindness, may so change him that he shall cease to be a foe, and then he's slain.

Charles Aleyn

Kindness is a language the dumb can speak, and the deaf can hear and understand.

Christian Nestell Bovee

Win hearts, and you have all men's hands and purses.

William Henry Burleigh

We cannot be just unless we are kindhearted.
Luc de Clapiers (Marquis de Vauvenargues)

He who confers a favor should at once forget it, if he is not to show a sordid, ungenerous spirit. To remind a man of a kindness conferred on him, and to talk of it, is little different from reproach.

Demosthenes

What do we live for, if it is not to make life less difficult to each other?
George Eliot (Mary Ann Evans)

When death, the great reconciler, has come, it is never our tenderness that we repent of, but our severity.
George Eliot (Mary Ann Evans)

Kindness is the only charm permitted to the aged; it is the coquetry of white hair.
Octave Feuillet

To speak kindly does not hurt the tongue.
French Proverb

Perfect obedience to the law of kindness would abolish government and the State.
Octavius Brooks Frothingham

A kind heart is a fountain of gladness, making everything in its vicinity freshen into smiles.

Washington Irving

To cultivate kindness is a valuable part of the business of life.

Samuel Johnson

If we were to make the conscious and frequent effort of treating others with consideration, the effects on us and on society as a whole would be amazing.

Henry Charles Link

Kind words prevent a good deal of that perverseness which rough and imperious usage often produces in generous minds.

John Locke

Ask yourself daily, to how many ill-minded persons you have shown a kind disposition.

Marcus Aurelius

Kindness: what a strange word to find on anybody's lips these days. It is like a style in clothes which is no longer worn, or like a musty language no longer spoken. What can one do with such a word? It is an instrument which has lost its usefulness. It is of no use either to the hero, or to the commune; it is an attribute neither of the lion nor of the ant. At best it is a feeble virtue; and it has had no part in history, for history is made by force. Nevertheless, it has a way of returning every now and then to earth, when one least expects it. The military bands stop a moment for breath, the hunters pause to sleep . . . and there is kindness again, nestling stubbornly in people's hearts, lifting a small peaceful voice, ready for the millennium.

Robert Nathan

Frankness and complete trust in the natural kindness of human nature will seldom fail, perhaps because it gives one even greater satisfaction to be helpful than helped.

Fulton Oursler

Kind words produce their own image in men's souls; and a beautiful image it is. They soothe and quiet and comfort the hearer. They shame him out of his sour, morose, unkind feelings. We have not yet begun to use kind words in such abundance as they ought to be used.

Blaise Pascal

I expect to pass through life but once. If therefore, there be any kindness I can show, or any good thing I can do to any fellow-being, let me do it now, and not defer or neglect it, as I shall not pass this way again.

William Penn

The last, best fruit which comes to late perfection, even in the kindliest soul, is tenderness toward the hard, forbearance toward the unforbearing, warmth of heart toward the cold, philanthropy toward the misanthropic.

Jean Paul Richter

Human kindness has never weakened the stamina or softened the fiber of a free people. A nation does not have to be cruel in order to be tough.

Franklin Delano Roosevelt

I had rather never receive a kindness, than never bestow one. Not to return a benefit is the greater sin, but not to confer it, is the earlier.

Seneca

The cheapest of all things is kindness, its exercise requiring the least possible trouble and self-sacrifice.

Samuel Smiles

You may find people ready enough to do the Samaritan without the oil and two-pence.

Sydney Smith

Kind hearts are more than coronets, and simple faith than Norman blood.

Alfred, Lord Tennyson

The best portion of a good man's life is his little, nameless, unremembered acts of kindness and of love.

William Wordsworth

See also: BENEFICENCE, CHARITY, HELP, MAGNANIMITY, PHILANTHROPY.

KING

The king will best govern his realm who reigneth over his people as a father doth over his children.

Agesilaus II

Royalty consists not in vain pomp, but in great virtues.

Agesilaus II

All precepts concerning kings are comprehended in these: remember thou art a man; remember thou art God's vicegerent.

Francis Bacon

He on whom Heaven confers a sceptre knows not the weight till he bears it.

Pierre Corneille

Wise kings generally have wise counsellors; and he must be a wise man himself who is capable of distinguishing one.

Diogenes

Kings' titles commonly begin by force, which time wears off and mellows into right; and power which in one age is tyranny is ripened in the next to true succession.

John Dryden

In a few years there will be only five kings in the world—the King of England and the four kings in a pack of cards.

Faruk I

Implements of war and subjugation are the last arguments to which kings resort.

Patrick Henry

In sovereignty it is a most happy thing not to be compelled, but so it is a most miserable thing not to be counselled.

Ben (Benjamin) Jonson

One of the strongest natural proofs of the folly of hereditary right in kings is, that nature disapproves it; otherwise she would not so frequently turn it into ridicule by giving mankind an ass in place of a lion.

Thomas Paine

Kings, in this chiefly, should imitate God; their mercy should be above all their works.

William Penn

Princes are never without flatterers to seduce them; ambition to deprave them; and desires to corrupt them.

Plato

The kingdom of God is the only absolute monarchy that is free from despotism.

Charles Simmons

The example of a vicious prince will corrupt an age, but that of a good one will not reform it.

Jonathan Swift

See also: DESPOTISM, GOVERNMENT, POWER.

KISS

A kiss is a lovely trick designed by nature to stop speech when words become superfluous.

Ingrid Bergman

It is the passion that is in a kiss that gives to it its sweetness; it is the affection in a kiss that sanctifies it.

Christian Nestell Bovee

Some say kissing is a sin; but if it was na lawful, lawyers would na allow it; if is was na holy, ministers would na do it; if it was na modest, maidens would na take it; if it was na plenty, puir folk would na get it.

Robert Burns

Eden revives in the first kiss of love.

George Gordon Byron (Lord Byron)

A long, long kiss—the kiss of youth and love.

George Gordon Byron (Lord Byron)

I felt the while a pleasing kind of smart;
The kiss went tingling to my panting heart.
When it was gone, the sense of it did stay;
The sweetness cling'd upon my lips all the day,
Like drops of honey, loth to fall away.

John Dryden

That farewell kiss which resembles greeting, that last glance of love which becomes the sharpest pang of sorrow.

George Eliot (Mary Ann Evans)

A kiss is the anatomical juxtaposition of two orbicular muscles in a state of contraction.

Cary Grant

Stolen kisses are always sweetest.

(James Henry) Leigh Hunt

Leave but a kiss in the cup, and I'll not look for wine.

Ben (Benjamin) Jonson

A soft lip would tempt you to eternity of kissing.

Ben (Benjamin) Jonson

A kiss can be a comma, a question mark or an exclamation point. That's basic spelling that every woman ought to know.

Jeanne Marie Bourgeois (Mistinguette)

I clasp thy waist; I feel thy bosom's beat.
O, kiss me into faintness, sweet and dim.

Alexander Smith

Dear as remembered kisses after death.

Alfred Lord Tennyson

Once he drew, with one long kiss, my whole soul through my lips.

Alfred, Lord Tennyson

I kissed my first woman and smoked my first cigarette on the same day; I have never had time for tobacco since.

Arturo Toscanini

A kiss from my mother made me a painter.

Benjamin West

Rather an honest slap than a false kiss.

Yiddish Proverb

See also: COURTSHIP, LOVE, ROMANCE.

KNOWLEDGE

What one knows is, in youth, of little moment; they know enough who know how to learn.

Henry Brooks Adams

A great deal of knowledge, which is not capable of making a man wise, has a natural tendency to make him vain and arrogant.

Joseph Addison

All knowledge and wonder (which is the seed of knowledge) is an impression of pleasure in itself.

Francis Bacon

Knowledge itself is power.

Francis Bacon

Reading maketh a full man; conference, a ready man: histories make men wise; poets, witty; the mathematics, subtle; natural philosophy, deep; moral philosophy, grave; logic and rhetoric, able to contend.

Francis Bacon

Some men think that the gratification of curiosity is the end of knowledge; some the love of fame; some the pleasure of dispute; some the necessity of supporting themselves by their knowledge; but the real use of all knowledge is this, that we should dedicate that reason which was given us by God to the use and advantage of man.

Francis Bacon

Knowledge that terminates in curiosity and speculation is inferior to that which is useful; and of all useful knowledge that is the most so which consists in a due care and just notion of ourselves.

Bernard of Clairvaux

That jewel knowledge is great riches, which is not plundered by kinsmen, nor carried off by thieves, nor decreased by giving.

Bhavabhuti

To the small part of ignorance that we arrange and classify we give the name knowledge.

Ambrose Gwinnett Bierce

I envy no man that knows more than myself, but pity them that know less.

Sir Thomas Browne

Knowledge conquered by labor becomes a possession,—a property entirely our own. A greater vividness and permanency of impression is secured, and facts thus acquired become registered in the mind in a way that mere imparted information can never produce.

Thomas Carlyle

The first step to knowledge is to know that we are ignorant.

Richard Cecil

As soon as a true thought has entered our mind, it gives a light which makes us see a crowd of other objects which we have never perceived before.

Vicomte François René de Chateaubriand

The essence of knowledge is, having it, to apply it; not having it, to confess your ignorance.

Confucius

Knowledge dwells in heads replete with thoughts of other men; wisdom, in minds attentive to their own.

William Cowper

One part of knowledge consists in being ignorant of such things as are not worthy to be known.

Crates

The more extensive a man's knowledge of what has been done, the greater will be his power of knowing what to do.

Benjamin Disraeli

Knowledge is the eye of desire and can become the pilot of the soul.

Will (William James) Durant

It's awfully hard for a woman to pretend not to know the things she ought not to know.

Robert Chambers (Bob) Edwards

What novelty is worth the sweet monotony where everything is known, and loved because it is known?

George Eliot (Mary Ann Evans)

He that sips of many arts, drinks of none.

Thomas Fuller

If you have knowledge, let others light their candles at it.

Thomas Fuller

It is knowledge that ultimately gives salvation.

Mohandas Karamchand (Mahatma) Gandhi

Knowledge of our duties is the most essential part of the philosophy of life. If you escape duty you avoid action. The world demands results.

George Washington Goethals

Man is not born to solve the problem of the universe, but to find out what he has to do; and to restrain himself within the limits of his comprehension.

Johann Wolfgang von Goethe

We know accurately only when we know little; with knowledge doubt increases.

Johann Wolfgang von Goethe

What is not fully understood is not possessed.

Johann Wolfgang von Goethe

Start some kind word on its travels. There is no telling where the good it may do will stop.

Sir Wilfred Thomason Grenfell

Many of the supposed increasers of knowledge have only given a new name, and often a worse, to what was well known before.
Augustus and Julius Hare

Knowledge is but folly unless it is guided by grace.
George Herbert

Knowledge and timber should not be much used until they are seasoned.
Oliver Wendell Holmes

The best part of our knowledge is that which teaches us where knowledge leaves off and ignorance begins.
Oliver Wendell Holmes

Only man among the creatures of the earth strives to penetrate the unknown and to understand the unknowable . . . This endless aerial pursuit is our fate, as truly as to bear offspring or to toil for bread. This passion is as genuine and as self-justifying as any other.
Oliver Wendell Holmes, Jr.

Other desires perish in their gratification, but the desire of knowledge never: the eye is not satisfied with seeing nor the ear with hearing.
Alfred Edward Housman

For the aims of my own career, I want to promote the increase of natural knowledge, and to forward the application of scientific methods of investigation to all the problems of life, in the conviction that there is no alleviation for the sufferings of mankind except veracity of thought and action, and the resolute facing of the world as it is, when the garment of make-believe is stripped off.
Thomas Henry Huxley

If a little knowledge is dangerous, where is the man who has so much as to be out of danger?
Thomas Henry Huxley

We face the future with a weapon in our hands that was not given to earlier rulers of the world. I mean scientific knowledge, and the capacity for increasing it indefinitely by scientific research.
Sir James Hopwood Jeans

The seeds of knowledge may be planted in solitude, but must be cultivated in public.
Samuel Johnson

When a king asked Euclid, whether he could not explain his art to him in a more compendious manner, he was answered, that there was no royal way to geometry. Other things may be seized by might, or purchased with money; but knowledge is to be gained only by study, and study to be prosecuted only in retirement.
Samuel Johnson

All wish to possess knowledge, but few, comparatively speaking, are willing to pay the price.
Juvenal

I keep six honest serving-men
(They taught me all I knew);
Their names are What and Why and When
And How and Where and Who.
Rudyard Kipling

What we know here is very little, but what we are ignorant of is immense.
Marquis Pierre Simon de Laplace

To me the pleasure of knowing is so great, so *wonderful*—nothing has meant so much to me in all my life, as certain knowledge [said Hermione]. Yes, it is the greatest thing in life—*to know*. It is really to be happy, to be *free*.
David Herbert Lawrence

The knowledge we have acquired ought not to resemble a great shop without order, and without an inventory; we ought to know what we possess, and be able to make it serve us in our need.
Baron Gottfried Wilhelm von Leibnitz

There is but one bond of peace that is both permanent and enriching: the increasing knowledge of the world in which experiment occurs.
Walter Lippmann

A taste of every sort of knowledge is necessary to form the mind, and is the only way to give the understanding its due improvement to the full extent of its capacity.
John Locke

All the knowledge that we mortals can acquire is not knowledge positive, but knowledge comparative, and subject to the errors and passions of humanity.
Edward G. Bulwer-Lytton (Baron Lytton)

Every generation enjoys the use of a vast hoard bequeathed to it by antiquity, and transmits that hoard, augmented by fresh acquisitions, to future ages.
Thomas Babington Macaulay

In many things it is not well to say, "Know thyself"; it is better to say, "Know others."
Menander of Athens

Fullness of knowledge always and necessarily means some understanding of the depths of our ignorance, and that is always conducive to both humility and reverence.
Robert Andrews Millikan

To know by rote is no knowledge; it is only a retention of what is entrusted to the memory. That which a man truly knows may be disposed of without regard to the author, or reference to the book from whence he had it.
Michel Eyquem de Montaigne

It is well for us to realize that the great increase in knowledge in the world does not necessarily make us better or wiser. We must know how to use that knowledge properly before we can fully profit by it. We must know whither to go before we rush ahead in our powerful car. We must, that is, have some idea of what the aim and object of life should be. Vast numbers of people today have no such notion, and never worry themselves about it. They live in an age of science, but the ideas that govern them and their actions belong to ages long past. It is natural that difficulties and conflicts should arise. A clever monkey may learn to drive a car, but he is hardly a safe chauffeur.
Jawaharlal Nehru

The wise man realizes how little he knows: it is the foolish person who imagines that he knows everything.
Jawaharlal Nehru

The brightest blaze of intelligence is of incalculably less value than the smallest spark of charity.
William Nevins

Never carry your shotgun or your knowledge at half-cock.
Austin O'Malley

Knowledge can be achieved only by minds which are freed from coercion in order that they may be faithful to evidence.
Ralph Barton Perry

Imparting knowledge is only lighting other men's candle at our lamp, without depriving ourselves of any flame.
Jane Porter

If you lack knowledge, what do you have? If you have knowledge what do you lack?
Proverb

It is wise to get knowledge and learning from every source—from a sot, a pot, a fool, a winter-mitten, or an old slipper.
François Rabelais

All I know is what I read in the papers.
Will (William Penn Adair) Rogers

We shall never know everything about anything, said Pascal. But the worst of it is to know that even everything about everything would leave us unsatisfied.
Jean Rostand

The end of all knowledge should be in virtuous action.
Sir Philip Sidney

Most men want knowledge, not for itself, but for the superiority which knowledge confers; and the means they employ to secure this superiority are as wrong as the ultimate object, for no man can ever end with being superior, who will not begin with being inferior.
Sydney Smith

Base-minded they that lack intelligence; for God himself for wisdom most is praised, and men to God thereby are highest raised.
Edmund Spenser

Knowledge is a comfortable and necessary retreat and shelter for us in advanced age, and if we do not plant it while young, it will give us no shade when we grow old.
Philip Dormer Stanhope (Lord Chesterfield)

The desire of knowledge, like the thirst of riches, increases ever with the acquisition of it.
Laurence Sterne

The great demand of the world is knowledge. The great problem is the equalization of intelligence, to put all knowledge in possession of every human being.
Lester Frank Ward

Knowledge has in our time, triumphed, and is triumphing, over prejudice and over bigotry. The civilized and Christian world is fast learning the great lesson, that difference of nation does not imply necessary hostility, and that all contact need not be war. The whole world is becoming a common field for intellect to act in. Energy of mind, genius, power, wheresoever it exists, may speak out in any tongue, and the world will hear it.

Daniel Webster

The word knowledge, strictly employed, implies three things, viz., truth, proof, and conviction.

Richard Whately

Knowledge, like religion, must be "experienced" in order to be known.

Edwin Percy Whipple

Knowledge . . . is finding out something for oneself with pain, with joy, with exultancy, with labor, and with all the little ticking, breathing moments of our lives, until it is ours as that only is ours which is rooted in the structure of our lives. Knowledge is a potent and subtle distillation of experience, a rare liquor, and it belongs to the person who has the power to see, think, feel, taste, smell, and observe for himself, and who has hunger for it.

Thomas Clayton Wolfe

See also: DISCOVERY, SCIENCE, UNDERSTANDING.

KOREA

[Ending the war] requires a personal trip to Korea. I shall make that trip. I shall go to Korea.

Dwight David Eisenhower

The attack upon Korea makes it plain beyond all doubt that Communism has passed beyond the use of subversion to conquer independent nations and will now use armed invasion and war.

Harry S Truman

Men of the armed forces in Korea, you will go down in history as the first army to fight under a flag of a world organization in the defense of human freedom. . . . Victory may be in your hands, but you are winning a greater thing than military victory, for you are vindicating the idea of freedom under international law.

Harry S Truman

See also: COMMUNISM, UNITED NATIONS, WAR.

L

LABOR

Alexander the Great, reflecting on his friends degenerating into sloth and luxury, told them that it was a most slavish thing to luxuriate, and a most royal thing to labor.

Isaac Barrow

If we would have anything of benefit, we must earn it, and earning it become shrewd, inventive, ingenious, active, enterprising.

Henry Ward Beecher

We don't consider manual work as a curse, or a bitter necessity, not even as a means of making a living. We consider it as a high human function, as the basis of human life, the most dignified thing in the life of the human being, and which ought to be free, creative. Men ought to be proud of it.

David Ben-Gurion

America . . . cannot develop citizens unless the workingmen possess industrial liberty; and industrial liberty is impossible if the right to organize be denied.

Louis Dembitz Brandeis

Don't assume that the interests of employer and employee are necessarily hostile. . . . The opposite is more apt to be the case.

Louis Dembitz Brandeis

The necessity of labor is a part of the primeval curse; and all the beauty, or glory, or dignity pertaining to it, depends on the ends to which it is the means.

Charles Astor Bristed

The true epic of our times is not "arms and the man," but "tools and the man," an infinitely wider kind of epic.

Thomas Carlyle

The fruit derived from labour is the sweetest of all pleasures.

Luc de Clapiers (Marquis de Vauvenargues)

A truly American sentiment recognises the dignity of labor and the fact that honor lies in honest toil.

(Stephen) Grover Cleveland

A man's best friends are his ten fingers.

Robert Collyer

Labor, even the most humble and the most obscure, if it is well done, tends to beautify and embellish the world.

Gabriele D'Annunzio

No way has been found for making heroism easy, even for the scholar. Labor, iron labor, is for him. The world was created as an audience for him; the atoms of which it is made are opportunities.

Ralph Waldo Emerson

Whatever there is of greatness in the United States, or indeed in any other country, is due to labor. The laborer is the author of all greatness and wealth. Without labor there would be no government, and no leading class, and nothing to preserve.

Ulysses Simpson Grant

Men give me some credit for genius. All the genius I have lies just in this: When I have a subject in hand, I study it profoundly. Day and night it is before me. I explore it in all its bearings. My mind becomes pervaded with it. Then the effort which I make the people are pleased to call the fruit of genius. It is the fruit of labor and thought.

Alexander Hamilton

Excellence in any department can be attained only by the labor of a lifetime; it is not to be purchased at a lesser price.

Samuel Johnson

The prosperity of a people is proportionate to the number of hands and minds usefully employed. To the community, sedition is a fever, corruption is a gangrene, and idleness is an atrophy. Whatever body or society wastes more than it acquires, must gradually decay; and every being that continues to be fed, and ceases to labor, takes away something from the public stock.

Samuel Johnson

Genius begins great works; labor alone finishes them.

Joseph Joubert

The labor of the body relieves us from the fatigues of the mind; and this it is which forms the happiness of the poor.

Duc François La Rochefoucauld

As regards bodily labor, even had man never fallen from the state of innocence, he would not have remained wholly unoccupied; but that which would then have been his free choice and his delight become afterwards compulsory, and the painful expiation for his disobedience.

Leo XIII (Gioacchino Vincenzo Pecci)

Toil and pleasure, in their nature opposites, are yet linked together in a kind of necessary connection.

Livy

Bowed by the weight of centuries he leans
Upon his hoe and gazes on the ground,
The emptiness of ages in his face,
And on his back the burden of the world.

Charles Edwin Markham

Love, therefore, labor; if thou shouldst not want it for food, thou mayest for physic. It is wholesome to the body and good for the mind; it prevents the fruit of idleness.

William Penn

The only form of labor . . . which gives the workingman a title to its fruits is that which a man exercises as his own master, and by which some new form or new value is produced.

Pius XI (Achille Ambrogio Damiano Ratti)

Excellence is never granted to man, but as a reward of labor. It argues, indeed, no small strength of mind to persevere in the habits of industry without the pleasure of perceiving those advantages, which, like the hand of a clock, while they make hourly approaches to their point, yet proceed so slowly as to escape observation.

Sir Joshua Reynolds

Nothing is denied to well-directed labor, and nothing is ever to be attained without it.

Sir Joshua Reynolds

I believe in the dignity of labor, whether with head or hand; that the world owes every man an opportunity to make a living.

John Davison Rockefeller, Jr.

It is only by labor that thought can be made healthy, and only by thought that labor can be made happy; and the two cannot be separated with impunity.

John Ruskin

Nature is just toward men. It recompenses them for their sufferings; it renders them laborious, because to the greatest toils it attaches the greatest rewards.

Charles de Secondat (Baron de Montesquieu)

Shun no toil to make yourself remarkable by some talent or other. Yet do not devote yourself to one branch exclusively. Strive to get clear notions about all. Give up to no science entirely, for science is but one.

Seneca

Without labor nothing prospers.

Sophocles

The guard of virtue is labor, and ease her sleep.

Torquato Tasso

Labor rids us of three great evils—irksomeness, vice, and poverty.

Voltaire (François Marie Arouet)

No race can prosper 'til it learns that there is as much dignity in tilling the field, as in writing a poem.

Booker Taliaferro Washington

Labor is the great producer of wealth; it moves all other causes.

Daniel Webster

Labor is one of the great elements of society—the great substantial interest on which we all stand. Not feudal service, or predial toil, or the irksome drudgery by one race of mankind subjected, on account of their color, to another; but labor, intelligent, manly, independent, thinking and acting for itself, earning its own wages, accumulating those wages into capital, educating childhood, maintaining worship, claiming the right of the elective franchise, and helping to uphold the great fabric of the State—that is American labor; and all my sympathies are with it, and my voice, till I am dumb, will be for it.

Daniel Webster

See also: CAPITALISM, EFFORT, EMPLOYMENT, INDUSTRY, UNIONS, WORK.

LABOR UNION: *see* UNIONS.

LAMB

Little lamb, who made thee?
Dost thou know who made thee?
Gave thee life, and bid thee feed
By the stream and o'er the mead;
Gave thee clothing of delight,
Softest clothing, woolly, bright.

William Blake

Though lions to their enemies, they were lambs to their friends.

Benjamin Disraeli

Like lambs, you do nothing but suck, and wag your tails.

Thomas Fuller

See also: ANIMAL, GENTLENESS.

LANGUAGE

Slovenly language corrodes the mind.

James Truslow Adams

A man's language is an unerring index of his nature.

Laurence Binyon

The language denotes the man; a coarse or refined character finds its expression naturally in a coarse or refined phraseology.

Christian Nestell Bovee

Language is properly the servant of thought, but not unfrequently becomes its master. The conceptions of a feeble writer are greatly modified by his style; a man of vigorous powers makes his style bend to his conceptions—a fact compatible enough with the acknowledgment of Dryden, that a rhyme had often helped him to an idea.

William Benton Clulow

Language is the armory of the human mind, and at once contains the trophies of its past and the weapons of its future conquests.

Samuel Taylor Coleridge

How can we appraise a proposal if the terms hurled at our ears can mean anything or nothing, and change their significance with the inflection of the voice? Welfare state, national socialism, radical, liberal, conservative, reactionary and a regiment of others—these terms in today's usage, are generally compounds of confusion and prejudice. If our attitudes are muddled, our language is often to blame. A good tonic for clearer thinking is a dose of precise, legal definition.

Dwight David Eisenhower

A man who is ignorant of foreign languages is ignorant of his own.

Johann Wolfgang von Goethe

Language is a solemn thing: it grows out of life—out of its agonies and ecstasies, its wants and its weariness. Every language is a temple in which the soul of those who speak it is enshrined.

Oliver Wendell Holmes

The function of language is twofold: to communicate emotion and to give information.

Aldous Leonard Huxley

Language is the dress of thought.

Samuel Johnson

Language is only the instrument of science, and words are but the signs of ideas.

Samuel Johnson

There is no tracing the connection of ancient nations but by language; therefore I am always sorry when any language is lost, for languages are the pedigree of nations.

Samuel Johnson

Language most shows a man; speak that I may see thee; it springs out of the most retired and inmost part of us.

Ben (Benjamin) Jonson

Language should do anything it is told, undertake any job required, not be a stubborn one-idea thing.

Dame Rose Macaulay

Scientists will have rifled the secrets of the moon and of Mars long before they will know the secret and subtle workings of the myriad-minded force which shapes the course of the language.

John Moore

A language is something infinitely greater than grammar and philology. It is the poetic testament of the genius of a race and a culture, and the living embodiment of the thoughts and fancies that have moulded them.

Jawaharlal Nehru

A living language is a throbbing, vital thing, ever changing, evergrowing and mirroring the people who speak and write it. It has its roots in the masses, though its superstructure may represent the culture of a few.

Jawaharlal Nehru

We have to make use of language, which is made up necessarily of pre-conceived ideas. Such ideas unconsciously held are the most dangerous of all.

Raymond Poincaré

England and America are two countries separated by the same language.

George Bernard Shaw

Language as well as the faculty of speech, was the immediate gift of God.

Noah Webster

The essence of language is that it utilizes those elements in experience most easily abstracted for conscious entertainment, and most easily reproduced in experience.

Alfred North Whitehead

Expression is the diffusion, in the environment, of something initially entertained in the experience of the expressor.

Alfred North Whitehead

Think like a wise man but communicate in the language of the people.

William Butler Yeats

See also: ACCENT, LITERATURE, SPEECH, WORD, WRITING.

LAUGHTER

If we consider the frequent reliefs we receive from laughter, and how often it breaks the gloom which is apt to depress the mind, one would take care not to grow too wise for so great a pleasure of life.

Joseph Addison

You grow up the day you have the first real laugh—at yourself.

Ethel Barrymore

I make myself laugh at everything, for fear of having to weep.

Pierre Augustin Caron de Beaumarchais

Laughter is caused by the spectacle of a human being responding mechanically to an unexpected situation.

Henri Bergson

A laugh, to be joyous, must flow from a joyous heart, for without kindness there can be no true joy.

Thomas Carlyle

No man who has once heartily and wholly laughed can be altogether and irreclaimably depraved.

Thomas Carlyle

The most utterly lost of all days, is that in which you have not once laughed.

Sébastien Roch Nicolas Chamfort

Laughter is the tonic, the relief, the surcease for pain.

Charles Spencer (Charlie) Chaplin

Equipped with the anti-toxin of laughter, one can live even in a standardized society without being too impressed by its standards.

Irwin Edman

He laughs best who laughs last.

English Proverb

People who believe in little laugh at little.

Leonard Feeney

Men show their character in nothing more clearly than by what they think laughable.

Johann Wolfgang von Goethe

Man is the only creature endowed with the power of laughter; is he not also the only one that deserves to be laughed at?

Fulke Greville (First Baron Brooke)

The loud laugh, that speaks the vacant mind.

Oliver Goldsmith

Alas for the worn and heavy soul, if, whether in youth or in age, it has outlived its privilege of spring time and sprightliness.

Nathaniel Hawthorne

Laughing is the sensation of feeling good all over, and showing it principally in one spot.

Bob (Leslie Townes) Hope

Maybe if we could all laugh alike, and laugh at the same time, this world of ours wouldn't be able to find so many things to squabble about.

> Bob (Leslie Townes) Hope

I like the laughter that opens the lips and the heart, that shows at the same time pearls and the soul.

> Victor Marie Hugo

A laugh is worth a hundred groans in any market.

> Charles Lamb

Beware of him who hates the laugh of a child.

> Johann Kaspar Lavater

The horse-laugh indicates coarseness or brutality of character.

> Johann Kaspar Lavater

Man alone suffers so excruciatingly in the world that he was compelled to invent laughter.

> Friedrich Wilhelm Nietzsche

That laughter costs too much which is purchased by the sacrifice of decency.

> Quintilian

Excellent authority tells us that the right laughter is medicine to weary bones.

> Carl Sandburg

The young man who has not wept is a savage, and the old man who will not laugh is a fool.

> George Santayana

Frequent and loud laughter is the characteristic of folly and ill manners; it is the manner in which the mob express their silly joy at silly things, and which they call being merry. In my mind there is nothing so ill-bred as audible laughter.

> Philip Dormer Stanhope (Lord Chesterfield)

Conversation never sits easier than when we now and then discharge ourselves in a symphony of laughter; which may not improperly be called the chorus of conversation.

> Sir Richard Steele

A good laugh is sunshine in a house.

> William Makepeace Thackeray

A hearty laugh gives one a dry cleaning, while a good cry is a wet wash.

> Puzant Kevork Thomajan

In laughter there is always a kind of joyousness that is incompatible with contempt or indignation.

> Voltaire (François Marie Arouet)

Nothing, no experience good or bad, no belief, no cause is in itself momentous enough to monopolize the whole of life to the exclusion of laughter.

> Alfred North Whitehead

Laugh, and the world laughs with you;
  Weep, and you weep alone,
For the sad old earth must borrow its mirth,
  But has trouble enough of its own.

> Ella Wheeler Wilcox

Weep before God—laugh before people.

> Yiddish Proverb

See also: CHEERFULNESS, MIRTH, SMILE.

LAW

In the search for ways to maintain our values and pursue them in an orderly way, we must look beyond the resources of law.

> Dean Gooderham Acheson

These written laws are just like spiders' webs; the small and feeble may be caught and entangled in them, but the rich and mighty force through and despise them.

> Anacharsis

We are going to have to decide what kind of people we are—whether we obey the law only when we approve of it, or whether we obey it no matter how distasteful we may find it.

> Harry Scott Ashmore

The result of the attempt to deal with evil socially rather than at its source in the individual, to substitute an outer for an inner control of appetite, has been a monstrous legalism, of which the Eighteenth Amendment is only the most notable example.

> Irving Babbitt

They are the best laws, by which the king has the greatest prerogative, and the people the best liberty.

> Francis Bacon

A mouse-trap: easy to enter but not easy to get out of.

> Arthur James Balfour

A law is valuable not because it is law, but because there is right in it.

> Henry Ward Beecher

Our business [the Supreme Court] is not to write laws to fit the day. Our task is to interpret the Constitution.

Hugo La Fayette Black

Law is the embodiment of the moral sentiment of the people.

Sir William Blackstone

Of all the parts of a law, the most effectual is the vindicatory; for it is but lost labor to say, "Do this, or avoid that," unless we also declare, "This shall be the consequence of your non-compliance." The main strength and force of a law consists in the penalty annexed to it.

Sir William Blackstone

If we desire respect for the law, we must first make the law respectable.

Louis Dembitz Brandeis

In all forms of Government the people is the true legislator.

Edmund Burke

In effect, to follow, not to force, the public inclination, to give a direction, a form, a technical dress, and a specific sanction, to the general sense of the community, is the true end of legislation.

Edmund Burke

In law nothing is certain but the expense.

Samuel Butler

The moment you step into the world of facts, you step into the world of limits. You can free things from alien or accidental laws, but not from the laws of their own nature.

Gilbert Keith Chesterton

Going to law is losing a cow for the sake of a cat.

Chinese Proverb

Possession is eleven points in the law.

Colley Cibber

Laws are silent in the midst of arms.

Cicero

True law is right reason conformably to nature, universal, unchangeable, eternal, whose commands urge us to duty, and whose prohibitions restrain us from evil.

Cicero

Reason is the life of law; nay, the common law itself is nothing else but reason.

Sir Edward Coke

Law and equity are two things that God hath joined together, but which man has put asunder.

Charles Caleb Colton

Men do not make laws. They do but discover them.

(John) Calvin Coolidge

Laws should be like clothes. They should be made to fit the people they are meant to serve.

Clarence Seward Darrow

When men are pure, laws are useless; when men are corrupt, laws are broken.

Benjamin Disraeli

Man became free when he recognized that he was subject to law.

Will (William James) Durant

The clearest way to show what the rule of law means to us in everyday life is to recall what has happened when there is no rule of law. The dread knock on the door in the middle of the night.

Dwight David Eisenhower

The greater the number of laws, the greater the number of offenses against them.

(Henry) Havelock Ellis

As the law dissolves all contracts which are without a valuable consideration, so a valuable consideration often dissolves the law.

Henry Fielding

Law never does anything constructive. We have had enough of legislators promising to do that which laws can not do.

Henry Ford

Ours is an accusatorial and not an inquisitorial system—a system in which the state must establish guilt by evidence independently and freely secured and may not by coercion prove its charge against an accused out of his own mouth.

Felix Frankfurter

Good laws make it easier to do right and harder to do wrong.

William Ewart Gladstone

The English laws punish vice; the Chinese laws do more, they reward virtue.

Oliver Goldsmith

Laws grind the poor, and rich men rule the law.

Oliver Goldsmith

Four out of five potential litigants will settle their disputes the first day they come together, if you will put the idea of arbitration into their heads.

Moses Henry Grossman

Laws are the very bulwarks of liberty; they define every man's rights, and defend the individual liberties of all men.

Josiah Gilbert Holland

The life of the law has not been logic; it has been experience.

Oliver Wendell Holmes, Jr.

Economic depression cannot be cured by legislative action or executive pronouncement. Economic wounds must be healed by the action of the cells of the economic body, the producers and consumers themselves.

Herbert Clark Hoover

It is impossible for men even to murder each other without statutes and maxims, and an idea of justice and honor. War has its laws as well as peace.

David Hume

The law is the standard and guardian of our liberty; it circumscribes and defends it; but to imagine liberty without a law, is to imagine every man with his sword in his hand to destroy him, who is weaker than himself; and that would be no pleasant prospect to those who cry out most for liberty.

Edward Hyde (Earl of Clarendon)

Law enforcement means more than putting on a uniform. It means learning about the Constitution, about our laws, about weaponry, about people. It means keeping up to date as our knowledge grows and our techniques and equipment improve. Many local law enforcement agencies cannot now supply the advanced training our men need.

Lyndon Baines Johnson

Penal laws—by which every man's danger becomes every man's safety, and by which, though all are restrained, yet all are benefited.

Samuel Johnson

To embarrass justice by a multiplicity of laws, or to hazard it by confidence in judges,

are the opposite rocks on which all civil institutions have been wrecked, and between which legislative wisdom has never yet found an open passage.

Samuel Johnson

It may be true that the law cannot make a man love me, but it can keep him from lynching me, and I think that's pretty important.

Martin Luther King, Jr.

The greatest of all injustice is that which goes under the name of law; and of all sorts of tyranny, the forcing the letter of the law against the equity is the most insupportable.

Sir Roger L'Estrange

To define law as an aggregate of rules, is to define human thought as an ensemble of the words in the dictionary.

Henry Levy-Ullman

The best way to get a bad law repealed is to enforce it strictly.

Abraham Lincoln

Let reverence for the laws become the political religion for the nations.

Abraham Lincoln

Laws are the sovereigns of sovereigns.

Louis XIV

The law of God is what we must do; the gospel is what God will give.

Martin Luther

Let but the public mind once become thoroughly corrupt, and all attempts to secure property, liberty, or life, by mere force of laws written on parchment, will be as vain as to put up printed notices in an orchard to keep off canker-worms.

Horace Mann

The law can make you quit drinking; but it can't make you quit being the kind that needs a law to make you quit drinking.

Donald Robert Perry (Don) Marquis

Multitudes of laws are signs, either of much tyranny in the prince, or much rebellious disobedience in the subject.

John Marston

The good need fear no law; it is his safety, and the bad man's awe.

Philip Massinger

Laws can discover sin, but not remove it.

John Milton

The laws keep up their credit, not because they are all just, but because they are laws. This is the mystical foundation of their authority.

Michel Eyquem de Montaigne

Laws are meant to fit existing conditions, and they are meant to help us to better ourselves. If conditions change, how can the old laws fit in? They must change with changing conditions, or else they become iron chains keeping us back while the world marches on. No law can be an "unchangeable law." It must be based on knowledge, and as knowledge grows, it must grow with it.

Jawaharlal Nehru

Please remember that law and sense are not always the same.

Jawaharlal Nehru

Whatever the legal aspect of the thing might be, there are moments when law is a feeble reed to rely upon.

Jawaharlal Nehru

The people's safety is the law of God.

James Otis

Where the law ends, there tyranny begins.

William Pitt

Law is experience developed by reason and applied continually to further experience.

Roscoe Pound

Petty laws breed great crimes.

Marie Louise de la Ramée (Ouida)

The excess of sentiment, which is misleading in philanthropy and economics, grows acutely dangerous when it interferes with legislation, or with the ordinary rulings of morality.

Agnes Repplier

Human nature is such that man does not accept rules unless they are imposed upon him by constituted authority.

Emery Reves

I believe that the law was made for man and not man for the law; that government is the servant of the people and not their master.

John Davison Rockefeller, Jr.

Society cannot exist without law and order, and cannot advance except through vigorous innovators.

Bertrand Arthur William Russell

The reason of the law is the law.

Sir Walter Scott

Laws only undertake to punish overt acts.

Charles de Secondat (Baron de Montesquieu)

We should never create by law what can be accomplished by morality.

Charles de Secondat (Baron de Montesquieu)

When I hear any man talk of an unalterable law, the only effect it produces on me is to convince me that he is an unalterable fool.

Sydney Smith

When the state is most corrupt, then the laws are most multiplied.

Tacitus

Men of the armed forces in Korea, you will go down in history as the first army to fight under a flag of a world organization in the defense of human freedom. . . . Victory may be in your hands, but you are winning a greater thing than military victory, for you are vindicating the idea of freedom under international law.

Harry S Truman

The law is merely an ever-inadequate human endeavor to divide justice, which is divine, into categories.

Peter Ustinov

A multitude of laws in a country is like a great number of physicians, a sign of weakness and malady.

Voltaire (François Marie Arouet)

If through some miracle it were possible to develop a superstructure of international cooperation and law, analogous to our Federal Union, the peoples of the world would in a few generations come to think of one another as neighbors and fellow citizens; and the perils of hyper-nationalism would disappear.

Earl Warren

The criminal law is not founded on the principle of vengeance; it uses evil only as the means of preventing greater evil.

Daniel Webster

Every instance of a man's suffering the penalty of the law, is an instance of the failure of that penalty in effecting its purpose, which is to deter from transgression.

Richard Whately

See also: CAPITAL PUNISHMENT, EQUITY, GOVERNMENT, JUDGE, JUSTICE, LAWYER, ORDER, POLITICS, STATESMANSHIP.

LAWYER

A lawyer who has not studied economics and sociology is very apt to become a public enemy.

Louis Dembitz Brandeis

What the lawyer needs to redeem himself is not more ability . . . but the moral courage in the face of financial loss and personal ill-will to stand for right and justice.

Louis Dembitz Brandeis

The trouble with law and government is lawyers.

Clarence Seward Darrow

A countryman between two lawyers is like a fish between two cats.

Benjamin Franklin

Every once in a while you meet a fellow in some honorable walk of life that was once admitted to the bar.

Frank McKinney (Kin) Hubbard

As to lawyers, their profession is supported by the indiscriminate defense of right and wrong.

Junius

What we lawyers want to do is to substitute courts for carnage, dockets for rockets, briefs for bombs, warrants for warheads, mandates for missiles.

Charles Sylvanus Rhyne

Our profession is good if practiced in the spirit of it; it is damnable fraud and iniquity when its true spirit is supplied by a spirit of mischief-making and money-getting. The love of fame is extinguished; every ardent wish for knowledge repressed; conscience put in jeopardy, and the best feelings of the heart indurated by the mean, money-catching, abominable practises, which cover with disgrace some of the modern practitioners of law.

Daniel Webster

See also: COURT, JUSTICE, LAW.

LEADERSHIP

And when we think we lead, we are most led.

George Gordon Byron (Lord Byron)

America has need of thousands of leaders who will never be elected President or even a governor of a state or president of a professional society, but who, quietly and without ostentation, nevertheless will exert true leadership in their several walks of life.

Harold Willis Dodds

Leadership is a word and a concept that has been more argued than almost any other I know. I am not one of the desk-pounding type that likes to stick out his jaw and look like he is bossing the show. I would far rather get behind and recognizing the frailties and the requirements of human nature, I would rather try to persuade a man to go along, because once I have persuaded him he will stick. If I scare him, he will stay just as long as he is scared, and then he is gone.

Dwight David Eisenhower

A platoon leader doesn't get his platoon to go by getting up and shouting and saying, "I am smarter, I am bigger. I am stronger. I am the leader." He gets men to go along with him because they want to do it for him and they believe in him.

Dwight David Eisenhower

The acts of men, who have come out to serve or lead, have always been misunderstood since the beginning of the world and none can help it.

Mohandas Karamchand (Mahatma) Gandhi

A leader is useless when he acts against the promptings of his own conscience.

Mohandas Karamchand (Mahatma) Gandhi

To put up with these misrepresentations and to stick to one's guns come what might—this is the essence of the gift of leadership.

Mohandas Karamchand (Mahatma) Gandhi

Charlatanism of some degree is indispensable to effective leadership.

Eric Hoffer

Leadership and learning are indispensable to each other.

John Fitzgerald Kennedy

Leadership is the other side of the coin of loneliness, and he who is a leader must always act alone. And acting alone, accept everything alone.

Ferdinand Edralin Marcos

Blindness in a leader is unpardonable.

Jawaharlal Nehru

A leader or a man of action in a crisis almost always acts subconsciously and then thinks of the reasons for his action.

Jawaharlal Nehru

The leader must know, must know that he knows, and must be able to make it abundantly clear to those about him that he knows.

Clarence Belden Randall

It [leadership in a democratic society] is the task of persuading people to sacrifice their short-run individual gratifications in order to achieve long-run community interests.

George F. Will

See also: COURAGE, GUIDANCE, HERO.

LEARNING

That learning is most requisite which unlearns evil.

Antisthenes

Learning teaches how to carry things in suspense, without prejudice, till you resolve.

Francis Bacon

A heap of ill-chosen erudition is but the luggage of antiquity.

Honoré de Balzac

You must learn day by day, year by year, to broaden your horizon. The more things you love, the more you are interested in, the more you enjoy, the more you are indignant about—the more you have left when anything happens.

Ethel Barrymore

Some will never learn anything because they understand everything too soon.

Sir Thomas Pope Blount

Acquire new knowledge whilst thinking over the old, and you may become a teacher of others.

Confucius

Seeing much, suffering much, and studying much, are the three pillars of learning.

Benjamin Disraeli

We cannot learn men from books.

Benjamin Disraeli

It is easy to learn something about everything, but difficult to learn everything about anything.

Nathaniel Emmons

I have learned silence from the talkative, toleration from the intolerant, and kindness from the unkind; yet strange, I am ungrateful to these teachers.

Kahlil Gibran

There is no lack of opportunity for learning among us. What is lacking is a respect of it . . . an honest respect such as we now have for technical competence or business success. . . . We honor learning, but do not believe in it. We reward it with lengthy obituaries and a wretched living wage. Rather than submit to it ourselves, we hire substitutes; rather than cultivate our own brains, we pick theirs. We spend as much time, and energy on short-cuts to learning and imitations of learning as we do on learning itself.

Alfred Whitney Griswold

The sweetest and most inoffensive path of life leads through the avenues of science and learning; and whoever can either remove any obstruction in this way, or open up any new prospect, ought, so far, to be esteemed a benefactor to mankind.

David Hume

The chief art of learning, as Locke has observed, is to attempt but little at a time. The widest excursions of the mind are made by short flights frequently repeated; the most lofty fabrics of science are formed by the continued accumulation of single propositions.

Samuel Johnson

I attribute the little I know to my not having been ashamed to ask for information, and to my rule of conversing with all descriptions of men on those topics that form their own peculiar professions and pursuits.

John Locke

The end of learning is to know God, and out of that knowledge to love him, and to imitate him, as we may the nearest, by possessing our souls of true virtue.

John Milton

Learning is a dangerous weapon, and apt to wound its master if it be wielded by a feeble hand, or by one not well acquainted with its use.

Michel Eyquem de Montaigne

We should not ask who is the most learned, but who is the best learned.

Michel Eyquem de Montaigne

The learning and knowledge that we have, is, at the most, but little compared with that of which we are ignorant.

Plato

A little learning is a dangerous thing!
Drink deep, or taste not the Pierian spring;
There shallow draughts intoxicate the brain,
And drinking largely sobers us again.

Alexander Pope

He who has no inclination to learn more will be very apt to think that he knows enough.

Sir John Powell

He who knoweth not what he ought to know, is a brute beast among men; he that knoweth no more than he hath need of, is a man among brute beasts; and he that knoweth all that may be known, is as a God among men.

Pythagoras

He who learns, and makes no use of his learning, is a beast of burden with a load of books. Does the ass comprehend whether he carries on his back a library or a bundle of faggots?

Saadi (Muslih-ud-Din)

The wisest mind hath something yet to learn.

George Santayana

Men learn while they teach.

Seneca

The true order of learning should be: first, what is necessary; second, what is useful; and third, what is ornamental. To reverse this arrangement is like beginning to build at the top of the edifice.

Lydia Howard Sigourney

Wear your learning, like your watch, in a private pocket. Do not pull it out merely to show that you have one. If asked what o'clock it is, tell it; but do not proclaim it hourly and unasked, like the watchman.

Philip Dormer Stanhope (Lord Chesterfield)

He that wants good sense is unhappy in having learning, for he has thereby only more ways of exposing himself; and he that has sense knows that learning is not knowledge, but rather the art of using it.

Sir Richard Steele

To be proud of learning, is the greatest ignorance.

Jeremy Taylor

The trouble about man is twofold. He cannot learn truths which are too complicated; he forgets truths which are too simple.

Dame Rebecca West

Learning makes a man fit company for himself.

Edward Young

See also: EDUCATION, INSTRUCTION, KNOWLEDGE, SCHOOL, STUDY, TEACHING, UNIVERSITY.

LEISURE

Leisure is a beautiful garment, but it will not do for constant wear.

Anonymous

The aim of education is the wise use of leisure.

Aristotle

The end of labor is to gain leisure.

Aristotle

He does not seem to me to be a free man who does not sometimes do nothing.

Cicero

Employ thy time well if thou meanest to gain leisure; and since thou art not sure of a minute, throw not away an hour. Leisure is time for doing something useful, and this leisure the diligent man will obtain, but the lazy man never, for a life of leisure and a life of laziness are two things.

Benjamin Franklin

Nearly all societies at nearly all times have had a leisure class—a class of persons who were exempt from toil. In modern times and especially in the United States the leisure class, at least in any identifiable phenomenon, has disappeared. To be idle is no longer considered rewarding or even entirely respectable.

John Kenneth Galbraith

More free time means more time to waste. The worker who used to have only a little time in which to get drunk and beat his wife now has time to get drunk, beat his wife—and watch TV.

Robert Maynard Hutchins

You cannot give an instance of any man who is permitted to lay out his own time, contriving not to have tedious hours.

Samuel Johnson

American society is shifting from a primary focus on work to one on leisure, from production-oriented to a consumption-oriented economy.

Robert Lee

Leisure offers a marvelous opportunity for freedom to be exercised, but where there is no commitment that freedom becomes aimlessness or apathy.

Robert Lee

Throughout the ages, man has dreamed of achieving a state in which he would be liberated from the burdens of labor. But now that the yearning for leisure has been largely fulfilled, we are in a quandary. We don't know quite how to face this new situation of living in a leisure society. We have so glorified labor that we find it difficult to live with leisure. Ironically, we approach with anxiety and restlessness a subject which is more appropriately associated with ease and relaxation.

Robert Lee

A workman ought to have leisure in proportion to the wear and tear of his strength.

Leo XIII (Gioacchino Vincenzo Pecci)

Back in the days when unremitting toil was the lot of all but the very few and leisure still a hopeless yearning, hard and painful as life was, it still felt real. People were in rapport with the small bit of reality allotted to them, the sense of the earth, the tang of the changing seasons, the consciousness of the eternal on-going of birth and death. Now, when so many have leisure, they become detached from themselves, not merely from the earth. From all widened horizons of our greater world a thousand voices call us to come near, to understand, and to enjoy, but our ears are not trained to hear them. The leisure is ours but not the skill to use it.

Robert Morrison MacIver

If the world were not so full of people, and most of them did not have to work so hard, there would be more time for them to get out and lie on the grass, and there would be more grass for them to lie on.

Donald Robert Perry (Don) Marquis

In this theater of man's life, it is reserved only for God and angels to be lookers-on.

Pythagoras

I am never less at leisure than when at leisure, nor less alone than when I am alone.

Scipio Africanus

There are two conflicting motifs that characterize American leisure time: first, a great sense of vacuity, of time emptied of meaningful activity; and second, an impression of determined frenzy to relax, to unwind, to do something different.

Robert Warren Spike

Leisure, itself the creation of wealth, is incessantly engaged in transmuting wealth into beauty by secreting the surplus energy which flowers in great architecture, great painting and great literature. Only in the atmosphere thus engendered floats that impalpable dust of ideas which is the real culture. A colony of ants or bees will never create a Parthenon.

Edith Newbold Jones Wharton

Leisure is not the opposite of work, it is the opportunity for free participation in the joyful activity and rest of those who are exploring the full potential of creation.

Colin Wilbur Williams

See also: IDLENESS, RECREATION, REST.

LENDING

Lend not beyond thy ability, nor refuse to lend out of thy ability; especially when it will help others more than it can hurt thee. If thy debtor be honest and capable, thou hast thy money again, if not with increase, with praise. If he prove insolvent do not ruin him to get that which it will not ruin thee to lose; for thou art but a steward, and another is thy owner, master, and judge.

William Penn

If you lend a person money it becomes lost for any purposes of your own. When you ask for it back again, you find a friend made an enemy by your own kindness. If you begin to press still further, either you must part with what you have lent or else you must lose your friend.

Plautus

If you lend money, you make a secret enemy; if you refuse it, an open one.

Voltaire (François Marie Arouet)

See also: BANK, BORROWING, CREDIT, MONEY.

LENIENCY

It is only necessary to grow old to become more indulgent. I see no fault committed that I have not committed myself.

Johann Wolfgang von Goethe

Lenity is a part of mercy, but she must not speak too loud for fear of waking justice.

Joseph Joubert

Lenity will operate with greater force in some instances than rigor. It is, therefore, my first wish to have all my conduct distinguished by it.

George Washington

See also: CLEMENCY, COMPASSION, MERCY.

LETTER

The test of a good letter is a very simple one. If one seems to hear the person talking, it is a good letter.

Arthur Christopher Benson

As water to a thirsty soul, so are letters from home to those in a foreign land.

Chinese New Year Motto

It is curious that the letters we desire to write most should often get delayed. The casual note, the routine letter is sent off and yet the letter which we are thinking of most remains unwritten.

Jawaharlal Nehru

To write a good love-letter, you ought to begin without knowing what you mean to say, and to finish without knowing what you have written.

Jean Jacques Rousseau

It is by the benefit of letters that absent friends are, in a manner, brought together.

Seneca

The best time to frame an answer to the letters of a friend is the moment you receive them; then the warmth of friendship and the intelligence received most forcibly cooperate.

William Shenstone

When the spirits sink too low, the best cordial is to read over all the letters of one's friends.

William Shenstone

Let your letter be written as accurately as you are able—I mean as to language, grammar, and stops; but as to the matter of it the less trouble you give yourself the better it will be. Letters should be easy and natural, and convey to the persons to whom we send just what we should say if we were with them.

Philip Dormer Stanhope (Lord Chesterfield)

A letter shows the man it is written to as well as the man it is written by.

Philip Dormer Stanhope (Lord Chesterfield)

See also: ABSENCE, MEMORY, LOVE, WRITING.

LEVELLER

Death and the cross are the two great levellers; kings and their subjects, masters and slaves, find a common level in two places—at the foot of the cross, and in the silence of the grave.

Charles Caleb Colton

Some persons are always ready to level those above them down to themselves, while they are never willing to level those below them up to their own position. But he that is under the influence of true humility will avoid both these extremes. On the one hand, he will be willing that all should rise just so far as their diligence and worth of character entitle them to; and on the other hand, he will be willing that his superiors should be known and acknowledged in their place, and have rendered to them all the honors that are their due.

Jonathan Edwards

Your levellers wish to level down as far as themselves, but they cannot bear levelling up to themselves.

Samuel Johnson

See also: COMMUNISM, DEMOCRACY, EQUALITY.

LEVITY

In infants, levity is a prettiness; in men, a shameful defect; in old age, a monstrous folly.

Duc François de La Rochefoucauld

Levity of behavior is the bane of all that is good and virtuous.

Seneca

Nothing like a little judicious levity.

Robert Louis Balfour Stevenson

See also: HUMOR, JESTING, LAUGHTER, MIRTH.

LIAR: *see* LYING.

LIBERAL

A liberal is one who has both feet firmly planted in the air.

Anonymous

A liberal is a man who is willing to spend somebody else's money.

Carter Glass

Broadmindedness is the result of flattening highmindedness out.

George Edward Bateman Saintsbury

See also: OPENMINDEDNESS, TOLERANCE.

LIBERALITY

Liberality consists less in giving much than in giving at the right moment.

Jean de La Bruyère

What we call liberality is often but the vanity of giving; we are more fond of the ostentation than of the generosity of the act.

Duc François de La Rochefoucauld

Frugality is good, if liberality be joined with it. The first is leaving off superfluous expenses; the last bestowing them to the benefit of others that need. The first without the last begets covetousness; the last without the first begets prodigality. Both together make an excellent temper. Happy the place where that is found.

William Penn

Some are unwisely liberal, and more delight to give presents than to pay debts.

Sir Philip Sidney

See also: BENEFICENCE, GENEROSITY, MAGNANIMITY, PHILANTHROPY.

LIBERTY

Absolute liberty is absence of restraint; responsibility is restraint; therefore, the ideally free individual is responsible to himself.

Henry Brooks Adams

A day, an hour of virtuous liberty is worth a whole eternity of bondage.

Joseph Addison

Liberty in itself is not government.

Bernard Mannes Baruch

To suppose that our civil and political liberties are secure because they are abstractly defined in written constitutions is to mistake the legal form for the living substance of freedom.

Carl Lotus Becker

There is no liberty to men whose passions are stronger than their religious feelings; there is no liberty to men in whom ignorance predominates over knowledge; there is no liberty to men who know not how to govern themselves.

Henry Ward Beecher

The people never give up their liberties but under some delusion.

Edmund Burke

What is liberty without wisdom and without virtue? It is the greatest of all possible evils, for it is folly, vice, and madness, without tuition or restraint.

Edmund Burke

Liberty in the most literal sense is the negation of law, for law is restraint, and the absence of restraint is anarchy.

Benjamin Nathan Cardozo

The spirit of liberty is not, as multitudes imagine, a jealousy of our own particular rights, but a respect for the rights of others, and an unwillingness that any one, whether high or low, should be wronged or trampled under foot.

William Ellery Channing

Liberty is a burden as well as a privilege; and the actual exercise of undictated and unguided free choice in every act of life would overburden all of us.

John Maurice Clark

Liberty, like charity, must begin at home.

James Bryant Conant

Reason and virtue alone can bestow liberty.

Anthony Ashley Cooper (Lord Shaftsbury)

The human race is in the best condition when it has the greatest degree of liberty.

Dante Alighieri

Oh, give me liberty! for even were paradise my prison, still I should long to leap the crystal walls.

John Dryden

Our nation was founded as an experiment in human liberty. Its institutions reflect the belief of our founders that men had their origin and destiny in God; that they were endowed by Him with inalienable rights and had duties prescribed by moral law, and that human institutions ought primarily to help men develop their God-given possibilities.

John Foster Dulles

When liberty destroys order, the hunger for order will destroy liberty.

Will (William James) Durant

True liberty consists only in the power of doing what we ought to will, and in not being constrained to do what we ought not to will.

Jonathan Edwards

If we must accept fate, we are not less compelled to assert liberty, the significance of the individual, the grandeur of duty, the power of character. We are sure, though we know not how, that necessity does comport with liberty, the individual with the world, my polarity with the spirit of the times.

Ralph Waldo Emerson

A Bible and a newspaper in every house, a good school in every district,—all studied and appreciated as they merit,—are the principal support of virtue, morality, and civil liberty.

Benjamin Franklin

I am a lover of my own liberty and so I would do nothing to restrict yours.

Mohandas Karamchand (Mahatma) Gandhi

There must be no tampering with the delicate machinery by which religious liberty and equality are secured, and no fostering of any spirit which would tend to destroy that machinery.

James Gibbons

Individualism always breeds tyranny, but personalism always breeds liberty, for a group of individuals is a herd, whereas a group of persons is a people.

Etienne Henry Gilson

Liberty lies in the hearts of men and women; when it dies there, no constitution, no law, no court can save it.

Learned Hand

The spirit of liberty is the spirit which is not too sure that it is right. The spirit of liberty is the spirit which seeks to understand the minds of other men and women. The spirit of liberty is the spirit which weighs their interests alongside its own bias. The spirit of liberty remembers that not even a sparrow falls to earth unheeded. The spirit of liberty is the spirit of Him who, nearly 2,000 years ago, taught mankind a lesson that it has never learned, but has never quite forgotten: that there may be a kingdom where the least shall be heard and considered side by side with the greatest.

Learned Hand

Is life so dear, or peace so sweet as to be purchased at the price of chains and slavery? Forbid it, Almighty God! I know not what course others may take, but, as for me, give me liberty or give me death.

Patrick Henry

If liberty with law is fire on the hearth, liberty without law is fire on the floor.

George Stillman Hillard

The spark of liberty in the mind and spirit of man cannot be long extinguished; it will break into flames that will destroy every coercion which seems to limit it.

Herbert Clark Hoover

In the past, personal and political liberty depended to a considerable extent upon governmental inefficiency. The spirit of tyranny was always more than willing; but its organization and material equipment were generally weak. Progressive science and technology have changed all this completely.

Aldous Leonard Huxley

We hold these truths to be self-evident, that all men are created equal; that they are endowed by their Creator with inalienable rights; and that among these are life, liberty, and the pursuit of happiness.

Thomas Jefferson

Let every nation know, whether it wishes us well or ill, that we shall pay any price, bear any burden, meet any hardship, support any friend, oppose any foe to assue the survival and the success of liberty.

John Fitzgerald Kennedy

Unless liberty flourishes in all lands, it cannot flourish in one.

John Fitzgerald Kennedy

Liberty is not idleness, it is an unconstrained use of time; it is the choice of work and of exercise. To be free, in a word, is not to be doing nothing, it is to be one's own master as to what one ought to do or not to do. What a blessing in this sense is liberty!

Jean de La Bruyère

Liberty is meaningless save in terms of law; and law demands authority and subordination as conditions of its life.

Harold Joseph Laski

Without equality, I say, there cannot be liberty.

Harold Joseph Laski

Liberty cannot extend to actions which present a clear and present danger to the existence of the democratic state itself, or to the established procedures for the succession of power within that state. But within these limits, it must be liberty for all.

Max Lerner

Our need today is the need of civil liberties not for a minority but for all.

Max Lerner

A useful definition of liberty is obtained only by seeking the principle of liberty in the main business of human life, that is to say, in the process by which men educate their responses and learn to control their environment.

Walter Lippmann

Liberty has restraints but no frontiers.

David Lloyd George

Liberty is not merely a privilege to be conferred; it is a habit to be acquired.

David Lloyd George

It is well observed by writers on civil polity that those people are more cruel and vindictive who have lost and recovered their liberty, than those who have preserved it as handed down by their fathers.

Niccolò Machiavelli

If freedom is no chimera, it means the intense claim to obey no one but reason.

Heinrich Mann

Give me the liberty to know, to think, to believe, and to utter freely, according to conscience, above all other liberties.

John Milton

Where liberty dwells, there is my country.

John Milton

The principle of liberty and equality, if coupled with mere selfishness, will make men only devils, each trying to be independent that he may fight only for his own interest. And here is the need of religion and its power, to bring in the principle of benevolence and love to men.

John Randolph

Liberty requires opportunity to make a living—a living which gives man not only enough to live by, but something to live for.

Franklin Delano Roosevelt

As liberty is not a fruit of all climates, it is not within the reach of all people.

Jean Jacques Rousseau

A country cannot subsist well without liberty, nor liberty without virtue.

Jean Jacques Rousseau

Free people, remember this maxim: we may acquire liberty, but it is never recovered if it is once lost.

Jean Jacques Rousseau

To live without let or hindrance would be life indeed, and so the spirit actually lives in its happier moments, in laughter or in quick thought. Yet there is a snare in this vital anarchy. It is like the liberty to sign cheques without possessing a bank account. You may write them for any amount; but it is only when a precise deposit limits your liberty that you may write them to any purpose.

George Santayana

There is no word which has received such a variety of significations, and has impressed the mind in so many different ways, as that of "liberty." Some have assumed it as the power of deposing him on whom they have conferred tyrannical authority; others, as the faculty of choosing him whom they ought to obey; others, as the privilege of bearing arms, and of exercising violence; others, again, as the right of being governed only by a man of their nation and by their own laws.

Charles de Secondat (Baron de Montesquieu)

The chief enemy of liberty is nationalism, the very thing which liberty itself created when it rescued nations from feudal tyranny or the overlordship of kings.

James Thomson Shotwell

Liberty consists in the right which God has given us, of doing, getting, and enjoying all the good in our power, according to the laws of God, of the State, and of our conscience. True liberty, therefore, can never interfere with the duties, rights, and interests of others.

Charles Simmons

There is not a truth to be gathered from history more certain, or more momentous, than this: that civil liberty cannot long be separated from religious liberty without danger, and ultimately without destruction to both. Wherever religious liberty exists, it will, first or last, bring in and establish political liberty. Wherever it is suppressed, the church establishment will, first or last, become the engine of despotism, and overthrow, unless it be itself overthrown, every vestige of political right.

Joseph Story

Christianity is the companion of liberty in all its conflicts, the cradle of its infancy, and the divine source of its claims.

Alexis de Tocqueville

Liberty, not communism, is the most contagious force in the world.

Earl Warren

Interwoven is the love of liberty with every ligament of the heart.

George Washington

Liberty and union, one and inseparable, now and forever.

Daniel Webster

The love of religious liberty is a stronger sentiment, when fully excited, than an attachment to civil freedom. Conscience, in the cause of religion, prepares the mind to act and to suffer, beyond almost all other causes. It sometimes gives an impulse so irresistible, that no fetters of power or of opinion can withstand it. History instructs us, that this love of religious liberty, made up of the clearest sense of right and the highest conviction of duty, is able to look the sternest despotism in the face, and, with means apparently inadequate, to shake principalities and powers.

Daniel Webster

Liberty is the one thing you can't have unless you give it to others.

William Allen White

See also: DEMOCRACY, FREEDOM, RIGHTS.

LIBRARY

Libraries are as the shrines where all the relics of saints, full of true virtue, and that without delusion or imposture, are preserved and reposed.

Francis Bacon

The true university of these days is a collection of books.

Thomas Carlyle

Next to acquiring good friends, the best acquisition is that of good books.

Charles Caleb Colton

The library is not a shrine for the worship of books. It is not a temple where literary incense must be burned or where one's devotion to the bound book is expressed in ritual. A library, to modify the famous metaphor of Socrates, should be the delivery room for the birth of ideas—a place where history comes to life.

Norman Cousins

A great library contains the diary of the human race. The great consulting room of a wise man is a library.

George Dawson

Over the door of a library in Thebes is the inscription "Medicine for the soul."

Diodorus Siculus

My books are my tools, and the greater their variety and perfection the greater the help to my literary work.

Tryon Edwards

Consider what you have in the smallest chosen library. A company of the wisest and wittiest men that could be picked out of all civil countries, in a thousand years, have set in best order the results of their learning and wisdom. The men themselves were hid and inaccessible, solitary, impatient of interruption, fenced by etiquette; but the thought which they did not uncover to their bosom friend is here written out in transparent words to us, the strangers of another age.

Ralph Waldo Emerson

What a place to be in is an old library! It seems as though all the souls of all the writers that have bequeathed their labors to these Bodleians were reposing here, as in some dormitory or middle state. I do not want to handle, to profane the leaves, their winding-sheets. I could as soon dislodge a shade. I seem to inhale learning, walking amid their foliage; and the odor of their old moth-scented coverings is fragrant as the first bloom of those sciential apples which grew amid the happy orchard.

Charles Lamb

The student has his Rome, his Florence, his whole glowing Italy, within the four walls of his library. He has in his books the ruins of an antique world and the glories of a modern one.

Henry Wadsworth Longfellow

See also: AUTHORSHIP, BOOK, LEARNING, LITERATURE, NOVEL, READING, STUDY.

LICENTIOUSNESS

The whore and gambler, by the state
Licensed, build that nation's fate.
The harlot's cry from street to street
Shall weave old England's winding sheet.

William Blake

Impure thoughts awaken impure feelings, lead to impure expressions, and beget impure actions, and these lead to imbecility both of body and mind, and to the ruin of all that is noble and pure in character.

Charles Simmons

Lewdness is a very broad way to death, ornamented with artful flowers, and begins to allure and seduce travelers at an early age. Parental watchfulness, guarding them from early childhood, should be diligent to keep them from this way to ruin.

Charles Simmons

Human brutes, like other beasts, find snares and poison in the provision of life, and are allured by their appetites to their destruction.

Jonathan Swift

See also: HARLOT, LUST, SENSUALITY, VICE.

LIFE

Life is activity, hence the deep-seated objections to negations.

James Truslow Adams

Though we seem grieved at the shortness of life in general, we are wishing every period of it at an end. The minor longs to be at age, then to be a man of business; then to make up an estate, then to arrive at honors, then to retire.

Joseph Addison

I don't want to own anything that won't fit into my coffin.

Fred Allen

The only time you live fully is from thirty to sixty.

(William) Hervey Allen

Every man's life is a fairy tale, written by God's fingers.

Hans Christian Andersen

The history of life on this planet is the history of the ways in which life has gained control over and freedom within its environment.

Wystan Hugh Auden

We live in deeds, not years; in thoughts, not breaths; in feelings, not in figures on the dial; we should count time by heart-throbs. He most lives who thinks most, feels the noblest, acts the best.

Gamaliel Bailey

The life of every man is a diary in which he means to write one story, and writes another; and his humblest hour is when he compares the volume as it is with what he hoped to make it.

Sir James Matthew Barrie

Age and youth look upon life from the opposite ends of the telescope; to the one it is exceedingly long, to the other exceedingly short.

Henry Ward Beecher

Life is not lost by dying! Life is lost minute by minute, day by dragging day, in all the thousand, small, uncaring ways.

Stephen Vincent Benét

We want bread and we want good bread . . . but man doesn't live by bread alone. Don't underestimate that fact. We've got to develop a way of living that is practical and successful. But it's got to be satisfactory in a cultural sense too.

Ralph Borsodi

I have only one life, and it is short enough. Why waste it on things I don't want most?

Louis Dembitz Brandeis

Be such a man, and live such a life, that if every man were such as you, and every life a life like yours, this earth would be God's Paradise.

Phillips Brooks

Don't believe the world owes you a living; the world owes you nothing—it was here first.

Robert Jones Burdette

Live as with God; and whatever be your calling, pray for the gift that will perfectly qualify you in it.

Horace Bushnell

All of the animals, excepting man, know that the principal business of life is to enjoy it.

Samuel Butler

Life is like playing a violin solo in public and learning the instrument as one goes on.

Samuel Butler

Life is the art of drawing sufficient conclusions from insufficient premises.

Samuel Butler

To live is like love, all reason is against it, and all healthy instinct for it.

Samuel Butler

Half the confusion in the world comes from not knowing how little we need . . . I live more simply now, and with more peace.

Richard Evelyn Byrd

One life; a little gleam of time between two eternities; no second chance for us forever more.

Thomas Carlyle

Our grand business in life is not to see what lies dimly at a distance, but to do what lies clearly at hand.

Thomas Carlyle

One of the most tragic things I know about human nature is that all of us tend to put off living. We are all dreaming of some magical rose garden over the horizon—instead of enjoying the roses that are blooming outside our windows today.

Dale Carnegie

The creed of the true saint is to make the most of life, and to make the best of it.

Edwin Hubbel Chapin

Let us so live that when we come to die even the undertaker will be sorry.

Samuel Langhorne Clemens (Mark Twain)

Whoever has lived long enough to find out what life is, knows how deep a debt of grati-

tude we owe to Adam, the first great benefactor of our race. He brought death into the world.

Samuel Langhorne Clemens (Mark Twain)

Hurried and worried until we're buried, and there's no curtain call,
Life's a very funny proposition, after all.

George Michael Cohan

How small a portion of our life it is that we really enjoy! In youth we are looking forward to things that are to come; in old age we are looking backward to things that are gone past; in manhood, although we appear indeed to be more occupied in things that are present, yet even that is too often absorbed in vague determinations to be vastly happy on some future day when we have time.

Charles Caleb Colton

For despite some of the horrors and barbarism of modern life which appall and grieve us, life in the twentieth century undeniably has—or has the potentiality of—such richness, joy and adventure as were unknown to our ancestors except in their dreams.

Arthur Holly Compton

It is the content of our lives that determines their value. If we limit ourselves to supply the means of living, in what way have we placed ourselves above the cattle that graze the fields.

Arthur Holly Compton

Life's a pretty precious and wonderful thing. You can't sit down and let it lap around you . . . you have to plunge into it; you have to dive through it! And you can't save it, you can't store it up; you can't horde it in a vault. You've got to taste it; you've got to use it. The more you use, the more you have . . . that's the miracle of it!

Kyle Samuel Crichton

It is not necessary to live, but to carve our names beyond that point, this is necessary.

Gabriele D'Annunzio

Few joys compare with that of pushing the battered dunce's book called Life under one's bolster; or, better yet, that of leaving one's Self, like a flower in a glass of water, to blush and revive unheeded amid the dark hours; hoping, if even against hope, that it may prove sweeter company in the morning.

Walter John de la Mare

What is called realism is usually a record of life at a low pitch and ebb viewed in the sunless light of day—so often a drab waste of grey and white, and an east wind blowing.
Walter John de la Mare

A man should live with his superiors as he does with his fire; not too near, lest he burn; not too far off, lest he freeze.
Diogenes

Live while you live, the epicure would say,
And seize the pleasures of the passing day.
Live while you live, the sacred preacher cries,
And give to God each moment as it flies.
Lord, in my views, let both united be.
I live in pleasure while I live in thee.
Philip Doddridge

I count all that part of my life lost which I spent not in communion with God, or in doing good.
John Donne

Life is like eating artichokes—you've got to go through so much to get so little.
Thomas Aloysius Dorgan

From the point of view of morals, life seems to be divided into two periods: in the first we indulge, in the second we preach.
Will (William James) Durant

He not busy being born is busy dying.
Bob Dylan

Life is hardly respectable if it has no generous task, no duties or affections that constitute a necessity of existence. Every man's task is his life-preserver.
Ralph Waldo Emerson

It is impossible to live pleasurably without living prudently, and honorably, and justly; or to live prudently, and honorably, and justly, without living pleasurably.
Epicurus

Life does not count by years. Some suffer a lifetime in a day, and so grow old between the rising and the setting of the sun.
Augusta Jane Evans

Dost thou love life? Then do not squander time, for that is the stuff life is made of.
Benjamin Franklin

The more the drive towards life is thwarted, the stronger is the drive towards destruction; the more life is realised, the less is the strength of destructiveness. *Destructiveness is the outcome of unlived life.*
Eric Fromm

I don't know a better preparation for life than a love of poetry and a good digestion.
Zona Gale

Life is but an endless series of experiments.
Mohandas Karamchand (Mahatma) Gandhi

The main purpose of life is to live rightly, think rightly, act rightly; the soul must languish when we give all our thoughts to the body.
Mohandas Karamchand (Mahatma) Gandhi

To enjoy life one should give up the lure of life.
Mohandas Karamchand (Mahatma) Gandhi

Life is the childhood of our immortality.
Johann Wolfgang von Goethe

A useless life is only an early death.
Johann Wolfgang von Goethe

The crab, more than any of God's creatures, has formulated the perfect philosophy of life. Whenever he is confronted by a great moral crisis in life, he first makes up his mind what is right, and then goes sideways as fast as he can.
Oliver Herford

That man lives twice who lives the first life well.
Robert Herrick

With most men life is like backgammon—half skill and half luck.
Oliver Wendell Holmes

The joy of life is to put out one's power in some natural and useful or harmless way. There is no other. And the real misery is not to do this.
Oliver Wendell Holmes, Jr.

A life spent, however victoriously, in securing the necessaries of life is no more than an elaborate furnishing and decoration of apartments for the reception of a guest who is never to come.
Alfred Edward Housman

The mintage of wisdom is to know that rest is rust, and that real life is love, laughter and work.

Elbert Green Hubbard

Life is not so bad, if you have plenty of luck, a good physique and not too much imagination.

Christopher William Bradshaw Isherwood

The great use of life is to spend it for something that outlasts it.

William James

Who can decide offhand which is absolutely better, to live or to understand life? We must do both alternately, and a man can no more limit himself to either than a pair of scissors can cut with a single one of its blades.

William James

Life, like every other blessing, derives its value from its use alone. Not for itself, but for a nobler end the eternal gave it; and that end is virtue.

Samuel Johnson

Life is an exciting business and most exciting when it is lived for others.

Helen Adams Keller

The best way to preserve life is to freeze it and dry it.

Walter William Kemmerer, Jr.

If life be miserable, it is painful to endure; if it be happy, it is frightful to lose.

Jean de La Bruyère

Man at his birth is tender and weak; at his death he is rigid and strong. . . . Thus rigidity and strength are the concomitants of death; softness and weakness are the concomitants of life.

Lao Tzu

Life, we learn too late, is in the living, in the tissue of each day and hour.

Stephen Butler Leacock

Live as if you expected to live an hundred years, but might die to-morrow.

Ann Lee

I would rather be ashes than dust! I would rather that my spark should burn out in a brilliant blaze than it should be stifled by dry-rot. I would rather be a superb meteor, every atom of me in magnificent glow, than a sleepy and permanent planet. The proper function of man is to live, not to exist. I shall not waste my days in trying to prolong them. I shall use my time.

Jack London

A new step in the sanctification of secular life is needed for the rejuvenation of the world. Not only will the spirit of Christ overflow into secular life, . . . as well as among monks dedicated to the search for perfection; but a kind of divine simplification will help people to realize that the perfection of human life does not consist in a stoic athleticism of virtue or in a humanly calculated application of holy recipes, but rather in a ceaselessly increasing love, despite our mistakes and weaknesses, between the Uncreated Self and the Created Self.

Jacques Maritain

It takes life to love Life.

Edgar Lee Masters

Life's a voyage that's homeward bound.

Herman Melville

Human life is basically a comedy. Even its tragedies often seem comic to the spectator, and not infrequently they actually have comic touches to the victim. Happiness probably consists largely in the capacity to detect and relish them.

Henry Louis Mencken

Life is but jest:
A dream, a doom;
A gleam, a gloom—
And then—good rest!

Life is but play;
A throb, a tear:
A sob, a sneer;
And then—good day.

Léon de Montenaeken

It is taken for granted that by lunch time the average man has been so beaten down by life that he will believe anything.

Christopher Darlington Morley

I look upon life as a party: One arrives long after it's started, and one's going to leave long before it's over, and it's as well, perhaps, not to try and be the life and soul of it, and not to try and take too much responsibility for it.

Robert Morley

Our sciences, our ideologies, and our arts are essential to humane living; and their expression in wholeness furthers and effectuates life.

Lewis Mumford

Our study of history has shown us that life is often very cruel and callous. To get excited over it, or merely to blame people, is foolish and does not help.

Jawaharlal Nehru

There are no simple congruities in life or history. The cult of happiness erroneously assumes them. It is possible to soften the incongruities of life endlessly by the scientific conquest of nature's caprices, and the social and political triumph over historic injustice. But all such strategies cannot finally overcome the fragmentary character of human existence. The final wisdom of life requires not the annulment of incongruity but the achievement of serenity within and above it.

Reinhold Niebuhr

Life is easier to take than you'd think; all that is necessary is to accept the impossible, do without the indispensable, and bear the intolerable.

Kathleen Norris

One thing led
To another and,
Before we knew it,
We were dead.

Michael O'Donoghue

The art of life lies in a constant readjustment to our surroundings.

Kakuzo Okakura

You may be important but your life's not. There's millions of it born every second. Life can cost too much even for a sucker to afford it—like everything else. And it's not sacred—only the you inside is. The rest is earth.

Eugene Gladstone O'Neill

Life must be dedicated to a destiny in order to have meaning.

José Ortega y Gasset

We are here to add what we can to, not to get what we can from, life.

Sir William Osler

We never live, but we ever hope to live.

Blaise Pascal

He that lives to live forever, never fears dying.

William Penn

The fear of life is the favorite disease of the twentieth century.

William Lyon Phelps

Each of us has come into this world as to a new city, in which he had no share before his birth.

Philo

The vanity of human life is like a rivulet, constantly passing away, and yet constantly coming on.

Alexander Pope

Fortune is a prize to be won. Adventure is the road to it. Chance is what may lurk in the shadows at the roadside.

William Sydney Porter (O. Henry)

Bestow thy youth so that thou mayst have comfort to remember it, when it hath forsaken thee, and not sigh and grieve at the account thereof. Whilst thou art young thou wilt think it will never have an end; but behold, the longest day hath his evening, and thou shalt enjoy it but once; it never turns again; use it therefore as the spring-time, which soon departeth, and wherein thou oughtest to plant and sow all provisions for a long and happy life.

Sir Walter Raleigh

Life is what our character wants it to be. We fashion it as a snail fashions its shell.

Jules Renard

Many think themselves to be truly God-fearing when they call this world a valley of tears. But I believe they would be more so, if they called it a happy valley. God is more pleased with those who think everything right in the world, than with those who think nothing right. With so many thousand joys, is it not black ingratitude to call the world a place of sorrow and torment?

Jean Paul Richter

A little work, a little sleep, a little love and it is all over.

Mary Roberts Rinehart

Man spends his life in reasoning on the past, complaining of the present, and trembling for the future.

Antoine Rivarol

Life is the game that must be played:
This truth at least, good friends, we know;
So live and laugh, nor be dismayed
As one by one the phantoms go.
Edwin Arlington Robinson

The poorest way to face life is to face it with a sneer.
Theodore Roosevelt

This solemn philosopher knows perfectly well that life is a pitiable farce; but this fool has no doubt that he is witnessing a magnificent adventure.
Jean Rostand

To succeed in giving life some weight without making it too heavy, that is the whole problem.
Jean Rostand

We owe almost everything that broadens or beautifies the lives of men to men who did not know how to live for themselves.
Jean Rostand

When life seems tolerable, we do not ask it to have meaning; it is the heart's upsets that make the mind too demanding.
Jean Rostand

To live is not merely to breathe, it is to act; it is to make use of our organs, senses, faculties, of all those parts of ourselves which give us the feeling of existence. The man who has lived longest is not the man who has counted most years, but he who has enjoyed life most. Such a one was buried a hundred years old, but he was dead from his birth. He would have gained by dying young; at least he would have lived till that time.
Jean Jacques Rousseau

There is no cure for birth and death save to enjoy the interval. The dark background which death supplies brings out the tender colours of life in all their purity.
George Santayana

There is a pathetic capacity in men to live nobly if only they would give one another the chance.
George Santayana

The first forty years of life give us the text; the next thirty supply the commentary.
Arthur Schopenhauer

I would so live as if I knew that I received my being only for the benefit of others.
Seneca

It is the bounty of nature that we live, but of philosophy that we live well; which is, in truth, a greater benefit than life itself.
Seneca

Life's evening will take its character from the day that preceded it.
Philip Nicholas Shuttleworth

Spiritual life and secure life do not go together. To save oneself one must struggle and take risks.
Ignazio Silone

It is always easier to go to heaven than to face the bewildering alternatives of contemporary life.
Lee Simonson

One learns in life to keep silent and draw one's own confusions.
Cornelia Otis Skinner

There are two things to aim at in life; first, to get what you want; and, after that, to enjoy it. Only the wisest of mankind achieve the second.
Logan Pearsall Smith

The end of life is to be like God, and the soul following God will be like him.
Socrates

To make good use of life, one should have in youth the experience of advanced years, and in old age the vigor of youth.
Stanislas I (Leszczyński)

There is nothing which must end, to be valued for its continuance. If hours, days, months, and years pass away, it is no matter what hour, day, month, or year we die. The applause of a good actor is due to him at whatever scene of the play he makes his exit.
Sir Richard Steele

Behold eighty-three years passed away! What cares! what agitation! what anxieties! what ill-will! what sad complications! and all without other result except great fatigue of body and mind, and disgust with regard to the past, and a profound sentiment of discouragement and despair with regard to the future.
Alexandre de Talleyrand-Périgord

Isn't life a terrible thing, thank God?
Dylan Thomas

The idea shared by many that life is a vale of tears is just as false as the idea shared by the great majority, the idea to which youth and health and riches incline you, that life is a place of entertainment.
Count Lev (Leo) Nikolaevich Tolstoi

To get all there is out of living we must employ our time wisely: never being in too much of a hurry to stop and sip life, but never losing our sense of the enormous value of a minute.
Robert Rawls Updegraff

Life is thick sown with thorns, and I know no other remedy than to pass quickly through them. The longer we dwell on our misfortunes, the greater is their power to harm us.
Voltaire (François Marie Arouet)

The shaping our own life is our own work. It is a thing of beauty, or a thing of shame, as we ourselves make it. We lay the corner and add joint to joint, we give the proportion, we set the finish. It may be a thing of beauty and of joy for ever. God forgive us if we pervert our life from putting on its appointed glory!
Henry Ware

It is good to be a part of life. Just as a sundial counts only the sunny hours, so does life know only that it is living.
Herbert George Wells

There are better things in life than fighting, but they are better only if their doers could have fought had they chosen.
Dame Rebecca West

Life is the only real counsellor; wisdom unfiltered through personal experience does not become a part of the moral tissue.
Edith Newbold Jones Wharton

The Book Of Life begins with a man and woman in a garden. It ends with Revelations.
Oscar Wilde

No one has learned the meaning of living until he has surrendered his ego to the service of his fellow men.
Walter Béran Wolfe

In masks outrageous and austere
The years go by in single file;
But none has merited my fear,
And none has quite escaped my smile.
Elinor Morton Wylie

The day when we plan seriously to start living either never comes or it comes too late.
Ida Alexa Ross Wylie

There appears to exist a greater desire to live long than to live well! Measure by man's desires, he cannot live long enough; measure by his good deeds, and he has not lived long enough; measure by his evil deeds, and he has lived too long.
Johann Georg von Zimmerman

See also: ACTION, AUTOBIOGRAPHY, BIOGRAPHY, MAN, PHILOSOPHY, SOUL, SPIRIT.

LIGHT

The first creation of God, in the works of the days was the light of sense; the last was the light of reason; and his Sabbath work, ever since, is the illumination of the spirit.
Francis Bacon

God appears, and God is Light,
To those poor souls who dwell in Night;
But does a Human Form display
To those who dwell in realms of Day.
William Blake

Light is the symbol of truth.
James Russell Lowell

Hail! holy light, offspring of heaven, first born!
John Milton

Lead, Kindly Light, amid the encircling gloom,
Lead Thou me on!
The night is dark, and I am far from home—
Lead Thou me on!
John Henry Newman

Light is the shadow of God.
Plato

The eye's light is a noble gift of heaven! All beings live from light; each fair created thing, the very plants, turn with a joyful transport to the light.
Johann Christoph Friedrich von Schiller

See also: DAY, MORNING, NIGHT, SUN.

LITERATURE

If I might control the literature of the household, I would guarantee the well-being of the church and state.

Francis Bacon

The great standard of literature, as to purity and exactness of style, is the Bible.

Hugh Blair

A country which has no national literature, or a literature too insignificant to force its way abroad, must always be, to its neighbors at least, in every important spiritual respect, an unknown and unestimated country.

Thomas Carlyle

Literature is but language; it is only a rare and amazing miracle by which a man really says what he means.

Gilbert Keith Chesterton

The study of literature nourishes youth, entertains old age, adorns prosperity, solaces adversity, is delightful at home, and unobtrusive abroad.

Cicero

Literature has now become a game in which the booksellers are the kings; the critics, the knaves; the public, the pack; and the poor author, the mere table or thing played upon.

Charles Caleb Colton

There, is first, the literature of knowledge; and, secondly, the literature of power. The function of the first is, to teach; of the second is, to move; the first is a rudder, the second an oar or a sail. The first speaks to the mere discursive understanding; the second speaks ultimately to the higher understanding or reason, but always through affections of pleasure and sympathy.

Thomas De Quincy

There is such a thing as literary fashion, and prose and verse have been regulated by the same caprice that cuts our coats and cocks our hats.

Benjamin Disraeli

Literature, has been, and probably always will be judged by moral standards.

Thomas Stearns Eliot

What I wish to affirm is that the whole of modern literature is corrupted by what I call secularism, that is simply unaware of, simply cannot understand, the primacy of the supernatural over the natural life: of something which I assume to be our primary concern.

Thomas Stearns Eliot

Literature happens to be the only occupation in which wages are not given in proportion to the goodness of the work done.

James Anthony Froude

The decline of literature indicates the decline of a nation; the two keep pace in their downward tendency.

Johann Wolfgang von Goethe

Literature is a fragment of a fragment; of all that ever happened, or has been said, but a fraction has been written, and of this but little is extant.

Johann Wolfgang von Goethe

Literary history is the great morgue where all seek the dead ones whom they love or to whom they are related.

Heinrich Heine

Let your literary compositions be kept from the public eye for nine years at least.

Horace

Such superiority do the pursuits of literature possess above every other occupation, that even he who attains but a mediocrity in them, merits the preeminence above those who excel the most in the common and vulgar professions.

David Hume

In science, read, by preference, the newest works; in literature, the oldest. The classic literature is always modern.

Edward G. Bulwer-Lytton (Baron Lytton)

In literature as in love, we are astonished at what is chosen by others.

André Maurois

The reason we constantly discover new truth in Shakespeare is that his complete understanding of the particular includes the universal.

Austin O'Malley

Great literature is simply language charged with meaning to the utmost possible degree.

Ezra Loomis Pound

Literature is news that stays news.

Ezra Loomis Pound

Literature is the immortality of speech.
August Wilhelm von Schlegel

Literature is a great staff, but a sorry crutch.
Sir Walter Scott

The literature of a people must spring from the sense of its nationality; and nationality is impossible without self-respect, and self-respect is impossible without liberty.
Harriet Elizabeth Beecher Stowe

Literature is that part of thought that is wrought out in the name of the beautiful.
David Swing

I never knew a man of letters ashamed of his profession.
William Makepeace Thackeray

All literature tends to be concerned with the question of reality.
Lionel Trilling

See also: AUTHORSHIP, BOOK, READING.

LITTLE THINGS: *see* TRIFLES.

LOGIC

Logic and rhetoric make men able to contend. Logic differeth from rhetoric as the fist from the palm; the one close, the other at large.
Francis Bacon

A paradox is a contradiction in which you take sides—both sides.
Gregory Bateson

Logic and metaphysics make use of more tools than all the rest of the sciences put together, and they do the least work.
Charles Caleb Colton

The mind has its own logic but does not often let others in on it.
Bernard Augustine De Voto

Ethics make one's soul mannerly and wise, but logic is the armory of reason, furnished with all offensive and defensive weapons.
Thomas Fuller

Logic is the science of the laws of thought as thought, that is, of the necessary conditions to which thought, in itself considered, is subject.
Sir William Hamilton

Whatever our characteristic American virtues are, logic isn't one of them. We share with the other English-speaking peoples a genius for living happily with contradictions, anomalies, and compromises.
Elizabeth Jackson

Logic works; metaphysics contemplates.
Joseph Joubert

It seems to me that logic is the art of convincing us of some truth; and eloquence a gift of the mind, which makes us master of the heart and spirit of others; which enables us to inspire them with or persuade them of whatever we please.
Jean de La Bruyère

It may be that dialectical theory finds its present truth in its own hopelessness.
Ronald David Laing

Syllogism is of necessary use, even to the lovers of truth, to show them the fallacies that are often concealed in florid, witty or involved discourses.
John Locke

It was a saying of the ancients, that "truth lies in a well"; and to carry on the metaphor, we may justly say, that logic supplies us with steps whereby we may go down to reach the water.
Isaac Watts

See also: ARGUMENT, METAPHYSICS, PHILOSOPHY, REASON, SCIENCE, TRUTH.

LONDON

London is roost for every bird.
Benjamin Disraeli

London—a nation, not a city.
Benjamin Disraeli

This downright earnestness of all things, this colossal uniformity, this machine-like movement, this troubled spirit in pleasure itself, this exaggerated London, smothers the imagination and rends the heart. . . . Send no poet to London.
Heinrich Heine

See also: CITY, ENGLAND.

LONELINESS

What is hell? Hell is oneself,
Hell is alone, the other figures in it
Merely projections. There is nothing to escape from

And nothing to escape to. One is always alone.

Thomas Stearns Eliot

In cities, no one is quiet but many are lonely; in the country, people are quiet but few are lonely.

Geoffrey Francis Fisher

All religion, all life, all art, all expression come down to this, to the effort of the human soul to break through its barrier of loneliness, of intolerable loneliness, and make some contact with another seeking soul, or with what all souls seek, which is (by any name) God.

Donald Robert Perry (Don) Marquis

People are lonely because they build walls instead of bridges.

Joseph Fort Newton

The whole world has always been full of that loneliness. The Loneliness does not come from the War. The War did not make it. It was the loneliness that made the War. It was the despair in all things for no longer having in them the grace of God.

William Saroyan

All this hideous doubt, despair, and dark confusion of the soul a lonely man must know, for he is united to no image save that which he creates himself.

Thomas Clayton Wolfe

Naked and alone we came into exile. . . .
Which of us has known his brother? Which of us has looked into his father's heart? . . .
Which of us is not forever a stranger and alone?

Thomas Clayton Wolfe

The surest cure for vanity is loneliness.

Thomas Clayton Wolfe

The whole conviction of my life now rests upon the belief that loneliness, far from being a rare and curious phenomenon, peculiar to myself and to a few other solitary men, is the central and inevitable fact of human existence.

Thomas Clayton Wolfe

See also: ABSENCE, DESOLATION, EMPTINESS, QUIET, SOLITUDE.

LOOKS

'Tis not my talent to conceal my thoughts, or carry smiles and sunshine in my face, when discontent sits heavy at my heart.

Joseph Addison

Features—the great soul's apparent seat.

William Cullen Bryant

What brutal mischief sits upon his brow!
He may be honest, but he looks damnation.

John Dryden

Looks are more expressive and reliable than words; they have a language which all understand, and language itself is to be interpreted by the look as well as tone with which it is uttered.

Tryon Edwards

A good face is a letter of recommendation, as a good heart is a letter of credit.

Edward G. Bulwer-Lytton (Baron Lytton)

How in the looks does conscious guilt appear.

Ovid

See also: APPEARANCE, FACE, IMPRESSION.

LOQUACITY

There is no elixir, balm, magisterium, opiate, unguent, ointment, local application, electuary, nor panacea, that can cure the excess of glottal activity in woman.

Anatole France

He who talks much cannot always talk well.

Carlo Goldoni

Every absurdity has a champion to defend it, for error is always talkative.

Oliver Goldsmith

They always talk who never think, and who have the least to say.

Matthew (Matt) Prior

Speaking much is a sign of vanity, for he that is lavish in words is a niggard in deed.

Sir Walter Raleigh

Nature has given us two ears, two eyes, and but one tongue, to the end that we should hear and see more than we speak.

Socrates

No fool can be silent at a feast.

Solon

See also: BABBLE, BORE, TALKING, TONGUE, VERBOSITY.

LOSS

Losing is like dying.

George Allen

Humanity may endure the loss of everything; all its possessions may be torn away without infringing its true dignity—all but the possibility of improvement.

Immanuel Hermann von Fichte

Show me a good loser and I'll show you a loser.

Vince Lombardi

When wealth is lost, nothing is lost; when health is lost, something is lost; when character is lost, all is lost.

German Motto

See also: ADVERSITY, GAIN, WASTE.

LOVE

Certain it is that there is no kind of affection so purely angelic as the love of a father to a daughter. He beholds her both with and without regard to her sex. In love to our wives, there is desire; to our sons, there is ambition; but in that to our daughters there is something which there are no words to express.

Joseph Addison

There is a Law that man should love his neighbor as himself. In a few hundred years it should be as natural to mankind as breathing or the upright gait; but if he does not learn it he must perish.

Alfred Adler

If there if anything better than to be loved, it is loving.

Anonymous

Love [God] and do what you will.

Augustine of Hippo

Nuptial love maketh mankind; friendly love perfecteth it; but wanton love corrupteth and embaseth it.

Francis Bacon

True love is eternal, infinite, and always like itself. It is equal and pure, without violent demonstrations: it is seen with white hairs and is always young in the heart.

Honoré de Balzac

Let no one who loves be called altogether unhappy.

Sir James Matthew Barrie

Of all the paths leading to a woman's love, pity is the straightest.

Francis Beaumont

We never know how much one loves till we know how much he is willing to endure and suffer for us; and it is the suffering element that measures love. The characters that are great, must, of necessity, be characters, that shall be willing, patient, and strong to endure for others. To hold our nature in the willing service of another, is the divine idea of manhood, of the human character.

Henry Ward Beecher

Young love is a flame; very pretty, often very hot and fierce, but still only light and flickering. The love of the older and disciplined heart is as coals, deep-burning, unquenchable.

Henry Ward Beecher

It is good that men should think; but it is indispensable that men should love.

Bernard Iddings Bell

The true measure of loving God is to love him without measure.

Bernard of Clairvaux

Love really has nothing to do with wisdom or experience or logic. It is the prevailing breeze in the land of youth.

Rudolph Block (Bruno Lessing)

The night has a thousand eyes,
    And the day but one;
Yet the light of the bright world dies,
    With the dying sun.

The mind has a thousand eyes,
    And the heart but one;
Yet the light of a whole life dies,
    When love is done.

Francis William Bourdillon

Our first love, and last love is self-love.

Christian Nestell Bovee

Love cannot be forced, love cannot be coaxed and teased. It comes out of Heaven, unasked and unsought.

Pearl Sydenstricker Buck

Love is a boy, by poets styl'd,
Then spare the rod, and spoil the child.
                          Samuel Butler

'Tis better to have loved and lost, than never to have lost at all.
                          Samuel Butler

Man's love is of man's life a part; it is woman's whole existence.
        George Gordon Byron (Lord Byron)

A man must love a thing very much if he not only practices it without any hope of fame or money, but even practices it without any hope of doing it well.
                Gilbert Keith Chesterton

The way to love anything is to realize that it might be lost.
                Gilbert Keith Chesterton

The man's courage is loved by the woman, whose fortitude again is coveted by the man. His vigorous intellect is answered by her infallible tact. Can it be true, as is so constantly affirmed, that there is no sex in souls? I doubt it exceedingly.
                Samuel Taylor Coleridge

Corporeal charms may indeed gain admirers, but there must be mental ones to retain them.
                    Charles Caleb Colton

Love is an alliance of friendship and animalism; if the former predominate it is a passion exalted and refined; if the latter, gross and sensual.
                    Charles Caleb Colton

Resignation, not mystic, not detached, but resignation open-eyed, conscious, and informed by love, is the only one of our feelings for which it is impossible to become a sham.
                          Joseph Conrad

We must know a person thoroughly before we can love.
                      Martial D'Auvergne

If nobody loves you, be sure it is your own fault.
                        Philip Doddridge

Love reckons hours for months, and days for years; and every little absence is an age.
                            John Dryden

A supreme love, a motive that gives a sublime rhythm to a woman's life, and exalts habit into partnership with the soul's highest needs, is not to be had where and how she wills: to know that high initiation, she must often tread where it is hard to tread, and feel the chill air, and watch through darkness.
              George Eliot (Mary Ann Evans)

Love, and you shall be loved. All love is mathematically just, as much as the two sides of an algebraic equation.
                      Ralph Waldo Emerson

Never self-possessed, or prudent, love is all abandonment.
                      Ralph Waldo Emerson

Love that has nothing but beauty to keep it in good health, is short-lived, and apt to have ague-fits.
                      Desiderius Erasmus

Bitterness imprisons life; love releases it. Bitterness paralyzes life; love empowers it. Bitterness sours life; love sweetens it. Bitterness sickens life; love heals it. Bitterness blinds life; love anoints its eyes.
                  Harry Emerson Fosdick

You've got to love what's lovable, and hate what's hateable. It takes brains to see the difference.
                      Robert Lee Frost

Affections, like the conscience, are rather to be led than drawn; and 'tis to be feared, they that marry where they do not love, will love where they do not marry.
                  (Sarah) Margaret Fuller

When two people loved each other they worked together always, two against the world, a little company. Joy was shared; trouble was split. You had an ally, somewhere, who was helping.
                          Paul Gallico

A coward is incapable of exhibiting love; it is the prerogative of the brave.
    Mohandas Karamchand (Mahatma) Gandhi

It is my firm belief that it is love that sustains the earth. There only is life where there is love. Life without love is death. Love is the reverse of the coin of which the obverse is Truth.
    Mohandas Karamchand (Mahatma) Gandhi

Love becomes lust the moment you make it a means for the satisfaction of animal needs.
Mohandas Karamchand (Mahatma) Gandhi

Love never claims, it ever gives. Love ever suffers, never resents, never revenges itself.
Mohandas Karamchand (Mahatma) Gandhi

Wherever you are confronted with an opponent, conquer him with love.
Mohandas Karamchand (Mahatma) Gandhi

That is the true season of love, when we believe that we alone can love, that no one could ever have loved so before us, and that no one will love in the same way after us.
Johann Wolfgang von Goethe

We are shaped and fashioned by what we love.
Johann Wolfgang von Goethe

First love is an instinct—at once a gift and a sacrifice. Every other is a philosophy—a bargain.
Arthur Sherburne Hardy

You can see them alongside the shuffleboard courts in Florida or on the porches of the old folks' homes up north: an old man with snow-white hair, a little hard of hearing, reading the newspaper through a magnifying glass; an old woman in a shapeless dress, her knuckles gnarled by arthritis, wearing sandals to ease her aching arches. They are holding hands, and in a little while they will totter off to take a nap, and then she will cook supper, not a very good supper, and they will watch television, each knowing exactly what the other is thinking, until it is time for bed. They may even have a good, soul-stirring argument, just to prove that they still really care. And through the night they will snore unabashedly, each resting content because the other is there. They are in love, they have always been in love, although sometimes they would have denied it. And because they have been in love they have survived everything that life could throw at them, even their own failures.
Ernest Havemann

The truth [is] that there is only one terminal dignity—love. And the story of a love is not important—what is important is that one is capable of love. It is perhaps the only glimpse we are permitted of eternity.
Helen Hayes

A man nearly always loves for other reasons than he thinks. A lover is apt to be as full of secrets from himself as is the object of his love from him.
Ben Hecht

Love and a cough cannot be hid.
George Herbert

There comes a time when the souls of human beings, women more even than men, begin to faint for the atmosphere of the affections they are made to breathe.
Oliver Wendell Holmes

Love, we say, is life; but love without hope and faith is agonizing death.
Elbert Green Hubbard

The first symptom of love in a young man, is timidity; in a girl, it is boldness. The two sexes have a tendency to approach, and each assumes the qualities of the other.
Victor Marie Hugo

The greatest happiness of life is the conviction that we are loved, loved for ourselves, or rather loved in spite of ourselves.
Victor Marie Hugo

The Bible speaks of a mysterious sin for which there is no forgiveness: this great unpardonable sin is the murder of the "love-life" in a human being.
Henrik Ibsen

A women is more considerate in affairs of love than a man; because love is more the study and business of her life.
Washington Irving

Love's like the measles, all the worse when it comes late in life.
Douglas William Jerrold

Love . . . is like a beautiful flower which I may not touch, but whose fragrance makes the garden a place of delight just the same.
Helen Adams Keller

Man while he loves is never quite depraved.
Charles Lamb

The heart of him who truly loves is a paradise on earth; he has God in himself, for God is love.
Félicité Robert de Lamennais

The reason why lovers are never weary of one another is this—they are always talking of themselves.

Duc François de La Rochefoucauld

True love is like a vision of ghosts; everybody talks about them but few have ever seen any.

Duc François de La Rochefoucauld

Love is an egotism of two.

Henri La Salle

As every lord giveth a certain livery to his servants, love is the very livery of Christ. Our Saviour, who is the Lord above all lords, would have his servants known by their badge, which is love.

Hugh Latimer

Love is a thing to be *learned*. It is a difficult, complex maintenance of individual integrity throughout the incalculable processes of inter-human polarity.

David Herbert Lawrence

To love is to place our happiness in the happiness of another.

Baron Gottfried Wilhelm von Leibnitz

Love gives itself; it is not bought.

Henry Wadsworth Longfellow

Faith, like light, should always be simple and unbending; while love, like warmth, should beam forth on every side and bend to every necessity of our brethren.

Martin Luther

Love is an image of God, and not a lifeless image, but the living essence of the divine nature which beams full of all goodness.

Martin Luther

It is the duty of men to love even those who injure them.

Marcus Aurelius

In love, as in war, a fortress that parleys is half taken.

Margaret of Valois

Love is not all; it is not meat or drink
Nor slumber nor a roof against the rain,
Not yet a floating spar to men that sink.

Edna St. Vincent Millay

Mutual love, the crown of all our bliss.

John Milton

Love is often a fruit of marriage.

Molière (Jean Baptiste Poquelin)

Reason is not what directs love.

Molière (Jean Baptiste Poquelin)

To love means to communicate to the other that you are all for him, that you will never fail him or let him down when he needs you, but that you will always be standing by with all the necessary encouragements. It is something one can communicate to another only if one has it.

Ashley Montagu

Love never reasons, but profusely gives; gives, like a thoughtless prodigal, its all, and trembles then lest it has done too little.

Hannah More

The worst thing an old man can be is a lover.

Thomas Otway

If a man loves a woman for her beauty, does he love her? No; for the small-pox, which destroys her beauty without killing her, causes his love to cease. And if any one loves me for my judgment or my memory, does he really love me? No; for I can lose these qualities without ceasing to be.

Blaise Pascal

The fundamental attitude of Catholics who want to convert the world is loving it. We shall love our neighbors and those far afield. We shall love our country, we shall love other people's. We shall love Catholics, the schismatics, the Protestants, the Anglicans, the indifferent, the Moslems, the pagans and the atheists. We shall love those who merit and those who do not merit to be loved. We shall love our time, our civilization, our technical science, our art, our sport, our world.

Paul VI (Giovanni Battista Montini)

Love is indeed heaven upon earth; since heaven above would not be heaven without it; for where there is not love, there is fear; but, "Perfect love casteth out fear." And yet we naturally fear most to offend what we most love.

William Penn

Love with old men is as the sun upon the snow, it dazzles more than it warms them.

John Petit-Senn

Two persons who love each other are in a place more holy than the interior of a church.

William Lyon Phelps

Those who love deeply never grow old; they may die of old age, but they die young.

Sir Arthur Wing Pinero

It is vain to try to conceal one's-self; the most discreet love allows its secret to escape by some slight token.

Jean Baptist Racine

The longest absence is less perilous to love than the terrible trials of incessant proximity.

Marie Louise de la Ramée (Ouida)

Love consists in this that two solitudes protect and touch and greet each other.

Rainer Maria Rilke

Nothing can of itself always be labeled as "wrong." One cannot, for instance, start from the position "sex relations before marriage" or "divorce" are wrong or sinful in themselves. They may be in 99 cases or even 100 cases out of 100, but they are not intrinsically so, for the only intrinsic evil is lack of love.

John Arthur Thomas Robinson

He who is intoxicated with wine will be sober again in the course of the night, but he who is intoxicated by the cup-bearer will not recover his senses until the day of judgment.

Saadi (Muslih-ud-Din)

Love does not consist in gazing at each other but in looking outward together in the same direction.

Antoine de Saint-Exupéry

A woman cannot love a man she feels to be her inferior; love without veneration and enthusiasm is only friendship.

George Sand (Baronne Dudevant)

Love is a brilliant illustration of a principle everywhere discoverable: namely, that human reason lives by turning the friction of material forces into the light of ideal goods. There can be no philosophic interest in disguising the animal basis of love, or in denying its spiritual sublimations, since all life is animal in its origin and all spiritual in its possible fruits.

George Santayana

I have enjoyed the happiness of the world; I have lived and loved.

Johann Christoph Friedrich von Schiller

Those who yield their souls captive to the brief intoxication of love, if no higher and holier feeling mingle with and consecrate their dream of bliss, will shrink trembling from the pangs that attend their waking.

August Wilhelm von Schlegel

Love is like the moon; when it does not increase it decreases.

Alexandre Joseph Pierre de Ségur

Love looks through a telescope; envy, through a microscope.

Henry Wheeler Shaw (Josh Billings)

The soul of woman lives in love.

Lydia Howard Sigourney

Take away love, and not physical nature only, but the heart of the moral world would be palsied.

Robert Southey

We attract hearts by the qualities we display: we retain them by the qualities we possess.

Jean Baptiste Antoine Suard

Love is the greatest thing that God can give us, for himself is love; and it is the greatest thing we can give to God, for it will also give ourselves, and carry with it all that is ours. The apostle calls it the bond of perfection; it is the old, the new, and the great commandment, and all the commandments, for it is the fulfilling of the law. It does the work of all the other graces without any instrument but its own immediate virtue.

Jeremy Taylor

It is better to have loved and lost, than not to love at all.

Alfred, Lord Tennyson

It is possible that a man can be so-changed by love as hardly to be recognized as the same person.

Terence

A lady of 47 who has been married 27 years and has six children knows what love really is and once described it for me like this: "Love is what you've been through with somebody."

James Grover Thurber

The life that goes out in love to all is the life that is full, and rich, and continually expanding in beauty and in power.

Ralph Waldo Trine

The real value of love is the increased general vitality it produces.

Paul Ambroise Valéry

As a source of reflection, love has no bounds: it is as profound as eternity, as lofty as the heavens, and as vast as the universe.

Comte Alfred Victor de Vigny

Love is a canvas furnished by Nature and embroidered by imagination.

Voltaire (François Marie Arouet)

Two sentiments alone suffice for man, were he to live the age of the rocks,—love, and the contemplation of the Deity.

Isaac Watts

I never could explain *why* I love anybody, or anything.

Walt (Walter) Whitman

That strange phenomenon love . . . pops up in the strangest places.

Thornton Niven Wilder

Love, though it expends itself in generosity and thoughtfulness, though it gives birth to visions and to great poetry, remains among the sharpest expressions of self interest. Not until it has passed through a long servitude, through its own self-hatred, through mockery, through great doubts, can it take its place among the loyalties. Many who have spent a lifetime in it can tell us less of love than the child that lost a dog yesterday.

Thornton Niven Wilder

See also: AFFECTION, COURTSHIP, DESIRE, DEVOTION, ESTEEM, LUST, MARRIAGE, ROMANCE, SEX, TENDERNESS.

LOYALTY

Loyalty . . . is a realization that America was born of revolt, flourished in dissent, became great through experimentation.

Henry Steele Commager

We must announce our loyalty . . . to those religious, political and humanitarian principles which seem best calculated to see a man or a nation through a period of darkness.

James Albert Michener

Up to a certain point it is good for us to know that there are people in the world who will give us love and unquestioned loyalty to the limit of their ability. I doubt, however, if it is good for us to feel assured of this without the accompanying obligation of having to justify this devotion by our behavior.

(Anna) Eleanor Roosevelt

Unless you can find some sort of loyalty, you cannot find unity and peace in your active living.

Josiah Royce

Loyalty means nothing unless it has at its heart the absolute principle of self-sacrifice.

(Thomas) Woodrow Wilson

See also: CONSTANCY, DEVOTION, FIDELITY.

LUCK

I never knew an early-rising, hard-working, prudent man, careful of his earnings, and strictly honest, who complained of bad luck. A good character, good habits, and iron industry are impregnable to the assaults of all the ill-luck that fools ever dreamed of.

Joseph Addison

As for what you're calling hard luck—well, we made New England out of it, that and codfish.

Stephen Vincent Benét

If your luck isn't what it should be write a "p" in front of it and try again.

Robert Chambers (Bob) Edwards

Shallow men believe in luck, believe in circumstances. It was somebody's name, or he happened to be there at the time, or it was so then, and another day it would have been otherwise. Strong men believe in cause and effect. The man was born to do it, and his father was born to be the father of him and of this deed, and by looking narrowly, you shall see there was no luck in the matter, but it was all a problem in arithmetic, or an experiment in chemistry.

Ralph Waldo Emerson

A pound of pluck is worth a ton of luck.

James Abram Garfield

There are no chances so unlucky from which clever people are not able to reap some advantage, and none so lucky that the foolish are not able to turn to their own disadvantage.

Duc François de La Rochefoucauld

The only sure thing about luck is that it will change.

Wilson Mizner

The only good luck many great men ever had was being born with the ability and determination to overcome bad luck.

Channing Pollock

Most people know that there is no such thing as luck, but it is difficult to find anyone who does not believe in it.

Raoul de Sales

Pitch a lucky man into the Nile, says the Arabian proverb, and he will come up with a fish in his mouth.

Nathaniel Parker Willis

Better an ounce of luck than a pound of gold.

Yiddish Proverb

Intelligence is not needed for luck, but luck is needed for intelligence.

Yiddish Proverb

See also: ACCIDENT, CARDS, CHANCE, DESTINY, DICE, FATE, FORTUNE, GAMBLING.

LUST

The conquest of lust is the highest endeavour of a man's or woman's existence.

Mohandas Karamchand (Mahatma) Gandhi

God's grace never descends upon a man who is a slave to lust.

Mohandas Karamchand (Mahatma) Gandhi

Woman must cease to consider herself the object of man's lust.

Mohandas Karamchand (Mahatma) Gandhi

When lust, by unchaste looks, loose gestures, and foul talk, but most by lewd and lavish acts of sin, lets in defilement to the inward parts, the soul grows clotted by contagion, embodies and imbrutes till she quite lose the divine property of her first being.

John Milton

Lust is an enemy to the purse, a foe to the person, a canker to the mind, a corrosive to the conscience, a weakness of the wit, a besotter of the senses, and, finally, a mortal bane to all the body.

Pliny the Elder

Lust is, of all the frailties of our nature, what most we ought to fear; the headstrong beast rushes along impatient of the course; nor hears the rider's call, nor feels the rein.

Nicholas Rowe

An enemy to whom you show kindness becomes your friend, excepting lust, the indulgence of which increases its enmity.

Saadi (Muslih-ud-Din)

Lust is a captivity of the reason and an enraging of the passions. It hinders business and distracts counsel. It sins against the body and weakens the soul.

Jeremy Taylor

See also: HARLOT, LICENTIOUSNESS, SEX.

LUXURY

Garrick showed Johnson his fine house, gardens, statues, pictures, etc., at Hampton Court. "Ah! David, David," said the doctor, "these are the things that make death terrible."

Julius Bate

I know it is more agreeable to walk upon carpets than to lie upon dungeon floors; I know it is pleasant to have all the comforts and luxuries of civilization; but he who cares only for these things is worth no more than a butterfly contented and thoughtless upon a morning flower; and who ever thought of rearing a tombstone to a last-summer's butterfly?

Henry Ward Beecher

War destroys men, but luxury destroys mankind; at once corrupts the body and the mind.

John Crowne

Unless we are accustomed to them from early youth, splendid chambers and elegant furniture had best be left to people who neither have nor can have any thoughts.

Johann Wolfgang von Goethe

The more we accommodate ourselves to plain things, and the less we indulge in those artificial delights which gratify pride and luxury, the nearer we approach to a state of innocency.

Matthew Henry

Luxury may possibly contribute to give bread to the poor; but if there were no luxury, there would be no poor.

Henry Home

You cannot spend money in luxury without doing good to the poor. Nay, you do more good to them by spending it in luxury than by giving; you make them exert industry, whereas, by giving it, you keep them idle.

Samuel Johnson

All luxury corrupts either the morals or the state.

Joseph Joubert

It was a shrewd saying, whoever said it, "That the man who first brought ruin on the Roman people was he who pampered them by largesses and amusements."

Plutarch

He repents on thorns that sleeps in beds of roses.

Francis Quarles

On the soft bed of luxury most kingdoms have expired.

Edward Young

See also: ELEGANCE, EXTRAVAGANCE, MONEY, PRODIGALITY, PROSPERITY, RICHES, WEALTH.

LYING

Truth is always consistent with itself, and needs nothing to help it out; it is always near at hand, sits upon our lips, and is ready to drop out before we are aware; a lie is troublesome, and sets a man's invention upon the rack, and one trick needs a great many more to make it good. It is like building upon a false foundation, which continually stands in need of props to shore it up, and proves at last more chargeable than to have raised a substantial building at first upon a true and solid foundation.

Joseph Addison

You can best reward a liar by believing nothing of what he says.

Aristippus

Never chase a lie. Let it alone, and it will run itself to death. I can work out a good

character much faster than any one can lie me out of it.

Lyman Beecher

The lie of fear is the refuge of cowardice, and the lie of fraud the device of the cheat. The inequalities of men and the lust of acquisition are a constant premium on lying.

Edward Bellamy

A lie may live and even wiggle after it has been spiked, but not beyond the sundown.

(Matthew) Heywood Campbell Broun

With a man, a lie is a last resort; with women, it's First Aid.

Frank Gelett Burgess

I do not mind lying, but I hate inaccuracy.

Samuel Butler

A lie should be trampled on and extinguished wherever found. I am for fumigating the atmosphere when I suspect that falsehood, like pestilence, breathes around me.

Thomas Carlyle

Terminological inexactitude.

Sir Winston Leonard Spencer Churchill

One of the striking differences between a cat and a lie is that a cat has only nine lives.

Samuel Langhorne Clemens (Mark Twain)

Every brave man is a man of his word; to such base vices he cannot stoop, and shuns more than death the shame of lying.

Pierre Corneille

A liar is always extravagant with his oaths.

Pierre Corneille

One ought to have a good memory when he has told a lie.

Pierre Corneille

A lie with a purpose is one of the worst kind, and the most profitable.

Finley Peter Dunne

Dare to be true; nothing can need a lie.

George Herbert

We lie loudest when we lie to ourselves.

Eric Hoffer

Sin has many tools, but a lie is the handle that fits them all.

Oliver Wendell Holmes

One lie engenders another. Once committed, the liar has to go on in his course of lying; it is the penalty of his transgression.

Francis Jacox

There is no worse lie than a truth misunderstood by those who hear it.

William James

It is always the best policy to speak the truth, unless of course you are an exceptionally good liar.

Jerome Klapka Jerome

It is sophistry to pretend that in a free country a man has some sort of inalienable or constitutional right to deceive his fellow men. . . . It may be inexpedient to arraign every public liar, as we try to arraign other swindlers. . . . But, in principle, there can be no immunity for lying in any of its protean forms.

Walter Lippmann

A lie in time saves nine.

Addison Mizner

After a tongue has once got the knack of lying, 'tis not to be imagined how impossible almost it is to reclaim it. Whence it comes to pass that we see some men, who are otherwise very honest, so subject to this vice.

Michel Eyquem de Montaigne

Lying is a hateful and accursed vice. We have no other tie upon one another, but our word. If we did but discover the horror and consequences of it, we should pursue it with fire and sword, and more justly than other crimes.

Michel Eyquem de Montaigne

We have seen a frightening increase, in the past decade, in the use of lie detectors employed by government representatives to induce persons under examination to be witnesses against themselves.

Vance Oakley Packard

There are people who lie simply for the sake of lying.

Blaise Pascal

When thou art obliged to speak, be sure to speak the truth; for equivocation is half way to lying, and lying is whole way to hell.

William Penn

Lying is a most disgraceful vice; it first despises God, and then fears men.

Plutarch

He who tells a lie is not sensible how great a task he undertakes; for he must be forced to invent twenty more to maintain one.

Alexander Pope

Who dares think one thing, and another tell,
My soul detests him as the gates of hell.

Alexander Pope

Lies are essential to humanity. They are perhaps as important as the pursuit of pleasure and moreover are necessary to that pursuit.

Marcel Proust

A lie has always a certain amount of weight with those whose wish to believe it.

Elliott Warren Rice

The liar's punishment is not in the least that he is not believed, but that he cannot believe anyone else.

George Bernard Shaw

The devil is the father of lies, but he neglected to patent the idea, and the business now suffers from competition.

Henry Wheeler Shaw (Josh Billings)

Lies which are told out of arrogance and ostentation, a man should detect in his own defense, because he should not be triumphed over. Lies which are told out of malice he should expose, both for his own sake and that of the rest of mankind, because every man should rise against a common enemy; but the officious liar, many have argued, is to be excused, because it does some man good, and no man hurt.

Sir Richard Steele

Although the devil be the father of lies, he seems, like other great inventors, to have lost much of his reputation by the continual improvements that have been made upon him.

Jonathan Swift

No man lies consistently, and he cannot lie about everything if he talks to you long.

(Thomas) Woodrow Wilson

See also: DISHONESTY, DECEIT, EQUIVOCATION, FALSEHOOD, FRAUD, HYPOCRISY.

M

MACHINE

It is the machines that make life complicated, at the same time that they impose on it a high tempo. . . . The idle curiosity, the mental vagabondage of the brooding, reflective mind, the machines will accept, but at high discount rates only; they put a premium on . . . promptness, regularity, precision, effortless adaptability to the accelerated movement and rhythm of modern life.

Carl Lotus Becker

The machine age has resulted in a transferring of the locus of the ideal of a larger and more evenly distributed happiness and leisure from heaven to earth.

John Dewey

One machine can do the work of fifty ordinary men. No machine can do the work of one extraordinary man.

Elbert Green Hubbard

Russia is straddling the centuries . . . pounding backward to Peter the Great and racing at the same time to overtake Henry Ford and Henry Kaiser before she has caught up with Thomas Jefferson.

Anne O'Hare McCormick

The cycle of the machine is now coming to an end . . . Man is at last in a position to transcend the machine, and to create a new biological and social environment, in which the highest possibilities of human existence will be realized, not for the strong and the lucky alone, but for all co-operating and understanding groups, associates, and communities.

Lewis Mumford

Modern Man is the victim of the very instruments he values most. Every gain in power, every mastery of natural forces, every scientific addition to knowledge, has proved potentially dangerous, because it has not been accompanied by equal gains in self-understanding and self-discipline.

Lewis Mumford

To curb the machine and limit art to handicraft is a denial of opportunity.

Lewis Mumford

In those countries where machinery has been developed to little or no purpose poverty reigns, ignorance is the prevailing condition, and civilization consequently far in the rear.

Carroll Davidson Wright

See also: CYBERNETICS, SCIENCE, TECHNOLOGY.

MADNESS

Great wits are sure to madness near alli'd
And thin partitions do their bounds divide.

John Dryden

The consummation of madness is, to do what, at the time of doing it, we intend to be afterward sorry for: the deliberate and intentional making of work for repentance.

William Nevins

Madness is consistent, which is more than can be said of poor reason. Whatever may be the ruling passion at the time continues so throughout the whole delirium, though it should last for life. Our passions and principles are steady in frenzy, but begin to shift and waver as we return to reason.

Laurence Sterne

See also: INSANITY, MENTAL HEALTH.

MAGNANIMITY

A brave man knows no malice; but forgets, in peace, the injuries of war, and gives his direst foe a friend's embrace.

William Cowper

Of all virtues magnanimity is the rarest; there are a hundred persons of merit for one who willingly acknowledges it in another.
William Hazlitt

A great mind will neither give an affront, nor bear it.
Henry Home

Magnanimity is sufficiently defined by its name; yet we may say of it, that it is the good sense of pride, and the noblest way of acquiring applause.
Duc François de La Rochefoucauld

If you desire to be magnanimous, undertake nothing rashly, and fear nothing thou undertakest. Fear nothing but infamy; dare anything but injury; the measure of magnanimity is to be neither rash nor timorous.
Francis Quarles

See also: BENEFICENCE, BENEVOLENCE, CHARITY, GENEROSITY, KINDNESS.

MAIDENHOOD

No padlock, bolts, or bars can secure a maiden so well as her own reserve.
Miguel de Cervantes Saavedra

The blushing beauties of a modest maid.
John Dryden

A child no more; a maiden now; a graceful maiden, with a gentle brow, and cheek tinged lightly, and a dove-like eye; and all hearts bless her, as she passes by.
Mary Botham Howitt

A loving maiden grows unconsciously more bold.
Jean Paul Richter

See also: INNOCENCE, MODESTY, VIRGINITY.

MAJORITY

One with the law is a majority.
(John) Calvin Coolidge

One and God make a majority.
Frederick Douglass

In matters of conscience, the law of the majority has no place.
Mohandas Karamchand (Mahatma) Gandhi

It is slavery to be amenable to the majority, no matter what its decisions are.
Mohandas Karamchand (Mahatma) Gandhi

It is a superstition and an ungodly thing to believe that an act of majority binds a minority.
Mohandas Karamchand (Mahatma) Gandhi

When there is complete freedom of opinion, that of the majority must prevail.
Mohandas Karamchand (Mahatma) Gandhi

We go by the major vote, and if the majority are insane, the sane must go to the hospital.
Horace Mann

The moment a mere numerical superiority by either states or voters in this country proceeds to ignore the needs and desires of the minority, and for their own selfish purpose or advancement, hamper or oppress that minority, or debar them in any way from equal privileges and equal rights—that moment will mark the failure of our constitutional system.
Franklin Delano Roosevelt

The voice of the majority is no proof of justice.
Johann Christoph Friedrich von Schiller

The thing we have to fear in this country, to my way of thinking, is the influence of the organized minorities, because somehow or other the great majority does not seem to organize. They seem to feel that they are going to be effective because of their known strength, but they give no expression of it.
Alfred Emanuel Smith

There is one body that knows more than anybody, and that is everybody.
Alexandre de Talleyrand-Périgord

It never troubles the wolf how many the sheep may be.
Virgil

See also: DEMOCRACY, MINORITY, POLITICS.

MALEVOLENCE

The malignity that never forgets or forgives is found only in base and ignoble natures, whose aims are selfish, and whose means are indirect, cowardly, and treacherous.
George Stillman Hillard

The violence and evil of our time have been, when viewed collectively, the work of loveless men; impotent men who lust after sadistic power to conceal their failure as lovers; repressed and frustrated men, lamed by unloving parents and seeking revenge by taking refuge in a system of thought or a mode of life into which love cannot intrude. . . . Those who are impotent to love, from Hitler downward, must seek a negative counterpart in hatred and disintegration.

Lewis Mumford

See also: ENEMY, HATE, MALICE.

MALICE

There is no malice like the malice of the renegade.

Thomas Babington Macaulay

Malice scorned, puts out itself; but argued, gives a kind of credit to a false accusation.

Philip Massinger

Malice sucks up the greater part of her own venom, and poisons herself.

Michel Eyquem de Montaigne

Malice drinks one half of its own poison.

Seneca

Malice, in its false witness, promotes its tale with so cunning a confusion, so mingles truths with falsehoods, surmises with certainties, causes of no moment with matters capital, that the accused can absolutely neither grant nor deny, plead innocence nor confess guilt.

Sir Philip Sidney

See also: ABUSE, ANGER, CALUMNY, CRUELTY, ENEMY, HATE, MEANNESS, MISCHIEF, RAGE, REVENGE, SLANDER, VENGEANCE, VILLAINY.

MAN

It is not what he has, or even what he does which expresses the worth of a man, but what he is.

Henri Frédéric Amiel

Man stands in his own shadow and wonders why it is dark.

Ancient Zen saying

Man perfected by society is the best of all animals; he is the most terrible of all when he lives without law, and without justice.

Aristotle

Man is an animal and until his immediate material and economic needs are satisfied, he cannot develop further.

Wystan Hugh Auden

Only man, with his conscious intelligence, has been able to continue his evolution after his biological development has finished.

Wyston Hugh Auden

Mankind is divisible into two great classes: hosts and guests.

Sir Max Beerbohm

Man is an animal which alone among the animals refuses to be satisfied by the fulfillment of animal desires.

Alexander Graham Bell

Man is a wealth grubber, man is a pleasure seeker; man is a power wielder; man is a thinker, and man is a creative lover.

Alexander Graham Bell

But man, never halting in his senseless career, flits ceaselessly from thought to thought; his heart always at sea, amidst a thousand embarrassments, knows neither what it wishes, nor what it does not wish: what it one day detests, the next it desires.

Nicolas Boileau-Despréaux

Of all the animals which fly in the air, walk on the ground, or swim in the sea, from Paris to Peru, from Japan to Rome, the most foolish animal in my opinion is man.

Nicolas Boileau-Despréaux

Behold man in his real character. He passes from white to black; he condemns in the morning what he maintained the evening before. Worrying all around, not less an enemy to himself, he changes every moment his opinions, as he does the fashion of his coat; the least puff of wind wheels him round; he is upset by the slightest rebuff: to-day in a helmet, to-morrow in a cowl.

Nicolas Boileau-Despréaux

Indisputably a great, good, handsome man is the first of created things.

Charlotte Brontë

Man is an animal that cooks his victuals.

Edmund Burke

Man is by his constitution a religious animal.

Edmund Burke

Half dust, half deity, alike unfit to sink or soar.

George Gordon Byron (Lord Byron)

He is of the earth, but his thoughts are with the stars. Mean and petty his wants and desires; yet they serve a soul exalted with grand, glorious aims,—with immortal longings,—with thoughts which sweep the heavens, and wander through eternity. A pigmy standing on the outward crest of this small planet, his far-reaching spirit stretches outward to the infinite, and there alone finds rest.

Thomas Carlyle

Show me the man you honor, and I will know what kind of a man you are, for it shows me what your ideal of manhood is, and what kind of a man you long to be.

Thomas Carlyle

Every man is a volume, if you know how to read him.

William Ellery Channing

There are times when one would like to hang the whole human race, and finish the farce.

Samuel Langhorne Clemens (Mark Twain)

To despise our own species is the price we must often pay for a knowledge of it.

Charles Caleb Colton

The way of a superior man is three-fold: virtuous, he is free from anxieties; wise, he is free from perplexities; bold, he is free from fear.

Confucius

No man is an island entire of itself; every man is part of the main. If a clod be washed away by the sea, Europe is the less, as well as if a promontory were, as well as if a manor of thy friends or thine own were. Any man's death diminishes me because I am involved in mankind, and therefore never send to know for whom the bell tolls; it tolls for thee.

John Donne

Among the forces which sweep and play throughout the universe, untutored man is but a wisp in the wind. Our civilization is still in a middle stage, scarcely beast, in that it is no longer wholly guided by instinct; scarcely human, in that it is not yet wholly guided by reason . . . We see man far removed from the lairs of the jungles, his innate instincts dulled by too near an approach to free-will, his free-will not sufficiently developed to replace his instincts and afford him perfect guidance. He is becoming too wise to hearken always to instincts and desires; he is still too weak to always prevail against them.

Theodore Dreiser

Perhaps man, having remade his environment, will turn around at last and begin to remake himself?

Will (William James) Durant

Man tries to make for himself in the fashion that suits him best a simplified and intelligible picture of the world.

Albert Einstein

The political freedoms we know, the American concept of democracy, certainly include a faith, related to some religion, that man is more than an animal, that he possesses a soul. If we have not that faith, then why should any of us admit that any other is born with equal rights to himself.

Dwight David Eisenhower

Human kind cannot bear very much reality.

Thomas Stearns Eliot

Every man is a divinity in disguise, a god playing the fool. It seems as if heaven had sent its insane angels into our world as to an asylum. And here they will break out into their native music, and utter at intervals the words they have heard in heaven; then the mad fit returns, and they mope and wallow like dogs!

Ralph Waldo Emerson

Of all the ways of defining man, the worst is the one which makes him out to be a rational animal.

Anatole France

Theologians and philosophers have been saying for a century that God is dead, but what we confront now is the possibility that man is dead, transformed into a thing, a producer, a consumer, an idolator of other things.

Erich Fromm

Man has reason, discrimination, and free-will such as it is. The brute has no such thing. It is not a free agent, and knows no distinction between virtue and vice, good and evil. Man, being a free agent, knows these distinctions, and when he follows his higher nature shows himself far superior to the brute, but when he follows his baser nature can show himself lower than the brute.

Mohandas Karamchand (Mahatma) Gandhi

Man is not all body but he is something infinitely higher. Of all the animal creation of God, man is the only animal who has been created in order that he may know his Maker. Man's aim in life is not therefore to add from day to day to his material prospects and to his material possessions but his predominant calling is from day to day to come nearer his own Maker.

Mohandas Karamchand (Mahatma) Gandhi

I mean to make myself a man, and if I succeed in that, I shall succeed in everything else.

James Abram Garfield

Man is an animal; but he is an animal plus something else. He is a mythic earth-tree, whose roots are in the ground, but whose top-most branches may blossom in the heavens.

Henry George

Man is greater than a world—than systems of worlds; there is more mystery in the union of soul with the body, than in the creation of a universe.

Henry Giles

The record of life runs thus: Man creeps into childhood,—bounds into youth,—sobers into manhood,—softens into age,—totters into second childhood, and slumbers into the cradle prepared for him,—thence to be watched and cared for.

Henry Giles

Man himself is the crowning wonder of creation; the study of his nature the noblest study the world affords.

William Ewart Gladstone

Man is to be trained chiefly by studying and by knowing man.

William Ewart Gladstone

There wouldn't be half as much fun in the world if it weren't for children and men, and there ain't a mite of difference between them under their skins.

Ellen Anderson Gholson Glasgow

One cannot always be a hero, but one can always be a man.

Johann Wolfgang von Goethe

It would indeed be the ultimate tragedy if the history of the human race proved to be nothing more noble than the story of an ape

playing with a box of matches on a petrol dump.

David Ormsby-Gore (Lord Harlech)

Man is a reasoning rather than a reasonable animal.

Alexander Hamilton

When man is a brute, he is the most sensual and loathsome of all brutes.

Nathaniel Hawthorne

A man can be destroyed but not defeated.

Ernest Hemingway

Whoever considers the study of anatomy, I believe, will never be an atheist; the frame of man's body, and coherence of his parts, being so strange and paradoxical, that I hold it to be the greatest miracle of nature.

Edward Herbert (Lord Herbert)

Those who think of man as essentially animal think of society as simply the jungle writ large—a jungle in which every animal survives or perishes by the relative sharpness of his claws, teeth, and brain.

Franklin Simpson Hickman

A small business may take men and events as they come; a large business must have a policy. The largest business of all (statecraft), must base its policy on some better-than-casual thought about human nature.

William Ernest Hocking

I think the best image for a man is an electric light—the spark feels isolated and independent but really is only a moment in a current.

Oliver Wendell Holmes, Jr.

Government, religion, property, books, are nothing but the scaffolding to build men. Earth holds up to her master no fruit like the finished man.

Baron Wilhelm von Humboldt

A man's a creature on a tightrope, walking delicately, equilibrated, with mind and consciousness and spirit at one end of his balancing pole and body and instinct and all that's unconscious and earthly and mysterious at the other. Balanced. Which is damnably difficult.

Aldous Leonard Huxley

Man has been called "the representative product of the universe"; and we will do well to remember that in this position his actions represent the worst of which nature is capable as well as the best.

Leo Vincent Jacks

Man, biologically considered, . . . is the most formidable of all the beasts of prey, and, indeed, the only one that preys systematically on its own species.

William James

Man wants but little here below, Nor wants that little long, said the poet; what a lie! Man wants almost unlimited quantities of almost everything, and he wants it till the day he dies.

Randall Jarrell

We are beginning to see man not as the smooth self-acting agent he pretends to be, but as he really is, a creature only dimly conscious of the various influences that mold his thought and action, and blindly resisting with all the means at his command the forces that are making for a higher and fuller consciousness.

Ernest Jones

What a deal of cold business doth a man misspend the better part of life in! In scattering compliments, tendering visits, gathering and venting news, following feasts and plays, making a little winter-love in a dark corner.

Ben (Benjamin) Jonson

The supreme reality of our time is our indivisibility as children of God and the common vulnerability of this planet.

John Fitzgerald Kennedy

Perhaps it is too soon, perhaps it will always be too soon, to try to formulate an adequate definition of man. Perhaps the fact that he is indefinable by his own mind is an essential fact about him.

Joseph Wood Krutch

The social sciences will never help us solve our problems as long as they continue to go on the assumption that whatever is true of a rat is true of a man. Indeed they will not be able to solve them so long as they assume that even a rat is adequately accounted for on the basis of mechanistic premises.

Joseph Wood Krutch

We have exalted man's importance by making his "welfare" the measure of all things; we have, at the same time, belittled him by assuming that he is, nevertheless, nothing in himself.

Joseph Wood Krutch

Bounded in his nature, infinite in his desires, man is a fallen god who has a recollection of heaven.

Alphonse de Lamartine

There are but three classes of men, the retrograde, the stationary, and the progressive.

Johann Kaspar Lavater

We believe in men not merely as production units, but as the children of God. We believe that the purpose of our society is not primarily to assure the "safety of the State" but to safeguard human dignity and the freedom of the individual.

David Eli Lilienthal

The miracle is that the universe created a part of itself [man] to study the rest of it, that this part, in studying itself, finds the rest of the universe in its own natural inner realities.

John Cunningham Lilly

Deep down I feel that creation of the universe out of nothingness and that of life out of inorganic state ultimately aimed at the creation of man. I believe that man is meant as a great experiment whose possible failure by man's own guilt would be paramount to the failure of creation itself. Whether this belief be true or not, man would be well advised if he behaved as though it were.

Thomas Mann

A man must stand erect, not be kept erect by others.

Marcus Aurelius

To say that a man is a person is to say that in the depth of his being he is more a whole than a part and more independent than servile. It is to say that he is a minute fragment of matter that is at the same time a universe, a beggar who participates in the absolute being, mortal flesh whose value is eternal and a bit of straw into which heaven enters.

Jacques Maritain

Men have dignity only in so far as they are rulers, only in so far as they share in the attempt to advance the common welfare. And, further, only as rulers have men a right to liberty.

Alexander Meiklejohn

In men whom men pronounce as ill
I find so much of goodness still.
In men whom men pronounce divine

I find so much of sin and blot;
I hesitate to draw the line
Between the two, when God has not.

> *Cincinnatus Hiner (Joaquin) Miller*

Assuredly man is a being wonderfully vain, changeable, and vacillating.

> *Michel Eyquem de Montaigne*

To create a man of truly human dimensions one needs the co-operation of a universal society; to create a universal society, one must begin and end with men who seek fullness of life. . . . These are two aspects of the same act; and with that act, a new world will come into being.

> *Lewis Mumford*

Men, in general, are but great children.

> *Napoleon I (Bonaparte)*

For us man is naturally more interesting than all the great animals that existed before him; he is interesting because he brought a new thing with him which the others do not seem to have had. This was mind—curiosity—the desire to find out and learn.

> *Jawaharlal Nehru*

History is not pleasant. Man, in spite of his great and vaunted progress, is still a very unpleasant and selfish animal.

> *Jawaharlal Nehru*

Indeed it is intelligence that separates man from the other animals. There is practically no difference between a man without any intelligence and an animal.

> *Jawaharlal Nehru*

It is very sad for a man to make himself servant to a single thing; his manhood all taken out of him by the hydraulic pressure of excessive business.

> *Theodore Parker*

It is of dangerous consequence to represent to man how near he is to the level of beasts, without showing him at the same time his greatness. It is likewise dangerous to let him see his greatness without his meanness. It is more dangerous yet to leave him ignorant of either; but very beneficial that he should be made sensible of both.

> *Blaise Pascal*

The state of man is changeableness, *ennui*, anxiety.

> *Blaise Pascal*

What a chimera is man! what a confused chaos! what a subject of contradiction! a professed judge of all things, and yet a feeble worm of the earth! the great depositary and guardian of truth, and yet a mere huddle of uncertainty! the glory and the scandal of the universe!

> *Blaise Pascal*

The most indisputable fact about man is that he is a union, and not a disjunction, of . . . contrasted aspects, which are complementaries and not mutually exclusive alternatives. Man is *both* lower and higher, *both* body and spirit, *both* outer and inner, *both* mechanical and purposive.

> *Ralph Barton Perry*

Man is but a tiny dot of light amidst the blind fury of the elements; the human mind is the dot of light that is proof against any tempest, and it is the only light we have.

> *Jules Henri Poincaré*

The proper study of mankind is man.

> *Alexander Pope*

For my part, I am not so sure at bottom that man is, as he says, the king of nature; he is far more its devastating tyrant. I believe he has many things to learn from animal societies, older than his own and of infinite variety.

> *Romain Rolland*

The ablest man I ever met is the man you think you are.

> *Franklin Delano Roosevelt*

There is no indispensable man.

> *Franklin Delano Roosevelt*

In making man, the universe presented itself at one stroke with a victim and a judge.

> *Jean Rostand*

Man is not a "dispossessed king" but a parvenu who possesses enough to make him afraid of his own power.

> *Jean Rostand*

Now the basest thought possible concerning man is, that he has no spiritual nature; and the foolish misunderstanding of him possible is, that he has, or should have, no animal nature. For his nature is nobly animal, nobly spiritual,—coherently and irrevocably so; neither part of it may, but at its peril, expel, despise, or defy the other.

> *John Ruskin*

There is an essential sanctity of the human personality, regardless of race or color or conditions of life. If that ideal is abandoned, the intellectual man goes to pieces, and that means the end of culture, and even of humanity.

Albert Schweitzer

Man is a social animal.

Seneca

Man is an animal that makes bargains; no other animal does this,—one dog does not change a bone with another.

Adam Smith

There is so much good in the worst of us, and so much bad in the best of us, that it behooves all of us not to talk about the rest of us.

Robert Louis Balfour Stevenson

A violent wind does not outlast the morning; a squall of rain does not outlast the day. Such is the course of nature. And if Nature herself cannot sustain her efforts long, how much less can man.

Tao Te Ching

The Dignity of Man and the Divine Destiny of Man are two things which it is at the moment impossible for me to accept with wholehearted enthusiasm.

James Grover Thurber

For some curious reason man has always assumed that his is the highest form of life in the Universe. There is, of course, nothing at all with which to sustain this view.

James Grover Thurber

Man, the aloof animal, has deteriorated in everything except mentality and in that he has done no more than barely hold his own for the past two thousand years.

James Grover Thurber

Man is able to break through the limitations of every definition of man, except that definition which refers to man's ability to change his nature.

Paul Tillich

When prehistoric man first lifted his shaggy hands off the ground and stood erect, the human race was in for trouble. People have been complaining of backaches ever since.

Time

For countless ages the sun rose and set, the moon waxed and waned, the stars shone in the Milky Way, but it was only with the coming of man that these things were understood. Man has unveiled secrets which might have been thought undiscoverable. Much has been achieved in the realm of art, science, literature, and religion. Is all this to end because so few are able to think of man rather than of this or that group of men?

U Thant

Every man is the creature of the age in which he lives; very few are able to raise themselves above the ideas of the times.

Voltaire (François Marie Arouet)

From now on, man will be compelled, by the fact of abundance, to organize for the benefit of man—not the exploitation of man. Otherwise, man will destroy himself.

Henry Agard Wallace

In my youth, I thought of writing a satire on mankind; but now in my age I think I should write an apology for them.

Horace Walpole

I am an acme of things accomplished, and I am encloser of things to be.

Walt (Walter) Whitman

When faith is lost, and honor dies, the man is dead.

John Greenleaf Whittier

How poor, how rich, how abject, how august, how complicate, how wonderful is man! distinguished link in being's endless chain! midway from nothing to the Deity! dim miniature of greatness absolute! an heir of glory! a frail child of dust! helpless immortal! insect infinite! a worm! a God!

Edward Young

See also: BACHELOR, BEARD, HUMAN NATURE, LIFE, MEN, SEXES.

MANKIND: *see* MAN.

MANNERS

The true art of being agreeable is to appear well pleased with all the company, and rather to seem well entertained with them than to bring entertainment to them. A man thus disposed may have not much learning, nor any wit; but if he has common sense, and

something friendly in his behavior, it conciliates men's minds more than the brightest
parts without this disposition.

Joseph Addison

Nothing is more reasonable and cheap than
good manners.

Anonymous

Good manners and good morals are sworn
friends and fast allies.

Cyrus Augustus Bartol

Always behave as if nothing had happened
no matter what has happened.

(Enoch) Arnold Bennett

Nothing, except what flows from the heart,
can render even external manners truly
pleasing.

Hugh Blair

There is a close connection between manners and clothes. You can't curtsy in a tight
skirt.

Mary Borden

Bad manners are a species of bad morals; a
conscientious man will not offend in that
way.

Christian Nestell Bovee

Manners are of more importance than laws.
Upon them, in a great measure, the laws depend. The law can touch us here and there,
now and then. Manners are what vex or
soothe, corrupt or purify, exalt or debase,
barbarize or refine, by a constant, steady,
uniform, insensible operation, like that of
the air we breathe in. They give their whole
form and color to our lives. According to
their quality, they aid morals, they supply
them, or they totally destroy them.

Edmund Burke

A man's own manner and character is what
most becomes him.

Cicero

He was of that nature which sets down every disinterested civility as a sign of weakness.

John Collier

Nowadays, manners are easy and life is
hard.

Benjamin Disraeli

Knowledge of men and manners, the freedom of habitudes, and conversation with the
best company of both sexes, is necessary to
the perfection of good manners.

John Dryden

Good manners are made up of petty sacrifices.

Ralph Waldo Emerson

I could better eat with one who did not respect the truth or the laws, than with a slov-
en and unpresentable person. Moral qualities rule the world, but at short distances the
senses are despotic.

Ralph Waldo Emerson

Comport thyself in life as at a banquet. If a
plate is offered thee, extend thy hand and
take it moderately; if it is to be withdrawn,
do not detain it. If it come not to thy side,
make not thy desire loudly known, but wait
patiently till it be offered thee.

Epictetus

In conversation use some, but not too much
ceremony; it teaches others to be courteous,
too. Demeanors are commonly paid back in
their own coin.

Thomas Fuller

After all, manners and methods change with
the times. We must grow with our years.
What was good enough for our babyhood
cannot be good enough for manhood.

Mohandas Karamchand (Mahatma) Gandhi

All the education young men receive will be
in vain if they do not learn good manners.

Mohandas Karamchand (Mahatma) Gandhi

The society of women is the element of
good manners.

Johann Wolfgang von Goethe

Unbecoming forwardness oftener proceeds
from ignorance than impudence.

Fulke Greville (First Baron Brooke)

What better school for manners than the
company of virtuous women; where the mutual endeavor to please must insensibly polish the mind, where the example of female
softness and modesty must communicate itself to their admirers, and where the delicacy of the sex puts every one on his guard
lest he give offence?

David Hume

Good manners are a part of good morals; and it is as much our duty as our interest to practise both.

John Hunter

Simplicity of manner is the last attainment. Men are very long afraid of being natural, from the dread of being taken for ordinary.

Francis Jeffrey (Lord Jeffrey)

Good breeding consists in having no particular mark of any profession, but a general elegance of manners.

Samuel Johnson

A man, whose great qualities want the ornament of exterior attractions, is like a naked mountain with mines of gold, which will be frequented only till the treasure is exhausted.

Samuel Johnson

There are peculiar ways in men, which discover what they are, through the most subtle feints and closest disguise. A blockhead cannot come in, nor go away, nor sit, nor rise, nor stand, like a man of sense.

Jean de La Bruyère

Fine manners are a stronger bond than a beautiful face. The former binds; the latter only attracts.

Alphonse de Lamartine

Nothing so much prevents our being natural as the desire of appearing so.

Duc François de La Rochefoucauld

The distinguishing trait of people accustomed to good society is a calm, imperturbable quiet which pervades all their actions and habits, from the greatest to the least. They eat in quiet, move in quiet, live in quiet, and lose even their money in quiet, while low persons cannot take up either a spoon or an affront without making an amazing noise about it.

Edward G. Bulwer-Lytton (Baron Lytton)

Manners easily and rapidly mature into morals.

Horace Mann

Manner is everything with some people, and something with everybody.

Conyers Middleton

Civility costs nothing, and buys everything.

Lady Mary Wortley Montagu

A well bred man is always sociable and complaisant.

Michel Eyquem de Montaigne

Better were it to be unborn than to be ill bred.

Sir Walter Raleigh

There is a deportment which suits the figure and talents of each person; it is always lost when we quit it to assume that of another.

Jean Jacques Rousseau

Rules of conduct, whatever they may be, are not sufficient to produce good results unless the ends sought are good.

Bertrand Arthur William Russell

There is not any benefit so glorious in itself, but it may yet be exceedingly sweetened and improved by the manner of conferring it. The virtue rests in the intent; the profit in the judicious application of the matter; but the beauty and ornament of an obligation lies in the manner of it.

Seneca

Good breeding is the result of much good sense, some good nature, and a little self-denial for the sake of others, and with a view to obtain the same indulgence from them.

Philip Dormer Stanhope (Lord Chesterfield)

The manner of a vulgar man has freedom without ease; the manner of a gentleman, ease without freedom.

Philip Dormer Stanhope (Lord Chesterfield)

A man's own good breeding is the best security against other people's ill manners.

Philip Dormer Stanhope (Lord Chesterfield)

Wisdom, valor, justice, and learning cannot keep in countenance a man that is possessed with these excellences, if he wants that inferior art of life and behavior called good breeding.

Sir Richard Steele

Good manners is the art of making those people easy with whom we converse; whoever makes the fewest persons uneasy, is the best bred man in company.

Jonathan Swift

We cannot always oblige, but we can always speak obligingly.

Voltaire (François Marie Arouet)

To be always thinking about your manners is not the way to make them good; the very perfection of manners is not to think about yourself.

Richard Whatley

See also: BEHAVIOR, CONDUCT, COURTESY, ETIQUETTE, GOOD BREEDING.

MARRIAGE

Marriage enlarges the scene of our happiness and of our miseries. A marriage of love is pleasant—of interest, easy, and where both meet, happy. A happy marriage has in it all the pleasures of friendship, all the enjoyments of sense and reason, and, indeed, all the sweets of life.

Joseph Addison

Two persons who have chosen each other out of all the species, with the design to be each other's mutual comfort and entertainment, have, in that action, bound themselves to be good-humored, affable, discreet, forgiving, patient, and joyful, with respect to each other's frailties and perfections, to the end of their lives.

Joseph Addison

Marriage is that relation between man and woman in which the independence is equal, the dependence mutual, and the obligation reciprocal.

Louis Kaufman Anspacher

Humble wedlock is far better than proud virginity.

Augustine of Hippo

He was reputed one of the wise men that made answer to the question when a man should marry? "A young man not yet, an elder man not at all."

Francis Bacon

A man finds himself seven years older the day after his marriage.

Francis Bacon

One should believe in marriage as in the immortality of the soul.

Honoré de Balzac

Marriage is our last, best chance to grow up.

Joseph Barth

Marriage is an institution the appreciation of which increases as one grows older.

Sir Thomas Beecham

Marriage, by making us more contented, causes us often to be less enterprising.

Christian Nestell Bovee

Married life ought to ensure youthfulness if your partner cares enough for you to be your critic.

Frank Gelett Burgess

The Christian religion, by confining marriage to pairs, and rendering the relation indissoluble, has by these two things done more toward the peace, happiness, settlement, and civilization of the world, than by any other part in this whole scheme of divine wisdom.

Edmund Burke

The bloom or blight of all men's happiness.

George Gordon Byron (Lord Byron)

Though women are angels, yet wedlock's the devil.

George Gordon Byron (Lord Byron)

I gravely doubt whether women were ever married by capture. I think they pretended to be; as they do still.

Gilbert Keith Chesterton

Husbands and wives talk of the cares of matrimony, and bachelors and spinsters bear them.

Wilkie Collins

That alliance may be said to have a double tie, where the minds are united as well as the body, and the union will have all its strength, when both the links are in perfection together.

Charles Caleb Colton

Married in haste, we repent at leisure.

William Congreve

There is no disparity in marriage like unsuitability of mind and purpose.

Charles John Huffman Dickens

Men marry to make an end; women to make a beginning.

Alexis Dupuy

In America, England and some other countries, marriage is often delayed for economic reasons. The repression sends thousands of young people to theaters and to the moving picture shows.

Sergei Mikhailovich Eisenstein

What greater thing is there for two human souls than to feel that they are joined for life—to strengthen each other in all labor, to rest on each other in all sorrow, to minister to each other in all pain, to be one with each other in silent, unspeakable memories at the moment of the last parting.

George Eliot (Mary Ann Evans)

Marriage is a natural thing in life, and to consider it derogatory in any sense is wholly wrong. The ideal is to look upon marriage as a sacrament and therefore to lead a life of self-restraint in the married state.

Mohandas Karamchand (Mahatma) Gandhi

The sanctity of marriage and the family relation make the corner-stone of our American society and civilization.

James Abram Garfield

Marriage has a biological basis, and would be far more often a success if its biology were generally understood and the knowledge acted upon.

John Burdon Sanderson Haldane

The man, at the head of the house, can mar the pleasure of the household, but he cannot make it. That must rest with the woman, and it is her greatest privilege.

Sir Arthur Helps

Marriage is something you have to give your whole mind to.

Henrik Ibsen

Wedlock's like wine, not properly judged of till the second glass.

Douglas William Jerrold

Marriage is the strictest tie of perpetual friendship, and there can be no friendship without confidence, and no confidence without integrity, and he must expect to be wretched, who pays to beauty, riches, or politeness that regard which only virtue and piety can claim.

Samuel Johnson

Were a man not to marry a second time, it might be concluded that his first wife had given him a disgust to marriage; but by taking a second wife, he pays the highest compliment to the first, by showing that she made him so happy as a married man, that he wishes to be so a second time.

Samuel Johnson

God has set the type of marriage everywhere throughout the creation. Every creature seeks its perfection in another. The very heavens and earth picture it to us.

Martin Luther

A successful marriage is an edifice that must be rebuilt every day.

André Maurois

A husband is a plaster that cures all the ills of girlhood.

Molière (Jean Baptiste Poquelin)

You cannot weld cake-dough to cast iron, nor a girl to an old man.

Austin O'Malley

If you would marry suitably, marry your equal.

Ovid

Marriages are best made of dissimilar material.

Theodore Parker

Never marry but for love; but see that thou lovest what is lovely.

William Penn

Marriage is the greatest educational institution on earth.

Channing Pollock

Men dream in courtship, but in wedlock wake.

Alexander Pope

In the career of female fame, there are few prizes to be obtained which can vie with the obscure state of a beloved wife, or a happy mother.

Jane Porter

Disagreeable suspicions are the usual fruits of a second marriage.

Jean Baptist Racine

Remember, that if thou marry for beauty, thou bindest thyself all thy life for that which perchance will neither last nor please thee one year; and when thou hast it, it will be to thee of no price at all; for the desire dieth when it is attained, and the affection perisheth when it is satisfied.

Sir Walter Raleigh

Marriage is not a union merely between two creatures—it is a union between two spirits;

and the intention of that bond is to perfect the nature of both, by supplementing their deficiencies with the force of contrast, giving to each sex those excellencies in which it is naturally deficient; to the one, strength of character and firmness of moral will; to the other, sympathy, meekness, tenderness; and just so solemn and glorious as these ends are for which the union was intended, just so terrible are the consequences if it be perverted and abused; for there is no earthly relationship which has so much power to ennoble and to exalt. There are two rocks, in this world of ours, on which the soul must either anchor or be wrecked—the one is God, and the other is the sex opposite.

Frederick William Robertson

If you would have the nuptial union last,
Let virtue be the bond that ties it fast.
Nicholas Rowe

From my experience, not one in twenty marries the first love; we build statues of snow, and weep to see them melt.
Sir Walter Scott

Men should keep their eyes wide open before marriage, and half shut afterward.
Magdeleine de Scudéry

The happiness of married life depends upon making small sacrifices with readiness and cheerfulness.
John Selden

Marriage with a good woman is a harbor in the tempest of life; with a bad woman, it is a tempest in the harbor.
John Petit-Senn

What God hath joined together no man shall put asunder: God will take care of that.
George Bernard Shaw

The whole world is strewn with snares, traps, gins and pitfalls for the capture of men by women.
George Bernard Shaw

A person's character is but half formed till after wedlock.
Charles Simmons

Marriage resembles a pair of shears, so joined that they cannot be separated; often moving in opposite directions, yet always punishing any one who comes between them.
Sydney Smith

A happy marriage is a new beginning of life, a new starting point for happiness and usefullness.
Arthur Penrhyn Stanley

Marriage is one long conversation chequered by disputes.
Robert Louis Balfour Stevenson

The reason why so few marriages are happy is because young ladies spend their time in making nets, not in making cages.
Jonathan Swift

There is more of good nature than of good sense at the bottom of most marriages.
Henry David Thoreau

God help the man who won't marry until he finds a perfect woman, and God help him still more if he finds her.
Benjamin Tillett

What a holler would ensue, if people had to pay the minister as much to marry them as they have to pay a lawyer to get them a divorce.
Claire Trevor

See also: BACHELOR, CHILDREN, DAUGHTER, FAMILY, FATHER, HOME, HUSBAND, LOVE, MOTHER, WIFE.

MARTYR

God discovers the martyr and confessor without the trial of flames and tortures, and will thereafter entitle many to the reward of actions which they never had the opportunity of performing.
Joseph Addison

I think the most uncomfortable thing about martyrs is that they look down on people who aren't.
Samuel Nathaniel Behrman

The blood shed on the Cross for the Redemption of mankind, as well as that which is shed invisibly every day in the Chalice of the Sacrament of the Altar, is naturally and supernaturally Jewish blood.
Léon Bloy

Fools love the martyrdom of fame.
George Gordon Byron (Lord Byron)

Christianity has made martyrdom sublime, and sorrow triumphant.
Edwin Hubbel Chapin

He that dies a martyr proves that he was not a knave, but by no means that he was not a fool; since the most absurd doctrines are not without such evidence as martyrdom can produce. A martyr, therefore, by the mere act of suffering, can prove nothing but his own faith.

Charles Caleb Colton

For some not to be martyred is a martyrdom.
John Donne

A martyr, a saint, is always made by the design of God, for His love of men, to warn them and to lead them, to bring them back to His ways. A martyrdom is never the design of man; for the true martyr is he who has become the instrument of God, who has lost his will in the will of God, not lost it but found it, for he has found freedom in submission to God. The martyr no longer desires anything for himself, not even the glory of martyrdom.

Thomas Stearns Eliot

The way of the world is, to praise dead saints, and persecute living ones.
Nathaniel Howe

The blood of the martyrs is the seed of the church.
Jerome (Eusebius Hieronymus)

Who falls for the love of God, shall rise a star.
Ben (Benjamin) Jonson

It is admirable to die the victim of one's faith; it is sad to die the dupe of one's ambition.
Alphonse de Lamartine

It is more difficult, and calls for higher energies of soul, to live a martyr than to die one.
Horace Mann

When we read, we fancy we could be martyrs; when we come to act, we cannot bear a provoking word.
Hannah More

It is the cause and not merely the death that makes the marytr.
Napoleon I (Bonaparte)

Even in this world they will have their judgment-day; and their names, which went down in the dust like a gallant banner trodden in the mire, shall rise again all glorious in the sight of nations.
Harriet Elizabeth Beecher Stowe

See also: FAITH, HEROISM, SACRIFICE, SAINT.

MARXISM

As a German and a Jew, Marx is authoritarian from head to heels.
Mikhail Aleksandrovich Bakunin

Marx was above all a revoluntionary, and his great aim in life was . . . the emancipation of the modern proletariat.
Friedrich Engels

If Socialism has become scientific, we owe this to Karl Marx.
Georgii Valentinovich Plekhanov

True or false, every Marxism which claims to be a systematized thought, even a philosophy of Marx, represents a complete alteration of his most profound intentions. The thought of Marx could not justify the birth of political ideology, that is the transformation of his sociological theses into norms of political action, neither as a sociological theory of a determined economic system. . . . This ideology could only be born as a perversion of the ethical presuppositions which confer on Marxist teaching an extraordinary force.
Maximilien Rubel

See also: COMMUNISM, RUSSIA.

MASTER

Such it hath been, and shall be, that many still must labor for the one; it is nature's doom.
George Gordon Byron (Lord Byron)

We must truly serve those whom we appear to command; we must bear with their imperfections, correct them with gentleness and patience, and lead them in the way to heaven.
François de Salignac de La-Mothe Fénelon

The eye of the master will do more work than both of his hands: not to oversee workmen, is to leave your purse open.
Benjamin Franklin

If thou art a master, sometimes be blind; if a servant, sometimes be deaf.
Thomas Fuller

See also: COMMANDER, OPPRESSION, SERVANT, SLAVERY, TYRANNY.

MATERIALISM

Love the soil. The work is hard and sometimes the return is little. . . . But you will
find in the good earth and fields a sure refuge from dangerous materialism.

John XXIII (Angelo Giuseppe Roncalli)

Men's ideas are the most direct emanations
of their material state.

Karl Marx

Material progress cannot go far or last long
unless it has its foundations in moral principles and high ideals.

Jawaharlal Nehru

See also: COMMUNISM, MARXISM, WEALTH.

MATHEMATICS

Pure mathematics do remedy and cure many
defects in the wit and faculties of individuals; for if the wit be dull, they sharpen it; if
too wandering they fix it; if too inherent in
the sense, they abstract it.

Francis Bacon

The structures with which mathematics
deals are more like lace, the leaves of trees,
and the play of light and shadow on a human face, than they are like buildings and
machines, the least of their representatives.
The best proofs in mathematics are short and
crisp like epigrams, and the longest have
swings and rhythms that are like music. The
structures of mathematics and the propositions about them are ways for the imagination to travel and the wings, or legs, or vehicles to take you where you want to go.

Scott Milross Buchanan

The study of mathematics cultivates the reason; that of the languages, at the same time,
the reason and the taste. The former gives
grasp and power to the mind; the latter both
power and flexibility. The former, by itself,
would prepare us for a state of certainties,
which nowhere exists; the latter, for a state
of probabilities, which is that of common
life. Each, by itself, does but an imperfect
work: in the union of both, is the best discipline for the mind, and the best mental
training for the world as it is.

Tryon Edwards

As far as the laws of mathematics refer to
reality, they are not certain; and as far as
they are certain, they do not refer to reality.

Albert Einstein

If a man's wits be wandering, let him study
the mathematics; for in demonstrations, if
his wit be called away ever so little, he must
begin again.

Samuel Johnson

There are two ways to teach mathematics.
One is to take real pains toward creating
understanding—visual aids, that sort of thing.
The other is the old British system of teaching until you're blue in the face.

James Roy Newman

Mathematics possesses not only truth, but
supreme beauty—a beauty cold and austere,
like that of sculpture.

Bertrand Arthur William Russell

See also: LOGIC, SCIENCE, STATISTICS, TECH-
NOLOGY.

MATURITY

By education most have been misled;
So they believe, because they were so bred.
The priest continues what the nurse began,
And thus the child imposes on the man.

John Dryden

By the age of twenty, any young man should
know whether or not he is to be a specialist
and just where his tastes lie. By postponing
the question we have set on immaturity a
premium which controls most American personality to its deathbed.

Robert Silliman Hillyer

To be mature means to face, and not evade,
every fresh crisis that comes.

Fritz Künkel

Men come to their meridian at various periods of their lives.

John Henry Newman

See also: ADULT, AGE, WISDOM.

MAXIM

It is more trouble to make a maxim than it is
to do right.

Samuel Langhorne Clemens (Mark Twain)

A maxim is a conclusion from observation of
matters of fact, and is merely speculative; a
principle carries knowledge within itself,
and is prospective.

Samuel Taylor Coleridge

A man of maxims only, is like a cyclops with
one eye, and that in the back of his head.

Samuel Taylor Coleridge

Pithy sentences are like sharp nails which force truth upon our memory.

Denis Diderot

The value of a maxim depends on four things: its intrinsic excellence or the comparative correctness of the principle it embodies; the subject to which it relates; the extent of its application; and the comparative ease with which it may be applied in practice.

Charles Hodge

Maxims are the condensed good sense of nations.

Sir James Mackintosh

All maxims have their antagonist maxims; proverbs should be sold in pairs, a single one being but a half truth.

William Mathews

Precepts or maxims are of great weight; and a few useful ones at hand do more toward a happy life than whole volumes that we know not where to find.

Seneca

See also: APHORISM, APOTHEGMS, PRINCIPLE, PROVERB.

MEAN

There are found some minds given to an extreme admiration of antiquity, others to an extreme love and appetite for novelty; but few so duly tempered that they can hold the mean, neither carping at what has been well laid down by the ancients, nor despising what is well introduced by the moderns.

Francis Bacon

There is a mean in all things; even virtue itself has stated limits; which not being strictly observed, it ceases to be virtue.

Horace

See also: COMPROMISE, EXTREMES, VIRTUE.

MEANNESS

I have great hope of a wicked man; slender hope of a mean one. A wicked man may be converted and become a prominent saint. A mean man ought to be converted six or seven times, one right after the other, to give him a fair start and put him on an equality with a bold, wicked man.

Henry Ward Beecher

Whoever is mean in his youth runs a great risk of becoming a scoundrel in riper years; meanness leads to villainy with fatal attraction.

Victor Cherbuliez

When a man's dog turns against him it is time for a wife to pack her trunk and go home to mama.

Samuel Langhorne Clemens (Mark Twain)

Superior men, and yet not always virtuous, there have been; but there never has been a mean man, and at the same time virtuous.

Confucius

See also: BASENESS, CRUELTY, MALICE, MISER, SELFISHNESS.

MEANS: see MEANS AND END.

MEANS AND END

There can be no end without means; and God furnishes no means that exempt us from the task and duty of joining our own best endeavors. The original stock, or wild olive tree of our natural powers, was not given us to be burnt or blighted, but to be grafted on.

Samuel Taylor Coleridge

Some men possess means that are great, but fritter them away in the execution of conceptions that are little; others, who can form great conceptions, attempt to carry them into execution with little means. These two descriptions of men might succeed if united, but kept asunder, both fail. It is a rare thing to find a combination of great means and of great conceptions in one mind.

Charles Caleb Colton

As the means, so the end.

Mohandas Karamchand (Mahatma) Gandhi

They say—"Means are after all means." I would say—"Means are after all everything."

Mohandas Karamchand (Mahatma) Gandhi

We must rest satisfied with a knowledge only of the means and if these are pure, we can fearlessly leave the end to take care of itself.

Mohandas Karamchand (Mahatma) Gandhi

The means should be such as lead to the end, otherwise they are wasted effort, and they might even result in even greater degradation, both outer and inner.

Jawaharlal Nehru

There is always a close and intimate relationship between the end we aim at and the means adopted to attain it. Even if the end is right but the means are wrong, it will vitiate the end or divert us in a wrong direction. Means and ends are thus intimately and inextricably connected and cannot be separated. That, indeed, has been the lesson of old taught us by many great men in the past, but unfortunately it is seldom remembered.

Jawaharlal Nehru

The end must justify the means.

Matthew Prior

All outward means of grace, if separate from the spirit of God, cannot profit, or conduce, in any degree, either to the knowledge or love of God. All outward things, unless he work in them and by them, are in vain.

John Wesley

See also: APPROACH, END, EXPEDIENCY.

MEDICINE

Cure the disease and kill the patient.

Francis Bacon

Nature, time, and patience are the three great physicians.

Henry George Bohn

Medicine is the only profession that labors incessantly to destroy the reason for its own existence.

James Bryce

The best of all medicines are rest and fasting.

Benjamin Franklin

When I began practice, if someone came to me with a pain in the lower right abdomen, I was relatively safe in assuming it was either appendicitis or green apples. Today, in addition to these two possibilities, it is also highly probable that the patient is suffering—really and acutely—from the fact that his wife of 40 years wants to leave him to join the Peace Corps or Richard Burton. Or the man might have Stockholder's Syndrome or Khrushchev Colic. It will be up to you to find out—you will get a very practical education in the symptoms of pressure.

Gunnar Gundersen

Twentieth century medical care cannot be given in 19th century hospitals. It is necessary that we proceed with a hospital modernization program without delay, not only in the interests of providing urgently needed health care, but also in the interest of economy.

Jacob K. Javits

The very success of medicine in a material way may now threaten the soul of medicine. Medicine is something more than the cold mechanical application of science to human disease. Medicine is the healing art. It must deal with individuals, their fears, their hopes and their sorrows. It must reach back further than a disease that the patient may have to those physical and emotional environmental factors which condition the individual for the reception of disease.

Walter Bramblette Martin

The bitterness of the potion, and the abhorrence of the patient are necessary circumstances to the operation. It must be something to trouble and disturb the stomach that must purge and cure it.

Michel Eyquem de Montaigne

No matter how complex or specialized medicine may become in the decades ahead . . . there always will have to be the equivalent of the family doctor.

Dwight Harrison Murray

We have not only multiplied diseases, but we have made them more fatal.

Richard Rush

The strain on existing hospitals, urban and rural, and public and private, has continued to worsen. The advent of medicare and medicaid have accentuated the trend.

William F. Ryan

See also: DISEASE, DOCTOR, HEALTH, MENTAL HEALTH, SICKNESS.

MEDIOCRITY

Mediocrity can talk; but it is for genius to observe.

Benjamin Disraeli

If every man worked at that for which nature fitted him, the cows will be well tended.

Jean Pierre Claris de Florian

How many minds you must leave as you find—in permanent mediocrity.

John Watson Foster

Mediocrity is now, as formerly, dangerous, commonly fatal, to the poet; but among even the successful writers of prose, those who rise sensibly above it are the very rarest exceptions.

William Ewart Gladstone

Persevering mediocrity is much more respectable, and unspeakably more useful, than talented inconstancy.

James Hamilton

Mediocrity is not allowed to poets, either by the gods or men.

Horace

Mediocrity is excellent to the eyes of mediocre people.

Joseph Joubert

There are certain things in which mediocrity is not to be endured, such as poetry, music, painting, public speaking.

Jean de La Bruyère

Nothing in the world is more haughty than a man of moderate capacity when once raised to power.

Freiherr von Wessenberg

See also: BORE, DULNESS, MAJORITY.

MEDITATION

By meditation I can converse with God, solace myself on the bosom of the Saviour, bathe myself in the rivers of divine pleasure, tread the paths of my rest, and view the mansions of eternity.

Anonymous

One of the rarest of all acquirements is the faculty of profitable meditation. Most human beings, when they fancy they are meditating, are, in fact, doing nothing at all, and thinking of nothing.

Andrew Kennedy Boyd

No soul can preserve the bloom and delicacy of its existence without lonely musings and silent prayer, and the greatness of this necessity is in proportion to the greatness of evil.

Frederic William Farrar

Meditation is the soul's perspective glass, whereby, in her long removes, she discerneth God, as if he were nearer at hand.

Owen Felltham

It is easier to go six miles to hear a sermon, than to spend one quarter of an hour in meditating on it when I come home.

Philip Henry

Meditation is that exercise of the mind by which it recalls a known truth, as some kind of creatures do their food, to be ruminated upon till all the valuable parts be extracted.

George Horne

It is not the number of books you read, nor the variety of sermons you hear, nor the amount of religious conversation in which you mix, but it is the frequency and earnestness with which you meditate on these things till the truth in them becomes your own and part of your being, that ensures your growth.

Frederick William Robertson

Meditation is the nurse of thought, and thought the food for meditation.

Charles Simmons

It seems to me a sad commentary on contemporary life and certainly public life, that we are so busy doing that we have little time for thinking; that we are so busy with so much that is transitory we give all too little to the intransitory and enduring. Perspective is the victim of pressure. Yet the truth lies in reflection and meditation.

Adlai Ewing Stevenson

Reading and conversation may furnish us with many ideas of men and things, yet it is our own meditation that must form our judgment.

Isaac Watts

'Tis greatly wise to talk with our past hours and ask them what report they bore to heaven, and how they might have borne more welcome news.

Owen D. Young

See also: CONTEMPLATION, PRAYER, THOUGHT.

MEEKNESS

Meekness is imperfect if it be not both active and passive, leading us to subdue our own passions and resentments, as well as to bear patiently the passions and resentments of others.

John Watson Foster

There will come a time when three words, uttered with charity and meekness, shall receive a far more blessed reward than three thousand volumes written with disdainful sharpness of wit.

Richard Hooker

Meekness cannot well be counterfeited. It is not insensibility, or unmanliness, or servility; it does not cringe, or whine. It is benevolence imitating Christ in patience, forbearance, and quietness. It feels keenly but not malignantly; it abounds in good will, and bears all things.

William Swan Plumer

The meek are not those who are never at all angry, for such are insensible; but those who, feeling anger, control it, and are angry only when they ought to be. Meekness excludes revenge, irritability, morbid sensitiveness, but not self-defence, or a quiet and steady maintenance of right.

Theophylactus

See also: DOCILITY, HUMILITY, PRIDE.

MEETING

The joy of meeting, not unmixed with pain.

Henry Wadsworth Longfellow

In life there are meetings which seem like a fate.

Edward R. Bulwer Lytton (Owen Meredith)

The joys of meeting pay the pangs of absence; else who could bear it?

Nicholas Rowe

Absence, with all its pains, is, by this charming moment, wiped away.

James Thomson

See also: ABSENCE, ACQUAINTANCE, PARTING, WELCOME.

MELANCHOLY

People of gloomy, uncheerful imaginations, will discover their natural tincture of mind in all their thoughts, words, and actions. As the finest wines have often the taste of the soil, so even the most religious thoughts often draw something that is peculiar from the constitution of the mind in which they arise. When folly or superstition strikes in with this natural depravity of temper, it is not in the power, even of religion itself, to preserve the character from appearing highly absurd and ridiculous.

Joseph Addison

Melancholy sees the worst of things—things as they might be, and not as they are. It looks upon a beautiful face, and sees but a grinning skull.

Christian Nestell Bovee

Melancholy is a fearful gift; what is it but the telescope of truth, which brings life near in utter darkness, making the cold reality too real?

George Gordon Byron (Lord Byron)

Whatever is highest and holiest is tinged with melancholy. The eye of genius has always a plaintive expression, and its natural language is pathos. A prophet is sadder than other men; and He who was greater than all the prophets was "a man of sorrows and acquainted with grief."

Lydia Maria Francis Child

Make not a bosom friend of a melancholy, sad soul. He will be sure to aggravate thine adversity and to lessen thy prosperity. He goes always heavily loaded, and thou must bear half.

François de Salignac de La Mothe-Fénelon

Melancholy attends the best joys of an ideal life.

(Sarah) Margaret Fuller

There is not a string attuned to mirth but has its chord of melancholy.

Edwin Paxton Hood

Melancholy, or low spirits, is that hysterical passion which forces unbidden sighs and tears. It falls upon a contented life, like a drop of ink on white paper, which is none the less a stain that it carries no meaning with it.

John Gibson Lockhart

The spirit of melancholy would often take its flight from us if only we would take up the song of praise.

Philip Bennett Power

It is impious in a good man to be sad.

Owen D. Young

See also: DESPONDENCY, SADNESS.

MEMORY

Memory is the cabinet of imagination, the treasury of reason, the registry of conscience, and the council chamber of thought.

Basil the Great

Memory can gleam, but never renew. It brings us joys faint as in the perfume of the flowers, faded and dried, of the summer that is gone.

Henry Ward Beecher

A memory without blot of contamination must be an exquisite treasure, an inexhaustible source of pure refreshment.

Charlotte Brontë

Joy's recollection is no longer joy, while sorrow's memory is sorrow still.

George Gordon Byron (Lord Byron)

Memory is the receptacle and sheath of all knowledge.

Cicero

Of all the faculties of the mind, memory is the first that flourishes, and the first that dies.

Charles Caleb Colton

Memory is the friend of wit, but the treacherous ally of invention; there are many books that owe their success to two things, —the good memory of those who write them, and the bad memory of those who read them.

Charles Caleb Colton

The joys I have possessed are ever mine; out of thy reach, behind eternity, hid in the sacred treasure of the past, but blest remembrance brings them hourly back.

John Dryden

They teach us to remember; why do not they teach us to forget? There is not a man living who has not, some time in his life, admitted that memory was as much of a curse as a blessing.

Francis Alexander Durivage

The secret of a good memory is attention, and attention to a subject depends upon our interest in it. We rarely forget that which has made a deep impression on our minds.

Tryon Edwards

Unless we remember we cannot understand.

Edward Morgan Forster

Memory depends very much on the perspicuity, regularity, and order of our thoughts. Many complain of the want of memory, when the defect is in their judgment; and others, by grasping at all, retain nothing.

(Sarah) Margaret Fuller

Memory is a very frail thing. The written word stands for ever.

Mohandas Karamchand (Mahatma) Gandhi

The memory of past favors, is like a rainbow, bright, vivid, and beautiful, but it soon fades away. The memory of injuries is engraved on the heart, and remains forever.

Thomas Chandler Haliburton

We must always have old memories and young hopes.

Arsène Houssaye

There is a remembrance of the dead, to which we turn even from the charms of the living. These we would not exchange for the song of pleasure or the bursts of revelry.

Washington Irving

The true art of memory is the art of attention.

Samuel Johnson

We consider ourselves as defective in memory, either because we remember less than we desire, or less than we suppose others to remember.

Samuel Johnson

Because of forgetting, the innocence of pleasure is perpetually reborn.

Jacob Klatzkin

Memory tempers prosperity, mitigates adversity, controls youth, and delights old age.

Lactantius

How can such deep-imprinted images sleep in us at times, till a word, a sound, awake them?

Gotthold Ephraim Lessing

Memories are all we really own.

Elias Lieberman

No one is likely to remember what is entirely uninteresting to him.

George Macdonald

What we learn with pleasure we never forget.

Charles Alfred Mercier

Experience teaches that a strong memory is generally joined to a weak judgment.

Michel Eyquem de Montaigne

To know by heart is no knowledge; that is merely to possess what has been committed to the memory. That which a man knows thoroughly and completely, he can make use of without referring to the author from which he may have borrowed some of the ideas, and without turning his eyes to his paper. It is a tedious and troublesome acquisition to depend on a book. In my opinion such knowledge serves merely for ornament, and not for foundation, on which any superstructure can be raised.

Michel Eyquem de Montaigne

If you have to keep reminding yourself of a thing, perhaps it isn't so.

Christopher Darlington Morley

Women and elephants never forget.

Dorothy Parker

The past is hidden somewhere outside the realm, beyond the reach of intellect in some material object (in the sensation which that material object will give us) which we do not suspect, and as for that object, it depends upon chance whether we come upon it or not before we ourselves die.

Marcel Proust

There is no man, however wise, who has not at some time in his youth said things or even done things whose memory he would wish to see expunged.

Marcel Proust

We find a little of everything in our memory; it is a kind of pharmacy or chemical laboratory in which chance guides our hand now to a calming drug and now to a dangerous poison.

Marcel Proust

Recollection is the only paradise from which we cannot be turned out.

Jean Paul Richter

The memory is a treasurer to whom we must give funds, if we would draw the assistance we need.

Nicholas Rowe

Memory is not wisdom; idiots can by rote repeat volumes. Yet what is wisdom without memory?

Martin Farquhar Tupper

See also: FORGETFULNESS, REMEMBRANCE.

MEN

If a woman wears gay colors, rouge and a startling hat, a man hesitates to take her out. If she wears a little turban and a tailored suit he takes her out and stares all evening at a woman in gay colors, rouge and a startling hat.

Baltimore Beacon

Good men do not always have grace and favor, lest they should be puffed up, and grow insolent and proud.

John Chrysostom

All great men are in some degree inspired.

Cicero

Men, by associating in large masses, as in camps and cities, improve their talents but impair their virtues; and strengthen their minds, but weaken their morals; thus a retrocession in the one, is too often the price they pay for a refinement of the other.

Charles Caleb Colton

The real difference between men is energy. A strong will, a settled purpose, an invincible determination, can accomplish almost anything; and in this lies the distinction between great men and little men.

Thomas Fuller

We do not commonly find men of superior sense amongst those of the highest fortune.

Juvenal

Nothing pleases men like renewing their ancient alliance with the brutes, and breaking off their more recent one with their fellowmen.

Walter Savage Landor

It is far easier to know men than to know man.

Duc François de La Rochefoucauld

Great men stand like solitary towers in the city of God, and secret passages, running deep beneath external nature, give their thoughts intercourse with higher intelligence, which strengthens and consoles them, and of which the laborers on the surface do not even dream.

Henry Wadsworth Longfellow

Lives of great men all remind us, we can make our lives sublime.

Henry Wadsworth Longfellow

We may judge of men by their conversation toward God, but never by God's dispensations toward them.

Ray Palmer

God divided man into men, that they might help each other.

Seneca

Men are but children, too, though they have gray hairs; they are only of a larger size.

Seneca

It is a folly to expect men to do all that they may reasonably be expected to do.

Richard Whately

See also: BACHELOR, FATHER, HUSBAND, MAN, SEXES.

MENTAL HEALTH

Mental hygiene is not concerned merely with those serious forms of mental disorder which require treatment in State hospitals; it is concerned with those other forms of mental disorders which do not necessarily mean the removal of the individual from his ordinary social environment.

Charles Macfie Campbell

We face a troubled world, its unhappy difficulties due in great, perhaps greatest part, to the mental, physical and moral maladjustments of its peoples . . . But mental hygiene has not as yet been far enough advanced to play its essential part. When it has been, and the coordinated efforts of those who heal the mind, of those who heal the body, and of those who heal the soul are brought to bear upon our world problems, shall we not see the beginnings of a brighter day—the rise of a finer and more stable civilization?

Central Hanover Bank and Trust Company

In the last analysis, the problem of mental health cannot be divorced from the general problem of the public health.

Albert Deutsch

We have traveled a long road upward from the ideal of repression to the ideal of prevention, from manacles to mental hygiene.

Albert Deutsch

A world of peace and freedom, from which the twin specters of war and insecurity will be banished, a world of equal opportunity, where people will be freed from stunting inhibitions and "guilt feelings" arising from outworn prejudices and taboos, a world where children may lead healthy, happy lives and grow into useful, well adjusted citizens, where the personality is permitted to develop naturally and freely, where the individual is given a sense of personal worth and dignity, and where his activities and ambitions are integrated with the development of group life—such is the goal toward which mental hygiene must strive.

Albert Deutsch

The problem of mental retardation is one which afflicts families throughout the United States from the very lowest income groups to the very highest. It is estimated that as many as 3 million Americans are mentally retarded, and about 11 percent of that number are so severely handicapped that they require institutional treatment of one sort or another.

Harley O. Staggers

Mentally ill and defective patients for whom treatment offers little promise need humane custodial care, both in institutions and in the community.

George Salvadore Stevenson

Such a stage of civilization as we have thus far reached has not been attained by a process of drifting, but only by the hardest kind of sustained effort over long periods of time. The primitive instincts with which man originally battled his way among the crude forces of nature have not perished. They still exist, but man must no longer be at their mercy. He must be able to recapture for socially constructive ends the energies that they represent. That is the lesson of mental hygiene.

William Alanson White

See also: INSANITY, PSYCHIATRY, PSYCHOLOGY, PSYCHOMETRICS, SICKNESS.

MERCY

Among the attributes of God, although they are all equal, mercy shines with even more brilliancy than justice.

Miguel de Cervantes Saavedra

Mercy among the virtues is like the moon among the stars,—not so sparkling and vivid as many, but dispensing a calm radiance that hallows the whole. It is the bow that rests upon the bosom of the cloud when the storm is past. It is the light that hovers above the judgment-seat.

Edwin Hubbel Chapin

Mercifulness makes us equal to the gods.
Claudian

Mercy to him that shows it, is the rule.
William Cowper

We hand folks over to God's mercy, and show none ourselves.
George Eliot (Mary Ann Evans)

Mercy more becomes a magistrate than the vindictive wrath which men call justice.
Henry Wadsworth Longfellow

The oils and herbs of mercy are so few.
Edna St. Vincent Millay

Teach me to feel another's woe,
   To hide the fault I see;
That mercy I to others show,
   That mercy show to me.
Alexander Pope

Mercy turns her back to the unmerciful.
Francis Quarles

Who will not mercy unto others show,
How can he mercy ever hope to have?
Edmund Spenser

Hate shuts her soul when dove-eyed mercy pleads.
Charles Sprague

Mercy is like the rainbow, which God hath set in the clouds; it never shines after it is night. If we refuse mercy here, we shall have justice in eternity.
Jeremy Taylor

See also: CLEMENCY, COMPASSION, FORGIVE-
NESS, PARDON, PITY.

MERIT

Mere bashfulness without merit, is awkward; and merit without modesty, insolent. But modest merit has a double claim to accept-ance, and generally meets with as many pa-trons as beholders.
Joseph Addison

The sufficiency of my merit, is to know that my merit is not sufficient.
Augustine of Hippo

Contemporaries appreciate the man rather than his merit; posterity will regard the mer-it rather than the man.
Charles Caleb Colton

I will not be concerned at other men's not knowing me; I will be concerned at my own want of ability.
Confucius

There's a proud modesty in merit; averse from asking, and resolved to pay ten times the gifts it asks.
John Dryden

It never occurs to fools that merit and good fortune are closely united.
Johann Wolfgang von Goethe

The art of being able to make a good use of moderate abilities wins esteem, and often confers more reputation than real merit.
Duc François de La Rochefoucauld

Eminence is to merit what fine attire is to a handsome person.
Duc François de La Rochefoucauld

The mark of extraordinary merit is to see those most envious of it constrained to praise.
Duc François de La Rochefoucauld

Men may have merit without rising to emi-nence, but no one has ever reached emi-nence without some degree of merit.
Duc François de La Rochefoucauld

True merit, like a river, the deeper it is, the less noise it makes.
Charles Montagu (1st Earl of Halifax)

If you wish your merit to be known, ac-knowledge that of other people.
Oriental Proverb

Charms strike the sight, but merit wins the soul.
Alexander Pope

Real merit of any kind, cannot long be concealed; it will be discovered, and noth-ing can depreciate it but a man exhibiting it himself. It may not always be rewarded as it ought; but it will always be known.
Philip Dormer Stanhope (Lord Chesterfield)

See also: EXCELLENCE, VIRTUE, WORTH.

MERRIMENT: see MIRTH.

MESSIAH

True Jews and true Christians have always expected a Messiah who should make them

love God, and by that love triumph over
their enemies.

Blaise Pascal

Like the dawning of the morning,
   On the mountain's golden heights,
Like the breaking of the moonbeams
   On the gloom of cloudy nights.
Like a secret told by angels,
   Getting known upon the earth,
Is the Mother's expectation
   Of Messias' speedy birth.

Frederick William Faber

See also: CHRIST, REDEMPTION.

METAPHYSICS

Metaphysicians are whetstones, on which to
sharpen dull intellects.

Henry Ward Beecher

On a metaphysician: A blind man in a dark
room—looking for a black hat—which isn't
there.

Charles Synge Christopher Bowen

Metaphysicians are musicians without musical ability.

Rudolph Carnap

Metaphysics is the anatomy of the soul.

Catherine Stanislas Jean de Boufflers

We have no strict demonstration of anything, except mathematical truths, but by
metaphysics. We can have no proof that is
properly demonstrative, of any one position
relating to the being and nature of God, his
creation of the world, the dependence of all
things on him, the nature of bodies and
spirits, the nature of our own souls, or any of
the great truths of morality and natural religion, but what is metaphysical.

Jonathan Edwards

It is in the light of our beliefs about the ultimate nature of reality that we formulate our
conceptions of right and wrong; and it is in
the light of our conceptions of right and
wrong that we frame our conduct.

Aldous Leonard Huxley

Metaphysics may be, after all, only the art
of being sure of something that is not so,
and logic only the art of going wrong with
confidence.

Joseph Wood Krutch

The perversion of the mind is only possible
when those who should be heard in its defense are silent.

Archibald MacLeish

Algebra is the metaphysics of arithmetic.

Laurence Sterne

When he that speaks, and he to whom he
speaks, neither of them understand what is
meant, that is metaphysics.

Voltaire (François Marie Arouet)

See also: LOGIC, MIND, PHILOSOPHY, SPECULA-
TION, THEORY.

METHOD

Irregularity and want of method are only
supportable in men of great learning or genius, who are often too full to be exact, and
therefore choose to throw down their pearls
in heaps before the reader, rather than be at
the pains of stringing them.

Joseph Addison

Method is like packing things in a box; a
good packer will get in half as much again
as a bad one.

Richard Cecil

The shortest way to do many things is to do
only one thing at a time.

Richard Cecil

The first idea of method is a progressive
transition from one step to another in any
course. If in the right course, it will be the
true method; if in the wrong, we cannot
hope to progress.

Samuel Taylor Coleridge

Method will teach you to win time.

Johann Wolfgang von Goethe

Every great man exhibits the talent of organization of construction, whether it be in a
poem, a philosophical system, a policy, or a
strategy. And without method there is no organization nor construction.

Edward G. Bulwer-Lytton (Baron Lytton)

Be methodical if you would succeed in business, or in anything. Have a work for every
moment, and mind the moment's work.
Whatever your calling, master all its bearings and details, its principles, instruments,
and applications. Method is essential if you
would get through your work easily and with
economy of time.

William Mathews

Method goes far to prevent trouble in business; for it makes the task easy, hinders confusion, saves abundance of time, and instructs those who have business depending, what to do and what to hope.

William Penn

Method facilitates every kind of business, and by making it easy makes it agreeable, and also successful.

Charles Simmons

Methods are the masters of masters.

Alexandre de Talleyrand-Périgord

See also: APPROACH, END, EXPEDIENCY.

METHODISM

The hymns sung are full of theology and personal experience. They reflect the Methodist confidence and joy in a salvation offered freely to all men. Many a humble believer has found his creed expressed in the songs he has learned in the society meetings, and there can be no doubt but that this emphasis on singing is one of Methodism's lasting influences and contributions.

Gerald Hamilton Kennedy

Methodism has always been a missionary-minded Church.

Gerald Hamilton Kennedy

The Methodism of the early days was good news for the poor, and was often resented by the rich.

Gerald Hamilton Kennedy

The Methodist movement was and is a singing fellowship.

Gerald Hamilton Kennedy

Methodism was born in a prayer meeting, but it learned to walk on a battlefield.

Halford Luccock and Paul Hutchinson

The Wesleys were utterly irregular; John Wesley was an ecclesiastical rebel of the first order. Methodism is the child of irregularity.

Halford Luccock and Paul Hutchinson

See also: CHRISTIANITY, SECT.

MEXICO

In a style uniquely its own, Mexico is forging an industrial nation which is the envy of many countries possessing greater natural advantages.

Michael Mansfield

See also: CANADA, CUBA, NATION.

MIDDLE AGE: see AGE, MIDDLE.

MIDDLE AGES

We owe to the Middle Ages the two worst inventions of humanity—romantic love and gun-powder.

André Maurois

To the man of the Middle Ages the world was itself the ultramundane and the supernatural.

José Ortega y Gasset

See also: AGE, THE; HISTORY.

MIDNIGHT

That hour, o' night's black arch the keystane.

Robert Burns

Oh, wild and wondrous midnight, there is a might in thee to make the charmed body almost like spirit, and give it some faint glimpses of immortality.

James Russell Lowell

Midnight brought on the dusky hour, friendliest to sleep and silence.

John Milton

Midnight,—strange mystic hour,—when the veil between the frail present and the eternal future grows thin.

Harriet Elizabeth Beecher Stowe

See also: DAY, NIGHT, SLEEP, STAR.

MIND

Old minds are like old horses; you must exercise them if you wish to keep them in working order.

John Quincy Adams

He who cannot contract the sight of his mind, as well as dilate it, wants a great talent in life.

Francis Bacon

All the choir of heaven and furniture of earth—in a word, all those bodies which compose the mighty frame of the world—have not any subsistence without a mind.

George Berkeley

Few minds wear out; more rust out.

Christian Nestell Bovee

Mind unemployed is mind unenjoyed.

Christian Nestell Bovee

The mind is like the body—the less its possessor is aware of it the more easy is its working.

Pearl Sydenstricker Buck

The human mind cannot create anything. It produces nothing until after having been fertilized by experience and meditation; its acquisitions are the germs of its production.

Comte Georges Louis Leclerc de Buffon

The more accurately we search into the human mind, the stronger traces we everywhere find of the wisdom of Him who made it.

Edmund Burke

My mind to me a kingdom is; such present joys therein I find, that it excels all other bliss that earth affords.

Geoffrey Chaucer

It is a great mistake to think anything too profound or rich for a popular audience. No train of thought is too deep or subtle or grand; but the manner of presenting it to their untutored minds should be peculiar. It should be presented in anecdote, or sparkling truism, or telling illustration, or stinging epithet, etc.; always in some concrete form, never in a logical, abstract, syllogistic shape.

Rufus Choate

Whatever that be which thinks, understands, wills, and acts, it is something celestial and divine.

Cicero

In the province of the mind, what is believed to be true is true or becomes true, within limits to be found experientially and experimentally. These limits are beliefs to be transcended. In the province of the mind there are no limits.

John Cunningham Lilly

The only catalogue of this world's goods that really counts is that which we keep in the silence of the mind.

Walter John de la Mare

The professional mind is so microscopic that it sometimes ceases to be binocular.

Bernard Augustine De Voto

A narrow mind begets obstinacy; we do not easily believe what we cannot see.

John Dryden

There is nothing so elastic as the human mind. Like imprisoned steam, the more it is pressed the more it rises to resist the pressure. The more we are obliged to do the more we are able to accomplish.

Tryon Edwards

A well cultivated mind is made up of all the minds of preceding ages; it is only the one single mind educated by all previous time.

Bernard Le Bovier de Fontenelle

To pass from a mirror-mind to a mind with windows is an essential element in the development of real personality.

Harry Emerson Fosdick

If thou desirest ease, in the first place take care of the ease of thy mind; for that will make all other sufferings easy. But nothing can support a man whose mind is wounded.

Thomas Fuller

We in vain summon the mind to intense application, when the body is in a languid state.

Gaius Cornelius Gallus

Man cannot develop his mind by simply writing and reading or making speeches all day long.

Mohandas Karamchand (Mahatma) Gandhi

Knowledge, wisdom, erudition, arts, and elegance, what are they, but the mere trappings of the mind, if they do not serve to increase the happiness of the possessor? A mind rightly instituted in the school of philosophy, acquires at once the stability of the oak, and the flexibility of the osier.

Oliver Goldsmith

There are few who need complain of the narrowness of their minds if they will only do their best with them.

Thomas Hobbes

As the mind must govern the hands, so in every society the man of intelligence must direct the man of labor.

Samuel Johnson

The end which at present calls forth our efforts will be found, when it is once gained, to be only one of the means to some remoter end. The natural flights of the human mind are not from pleasure to pleasure, but from hope to hope.

Samuel Johnson

The human mind is our fundamental resource.
John Fitzgerald Kennedy

How . . . can the consciousness be dismissed as an epiphenomenon when only by virtue of this epiphenomenon could it be perceived to be an epiphenomenon—or anything else?
Joseph Wood Krutch

As the fire-fly only shines when on the wing, so it is with the human mind—when at rest, it darkens.
Letitia Elizabeth Landon

Commonplace minds usually condemn what is beyond the reach of their understanding.
Duc François de La Rochefoucauld

The defects of the mind, like those of the face, grow worse as we grow old.
Duc François de La Rochefoucauld

Little minds are too much hurt by little things; great minds are quite conscious of them, and despise them.
Duc François de La Rochefoucauld

A mind once cultivated will not lie fallow for half an hour.
Edward G. Bulwer-Lytton (Baron Lytton)

Our minds have unbelievable power over our bodies.
André Maurois

The biggest human brain on record was that of an idiot; one of the smallest was that of the gifted French writer Anatole France.
Ashley Montagu

The human mind refuses to imprison itself and continues to reach out for that fruit of knowledge which it well knows is beyond reach.
Jawaharlal Nehru

The mind is like the stomach. It is not how much you put into it that counts, but how much it digests.
Albert Jay Nock

The immature mind hops from one thing to another; the mature mind seeks to follow through.
Harry Allen Overstreet

A . . . program for the unrigid mind was once given me by a friend who himself had it from an old sea captain. I cannot refrain from passing it on. What we need if we want to stay flexible and young in our minds, the old captain said, is to be "limber, loving, and a little loony."
Harry Allen Overstreet

The mind ought sometimes to be diverted that it may return to better thinking.
Phaedrus

At a certain age some people's minds close up; they live on their intellectual fat.
William Lyon Phelps

The great business of man is to improve his mind, and govern his manners; all other projects and pursuits, whether in our power to compass or not, are only amusements.
Pliny the Elder

The best way to prove the clearness of our mind, is by showing its faults; as when a stream discovers the dirt at the bottom, it convinces us of the transparency and purity of the water.
Alexander Pope

Strength of mind is exercise, not rest.
Alexander Pope

Our minds are like our stomachs; they are whetted by the change of their food, and variety supplies both with fresh appetite.
Quintilian

The mind is but a barren soil; a soil which is soon exhausted, and will produce no crop, or only one, unless it be continually fertilized and enriched with foreign matter.
Sir Joshua Reynolds

What the country needs is dirtier fingernails and cleaner minds.
Will (William Penn Adair) Rogers

Nowhere does the mind better demonstrate its power than where it excludes itself in order to try to understand itself.
Jean Rostand

The trivialities of a great mind interest me more than the treasures of a mediocre one.
Jean Rostand

The mind grows narrow in proportion as the soul grows corrupt.

Jean Jacques Rousseau

The mind is chameleon-like in one respect, it receives hues from without; but it is unlike it in another respect, for it retains them.

Bayle St. John

As the soil, however rich it may be, cannot be productive without culture, so the mind without cultivation can never produce good fruit.

Seneca

The mind itself must, like other things, sometimes be unbent; or else it will be either weakened or broken.

Sir Philip Sidney

It is the mind that maketh good or ill, that maketh wretch or happy, rich or poor.

Edmund Spenser

Our species is the only creative species, and it has only one creative instrument, the individual mind and spirit of a man. Nothing was ever created by two men. There are no good collaborations, whether in music, in art, in poetry, in mathematics, in philosophy. Once the miracle of creation has taken place, the group can build and extend it, but the group never invents anything. The preciousness lies in the lonely mind of man.

John Ernst Steinbeck

I find, by experience, that the mind and the body are more than married, for they are most intimately united; and when the one suffers, the other sympathizes.

Philip Dormer Stanhope (Lord Chesterfield)

A weak mind is like a microscope, which magnifies trifling things, but cannot receive great ones.

Philip Dormer Stanhope (Lord Chesterfield)

Sublime is the dominion of the mind over the body, that for a time can make flesh and nerve impregnable, and string the sinews like steel, so that the weak become so mighty.

Harriet Elizabeth Beecher Stowe

If we work marble, it will perish; if we work upon brass, time will efface it; if we rear temples, they will crumble into dust; but if we work upon immortal minds and instill into them just principles, we are then en-graving that upon tablets which no time will efface, but will brighten and brighten to all eternity.

Daniel Webster

I not only use all the brains I have, but all I can borrow.

(Thomas) Woodrow Wilson

Where brains are what you need, force will not succeed.

Yiddish Proverb

See also: HEAD, INTELLECT, INTELLIGENCE, PSYCHIATRY, PSYCHOLOGY, PSYCHOMETRICS, REASON, UNDERSTANDING.

MINISTER

The proud he tamed; the penitent he cheered;
Nor to rebuke the rich offender, feared;
His preaching much, but more his practice wrought,
A living sermon of the truths he taught.

John Dryden

Men of God have always, from time to time, walked among men, and made their commission felt in the heart and soul of the commonest hearer.

Ralph Waldo Emerson

It was said of one who preached very well, and lived very ill, that when he was out of the pulpit, it was a pity he should ever go in; and when in the pulpit, it was a pity he should ever come out.

Thomas Fuller

The minister is to be a real man, a live man, a true man, a simple man, great in his love, in his life, in his work, in his simplicity, in his gentleness.

John Hall

The life of a pious minister is visible rhetoric.

Herman Hooker

The Christian ministry is the worst of all trades, but the best of all professions.

John Newton

"Three things," says Luther, "make a Divine—prayer, meditation, and trials." These make a Christian; but a Christian minister needs three more, talent, application, and acquirements.

Charles Simmons

If there were not a minister in every parish, you would quickly find cause to increase the number of constables; and if churches were not employed as places to hear God's law, there would be need of them to be prisons for law-breakers.

Robert South

See also: CLERGY, CHURCH.

MINORITY

Every new opinion, at its starting, is precisely in a minority of one.

Thomas Carlyle

Governments exist to protect the rights of minorities. The loved and the rich need no protection,—they have many friends and few enemies.

Wendell Phillips

Votes should be weighed, not counted.

Johann Christoph Frederich von Schiller

The smallest number, with God and truth on their side, are weightier than thousands.

Charles Simmons

See also: ARISTOCRACY, DEMOCRACY, GOVERN-
MENT, PARTY, POLITICS.

MIRACLES

In those parts of the world where learning and science has pervailed, miracles have ceased; but in those parts of it as are barbarous and ignorant, miracles are still in vogue.

Ethan Allen

Nothing can save us that is possible:
We who must die demand a miracle.

Wystan Hugh Auden

Every believer is God's miracle.

Gamaliel Bailey

Miracles are the swaddling clothes of infant churches.

Thomas Fuller

A Miracle: An event described by those to whom it was told by men who did not see it.

Elbert Green Hubbard

A miracle I take to be a sensible operation, which being above the comprehension of the spectator, and in his opinion contrary to the established course of nature, is taken by him to be divine.

John Locke

Miracles seldom occur, except in the imaginations of the faithful.

Jawaharlal Nehru

A miracle is a work exceeding the power of any created agent, consequently being an effect of the divine omnipotence.

Robert South

See also: CHRIST, GOD, MYSTERY.

MIRTH

Man is the merriest species of the creation; all above or below him are serious.

Joseph Addison

An ounce of mirth is worth a pound of sorrow.

Richard Baxter

Mirthfulness is in the mind, and you cannot get it out. It is the blessed spirit that God has set in the mind to dust it, to enliven its dark places, and to drive asceticism, like a foul fiend, out of the back-door. It is just as good, in its place, as conscience or veneration. Praying can no more be made a substitute for smiling than smiling can for praying.

Henry Ward Beecher

Unseasonable mirth always turns to sorrow.

Miguel de Cervantes Saavedra

Fun gives you a forcible hug, and shakes laughter out of you, whether you will or no.

David Garrick

There is nothing like fun, is there? I haven't any myself, but I do like it in others. We need all the counter-weights we can muster to balance the sad relations of life. God has made sunny spots in the heart; why should we exclude the light from them?

Thomas Chandler Haliburton

Merriment is always the effect of a sudden impression. The jest which is expected is already destroyed.

Samuel Johnson

Nothing is more hopeless than a scheme of merriment.

Samuel Johnson

Old Times have bequeathed us a precept, to be merry and wise, but who has been able to observe it?

Samuel Johnson

Who cannot make one in the circle of harm-less merriment may be suspected of pride, hypocrisy, or formality.

Johann Kaspar Lavater

I love such mirth as does not make friends ashamed to look upon one another next morning; or men, that cannot well bear it, to repent of the money they spend when they be warmed with drink; and take this for a rule, you may pick out such times and such companies, that you may make yourself mer-rier for a little than a great deal of money, for "it is the company and not the charge that makes the feast."

Izaak Walton

Care to our coffin adds a nail, no doubt; and every grin, so merry, draws one out.

John Wolcot (Peter Pindar)

See also: HAPPINESS, JOY, LAUGHTER.

MISCHIEF

The sower of the seed is assuredly the au-thor of the whole harvest of mischief.

Demosthenes

He that may hinder mischief, yet permits it, is an accessory.

Edward Augustus Freeman

Few men are so clever as to know all the mischief they do.

Duc François de La Rochefoucauld

It is difficult to say who do you the most mis-chief, enemies with the worst intentions, or friends with the best.

Edward G. Bulwer-Lytton (Baron Lytton)

Only one-third of the people of the world are asleep at any given moment. The other two-thirds are awake and probably stirring up mischief somewhere.

(David) Dean Rusk

The opportunity to do mischief is found a hundred times a day, and that of doing good once a year.

Voltaire (François Marie Arouet)

See also: CRIME, MALICE, TROUBLE.

MISER

There is not in nature anything so remotely distant from God, or so extremely opposite to him, as a greedy and griping niggard.

Isaac Barrow

A mere madness—to live like a wretch that he may die rich.

Richard Eugene Burton

To cure us of our immoderate love of gain, we should seriously consider how many goods there are that money will not pur-chase, and these the best; and how many evils there are that money will not remedy, and these the worst.

Charles Caleb Colton

A thorough miser must possess considerable strength of character to bear the self-denial imposed by his penuriousness. Equal sacri-fices, endured voluntarily, in a better cause, would make a saint or a martyr.

William Benton Clulow

The word "miser," so often used as expres-sive of one who is grossly covetous and sav-ing, in its origin signifies one that is miser-able, the very etymology of the word thus indicating the necessary unhappiness of the miser spirit.

Tryon Edwards

There are sordid souls, incrusted with mud and dirt, in love with gain and filthy lucre, as noble spirits are with glory and virtue; ca-pable of enjoying one single pleasure, that of acquiring money, and grasping it; in search of and greedy after ten per cent, thinking of nothing but their debtors, always uneasy about the fall in the funds, or abatement in the value of money, plunged deep and as it were sunk in the abyss of contracts, titles, and parchments. Such people are neither re-lations, friends to any one, citizens, nor Christians, nor perhaps human beings: they have riches.

Jean de La Bruyère

Misers mistake gold for good, whereas it is only a means of obtaining it.

Duc François de La Rochefoucauld

The miser, starving his brother's body, starves also his own soul, and at death shall creep out of his great estate of injustice, poor and naked and miserable.

Theodore Parker

How vilely he has lost himself who becomes a slave to his servant, and exalts him to the dignity of his Maker! Gold is the God, the wife, the friend of the money-monger of the world.

William Penn

The miser is as much in want of that which he has, as of that which he has not.

Publilius Syrus

A miser grows rich by seeming poor; an extravagant man grows poor by seeming rich.

William Shenstone

Groan under gold, yet weep for want of bread.

Edward Young

See also: AVARICE, COVETOUSNESS, FRUGALITY, GOLD, MONEY, SELFISHNESS.

MISERY

A misery is not to be measured from the nature of the evil, but from the temper of the sufferer.

Joseph Addison

It is often better to have a great deal of harm happen to one than a little: a great deal may rouse you to remove what a little will only accustom you to endure.

Fulke Greville (First Baron Brooke)

Great misery may lodge in a little bosom.

Heinrich Heine

There are a good many real miseries in life that we cannot help smiling at, but they are the smiles that make wrinkles and not dimples.

Oliver Wendell Holmes

We should pass on from crime to crime, heedless and remorseless, if misery did not stand in our way, and our own pains admonish us of our folly.

Samuel Johnson

If you wish to be miserable, think about yourself; about what you want, what you like, what respect people ought to pay you, what people think of you; and then to you nothing will be pure. You will spoil everything you touch; you will make sin and misery for yourself out of everything God sends you; you will be as wretched as you choose.

Charles Kingsley

Misery loves company, but company does not reciprocate.

Addison Mizner

Man is so great that his greatness appears even in his consciousness of misery. A tree does not know itself to be miserable. It is true that it is misery indeed to know one's self to be miserable; but then it is greatness also. In this way all man's miseries go to prove his greatness. They are the miseries of a mighty potentate, of a dethroned monarch.

Blaise Pascal

Notwithstanding the sight of all the miseries which wring us and threaten our destruction, we have still an instinct that we cannot repress, which elevates us above our sorrows.

Blaise Pascal

Misery so little appertains to our nature, and happiness so much so, that we lament over that which has pained us, but leave unnoticed that which has rejoiced us.

Jean Paul Richter

Man is only miserable so far as he thinks himself so.

Jacopo Sannazaro

No scene of life but teems with mortal woe.

Sir Walter Scott

Half the misery in the world comes of want of courage to speak and to hear the truth plainly, and in a spirit of love.

Harriet Beecher Stowe

See also: ADVERSITY, AFFLICTION, PAIN.

MISFORTUNE

A soul exasperated by its ills, falls out with everything, with its friend and itself.

Joseph Addison

Evil events come from evil causes; and what we suffer, springs, generally, from what we have done.

Aristophanes

After all, our worst misfortunes never happen, and most miseries lie in anticipation.

Honoré de Balzac

Misfortune makes of certain souls a vast desert through which rings the voice of God.

Honoré de Balzac

The greatest misfortune of all is, not to be able to bear misfortune.

Bias of Priene

For truly in adverse fortune the worst sting of misery is to *have been* happy.

Boethius

He that is down needs fear no fall.

John Bunyan

Most of our misfortunes are more supportable than the comments of our friends upon them.

Charles Caleb Colton

By speaking of our misfortunes we often seem to get relief.

Pierre Corneille

By struggling with misfortunes, we are sure to receive some wounds in the conflict; but a sure method to come off victorious is by running away.

Oliver Goldsmith

The effect of great and inevitable misfortune is, to elevate those souls which it does not deprive of all virtue.

Elisabeth Charlotte Pauline Guizot

It is well to treasure the memories of past misfortunes; they constitute our bank of fortitude.

Eric Hoffer

Little minds are tamed and subdued by misfortune; but great minds rise above it.

Washington Irving

Misfortune is never mournful to the soul that accepts it; for such do always see that in every cloud is an angel's face.

Jerome (Eusebius Hieronymus)

Depend upon it, that if a man talks of his misfortune there is something in them that is not disagreeable to him: for where there is nothing but pure misery, there never is any mention of it.

Samuel Johnson

The only real misfortune that can befall man is to find himself in fault, and to have done something of which he need be ashamed.

Jean de La Bruyère

Let us be of good cheer, remembering that the misfortunes hardest to bear are those which never happen.

James Russell Lowell

Who hath not known ill-fortune never knew himself, or his own virtue.

David Mallet

Misfortune sprinkles ashes on the head of the man, but falls like dew on the head of the woman, and brings forth germs of strength of which she herself had no conscious possession.

Anna Cora Mowatt

When I was happy I thought I knew men, but it was fated that I should know them only in misfortune.

Napoleon I (Bonaparte)

Personal misfortune is of little account in this world of sorrow and strife, which demands from us all our strength in the struggles that convulse it.

Jawaharlal Nehru

I never knew a man who could not bear the misfortunes of another perfectly like a Christian.

Alexander Pope

If all the misfortunes of mankind were cast into a public stock, in order to be equally distributed among the whole species, those who now think themselves the most unhappy would prefer the share they are already possessed of before that which would fall to them by such a division.

Socrates

Almost all of life's misfortunes are rooted in our misconception of what happens to us. To know men thoroughly, to judge what happens sanely, is therefore a great step towards happiness.

Stendhal (Marie Henri Beyle)

It is seldom that God sends such calamities upon man as men bring upon themselves and suffer willingly.

Jeremy Taylor

Sorrow's crown of sorrow is remembering happier things.

Alfred, Lord Tennyson

See also: ADVERSITY, LOSS, SUFFERING.

MISTAKE

It is only an error in judgment to make a mistake, but it shows infirmity of character to adhere to it when discovered.

Christian Nestell Bovee

Any man may make a mistake, but none but a fool will continue in it.

Cicero

The young fancy that their follies are mistaken by the old for happiness; and the old fancy that their gravity is mistaken by the young for wisdom.
Charles Caleb Colton

A full and candid admission of one's mistake should make one proof against its repetition.
Mohandas Karamchand (Mahatma) Gandhi

I believe that if in spite of the best of intentions one is led into committing mistakes, they do not really result in harm to the world or, for the matter of that, any individual.
Mohandas Karamchand (Mahatma) Gandhi

No man ever became great or good except through many and great mistakes.
William Ewart Gladstone

The greatest mistake you can make in this life is to be continually fearing you will make one.
Elbert Green Hubbard

No persons are more frequently wrong, than those who will not admit they are wrong.
Duc François de La Rochefoucauld

When a fellow makes the same mistake twice he's got to throw up both hands and own up to carelessness or cussedness.
George Horace Lorimer

We learn wisdom from failure much more than from success; we often discover what will do, by finding out what will not do; and probably he who never made a mistake never made a discovery.
Samuel Smiles

The only people who make no mistakes are dead people. I saw a man last week who has not made a mistake for four thousand years. He was a mummy in the Egyptian department of the British Museum.
Heman Lincoln Wayland

See also: DELUSION, ERROR, WRONG.

MOB

A crowd always thinks with its sympathy, never with its reason.
William Rounseville Alger

It is an easy and vulgar thing to please the mob, and not a very arduous task to astonish them; but to benefit and improve them is a work fraught with difficulty, and teeming with danger.
Charles Caleb Colton

A mob is usually a creature of very mysterious existence, particularly in a large city. Where it comes from, or whither it goes, few men can tell. Assembling and dispersing with equal suddenness, it is as difficult to follow to its various sources as the sea itself; nor does the parallel stop here, for the ocean is not more fickle and uncertain, more terrible when roused, more unreasonable or more cruel.
Charles John Huffam Dickens

A mob is the scum that rises upmost when the nation boils.
John Dryden

A mob is a society of bodies, voluntarily bereaving themselves of reason, and traversing its work. The mob is man, voluntarily descending to the nature of the beast. Its fit hour of activity is night; its actions are insane, like its whole constitution.
Ralph Waldo Emerson

The greatest obstacle is that we have not yet emerged from the mobocratic stage. But my consolation lies in the fact that nothing is so easy as to train mobs, for the simple reason that they have no mind, no premeditation. They act in a frenzy. They repent quickly.
Mohandas Karamchand (Mahatma) Gandhi

Every numerous assembly is a mob; everything there depends on instantaneous turns.
Jean de Gondi (Cardinal de Retz)

Get together a hundred or two men, however sensible they may be, and you are very likely to have a mob.
Samuel Johnson

Let there be an entire abstinence from intoxicating drinks throughout this country during the period of a single generation, and a mob would be as impossible as combustion without oxygen.
Horace Mann

As a goose is not alarmed by hissing, nor a sheep by bleating; so neither be you terrified by the voice of a senseless multitude.
Tyrius Maximus

License they mean, when they cry liberty.
John Milton

There is nothing so little to be expected or hoped for from this many-headed monster, when incensed, as humanity and good nature; it is much more capable of alarm and fear.

Michel Eyquem de Montaigne

A mob is a sort of bear; while your ring is through its nose, it will even dance under your cudgel; but should the ring slip, and you lose your hold, the brute will turn and rend you.

Jane Porter

Human affairs are not so happily arranged that the best things please the most men. It is the proof of a bad cause when it is applauded by the mob.

Seneca

See also: COMMON MAN, CROWD, POPULACE.

MODERATION

I knew a wise man who had for a byword, when he saw men hasten to a conclusion, "stay a little, that we may come to the end sooner."

Francis Bacon

There is a German proverb which says that "Take it easy," and "Live long," are brothers.

Christian Nestell Bovee

The pursuit, even of the best things, ought to be calm and tranquil.

Cicero

Moderation is the inseparable companion of wisdom, but with it genius has not even a nodding acquaintance.

Charles Caleb Colton

The superior man wishes to be slow in his words, and earnest in his conduct.

Confucius

What is the spirit of moderation? It is the temper which does not press a partisan advantage to its bitter end, which can understand and will respect the other side.

Learned Hand

In adversity assume the countenance of prosperity, and in prosperity moderate the temper and desires.

Livy

To go beyond the bounds of moderation is to outrage humanity.

Blaise Pascal

Moderation, which consists in an indifference about little things, and in a prudent and well-proportioned zeal about things of importance, can proceed from nothing but true knowledge, which has its foundation in self-acquaintance.

William Pitt (Lord Chatham)

Everything that exceeds the bounds of moderation, has an unstable foundation.

Seneca

It is certainly a very important lesson, to learn how to enjoy ordinary things, and to be able to relish your being, without the transport of some passion, or the gratification of some appetite.

Sir Richard Steele

The choicest pleasures of life lie within the ring of moderation.

Martin Farquhar Tupper

See also: SELF-CONTROL, TEMPERANCE.

MODESTY

Modesty is not only an ornament, but also a guard to virtue.

Joseph Addison

Modesty is the conscience of the body.

Honoré de Blazac

Modesty is the citadel of beauty and virtue.

Demades

Modesty is the color of virtue.

Diogenes

Make no display of your talents or attainments; for every one will clearly see, admire, and acknowledge them, so long as you cover them with the beautiful veil of modesty.

Nathaniel Emmons

A false modesty is the meanest species of pride.

Edward Gibbon

Modesty is the chastity of merit, the virginity of noble souls.

Emile de Girardin

Modesty seldom resides in a breast that is not enriched with nobler virtues.

Oliver Goldsmith

Modesty is a shining light; it prepares the mind to receive knowledge, and the heart for truth.

François Pierre Guizot

As lamps burn silent, with unconscious light,
So modest ease in beauty shines most bright;
Unaiming charms with edge resistless fall,
And she who means no mischief does it all.

Aaron Hill

An egotist will always speak of himself, either in praise or in censure; but a modest man ever shuns making himself the subject of his conversation.

Jean de La Bruyère

False modesty is the refinement of vanity. It is a lie.

Jean de La Bruyère

Men are too much occupied with themselves to have leisure to know others thoroughly, or to discern their real character; hence it happens that with a great merit and a greater modesty, one may be a long time lost sight of.

Jean de La Bruyère

If you are always shy, people will end by imagining that you have a modest nature: and that, since it will flatter their own self-esteem, will make you extremely popular.

Harold Nicolson

The modest man has everything to gain, and the arrogant man everything to lose, for modesty has always to deal with generosity, and arrogance with envy.

Antoine Rivarol

Modesty once extinguished knows not how to return.

Seneca

A modest person seldom fails to gain the good will of those he converses with, because nobody envies a man who does not appear to be pleased with himself.

Sir Richard Steele

There are as many kinds of modesty as there are races. To the English woman it is a duty; to the French woman a propriety.

Hippolyte Adolphe Taine

Modesty and humility are the sobriety of the mind, as temperance and chastity are of the body.

Benjamin Whichote

See also: BLUSH, DECENCY, HUMILITY.

MOHAMMEDANISM

At the outset let it be said that Muhammad was one of the great figures of history whose overmastering conviction was that there was one God alone and that there should be one community of believers. His ability as a statesman faced with problems of extraordinary complexity is truly amazing. With all the power of armies, police, and civil service no Arab has ever succeeded in holding his countrymen together as he did.

Alfred Guillaume

The Muslim is not to fear death, for it is the gate of Paradise: patience and trust are incumbent on him. He must endure with fortitude the troubles and trials of life, and must put his trust in God at all times. This in the briefest possible terms is the moral basis of Islam, and only the prejudiced can deny that it has produced, and still produces, men of the highest character and integrity.

Alfred Guillaume

Muslims are prone to quote verses from the Qurân in all the manifold circumstances of life.

Alfred Guillaume

The conversion to Islâm, within a hundred years, of such nations as the Egyptian, the Syrian, and the Persian, can hardly be attributed to anything but the latent talents, the formerly suppressed energy of the Arabian race having found a favourable soil for its development.

Christiaan Snouck Hurgronje

Mohammed's fragmentary and unsystematic accounts of sacred history were freely drawn from Jewish and Christian sources and covered the whole period from the creation of the world until the first centuries of the Christian era.

Christiaan Snouck Hurgronje

There are more than two hundred million people who call themselves after the name of Mohammed, would not relinquish that name at any price, and cannot imagine a greater blessing for the remainder of humanity than to be incorporated into their communion. Their ideal is no less than that the whole earth should join in the faith that there is no god but Allah and that Mohammed is Allah's last and most perfect messenger, who brought the latest and final revelation of Allah to humanity in Allah's own words.

Christiaan Snouck Hurgronje

The kingdoms and the crowns which the Moslems have lost in the course of history are far less important than the kingdom of the free and searching mind which they have lost in the process of intellectual stagnation.

Mohammad Ayub Khan

See also: HINDUISM, INDIA, RELIGION.

MONEY

Money is like manure, of very little use except to be spread.

Francis Bacon

Money speaks sense in a language all nations understand.

Aphra Behn

Money is a good servant, but a poor master.

Dominique Bouhours

It's a good thing to know how to satisfy your own conscience and make the cash register ring also.

Arthur Brisbane

You will find out, if you want to make any money, that it is not always wise to be disturbed by what we call evil, though its existence must be admitted.

Arthur Brisbane

For money has a power above
The stars and fate, to manage love.

Samuel Butler

To despise money is to dethrone a king.

Sébastien Roch Nicolas Chamfort

Our incomes are like our shoes; if too small, they gall and pinch us; but if too large, they cause us to stumble and to trip.

Charles Caleb Colton

Money itself isn't the primary factor in what one does. A person does things for the sake of accomplishing something. Money generally follows.

Henry Crown

Gold is the fool's curtain, which hides all his defects from the world.

Owen Felltham

Make money your god, it will plague you like the devil.

Henry Fielding

Money never made a man happy yet, nor will it. There is nothing in its nature to produce happiness. The more a man has, the more he wants. Instead of its filling a vacuum, it makes one. If it satisfies one want, it doubles and trebles that want another way. That was a true proverb of the wise man, rely upon it: "Better is little with the fear of the Lord, than great treasure, and trouble therewith."

Benjamin Franklin

The use of money is all the advantage there is in having it.

Benjamin Franklin

Never ask of money spent
Where the spender thinks it went.
Nobody was ever meant
To remember or invent
What he did with every cent.

Robert Lee Frost

It is my opinion that a man's soul may be buried and perish under a dung-heap, or in a furrow of the field, just as well as under a pile of money.

Nathaniel Hawthorne

The first panacea for a mismanaged nation is inflation of the currency.

Ernest Hemingway

Money spent on myself may be a millstone about my neck; money spent on others may give me wings like the angels.

Roswell Dwight Hitchcock

Put not your trust in money, but put your money in trust.

Oliver Wendell Holmes

Money is a handmaiden, if thou knowest how to use it; a mistress, if thou knowest not.

Horace

Money never made a fool of anybody; it only shows 'em up.

Frank McKinney (Kin) Hubbard

The safest way to double your money is to fold it over once and put it in your pocket.

Frank McKinney (Kin) Hubbard

Money and time are the heaviest burdens of life, and the unhappiest of all mortals are those who have more of either than they know how to use.

Samuel Johnson

The covetous man never has money; the prodigal will have none shortly.

Ben (Benjamin) Jonson

The so-called free world constitutes the kingdom of the dollar.

Nikita Sergeevich Khrushchev

It's good to have money and the things that money can buy, but it's good, too, to check up once in a while and make sure that you haven't lost the things that money can't buy.

George Horace Lorimer

Money degrades all the gods of man and converts them into commodities.

Karl Marx

Money is man's work and being, alienated from himself, and this alien being rules him, and he prays to it.

Karl Marx

Money is like a sixth sense—and you can't make use of the other five without it.

(William) Somerset Maugham

A man's treatment of money is the most decisive test of his character—how he makes it and how he spends it.

James Moffatt

There is a vast difference in one's respect for the man who has made himself, and the man who has only made his money.

Dinah Maria Mulock

Many of the greatest creations of man have been inspired by the desire to make money. When George Frederick Handel was on his beam ends, he shut himself up for twenty-one days and emerged with the complete score of Messiah—and hit the jackpot.

David Mackenzie Ogilvy

Covetous men need money least, yet most affect and seek it; prodigals who need it most, do least regard it.

Theodore Parker

No man needs money so much as he who despises it.

Jean Paul Richter

By doing good with his money, a man, as it were, stamps the image of God upon it, and makes it pass current for the merchandise of heaven.

John Rutledge

Money does all things for reward. Some are pious and honest as long as they thrive upon it, but if the devil himself gives better wages, they soon change their party.

Seneca

Wealth is a very dangerous inheritance, unless the inheritor is trained to active benevolence.

Charles Simmons

Solvency is entirely a matter of temperament and not of income.

Logan Pearsall Smith

All love has something of blindness in it, but the love of money especially.

Robert South

Money has little value to its possessor unless it also has value to others.

(Amasa) Leland Stanford

Money is the life blood of the nation.

Jonathan Swift

A wise man should have money in his head, not in his heart.

Jonathan Swift

Money is not required to buy one necessity of the soul.

Henry David Thoreau

Money is a new form of slavery, and distinguishable from the old simply by the fact that it is impersonal—that there is no human relation between master and slave.

Count Lev (Leo) Nikolaevich Tolstoi

Make all you can, save all you can, give all you can.

John Wesley

What this country needs is a good five-cent nickel.

Ed (Edwin Leopold) Wynn

He who'll pay has the say.

Yiddish Proverb

Money answers all questions.

Yiddish Proverb

Money attracts money.

Yiddish Proverb

Money won, virtue gone.

Yiddish Proverb

See also: GOLD, RICHES, WEALTH.

MONOMANIA

Adhesion to one idea is monomania; to a few it is slavery.

Christian Nestell Bovee

The greatest part of mankind labor under one delirium or another; and Don Quixote differed from the rest, not in madness, but in the species of it. The covetous, the prodigal, the superstitious, the libertine, and the coffee-house politician, are all Quixotes in their several ways.

Henry Fielding

The man with but one idea in his head, is sure to exaggerate that to top-heaviness, and thus he loses his equilibrium.

Aaron Hill

See also: FANATICISM, INSANITY, PREJUDICE.

MONOTONY

Monotony is the law of nature. Look at the monotonous manner in which the sun rises. And imagine the catastrophe that would befall the universe, if the sun became capricious and went in for a variety of pastime. But there it a monotony that sustains and a monotony that kills. The monotony of necessary occupation is exhilarating and life-giving. An artist never tires of his art. A spinner who has mastered his art will certainly be able to do sustained work without fatigue. There is a music about the spindle which the practised spinner catches without fail.

Mohandas Karamchand (Mahatma) Gandhi

Everything has been said.

Jean de La Bruyère

See also: BORE, DULNESS, VARIETY.

MONUMENT

If I have done any deed worthy of remembrance, that deed will be my monument. If not, no monument can preserve my memory.

Agesilaus II

Tombs are the clothes of the dead; a grave is but a plain suit; a rich monument is an embroidered one.

Thomas Fuller

No man who needs a monument ever ought to have one.

Nathaniel Hawthorne

They only deserve a monument who do not need one; that is, who have raised themselves a monument in the minds and memories of men.

William Hazlitt

Monuments are the grappling-irons that bind one generation to another.

Joseph Joubert

Monuments! what are they? the very pyramids have forgotten their builders, or to whom they were dedicated. Deeds, not stones, are the true monuments of the great.

John Lothrop Motley

Virtue alone outbuilds the pyramids; her monument shall last when Egypts fall.

Edward Young

See also: ART, CIVILIZATION, CULTURE, DEATH, EPITAPH, GRAVE, HISTORY, POSTERITY, RUINS.

MOON

The moving moon went up the sky,
And nowhere did abide;
Softly she was going up,
And a star or two beside.

Samuel Taylor Coleridge

No one really expects life to be found on the moon.

Walter William Kemmerer, Jr.

The lovely and luminous moon has become a public issue. For quite a few thousand years it was a private issue; it figured in purely bilateral negotiations between lovers; poets from attic windows issued the statements about the moon, and they made better reading than the handouts now being issued by Assistant Secretaries of Defense.

Eric Sevareid

That orbed maiden with white fire laden,
Whom mortals call the moon.

Percy Bysshe Shelley

See also: EVENING, NIGHT, SKY, STAR.

MORALE

Morale is the most important thing that a human being has, whether he is tackling a job or whether he is going to war or whether he is trying to gain a peace. It is the belief in the spirit, and when you know someone is with you, if the poeple sitting alongside you are ready to support what you say, what you do, you believe together, you have got a strength that is very hard to defeat. It is the strength of a democracy in war.

Dwight David Eisenhower

You cannot attain success without the people's co-operation; you cannot attain success without raising the morale of the people for the task. If the people think that the country is going ahead, their morale goes up and thereby their capacity to work increases. If the people think that we are where we were or worse, their morale goes down, their desire to help goes down, their capacity to work goes down and this affects you and me and everybody else and all our work suffers.

Jawaharlal Nehru

See also: CONFIDENCE, HOPE, ZEAL.

MORALITY

Discourses on morality and reflection on human nature, are the best means we can make use of to improve our minds, gain a true knowledge of ourselves, and recover our souls out of the vice, ignorance, and prejudice which naturally cleave to them.

Joseph Addison

Man's advance in control over his environment is making it more and more difficult for him, at least in the industrialized countries with a high standard of living, like America or England, to lead a naturally good life, and easier and easier to lead a morally bad one.

Wystan Hugh Auden

People committing acts in obedience to law or habit are not being moral.

Wystan Hugh Auden

Is it not remarkable that the greatest atrocities of life—I think of the capitalistic system and of the war—can justify themselves on purely moral principles? The devil may also make use of morality.

Karl Barth

Some would divorce morality from religion; but religion is the root without which morality would die.

Cyrus Augustus Bartol

Every young man would do well to remember that all successful business stands on the foundation of morality.

Henry Ward Beecher

A truth that's told with bad intent
Beats all the lies you can invent.
It is right it should be so;
Man was made for Joy and Woe;
And when this we rightly know,
Thro' the World we safely go,
Joy and woe are woven fine,
A clothing for the soul divine.

William Blake

The divorcement of morals and piety is characteristic of all pagan religions.

David James Burrell

Morality is the vestibule of religion.

Edwin Hubbel Chapin

The more knowledge man has the more sensible he will be of the benefits of morality.

Cadwallader Colden

Too many moralists begin with a dislike of reality: a dislike of men as they are.

Clarence Shepard Day, Jr.

Moral vanity is the snare of good people.

Margaret Deland

Conventional morality is a drab morality, in which the only fatal thing is to be conspicuous.

John Dewey

Two points of danger beset mankind; namely, making sin seem either too large or too small.

Mary Baker Eddy

There can by no high civility without a deep morality.

Ralph Waldo Emerson

As soon as we lose the moral basis, we cease to be religious. There is no such thing as religion overriding morality. Man, for instance, cannot be untruthful, cruel or incontinent and claim to have God on his side.

Mohandas Karamchand (Mahatma) Gandhi

Increase of material comforts, it may be generally laid down, does not in any way whatsoever conduce to moral growth.

Mohandas Karamchand (Mahatma) Gandhi

Morality is the basis of things and truth is the substance of all morality.

Mohandas Karamchand (Mahatma) Gandhi

In matters of prudence last thoughts are best; in matters of morality, first thoughts.

Robert Hall

What is moral is what you feel good after and what is immoral is what you feel bad after.

Ernest Hemingway

Moralizing and morals are two entirely different things and are always found in entirely different people.

Don Herold

Atheistic morality is not impossible, but it will never answer our purpose. The morality that holds the great masses of sinewy people together must be very firmly rooted in an honest, downright personal faith and fear.

Roswell Dwight Hitchcock

The moral experience of men has everywhere and in all ages been the same.

John Haynes Holmes

More important than any single moral principle is the training of the individual will, particularly in childhood, for character must exist before intelligence can function, and self-mastery is the essence of character.

Frank Snowden Hopkins

I have never found a thorough, pervading, enduring morality but in those who feared God.

Friedrich Heinrich Jacobi

The morality of an action depends upon the motive from which we act. If I fling a half crown to a beggar with intention to break his head, and he picks it up and buys victuals with it, the physical effect is good; but with respect to me, the action is very wrong.

Samuel Johnson

Turning the other cheek is a kind of moral jiu-jitsu.

Gerald Stanley Lee

I am very doubtful whether history shows us one example of a man who, having stepped outside rational morality and attained power, has used that power benevolently.

Clive Staples Lewis

To give a man a full knowledge of true morality, I would send him to no other book than the New Testament.

John Locke

Men are not made religious by performing certain actions which are externally good, but they must first have righteous principles, and then they will not fail to perform virtuous actions.

Martin Luther

I restrict myself within bounds in saying, that, so far as I have observed in this life, ten men have failed from defect in morals where one has failed from defect in intellect.

Horace Mann

Christian morality assumes to itself no merit—it sets up no arrogant claim to God's favor—it pretends not to "open the gates of heaven"; it is only the handmaid in conducting the Christian believer in his road toward them.

Richard Mant

Learn what a people glory in, and you may learn much of both the theory and practice of their morals.

James Martineau

Where social improvements originate with the clergy, and where they bear a just share of the toil, the condition of morals and manners cannot be very much depressed.

James Martineau

It is difficult to moralise about any matter, as ideas of conventional morality differ from age to age and country to country.

Jawaharlal Nehru

Political surrender leads almost inevitably to moral surrender also.

Jawaharlal Nehru

The masters have been abolished; the morality of the common man has triumphed.

Friedrich Wilhelm Nietzsche

Morality is the best of all devices for leading mankind by the nose.

Friedrich Wilhelm Nietzsche

Morality is what is left of fear forgotten.

Jean Rostand

Moral rights and obligations must have an objective foundation, a metaphysical foundation. If not, they remain mere abstractions, mere creations of the human mind. An adequate foundation exists only in God.

John Augustine Ryan

A passion for the primitive is a sign of archaism in morals.

George Santayana

An Englishman thinks he is moral when he is only uncomfortable.

George Bernard Shaw

The great mistake of my life has been that I tried to be moral without faith in Jesus; but I have learned that true morality can only keep pace with trust in Christ as my Saviour.

Gerrit Smith

Wrong is wrong only when you are at liberty to choose.

Sir Rabindranth Tagore

The spiritual and moral coordination of the world is the real issue of tomorrow.

Dorothy Thompson

All sects are different, because they come from men; morality is everywhere the same, because it comes from God.

Voltaire (François Marie Arouet)

Let us with caution indulge the supposition that morality can be maintained without religion. Reason and experience both forbid us to expect that national morality can prevail in exclusion of religious principle.

George Washington

Heat water to the highest degree, you cannot make wine of it; it is water still; so, let morality be raised to the highest, it is nature still; it is old Adam put in a better dress.

Thomas Watson

We deny the doctrine of the ancient Epicureans, that pleasure is the supreme good; of Hobbes, that moral rules are only the work of men's mutual fear; of Paley, that what is expedient is right, and that there is no difference among pleasures except their intensity and duration; and of Bentham, that the rules of human action are to be obtained by counting up the pleasures which actions produce. And we maintain with Plato, that reason has a natural and rightful authority over desire and affection; with Butler, that there is a difference of kind in our principles of action; and with the general voice of mankind, that we must do what is right at whatever cost of pain and loss. What we ought to do, that we should do, and that we must do, though it bring pain and loss. And why? Because it is right.

William Whewell

All the things I really like to do are either immoral, illegal, or fattening.

Alexander Woollcott

See also: BEHAVIOR, CONDUCT, HONESTY, RECTITUDE, RIGHT AND WRONG, VIRTUE.

MORNING

It is well to be up before daybreak, for such habits contribute to health, wealth, and wisdom.

Aristotle

Its brightness, mighty divinity! has a fleeting empire over the day, giving gladness to the fields, color to the flowers; the season of the loves; harmonious hour of wakening birds.

Pedro Calderón de la Barca

I see the spectacle of morning from the hilltop over against my house, from daybreak to sunrise, with emotions an angel might share. The long, slender bars of cloud float, like fishes, in the sea of crimson light. From the earth, as a shore, I look out into that silent sea. I seem to partake its rapid transformations; the active enchantment reaches me, and I dilate and conspire with the morning wind.

Ralph Waldo Emerson

The early morning hath gold in its mouth.

Benjamin Franklin

The breezy call of incense-breathing morn.

Thomas Gray

In saffron-colored mantle, from the tides of ocean rose the morning to bring light to gods and men.

Homer

Morn in the white-wake of morning star, Came furrowing all the Orient into gold.

Alfred, Lord Tennyson

Lose an hour in the morning, and you will be all day hunting for it.

Richard Whately

See also: DAY, DAWN, DEW, SUNRISE.

MOROSENESS

Men possessing minds which are morose, solemn, and inflexible, enjoy, in general, a greater share of dignity than of happiness.

Francis Bacon

There is no mockery like the mockery of that spirit which looks around in the world and believes that all is emptiness.

Edwin Hubbel Chapin

Moroseness is the evening of turbulence.

Walter Savage Landor

The morose man takes both narrow and selfish views of life and the world; he is either envious of the happiness of others, or denies its existence.

Charles Simmons

See also: COMPLAINT, DESPONDENCY, MELANCHOLY, PESSIMISM, SADNESS.

MORTALITY

The fear of death often proves mortal, and sets people on methods, to save their lives, which infallibly destroy them. This is a reflection made upon observing that there are more thousands killed in a flight, than in a battle; and may be applied to those multitudes of imaginary sick persons that break their constitutions by physic, and throw themselves into the arms of death, by endeavoring to escape it.

Joseph Addison

Lo! as the wind is, so is mortal life; a moan, a sigh, a sob, or a storm, a strife.

Sir Edwin Arnold

All things that belong to you die as you do, but mortality in some you do not observe; they last so long, as you pass by so suddenly.

Dante Alighieri

When we see our enemies and friends gliding away before us, let us not forget that we are subject to the general law of mortality, and shall soon be where our doom will be fixed forever.

Samuel Johnson

Man weeps to think that he will die so soon; woman, that she was born so long ago.

Henry Louis Mencken

It's all a world where bugs and emperors
Go singularly back to the same dust,
Each in his time.

Edwin Arlington Robinson

All men think all mortal but themselves.

Owen D. Young

See also: DEATH, GRAVE, LIFE, MAN.

MOTHER

All that I am my mother made me.

John Quincy Adams

The future of society is in the hands of the mothers. If the world was lost through woman, she alone can save it.

Louis de Beaufort

The mother's heart is the child's schoolroom.

Henry Ward Beecher

I think it must somewhere be written, that the virtues of mothers shall be visited on their children, as well as the sins of the fathers.

Charles John Huffam Dickens

There is in all this cold and hollow world no fount of deep, strong, deathless love, save that within a mother's heart.

Felicia Dorothea Browne Hemans

What are Raphael's Madonnas but the shadow of a mother's love, fixed in permanent outline forever?

Thomas Wentworth Storrow Higginson

A man never sees all that his mother has been to him till it's too late to let her know that he sees it.

William Dean Howells

The old-time mother who used to wonder where her boy was now has a grandson who wonders where his mother is.

Frank McKinney (Kin) Hubbard

A father may turn his back on his child; brothers and sisters may become inveterate enemies; husbands may desert their wives, and wives their husbands. But a mother's love endures through all; in good repute, in bad repute, in the face of the world's condemnation, a mother still loves on, and still hopes that her child may turn from his evil ways, and repent; still she remembers the infant smiles that once filled her bosom with rapture, the merry laugh, the joyful shout of his childhood, the opening promise of his youth; and she can never be brought to think him all unworthy.

Washington Irving

God could not be everywhere, and therefore he made mothers.

Jewish Proverb

I would desire for a friend the son who never resisted the tears of his mother.
Jean Charles Dominique Lacretelle

The loss of a mother is always severely felt: even though her health may incapacitate her from taking any active part in the care of her family, still she is a sweet rallying-point, around which affection and obedience, and a thousand tender endeavors to please, concentrate; and dreary is the blank when such a point is withdrawn.
Alphonse de Lamartine

Children are what the mothers are; no fondest father's fondest care can so fashion the infant's heart, or so shape the life.
Walter Savage Landor

All that I am, or hope to be, I owe to my angel mother.
Abraham Lincoln

Even He that died for us upon the cross, in the last hour, in the unutterable agony of death, was mindful of his mother, as if to teach us that this holy love should be our last worldly thought,—the last point of earth from which the soul should take its flight for heaven.
Henry Wadsworth Longfellow

When Eve was brought unto Adam, he became filled with the Holy Spirit, and gave her the most sanctified, the most glorious of appellations. He called her Eva, that is to say, the Mother of All. He did not style her wife, but simply mother,—mother of all living creatures. In this consists the glory and the most precious ornament of woman.
Martin Luther

Nature's loving proxy, the watchful mother.
Edward G. Bulwer-Lytton (Baron Lytton)

Children, look in those eyes, listen to that dear voice, notice the feeling of even a single touch that is bestowed upon you by that gentle hand! Make much of it while yet you have that most precious of all good gifts, a loving mother. Read the unfathomable love of those eyes; the kind anxiety of that tone and look, however slight your pain. In after life you may have friends, fond, dear friends, but never will you have again the inexpressible love and gentleness lavished upon you, which none but a mother bestows.
Thomas Babington Macaulay

It is the general rule, that all superior men inherit the elements of superiority from their mothers.
Jules Michelet

Let France have good mothers, and she will have good sons.
Napoleon I (Bonaparte)

Intolerable . . . is the abuse whereby mothers of families, because of the insufficiency of the father's salary, are forced to engage in gainful occupations outside the domestic walls to the neglect of their own proper cares and duties, particularly the education of their children.
Pius XI (Achille Ambrogio Damiano Ratti)

No joy in nature is so sublimely affecting as the joy of a mother at the good fortune of her child.
Jean Paul Richter

Stories first heard at a mother's knee are never wholly forgotten,—a little spring that never quite dries up in our journey through scorching years.
Giovanni Ruffini

Observe how soon, and to what a degree, a mother's influence begins to operate! Her first ministration for her infant is to enter, as it were, the valley of the shadow of death, and win its life at the peril of her own! How different must an affection thus founded be from all others!
Lydia Howard Sigourney

If you would reform the world from its errors and vices, begin by enlisting the mothers.
Charles Simmons

An ounce of mother is worth a pound of clergy.
Spanish Proverb

See also: BIRTH, FAMILY, FATHER, HOME, MARRIAGE, PARENT, WIFE, WOMAN.

MOTION PICTURE

Fundamentally I feel that there is as much difference between the stage and the films as between a piano and a violin. Normally you can't become a virtuoso in both.
Ethel Barrymore

People in Hollywood can't face the truth in themselves or in others. This town is filled with people who make adventure pictures and who have never left this place. They make religious pictures and they haven't been in a church or a synagogue in years. They make pictures about love and they haven't been in love—ever.

Richard Edwin Brooks

A wide screen just makes a bad film twice as bad.

Samuel Goldwyn

Hollywood continued to furnish the heroes and heroines of our time. The ubiquitous cinema screen projected their images throughout the world. Sex is the ersatz, or substitute, religion of the 20th century. These were its priests and priestesses. They were the American Dream, soon to be in technicolor—a Dream in terms of material satisfactions and sensual love, whose requisite happy ending was always a long drawn-out embrace.

Malcolm Muggeridge

We seem to pay too much attention to the cinema. It is undoubtedly an excellent medium for many good things but unfortunately it has not proved to be particularly inspiring.

Jawaharlal Nehru

Hollywood money isn't money. It is congealed snow.

Dorothy Parker

See also: ACTOR AND ACTRESS, SHOWMANSHIP, TELEVISION, THEATER, TRAGEDY.

MOTIVE

Never ascribe to an opponent motives meaner than your own.

Sir James Matthew Barrie

If a man speaks or acts with pure thought, happiness follows him like a shadow that never leaves him.

Buddha

The true motives of our actions, like the real pipes of an organ, are usually concealed; but the gilded and hollow pretext is pompously placed in the front for show.

Charles Caleb Colton

The moment there is suspicion about a person's motives, everything he does becomes tainted.

Mohandas Karamchand (Mahatma) Gandhi

Numerous examples have convinced me that God ultimately saves him whose motive is pure.

Mohandas Karamchand (Mahatma) Gandhi

Though a good motive cannot sanctify a bad action, a bad motive will always vitiate a good action. In common and trivial matters we may act without motive, but in momentous ones the most careful deliberation is wisdom.

William Jay

The morality of an action depends upon the motive from which we act.

Samuel Johnson

The two great movers of the human mind are the desire of good, and the fear of evil.

Samuel Johnson

It is motive alone that gives character to the actions of men.

Jean de La Bruyère

We would often be ashamed of our noblest actions if the world were acquainted with the motives that impelled us.

Duc François de La Rochefoucauld

The road is long from the intention to the completion.

Molière (Jean Baptiste Poquelin)

He that does good for good's sake, seeks neither praise nor reward, but he is sure of both in the end.

William Penn

It is not the incense, or the offering which is acceptable to God, but the purity and devotion of the worshiper.

Seneca

The four great motives which move men to social activity are hunger, love, vanity, and fear of superior powers.

William Graham Sumner

Motives and purposes are in the brain and heart of man. Consequences are in the world of fact.

William Graham Sumner

The noblest motive is the public good.

Virgil

See also: AIM, DESIRE, END, IMPULSE, INTENTION, OBJECTIVE, PURPOSE.

MURDER

Blood, though it sleep a time, yet never dies.

George Chapman

Nor cell, nor chain, nor dungeon speaks to the murderer like the voice of solitude.

Charles Robert Maturin

One murder made the villain; millions the hero. Princes were privileged to kill, and numbers sanctified the crime.

Beilby Porteus

Every unpunished murder takes away something from the security of every man's life.

Daniel Webster

See also: CAPITAL PUNISHMENT, CRIME.

MUSEUM

Art galleries and museums in a great city are like windows which look out on the broader, richer and deeper things of life.

Jawaharlal Nehru

I suppose it is some kind of congealed history or a bit of the past locked up in your cabinets and placed so that you may have a glimpse of it. It is a place where you collect beautiful objects and it is good to have beautiful objects for people to look at.

Jawaharlal Nehru

See also: ART, HISTORY, MONUMENT, RUINS.

MUSIC

Music is the only sensual gratification in which mankind may indulge to excess without injury to their moral or religious feelings.

Joseph Addison

Psychologists have found that music does things to you whether you like it or not. Fast tempos invariably raise your pulse, respiration and blood pressure; slow music lowers them.

Doron Kemp Antrin

Music washes away from the soul the dust of every-day life.

Berthold Auerbach

All human activity must pass through its periods of rise, ripeness, and decline, and music has been, to a certain extent, fortunate in that it is the last of the great arts to suffer this general experience.

Sir Thomas Beecham

Composers should write tunes that chauffeurs and errand boys can whistle.

Sir Thomas Beecham

The English may not like music, but they absolutely love the noise it makes.

Sir Thomas Beecham

If an opera cannot be played by an organ-grinder—as Puccini's and Verdi's melodies were played—then that opera is not going to achieve immortality.

Sir Thomas Beecham

In old music you stand alone, alone and naked, and every note you play has got to be perfect. No one notices in modern music how many wrong notes you play. The cry today is "Down with Mozart, to hell with anyone who can write a tune. Give us discord."

Sir Thomas Beecham

Movie music is noise. It's even more painful than my sciatica.

Sir Thomas Beecham

Music is the mediator between the spiritual and the sensual life. Although the spirit be not master of that which it creates through music, yet it is blessed in this creation, which, like every creation of art, is mightier than the artist.

Ludwig van Beethoven

In the germ, when the first trace of life begins to stir, music is the nurse of the soul; it murmurs in the ear, and the child sleeps; the tones are companions of his dreams,— they are the world in which he lives.

Antoine Bettini

Music is the fourth great material want of our nature,—first food, then raiment, then shelter, then music.

Christian Nestell Bovee

Among the instrumentalities of love and peace, surely there can be no sweeter, softer, more effective voice than that of gentle peace-breathing music.

Elihu Burritt

The meaning of song goes deep. Who is there that, in logical words, can express the effect music has on us? A kind of inarticulate, unfathomable speech, which leads us to the edge of the infinite, and lets us for moments gaze into that!

> *Thomas Carlyle*

Music is well said to be the speech of angels.

> *Thomas Carlyle*

One must feel occasionally that the sounds of music are arranged in such a way as to compose the soul and mind for the concentrated joy of a moment of silence, a vacant interval in time made perfectly endurable for the restless spirit of man.

> *Clarence Cason*

Music is the child of prayer, the companion of religion.

> *Vicomte François René de Chateaubriand*

The best sort of music is what it should be—sacred; the next best, the military, has fallen to the lot of the devil.

> *Samuel Taylor Coleridge*

Music has charms to soothe the savage breast, to soften rocks, and bend the knotted oak.

> *William Congreve*

O Music! miraculous art! . . . A blast of thy trumpet, and millions rush forward to die; a peal of thy organ, and uncounted nations sink down to pray.

> *Benjamin Disraeli*

When men have a faith they sing. Lacking it, living music has never yet been fabricated.

> *Edwin Olin Downes*

There is no feeling, except the extremes of fear and grief, that does not find relief in music.

> *George Eliot (Mary Ann Evans)*

Music, in the best sense, does not require novelty; nay, the older it is, and the more we are accustomed to it, the greater its effect.

> *Johann Wolfgang von Goethe*

Music is a friend of labor; it lightens the task by refreshing nerves and spirit.

> *William Green*

A good ear for music, and a taste for music are two very different things which are often confounded; and so is comprehending and enjoying every object of sense and sentiment.

> *Fulke Greville (First Baron Brooke)*

I occasionally play works by contemporary composers and for two reasons. First to discourage the composer from writing any more and secondly to remind myself how much I appreciate Beethoven.

> *Jascha Heifetz*

There is something marvelous in music. I might almost say it is, in itself, a marvel. Its position is somewhere between the region of thought and that of phenomena; a glimmering medium between mind and matter, related to both and yet differing from either. Spiritual, and yet requiring rhythm; material, and yet independent of space.

> *Heinrich Heine*

Music expresses that which cannot be said and on which it is impossible to be silent.

> *Victor Marie Hugo*

After silence that which comes nearest to expressing the inexpressible is music.

> *Aldous Leonard Huxley*

Let me have music dying, and I seek no more delight.

> *John Keats*

Music is only useful if it is good music, whether light or serious. Unless it provides one with some vital experience which no other art can convey, it is not only useless but a nuisance.

> *Constant Lambert*

Music moves us, and we know not why; we feel the tears, but cannot trace their source. Is it the language of some other state, born of its memory? For what can wake the soul's strong instinct of another world like music?

> *Letitia Elizabeth Landon*

We love music for the buried hopes, the garnered memories, the tender feelings it can summon at a touch.

> *Letitia Elizabeth Landon*

Hidden in a brief adagio
There is a sermon on the transient hour;
And lured from inner depths by sweep of
     bow
May be a vision of the perfect flower,
Immortal blossom of divine intent
Whose humblest seed explains the firmament.

> *Elias Lieberman*

Music itself is the purest expression of emotion. To me, emotion is the guts of theater.

With music you can say in one moment what an author would take a whole scene to tell you in a drama.

Joshua Logan

Music is the art of the prophets, the only art that can calm the agitations of the soul; it is one of the most magnificent and delightful presents God has given us.

Martin Luther

Music is a discipline, and a mistress of order and good manners, she makes the people milder and gentler, more moral and more reasonable.

Martin Luther

Music is one of the fairest and most glorious gifts of God, to which Satan is a bitter enemy, for it removes from the heart the weight of sorrow, and the fascination of evil thoughts.

Martin Luther

Next to theology I give to music the highest place and honor. And we see how David and all the saints have wrought their godly thoughts into verse, rhyme, and song.

Martin Luther

Music is the harmonious voice of creation; an echo of the invisible world; one note of the divine concord which the entire universe is destined one day to sound.

Giuseppe Mazzini

I live with music like a monk who prays every moment, including the night when he gets up to say "Ave Maria." It is no more or no less. Simply utter devotion. The utmost devotion.

Dimitri Mitropoulos

Music, of all the liberal arts has the greatest influence over the passions, and is that to which the legislator ought to give the greatest encouragement.

Napoleon I (Bonaparte)

Music, I feel, must be emotional first and intellectual second.

Maurice Joseph Ravel

I cannot tell you how much I love to play for people. Would you believe it—sometimes when I sit down to practice and there is no one else in the room, I have to stifle an impulse to ring for the elevator man and offer him money to come in and hear me.

Artur Rubinstein

The history of a country is written in its popular songs.

Sigmund Spaeth

It is not necessary to understand music; it is only necessary that one enjoy it.

Leopold Antoni Stanislaw Stokowski

The trouble with music appreciation in general is that people are taught to have too much respect for music; they should be taught to love it instead.

Igor Fedorovich Stravinsky

Explain it as we may, a martial strain will urge a man into the front rank of battle sooner than an argument, and a fine anthem excite his devotion more certainly than a logical discourse.

Henry Theodore Tuckerman

Lord, what music hast thou provided for thy saints in heaven, when thou affordest bad men such music on earth!

Izaak Walton

See also: ART, JAZZ, POETRY, SONG, VOICE.

MUTABILITY

What shadows we are, and what shadows we pursue!

Edmund Burke

Mutability is the badge of infirmity. It is seldom that a man continues to wish and design the same thing for two days alike.

Pierre Charron

Man must be prepared for every event of life, for there is nothing that is durable.

Menander of Athens

Clocks will go as they are set; but man, irregular man, is never constant, never certain.

Thomas Otway

In human life there is constant change of fortune; and it is unreasonable to expect an exemption from the common fate. Life itself decays, and all things are daily changing.

Plutarch

The blessings of health and fortune, as they have a beginning, so they must also have an end. Everything rises but to fall, and increases but to decay.

Sallust

See also: CHANGE, EVOLUTION, INCONSTANCY, INSTABILITY, UNCERTAINTY, VARIETY.

MYSTERY

The philosopher aspires to explain away all mysteries, to dissolve them into light. Mystery on the other hand is demanded and pursued by the religious instinct; mystery constitutes the essence of worship.

Henri Frédéric Amiel

A good parson once said, that where mystery begins, religion ends. Cannot I say, as truly at least, of human laws, that where mystery begins, justice ends?

Edmund Burke

The lucrative business of mystery.

Edmund Burke

We injure mysteries, which are matters of faith, by any attempt at explanation, in order to make them matters of reason. Could they be explained, they would cease to be mysteries; and it has been well said that a thing is not necessarily against reason, because it happens to be above it.

Charles Caleb Colton

A mystery is something of which we know that it is, though we do not know how it is.

Joseph Cook

He had lived long enough to know that it is unwise to wish everything explained.

Benjamin Disraeli

All is mystery; but he is a slave who will not struggle to penetrate the dark veil.

Benjamin Disraeli

Mystery is but another name for our ignorance; if we were omniscient, all would be perfectly plain.

Tryon Edwards

The most beautiful experience we can have is the mysterious. It is the fundamental emotion which stands at the cradle of true art and true science.

Albert Einstein

While reason is puzzling itself about mystery, faith is turning it to daily bread, and feeding on it thankfully in her heart of hearts.

Frederic Dan Huntington

Each particle of matter is an immensity; each leaf a world; each insect an inexplicable compendium.

Johann Kaspar Lavater

Like a morning dream, life becomes more and more bright the longer we live, and the reason of everything appears more clear. What has puzzled us before seems less mysterious, and the crooked paths look straighter as we approach the end.

Jean Paul Richter

It is the dim haze of mystery that adds enchantment to pursuit.

Antoine Rivarol

As defect of strength in us makes some weights to be immovable, so likewise, defect of understanding makes some truths to be mysterious.

Thomas Sherlock

See also: ADVENTURE, DOUBT, FAITH, MIRA-CLES, QUESTION.

MYSTICISM

I myself am just at present a Mystic, following the advice of my physician to avoid stimulants to thought.

Heinrich Heine

The mystic tries to rid himself of self, and in the process usually becomes obsessed with it.

Jawaharlal Nehru

Religion merges into mysticism and metaphysics and philosophy. There have been great mystics, attractive figures, who cannot easily be disposed of as self-deluded fools. Yet mysticism (in the narrow sense of the word) irritates me; it appears to be vague and soft and flabby, not a rigorous discipline of the mind but a surrender of mental faculties and a living in a sea of emotional experience. The experience may lead occasionally to some insight into inner and less obvious processes, but it is also likely to lead to self-delusion.

Jawaharlal Nehru

See also: HEAVEN, MEDITATION, METAPHYSICS, PHILOSOPHY, RELIGION.

MYTHOLOGY

Mythology is not religion. It may rather be regarded as the ancient substitute, the poetical counterpart for dogmatic theology.

Augustus and Julius Hare

Mythology is the religious sentiment growing wild.

Friedrich Wilhelm Joseph von Schelling

The heathen mythology not only was not true, but it was not even supported as true; it not only deserved no faith, but it demanded none. The very pretension to truth, the very demand of faith, were characteristics of Christianity.

Richard Whately

See also: FABLE, FICTION, RELIGION.

N

NAME

Some to the fascination of a name surrender judgment hoodwinked.

William Cowper

Favor or disappointment has been often conceded, as the name of the claimant has affected us; and the accidental affinity or coincidence of a name, connected with ridicule or hatred, with pleasure or digust, has operated like magic.

Benjamin Disraeli

A name is a kind of face whereby one is known.

Thomas Fuller

A man's name is not like a mantle which merely hangs about him, and which one perchance may safely twitch and pull, but a perfectly fitting garment, which, like the skin, has grown over him, at which one cannot rake and scrape without injuring the man himself.

Johann Wolfgang von Goethe

A good name lost is seldom regained. When character is gone, all is gone, and one of the richest jewels of life is lost forever.

Joel Hawes

Great names debase, instead of raising those who know not how to use them.

Duc François de La Rochefoucauld

One of the greatest artifices the devil uses to engage men in vice and debauchery, is to fasten names of contempt on certain virtues, and thus fill weak souls with a foolish fear of passing for scrupulous, should they desire to put them in practice.

Blaise Pascal

Some men do as much begrudge others a good name, as they want one themselves; and perhaps that is the reason of it.

William Penn

A person with a bad name is already half-hanged.

Proverb

A virtuous name is the precious, only good, for which queens and peasants' wives must contest together.

Johann Christoph Friedrich von Schiller

See also: HONOR, NICKNAME, PROPAGANDA.

NATION

In the youth of a state, arms do flourish; in the middle age, learning; and then both of them together for a time; in the declining age, mechanical arts and merchandise.

Francis Bacon

A nation is a totality of men united through community of fate into a community of character.

Otto Bauer

A day of small nations has long passed away. The day of Empires has come.

Joseph Chamberlain

A nation's character is the sum of its splendid deeds; they constitute one common patrimony, the nation's inheritance. They awe foreign powers, they arouse and animate our own people.

Henry Clay

The greatest asset of any nation is the spirit of its people, and the greatest danger that can menace any nation is the breakdown of that spirit—the will to win and the courage to work.

George Bruce Cortelyou

Individuals may form communities, but it is institutions alone that can create a nation.

Benjamin Disraeli

A nation is a work of art and a work of time.

Benjamin Disraeli

Wise men forever have known that a nation lives on what its body assimilates, as well as on what its mind acquires as knowledge.

Mary Frances (Kennedy) Fisher

The great lack of the nations that are the generative spots of world infection is, I suggest, not only capital investment, perhaps not primarily capital investment, but investment in people, their health, education and training.

Abe Fortas

I believe that a nation that is capable of limitless sacrifice is capable of rising to limitless heights.

Mohandas Karamchand (Mahatma) Gandhi

Nations are born out of travail and suffering.

Mohandas Karamchand (Mahatma) Gandhi

Territory is but the body of a nation. The people who inhabit its hills and valleys are its soul, its spirit, its life.

James Abram Garfield

No nation can be destroyed while it possesses a good home life.

Josiah Gilbert Holland

The basic resource of a nation is its people. Its strength can be no greater than the health and vitality of its population. Preventable sickness, disability and physical or mental incapacity are matters of both individual and national concern.

John Fitzgerald Kennedy

The greatest art of the world was the work of little nations. The most enduring literature of the world came from little nations. The heroic deeds that thrill humanity through generations were the deeds of little nations fighting for their freedom and, yes, the salvation of mankind came through a little nation.

John Fitzgerald Kennedy

There are more important goals than winning contests, and that is to improve on a broad level the health and vitality of all of our people.

John Fitzgerald Kennedy

Throughout the world the people of the newly developing nations are struggling for economic and social progress which reflects their deepest desires. Our own freedom, and the future of freedom around the world,

depend, in a very real sense, on their ability to build growing and independent nations where men can live in dignity, liberated from the bonds of hunger, ignorance, and poverty.

John Fitzgerald Kennedy

The frenzy of nations is the statesmanship of fate.

Edward G. Bulwer-Lytton (Baron Lytton)

I remember what the English were like before the First World War; we behaved the same way on the Continent. We had taken responsibility for the world for a hundred years from the Napoleonic Wars. Our people got used to it at last and were very above themselves. We made ourselves very disliked. America will probably do the same thing. No one learns from anyone else's experience. They just have to go through it.

(William) Somerset Maugham

Today the nations of the world may be divided into two classes—the nations in which the government fears the people, and the nations in which the people fear the government.

Amos Richards Eno Pinchot

The best protection of a nation is its men; towns and cities cannot have a surer defense than the prowess and virtue of their inhabitants.

François Rabelais

A nation, like a person, has a mind—a mind that must be kept informed and alert, that must know itself, that understands the hopes and the needs of its neighbors—all the other nations that live within the narrowing circle of the world.

Franklin Delano Roosevelt

Political internationalism without economic internationalism is a house built upon sand. For no nation can reach its fullest development alone.

Wendell Lewis Willkie

See also: AMERICA, AUSTRALIA, CANADA, CHINA, CUBA, EGYPT, ENGLAND, FRANCE, GERMANY, GREECE, INDIA, IRELAND, ISRAEL, ITALY, JAPAN, MEXICO, NETHERLANDS, POLAND, RUSSIA, VIETNAM.

NATIONALISM

The root problem is very simply stated: if there were no sovereign independent states, if the states of the civilized world were organized in some sort of federalism, as the states of the American Union, for instance, are organized, there would be no international war as we know it. . . . The main obstacle is nationalism.

Sir Norman Angell

National interest in the nation, common interest in the community. That is what I, now as yesterday, have the duty to represent, to make valid and even to impose if the public welfare demands it. These are my obligations, and I will not fail.

Charles André Joseph Marie de Gaulle

Nationalism is an infantile disease. It is the measles of mankind.

Albert Einstein

National memories lie deeper in man's heart than we generally imagine.

Heinrich Heine

We are in the midst of a great transition from narrow nationalism to international partnership.

Lyndon Baines Johnson

See also: CITIZENSHIP, PATRIOTISM.

NATURE

Nature is commanded by obeying her.

Francis Bacon

In nature things move violently to their place, and calmly in their place.

Francis Bacon

To say that the nature of things may be *incoherent*, but we shall approach the truth about it precisely so far as our thoughts become coherent, sounds very much like nonsense.

Brand Blanshard

The ignorant man marvels at the exceptional; the wise man marvels at the common; the greatest wonder of all is the regularity of nature.

George Dana Boardman

Nature always springs to the surface and manages to show what she is. It is vain to stop or try to drive her back. She breaks through every obstacle, pushes forward, and at last makes for herself a way.

Nicolas Boileau-Despréaux

Nature's laws affirm instead of prohibiting. If you violate her laws you are your own prosecuting attorney, judge, jury, and hangman.

Luther Burbank

There is no other door to knowledge than the door Nature opens; and there is no truth except the truths we discover in nature.

Luther Burbank

Nature is the time-vesture of God that reveals him to the wise, and hides him from the foolish.

Thomas Carlyle

Hill and valley, seas and constellations, are but stereotypes of divine ideas appealing to, and answered by the living soul of man.

Edwin Hubbel Chapin

I follow nature as the surest guide, and resign myself, with implicit obedience, to her sacred ordinances.

Cicero

We talk of our mastery of nature, which sounds very grand; but the fact is we respectfully adapt ourselves, first, to her ways.

Clarence Shepard Day

Nature gives to every time and season some beauties of its own; and from morning to night, as from the cradle to the grave, is but a succession of changes so gentle and easy that we can scarcely mark their progress.

Charles John Huffam Dickens

Surely there is something in the unruffled calm of nature that overawes our little anxieties and doubts: the sight of the deep-blue sky, and the clustering stars above, seem to impart a quiet to the mind.

Jonathan Edwards

Nature and revelation are alike God's books; each may have mysteries, but in each there are plain practical lessons for every-day duty.

Tryon Edwards

Nature is no sentimentalist—does not cosset or pamper us. We must see that the world is rough and surly, and will not mind drowning a man or a woman, but swallows your ships like a grain of dust. The cold, inconsiderate of persons, tingles your blood, benumbs your feet, freezes a man like an apple. The diseases, the elements, fortune, gravity, lightning, respect no persons.

Ralph Waldo Emerson

Nature is too thin a screen; the glory of the One breaks in everywhere.

Ralph Waldo Emerson

We cannot impose our wills on nature unless we first ascertain what her will is. Working without regard to law brings nothing but failure; working with law enables us to do what seemed at first impossible.

Ralph Tyler Flewelling

Nature does not complete things. She is chaotic. Man must finish, and he does so by making a garden and building a wall.

Robert Lee Frost

Nature knows no pause in progress and development, and attaches her curse on all inaction.

Johann Wolfgang von Goethe

Nature is the living, visible garment of God.

Johann Wolfgang von Goethe

Man is no law-giver to nature, he is an absorber. She it is who stands firm; he it is who must accommodate himself.

William James

A man finds in the productions of nature an inexhaustible stock of material on which he can employ himself, without any temptations to envy or malevolence, and has always a certain prospect of discovering new reasons for adoring the sovereign author of the universe.

Samuel Johnson

Nature and wisdom always say the same.

Juvenal

Nature—a thing which science and art never appear to see with the same eyes. If to an artist nature has a soul, why, so has a steam-engine. Art gifts with soul all matter that it contemplates; science turns all that is already gifted with soul into matter.

Edward G. Bulwer-Lytton (Baron Lytton)

In contemplation of created things, by steps we may ascend to God.

John Milton

Nature has perfections, in order to show that she is the image of God; and defects, to show that she is only his image.

Blaise Pascal

Of all things under the sun that a man may love, the living world he loves most purely.

Donald Culross Peattie

It were happy if we studied nature more in natural things; and acted according to nature, whose rules are few, plain, and most reasonable.

William Penn

Looks through nature up to nature's God.

Alexander Pope

Living on intimate terms with nature, one inadvertently becomes different from other people. Her silent language penetrates, saturates, persuades one gently of the insufficiency of all human speech.

Jean Rostand

Whether man is disposed to yield to nature or to oppose her, he cannot do without a correct understanding of her language.

Jean Rostand

Everything made by man may be destroyed by man: there are no ineffaccable characters except those engraved by nature; and nature makes neither princes, nor rich men, nor great lords.

Jean Jacques Rousseau

Whatever you are by nature, keep to it; never desert your own line of talent. Be what nature intended you for, and you will succeed; be anything else and you will be ten thousand times worse than nothing.

Sydney Smith

The power of nature is the power of God.

Baruch (Benedict) Spinoza

Nature is man's teacher. She unfolds her treasures to his search, unseals his eye, illumes his mind, and purifies his heart; an influence breathes from all the sights and sounds of her existence.

Alfred Billings Street

Nature is avariciously frugal; in matter, it allows no atom to elude its grasp; in mind, no thought or feeling to perish. It gathers up the fragments that nothing be lost.

David Thomas

It is a false dichotomy to think of nature and man. Mankind is that factor in nature which exhibits in its most intense form the plasticity of nature.

Alfred North Whitehead

See also: AUTUMN, CLOUD, COUNTRY, DAY, DEW, EARTH, EVENING, FLOWER, LIFE, MORNING, NIGHT, RAIN, RAINBOW, SEA, SPRING, STAR, SUMMER, SUN, SUNRISE, SUNSET, TREE, TWILGHT, WIND, WORLD.

NAVY

The royal navy of England hath ever been its greatest defence and ornament; it is its ancient and natural strength; the floating bulwark of the island.

Sir William Blackstone

Britannia needs no bulwarks,
  No towers along the steep;
Her march is o'er the mountain waves,
  Her home is one the deep.

Thomas Campbell

May the great God, whom I worship, grant to my country and for the benefit of Europe in general, a great and glorious victory, and may no misconduct in anyone tarnish it, and may humanity after the victory be the predominant feature of the British fleet.

Horatio Nelson

See also: ARMY, SEA, SOLDIER, WAR.

NAZISM

Every German who did not spend the entire Nazi era in prison camps must feel responsible and must atone for the sins committed by the murderers in German uniforms and in the name of Germany.

Heinrich Albertz

This bloodthirsty guttersnipe must launch his mechanical armies upon new fields of slaughter, pillage and devastation . . . Any man or state who fights against Nazidom will have our aid. Any man or state who marches with Hitler is our foe.

Sir Winston Leonard Spencer Churchill

We are barbarians. We want to be barbarians. It is an honorable title.

Adolf Hitler

See also: GENOCIDE, GERMANY, TYRANNY.

NECESSITY

Necessity is the mother of invention.

George Farquhar

Necessity never made a good bargain.

Benjamin Franklin

Necessity may render a doubtful act innocent, but it cannot make it praiseworthy.

Joseph Joubert

We cannot conquer fate and necessity, yet we can yield to them in such a manner as to be greater than if we could.

Walter Savage Landor

There is no contending with necessity, and we should be very tender how we censure those that submit to it. 'Tis one thing to be at liberty to do what we will, and another thing to be tied up to do what we must.

Sir Roger L'Estrange

Necessity is blind until it becomes conscious. Freedom is the consciousness of necessity.

Karl Marx

And with necessity, the tyrant's plea, excused his devilish deeds.

John Milton

Necessity, that great refuge and excuse for human frailty, breaks through all law; and he is not to be accounted in fault whole crime is not the effect of choice, but force.

Blaise Pascal

Necessity is the argument of tyrants: it is the creed of slaves.

William Pitt

Necessity of action takes away the fear of the act, and makes bold resolution the favorite of fortune.

Francis Quarles

Our necessities are few but our wants are endless.

Henry Wheeler Shaw (Josh Billings)

A people never fairly begins to prosper till necessity is treading on its heels. The growing want of room is one of the sources of civilization. Population is power, but it must be a population that, in growing, is made daily apprehensive of the morrow.

William Gilmore Simms

Nothing in the universe is contingent, but all things are conditioned to exist and operate in a particular manner by the necessity of the divine nature.

Baruch (Benedict) Spinoza

What was once to me mere matter of the fancy, now has grown to be the necessity of heart and life.

Alfred, Lord Tennyson

The argument of necessity is not only the tyrant's plea, but the patriot's defense, and the safety of the state.

James Wilson

See also: DESTINY, DETERMINISM, FATE, FORCE, OBLIGATION.

NEED

From each according to his abilities, to each according to his needs.

Karl Marx

When the need is highest, God is nighest.

Yiddish Proverb

See also: NECESSITY, POVERTY, WANT.

NEGLECT

A wise and salutary neglect.

Edmund Burke

Negligence is the rust of the soul, that corrodes through all her best resolves.

Owen Felltham

A little neglect may breed great mischief; for want of a nail the shoe was lost; for want of a shoe the horse was lost, and for want of a horse the rider was lost, being overtaken and slain by an enemy, all for want of a little care about a horse-shoe nail.

Benjamin Franklin

The best ground, untilled and neglected, soonest runs out into rank weeds. A man of knowledge that is either negligent or uncorrected cannot but grow wild and godless.

Joseph Hall

He that thinks he can afford to be negligent, is not far from being poor.

Samuel Johnson

See also: DELAY, IDLENESS, PROCRASTINATION.

NEGOTIATION

So let us begin anew—remembering on both sides that civility is not a sign of weakness, and sincerity is always subject to proof. Let us never negotiate out of fear. But let us never fear to negotiate.

John Fitzgerald Kennedy

See also: BUSINESS, FOREIGN POLICY, PEACE, WAR.

NEGRO

My mother bore me in the southern wild,
And I am black, but O! my soul is white;
White as an angel is the English child,
But I am black, as if bereav'd of light.

William Blake

The bleak record of public education for ghetto children is growing worse. In the critical skills—verbal and reading ability—Negro students are falling farther behind whites with each year of school completed. The high unemployment and underemployment rate for Negro youth is evidence, in part, of the growing educational crisis.

Commission on Civil Disorder, 1968

I have almost reached the regrettable conclusion that the Negro's great stumbling block in the stride toward freedom is not the White Citizens Counciler or the Ku Klux Klanner, but the white moderate who is more devoted to order than to justice; who prefers a negative peace, which is the absence of tension, to a positive peace, which is the presence of justice.

Martin Luther King, Jr.

Like anybody, I would like to live a long life. Longevity has its place. But I'm not concerned about that now. I just want to do God's will.

And He's allowed me to go up to the mountain. And I've looked over, and I've seen the promised land.

I may not get there with you, but I want you to know tonight that we as a people will get to the promised land.

So I'm happy tonight. I'm not worried about anything. I'm not fearing any man. Mine eyes have seen the glory of the coming of the Lord.

Martin Luther King, Jr.

We owe to the Negro our love because of the martyrdom to which we have subjected him.

Meyer London

Sports cracked or ignored every kind of social and ethnic barrier. Negroes were unknown in baseball and pro football before World War II. There was no rule saying they were unacceptable. They just weren't. Today, neither of these games could be played at their current levels of excitement and proficiency without Negro ball players.

Harold Rosenthal

The white man cannot keep the Negro in the ditch without sitting down there with him.

Booker Taliaferro Washington

Negro citizens have as their first priority the immediate problem of survival in this country. They are therefore concerned about the rat and the job tomorrow.

Whitney Moore Young, Jr.

See also: AFRICA, BLACK POWER, RACISM.

NEIGHBOR

It is discouraging to try to be a good neighbor in a bad neighborhood.

William Richards Castle

Your own safety is at stake when your neighbor's house is in flames.

Horace

In the field of world policy I would dedicate this nation to the policy of the good neighbor.

Franklin Delano Roosevelt

See also: BROTHERHOOD, FRIENDSHIP, JUSTICE, LOVE, MAN.

NETHERLANDS

The whole of Holland is proof of what man can create on the most thankless soil.

Theodor Herzl

In the struggle against sea and Inquisition, the people of the Netherlands grew more vigorous than the furious elements.

Luigi Luzzatti

Holland, that scarce deserves the name of land,
As but the off-scouring of the British sand;
And so much earth as was contributed
By English pilot, when they heaved the lead.

Andrew Marvell

See also: NATION, UNITED NATIONS.

NEUROSIS

During the Renaissance there was no neurosis because people were surrounded by beauty—which was like spiritual food to them. But today everybody is neurotic because they are surrounded by ugliness.

Salvador Dali

Neurosis appears to be a human privilege.

Sigmund Freud

See also: MEDICINE, MENTAL HEALTH, MIND, PSYCHIATRY, PSYCHOLOGY.

NEUTRALITY

The cold neutrality of an impartial judge.

Edmund Burke

Neutral men are the devil's allies.

Edwin Hubbel Chapin

Neutrality is no favorite with Providence, for we are so formed that it is scarcely possible for us to stand neuter in our hearts, although we may deem it prudent to appear so in our actions.

Charles Caleb Colton

There is in some men a dispassionate neutrality of mind, which, though it generally passes for good temper, can neither gratify nor warm us; it must indeed be granted that these men can only negatively offend; but then it should also be remembered that they cannot positively please.

Fulke Greville (First Baron Brooke)

Neutrality in things good or evil is both odious and prejudicial, but in matters of an indifferent nature, is safe and commendable.

Joseph Hall

Neutrality, as a lasting principle, is an evidence of weakness.

Lajos Kossuth

A wise neuter joins with neither, but uses both as his honest interest leads him.

William Penn

See also: OPENMINDEDNESS, TOLERATION.

NEW TESTAMENT: see GOSPEL.

NEW YORK

New York has absolutely everything today except the past.

Louis Auchincloss

Not only is New York City the nation's melting pot, it is also the casserole, the chafing dish, and the charcoal grill.

John Vliet Lindsay

In dress, habits, manners, provincialism, routine and narrowness, he acquired that charming insolence, that irritating completeness, that sophisticated crassness, that overbalanced poise that makes the Manhattan gentleman so delightfully small in his greatness.

William Sydney Porter (O. Henry)

See also: AMERICANA, CITY, GHETTO.

NEWNESS

Men reject their prophets and slay them, but they love their martyrs and honor those whom they have slain.

Fëdor Mikhailovich Dostoevski

It is the customary fate of new truths to begin as heresies and to end as superstitions.

Thomas Henry Huxley

There is nothing more difficult to take in hand, more perilous to conduct, or more uncertain in its success, than to take the lead in the introduction of a new order of things.

Niccolò Machiavelli

What is new is not always true, and what is true is not always new.

William Walters Sargant

See also: INNOVATION, NOVELTY.

NEWS

NEWS is that which comes from the North, East, West and South, and if it comes from only one point of the compass, then it is a class publication and not news.

Benjamin Disraeli

Ill news is winged with fate, and flies apace.

John Dryden

Each mind is pressed, and open every ear, to hear new tidings, though they no way joy us.

Edward Fairfax

A map does not exhibit a more distinct view of the situation and boundaries of every country, than its news does a picture of the genius and morals of its inhabitants.

Oliver Goldsmith

News, the manna of a day.

Mary Anne Everett Greene

Evil news rides post, while good news bates.

John Milton

I hope that . . . television, radio, and the press first recognize the great responsibility they have to report all the news and second recognize that they have a right and a responsibility if they are against a candidate to give him the shaft but also to recognize if they give the shaft, (to) put one lonely reporter on the campaign who will report what the candidate says now and then.

Richard Milhous Nixon

Like officials in Washington, we suffer from Afghanistanism. If it's far away, it's news, but if it's close at home, it's sociology.

James Barrett Reston

When ill news comes too late to be serviceable to your neighbor, keep it to yourself.

Johann Georg von Zimmermann

See also: COMMUNICATIONS MEDIA, JOURNALISM, NEWSPAPER, PUBLIC OPINION.

NEWSPAPER

It seems really as if our newspapers were busy to spread superstition. Omens and dreams, and prodigies are recorded, as if they were worth minding. The increasing fashion for printing wonderful tales of crimes and accidents is worse than ridiculous, as it corrupts both the public taste and morals. It multiplies fables and crimes, and thus makes shocking things familiar while it withdraws popular attention from familiar truth, because it is not shocking. Surely, extraordinary events have not the best title to our studious attention. To study nature or man, we ought to know things that are in the ordinary course, not the unaccountable things that happen out of it.

Fisher Ames

From the American newspapers you'd think America was populated solely by naked women and cinema stars.

Viscountess Nancy Langhorne Astor

A newspaper is a circulating library with high blood pressure.

Arthur (Bugs) Baer

Newspapers are the schoolmasters of the common people—a greater treasure to them than uncounted millions of gold.

Henry Ward Beecher

Perhaps the quickest and best phrasemaker who ever inhabited the White House,

F.D.R. was a president after a newsman's heart. He talked in headline phrases. He acted, he emoted; he was angry, he was smiling. He was persuasive, he was demanding; he was philosophical, he was elemental. He was sensible, he was unreasonable; he was benevolent, he was malicious. He was satirical, he was soothing; he was funny, he was gloomy. He was exciting. He was human. He was copy.

Jack Bell

The paper which obtains a reputation for publishing authentic news and only that which is fit to print, . . . will steadily increase its influence.

Andrew Carnegie

Take away the newspaper and this country of ours would become a scene of chaos.

Harry Chandler

A newspaper should be the maximum of information, and the minimum of comment.

Richard Cobden

Newspapers are the world's cyclopaedia of life; telling us everything from every quarter of the globe. They are a universal whispering gallery for mankind, only their whispers are sometimes thunders.

Tryon Edwards

Newspapers are the world's mirrors.

James Ellis

A ration of one newspaper a day ought to be enough for anyone who still prefers to retain a little mental balance.

Clifton Fadiman

In these times we fight for ideas, and newspapers are our fortresses.

Heinrich Heine

Of all the amusements that can possibly be imagined for a hard-working man, after a day's toil, or in its intervals, there is nothing like reading an entertaining newspaper. It relieves his home of its dullness or sameness, and transports him to a gayer and livelier and more diversified and interesting scene. It accompanies him in his next day's work, and if the paper be anything above the very idlest and lightest, it gives him something to think of besides the mechanical drudgery of his every-day occupation—something he can enjoy while absent, and look forward with pleasure to return to.

Sir John Frederick William Herschel

A newspaper is the history for one day of the world in which we live, and with which we are consequently more concerned than with those which have passed away, and exist only in remembrance.

George Horne

These papers of the day have uses more adequate to the purposes of common life than more pompous and durable volumes.

Samuel Johnson

While news is important, news interpretation is far more important.

H. V. Kaltenborn (Hans von Kaltenborn)

The newspaper is an institution developed by modern civilization to present the news of the day, to foster commerce and industry, to inform and lead public opinion, and to furnish that check upon government which no constitution has ever been able to provide.

Robert Rutherford McCormick

A good newspaper, I suppose, is a nation talking to itself.

Arthur Miller

As a mental discipline the reading of newspapers is hurtful. What can be worse for the mind than to think of forty things in ten minutes.

Theodore Thornton Munger

I fear three newspapers more than a hundred thousand bayonets.

Napoleon I (Bonaparte)

Newspapers have developed what might be called a *vested interest in catastrophe.* If they can spot a fight, they will play up that fight. If they can uncover a tragedy, they will headline that tragedy.

Harry Allen Overstreet

The newspaper press is the people's university. Half the readers of Christendom read little else.

James Parton

I prefer to be loved rather than disliked. But I don't think you can really write the news in Washington and be loved.

Drew Pearson

We live under a government of men and morning newspapers.

Wendell Phillips

Just as it is the automobile manufacturer's business to sell transportation, so it is the newspaper owner's business to sell information and not advice nor propaganda.

Walter Boughton Pitkin

The death of any newspaper anywhere leaves us all the poorer.

Nelson Aldrich Rockefeller

All I know is what I read in the papers.

Will (William Penn Adair) Rogers

The careful reader of a few good newspapers can learn more in a year than most scholars do in their great libraries.

Franklin Benjamin Sanborn

The newspaper is the great educator of the nineteenth century. There is no force compared with it. It is book, pulpit, platform, forum, all in one.

Thomas de Witt Talmage

A short term on a newspaper is better than a long term in school.

Charles Washburn

To write weekly, to write daily, to write shortly, to write for busy people catching trains in the morning or for tired people coming home in the evening, is a heartbreaking task for men who know good writing from bad.

(Adeline) Virginia Woolf

See also: FREEDOM OF THE PRESS, JOURNALISM, NEWS, PRESS.

NICKNAME

Nicknames stick to people, and the most ridiculous are the most adhesive.

Thomas Chandler Haliburton

There is also an evil name or report, light, indeed, and easy to raise, but difficult to carry, and still more difficult to get rid of.

Hesiod

A good name will wear out; a bad one may be turned; a nickname lasts forever.

Johann Georg von Zimmermann

See also: FRIENDSHIP, NAME, SLANG.

NIGHT

In her starry shade of dim and solitary loveliness, I learn the language of another world.

George Gordon Byron (Lord Byron)

Night is the mother of thoughts.

John Florio

Oh, treacherous night! thou lendest thy ready veil to every treason, and teeming mischiefs thrive beneath thy shade.

Aaron Hill

The day is done, and darkness falls from the wings of night.

Henry Wadsworth Longfellow

Quiet night, that brings rest to the laborer, is the outlaw's day, in which he rises early to do wrong, and when his work is ended, dares not sleep.

Philip Massinger

Night's silent reign had robbed the world of light, to lend, in lieu, a greater benefit, repose and sleep, when every mortal whom care or grief permitted, took their rest.

Sir Thomas Erskine May

Why does the evening, why does the night, put warmer love in our hearts? Is it the nightly pressure of helplessness? Or is it the exalting separation from the turmoils of life, that veiling of the world in which, for the soul, nothing remains but souls?

Jean Paul Richter

The worm of conscience is the companion of the owl. The light is shunned by sinners and evil spirits only.

Johann Christoph Friedrich von Schiller

The night is made for tenderness so still that the low whisper, scarcely audible, is heard like music, and so deeply pure that the fond thought is chastened as it springs and on the lip is made holy.

Nathaniel Parker Willis

This sacred shade and solitude, what is it? It is the felt presence of the Deity. Few are the faults we flatter when alone; vice sinks in her allurements, in ungilt, and looks, like other objects, black by night. By night an atheist half believes a God.

Edward Young

See also: DAY, EVENING, MIDNIGHT, STAR, SUNSET, TWILIGHT.

NOBILITY

He who is lord of himself, and exists upon his own resources, is a noble but a rare being.

Sir Samuel Egerton Brydges

A fool, indeed, has great need of a title; it teaches men to call him count or duke, and thus forget his proper name of fool.

John Crowne

All nobility, in its beginnings, was somebody's natural superiority.

Ralph Waldo Emerson

Virtue is the first title of nobility.

Molière (Jean Baptiste Poquelin)

It is not wealth, nor ancestry, but honorable conduct and a noble disposition that make men great.

Ovid

If a man be endued with a generous mind, this is the best kind of nobility.

Plato

Man's nobility is his belief in it.

Jean Rostand

It is better to be nobly remembered, than nobly born.

John Ruskin

Talent and worth are the only eternal grounds of distinction. To these the Almighty has affixed his everlasting patent of nobility. Knowledge and goodness–these make degrees in heaven and they must be the graduating scale of a true democracy.

Catherine Maria Sedgwick

The origin of all men is the same and virtue is the only nobility.

Seneca

Nobility should be elective, not hereditary.

Johann Georg von Zimmermann

See also: ARISTOCRACY, DIGNITY, EMINENCE, GREATNESS, TITLE.

NOISE

A noisy man is always in the right.

William Cowper

It is with narrow-souled people as with narrow-necked bottles; the less they have in them, the more noise they make in pouring it out.

Alexander Pope

See also: BLUSTERING, SILENCE, SOUND.

NONCONFORMITY

Conformity keeps tradition alive; nonconformity breaks through tradition and, if directed by reason, helps to free us from the errors of the past.

Franz Boas

Radio and TV stations often fear their advertisers, who in turn fear non-conformists.

William Orville Douglas

The dissenter is every human being at those moments of his life when he resigns momentarily from the herd and thinks for himself.

Archibald MacLeish

See also: CHANGE, INNOVATION, LIBERAL, NOVELTY, OPENMINDEDNESS, PROGRESS, REFORM.

NONSENSE

To write or talk concerning any subject, without having previously taken the pains to understand it, is a breach of the duty which we owe to ourselves, though it may be no offence against the laws of the land. The privilege of talking and even publishing nonsense is necessary in a free state; but the more sparingly we make use of it the better.

Samuel Taylor Coleridge

Nonsense and noise will oft prevail,
When honor and affection fail.

William Lloyd

Nonsense is to sense, as shade to light; it heightens effect.

Frederick Saunders

I find that nonsense, at times, is singularly refreshing.

Charles Maurice de Talleyrand-Périgord

See also: ABSURDITY, FOLLY, JESTING.

NORMALITY

The only glory most of us have to hope for is the glory of being normal.

Katharine Fullerton Gerould

All the world is queer save thee and me, and even thou art a little queer.

Robert Owen

See also: DISEASE, INSANITY, MENTAL HEALTH, PSYCHOLOGY.

NOSE

He that has a great Nose thinks every body is speaking of it.

Thomas Fuller

If the nose of Cleopatra had been a little shorter the whole face of the world would have been changed.

Blaise Pascal

Plain as a nose in a man's face.

François Rabelais

See also: APPEARANCE, EYE, FACE, LOOKS.

NOVEL

We must have books for recreation and entertainment, as well as for instruction and for business; the former are agreeable, the latter useful, and the human mind requires both. The canon law and the codes of Justinian shall have due honor and reign at the universities, but Homer and Virgil need not therefore be banished. We will cultivate the olive and the vine, but without eradicating the myrtle and the rose.

Honoré de Balzac

Novel reading tends to destroy a relish for history, philosophy, and other useful knowledge. Novels give false notions of life, which are dangerous and injurious.

James Beattie

It cannot but be injurious to the human mind never to be called into effort; the habit of receiving pleasure without any exertion of thought, by the mere excitement of curiosity and sensibility, may be justly ranked among the worst effects of habitual novel reading. Like idle morning visitors, the brisk and breathless periods hurry in and hurry off in quick and profitless succession—each, indeed, for the moment of its stay preventing the pain of vacancy, while it indulges the love of sloth; but, altogether, they leave the mistress of the house—the soul—flat and exhausted, incapable of attending to her own concerns, and unfitted for the conversation of more rational guests.

Samuel Taylor Coleridge

Novels may teach us as wholesome a moral as the pulpit. There are "sermons in stones," in healthy books, and "good in everything."

Charles Caleb Colton

Above all things, never let your son touch a novel of romance. How delusive, how destructive are those pictures of consummate bliss! They teach the youthful to sigh after beauty and happiness that never existed; to despise the little good that fortune has mixed in our cup, by expecting more than she ever gave; and in general—take the word of a man who has seen the world, and studied it more by experience than by precept—take my word for it, I say, that such books teach us very little of the world.

Oliver Goldsmith

The primary aim of the novel . . . is the representation of human beings at their follies and villainies, and no other art form clings to that aim so faithfully.

Henry Louis Mencken

Legitimately produced, and truly inspired, fiction interprets humanity, informs the understanding, and quickens the affections. It reflects ourselves, warns us against prevailing social follies, adds rich specimens to our cabinets of character, dramatizes life for the unimaginative, daguerreotypes it for the unobservant, multiplies experience for the isolated or inactive, and cheers age, retirement, and invalidism with an available and harmless solace.

Henry Theodore Tuckerman

Novels do not force their readers to sin, but only instruct them how to sin.

Johann Georg von Zimmermann

See also: BOOK, FICTION, LITERATURE, NOVELIST, ROMANCE.

NOVELIST

The object of the novelist is to keep the reader entirely oblivious of the fact that the author exists—even of the fact that he is reading a book.

Ford Maddox Ford

The function of the novelist of this present day is to comment upon life as he sees it.

Frank (Benjamin Franklin) Norris

The business of the novelist is not to relate great events, but to make small ones interesting.

Arthur Schopenhauer

See also: AUTHORSHIP, NOVEL.

NOVELTY

Curiosity, from its nature, is a very active principle; it quickly runs over the greatest part of its objects, and soon exhausts the variety common to be met with in nature. Some degree of novelty must be one of the materials in almost every instrument which works upon the mind; and curiosity blends itself, more or less, with all our pleasures.

Edmund Burke

There is nothing new under the sun.

George Michael Cohan

The earth was made so various, that the mind of desultory man, studious of change, and pleased with novelty, might be indulged.

William Cowper

Such is the nature of novelty that where anything pleases it becomes doubly agreeable if new; but if it displeases, it is doubly displeasing on that very account.

David Hume

Before I translated the New Testament out of the Greek, all longed after it; when it was done, their longing lasted scarce four weeks. Then they desired the books of Moses; when I had translated these, they had enough thereof in a short time. After that, they would have the Psalms; of these they were soon weary, and desired other books. So it will be with the book of Ecclesiastes, which they now long for, and about which I have taken great pains. All is acceptable until our giddy brains be satisfied; afterwards we let familiar things lie, and seek after new.

Martin Luther

In science, as in common life, we frequently see that a novelty in system, or in practise, cannot be duly appreciated till time has sobered the enthusiasm of its advocates.

Maud

It is not only old and early impressions that deceive us; the charms of novelty have the same power.

Blaise Pascal

Novelty is the great parent of pleasure.

Robert South

Novelty has charms that our minds can hardly withstand. The most valuable things, if they have for a long while appeared among us, do not make any impression as they are good, but give us a distaste as they are old. But when the influence of this fantastical humor is over, the same men or things will come to be admired again, by a happy return of our good taste.

William Makepeace Thackeray

See also: DISCOVERY, INNOVATION, NONCONFORMITY, ORIGINALITY, VARIETY.

NUCLEAR ENERGY

We are convinced that parallel to the formation of a regional common market we must take concrete steps to begin a process of inter-American integration built around the utilization of atomic energy.

Arthur Costa e Silva

The discovery of nuclear chain reaction need not bring about the destruction of mankind any more than the discovery of matches.

Albert Einstein

Since I do not foresee that atomic energy is to be a great boon for a long time, I have to say that for the present it is a menace. Perhaps it is well that it should be. It may intimidate the human race into bringing order into its international affairs, which, without the pressure of fear, it would not do.

Albert Einstein

Some recent work by E. Fermi and L. Szilard, which has been communicated to me in manuscript, leads me to expect that the element uranium may be turned into a new and important source of energy in the immediate future. [Letter to Franklin D. Roosevelt, August 2, 1939.]

Albert Einstein

The real vision of the atomic future rests not in the material abundance which it should eventually bring for man's convenience and comfort in living. It lies in finding at last, through the common use of such abundance, a way to make the nations of the world friendly neighbors on the same street.

Dwight David Eisenhower

The man who made the greatest contribution to the American development of the atom bomb was Adolf Hitler. For it was his racial theories which drove such men and women as Einstein, Meitner, Bohr, Fermi and countless others from Germany and its allies, or conquered countries. The theoretical physicists, chemists and mathematicians who were exiled . . . provided the nucleus around which the American and British teams rallied to produce the atom bomb. As anyone who has even skimmed through the name index . . . must know, the Manhattan Project was truly an international accomplishment.

James Byron Kelley

It would be madness to let the purposes or the methods of private enterprise set the habits of the age of atomic energy.

Harold Joseph Laski

The fear that atomic energy will become a weapon of universal destruction rather than a tool of planetary health and prosperity is a realistic fear—indispensable; as a matter of fact, for the planning of new strategies to master the social and economic dangers of our day.

Joshua Loth Liebman

I have no doubt that just as we were affected by the advent of steam and electric power, the advent of atomic power in the next ten, fifteen or twenty years, will make a vast difference to the running of all our factories.

Jawaharlal Nehru

It is obvious that all this technological and scientific progress in the world unless it is balanced by some kind of moral standards and ethical values, is likely to lead to destruction. That is why we are so concerned over the basic question presented by atomic energy. Use it for evil, and it will destroy the world; use it for good, and it will raise the world to unknown standards of progress and happiness.

Jawaharlal Nehru

Disintegration of the atom.
From now on, all animals, all plants, everything alive is at the mercy of human error or stupidity.

Jean Rostand

For years man dreamed of freeing the energy stored in the atom. Hardly has he realized his dream than he begins to groan at its danger: were we then so naïve as to think we were going to play with harmless toys right to the end?

Jean Rostand

Since the discovery of atomic disintegration, it has become incumbent on humanity to live under threat of death. Why shouldn't the feeling of lethal danger, which is so productive for the individual, be so for the species, as well?

Jean Rostand

The awareness that we are all human beings together has become lost in war and politics. . . . At this stage we have the choice of two risks. The one consists in continuing the mad atomic arms race with the danger of unavoidable atomic war in the near future. The other is in the renunciation of nuclear weapons, and the hope that America and the Soviet Union, and the peoples associated with them, will manage to live in peace. The first holds no hope of a prosperous future; the second does. We must risk the second.

Albert Schweitzer

Depite the atomic bomb we are seeking the dawn and not the twilight of the world.

Harlow Shapley

The powers of the atom unleashed by science are too startling, too intoxicating, and at the same time too useful as human tools for any of us to wish to abandon the astonishing new technology. But, if we will not abandon it, we must master it.

Adlai Ewing Stevenson

We turned the switch, we saw the flashes, we watched them for about ten minutes— and then we switched everything off and went home. That night I knew that the world was headed for sorrow. [Describing an experiment in uranium fission made March 3, 1939.]

Leo Szilard

See also: NUCLEAR WARFARE, RADIATION, SCIENCE, TECHNOLOGY.

NUCLEAR WARFARE

Some substantial and respected persons have advocated the use of atom bombs— small ones, that is. The other day a representative of a respected and well-known national organization came to my office to urge the use of atom bombs in the Vietnam war. The demand that we use atomic weapons will increase as our casualty lists grow.

George David Aiken

We've opened a door—maybe a treasure-house, maybe only the realization of a maniac's dream of destruction.

Sir John Anderson

We develop weapons, not to wage war, but to prevent war. Only in the clear light of this greater truth can we properly examine the lesser matter of the testing of our nuclear weapons.

Dwight David Eisenhower

We go ahead with this hydrogen bomb, not to make a bigger bank, not to cause more destruction, (but) to find out ways and means in which you can limit it, make it useful in defensive purposes, of shooting against a fleet of airplanes that are coming over, to reduce fall-out, to make it more of a military weapon and less one just of mass destruction.

Dwight David Eisenhower

The United States pledges . . . its determination to help solve the fearful atomic dilemma—to devote its entire heart and mind to find the way by which the miraculous inventiveness of man shall not be dedicated to his death, but consecrated to his life.

Dwight David Eisenhower

People who talk of outlawing the atomic bomb are mistaken—what needs to be outlawed is war.

Leslie Richard Groves

Bombs do not choose. They will hit everything. I will not hesitate to give orders . . . to crush military bases of the North Atlantic bloc located in Greece. And they would not, of course, have any mercy on the olive groves or on the Acropolis, because bombs do not differentiate . . . Perhaps someone is counting on declaring some cities to be "open" as they managed to do in the last war. . . . In the future, if nuclear weapons are unleashed there will be no front and no rear.

Nikita Sergeevich Khrushchev

Let there be more corn and more meat and let there be no hydrogen bombs at all.

Nikita Sergeevich Khrushchev

The atomic bomb may help to decide a future war; like any other weapon it solves none of the problems which make for war.

Hans Kohn

At first it [the first atomic explosion] was a giant column that soon took the shape of a supramundane mushroom.

William Leonard Laurence

The Atomic Age began at exactly 5:30 Mountain War Time on the morning of July 16, 1945, on a stretch of semi-desert land about fifty airline miles from Alamogordo, New Mexico.

At that great moment in history, ranking with the moment in the long ago when man first put fire to work for him and started on his march to civilization, the vast energy locked within the hearts of the atoms of matter was released for the first time in a burst of flame such as had never before been seen on this planet. . . .

A great ball of fire about a mile in diameter, changing colors as it kept shooting upward, from deep purple to orange, expanding, an elemental force freed from its bonds after being chained for billions of years.

William Leonard Laurence

As the bomb fell over Hiroshima and exploded, we saw an entire city disappear. I wrote in my log the words: "My God, what have we done?"

Robert Lewis

The hydrogen bomb is history's exclamation point. It ends an age-long sentence of manifest violence!

(Herbert) Marshall McLuhan

The hydrogen bomb does not recognize national boundaries.

Brien McMahon

With a 3-minute warning, 15-minute warning or no warning at all, we could still absorb a surprise [nuclear] attack and strike back with sufficient power to destroy the attacker.

Robert Strange McNamara

These experiments show man is unleasing power which can ultimately get out of control.

Jawaharlal Nehru

Idealists maintain that all nations should share the atomic bomb. Pessimists maintain that they will.

Punch

All of us know that space and time have been annihilated on this small, small spaceship we call 'planet earth.' We can blow it up. We can annihilate the thin envelope of soil on which our nourishment depends, and contaminate the thin layer of air we breathe. This apocalyptic risk exists simply because our modern means of science have made neighbors of us all.

Adlai Ewing Stevenson

We are all standing shoulder to shoulder— with a hydrogen bomb ticking in our pockets.

Adlai Ewing Stevenson

Almost two months have passed since the atomic bomb was used against Japan. That bomb did not win the war, but it certainly shortened the war. We know that it saved the lives of untold thousands of American and Allied soldiers who would otherwise have been killed in battle.

Harry S Truman

Sixteen hours ago an American airplane dropped one bomb on Hiroshima. . . . It is a harnessing of the basic power of the universe. The force from which the sun draws its powers has been loosed against those who brought war to the Far East.

Harry S Truman

This is indeed The Year Atomic Bomb One. It has opened most ominously. We must waste no time if we plan to be alive in A.B. 5 or A.B. 10.

Harold Clayton Urey

Nothing could have been more obvious to the people of the early twentieth century than the rapidity with which war was becoming impossible. And as certainly they did not see it. They did not see it until the atomic bombs burst in their fumbling hands.

Herbert George Wells

I personally wish we would quit rattling the atom bomb.

Charles Erwin Wilson

See also: ARMS, ARMY, GUN, NAVY, NUCLEAR ENERGY, RADIATION, WAR.

O

OATH

Of all men, a philosopher should be no swearer; for an oath, which is the end of controversies in law, cannot determine any here, where reason only must decide.

Sir Thomas Browne

Oaths are but words, and words but wind.

Samuel Butler

Rash oaths, whether kept or broken, frequently lead to guilt.

Samuel Johnson

See also: ASSERTION, CURSE, PROMISE, VOW.

OBEDIENCE

Obedience is the mother of success and is wedded to safety.

Aeschylus

Wicked men obey from fear; good men, from love.

Aristotle

"Theirs not to make reply, theirs not to reason why," may be a good enough motto for men who are on their way to be shot. But from such men expect no empires to be built, no inventions made, no great discoveries brought to light.

Bruce Barton

Thirty years of our Lord's life are hidden in these words of the gospel: "He was subject unto them."

Jacques Bénigne Bossuet

There are two kinds of men who never amount to much: those who cannot do what they are told, and those who can do nothing else.

Cyrus Hermann Kotzschmar Curtis

The best way to insure implicit obedience is to commence tyranny in the nursery.

Benjamin Disraeli

It is vain thought to flee from the work that God appoints us, for the sake of finding a greater blessing, instead of seeking it where alone it is to be found—in loving obedience.

George Eliot (Mary Ann Evans)

Obedience to God is the most infalliable evidence of sincere and supreme love to him.

Nathaniel Emmons

Let thy child's first lesson be obedience, and the second may be what thou wilt.

Thomas Fuller

The first law that ever God gave to man, was a law of obedience; it was a commandment pure and simple, wherein man had nothing to inquire after or to dispute, for as much as to obey is the proper office of a rational soul acknowledging a heavenly superior and benefactor. From obedience and submission spring all other virtues, as all sin does from self-opinion and self-will.

Michel Eyquem de Montaigne

One very common error misleads the opinion of mankind, that authority is pleasant, and submission painful. In the general course of human affairs the very reverse of this is nearer to the truth. Command is anxiety; obedience is ease.

William Paley

Obedience is not truly performed by the body, if the heart is dissatisfied.

Saadi (Muslih-ud-Din)

We are born subjects, and to obey God is perfect liberty. He that does this shall be free, safe, and happy.

Seneca

A slave is bound to obey his master's orders, given solely in the master's interest. A son obeys his father's orders, given in his own interest. A subject obeys the order of the sovereign power, given for the common interest, wherein he is included.

> Baruch (Benedict) Spinoza

The only safe ruler is he who has learned to obey willingly.

> Thomas à Kempis

See also: DEFERENCE, DISOBEDIENCE, DUTY, HUMILITY, SUBMISSION.

OBJECTIVE

We succeed only as we identify in life, or in war, or in anything else, a single overriding objective, and make all other considerations bend to that one objective.

> Dwight David Eisenhower

No wind makes for him that hath no intended port to sail unto.

> Michel Eyquem de Montaigne

See also: AIM, END, INTENTION, PURPOSE.

OBLIGATION

To owe an obligation to a worthy friend, is a happiness, and can be no disparagement.

> Pierre Charron

When some men discharge an obligation you can hear the report for miles around.

> Samuel Langhorne Clemens (Mark Twain)

It is well known to all great men, that by conferring an obligation they do not always procure a friend, but are certain of creating many enemies.

> Henry Fielding

Obligation is thraldom, and thraldom is hateful.

> Thomas Hobbes

An extraordinary haste to discharge an obligation, is a sort of ingratitude.

> Duc François de La Rochefoucauld

What do I owe to my times, to my country, to my neighbors, to my friends? Such are the questions which a virtuous man ought often to ask himself.

> Johann Kaspar Lavater

I am fettered by a thousand little obligations resulting from my independence.

> Jean Rostand

Man owes not only his services, but himself to God.

> Thomas Secker

In some there is a kind of graceless modesty that makes a man ashamed of requiting an obligation, because it is a confession that he has received one.

> Seneca

See also: BORROWING, DEBT, DUTY, NECESSITY, RESPONSIBILITY.

OBLIVION

Fame is a vapor; popularity an accident; riches take wings; the only certainty is oblivion.

> Horace Greeley

Oblivion is the rule, and fame the exception of humanity.

> Antoine Rivarol

Oblivion is the flower that grows best on graves.

> George Sand

See also: DEATH, FORGETFULNESS, GRAVE, OBSCURITY.

OBSCENITY

Sex and obscenity are not synonymous. Obscene material is material which deals with sex in a manner appealing to prurient interest.

> William Joseph Brennan, Jr.

What is obscenity to one person is but a subject of scientific inquiry to another.

> Edmund Louis Palmieri

See also: CENSORSHIP, PORNOGRAPHY.

OBSCURITY

There is no defence against reproach but obscurity; it is a kind of concomitant to greatness, as satires and invectives were an essential part of a Roman triumph.

> Joseph Addison

The obscure is the principal ingredient of the sublime.

> Benjamin Disraeli

How many wonderful men, and who possessed the noblest genius, have died without ever being spoken of! How many live at the present moment of whom men do not speak, and of whom they will never speak!

> Jean de La Bruyère

Thus let me live, unseen, unknown;
  Thus unlamented let me die,

Steal from the world, and not a stone
Tell where I lie.

> *Alexander Pope*

Who is the Forgotten Man? He is the clean, quiet, virtuous, domestic citizen, who pays his debts and his taxes and is never heard of out of his little circle.

> *William Graham Sumner*

See also: CONCEALMENT, MYSTERY, OBLIVION, PRIVACY, SECRECY.

OBSERVATION

Each one sees what he carries in his heart.

> *Johann Wolfgang von Goethe*

Objects imperfectly discerned take forms from the hope or fear of the beholder.

> *Samuel Johnson*

He alone is an acute observer, who can observe minutely without being observed.

> *Johann Kaspar Lavater*

General observations drawn from particulars are the jewels of knowledge, comprehending great store in a little room.

> *John Locke*

It is the close observation of little things which is the secret of success in business, in art, in science, and in every pursuit in life. Human knowledge is but an accumulation of small facts, made by successive generations of men,—the little bits of knowledge and experience carefully treasured up and growing at length into a mighty pyramid.

> *Samuel Smiles*

See also: ATTENTION, EXPERIENCE, EYE, PERCEPTION, SCIENCE.

OBSTINACY

Obstinacy is will asserting itself without being able to justify itself. It is persistence without a reasonable motive. It is the tenacity of self-love substituted for that of reason and conscience.

> *Henri Frédéric Amiel*

Obstinacy and vehemency in opinion are the surest proofs of stupidity.

> *Bruce Barton*

Obstinacy is certainly a great vice; and in the changeful state of political affairs is frequently the cause of great mischief. It happens, however, very unfortunately, that almost the whole line of the great and masculine virtues—constancy, gravity, magnanimity, fortitude, fidelity, and firmness—are closely allied to this disagreeable quality, of which you have so just an abhorrence; and in their excess, all these virtues very easily fall into it.

> *Edmund Burke*

Obstinacy is the strength of the weak. Firmness founded upon principle, upon truth and right, order and law, duty and generosity, is the obstinacy of sages.

> *Johann Kaspar Lavater*

Obstinacy and heat in argument are surest proofs of folly. Is there anything so stubborn, obstinate, disdainful, contemplative, grave, serious, as an ass?

> *Michel Eyquem de Montaigne*

There are few, very few, that will own themselves in a mistake.

> *Jonathan Swift*

See also: FIRMNESS, INDEPENDENCE, PERVERSENESS, REBELLION, SELF-WILL.

OCCUPATION

Most of the trades, professions, and ways of living among mankind, take their original either from the love of pleasure, or the fear of want. The former, when it becomes too violent, degenerates into luxury, and the latter into avarice.

> *Joseph Addison*

The crowning fortune of a man is to be born with a bias to some pursuit which finds him in employment and happiness.

> *Ralph Waldo Emerson*

Every Egyptian was commanded by law annually to declare by what means he maintained himself; and if he omitted to do it, or gave no satisfactory account of his way of living, he was punishable with death. This law Solon brought from Egypt to Athens, where it was inviolably observed as a most equitable regulation.

> *Herodotus*

The ugliest of trades have their moments of pleasure. Now, if I were a gravedigger, or even a hangman, there are some people I could work for with a great deal of enjoyment.

> *Douglas William Jerrold*

See also: BUSINESS, EMPLOYMENT, LABOR, PROFESSION, TRADE, WORK.

OFFENSE

Who fears to offend takes the first step to please.

Colley Cibber

When any one has offended me, I try to raise my soul so high that the offense cannot reach it.

René Descartes

A very small offence may be a just cause for great resentment; it is often much less the particular instance which is obnoxious to us, than the proof it carries with it of the general tenor and disposition of the mind from whence it sprung.

Fulke Greville (First Baron Brooke)

Offenses ought to be pardoned, for few offend willingly, but only as led by some excitement.

Hegesippus

At every trifle scorn to take offence;
That always shows great pride, or little sense.

Alexander Pope

That man who offends you—either he was born of a race different from yours or else he is your strayed brother: doesn't he, in either case, deserve your compassion?

Jean Rostand

See also: CRIME, IMPERTINENCE, IMPUDENCE, INJURY, INSULT, SIN, VICE, WRONG.

OFFICE

Ministers fall like buttered bread: usually with the good side down.

Ludwig Börne

No matter how humble a man's beginnings, he achieves the stature of the office to which he is elected.

Nikita Sergeevich Khrushchev

If ever this free people, if this government itself is ever utterly demoralized, it will come from this incessant human wriggle and struggle for office, which is but a way to live without work.

Abraham Lincoln

Five things are requisite to a good officer—ability, clean hands, despatch, patience, and impartiality.

William Penn

Every man who takes office in Washington either grows or swells.

(Thomas) Woodrow Wilson

See also: AUTHORITY, DUTY, PRESIDENT, POLITICIAN, POLITICS.

OLD AGE: see AGE, OLD.

OMNIPOTENCE

Who guides below and rules above, the great disposer and the mighty king; than he none greater; next him none can be, or is, or was; supreme, he singly fills the throne.

Horace

God veiled in majesty, alone gives light and life to all; bids the great systems move, and changing seasons in their turns advance, unmoved, unchanged himself.

Thomas Somerville

See also: GOD, OMNIPRESENCE, OMNISCIENCE, POWER, PROVIDENCE.

OMNIPRESENCE

God oft descends to visit men, unseen, and through their habitations walks, to mark their doings.

John Milton

Where one is present, God is the second, and where there are two, God is the third.

Mohammed

Yes, thou art ever present, power divine; not circumscribed by time, nor fixed by space, confined to altars, nor to temples bound. In wealth, in want, in freedom, or in chains, in dungeons or on thrones, the faithful find thee.

Hannah More

See also: GOD, OMNIPOTENCE.

OMNISCIENCE

We cannot too often think there is a never-sleeping eye, which reads the heart, and registers our thoughts.

Francis Bacon

What can escape the eye of God, all seeing, or deceive his heart, omniscient!

John Milton

In all thy actions, think God sees thee; and in all his actions labor to see him.

Francis Quarles

See also: GOD, KNOWLEDGE, OMNIPOTENCE.

OPENMINDEDNESS

An open mind is all very well in its way, but it ought not to be so open that there is no keeping anything in or out of it. It should be capable of shutting its doors sometimes, or it may be found a little draughty.

Samuel Butler

Minds are like parachutes. They only function when they are open.

Thomas Robert Dewar

See also: LIBERAL, NEUTRALITY, TOLERATION.

OPINION

He who is master of all opinions can never be the bigot of any.

William Rounseville Alger

The ambitious man grasps at opinion as necessary to his designs; the vain man sues for it as a testimony to his merit; the honest man demands it as his due; and most men consider it as necessary to their existence.

Cesare Bonesana (Marchese di Beccaria)

I could never divide myself from any man upon the difference of opinion, or be angry with his judgment for not agreeing in that from which, within a few days, I might dissent myself.

Sir Thomas Browne

One of the mistakes in the conduct of human life is, to suppose that other men's opinions are to make us happy.

Richard Eugene Burton

An obstinate man does not hold opinions—they hold him.

Joseph Butler

It is not only arrogant, but profligate, for a man to disregard the world's opinion of himself.

Cicero

No liberal man would impute a charge of unsteadiness to another for having changed his opinion.

Cicero

It were not best that we should all think alike; it is difference of opinion that makes horseraces.

Samuel Langhorne Clemens (Mark Twain)

The masses procure their opinions ready made in open market.

Charles Caleb Colton

Predominant opinions are generally the opinions of the generation that is vanishing.

Benjamin Disraeli

He that never changes his opinions, never corrects his mistakes, and will never be wiser on the morrow than he is to-day.

Tryon Edwards

To force opinion is like pushing the magnetized needle round by brute strength until it points to where we wish the North Star stood, rather than to where it really is.

Dorothy Canfield Fisher

The eyes of other people are the eyes that ruin us. If all but myself were blind, I should want neither fine clothes, fine houses, nor fine furniture.

Benjamin Franklin

As our inclinations, so our opinions.

Johann Wolfgang von Goethe

The men of the past had convictions, while we moderns have only opinions.

Heinrich Heine

A man's opinions are generally of much more value than his arguments.

Oliver Wendell Holmes

One of the commonest ailments of the present day is premature formation of opinion.

Frank McKinney (Kin) Hubbard

All power, even the most despotic, rests ultimately on opinion.

David Hume

Error of opinion may be tolerated where reason it left free to combat it.

Thomas Jefferson

Those who never retract their opinions love themselves more than they love truth.

Joseph Joubert

As for the differences of opinion upon speculative questions, if we wait till they are reconciled, the action of human affairs must be suspended forever. But neither are we to look for perfection in any one man, nor for agreement among many.

Junius

I would submit there is more respect to be won in the opinion of the world by a resolute and courageous liquidation of unsound positions than in the most stubborn pursuit of extravagant or unpromising objectives.

George Frost Kennan

He who has no opinion of his own, but depends upon the opinion and taste of others, is a slave.

Friedrich Klopstock

Those who, without being thoroughly acquainted with our real character, think ill of us, do us no wrong; it is not we whom they attack, but the phantom of their own imagination.

Jean de La Bruyère

We think very few people sensible, except those who are of our opinion.

Duc François de La Rochefoucauld

It is the inclination and tendency of the heart which finally determines the opinions of the mind.

Christoph Ernest Luthardt

Do not think of knocking out another person's brains because he differs in opinion from you. It would be as rational to knock yourself on the head because you differ from yourself ten years ago.

Horace Mann

Opinion is the main thing which does good or harm in the world. It is our false opinions of things which ruin us.

Marcus Aurelius

Follow your own bent, no matter what people say.

Karl Marx

There never was in the world two opinions alike, no more than two hairs or two grains. The most universal quality is diversity.

Michel Eyquem de Montaigne

One has to face the modern world with its good as well as its bad and it is better, on the whole, I think, that we give licence rather than suppress the normal flow of opinion.

Jawaharlal Nehru

Ultimately what we really are matters more than what other people think of us.

Jawaharlal Nehru

I will utter what I believe to-day, if it should contradict all I said yesterday.

Wendell Phillips

There is, and always has been, one tremendous ruler of the human race—and that ruler is that combination of the opinions of all, the leveling up of universal sense which is called public sentiment. That is the ever-present regulator and police of humanity.

Thomas Brackett Reed

It is more true to say that our opinions depend upon our lives and habits, than to say that our lives and habits depend on our opinions.

Frederick William Robertson

The feeble tremble before opinion, the foolish defy it, the wise judge it, the skillful direct it.

Madame Roland

Human opinion would be quite different if everyone would risk his own: fear prevents some people from including themselves in the poll.

Jean Rostand

One has of course the right to change opinion, but on condition of not fraudulently adjusting the new to the old.

Jean Rostand

Among the best men are diversities of opinions; which should no more, in true reason, breed hatred, than one that loves black should be angry with him that is clothed in white; for thoughts are the very apparel of the mind.

Sir Philip Sidney

No errors of opinion can possibly be dangerous in a country where opinion is left free to grapple with them.

William Gilmore Simms

Wind puffs up empty bladders; opinion, fools.

Socrates

If a man should register all his opinions upon love, politics, religion, learning, etc., beginning from his youth, and so go on to old age, what a bundle of inconsistencies and contradictions would appear at last.

Jonathan Swift

What I admire in Columbus is not his having discovered a world, but his having gone to search for it on the faith of an opinion.

Anne Robert Jacques Turgot

The history of human opinion is scarcely anything more than the history of human errors.

> *Voltaire (François Marie Arouet)*

We are too much inclined to under-rate the power of moral influence, the influence of public opinion, and the influence of the principles to which great men—the lights of the world and of the present age—have given their sanction.

> *Daniel Webster*

See also: BELIEF, CREED, DOCTRINE, FANCY, IDEA, IMPRESSION, JUDGMENT, PHILOSOPHY, PREJUDICE, PUBLIC OPINION, SENTIMENT, THEORY.

OPPORTUNITY

A wise man will make more opportunities than he finds.

> *Francis Bacon*

There is an hour in each man's life appointed to make his happiness, if then he sieze it.

> *Francis Beaumont and John Fletcher*

Some of us miss opportunity because we are too dull to try. Others let opportunity go by, too much startled when they see it to take hold of it.

> *Arthur Brisbane*

You will never "find" time for anything. If you want time you must make it.

> *Charles Buxton*

Too many people are thinking of security instead of opportunity; they seem more afraid of life than of death.

> *James Francis Byrnes*

A word spoken in season, at the right moment, is the matter of ages.

> *Thomas Carlyle*

The best men are not those who have waited for chances but who have taken them; besieged the chance; conquered the chance; and made chance the servitor.

> *Edwin Hubbel Chapin*

The sure way to miss success is to miss the opportunity.

> *Philarète Chasles*

Every one has a fair turn to be as great as he pleases.

> *Jeremy Collier*

When heaven half opens its arms, he who is faint-hearted deserves not anything. It is this want of faith that often keeps heaven from bestowing its blessings; and even when they come down, it is apt to send them away.

> *Pierre Corneille*

Next to knowing when to seize an opportunity, the most important thing in life is to know when to forego an advantage.

> *Benjamin Disraeli*

All that is valuable in human society depends upon the opportunity for development accorded the individual.

> *Albert Einstein*

Occasion may be the bugle call that summons an army to battle, but the blast of a bugle can never make soldiers nor win battles.

> *James Abram Garfield*

The very essence of equality of opportunity and of American individualism . . . demands economic justice as well as political and social justice. It is no system of laissez faire.

> *Herbert Clark Hoover*

To improve the golden moment of opportunity and catch the good that is within our reach, is the great art of life.

> *Samuel Johnson*

If you can fill the unforgiving minute
    With sixty seconds' worth of distance run,
Yours is the Earth and everything that's in it,
    And—which is more—you'll be a Man, my son!

> *Rudyard Kipling*

To be a great man it is necessary to turn to account all opportunities.

> *Duc François de La Rochefoucauld*

Who makes quick use of the moment, is a genius of prudence.

> *Johann Kaspar Lavater*

The public man needs but one patron, namely, the lucky moment.

> *Edward G. Bulwer-Lytton (Baron Lytton)*

Our opportunities to do good are our talents.

> *Cotton Mather*

A philosopher being asked what was the first thing necessary to win the love of a woman, answered: "Opportunity."

Thomas Moore

Vigilance in watching opportunity; tact and daring in seizing upon opportunity; force and persistence in crowding opportunity to its utmost of possible achievement—these are the martial virtues which must command success.

Austin Phelps

No man possesses a genius so commanding that he can attain eminence, unless a subject suited to his talents should present itself, and an opportunity occur for their development.

Pliny the Elder

Do not wait for extraordinary circumstances to do good; try to use ordinary situations.

Jean Paul Richter

The May of life blooms only once.

Johann Christoph Friedrich von Schiller

If we do not watch, we lose our opportunities; if we do not make haste, we are left behind; our best hours escape us, the worst are come. The purest part of our life runs first, and leaves only the dregs at the bottom; and that time which is good for nothing else we dedicate to virtue, and only propose to begin to live at an age that very few people arrive at.

Seneca

It is less important to redistribute wealth than it is to redistribute opportunity.

Arthur Hendrick Vandenberg

There can be no equality of opportunity, the first essential of justice in the body politic, if men and women and children be not shielded in their lives, their very vitality, from the consequences of great industrial and social processes which they cannot alter, control, or singly cope with.

(Thomas) Woodrow Wilson

Miss not the occasion; by the forelock take that subtle power, the never-halting time.

William Wordsworth

See also: CHANCE, CIRCUMSTANCE, ENVIRONMENT, FORTUNE, LUCK.

OPPOSITION

Like the course of the heavenly bodies, harmony in national life is a resultant of the struggle between contending forces.

Louis Dembitz Brandeis

He that wrestles with us, strengthens our nerves, and sharpens our skill. Our antagonist is our helper.

Edmund Burke

No government can long be secure without a formidable opposition.

Benjamin Disraeli

Nature is upheld by antagonism. Passions, resistance, danger, are educators. We acquire the strength we have overcome.

Ralph Waldo Emerson

A strenuous soul hates cheap success; it is the ardor of the assailant that makes the vigor of the defendant.

Ralph Waldo Emerson

It is not the victory that makes the joy of noble hearts, but the combat.

Charles Forbes (Comte de Montalembert)

The coldest bodies warm with opposition; the hardest sparkle in collision.

Junius

Don't be afraid of opposition. Remember, a kite rises against, not with, the wind.

Hamilton Wright Mabie

The greater the obstacle, the more glory in overcoming it; and difficulties are but the maids of honor to set off the virtue.

Molière (Jean Baptiste Poquelin)

A certain amount of opposition is a great help to a man; it is what he wants and must have to be good for anything. Hardship and opposition are the native soil of manhood and self-reliance.

John Neal

I am grateful to those who, by their opposition, often help me to remain true to myself.

Jean Rostand

Opposition inflames the enthusiast, never converts him.

Johann Christoph Friedrich von Schiller

It is not ease but effort,—not facility, but difficulty, that makes men. There is, perhaps, no station in life in which difficulties have not to be encountered and overcome before any decided measure of success can be achieved.

Samuel Smiles

See also: AGITATION, ARGUMENT, CONTENTION, CONTRADICTION, CONTROVERSY, DIFFERENCE, REBELLION, REVOLUTION, WAR.

OPPRESSION

It is bad to be oppressed by a minority, but it is worse to be oppressed by a majority. For there is a reserve of latent power in the masses which, if it is called into play, the minority can seldom resist. But from the absolute will of an entire people there is no appeal, no redemption, no refuge but treason.

John Dalberg-Acton (Lord Acton)

An extreme rigor is sure to arm everything against it.

Edmund Burke

French Jews, let us be the first to come to the aid of our Christian brothers. . . . A permanent committee in each country, with eyes open to all victims of fanaticism, regardless of religion, must be created and supported.

Adophe (Isaac Moise) Crémieux

No other offense has ever been visited with such severe penalties as seeking to help the oppressed.

Clarence Seward Darrow

There is no happiness for him who oppresses and persecutes; there can be no repose for him. For the sighs of the unfortunate cry for vengeance to heaven.

Johann Heinrich Pestalozzi

I never could believe that Providence had sent a few men into the world, ready booted and spurred to ride, and millions ready saddled and bridled to be ridden.

Richard Rumbold

Power exercised with violence has seldom been of long duration, but temper and moderation generally produce permanence in all things.

Seneca

A desire to resist oppression is implanted in the nature of man.

Tacitus

See also: ABUSE, CRUELTY, DESPOTISM, PERSECUTION, SLAVERY, TYRANNY.

OPTIMISM

What passes for optimism is most often the effect of an intellectual error.

Raymond Aron

Optimism is the content of small men in high places.

Francis Scott Key Fitzgerald

I am an irrepressible optimist. No scientist starts his experiments with a faint heart. I belong to the tribe of Columbus and Stevenson, who hoped against hope in the face of heaviest odds. The days of miracles are not gone. They will abide so long as God abides.

Mohandas Karamchand (Mahatma) Gandhi

Two men look out through the same bars:
One sees the mud, and one the stars.

Frederick Langbridge

Every cloud has its silver lining but it is sometimes a little difficult to get it to the mint.

Donald Robert Perry (Don) Marquis

An optimist is a guy that has never had much experience.

Donald Robert Perry (Don) Marquis

In these times you have to be an optimist to open your eyes when you awake in the morning.

Carl Sandburg

An optimist is a person who sees a green light everywhere, while the pessimist sees only the red stop light . . . But the truly wise person is color-blind.

Albert Schweitzer

See also: CHEERFULNESS, PESSIMISM.

ORATORY

Orators are most vehement when they have the weakest cause, as men get on horseback when they cannot walk.

Cicero

There is no power like that of true oratory. Caesar controlled men by exciting their fears; Cicero, by captivating their affections and swaying their passions. The influence of the one perished with its author; that of the other continues to this day.

Henry Clay

A man never becomes an orator if he has anything to say.

Finley Peter Dunne

An orator or author is never successful till he has learned to make his words smaller than his ideas.

Ralph Waldo Emerson

The effective public speaker receives from his audience in vapor, what he pours back on them in a flood.

William Ewart Gladstone

All epoch-making revolutionary events have been produced not by the written but by the spoken word.

Adolf Hitler

The passions are the only orators that always succeed. They are, as it were, nature's art of eloquence, fraught with infallible rules. Simplicity, with the aid of the passions, persuades more than the utmost eloquence without it.

Duc François de La Rochefoucauld

What too many orators want in depth, they give you in length.

Charles de Secondat (Baron de Montesquieu)

To be an orator, you have to use your own words and be on fire with them. To be a talker—somebody else can write your words and you can read them.

Fulton John Sheen

Oratory is the power to talk people out of their sober and natural opinions.

Horatio Smith (Paul Chatfield)

In oratory, the greatest art is to conceal art.

Jonathan Swift

See also: PUBLIC SPEAKING, RHETORIC, SPEECH.

ORDER

Order means light and peace, inward liberty and free command over one's self; order is power.

Henri Frédéric Amiel

Good order is the foundation of all good things.

Edmund Burke

Set all things in their own peculiar place
And know that order is the greatest grace.

John Dryden

A place for everything, everything in its place.

Benjamin Franklin

He who has no taste for order, will be often wrong in his judgment, and seldom considerate or conscientious in his actions.

Johann Kaspar Lavater

Order is heav'n's first law.

Alexander Pope

Order is the sanity of the mind, the health of the body, the peace of the city, the security of the state. As the beams to a house, as the bones to the body, so is order to all things.

Robert Southey

See also: DISCIPLINE, EFFICIENCY, LAW.

ORIGINALITY

The merit of originality is not novelty, it is sincerity. The believing man is the original man; he believes for himself, not for another.

Thomas Carlyle

Every human being is intended to have a character of his own; to be what no other is, and to do what no other can do.

William Ellery Channing

What a good thing Adam had—when he said a good thing, he knew nobody had said it before.

Samuel Langhorne Clemens (Mark Twain)

The originality of a subject is in its treatment.

Benjamin Disraeli

If you would create something, you must be something.

Johann Wolfgang von Goethe

Originality is simply a pair of fresh eyes.

Thomas Wentworth Storrow Higginson

He who thinks for himself, and rarely imitates, is a free man.

Friedrich Gottlieb Klopstock

It is better to create than to be learned; creating is the true essence of life.

Barthold Georg Niebuhr

Originality is nothing but judicious imitation. The most original writers borrowed one from another. The instruction we find in books is like fire. We fetch it from our neighbor's, kindle it at home, communicate it to others, and it becomes the property of all.

Voltaire (François Marie Arouet)

See also: CREATIVITY, DISCOVERY, FASHION, INNOVATION, INVENTION, NOVELTY.

ORNAMENT

Ornaments were invented by modesty.

Joseph Joubert

All finery is a sign of littleness.

Johann Kaspar Lavater

Excess in apparel is another costly folly. The very trimming of the vain world would clothe all the naked ones.

William Penn

We all originally came from the woods; it is hard to eradicate from any of us the old taste for the tattoo and the war-paint; and the moment that money gets into our pockets, it somehow or another breaks out in ornaments on our person, without always giving refinement to our manners.

Edwin Percy Whipple

See also: APPEARANCE, ART, DRESS, FASHION, LOOKS, OSTENTATION.

OSTENTATION

An ostentatious man will rather relate a blunder or an absurdity he has committed, than be debarred from talking of his own dear person.

Joseph Addison

Whatever is done without ostentation, and without the people being witnesses of it, is, in my opinion, most praiseworthy: not that the public eye should be entirely avoided, for good actions desire to be placed in the light; but notwithstanding this, the greatest theatre for virtue is conscience.

Cicero

Ostentation is the signal flag of hypocrisy. The charlatan is verbose and assumptive;

the Pharisee is ostentatious, because he is a hypocrite. Pride is the master sin of the devil, and the devil is the father of lies.

Edwin Hubbel Chapin

Do what good thou canst unknown, and be not vain of what ought rather to be felt than seen.

William Penn

See also: BOASTING, ORNAMENT, PRETENSION, PRIDE.

OWNERSHIP

The instinct of ownership is fundamental in man's nature.

William James

The right to possess private property is derived from nature, not from man; and the State has by no means the right to abolish it, but only to control its use and bring it into harmony with the interests of the public good.

Leo XIII (Gioacchino Vincenzo Pecci)

It is rightly contended that certain forms of property must be reserved to the State, since they carry with them an opportunity of domination too great to be left to private individuals without injury to the community at large.

Pius XI (Achille Ambrogio Damiano Ratti)

Every man holds his property subject to the general right of the community to regulate its use to whatever degree the public welfare may require it.

Theodore Roosevelt

See also: CAPITALISM, PROPERTY.

OX

The years like great black oxen tread the world,
And God the herdsman goads them on behind,
And I am broken by their passing feet.

William Butler Yeats

An ox for a penny! But what if you don't have the penny!

Yiddish Proverb

You can't get two skins off one ox.

Yiddish Proverb

See also: ANIMAL.

OXFORD

Oxford is on the whole more attractive than Cambridge to the ordinary visitor; and the traveller is therefore recommended to visit Cambridge first, or to omit it altogether if he cannot visit both.

Karl Baedeker

I speak not of this college or of that, but of the University as a whole; and, gentlemen, what a *whole* Oxford is!

Sir John Duke Coleridge

See also: EDUCATION, ENGLAND, UNIVERSITY.

P

PAIN

Pain is the outcome of sin.

Buddha

Pain is the deepest thing we have in our nature, and union through pain and suffering has always seemed more real and holy than any other.

Arthur Henry Hallam

Pain spiritualizes even beasts.

Heinrich Heine

The same refinement which brings us new pleasures, exposes us to new pains.

Edward G. Bulwer-Lytton (Baron Lytton)

Pain itself is not without its alleviations. It is seldom both violent and long-continued; and its pauses and intermissions become positive pleasures. It has the power of shedding a satisfaction over intervals of ease, which few enjoyments exceed.

William Paley

Bodily pain affects man as a whole down to the deepest layers of his moral being. It forces him to face again the fundamental questions of his fate, of his attitude toward God and fellow men, of his individual and collective responsibility and of the sense of his pilgrimage on earth.

Pius XII (Eugenio Pacelli)

. . . that anguish which lies in knowing that the creature one adores is in some place of enjoyment where oneself is not and cannot follow.

Marcel Proust

Pain and pleasure, like light and darkness, succeed each other; and he only who knows how to accommodate himself to their returns, and can wisely extract the good from the evil, knows how to live.

Laurence Sterne

Pain adds rest unto pleasure, and teaches the luxury of health.

Martin Farquhar Tupper

The only folks who give us pain are those we love the best.

Ella Wheeler Wilcox

The greatest pain is that which you can't tell others.

Yiddish Proverb

See also: AFFLICTION, DISEASE, GRIEF, MISERY, SICKNESS, SORROW, SUFFERING.

PAINTING

There is a logic of colors, and it is with this alone, and not with the logic of the brain, that the painter should conform.

Paul Cézanne

When I am finishing a picture I hold some God-made object up to it—a rock, a flower, the branch of a tree or my hand—as a kind of final test. If the painting stands up beside a thing man cannot make, the painting is authentic. If there's a clash between the two, it is bad art.

Marc Chagall

Painting is complete as a distraction. I know of nothing which, without exhausting the body, more completely absorbs the mind. Whatever the worries of the hour . . . once the picture has begun to flow along, there is no room for them. They pass out into shadows and darkness. All one's mental light . . . becomes concentrated on the task.

Sir Winston Leonard Spencer Churchill

I do not paint a portrait to look like the subject, rather does the person grow to look like his portrait.

Salvador Dali

The masters painted for joy, and knew not that virtue had gone out of them. They could not paint the like in cold blood. The masters of English lyric wrote their songs so. It was a fine efflorescence of fine powers.

Ralph Waldo Emerson

A room with pictures and a room without pictures, differ nearly as much as a room with windows and a room without windows; for pictures are loopholes of escape to the soul, leading it to other scenes and spheres, where the fancy for a moment may revel, refreshed and delighted. Pictures are consolers of loneliness, and a relief to the jaded mind, and windows to the imprisoned thought; they are books, histories, and sermons—which we can read without the trouble of turning over the leaves.

Sir John Gilbert

A picture is a poem without words.

Horace

Would that we could at once paint with the eyes! In the long way from the eye, through the arm, to the pencil, how much is lost!

Gotthold Ephraim Lessing

There is nothing more difficult for a truly creative painter than to paint a rose, because before he can do so he has first to forget all the roses that were ever painted.

Henri Matisse

There are painters who transform the sun into a yellow spot, but there are others who, thanks to their art and intelligence, transform a yellow spot into the sun.

Pablo Picasso

Style in painting is the same as in writing,—a power over materials, whether words or colors, by which conceptions or sentiments are conveyed.

Sir Joshua Reynolds

A room hung with pictures, is a room hung with thoughts.

Sir Joshua Reynolds

Every time I paint a portrait I lose a friend.

John Singer Sargent

Painting is silent poetry, and poetry is a speaking picture.

Simonides of Ceos

See also: ART, CARICATURE, CREATIVITY.

PANIC

A panic is a sudden desertion of us, and a going over to the enemy of our imagination.

Christian Nestell Bovee

Panic is the most demoralising state anyone can be in. There never is any cause for panic. One must keep heart whatever happens. War is an unmitigated evil. But it certainly does one good thing, it drives away fear and brings bravery to the surface.

Mohandas Karamchand (Mahatma) Gandhi

A panic is the stampede of our self-possession.

Antoine Rivarol

Panic is mass hysteria. And hysteria, contrary to the popular impression, is most often seen in persons superficially both cool and collected.

Philip Wylie

See also: DEPRESSION, FEAR, MOB, RIOT.

PANTHEISM

Pantheists are only Atheists ashamed.

Heinrich Heine

All are but parts of one stupendous whole, Whose body nature is, and God the soul.

Alexander Pope

He is made one with Nature: there is heard His voice in all her music, from the moan Of thunder to the song of night's sweet bird.

Percy Bysshe Shelley

See also: GOD, NATURE, OMNIPRESENCE.

PARADISE

For the pious, Paradise exists everywhere.

Benjamin Disraeli

All Indo-European antiquity had placed paradise in the beginning; all its poets had swept a vanished golden age. Israel placed the age of gold in the future.

Joseph Ernest Renan

Remembrance is the only paradise out of which we cannot be driven away. Indeed our first parents were not to be deprived of it.

Jean Paul Richter

The heathen nations have only a lost paradise behind them; the Jews have one also before them.

Johann Karl Rosenkranz

See also: ANGEL, ETERNITY, HEAVEN.

PARDON

They never pardon who commit the wrong.
John Dryden

God will pardon: that's His business.
Heinrich Heine

We pardon as long as we love.
Duc François de La Rochefoucauld

Pardon is the virtue of victory.
Giuseppe Mazzini

To pardon those absurdities in ourselves which we cannot suffer in others, is neither better nor worse than to be more willing to be fools ourselves than to have others so.
Alexander Pope

See also: CLEMENCY, FORGIVENESS, MERCY.

PARENT

The joys of parents are secret, and so are their griefs and fears.
Francis Bacon

It is the intimations of mortality, not immortality, that devastate parents in the presence of their young.
John Mason Brown

The thing that impresses me most about America is the way parents obey their children.
Edward VIII (Duke of Windsor)

Unblessed is the son who does not honor his parents; but if reverent and obedient to them, he will receive the same from his own children.
Euripides

How many hopes and fears, how many ardent wishes and anxious apprehensions are twisted together in the threads that connect the parent with the child!
Samuel Griswold Goodrich

The most important thing a father can do for his children is to love their mother.
Theodore Martin Hesburgh

When thou art contemplating some base deed, let the presence of thy infant son act as a check on thy headlong course to sin.
Juvenal

Parents wonder why the streams are bitter, when they themselves have poisoned the fountain.
John Locke

The family circle has widened. The world-pool of information fathered by electric media—movies, Telstar, flight—far surpasses any possible influence mom and dad can now bring to bear. Character no longer is shaped by only two earnest, fumbling experts. Now all the world's a sage.
(Herbert) Marshall McLuhan

When men abandon the upbringing of their children to their wives, a loss is suffered by everyone, but perhaps most of all by themselves. For what they lose is the possibility of growth in themselves for being human which the stimulation of bringing up one's children gives.
Ashley Montagu

The sacred books of the ancient Persians say: If you would be holy instruct your children, because all the good acts they perform will be imputed to you.
Charles de Secondat (Baron de Montesquieu)

Children aren't happy with nothing to ignore,
And that's what parents were created for.
Ogden Nash

What God is to the world, parents are to their children.
Philo

If parents would only realize how they bore their children!
George Bernard Shaw

The more people have studied different methods of bringing up children the more they have come to the conclusion that what good mothers and fathers instinctively feel like doing for their babies is usually best after all.
Benjamin McLane Spock

See also: ANCESTRY, BIRTH, CHILDREN, DAUGHTER, FAMILY, FATHER, MOTHER.

PARTING

In every parting there is an image of death.
George Eliot (Mary Ann Evans)

Could we see when and where we are to meet again, we would be more tender when we bid our friends good-by.
Marie Louise de la Ramée (Ouida)

Never part without loving words to think of during your absence. It may be that you will not meet again in life.
Jean Paul Richter

Alienation from self and from one's fellow men has its roots in separation from God.

Fulton John Sheen

See also: ABSENCE, FAREWELL, SOLITUDE.

PARTY

Party standards are the shadows in which patriotism is buried.

Jacques Henri Bernardin de Saint-Pierre

There is little to be expected from political parties. They are prone to subordinate everything to party success or to party expediency.

William Edgar Borah

The United States cannot successfully bring about a coalition for peace unless the two major political parties cooperate on major policies.

John Foster Dulles

If a political party does not have its foundation in the determination to advance a cause that is right and that is moral, then it is not a political party, it is merely a conspiracy, which is to seize power.

Dwight David Eisenhower

He serves his party best who serves the country best.

Rutherford Birchard Hayes

Political parties, founded as organs of the people, are becoming organs of the state, which in its turn again rules its subjects in an authoritarian fashion.

Karl Jaspers

In the Democratic party even the old seem young—but in the Republican party, even the young seem old.

Lyndon Baines Johnson

Of all kinds of credulity, the most obstinate is that of party-spirit; of men, who, being numbered, they know not why, in any party, resign the use of their own eyes and ears, and resolve to believe nothing that does not favor those whom they profess to follow.

Samuel Johnson

He knows very little of mankind, who expects, by any facts or reasoning, to convince a determined party-man.

Johann Kaspar Lavater

One thing I certainly never was made for, and that is to put principles on and off at the

dictation of a party, as a lackey changes his livery at his master's command.

Horace Mann

Party is the madness of many, for the gain of a few.

Alexander Pope

There is among you the man who is not bound by party lines. You vote according to your common sense and your calm judgment after hearing each party set forth its program. To you I say that the strength of this independent thought is the great contribution of the American political system.

Franklin Delano Roosevelt

The whole history of reparations has been a fight by the politicians to get paid, and a fight by the industrialists to prevent themselves being paid.

Josiah Charles Stamp

The man who can make two ears of corn, or two blades of grass, grow on the spot where only one grew before, would deserve better of mankind, and render more essential service to the country, than the whole race of politicians put together.

Jonathan Swift

The political parties that I would call great, are those which cling more to principles than to consequences; to general, and not to special cases; to ideas, and not to men. Such parties are usually distinguished by a nobler character, more generous passions, more genuine convictions, and a more bold and open conduct than others.

Alexis de Tocqueville

If we mean to support the liberty and independence which have cost us so much blood and treasure to establish, we must drive far away the demon of party spirit and local reproach.

George Washington

See also: DEMOCRATIC PARTY, FACTION, GOVERNMENT, REPUBLICAN PARTY.

PASSION

The passions are like fire, useful in a thousand ways and dangerous only in one, through their excess.

Christian Nestell Bovee

In doing good, we are generally cold, and languid, and sluggish; and of all things afraid of being too much in the right. But the works of malice and injustice are quite in another style. They are finished with a bold masterly hand, touched as they are with the spirit of those vehement passions that call forth all our energies whenever we oppress and persecute.

Edmund Burke

He only employs his passion who can make no use of his reason.

Cicero

What profits us, that we from heaven derive a soul immortal, and with looks erect survey the stars, if, like the brutal kind, we follow where passions lead the way?

Claudian

Our headstrong passions shut the door of our souls against God.

Confucius

An evil passion may give great physical and intellectual powers a terrible efficiency.

Charles William Eliot

Passion, though a bad regulator, is a powerful spring.

Ralph Waldo Emerson

Chastise your passions, that they may not chastise you. No one who is a lover of money, of pleasure, or of glory, is likewise a lover of mankind. Riches are not among the number of things that are good. It is not poverty that causes sorrow, but covetous desires. Deliver yourself from appetite, and you will be free. He who is discontented with things present and allotted, is unskilled in life.

Epictetus

It is the passions of men that both do and undo everything. They are the winds that are necessary to put every thing in motion, though they often cause storms.

Bernard Le Bovier de Fontenelle

Men are not blindly betrayed into corruption, but abandon themselves to their passions with their eyes open; and lose the direction of truth, because they do not attend to her voice, not because they do not understand it.

Samuel Johnson

If we resist our passions, it is more through their weakness than from our strength.

Duc François de La Rochefoucauld

He submits to be seen through a microscope, who suffers himself to be caught in a fit of passion.

Johann Kaspar Lavater

What a mistake to suppose that the passions are strongest in youth! The passions are not stronger, but the control over them is weaker! They are more easily excited, they are more violent and apparent; but they have less energy, less durability, less intense and concentrated power than in maturer life.

Edward G. Bulwer-Lytton (Baron Lytton)

The passionate are like men standing on their heads; they see all things the wrong way.

Plato

The ruling passion, be it what it will,
The ruling passion conquers reason still.

Alexander Pope

All passions are good or bad, according to their objects: where the object is absolutely good, there the greatest passion is too little; where absolutely evil, there the least passion is too much; where indifferent, there a little is enough.

Francis Quarles

The only praiseworthy indifference is an acquired one; we must feel as well as control our passions.

Jean Paul Richter

The passions of mankind are partly protective, partly beneficent, like the chaff and grain of the corn, but none without their use, none without nobleness when seen in balanced unity with the rest of the spirit which they are charged to defend.

John Ruskin

Passions make us feel, but never see clearly.
Charles de Secondat (Baron de Montesquieu)

Passion is the great mover and spring of the soul: when men's passions are strongest, they may have great and noble effects; but they are then also apt to fall into the greatest miscarriages.

Thomas Sprat

Almost all men are born with every passion to some extent, but there is hardly a man who has not a dominant passion to which the others are subordinate. Discover this governing passion in every individual; and when you have found the master passion of a man, remember never to trust to him where that passion is concerned.

Philip Dormer Stanhope (Lord Chesterfield)

Men spend their lives in the service of their passions, instead of employing their passions in the service of their life.

Sir Richard Steele

Our passions are like convulsion fits, which, though they make us stronger for the time, leave us the weaker ever after.

Jonathan Swift

The passions are the winds that fill the sails of the vessel. They sink it at times; but without them it would be impossible to make way. Many things that are dangerous here below, are still necessary.

Voltaire (François Marie Arouet)

True passion is a consuming flame, and either it must find fruition or it will burn the human heart to dust and ashes.

William Winter

See also: ANGER, DESIRE, EMOTION, ENTHUSIASM, FEELINGS, LUST, RAGE.

PASSOVER

Historically the profoundest meaning of Passover is something which sets Judaism apart from other religions. It marks the birth of a nation. Out of a mass of slaves, Moses fashioned a nation and gave them a faith. From that day to this, Jews have never ceased to be a people.

Philip Sidney Bernstein

If a poll were to be taken among Jews, Passover would be chosen the most popular festival. For, gladsome as is Purim, radiant as is Chanukah, charming as is Succos, inspiring as are the holy days, none has that combination of ceremonial loveliness, treasured family associations, springtime exuberance, hallowed national memories and hopes which are contained in Passover.

Philip Sidney Bernstein

The head of the house sits at the table and reads from a strange book called *Haggadah,* which contains a marvelous mixture of age-old legends, miracles of the Exodus, curious discussions, prayers, and festive songs. The head of the house reads this book with an old, traditional chant; time and again the others at the table join him in chorus. The

chant's melody is a fearfully hearty one; it lulls and soothes, and at the same time it rouses and calls, so that even those Jews who have long drifted from the faith of their fathers and look for strange joys and foreign honors are touched when the old, familiar Passover sounds chance to fall upon their ears.

Heinrich Heine

Passover affirms the great truth that liberty is the inalienable right of every human being.

Morris Joseph

The eight days of the festival pass by as a sweet dream. Matsoh and beet soup, dumplings and pancakes are eaten and eaten; the children play games with nuts.

Hayyim Schauss

Pesach [Passover] has had a long history and has had many evolutions in the course of its career; but it retains to this day one quality it possessed from the very beginning of time. It is a family festival. Here in America, Pesach is the holiday which unites all members of the family and brings them together at one table, at one joyful feast.

Hayyim Schauss

Pesach, usually called Passover, is first in the calendar of Jewish festivals. It is the greatest of Jewish festivals. For over two thousand years it has been more than a holiday; it has been *the* holiday, the festival of redemption.

Hayyim Schauss

These are days of freedom for the Jewish lad, days filled with longing and expectation. Indoors one is on the threshold of Pesach; outdoors on the threshold of spring. The nights are still cold, but the sun shines with increasing warmth during the day and the winter's mud slowly dries up. Mild winds caress the skin, harbingers of spring. They bring the joyful message of a world becoming youthful and green.

Hayyim Schauss

See also: HANUKKAH, ISRAEL, JUDAISM, YOM KIPPUR.

PAST

The past has little serious value save as a guide to what may come.

Brooks Adams

The present contains nothing more than the past, and what is found in the effect was already in the cause.

Henri Bergson

Many are always praising the by-gone time, for it is natural that the old should extol the days of their youth; the weak, the time of their strength; the sick, the season of their vigor; and the disappointed, the spring-tide of their hopes.

Caleb Bingham

The true past departs not; no truth or goodness realized by man ever dies, or can die; but all is still here, and, recognized or not, lives and works through endless changes.

Thomas Carlyle

Study the past if you would divine the future.

Confucius

The past is never dead. It's not even past.

William Faulkner

It is delightful to transport one's self into the spirit of the past, to see how a wise man has thought before us, and to what a glorious height we have at last reached.

Johann Wolfgang von Goethe

Nothing changes more constantly than the past; for the past that influences our lives does not consist of what actually happened, but of what men believe happened.

Gerald White Johnson

O God! Put back Thy universe and give me yesterday.

Henry Arthur Jones

It is to live twice, when we can enjoy the recollections of our former life.

Martial

Some are so very studious of learning what was done by the ancients, that they know not how to live with the moderns.

William Penn

The past—the death no one can take away from us.

Jean Rostand

Those who do not remember the past are condemned to relive it.

George Santayana

So sad, so fresh, the days that are no more.

Alfred, Lord Tennyson

We ought not to look back unless it is to derive useful lessons from past errors, and for the purpose of profiting by dear bought experience.

George Washington

There was a time when meadow, grove, and
  stream,
The earth, and every common sight,
To me did seem
Apparelled in celestial light,
The glory and the freshness of a dream.
It is not now as it hath been of yore—
Turn wheresoe'er I may,
By night or day,
The things which I have seen I now can see
  no more.

William Wordsworth

See also: ANTIQUITY, PRESENT, FUTURE, TIME.

PATIENCE

Patience is passion tamed.

Lyman Abbott

Patience is so like fortitude that she seems either her sister or her daughter.

Aristotle

Not through patience, but through impatience, are peoples liberated.

Ludwig Börne

Never think that God's delays are God's denials. Hold on; hold fast; hold out. Patience is genius.

Comte Georges Louis Leclerc de Buffon

Our patience will achieve more than our force.

Edmund Burke

It is not necessary for all men to be great in action. The greatest and sublimest power is often simple patience.

Horace Bushnell

To bear is to conquer our fate.

Thomas Campbell

Patience is power; with time and patience the mulberry leaf becomes silk.

Chinese Proverb

Patience is the art of hoping.

Luc de Clapiers (Marquis de Vauvenargues)

Patient waiting is often the highest way of doing God's will.

Jeremy Collier

Beware the fury of a patient man.

John Dryden

It's easy finding reasons why other folks should be patient.

George Eliot (Mary Ann Evans)

He that can have patience, can have what he will.

Benjamin Franklin

To lose patience is to lose the battle.

Mohandas Karamchand (Mahatma) Gandhi

There is no great achievement that is not the result of patient working and waiting.

Josiah Gilbert Holland

Lack of pep is often mistaken for patience.

Elbert Green Hubbard

He surely is most in need of another's patience, who has none of his own.

Johann Kaspar Lavater

Patience and time do more than strength or passion.

Jean de La Fontaine

To know how to wait is the great secret of success.

Joseph Marie de Maistre

They also serve who only stand and wait.

John Milton

Patience is bitter, but its fruit is sweet.

Jean Jacques Rousseau

There's no music in a "rest," but there's the making of music in it. And people are always missing that part of the life melody, always talking of perseverance and courage and fortitude; but patience is the finest and worthiest part of fortitude, and the rarest, too.

John Ruskin

Accustom yourself to that which you bear ill, and you will bear it well.

Seneca

If we could have a little patience, we should escape much mortification; time takes away as much as it gives.

Marquise de Sévigné

Everything comes if a man will only wait.

Tancred

See also: ENDURANCE, FORBEARANCE, FORTITUDE, PERSEVERANCE, WAITING.

PATRIOTISM

No man can be a patriot on an empty stomach.

William Cowper Brann

The religion of Hell is patriotism, and the government is an enlightened democracy.

James Branch Cabell

Surely the hero whose name is splashed in headlines for some singular spectacular deed of valor is not more a patriot than the unknown, steadfast citizen who year after year quietly and unselfishly benefits his nation.

Albert Carr

Bearing ourselves humbly before God, but conscious that we serve an unfolding purpose, we are ready to defend our native land.

Sir Winston Leonard Spencer Churchill

Patriotism is easy to understand in America; it means looking out for yourself by looking our for your country.

(John) Calvin Coolidge

The age of virtuous politics is past, and we are deep in that of cold pretence. Patriots are grown too shrewd to be sincere, and we too wise to trust them.

William Cowper

Of all the nations of today the future will say that there were two kinds: those that were intelligent, courageous, decisive and tireless in their support of high principle— and those that disappeared from the earth. The true patriots of today are those who are giving their best to assure that our own country will always be found in the first of these two categories.

Dwight David Eisenhower

It is tragic, indeed, when any portion of the nation's authority shows more concern for draftcard burners and unkempt demonstrators than for our brave young men who are fighting and dying on the battlefields of the world to defend and hold secure for all of us every right and privilege which free men hold dear.

Orval Eugene Faubus

There never can be any conflict between the real interest of one's country and that of one's religion. Where there appears to be any, there is something wrong with one's religion; i.e., one's morals. True religion means good thought and good conduct. True patriotism also means good thought and good conduct. To set up a comparison between two synonymous things is wrong.

Mohandas Karamchand (Mahatma) Gandhi

Of the whole sum of human life no small part is that which consists of a man's relations to his country, and his feelings concerning it.

William Ewart Gladstone

I only regret that I have but one life to lose for my country.

Nathan Hale

Our country's welfare is our first concern, and who promotes that best, best proves his duty.

William Havard

It seems like the less a statesman amounts to, the more he loves the flag.

Frank McKinney (Kin) Hubbard

Patriotism is the last refuge of a scoundrel!

Samuel Johnson

Ask not what your country can do for you: Ask what you can do for your country.

John Fitzgerald Kennedy

With a good conscience our only sure reward, with history the final judge of our deeds, let us go forth to lead the land we love, asking His blessing and His help, but knowing that here on earth God's work must truly be our own.

John Fitzgerald Kennedy

Patriotism like love is a most imperfect passion.

(Nicholas) Vachel Lindsay

Duty, honor, country: Those three hallowed words reverently dictate what you ought to be, what you can be, what you will be. They are your rallying point to build courage when courage seems to fail, to regain faith when there seems to be little cause for faith, to create hope when hope becomes forlorn.

Douglas MacArthur

Let all parties perish, ours along with the others, so long as our country is safe.

Benito Mussolini

When the nation is in peril, the first duty of every citizen is to give his or her service to the nation without fear or expectation of reward.

Jawaharlal Nehru

If patriotism is "the last refuge of a scoundrel," it is not merely because evil deeds may be performed in the *name* of patriotism, . . . but because patriotic fervor can obliterate moral distinctions altogether.

Ralph Barton Perry

Those who have not risen to the level of patriotism are not likely to rise to higher levels.

Ralph Barton Perry

Cut an American into a hundred pieces and boil him down, you will find him all Fourth of July.

Wendell Phillips

Millions for defence, but not one cent for tribute.

Charles Cotesworth Pinckney

A man's feet must be planted in his country, but his eyes should survey the world.

George Santayana

Breathes there the man with soul so dead,
Who never to himself hath said,
This is my own, my native land!

Sir Walter Scott

Patriotism is your conviction that this country is superior to all other countries because you were born in it.

George Bernard Shaw

You'll never have a quiet world till you knock the patriotism out of the human race.

George Bernard Shaw

The proper means of increasing the love we bear to our native country, is to reside some time in a foreign one.

William Shenstone

For a man to love his country truly, he must also know how to love mankind, and this love must be the sustaining force in the search for world order.

Adlai Ewing Stevenson

The real patriots are those who love America as she is, but who want the beloved to be more lovable. This is not treachery. This, as every parent, every teacher, every friend must know, is the truest and noblest affection.

Adlai Ewing Stevenson

After what I owe to God, nothing should be more dear or more sacred than the love and respect I owe to my country.

François Auguste de Thou

National enthusiasm is the great nursery of genius.

Henry Theodore Tuckerman

The noblest motive is the public good.

Virgil

Let our object be our country, our whole country, and nothing but our country. And, by the blessing of God, may that country itself become a vast and splendid monument, not of oppression and terror, but of wisdom, of peace, and of liberty, upon which the world may gaze with admiration forever.

Daniel Webster

Liberty and union, now and forever, one and inseparable.

Daniel Webster

Patriotism is the finest flower of western civilization as well as the refuge of the scoundrel.

Leonard Sydney Woolf

Patriotism is not, as sentimentalists like to assert, one of the profoundest of man's noblest instincts.

Ida Alexa Ross Wylie

See also: CITIZENSHIP, DUTY, FATHERLAND, HERO, NATION, SOLDIER, WAR.

PEACE

Peace is positive, and it has to be waged with all our thought, energy, and courage and with the conviction that war is not inevitable.

Dean Gooderham Acheson

I am not very keen for doves or hawks. I think we need more owls.

George Aiken

Antarctica shall be used for peaceful purposes only. There shall be prohibited, *inter alia*, any measure of a military nature, such as the establishment of military bases and fortifications, the carrying out of military maneuvers, as well as the testing of any type of weapons [Article 1].

Antarctica Pact

I believe it is peace for our time . . . peace with honour.

Neville Chamberlain

After the end of the World War of 1914 there was a deep conviction and almost universal hope that peace would reign in the world. This heart's desire of all the peoples could easily have been gained by steadfastness in righteous convictions, and by reasonable common sense and prudence.

Sir Winston Leonard Spencer Churchill

In this solemn hour it is a consolation to recall and dwell upon our repeated efforts for peace. All have been ill-starred, but all have been faithful and sincere. This is of the highest moral value.

Sir Winston Leonard Spencer Churchill

Peace rules the day, where reason rules the mind.

Wilkie Collins

No world settlement that affords nations only a place on relief rolls will provide the basis for a just and durable peace.

William Orville Douglas

Peace cannot be kept by force. It can only be achieved by understanding.

Albert Einstein

Especially important it is to realize that there can be no assured peace and tranquility for any one nation except as it is achieved for all. So long as want, frustration, and a sense of injustice prevail among significant sections of earth, no other section can be wholly released from fear.

Dwight David Eisenhower

I have said time and again there is no place on this earth to which I would not travel, there is no chore I would not undertake if I had any faintest hope that, by so doing, I would promote the general cause of world peace.

Dwight David Eisenhower

Nothing can bring you peace but yourself; nothing can bring you peace but the triumph of principles.

Ralph Waldo Emerson

Only the just man enjoys peace of mind.

Epicurus

Universal peace will be realized, not because man will become better, but because a new order of things, a new science, new economic necessities, will impose peace.

Anatole France

Each one has to find his peace from within. And peace to be real must be unaffected by outside circumstances.

Mohandas Karamchand (Mahatma) Gandhi

The way of peace is the way of truth. Truthfulness is even more important than peacefulness.

Mohandas Karamchand (Mahatma) Gandhi

The way to peace in this turbulent age is to keep to that national vision, to work with all our might for the establishment of a structure of law that will be reliable and just to all nations. For though law alone cannot assure world peace, there can be no peace without it. Our national power and all our energies should operate in the light of that truth. Power not ruled by law is a menace, but law not served by power is a delusion.

Arthur J. Goldberg

Peace is to be desired, and is blessed when it secures us from the suspicions of our neighbours, does not add to our danger, when it leads men to rest in quiet, and lessens their expenses; but when the very opposite of all this takes place, it is then, under the treacherous name of peace, nothing else than destructive war, it is under the name of healthful medicine deadly poison.

Francesco Guicciardini

Peace is such a precious jewel that I would give anything for it but truth.

Matthew Henry

Peace has its victories no less than war, but it doesn't have as many monuments to unveil.

Frank McKinney (Kin) Hubbard

The door of peace must be kept wide open for all who wish to avoid the scourge of war, but the door of agression must be closed and bolted if man is to survive.

Lyndon Baines Johnson

If we cannot end our differences, at least we can help make the world safe for diversity. For, in the final analysis, our most basic common link is that we all inhabit this small planet. We all breathe the same air. We all cherish our children's future. And we are all mortal.

John Fitzgerald Kennedy

Never have the nations of the world had so much to lose or so much to gain. Together we shall save our planet or together we shall perish in its flames. Save it we can and save it we must, and then shall we earn the eternal thanks of mankind and, as peacemakers, the eternal blessing of God.

John Fitzgerald Kennedy

Where nature makes natural allies of us all, we can demonstrate that beneficial relations are possible even with those with whom we most deeply disagree, and this must someday be the basis of world peace and world law.

John Fitzgerald Kennedy

The currency with which you pay for peace is made up of manly courage, fearless virility, readiness to serve justice and honor at any cost, and a mind and a heart attuned to sacrifice.

William Franklin (Frank) Knox

I am a man of peace. God knows how I love peace. But I hope I shall never be such a coward as to mistake oppression for peace.

Lajos Kossuth

When we do not find peace within ourselves, it is vain to seek for it elsewhere.

Duc François de La Rochefoucauld

There is always a bond of peace that is both permanent and enriching; the increasing knowledge of the world in which experiment occurs.

Walter Lippmann

Peace is indivisible.

Maksim Maksimovich Litvinov

The responsibility for making peace rests, above all, on the country that is most nearly normal as the war ends.

Anne O'Hare McCormick

If man does find the solution for world peace it will be the most revolutionary reversal of his record we have ever known.

George Catlett Marshall

Peace hath her victories, no less renowned than war.

John Milton

If nations could overcome the mutual fear and distrust whose somber shadow is now thrown over the world, and could meet with confidence and good will to settle their possible differences, they would easily be able to establish a lasting peace.

Fridtjof Nansen

If they want peace, nations should avoid the pin-pricks that precede cannon-shots.

Napoleon I (Bonaparte)

The man who has got everything he wants is all in favour of peace and order.

Jawaharlal Nehru

Peace cannot suddenly descend from the heavens. It can only come when the root-causes of trouble are removed.

Jawaharlal Nehru

May we be permitted to express the hope that this truce become an armistice, and that the armistice be the occasion for sincere negotiations, negotiations which will lead to peace [in Vietnam].

Paul VI (Giovanni Battista Montini)

Peace in the present time is based more on fear than on friendship. It is maintained more by terror of deadly weapons than by mutual harmony and faith among peoples. And if tomorrow peace were broken—God forbid—all humanity could be destroyed.

Paul VI (Giovanni Battista Montini)

True peace is not that hypocritical propaganda aimed at lulling the adversary to sleep and concealing one's own preparation for war. Peace does not consist in pacifist rhetoric that refuses the indispensable, patient, and which tiresome negotiations are the only efficacious means.

It is not based merely on the precarious balance of opposing economic interests, nor on the dream of proud supremacy. But true peace is based on the abolition, or at least on the mitigation, of the causes that endanger its security, as nationalistic or ideological pride, the arms race, lack of confidence in

the methods or in the organizations that have been constituted to render the relations among nations orderly and friendly.

Peace in truth, in justice, in freedom, in love—this is the peace we pray for.

Paul VI (Giovanni Battista Montini)

True peace . . . is still the result of the harmony built into human society by its Divine Founder, and which can be realized by men as they thirst for ever greater justice, based on the firm determination to respect the liberty and dignity of men and people.

Paul VI (Giovanni Battista Montini)

Five great enemies to peace inhabit with us: viz., avarice, ambition, envy, anger, and pride. If those enemies were to be banished, we should infallibly enjoy perpetual peace.

Petrarch

The blame for the danger to world peace lies not in the world population but in the political leaders of that population.

Franklin Delano Roosevelt

More than an end to war, we want an end to the beginnings of all wars—yes, an end to this brutal, inhuman and thoroughly impractical method of settling the differences between governments.

Franklin Delano Roosevelt

We can gain no lasting peace if we approach it with suspicion and mistrust—or with fear.

Franklin Delano Roosevelt

We have learned that we cannot live alone, at peace; that our own well-being is dependent upon the well-being of other nations, far away.

Franklin Delano Roosevelt

Peace is rarely denied to the peaceful.

Johann Christoph Friedrich von Schiller

We do hope and pray, through the valor, the dedication, the service of our men and women of our armed forces, we shall soon have the victory for which all of us in Vietnam and all over the world are praying and hoping; for less than victory is inconceivable.

Francis Joseph Spellman

Lovely concord and most sacred peace doth nourish virtue, and fast friendship breed.

Edmund Spenser

If any foreign minister begins to defend to the death a "peace conference" you can be sure his Government has already placed its orders for new battleships and airplanes.

Joseph Stalin

Peace is the one condition of survival in this nuclear age.

Adlai Ewing Stevenson

The alternative to peace is not war. It is annihilation.

Raymond Gram Swing

We realize that the peace we enjoy is the absence of war, rather than the presence of confidence, understanding and generous conduct.

Raymond Gram Swing

Christ preached peace when he preached love, when he preached the oneness of the Father with the brothers who are many. And this was the truth of peace. Christ never held that peace was the best policy. For policy is not truth.

Sir Rabindranath Tagore

They have not wanted Peace at all; they have wanted to be spared war—as though the absence of war was the same as peace.

Dorothy Thompson

Peace is the happy, natural state of man; war, his corruption, his disgrace.

James Thomson

Peace has to be built on power for good. Justice and good will and good deeds are not enough.

Harry S Truman

I am convinced that if peace were soon restored there would be a rebirth of faith in our ability to promote the well-being of all.

U Thant

Is it too much to hope that what is made possible for just a couple of days by the occurrence of common holidays, may soon prove feasible for a longer period by the new commitments that peace requires, so that an atmosphere may be created which is necessary for meaningful talks to be held in the quest for a peaceful solution?

U Thant

With peace in crime, ah! who can flatter himself?

Voltaire (François Marie Arouet)

If peace is the overriding concern of the human race, we ought to be willing to bend our best energies and intellect to a consideration of how the ethical insights of each nation are translated into a charter of peace for all nations.

Earl Warren

To be prepared for war is one of the most effectual means of preserving peace.

George Washington

It must be a peace without victory. Only a peace between equals can last: only a peace, the very principle of which is equality, and a common participation in a common benefit.

(Thomas) Woodrow Wilson

See also: ORDER, QUIET, PEACE CORPS, UNITED NATIONS, WAR.

PEACE CORPS

As volunteer services become more universal, the status of persons who have completed tours becomes more significant. Certainly the record of the Peace Corps shows that this experience leads to profound career changes and, in an impressive number of cases, a lifetime now devoted to service.

Robert Calvert, Jr.

The Congress of the United States declares that it is the policy of the United States and the purpose of this Act to promote world peace and friendship through a Peace Corps, which shall make available to interested countries and areas men and women of the United States qualified for service abroad and willing to serve, under conditions of hardship if necessary, to help the peoples of such countries and areas in meeting their needs for trained manpower, and to help promote a better understanding of the American people on the part of the peoples served and a better understanding of other peoples on the part of the American people. [Public Law 87-283; 87th Congress, H.R. 7500; September 22; Stat. 612. "Declaration of Purpose".]

Eighty-Seventh Congress, 1961

No group, no organization, contributes more to the cause of peace, in my judgment, than the Peace Corps.

Lyndon Baines Johnson

The Peace Corps is the point of the lance. In Latin America, it is the human cutting edge of the Alliance for Progress, the focus of ideas and people in action.

Jack Hood Vaughn

Fortunately, not many people took the Peace Corps seriously during its first five years. . . . In the American mind, it took its place somewhere between the boy scouts and motherhood. Overseas, it was generally seen either as a peculiar but relatively benevolent combination of propaganda and charity, somewhat galling but to be accepted and put to use, or as a special scheme of John F. Kennedy, therefore to be respected.

Harris Llewellyn Wofford, Jr.

The Peace Corps is, perhaps, more alive than any other government bureaucracy because it is, in fact, comprised of ten to fifteen thousand Volunteers, who bring to the Peace Corps the same challenge and independence that they bring to the host countries.

Harris Llewellyn Wofford, Jr.

The Peace Corps was permitted to go its own way, to experiment and to find itself, to grow up with a freedom probably unique in the history of bureaucracies. It has even been described as an antibureaucratic bureaucracy, an organization for those who do not want to be organization men.

Harris Llewellyn Wofford, Jr.

See also: AMERICA, FOREIGN AID, PEACE.

PEDANTRY

A man who has been brought up among books, and is able to talk of nothing else, is a very indifferent companion, and what we call a pedant. But we should enlarge the title, and give it to every one that does not know how to think out of his profession and particular way of life.

Joseph Addison

Brimful of learning, see the pedant stride,
Bristling with horrid Greek, and puffed with pride!
A thousand authors he in vain has read,
And with their maxims stuffed his empty head;
And thinks that without Aristotle's rules,
Reason is blind, and common sense a fool!

Nicolas Boileau-Despréaux

Pedantry crams our heads with learned lumber, and takes out our brains to make room for it.

Charles Caleb Colton

Pedantry and bigotry are millstones, able to sink the best book which carries the least part of their dead weight. The temper of the pedagogue suits not with the age; and the world, however it may be taught, will not be tutored.

Anthony Ashley Cooper (Lord Shaftesbury)

Pedantry, in the common acceptation of the word, means an absurd ostentation of learning, and stiffness of phraseology, proceeding from a misguided knowledge of books, and a total ignorance of men.

Henry Mackenzie

Deep versed in books, and shallow in himself.

John Milton

Diligent as one must be in learning, one must be as diligent in forgetting; otherwise the process is one of pedantry, not culture.

Albert Jay Nock

The boastful blockhead ignorantly read,
With loads of learned lumber in his head.

Alexander Pope

A well-read fool is the most pestilent of blockheads; his learning is a flail which he knows how to handle, and with which he breaks his neighbor's shins as well as his own. Keep a fellow of this description at arm's length, as you value the integrity of your bones.

Stanislas I (Leszczyński)

The most annoying of all blockheads is a well-read fool.

Bayard Taylor

See also: BORE, KNOWLEDGE, OSTENTATION.

PEN

Scholars are men of peace; they bear no arms, but their tongues are sharper than the sword; their pens carry further and give a louder report than thunder. I had rather stand in the shock of a basilisk than in the fury of a merciless pen.

Sir Thomas Browne

Oh, nature's noblest gift,—my gray goose-quill!

George Gordon Byron (Lord Byron)

Take away the sword; states can be saved without it; bring the pen!

Edward G. Bulwer-Lytton (Baron Lytton)

There are only two powers in the world, the sword and the pen; and in the end the former is always conquered by the latter.

Napoleon I (Bonaparte)

Consider a pen. . . . It comes new and shining into your hand. It gets blackened working for you. You let it rust, And when it is worn out and can no longer serve you, you discard it with scorn. Remarkable, is it not? A pen has about the same fate as a good servant of the rich, or as a laborer in a factory.

Morris Winchevesky

See also: AUTHORSHIP, NOVELIST, POET.

PENANCE

Penances with me are no mechanical acts. They are done in obedience to the Inner Voice.

Mohandas Karamchand (Mahatma) Gandhi

Quoth he, "The man hath penance done,
And penance more will do."

Samuel Taylor Coleridge

When the scourge
Inexorably, and the torturing hour
Calls us to penance.

John Milton

See also: RETRIBUTION, SUFFERING.

PEOPLE

When dealing with people, remember you are not dealing with creatures of logic, but with creatures of emotion, creatures bristling with prejudice and motivated by pride and vanity.

Dale Carnegie

There are three kinds of people in the world, the wills, the wont's and the can'ts. The first accomplish everything; the second oppose everything; the third fail in everything.

Eclectic Magazine

He who uses the word people refers to more than one thing; it is a vast expression, and one would be astonished to see what it embraces, and how far it extends. There is the people opposed to the great,—that is the populace and the many: there is the people opposed to the wise, the able, the virtuous,—these include the great as well as the little.

Jean de La Bruyère

Most people judge others either by the company they keep, or by their fortune.

Duc François de La Rochefoucauld

You may deceive all the people part of the time, and part of the people all the time, but not all the people all the time.

Abraham Lincoln

The world may be divided into people that read, people that write, people that think, and fox-hunters.

William Shenstone

Local assemblies of the people constitute the strength of free nations. Municipal institutions are to liberty, what primary schools are to science: they bring it within the people's reach, and teach them how to use and enjoy it. A nation may establish a system of free government, but without the spirit of municipal institutions it cannot have the spirit of liberty.

Alexis de Tocqueville

See also: CROWD, MAN, MOB, POPULACE.

PERCEPTION

Make a point never so clear, and it is great odds that a man whose habits, and the bent of whose mind lie a contrary way shall be unable to comprehend it;—so weak a thing is reason in competition with inclination.

George Berkeley

To see what is right, and not do it, is want of courage, or of principle.

Confucius

Penetration seems a kind of inspiration; it gives me an idea of prophecy.

Fulke Greville (First Baron Brooke)

Simple creatures, whose thoughts are not taken up, like those of educated people, with the care of a great museum of dead phrases, are very quick to see the live facts which are going on about them.

Oliver Wendell Holmes

The clearsighted do not rule the world, but they sustain and console it.

Agnes Repplier

The dullest man sees the most things as the same; the livest man sees the most differences, and a completely live man tends . . . to find in even random objects a precious order and degree of being, as if the universe were here only that it might contain them.

Mark Van Doren

See also: APPRECIATION, DISCERNMENT, JUDG-
MENT, OBSERVATION, POINT OF VIEW,
UNDERSTANDING.

PERFECTION

This is the very perfection of a man, to find out his own imperfection.

Augustine of Hippo

Bachelor's wives and old maid's children are always perfect.

Sébastien Roch Nicolas Chamfort

To arrive at perfection, a man should have very sincere friends or inveterate enemies; because he would be made sensible of his good or ill conduct, either by the censures of the one or the admonitions of the other.

Diogenes

Among the other excellencies of man, this is one, that he can form the image of perfection much beyond what he has experience of in himself, and is not limited in his conception of wisdom and virtue.

David Hume

It is reasonable to have perfection in our eye that we may always advance toward it, though we know it can never be reached.

Samuel Johnson

Perfection does not exist; to understand it is the triumph of human intelligence; to expect to possess it is the most dangerous kind of madness.

(Louis Charles) Alfred de Musset

He that seeks perfection on earth leaves nothing new for the saints to find in heaven; as long as men teach, there will be mistakes in divinity; and as long as they govern, errors in state.

Francis Osborn

Faultily faultless, icily regular, splendidly null, dead perfection; no more.

Alfred, Lord Tennyson

Perfection is attained by slow degrees; it requires the hand of time.

Voltaire (François Marie Arouet)

See also: EXCELLENCE, GOODNESS, IDEAL.

PERFUME

A woman smells best when she hath no perfume at all.

Robert Burton

I counted two-and-seventy stenches,
All well defined, and several stinks. . . .
The river Rhine, it is well known,
Doth wash your city of Cologne;
But tell me, nymphs! what power divine
Shall henceforth wash the river Rhine?

Samuel Taylor Coleridge

Perfumes are the feelings of flowers.

Heinrich Heine

See also: DRESS, ORNAMENT, WOMAN.

PERSECUTION

Persecution is a bad and indirect way to plant religion.

Sir Thomas Browne

In all places, and in all times, those religionists who have believed too much, have been more inclined to violence and persecution than those who have believed too little.

Charles Caleb Colton

Persistent people begin their success where others end in failure.

Edward Eggleston

The way of the world is, to praise dead saints, and persecute living ones.

Nathaniel Howe

Wherever you see persecution, there is more than a probability that truth is on the persecuted side.

Hugh Latimer

There is nothing more unreasonable, more inconsistent with the rights of human nature, more contrary to the spirit and precepts of the Christian religion, more iniquitous and unjust, more impolitic, than persecution. It is against natural religion, against revealed religion, and against sound policy.

William Murray (Lord Mansfield)

We cannot drive scientists into our laboratories, but, if we tolerate reckless or unfair attacks, we can certainly drive them out.

Harry S Truman

Persecution is not wrong because it is cruel, but cruel because it is wrong.

Richard Whately

See also: ANTI-SEMITISM, OPPRESSION, RACISM, SLAVERY, TYRANNY.

PERSEVERANCE

The difference between perseverance and obstinacy is, that one often comes from a strong will, and the other from a strong won't.

Henry Ward Beecher

We make way for the man who boldly pushes past us.

Christian Nestell Bovee

Persistence is a great and necessary virtue.

Louis Dembitz Brandeis

By gnawing through a dyke, even a rat may drown a nation.

Edmund Burke

Every noble work is at first impossible.

Thomas Carlyle

We shall not fail or falter; we shall not weaken or tire. Neither the sudden shock of battle, nor the long-drawn trials of vigilance and exertion will wear us down. Give us the tools, and we will finish the job.

Sir Winston Leonard Spencer Churchill

Perpetual pushing and assurance put a difficulty out of countenance, and make a seeming impossibility give way.

Jeremy Collier

Perseverance and audacity generally win.

Madame Dorothée Deluzy

Glory lies in the attempt to reach one's goal and not in reaching it.

Mohandas Karamchand (Mahatma) Gandhi

Perseverance opens up treasures which bring perennial joy.

Mohandas Karamchand (Mahatma) Gandhi

Perseverance is the most overrated of traits, if it is unaccompanied by talent; beating your head against a wall is more likely to produce a concussion in the head than a hole in the wall.

Sydney Justin Harris

There is no royal road to anything. One thing at a time, and all things in succession. That which grows slowly endures.

Josiah Gilbert Holland

There is no failure except in no longer trying. There is no defeat except from within, no really insurmountable barrier save our own inherent weakness of purpose.

Elbert Green Hubbard

The heights by great men reached and kept
  Were not attained by sudden flight,
But they, while their companions slept,
  Were toiling upward in the night.

Henry Wadsworth Longfellow

The falling drops at last will wear the stone.

Lucretius

The virtue lies in the struggle, not in the prize.

Richard Monckton Milnes

Victory belongs to the most persevering.

Napoleon I (Bonarparte)

Some men give up their designs when they have almost reached the goal; while others, on the contrary, obtain a victory by exerting, at the last moment, more vigorous efforts than before.

Polybius

No rock so hard but that a little wave may beat admission in a thousand years.

Alfred, Lord Tennyson

Hard pounding, gentlemen; but we will see who can pound the longest.

Arthur Wellesley (First Duke Wellington)

Even in social life, it is persistency which attracts confidence more than talents and accomplishments.

Henry Benjamin Whipple

See also: CONSTANCY, ENDURANCE, LABOR, RESOLUTION, WORK.

PERSONALITY

If you have anything really valuable to contribute to the world it will come through the expression of your own personality—that single spark of divinity that sets you off and makes you different from every other living creature.

Bruce Barton

Everyone is a moon, and has a dark side which he never shows to anybody.

Samuel Langhorne Clemens (Mark Twain)

It is the hard environment that develops personality.

Sir Wilfred Thomason Grenfell

Man must build his culture about the complete human personality. . . . Whatever nourishes the personality, humanizes it, refines it, deepens it, intensifies its aptitude and broadens its field of action is good; whatever limits it or thwarts it, whatever sends it back into tribal patterns and limits its capacity for human co-operation and communion must be counted as bad.

Lewis Mumford

Personality is to man what perfume is to a flower.

Charles M. Schwab

See also: CHARACTER, INDIVIDUALITY.

PERVERSENESS

Some men, like spaniels, will only fawn the more when repulsed, but will pay little heed to a friendly caress.

Abd-el-Kader

Stiff in opinion; always in the wrong.

John Dryden

Some men put me in mind of half-bred horses, which often grow worse in proportion as you feed and exercise them for improvement.

Fulke Greville (First Baron Brooke)

We have all a propensity to grasp at forbidden fruit.

Latin Proverb

The worst things are the perversions of good things. Abused intellectual gifts make the dangerous villain; abused sensibilities make the accomplished tempter; abused affections engender the keenest of all misery.

James McCosh

So remarkably perverse is the nature of man, that he despises those that court him, and admires whoever will not bend before him.

Thucydides

See also: DISOBEDIENCE, WICKEDNESS.

PESSIMISM

A pessimist is one who feels bad when he feels good for fear he'll feel worse when he feels better.

Anonymous

The optimist proclaims that we live in the best of all possible worlds; and the pessimist fears this is so.

James Branch Cabell

Away with pessimism! Let us work at whatsoever is pure, whatsoever is constructive, and not parade our failings and our sins.

Sir Wilfred Thomason Grenfell

Cheer up, the worst is yet to come.

Philander Chase Johnson

It is folly to be merely optimistic and not to see facts as they are. But it is at least as great folly to be pessimistic and imagine all kinds of evil happenings overtaking us.

Jawaharlal Nehru

My pessimism goes to the point of suspecting the sincerity of the pessimists.

Edmond Rostand

A pessimist is a man who thinks everybody as nasty as himself, and hates them for it.

George Bernard Shaw

See also: CYNICISM, DESPAIR, MOROSENESS.

PHILANTHROPY

Philanthropy is an American habit and the modern foundation is an American invention. To make human beings healthier, happier, wiser, more conscious of the rich possibilities of human existence and more capable of realizing them.

Charles Dollard

Not for himself, but for the world he lives.

Lucan

Where there is the most love to God, there will be there the truest and most enlarged philanthropy.

Robert Southey

See also: BENEFICIENCE, CHARITY, GENEROSITY, GOODNESS, HELP.

PHILISTINISM

Philistine must have originally meant, in the mind of those who invented the nickname, a strong, dogged, unenlightened opponent of the chosen people, of the children of the light.

Matthew Arnold

Philistinism!—We have not the expression in English. Perhaps we have not the word because we have so much of the thing.

Matthew Arnold

See also: VULGARITY.

PHILOSOPHER

A "new thinker," when studied closely, is merely a man who does not know what other people have thought.

Frank Moore Colby

The first business of a philosopher is, to part with self-conceit.

Epictetus

To ridicule philosophy, that is really to act the philosopher.

Blaise Pascal

Between the laughing and the weeping philosopher there is no opposition: *the same facts* that make one laugh make one weep. No whole-hearted man, no sane art, can be limited to either mood.

George Santayana

The philosopher is Nature's pilot. And there you have our difference: to be in hell is to drift: to be in heaven is to steer.

George Bernard Shaw

To be a philosopher is not merely to have subtle thoughts; but so to love wisdom as to live according to its dictates.

Henry David Thoreau

The besetting sin of philosophers is that, being men, they endeavor to survey the universe from the standpoint of gods.

Alfred North Whitehead

See also: LIFE, PHILOSOPHY.

PHILOSOPHY

Philosophy: unintelligible answers to insoluble problems.

Henry Brooks Adams

A philosophic attitude towards the problems of life can alone save us from the perils of an easy, seductive, and false dogmatism, whether it be of theology, science, economics, politics, or anything else.

James Truslow Adams

Philosophy is the science which considers truth.

Aristotle

Philosophy, when superficially studied, excites doubt; when thoroughly explored, it dispels it.

Francis Bacon

Philosophy is a proud, sullen detector of the poverty and misery of man. It may turn him from the world with a proud, sturdy contempt; but it cannot come forward and say, here are rest, grace, pardon, peace, strength, and consolation.

Richard Cecil

A small inkling of philosophy leads man to despise learning; much philosophy leads man to esteem it.

Sébastien Roch Nicolas Chamfort

Philosophy, if rightly defined, is nothing but the love of wisdom.

Cicero

To study philosophy is nothing but to prepare one's self to die.

Cicero

It is not a head merely, but a heart and resolution, which complete the real philosopher.

Anthony Ashley Cooper (Lord Shaftesbury)

True philosophy invents nothing; it merely establishes and describes what is.

Victor Cousin

To be a husbandman, is but a retreat from the city; to be a philosopher, from the world; or rather a retreat from the world as it is man's, into the world as it is God's.

Abraham Cowley

The chief intellectual characteristic of the present age is its despair of any constructive philosophy.

John Dewey

The moment philosophy supposes it can find a final and comprehensive solution, it ceases to be inquiry and becomes bitter apologetics or propaganda.

John Dewey

Philosophy recovers itself when it ceases to be the device for dealing with the problems of philosophers and becomes the method, cultivated by philosophers for dealing with the problems of men.

John Dewey

Philosophy is as far separated from impiety as religion is from fanaticism.

Denis Diderot

All philosophy worthy of the name will be found first of all to be an answer to the fundamental questions which man asks about himself or about the world, and, in the second place, will be found not to require more intellectual effort than poetry.

Ernest Dimnet

That philosophy, or reflection, should begin with Man is natural, for we are conscious of ourselves before being conscious of anything else.

Ernest Dimnet

Christianity is a philosophy of principles rather than of rules and so is fitted for universal extension and acceptance.

Tryon Edwards

All philosophy lies in two words, sustain and abstain.

Epictetus

Philosophy goes no further than probabilities, and in every assertion keeps a doubt in reserve.

James Anthony Froude

Philosophy triumphs easily over past and over future evils, but present evils triumph over philosophy.

Duc François de La Rochefoucauld

Philosophy consists largely of one philosopher arguing that all others are jackasses. He usually proves it, and I should add that he also usually proves that he is one himself.

Henry Louis Mencken

Admiration is the foundation of all philosophy; investigation the progress; and ignorance the end.

Michel Eyquem de Montaigne

Philosophy has been called the knowledge of our knowledge; it might more truly be called the knowledge of our ignorance, or in the language of Kant, the knowledge of the limits of our knowledge.

Friedrich Max Müller

Inertia rides and riddles me;
The which is called philosophy.

Dorothy Parker

Philosophy is the art of living.

Plutarch

I should never trust a system into which all the facts could be fitted—nor should I think any better of one that couldn't admit them all.

Jean Rostand

It is the bounty of nature that we live, but of philosophy, that we live well; which is, in truth, a greater benefit than life itself.

Seneca

Philosophy is the art and law of life, and it teaches us what to do in all cases, and, like good marksmen, to hit the white at any distance.

Seneca

Philosophy hath given us several plausible rules for attaining peace and tranquillity of mind, but they fall very much short of bringing men to it.

John Tillotson

He who seeks philosophy in divinity, seeks the dead among the living; and he that seeks divinity in philosophy, seeks the living among the dead.

Ralph Venning

The discovery of what is true, and the practice of that which is good, are the two most important objects of philosophy.

Voltaire (François Marie Arouet)

Philosophy is the attempt to make manifest the fundamental evidence as to the nature of things.

Alfred North Whitehead

Philosophy may teach us to bear with equanimity the misfortunes of our neighbors.

Oscar Wilde

No stream rises higher than its source. Whatever man might build could never express or reflect more than he was. It was no more than what he felt. He could record neither more nor less than he had learned of life when the buildings were built. . . . His philosophy, true or false, is there.

Frank Lloyd Wright

See also: BELIEF, LOGIC, METAPHYSICS, PHILOS-
OPHER, REASON, SPECULATION, STOI-
CISM, THEORY.

PHYSICIAN: *see* DOCTOR.

PIETY

All is vanity which is not honest, and there is no solid wisdom but in true piety.
John Evelyn

Let us learn upon earth, those things which can prepare us for heaven.
Jerome (Eusebius Hieronymus)

I do not doubt but that genuine piety is the spring on peace of mind: it enables us to bear the sorrows of life, and lessens the pangs of death: the same cannot be said of hypocrisy.
Jean de La Bruyère

Among the many strange servilities mistaken for pieties one of the least lovely is that which hopes to flatter God by despising the world and villifying human nature.
George Henry Lewes

Piety is the only proper and adequate relief of decaying man. He that grows old without religious hopes, as he declines into imbecility, and feels pains and sorrows crowding upon him, falls into a gulf of bottomless misery, in which every reflection must plunge him deeper and deeper.
Samuel Johnson

See also: DEVOTION, HOLINESS, PRAYER, RELIGION, SAINT, WORSHIP.

PITY

Pity makes the world soft to the weak and noble for the strong.
Sir Edwin Arnold

Of all the paths that lead to a woman's love, pity is the straightest.
Francis Beaumont and John Fletcher

Pity is best taught by fellowship in woe.
Samuel Taylor Coleridge

Let no one underestimate the need of pity. We live in a stony universe whose hard, brilliant forces rage fiercely.
Theodore Dreiser

It is through pity that we remain truly a man.
Anatole France

Pity is not natural to man. Children and savages are always cruel. Pity is acquired and improved by the cultivation of reason. We may have uneasy sensations from seeing a creature in distress, without pity; but we have not pity unless we wish to relieve him. When I am on my way to dine with a friend, and, finding it late, bid the coachman make haste, when he whips his horses I may feel unpleasantly that the animals are put to pain, but I do not wish him to desist; no, sir, I wish him to drive on.
Samuel Johnson

Pity is the feeling which arrests the mind in the presence of whatsoever is grave and constant in human sufferings and unites it with the human sufferer.
James Joyce

Pity's a scent sachet that serves to stop your nose.
Jules Romains

It is not in man to put himself in the place of people who are more happy than he is, but only of those who are more to be pitied.
Jean Jacques Rousseau

We pity in others only those evils which we have ourselves experienced.
Jean Jacques Rousseau

Pity, more than any other feeling, is a "learned" emotion; a child will have it least of all. Pity comes from infinite accumulations of man's memory, from the angiush, pain, and suffering of life, from the full deposit of experience, from the forgotten faces, the lost men, and from the million strange and haunting visages of time.
Thomas Clayton Wolfe

See also: COMPASSION, KINDNESS, MERCY.

PLACE

Whatever the place allotted to us by Providence, that for us is the post of honor and duty. God estimates us not by the position we are in, but by the way in which we fill it.
Tryon Edwards

Where you are is of no moment, but only what you are doing there. It is not the place that ennobles you, but you the place; and this only by doing that which is great and noble.
Petrarch

He who thinks his place below him, will certainly be below his place.

John Faucit Saville

See also: OFFICE, RANK, STATION, TITLE.

PLAGIARISM

They lard their lean books with the fat of others' works.

Robert Burton

Plagiarists are always suspicious of being stolen from.

Samuel Taylor Coleridge

If we steal thoughts from the moderns, it will be cried down as plagiarism; if from the ancients, it will be cried up as erudition. But in this respect every author is a Spartan, more ashamed of the discovery than of the depredation.

Charles Caleb Colton

Most plagiarists, like the drone, have not the taste to select, the industry to acquire, nor the skill to improve, but impudently pilfer the honey ready prepared, from the hive.

Charles Caleb Colton

Plagiarists have, at least, the merit of preservation.

Benjamin Disraeli

It has come to be practically a sort of rule in literature, that a man, having once shown himself capable of original writing, is entitled, thenceforth, to steal from the writings of others at discretion. Thought is the property of him who can entertain it and of him who can adequately place it. A certain awkwardness marks the use of borrowed thoughts; but as soon as we have learned what to do with them, they become our own.

Ralph Waldo Emerson

Borrowed thoughts, like borrowed money, only show the poverty of the borrower.

Marguerite Gardiner (Lady Blessington)

Nothing is sillier than this charge of plagiarism. There is no sixth commandment in art. The poet dare help himself wherever he lists—wherever he finds material suited to his work. He may even appropriate entire columns with their carved capitals, if the temple he thus supports be a beautiful one. Goethe understood this very well, and so did Shakespeare before him.

Heinrich Heine

It is not strange that remembered ideas should often take advantage of the crowd of thoughts and smuggle themselves in as original. Honest thinkers are always stealing unconsciously from each other. Our minds are full of waifs and estrays which we think our own. Innocent plagiarism turns up everywhere.

Oliver Wendell Holmes

Literature is full of coincidences, which some love to believe are plagiarisms. There are thoughts always abroad in the air which it takes more wit to avoid than to hit upon.

Oliver Wendell Holmes

No earnest thinker is a plagiarist pure and simple. He will never borrow from others that which he has not already, more or less, thought out for himself.

Charles Kingsley

Horace or Boileau have said such a thing, before. I take your word for it, but I said it as my own; and may I not have the same just thoughts after them, as others may have after me?

Jean de La Bruyère

Take the whole range of imaginative literature, and we are all wholesale borrowers. In every matter that relates to invention, to use, or beauty or form, we are borrowers.

Wendell Phillips

Steal! to be sure they may, and, egad, serve your best thoughts as gipsies do stolen children—disfigure them to make them pass for their own.

Richard Brinsley Sheridan

Keep your hands from literary picking and stealing. But if you cannot refrain from this kind of stealth, abstain from murdering what you steal.

Augustus Montague Toplady

All the makers of dictionaries, and all compilers who do nothing else than repeat backwards and forwards the opinions, the errors, the impostures, and the truths already printed, we may term plagiarists; but they are honest plagiarists, who do not arrogate the merit of invention. Call them, if you please, book-makers, not authors; rather secondhand dealers than plagiarists.

Voltaire (François Marie Arouet)

See also: DISHONESTY, IMITATION, LITERATURE, WRITING.

PLAYWRIGHT: *see* THEATER.

PLEASING

And sure he must have more than mortal Skill,
Who pleases any one against his Will.

William Congreve

The art of pleasing consists in being pleased. To be amiable is to be satisfied with one's self and others.

William Hazlitt

We all live in the hope of pleasing somebody; and the pleasure of pleasing ought to be greatest, and always will be greatest, when our endeavors are exerted in consequence of our duty.

Samuel Johnson

If you wish to please people, you must begin by understanding them.

Charles Reade

See also: CHARM, CHEERFULNESS, PLEASURE.

PLEASURE

The man of pleasure little knows the perfect joy he loses for the disappointing gratifications which he pursues.

Joseph Addison

Consider pleasures as they depart, not as they come.

Aristotle

In diving to the bottom of pleasures we bring up more gravel than pearls.

Honoré de Balzac

The worst of enemies are flatterers, and the worst of flatterers are pleasures.

Jacques Bénigne Bossuet

No state can be more destitute than that of a person, who, when the delights of sense forsake him, has no pleasures of the mind.

James Burgh

To make pleasures pleasant shorten them.

Charles Buxton

There is no sterner moralist than pleasure.
George Gordon Byron (Lord Byron)

Mental pleasures never cloy; unlike those of the body, they are increased by repetition, approved by reflection, and strengthened by enjoyment.

Charles Caleb Colton

Pleasure's couch is virtue's grave.
Augustine Joseph Hickey Duganne

All pleasure must be bought at the price of pain. The difference between false and true pleasure is this: for the true, the price is paid before you enjoy it; for the false, after you enjoy it.

John Watson Foster

Choose such pleasures as recreate much and cost little.

Thomas Fuller

Every perfect action is accompanied by pleasure. By that you can tell that you ought to do it.

André Gide

Pleasure, after all, is at best an intensely exquisite, convulsive pain!

Heinrich Heine

Fly the pleasure that bites to-morrow.
George Herbert

Pleasure is very seldom found where it is sought. Our brightest blazes of gladness are commonly kindled by unexpected sparks.

Samuel Johnson

The most delicate, the most sensible of all pleasures, consists in promoting the pleasure of others.

Jean de La Bruyère

The greatest pleasure I know, is to do a good action by stealth, and have it found out by accident.

Charles Lamb

He who can at all times sacrifice pleasure to duty approaches sublimity.

Johann Kaspar Lavater

The sweetest pleasures are those which do not exhaust hope.

Gaston Pierre Marc de Lévis

All worldly pleasure is correspondent to a like measure of anxiety.

Francis Osborn

We tire of those pleasures we take, but never of those we give.

John Petit-Senn

He buys honey too dear who licks it from thorns.

Proverb

Enjoy present pleasures in such a way as not to injure future ones.

Seneca

There are two things to aim at in life: first, to get what you want; and, after that, to enjoy it. Only the wisest of mankind achieve the second.

Logan Pearsall Smith

All fits of pleasure are balanced by an equal degree of pain or languor; 'tis like spending this year, part of the next year's revenue.

Jonathan Swift

There is little pleasure in the world that is true and sincere beside the pleasure of doing our duty and doing good. I am sure no other is comparable to this.

John Tillotson

See also: AMUSEMENT, COMFORT, DELIGHT, DIVERSION, ENJOYMENT, HAPPINESS, INDULGENCE, JOY, RECREATION.

POET

A poet can write about a man slaying the dragon, but not about a man pushing a button that releases a bomb.

Wystan Hugh Auden

A poet is, before anything else, a person who is passionately in love with language.

Wystan Hugh Auden

Poets are all who love, who feel great truths,
And tell them.

Philip James Bailey

The poet's voice need not merely be the record of man, it can be one of the props, the pillars to help him endure and prevail.

William Faulkner

I believe that every English poet should read the English classics, master the rules of grammar before he attempts to bend or break them, travel abroad, experience the horror of sordid passion, and—if he is lucky enough—know the love of an honest woman.

Robert Ranke Graves

Sad is his lot, who, once at least in his life, has not been a poet.

Alphonse de Lamartine

All that is best in the great poets of all countries, is not what is national in them, but what is universal.

Henry Wadsworth Longfellow

When will poets learn that a grassblade of their own raising is worth a barrow-load of flowers from their neighbor's garden?

James Russell Lowell

He who, in an enlightened and literary society, aspires to be a great poet, must first become a little child.

Thomas Babington Macaulay

The poet has realized that he has his own way, which is neither scientific or philosophical, of knowing the world.

Jacques Maritain

Poets utter great and wise things which they do not themselves understand.

Plato

The function of the poet is not to be inspired himself, but to create inspiration in his readers.

Paul Ambroise Valéry

See also: AUTHORSHIP, POETRY.

POETRY

[Poetry] a criticism of life under the conditions fixed for such a criticism by the laws of poetic truth and poetic beauty.

Matthew Arnold

It's silly to suggest the writing of poetry as something ethereal, a sort of soul-crashing emotional experience that wrings you. I have no fancy ideas about poetry. It doesn't come to you on the wings of a dove. It's something you work hard at.

Louise Bogan

Whatever we conceive well we express clearly, and words flow with ease.

Nicolas Boileau-Despréaux

Poetry is the art of substantiating shadows, and of lending existence to nothing.

Edmund Burke

Poetry, good sir, in my opinion, is like a tender virgin, very young, and extremely beautiful, whom divers others virgins—namely, all the other sciences—make it their business to enrich, polish and adorn; and to her it belongs to make use of them all, and on her part to give a lustre to them all.

Miguel de Cervantes Saavedra

Poetry has been to me its own exceeding great reward: it has given me the habit of wishing to discover the good and beautiful in all that meets and surrounds me.

Samuel Taylor Coleridge

Writing free verse is like playing tennis with the net down.

Robert Lee Frost

Thoughts that breathe, and words that burn.

Thomas Gray

Poetry is emotion put into measure. The emotion must come by nature, but the measure can be acquired by art.

Thomas Hardy

An artist that works in marble or colors has them all to himself and his tribe, but the man who moulds his thoughts in verse has to employ the materials vulgarized by everybody's use, and glorify them by his handling.

Oliver Wendell Holmes

Poetry is not the thing said but a way of saying it.

Alfred Edward Housman

Poetry cannot be translated; and, therefore, it is the poets that preserve the languages; for we would not be at the trouble to learn a language if we could have all that is written in it just as well in a translation. But as the beauties of poetry cannot be preserved in any language except that in which it was originally written, we learn the language.

Samuel Johnson

You arrive at truth through poetry; I arrive at poetry through truth.

Joseph Joubert

When power leads man toward arrogance, poetry reminds him of his limitations. When power narrows the areas of man's concern, poetry reminds him of the richness and diversity of his existence. When power corrupts, poetry cleanses.

John Fitzgerald Kennedy

In these days of nuclear energy, can the earthenware lamp of the poet still suffice? Yes, if its clay reminds us of our own. And it

is sufficient mission for the poet to be the guilt conscience of his time.

Alexis Léger

Indifference to poetry is one of the most conspicuous characteristics of the human race.

Robert Lynd

By poetry we mean the art of employing words in such a manner as to produce an illusion on the imagination; the art of doing by means of words, what the painter does by means of colors.

Thomas Babington Macaulay

A poem should be equal to:
Not true

Archibald MacLeish

A poem should be palpable and mute
As a globed fruit

Archibald MacLeish

A poem should not mean
But be.

Archibald MacLeish

Poetry alone imagines, and imagining creates the world that men can wish to live in and make true.

Archibald MacLeish

Poetry, which owes no man anything, owes nevertheless one debt . . . an image of mankind in which men can again believe.

Archibald MacLeish

Publishing a volume of verse is like dropping a rose-petal down the Grand Canyon and waiting for the echo.

Donald Robert Perry (Don) Marquis

Poetry is an art in which the artist by means of rhythm and great sincerity can convey to others the sentiment which he feels about life.

John Masefield

Since the printing press came into being, poetry has ceased to be the delight of the whole community of man; it has become the amusement and delight of the few.

John Masefield

We have more poets than judges and interpreters of poetry. It is easier to write an indifferent poem than to understand a good one.

Michel Eyquem de Montaigne

The greatest poem ever known
Is one all poets have outgrown:
The poetry, innate, untold,
Of being only four years old.
Christopher Darlington Morley

Poetry comes nearer to vital truth than history.
Plato

Truth shines the brighter clad in verse.
Alexander Pope

The office of poetry is not to make us think accurately, but feel truly.
Frederick William Robertson

Poetry is a language which tells us, through a more or less emotional reaction, something that cannot be said.
Edwin Arlington Robinson

He who finds elevated and lofty pleasure in the feeling of poetry is a true poet, though he never composed a line of verse in his entire lifetime.
George Sand (Baronne Dudevant)

Poetry is the record of the best and happiest moments of the happiest and best minds.
Percy Bysshe Shelley

They learn in suffering what they teach in song.
Percy Bysshe Shelley

The important thing about a poem is the reader.
Mark Van Doren

One merit of poetry few persons will deny; it says more, and in fewer words, than prose.
Voltaire (François Marie Arouet)

Poetry is most just to its divine origin, when it administers the comforts and breathes the thoughts of religion.
William Wordsworth

See also: BALLAD, BOOK, FANCY, IMAGINATION, LITERATURE, MUSIC, POET, READING, SONG, WORD, WRITING.

POINT OF VIEW

Two men look out through the same bars:
One sees the mud, and one the stars.
Frederick Langbridge

When a man wants to murder a tiger he calls it sport: when the tiger wants to murder him he calls it ferocity.
George Bernard Shaw

Who has the longer view of things, anyway, a prime minister in a closet or a man on a barn roof?
Elwyn Brooks White

See also: APPROACH, IDEA, METHOD, PERCEPTION, PURPOSE.

POLAND

The Pole will wield the pen as skillfully as the lance, and will show himself as brave in the fields of knowledge as on the tried fields of battle.
Heinrich Heine

The honest Jew loves his country like a Pole!
Adam Mickiewicz

See also: NATION, UNITED NATIONS.

POLICE

The Commission believes there is a grave danger that some communities may resort to the indiscriminate and excessive use of force. The harmful effects of overreaction are incalculable. The Commission condemns moves to equip police departments with mass destruction weapons, such as automatic rifles, machine guns and tanks. Weapons which are designed to destroy, not to control, have no place in densely populated urban communities.
Commission on Civil Disorder, 1968

To some Negroes police have come to symbolize white power, white racism and white repression. And the fact is that many police do reflect and express these white attitudes. The atmosphere of hostility and cynicism is reinforced by a widespread belief among Negroes in the existence of police brutality and in a "double standard" of justice and protection—one for Negroes and one for whites.
Commission on Civil Disorder, 1968

See also: CRIME, GUN, LAW, ORDER.

POLICY

Policy consists in serving God in such a manner as not to offend the devil.
Thomas Fuller

Let us understand the distinction between policy and creed. A policy may be changed, a creed cannot. But either is as good as the other whilst it is held.

Mohandas Karamchand (Mahatma) Gandhi

Measures, not men, have always been my mark.

Oliver Goldsmith

See also: APPROACH, CAUTION, DISCRETION, EXPEDIENCY, MEANS AND END, METHOD, PHILOSOPHY, POINT OF VIEW.

POLITENESS

If a man be gracious and courteous to strangers, it shows he is a citizen of the world.

Francis Bacon

In all the affairs of life, social as well as political, courtesies of a small and trivial character are the ones which strike deepest to the grateful and appreciating heart.

Henry Clay

As charity covers a multitude of sins before God, so does politeness before men.

Fulke Greville (First Baron Brooke)

Politeness comes from within, from the heart: but if the forms of politeness are dispensed with, the spirit and the thing itself soon die away.

John Hall

Politeness is fictitious benevolence. It supplies the place of it among those who see each other only in public, or but little. The want of it never fails to produce something disagreeable to one or other.

Samuel Johnson

The true effect of genuine politeness seems to be rather ease than pleasure.

Samuel Johnson

Politeness does not always evince goodness equity, complaisance, or gratitude, but it gives at least the appearance of these qualities, and makes man appear outwardly as he should be within.

Jean de La Bruyère

Politeness is not always the sign of wisdom, but the want of it always leaves room for the suspicion of folly.

Walter Savage Landor

There is no policy like politeness; and a good manner is the best thing in the world, either to get a good name, or supply the want of it.

Edward G. Bulwer-Lytton (Baron Lytton)

Politeness has been well defined as benevolence in small things.

Thomas Babington Macaulay

There is no policy like politeness, since a good manner often succeeds where the best tongue has failed.

Elias Lyman Magoon

To the acquisition of the rare quality of politeness, so much of an enlightened understanding is necessary that I cannot but consider every book in every science, which tends to make us wiser, and of course better men, as a treatise on a more enlarged system of politeness.

Neil Munro

Bowing, ceremonious, formal compliments, stiff civilities, will never be politeness; that must be easy, natural, unstudied; and what will give this but a mind benevolent and attentive to exert that amiable disposition in trifles to all you converse and live with?

William Pitt (Lord Chatham)

Men, like bullets, go farthest when they are smoothest.

Jean Paul Richter

Politeness goes far, yet costs nothing.

Samuel Smiles

Politeness is good nature regulated by good sense.

Sydney Smith

Do not press your young children into book learning; but teach them politeness, including the whole circle of charities which spring from the consciousness of what is due to their fellow-beings.

Johann Kaspar Spurzheim

True politeness is perfect ease and freedom. It simply consists in treating others just as you love to be treated yourself.

Philip Dormer Stanhope (Lord Chesterfield)

There are two kinds of politeness; one says, "See how polite I am"; the other, "I would make you happy."

Charles Tomlinson

See also: COURTESY, MANNERS.

POLITICIAN

A politician is an animal who can sit on a fence and yet keep both ears to the ground.

Anonymous

A politician thinks of the next election; a statesman of the next generation. A politician looks for the success of his party; a statesman for that of his country. The statesman wishes to steer.

James Freeman Clarke

Since a politician never believes what he says, he is surprised when others believe him.

Charles André Joseph Marie de Gaulle

I have never seen difficulties that prevented leading politicians of great maturity and strong personalities from getting together when they felt it made sense.

Dag Hammarskjold

Politicians are the same all over. They promise to build a bridge even where there is no river.

Nikita Sergeevich Khrushchev

Although I myself do not drink, I always make a point of shaking hands with bartenders whenever I come across them, because their recommendations, voiced at that moment when men's minds are highly receptive to ideas, carry much weight in a community.

Joseph William Martin

The proper memory for a politician is one that knows what to remember and what to forget.

John Morley

A politician is a person who approaches every subject with an open mouth.

Adlai Ewing Stevenson

A politician is a man who understands government, and it takes a politician to run a government. A statesman is a politician who's been dead 10 or 15 years.

Harry S Truman

See also: GOVERNMENT, PARTY, POLITICS.

POLITICS

Knowledge of human nature is the beginning and the end of political education.

Henry Brooks Adams

Politics is and has always been an imitation of war aimed at exorcising war.

Max Ascoli

In any assembly the simplest way to stop the transacting of business and split the ranks is to appeal to a principle.

Jacques Martin Barzun

The most striking defect of our system of government is that it divides political power and thereby conceals political responsibility.

Carl Lotus Becker

Politics are not an exact science.

Otto Eduard Leopold von Bismarck

To be a chemist you must study chemistry; to be a lawyer or a physician you must study law or medicine; but to be a politician you need only to study your own interests.

Paul Blouet (Max O'Rell)

In politics, merit is rewarded by the possessor being raised, like a target, to a position to be fired at.

Christian Nestell Bovee

This is the first Convention of a space age— where a candidate can promise the moon and mean it.

David Brinkley

Nowhere are prejudices more mistaken for truth, passion for reason, and invective for documentation than in politics. That is a realm, peopled only by villians or heroes, in which everything is black or white and gray is a forbidden color.

John Mason Brown

The humblest in all the land, when clad in the armor of a righteous cause, is stronger than all the hosts of error.

William Jennings Bryan

Some have said that it is not the business of private men to meddle with government,—a bold and dishonest saying, which is fit to come from no mouth but that of a tyrant or a slave. To say that private men have nothing to do with government is to say that private men have nothing to do with their own happiness or misery; that people ought not to concern themselves whether they be naked or clothed, fed or starved, deceived or instructed, protected or destroyed.

Cato the Elder

The people have plenty of confidence. The place where confidence and courage are needed is in our political leaders.
Raymond Clapper

In politics experiments mean resolutions.
Benjamin Disraeli

In politics nothing is contemptible.
Benjamin Disraeli

Real politics are the possession and distribution of power.
Benjamin Disraeli

There is no gambling like politics.
Benjamin Disraeli

This career of plundering and blundering.
Benjamin Disraeli

There has been an appreciable longtime improvement in the level of political morals. . . . Our government is now so huge and affects our lives so directly that we cannot be content with merely a moderately decent level of behavior on the part of our public officials. . . . What could be tolerated when government was small cannot be endured when government is big.
Paul Howard Douglas

In the name of all that's American, how can any good citizen feel superior to politics? We achieved our independence by politics. We freed the slaves by politics. We are taxed by politics. Our businesses flourish or wither by politics.
Charles Leroy Edson

Politics is a profession; a serious, complicated and, in its true sense, a noble one.
Dwight David Eisenhower

Every political question is becoming a social question, and every social question is becoming a religious question.
Richard Theodore Ely

The day of the political boss, if it isn't past, well, its darn close to being past. More and more people are independent enough, however they register, to vote for the man they think can provide the leadership they need. And these days, they know what's going on.
Daniel Jackson Evans

I believe that politics is a science. It's a scientific approach to handling human beings.
James Aloysius Farley

Cicero was in politics a moderate of the most violent description.
Anatole France

I think the political life must be an echo of private life and that there cannot be any divorce between the two.
Mohandas Karamchand (Mahatma) Gandhi

Politics bereft of religion are a death-trap because they kill the soul.
Mohandas Karamchand (Mahatma) Gandhi

Pouring ridicule on one's opponent is an approved method in "civilized politics."
Mohandas Karamchand (Mahatma) Gandhi

Real political issues cannot be manufactured by the leaders of parties, and cannot be evaded by them. They declare themselves, and come out of the depths of that deep which we call public opinion.
James Abram Garfield

How little do politics affect the life, the moral life of a nation. One single good book influences the people a vast deal more.
William Ewart Gladstone

I hate all bungling as I do sin, but particularly bungling in politics, which leads to the misery and ruin of many thousands and millions of people.
Johann Wolfgang von Goethe

Modern political ideas are very largely the creation of the Jewish prophets, who foresaw the new Jerusalem in the future, at a time when their contemporaries of other nations had no particular hopes for the betterment of humanity.
John Burdon Sanderson Haldane

The end of all political effort must be the well-being of the individual in a life of safety and freedom.
Dag Hammarskjold

Conferences at the top level are always courteous. Name-calling is left to the Foreign Ministers.
Averell W. Harriman

If you wish the sympathy of broad masses then you must tell them the crudest and most stupid things.
Adolf Hitler

Politics is the most practical of the arts. It is most concerned with 'hard facts'; for what facts are harder than the facts of human interest and passion? Yet it is, and always has been, the most theoretical . . . conducted on the basis of some theory, theological or other, of authority and the obligation of obedience.

William Ernest Hocking

The purification of politics is an iridescent dream.

John James Ingalls

We shall have to fight the politician, who remembers only that the unborn have no votes and that since posterity has done nothing for us we need do nothing for posterity.

William Ralph Inge

I am not able—nor even the least interested in trying—to define my political philosophy by the choice of a one-word or two-word label. . . . At the heart of my own beliefs is a rebellion against this very process of classifying, labeling, and filing Americans under headings: regional, economic, occupational, religious, racial, or otherwise. I bridle at the very casualness with which we have come to ask each other, "What is your political philosophy?"

Lyndon Baines Johnson

The violation of party faith, is, of itself, too common to excite surprise or indignation. Political friendships are so well understood that we can hardly pity the simplicity they deceive.

Junius

Politics is very much like taxes—everybody is against them, or everybody is for them as long as they don't apply to him.

Fiorello Henry La Guardia

Before you can begin to think about politics at all, you have to abandon the notion that here is a war between good men and bad men.

Walter Lippmann

No quarrel ought ever to be converted into a policy.

David Lloyd George

A new form of "politics" is emerging, and in ways we haven't yet noticed. The living room has become a voting booth. Participation via television in Freedom Marches, in war, revolution, pollution, and other events is changing everything.

(Herbert) Marshall McLuhan

A political war is one in which everyone shoots from the lip.

Raymond Moley

In politics where immediate success is attained by saying what people can be made to believe, rather than what is demonstrably true, accent is generally placed on the desirable rather than on the possible.

Raymond Moley

Able young people should be encouraged to run for office. They should receive adequate campaign funds from the party and from public-spirited citizens, without making commitments in return.

Wayne Lyman Morse

People vote their resentment, not their appreciation. The average man does not vote *for* anything, but *against* something.

William Bennett Munro

Politics is the diversion of trivial men who, when they succeed at it, become important in the eyes of more trivial men.

George Jean Nathan

The politics of courts are so mean that private people would be ashamed to act in the same way; all is trick and finesse, to which the common cause is sacrificed.

Horatio Nelson (Lord Nelson)

With all the temptations, dangers, and degradations that beset it, politics is still, I think, the noblest career that any man can choose.

Frederick Scott Oliver

Politics is the science of exigencies.

Theodore Parker

Great political questions stir the deepest nature of one half the nation, but they pass far above and over the heads of the other half.

Wendell Phillips

There is an infinity of political errors which, being once adopted, become principles.

Guillaume Thomas François Raynal

How a minority, reaching majority, seizing authority, hates a minority.

Leonard Harman Robbins

Politics is a perpetual emergency.
Ralph Leclerq Roeder

There is no more independence in politics than there is in jail.
Will (William Penn Adair) Rogers

My hat's in the ring. The fight is on and I'm stripped to the buff.
Theodore Roosevelt

He knows nothing; and he thinks he knows everything. That points clearly to a political career.
George Bernard Shaw

An independent is a person who wants to take the politics out of politics.
Adlai Ewing Stevenson

Nothing is more deceitful than the statements that what we need in politics is the business man. Politics are a business—at least they are a field in which experience tells for usefulness and effectiveness—and a man who has devoted his entire life to the successful establishment of a business is generally not the man who will be useful to the public in the administration of public business.
William Howard Taft

I'm not going to give up. This is my first race (for political office) and now I know how the game is played.
Shirley Temple

Politics is the art of government.
Harry S Truman

Any national administration in a modern complex industrial society must exercise vast powers. The United States cannot be divided into forty-eight separate economic units. We cannot, for instance, have forty-eight different minimum wage laws. . . . The issue today is not the issue of states' rights versus federal power. The issue is government administered under law.
Wendell Lewis Willkie

Politics I conceive to be nothing more than the science of the ordered progress of society along the lines of greatest usefulness and convenience to itself.
(Thomas) Woodrow Wilson

I resent at any time or at any place the attitude that the safety of this country depends on any man holding his job. No man has

achieved that strength, and this country has not deteriorated to that weakness.
Owen D. Young

See also: DEMOCRATIC PARTY, FACTION, GOVERNMENT, OFFICE, PARTY, REPUBLICAN PARTY, STATESMANSHIP.

POOR: *see* POVERTY.

POPE

A little skill in antiquity inclines a man to popery; but depth in that study brings him about again to our Christian religion.
Thomas Fuller

It often happens that I wake at night and begin to think about a serious problem and decide I must tell the Pope about it. Then I wake up completely and remember that I am the Pope.
John XXIII (Angelo Giuseppe Roncalli)

The Pope derives his institutions neither from divine nor from human right, but is a self-chosen human creature and intruder.
Martin Luther

I am moved to obedience to that See not only by what learned and holy men have written, but by this fact especially, that we shall find that on the one hand every enemy of the Christian faith makes war on that See, and that, on the other hand, no one has ever declared himself an enemy of that See who has not also shortly shown most evidently that he was the enemy of the Christian religion.
Sir Thomas More

He for eighteen hundred years has lived in the world; he has seen all fortunes, he has encountered all adversaries, he has shaped himself for all emergencies. If ever there was a power on earth who had an eye for the times, who has confined himself to the practicable, and has been happy in his anticipations, whose words have been facts, and whose commands prophecies, such is he in the history of ages, who sits from generation to generation in the chair of the apostles, as the vicar of Christ, and the doctor of his Church.
John Henry Newman

See also: CATHOLICISM, REFORMATION.

POPULACE

The multitude is always in the wrong.
Wentworth Dillon (Earl of Roscommon)

The multitude which is not brought to act as unity, is confusion. That unity which has not its origin in the multitude is tyranny.

Blaise Pascal

There are occasions when the general belief of the people, even though it be groundless, works its effect as sure as truth itself.

Johann Christoph Friedrich von Schiller

See also: COMMON MAN, CROWD, MAN, MOB, NATION, PEOPLE, PUBLIC, SOCIETY, STATE.

POPULARITY

Popular opinion is the greatest lie in the world.

Thomas Carlyle

I put no account on him who esteems himself just as the popular breath may chance to raise him.

Johann Wolfgang von Goethe

Those who are commended by everybody must be very extraordinary men, or, which is more probable, very inconsiderable men.

Fulke Greville (First Baron Brooke)

The common people are but ill judges of a man's merits; they are slaves to fame, and their eyes are dazzled with the pomp of titles and large retinue. No wonder, then, that they bestow their honors on those who least deserve them.

Horace

A generous nation is grateful even for the preservation of its rights, and willingly extends the respect due to the office of a good prince into an affection for his person.

Junius

Seek not the favor of the multitude; it is seldom got by honest and lawful means. But seek the testimony of the few; and number not voices, but weigh them.

Immanuel Kant

Whatever is popular deserves attention.

Sir James Mackintosh

Popularity is exhausting. The life of the party almost always winds up in a corner with an overcoat over him.

Wilson Mizner

True popularity is not the popularity which is followed after, but the popularity which follows after.

William Murray (Lord Mansfield)

Avoid popularity; it has many snares, and no real benefit.

William Penn

Be as far from desiring the popular love as fearful to deserve the popular hate; ruin dwells in both; the one will hug thee to death; the other will crush thee to destruction: to escape the first, be not ambitious; avoid the second, be not seditious.

Francis Quarles

See also: APPLAUSE, FAME, PRAISE.

POPULATION

In October, 1838—that is fifteen months after I had begun my systematic enquiry—I happened to read for amusement Malthus on *Population*, and being well prepared to appreciate the struggle for existence which everywhere goes on from long-continued observation of the habits of animals and plants, it at once struck me that under these circumstances favourable variations would tend to be preserved, and unfavourable ones to be destroyed.

Charles Robert Darwin

Many governments lack a full appreciation of the enormous impact of fast growing populations on the life of their peoples, not only on their food supply but in their entire development effort.

William Steen Gaud

The hungry world cannot be fed until and unless the growth of its resources and the growth of its population come into balance. Each man and woman—and each nation—must make decisions of conscience and policy in the face of this great problem.

Lyndon Baines Johnson

Population, when unchecked, increases in a geometrical ratio.

Thomas Robert Malthus

The human population of the entire world should be kept well under a hundred million. . . . If the world were not so full of people, and most of them did not have to work so hard, there would be more time for them to get out and lie on the grass, and there would be more grass for them to lie on.

Donald Robert Perry (Don) Marquis

We have been God-like in our planned breeding of our domesticated plants and animals, but we have been rabbit-like in our unplanned breeding of ourselves.

Arnold Joseph Toynbee

See also: BIRTH CONTROL, HUNGER, POVERTY, NATION, UNITED NATIONS.

PORNOGRAPHY

The bulk of pornography is badly written, tedious, and boring; but by no means all. Men of the literary standing of Goethe and Maupassant have lent their pens to its production, and Alfred de Musset wrote *Gamiani* to demonstrate that the French language was capable of being used to produce a book of the utmost license without employing a coarse word or inelegant expression. Indeed a great deal of pornography is quite readable taken in small doses, although the difficulties of the pornographer's task—the repeated presentation of sexual incidents which must rise to a crescendo of excitement—are all too apparent.

Alec Craig

A definition of pornography in the sense of reprehensible sexual writing that all right-minded people are supposed to want suppressed by law has become almost classic.

Alec Craig

There is evidence that pornography is sometimes associated with crime and depravity, but there is little evidence that this association is a causal relationship. When books are blamed for evil consequences and antisocial conduct, the fault is generally with the reader rather than with the book.

Alec Craig

There is a large volume of writing devoted to sexual subject matter which makes no pretense to be a contribution to literature and which claims no scientific or artistic merit. Its publication meets no intellectual or social interest except perhaps that of the psychiatrist. If by some chance it escapes oblivion it can do no more than satisfy some historical curiosity regarding the manners of the time or the private character of a great name.

Alec Craig

When considering the extent to which readers are likely to be susceptible to the normal or abnormal stimulus given by pornography account should be taken of the extent to which they may be immunized by media of communication other than printing, for though obscenity laws may make pornographic books expensive and difficult to obtain, acquaintance with pornographic material and attitudes is by no means restricted.

Alec Craig

See also: CENSORSHIP, OBSCENITY.

POSITION

In general, it is not very difficult for little minds to attain splendid situations. It is much more difficult for great minds to attain the place to which their merit fully entitles them.

Baron Friedrich Melchior von Grimm

The higher we rise, the more isolated we become; all elevations are cold.

Catherine Stanislas Jean de Boufflers

See also: PLACE, RANK, STATION.

POSITIVENESS

Positiveness is a most absurd foible. If you are in the right, it lessens your triumph; if in the wrong, it adds shame to your defeat.

Laurence Sterne

Positiveness is a good quality for preachers and orators, because whoever would obtrude his thoughts and reasons upon a multitude will convince others the more, as he appears convinced himself.

Jonathan Swift

Every one of his opinions appears to himself to be written with sunbeams.

Isaac Watts

Positive views of truth and duty are those that impress the mind and lead to action; negation dwells mostly in cavil and denial.

Richard Whately

See also: CERTAINTY, CONFIDENCE, DECISION, DOGMATISM, FANATICISM, RESOLUTION.

POSSESSIONS

Man should not consider his outward possessions as his own, but as common to all, so as to share them without hesitation when others are in need.

Thomas Aquinas

They who have nothing have little to fear,
Nothing to lose or to gain.
Madison Julius Cawein

Attainment is followed by neglect, and possession by disgust. The malicious remark of the Greek epigrammatist on marriage may apply to every other course of life—that its two days of happiness are the first and the last.

Samuel Johnson

In all worldly things that a man pursues with the greatest eagerness and intention of mind, he finds not half the pleasure in the actual possession of them as he proposed to himself in the expectation.

Robert South

No possessions are good but by the good use we make of them; without which wealth, power, friends, and servants, do but help to make our lives more unhappy.
Sir William Temple

See also: CAPITALISM, OWNERSHIP, PROPERTY, RICHES, WEALTH.

POSSIBILITY

The world is moving so fast these days that the man who says it can't be done is generally interrupted by someone doing it.
Elbert Green Hubbard

It is a most mortifying reflection for a man to consider what he has done, compared to what he might have done.
Samuel Johnson

See also: ABILITY, CHANCE, POWER, STRENGTH, TALENT.

POSTERITY

I would much rather that posterity should inquire why no statues were erected to me, than why they were.
Cato the Elder

Time will unveil all things to posterity; it is a chatterer and speaks to those who do not question it.
Euripides

We are too careless of posterity, not considering that as they are so the next generation will be.
William Penn

Why should we put ourselves out of the way to do anything for posterity? What has posterity done for us?

Sir Boyle Roche

Of this our ancestors complained, we ourselves do so and our posterity will equally lament because goodness has vanished and evil habits prevail while human affairs grow worse and worse sinking into an abyss of wickedness.

Seneca

Posterity preserves only what will pack into small compass. Jewels are handed down from age to age; less portable valuables disappear.

Edward John Stanley

It is pleasant to observe how free the present age is in laying taxes on the next. "Future ages shall talk of this; they shall be famous to all posterity"; whereas their time and thoughts will be taken up about present things, as ours are now.

Jonathan Swift

See also: CHILDREN, FUTURE, PROGRESS.

POVERTY

Poverty is only contemptible when it is felt to be so. Doubtless the best way to make our poverty respectable is to seem never to feel it as an evil.
Christian Nestell Bovee

Spinoza, greatest abstract philosopher, left his sister a bed and a small silver pen knife, no money, no land, no house, but his thought has taught the world's greatest thinking men.

Arthur Brisbane

Most of our realists and sociologists talk about a poor man as if he were an octopus or an alligator.
Gilbert Keith Chesterton

The real wants of nature are the measure of enjoyments, as the foot is the measure of the shoe. We can call only the want of what is necessary, poverty.

Clement I

Employment problems have drastic social impact in the ghetto. Men who are chronically unemployed or employed in the lowest status jobs are often unable or unwilling to remain with their families. The handicap imposed on children growing up without fathers in an atmosphere of poverty and deprivation is increased as mothers are forced to work to provide support.

The culture of poverty that results from unemployment and family breakup generates a system of ruthless, exploitative relationships within the ghetto. Prostitution, dope addiction and crime create an environmental "jungle" characterized by personal insecurity and tension. Children growing up under such conditions are likely participants in civil disorder.

Commission on Civil Disorder, 1968

In a terrible crisis there is only one element more helpless than the poor, and that is the rich.

Clarence Seward Darrow

When we have only a little we should be satisfied; for this reason, that those best enjoy abundance who are contented with the least.

Epicurus

Poverty possesses this disease, that through want it teaches man to do evil.

Euripides

Poverty is not essentially a lack of money; nor is the mere lack of money poverty. Rather, poverty is the lack of ability, in any given set of circumstances, to get whatever is necessary for comfortable living.

Edward Hubert Faulkner

The cure for "Materialism" is to have enough for everybody and to spare. When people are sure of having what they need they cease to think about it.

Henry Ford

I thank fate for having made me born poor. Poverty taught me the true value of the gifts useful to life.

Anatole France

Poverty often deprives a man of all spirit and virtue; it is hard for an empty bag to stand upright.

Benjamin Franklin

The past theory has been that the only way to cure poverty is to make everybody a productive citizen, a participant in economy. But the people who are poor in the United States are those who are *excluded* from participating in the economy—by personal dis-

qualification or moral disqualification or educational disqualification or physical disqualification.

John Kenneth Galbraith

The curse of the poor has destroyed nations, has deprived kings of their crowns and the rich of their riches. Retributive justice is inexorable. The blessings of the poor have made kingdoms flourish.

Mohandas Karamchand (Mahatma) Gandhi

Riches are no test of goodness. Indeed poverty is the only test. A good man voluntarily embraces poverty.

Mohandas Karamchand (Mahatma) Gandhi

For every talent that poverty has stimulated it has blighted a hundred.

John William Gardner

To be poor, and seem to be poor, is a certain way never to rise.

Oliver Goldsmith

Want of prudence is too frequently the want of virtue; nor is there on earth a more powerful advocate for vice than poverty.

Oliver Goldsmith

It is one of the ironies in meagre lives that the less there is to lose, the greater is the fear of losing it.

Joseph Gollomb

Poverty, labor, and calamity are not without their luxuries, which the rich, the indolent, and the fortunate in vain seek for.

William Hazlitt

In America today we are nearer a final triumph over poverty than in any land. The poorhouse has vanished from amongst us.

Herbert Clark Hoover

It's no disgrace to be poor, but it might as well be.

Frank McKinney (Kin) Hubbard

The prevalent fear of poverty among the educated classes is the worst moral disease from which our civilisation suffers.

William James

Born poor, but of honored and humble people, I am particularly proud to die poor.

John XXIII (Angelo Giuseppe Roncalli)

This Administration today, here and now, declares unconditional war on poverty in America, and I urge this Congress and all Americans to join with me in that effort. It will not be a short or easy struggle, no single weapon or strategy will suffice, but we shall not rest until that war is won. The richest nation on earth can afford to win it.

Lyndon Baines Johnson

At its heart, the law enforcement problem has always been—and will remain—a human problem. Wretched living conditions produced high crime rates a century ago in immigrant neighborhoods. Today, slum conditions are producing equally serious crime problems among the new immigrants to our cities.

Lyndon Baines Johnson

Very often a lack of jobs and money is not the cause of poverty, but the symptom. The cause may lie deeper, in our failure to give our fellow citizens a fair chance to develop their own capabilities, in a lack of medical care and housing, in a lack of decent communities in which to live and bring up their children. But whatever the cause, our joint federal-local effort must pursue poverty, pursue it wherever it exists. In city slums, in small towns, in sharecroppers' shacks or in migrant worker camps, on Indian reservations, among whites as well as Negroes, among the young as well as the aged, in the boom towns and in the depressed areas.

Lyndon Baines Johnson

Poverty, in large cities, has very different appearances. It is often concealed in splendor, and often in extravagance. It is the care of a great part of mankind to conceal their indigence from the rest. They support themselves by temporary expedients, and every day is lost in contriving for to-morrow.

Samuel Johnson

To those people in the huts and villages across the globe struggling to break the bonds of mass misery, we pledge our best efforts to help them help themselves, for whatever period is required—not because the Communists may be doing it, not because we seek their votes, but because it is right. If a free society cannot help the many who are poor, it cannot save the few who are rich.

John Fitzgerald Kennedy

The day of the silent poor is over. There is anger and bitterness in the contemporary slum and occasionally it is irrational. Yet even if surges of rage that grip the oppressed complicate solutions, they are evidence that resignation and apathy are finished. The slum dweller is giving notice that he is only a temporary resident, that slums in an affluent society are as anachronistic in 1966 as horse cars on Fifth Ave.

Martin Luther King, Jr.

He is poor whose expenses exceed his income.

Jean de La Bruyère

Lord God, I thank you that you have been pleased to make me a poor and indigent man upon earth. I have neither house nor land nor money to leave behind me.

Martin Luther

The war on hunger is everybody's business because it means a world of hunger and chaos in which none of us will be safe and in which individual liberty and security under law could be wiped out.

But the trouble is that everybody's business is nobody's clear responsibility.

George Stanley McGovern

Half a century on my back, and still a pauper!

Karl Marx

Pauperism is the hospital of the labor army.

Karl Marx

The human race has lived for ages in a scarcity economy. Poverty, privation and hardship have been taken for granted. Machine mass production opens up new social vistas. Poverty can be abolished.

Scott Nearing

The child was diseased at birth, stricken with a hereditary ill that only the most vital men are able to shake off. I mean poverty—the most deadly and prevalent of all diseases.

Eugene Gladstone O'Neill

Not to be able to bear poverty is a shameful thing; but not to know how to chase it away by work is a more shameful thing yet.

Pericles

Poverty is not dishonorable in itself, but only when it comes from idleness, intemperance, extravagance, and folly.

Plutarch

The isolation and alienation of the poor in the inner city are significant factors of poverty. Urban life with its overcrowding, dirt, and impersonality has a dislocating effect on the individual moving to the city from the country, and a disruptive effect on normal social patterns.

Winston Lewis Prouty

Americans over the age of 65 constitute the largest single group trapped by poverty. Thousands are having their first encounter with want since the depression years of the 1930's. Their encounter is with a poverty which is the cruelest of all.

Winston Lewis Prouty

Never mind that one more upward spiral of the arms race would probably leave both sides with no more real security than they have now. Never mind that after both sides have an anti-missile system the race will then start all over to produce new, more expensive and more sophisticated missiles that can penetrate the antimissile systems. Never mind that the costs will cut even deeper into the poverty programs. The Administration must not be vulnerable to political attack. It must have an effective antipolitical missile system even if it cannot get an effective anti-ballistic missile system. And let the poor eat missiles and live in shelters.

James Barrett Reston

It is only luxury and avarice that make poverty grievous to us; for it is a very small matter that does our business; and when we have provided against cold, hunger, and thirst, all the rest is but vanity and excess.

Seneca

As you say, I am honoured and famous and rich. But as I have to do all the hard work, and suffer an increasing multitude of fools gladly, it does not feel any better than being reviled, infamous and poor, as I used to be.

George Bernard Shaw

Poverty does not produce unhappiness: it produces degradation.

George Bernard Shaw

He travels safe and not unpleasantly, who is guarded by poverty and guided by love.

Sir Philip Sidney

Poverty is no disgrace to a man but it is confoundedly inconvenient.

Sydney Smith

Since 1960 the wealth of the wealthy has been growing at two and three times the speed of the national income of the poorest group.

Adlai Ewing Stevenson

Virtue often trips and falls on the sharp-edged rock of poverty.

Eugène Sue

Peace will never be entirely secure until men everywhere have learned to conquer poverty without sacrificing liberty to security.

Norman Mattoon Thomas

An avowal of poverty is no disgrace to any man; to make no effort to escape it is indeed disgraceful.

Thucydides

I've never been poor, only broke. Being poor is a frame of mind. Being broke is only a temporary situation.

Mike Todd

If we succeed in getting rid of war, as we have already succeeded in getting rid of pestilence, the problem of the pauper two-thirds of mankind will become imperative.

Arnold Joseph Toynbee

It would be a considerable consolation to the poor and discontented, could they but see the means whereby the wealth they covet has been acquired, or the misery that it entails.

Johann Georg von Zimmermann

See also: ADVERSITY, CITY, CRIME, DEPRESSION, GHETTO, HARDSHIP, NEGRO, RICH AND POOR, RIOT, WANT.

POWER

Nothing destroys authority so much as the unequal and untimely interchange of power, pressed too far and relaxed too much.

Francis Bacon

All human power is a compound of time and patience.

Honoré de Balzac

Power must always feel the check of power.

Louis Dembitz Brandeis

Unwillingness to surrender power is the curse of civilization, the root of ages of trouble. Some men find the appetite irresistible.

They will sacrifice everything else to hold their power.

Raymond Clapper

To know the pains of power, we must go to those who have it; to know its pleasures, we must go to those who are seeking it. The pains of power are real; its pleasures imaginary.

Charles Caleb Colton

Power is an emotionally charged word. When we possess it we call it *influence,* but when it is held by someone else we are content to use the ugly word. Yet there is nothing wrong with power; it takes power to get things done. Power is the application of intelligence to force. A river may be a terrific force, but it develops power only when directed through a turbine.

Arthur Fisher Corey

It is not possible to found a lasting power upon injustice, perjury, and treachery.

Demosthenes

All power is a trust.

Benjamin Disraeli

Power, to its last particle, is duty.

John Watson Foster

Power is of two kinds. One is obtained by the fear of punishment and the other by art of love. Power based on love is a thousand times more effective and permanent than the one derived from fear of punishment.

Mohandas Karamchand (Mahatma) Gandhi

Beware of dissipating your powers; strive constantly to concentrate them. Genius thinks it can do whatever it sees others doing, but it is sure to repent of every ill-judged outlay.

Johann Wolfgang von Goethe

Power is a relative thing, and no nation, or group of nations, can become relatively stronger without making other nations relatively weaker. If each nation had sought to excel in the arts, in learning or well-being, its success would not have meant failure for the others. But with each nation . . . aiming at an increase in power, we have entered an era of perpetual warfare . . . burdensome and fruitless.

Glenn E. Hoover

Responsibilities gravitate to the person who can shoulder them; power flows to the man who knows how.

Elbert Green Hubbard

Power? The only power I've got is nuclear— and I can't use that.

Lyndon Baines Johnson

The men who create power make an indispensable contribution to the nation's greatness. But the men who question power make a contribution just as indispensable, especially when that questioning is disinterested. For they determine whether we use power or power uses us.

John Fitzgerald Kennedy

We have more power than will; and it is often by way of excuse to ourselves that we fancy things are impossible.

Duc François de La Rochefoucauld

Grim experience taught men that power is poisonous to its possessors; that no dynasty and no class can exclusively control the engines of power without ultimately confusing their private interest with the public well-being.

Harold Joseph Laski

We cannot live by power, and a culture that seeks to live by it becomes brutal and sterile. But we can die without it.

Max Lerner

Power is so characteristically calm, that calmness in itself has the aspect of power, and forbearance implies strength.

Edward G. Bulwer-Lytton (Baron Lytton)

The history of political thought is the history of the moral evaluation of political power.

Hans Joachim Morgenthau

Man is born to seek power, yet his actual condition makes him a slave to the power of others.

Hans Joachim Morgenthau

Even in war moral power is to physical as three parts out of four.

Napoleon I (Bonaparte)

Justice without power is inefficient; power without justice is tyranny. Justice without power is opposed, because there are always wicked men. Power without justice is soon questioned. Justice and power must therefore be brought together, so that whatever is just may be powerful, and whatever is powerful may be just.

Blaise Pascal

Power is ever stealing from the many to the few. The manna of popular liberty must be gathered each day, or it is rotten.

Wendell Phillips

It is patent in our days that not alone is wealth accumulated, but immense power and despotic economic domination are concentrated in the hands of a few, and that those few are frequently not the owners but only the trustees and directors of invested funds which they administer at their good pleasure.

Pius X (Giuseppe Melchiorre Sarto)

It is an observation no less just than common, that there is no stronger test of a man's real character than power and authority, exciting as they do every passion, and discovering every latent vice.

Plutarch

A few great minds are enough to endow humanity with monstrous power, but a few great hearts are not enough to make us worthy of using it.

Jean Rostand

The basis of international anarchy is men's proneness to fear and hatred. This is also the basis of economic disputes; for the love of power, which is at their root, is generally an embodiment of fear. Men desire to be in control because they are afraid that the control of others will be used unjustly to their detriment.

Bertrand Arthur William Russell

Power acquired by guilt has seldom been directed to any good end or useful purpose.

Tacitus

Since nothing is settled until it is settled right, no matter how unlimited power a man may have, unless he exercises it fairly and justly his actions will return to plague him.

Frank Arthur Vanderlip

There must be, not a balance of power, but a community of power; not organized rivalries, but an organized common peace.

(Thomas) Woodrow Wilson

See also: ABILITY, AUTHORITY, COMMANDER,
EFFICIENCY, FORCE, GOVERNMENT,
INFLUENCE, STRENGTH.

PRACTICE

Indeed, I hold that what cannot be proved in practice cannot be sound in theory.

Mohandas Karamchand (Mahatma) Gandhi

An ounce of practice is more than tons of preaching.

Mohandas Karamchand (Mahatma) Gandhi

See also: EXAMPLE, EXPERIENCE, PROGRESS.

PRAISE

Praise undeserved is satire in disguise.

Henry Broadhurst

Praise is a debt we owe to the virtues of others, and is due to our own from all whom malice has not made mutes, or envy struck dumb.

Sir Thomas Browne

We are all excited by the love of praise, and it is the noblest spirits that feel it most.

Cicero

Expect not praise without envy until you are dead. Honors bestowed on the illustrious dead have in them no admixture of envy; for the living pity the dead; and pity and envy, like oil and vinegar, assimilate not.

Charles Caleb Colton

The praises of others may be of use in teaching us, not what we are, but what we ought to be.

Augustus and Julius Hare

True praise is frequently the lot of the humble; false praise is always confined to the great.

Henry Home

Praise, like gold and diamonds, owes its value only to its scarcity. It becomes cheap as it becomes vulgar, and will no longer raise expectation or animate enterprise.

Samuel Johnson

Praise is sometimes a good thing for the diffident and despondent. It teaches them properly to rely on the kindness of others.

Letitia Elizabeth Landon

No ashes are lighter than those of incense, and few things burn out sooner.

Walter Savage Landor

When we disclaim praise, it is only showing our desire to be praised a second time.

Duc François de La Rochefoucauld

How a little praise warms out of a man the good that is in him, as the sneer of contempt which he feels is unjust chills the ardor to excel.

Edward G. Bulwer-Lytton (Baron Lytton)

The most agreeable recompense which we can receive for things which we have done is to see them known, to have them applauded with praises which honor us.

Molière (Jean Baptiste Poquelin)

A man's accusations of himself are always believed, his praises never.

Michel Eyquem de Montaigne

Those who are greedy of praise prove that they are poor in merit.

Plutarch

Damn with faint praise.

Alexander Pope

His praise is lost who waits till all commend.

Alexander Pope

Think not those faithful who praise all your words and actions, but those who kindly reprove your faults.

Socrates

Whenever you commend, add your reasons for doing so; it is this which distinguishes the approbation of a man of sense from the flattery of sycophants and admiration of fools.

Sir Richard Steele

The more you speak of yourself, the more you are likely to lie.

Johann Georg von Zimmermann

See also: APPLAUSE, COMPLIMENT, FLATTERY, POPULARITY.

PRAYER

Prayer is the wing wherewith the soul flies to heaven, and meditation the eye wherewith we see God.

Ambrose of Milan

People would be surprised to know how much I learned about prayer from playing poker.

Mary Hunter Austin

Prayer is a virtue that prevaileth against all temptations.

Bernard of Clairvaux

God hears no more than the heart speaks; and if the heart be dumb, God will certainly be deaf.

Thomas Brooks

The greatest prayer is patience.

Buddha

He who runs from God in the morning will scarcely find Him the rest of the day.

John Bunyan

In prayer it is better to have a heart without words, than words without a heart.

John Bunyan

Prayer is a binding necessity in the lives of men and nations.

Alexis Carrell

He prayeth best who loveth best.

Samuel Taylor Coleridge

We should pray with as much earnestness as those who expect everything from God; and should act with as much energy as those who expect everything from themselves.

Charles Caleb Colton

The end of our prayers is often gained by an answer very different from what we expect. "Lord, what wilt thou have me to do?" was the question of Paul; and a large part of the answer was, "I will show him how great things he must suffer."

Tryon Edwards

Is not prayer a study of truth, a sally of the soul into the unfound infinite? No man ever prayed heartily without learning something.

Ralph Waldo Emerson

Begin your day with prayer and make it so soulful that it may remain with you until the evening. Close the day with prayer so that you may have a peaceful night free from dreams and nightmares. Do not worry about the form of prayer. Let it be any form, it should be such as can put you into communion with the divine. Only, whatever be the form, let not the spirit wander while the words of prayer run out of your mouth.

Mohandas Karamchand (Mahatma) Gandhi

Prayer is a confession of one's own unworthiness and weakness.

Mohandas Karamchand (Mahatma) Gandhi

Prayer is the key of the morning and the bolt of the evening.

Mohandas Karamchand (Mahatma) Gandhi

Worship or prayer is no flight of eloquence; it is no lip-homage. It springs from the heart. If, therefore, we achieve that purity of the heart when it is emptied of all but love, if we keep all the chords in proper tune, they "trembling pass in music out of sight." Prayer needs no speech. It is in itself independent of any sensuous effort. I have not the slightest doubt that prayer is an unfailing means of cleansing the heart of passions. But it must be combined with the utmost humility.

Mohandas Karamchand (Mahatma) Gandhi

You pray in your distress and in your need; would that you might pray also in the fullness of your joy and in your days of abundance.

Kahlil Gibran

Certain thoughts are prayers. There are moments when, whatever be the attitude of the body, the soul is on its knees.

Victor Marie Hugo

I have lived to thank God that all my prayers have not been answered.

Jean Ingelow

To saints their very slumber is a prayer.

Jerome (Eusebius Hieronymous)

The ivory tower was an esthete's creation; others are modelled on ethic principles. Their inhabitants don't fiddle while Rome burns, they pray.

Arthur Koestler

I have been driven many times to my knees by the overwhelming conviction that I had nowhere else to go. My own wisdom, and that of all about me, seemed insufficient for the day.

Abraham Lincoln

The fewer words the better prayer.

Martin Luther

The prayer that begins with trustfulness, and passes on into waiting, will always end in thankfulness, triumph, and praise.

Alexander Maclaren

God warms his hands at man's heart when he prays.

John Masefield

The Lord's Prayer is not, as some fancy, the easiest, the most natural of all devout utterances. It may be committed to memory quickly, but it is slowly learned by heart.

(John) Frederick Denison Maurice

Trouble and perplexity drive me to prayer, and prayer drives away perplexity and trouble.

Philip Melanchthon

Human life is a constant want, and ought to be a constant prayer.

Samuel Osgood

Practise in life whatever you pray for, and God will give it to you more abundantly.

Edward Bouverie Pusey

Heaven is never deaf but when man's heart is dumb.

Francis Quarles

What men usually ask for when they pray to God is, that two and two may not make four.

Russian Proverb

The answer to our prayer may be the echo of our resolve.

Sir Herbert Louis Samuel

The first petition that we are to make to Almighty God is for a good conscience, the next for health of mind, and then of body.

Seneca

Pray as if everything depended on God, and work as if everything depended upon man.

Francis Joseph Spellman

The body of our prayer is the sum of our duty; and as we must ask of God whatsoever we need, so we must watch and labor for all that we ask.

Jeremy Taylor

The Lord's Prayer is short and mysterious, and, like the treasures of the Spirit, full of wisdom and latent senses: it is not improper to draw forth those excellencies which are intended and signified by every petition, that by so excellent an authority we may know what it is lawful to beg of God.

Jeremy Taylor

Prayer is not overcoming God's reluctance; it is laying hold of His highest willingness.

Richard Chenevix Trench

The Lord's Prayer contains the sum total of religion and morals.

Arthur Wellesley (First Duke Wellington)

The simple heart that freely asks in love, obtains.

John Greenleaf Whittier

Pray to God, at the beginning of all your works, that so you may bring them all to a good ending.

Xenophon

See also: DEVOTION, MEDITATION, PIETY, WORSHIP.

PREACHING

I preached as never sure to preach again,
And as a dying man to dying men.

Richard Baxter

The world is dying for want, not of good preaching, but of good hearing.

George Dana Boardman

For the preacher's merit or demerit,
It were to be wished the flaws were fewer
In the earthen vessel, holding treasure,
Which lies as safe in a golden ewer;
But the main thing is, does it hold good
    measure?
Heaven soon sets right all other matters!

Robert Browning

And pulpit, drum ecclesiastic,
Was beat with fist, instead of a stick.

Samuel Butler

It requires as much reflection and wisdom to know what is not to be put into a sermon, as what is.

Richard Cecil

To love to preach is one thing—to love those to whom we preach, quite another.

Richard Cecil

Let your sermon grow out of your text, and aim only to develop and impress its thought. Of a discourse that did not do this it was once wittily said, "If the text had the small-pox, the sermon would never catch it."

Tryon Edwards

I would have every minister of the Gospel address his audience with the zeal of a friend, with the generous energy of a father, and with the exuberant affection of a mother.

François de Salignac de La Mothe-Fénelon

Grant that I may never rack a Scripture similie beyond the true intent thereof, lest, instead of sucking milk, I squeeze blood out of it.

Thomas Fuller

A strong and faithful pulpit is no mean safeguard of a nation's life.

John Hall

The defects of a preacher are soon spied. Let him be endued with ten virtues, and have but one fault, and that one fault will eclipse and darken all his virtues and gifts, so evil is the world in these times.

Martin Luther

A preacher should have the skill to teach the unlearned simply, roundly, and plainly; for teaching is of more importance than exhorting.

Martin Luther

Some plague the people with too long sermons; for the faculty of listening is a tender thing, and soon becomes weary and satiated.

Martin Luther

I love a serious preacher, who speaks for my sake and not for his own; who seeks my salvation, and not his own vainglory. He best deserves to be heard who uses speech only to clothe his thoughts, and his thoughts only to promote truth and virtue. Nothing is more detestable than a professed declaimer, who retails his discourses as a quack does his medicine.

Jean Baptiste Massillon

Only the sinner has a right to preach.

Christopher Darlington Morley

My grand point in preaching is to break the hard heart, and to heal the broken one.

John Newton

Sermons are like pie-crust, the shorter the better.

Austin O'Malley

Genius is not essential to good preaching, but a live man is.

Austin Phelps

Pulpit discourses have insensibly dwindled from speaking to reading; a practice of itself sufficient to stifle every germ of eloquence.

Sydney Smith

Many a meandering discourse one hears, in which the preacher aims at nothing, and—hits it.

Richard Whately

To preach more than half an hour, a man should be an angel himself or have angels for hearers.

George Whitefield

See also: ADVICE, CHURCH, CLERGY, INSTRUCTION, MINISTER, TEACHING.

PRECEDENT

A precedent embalms a principle.

Benjamin Disraeli

One precedent creates another. They soon accumulate, and constitute law. What yesterday was fact, to-day is doctrine. Examples are supposed to justify the most dangerous measures; and where they do not suit exactly, the defect is supplied by analogy.

Junius

The lawless science of the law, that codeless myriad of precedent, that wilderness of single instances.

Alfred, Lord Tennyson

See also: AUTHORITY, CUSTOM, HISTORY, LAW, TRADITION.

PRECEPT

The practices of good men are more subject to error than their speculations. I will, then, honor good examples, but endeavor to live according to good precepts.

Joseph Hall

He that lays down precepts for the government of our lives and moderating our passions, obliges human nature not only in the present but in all succeeding generations.

Seneca

Precepts are the rules by which we ought to square our lives. When they are contracted into sentences, they strike the affections; whereas admonition is only blowing of the coal.

Seneca

Most precepts that are given are so general that they cannot be applied, except by an exercise of as much discretion as would be sufficient to frame them.

Richard Whately

See also: ADVICE, LAW, PRINCIPLE.

PREFACE

Go, little book; God send thee good passage, and specially let this be thy prayer, unto them all that thee will read or hear, where thou art wrong, after their help to call, thee to correct in any part, or all.

Geoffrey Chaucer

A good preface is as essential to put the reader into good humor, as a good prologue is to a play, or a fine symphony to an opera, containing something analogous to the work itself; so that we may feel its want as a desire not elsewhere to be gratified. The Italians call the preface "the sauce of the book;" and, if well-seasoned, it creates an appetite in the reader to devour the book itself.

Benjamin Disraeli

See also: BOOK, LITERATURE, INDEX.

PREJUDICE

The prejudices of ignorance are more easily removed than the prejudices of interest; the first are all blindly adopted, the second willfully preferred.

George Bancroft

A prejudice is a vagrant opinion without visible means of support.

Ambrose Gwinnett Bierce

Even when we fancy we have grown wiser, it is only, it may be, that new prejudices have displaced old ones.

Christian Nestell Bovee

The great obstacle to progress is prejudice.

Christian Nestell Bovee

I'm quite sure that . . . I have no race prejudices, and I think I have no color prejudices nor creed prejudices. Indeed, I know it. I can stand any society. All I care to know is that a man is a human being—that is enough for me; he can't be any worse.

Samuel Langhorne Clemens (Mark Twain)

There are only two ways to be quite unprejudiced and impartial. One is to be completely ignorant. The other is to be completely indifferent. Bias and prejudice are attitudes to be kept in hand, not attributes to be avoided.

Charles Pelham Curtis

Prejudice, which sees what it pleases, cannot see what is plain.

Aubrey Thomas de Vere

Ignorance is less remote from the truth than prejudice.

Denis Diderot

To divest one's self of some prejudices, would be like taking off the skin to feel the better.

Fulke Greville (First Baron Brooke)

Agnosticism, being a refusal to make up one's mind at all, is surely the very opposite of prejudice, which is the making-up of one's mind before hearing the evidence.

John Burdon Sanderson Haldane

Prejudice is never easy unless it can pass itself off for reason.

William Hazlitt

To lay aside all prejudices, is to lay aside all principles. He who is destitute of principles is governed by whims.

Friedrich Heinrich Jacobi

Opinions grounded on prejudice are always sustained with the greatest violence.

Francis Jeffrey (Lord Jeffrey)

The Negro says, "Now." Others say, "Never." The voice of responsible Americans . . . says "Together." There is no other way. Until justice is blind to color, until education is unaware of race, until opportunity is unconcerned with the color of men's skins, emancipation will be a proclamation but not a fact.

Lyndon Baines Johnson

Prejudice squints when it looks, and lies when it talks.

Laure Permon Junot (Duchesse d'Abrantès)

I hope that no American, considering the really critical issues facing this country, will waste his franchise and throw away his vote by voting either for me or against me solely on account of my religious affiliation. It is not relevant.

John Fitzgerald Kennedy

Every one is forward to complain of the prejudices that mislead other men and parties, as if he were free, and had none of his own. What now is the cure? No other but this, that every man should let alone others' prejudices and examine his own.

John Locke

He who knows only his own side of the case knows little of that.

John Stuart Mill

Every period of life has its peculiar prejudice; whoever saw old age that did not applaud the past, and condemn the present times?

Michel Eyquem de Montaigne

Everyone is a prisoner of his own experiences. No one can eliminate prejudices—just recognize them.

Edward Roscoe Murrow

It is difficult to discover a just balance between one's hopes and fears or to prevent one's wishes colouring the thinking of one's mind. Our desires seek out supporting reasons and tend to ignore facts and arguments that do not fit in with them.

Jawaharlal Nehru

When minds are closed they become impervious to reason.

Jawaharlal Nehru

There is nothing stronger than human prejudice. A crazy sentimentalism, like that of Peter the Hermit, hurled half of Europe upon Asia, and changed the destinies of kingdoms.

Wendell Phillips

Never try to reason the prejudice out of a man. It was not reasoned into him, and cannot be reasoned out.

Sydney Smith

When we destroy an old prejudice we have need of a new virtue.

Madame de Staël

Human nature is so constituted, that all see, and judge better, in the affairs of other men, than in their own.

Terence

Prejudice is the reason of fools.

Voltaire (François Marie Arouet)

Prejudices are what rule the populace.

Voltaire (François Marie Arouet)

See also: ANTI-SEMITISM, BIGOTRY, FANATICISM, INTOLERANCE, NEGRO, OPINION, RACE, RACISM, SEGREGATION.

PRESBYTERIANISM: *see* CALVINISM.

PRESENT

Since Time is not a person we can overtake when he is gone, let us honor him with mirth and cheerfulness of heart while he is passing.

Johann Wolfgang von Goethe

Duty and to-day are ours, results and futurity belong to God.

Horace Greeley

Abridge your hopes in proportion to the shortness of the span of human life; for while we converse, the hours, as if envious of our pleasure, fly away; enjoy therefore the present time, and trust not too much to what to-morrow may produce.

Horace

The future is purchased by the present.

Samuel Johnson

Let us enjoy the fugitive hour. Man has no harbor, time has no shore, it rushes on and carries us with it.

Alphonse de Lamartine

Trust no Future, howe'er pleasant!
  Let the dead Past bury its dead!
Act—act in the living Present!
  Heart within, and God o'erhead!

Henry Wadsworth Longfellow

Every man's life lies within the present; for the past is spent and done with, and the future is uncertain.

Marcus Aurelius

Let any man examine his thoughts, and he will find them ever occupied with the past or the future. We scarcely think at all of the present; or if we do, it is only to borrow the light which it gives for regulating the future. The present is never our object; the past and the present we use as means; the future only is our end. Thus, we never live, we only hope to live.

Blaise Pascal

Look upon every day as the whole of life, not merely as a section; and enjoy and improve the present without wishing, through haste, to rush on to another.

Jean Paul Richter

Man, living, feeling man, is the easy sport of the over-mastering present.

Johann Christoph Friedrich von Schiller

See also: EXISTENCE, EXISTENTIALISM, FUTURE, PAST, TIME.

PRESIDENT

This is what I mean to people—sense and honesty and fairness and a decent amount of progress. I don't think the people want to be listening to a Roosevelt, sounding as if he were one of the Apostles, or the partisan yipping of Truman . . . So there's no use my making compromises with the truth, supposedly for the party, because if I were caught in one falsehood, and what I stand for in people's eyes got tarnished, then not just me but the whole Republican gang would be finished.

Dwight David Eisenhower

President means chief servant.

Mohandas Karamchand (Mahatma) Gandhi

An assasin's bullet has thrust upon me the awesome burden of the Presidency. I am here today to say I need your help. I cannot bear this burden alone. I need the help of all Americans, in all America.

Lyndon Baines Johnson

The greatest leader [John F. Kennedy] of our time has been struck down by the foulest deed of our time . . . No words are sad enough to express our sense of loss. No words are strong enough to express our determination to continue the forward thrust of America that he began.

Lyndon Baines Johnson

I think this is the most extraordinary collection of talent, of human knowledge, that has ever been gathered together at the White House—with the possible exception of when Thomas Jefferson dined alone.

John Fitzgerald Kennedy

He [John F. Kennedy] was a young lion, treading his way with a proud grace until a murderous hate stopped him in his path, and after that there was darkness.

Max Lerner

I have a theory that in the United States those who seek the Presidency never win it. Circumstances rather than a man's ambition determine the result. If he is the right man for the right time, he will be chosen.

Richard Milhous Nixon

I wanted to be a sports writer, but it took me too long to turn out my stuff. I found I could become Vice-President faster than I could become a newspaper man.

Richard Milhous Nixon

What a terrible thing [the assassination of John F. Kennedy] has happened to us all To you there, to us here, to all everywhere. Peace who was becoming bright-eyed, now sits in the shadow of death; her handsome champion has been killed as he walked by her very side. Her gallant boy is dead. What a cruel, foul, and most unnatural murder! We mourn here with you, poor, sad American people.

Sean O'Casey

Thinking of him [John F. Kennedy], we all see so vividly what we admire in a human life, and what are the great causes we care about. The impact of his example will help and inspire men and women for time yet to come.

Arthur Michael Ramsey

President Kennedy was so contemporary a man—so involved in our world—so immersed in our times—so responsive to its challenges—so intense a participant in the great events and great decisions of our day, that he seemed the very symbol of the vitality and exuberance that is the essence of life itself.

Adlai Ewing Stevenson

Any man who has had the job I've had and didn't have a sense of humor wouldn't still be here.

Harry S Truman

Hell, no. I'm glad to be rid of it. One really can't enjoy being President of the greatest republic in the history of the world. It's just too big a job for any one man to control it.

Harry S Truman

See also: AUTHORITY, DUTY, GOVERNMENT, NATION, OFFICE, PATRIOTISM.

PRESS

The press is good or evil according to the character of those who direct it. It is a mill that grinds all that is put into its hopper. Fill the hopper with poisoned grain and it will grind it to meal, but there is death in the bread.

William Cullen Bryant

The day of the printed word is far from ended. Swift as is the delivery of the radio bulletin, graphic as is television's eyewitness picture, the task of adding meaning and clarity remains urgent. People cannot and need not absorb meanings at the speed of light.

Erwin D. Canham

I would publish no book which would destroy a man's simple faith in God without providing an adequate substitute. I would publish no book which would destroy the institution of marriage without providing a substitute order of society which would be protective of the younger generation. All else I would cheerfully publish.

George H. Doran

In the long, fierce struggle for freedom of opinion, the press, like the Church, counted its martyrs by thousands.

James Abram Garfield

Let there be a fresh breeze of new honesty, new idealism, new integrity. And there, gentlemen, is where you come in. You have typewriters, presses and a huge audience. How about raising hell?

Jenkin Lloyd Jones

The press is our chief ideological weapon. Its duty is to strike down the enemies of the working class, the foes of the working people.

Nikita Sergeevich Khrushchev

When the press is the echo of sages and reformers, it works well; when it is the echo of turbulent cynics, it merely feeds political excitement.

Alphonse de Lamartine

This country is not priest-ridden, but press-ridden.

Henry Wadsworth Longfellow

What gunpowder did for war, the printing-press has done for the mind; the statesman is no longer clad in the steel of special education, but every reading man is his judge.

Wendell Phillips

See also: FREEDOM OF THE PRESS, JOURNALISM, NEWS, NEWSPAPER.

PRETENSION

True glory strikes root, and even extends itself; all false pretensions fall as do flowers, nor can any feigned thing be lasting.

Cicero

We are only vulnerable and ridiculous through our pretensions.

Delphine de Girardin

Where there is much pretension, much has been borrowed; nature never pretends.

Johann Kaspar Lavater

Pretences go a great way with men that take fair words and magisterial looks for current payment.

Sir Roger L'Estrange

We had better appear what we are, than affect to appear what we are not.

Duc François de La Rochefoucauld

Above all things it is, in my opinion, to play the fool egregiously to show off one's learning before the ignorant, to speak always with affected gravity. You should let yourself down to the level of those with whom you are conversing, and sometimes to pretend ignorance. Laying aside mental vigour and subtlety in the common intercourse of life, it is enough if you preserve decency and order in it. In short, creep along the ground if the world wish it.

Michel Eyquem de Montaigne

It is no disgrace not to be able to do everything; but to undertake or pretend to do what you are not made for, is not only shameful, but extremely troublesome and vexatious.

Plutarch

When you see a man with a great deal of religion displayed in his shop window, you may depend upon it he keeps a very small stock of it within.

Charles Haddon Spurgeon

The only good in pretending is the fun we get out of fooling ourselves that we fool somebody.

Booth Tarkington

See also: AFFECTATION, BOASTING, CONCEIT, FALSEHOOD, OSTENTATION.

PREVENTION

Preventives of evil are far better than remedies; cheaper and easier of application, and surer in result.

Tryon Edwards

Who would not give a trifle to prevent what he would give a thousand worlds to cure?

Edward Young

Laws act after crimes have been committed; prevention goes before them both.

Johann Georg von Zimmermann

See also: CAUTION, FORETHOUGHT.

PRIDE

When shall we learn to be proud? For only pride is creative.

Randolph Silliman Bourne

I think it humanly impossible for anyone to think of his own name as a word of little importance.

Frank Case

There is this paradox in pride—it makes some men ridiculous, but prevents others from becoming so.

Charles Caleb Colton

The proud are ever most provoked by pride.

William Cowper

Much that passes for pride in the behavior of the great comes from the fear of the betrayal of emotions that belong to a simpler manner of life.

Samuel McChord Crothers

Pride the first peer and president of hell.

Daniel Defoe

There is no greater pride than in seeking to humiliate ourselves beyond measure! and sometimes there is no truer humility than to attempt great works for God.

Jean Du Vergier de Hauranne

As Plato entertained some friends in a room where there was a couch richly ornamented, Diogenes came in very dirty, as usual, and getting upon the couch, and trampling on it, said, "I trample upon the pride of Plato." Plato mildly answered, "But with greater pride, Diogenes!"

Desderius Erasmus

Pride breakfasted with plenty, dined with poverty, and supped with infamy.

Benjamin Franklin

Pride is increased by ignorance; those assume the most who know the least.

John Gay

There was one who thought himself above me, and he was above me until he had that thought.

Elbert Green Hubbard

The seat of pride is in the heart, and only there; and if it be not there, it is neither in the look, nor in the clothes.

Edward Hyde (Lord Clarendon)

Pride is a vice, which pride itself inclines every man to find in others, and to overlook in himself.

Samuel Johnson

Pride is seldom delicate; it will please itself with very mean advantages.

Samuel Johnson

I frankly confess I have a respect for family pride. If it be a prejudice, it is prejudice in its most picturesque shape. But I hold it is connected with some of the noblest feelings in our nature.

Letitia Elizabeth Landon

Nature has given us pride to spare us the pain of being conscious of our imperfections.

Duc François de La Rochefoucauld

The vices I am talking of is Pride of Self-Conceit: and the virtue opposite to it, in Christian morals, is called Humility. You may remember, when I was talking about sexual morality, I warned you that the centre of Christian morals did not lie there. Well, now we have come to the centre. According to Christian teachers, the essential vice, the utmost evil, is Pride. Unchastity, anger, greed, drunkenness, and all that, are mere flea-bites in comparison: it was through Pride that the devil became the devil: Pride leads to every other vice: it is the complete anti-God state of mind.

Clive Staples (C. S.) Lewis

When pride and presumption walk before, shame and loss follow very closely.

Louis XI

To be proud and inaccessible is to be timid and weak.

Jean Baptiste Massillon

Pride counterbalances all our miseries, for it either hides them, or if it discloses them, boasts of that disclosure. Pride has such a thorough possession of us, even in the midst of our miseries and faults, that we are prepared to sacrifice life with joy, if it may but be talked of.

Blaise Pascal

Of all the causes which conspire to blind
Man's erring judgment, and misguide the
      mind,
What the weak head with strongest bias
      rules,
Is pride, the never-failing vice of fools.

Alexander Pope

Pride defeats its own end, by bringing the man who seeks esteem and reverence into contempt.

Henry St. John (Lord Bolingbroke)

Pride may be allowed to this or that degree, else a man cannot keep up his dignity. In gluttony there must be eating, in drunkenness there must be drinking; 'tis not the eating, and 'tis not the drinking that must be blamed, but the excess. So in pride.

John Selden

Men are sometimes accused of pride merely because their accusers would be proud themselves if they were in their places.

William Shenstone

If a man has a right to be proud of anything, it is of a good action done as it ought to be, without any base interest lurking at the bottom of it.

Laurence Sterne

We can believe almost anything if it be necessary to protect our pride.

Douglas Armour Thom

The infinitely little have a pride infinitely great.

Voltaire (François Marie Arouet)

See also: ARROGANCE, BOASTING, CONCEIT, EGOTISM, SNOB, VANITY.

PRINCIPLE

Always vote for a principle, though you vote alone, and you may cherish the sweet reflection that your vote is never lost.

John Quincy Adams

It is easier to fight for one's principles than to live up to them.

Alfred Adler

It is no simple matter to pause in the midst of one's maturity, when life is full of function, to examine what are the principles which control that functioning.

Pearl Sydenstricker Buck

He who merely knows right principles is not equal to him who loves them.

Confucius

A man who prides himself upon acting upon principle is likely to be a man who insists upon having his own way without learning from experience what is the better way.

John Dewey

The value of a principle is the number of things it will explain; and there is no good theory of a disease which does not at once suggest a cure.

Ralph Waldo Emerson

No single principle can answer all of life's complexities.

Felix Frankfurter

There are eternal principles which admit of no compromise; and one must be prepared to lay down one's life in the practice of them.

Mohandas Karamchand (Mahatma) Gandhi

We must be prepared to displease the dearest ones for the sake of principle.

Mohandas Karamchand (Mahatma) Gandhi

Work and struggle and never accept an evil that you can change.

André Gide

Many men do not allow their principles to take root, but pull them up every now and then, as children do the flowers they have planted, to see if they are growing.

Henry Wadsworth Longfellow

Back of every noble life there are principles which have fashioned it.

George Horace Lorimer

A principle is one thing; a maxim or rule is another. A principle requires liberality; a rule says, "one tenth." A principle says, "forgive"; a rule defines "seven times."

Frederick William Robertson

It is not talking nonsense that offends, but talking it in the name of principles.

Jean Rostand

Our principles are the springs of our actions; our actions, the springs of our happiness or misery. Too much care, therefore, cannot be taken in forming our principles.

Philip Skelton

The clearest statement of principle goes bad if it is repeated too often. It ceases to be a statement and becomes a slogan.

Virgil Thomson

The change we personally experience from time to time, we obstinately deny to our principles.

Johann Georg von Zimmermann

See also: BELIEF, CREED, DOCTRINE, LAW, MAXIM, OPINION, PRECEDENT, PRECEPT, THEORY.

PRIVACY

The forces allied against the individual have never been greater.

William Orville Douglas

The principle that a man's home is his castle is under new attack. For centuries the law of trespass protected a man's lands and his home. But in this age of advanced technology, thick walls and locked doors cannot guard our privacy or safeguard our personal freedom. Today we need a strong law—suited to modern conditions—to protect us from those who would trespass upon our conversations.

Lyndon Baines Johnson

Society is continually pushing in on the individual. He has only a few areas in which he can be himself, free from external restraint or observation.

Edward Vaughan Long

See also: PSYCHOMETRICS, SOLITUDE, SPYING, WIRETAPPING.

PROCRASTINATION

Everything comes to him who waits—among other things—death.

Francis Herbert Bradley

There is no fun in having nothing to do; the fun is having lots to do and not doing it.

Francis Herbert Bradley

Never do to-day what you can put off till to-morrow. Delay may give clearer light as to what is best to be done.

Aaron Burr

Indulge in procrastination, and in time you will come to this, that because a thing ought to be done, therefore you can't do it.

Charles Buxton

Delay not till to-morrow to be wise;
To-morrow's sun to thee may never rise.

William Congreve

Never put off till to-morrow that which you can do to-day.

Benjamin Franklin

Even if you're on the right track—
You'll get run over if you just sit there.
Arthur Godfrey

Putting off an easy thing makes it hard, and putting off a hard one makes it impossible.
George Horace Lorimer

Procrastination is the art of keeping up with yesterday.
Donald Robert Perry (Don) Marquis

See also: DELAY, TOMORROW.

PRODIGALITY

The injury of prodigality leads to this, that he that will not economize will have to agonize.
Confucius

The difference between the covetous man and the prodigal, is, that the former never has money, and the latter will have none shortly.
Ben (Benjamin) Jonson

The prodigal robs his heir, the miser robs himself. The middle way is, justice to ourselves and others.
Jean de La Bruyère

See also: EXTRAVAGANCE, GAMBLING, WASTE.

PROFANITY

It chills my blood to hear the blest Supreme
Rudely appealed to on each trifling theme.
Maintain your rank, vulgarity despise.
To swear is neither brave, polite, nor wise.
William Cowper

The devil tempts men through their ambition, their cupidity or their appetite, until he comes to the profane swearer, whom he catches without any bait or reward.
Horace Mann

Nothing is a greater, or more fearful sacrilege than to prostitute the great name of God to the petulancy of an idle tongue.
Jeremy Taylor

The foolish and wicked practice of profane cursing and swearing is a vice so mean and low, that every person of sense and character detests and despises it.
George Washington

See also: CURSE, IMPURITY, OATH.

PROFESSION

I hold every man a debtor to his profession.
Francis Bacon

In all professions each affects a look and an exterior to appear what he wishes the world to believe that he is. Thus we may say that the whole world is made up of appearances.
Duc François de La Rochefoucauld

See also: LABOR, OCCUPATION, TRADE.

PROGRESS

Intellectually, as well as politically, the direction of all true progress is toward greater freedom, and along an endless succession of ideas.
Christian Nestell Bovee

Progress is the law of life; man is not man as yet.
Robert Browning

By the disposition of a stupendous wisdom, moulding together the great mysterious incorporation of the human race, the whole, at one time, is never old, or middle-aged, or young, but moves on through the varied tenor of perpetual decay, fall, renovation, and progression.
Edmund Burke

Intercourse is the soul of progress.
Charles Buxton

Generations are as the days of toilsome mankind. What the father has made, the son can make and enjoy, but he has also work of his own appointed to him. Thus all things wax and roll onwards—arts, establishments, opinions; nothing is ever completed, but completing.
Thomas Carlyle

I have always considered that the substitution of the internal combustion engine for the horse marked a very gloomy milestone in the progress of mankind.
Sir Winston Leonard Spencer Churchill

If a man is not rising upward to be an angel, depend upon it, he is sinking downward to be a devil. He cannot stop at the beast.
Samuel Taylor Coleridge

He that is good, will infallibly become better, and he that is bad, will as certainly become worse; for vice, virtue, and time, are three things that never stand still.

Charles Caleb Colton

Behold the turtle. He makes progress only when he sticks his neck out.

James Bryant Conant

We cannot believe that the church of God is already possessed of all that light which God intends to give it; nor that all Satan's lurking-places have already been found out.

Jonathan Edwards

The path of human progress is not along the path of hatreds; it is not along the path of the extremes. It is along the path that represents the road where people of good will and real sensibilities can get together and say, "Here is a way we can go together."

Dwight David Eisenhower

What we call Progress is the exchange of one Nuisance for another Nuisance.

(Henry) Havelock Ellis

Progress is the activity of to-day and the assurance of to-morrow.

Ralph Waldo Emerson

If virtue promises happiness, prosperity and peace, then progress in virtue is progress in each of these; for to whatever point the perfection of anything brings us, progress is always an approach toward it.

Epictetus

The fact of progress is written plain and large on the page of history; but progress is not a law of nature. The ground gained by one generation may be lost by the next.

Herbert Albert Laurens Fisher

All that is human must retrograde if it do not advance.

Edward Gibbon

Nature knows no pause in progress and development, and attaches her curse on all inaction.

Johann Wolfgang von Goethe

I find the great thing in this world is not so much where we stand, as in what direction we are moving.

Oliver Wendell Holmes

Progress—the onward stride of God.

Victor Marie Hugo

The religion of inevitable progress—which is, in the last analysis, the hope and faith (in the teeth of all human experience) that one can get something for nothing.

Aldous Leonard Huxley

There is no law of progress. Our future is in our own hands, to make or to mar. It will be an uphill fight to the end, and would we have it otherwise? Let no one suppose that evolution will ever exempt us from struggles. "You forget," said the Devil, with a chuckle, "that I have been evolving too."

William Ralph Inge

Mankind does nothing save through initiatives on the part of inventors, great and small, and imitation by the rest of us—these are the sole factors active in human progress.

William James

The mere absence of war is not peace. The mere absence of recession is not growth.

John Fitzgerald Kennedy

The cruelties and obstacles of this swiftly changing planet will not yield to the obsolete dogmas and outworn slogans; they cannot be moved by those who cling to a present that is already dying, who prefer the illusion of security to the excitement and danger that come with even the most peaceful progress.

Robert Francis Kennedy

I look forward to a time when man shall progress upon something worthier and higher than his stomach.

Jack London

Progress is the real cure for an over-estimate of ourselves.

George Macdonald

Let us labor for that larger comprehension of truth, and that more thorough repudiation of error, which shall make the history of mankind a series of ascending developments.

Horace Mann

All the grand agencies which the progress of mankind evolves are the aggregate result of countless wills, each of which, thinking merely of its own end, and perhaps fully gaining it, is at the same time enlisted by Providence in the secret service of the world.

James Martineau

The moral law of the universe is progress. Every generation that passes idly over the earth without adding to that progress remains uninscribed upon the register of humanity, and the succeeding generation tramples its ashes as dust.

Giuseppe Mazzini

We are never present with, but always beyond ourselves. Fear, desire, and hope are still pushing us on toward the future.

Michel Eyquem de Montaigne

Mankind never loses any good thing, physical, intellectual, or moral, till it finds a better, and then the loss is a gain. No steps backward, is the rule of human history. What is gained by one man is invested in all men, and is a permanent investment for all time.

Theodore Parker

By a peculiar prerogative, not only each individual is making daily advances in the sciences, and may make advances in morality, but all mankind together are making a continual progress in proportion as the universe grows older; so that the whole human race, during the course of so many ages, may be considered as one man, who never ceases to live and learn.

Blaise Pascal

Humanity, let us say, is like people packed in an automobile which is travelling down hill without lights on a dark night at terrific speed and driven by a four-year-old child. The signposts along the way are all marked, "Progress."

Edward Plunkett (Lord Dunsany)

The test of our progress is not whether we add more to the abundance of those who have much; it is whether we provide enough for those who have too little.

Franklin Delano Roosevelt

An individual's deeds are of no use except to himself, or—through their results—to the community. We progress either for ourselves, alone, or for all.

Jean Rostand

He is only advancing in life, whose heart is getting softer, his blood warmer, his brain quicker, and his spirit entering into living peace.

John Ruskin

The true law of the race is progress and development. Whenever civilization pauses in the march of conquest, it is overthrown by the barbarian.

William Gilmore Simms

That past which is so presumptuously brought forward as a precedent for the present, was itself founded on some past that went before it.

Madame de Staël

Social progress is based on the annihilation of individualism.

Wilhelm Stekel

I know there are utopians who believe that human progress is inevitable, a divine trajectory irreversible in its upward motion. Let me just point out to them that in the last few thousand years we have blazed what I consider to be a trail of questionable glory—from Abraham and Isaac to Dennis the Menace.

Adlai Ewing Stevenson

The art of progress is to preserve order amid change, and to preserve change amid order. Life refuses to be embalmed alive.

Alfred North Whitehead

See also: IMPROVEMENT, REFORM, SCIENCE.

PROMISE

A mind conscious of integrity scorns to say more than it means to perform.

Robert Burns

Every brave man is a man of his word.

Pierre Corneille

Above all keep yourselves pure and clean, and learn to keep your promises even at the cost of life.

Mohandas Karamchand (Mahatma) Gandhi

Breach of promise is a base surrender of truth.

Mohandas Karamchand (Mahatma) Gandhi

Breach of promise is no less an act of insolvency than a refusal to pay one's debt.

Mohandas Karamchand (Mahatma) Gandhi

We promise according to our hopes, but perform according to our selfishness and our fears.

Duc François de La Rochefoucauld

Magnificent promises are always to be suspected.

> Theodore Parker

He who is most slow in making a promise is the most faithful in its performance.

> Jean Jacques Rousseau

He who promises runs in debt.

> Talmud

See also: DEBT, OATH, OBLIGATION, VOW.

PROMPTNESS

Deliberate with caution, but act with decision and promptness.

> Charles Caleb Colton

Timely service, like timely gifts, is doubled in value.

> George Macdonald

Promptitude is not only a duty, but is also a part of good manners; it is favorable to fortune, reputation, influence, and usefulness; a little attention and energy will form the habit, so as to make it easy and delightful.

> Charles Simmons

Promptness is the soul of business.

> Philip Dormer Stanhope (Lord Chesterfield)

See also: DISPATCH, HASTE, PUNCTUALITY.

PROOF

Hume took unwearied pains to prove that nothing could be proved.

> Edward Bellamy

I come from a State that raises corn and cotton and cockleburs and Democrats, and frothy eloquence neither convinces nor satisfies me. I am from Missouri. You have got to show me.

> Willard Duncan Vandiver

See also: EVIDENCE, FACT.

PROPAGANDA

Slogans are both exciting and comforting, but they are also powerful opiates for the conscience.

> James Bryant Conant

Some of mankind's most terrible misdeeds have been committed under the spell of certain magic words or phrases.

> James Bryant Conant

We have made the Reich by propaganda.

> Joseph Paul Goebbels

See also: ADVERTISING, NEWS, PUBLICITY.

PROPERTY

Property is merely the art of democracy. It means that every man should have something that he can shape in his own image.

> Gilbert Keith Chesterton

The accumulation of property is no guarantee of the development of character, but the development of character, or of any other good whatever, is impossible without property.

> William Graham Sumner

Property is dear to men not only for the sensual pleasure it can afford, but also because it is the bulwark of all they hold dearest on earth, and above all else, because it is the safeguard of those they love most against misery and all physical distress.

> William Graham Sumner

Material blessings, when they pass beyond the category of need, are weirdly fruitful of headache.

> Philip Wylie

See also: OWNERSHIP, POSSESSIONS, WEALTH.

PROSPERITY

All sunshine makes the desert.

> Arabian Proverb

Prosperity doth best discover vice, but adversity doth best discover virtue.

> Francis Bacon

Watch lest prosperity destroy generosity.

> Henry Ward Beecher

In prosperity prepare for a change; in adversity hope for one.

> James Burgh

In prosperity, let us take great care to avoid pride, scorn, and arrogance.

> Cicero

It is a frail mind that does not bear prosperity as well as adversity with moderation.

> Cicero

Prosperity is only an instrument to be used, not a deity to be worshipped.

> (John) Calvin Coolidge

The mind that is much elevated and insolent with prosperity, and cast down by adversity, is generally abject and base.

Epicurus

Everything in the world may be endured, except continual prosperity.

Johann Wolfgang von Goethe

The human race has had long experience and a fine tradition in surviving adversity. But we now face a task for which we have little experience, the task of surviving prosperity.

Alan Gregg

Men have no greater enemy than too great prosperity; for in consequence of it they are no longer their own masters; they become licentious and bold in the ways of wickedness, and ready to destroy their own good by running after novelties.

Francesco Guicciardini

As riches and favor forsake a man, we discover him to be a fool but nobody could find it out in his prosperity.

Jean de La Bruyère

The prosperous man is never sure that he is loved for himself.

Lucan

While prosperous you can number many friends; but when the storm comes you are left alone.

Ovid

Nothing is harder to direct than a man in prosperity; nothing more easily managed than one in adversity.

Plutarch

Prosperity makes friends, adversity tries them.

Publilius Syrus

If on this new continent we merely build another country of great but unjustly divided material prosperity, we shall have done nothing.

Theodore Roosevelt

The good things which belong to prosperity may be wished; but the good things which belong to adversity are to be admired.

Seneca

When God has once begun to tread upon the prosperous, He destroys them altogether. This is the end of the mighty.

Seneca

Who feels no ills, should, therefore, fear them; and when fortune smiles, be doubly cautious, lest destruction come remorseless on him, and he fall unpitied.

Sophocles

Prosperity is the touchstone of virtue; for it is less difficult to bear misfortunes, than to remain uncorrupted by pleasure.

Tacitus

One is never more on trial than in the moment of excessive good fortune.

Lewis (Lew) Wallace

It appears more difficult to find a man that bears prosperity well, than one that bears adversity well; for prosperity creates presumption in most men, but adversity brings sobriety to all.

Xenophon

Take care to be an economist in prosperity: there is no fear of your being one in adversity.

Johann Georg von Zimmermann

See also: FORTUNE, MONEY, POSSESSIONS, PROPERTY, RICHES, WEALTH.

PROTESTANTISM

The true force of Protestantism was its signal return to the individual conscience—to the method of Jesus.

Matthew Arnold

Religion shows a rosy color'd face,
Not hatter'd out with drudging works of grace;
A down-hill Reformation rolls apace.
What flesh and blood would crowd the narrow gate,
Or, till they waste their pamper'd paunches, wait?
All would be happy at the cheapest rate.

John Dryden

The religion of the Scotch Protestants is simply pork-eating Judaism.

Heinrich Heine

The Protestant principle, that "God alone is Lord of the conscience," has done more to give the mind power, and to strike off its chains, than any principle of mere secular policy in the most perfect "Bill of Rights."

Gardiner Spring

See also: CHRISTIANITY; REFORMATION, THE.

PROVERB

The genius, wit, and spirit of a nation are discovered in its proverbs.

Francis Bacon

Short sentences drawn from long experiences.

Miguel de Cervantes Saavedra

Proverbs were anterior to books, and formed the wisdom of the vulgar, and in the earliest ages were the unwritten laws of morality.

Benjamin Disraeli

Proverbs are the literature of reason, or the statements of absolute truth, without qualification. Like the sacred books of each nation, they are the sanctuary of its intuitions.

Ralph Waldo Emerson

A proverb has three characteristics: few words, right sense, fine image.

Moses ben Jacob Ibn-Ezra

Proverbs may be said to be the abridgments of wisdom.

Joseph Joubert

The proverbial wisdom of the populace in the street, on the roads, and in the markets, instructs the ear of him who studies man more fully than a thousand rules ostentatiously displayed.

Johann Kaspar Lavater

Proverbs, it has well been said, should be sold in pairs, a single one being but half a truth.

William Mathews

Proverbs are but rules, and rules do not create character. They prescribe conduct, but do not furnish a full and proper motive. They are usually but half truths, and seldom contain the principle of the action they teach.

Theodore Thornton Munger

Proverbs are somewhat analogous to those medical formulas which, being in frequent use, are kept ready made up in the chemists' shops, and which often save the framing of a distinct prescription.

Richard Whately

See also: APHORISM, APOTHEGM, QUOTATION.

PROVIDENCE

God hangs the greatest weights upon the smallest wires.

Francis Bacon

Some one has said that in war providence is on the side of the strongest regiments. And I have noticed that providence is on the side of clear heads and honest hearts;—and wherever a man walks faithfully in the ways that God has marked out for him, providence, as the Christian says,—luck, as the heathen says,—will be on that man's side. In the long run you will find that God's providence is in favor of those that keep his laws, and against those that break them.

Henry Ward Beecher

In the huge mass of evil as it rolls and swells, there is ever some good working toward deliverance and triumph.

Thomas Carlyle

Providence is a greater mystery than revelation. The state of the world is more humiliating to our reason than the doctrines of the Gospel. A reflecting Christian sees more to excite his astonishment, and to exercise his faith, in the state of things between Temple Bar and St. Paul's, than in what he reads from Genesis to Revelations.

Richard Cecil

The longer I live, the more faith I have in Providence, and the less faith in my interpretation of Providence.

Jeremiah Day

We are not to lead events, but follow them.

Epictetus

The longer I live, the more convincing proofs I see of this truth, that God governs in the affairs of man; and if a sparrow cannot fall to the ground without his notice, is it probable that an empire can rise without his aid?

Benjamin Franklin

What in me is dark
Illumine, what is low raise and support;
That to the height of this great argument
I may assert Eternal Providence,
And justify the ways of God to men.

John Milton

Who finds not Providence all good and wise,
Alike in what it gives and what denies?

Alexander Pope

I once asked a hermit in Italy how he could venture to live alone, in a single cottage, on the top of a mountain, a mile from any habitation? He replied, that Providence was his next-door neighbor.

Laurence Sterne

See also: ECONOMY, FORETHOUGHT, FRUGAL-ITY, GOD, PRUDENCE.

PRUDENCE

Men of sense often learn from their enemies. Prudence is the best safeguard. This principal cannot be learned from a friend, but an enemy extorts it immediately. It is from their foes, not their friends, that cities learn the lesson of building high walls and ships of war. And this lesson saves their children, their homes, and their properties.

Aristophanes

If the prudence of reserve and decorum dictates silence in some circumstances, in others prudence of a higher order, may justify us in speaking our thoughts.

Edmund Burke

It is by the goodness of God that in our country we have those three unspeakable precious things: freedom of speech, freedom of conscience, and the prudence never to practice either.

Samuel Langhorne Clemens (Mark Twain)

The rules of prudence, in general, like the laws of the stone tables, are for the most part prohibitive. Thou shalt not, is their characteristic formula; and it is an especial part of Christian prudence that it should be so.

Samuel Taylor Coleridge

There is nothing more imprudent than excessive prudence.

Charles Caleb Colton

The one prudence in life is concentration; the one evil is dissipation.

Ralph Waldo Emerson

The prudence of the best heads is often defeated by the tenderness of the best of hearts.

Henry Fielding

That man is prudent who neither hopes nor fears anything from the uncertain events of the future.

Anatole France

Those who, in the confidence of superior capacities or attainments, neglect the common maxims of life, should be reminded that nothing will supply the want of prudence; but that negligence and irregularity, long continued, will make knowledge useless, wit ridiculous, and genius contemptible.

Samuel Johnson

No other protection is wanting, provided you are under the guidance of prudence.

Juvenal

There is no amount of praise which is not heaped on prudence; yet there is not the most insignificant event of which it can make us sure.

Duc François de La Rochefoucauld

The richest endowments of the mind are temperance, prudence, and fortitude. Prudence is a universal virtue, which enters into the composition of all the rest; and where she is not, fortitude loses its name and nature.

Voltaire (François Marie Arouet)

See also: CAUTION, COMMON SENSE, DISCRETION, INTELLIGENCE, SENSE, WISDOM.

PSALM

I may truly name this book the anatomy of all parts of the soul; for no one can feel a movement of the spirit which is not reflected in this mirror. All the sorrows, troubles, fears, doubts, hopes, pains, perplexities, stormy outbreaks, by which the souls of men are tossed, are depicted here to the very life.

John Calvin

Let all the world in ev'ry corner sing
    My God and King.
The heav'ns are not too hight,
His praise may thither fly;
The earth is not too low,
His praises there may grow.
Let all the world in ev'ry corner sing
    My God and King.
The Church with psalms must shout,
No door can keep them out:
But above all, the heart
Must bear the longest part.

George Herbert

See also: BIBLE, ISRAEL, PRAYER, SONG.

PSYCHIATRY

It has long been a matter of fascination to me that Jews who have cut themselves off from all ties with their religious heritage still will often serve the culinary customs of their ancestors. A psychiatrist once told me the story of a young Jewish agnostic who had completely convinced himself that the religion of his fathers was stuff and nonsense. He visited the psychiatrist, however, because every time he ate pork he became deathly ill.

Steve Allen

The community needs psychiatric consultation in planning and operating its various services and agencies in order to insure mentally hygienic conditions in schools, recreation, industry, etc., and in order to modify those conditions that are threats to mental health.

George Salvadore Stevenson

See also: INSANITY, MENTAL HEALTH, MIND, PSYCHOLOGY, PSYCHOMETRICS.

PSYCHOANALYSIS: *see* PSYCHOLOGY.

PSYCHOLOGY

A wonderful discovery—psychoanalysis. Makes quite simple people feel they're complex.

Samuel Nathaniel Behrman

Anybody who is 25 or 30 years old has physical scars from all sorts of things, from tuberculosis to polio. It's the same with the mind.

Moses Ralph Kaufman

Psychoanalysis has changed American psychiatry from a diagnostic to a therapeutic science, not because so many patients are cured by the psychoanalytic technique, but because of the new understanding of psychiatric patients it has given us and the new and different concept of illness and health.

Karl Augustus Menninger

Every medical doctor needs to be also a doctor of the soul and . . . the parish minister needs to be a good psychologist as well as a good religionist.

Winfred Rhoades

See also: MENTAL HEALTH, MIND, PSYCHIATRY, PSYCHOMETRICS.

PSYCHOMETRICS

As long as learning is connected with earning, as long as certain jobs can only be reached through exams, so long must we take the examination system seriously. If another ladder to employment was contrived, much so-called education would disappear, and no one would be a penny the stupider.

Edward Morgan Forster

The invention of I.Q. did a great disservice to creativity in education. . . . Individuality, personality, originality, are too precious to be meddled with by amateur psychiatrists whose patterns for a "wholesome personality" are inevitably their own.

Joel Henry Hildebrand

I can only confess to a degree of disquiet over the possibilities for manipulation and exploitation of my fellow human beings inherent in the administrative use of personality tests and clinical diagnoses of adjustment for purposes of placement . . . The critical point is whether management has any moral right to invade the personality.

Douglas Murray McGregor

See also: MIND, PSYCHOLOGY.

PUBLIC

The public is wiser than the wisest critic.

George Bancroft

It it has to choose who is to be crucified, the crowd will always save Barabbas.

Jean Cocteau

The public wishes itself to be managed like a woman; one must say nothing to it except what it likes to hear.

Johann Wolfgang von Goethe

The public, with its mob yearning to be instructed, edified and pulled by the nose, demands certainties; . . . but there are no certainties.

Henry Louis Mencken

In a free and republican government, you cannot restrain the voice of the multitide. Every man will speak as he thinks, or, more properly, without thinking, and consequently will judge of effects without attending to their causes.

George Washington

Very few public men but look upon the public as their debtors and their prey; so much for their pride and honesty.

Johann Georg von Zimmerman

See also: MAN, MOB, NATION, PEOPLE, POPULACE, SOCIETY, STATE.

PUBLIC OPINION

Public opinion is, with multitides, a second conscience; with some, the only one.
William Rounseville Alger

Private opinion is weak, but public opinion is almost omnipotent.
Henry Ward Beecher

Popular opinion is the greatest lie in the world.
Thomas Carlyle

The institution that fails to win public support has no right to exist as such.
Mohandas Karamchand (Mahatma) Gandhi

Public opinion alone can keep a society pure and healthy.
Mohandas Karamchand (Mahatma) Gandhi

The voice of the people is the voice of God.
Mohandas Karamchand (Mahatma) Gandhi

I do not regret having braved public opinion, when I knew it was wrong and was sure it would be merciless.
Horace Greeley

A statesman should follow public opinion as a coachman follows his horses; having firm hold on the reins, and guiding them.
Julius Charles Hare

Social opinion is like a sharp knife. There are foolish people who regard it only with terror, and dare not touch or meddle with it; there are more foolish people, who, in rashness or defiance, seize it by the blade, and get cut and mangled for their pains; and there are wise people, who grasp it discreetly and boldly by the handle, and use it to carve out their own purposes.
Anna Brownell Murphy Jameson

Where mass opinion dominates the government, there is a morbid derangement of the true functions of power. . . . The prevailing public opinion has been destructively wrong at the critical junctures. The people have imposed a veto upon the judgments of informed and responsible officials.
Walter Lippmann

There is no tyranny so despotic as that of public opinion among a free people.
Donn Piatt

Each man in his sphere, however narrow or extended, will find that his fellowmen weigh his character and his abilities often, and unconsciously stamp him with their estimate: and that the average resultant of these frequent estimates is just.
Edwards Pierrepont

Public opinion, or public sentiment, is able to sustain, or to pull down any law of the commonwealth.
Charles Simmons

Let a man proclaim a new principle. Public sentiment will surely be on the other side.
Thomas Brackett Reed

Public opinion is a weak tyrant compared with our private opinion. What a man thinks of himself, that it is which determines, or rather indicates his fate.
Henry David Thoreau

See also: OPINION, REPUTATION.

PUBLIC SPEAKING

An after-dinner speech is like a love letter. Ideally, you should begin by not knowing what you are going to say, and end by not knowing what you've said.
William Allen Jowitt (First Earl Jowitt)

I know that one is able to win people far more by the spoken than by the written word, and that every great movement on this globe owes its rise to the great speakers and not to the great writers.
Adolf Hitler

See also: ORATORY, PREACHING, SPEECH.

PUBLICITY

I have often wondered if newspaper publicity would not have had thirteen original colonies fighting among themselves if we had been present at their conference at the time of the Revolution.
William Hard

Whenever, wherever, or however you tell a number of people the same thing at the same time—and with any enthusiasm beyond the mere pleasure of the occasion—it can be called Publicity.
Christopher Darlington Morley

Publicity, *publicity*, PUBLICITY is the greatest moral factor and force in our public life.

Joseph Pulitzer

See also: ADVERTISING, COMMERCIAL, PRESS.

PUNCTUALITY

The most indispensable qualification of a cook is punctuality. The same must be said of guests.

Anthelme Brillat-Savarin

Strict punctuality is, perhaps, the cheapest virtue which can give force to an otherwise utterly insignificant character.

John Frederick Boyes

Appointments once made, become debts. If I have made an appointment with you, I owe you punctuality; I have no right to throw away your time, if I do my own.

Richard Cecil

Method is the very hinge of business; and there is no method without punctuality.

Richard Cecil

I could never think well of a man's intellectual or moral character, if he was habitually unfaithful to his appointments.

Nathaniel Emmons

Want of punctuality is a want of virtue.

John Mitchell Mason

Nothing inspires confidence in a business man sooner than punctuality, nor is there any habit which sooner saps his reputation than that of being always behind time.

William Mathews

I have always been a quarter of an hour before my time, and it has made a man of me.

Horatio Nelson (Lord Nelson)

See also: DISPATCH, HASTE, PROMPTNESS.

PUNISHMENT

Punishment is justice for the unjust.

Augustine of Hippo

The exposition of future punishment in God's word is not to be regarded as a threat, but as a merciful declaration. If in the ocean of life, over which we are bound to eternity, there are these rocks and shoals, it is no cruelty to chart them down; it is an eminent and prominent mercy.

Henry Ward Beecher

It is better that ten guilty persons escape than one innocent suffer.

Sir William Blackstone

The public has more interest in the punishment of an injury than he who receives it.

Cato the Elder

God in on the side of virtue; for whoever dreads punishment suffers it, and whoever deserves it dreads it.

Charles Caleb Colton

The certainty of punishment, even more than its severity, is the preventive of crime.

Tryon Edwards

The work of eradicating crimes is not by making punishment familiar, but formidable.

Oliver Goldsmith

Punishment is lame, but it comes.

George Herbert

Society does not punish those who sin, but those who sin and conceal not cleverly.

Elbert Green Hubbard

We are not punished for our sins, but by them.

Elbert Green Hubbard

Never was the voice of conscience silenced without retribution.

Anna Brownell Murphy Jameson

Even legal punishments lose all appearance of justice, when too strictly inflicted of men compelled by the last extremity of distress to incur them.

Junius

One man meets an infamous punishment for that crime which confers a diadem upon another.

Juvenal

If punishment makes not the will supple it hardens the offender.

John Locke

Jails and prisons are the complement of schools; so many less as you have of the latter, so many more you must have of the former.

Horace Mann

The object of punishment is the prevention of evil; it can never be made impulsive to good.

Horace Mann

We do not aim to correct the man we hang; we correct and warn others by him.

Michel Eyquem de Montaigne

It is as expedient that a wicked man be punished as that a sick man be cured by a physician; for all chastisement is a kind of medicine.

Plato

There is no greater punishment than that of being abandoned to one's self.

Pasquier Quesnel

To conclude, frequency of punishment is always a sign of weakness or supineness in a government. There is no knave that may not be made good for something. No one ought to be put to death, even for the sake of example, except the man who cannot be preserved without danger.

Jean Jacques Rousseau

We will not punish a man because he hath offended, but that he may offend no more; nor does punishment ever look to the past, but to the future; for it is not the result of passion, but that the same thing may be guarded against in time to come.

Seneca

To make punishments efficacious, two things are necessary; they must never be disproportioned to the offence, and they must be certain.

William Gilmore Simms

The punishment of criminals should be of use; when a man is hanged he is good for nothing.

Voltaire (François Marie Arouet)

This, it seems to me, is the most severe punishment—finding out you are wrong.

Walter Winchell

See also: CAPITAL PUNISHMENT, CRIME, DISCIPLINE, JUSTICE, LAW, RETRIBUTION.

PUNS

And torture one poor word ten thousand ways.

John Dryden

A pun is a noble thing per se. It fills the mind; it is as perfect as a sonnet; better.

Charles Lamb

Punning, like poetry, is something every person belittles and everyone attempts.

Louis Untermeyer

See also: HUMOR, JESTING.

PURITY

Purity consists first of all in possessing a pure heart but what there is in the heart comes out also and is shown in outward acts and outward behaviour.

Mohandas Karamchand (Mahatma) Gandhi

Purity of personal life is the one indispensable condition for building up a sound education.

Mohandas Karamchand (Mahatma) Gandhi

My strength is as the strength of ten,
Because my heart is pure.

Alfred, Lord Tennyson

See also: CHASTITY, INNOCENCE, MAIDENHOOD, MODESTY, PERFECTION, VIRTUE.

PURPOSE

The good man is the man who, no matter how morally unworthy he has been, is moving to become better.

John Dewey

The secret of success is constancy to purpose.

Benjamin Disraeli

It is better by a noble boldness to run the risk of being subject to half of the evils we anticipate, than to remain in cowardly listlessness for fear of what may happen.

Herodotus

Only the consciousness of a purpose that is mightier than any man and worthy of all men can fortify and inspirit and compose the souls of men.

Walter Lippmann

Lack of something to feel important about is almost the greatest tragedy a man may have.

Arthur Ernest Morgan

Man's chief purpose . . . is the creation and preservation of values.

Lewis Mumford

A person is really alive only when he is moving forward to something more.

> *Winfred Rhoades*

Nature has no particular goal in view, and final causes are mere human figments.

> *Baruch (Benedict) Spinoza*

Man proposes, but God disposes.

> *Thomas à Kempis*

See also: AIM, AMBITION, DECISION, IDEAL, INTENTION, OBJECTIVE, RESOLUTION.

PURSUIT

Like one that on a lonesome road
Doth walk in fear and dread,
And having once turned round walks on,
And turns no more his head;
Because he knows a frightful fiend
Doth close behind him tread.

> *Samuel Taylor Coleridge*

The rapture of pursuing is the prize the vanquished gain.

> *Henry Wadsworth Longfellow*

I take it to be a principal rule of life, not to be too much addicted to one thing.

> *Terence*

See also: ANTICIPATION, COURTSHIP, INQUIRY, ZEAL.

Q

QUAKERS

He [Oliver Cromwell] said: "I see there is a people risen, that I cannot win either with gifts, honours, offices or places; but all other sects and people I can."

George Fox

Justice Bennet of Derby, was the first that called us Quakers, because I bid them tremble at the word of the Lord. This was in the year 1650.

George Fox

We should all then, like the Quakers, live without an order of priests, moralize for ourselves, follow the oracles of conscience, and say nothing about what no man can understand, nor therefore believe.

Thomas Jefferson

See also: CHRISTIANITY, PROTESTANTISM, SECT.

QUALITY

It is the quality of our work which will please God and not quantity.

Mohandas Karamchand (Mahatma) Gandhi

Strength of numbers is the delight of the timid. The valiant of spirit glory in fighting alone. Be you one or many, this valour is the only true valour, all else is false. And the valour of the spirit cannot be achieved without Sacrifice, Determination, Faith and Humility.

Mohandas Karamchand (Mahatma) Gandhi

I think there is only one quality worse than hardness of heart and that is softness of head.

Theodore Roosevelt

See also: ABILITY, CHARACTER, VALUE, WORTH.

QUARREL

So also those false alarms of strife
Between the husband and the wife,
And little quarrels often prove
To be but new recruits of love;
When those who're always kind of coy,
In time must either tire or cloy.

Samuel Butler

Quarrels would not last long if the wrong was all on one side.

Duc François de La Rochefoucauld

When chickens quit quarrelling over their food they often find that there is enough for all of them. I wonder if it might not be the same with the human race.

Donald Robert Perry (Don) Marquis

See also: ANGER, ARGUMENT, CONTENTION, ENEMY, OPPOSITION.

QUESTION

I am prejudiced in favor of him who, without impudence, can ask boldly. He has faith in humanity, and faith in himself. No one who is not accustomed to give grandly can ask nobly and with boldness.

Johann Kaspar Lavater

Man will not live without answers to his questions.

Hans Joachim Morgenthau

No man really becomes a fool until he stops asking questions.

Charles Proteus Steinmetz

We must not expect simple answers to far-reaching questions. However far our gaze penetrates, there are always heights beyond which block our vision.

Alfred North Whitehead

See also: CURIOSITY, DOUBT, INQUIRY, INQUISITIVENESS, UNCERTAINTY.

QUIET

The good and the wise lead quiet lives.

Euripides

To have a quiet mind is to possess one's mind wholly; to have a calm spirit is to command one's self.

Hamilton Wright Mabie

The holy time is quiet as a Nun
Breathless with adoration.

William Wordsworth

See also: PEACE, REPOSE, REST, SILENCE.

QUOTATION

When a thing has been said and well said, have no scruple: take it and copy it. Give references? Why should you? Either your readers know where you have taken the passage and the precaution is needless, or they do not know and you humiliate them.

Anatole France

Certain brief sentences are peerless in their ability to give one the feeling that nothing remains to be said.

Jean Rostand

Now we sit through Shakespeare in order to recognize the quotations.

Orson Welles

See also: APOTHEGM, MAXIM, PROVERB.

R

RACE

The fear I heard in my father's voice . . . when he realized that I really *believed* I could do anything a white boy could do, and had every intention of proving it, was not at all like the fear I heard when one of us was ill or had fallen down the stairs or strayed too far from the house. It was another fear, a fear that the child, in challenging the white world's assumptions, was putting himself in the path of destruction.

James Baldwin

If we were to select the most intelligent, imaginative, energetic and emotionally stable third of mankind, all races would be represented.

Franz Boas

Nobody has ever given satisfactory proof of an inherent inequality of races.

Franz Boas

There is in America today a generation of white youth that is truly worthy of a black man's respect, and this is a rare event in the foul annals of American history.

Eldridge Cleaver

The racist conscience of America is such that murder does not register as murder, really, unless the victim is white.

Eldridge Cleaver

Ontology—once it was finally admitted as leaving experience by the wayside—does not permit us to understand the being of the black man. For not only must the black man be black; he must be black in relation to the white man.

Frantz Fanon

At the best, however, belief in race dogma is just the same as national chauvinism, a symptom of immaturity, lack of experience, and in general of an intellectually poor individuality.

Friedrich Otto Hertz

At the heart of racism is the religious assertion that God made a creative mistake when He brought some people into being.

George Dennis Sale Kelsey

I have a dream that one day on the red hills of Georgia, the sons of former slaves and the sons of former slave-owners will be able to sit together at the table of brotherhood. . . . That one day even the State of Mississippi, a state sweltering with the heat of injustice, sweltering with the heat of oppression, will be transformed into an oasis of freedom and justice. . . . That my four little children will one day live in a nation where they will not be judged by the color of their skin but by the content of their character.

Martin Luther King, Jr.

I want to be the white man's brother, not his brother-in-law.

Martin Luther King, Jr.

The Negro lives on a lonely island of poverty in the midst of a vast ocean of material prosperity and finds himself an exile in his own land.

Martin Luther King, Jr.

Race is a fiction . . . human races are not pure, i.e., strictly speaking, there is no such thing as a race.

Bernard Lazare

With the mingling of races there is increasing life and vigor.

Leone Levi

I have one criticism (about) Negro troops who fought under my command in the Korean War. They didn't send me enough of them.

Douglas MacArthur

Our nation was born in genocide when it embraced the doctrine that the original American, the Indian, was an inferior race.

Malcolm X.

An adequate explanation of racial antagonisms can be found in impulses and motives that are independent of race.

John Houldsworth Oldham

"Race" is the cheap explanation tyros offer for any collective trait that they are too stupid or too lazy to trace to its origin in the physical environment, the social environment, or historical conditions.

Edward Alsworth Ross

The sin of racial pride still represents the most basic challenge to the American conscience. We cannot dodge this challenge without renouncing our highest moral pretentions.

Arthur Meier Schlesinger

A heavy guilt rests upon us for what the whites of all nations have done to the colored peoples. When we do good to them, it is not benevolence—it is atonement.

Albert Schweitzer

Can one preach at home inequality of races and nations and advocate abroad good-will towards all men?

Dorothy Thompson

Neither race nor environment, taken by itself, can be the positive factor which, within the last six thousand years, has shaken humanity out of its static repose on the level of primitive society and started it on the hazardous quest of civilization.

Arnold Joseph Toynbee

See also: AFRICA, BLACK POWER, NEGRO, PREJUDICE, RACISM, SOCIETY.

RACISM

The time is past when Christians in America can take a long spoon and hand the gospel to the black man out the back door.

Mordecai Wyatt Johnson

The importance that this Southern Negro sees in the elections in the United States is not who is elected President, all he wants to know is who's going to be Sheriff. That's the person who's going to be on his back. I'm not talking about Negroes in the universi-

ties, I'm talking about the ordinary **Negro** whose life is just one risk after another.

James Madison Nabrit, Jr.

Dr. King was a symbol of the nonviolent civil rights protest movement. He was a man of peace, of dedication, of great courage. His senseless assassination solves nothing. It will not stay the civil rights movement; it will instead spur it to greater activity. It is to be hoped that this tragedy will help move the American people to prompt action to expunge racism from our national life. If such action is taken forthwith, the sacrifice of this great and good man will not have been in vain.

Roy Wilkins

See also: BIGOTRY, PREJUDICE, RACE.

RADIATION

It has long been recognized, of course, that the wide range of diagnostic and therapeutic X-ray devices used in medicine, while they are of inestimable value in modern medical care, still afford great risks if defective or misused.

E. L. (Bob) Bartlett

We have developed, in this country and abroad, a vast wealth of information as to what irradiation does to living cells—human and nonhuman—and this knowledge is being expanded upon every day in both private and public research laboratories.

Jennings Randolph

See also: NUCLEAR ENERGY, TECHNOLOGY.

RADIO: see TELEVISION.

RAGE

Rage is essentially vulgar, and never more vulgar than when it proceeds from mortified pride, disappointed ambition, or thwarted wilfulness.

William Hart Coleridge

'Tis in my head; 'tis in my heart; 'tis everywhere; it rages like a madness, and I most wonder how my reason holds.

Thomas Otway

When transported by rage, it is best to observe its effects on those who deliver themselves up to the same passion.

Plutarch

See also: ANGER, EMOTION, HATE, PASSION, RESENTMENT.

RAILLERY

The raillery which is consistent with good breeding is a gentle animadversion on some foible, which, while it raises the laugh in the rest of the company, doth not put the person rallied out of countenance, or expose him to shame or contempt. On the contrary, the jest should be so delicate that the object of it should be capable of joining in the mirth it occasions.

Henry Fielding

Raillery is sometimes more insupportable than wrong; because we have a right to resent injuries, but it is ridiculous to be angry at a jest.

Duc François de La Rochefoucauld

If nettled by severe raillery, conceal the sting if you would escape a repetition of the evil.

Sir Roger L'Estrange

Raillery is a mode of speaking in favor of one's wit against one's good nature.

Charles de Secondat (Baron de Montesquieu)

Good humor is the best shield against the darts of satirical raillery.

Charles Simmons

See also: HUMOR, IRONY, JESTING, RIDICULE, SARCASM, SATIRE.

RAIN

We knew it would rain, for the poplars showed
The white of their leaves, the amber grain
Shrunk in the wind—and the lightning now
Is tangled in tremulous skeins of rain!

Thomas Bailey Aldrich

The thirsty earth soaks up the rain,
And drinks, and gapes, for drink again.

Abraham Cowley

Clouds dissolved the thirsty ground supply.

Wentworth Dillon (Earl of Roscommon)

Fall on me like a silent dew,
Or like those maiden showers
Which, by the peep of day, doe strew
A baptime o're the flowers.

Robert Herrick

The hooded clouds, like friars,
Tell their beads in drops of rain.

Henry Wadsworth Longfellow

The kind refresher of the summer heats.

Edward Thomson

See also: CLOUD, NATURE, RAINBOW.

RAINBOW

Be thou the rainbow to the storms of life,
The evening beam that smiles the clouds away,
And tints to-morrow with prophetic ray!

George Gordon Byron (Lord Byron)

That gracious thing, made up of tears and light.

Samuel Taylor Coleridge

That smiling daughter of the storm.

Charles Caleb Colton

My heart leaps up when I behold
A rainbow in the sky:
So was it when my life began;
So is it now I am a man;
So be it when I shall grow old,
Or let me die.
The child is father of the man;
And I could wish my days to be
Bound each to each by natural piety.

William Wordsworth

See also: NATURE, RAIN, SUN.

RANK

The rank is but the guinea's stamp,
The man's the gowd for a'that.

Robert Burns

Every error of the mind is the more conspicuous, and culpable, in proportion to the rank of the person who commits it.

Juvenal

Rank is a great beautifier.

Edward G. Bulwer-Lytton (Baron Lytton)

Distinction of rank is necessary for the economy of the world, and was never called in question, but by barbarians and enthusiasts.

Nicholas Rowe

Rank and riches are chains of gold, but still chains.

Giovanni Ruffini

To be vain of one's rank or place, is to show that one is below it.

Stanislas I (Leszczyński)

I weigh the man, not his title; 'tis not the king's stamp can make the metal better.

William Wycherley

See also: ANCESTRY, ARISTOCRACY, BIRTH, NOBILITY, OFFICE, PLACE, POSITION, STATION, TITLE.

RASHNESS

Cotton Mather used to say there was a gentleman mentioned in the nineteenth chapter of Acts, to whom he was more deeply indebted than almost any other person. And that was the town clerk of Ephesus, whose counsel was to do nothing rashly. Upon any proposal of consequence it was usual with him to say, "Let us first consult with the town clerk of Ephesus." What mischief, trouble, and sorrow would be avoided in the world were the people more in the habit of consulting this gentleman.

Francis Bacon

Rashness is the characteristic of ardent youth, and prudence that of mellowed age.

Cicero

Some act first, think afterward, and then repent forever.

Charles Simmons

See also: FOLLY, HASTE, IMPULSE, INDISCRETION, RECKLESSNESS.

READING

Reading is a basic tool in the living of a good life.

Mortimer Jerome Adler

One must be rich in thought and character to owe nothing to books, though preparation is necessary to profitable reading; and the less reading is better than more:—book-stuck men are of all readers least wise, however knowing or learned.

Amos Bronson Alcott

Reading maketh a full man; conference a ready man; and writing an exact man; and, therefore, if a man write little, he had need have a great memory; if he confer little, he had need have a present wit; and if he read little, he had need have much cunning, to seem to know that he doth not.

Francis Bacon

When I am dead, I hope it may be said:
"His sins were scarlet, but his books were read."

Hilaire Belloc

It is well to read everything of something, and something of everything.

Henry Peter Brougham (Lord Brougham)

To read without reflecting, is like eating without digesting.

Edmund Burke

It was from my own early experience that I decided there was no use to which money could be applied so productive of good to boys and girls who have good within them and ability and ambition to develop it as the founding of a public library.

Andrew Carnegie

They that have read about everything are thought to understand everything too; but it is not always so. We are of the ruminating kind, and it is not enough to cram ourselves with a great load of collections. Unless we chew them over again, they will not give us strength and nourishment.

William Ellery Channing

Force yourself to reflect on what you read, paragraph by paragraph.

Samuel Taylor Coleridge

By reading, we enjoy the dead; by conversation, the living; and by contemplation, ourselves. Reading enriches the memory; conversation polishes the wit; and contemplation improves the judgment. Of these, reading is the most important, as it furnishes both the others.

Charles Caleb Colton

Every book salesman is an advance agent for culture and for better citizenship, for education and for the spread of intelligence.

Frank Crane

If a book is dull, that is a matter between itself and its maker; but if it makes me duller than I should otherwise have been, I have a grievance.

Samuel McChord Crothers

We should be as careful of the books we read, as of the company we keep. The dead very often have more power than the living.

Tryon Edwards

Reading, after a certain age, diverts the mind too much from its creative pursuits. Any man who reads too much and uses his own brain too little falls into lazy habits of thinking.

Albert Einstein

Reading should be in proportion to thinking, and thinking in proportion to reading.

Nathaniel Emmons

The teaching of reading—all over the United States, in all the schools, in all the text books—is totally wrong and flies in the face of all logic and common sense. Johnny couldn't read . . . for the simple reason that nobody ever showed him how. Johnny's only problem was that he was unfortunately exposed to an ordinary American school.

Rudolf Franz Flesch

Leibnitz has obtained this fruit from his great reading, that he has a mind better exercised for receiving all sorts of ideas, more susceptible of all forms, more accessible to that which is new and even opposed to him, more indulgent to human weakness, more disposed to favorable interpretations, and more industrious to find them.

Bernard Le Bovier de Fontenelle

A man of ability, for the chief of his reading, should select such works as he feels are beyond his own power to have produced. What can other books do for him but waste his time or augment his vanity?

John Watson Foster

Every reader if he has a strong mind, reads himself into the book, and amalgamates his thoughts with those of the author.

Johann Wolfgang von Goethe

There are three classes of readers: some enjoy without judgment; others judge without enjoyment; and some there are who judge while they enjoy, and enjoy while they judge. The latter class reproduces the work of art on which it is engaged. Its numbers are very small.

Johann Wolfgang von Goethe

The first time I read an excellent work, it is to me just as if I had gained a new friend; and when I read over a book I have perused before, it resembles the meeting with an old one.

Oliver Goldsmith

Read much, but not many works.

Sir William Hamilton

By conversing with the mighty dead we imbibe sentiment with knowledge. We become strongly attached to those who can no longer either hurt or serve us, except through the

influence which they exert over the mind. We feel the presence of that power which gives immortality to human thoughts and actions, and catch the flame of enthusiasm from all nations and ages.

William Hazlitt

There is a gentle, but perfectly irresistible coercion in a habit of reading well directed, over the whole tenor of a man's character and conduct, which is not the least effectual because it works insensibly and because it is really the last thing he dreams of.

Sir John Frederick William Herschel

Had I read as much as others, I had remained as ignorant as they.

Thomas Hobbes

Anybody that's got time to read half of the new books has got entirely too much time.

Frank McKinney (Kin) Hubbard

To destroy the Western tradition of independent thought it is not necessary to burn the books. All we have to do is to leave them unread for a couple of generations.

Robert Maynard Hutchins

Reading is one of our bad habits . . . We read, most of the time, not because we wish to instruct ourselves, not because we long to have our feelings touched and our imagination fired, but . . . because we have time to spare.

Aldous Leonard Huxley

The foundation of knowledge must be laid by reading. General principles must be had from books, which, however, must be brought to the test of real life. In conversation you never get a system. What is said upon a subject is to be gathered from a hundred people. The parts of a truth, which a man gets thus, are at such a distance from each other, that he never attains to a full view.

Samuel Johnson

One ought to read just as inclination takes him, for what he reads as a task will do him little good.

Samuel Johnson

What is twice read is commonly better remembered than what is transcribed.

Samuel Johnson

Stupid people read a book and do not understand it: second-rate minds think that they understand it perfectly: master spirits sometimes do not understand it entirely: that appears to them obscure which is obscure, as that seems clear which is clear. Witlings try to look upon that as obscure which is not so, and not to understand what is perfectly intelligible.

Jean de La Bruyère

The wise man reads both books and life itself.

Lin Yutang

A page digested is better than a volume hurriedly read.

Thomas Babington Macaulay

As you grow ready for it, somewhere or other, you will find what is needful for you in a book.

George Macdonald

Resolve to edge in a little reading every day, if it is but a single sentence. If you gain fifteen minutes a day, it will make itself felt at the end of the year.

Horace Mann

There is no more merit in having read a thousand books than in having ploughed a thousand fields.

(William) Somerset Maugham

Deep versed in books, but shallow in himself.

John Milton

No entertainment is so cheap as reading, nor any pleasure so lasting.

Lady Mary Wortley Montagu

I divide all readers into two classes: those who read to remember and those who read to forget.

William Lyon Phelps

He picked something valuable out of everything he read.

Pliny the Elder

The best teacher is not life, but the crystallized and distilled experience of the most sensitive, reflective, and most observant of our human beings, and this experience you will find preserved in our great books and nowhere else.

Nathan Marsh Pusey

In spite of the wide increase of literacy, we are beginning to rely so much on pictured announcements that we shall soon forget how to read.

Max Radin

Do not give him pieces to recite from tragedies or comedies, nor teach him, as they say, to declaim. Teach him to speak without stammering, distinctly, to articulate clearly, to pronounce with precision and without affectation, to understand and follow grammatical accent and prosody, to speak with sufficient loudness to be heard, but never more than is necessary; a defect generally found in children brought up in schools; in short, nothing too much.

Jean Jacques Rousseau

There was so much of splendor and of glory,
There was so much of wonder and delight,
That there can be no ending of our story
Although the book is closed and it is night.

Margaret Elizabeth Sangster

Reading made Don Quixote a gentleman, but believing what he read made him mad.

George Bernard Shaw

It is manifest that all government of action is to be gotten by knowledge, and knowledge, best, by gathering many knowledges, which is reading.

Sir Philip Sidney

What blockheads are those wise persons, who think it necessary that a child should comprehend everything it reads.

Robert Southey

Reading is seeing by proxy.

Herbert Spencer

Insist on reading the great books, on marking the great events of the world. Then the little books can take care of themselves, and the trivial incidents of passing politics and diplomacy may perish with the using.

Arthur Penrhyn Stanley

We read too much; we have forgotten how to listen.

(Joseph) Lincoln Steffens

Reading is the work of the alert mind, is demanding, and under ideal conditions produces finally a sort of ecstasy. This gives the experience of reading a sublimity and power unequaled by any other form of communication.

Elwyn Brooks White

If one cannot enjoy reading a book over and over again, there is no use in reading it at all.

Oscar Wilde

I would never read a book if it were possible for me to talk half an hour with the man who wrote it.

(Thomas) Woodrow Wilson

Get a habit, a passion for reading; not flying from book to book, with the squeamish caprice of a literary epicure; but read systematically, closely, thoughtfully, analyzing every subject as you go along, and laying it up carefully and safely in your memory. It is only by this mode that your information will be at the same time extensive, accurate, and useful.

William Wirt

Never read a book through merely because you have begun it.

John Witherspoon

The man whom neither riches nor luxury nor grandeur can render happy may, with a book in his hand, forget all his troubles under the friendly shade of every tree, and may experience pleasures as infinite as they are varied, as pure as they are lasting, as lively as they are unfading, and as compatible with every public duty as they are contributory to private happiness.

Johann Georg von Zimmermann

See also: BOOK, LEARNING, NEWSPAPER.

REALISM

Boys like romantic tales; but babies like realistic tales—because they find them romantic. In fact, a baby is about the only person, I should think, to whom a modern realistic novel could be read without boring him.

Gilbert Keith Chesterton

The realist is the man, who having weighed all the visible factors in a given situation and having found that the odds are against him, decides that fighting is useless.

Raoul de Sales

Most advocates of realism in this world are hopelessly unrealistic.

Jawaharlal Nehru

See also: FACT, REALITY, TRUTH.

REALITY

Facts are facts and will not disappear on account of your likes.

Jawaharlal Nehru

The non-recognition of realities naturally leads to artificial policies and programmes.

Jawaharlal Nehru

A theory must be tempered with reality.

Jawaharlal Nehru

The world of reality has its limits; the world of imagination is boundless. Not being able to enlarge the one, let us contract the other: for it is from their difference alone that all the evils arise which render us really unhappy.

Jean Jacques Rousseau

No matter how thin you slice it, it's still boloney.

Alfred Emanuel Smith

See also: EXISTENCE, EXISTENTIALISM, PHILOSOPHY, REALISM, TRUTH.

REASON

Man is a creature of impulse, emotion, action rather than reason. Reason is a very late development in the world of living creatures, most of whom, as far as we know, get along admirably in daily life without it.

James Truslow Adams

The voice of reason is more to be regarded than the bent of any present inclination; since inclination will at length come over to reason, though we can never force reason to comply with inclination.

Joseph Addison

"Theirs not to make reply, theirs not to reason why," may be a good enough motto for men who are on their way to be shot. But from such men expect no empires to be builded, no inventions made, no great discoveries brought to light.

Bruce Barton

If we would guide by the light of reason, we must let our minds be bold.

Louis Dembitz Brandeis

It is good sense, reason that produces everything: virtue, genius, wit, talent, and taste. What is virtue? reason in practice. Talent? reason enveloped in glory. Wit? reason which

is chastely expressed. Taste is nothing else than good sense delicately put in force, and genius is reason in its most sublime form
Marie Joseph de Chénier

Wise men are instructed by reason; men of less understanding, by experience; the most ignorant, by necessity; and beasts by nature.
Cicero

It has been my object and unquenched desire, to kindle young minds, and to guard them against the temptations of scorners, by showing that the scheme of Christianity, though not discoverable by human reason, is yet in accordance with it; that link follows link by necessary consequence; that religion passes out of the ken of reason only where the eye of reason has reached its own horizon; and that faith is then but its continuation; even as the day softens away into the sweet twilight, and twilight, hushed and breathless, steals into the darkness.
Samuel Taylor Coleridge

There are few things reason can discover with so much certainty and ease as its own insufficiency.
Jeremy Collier

The soundest argument will produce no more conviction in an empty head, than the most superficial declamation; a feather and a guinea fall with equal velocity in a vacuum.
Charles Caleb Colton

We have lost confidence in reason because we have learned that man is chiefly a creature of habit and emotion.
John Dewey

He that will not reason is a bigot; he that cannot reason is a fool; and he that dares not reason is a slave.
William Drummond

Reason of course, is weak, when measured against its neverending task. Weak indeed, compared with the follies and passions of mankind, which, we must admit, almost entirely control our human destinies, in great things and small.
Albert Einstein

Neither great poverty nor great riches will hear reason.
Henry Fielding

"It stands to reason" is a formula that gives its user the unfair advantage of at once invoking reason and refusing to listen to it.
Henry Watson Fowler

The golden rule is to test everything in the light of reason and experience, no matter from whom it comes.
Mohandas Karamchand (Mahatma) Gandhi

I reject any religious doctrine that does not appeal to reason and is in conflict with morality.
Mohandas Karamchand (Mahatma) Gandhi

Let us not dream that reason can ever be popular. Passions, emotions, may be made popular, but reason remains ever the property of the few.
Johann Wolfgang von Goethe

. . . be faithful to reason . . . There is no real greatness except that which issues from reason. Light surpasses in beauty both form and color.
Édouard Herriot

Most people reason dramatically, not quantitatively.
Oliver Wendell Holmes, Jr.

Irrationally held truths may be more harmful than reasoned errors.
Thomas Henry Huxley

Your giving a reason for it will not make it right. You may have a reason why two and two should make five, but they will still make but four.
Samuel Johnson

He is not a reasonable man who by chance stumbles upon reason, but he who derives it from knowledge, from discernment, and from taste.
Duc François de La Rochefoucauld

It is the mind, or reason, which is the predominant element in us who are human creatures; it is this which renders a human being human, and distinguishes him essentially and generically from the brute.
Leo XIII (Gioacchino Vincenzo Pecci)

We are a people with a faith in reason, and when we lose that faith and substitute for it faith in weapons we become weak and are lost, even with our superatomic weapons.
David Eli Lilienthal

He that takes away reason to make way for revelation puts out the light of both, and does much the same as if he would persuade a man to put out his eyes the better to receive the remote light of an invisible star by a telescope.

John Locke

Human reason is like a drunken man on horseback; set it up on one side, and it tumbles over on the other.

Martin Luther

Philosophers have done wisely when they have told us to cultivate our reason rather than our feelings, for reason reconciles us to the daily things of existence; our feelings teach us to yearn after the far, the difficult, the unseen.

Edward G. Bulwer-Lytton (Baron Lytton)

If you make people think they're thinking, they'll love you; but if you really make them think, they'll hate you.

Donald Robert Perry (Don) Marquis

To despise the animal basis of life, to seek value only at the level of conscious intelligence and rational effort, is ultimately to lose one's sense of cosmic relationships.

Lewis Mumford

The three most important events of human life are equally devoid of reason—birth, marriage and death.

Austin O'Malley

The weakness of human reason appears more evidently in those who know it not, than in those who know it.

Blaise Pascal

Faith evermore looks upward and descries objects remote; but reason can discover things only near, and sees nothing that is above her.

Francis Quarles

Most of our so-called reasoning consists in finding arguments for going on believing as we already do.

James Harvey Robinson

Reason's weakness is the belief that it has the capacity to convince unreason.

Jean Rostand

When my reason is afloat, my faith cannot long remain in suspense, and I believe in God as firmly as in any other truth whatever; in short, a thousand motives draw me to the consolatory side, and add the weight of hope to the equilibrium of reason.

Jean Jacques Rousseau

Real life is, to most men, a long second-best, a perpetual compromise between the ideal and the possible; but the world of pure reason knows no compromise, no practical limitations, no barrier to the creative activity.

Bertrand Arthur William Russell

Reason, alas, does not remove mountains. It only tries to walk around them, and see what is on the other side.

George William Russell

In me past, present, future meet—
To hold long chiding conference.
My lusts usurp the present tense—
And strangle Reason in his seat.

Siegfried Sassoon

Reason is the triumph of the intellect, faith of the heart; and whether the one or the other shall best illumine the dark mysteries of our being, they only are to be despaired of who care not to explore.

James Schouler

When a man has not a good reason for doing a thing, he has one good reason for letting it alone.

Sir Walter Scott

Wouldst thou subject all things to thyself? Subject thyself to thy reason.

Seneca

We think so because other people all think so; or because—or because—after all, we do think so; or because we were told so, and think we must think so; or because we once thought so, and think we still think so; or because, having thought so, we think we will think so.

Henry Sidgwick

Reason only controls individuals after emotion and impulse have lost their impetus.

Carlton Simon

The Bible leaves reason absolutely free.

Baruch (Benedict) Spinoza

Reason can do much to restrain and moderate the passions, but . . . the road which reason herself points out is very steep, so that such as persuade themselves that the multitude of men distracted by politics can ever be induced to live according to the bare dictate of reason, must be dreaming of the poetic golden age, or of a state-play.

Baruch (Benedict) Spinoza

True virtue is life under the direction of reason.

Baruch (Benedict) Spinoza

It is useless to attempt to reason a man out of a thing he was never reasoned into.

Jonathan Swift

He that speaketh against his own reason speaks against his own conscience, and therefore it is certain that no man serves God with a good conscience who serves him against his reason.

Jeremy Taylor

We have, on the face of it, loved, honored and obeyed reason more in the last century and a half than at any other epoch, and yet cumulatively and collectively, in the grand total of all our individual lives, we have produced more unreason, bigger and fiercer wars, than any other age in history.

Laurens Van der Post

Reason can no more influence the will, and operate as a motive, than the eyes which show a man his road can enable him to move from place to place, or than a ship provided with a compass can sail without a wind.

Richard Whately

Reason never has failed men. Only force and repression have made the wrecks in the world.

William Allen White

Reason is progressive; instinct is complete; swift instinct leaps; slow reason feebly climbs.

Edward Young

See also: COMMON SENSE, INTELLECT, INTELLIGENCE, JUDGMENT, LOGIC, MIND, PHILOSOPHY, SCIENCE, SENSE, WISDOM.

REBELLION

Men seldom, or rather never for a length of time, and deliberately, rebel against anything that does not deserve rebelling against.

Thomas Carlyle

Rebellion against tyrants is obedience to God.

Benjamin Franklin

Any people anywhere being inclined and having the power, have the right to rise up and shake off the existing government, and form a new one that suits them better. This is a most valuable, a most sacred right—a right which we hope and believe is to liberate the world.

Abraham Lincoln

There is little hope of equity where rebellion reigns.

Sir Philip Sidney

See also: DISOBEDIENCE, REVOLUTION.

RECKLESSNESS

Who falls from all he knows of bliss, cares little into what abyss.

George Gordon Byron (Lord Byron)

Over-daring is as great a vice as overfearing.

Ben (Benjamin) Jonson

See also: FOLLY, HASTE, IMPULSE, INDISCRETION, RASHNESS.

RECOMPENSE

There never was a person who did anything worth doing that did not receive more than he gave.

Henry Ward Beecher

Recompense injury with justice, and unkindness with kindness.

Confucius

There are minds so impatient of inferiority that their gratitude is a species of revenge, and they return benefits, not because recompense is a pleasure, but because obligation is a pain.

Samuel Johnson

See also: COMPENSATION, MERIT, REWARD.

RECREATION

The bow cannot possibly always stand bent, nor can human nature or human frailty subsist without some lawful recreation.

Miguel de Cervantes Saavedra

In our recreation we may try to live a primitive life. Having motored hundreds of miles over hard highways, we arrive at the cabin in the wildwood, cook Chicago bacon on a stove using oil from Texas refined in New Jersey, and go fishing with an outboard motor made in Michigan. . . . Though we want to be free from the ring of the telephone and to use the sun as our clock, we must take care that the milk we drink is pasteurized. Thus the American frees himself from technology!

Arthur Holly Compton

I have never been able to understand why pigeon-shooting at Hurlingham should be refined and polite, while a rat-killing match in White-chapel is low.

Thomas Henry Huxley

He that will make a good use of any part of his life must allow a large part of it to recreation.

John Locke

Recreation is not the highest kind of enjoyment, but in its time and place is quite as proper as prayer.

Samuel Irenaeus Prime

See also: AMUSEMENT, DIVERSION, PLEASURE.

RECTITUDE

A straight line is the shortest in morals as in mathematics.

Maria Edgeworth

If you would convince a man that he does wrong, do right. Men will believe what they see. Let them see.

Henry David Thoreau

The man who is so conscious of the rectitude of his intentions as to be willing to open his bosom to the inspection of the world, is in possession of one of the strongest pillars of a decided character. The course of such a man will be firm and steady, because he has nothing to fear from the world, and is sure of the approbation and support of Heaven.

William Wirt

See also: HONESTY, RIGHT AND WRONG.

REDEMPTION

Christ is redemption to us, only as he actually redeems and delivers our nature from sin. If he is not the law and spring of a new spirit of life, he is nothing to us. "As many as are led by the Spirit of God, they are the sons of God,"—as many; no more.

Horace Bushnell

By Christ's purchasing redemption, two things are intended: his satisfaction and his merit; the one pays our debt, and so satisfies; the other procures our title, and so merits. The satisfaction of Christ is to free us from misery; the merit of Christ is to purchase happiness for us.

Jonathan Edwards

Underneath all the arches of Bible history, throughout the whole grand temple of the Scriptures, these two voices ever echo, man is ruined; man is redeemed.

Cyrus David Foss

We want to be saved, but not from our sins. . . . We are willing to be saved from poverty, from war, from ignorance, from disease, from economic insecurity; such types of salvation leave our individual whims and passions and concupiscences untouched.

Fulton John Sheen

See also: CHRIST, CHRISTIANITY, CROSS, EASTER, FORGIVENESS, RESURRECTION, SIN.

REFINEMENT

That alone can be called true refinement which elevates the soul of man, purifying the manners by improving the intellect.

Samuel Taylor Coleridge

If refined sense and exalted sense be not so useful as common sense, their rarity, their novelty, and the nobleness of their objects make some compensation, and render them the admiration of mankind; as gold, though less serviceable than iron, acquires from its scarcity a value which is much superior.

David Hume

Too great refinement is false delicacy, and true delicacy is solid refinement.

Duc François de La Rochefoucauld

Many refined people will not kill a fly, but eat an ox.

Isaac Loeb Peretz

See also: CULTIVATION, COURTESY, DECENCY, ETIQUETTE, GOOD BREEDING, MANNERS, POLITENESS.

REFLECTION

There is one art of which every man should be a master—the art of reflection. If you are not a thinking man, to what purpose are you a man at all?

Samuel Taylor Coleridge

The object of reflection is invariably the discovery of something satisfying to the mind which was not there at the beginning of the search.

Ernest Dimnet

Knowledge is acquired by study and observation, but wisdom cometh by opportunity of leisure; the ripest thought comes from the mind which is not always on the stretch, but fed, at times, by a wise passiveness.

William Mathews

They only babble who practise not reflection. I shall think; and thought is silence.

Richard Brinsley Sheridan

We are told, "Let not the sun go down on your wrath," but I would add, never act or write till it has done so. This rule has saved me from many an act of folly. It is wonderful what a different view we take of the same event four-and-twenty hours after it has happened.

Sydney Smith

The system [of Nature] is not only more complex than we think, but more complex than we *can* think.

The Wild Kingdom

The advice of a scholar, whose piles of learning were set on fire by imagination, is never to be forgotten. Proportion an hour's reflection to an hour's reading, and so dispirit the book into the student.

Robert Eldridge Aris Willmott

See also: CONTEMPLATION, MEDITATION.

REFORM

He who reforms himself, has done much toward reforming others; and one reason why the world is not reformed, is, because each would have others make a beginning, and never thinks of himself doing it.

Thomas Adams

Reform like charity must begin at home. Once well at home, it will radiate outward, irrepressible, into all that we touch and handle, speak and work, ever kindling new light by incalculable contagion, spreading in geometric ratio, far and wide, doing only good wherever it spreads, and not evil.

Thomas Carlyle

Public reformers had need first practice on their own hearts that which they propose to try on others.

Charles I

It has been the fate of all bold adventurers and reformers, to be esteemed insane.

George Barrell Cheever

Nothing so needs reforming as other people's habits.

Samuel Langhorne Clemens (Mark Twain)

We are reformers in spring and summer; in autumn and winter we stand by the old—reformers in the morning, conservatives at night. Reform is affirmative, conservatism is negative; conservatism goes for comfort, reform for truth.

Ralph Waldo Emerson

How important, often, is the pain of guilt, as a stimulant to amendment and reformation.

John Watson Foster

One vicious habit each year rooted out, in time might make the worst man good.

Benjamin Franklin

Reform must come from within, not from without. You cannot legislate for virtue.

James Gibbons

Reforms are made by the vigor and courage and the self-sacrifice and the emotional convictions of young men, who did not know enough to be afraid, and who feel much more deeply than they think.

Lafcadio Hearn

It is well known what strange work there has been in the world, under the name and pretence of reformation; how often it has turned out to be, in reality, deformation; or, at best, a tinkering sort of business, where, while one hole has been mended, two have been made.

George Horne

I think I am better than the people who are trying to reform me.

Edgar Watson Howe

To reform a man, you must begin with his grandmother.

Victor Marie Hugo

We are standing at the end of an era of debunking . . . We carried it too far. In our efforts to smash false facades, we smashed some of the solid old foundations.

William Bradford Huie

It is easier to enrich ourselves with a thousand virtues, than to correct ourselves of a single fault.

Jean de La Bruyère

Reform should be more than a test of our beliefs. . . . It need not mean abandoning our fundamental principles, but rather a re-examination of them to determine whether we are following the dead letter or the living spirit which they embody.

Anne Spencer Morrow Lindbergh

We must reshape our institutions, our technology, our bureaucracy, and our political process so that they become our servants, not our masters.

George Stanley McGovern

Long is the way and hard, that out of hell leads up to light.

John Milton

The big fallacy of reform is thinking that it's going to succeed. What really provides stamina for this kind of work is the knowledge that you will never succeed, that basically all you're trying to do is to reduce our problems to the level of tolerability.

Ralph Nader

Most reformers, like a pair of trousers on a windy clothesline, go through a vast deal of vehement motion, but stay in the same place.

Austin O'Malley

Social reconstruction must be preceded by a profound renewal of the Christian spirit . . . Otherwise, all our efforts will be futile, and our social edifice will be built, not upon a rock, but upon shifting sands.

Pius XI (Achille Ambrogio Damiano Ratti)

The true reformer purifies and enlarges the heritage of mankind and does not belittle, still less deny it.

Sir Sarvepalli Radhakrishnan

Reformation is a work of time. A national taste, however wrong it may be, cannot be totally changed at once; we must yield a little to the prepossession which has taken hold on the mind, and we may then bring people to adopt what would offend them, if endeavored to be introduced by violence.

Sir Joshua Reynolds

The lunatic fringe in all reform movements.

Theodore Roosevelt

Conscious remorse and anguish must be felt, to curb desire, to break the stubborn will, and work a second nature in the soul.

Nicholas Rowe

Necessity reforms the poor, and satiety the rich.

Tacitus

There is a boldness, a spirit of daring, in religious reformers, not to be measured by the general rules which control men's purposes and actions.

Daniel Webster

See also: IMPROVEMENT; PROGRESS; REFORMATION, THE; REPENTANCE.

REFORMATION, THE

It cannot be denied that corruption of morals prevailed in the sixteenth century to such an extent as to call for a sweeping reformation, and that laxity of discipline invaded even the sanctuary.

James Gibbons

Here I stand; I can do no otherwise. God help me. Amen!

Martin Luther

The Reformation was in large measure a reaffirmation of the Old Testament and of Judaism.

Tomáš Garrigue Masaryk

The Reformation was cradled in the printing-press, and established by no other instrument.

Agnes Strickland

See also: CHRISTIANITY, PROTESTANTISM.

REGRET

Regret is an appalling waste of energy; you can't build on it; it's only good for wallowing in.

Katherine Mansfield

What 'twas weak to do
'Tis weaker to lament, once being done.

Percy Bysshe Shelley

O last regret, regret can die!

Alfred, Lord Tennyson

See also: GRIEF, REMORSE, REPENTANCE.

REGULATION

It was hard enough to keep the government pure when only a few industries were regulated. . . . But in future, if virtually all economic life is drawn into the governmental web, who will be left to defend the interests of the general public?

Paul Howard Douglas

The conceit of the present generation of reformers is the "freedom" of uniformity. Russian style or American style. . . . Whether education "to be like Stalin" or to "adjust to the group" after the notion of John Dewey, the tendency of these gigantic states is toward a sheep-population, though achieved in Russia by harsh compulsion, in America by contagion and attraction.

Russell Amos Kirk

We see almost daily evidence that in the very steps we take to defeat communism we may imitate that very regimentation of thinking, and that very domination of private affairs by politicians and political methods against which we have set out to fight.

David Eli Lilienthal

See also: GOVERNMENT, LAW, ORDER, RULE.

RELATIVITY

When a man sits with a pretty girl for an hour, it seems like a minute. But let him sit on a hot stove for a minute—and it's longer than any hour. That's relativity.

Albert Einstein

Children's griefs are little, certainly; but so is the child, so is its endurance, so is its field of vision, while its nervous impressionability is keener than ours. Grief is a matter of relativity; the sorrow should be estimated by its proportion to the sorrower; a gash is as painful to one as an amputation to another.

Francis Thompson

See also: POINT OF VIEW, SCIENCE.

RELIGION

Those who make religion to consist in the contempt of this world and its enjoyments, are under a very fatal and dangerous mistake. As life is the gift of heaven, it is religion to enjoy it. He, therefore, who can be happy in himself, and who contributes all in his power toward the happiness of others, answers most effectually the ends of his cre-ation, is an honor to his nature, and a pattern to mankind.

Joseph Addison

True religion and virtue give a cheerful and happy turn to the mind; admit of all true pleasures, and even procure for us the highest.

Joseph Addison

The true meaning of religion is thus not simply morality, but morality touched by emotion.

Matthew Arnold

If I did not feel . . . and hope that some day—perhaps millions of years hence—the Kingdom of God would overspread the whole world . . . then I would give my office over this morning to anyone who would take it.

Stanley Baldwin

One's religion is whatever he is most interested in, and yours is Success.

Sir James Matthew Barrie

It is one thing to take God and heaven for your portion, as believers do, and another thing to be desirous of it as a reserve, when you can keep the world no longer. It is one thing to submit to heaven, as a lesser evil than hell; and another thing to desire it as a greater good than earth. It is one thing to lay up treasures and hopes in heaven, and seek it first; and another thing to be contented with it in our necessity, and to seek the world before it, and give God what the flesh can spare. Thus differeth the religion of serious Christians and of carnal, worldly hypocrites.

Richard Baxter

Many would like religion as a sort of lightning rod to their houses, to ward off, by and by, the bolts of divine wrath.

Henry Ward Beecher

Religion—a daughter of Hope and Fear, explaining to Ignorance the nature of the Unknowable. Impiety—your irreverence toward my deity.

Ambrose Gwinnett Bierce

The best perfection of a religious man is to do common things in a perfect manner.

Bonaventure (Giovanni di Fidanza)

There are critics who will welcome any philosophy, no matter how extravagant, provided it does not eventuate in theism; and will reject, without careful examination, any philosophy, no matter how reasonable, if it be inclined to find some truth in religion.

Edgar Sheffield Brightman

While men believe in the possibilities of children being religious, they are largely failing to make them so, because they are offering them not a child's but a man's religion—men's forms of truth and men's forms of experience.

Phillips Brooks

The tragedy is that with loss of faith in religion so many people have lost faith in the possibility of a unifying creed of any kind.

William Adams Brown

Nothing is so fatal to religion as indifference, which is, at least, half infidelity.

Edmund Burke

We know, and, what is better, we feel inwardly, that religion is the basis of civil society, and the source of all good and of all comfort.

Edmund Burke

The noblest charities, the best fruits of learning, the richest discoveries, the best institutions of law and justice, every greatest thing the world has seen, represents, more or less directly, the fruitfulness and creativeness of religion.

Horace Bushnell

The submergence of self in the pursuit of an ideal, the readiness to spend oneself without measure, prodigally, almost ecstatically, for something intuitively apprehended as great and noble, spend oneself knowing not why—some of us like to believe that this is what religion means.

Benjamin Nathan Cardozo

Religion cannot pass away. The burning of a little straw may hide the stars of the sky, but the stars are there, and will reappear.·

Thomas Carlyle

A man who puts aside his religion because he is going into society, is like one taking off his shoes because he is about to walk upon thorns.

Richard Cecil

It was religion, which, by teaching men their near relation to God, awakened in them the consciousness of their importance as individuals. It was the struggle for religious rights, which opened their eyes to all their rights. It was resistance to religious usurpation which led men to withstand political oppression. It was religious discussion which roused the minds of all classes to free and vigorous thought. It was religion which armed the martyr and patriot in England against arbitrary power; which braced the spirits of our fathers against the perils of the ocean and wilderness, and sent them to found here the freest and most equal state on earth.

William Ellery Channing

Too many persons seem to use their religion as a diver does his bell, to venture down into the depths of worldliness with safety, and there grope for pearls, with just so much of heaven's air as will keep them from suffocating, and no more; and some, alas! as at times is the case with the diver, are suffocated in the experiment.

George Barrell Cheever

It is the test of a good religion whether you can joke about it.

Gilbert Keith Chesterton

Piety and holiness will propitiate the Gods.

Cicero

You have no security for a man who has no religious principle.

Richard Cobden

Depend upon it religion is, in its essence, the most gentlemanly thing in the world. It will alone gentilize, if unmixed with cant; and I know nothing else that will, alone.

Samuel Taylor Coleridge

Men will wrangle for religion; write for it; fight for it; die for it; anything but live for it.

Charles Caleb Colton

Where true religion has ' prevented one crime, false religions have afforded a pretext for a thousand.

Charles Caleb Colton

There can be no conflict between science and religion. Science is a reliable method of finding truth. Religion is the search for a satisfying way of life. Science is growing; yet a world that has science needs, as never before, the inspiration that religion offers.

Arthur Holly Compton

God is for men and religion for women.

Joseph Conrad

If I could choose what of all things would be at the same time the most delightful and useful to me, I should prefer a firm religious belief to every other blessing; for this makes life a discipline of goodness; creates new hopes when all earthly ones vanish; throws over the decay of existence the most gorgeous of all lights; awakens life even in death; makes even torture and shame the ladder of ascent to paradise; and far above all combinations of earthly hopes, calls up the most delightful visions of the future, the security of everlasting joys, where the sensualist and the sceptic view only gloom, decay, annihilation, and despair.

Sir Humphrey Davy

The future of religion is connected with the possibility of developing a faith in the possibilities of human experience and human relationships that will create a vital sense of the solidarity of human interests and inspire action to make that sense a reality.

John Dewey

It seems to me that the chief danger to religion lies in the fact that it has become so respectable.

John Dewey

Religion should be the rule of life, not a casual incident in it.

Benjamin Disraeli

The soul of a civilization is its religion, and it dies with its faith.

Will (William James) Durant

Religion flourishes vastly only in a world conceived in terms of caste.

Max Forrester Eastman

What we need in religion, is not new light, but new sight; not new paths, but new strength to walk in the old ones; not new duties, but new strength from on high to fulfill those that are plain before us.

Tryon Edwards

I cannot believe that God plays dice with the cosmos!

Albert Einstein

All religions, arts and sciences are branches of the same tree.

Albert Einstein

The most beautiful and most profound emotion we can experience is the sensation of the mystical. It is the power of all true science . . . To know that what is impenetrable to us really exists, manifesting itself as the highest wisdom and the most radiant beauty which our dull faculties can comprehend only in their most primitive forms—this knowledge, this feeling, is at the center of true religiousness.

Albert Einstein

Science without religion is lame, religion without science is blind.

Albert Einstein

Religion is the sum of the expansive impulses of a being.

(Henry) Havelock Ellis

Unless we place our religion and our treasure in the same thing religion will always be sacrificed.

Epictetus

The loss of popular respect for religion is the dry rot of social institutions. The idea of God as the Creator and Father of all mankind is in the moral world, what gravitation is in the natural; it holds all together and causes them to revolve around a common center. Take this away, and men drop apart; there is no such thing as collective humanity, but only separate molecules, with no more cohesion than so many grains of sand.

Henry Martyn Field

Religious contention is the devil's harvest.

Charles Fontaine

There need not be in religion, or music, or art, or love, or goodness, anything that is against reason; but never while the sun shines will we get great religion, or music, or art, or love, or goodness, without going beyond reason.

Harry Emerson Fosdick

Religion means faith that man's ideals are achievable and will be achieved.

Jerome New Frank

If men are so wicked with religion, what would they be without it!

Benjamin Franklin

If we think of religion only as a means of escaping what we call the wrath to come, we shall not escape it; we are under the burden of death, if we care only for ourselves.

James Anthony Froude

Sacrifice is the first element of religion, and resolves itself in theological language into the love of God.

James Anthony Froude

Measure not men by Sundays, without regarding what they do all the week after.

Thomas Fuller

No religion which is narrow and which cannot satisfy the test of reason will survive the coming reconstruction of society in which the values will have changed and character, not possession of wealth, title or birth, will be the test of merit.

Mohandas Karamchand (Mahatma) Gandhi

Religion deals with the science of the soul. Great as the other forces of the world are, if there is such a thing as God, soul-force is the greatest of all. We know as a matter of fact that the greater the force the finer it is. Hitherto electricity has held the field among the finer physical powers. And yet nobody has seen it except through its wonderful results. Scientific speculation dares to talk of a force finer even than that of electricity. But no instrument devised by man has been able to know anything positive of soul-force or spiritual force. It is on that force that the true religious reformer has hitherto relied.

Mohandas Karamchand (Mahatma) Gandhi

The Christian religion is one that diffuses among the people a pure, benevolent, and universal system of ethics, adapted to every condition of life, and recommended as the will and reason of the Supreme Deity, and enforced by sanctions of eternal punishment.

Edward Gibbon

There is no religion so foolish that it has not made converts and engendered fiery convictions.

André Gide

To swallow and follow, whether old doctrine or new propaganda, is a weakness still dominating the human mind.

Charlotte Perkins Gilman

Nothing can be hostile to religion which is agreeable to justice.

William Ewart Gladstone

True religion teaches us to reverence what is under us, to recognize humility, poverty, wretchedness, suffering, and death, as things divine.

Johann Wolfgang von Goethe

Religion presents few difficulties to the humble; many to the proud; insuperable ones to the vain.

Augustus and Julius Hare

Religion is the answer to that cry of reason which nothing can silence; that aspiration of the soul which no created thing can meet; of that want of the heart which all creation cannot supply.

Isaac Thomas Hecker

Religion is bigger than any church or any creed or any faith, and its business is the development of a wiser and a better humanity.

Ellwood Hendrick

Nothing exposes religion more to the reproach of its enemies than the worldliness and hard-heartedness of its professors.

Matthew Henry

I would give nothing for that man's religion, whose very dog, and cat are not the better for it.

Rowland Hill

Religion is not a dogma, not an emotion, but a service. Our redemption is not of the head alone, nor of the heart alone, but preeminently of the life, as the only infallible criterion of what we really are. Not belief, not emotion, but obedience is the test. Mere belief would make religion a mere theology. Mere emotion would make it a mere excitement. While the true divine of it is a life, begotten of grace in the depths of the human soul, subduing to Christ all the powers of the heart and life, and incarnating itself in patient, steady, sturdy service—doing the will of God.

Roswell Dwight Hitchcock

When men cease to be faithful to God, he who expects to find them so to each other will be much disappointed.

George Horne

A religion that never suffices to govern a man, will never suffice to save him. That which does not distinguish him from a sinful world, will never distinguish him from a perishing world.

John Howe

Such as men themselves are, such will God appear to them to be; and such as God appears to them to be, such will they show themselves in their dealings with their fellow men.

William Ralph Inge

Many people think they have religion when they are troubled with dyspepsia.

Robert Green Ingersoll

Religion is a man's total reaction upon life.

William James

Religion is a monumental chapter in the history of human egotism.

William James

A life that will bear the inspection of men and of God, is the only certificate of true religion.

Samuel Johnson

No creed is final. Such a creed as mine must grow and change as knowledge grows and changes.

Sir Arthur Keith

It has been said that true religion will make a man a more thorough gentleman than all the courts in Europe. And it is true that you may see simple laboring men as thorough gentlemen as any duke, simply because they have learned to fear God; and, fearing him, to restrain themselves, which is the very root and essence of all good breeding.

Charles Kingsley

What I want is, not to possess religion, but to have a religion that shall possess me.

Charles Kingsley

A genuine knowledge or vision of God means the largest possible increase of life.

Raymond Collyer Knox

The highest aim of religion, it is always to be remembered, is not to condemn and to destroy, but to fulfill.

Raymond Collyer Knox

My principles in respect of religious interest are two, one is, that the Church shall not meddle with politics, and the government shall not meddle with religion.

Lajos Kossuth

All the naturalistic religions are founded upon the assumption that nature—which

"never did betray the heart that loved her"—is discoverable and ready to serve as an infallible guide.

Joseph Wood Krutch

Certain transcendental experiences seem to me to be the original wellspring of all religions. Some psychotic people have transcendental experiences. . . . I am not saying, however, that psychotic experience necessarily contains this element more manifestly than sane experience.

Ronald David Laing

I have lived long enough to know what I did not at one time believe—that no society can be upheld in happiness and honor without the sentiment of religion.

Marquis Pierre Simon de Laplace

All belief that does not render us more happy, more free, more loving, more active, more calm, is, I fear, an erroneous and superstitious belief.

Johann Kaspar Lavater

The best religion is humanity, the best divine service, love thy neighbor as thyself. The motto which we inscribe on our banner is the fatherhood of God and the brotherhood of man.

Max Menahem Lilienthal

If the philosophers teach that religious experience is a purely psychological phenomenon, related to nothing beyond each man's psychic condition, then they will give educated men a bad intellectual conscience if they have religious experiences. The philosophers cannot give them religion. But they can keep them away from it.

Walter Lippmann

Religion may be the most immoral thing in the world. It is, when it is a religion which brings comfort without rebuke, when it gives satisfaction without conviction of sin.

Halford Edward Luccock

And as the strict observance of religious worhsip is the cause why states rise to eminence, so contempt for religion brings ruin on them. For where the fear of God is wanting, destruction is sure to follow, or else it must be sustained by the fear felt for their prince, who may thus supply the want of religion in his subjects. Whence it arises that the kingdoms, that depend only on the virtue of a mortal, have a short duration; it is seldom that the virtue of the father survives in the son.

Niccolò Machiavelli

A ritual religion is generally light and gay, not serious in its spirit; all religions being so, which cast responsibility into outward observances.

Harriet Martineau

The first requisite for the people's happiness is the abolition of religion.

Karl Marx

Religion is the sigh of the oppressed creature, the feeling of a heartless world, just as it is the spirit of unspiritual conditions. It is the opium of the people.

Karl Marx

It will cost something to be religious: it will cost more to be not so.

John Mitchell Mason

Religion would not have enemies, if it were not an enemy to their vices.

Jean Baptiste Massillon

Man has never been the same since God died.

Edna St. Vincent Millay

I conceive the essential task of religion to be "to develop the consciences, the ideals, and the aspirations of mankind."

Robert Andrews Millikan

If we were to be hired to religion, it is able to outbid the corrupted world with all it can offer us, being so much richer of the two in everything where reason is admitted to be a judge of the value.

Charles Montagu (Earl of Halifax)

Science is only an episode of religion—and an unimportant one at that.

Christian Morganstern

To be thoroughly religious, one must, I believe, be sorely disappointed. One's faith in God increases as one's faith in the world decreases. The happier the man, the farther he is from God.

Goerge Jean Nathan

Religion is a candle inside a multicolored lantern. Everyone looks through a particular color, but the candle is always there.

Mohammed Neguib

In the name of religion many great and fine deeds have been performed. In the name of religion also, thousands and millions have been killed, and every possible crime has been committed.

Jawaharlal Nehru

It is strange that any one should be so foolish as to think that religion and faith can be thrust down a person's throat at the point of the sword or a bayonet.

Jawaharlal Nehru

Often in history we see that religion, which was meant to raise us and make us better and nobler, has made people behave like beasts. Instead of bringing enlightenment of them, it has often tried to keep them in the dark; instead of broadening their minds, it has frequently made them narrow-minded and intolerant of others.

Jawaharlal Nehru

There can be no doubt that the founders of the great religions have been among the greatest and noblest men that the world has produced.

Jawaharlal Nehru

No sciences are better attested than the religion of the Bible.

Sir Isaac Newton

Religion is the best armor in the world, but the worst cloak.

John Newton

The final test of religious faith . . . is whether it will enable men to endure insecurity without complacency or despair, whether it can so interpret the ancient verities that they will not become mere escape hatches from responsibilities but instruments of insights into what civilization means.

Reinhold Niebuhr

A vital religion proves itself both by moral responsibility in creating tolerable forms of community and justice, and by a humble awareness of human imperfectibility. Above all, it preserves a sense of ultimate majesty and meaning, transcending all our little majesties and partial meanings.

Reinhold Niebuhr

It usually takes as many generations to make a religious convert as to make a gentleman.

Austin O'Malley

Religion, in some quarters, is being identified with the cult of success, and prayer as but a means to promotion to the presidency of the company. This is not a worthy approach to the Eternal.

Garfield Bromley Oxnam

If we subject everything to reason, our religion will have nothing mysterious or supernatural; if we violate the principles of reason, our religion will be absurd and ridiculous.

Blaise Pascal

Religion is the fear and love of God; its demonstration is good works; and faith is the root of both, for without faith we cannot please God; nor can we fear and love what we do not believe.

William Penn

If you are not right toward God, you can never be so toward man; and this is forever true, whether wits and rakes allow it or not.

William Pitt (Lord Chatham)

When a man is beset by some trouble, it is then that he remembers there is a god, and that he is only a man.

Pliny the Elder

The only impregnable citadel of virtue is religion; for there is no bulwark of mere morality, which some temptation may not overtop or undermine and destroy.

Jane Porter

It was an admirable and true saying of Plutarch, "That a city may as well be built in the air, as a commonwealth or kingdom be either constituted or preserved without the support of religion."

Beilby Porteus

Creeds grow so thick along the way their boughs hide God.

Lizette Woodworth Reese

Religion is a sum of scruples which impede the free exercise of our faculties.

Salomon Reinach

In a modern civilization, all three—religion, democracy, and international good faith—complement each other.

Where freedom of religion has been attacked, the attack has come from sources opposed to democracy. Where democracy has been overthrown, the spirit of free worship has disappeared. And where religion and democracy have vanished, good faith and reason in international affairs have given way to strident ambition and brute force.

Franklin Delano Roosevelt

Philosophy can do nothing which religion cannot do better than she; and religion can do a great many other things which philosophy cannot do at all.

Jean Jacques Rousseau

The religion that makes the purest and happiest homes will always be the best for any country. If Christianity does that, it is the best of all religions.

John Ruskin

Religion is the indispensable basis of democracy.

John Augustine Ryan

If your whole life is guided by religion, the hearts of others may be touched by this mute language, and may open to the reception of that spirit which dwells in you.

Friedrich Ernst Daniel Schleiermacher

Day by day we should weigh what we have granted to the spirit of the world against what we have denied to the spirit of Jesus, in thought and especially in deed.

Albert Schweitzer

In disputes about common things, as every one feels that he may be mistaken, stubbornness and obstinacy are never carried to an extreme; but in those which we have respecting religion, as every one naturally feels sure that his opinion is the true one, we are highly indignant against those who, instead of changing, are obstinately bent on making us change.

Charles de Secondat (Baron de Montesquieu)

The pious man and the atheist always talk of religion; the one of what he loves, and the other of what he fears.

Charles de Secondat (Baron de Montesquieu)

There is only one religion, though there are a hundred versions of it.

George Bernard Shaw

What I mean by a religious person is one who conceives himself or herself to be the instrument of some purpose in the universe which is a high purpose, and is the motive power of evolution—that is, of a continual ascent in organization and power and life, and extension of life.

George Bernard Shaw

Religion is so far from barring men any innocent pleasure, or comfort of human life, that it purifies the pleasures of it, and renders them more grateful and generous; and besides this, it brings mighty pleasures of its own, those of a glorious hope, a serene mind, a calm and undisturbed conscience, which do far out-relish the most studied and artificial luxuries.

James Shirley

True religion is far more a matter of character than a question of cult and creed.

Isidore Singer

No man's religion ever survives his morals.

Robert South

To see in moralizing the final aim in religion is to be ignorant of what religion is.

Oswald Spengler

Until religion passes out of the area which must be occupied by faith and its truths achieve something like mathematical verification, we must face the fact that our beliefs may not correspond to reality.

Willard Learoyd Sperry

A religious life is a struggle and not a hymn.

Madame de Staël

The important thing is not that people go more to church, listen to evangelists and join churches. The important thing is that the younger generation asks the right questions . . . the meaning of our life, the conflicts of our existence, the way to deal with anxiety in our life, the feeling of guilt, the feeling of emptiness.

Paul Tillich

As far as our present knowledge goes, religion appears to be universal among men. There is no community of which we can say with certainty that it is without religion.

Crawford Howell Toy

The task and triumph of religion is to make men and nations true and just and upright in all their dealings, and to bring all law as well as all conduct into subjection and conformity to the law of God.

Henry Jackson Van Dyke

Religion finds the love of happiness and the principles of duty separated in us; and its mission—its masterpiece is, to reunite them.

Alexandre Vinet

If it is said that the churches should only be concerned with spiritual matters, the answer is surely that concern for the victims of injustice and conflict is a most spiritual matter.

Willem Adolf Visser t'Hooft

The tolerance of all religions is a law of nature, stamped on the hearts of all men. For by what right should a created being compel another being to think as he does? But when a people has become an associated body, when religion has become a law of the state, we must submit to that law.

Voltaire (François Marie Arouet)

Of all the dispositions and habits which lead to political prosperity, religion and morality are indispensable supports. In vain would that man claim the tribute of patriotism, who should labor to subvert these great pillars of human happiness, these firmest props of the duties of men and citizens.

George Washington

Religion is as necessary to reason as reason is to religion. The one cannot exist without the other. A reasoning being would lose his reason, in attempting to account for the great phenomena of nature, had he not a Supreme Being to refer to; and well has it been said, that if there had been no God, mankind would have been obliged to imagine one.

George Washington

The church, still bound to the image of God as the King of kings, adopted a religion about Jesus instead of the religion of Jesus.

Alan Watts

A man with no sense of religious duty is he whom the Scriptures describes in so terse but terrific a manner, as "living without hope and without God in the world." Such a man is out of his proper being, out of the circle of all his duties, out of the circle of all his happiness, and away, far, far away from the purposes of his creation.

Daniel Webster

Religion is the first thing and the last thing, and until a man has found God and been found by God, he begins at no beginning, he works to no end.

Herbert George Wells

If our religion is not true, we are bound to change it; if it is true, we are bound to propagate it.

Richard Whately

You must make your own religion, and it is only what you make yourself which will be of any use to you.

William Hale White (Mark Rutherford)

Religion will not regain its old power until it can face change in the same spirit as does science.

Alfred North Whitehead

Those theologians do religion a bad service, who emphasize infinitude at the expense of the finite transitions within history.

Alfred North Whitehead

I would rather think of my religion as a gamble than to think of it as an insurance premium.

Stephen Samuel Wise

See also: BELIEF, CHURCH, CREED, FAITH, HOLINESS, PIETY, WORSHIP.

REMEMBRANCE

I cannot sing the old songs
I sang long years ago,
For heart and voice would fail me,
And foolish tears would flow.

Charlotte Barnard

The greatest comfort of my old age, and that which gives me the highest satisfaction, is the pleasing remembrance of the many benefits and friendly offices I have done to others.

Cato the Elder

The world does not require so much to be informed as reminded.

Hannah More

Every one can remember that which has interested himself.

Plautus

Remembrance is the only paradise out of which we cannot be driven away.

Jean Paul Richter

The sweet remembrance of the just
Shall flourish when he sleeps in dust.

Nahum Tate and Nicholas Brady

See also: MEMORY, PAST.

REMORSE

Remorse begets reform.

William Cowper

Not sharp revenge, nor hell itself can find
A fiercer torment than a guilty mind.

John Dryden

Remorse is the echo of a lost virtue.

Edward G. Bulwer-Lytton (Baron Lytton)

Remorse is beholding heaven and feeling hell.

Thomas Moore

Remorse is surgical in action; it cuts away foul tissues of the mind.

Christopher Darlington Morley

Remorse goes to sleep when we are in the enjoyment of prosperity, and makes itself felt in adversity.

Jean Jacques Rousseau

'Tis when the wound is stiffening with the cold,
The warrior first feels pain—'tis when the heat
And fiery fever of the soul is past,
The sinner feels remorse.

Sir Walter Scott

See also: GRIEF, GUILT, REGRET, REPENTANCE, RETRIBUTION, SORROW.

REPARTEE

Repartee is what you wish you'd said.

(Matthew) Heywood Campbell Broun

Repartee is perfect, when it effects its purpose with a double edge. Repartee is the highest order of wit, as it bespeaks the coolest yet quickest exercise of genius at a moment when the passions are roused.

Charles Caleb Colton

Repartee is a duel fought with the points of jokes.

Max Forrester Eastman

The impromptu reply is the touchstone of the man of wit.

Molière (Jean Baptiste Poquelin)

See also: CONVERSATION, TALKING, WIT.

REPENTANCE

Repentance is the relinquishment of any practice from the conviction that it has offended God. Sorrow, fear, and anxiety are properly not parts, but adjuncts of repentance, yet they are too closely connected with it to be separated.

Joseph Addison

True repentance is to cease from sinning.

Ambrose of Milan

The best part of repentance is little sinning.

Arabian Proverb

Bad men are full of repentance.

Aristotle

There is one case of death-bed repentance recorded, that of the penitent thief, that none should despair; and only one that none should presume.

Augustine of Hippo

Of all acts of man repentance is the most divine. The greatest of all faults is to be conscious of none.

Thomas Carlyle

Death-bed repentance is burning the candle of life in the service of the devil, then blowing the snuff in the face of heaven.

Lorenzo Dow

Repentance, without amendment, is like continually pumping without mending the leak.

Lewis Weston Dillwyn

If you would be good, first believe you are bad.

Epictetus

Great is the difference betwixt a man's being frightened at, and humbled for his sins.

Thomas Fuller

Our greatest glory consists not in never falling, but in rising every time we may fall.

Oliver Goldsmith

When the soul has laid down its faults at the feet of God, it feels as though it had wings.

Eugénie de Guérin

It is never too late with us, so long as we are aware of our faults and bear them impatiently.

Friedrich Heinrich Jacobi

It is a common error, and the greater and more mischievous for being so common, to believe that repentance best becomes and most concerns dying men. Indeed, what is necessary every hour of our life is necessary in the hour of death too, and as long as one lives he will have need of repentance, and therefore it is necessary in the hour of death too; but he who hath constantly exercised himself in it in his health and vigor, will do it with less pain in his sickness and weakness; and he who hath practised it all his life, will do it with more ease and less perplexity in the hour of his death.

Samuel Johnson

Repentance is a hearty sorrow for our past misdeeds, and is a sincere resolution and endeavor, to the utmost of our power, to conform all our actions to the law of God. It does not consist in one single act of sorrow, but in doing works meet for repentance; in a sincere obedience to the law of Christ for the remainder of our lives.

John Locke

To do so no more is the truest repentance.

Martin Luther

What is past is past. There is a future left to all men who have the virtue to repent, and the energy to atone.

Edward G. Bulwer-Lytton (Baron Lytton)

Repentance is not only grief on account of this or that particular act; it is a deep-seated sorrow on account of the discrepancy between the outward acts of the will and that ideal which is presented to the conscience in the new Adam the typical the Christian man.

Hans Lassen Martensen

The golden key that opens the palace of eternity.

John Milton

Repentance is nothing else but a renunciation of our will, and a controlling of our fancies, which lead us which way they please.

Michel Eyquem de Montaigne

He that waits for repentance, waits for that which cannot be had as long as it is waited for. It is absurd for a man to wait for that which he himself has to do.

William Nevins

There is a greater depravity in not repenting of sin when it has been committed, than in committing it at first. To deny, as Peter did, is bad; but not to weep bitterly, as he did, when we have denied, is worse.

Edward Payson

Most people repent of their sins by thanking God they ain't so wicked as their neighbors.

Henry Wheeler Shaw (Josh Billings)

It is the greatest and dearest blessing that ever God gave to men, that they may repent; and therefore to deny or to delay it is to refuse health when brought by the skill of the physician—to refuse liberty offered to us by our gracious Lord.

Jeremy Taylor

Late repentance is seldom true, but true repentance is never too late.

Ralph Venning

The vain regret that steals above the wreck of squandered hours.

John Greenleaf Whittier

See also: REGRET, REMORSE, SORROW.

REPETITION

Repetition may not entertain but it teaches.

Frédéric Bastiat

Men get opinions as boys learn to spell,
By reiteration chiefly.

Elizabeth Barrett Browning

There is no absurdity so palpable but that it may be firmly planted in the human head if you only begin to inculcate it before the age of five, by constantly repeating it with an air of great solemnity.

Arthur Schopenhauer

See also: LOQUACITY, VERBOSITY.

REPOSE

Thou hast created us for thyself, and our heart cannot be quieted till it may find repose in thee.

Augustine of Hippo

Repose and cheerfulness are the badge of the gentleman—repose in energy. The Greek battle pieces are calm; the heroes, in whatever violent actions engaged, retain a serene aspect.

Ralph Waldo Emerson

There is no mortal truly wise and restless at once; wisdom is the repose of minds.

Johann Kaspar Lavater

There is a repose which comes from adjustment to present conditions, acceptance of present limitations, and victorious recognition of the far-off peace.

Hamilton Wright Mabie

Have you known how to compose your manners? You have done a great deal more than he who has composed books. Have you known how to take repose? You have done more than he who has taken cities and empires.

Michel Eyquem de Montaigne

Repose is agreeable to the human mind; and decision is repose. A man has made up his opinions; he does not choose to be disturbed; and he is much more thankful to the man who confirms him in his errors, and leaves him alone, than he is to the man who refutes him, or who instructs him at the expense of his tranquillity.

Sydney Smith

See also: BED, PEACE, QUIET, SLEEP.

REPROOF

The silent upbraiding of the eye is the very poetry of reproach; it speaks at once to the imagination.

Clara Lucas Balfour

Aversion from reproof is not wise. It is a mark of a little mind. A great man can afford to lose; a little, insignificant fellow is afraid of being snuffed out.

Richard Cecil

No reproach is like that we clothe in a smile, and present with a bow.

Edward G. Bulwer-Lytton (Baron Lytton)

Reproof is a medicine like mercury or opium; if it be improperly administered, it will do harm instead of good.

Horace Mann

Whenever anything is spoken against you that is not true, do not pass by or despise it because it is false; but forthwith examine yourself, and consider what you have said or done that may administer a just occasion of reproof.

Plutarch

Fear not the anger of the wise to raise;
Those best can bear reproof who merit
      praise.

Alexander Pope

Reprove thy friend privately; commend him
publicly.

Solon

Many men are angry with them that tell
them of their faults, when they should be
angry only with the faults that are told
them.

Ralph Venning

See also: CENSURE, CRITICISM.

REPUBLIC

It is the weakness and danger of republics,
that the vices as well as virtues of the people are represented in their legislation.

Helen Maria Hunt Jackson

Equal and exact justice to all: peace, commerce and honest friendship with all nations, and the entangling alliances with
none; the support of State governments in
all their rights, as the most competent administration of our domestic concerns, are
the surest bulwarks against antirepublican
tendencies.

Thomas Jefferson

At twenty, every one is republican.

Alphonse de Lamartine

Republics come to an end by luxurious habits; monarchies by poverty.

Charles de Secondat (Baron de Montesquieu)

Republicanism is not the phantom of a deluded imagination. On the contrary, under
no form of government are laws better supported, liberty and property better secured,
or happiness more effectually dispensed to
mankind.

George Washington

See also: COMMUNISM, DEMOCRACY, EQUALITY,
      FREEDOM, GOVERNMENT, STATE.

REPUBLICAN PARTY

Southern Republicans must not climb aboard
the sink-ship of racial injustice. . . . Any republican victory that would come courting
racists black, or white, would be a defeat for
our future in the South and our party in the
nation.

Richard Milhous Nixon

The trouble with the Republican party is
that it has not had a new idea in 30 years.

(Thomas) Woodrow Wilson

See also: DEMOCRATIC PARTY, PARTY.

REPUTATION

Reputation is sometimes as wide as the horizon, when character is but the point of a
needle. Character is what one really is; reputation what others believe him to be.

Henry Ward Beecher

My gifts are small. I've used them very well
and discreetly, never straining them, and
the result is that I have made a charming little reputation.

Sir Max Beerbohm

The two most precious things this side the
grave are our reputation and our life. But it
is to be lamented that the most contemptible whisper may deprive us of the one, and
the weakest weapon of the other. A wise
man, therefore, will be more anxious to deserve a fair name than to possess it, and this
will teach him so to live, as not to be afraid
to die.

Charles Caleb Colton

An honest reputation is within the reach of
all; they obtain it by social virtues and doing
their duty. This kind of reputation, though
neither brilliant nor startling, is often the
most conducive to happiness.

Charles Pinot Duclos

A reputation once broken may possibly be
repaired, but the world will always keep
their eyes on the spot where the crack was.

Joseph Hall

A man's reputation is not in his own keeping, but lies at the mercy of the profligacy of
others. Calumny requires no proof.

William Hazlitt

Nothing is so uncertain as general reputation. A man injures me from humor, passion,
or interest; hates me because he has injured
me; and speaks ill of me because he hates
me.

Henry Home (Lord Kames)

Many a man's reputation would not know his
character if they met on the street.

Elbert Green Hubbard

Good will, like a good name, is got by many actions, and lost by one.

Francis Jeffrey (Lord Jeffrey)

The blaze of reputation cannot be blown out, but it often dies in the socket.

Samuel Johnson

Whatever ignominy we may have incurred, it is almost always in our power to restore our reputation.

Duc François de La Rochefoucauld

One may be better than his reputation, but never better than his principles.

Nicolas Valentin de Latena

Reputation: what others are not thinking about you.

Thomas Lansing (Tom) Masson

Reputation is what men and women think of us; character is what God and angels know of us.

Thomas Paine

Reputation is rarely proportioned to virtue. We have seen a thousand people esteemed, either for the merit they had not yet attained or for what they no longer possessed.

Seigneur de Saint-Évremond

A broken reputation is like a broken vase—it may be mended, but it always shows where the break was!

Henry Wheeler Shaw (Josh Billings)

The way to gain a good reputation, is, to endeavor to be what you desire to appear.

Socrates

A good name is properly that reputation of virtue which every man may challenge as his right and due in the opinion of others, till he has made forfeit of it by the viciousness of his actions.

Robert South

There are few persons of greater worth than their reputation; but how many are there whose worth is far short of their reputation!

Stanislas I (Leszczyński)

The reputation of a man is like his shadow, gigantic when it precedes him, and pigmy in its proportions when it follows.

Alexandre de Talleyrand-Périgord

In all the affairs of this world, so much reputation is, in reality, so much power.

John Tillotson

Associate with men of good quality, if you esteem your own reputation; it is better to be alone than in bad company.

George Washington

We should be careful to deserve a good reputation by doing well; and when that care is once taken, not to be over-anxious about the success.

John Wilmot (Earl of Rochester)

See also: CALUMNY, DISGRACE, FAME, HONOR.

RESEARCH

I think research without test is perfectly useless, a waste of money.

Dwight David Eisenhower

Research is an organized method for keeping you reasonably dissatisfied with what you have.

Charles Franklin Kettering

See also: INQUIRY, INVENTION, SCIENCE.

RESENTMENT

Resentment is, in every stage of the passion, painful, but it is not disagreeable, unless in excess.

Henry Home (Lord Kames)

Resentment is a union of sorrow with malignity; a combination of a passion which all endeavor to avoid with a passion which all concur to detest.

Samuel Johnson

Resentment seems to have been given us by nature for defence, and for defence only; it is the safeguard of justice, and the security of innocence.

Adam Smith

See also: ANGER, DISCONTENTMENT, HATE, REBELLION.

RESERVE

Reserve may be pride fortified in ice; dignity is worth reposing on truth.

William Rounseville Alger

Reserve is the truest expression of respect toward those who are its objects.

Thomas De Quincey

There is nothing more allied to the barbarous and savage character than sullenness, concealment, and reserve.

Parke Godwin

Persons extremely reserved are like old enamelled watches, which had painted covers that
hindered your seeing what o'clock it was.

Horace Walpole

See also: CONCEALMENT, DIGNITY, MODESTY,
SILENCE.

RESIGNATION

The truest kinship with humanity would lie
in doing as humanity has always done, accepting with sportsmanlike relish the estate
to which we are called, the star of our happiness, and the fortunes of the land of our
birth.

Gilbert Keith Chesterton

Remember you are but an actor in a drama
of such sort as the author chooses. If it be
his pleasure that you should act a poor man,
see that you act it well; or a cripple, or a
ruler, or a private citizen. For this is your
business, to act well the given part; but to
choose it belongs to another.

Epictetus

There is but one way to tranquility of mind
and happiness, and that is to account no external things thine own, but to commit all to
God.

Epictetus

O Lord, I do most cheerfully commit all
unto Thee.

Francois de Salignac de La Mothe-Fénelon

It is not where we have gathered up our
brighter hopes, that the dawn of happiness
breaks. It is not where we have glanced our
eye with affright, that we find the deadliest
gloom. What should this teach us? To bow to
the great and only source of light, and live
humbly and with confiding resignation.

Johann Wolfgang von Goethe

We cannot conquer fate and necessity, yet
we can yield to them in such a manner as to
be greater than if we could.

Walter Savage Landor

Let God do with me what He will, anything
He will; and, whatever it be, it will be either heaven itself, or some beginning of it.

William Mountford

It was a philosophical maxim, that a wise
moral man could not be injured, or miserable. But it is much more true of him who
has that divine wisdom of Christian resignation, which twines and enwraps all his
choices with God's; and is neither at the
pains nor the hazards of his own election,
but is secure, unless omniscience can be deceived and omnipotence defeated, that he
shall have what is really best for him.

Ray Palmer

All we have is the Almighty's, and shall not
God have his own when he calls for it?

William Penn

"My will, not thine, be done," turned paradise into a desert. "Thy will, not mine, be
done," turned the desert into a paradise,
and made Gethsemane the gate of heaven.

Edmond Dehaut de Pressensé

When we have not what we love, we must
love what we have.

Roger de Rabutin (Comte de Bussy)

Every man has his chain and clog, only it is
looser and lighter to one than to another;
and he is more at ease who takes it up and
carries it than he who drags it.

Seneca

Resignation is putting God between ourselves and our troubles.

Anne Sophie Swetchine

Vulgar minds refuse to crouch beneath their
load; the brave bear theirs without repining.

James Thomson

Resignation is the courage of Christian sorrow.

Alexandre Vinet

See also: ENDURANCE, FORTITUDE, PATIENCE,
PHILOSOPHY, STOICISM, SUBMISSION.

RESOLUTION

Men die that might just as well live if they
had resolved to live.

George Miller Beard

The block of granite which is an obstacle in
the pathway of the weak, becomes a
stepping-stone in the pathway of the strong.

Thomas Carlyle

There is nothing impossible in all the world
except that the heart of man is wanting in
resolution.

Confucius

A good intention clothes itself with power.

Ralph Waldo Emerson

He who is firm and resolute in will moulds the world to himself.

Johann Wolfgang von Goethe

You may be whatever you resolve to be. Determine to be something in the world, and you will be something. "I cannot," never accomplished anything; "I will try," has wrought wonders.

Joel Hawes

Either I will find a way, or I will make one.

Sir Philip Sidney

See also: CONSTANCY, COURAGE, DECISION, DETERMINATION, FIRMNESS, PERSEVERANCE, PURPOSE.

RESPECT

A man's real life is that accorded to him in the thoughts of other men by reason of respect or natural love.

Joseph Conrad

I must respect the opinions of others even if I disagree with them.

Herbert Henry Lehman

See also: COURTESY, DEFERENCE, MANNERS.

RESPECTABILITY

To secure respect for law, we must make the law respectable.

Louis Dembitz Brandeis

The hat is the *ultimum moriens* of respectability.

Oliver Wendell Holmes

Respectable means rich, and decent means poor. I should die if I heard my family called decent.

Thomas Love Peacock

The more things a man is ashamed of, the more respectable he is.

George Bernard Shaw

See also: APPEARANCE, GOOD BREEDING.

RESPONSIBILITY

All men, if they work not as in the great taskmaster's eye, will work wrong, and work unhappily for themselves and for you.

Thomas Carlyle

Every human being has a work to carry on within, duties to perform abroad, influences to exert, which are peculiarly his, and which no conscience but his own can teach.

William Ellery Channing

Responsibility is the thing people dread most of all. Yet it is the one thing in the world that develops us, gives us manhood or womanhood fibre.

Frank Crane

There can be no stable and balanced development of the mind, apart from the assumption of responsibility.

John Dewey

On its highest level man's contemporary desire to escape responsibility expresses itself not in emphasis on luck, or in emotional submission to fate, but in a thoroughgoing deterministic theory, ascribing all personal qualities to heredity and environment.

Harry Emerson Fosdick

Much misconstruction and bitterness are spared to him who thinks naturally upon what he owes to others rather than what he ought to expect from them.

Élisabeth Charlotte Pauline de Guizot

Responsibility walks hand in hand with capacity and power.

Josiah Gilbert Holland

Of those to whom much is given, much is required. And when at some future date the high court of history sits in judgment on each one of us—recording whether in our brief span of service we fulfilled our responsibilities to the state—our success or failure, in whatever office we may hold, will be measured by the answers to four questions— were we truly men of courage . . . were we truly men of judgment . . . were we truly men of integrity . . . were we truly men of dedication?

John Fitzgerald Kennedy

This nation was not founded solely on the principle of citizen rights. Equally important—though too often not discussed—is the citizen's responsibility. For our privileges can be no greater than our obligations. The protection of our rights can endure no longer than the performance of our responsibilities. Each can be neglected only at the peril of the other.

John Fitzgerald Kennedy

The feeling of a direct responsibility of the individual to God is almost wholly a creation of Protestantism.

John Stuart Mill

Responsibility educates.

Wendell Phillips

Responsibility is measured, not by the amount of injury resulting from wrong action, but by the distinctness with which conscience has the opportunity of distinguishing between the right and the wrong.

Frederick William Robertson

The most important thought I ever had was that of my individual responsibility to God.

Daniel Webster

See also: DUTY, INTEGRITY, OBLIGATION.

REST

Repose is good when it is rest, when we have chosen it . . . it is not good when it is our sole occupation.

Ludwig Börne

Absence of occupation is not rest;
A mind quite vacant is a mind distressed.

William Cowper

Rest is not quitting the busy career; rest is the fitting of self to its sphere.

John Sullivan Dwight

Too much rest itself becomes a pain.

Homer

Some seek bread; and some seek wealth and ease; and some seek fame, but all are seeking rest.

Frederick Langbridge

Certainly work is not always required of a man. There is such a thing as a sacred idleness—the cultivation of which is now fearfully neglected.

George Macdonald

Alternate rest and labor long endure.

Ovid

Rest is the sweet sauce of labor.

Plutarch

When I rest I rust.

Fritz Thyssen

See also: BED, PEACE, QUIET, RECREATION, REPOSE, SLEEP.

RESTLESSNESS

The mind is found most acute and most uneasy in the morning. Uneasiness is, indeed, a species of sagacity—a passive sagacity. Fools are never uneasy.

Johann Wolfgang von Goethe

Always driven toward new shores, or carried hence without hope of return, shall we never, on the ocean of age, cast anchor for even a day?

Alphonse de Lamartine

So when a raging fever burns,
We shift from side to side by turns;
And 'tis a poor relief we gain
To change the place, but keep the pain.

Isaac Watts

See also: AGITATION, AMBITION, DISCONTENTMENT, INSTABILITY, IRRESOLUTION.

RESTRAINT

Wou'd I were free from this restraint,
   Or else had hopes to win her;
Wou'd she cou'd make of me a saint,
   Or I of her a sinner.

William Congreve

Restraint never ruins one's health.

Mohandas Karamchand (Mahatma) Gandhi

Restraint self-imposed is no compulsion.

Mohandas Karamchand (Mahatma) Gandhi

The very first step in self-restraint is the restraint of thoughts.

Mohandas Karamchand (Mahatma) Gandhi

See also: MODERATION, TEMPERANCE, WILL.

RESULT

Results! Why, man, I have gotten a lot of results. I know several thousand things that won't work.

Thomas Alva Edison

No action, whether foul or fair,
Is ever done, but it leaves somewhere
A record, written by fingers ghostly
As a blessing or a curse, and mostly
In the greater weakness or greater strength
Of the acts which follow it.

Henry Wadsworth Longfellow

   Such souls
Whose sudden visitations daze the world,
Vanish like lightning; but they leave behind

A voice that in the distance far away
Wakens the slumbering ages.

Sir Henry Taylor

See also: BEGINNING, CAUSE, MEANS AND END.

RESURRECTION

I do believe, that die I must,
And be return'd from out my dust:
I do believe, that when I rise,
Christ I shall see, with these same eyes.

Robert Herrick

This only can be said:
He loved us all; is dead;
 May rise again.
But if He rise not? Over the far main,
The sun of glory falls indeed: the stars are
 plain.

Lionel Pigot Johnson

The diamond that shines in the Saviour's crown shall beam in unquenched beauty, at last, on the forehead of every human soul, risen through grace to the immortality of heaven.

Martin Luther

See also: CHRIST, EASTER, HEAVEN, IMMORTAL-
  ITY, REDEMPTION.

RETIREMENT

Before you think of retiring from the world, be sure you are fit for retirement; in order to which it is necessary that you have a mind so composed by prudence, reason, and religion, that it may bear being looked into; a turn to rural life, and a love for study.

James Burgh

Depart from the highway, and transplant thyself in some enclosed ground, for it is hard for a tree that stands by the wayside to keep its fruit until it be ripe.

John Chrysostom

I will be more than delighted when the time comes that I can retire to a cabin somewhere and take it easy and let others worry about budgets and all the other things that are constantly on my desk.

Dwight David Eisenhower

A man who can retire from the world to seek entertainment in his closet, has a thousand advantages of which other people have no idea. He is master of his own company and pleasures, and can command either the one or the other according to his circum-

stances or temper. All nature is ready for his view, and all ages appear at his call. He can transport himself to the most distant regions, and enjoy the best and politest company that ever the world afforded.

Hibernicus' Letters

Don't think of retiring from the world until the world will be sorry that you retire. I hate a fellow whom pride or cowardice or laziness drive into a corner, and who does nothing when he is there but sit and growl. Let him come out as I do, and bark.

Samuel Johnson

Nature I'll court in her sequestered haunts,
By mountain, meadow, streamlet, grove, or
 cell;
Where the poised lark his evening ditty
 chaunts,
And health and peace, and contemplation
 dwell.

Tobias George Smollett

See also: AGE, OLD; IDLENESS; LEISURE; REST;
  SOLITUDE.

RETRIBUTION

God is a sure paymaster. He may not pay at the end of every week, or month, or year, but remember He pays in the end.

Anne of Austria

Retribution is one of the grand principles in the divine administration of human affairs; a requital is imperceptible only to the wilfully unobservant. There is everywhere the working of the everlasting law of requital: man always gets as he gives.

John Watson Foster

God's mill grinds slow but sure.

George Herbert

The more pure and righteous a moral being is, the more squarely must he antagonize, the more intensely must he hate, the more surely must he punish impurity and unrighteousness. Volcanic fire inside the globe, and forked lightning outside of it, are faint emblems of holy wrath. When a thoroughly bad man stands revealed only lightning is logical. He that sows the wind ought to reap the whirlwind.

Roswell Dwight Hitchcock

Man never fastened one end of a chain around the neck of his brother, that God did

not fasten the other end round the neck of
the oppressor.

Alphonse de Lamartine

The blind and cowardly spirit of evil is
forever telling you that evil things are pardonable, and you shall not die for them; and
that good things are impossible, and you
need not live for them. And, if you believe
these things, you will find some day, to your
cost, that they are untrue.

John Ruskin

Life resembles the banquet of Damocles;
the sword is ever suspended.

Voltaire (François Marie Arouet)

See also: HELL, JUDGMENT, JUSTICE, MERIT,
PUNISHMENT, REWARD.

RETROSPECTION

Often a retrospect delights the mind.

Dante Alighieri

He possesses dominion over himself, and is
happy, who can every day say, "I have
lived." Tomorrow the heavenly Father may
either involve the world in dark clouds, or
cheer it with clear sunshine; he will not,
however, render ineffectual the things which
have already taken place.

Horace

Of no day can the retrospect cause pain to a
good man, nor has one passed away which he
is unwilling to remember: the period of his
life seems prolonged by his good acts; and
we may be said to live twice, when we can
reflect with pleasure on the days that are
gone.

Martial

The thought of our past years in me doth
breed perpetual benediction.

William Wordsworth

See also: MEDITATION, MEMORY, REFLECTION,
REMEMBRANCE, REVERIE.

REVELATION

'Tis revelation satisfies all doubts,
Explains all mysteries except her own,
And so illuminates the path of life,
That fools discover it, and stray no more.

William Cowper

Revelation, like creation, must be fluent.

Charles William Eliot

Nature is a revelation of God;
Art a revelation of man.

Henry Wadsworth Longfellow

Revelation may not need the help of reason,
but man does, even when in possession of
revelation. Reason is the candle in the man's
hand which enables him to see what revelation is.

William Gilmore Simms

See also: BIBLE, CHRISTIANITY, GOSPEL, MO-
HAMMEDANISM, RELIGION.

REVENGE

He that studieth revenge keepeth his own
wounds green, which otherwise would heal
and do well.

Francis Bacon

Sweet is revenge—especially to women.

George Gordon Byron (Lord Byron)

Revenge is an act of passion; vengeance of
justice. Injuries are revenged; crimes are
avenged.

Joseph Joubert

Revenge is the abject pleasure of an abject
mind.

Juvenal

Revenge is a common passion; it is the sin of
the uninstructed. The savage deems it noble; but the religion of Christ, which is the
sublime civilizer, emphatically condemns it.
Why? Because religion ever seeks to ennoble man; and nothing so debases him as revenge.

Edward G. Bulwer-Lytton (Baron Lytton)

A spirit of revenge is the very spirit of the
devil; than which nothing makes a man
more like him, and nothing can be more opposite to the temper Christianity was designed to promote. If your revenge be not
satisfied, it will give you torment now; if it
be, it will give you greater hereafter. None
is a greater self-tormentor than a malicious
and revengeful man, who turns the poison of
his own temper in upon himself.

John Mitchell Mason

Revenge, at first though sweet,
Bitter ere long back on itself recoils.

John Milton

If you are affronted it is better to pass it by
in silence, or with a jest, though with some

dishonor, than to endeavor revenge. If you can keep reason above passion, that and watchfulness will be your best defenders.

Joseph Fort Newton

The best manner of avenging ourselves is by not resembling him who has injured us.

Jane Porter

Hath any wronged thee? Be bravely revenged. Slight it, and the work is begun; forgive it, and it is finished. He is below himself that is not above any injury.

Francis Quarles

Revenge is barren of itself; itself is the dreadful food it feeds on; its delight is murder; its satiety despair.

Johann Christoph Friedrich von Schiller

See also: HATE, INJURY, MALICE, PUNISHMENT, RESENTMENT, VENGEANCE.

REVERENCE

Reverence is an ennobling sentiment; it is felt to be degrading only by the vulgar mind, which would escape the sense of its own littleness by elevating itself into an antagonist of what is above it. He that has no pleasure in looking up is not fit so much as to look down.

Washington Allston

The soul of the Christian religion is reverence.

Johann Wolfgang von Goethe

The Turks carefully collect every scrap of paper that comes in their way, because the name of God may be written thereon.

Jean Paul Richter

See also: ADMIRATION, DEFERENCE, DEVOTION, PIETY, RESPECT, RELIGION.

REVERIE

Reverie, which is thought in its nebulous state, borders closely upon the land of sleep, by which it is bounded as by a natural frontier.

Victor Marie Hugo

Reverie is when ideas float in our mind without reflection or regard of the understanding.

John Locke

To lose one's self in reverie, one must be either very happy, or very unhappy. Reverie is the child of extremes.

Antoine Rivarol

Both mind and heart, when given up to reverie and dreaminess, have a thousand avenues open for the entrance of evil.

Charles Simmons

In that sweet mood when pleasant thoughts bring sad thoughts to the mind.

William Wordsworth

See also: DREAM, FANCY, RETROSPECTION.

REVOLUTION

The surest way to prevent seditions is to take away the matter of them; for if there be fuel prepared, it is hard to tell whence the spark shall come that shall set it on fire.

Francis Bacon

Revolution: in politics, an abrupt change in the form of misgovernment.

Ambrose Gwinnett Bierce

Times and occasions and provocations will teach their own lessons. But with or without right, a revolution will be the very last resource of the thinking and the good.

Edmund Burke

I began revolution with 82 men. If I had [to] do it again, I do it with 10 or 15 men and absolute faith. It does not matter how small you are if you have faith and plan of action.

Fidel Castro

It is far more easy to pull down than to build up, and to destroy than to preserve. Revolutions have on this account been falsely supposed to be fertile of great talent; as the dregs rise to the top during a fermentation, and the lightest things are carried highest by the whirlwind.

Charles Caleb Colton

America is fitted by tradition for directing and guiding revolutions. We won our freedom by revolution and set the example which today inspires the peasants of Asia. We cannot remake the world in our image; but we can help those who are seeking an escape from squalor to find alternatives to communism.

William Orville Douglas

The world is in a revolution which cannot be bought off with dollars. . . . A fire is gathering for a mighty effort.

William Orville Douglas

Too long denial of guaranteed right is sure to lead to revolution—bloody revolution, where suffering must fall upon the innocent as well as the guilty.

Ulysses Simpson Grant

The working of revolutions misleads me no more; it is as necessary to our race as its waves to the stream, that it may not be a stagnant marsh. Ever renewed in its forms, the genius of humanity blossoms.

Johann Gottfried von Herder

Revolution is the larva of civilization.

Victor Marie Hugo

All experience hath shown that mankind are more disposed to suffer, while evils are sufferable, than to right themselves by abolishing the forms to which they are accustomed.

Thomas Jefferson

It is commonly assumed that revolutions are periods of accelerated social evolution, but the assumption is doubtful.

Alvin Saunders Johnson

The republics of this hemisphere have shown that deep social change is compatible with peace, is consistent with democracy and is consonant with individual liberty. Great changes can be wrought by reason and not by rifles, by builders and not bullets.

Lyndon Baines Johnson

Let them call it mischief; when it's past and prospered, it will be virtue.

Ben (Benjamin) Jonson

Nothing has ever remained of any revolution but what was ripe in the conscience of the masses.

Alexandre Auguste Ledru-Rollin

We deplore the outrages which accompany revolutions. But the more violent the outrages, the more assured we feel that a revolution was necessary! The violence of these outrages will always be proportioned to the ferocity and ignorance of the people: and the ferocity and ignorance of the people will be proportioned to the oppression and degradation under which they have been accustomed to live.

Thomas Babington Macaulay

For men are willing enough to change their prince, thinking that they will thereby better their condition, and that induces them to re-

bel, but they find themselves mistaken, for experience often proves that they have changed for the worse.

Niccolò Machiavelli

Revolution is not a dinner party, nor an essay, nor a painting, nor a piece of embroidery; it cannot be advanced softly, gradually, carefully, considerately, respectfully, politely, plainly and modestly.

Mao Tse-tung

Great revolutions are the work rather of principles than of bayonets, and are achieved first in the moral, and afterwards in the material sphere.

Giuseppe Mazzini

Revolutions begin in the best heads, and run steadily down to the populace.

Prince Klemens von Metternich

Those who give the first shock to a state are naturally the first to be overwhelmed in its ruin. The fruits of public commotion are seldom enjoyed by the man who was the first to set it a-going; he only troubles the water for another's net.

Michel Eyquem de Montaigne

Who does more earnestly long for a change than he who is uneasy in his present circumstances? And who run to create confusions with so desperate a boldness, as those who have nothing to lose, hope to gain by them?

Sir Thomas More

Revolutions are like the most noxious dungheaps, which bring into life the noblest vegetables.

Napoleon I (Bonaparte)

Political convulsions, like geological upheavings, usher in new epochs of the world's progress.

Wendell Phillips

There is a revolution coming. It will not be like revolutions of the past. It will originate with the individual and with culture, and it will change the political structure only as its final act. It will not require violence to succeed, and it cannot be successfully resisted by violence.

Charles Alan Reich

The best security against revolution is in constant correction of abuses and the introduction of needed improvements. It is the neglect of timely repair that makes rebuilding necessary.

Richard Whately

See also: ANARCHY, COMMUNISM, REBELLION, RIOT, VIOLENCE, WAR.

REWARD

He who wishes to secure the good of others has already secured his own.

Confucius

Blessings ever wait on virtuous deeds,
And though a late, a sure reward succeeds.

William Congreve

It is the amends of a short and troublesome life, that doing good and suffering ill entitles man to a longer and better.

William Penn

We utter a word of praise for various systems devised and attempted in practice, by which an increased wage is paid in view of increased family burdens.

Pius XI (Achille Ambrogio Damiano Ratti)

No man, who continues to add something to the material, intellectual, and moral well being of the place in which he lives, is left long without proper reward.

Booker Taliaferro Washington

See also: COMPENSATION, RECOMPENSE.

RHETORIC

All a rhetorician's rules teach nothing but to name his tools.

Samuel Butler

A hundred years ago our affairs for good or evil were wielded triumphantly by rhetoricians. Now our affairs are hopelessly muddled by strong, silent men.

Gilbert Keith Chesterton

Rhetoric is nothing but reason well dressed, and argument put in order.

Jeremy Collier

The florid, elevated, and figurative way is for the passion; for love and hatred, fear and anger, are begotten in the soul by showing their objects out of their true proportion, either greater than the life, or less; but instruction is to be given by showing them what they naturally are. A man is to be cheated into passion, but reasoned into truth.

John Dryden

The best rules of rhetoric are, to speak intelligently; speak from the heart; have something to say, say it; and stop when you've done.

Tryon Edwards

All the arts of rhetoric, besides order and clearness, are for nothing else but to insinuate wrong ideas, move the passions, and thereby mislead the judgment.

John Locke

There is truth and beauty in rhetoric; but it oftener serves ill turns than good ones.

William Penn

Mere rhetoric, in serious discourses, is like flowers in corn, pleasing to those who look only for amusement, but prejudicial to him who would reap profit from it.

Jonathan Swift

See also: ELOQUENCE, ORATORY, SPEECH.

RICH AND POOR

There are two things needed in these days; first, for rich men to find out how poor men live; and second, for poor men to know how rich men work.

Edward Atkinson

The greatest and the most amiable privilege which the rich enjoy over the poor is that which they exercise the least,—the privilege of making others happy.

Charles Caleb Colton

If we permit extremes of wealth for a few and enduring poverty for many, we shall create a social explosiveness and a demand for revolutionary change.

Dwight David Eisenhower

No doctrine has shocked me more than the common American formula that he who has much money must be admirable and that he who has none ought to apologize.

John Erskine

A rich man is nothing but a poor man with money.

William Claude Fields

Few things have been more productive of controversy over the ages than the suggestion that the rich should, by one device or another, share their wealth with those who are not.

John Kenneth Galbraith

Riches, honors, and pleasures are the sweets which destroy the mind's appetite for heavenly food; poverty, disgrace, and pain are the bitters which restore it.

George Horne

I take him to be the only rich man that lives upon what he has, owes nothing, and is contented; for there is no determinate sum of money, nor quantity of estate that can denote a man rich, since no man is truly rich that has not so much as perfectly satiates his desire of having more; for the desire of more is want, and want is poverty.

John Howe

We give our money and go back to our homes and maybe our swimming pools and wonder, Why don't they keep quiet, why don't they go away?

Robert Francis Kennedy

He is rich whose income is more than his expenses; and he is poor whose expenses exceed his income.

Jean de La Bruyère

Wherever there is excessive wealth, there is also in its train excessive poverty, as where the sun is highest, the shade is deepest.

Walter Savage Landor

We could be known as the generation which put a man on the moon while standing ankle-deep in garbage.

Ralph Locher

It is wrong to say that God made rich and poor; He made only male and female, and He gave them the whole earth for their inheritance.

Thomas Paine

Gentlemen of the press, it is up to you to place before our eyes the story of the efforts exerted to promote mutual assistance among peoples, as well as the spectacle of the miseries which men tend to forget in order to quiet their consciences. Thus at least the wealthy will know that the poor stand outside their doors waiting to receive some leftovers from their banquets.

Paul VI (Giovanni Battista Montini)

Wealth . . . must be so distributed . . . that the common good of all . . . be thereby promoted. This sacred law is violated by an irresponsible wealthy class who, in the excess of their good fortune, deem it a just state of things that they should receive everything and the laborer nothing; it is violated also by a propertyless wage-earning class who demand for themselves all the fruits of production, as being the work of their hands.

Pius XI (Achille Ambrogio Damiano Ratti)

Nothing is so hard for those who abound in riches as to conceive how others can be in want.

Jonathan Swift

The big house on the hill surrounded by mud huts has lost its awesome charm.

Wendell Lewis Willkie

See also: POVERTY, RICHES, SLUM, WEALTH.

RICHES

Riches are apt to betray a man into arrogance.

Joseph Addison

A great estate is a great disadvantage to those who do not know how to use it, for nothing is more common than to see wealthy persons live scandalously and miserably; riches do them no service in order to virtue and happiness; it is precept and principle, not an estate, that makes a man good for something.

Marcus Aurelius

Riches are a good handmaid, but the worst mistress.

Francis Bacon

Never respect men merely for their riches, but rather for their philanthropy; we do not value the sun for its height, but for its use.

Gamaliel Bailey

Riches are not an end of life, but an instrument of life.

Henry Ward Beecher

Of all the riches that we hug, of all the pleasures we enjoy, we can carry no more out of this world than out of a dream.

James Bonnell

The use we make of our fortune determines as to its sufficiency. A little is enough if used wisely, and too much if expended foolishly.

Christian Nestell Bovee

Misery assails riches, as lightning does the highest towers; or as a tree that is heavy laden with fruit breaks its own boughs, so do riches destroy the virtue of their possessor.

Richard Eugene Burton

Public sentiment will come to be, that the man who dies rich dies disgraced.

Andrew Carnegie

Man was born to be rich, or grows rich by the use of his faculties, by the union of thought with nature. Property is an intellectual production. The game requires coolness, right reasoning, promptness, and patience in the players. Cultivated labor drives out brute labor.

Ralph Waldo Emerson

Riches without charity are nothing worth. They are a blessing only to him who makes them a blessing to others.

Henry Fielding

The pride of dying rich raises the loudest laugh in hell.

John Watson Foster

Riches amassed in haste will diminish, but those collected by little and little will multiply.

Johann Wolfgang von Goethe

There is a burden of care in getting riches; fear in keeping them; temptation in using them; guilt in abusing them; sorrow in losing them; and a burden of account at last to be given concerning them.

Matthew Henry

If I have but enough for myself and family, I am steward only for myself and them; if I have more, I am but a steward of that abundance for others.

George Herbert

Riches are valuable at all times and to all men, because they always purchase pleasures such as men are accustomed to and desire: nor can anything restrain or regulate the love of money but a sense of honor and virtue, which, if not equal at all times, will naturally abound most in ages of knowledge and refinement.

David Hume

I don't think you can spend yourself rich.

George Humphrey

One cause, which is not always observed, of the insufficiency of riches, is that they very seldom make their owner rich.

Samuel Johnson

Riches exclude only one inconvenience, and that is poverty.

Samuel Johnson

Riches are gotten with pain, kept with care, and lost with grief. The cares of riches lie heavier upon a good man than the inconveniences of an honest poverty.

Sir Roger L'Estrange

Riches are the pettiest and least worthy gifts which God can give a man. What are they to God's Word, to bodily gifts, such as beauty and health; or to the gifts of the mind, such as understanding, skill, wisdom! Yet men toil for them day and night, and take no rest. Therefore God commonly gives riches to foolish people to whom he gives nothing else.

Martin Luther

To have what we want is riches, but to be able to do without is power.

George Macdonald

The rich are the real outcasts of society, and special missions should be organized for them.

Norman Macleod

Plenty and indigence depend upon the opinion every one has of them; and riches, like glory or health, have no more beauty or pleasure, than their possessor is pleased to lend them.

Michel Eyquem de Montaigne

There is no less merit in keeping what we have got, than in first acquiring it. Chance has something to do with the one, while the other will always be the effect of skill.

Ovid

That plenty should produce either covetousness or prodigality is a perversion of providence; and yet the generality of men are the worse for their riches.

William Penn

Rich men die but banks are immortal.

Wendell Phillips

To whom can riches give repute, or trust, Content, or pleasure, but the good and just?

Alexander Pope

Wouldst thou multiply thy riches?—diminish them wisely. Or wouldst thou make thine estate entire?—divide it charitably. Seeds that are scattered increase, but hoarded up they perish.

Francis Quarles

We see how much a man has, and therefore we envy him; did we see how little he enjoys, we should rather pity him.

Jeremiah Seed

We are so vain as to set the highest value upon those things to which nature has assigned the lowest place. What can be more coarse and rude in the mine than the precious metals, or more slavish and dirty than the people that dig and work them? And yet they defile our minds more than our bodies, and make the possessor fouler than the artificer of them. Rich men, in fine, are only the greater slaves.

Seneca

It is the wretchedness of being rich that you have to live with rich people.

Logan Pearsall Smith

For generations English society has been wide open to, defenceless against, rich and determined men.

Sir Charles Percy Snow

If a rich man is proud of his wealth, he should not be praised until it is known how he employs it.

Socrates

He is richest who is content with the least, for content is the wealth of nature.

Socrates

Satiety comes of riches, and contumaciousness of satiety.

Solon

Leisure and solitude are the best effect of riches, because the mother of thought. Both are avoided by most rich men, who seek company and business, which are signs of being weary of themselves.

Sir William Temple

Worldly riches are like nuts; many clothes are torn in getting them, many a tooth broke in cracking them, but never a belly filled with eating them.

Ralph Venning

I have a rich neighbor that is always so busy that he has no leisure to laugh; the whole business of his life is to get money, more money, that he may still get more. He considers not that it is not in the power of riches to make a man happy; for it was wisely said that "there be as many miseries beyond riches as on this side of them."

Izaak Walton

To value riches is not to be covetous. They are the gift of God, and, like every gift of his, good in themselves, and capable of a good use. But to over-value riches, to give them a place in the heart which God did not design them to fill, this is covetousness.

Heman Lincoln Wayland

The larger the income, the harder it is to live within it.

Richard Whately

See also: POVERTY, RICH AND POOR, WEALTH.

RIDICULE

Cervantes smiled Spain's chivalry away.

George Gordon Byron (Lord Byron)

It was the saying of an ancient sage that humor was the only test of gravity, and gravity of humor; for a subject that would not bear raillery was suspicious, and a jest that would not bear a serious examination was certainly false wit.

Anthony Ashley Cooper (Lord Shaftesbury)

Scoff not at the natural defects of any which are not in their power to amend. It is cruel to beat a cripple with his own crutches!

Thomas Fuller

Man learns more readily and remembers more willingly what excites his ridicule than what deserves esteem and respect.

Horace

If there be any one habit which more than another is the dry-rot of all that is high and generous in youth, it is the habit of ridicule.

Letitia Elizabeth Landon

He who brings ridicule to bear against truth finds in his hand a blade without a hilt. The most sparkling and pointed flame of wit flickers and expires against the incombustible walls of her sanctuary.

Walter Savage Landor

Your sayer of smart things has a bad heart.

Blaise Pascal

Mockery is the weapon of those who have no other.

Hubert Pierlot

Ridicule is the weapon most feared by enthusiasts of every description; from its predominance over such minds it often checks what is absurd, but fully as often smothers that which is noble.

Sir Walter Scott

Ridicule is the first and last argument of fools.

Charles Simmons

Learn from the earliest days to inure your principles against the perils of ridicule: you can no more exercise your reason if you live in the constant dread of laughter, than you can enjoy your life if you are in the constant terror of death.

Sydney Smith

It has been said that ridicule is the best test of truth, for that it will not stick where it is not just. I deny it. A truth viewed in a certain light, and attacked in certain words, by men of wit and humor, may, and often doth, become ridiculous, at least so far that the truth is only remembered and repeated for the sake of the ridicule.

Philip Dormer Stanhope (Lord Chesterfield)

Ridicule is a weak weapon when levelled at strong minds, but common men are cowards and dread an empty laugh.

Martin Farquhar Tupper

Reason is the test of ridicule—not ridicule the test of truth.

William Warburton

Vices, when ridiculed
 First lose the horror they ought to raise,
Grow by degrees approved,
 And almost aim at praise.

William Whitehead

See also: ABSURDITY, CARICATURE, CRITICISM, IRONY, RAILLERY, SARCASM.

RIGHT AND WRONG

Let a man try faithfully, manfully to be right, he will daily grow more and more right. It is at the bottom of the condition on which all men have to cultivate themselves.

Thomas Carlyle

I would rather be right than be president.

Henry Clay

Right is might, and ever was, and ever shall be so. Holiness, meekness, patience, humility, self-denial, and self-sacrifice, faith, love,—each is might, and every gift of the spirit is might.

Augustus and Julius Hare

Whatever is physiologically right, is morally right; and whatever is physiologically wrong is morally wrong.

Mark Hopkins

I refuse to accept the cynical notion that nation after nation must spiral down a militaristic stairway into the hell of thermonuclear destruction. I believe that unarmed truth and unconditional love will have the final word in reality. This is why right, temporarily defeated, is stronger than evil triumphant.

Martin Luther King, Jr.

When everybody is wrong, everybody is right.

Pierre Claude Nivelle de La Chausée

Let us have faith that right makes might, and in that faith, let us to the end, dare to do our duty, as we understand it.

Abraham Lincoln

The conviction of being right which is, in my eyes, the infallible sign of error.

Jean Rostand

See also: HONESTY, MORALITY, RECTITUDE.

RIGHTS

Many a person seems to think it isn't enough for the government to guarantee him the pursuit of happiness. He insists it also run interference for him.

Anonymous

The fears of one class of men are not the measure of the rights of another.

George Bancroft

How can you have states' rights when you keep running to Washington for money?

Bernard Mannes Baruch

The right of the people to assemble and consult for the public good is exercised with little let or hindrance. . . . But where the people chiefly assembly is in front of their radios to consult with disembodied voices that announce and comment on news collected by corporations organized for private profit.

Carl Lotus Becker

The makers of our Constitution . . . sought to protect Americans. . . . They conferred, as against the government, the right to be left alone—the most comprehensive of rights and the right most valued by civilized men. To protect that right, every unjustifiable intrusion by the government upon the privacy of the individial, whatever the means employed, must be deemed a violation of the Fourth Amendment. And the use, as evidence in a criminal proceeding, of facts ascertained by such intrusion must be deemed a violation of the Fifth.

Louis Dembitz Brandeis

Today, as rarely before, case after case comes to the Court which finds the individual battling to vindicate a claim under the Bill of Rights against the powers of government, federal and state.

William Joseph Brennan, Jr.

In our land, the citizen is the power, and every citizen should have his share.

Richard James Cushing

The right to think is the real difference between us and the enemy; it is likely to give us ultimate victory in the cold war—or in a hot war, if that should break out.

Elmer Holmes Davis

The fences have been broken down . . . The Bill of Rights—with the judicial gloss it has acquired—plainly is not adequate to protect the individual against the growing bureaucracy.

William Orville Douglas

In free countries, the agent may never become the master; if human rights and freedoms are to flourish, government must operate with its powers sharply defined and limited by the governed. . . . But the dividing line between government's functions, on the one hand, and the individual's rights, privileges and inescapable responsibilities never is completely fixed; never is static. It oscillates constantly in a middle area between centralized authority and individual liberty, as economic, social and political conditions require more or less action by government.

Dwight David Eisenhower

In fact the right to perform one's duties is the only right that is worth living for and dying for. It covers all legitimate rights.

Mohandas Karamchand (Mahatma) Gandhi

Rights accrue automatically to him who duly performs his duties.

Mohandas Karamchand (Mahatma) Gandhi

"Freedom from fear" could be said to sum up the whole philosophy of human rights.

Dag Hammarskjold

Men have as exaggerated an idea of their rights as women have of their wrongs.

Edgar Watson Howe

We hold these truths to be self-evident that all men are created equal, that they are endowed by their Creator with certain unalienable Rights, that among these are Life, Liberty, and the pursuit of Happiness.

Thomas Jefferson

I do not say that all men are equal in their ability, character and motivation. I do say that every American should be given a fair chance to develop all the talents they may have.

John Fitzgerald Kennedy

In giving rights to others which belong to them, we give rights to ourselves and to our country.

John Fitzgerald Kennedy

Let the word go forth from this time and place, to friend and foe alike, that the torch has been passed to a new generation of Americans—born in this century, tempered by war, disciplined by a hard and bitter peace, proud of our ancient heritage—and unwilling to witness or permit the slow undoing of those human rights to which this nation has always been committed, and to which we are committed today at home and around the world.

John Fitzgerald Kennedy

One hundred years of delay have passed since President Lincoln freed the slaves, yet their heirs, their grandsons, are not fully free. They are not yet freed from the bonds of injustice.

John Fitzgerald Kennedy

When the universal values of human dignity, truth, and justice under law have been guaranteed to all men—we will have created an enduring peace for ourselves, our children, and the priceless institutions of our way of life.

John Fitzgerald Kennedy

The world is very different now. For man holds in his mortal hands the power to abolish all forms of human poverty and all forms of human life. And yet the same revolutionary beliefs for which our forebears fought are still at issue around the globe—the belief that the rights of man come not from the generosity of the state but from the hand of God.

John Fitzgerald Kennedy

Man precedes the State, and possesses, prior to the formation of any State, the right of providing for the sustenance of his body.

Leo XIII (Gioacchino Vincenzo Pecci)

There is no right without a parallel duty, no liberty without the supremacy of the law, no high destiny without earnest perseverance, no greatness without self-denial.

Francis Lieber

Nobody can justify . . . an unrestricted right of anyone to utter anything he likes at any time he chooses. There can, for example, be no right, as Mr. Justice Holmes said, to cry "Fire" in a crowded theater.

Walter Lippmann

Neither Pagan nor Mahometan nor Jew ought to be excluded from the civil rights of the Commonwealth because of his religion. . . . If we allow the Jews to have . . . dwellings amongst us, why should we not allow them to have synagogs?

John Locke

We need to rectify this mockery of justice and seek to realine the imbalanced scales of justice that all too often subjugate the rights and safety of society to the privileged exploitations and atrocities by the criminal.

John L. McClellan

One of the grandest things in having rights is, that though they are your rights you may give them up.

George Macdonald

I want to see civil rights leaders take great care against overheating the ghettos . . . This could escalate into a race war in this nation which could become catastrophic to the Negroes and to America.

Asa Philip Randolph

From the equality of rights springs identity of our highest interests; you cannot subvert your neighbor's rights without striking a dangerous blow at your own.

Carl Schurz

No man has a right to do as he pleases, except when he pleases to do right.

Charles Simmons

Never, with the Bible in our hands, can we deny rights to another, which, under the same circumstances, we would claim for ourselves.

Gardiner Spring

We must reduce hunger and want and disease and the shocking difference between what life holds for a child in a developed country and what it holds for a child in an underdeveloped country. We must finish once and for all with the myth of inequality of races and peoples, with the scandal of discrimination, with the shocking violations of human rights and the cynical violations of political rights.

Adlai Ewing Stevenson

The Fourth Amendment and the personal rights it secures have a long history. At the very core stands the right of a man to retreat into his own home and there be free from unreasonable governmental intrusion.

Potter Stewart

The growth of the American conscience during the years of my adult life in the field of what we now call civil rights . . . has been the single most encouraging moral symptom in American society. We have a long way to go before we end racial discrimination once and for all, but the progress made strengthens my faith, even in moments of depression, that an appeal to the American conscience and intelligence is by no means wasted effort.

Norman Mattoon Thomas

In the cause of freedom, we have to battle for the rights of people with whom we do not agree; and whom, in many cases, we may not like. These people test the strength of the freedoms which protect all of us. If we do not defend their rights, we endanger our own.

Harry S Truman

The right is more precious than peace, and we shall fight for the things which we have always carried nearest to our hearts—for democracy, for the right of those who submit to authority to have a voice in their own government, for the rights and liberties of small nations, for a universal dominion of right by such a concert of free people as shall bring peace and safety to all nations and make the world itself at last free.

(Thomas) Woodrow Wilson

Senseless rebellion against authority proves nothing except perhaps the poor judgment or immaturity of the rebel. This is particularly true when the rebellion is itself supposed to manifest some type of protest against restraints on civil liberties or civil rights. Two wrongs still do not make a right, and it is the height of asininity to suppose that the cause of civil rights is furthered by persons who engage in civil wrongs or criminal conduct.

Louis Crosby Wyman

See also: DEMOCRACY, EQUITY, JUSTICE.

RIOT

No nation, no matter how enlightened, can endure criminal violence. If we cannot control it we are admitting to the world and to ourselves that our laws are no more than a facade that crumbles when the winds of crisis rise.

Alan Bible

Numerous Negro counter-rioters walked the streets urging rioters to "cool it." The typical counter-rioter was better educated and had higher income than either the rioter or the noninvolved.

Commission on Civil Disorder, 1968

The typical rioter was a teenager or young adult, a lifelong resident of the city in which he rioted, a high school dropout; he was, nevertheless, somewhat better educated than his nonrioting Negro neighbor, and was usually underemployed or employed in a menial job. He was proud of his race, extremely hostile to both whites and middle-class Negroes and, although informed about politics, highly distrustful of the political system.

Commission on Civil Disorder, 1968

The urban disorders of the summer of 1967 were not caused by nor were they the consequence of, any organized plan or "conspiracy."

Commission on Civil Disorder, 1968

Violence cannot build a better society. Disruption and disorder nourish repression, not justice. They strike at the freedom of every citizen. The community cannot—it will not—tolerate coercion and mob rule.

Commission on Civil Disorder, 1968

We are fooling ourselves if we believe that placing a priority on riot control will solve the fundamental social problems that serve as a catalyst for urban unrest and crime. I support legislation aimed at strengthening local law-enforcement agencies in order to protect our citizens against the tragedy of riots and against organized crime. But, to me, it is of crucial importance that our society be mobilized to attack the basic cause of this problem: personal despair. I believe these muggings are further evidence that through the war against poverty and related programs, we must assure all citizens the opportunity to lead productive lives. In my judgment, this is the only way to make our cities truly safe for all citizens.

Leonard Farbstein

[The Federal Antiriot Act] is not a solution to our urban problems. But it does give the Federal Government the power to act against those who might move around the country, inciting and joining in the terror of riots.

Lyndon Baines Johnson

The poor suffer twice at the rioter's hands. First, his destructive fury scars their neighborhood; second, the atmosphere of accommodation and consent is changed to one of hostility and resentment.

Lyndon Baines Johnson

The summer of 1967 will be recorded as one of the most violent in the history of this Nation. This was a summer when racial unrest reached the point where violence was so common that it was news when it was quiet in our cities.

Walter F. Mondale

If we resort to lawlessness, the only thing we can hope for is civil war, untold bloodshed, and the end of our dreams.

Archie Lee Moore

One speaks of the possibility of violence with caution. Too often, to predict the possibility of violence is interpreted as an incitement to violence. But I infinitely prefer to be called an alarmist than to stand by, a silent witness to impending crisis.

Whitney Moore Young, Jr.

See also: BLACK POWER, CITY, POVERTY, SLUM, VIOLENCE.

RISK

People avoid action often because they are afraid of the consequences, for action means risk and danger. Danger seems terrible from a distance: it is not so bad if you have a close look at it. And often it is a pleasant companion, adding to the zest and delight of life.

Jawaharlal Nehru

The policy of being too cautious is the greatest risk of all.

Jawaharlal Nehru

Everything is sweetened by risk.

Alexander Smith

See also: BRAVERY, DANGER, FEAR.

RIVALRY

It is the privilege of posterity to set matters right between those antagonists who, by their rivalry for greatness, divided a whole age.

Joseph Addison

In ambition, as in love, the successful can afford to be indulgent toward their rivals. The prize our own, it is graceful to recognize the merit that vainly aspired to it.

Christian Nestell Bovee

Nothing is ever done beautifully which is done in rivalship; or nobly, which is done in pride.

John Ruskin

See also: CONTENTION, ENVY, JEALOUSY.

RIVER

Dark brown is the river,
  Golden is the sand,
It flows along for ever,
  With trees on either hand.

Robert Louis Balfour Stevenson

Rivers are roads which move, and carry us whither we wish to go.

Blaise Pascal

The river glideth at his own sweet will.

William Wordsworth

See also: NATURE, RAIN, SEA, WATER.

ROGUERY

A rogue is a roundabout fool.

Samuel Taylor Coleridge

Rogues are always found out in some way. Whoever is a wolf will act as a wolf; that is the most certain of all things.

Charles Fontaine

After long experience of the world, I affirm before God, that I never knew a rogue who was not unhappy.

Junius

See also: BASENESS, CRIME, DECEIT, DISHONES-TY, FRAUD, MISCHIEF, VILLAINY.

ROMANCE

I despair of ever receiving the same degree of pleasure from the most exalted performances of genius which I felt in childhood from pieces which my present judgment regards as trifling and contemptible.

Edmund Burke

Romance has been elegantly defined as the offspring of fiction and love.

Benjamin Disraeli

Romance is the poetry of literature.

Albertine Adrienne de Saussure Necker

In this commonplace world every one is said to be romantic who either admires a finer thing or does one.

Alexander Pope

Lessons of wisdom have never such power over us as when they are wrought into the heart through the groundwork of a story which engages the passions.

Laurence Sterne

See also: ALLEGORY, FABLE, FICTION, LOVE, NOVEL, POETRY, READING.

ROME

Rome would always rule, and when her legions fell, she sent dogmas into the provinces. Like a giant spider, she sat in the center of the Latin world, and spun over it her endless web.

Heinrich Heine

God was on the Roman side.

Flavius Josephus

Great are their possessions, the people that won them are greater still!

Flavius Josephus

See the wild waste of all-devouring years,
How Rome her own sad sepulchre appears,
With nodding arches, broken temples
    spread,
The very tombs now vanish's like their dead.
                    Alexander Pope

See also: CITY, GREECE, ITALY, RUINS.

ROSE

Who reaches with a clumsy hand for a rose
must not complain if the thorns scratch.
                    Heinrich Heine

Go, lovely rose!
    Tell her that wastes her time, and me
That now she knows,
    When I resemble her to thee,
    How sweet, and fair, she seems to be.
                    Edmund Waller

How fair is the Rose! what a beautiful flow-
    er.
    The glory of April and May!
But the leaves are beginning to fade in an
    hour,
    And they wither and die in a day.
Yet the Rose has one powerful virtue to
    boast,
    Above all the flowers of the field:
When its leaves are all dead, and fine col-
    ours are lost,
    Still how sweet a perfume it will yield!
                    Isaac Watts

See also: FLOWER, NATURE.

ROUTINE

Keep out of ruts; a rut is something which
If traveled in too much, becomes a ditch.
                    Arthur Guiterman

We need some imaginative stimulus, some
not impossible ideal such as may shape
vague hope, and transform it into effective
desire, to carry us year after year, without
disgust, through the routine-work which is so
large a part of life.
                    Walter Horatio Pater

See also: ORDER, REPETITION.

RUINS

Cicero was not so eloquent as thou, thou
nameless column with the buried base.
                    George Gordon Byron (Lord Byron)

Mile-stones on the road of time.
                    Sébastian Roch Nicolas Chamfort

Black-letter record of the ages.
                    Denis Diderot

Men moralize among ruins.
                    Benjamin Disraeli

We do not understand ruins, until we ourselves have become ruins.
                    Heinrich Heine

The legendary tablets of the past.
                    Sir Walter Scott

See also: ANTIQUITY, GREECE, HISTORY, ROME.

RULE

To rule is an art, not a science.
                    Ludwig Börne

A smile for a friend and a sneer for the
world, is the way to govern mankind.
                    Benjamin Disraeli

All who know well how to obey will know
also how to rule.
                    Flavius Josephus

See also: AUTHORITY, GOVERNMENT, LAW, OR-
    DER, POWER, PRECEPT.

RUMOR

Rumor was the messenger of defamation,
and so swift, that none could be first to tell
an evil tale.
                    Robert Pollok

When rumours increase, and when there is
abundance of noise and clamor, believe the
second report.
                    Alexander Pope

The flying rumours gather'd as they roll'd,
Scarce any tale was sooner heard than told;
And all who told it added something new,
And all who heard it made enlargements
    too.
                    Alexander Pope

He that easily believes rumors has the principle within him to augment rumors. It is

strange to see the ravenous appetite with which some devourers of character and happiness fix upon the sides of the innocent and unfortunate.

Jane Porter

See also: BABBLE, BUSYBODY, GOSSIP, SCANDAL, SLANDER, TALKING, TONGUE.

RUSSIA

I cannot forecast to you the action of Russia. It is a riddle wrapped in a mystery inside an enigma: but perhaps there is a key. That key is Russian national interest.

Sir Winston Leonard Spencer Churchill

We say the name of God, but that is only habit. We are atheists.

Nikita Sergeevich Khrushchev

Whether you like it or not, history is on our side. We will bury you!

Nikita Sergeevich Khrushchev

See also: COLD WAR, COEXISTENCE, COMMUNISM, NATION, REVOLUTION.

S

SABBATH

There are many persons who look on Sunday as a sponge to wipe out the sin of the week.

Henry Ward Beecher

The keeping of one day in seven holy, as a time of relaxation and refreshment as well as public worship, is of inestimable benefit to a state, considered merely as a civil institution.

Sir William Blackstone

Of all the days that's in the week
 I dearly love but one day—
And that's the day that comes betwixt
A Saturday and Monday.

Henry Carey

I feel as if God had, by giving the Sabbath, given fifty-two springs in every year.

Samuel Taylor Coleridge

There is a Sunday conscience, as well as a Sunday coat; and those who make religion a secondary concern put the coat and conscience carefully by to put on only once a week.

Charles John Huffam Dickens

To say nothing of the divine law, on mere worldly grounds it is plain that nothing is more conducive to the health, intelligence, comfort, and independence of the working classes, and to our prosperity as a people than our Christian American Sabbath.

Tryon Edwards

The Sunday is the core of our civilization, dedicated to thought and reverence. It invites to the noblest solitude and to the noblest society.

Ralph Waldo Emerson

Without a Sabbath, no worship; without worship, no religion; and without religion, no permanent freedom.

Charles Forbes (Comte de Montalembert)

A holiday Sabbath is the ally of despotism.

John Hallam

Sunday is the golden clasp that binds together the volume of the week.

Henry Wadsworth Longfellow

He who ordained the Sabbath loves the poor.

James Russell Lowell

If the Sunday had not been observed as a day of rest during the last three centuries, I have not the slightest doubt that we should have been at this moment a poorer people and less civilized.

Thomas Babington Macaulay

Where there is no Christian Sabbath, there is no Christian morality; and without this, free institutions cannot long be sustained.

John McLean

Perpetual memory of the Maker's rest.

Richard Mant

I never knew a man escape failures, in either mind or body, who worked seven day in a week.

Sir Robert Peel

Break down Sunday, close the churches, open the bars and the theatres on that day, and where would values be? What was real estate worth in Sodom?

Heman Lincoln Wayland

See also: HOLIDAY, RELIGION, REST.

SACRIFICE

Our virtues are dearer to us the more we have had to suffer for them. It is the same with our children. All profound affection admits a sacrifice.
Luc de Clapiers (Marquis de Vauvenargues)

The mice which helplessly find themselves between the cat's teeth acquire no merit from their enforced sacrifice.
Mohandas Karamchand (Mahatma) Gandhi

No sacrifice is worth the name unless it is a joy. Sacrifice and a long face go ill together. Sacrifice is 'making sacred'. He must be a poor specimen of humanity who is in need of sympathy for his sacrifice.
Mohandas Karamchand (Mahatma) Gandhi

That sacrifice which causes pain, loses its sacred character and will break down under stress. One gives up things that one considers to be injurious and therefore there should be pleasure attendant upon the giving up.
Mohandas Karamchand (Mahatma) Gandhi

We can offer up much in the large, but to make sacrifices in little things is what we are seldom equal to.
Johann Wolfgang von Goethe

See also: HEROISM, LOVE, MARTYR.

SADNESS

One cannot be deeply responsive to the world without being saddened very often.
Eric Fromm

Take my word for it, the saddest thing under the sky is a soul incapable of sadness.
Comtesse de Gasparin

A feeling of sadness and longing,
  That is not akin to pain,
And resembles sorrow only
  As the mist resembles the rain.
Henry Wadsworth Longfellow

I wonder many times that ever a child of God should have a sad heart, considering what the Lord is preparing for him.
Samuel Rutherford

  Dreary! weary!
  Weary! dreary!
Sighs my soul this lonely night.
  Farewell gladness!

  Welcome sadness!
Vanished are my visions bright.
Abram Joseph Ryan

We look before and after,
  And pine for what is not,
Our sincerest laughter
  With some pain is fraught:
Our sweetest songs are those that tell of saddest thought.
Percy Bysshe Shelley

'Tis impious in a good man to be sad.
Edward Young

See also: DEPRESSION, DESPAIR, DESPONDENCY, GRIEF, MELANCHOLY, SORROW, TEAR, UNHAPPINESS.

SAINT

The elect are whosoever will, and the non-elect, whosoever won't.
Henry Ward Beecher

We have relegated the Saints to a pink and blue and gold world of plaster statuary that belongs to the past; it is a hangover, a relic, of the Dark Ages when men were the children of fantasy's magic. We are content to place a statue of Francis of Assisi in the middle of a bird bath and let the whole business of the Saints go at that.
Chauncie Kilmer Myers

A saint is a man of convictions, who has been dead a hundred years, canonized now, but cannonaded while living.
Heman Lincoln Wayland

See also: GOODNESS, HOLINESS, MARTYR, PIETY, PURITY, SAINT AND SINNER.

SAINT AND SINNER

The sinner has a better chance than the saint of being hereafter remembered. We, in whom original sin preponderates, find him easier to understand. He is near to us, clear to us. The saint is remote, dim. A very great saint may, of course, be remembered through some sheer force of originality in him; and then the very mystery that involves him for us makes him the harder to forget: he haunts us the more surely because we shall never understand him. But the ordinary saints grow faint to posterity; whilst quite ordinary sinners pass vividly down the ages.
Sir Max Beerbohm

The greatest saints and sinners have been
made
The proselytes of one another's trade.

Samuel Butler

See also: HOLINESS, MARTYR, SAINT, VIRTUE
AND VICE.

SALESMANSHIP: *see* SELLING.

SARCASM

At the best, sarcasms, bitter irony, scathing
wit, are a sort of sword-play of the mind.
You pink your adversary, and he is forthwith
dead; and then you deserve to be hung for
it.

Christian Nestell Bovee

Sarcasm is the language of the devil; for
which reason I have long since as good as
renounced it.

Thomas Carlyle

A graceful taunt is worth a thousand insults.

Louis Nizer

Sarcasm poisons reproof.

Edward Wigglesworth

See also: CRITICISM, HUMOR, IRONY, RIDICULE,
SATIRE, SNEER.

SATAN: *see* DEVIL.

SATIETY

With pleasure drugged, he almost longed
for woe.

George Gordon Byron (Lord Byron)

Some are cursed with the fulness of satiety;
and how can they bear the ills of life, when
its very pleasures fatigue them?

Charles Caleb Colton

With much we surfeit; plenty makes us
poor.

Michael Drayton

Satiety comes of too frequent repetition;
and he who will not give himself leisure to
be thirsty can never find the true pleasure
of drinking.

Michel Eyquem de Montaigne

See also: CONTENTMENT, LUXURY, RICH AND
POOR, RICHES, WEALTH.

SATIRE

A satire should expose nothing but what is
corrigible, and should make a due discrimi-

nation between those that are, and those
that are not the proper objects of it.

Joseph Addison

To lash the vices of a guilty age.

Charles Churchill

Satire is a lonely and introspective occupation, for nobody can describe a fool to the
life without much patient self-inspection.

Frank Moore Colby

The end of satire is the amendment of vices
by correction, and he who writes honestly is
no more an enemy to the offender, than the
physician is to the patient when he prescribes harsh remedies.

John Dryden

In the present state of the world it is difficult not to write lampoons.

Juvenal

Satire should, like a polished razor keen,
Wound with a touch that's scarcely felt or
seen.

Lady Mary Wortley Montagu

We smile at the satire expended upon the
follies of others, but we forget to weep at
our own.

Albertine Adrienne Necker de Saussure

Damn with faint praise, assent with civil
leer,
And without sneering, teach the rest to
sneer;
Willing to wound, and yet afraid to strike,
Just hint a fault, and hesitate dislike;
Alike reserv'd to blame, or to commend,
A tim'rous foe, and a suspicious friend.

Alexander Pope

It is as hard to satirize well a man of distinguished vices, as to praise well a man of distinguished virtues.

Jonathan Swift

Satire lies respecting literary men during
their life, and eulogy does so after their
death.

Voltaire (François Marie Arouet)

Satire is the last flicker of originality in a
passing epoch as it faces the onrush of stale-
ness and boredom. Freshness has gone; bitterness remains.

Alfred North Whitehead

Satire! thou shining supplement of public laws.

Edward Young

See also: CARICATURE, CRITICISM, HUMOR, IRONY, LEVITY, RAILLERY, RIDICULE, SARCASM, WIT.

SCANDAL

Scandal is the sport of its authors, the dread of fools, and the contempt of the wise.

William Benton Clulow

As to people saying a few idle words about us, we must not mind that, any more than the old church steeple minds the rooks cawing about it.

George Eliot (Mary Ann Evans)

Great numbers of moderately good people think it fine to talk scandal; they regard it as a sort of evidence of their own goodness.

Frederick William Faber

There is a lust in a man, no charm can tame,
Of loudly publishing his neighbor's shame;
On eagle's wings immortal scandals fly,
While virtuous actions are but born and die.

Stephen Harvey

Praise undeserved is scandal in disguise.

Alexander Pope

Believe that story false that ought not to be true.

Richard Brinsley Sheridan

There are a set of malicious, prating, prudent gossips, both male and female, who murder characters to kill time; and will rob a young fellow of his good name before he has years to know the value of it.

Richard Brinsley Sheridan

Scandal is what one-half the world takes pleasure in inventing, and the other half in believing.

Horatio Smith (Paul Chatfield)

In scandal, as in robbery, the receiver is always as bad as the thief.

Philip Dormer Stanhope (Lord Chesterfield)

The improbability of a malicious story serves to help forward the currency of it, because it increases the scandal. So that, in such instances, the world is like the one who said he believed some things because they were absurd and impossible.

Laurence Sterne

Scandal is but amusing ourselves with the faults, foibles, follies and reputations of our friends.

Royall Tyler

See also: BABBLE, DISGRACE, GOSSIP, INFAMY, REPUTATION, RUMOR, SHAME, SLANDER, TATTLING.

SCHOOL: see EDUCATION.

SCIENCE

Every great scientific truth goes through three stages. First, people say it conflicts with the Bible. Next they say it had been discovered before. Lastly, they say they always believed it.

Louis Agassiz

When man seized the loadstone of science, the loadstar of superstition vanished in the clouds.

William Rounseville Alger

Great discoveries and improvements invariably involve the co-operation of many minds. I may be given credit for having blazed the trail but when I look at the subsequent developments I feel the credit is due to others rather than to myself.

Alexander Graham Bell

The sciences are of sociable disposition, and flourish best in the neighborhood of each other; nor is there any branch of learning but may be helped and improved by assistance drawn from other arts.

Sir William Blackstone

Science is an allegory that asserts that the relations between the parts of reality are similar to the relations between terms of discourse.

Scott Milrose Buchanan

The tendency of modern science is to reduce proof to absurdity by continually reducing absurdity to proof.

Samuel Butler

Ours is not yet an age of science, for the character of the age is writ by man's behavior.

Anton Julius Carlson

As crude a weapon as the cave man's club, the chemical barrage has been hurled against the fabric of life.

Rachel Louise Carson

Modern science is standing on tiptoe, ready to open the doors of a golden age.

Sir Winston Leonard Spencer Churchill

Every great advance in science has issued from a new audacity of imagination.

John Dewey

The intellectual content of religions has always finally adapted itself to scientific and social conditions after they have become clear. . . . For this reason I do not think that those who are concerned about the future of a religious attitude should trouble themselves about the conflict of science with traditional doctrines.

John Dewey

Science, which was to be the midwife of progress, became the angel of death, killing with a precision and a rapidity that reduced the wars of the middle ages to the level of college athletics.

Will (William James) Durant

In war it serves that we may poison and mutilate each other. In peace it has made our lives hurried and uncertain. Instead of freeing us in great measure from spiritually exhausting labor, it has made men into slaves of machinery, who for the most part complete their monotonous long day's work with disgust and must continually tremble for their poor rations.

Albert Einstein

It stands to the everlasting credit of science that by acting on the human mind it has overcome man's insecurity before himself and before nature.

Albert Einstein

The most beautiful thing we can experience is the mysterious. It is the source of all true art and science. He to whom this emotion is a stranger, who can no longer pause to wonder and stand rapt in awe, is as good as dead: his eyes are closed. . . . To know that what is impenetrable to us really exists, manifesting itself as the highest wisdom and the most radiant beauty which our dull faculties can comprehend only in their most primitive forms—this knowledge, this feeling, is at the center of true religiousness. In this sense, and in this sense only, I belong in the ranks of devoutly religious men.

Albert Einstein

Science is the century-old endeavor to bring together by means of systematic thought the perceptible phenomena of this world into as thorough-going an association as possible. To put it boldly, it is the attempt at the posterior reconstruction of existence by the process of conceptualization.

Albert Einstein

Science surpasses the old miracles of mythology.

Ralph Waldo Emerson

The Sciences are beneficent. They prevent men from thinking.

Anatole France

The person who thinks there can be any real conflict between science and religion must be either very young in science or very ignorant in religion.

Philip Henry

As knowledge advances, science ceases to scoff at religion; and religion ceases to frown on science. The hour of mockery by the one, and of reproof by the other, is passing away. Henceforth, they will dwell together in unity and good-will. They will mutually illustrate the wisdom, power, and grace of God. Science will adorn and enrich religion; and religion will ennoble and sanctify science.

Science—in other words, knowledge—is not the enemy of religion; for, if so, then religion would mean ignorance; but it is often the antagonist of school-divinity.

Oliver Wendell Holmes

It is certain that a serious attention to the sciences and liberal arts softens and humanizes the temper, and cherishes those fine emotions in which true virtue and honor consist. It very rarely happens that a man of taste and learning is not, at least, an honest man, whatever frailties may attend him.

David Hume

Science is for the most part agnostic about the existence of a personal God, but it is positive in rejecting much that has been falsely taught and believed about God.

William Ralph Inge

A great step was taken when the flash of lightning and the peal of thunder were explained, not as the wrath of the gods, but as the operation of physical forces under atmospheric conditions.

Joseph Jastrow

All men will benefit if we can invoke the wonders of science instead of its terrors.

John Fitzgerald Kennedy

We are just in the kindergarten of uncovering things; and there is no down curve in science.

Charles Franklin Kettering

It is generally as painful to us to discard old beliefs as for the scientists to discard the old laws of physics and accept new theories.

Lin Yutang

The tragedy of scientific man is that he has found no way to guide his own discoveries to a constructive end. He has devised no weapon so terrible that he has not used it. He has guarded none so carefully that his enemies have not eventually obtained it and turned it against him. . . . His security today and tomorrow seems to depend on building weapons which will destroy him tomorrow.

Charles Augustus Lindbergh

Art and science have their meeting point in method.

Edward G. Bulwer-Lytton (Baron Lytton)

Science, at bottom, is really anti-intellectual. It always distrusts pure reason, and demands the production of objective fact.

Henry Louis Mencken

The study of science teaches young men to think, while study of the classics teaches them to express thought.

John Stuart Mill

Science cannot determine origin, and so cannot determine destiny. As it presents only a sectional view of creation, it gives only a sectional view of everything in creation.

Theodore Thornton Munger

New technology is needed to balance the costs and injustices of old technology.

Ralph Nader

Physical science reads through its sense of touch like a blind man, and the supply of books in braille type on the spiritual life is very small.

Austin O'Malley

Science will never be able to reduce the value of a sunset to arithmetic. Nor can it reduce friendship or statesmanship to a formula. Laughter and love, pain and loneliness, the challenge of accomplishment in living, and the depth of insight into beauty and truth: these will always surpass the scientific mastery of nature.

Louis Orr

Science is made by man for man; it must therefore come out of the sphere of research and reflect on man and through man on human society and on universal history.

Paul VI (Giovanni Battista Montini)

Those who speak of the incompatibility of science and religion either make science say that which it never said or make religion say that which it never taught.

Pius XI (Achille Ambrogio Damiano Ratti)

Human science is an uncertain guess.

Matthew Prior

In proportion as science increases her power, science feels less assured of her knowledge. Like a person afflicted with a "failure neurosis," science finds occasion for her gravest doubts in her greatest triumphs.

Jean Rostand

Judging by the way things are going, I foresee that we shall soon be told that certain scientific errors are more valuable than the truth.

Jean Rostand

Science had better not free the minds of men too much, before it has tamed their instincts.

Jean Rostand

Science must shake the yoke of all philosophies, including the one of which she is leader.

Jean Rostand

Science: the only way of serving men without becoming a party to their passions.

Jean Rostand

Although this may seem a paradox, all exact science is dominated by the idea of approximation.

Bertrand Arthur William Russell

If rational men cooperated and used their scientific knowledge to the full, they could now secure the economic welfare of all.

Bertrand Arthur William Russell

Men sometimes speak as though the progress of science must necessarily be a boon to mankind, but that, I fear, is one of the comfortable nineteenth century delusions which our more disillusioned age must discard.

Bertrand Arthur William Russell

It is the unscientific who are the materialists, whose intellect is not quickened, and the divinity which is everywhere eludes their stupid gaze.

George William Russell

Science is convinced there's no intelligent life in our solar system.

San Francisco Chronicle

Science is nothing but developed perception, interpreted intent, common sense rounded out and minutely articulated.

George Santayana

At their best, at their most creative, science and engineering are attributes of liberty—noble expressions of man's God-given right to investigate and explore the universe without fear of social or political or religious reprisals.

David Sarnoff

The fairest thing we can experience is the mysterious. It is the fundamental emotion which stands at the cradle of true science. He who knows it not, and can no longer wonder, no longer feel amazement, is as good as dead. We all had this priceless talent when we were young. But as time goes by, many of us lose it. The true scientist never loses the faculty of amazement. It is the essence of his being.

Hans Selye

Science is always wrong. It never solves a problem without creating ten more.

George Bernard Shaw

Science is organized knowledge.

Herbert Spencer

Learning is the dictionary, but sense the grammar of science.

Laurence Sterne

What are the sciences but maps of universal laws; and universal laws but the channels of universal power; and universal power but the outgoings of a supreme universal mind?

Edward Thomson

Science is a collection of successful recipes.

Paul Ambroise Valéry

Have we not all felt the shrinkage of the much vaunted miracles of science into the veriest kitchen utensils of comfort-worshipping society?

Henry van Dyke

I have come to have very profound and deep-rooted doubts whether Science, as practiced at present by the human race, will ever do anything to make the world a better and happier place to live in, or will ever stop contributing to our general misery.

Hendrik Willem van Loon

Science keeps on assidously transforming the world, and trusts to luck that the transformations will be benign, beneficial to the majority.

Henry Agard Wallace

Biologists can be just as sensitive to heresy as theologians.

Herbert George Wells

In the scientific world I find just that disinterested devotion to great ends that I hope will spread at last through the entire range of human activity.

Herbert George Wells

See also: COMMUNICATIONS MEDIA, COMPUT-
ER, CYBERNETICS, FACT, INQUIRY,
KNOWLEDGE, LOGIC, REASON, TECH-
NOLOGY, TRUTH.

SCIENTIST

The scientist ought not to occupy any special privileged position as a citizen, and he must certainly not expect to dictate how his work should be used. A dictatorship of scientists would be just as bad as any other dictatorship.

Sir Edward Victor Appleton

Increasingly and of necessity the brilliant scientist in one subject is a layman in another. The task of being a master in his own subject exhausts his capacities.

Gerald Heard

A scientist worthy of the name, above all a mathematician, experiences in his work the same impression as an artist; his pleasure is as great and of the same nature.

Jules Henri Poincaré

I believe scientists have something to give which our kind of existential society is desperately short of: so short of, that it fails to recognise of what it is starved. That is foresight.

Sir Charles Percy Snow

Listening to American and Soviet scientists, trying to study the way in which you both do your government science, I am struck, not by the differences, but by the similarities.

Sir Charles Percy Snow

Some of the most intelligent people in the world cannot really comprehend the nature—and the fallibility—of scientific judgment. So that, over the hard core of the argument on nuclear testing, just as over the major scientific arguments of the 1939-45 war, politicians, responsible in form for the final decision, have in the long run to trust their scientists. Of course, it is not always easy to know which scientists to trust.

Sir Charles Percy Snow

Various kinds of fear distort scientific judgments, just as they do other judgments: but, most of all, the self-deceiving factor seems to be a set of euphorias. The euphoria of gadgets; the euphoria of secrecy. They are usually, but not invariably, combined. They are the origin of 90 per cent of ill-judged scientific choices. Any scientist who is prone to these euphorias ought to be kept out of government decisions or choice-making, at almost any cost.

Sir Charles Percy Snow

See also: RESEARCH, SCIENCE, TECHNOLOGY.

SCOTLAND

Scots, wha hae wi' Wallace bled,
Scots, wham Bruce has aften led,
Welcome to your gory bed,
Or to victorie.

Robert Burns

A Scotchman must be a very sturdy moralist who does not love Scotland better than the truth.

Samuel Johnson

O Caledonia! stern and wild,
Meet nurse for a poetic child!
Land of brown heath and shaggy wood;
Land of the mountain and the flood!

Sir Walter Scott

See also: ENGLAND, NATION, UNITED NATIONS.

SCRIPTURE: *see* BIBLE.

SEA

The sea and its resources constitute one of man's last frontiers, a source of staggering amounts of both food and wealth. While we are very much aware that the potential is great, we cannot say with certainty how great it is; neither do we know how best to utilize it and to manage it. Even more disturbing to me is that the United States is far back in the pack in the race to put the sea's treasures to use. Other countries are far ahead of us.

Edward Lewis (Bob) Bartlett

Roll on, thou deep and dark blue ocean—
　　roll!
Ten thousand fleets sweep over them in
　　vain;
Man marks the earth with ruin—his control
Stops with the shore.

George Gordon Byron (Lord Byron)

The sea never changes and its works, for all the talk of men, are wrapped in mystery.

Joseph Conrad

Praise the sea, but keep on the land.

George Herbert

Surely oak and threefold brass surrounded his heart who first trusted a frail vessel to the merciless ocean.

Horace

The noises of the sea were constantly changing, rising and falling, with the stupendous modulations of an orchestra played by giants.

Liam O'Flaherty

Whoever commands the sea, commands the trade, whoever commands the trade of the world, commands the riches of the world, and consequently the world itself.

Sir Walter Raleigh

See also: NATURE, RIVER.

SECRECY

There is a skeleton in every house.

Anonymous

Talkers and futile persons, are commonly vain and credulous withal; for he that talketh what he knoweth will also talk what he knoweth not; therefore set it down, that a habit of secrecy is both politic and moral.

Francis Bacon

Never confide your secrets to paper; it is
like throwing a stone in the air, you do not
know where it may fall.

Pedro Calderón de la Barca

None are so fond of secrets as those who do
not mean to keep them. Such persons covet
secrets as spendthrifts do money, for the
purpose of circulation.

Charles Caleb Colton

Secrets with girls, like guns with boys are
never valued till they make a noise.

George Crabbe

There is as much responsibility in imparting
your own secrets, as in keeping those of
your neighbor.

George Darley

He who trusts secrets to a servant makes
him his master.

John Dryden

Three may keep a secret, if two of them are
dead.

Benjamin Franklin

The truly wise man should have no keeper
of his secret but himself.

François Pierre Guillaume Guizot

People addicted to secrecy are so without
knowing why; they are not so for cause, but
for secrecy's sake.

William Hazlitt

To keep your secret is wisdom; but to expect others to keep it is folly.

Oliver Wendell Holmes

A secret is too little for one, enough for two,
and too much for three.

Jeremiah Brown Howell

To tell our own secrets is generally folly, but
that folly is without guilt; to communicate
those with which we are intrusted is always
treachery, and treachery for the most part
combined with folly.

Samuel Johnson

A secret in his mouth is like a wild bird put
into a cage; whose door no sooner opens,
but it is out.

Ben (Benjamin) Jonson

A man can keep the secret of another better
than his own: a woman, on the contrary,
keeps her own better than that of another.

Jean de La Bruyère

When a secret is revealed, it is the fault of
the man who has intrusted it.

Jean de La Bruyère

Trust him not with your secrets, who, when
left alone in your room, turns over your papers.

Johann Kaspar Lavater

I will govern my life and my thoughts as if
all the world were to see the one and to
read the other; for what does it signify to
make anything a secret to my neighbor,
when to God all our privacies are open?

Seneca

What is mine, even to my life, is hers I love;
but the secret of my friend is not mine.

Sir Philip Sidney

It is said that he or she who admits the possession of a secret, has already half revealed
it. It is a great deal gained toward the acquisition of a treasure, to know exactly
where it is.

William Gilmore Simms

If a fool knows a secret, he tells it because
he is a fool: if a knave knows one, he tells it
whenever it is his interest to tell it. But
women and young men are very apt to tell
what secrets they know, from the vanity of
having been trusted. Trust none of these
whenever you can help it.

Philip Dormer Stanhope (Lord Chesterfield)

Secrecy is the chastity of friendship.

Jeremy Taylor

Conceal your domestic ills.

Thales

I usually get my stuff from people who
promised somebody else that they would
keep it a secret.

Walter Winchell

See also: CONCEALMENT, CONSPIRACY, EQUIVO-
CATION, MYSTERY, OBSCURITY, PRI-
VACY, RESERVE, SILENCE, SPYING,
WIRETAPPING.

SECT

Sects and Christians that desire to be known by the undue prominence of doing some single feature of Christianity, are imperfect just in proportion to the distinctness of their peculiarities. The power of Christian truth is in its unity and sympathy, and not in the saliency or brilliancy of any of its special doctrines. The spirit of Christ is the greatest essential truth.

Henry Ward Beecher

In England there are sixty different religions, and only one sauce.

Francesco Caraccioli

The more men have multiplied the forms of religion, the more vital Godliness has declined.

Nathaniel Emmons

I do not want the walls of separation between different orders of Christians to be destroyed, but only lowered, that we may shake hands a little easier over them.

Rowland Hill

The effective strength of sects is not to be ascertained merely by counting heads.

Thomas Babington Macaulay

It is written, that the coat of our Saviour was without seam; whence some would infer, that there should be no division in the church of Christ. It should be so indeed; yet seams in the same cloth neither hurt the garment, nor misbecome it; and not only seams, but schisms will be while men are fallible.

John Milton

What are all the forms of religion, compared with the true and holy life of the devoted Christian?

Edward Thomson

We established missions in Asia and Africa and in the isles of the sea . . . and most of this prodigious labor was accomplished through denominational zeal. But once the far-flung missions were established much of the denominational emphasis was necessarily transcended. It takes no great sense of humor to see the absurdity of Southern Presbyterianism in Northern China or of Japanese

Dutch Reformed Christians. . . . Ecumenicity became a fact before it was a doctrine.

David Elton Trueblood

See also: ANGLICANISM, BAPTISTS, BIGOTRY, BUDDHISM, CALVINISM, CATHOLICISM, CHRIST, CHRISTIANITY, CREED, DOGMATISM, FACTION, FANATICISM, HINDUISM, JEWS, JUDAISM, METHODISM, MOHAMMEDANISM, PARTY, QUAKERS, RELIGION.

SECURITY

Security is mostly a superstition. It does not exist in nature, nor do the children of men as a whole experience it. Avoiding danger is no safer in the long run than outright exposure. Life is either a daring adventure, or nothing. Serious harm, I am afraid, has been wrought to our generation by fostering the idea that they would live secure in a permanent order of things. They have expected stability and find none within themselves or in their universe. Before it is too late they must learn and teach others that only by brave acceptance of change and all-time crisis-ethics can they rise to the height of superlative responsibility.

Helen Adams Keller

The virtue of a state is its security.

Baruch (Benedict) Spinoza

See also: CERTAINTY, CONFIDENCE.

SEDITION

The causes and motives of sedition are: innovation in religion; taxes; alteration of laws and customs; breaking of privileges; general oppression; advancement of unworthy persons, strangers; dearths; disbanded solders; factions grown desperate; and whatsoever in offending a people joineth them in a common cause.

Francis Bacon

Sedition is bred in the lap of luxury, and its chosen emissaries are the beggared spendthrift and the impoverished libertine.

George Bancroft

See also: REBELLION, REVOLUTION, TREASON.

SEGREGATION

Pervasive discrimination and segregation in employment, education and housing have resulted in the continuing exclusion of great numbers of Negroes from the benefits of economic progress.

Commission on Civil Disorder, 1968

I . . . ask every member of Congress to set aside sectional and political ties, and to look at this issue from the viewpoint of the nation. I ask you to look into your hearts—not in search of charity, for the Negro neither wants nor needs condescension—but for the one plain, proud and priceless quality that unites us all as Americans: a sense of justice. In this year of the Emancipation centennial, justice requires us to insure the blessings of liberty for all Americans and their posterity—not merely for reasons of economic efficiency, world diplomacy and domestic tranquility—but, above all, because it is right.

John Fitzgerald Kennedy

No one has been barred on account of his race from fighting or dying for America— there are no "white" or "colored" signs on the foxholes or graveyards of battle.

John Fitzgerald Kennedy

We come then to the question presented: does segregation of children in public schools solely on the basis of race, even though the physical facilities and other "tangible" factors may be equal, deprive the children of the minority group of equal education opportunities? We believe that it does . . . We conclude that in the field of public education the doctrine of "separate but equal" has no place [Unanimous decision outlawing Negro segregation in public schools].

United States Supreme Court

See also: BLACK POWER, EQUALITY, GHETTO, JUSTICE, NEGRO, RACE, RACISM.

SELECTIVE SERVICE: *see* DRAFT.

SELF

The very heart and root of sin is an independent spirit. We erect the idol self, and not only wish others to worship, but worship it ourselves.

Richard Cecil

One realm we have never conquered—the pure present. One great mystery of time is terra incognita to us—the instant. The most superb mystery we have hardly recognized— the immediate, instant self. The quick of all

the universe, of all creation, is the incarnate, carnal self.

David Herbert Lawrence

Self is the only prison that can ever bind the soul.

Henry van Dyke

If you live only for yourself you are always in immediate danger of being bored to death with the repetition of your own views and interests.

Walter Béran Wolfe

See also: EGOTISM, SELFISHNESS.

SELF-APPROBATION

We follow the world in approving others: we go far before it in approving ourselves.

Charles Caleb Colton

One self-approving hour whole years outweighs
Of stupid starers and of loud huzzas.

Alexander Pope

Self-approbation, when found in truth and a good conscience, is a source of some of the purest joys known to man.

Charles Simmons

See also: BOASTING, CONCEIT, EGOTISM, PRIDE, SELF-PRAISE, SELF-RESPECT, SELF-RIGHTEOUSNESS, SNOB, VANITY.

SELF-CONFIDENCE

He who places implicit confidence in his genius will find himself some day utterly defeated and deserted.

Benjamin Disraeli

The history of the world is full of men who rose to leadership, by sheer force of self-confidence, bravery and tenacity.

Mohandas Karamchand (Mahatma) Gandhi

Man often becomes what he believes himself to be. If I keep on saying to myself that I cannot do a certain thing, it is possible that I may end by really becoming incapable of doing it. On the contrary, if I have the belief that I can do it, I shall surely acquire the capacity to do it even if I may not have it at the beginning.

Mohandas Karamchand (Mahatma) Gandhi

There are admirable potentialities in every human being. Believe in your strength and your youth. Learn to repeat endlessly to yourself: "It all depends on me."

André Gide

The worst of poisons: to mistrust one's power.

Heinrich Heine

Self-confidence is of more importance in conversation than ability.

Duc François de La Rochefoucauld

See also: CONFIDENCE, SELF-RELIANCE.

SELF-CONSCIOUSNESS

Self-consciousness, extending to pride, if properly directed, can become a safe moral principle.

Berthold Auerbach

There is nothing the average male dislikes so much as to be made self-conscious, and the desire to avoid this at all costs lies at the root of most of his pleasures and many of his failures.

Susan Ertz

See also: BASHFULNESS.

SELF-CONTEMPT

Of all afflictions, the worst is self-contempt.

Berthold Auerbach

Perhaps the only true dignity of man is his capacity to despise himself.

George Santayana

See also: HUMILITY, MEEKNESS, SELF-DENIAL.

SELF-CONTROL

We cannot kindle when we will
  The fire which in the heart resides,
The spirit bloweth and is still,
  In mystery our soul abides:
But tasks in hours of insight will'd
Can be through hours of gloom fulfill'd.

Matthew Arnold

Who to himself is law, no law doth need.

George Chapman

It is the man who is cool and collected, who is master of his countenance, his voice, his actions, his gestures, of every part, who can work upon others at his pleasure.

Denis Diderot

Complete extinction of impure thought is impossible without ceaseless penance. There

is only one way to achieve this. The moment an impure thought arises, confront it with a pure one. This is possible only with God's grace and God's grace come through ceaseless communion with Him and complete self-surrender.

Mohandas Karamchand (Mahatma) Gandhi

The mind may wander, but let not the senses wander with it. If the senses wander where the mind takes them, one is done for. But he who keeps control of the physical senses will some day be able to bring impure thoughts under control.

Mohandas Karamchand (Mahatma) Gandhi

Not to have control over the senses is like sailing in a rudderless ship, bound to break to pieces on coming in contact with the very first rock.

Mohandas Karamchand (Mahatma) Gandhi

To conquer the subtle passion seems to me to be harder far than the physical conquest of the world by the force of arms.

Mohandas Karamchand (Mahatma) Gandhi

No one who cannot master himself is worthy to rule, and only he can rule.

Johann Wolfgang von Goethe

Those who can command themselves command others.

William Hazlitt

No conflict is so severe as his who labors to subdue himself.

Thomas à Kempis

The most precious of all possessions, is power over ourselves; power to withstand trial, to bear suffering, to front danger; power over pleasure and pain; power to follow our convictions, however resisted by menace and scorn; the power of calm reliance in scenes of darkness and storms. He that has not a mastery over his inclinations; he that knows not how to resist the importunity of present pleasure or pain, for the sake of what reason tells him is fit to be done, wants the true principle of virtue and industry, and is in danger of never being good for anything.

John Locke

For me, life can hold no higher adventure than to see man learn to control his own nature as he now controls the atoms.

Walter Boughton Pitkin

No man is free who cannot command himself.

Pythagoras

Most powerful is he who has himself in his own power.

Seneca

It is the whole history of mankind that power lacking the inner strength of self-restraint will be eventually cast down.

Adlai Ewing Stevenson

See also: ABSTINENCE, ASCETICISM, CAUTION, DISCRETION, EQUANIMITY, FASTING, MODERATION, PRUDENCE, TEMPERANCE, VIRTUE.

SELF-DECEPTION

Nothing is so easy as to deceive one's self, for what we wish we readily believe; but such expectations are often inconsistent with the reality of things.

Demosthenes

Who has deceived thee so often as thyself?

Benjamin Franklin

No man was ever so much deceived by another, as by himself.

Fulke Greville (First Baron Brooke)

The coward reckons himself cautious; the miser thinks himself frugal.

Henry Home (Lord Kames)

See also: CONCEIT, DELUSION, ERROR, ILLUSION, MENTAL HEALTH.

SELF-DEFENSE

Self-defence is nature's eldest law.

John Dryden

Self-defence is, according to the law of nature, common to all men, and approved of by God Almighty, and by the consent of all nations, having come into existence at the same time with the world, and about to last as long as the world lasts; and which cannot be annulled either by civil or canonical laws based on the will of men; which being written on parchment, cannot do away with a law not made by man, but by Nature herself, written, engraved, and fixed in the breasts and minds of every generation of men.

Francesco Guicciardini

If a madman were to come into this room with a stick in his hand no doubt we should pity the state of his mind, but our primary consideration would be to take care of ourselves. We should knock him down first, and pity him afterward.

Samuel Johnson

See also: CITY, CRIME, GHETTO, GUN, MURDER.

SELF-DENIAL

Contempt of all outward things that come in competition with duty fulfils the ideal of human greatness. It is sanctioned by conscience, that universal and eternal lawgiver, whose chief principle is, that everything must be yielded up for right.

William Ellery Channing

He is one of the noblest conquerors who carries on a successful warfare against his own appetites and passions, and has them under wise and full control.

Tryon Edwards

Whoever will labor to get rid of self, to deny himself according to the instructions of Christ, strikes at once at the root of every evil, and finds the germ of every good.

François de Salignac de La Mothe-Fénelon

Shall we call ourselves benevolent, when the gifts we bestow do not cost us a single privation?

Baron Joseph Marie de Gerando

Self-abnegation, that rare virtue, that good men preach and good women practice.

Oliver Wendell Holmes

The very act of faith by which we receive Christ is an act of utter renunciation of self and all its works, as a ground of salvation. It is really a denial of self, and a grounding of arms in the last citadel into which it can be driven, and is, in its principle, inclusive of every subsequent act of self-denial by which sin is forsaken or overcome.

Mark Hopkins

The more a man denies himself, the more he shall obtain from God.

Horace

One secret act of self-denial, one sacrifice of inclination to duty, is worth all the mere good thoughts, warm feelings, passionate prayers in which idle people indulge themselves.

John Henry Newman

Self-denial is indispensable to a strong character, and the loftiest kind thereof comes only of a religious stock—from consciousness of obligation and dependence on God.

Theodore Parker

I often think the doctrines of fasting in Lent and having meatless days are old fashioned. . . . It might be better to give up television. That would be a more meaningful self-denial in this day and age.

Arthur Michael Ramsey

'Tis much the doctrine of the times that men should not please themselves, but deny themselves everything they take delight in; not look upon beauty, wear no good clothes, eat no good meat, etc., which seems the greatest accusation that can be upon the Maker of all good things. If they are not to be used, why did God make them?

John Selden

The worst education which teaches self-denial, is better than the best which teaches everything else and not that.

John Sterling

When you give, take to yourself no credit for generosity, unless you deny yourself something in order that you may give.

Henry Taylor

See also: ABSTINENCE, ASCETICISM, MODERATION, SACRIFICE, TEMPERANCE.

SELF-ESTEEM

Half of the harm that is done in this world
Is due to people who want to feel important.
They don't mean to do harm—but the harm
    does not interest them.
Or they do not see it, or they justify it
Because they are absorbed in the endless
    struggle
To think well of themselves.

Thomas Stearns Eliot

The average man plays to the gallery of his own self-esteem.

Elbert Green Hubbard

Of all the traps and pitfalls in life, self-esteem is the deadliest, and the hardest to

overcome; for it is a pit designed and dug by our own hands, summed up in the phrase, "It's no use—I can't do it." . . . It is that good hard second look—taken not just for one's own sake but everyone else's too—that very often reveals that the "impossible" task is quite possible after all.

Maxwell Maltz

Oft-times nothing profits more
Than self-esteem, grounded on just and right
Well manag'd.

John Milton

The most difficult secret for a man to keep is his own opinion of himself.

Marcel Pagnol

See also: CONCEIT, PRIDE, SELF-CONCEIT, SELF-LOVE, SELF-PRAISE, SELF-RESPECT.

SELF-EXAMINATION

The superior man will watch over himself when he is alone. He examines his heart that there may be nothing wrong there, and that he may have no cause of dissatisfaction with himself.

Confucius

It belongs to every large nature, when it is not under the immediate power of some strong unquestioning emotion, to suspect itself, and doubt the truth of its own impressions, conscious of possibilities beyond its own horizon.

George Eliot (Mary Ann Evans)

Never let us be discouraged with ourselves. It is not when we are conscious of our faults that we are the most wicked; on the contrary, we are less so. We see by a brighter light; and let us remember for our consolation, that we never perceive our sins till we begin to cure them.

François de Salignac de La Mothe-Fénelon

If any speak ill of thee, fly home to thy own conscience and examine thy heart. If thou art guilty, it is a just correction; if not guilty, it is a fair instruction.

George Herbert

I study myself more than any other subject; it is my metaphysic, and my physic.

Michel Eyquem de Montaigne

Let not sleep fall upon thy eyes till thou hast thrice reviewed the transactions of the past day. Where have I turned aside from rectitude? What have I been doing? What have I left undone, which I ought to have done? Begin thus from the first act, and proceed; and, in conclusion, at the ill which thou hast done, be troubled, and rejoice for the good.

Pythagoras

We should every night call ourselves to an account: What infirmity have I mastered today? what passions opposed? what temptation resisted? what virtue acquired? Our vices will abate of themselves if they be brought every day to the shrift.

Seneca

Observe thyself as thy greatest enemy would do, so shalt thou be thy greatest friend.

Jeremy Taylor

Though not always called upon to condemn ourselves, it is always safe to suspect ourselves.

Richard Whately

Never lose sight of this important truth, that no one can be truly great until he has gained a knowledge of himself, a knowledge which can only be acquired by occasional retirement.

Johann Georg von Zimmermann

See also: REFLECTION, SELF-KNOWLEDGE.

SELF-HELP

Welcome evermore to gods and men is the self-helping man.

Ralph Waldo Emerson

Manliness consists in making circumstances subserve to ourselves. Those who will not heed themselves perish. To understand this principle is not to be impatient, not to reproach fate, not to blame others. He who understands the doctrine of self-help blames himself for failure.

Mohandas Karamchand (Mahatma) Gandhi

Self-help is the capacity to stand on one's legs without anybody's help. This does not mean indifference to or rejection of outside help, but it means the capacity to be at peace with oneself, to preserve one's self-respect, when outside help is not forthcoming or is refused.

Mohandas Karamchand (Mahatma) Gandhi

Help thyself, and God will help thee.

George Herbert

God gives every bird its food, but he does not throw it into the nest.

Josiah Gilbert Holland

See also: CONFIDENCE, SELF-RELIANCE.

SELF-IMPROVEMENT

There is no use whatever trying to help people who do not help themselves. You cannot push anyone up a ladder unless he be willing to climb himself.

Andrew Carnegie

One of the best exercises of meekness we can perform is . . . in never fretting at our own imperfections. . . . We correct ourselves much better by a calm and steady repentance than by one that is harsh, turbulent, and passionate.

Francis of Sales

Turning attention to oneself in the earnest endeavor to improve oneself may only increase obsession with oneself, which is the root of the mischief. . . . To be whole persons we must get ourselves off our hands.

Harry Emerson Fosdick

Each year, one vicious habit rooted out in time ought to make the worst man good.

Benjamin Franklin

People seldom improve, when they have no other model but themselves to copy after.

Oliver Goldsmith

Begin to be now what you will be hereafter.

Jerome (Eusebius Hieronymus)

If we do not *better* our civilization, our way of life, and our democracy, there will be no use trying to "save" them by fighting; they will crumble away under the very feet of our armies.

Anne Spencer Morrow Lindbergh

The improvement of our way of life is more important than the spreading of it. If we make it satisfactory enough, it will spread automatically. If we do not, no strength of arms can permanently impose it.

Charles Augustus Lindbergh

In each of us personality and freedom of independence increase together. For man is a being in movement. If he does not augment, he has nothing, and he loses what he had; he must fight for his being.

Jacques Maritain

If there is literally enough force in you to blow up the greatest city in the world, there is also literally enough power in you to overcome every obstacle in your life.

Norman Vincent Peale

You will find that the mere resolve not to be useless, and the honest desire to help other people, will, in the quickest and delicatest ways, improve yourself.

John Ruskin

See also: IMPROVEMENT, PROGRESS, REFORM.

SELF-INTEREST

Self-interest, that leprosy of the age, attacks us from infancy, and we are startled to observe little heads calculate before knowing how to reflect.

Delphine de Girardin

Self-interest speaks all kinds of languages, and plays all kinds of parts, even that of the disinterested.

Duc François de La Rochefoucauld

The modern trouble is in a low capacity to believe in precepts which restrict and restrain private interests and desires.

Walter Lippmann

The world is governed only by self-interest.

Johann Christoph Friedrich von Schiller

Self-interest is the enemy of all true affection.

Tacitus

See also: EGOTISM, SELF, SELF-LOVE.

SELFISHNESS

Deliver me, O Lord, from that evil man, myself.

Thomas Brooks

The selfish man suffers more from his selfishness than he from whom that selfishness withholds some important benefit.

Ralph Waldo Emerson

Selfishness is the root and source of all natural and moral evils.

Nathaniel Emmons

So long as we are full of self we are shocked at the faults of others. Let us think often of our own sin, and we shall be lenient to the sins of others.

François de Salignac de La Mothe-Fénelon

That household god, a man's own self.

John Flavel

That man who lives for self alone
Lives for the meanest mortal known.

Cincinnatus Hiner (Joaquin) Miller

The man who lives by himself and for himself is apt to be corrupted by the company he keeps.

Charles Henry Parkhurst

Some people think that all the world should share their misfortunes, though they do not share in the sufferings of any one else.

Achille Poincelot

It is very natural for a young friend and a young lover to think the persons they love have nothing to do but to please them.

Alexander Pope

He who lives only to benefit himself confers on the world a benefit when he dies.

Tertullian

A man is called selfish, not for pursuing his own good, but for neglecting his neighbor's.

Richard Whately

Selfishness is not living as one wishes to live; it is asking others to live as one wishes to live. And unselfishness is letting other people's lives alone, not interfering with them. Selfishness always aims at creating around it an absolute uniformity of type. Unselfishness recognizes infinite variety of type as a delightful thing, accepts it, acquiesces in it, enjoys it.

Oscar Wilde

See also: AVARICE,   COVETOUSNESS,   EGOTISM, INTEREST, MEANNESS, MISER.

SELF-KNOWLEDGE

Resolve to be thyself: and know, that he
Who finds himself, loses his misery.

Matthew Arnold

The precept, "Know yourself," was not solely intended to obviate the pride of mankind; but likewise that we might understand our own worth.

Cicero

He that knows himself, knows others; and he that is ignorant of himself, could not write a very profound lecture on other men's heads.

Charles Caleb Colton

To reach perfection, we must be made sensible of our failings, either by the admonitions of friends, or the invectives of enemies.
Diogenes

Self-knowledge is best learned, not by contemplation, but action. Strive to do your duty, and you will soon discover of what stuff you are made.
Johann Wolfgang von Goethe

He knows the universe, and knows not himself.
Jean de La Fontaine

"Know thyself" means this, that you get acquainted with what you know, and what you can do.
Menander of Athens

Trust not yourself, but your defects to know,
Make use of every friend and every foe.
Alexander Pope

Where politics, morals, or philosophy are concerned, I view with suspicion the judgment of those who know nothing about their own composition.
Jean Rostand

Other men's sins are before our eyes; our own are behind our back.
Seneca

The highest and most profitable learning is the knowledge of ourselves. To have a low opinion of our own merits, and to think highly of others, is an evidence of wisdom. All men are frail, but you should consider none so frail as yourself.
Thomas à Kempis

See also: INTELLIGENCE, KNOWLEDGE, MEDITATION, REFLECTION, SELF-EXAMINATION, UNDERSTANDING, WISDOM.

SELF-LOVE

It is the nature of extreme self-lovers, as they will set a house on fire, and it were but to roast their eggs.
Francis Bacon

Self-love is, in almost all men, such an overweight that they are incredulous of a man's habitual preference of the general good to his own; but when they see it proved by sacrifices of ease, wealth, rank, and of life itself, there is no limit to their admiration.
Ralph Waldo Emerson

All other love is extinguished by self-love; beneficence, humanity, justice, and philosophy sink under it.
Epicurus

Self-love is a cup without any bottom; you might pour all the great lakes into it, and never fill it up.
Oliver Wendell Holmes

The most amiable people are those who least wound the self-love of others.
Jean de La Bruyère

The greatest of all flatterers is self-love.
Duc François de La Rochefoucauld

Self-love, as it happens to be well or ill conducted, constitutes virtue and vice.
Duc Francois de La Rochefoucauld

The cause of all the blunders committed by man arises from excessive self-love. He who intends to be a great man ought to love neither himself nor his own things, but only what is just, whether it happens to be done by himself or by another.
Plato

Our self-love is ever ready to revolt from our better judgment, and join the enemy within.
Sir Richard Steele

Of all mankind each loves himself the best.
Terence

Offended self-love never forgives.
Louis Jean Baptiste Etienne Vigée

Self-love is the instrument of our preservation; it resembles the provision for the perpetuity of mankind—it is necessary, it is dear to us, it gives us pleasure, and we must possess it.
Voltaire (François Marie Arouet)

To love one's self is the beginning of a lifelong romance.
Oscar Wilde

It is falling in love with our own mistaken ideas that makes fools and beggars of half mankind.
Edward Young

See also: CONCEIT, EGOTISM, SELF-INTEREST, SELFISHNESS, SNOB, VANITY.

SELF-PITY

I am a lone lorn creetur and everythink goes contrairy with me.

Charles John Huffam Dickens

To feel sorry for oneself is one of the most disintegrating things the individual can do to himself.

Winfred Rhoades

See also: EGOTISM, PITY, SELF, SELF-INTEREST.

SELF-PRAISE

The advantage of doing one's praising for oneself is that one can lay it on so thick and exactly in the right places.

Samuel Butler

A man's accusations of himself are always believed; his praises of self never.

Michel Eyquem de Montaigne

A man's praises have very musical and charming accents in the mouth of another, but sound very flat and untunable in his own.

Xenophon

See also: BOASTING, CONCEIT, EGOTISM, SELF-LOVE, SELF-RIGHTEOUSNESS.

SELF-RELIANCE

Doubt whom you will, but never doubt yourself.

Christian Nestell Bovee

Self-reliance and self-respect are about as valuable commodities as we can carry in our pack through life.

Luther Burbank

Trust in God, but keep your powder dry.

Oliver Cromwell

The best lightning-rod for your protection is your own spine.

Ralph Waldo Emerson

If you would have a faithful servant, and one that you like, serve yourself.

Benjamin Franklin

The supreme fall of falls is this, the first doubt of one's self.

Comtesse de Gasparin

The man who cannot enjoy his own natural gifts in silence, and find his reward in the exercise of them, will generally find himself badly off.

Johann Wolfgang von Goethe

More powerful than all the success slogans ever penned by human hand is the realization for every man that he has but one boss. That boss is the man—he—himself.

Gabriel Heatter

Look well into thyself; there is a source of strength which will always spring up if thou wilt always look there.

Marcus Aurelius

There is no man so low down that the cure for his condition does not lie strictly within himself.

Tom (Thomas Lansing) Masson

Of the many hard lessons that I had learnt, the hardest and the most painful now faced me; that it is not possible in any vital matter to rely on any one. One must journey through life alone; to rely on others is to invite heartbreak.

Jawaharlal Nehru

Time and I against any two.

Philip II of Macedonia

The man who makes everything that leads to happiness depend upon himself, and not upon other men, has adopted the very best plan for living happily. This is the man of moderation, the man of manly character and of wisdom.

Plato

They can conquer who believe they can.

Virgil

See also: CONFIDENCE, INDEPENDENCE, RESPONSIBILITY, SELF-CONFIDENCE.

SELF-RESPECT

The reverence of man's self, is, next to religion, the chiefest bridle of all vices.

Francis Bacon

All must respect those who respect themselves.

Benjamin Disraeli

Dignity of the soul and self-respect are interpreted differently by different persons. I am aware that self-respect is often misinterpreted. The over-sensitive man may see disrespect or hurt in almost everything. Such a man does not really understand what self-respect is.

Mohandas Karamchand (Mahatma) Gandhi

Self-respect cannot be hunted. It cannot be purchased. It is never for sale. It cannot be fabricated out of public relations. It comes to us when we are alone, in quiet moments, in quiet places, when we suddenly realize that, knowing the good, we have done it; knowing the beautiful, we have served it; knowing the truth, we have spoken it.
Alfred Whitney Griswold

Self-respect,—that corner-stone of all virtue.
Sir John Frederick William Herschel

I care not so much what I am in the opinion of others as what I am in my own; I would be rich of myself and not by borrowing.
Michel Eyquem de Montaigne

Above all things, reverence yourself.
Pythagoras

To have a respect for ourselves guides our morals; and to have a deference for others governs our manners.
Laurence Sterne

Self-reverence, self-knowledge, self-control, these three alone lead life to sovereign power.
Alfred, Lord Tennyson

See also: CONSCIENCE, DIGNITY, PRIDE, SELF-APPROBATION, SELF-PRAISE.

SELF-RIGHTEOUSNESS

Self-righteousness is the devil's masterpiece to make us think well of ourselves.
Thomas Adams

Regret not that which is past; and trust not to thine own righteousness.
Anthony of Padua

If there be ground for you to trust in your own righteousness, then, all that Christ did to purchase salvation, and all that God did to prepare the way for it is in vain.
Jonathan Edwards

If you have fasted two days, do not think yourself better than one who has not fasted. You fast and are peevish; the other eats and is pleasant.
Jerome (Eusebius Hieronymus)

See also: CONCEIT, EGOTISM, VANITY.

SELF-SACRIFICE

No person . . . shall be compelled in any criminal case to be a witness against himself [Amendment V].
Constitution of the United States

They will let you live only when you learn to die.
Theodor Herzl

Only he can understand what a farm is, what a country is, who shall have sacrificed part of himself to his farm or his country, sought to save it, struggled to make it beautiful.
Antoine de Saint-Exupéry

See also: CITIZENSHIP, CHRISTIAN, HEROISM, LOVE, SACRIFICE.

SELLING

Just so long as I can forget myself and what I am going to make out of a sale, and keep my mind on the other person and what *he* will get out of the sale, I have no fear of creating the impression that I am high pressure.
Frank Bettger

The most important secret of salesmanship is to find out what the other fellow wants, then help him find the best way to get it.
Frank Bettger

Selling can never be reduced to an exact science any more than medicine can be reduced to an exact science, but it is amazing how many things about selling can be measured and forecast.
Frank Bettger

You must keep everlastingly going to be a successful big game salesman. You ride the hunting grounds from early morning to dusk, getting your saddle sores, and at times tearing your hands and face.
But, if you are well prepared in advance, with good equipment, the right guides, hounds, and fighters ahead, you will get your share of kills at last.
Ray Hickok

Gentlemen, after all, this business of selling narrows down to one thing—just *one* thing . . . seeing the people! Show me any man of ordinary ability who will go out and earnestly tell his story to four or five people every day, and I will show you a man who just can't help making good!

Walter Le Mar Talbot

Most sales stories are not, in my experience, neat little incidents clearly defined by themselves as are the patterns in a mosaic but a serial story, if you will, a series of stories that climaxes into the signature on the dotted line.

Sidney Weil

Salesmanship is an American specialty. It typifies the competitive spirit of our economy. Nowhere else in the world have so many executives come up through the selling ranks. It is not surprising that the salesman has been the first business casualty in every country the communists have conquered. Freedom of choice and competition, which he symbolizes, are directly contrary to all that communism stands for.

Robert A. Whitney

See also: ADVERTISING, COMMERCIAL.

SENSE

If Poverty is the Mother of Crimes, want of Sense is the Father.

Jean de La Bruyère

Good sense which only is the gift of Heaven,
And though no science, fairly worth the seven.

Alexander Pope

Of plain, sound sense, life's current coin is made.

Edward Young

See also: COMMON SENSE, DISCERNMENT, DISCRETION, INTELLIGENCE, JUDGMENT, PERCEPTION, PRUDENCE, REASON, UNDERSTANDING, WISDOM.

SENSIBILITY

Sight, indeed, unlike touch and smell, is not a local sensibility: it seems to flood one's whole being with the lustrous scene it bestows.

Walter John de la Mare

Laughter and tears are meant to turn the wheels of the same machinery of sensibility; one is wind-power, and the other water-power; that is all.

Oliver Wendell Holmes

Sensibility is the power of woman.

Johann Kaspar Lavater

For every one pupil who needs to be guarded from a weak excess of sensibility there are three who need to be awakened from the slumber of cold vulgarity. The task of the modern educator is not to cut down jungles but to irrigate deserts.

Clive Staples (C. S.) Lewis

And the heart that is soonest awake to the flowers
Is always the first to be touch'd by the thorns.

Thomas Moore

See also: APPRECIATION, CULTIVATION, DELICACY, EMOTION, FEELINGS, REFINEMENT, SENSITIVENESS, SYMPATHY.

SENSITIVENESS

Quick sensitiveness is inseparable from a ready understanding.

Joseph Addison

Sensitiveness is closely allied to egotism. Indeed excessive sensitiveness is only another name for morbid self-consciousness. The cure for it is to make more of our objects, and less of ourselves.

Christian Nestell Bovee

That chastity of honor which felt a stain like a wound.

Edmund Burke

There are moments when petty slights are harder to bear than even a serious injury. Men have died of the festering of a gnat-bite.

William Danby

See also: SENSIBILITY.

SENSUALITY

The body of a sensualist is the coffin of a dead soul.

Christian Nestell Bovee

Sensuality is the grave of the soul.

William Ellery Channing

A youth of sensuality and intemperance delivers over a worn-out body to old age.

Cicero

Those wretches who never have experienced the sweets of wisdom and virtue, but spend all their time in revels and debauches, sink downward day after day, and make their whole life one continued series of errors. They taste no real or substantial pleasure; but, resembling so many brutes, with eyes always fixed on the earth, and intent upon their loaden tables, they pamper themselves in luxury and excess.

Plato

If sensuality were happiness, beasts were happier than men; but human felicity is lodged in the soul, not in the flesh.

Seneca

All sensuality is one, though it takes many forms, as all purity is one. It is the same whether a man eat, or drink, or cohabit, or sleep sensually. They are but one appetite, and we only need to see a person do any one of these things to know how great a sensualist he is.

Henry David Thoreau

See also: HARLOT, LICENTIOUSNESS, LUST, VICE, VOLUPTUOUSNESS.

SENTIMENT

Nature has cast men in so soft a mould,
That but to hear a story, feigned for
    pleasure,
Of some sad lover's death, moistens my
    eyes,
And robs me of my manhood.

John Dryden

Cure the drunkard, heal the insane, mollify the homicide, civilize the Pawnee, but what lessons can be devised for the debaucher of sentiment?

Ralph Waldo Emerson

Sentiment is intellectualized emotion; emotion precipitated, as it were, in pretty crystals by the fancy.

James Russell Lowell

Sentiment has a kind of divine alchemy, rendering grief itself the source of tenderest thoughts and far-reaching desires, which the sufferer cherishes as sacred treasures.

Sir Thomas Noon Talfourd

See also: ASSERTION, BELIEF, EMOTION, FEELINGS, OPINION, SENSIBILITY.

SENTIMENTALITY

Sentimentality—that's what we call the sentiment we don't share.

Graham Greene

The sentimental people fiddle harmonics on the string of sensualism.

Edward R. Bulwer Lytton (Owen Meredith)

See also: EMOTION, FEELINGS, HEART, SENTIMENT, SENTIMENTALITY.

SERIOUSNESS

Nobody speaks in earnest, Sir; there is no serious conversation.

Samuel Johnson

Nothing is serious for the mind; for the heart, anything may become so.

Jean Rostand

See also: GRAVITY.

SERMON: *see* PREACHING.

SERVANT

Be not too familiar with thy servants; at first it may beget love, but in the end 'twill breed contempt.

Thomas Fuller

If thou hast a loitering servant, send him of thy errand just before his dinner.

Thomas Fuller

Choose none for thy servant who have served thy betters.

George Herbert

More knowledge may be gained of a man's real character by a short conversation with one of his servants than from a formal and studied narrative, begun with his pedigree and ended with his funeral.

Samuel Johnson

See also: EMPLOYMENT, OCCUPATION, SERVICE, SLAVERY.

SERVICE

All service is the same with God.

Robert Browning

Service without humility is selfishness and egotism.

Mohandas Karamchand (Mahatma) Gandhi

A truly religious person becomes a citizen of the world but the service of one's own country is the stepping-stone to the service of humanity. And where service is rendered to the country consistently with the welfare of the world it finally leads to self-realization.

Mohandas Karamchand (Mahatma) Gandhi

The service we render to others is really the rent we pay for our room on this earth.

Sir Wilfred Thomason Grenfell

See also: USEFULNESS.

SEVERITY

Severity breedeth fear, but roughness breedeth hate. Even reproofs from authority ought to be grave, and not taunting.

Francis Bacon

Severity is allowable where gentleness has no effect.

Pierre Corneille

See also: ABUSE, CRUELTY, VIOLENCE.

SEX

The omnipresence process of sex, as it is woven into the whole texture of our man's or woman's body, is the pattern of all the process of our life.

(Henry) Havelock Ellis

Certainly no aspect of human biology in our current civilization stands in more need of scientific knowledge . . . than that of sex.

Alan Gregg

The principal reason for sex deification is loss of belief in God. Once men lose God, they lose the purpose of life; and when the purpose of living is forgotten, the universe becomes meaningless. Man then tries to forget his emptiness in the intensity of a momentary experience.

Fulton John Sheen

Sex has become one of the most discussed subjects of modern times. The Victorians pretended it did not exist; the moderns pretend that nothing else exists.

Fulton John Sheen

See also: COURTSHIP, MEN, SEXES, WOMAN.

SEXES

No improvement that takes place in either of the sexes, can be confined to itself; each is a universal mirror to each; and the respective refinement of the one, will be in reciprocal proportion to the polish of the other.

Charles Caleb Colton

The sexes were made for each other, and only in the wise and loving union of the two is the fulness of health and duty and happiness to be expected.

William Hall

The evidence indicates that woman is, on the whole, biologically superior to man.

Ashley Montagu

Though women *are* more emotional than men, men are emotionally weaker than women; that is, men break more easily under emotional strain than women do. Women . . . bend more easily, and are more resilient.

Ashley Montagu

Each loves itself, but not itself alone,
Each sex desires alike, till two are one,
Nor ends the pleasure with the fierce embrace;
They love themselves a third time in their race.

Alexander Pope

See also: BACHELOR, LOVE, LUST, MAN, MARRIAGE, MEN, WIFE, WOMAN.

SHAME

While shame keeps watch virtue is not wholly extinguished from the heart, nor will moderation be utterly exiled from the mind of tyrants.

Edmund Burke

It is the guilt, not the scaffold, which constitutes the shame.

Pierre Corneille

Shame is nature's hasty conscience.

Maria Edgeworth

Be assured that when once a woman begins to be ashamed of what she ought not to be ashamed of, she will not be ashamed of what she ought.

Livy

I regard that man as lost, who has lost his sense of shame.

Plautus

Shame may restrain what law does not prohibit.

Seneca

We live in an atmosphere of shame. We are ashamed of everything that is real about us; ashamed of ourselves, of our relatives, of our incomes, of our accents, of our opinion, of our experience, just as we are ashamed of our naked skins.

George Bernard Shaw

I never wonder to see men wicked, but I often wonder to see them not ashamed.

Jonathan Swift

Where there's no shame before men, there's no fear of God.

Yiddish Proverb

See also: CONSCIENCE, DISGRACE, GUILT, INFAMY, REMORSE, SCANDAL.

SHOWMANSHIP

The showmanship idea of yesterday was to give the public what it wanted. This is a fallacy. You don't know what they want and they don't know what they want.

Samuel Lionel Rothafel

See also: ACTOR AND ACTRESS, ADVERTISING, MOTION PICTURES, THEATER.

SICKNESS

Some maladies are rich and precious and only to be acquired by the right of inheritance or purchased with gold.

Nathaniel Hawthorne

We have all had illnesses in our families. Some of them can be so serious that over a period of even a few weeks one's life savings could be wiped out. This is happening to a high percentage of the families in this country today. An individual has a heart attack at an elderly age. Sometimes, even if his income is $6,000, $7,000, or even $10,000 a year, it can wipe out his savings entirely in 2 or 3 weeks.

Robert Francis Kennedy

When a man is laboring under the pain of any distemper, it is then that he recollects there is a God, and that he himself is but a man. No mortal is then the object of his envy, his admiration, or his contempt; and, having no malice to gratify, the tales of slander excite him not.

Pliny the Elder

I enjoy convalescence. It is the part that makes the illness worth while.

George Bernard Shaw

Few spirits are made better by the pain and languor of sickness; as few great pilgrims become eminent saints.

Thomas à Kempis

See also: AFFLICTION, DISEASE, HEALTH, MEDICINE, PAIN, SUFFERING.

SILENCE

Silence never shows itself to so great an advantage as when it is made the reply to calumny and defamation.

Joseph Addison

As we must render an account of every idle word, so we must of our idle silence.

Ambrose of Milan

Silence is the virtue of fools.

Francis Bacon

He has observ'd the golden rule,
Till he's become the golden fool.

William Blake

Silence is the understanding of fools and one of the virtues of the wise.

Chevalier Bernard de Bonnard

Silence is a virtue in those who are deficient in understanding.

Dominique Bouhours

Silence, when nothing need be said, is the eloquence of discretion.

Christian Nestell Bovee

Silence is the element in which great things fashion themselves together; that at length they may emerge, full-formed and majestic, into the delights of life, which they are thenceforth to rule.

Thomas Carlyle

This is such a serious world that we should never speak at all unless we have something to say.

Thomas Carlyle

I think the first virtue is to restrain the tongue; he approaches nearest to the gods who knows how to be silent, even though he is in the right.

Cato the Elder

A man's profundity may keep him from opening on a first interview, and his caution on a second; but I should suspect his emptiness, if he carried on his reserve to a third.

Charles Caleb Colton

If you don't say anything, you won't be called on to repeat it.

(John) Calvin Coolidge

I like better for one to say some foolish thing upon important matters than to be silent. That becomes the subject of discussion and dispute, and the truth is discovered.

Denis Diderot

Silence in times of suffering is the best.

John Dryden

Blessed is the man who, having nothing to say, abstains from giving wordy evidence of the fact.

George Eliot (Mary Ann Evans)

What a strange power there is in silence! How many resolutions are formed, how many sublime conquests effected, during that pause when lips are closed, and the soul secretly feels the eye of her Maker upon her! They are the strong ones of earth who know how to keep silence when it is a pain and grief unto them, and who give time to their own souls to wax strong against temptation.

Ralph Waldo Emerson

A judicious silence is always better than truth spoken without charity.

Francis of Sales

Fellows who have no tongues are often all eyes and ears.

Thomas Chandler Haliburton

We listen too much to the telephone and we listen too little to nature. The wind is one of my sounds. A lonely sound, perhaps, but soothing. Everybody should have his personal sounds to listen for—sounds that will make him exhilarated and alive, or quiet and calm. . . . As a matter of fact, one of the greatest sounds of them all—and to me it is a sound—is utter, complete silence.

André Kostelanetz

Whatever success I have had may perhaps be attributable to three things. One is silence; the second is more silence; while the third is still more silence.

Ivar Kreuger

Silence is the safest course for him who distrusts himself.

Duc François de La Rochefoucauld

The main reason why silence is so efficacious an element of repute is, first, because of that magnification which proverbially belongs to the unknown; and, secondly, because silence provokes no man's envy, and wounds no man's self-love.

Edward G. Bulwer-Lytton (Baron Lytton)

If you keep your mouth shut you will never put your foot in it.

Austin O'Malley

Silence is a figure of speech, unanswerable, short, cold, but terribly severe.

Theodore Parker

He can never speak well, who knows not how to hold his peace.

Plutarch

It is better either to be silent, or to say things of more value than silence. Sooner throw a pearl at hazard than an idle or useless word; and do not say a little in many words, but a great deal in a few.

Pythagoras

If thou desire to be held wise, be so wise as to hold thy tongue.

Francis Quarles

A silent man is easily reputed wise. The unknown is always wonderful. A man who suffers none to see him in the common jostle and undress of life easily gathers round him a mysterious veil of unknown sanctity, and men honor him for a saint.

Frederick William Robertson

Of all virtues, Zeno made choice of silence; for by it, said he, I hear other men's imperfections, and conceal my own.

Rule of Life

Nothing is so good for an ignorant man as silence; if he were sensible of this he would not be ignorant.

Saadi (Muslih-ud-Din)

Silence is one of the hardest arguments to refute.

Henry Wheeler Shaw (Josh Billings)

Silence and reserve suggest latent power. What some men think has more effect than what others say.

Philip Dormer Stanhope (Lord Chesterfield)

A good word is an easy obligation; but not to speak ill requires only our silence, which costs us nothing.

John Tillotson

See also: PEACE, QUIET, RESERVE, SECRECY.

SIMILARITY: *see* COMPARISON.

SIMPLICITY

Elegance of language may not be in the power of all of us; but simplicity and straightforwardness are. Write much as you would speak; speak as you think. If with your inferiors, speak no coarser than usual; if with your superiors, no finer. Be what you say; and, within the rules of prudence, say what you are.

Henry Alford

When thought is too weak to be simply expressed, it is a clear proof that it should be rejected.

Luc de Clapiers (Marquis de Vauvenargues)

Nothing is more simple than greatness; indeed, to be simple is to be great.

Ralph Waldo Emerson

The greatest truths are the simplest; and so are the greatest men.

Augustus and Julius Hare

Simplicity of character is the natural result of profound thought.

William Hazlitt

Give me a look, give me a face,
That makes simplicity a grace;
Robes loosely flowing, hair as free:
Such sweet neglect more taketh me
Than all th' adulteries of art;
They strike mine eyes, but not my heart.

Ben (Benjamin) Jonson

Affected simplicity is a subtle deception.

Duc François de La Rochefoucauld

In character, in manners, in style, in all things, the supreme excellence is simplicity.

Henry Wadsworth Longfellow

It is the essence of genius to make use of the simplest ideas.

Charles Pierre Péguy

A childlike mind, in its simplicity, practices that science of good to which the wise may be blind.

Johann Christoph Friedrich von Schiller

Simplicity, of all things, is the hardest to be copied.

Sir Richard Steele

Purity and simplicity are the two wings with which man soars above the earth and all temporary nature. Simplicity is in the intention; purity in the affection: simplicity turns to God; purity unites with and enjoys him.

Thomas à Kempis

Simplicity is making the journey of this life with just baggage enough.

Charles Dudley Warner

Five lines where three are enough is stupidity. Nine pounds where three are sufficient is stupidity. But to eliminate expressive words that intensify or vivify meaning in speaking or writing is not simplicity; nor is similar elimination in architecture simplicity —it, too, may be stupidity.

Frank Lloyd Wright

See also: BREVITY, CANDOR, CHILDREN, CREDULITY, IGNORANCE, INNOCENCE, SINCERITY.

SIN

As sins proceed they ever multiply; and like figures in arithmetic, the last stands for more than all that went before it.

Sir Thomas Browne

One leak will sink a ship, and one sin will destroy a sinner.

John Bunyan

Whatever disunites man from God disunites man from man.

Edmund Burke

The deadliest sin were the consciousness of no sin.

Thomas Carlyle

A belief in a supernatural source of evil is not necessary; men alone are quite capable of every wickedness.

Joseph Conrad

It is not true that there are no enjoyments in the ways of sin; there are, many and various. But the great and radical defect of them all is, that they are transitory and unsubstantial, at war with reason and conscience, and always leave a sting behind. We are hungry, and they offer us bread; but it is poisoned bread. We are thirsty, and they offer us drink; but it is from deadly fountains. They may and often do satisfy us for the moment; but it is death in the end. It is only the bread of heaven and the water of life that

can so satisfy that we shall hunger no more
and thirst no more forever.

Tryon Edwards

All sins are committed in secrecy. The moment we realise that God witnesses even
our thoughts, we shall be free.

Mohandas Karamchand (Mahaima) Gandhi

I do not seek redemption from the consequences of my sin. I seek to be redeemed
from sin itself, or rather from the very
thought of sin. Until I have attained that
end I shall be content to be restless.

Mohandas Karamchand (Mahatma) Gandhi

Sins are like circles in the water when a
stone is thrown into it; one produces another. When anger was in Cain's heart, murder
was not far off.

Philip Henry

Sin is not offense against God, but against
our humanity.

Emil Gustav Hirsch

What is human sin but the abuse of human
appetites, of human passions, of human faculties, in themselves all innocent?

Roswell Dwight Hitchcock

Adam ate the apple, and our teeth still ache.

Hungarian Proverb

Bad men hate sin through fear of punishment; good men hate sin through their love
of virtue.

Juvenal

God may forgive you your sins, but your nervous system won't.

Alfred Habdank Skarbek Korzybski

Every one has a besetting sin to which he
returns.

Jean de La Fontaine

Sin is a queer thing. It isn't the breaking of
divine commandments. It is the breaking of
one's own integrity.

David Herbert Lawrence

Sin is first pleasing, then it grows easy, then
delightful, then frequent, then habitual,
then confirmed; then the man is impenitent,
then he is obstinate, then he is resolved never to repent, and then he is ruined.

Robert Leighton

Anything that's natural can't be sinful—it
may be inconvenient, but it's not sinful.

Madeleine L'Engle

The recognition of sin is the beginning of
salvation.

Martin Luther

Sin is, essentially, a departure from God.

Martin Luther

There are some sins which are more justly to
be denominated surprises than infidelities.
To such the world should be lenient, as,
doubtless, Heaven is forgiving.

Jean Baptiste Massillon

Of Man's first disobedience, and the fruit
Of that forbidden tree whose mortal taste
Brought death into the world, and all our
woe.

John Milton

How immense appear to us the sins that we
have not committed.

Albertine Adrienne Necker de Saussure

If thou wouldst conquer thy weakness thou
must never gratify it. No man is compelled
to evil; only his consent makes it his. It is no
sin to be tempted; it is to yield and be overcome.

William Penn

If I were sure God would pardon me, and
men would not know my sin, yet I should be
ashamed to sin, because of its essential baseness.

Plato

Sin is any want of conformity unto, or transgression of the law of God.

Shorter Catechism

There is a vast difference between sins of
infirmity and those of presumption, as vast
as between inadvertency and deliberation.

Robert South

No sin is small. It is against an infinite God,
and may have consequences immeasurable.
No grain of sand is small in the mechanism
of a watch.

Jeremy Taylor

Sins of the mind have less infamy than those
of the body, but not less malignity.

Benjamin Whichcote

This is the unpardonable sin: to talk discouragingly to human souls hungering for hope.
Ella Wheeler Wilcox

See also: BASENESS, CRIME, DEPRAVITY, ERROR, GUILT, MISCHIEF, OFFENSE, RIGHT AND WRONG, ROGUERY, VICE, VILLAINY, WICKEDNESS, WRONG.

SINCERITY

A man often hopes that his friends are more sincere than himself.
William Allingham

Sincerity and truth are the basis of every virtue.
Confucius

Sincerity is no test of truth—no evidence of correctness of conduct. You may take poison sincerely believing it the needed medicine, but will it save your life?
Tryon Edwards

Self-suffering is the truest test of sincerity.
Mohandas Karamchand (Mahatma) Gandhi

We need expect little sincerity or trustworthy aid from him who is convinced that double-dealing and deceit are the principles that guide all men in their conduct through life.
Francesco Guicciardini

Sincerity, thou first of virtues, let no mortal leave thy onward path, although the earth should gape, and from the gulf of hell destruction rise, to take dissimulation's winding way.
Henry Home (Lord Kames)

Sincerity is the indispensable ground of all conscientiousness, and by consequence of all heartfelt religion.
Immanuel Kant

Men of weak character cannot be sincere.
Duc François de La Rochefoucauld

It is not the dress that makes the monk. Many are dressed like monks who are inwardly anything but monks: and some wear Spanish caps who have but little of the valour of the Spaniard in them.
François Rabelais

To be sincere with ourselves is better and harder than to be painstakingly accurate with others.
Agnes Repplier

The shortest and surest way to live with honor in the world, is to be in reality what we would appear to be; all human virtues increase and strengthen themselves by the practice and experience of them.
Socrates

Inward sincerity will of course influence the outward deportment; where the one is wanting, there is great reason to suspect the absence of the other.
Laurence Sterne

Sincerity is to speak as we think, to do as we pretend and profess, to perform what we promise, and really to be what we would seem and appear to be.
John Tillotson

A little sincerity is a dangerous thing, and a great deal of it is absolutely fatal.
Oscar Wilde

See also: TRUTH.

SINGULARITY

Singularity is laudable, when in contradiction to a multitude, it adheres to the dictates of morality and honor. In concerns of this kind it is to be looked upon as heroic bravery, in which a man leaves the species only as he soars above it.
Joseph Addison

Let those who would affect singularity with success, first determine to be very virtuous, and they will be sure to be very singular.
Charles Caleb Colton

He who would be singular in his apparel had need have something superlative to balance that affectation.
Owen Felltham

See also: DEVIATION, DISTINCTION, ECCENTRICITY, HIPPIE, INDIVIDUALITY, INNOVATION, NONCONFORMITY, ORIGINALITY, SELF-RELIANCE.

SIZE

All the great things have been done by little nations.
Benjamin Disraeli

Some of the greatest military feats have been performed by small armies.
Benjamin Disraeli

We do not think ourselves worse than the elephant for being smaller and shorter lived.

George Santayana

A dwarf is small, even if he stands on a mountain; a collossus keeps his height, even if he stands in a well.

Seneca

The history of almost every civilization furnishes examples of geographical expansion coinciding with deterioration in quality.

Arnold Joseph Toynbee

See also: BIGNESS, GREATNESS.

SKEPTICISM

Scepticism has never founded empires, established principles, or changed the world's heart. The great doers in history have always been men of faith.

Edwin Hubbel Chapin

Skepticism becomes the mark and even the pose of the educated mind. It is not longer directed against this and that article of the older creeds but is rather a bias against any kind of far-reaching ideas, and a denial of systematic participation on the part of such ideas in the intelligent direction of affairs.

John Dewey

Scepticism is slow suicide.

Ralph Waldo Emerson

Skeptics laugh in order not to weep.

Anatole France

The great trouble with the scepticism of the age is, that it is not thorough enough. It questions everything but its own foundations.

John Bannister Gibson

A skeptic who turns dogmatist has decided it is high time to take it easy.

Henry Stanley Haskins

Skeptics are generally ready to believe anything provided it is only sufficiently improbable; it is at matters of fact that such people stumble.

Karl Ludwig von Knebel

The skeptic—and this is fortunate for him—is not obliged to explain how human dilemma arose. It is indeed one of the advantages of his position that it enables him to shirk that

obligation which others seem to feel—that of accounting for all phenomena by some explanation, however improbable.

Joseph Wood Krutch

Great intellects are skeptical.

Friedrich Wilhelm Nietzsche

I prefer credulity to skepticism and cynicism, for there is more promise in almost anything than in nothing at all.

Ralph Barton Perry

The sceptical writers are a set whose business is to prick holes in the fabric of knowledge wherever it is weak and faulty; and when these places are properly repaired, the whole building becomes more firm and solid than it was before.

Thomas Reid

By the spirit of the age . . . the man of today is forced into skepticism about his own thinking, in order to make him receptive to truth which comes to him from authority. . . . Truth taken over by skepticism which has become believing . . . is not capable of uniting itself with him to the very marrow of his being.

Albert Schweitzer

Every person who has mastered a profession is a sceptic concerning it.

George Bernard Shaw

Free thinkers are generally those who never think at all.

Laurence Sterne

Every man is occasionally visited by the suspicion that the planet on which he is riding is not really going anywhere; that the Force which controls its measured eccentricities hasn't got anything special in mind.

James Grover Thurber

The thorough sceptic is a dogmatist. He enjoys the delusion of complete futility.

Alfred North Whitehead

See also: AGNOSTICISM, DOUBT, UNBELIEF.

SKILL: *see* ABILITY.

SLANDER

Next to the slanderer, we detest the bearer of the slander to our ears.

Mary Catherwood

Slander cannot make the subject of it either better or worse. It may represent us in a false light, or place a likeness of us in a bad one, but we are always the same. Not so the slanderer, for calumny always makes the calumniator worse, but the calumniated never.

Charles Caleb Colton

Who stabs my name would stab my person, too, did not the hangman's axe lie in the way.

John Crowne

The way to check slander is to despise it; attempt to overtake and refute it, and it will outrun you.

Alexandre Dumas (pére)

The slanderer and the assassin differ only in the weapon they use; with the one it is the dagger, with the other the tongue. The former is worse than the latter, for the last only kills the body, while the other murders the reputation and peace.

Tryon Edwards

If any one tells you a person speaks ill of you, do not make excuse about what is said, but answer: "He was ignorant of my other faults else he would not have mentioned these alone."

Epictetus

The slander of some people is as great a recommendation as the praise of others.

Henry Fielding

I hate the man who builds his name
On ruins of another's fame.

John Gay

There would not be so many open mouths if there were not so many open ears.

Joseph Hall

When will talkers refrain from evil-speaking? When will listeners refrain from evil-hearing.

Augustus and Julius Hare

The slanderer inflicts wrong by calumniating the absent; and he who gives credit to the calumny before he knows its truth, is equally guilty.

Herodotus

Slander is the revenge of a coward, and dissimulation his defence.

Samuel Johnson

Have patience awhile; slanders are not long-lived. Truth is the child of time; ere long she shall appear to vindicate thee.

Immanuel Kant

No one is safe from slander. The best way is to pay no attention to it, but live in innocence and let the world talk.

Molière (Jean Baptiste Poquelin)

Never throw mud. You may miss your mark, but you must have dirty hands.

Joseph Parker

Believe nothing against another, but on good authority; nor report what may hurt another, unless it be a greater hurt to some other to conceal it.

William Penn

Some residue is always left in us of the trivial slanders our hearts have indulged in about those we love.

Jean Rostand

Slanderers are like flies, that pass all over a man's good parts to light only on his sores.

Rule of Life

Oh! many a shaft, at random sent,
Finds mark the archer little meant;
And many a word, at random spoken,
May soothe or wound a heart that's broken.

Sir Walter Scott

A slander is like a hornet; if you cannot kill it dead the first blow, better not strike at it.

Henry Wheeler Shaw (Josh Billings)

The worthiest people are the most injured by slander, as it is the best fruit which the birds have been pecking at.

Jonathan Swift

See also: ABUSE, BABBLE, CALUMNY, DETRACTION, GOSSIP, INJURY, REPUTATION, RUMOR, SCANDAL, TATTLING.

SLANG

Slang is the speech of him who robs the literary garbage cans on their way to the dump.

Ambrose Gwinnett Bierce

Slang is just sport-model language stripped down to get more speed with less horsepower.

Buffalo Evening News

Slang is a token of man's lively spirit ever at work in unexpected places. . . . For slang, after all, is a kind of metaphor and metaphor, we have agreed, is a kind of poetry; you might say indeed that slang is a poor-man's poetry.

John Moore

Slang is a language that rolls up its sleeves, spits on its hands and goes to work.

Carl Sandburg

See also: LANGUAGE, NICKNAME, WORD.

SLAVERY

Slavery in all its forms, in all its degrees, is a violation of divine law, and a degradation of human nature.

Jacques Pierre Brissot

There is a law above all human enactments, written upon the heart by the finger of God; and while men despise fraud, and loathe rapine, and abhor blood, they shall reject with indignation the wild and guilty phantasy, that man can hold property in man.

Henry Brougham (Baron Brougham)

Slavery is a state so improper, so degrading, so ruinous to the feelings and capacities of human nature, that it ought not to be suffered to exist.

Edmund Burke

Here lies the evil of slavery: Its whips, imprisonments, and even the horrors of the middle passage, are not to be named, in comparison with the extinction of the proper consciousness of a human being—with the degradation of a man into a brute.

William Ellery Channing

Slavery is an atrocious debasement of human nature.

Benjamin Franklin

A slave, to be free, must continuously rise against his slavery, and be locked up in his master's cell for his rebellion. The cell-door is the door to freedom.

Mohandas Karamchand (Mahatma) Gandhi

When a slave begins to take pride in his fetters and hugs them like precious ornaments, the triumph of the slave-owner is complete.

Mohandas Karamchand (Mahatma) Gandhi

The man who gives me employment, which I must have or suffer, that man is my master, let me call him what I will.

Henry George

Those are men-stealers who abduct, keep, sell, or buy slaves or freemen.

Hugo Grotius

Slavery is not only opposed to all the principles of morality, but, as it appears to me, is pregnant with appalling and inevitable danger to the Republic.

Baron Wilhelm von Humboldt

The abolition of domestic slavery is the greatest object of desire in these colonies, where it was unhappily introduced in their infant state.

Thomas Jefferson

The whole commerce between master and slave is a perpetual exercise of the most boisterous passions; the most unremitting despotism on the one part, and degrading submission on the other. The man must be a prodigy who can retain his manners and morals undepraved by such circumstances. The hour of emancipation must come; but whether it will be brought on by the generous energies of our own minds, or by the bloody scenes of St. Domingo, is a leaf of our history not yet turned over. The Almighty has no attribute which can take sides with us in such a contest.

Thomas Jefferson

Not only does the Christian religion, but Nature herself, cry out against the state of slavery.

Leo X (Giovanni de Medici)

Every man has a property in his own person; this nobody has a right to but himself.

John Locke

We have found that this evil, slavery, has preyed upon the very vitals of the Union, and has been prejudicial to all the States in which it has existed.

James Monroe

It was with the Jews that the revolt of the slaves begins in the sphere of morals.

Friedrich Wilhelm Nietzsche

It is injustice to permit slavery to remain for a single hour.

William Pitt

Slavery is a system of the most complete injustice.

Plato

Englishmen will never be slaves; they are free to do whatever the Government and public opinion allow them to do.

George Bernard Shaw

Slavery is a system of outrage and robbery.

Socrates

The true slave is he who is led away by his pleasures and can neither see what is good for him nor act accordingly.

Baruch (Benedict) Spinoza

Where slavery is, there liberty cannot be; and where liberty is, there slavery cannot be.

Charles Sumner

I can only say that there is not a man living who wishes more sincerely than I do to see a plan adopted for the abolition of slavery.

George Washington

From my earliest youth I have regarded slavery as a great moral and political evil. I think it unjust, repugnant to the natural equality of mankind, founded only in superior power; a standing and permanent conquest by the stronger over the weaker. The religion of Christ is a religion of kindness, justice, and brotherly love:—but slavery is not kindly affectionate; it does not seek another's and not its own; it does not let the oppressed go free; it is but a continual act of oppression.

Daniel Webster

That execrable sum of all villainies commonly called the slave-trade.

John Wesley

See also: OPPRESSION, PERSECUTION, TYRANNY.

SLEEP

Sleep is a death, O make me try,
By sleeping what it is to die.
And as gently lay my head
On my grave, as now my bed.

Sir Thomas Browne

[Sleep is] so like death, I dare not trust it without my prayers.

Sir Thomas Browne

Of all the thoughts of God that are
Borne inward into souls afar,
Along the Psalmist's music deep,

Now tell me if that any is,
For gift or grace, surpassing this:
"He giveth his beloved—sleep?"

Elizabeth Barrett Browning

Sleep is sweet to the labouring man.

John Bunyan

Blessings on him who first invented sleep. It covers a man all over, thoughts and all, like a cloak. It is meat for the hungry, drink for the thirsty, heat for the cold, and cold for the hot. It makes the shepherd equal to the monarch, and the fool to the wise. There is but one evil in it, and that is that it resembles death, since between a dead man and a sleeping man there is but little difference.

Miguel de Cervantes Saavedra

Nor has the man of science, in spite of the knowledge and instruments he can bring to his enquiry, yet been able to explore and to explain the mystery of sleep.

Walter John de la Mare

Sleep, however, is in general so usual and so easy a refuge that its strangeness and mystery are apt to be as little heeded as are its incalculable value and its gifts of grace.

Walter John de la Mare

What the will and reason are powerless to remove, sleep melts like snow in water.

Walter John de la Mare

It is a delicious moment, certainly, that of being well nestled in bed and feeling that you shall drop gently to sleep. The good is to come, not past; the limbs are tired enough to render the remaining in one posture delightful; the labor of the day is gone. A gentle failure of the perceptions creeps over you; the spirit of consciousness disengages itself once more, and with slow and hushing degrees, like a mother detaching her hand from that of a sleeping child, the mind seems to have a balmy lid closing over it, like the eye —it is closed—the mysterious spirit has gone to take its airy rounds.

(James Henry) Leigh Hunt

For I am weary, and am over wrought
With too much toil, with too much care distraught,
And with the iron crown of anguish crowned.
Lay thy soft hand upon my brow and cheek,
O peaceful Sleep!

Henry Wadsworth Longfellow

To do each day two things one dislikes is a precept I have followed scrupulously: every day I have got up and I have gone to bed.

(William) Somerset Maugham

Sleep, thou repose of all things; thou gentlest of the duties; thou peace of the mind, from which care flies; who dost soothe the hearts of men wearied with the toils of the day, and refittest them for labor.

Ovid

Sleep, the antechamber of the grave.

Jean Paul Richter

God gives sleep to the bad, in order that the good may be undisturbed.

Saadi (Muslih-ud-Din)

Sleep means reexperiencing one's past, forgetting one's present, and pre-feeling one's future.

Wilhelm Stekel

When one begins to turn in bed, it is time to turn out.

Arthur Wellesley (1st Duke Wellington)

See also: BED, DEATH, NIGHT, QUIET, PEACE, REPOSE, REST.

SLOGAN

Slogans are both exciting and comforting, but they are also powerful opiates for the conscience.

James Bryant Conant

See also: ADVERTISING, PROPAGANDA.

SLOTH

Flee sloth, for the indolence of the soul is the decay of the body.

Cato the Elder

Sloth never arrived at the attainment of a good wish.

Miguel de Cervantes Saavedra

Sloth, if it has prevented many crimes, has also smothered many virtues.

Charles Caleb Colton

See also: IDLENESS, INACTIVITY, INDOLENCE.

SLUM

The enemy today within our gates is slum-ism. We must make our declaration of war against slumism. It is a war in which all of us must enlist. And our goal can be nothing than total victory.

Hubert Horatio Humphrey

The latent manpower wasting away in the slums is urgently needed. The supply of capable people may be the limiting factor in our industrial growth rate.

Stephen Flaherty Keating

See also: CITY, GHETTO, POVERTY, RACISM, RICH AND POOR, SEGREGATION.

SMILE

A smile is the whisper of a laugh.

Anonymous

Something of a person's character may be discovered by observing how he smiles. Some people never smile; they only grin.

Christian Nestell Bovee

Thinking a smile all the time will keep your face youthful.

Frank Gelett Burgess

Wrinkles should merely indicate where smiles have been.

Samuel Langhorne Clemens (Mark Twain)

A woman has two smiles that an angel might envy—the smile that accepts a lover before words are uttered, and the smile that lights on the first-born babe, and assures it of a mother's love.

Thomas Chandler Haliburton

There are many kinds of smiles, each having a distinct character. Some announce goodness and sweetness, others betray sarcasm, bitterness, and pride; some soften the countenance by their languishing tenderness, others brighten by their spiritual vivacity.

Johann Kaspar Lavater

A face that cannot smile is never good.

Martial

It's full of worth and goodness too, with manly kindness blent,
It's worth a million dollars and it doesn't cost a cent.

Wilbur D. Nesbit

Eternal smiles his emptiness betray,
As shallow streams run dimpling all the way.

Alexander Pope

See also: AMIABILITY, CHEERFULNESS, COM-
PLACENCY, DELIGHT, GOOD HUMOR,
GOOD NATURE, HAPPINESS, HUMOR,
JESTING, JOY, LAUGHTER, MIRTH,
NONSENSE, PLEASURE, WIT.

SMOG: *see* AIR POLLUTION.

SMOKING

The sweet post-prandial cigar.
> *Robert Williams Buchanan*

Tobacco, divine, rare, superexcellent tobacco, which goes far beyond all the panaceas, potable gold and philospher's stones, a sovereign remedy to all diseases.
> *Robert Burton*

Despite the fact that the Surgeon General's report on smoking and health showed no evidence that smoking early in life is a symbol of growing up, nearly every smoker my own colleagues and I have interviewed over the past ten years reported that this was indeed the original reason for taking up the custom.
> *Arthur Homer Cain*

In a way, smoking cigarettes is somewhat like acquiring a taste for persimmons: one must willfully overcome an aversion to them before he can start enjoying them.
> *Arthur Homer Cain*

The production, packaging, distribution, and advertising of cigarettes is an enormously complicated industry and one which contributes substantially to the national income through taxation (3.3 billion dollars) and by providing work and a higher standard of living in many parts of the country.
> *Arthur Homer Cain*

The smoking of cigarettes is a fact of life throughout the world—regardless of the current controversy concerning its possible adverse effects on the human body.
> *Arthur Homer Cain*

I have a horror of smoking as I have of wines. Smoking I consider to be a vice. It deadens one's conscience and is often worse than drink, in that it acts imperceptibly. It is a habit which is difficult to get rid of when once it seizes hold of a person. It is an expensive vice. It fouls the breath, discolours the teeth and sometimes even causes cancer. It is an unclean habit.
> *Mohandas Karamchand (Mahatma) Gandhi*

Smoking is in a way a greater curse than drink, in as much as the victim does not realise its evil in time. It is not regarded as a sign of barbarism, it is even acclaimed by civilised people. I can only say, let those who can, give it up and set the example.
> *Mohandas Karamchand (Mahatma) Gandhi*

Tobacco is a dirty weed. I like it.
It satisfies no normal need. I like it.
It makes you thin, it makes you lean,
It takes the hair right off your bean.
It's the worst darn stuff I've ever seen.
> I like it.
> *Graham Lee Hemminger*

The man who smokes, thinks like a sage and acts like a samaritan.
> *Edward G. Bulwer-Lytton (Baron Lytton)*

Although a million adult smokers stop smoking every year, a million youngsters are coming along to take up the habit.
> *John Emerson Moss*

I can say, in reporting on the World Conference on Smoking and Health, that many other countries of the world have gone much further than we have in regulating and curtailing cigarette advertizing. The evidence is overwhelming—it is undisputed now—that cigarette smoking not only shortens life, not only is a cause of many of the killing diseases that we know, but it has become the Nation's No. 1 health hazard. In making that statement, I am quoting the Surgeon General of the United States. Not only do people die sooner; they become sick and lose time from work, as well. In the United States, more days lost from work are attributable to cigarette smoking than to any other cause.
> *John Emerson Moss*

The habitual use of tobacco is related primarily to psychological and social drives, reinforced and perpetuated by the pharmacological actions of nicotine.
> *United States Department of*
> *Health, Education and Welfare*

See also: ALCOHOL, CANCER, DRINK, HEALTH.

SNAKE

Man spurns the worm, but pauses ere he wake
The slumbering venom of the folded snake.
> *George Gordon Byron (Lord Byron)*

A snake lurks in the grass.
> *Virgil*

See also: ANIMAL.

SNEER

There was a laughing devil in his sneer,
Which raised emotions both of rage and
    fear;
And where his frown of hatred darkly fell,
Hope withering fled, and mercy sighed fare-
    well.
                George Gordon Byron (Lord Byron)

The most insignificant people are the most
apt to sneer at others. They are safe from
reprisals, and have no hope of rising in their
own esteem but by lowering their neighbors.
                            William Hazlitt

Damn with faint praise, assent with civil
    leer,
And without sneering, teach the rest to
    sneer.
                            Alexander Pope

Who can refute a sneer? It is independent
of proof, reason, argument, or sense, and
may as well be used against facts and truth,
as against falsehood.
                            Charles Simmons

I fancy that it is just as hard to do your duty
when men are sneering at you as when they
are shooting at you.
                (Thomas) Woodrow Wilson

See also: CONTEMPT, CYNICS, IRONY, JEERING,
        MISANTHROPY, RIDICULE, SARCASM.

SNOB

Snobbery is the pride of those who are not
sure of their position.
                            Berton Braley

He who meanly admires a mean thing is a
Snob—perhaps that is a safe definition of the
character.
                William Makepeace Thackeray

See also: AFFECTATION, ARISTOCRACY, ARRO-
        GANCE, CONCEIT, EGOTISM, PRETEN-
        SION, PRIDE, SELF-RIGHTEOUSNESS.

SOCIABILITY

Half of the secret of getting along with people is consideration of their views; the other
half is tolerance in one's own views.
                            Daniel Frohman

If we wish to give pleasure in company, the
course to be pursued is, that we should

think less of showing off our own abilities
than of giving others an opportunity of shining; he who leaves you satisfied with himself
and with the display of his mental powers, is
sure to be perfectly satisfied with you. Men
care not to admire you, they wish to please;
they seek much less to be instructed, or
even amused, than to be appreciated and
applauded; the most delicate species of
pleasure is to give it to others.
                            Jean de La Bruyère

We are more sociable, and get on better
with people by the heart than the intellect.
                            Jean de La Bruyère

Rascals are always sociable, and the chief
sign that a man has any nobility in his character is the little pleasure he takes in other's
company.
                        Arthur Schopenhauer

See also: CONVIVIALITY.

SOCIALISM

We are in for some kind of socialism, call it
by whatever name we please.
                            John Dewey

I am flatly opposed to the socialization of
medicine. The great need for hospital and
medical services can best be met by the initiative of private plans . . . (however) federal government can do so many helpful
things and still avoid the socialization of
medicine.
                    Dwight David Eisenhower

Social service to be effective has to be rendered without noise. It is best performed
when the left hand knoweth not what the
right is doing.
        Mohandas Karamchand (Mahatma) Gandhi

What the vast mass of mankind does for self
or at best for family, a social servant does for
general good.
        Mohandas Karamchand (Mahatma) Gandhi

The ideal social state is not that in which
each gets an equal amount of wealth, but in
which each gets in proportion to his contribution to the general stock.
                            Henry George

What is characteristic of socialism is the joint
ownership by all members of the community
of the instruments and means of production,
which carries with it the consequence that

the division of all the produce among the body of owners must be a public act performed according to the rules laid down by the community.

John Stuart Mill

We are not going to perpetuate poverty by substituting a permanent dole for a pay check. There is no humanity or charity in destroying self reliance, dignity and self respect . . . the very substance of moral fiber. We seek reforms that will, wherever possible, change relief check to pay check.

Ronald Reagan

The agrarian, like the communist, would bring all above him down to his own level, or raise himself to theirs, but is not anxious to bring those below him up to himself.

Charles Simmons

Socialism is a stage in social development from a society guided by the dictatorship of the proletariat to a society wherein the state will have ceased to exist.

Joseph Stalin

I'm no more in favor of socialism than anybody else, and I particularly dislike things which creep. But, if I don't like "creeping socialism," there's something else I dislike just as much—and that's galloping reaction.

Adlai Ewing Stevenson

Many people consider the things government does for them to be social progress, but they regard the things government does for others as socialism.

Earl Warren

See also: COMMUNISM, GOVERNMENT.

SOCIAL WELFARE: *see* SOCIALISM.

SOCIETY

The only worthwhile achievements of man are those which are socially useful.

Alfred Adler

The pressure of social influence about us is enormous, and no single arm can resist it.

Felix Adler

Our society distributes itself into Barbarians, Philistines, and Populace.

Matthew Arnold

No social system will bring us happiness, health, and prosperity unless it is inspired by something greater than materialism.

Clement Richard Atlee

Man was formed for society.

Sir William Blackstone

In and of itself, color has no meaning. But the white world has given it meaning—political, social, economic, historical, physiological and philosophical . . . an order is thereby established.

H. Rap Brown

Society is composed of two great classes: those who have more dinners than appetite, and those who have more appetite than dinners.

Sébastien Roch Nicolas Chamfort

This is our basic conclusion: Our Nation is moving toward two societies, one black, one white—separate and unequal.

Commission on Civil Disorder, 1968

It is a community of purpose that constitutes society.

Benjamin Disraeli

It is not social change alone which is the challenge. It is the rate of change. That rate of change has been vastly accelerated by numerous factors. Peril lies not in change but in that tremendous rate of change.

William Orville Douglas

I think it's quite sad that our species—which has so much hubris—is basically thrown back on nothing but luck. Our future is all a flip of the coin . . . a cut of the cards. Is the weather going to hold for another year or two, or isn't it?

Paul Ehrlich

Society undergoes continual changes; it is barbarous, it is civilized, it is Christianized, it is rich, it is scientific; but this change is not amelioration. For everything that is given something is taken. Society acquires new arts, and loses old instincts. The civilized man has built a coach, but has lost the use of his feet; he has a fine Geneva watch, but cannot tell the hour by the sun.

Ralph Waldo Emerson

I must try to live in society and yet remain untouched by its pitfalls.

Mohandas Karamchand (Mahatma) Gandhi

What an argument in favor of social connections is the observation that, by communicating our grief we have less, and by communicating our pleasures we have more.

Fulke Greville (First Baron Brooke)

Society has only one law, and that is custom. Even religion is socially powerful only so far as it has custom on its side.

Philip Gilbert Hamerton

In the pioneer days of our history it was easy to love one's neighbor and respect his rights, when possibly the neighbor lived at a distance of four or five miles and the relations were not intimate enough to occasion a clash of interests. Now one finds that society rather than another individual is his neighbor.

John Grier Hibben

Society is like a lawn, where every roughness is smoothed, every bramble eradicated, and where the eye is delighted by the smiling verdure of a velvet surface. He, however, who would study nature in its wildness and variety, must plunge into the forest, must explore the glen, must stem the torrent, and dare the precipice.

Washington Irving

The uprooting of human beings from the land, the concentration in cities, the breakdown of the authority of the family, of tradition, and of moral conventions, the complexity and the novelty of modern life, and finally the economic insecurity of our industrial system have called into being the modern social worker. They perform a function in modern society which is not a luxury but an absolute necessity.

Walter Lippmann

We are a kind of chameleons, taking our hue—the hue or our moral character, from those who are about us.

John Locke

Society is a wall of very strong mosonry, as it now stands; it may be sapped in the course of a thousand years, but stormed in a day—no! You dash your head against it—you scatter your brains, and you dislodge a stone. Society smiles in scorn, effaces the stain, and replaces the stone.

Edward G. Bulwer-Lytton (Baron Lytton)

We do have an affluent society that is unmatched and unparalleled in world history.

We are surrounded by abundance—goods, conveniences, and comforts. In spite of all the clamor about poverty, opportunity is present everywhere, and we are living in a marvelous age—indeed, in a golden age economically. But, unhappily, with all of our great affluence and greatness, crime abounds and flourishes throughout the land.

John L. McClellan

Man . . . can develop into an individual only in society.

Karl Marx

The change from the individual life of the animal to the group life of civilized man, which becomes a life of ever-expanding complexity as our scientific civilization advances, would obviously be impossible unless the individual learned in ever-increasing measure to subordinate his impulses and interests to the furtherance of the group life.

Robert Andrews Millikan

The very extension of the range of community in our time, through national and world-wide organizations, only increases the need for building up, as never before, the intimate cells, the basic tissue, of social life; the family and the home, the neighborhood and the city, the work-group and the factory.

Lewis Mumford

Social problems can no longer be solved by class warfare any more than international problems can be solved by wars between nations. Warfare is negative and will sooner or later lead to destruction, while good will and cooperation are positive and supply the only safe basis for building a better future.

Fridtjof Nansen

It is a little dangerous to live in a society which is closed up like a shell. We petrify there and grow unaccustomed to fresh air and fresh ideas.

Jawaharlal Nehru

Wisdom and foresight would demonstrate that in the long run the best way of profiting oneself is to profit society as a whole of which one is a member.

Jawaharlal Nehru

Bourgeois democrats are inclined to believe that freedom is primarily a necessity for the individual, and that community and social order are necessary only because there are many individuals in a small world, so that minimal restrictions are required to prevent confusion. Actually the community requires freedom as much as the individual; and the individual requires order as much as does the community.

Reinhold Niebuhr

We must have the press of the crowd to draw virtue from us.

Angelo Patri

Society—the only field where the sexes have ever met on terms of equality, the arena where character is formed and studied, the cradle and the realm of public opinion, the crucible of ideas, the world's university, at once a school and a theatre, the spur and the crown of ambition, the tribunal which unmasks pretension and stamps real merit, the power that gives government leave to be, and outruns the lazy church in fixing the moral sense.

Wendell Phillips

Clearly the ideal situation would be that in which society would increasingly respect the individual, who would, in turn, increasingly respect society.

Jean Rostand

Society is the master and man is the servant; and it is entirely according as society proves a good or bad master, whether he turns out a bad or a good servant.

George Augustus Henry Sala

In a healthy society the public instinctively runs to help the police; the criminal is felt to be everybody's enemy; there is an implicit brotherhood amongst peaceful citizens, who if attacked may confidently cry *Help, Help,* or *Stop Thief.*

George Santayana

Man is a social animal. . . . Men can provide for their wants much more easily by mutual help, and only by uniting their forces can they escape from the dangers that beset them.

Baruch (Benedict) Spinoza

The good of society as a whole cannot be better served than by the preservation against arbitrary restraint of the liberties of its constituent members.

George Sutherland

There are four varieties in society; the lovers, the ambitious, observers, and fools. The fools are the happiest.

Hippolyte Adolphe Taine

Societies can bear an amazing amount of corruption and still produce high cultures.

Allen Tate

A schism in the souls of human beings will be found to underlie any schism that reveals itself on the surface of the society which is the common ground of these human actors' respective fields of activity.

Arnold Joseph Toynbee

Society is the offspring of leisure; and to acquire this forms the only rational motive for accumulating wealth, notwithstanding the cant that prevails on the subject of labor.

Henry Theodore Tuckerman

I believe that we already have a science of society—a very young and very incomplete science, but one that is steadily growing and that is capable of indefinite extension.

Beatrice Webb

Other people are quite dreadful. The only possible society is oneself.

Oscar Wilde

To get into the best society nowadays, one has either to feed people, amuse people, or shock people.

Oscar Wilde

It is fitting that technological society, which dwarfs men by things, should have found so mean an instrument [as Richard Nixon].

Shelden S. Wolin

See also: ASSOCIATES, COMPANIONSHIP, CONVIVIALITY, HUMANITY, MAN, PEOPLE.

SOLDIER

Soldiers that carry their lives in their hands, should carry the grace of God in their hearts.

Richard Baxter

He is the true soldier who knows how to die and stand his ground in the midst of a hail of bullets.

Mohandas Karamchand (Mahatma) Gandhi

A true soldier does not argue, as he marches, how success is going to be ultimately achieved. But he is confident that if he only plays the humble part well, somehow or other the battle will be won.

Mohandas Karamchand (Mahatma) Gandhi

I want to see you shoot the way you shout.

Theodore Roosevelt

Soldiers are citizens of death's gray land.
Siegfried Sassoon

Dost thou know the fate of soldiers? They are but ambition's tools, to cut a way to her unlawful ends. And when they are worn, hacked, hewn with constant service, thrown aside, to rust in peace and rot in hospitals.
Thomas Southerne

Policy goes beyond strength, and contrivance before action; hence it is that direction is left to the commander, and execution to the soldier, who is not to ask Why? but to do what he is commanded.
Xenophon

Ignorance, poverty and vanity make many soldiers.
Johann George von Zimmermann

Soldiers are the only carnivorous animals that live in a gregarious state.
Johann George von Zimmermann

See also: ARMY, NAVY, WAR.

SOLITUDE

In Genesis it says that it is not good for a man to be alone, but sometimes it is a great relief.
John Barrymore

It would do the world good if every man in it would compel himself occasionally to be absolutely alone. Most of the world's progress has come out of such loneliness.
Bruce Barton

The right to be alone—the most comprehensive of rights, and the right most valued by civilized man.
Louis Dembitz Brandeis

An entire life of solitude contradicts the purpose of our being, since death itself is scarcely an idea of more terror.
Edmund Burke

In solitude, where we are least alone.
George Gordon Byron (Lord Byron)

There is a pleasure in the pathless woods,
There is a rapture on the lonely shore,
There is society, where none intrudes,
By the deep Sea, and music in its roar.
George Gordon Byron (Lord Byron)

Solitude shows us what we should be; society shows us what we are.
Richard Cecil

I praise the Frenchman, his remark was shrewd—
"How sweet, how passing sweet is solitude!"
But grant me still a friend in my retreat,
Whom I may whisper—Solitude is sweet.
William Cowper

Conversation enriches the understanding, but solitude is the school of genius.
Edward Gibbon

The strongest man in the world is he who stands most alone.
Henrik Ibsen

Half the pleasure of solitude comes from having with us some friend to whom we can say how sweet solitude is.
William Jay

The love of retirement has in all ages adhered closely to those minds which have been most enlarged by knowledge, or elevated by genius. Those who enjoyed everything generally supposed to confer happiness have been forced to seek it in the shades of privacy.
Samuel Johnson

I really only have Perfect Fun with myself. Other people won't stop and look at the things I want to look at or, if they do, they stop to please me or to humor me or to keep the peace.
Katherine Mansfield

It is the mark of a superior man that, left to himself, he is able endlessly to amuse, interest and entertain himself out of his personal stock of meditations, ideas, criticisms, memories, philosophy, humor and what not.
George Jean Nathan

Until I truly loved I was alone.
Caroline Elizabeth Sarah Norton

You cannot build up a character in a solitude; you need a formed character to stand a solitude.
Austin O'Malley

The thoughtful Soul to Solitude retires.
Omar Khayyám

Thus let me live, unseen, unknown,
  Thus unlamented let me die;
Steal from the world, and not a stone
  Tell where I lie.
Alexander Pope

That which happens to the soil when it ceases to be cultivated, happens to man himself when he foolishly forsakes society for solitude; the brambles grow up in his desert heart.

Antoine Rivarol

Solitude is one of the highest enjoyments of which our nature is susceptible. It is also, when too long continued, capable of being made the most severe, indescribable, unendurable source of anguish.

Henry Scott (Earl of Deloraine)

No doubt solitude is wholesome, but so is abstinence after a surfeit. The true life of man is in society.

William Gilmore Simms

Solitude cherishes great virtues and destroys little ones.

Sydney Smith

In solitude the mind gains strength, and learns to lean upon itself; in the world it seeks or accepts of a few treacherous supports—the feigned compassions of one, the flattery of a second, the civilities of a third, the friendship of a fourth; they all deceive, and bring the mind back to retirement, reflection, and books.

Laurence Sterne

A wise man is never less alone than when he is alone.

Jonathan Swift

Leisure and solitude are the best effect of riches, because mother of thought. Both are avoided by most rich men, who seek company and business; which are signs of their being weary of themselves.

Sir William Temple

Those beings only are fit for solitude, who like nobody, and are liked by nobody.

Johann Georg von Zimmermann

See also: ABSENCE, DESOLATION, LONELINESS, QUIET, REST, RETIREMENT.

SONG

The best days of the church have always been its singing days.

Theodore Ledyard Cuyler

A song will outlive all sermons in the memory.

Henry Giles

Behold her, single in the field,
    Yon solitary Highland Lass!
Reaping and singing by herself;
    Stop here, or gently pass!

William Wordsworth

See also: BALLAD, JAZZ, POETRY, MUSIC.

SOPHISTRY

The juggle of sophistry consists, for the most part, in using a word in one sense in the premises, and in another sense in the conclusion.

Samuel Taylor Coleridge

Some men weave their sophistry till their own reason is entangled.

Samuel Johnson

Casuistry is useful for purposes of defense, and a skillful apologist can explain away much.

Vernon Louis Parrington

See also: ARGUMENT, ERROR, FALSEHOOD, PEDANTRY, SKEPTICISM, SUBTLETY.

SORROW

Wherever souls are being tried and ripened, in whatever commonplace and homely way, there God is hewing out the pillars for His temple.

Phillips Brooks

Sorrow was made for man, not for beasts; yet if men encourage melancholy too much, they become no better than beasts.

Miguel de Cervantes Saavedra

One can never be the judge of another's grief. That which is a sorrow to one, to another is joy. Let us not dispute with any one concerning the reality of his sufferings; it is with sorrows as with countries—each man has his own.

Vicomte François René de Chateaubriand

To forecast our sorrows is only to increase the suffering without increasing our strength to bear them. Many of life's noblest enterprises might never have been undertaken if all the difficulties and defects could be foreseen.

Theodore Ledyard Cuyler

With sorrow comes experience, and that cruel knowledge of life which teaches us to guard against our hopes.

Emile Gaboriau

The capacity of sorrow belongs to our gran-•
deur; and the loftiest of our race are those
who have had the profoundest griefs because they have had the profoundest sympathies.

Henry Giles

The sorrow which calls for help and comfort
is not the greatest, nor does it come from
the depths of the heart.

Baron Wilhelm von Humboldt

Sorrow is our John the Baptist, clad in grim
garments, with rough arms, a son of the wilderness, baptizing us with bitter tears,
preaching repentance; and behind him
comes the gracious, affectionate, healing
Lord, speaking peace and joy to the soul.

Frederic Dan Huntington

Social sorrow loses half its pain.

Samuel Johnson

Sorrow is a kind of rust of the soul which every new idea contributes in its passage to
scour away. It is the putrefaction of stagnant
life, and is remedied by exercise and motion.

Samuel Johnson

The world is so full of care and sorrow that
it is a gracious debt we owe to one another
to discover the bright crystals of delight hidden in somber circumstances and irksome
tasks.

Helen Adams Keller

The mind profits by the wreck of every passion, and we may measure our road to wisdom by the sorrows we have undergone.

Edward G. Bulwer-Lytton (Baron Lytton)

Sorrows humanize our race; tears are the
showers that fertilize the world.

Edward R. Bulwer Lytton (Owen Meredith)

Earth hath no sorrow that heaven cannot
heal.

Thomas Moore

A coal fire softens iron, and sorrow softens a
man's heart, but both revert to the original
hardness.

Austin O'Malley

Sorrow is the source of literature, joy is the
source of virtue.

Austin O'Malley

Life, with all its sorrows, cares, perplexities
and heartbreaks, is more interesting than bo-
vine placidity, hence more desirable. The
more interesting it is, the happier it is.

William Lyon Phelps

She would have made a splendid wife, for
crying only made her eyes more bright and
tender.

William Sydney Porter (O. Henry)

He that hath pity on another man's sorrow
shall be free from it himself; and he that delighteth in, and scorneth the misery of another shall one time or other fall into it himself.

Sir Walter Raleigh

To withhold from a child some knowledge—
apportioned to his understanding—of the
world's sorrows and wrongs is to cheat him
of his kinship with humanity.

Agnes Repplier

A small sorrow distracts; a great one makes
us collected.

Jean Paul Richter

Light griefs do speak, while sorrow's tongue
is bound.

Seneca

The deeper the sorrow the less tongue it
has.

Talmud

I shall not let a sorrow die
  Until I find the heart of it,
Nor let a wordless joy go by
  Until it talks to me a bit.

Sara Teasdale

Never morning wore to evening, but some
heart did break.

Alfred, Lord Tennyson

Those touches of manhood, of nature, of sorrow, of pride, of generosity and pity, which
make the whole world kin, tell us specifical-
ly and with emphasis that we are of one
family, and should be of one household
forever.

Henry Watterson

Where there is sorrow, there is holy ground.

Oscar Wilde

See also: AFFLICTION, GRIEF, SADNESS, SUFFER-
ING, TEARS, UNHAPPINESS.

SOUL

The soul, considered with its Creator, is like one of those mathematical lines that may draw nearer to another for all eternity without a possibility of touching it; and can there be a thought so transporting as to consider ourselves in these perpetual approaches to Him, who is not only the standard of perfection, but of happiness?

Joseph Addison

The wealth of a soul is measured by how much it can feel; its poverty by how little.

William Rounseville Alger

Everything here, but the soul of man, is a passing shadow. The only enduring substance is within. When shall we awake to the sublime greatness, the perils, the accountableness, and the glorious destinies of the immortal soul?

William Ellery Channing

Whatever that be which thinks, which understands, which wills, which acts, it is something celestial and divine, and on that account must necessarily be eternal.

Cicero

Either we have an immortal soul, or we have not. If we have not, we are beasts; the first and wisest of beasts it may be; but still beasts. We only differ in degree, and not in kind; just as the elephant differs from the slug. But by the concession of the materialists, we are not of the same kind as beasts; and this also we say from our own consciousness. Therefore, methinks, it must be the possession of a soul within us that makes the difference.

Samuel Taylor Coleridge

A fiery soul, which, working out its way,
Fretted the pigmy body to decay,
And o'er-informed the tenement of clay.

John Dryden

The problem of restoring to the world original and eternal beauty is solved by the redemption of the soul.

Ralph Waldo Emerson

Dust thou art, to dust returnest,
Was not spoken of the soul.

Henry Wadsworth Longfellow

The soul can split the sky in two,
And let the face of God shine through.

Edna St. Vincent Millay

Had I no other proof of the immortality of the soul than the oppression of the just and the triumph of the wicked in this world, this alone would prevent my having the least doubt of it. So shocking a discord amidst a general harmony of things would make me naturally look for a cause; I should say to myself we do not cease to exist with this life; everything reassumes its order after death.

Jean Jacques Rousseau

The mind is never right but when it is at peace within itself; the soul is in heaven even while it is in the flesh, if it be purged of its natural corruptions, and taken up with divine thoughts and contemplations.

Seneca

See also: CONSCIENCE, EMOTION, ETERNITY, FEELINGS, HEART, IMMORTALITY, INTELLECT, MIND, SPIRIT.

SOUL AND BODY

How can I, who knows the body to be perishable and the soul to be imperishable, mourn over the separation of body from soul?

Mohandas Karamchand (Mahatma) Gandhi

All of us have mortal bodies, composed of perishable matter, but the soul lives forever: it is a portion of the Deity housed in our bodies.

Flavius Josephus

The soul has more diseases than the body.

Henry Wheeler Shaw (Josh Billings)

See also: BODY, MORTALITY, SOUL.

SOUND

What a blessing it would be if we could open and shut our ears as easily as we do our eyes.

Georges Christophe

Verse sweetens toil, however rude the sound.

Orrin Philip Gifford

The murmur that springs
From the growing of grass.

Edgar Allan Poe

The sound must seem an echo to the sense.

Alexander Pope

See also: MUSIC, NOISE, VOICE.

SPACE

A civilian-setting for the administration of space for the testing of missiles designed for of our nation that outer space be devoted to peaceful and scientific purposes.

Dwight David Eisenhower

I propose that we agree that outer space should be used only for peaceful purposes. We face a decisive moment in history in relation to this matter. Both the Soviet Union and the United States are now using outer space for the testing of missiles designed for military purposes. The time to stop is now.

Dwight David Eisenhower

I could have gone on flying through space forever.

Yuri Gagarin

Make no mistake about it. The first man who will walk on the moon has already been born. I hope in America.

James Maurice Gavin

The moon and other celestial bodies should be free for exploration and use by all countries. No country should be permitted to advance a claim of sovereignty.

Lyndon Baines Johnson

In a field where the United States and the Soviet Union have a special capacity—in the field of space—there is room for new cooperation, for further joint efforts in the regulation and exploration of space. I include among these possibilities a joint expedition to the moon.

John Fitzgerald Kennedy

God has no intention of setting a limit to the efforts of man to conquer space.

Pius XII (Eugenio Pacelli)

The exploration and use of outer space, including the moon and other celestial bodies, shall be carried out for the benefit and in the interests of all countries, irrespective of their degree of economic or scientific development, and shall be the province of all mankind [Article 1].

Treaty on Exploration and Use of Space

For my confirmation, I didn't get a watch and my first pair of long pants, like most Lutheran boys. I got a telescope. My mother thought it would make the best gift.

Wernher Von Braun

There is beauty in space, and it is orderly. There is no weather, and there is regularity. It is predictable. . . . Everything in space obeys the laws of physics. If you know these laws, and obey them, space will treat you kindly. And don't tell me man doesn't belong out there. Man belongs wherever he wants to go—and he'll do plenty well when he gets there.

Wernher Von Braun

See also: CYBERNETICS, MOON, SCIENCE, TECHNOLOGY.

SPECIALTY

Let everyone ascertain his special business or calling, and then stick to it, if he would be successful.

Benjamin Franklin

No one can exist in society without some specialty. Eighty years ago it was only necessary to be well dressed and amiable; today a man of this kind would be too much like the garçons at the cafés.

Hippolyte Adolphe Taine

See also: OCCUPATION, TALENT, TRADE.

SPECULATION

The narrower the mind, the broader the statement.

Proctor Fyffe (Ted) Cook

The besetting evil of our age is the temptation to squander and dilute thought on a thousand different lines of inquiry.

Sir John Frederick William Herschel

Conjecture as to things useful is good; but conjecture as to what it would be useless to know, such as whether men ever went upon all-fours, is very idle.

Samuel Johnson

A man cannot administer great corporations which employ armies of men and serve large communities if his judgment is diluted and distracted by huge speculative transactions. . . . A man cannot be a good doctor and keep telephoning to his broker between visits to his patients, nor a good lawyer with one eye on the ticker.

Walter Lippmann

Artificial inflation of stocks must be considered a crime as serious as counterfeiting, which it closely resembles.

André Maurois

SPEECH

Discretion of speech is more than eloquence; and to speak agreeably to him with
whom we deal is more than to speak in good
words, or in good order.

Francis Bacon

A constant governance of our speech, according to duty and reason, is a high instance and a special argument of a thoroughly sincere and solid goodness.

Isaac Barrow

If a political candidate can't get up and
make a speech of his own, if he has to hire a
press agent to write it for him, then why not
let the press agent be the candidate?

Raymond Clapper

A superior man is modest in his speech, but
exceeds in his actions.

Confucius

Think all you speak, but speak not all you
think. Thoughts are your own; your words
are so no more.

Patrick Delany

As a vessel is known by the sound, whether
it be cracked or not, so men are proved by
their speeches whether they be wise or foolish.

Demosthenes

Half the sorrows of women would be avert-
ed if they could repress the speech they
know to be useless—nay, the speech they
have resolved not to utter.

George Eliot (Mary Ann Evans)

Half the world is composed of people who
have something to say and can't, and the
other half who have nothing to say and keep
on saying it.

Robert Lee Frost

We make ourselves a place apart
    Behind light words that tease and flout,
But oh, the agitated heart
    Till someone find us really out.

Robert Lee Frost

Speech is silvern, silence is golden; speech
is human, silence is divine.

German Proverb

The obvious duty of a toastmaster is to be so
infernally dull that the succeeding speakers
will appear brilliant by contrast.

Clarence Budington Kelland

We seldom repent of speaking little, very
often of speaking too much; a vulgar and
trite maxim, which all the world knows, but
which all the world does not practise.

Jean de La Bruyère

We speak little if not egged on by vanity.

Duc François de La Rochefoucauld

If you your lips would keep from slips,
    Five things observe with care;
To whom you speak, of whom you speak,
    And how, and when, and where.

William Edward Norris

Many public speakers are good extemporaneous listeners.

Edgar Wilson (Bill) Nye

A good speech is a good thing, but the verdict is the thing.

Daniel O'Connell

Speeches cannot be made long enough for
the speakers, nor short enough for the hearers.

James Perry

I sometimes marvel at the extraordinary docility with which Americans submit to
speeches.

Adlai Ewing Stevenson

Speech is a faculty given to man to conceal
his thoughts.

Alexandre de Talleyrand-Périgord

There is a wide difference between speaking to deceive, and being silent to be impenetrable.

Voltaire (François Marie Arouet)

There is but one pleasure in life equal to
that of being called to make an after-dinner
speech, and that is not being called on to
make one.

Charles Dudley Warner

Never rise to speak till you have something
to say; and when you have said it, cease.

John Witherspoon

See also: PUBLIC SPEAKING, TALKING.

SPEECH, FREEDOM OF:
see FREEDOM OF SPEECH.

SPIRIT

A man of a right spirit is not a man of narrow and private views, but is greatly interested and concerned for the good of the community to which he belongs, and particularly of the city or village in which he resides, and for the true welfare of the society of which he is a member.

Jonathan Edwards

The life of the spirit, the veritable life, is intermittent and only the life of the mind is constant.

Antoine de Saint-Exupéry

He that loseth wealth, loseth much; he that loseth friends, loseth more; but he that loseth his spirit loseth all.

Spanish Maxim

High spirit in man is like a sword, which, though worn to annoy his enemies, yet is often troublesome to his friends: he can hardly wear it so inoffensively but it is apt to incommode one or other of the company: it is more properly a loaded pistol, which accident alone may fire and kill one.

William Shenstone

Spirit is now a very fashionable word; to act with spirit, to speak with spirit, means only to act rashly, and to talk indiscreetly. An able man shows his spirit by gentle words and resolute actions; he is neither hot nor timid.

Philip Dormer Stanhope (Lord Chesterfield)

See also: COURAGE, EMOTION, ENERGY, ENTERPRISE, ENTHUSIASM, FEELINGS, LIFE, SOUL, VIVACITY, ZEAL.

SPORTS

There is a need to feel our bodies have a skill and energy of their own, apart from the man-made machines they may drive. There is the desire to find in sport a companionship with kindred people. I have found all these.

Roger Gilbert Bannister

What I admire in the order to which you belong is that they do live in the air; that they excel in athletic sports; that they can only speak one language; and that they never read. This is not a complete education, but it is the highest education since the Greek.

Benjamin Disraeli

Winning is not the main thing, it is the only thing.

Vince Lombardi

When a man wants to murder a tiger he calls it sport: when the tiger wants to murder him he calls it ferocity.

George Bernard Shaw

See also: AUTOMOBILE RACING, BASEBALL, BASKETBALL, BOXING, EXERCISE, FISHING, FOOTBALL, RECREATION.

SPRING

Spring hangs her infant blossoms on the trees,
Rock'd in the cradle of the western breeze.

William Cowper

So then the year is repeating its old story again. We are come once more, thank God! to its most charming chapter. The violets and the May flowers are as its inscriptions or vignettes. It always makes a pleasant impression on us, when we open again at these pages of the book of life.

Johann Wolfgang von Goethe

Now the bright morning-star, Day's harbinger,
Comes dancing from the east, and leads with her
The flowery May, who, from her green lap, throws
The yellow cowslip, and the pale primrose.
Hail, bounteous May, that dost inspire
Mirth and youth, and warm desire!
Woods and groves are of thy dressing;
Hill and dale doth boast thy blessing.
Thus we salute thee with our early song,
And welcome thee and wish thee long.

John Milton

Now fades the last long streak of snow,
Now burgeons every maze of quick
About the flowering squares, and thick
By ashen roots the violets blow.

Alfred, Lord Tennyson

See also: APRIL, AUTUMN, FLOWER, LOVE, NATURE, SUMMER, WINTER.

SPYING

A hallmark of totalitarian societies is that the people are apprehensive of being overheard or spied upon.

American Civil Liberties Union

In cities where wiretapping was known to exist there was generally a sense of insecurity among professional people and people engaged in political life. Prominent persons were consequently afraid to use their telephones despite the fact that they were not engaged in any wrongdoing. It was clear that freedom of communication and the atmosphere of living in a free society without fear were handicapped by the presence of spying ears.

Samuel Dash

The total ultimate impact of all this managerial reliance upon psychologic spies, lie detectors, hidden cameras, undercover agents, bugging, health reports, controls, police dogs, and fingerprinting is appalling to contemplate.

Vance Oakley Packard

Virtually all of the few real American spies who have been caught supplying secrets to the Soviets were elaborately careful to be tight-lipped and to pose as loyal Americans possessing only the most orthodox of opinions.

Vance Oakley Packard

See also: PRIVACY, WIRETAPPING.

STAMMERING

And when you stick on conversation's burs,
Don't strew your pathway with those dreadful *urs.*

Oliver Wendell Holmes

What has influenced my life more than any other single thing has been my stammer. Had I not stammered I would probably . . . have gone to Cambridge as my brothers did, perhaps have become a don and every now and then published a dreary book about French literature.

(William) Somerset Maugham

Demosthenes overcame and rendered more distinct his inarticulate and stammering pronunciation by speaking with peebles in his mouth.

Plutarch

See also: PUBLIC SPEAKING, SPEECH.

STANDARD

If you think of "standardization" as the best that you know today, but which is to be improved tomorrow—you get somewhere.

Henry Ford

Let us raise a standard to which the wise and honest can repair.

George Washington

See also: EFFICIENCY, METHOD, ORDER.

STAR

And you, ye stars,
Who slowly begin to marshal,
As of old, in the fields of heaven,
Your distant, melancholy lines!

Matthew Arnold

Ye stars, that are the poetry of heaven!
George Gordon Byron (Lord Byron)

A star is beautiful; it affords pleasure, not from what it is to do, or to give, but simply by being what it is. It befits the heavens; it has congruity with the mighty space in which it dwells. It has repose; no force distrubs its eternal peace. It has freedom; no obstruction lies between it and infinity.

Thomas Carlyle

When I gaze into the stars, they look down upon me with pity from their serene and silent spaces, like eyes glistening with tears over the little lot of man. Thousands of generations, all as noisy as our own, have been swallowed up by time, and there remains no record of them any more. Yet Arcturus and Orion, Sirius and Pleiades, are still shining in their courses, clear and young, as when the shepherd first noted them in the plain of Shinar!

Thomas Carlyle

These preachers of beauty, which light the world with their admonishing smile.
Ralph Waldo Emerson

Stars in which one no longer believes grow pale.

Heinrich Heine

Let not the dark thee cumber:
What though the moon does slumber?
    The stars of night
    Will lend thee their light
Like tapers clear without number.

Robert Herrick

Bright Star! would I were steadfast as thou
art.

John Keats

Silently one by one, in the infinite meadows
of heaven,
Blossomed the lovely stars, the forget-me-
nots of the angels.

Henry Wadsworth Longfellow

See also: EVENING, NIGHT.

STATE

A state without the means of some change is
without the means of its conservation.

Edmund Burke

If the moral and physical fiber of its manhood and its womanhood is not a state concern, the question is, what is?

Benjamin Nathan Cardozo

In a free country there is much clamor with
little suffering: in a despotic state there is
little complaint but much suffering.

Lazare Hippolyte Carnot

A state to prosper, must be built on foundations of a moral character, and this character
is the principal element of its strength, and
the only guaranty of its permanence and
prosperity.

Jabez Lamar Monroe Curry

People are the roots, the state is the fruit. If
the roots are sweet, the fruits are bound to
be sweet.

Mohandas Karamchand (Mahatma) Gandhi

Submission, therefore, to a state wholly or
largely unjust is an immoral barter for liberty.

Mohandas Karamchand (Mahatma) Gandhi

It is the needs and the initiative of individuals that have made the state, and continue
to make it. This implies that the individual is
prior to the state; it also implies that the
state is prior to the completed individual.
He needs the state to become the person
that he has it in him to become.

William Ernest Hocking

The state ought not to be that great levia-
than before whom the free soul is compelled
to bow down.

Howard Mumford Jones

What constitutes a state? Not high raised
battlement, or labored mound, thick wall, or

moated gate; not cities, proud with spires
and turrets crowned, nor bays and broad-
armed ports, where, laughing at the storm,
rich navies ride, nor starred and spangled
courts. No! men, high-minded men, with
powers as far above all brutes endowed as
beasts excel cold rocks and brambles; men,
who their duties know, but know their
rights, and knowing dare maintain—these
constitute a state.

William Jones of Nayland

The worth of a state, in the long run, is the
worth of the individuals composing it.

John Stuart Mill

The state, it cannot too often be repeated,
does nothing, and can give nothing, which it
does not take from somebody.

William Graham Sumner

One should get rid of suspicion and fear so
unworthy of state authority. The greatest offense of state authority is fear of people who
should not be feared but who should be
loved.

Stefan Wyszynski

See also: GOVERNMENT, NATION, REPUBLIC.

STATESMANSHIP

True statesmanship is the art of changing a
nation from what it is into what it ought to
be.

William Rounseville Alger

Why don't you show us a statesman who can
rise up to the emergency, and cave in the
emergency's head?

Charles Farrar Browne (Artemus Ward)

The great difference between the real
statesman and the pretender is, that the one
sees into the future, while the other regards
only the present; the one lives by the day,
and acts on expediency; the other acts on
enduring principles and for immortality.

Edmund Burke

What morality requires, true statesmanship
should accept.

Edmund Burke

The three great ends for a statesman are, security to possessors, facility to acquirers, and
liberty and hope to the people.

Samuel Taylor Coleridge

It is curious that we pay statesmen for what they say, not for what they do, and judge them from what they do, not from what they say. Hence they have one code of maxims for professions, and another for practice, and make up their consciences as the Neapolitans do their beds, with one set of furniture for show, and another for use.

Charles Caleb Colton

The world is weary of statesmen whom democracy has degraded into politicians.

Benjamin Disraeli

The true genius that conducts a state is he, who doing nothing himself, causes everything to be done; he contrives, he invents, he forsees the future; he reflects on what is past; he distributes and proportions things; he makes early preparations; he incessantly arms himself to struggle against fortune, as a swimmer against a rapid stream of water; he is attentive night and day, that he may leave nothing to chance.

François de Salignac de La Mothe-Fénelon

If I had wished to raise up a race of statesmen higher than politicians, animated not by greed or selfishness, by policy or party, I would familiarize the boys of the land with the characters of the Bible.

John Hall

Honest statesmanship is the wise employment of individual meannesses for the public good.

Abraham Lincoln

The politician says: "I will give you what you want." The statesman says: "What you think you want is this. What it is possible for you to get is that. What you really want, therefore, is the following."

Walter Lippmann

The statesman shears the sheep, the politician skins them.

Austin O'Malley

You can always get the truth from an American statesman after he has turned seventy or given up all hope of the Presidency.

Wendell Phillips

Statesmanship consists sometimes not so much in knowing what to do ultimately as in what to do now.

Adlai Ewing Stevenson

See also: GOVERNMENT, KING, POLITICIAN,

STATES' RIGHTS: *see* RIGHTS.

STATION

The place should not honor the man, but the man the place.

Agesilaus II

Whom the grandeur of his office elevates over other men will soon find that the first hour of his new dignity is the last of his independence.

Henri François d'Aguesseau

Men in great places are thrice servants: servants of the sovereign or state, servants of fame, and servants of business; so as they have no freedom, neither in their persons, in their actions, or in their times.

Francis Bacon

A true man never frets about his place in the world, but just slides into it by the gravitation of his nature, and swings there as easily as a star.

Edwin Hubbel Chapin

Great duties could alone confer great station.

Benjamin Disraeli

Whatever the place allotted us by providence, that is for us the post of honor and duty. God estimates us not by the position we are in, but by the way in which we fill it.

Tryon Edwards

Every man whom chance alone has, by some accident, made a public character, hardly ever fails of becoming, in a short time, a ridiculous private one.

Jean de Gondi (Cardinal de Retz)

Men and statues that are admired in an elevated situation, have a very different effect on us when we approach them; the first appear less than we imagined them, the last bigger.

Fulke Greville (First Baron Brooke)

What people say behind your back is your standing in the community in which you live.

Edgar Watson Howe

Eminent stations make great men more great, and little ones less.

Jean de La Bruyère

How happy the station which every moment furnishes opportunities of doing good to thousands! How dangerous that which every moment exposes to the injuring of millions!

Jean de La Bruyère

It is of great advantage that man should know his station, and not erroneously imagine that the whole universe exists only for him.

Maimonides

Our distinctions do not lie in the places we occupy, but in the grace and dignity with which we fill them.

William Gilmore Simms

See also: OFFICE, PLACE, RANK.

STATISTICS

Statistics are no substitute for judgment.

Henry Clay

There are three kinds of lies; lies, damned lies, and statistics.

Benjamin Disraeli

He uses statistics as a drunken man uses lamp-posts for support rather than illumination.

Andrew Lang

Facts and figures illustrating [economic] progress fly across frontiers like guided missiles directed at people's minds. And, of course, those who lag behind in such progress are the most exposed to this propaganda.

Pierre Mendès-France

There is no portion of our time that is our time, and the rest God's; there is no portion of money that is our money, and the rest God's money. It is all His; He made it all, gives it all, and He has simply trusted it to us for His service. A servant has two purses, the master's and his own, but we have only one.

Adolphe Monod

Statistics are mendacious truths.

Lionel Strachey

See also: ECONOMICS, FACT, MATHEMATICS.

STATUS: see STATION.

STERILIZATION

It is better for all the world, if instead of waiting to execute degenerate offspring for crime, or let them starve for their imbecility, society can prevent those who are manifestly unfit from continuning their kind. The principle that sustains compulsory vaccination is broad enough to cover cutting the Fallopian tubes.

Oliver Wendell Holmes

Regulations in my state of Connecticut permit an administrative board of three, upon a majority vote, to sterilize a person. Under the statute no notice need be given. The prospective victim cannot appeal the order or even demand an opportunity to be heard.

Vance Oakley Packard

See also: ABORTION, BIRTH CONTROL, MORALITY, LIFE, POPULATION.

STOICISM

'Tis pride, rank pride, and haughtiness of soul; I think the Romans call it stoicism.

Joseph Addison

There are two ways of escaping from suffering; the one by rising above the causes of conflict, the other by sinking below them. The one is the religious method; the other is the vulgar, worldly method. The one is Christian elevation; the other is stoicism.

Henry Ward Beecher

To feel for none is the true social art of the world's stoics—men without a heart.

George Gordon Byron (Lord Byron)

See also: ASCETICISM, ENDURANCE, EQUANIMITY, FORTITUDE, INDIFFERENCE, PATIENCE, PHILOSOPHY, RESIGNATION, SELF-CONTROL.

STORYTELLING

A good storyteller is a person who has a good memory and hopes other people haven't.

Irvin Shrewsbury Cobb

No story is the same to us after the lapse of time: or rather we who read it are no longer the same interpreters.

George Eliot (Mary Ann Evans)

But that is another story.

Rudyard Kipling

Stories now, to suit a public taste, must be half epigram, half pleasant vice.

James Russell Lowell

I cannot tell how the truth may be;
I say the tale as it was said to me.

Sir Walter Scott

Story-telling is subject to two unavoidable defects—frequent repetition and being soon exhausted; so that whoever values this gift in himself, has need of a good memory, and ought frequently to shift his company.

Jonathan Swift

See also: ANECDOTE, BALLAD, CONVERSATION, FICTION, LITERATURE, NOVEL, TALKING, WRITING.

STRENGTH

The strongest are those who renounce their own times and become a living part of those yet to come. The strongest, and the rarest.

Milovan Djilas

Strength does not come from physical capacity. It comes from an indomitable will.

Mohandas Karamchand (Mahatma) Gandhi

Strength is born in the deep silence of long-suffering hearts; not amidst joy.

Felicia Dorothea Browne Hemans

Strength, wanting judgment and policy to rule, overturneth itself.

Horace

Strength alone knows conflict; weakness is below even defeat, and is born vanquished.

Anne Sophie Swetchine

See also: ENDURANCE, ENERGY, FORCE, HEALTH, POWER.

STRESS

Don't be afraid to enjoy the stress of a full life nor too naive to think you can do so without some intelligent thinking and planning. Man should not try to avoid stress any more than he would shun food, love or exercise.

Hans Selye

See also: ACCENT, ADVERSITY, NEUROSIS.

STUDENT

Don't despair of a student if he has one clear idea.

Nathaniel Emmons

I hold it to be quite wrong on the part of students and pupils to take part in political demonstrations and party politics. Such fer-

ment interferes with serious study and unfits students for solid work as future citizens.

Mohandas Karamchand (Mahatma) Gandhi

A student has no business to multiply delicacies and luxuries of opinion.

Mohandas Karamchand (Mahatma) Gandhi

A student, no matter how wise or old he is, surrenders when he joins a school or a college, the right of rejecting its discipline.

Mohandas Karamchand (Mahatma) Gandhi

The students' minds must not be caged, nor for that matter those of the teachers.

Mohandas Karamchand (Mahatma) Gandhi

There is an unspeakable pleasure attending the life of a voluntary student.

Oliver Goldsmith

A few books, well studied, and thoroughly digested, nourish the understanding more than hundreds but gargled in the mouth, as ordinary students use.

Francis Osborne

It is a great mistake of many ardent students that they trust too much to their books, and do not draw from their own resources—forgetting that of all sophists our own reason is that which abuses us least.

Jean Jacques Rousseau

See also: EDUCATION, STUDY, UNIVERSITY.

STUDY

Our delight in any particular study, art, or science rises and improves in proportion to the application which we bestow upon it. Thus, what was at first an exercise becomes at length an entertainment.

Joseph Addison

I would live to study, and not study to live.

Francis Bacon

Studies teach not their own use; that is a wisdom without them and above them, won by observation.

Francis Bacon

There are more men ennobled by study than by nature.

Cicero

The understanding is more relieved by change of study than by total inactivity.

William Benton Clulow

He that studies only men, will get the body of knowledge without the soul; and he that studies only books, the soul without the body. He that to what he sees, adds observation, and to what he reads, reflection, is in the right road to knowledge, provided that in scrutinizing the hearts of others, he neglects not his own.

Charles Caleb Colton

Desultory studies are erased from the mind as easily as pencil marks; classified studies are retained like durable ink.

Peter Cooper

The love of study, a passion which derives great vigor from enjoyment, supplies each day, each hour, with a perpetual round of independent and rational pleasure.

Edward Gibbon

Impatience of study is the mental disease of the present generation.

Samuel Johnson

Mankind have a great aversion to intellectual labor, but, even supposing knowledge to be easily attainable, more people would be content to be ignorant than would take even a little trouble to acquire it.

Samuel Johnson

As there is a partiality to opinions, which is apt to mislead the understanding, so there is also a partiality to studies, which is prejudicial to knowledge.

John Locke

There is no study that is not capable of delighting us after a little application to it.

Alexander Pope

Whatever study tends neither directly nor indirectly to make us better men and citizens is at best but a specious and ingenious sort of idleness, and the knowledge we acquire by it only a creditable kind of ignorance, nothing more.

Henry St. John (Lord Bolingbroke)

To the man who studies to gain a thorough insight into science, books and study are merely the steps of the ladder by which he climbs to the summit; as soon as a step has been advanced he leaves it behind. The majority of mankind, however, who study to fill their memory with facts do not use the steps of the ladder to mount upward, but take them off and lay them on their shoulders in order that they may take them along, delighting in the weight of the burden they are carrying. They ever remain below because they carry what should carry them.

Arthur Schopenhauer

If you devote your time to study, you will avoid all the irksomeness of this life, nor will you long for the approach of night, being tired of the day; nor will you be a burden to yourself, nor your society insupportable to others.

Seneca

Shun no toil to make yourself remarkable by some one talent. Yet do not devote yourself to one branch exclusively. Strive to get clear notions about all. Give up no science entirely, for all science is one.

Seneca

The more we study the more we discover our ignorance.

Percy Bysshe Shelley

I study much, and the more I study the oftener I go back to those first principles which are so simple that childhood itself can lisp them.

Anne Sophie Swetchine

His studies were pursued but never effectually overtaken.

Herbert George Wells

See also: BOOK, EDUCATION, INQUIRY, LEARNING, OBSERVATION, READING, SELF-IMPROVEMENT.

STYLE

Style is the gossamer on which the seeds of truth float through the world.

George Bancroft

Word has somehow got around that the split infinitive is always wrong. This is of a piece with the outworn notion that it is always wrong to strike a lady.

Robert Charles Benchley

The least degree of ambiguity, which leaves the mind in suspense as to the meaning, ought to be avoided with the greatest care.

Hugh Blair

Style is a man's own; it is a part of his nature.

Comte Georges Louis Leclerc de Buffon

A man's style in any art should be like his dress—it should attract as little attention as possible.

Samuel Butler

Perspicuity is the frame-work of profound thoughts.

Luc de Clapiers (Marquis de Vauvenargues)

Intense study of the Bible will keep any man from being vulgar in point of style.

Samuel Taylor Coleridge

Words in prose ought to express the intended meaning; if they attract attention to themselves, it is a fault; in the very best styles you read page after page without noticing the medium.

Samuel Taylor Coleridge

If a man really has an idea he can communicate it; and if he has a clear one, he will communicate it clearly.

Nathaniel Emmons

A sentence well couched takes both the sense and the understanding.

Owen Felltham

A man's style is nearly as much a part of himself as his face, or figure, or the throbbing of his pulse; in short, as any part of his being which is subjected to the action of his will.

François de Salignac de La Mothe-Fénelon

Simple style is like white light. It is complex but its complexity is not obvious.

Anatole France

Generally speaking, an author's style is a faithful copy of his mind. If you would write a lucid style, let there first be light in your own mind; and if you would write a grand style, you ought to have a grand character.

Johann Wolfgang von Goethe

Style is a way in which great minds think.

Frank Harris

The lively phraseology of Montesquieu was the result of long meditation. His words, as light as wings, bear on them grave reflections.

Joseph Joubert

If I am ever obscure in my expressions, do not fancy that therefore I am deep. If I were really deep, all the world would understand, though, they might not appreciate. The perfectly popular style is the perfectly scientific one. To me an obscurity is a reason for suspecting a fallacy.

Charles Kingsley

Clear writers, like clear fountains, do not seem so deep as they are; the turbid looks most profound.

Walter Savage Landor

Obscurity and affectation are the two great faults of style. Obscurity of expression generally springs from confusion of ideas; and the same wish to dazzle, at any cost, which produces affectation in the manner of a writer, is likely to produce sophistry in his reasoning.

Thomas Babington Macaulay

A pure style in writing results from the rejection of everything superfluous.

Albertine Adrienne Necker de Saussure

The old prose writers wrote as if they were speaking to an audience; among us, prose is invariably written for the eye alone.

Barthold Georg Niebuhr

When we meet with a natural style we are surprised and delighted, for we expected to find an author, and have found a man.

Blaise Pascal

In what he leaves unsaid I discover a master of style.

Johann Christoph Friedrich von Schiller

Long sentences in a short composition are like large rooms in a little house.

William Shenstone

There is a certain majesty in plainness; as the proclamation of a prince never frisks it in tropes or fine conceits, in numerous and well-turned periods, but commands in sober natural expressions.

Robert South

Style is the dress of thoughts; let them be ever so just, if your style is homely, coarse, and vulgar, they will appear to as much disadvantage, and be as ill received, as your person, though ever so well proportioned, would be if dressed in rags, dirt, and tatters.

Philip Dormer Stanhope (Lord Chesterfield)

Style may be defined, "proper words in proper places."

Jonathan Swift

A great writer possesses, so to speak, an individual and unchangeable style, which does not permit him easily to preserve the anonymous.

Voltaire (François Marie Arouet)

Any style formed in imitation of some model must be affected and straightlaced.

Edwin Percy Whipple

In composing, think much more of your matter than your manner. Spirit, grace, and dignity of manner are of great importance, both to the speaker and writer; but of infinitely more importance are the weight and worth of matter.

William Wirt

See also: ELOQUENCE, FASHION, LANGUAGE, LITERATURE, ORATORY, ORIGINALITY, RHETORIC, SPEECH, WRITING.

SUBLIMITY

One source of sublimity is infinity.

Edmund Burke

The truly sublime is always easy, and always natural.

Edmund Burke

Sublimity is Hebrew by birth.

Samuel Taylor Coleridge

The sublime, when it is introduced at a seasonable moment, has often carried all before it with the rapidity of lightning, and shown at a glance the mighty power of genius.

Longinus

From the sublime to the ridiculous there is but one step.

Napoleon I (Bonaparte)

See also: BEAUTY, EXCELLENCE, GREATNESS.

SUBMISSION

The strength of a man consists in finding out the way God is going, and going in that way too.

Henry Ward Beecher

Submission to God is the only balm that can heal the wounds he gives us.

Nathaniel Emmons

Submission to convention in trivial matters in which there is no danger of deceiving others of oneself is often desirable and even necessary. But submission in matters of religion, especially where there is a positive repugnance from within and a danger of deceiving our neighbours and ourselves, cannot but be debasing.

Mohandas Karamchand (Mahatma) Gandhi

What is readily yielded to courtesy is never yielded to force. Submission to a courteous request is religion, submission to force is irreligion.

Mohandas Karamchand (Mahatma) Gandhi

That is best which God sends; it was his will; it is mine.

Edward R. Bulwer Lytton (Owen Meredith)

Subjection, but requir'd with gentle sway,
And by her yielded, by him best receiv'd
Yielded with coy submission, modest pride,
And sweet reluctant amorous delay.

John Milton

Patience, says another, is an excellent remedy for grief, but submission to the hand of him that sends it is a far better.

Charles Simmons

Men are especially intolerant of serving, and being ruled by, their equals.

Baruch (Benedict) Spinoza

As thou wilt; what thou wilt; when thou wilt.

Thomas à Kempis

God is too great to be withstood, too just to do wrong, too good to delight in any one's misery. We ought, therefore, quietly to submit to his dispensations as the very best.

Daniel Wilson

See also: DOCILITY, HUMILITY, MEEKNESS, OBEDIENCE, PATIENCE, RESIGNATION.

SUBSIDY

A subsidy is a formula for handing you back your own money with a flourish that makes you think it's a gift.

Joel Foote Bingham

See also: CHARITY, FOREIGN AID, GIFT, HELP.

SUBTLETY

Cunning is the dwarf of wisdom.

William Rounseville Alger

Subtlety may deceive you; integrity never will.

Oliver Cromwell

Cunning pays no regard to virtue, and is but the low mimic of wisdom.

> *Henry St. John (Lord Bolingbroke)*

See also: CLEVERNESS, CUNNING.

SUBURBIA: *see* CITY.

SUCCESS

If you wish success in life, make perseverance your bosom friend, experience your wise counselor, caution your elder brother, and hope your guardian genius.

> *Joseph Addison*

The reason some men do not succeed is because their wishbone is where their backbone ought to be.

> *Anonymous*

Our business in life is not to get ahead of other people, but to get ahead of ourselves.

> *Maltbie Davenport Babcock*

Not what men do worthily, but what they do successfully, is what history makes haste to record.

> *Henry Ward Beecher*

Perhaps historians may yet discover that success is just a form of amusement, mostly sacred to those who have not brains enough to attain it.

> *Thomas Beer*

The only infallible criterion of wisdom to vulgar judgments—success.

> *Edmund Burke*

I believe the true road to preeminent success in any line is to make yourself master of that line.

> *Andrew Carnegie*

Put all good eggs in one basket and then watch that basket.

> *Andrew Carnegie*

All you need in this life is ignorance and confidence, and then Success is sure.

> *Samuel Langhorne Clemens (Mark Twain)*

He that would make sure of success should keep his passion cool, and his expectation low.

> *Jeremy Collier*

He that has never known adversity, is but half acquainted with others, or with himself.

Constant success shows us but one side of the world. For, as it surrounds us with friends, who will tell us only our merits, so it silences those enemies from whom alone we can learn our defects.

> *Charles Caleb Colton*

To know a man, observe how he wins his object, rather than how he loses it; for when we fail, our pride supports; when we succeed, it betrays us.

> *Charles Caleb Colton*

The simple virtues of willingness, readiness, alertness and courtesy will carry a young man farther than mere smartness.

> *Henry Pomeroy Davison*

Success has a great tendency to conceal and throw a veil over the evil deeds of men.

> *Demosthenes*

The road to success is filled with women pushing their husbands along.

> *Thomas Robert Dewar*

Success is counted sweetest by those who ne'er succeed.

> *Emily Elizabeth Dickinson*

Success is the child of Audacity.

> *Benjamin Disraeli*

Never one thing and seldom one person can make for a success. It takes a number of them merging into one perfect whole.

> *Marie Dressler*

Nothing succeeds like success.

> *Alexandre Dumas (père)*

Possessions, outward success, publicity, luxury—to me these have always been contemptible. I believe that a simple and unassuming manner of life is best for everyone, best both for the body and the mind.

> *Albert Einstein*

A successful man is he who receives a great deal from his fellowmen, usually incomparably more than corresponds to his service to them. The value of a man, however, should be seen in what he gives and not in what he is able to receive.

> *Albert Einstein*

Success against the odds is the American ideal.

> *Edwin Rogers Embree*

Had I succeeded well, I had been reckoned among the wise; our minds are so disposed to judge from the event.

Euripides

Success is little more than a chemical compound of man with moment.

Philip Guedalla

Somebody said it couldn't be done, but he with a chuckle replied that "maybe it couldn't," but he would be one who wouldn't say so till he'd tried.

Edgar Albert Guest

We do not know, is most cases, how far social failure and success are due to heredity, and how far to environment. But environment is the easier of the two to improve.

John Burdon Sanderson Haldane

Like the British Constitution, she owes her success in practice to her inconsistencies in principle.

Thomas Hardy

Moderation is commonly firm, and firmness is commonly successful.

Samuel Johnson

Success produces confidence; confidence relaxes industry, and negligence ruins the reputation which accuracy had raised.

Ben (Benjamin) Jonson

Success serves men as a pedestal; it makes them look larger, if reflection does not measure them.

Joseph Joubert

The eminently successful man should beware of the tendency of wealth to chill and isolate.

Otto Herman Kahn

We can do anything we want to do if we stick to it long enough.

Helen Adams Keller

Few things are impracticable in themselves, and it is for want of application, rather than of means, that men fail of success.

Duc François de La Rochefoucauld

The man who succeeds above his fellows is the one who, early in life, clearly discerns his object, and towards that object habitually directs his powers. Even genius itself is but fine observation strengthened by fixity of purpose. Every man who observes vigilantly and resolves steadfastly grows unconsciously into genius.

Edward G. Bulwer-Lytton (Baron Lytton)

The greedy search for money or success will almost always lead men into unhappiness. Why? Because that kind of life makes them depend upon things outside themselves.

André Maurois

In the battle for existence, talent is the punch, and tact is the clever footwork.

Wilson Mizner

How shall we pass most swiftly from point to point, and be present always at the focus where the greatest number of vital forces unite in their purest energy? To maintain this ecstasy is success in life.

Walter Horatio Pater

I can give you a six-word formula for success: "Think things through—then follow through."

Edward Vernon (Eddie) Rickenbacker

The most important single ingredient in the formula of success is the knack of getting along with people.

Theodore Roosevelt

I have always observed, that to succeed in the world we must be foolish in appearance, but in reality wise.

Charles de Secondat (Baron de Montesquieu)

In most things success depends on knowing how long it takes to succeed.

Charles de Secondat (Baron de Montesquieu)

The surest way not to fail is to determine to succeed.

Richard Brinsley Sheridan

The flavor of social success is delicious, though it is scorned by those to whose lips the cup has not been proffered.

Logan Pearsall Smith

People judge, for the most part, by the success. Let a man show all the good conduct that is possible, if the event does not answer, ill fortune passes for a fault, and is justified by a very few persons.

Seigneur de Saint-Évremond

Nothing succeeds so well as success.

Alexandre de Talleyrand-Périgord

The successful businessman must be able to foresee possibilities, to estimate with sagacity the outcome in the future.

Frank William Taussig

It is success that colors all in life: success makes fools admired, makes villains honest: all the proud virtue of this vaunting world fawns on success and power, howe'er acquired.

James Thomson

Mere success is one of the worst arguments in the world of a good cause, and the most improper to satisfy conscience: and yet in the issue it is the most successful of all other arguments, and does in a very odd, but effectual, way, satisfy the consciences of a great many men, by showing them their interest.

John Tillotson

In history as in life it is success that counts. Start a political upheaval and let yourself be caught, and you will hang as a traitor. But place yourself at the head of a rebellion and gain your point, and all future generations will worship you as the Father of their Country.

Hendrik Willem van Loon

I have learned that success is to be measured not so much by the position that one has reached in life as by the obstacles which he has overcome while trying to succeed.

Booker Taliaferro Washington

Life has a way of overgrowing its achievements as well as its ruins.

Edith Newbold Jones Wharton

There is no moment when a man so surely has the world by the tail as when he strolls down the midway swinging a prize cane.

Elwyn Brooks White

Nothing recedes like success.

Walter Winchell

See also: FAME, POSITION, POWER, PROSPERITY, VICTORY, WEALTH.

SUFFERING

Night brings out stars, as sorrow shows us truths.

Gamaliel Bailey

God washes the eyes by tears until they can behold the invisible land where tears shall come no more.

Henry Ward Beecher

To be born is to suffer: to grow old is to suffer: to die is to suffer: to lose what is loved is to suffer: to be tied to what is not loved is to suffer: to endure what is distasteful is to suffer. In short, all the results of individuality, of separate self-hood, necessarily involve pain or suffering.

Subhadra Bhikshu

Suffering without understanding in this life is a heap worse than suffering when you have at least the grain of an idea what it's all for.

Mary Ellen Chase

The salvation of the world is in man's suffering.

William Faulkner

The appeal of reason is more to the head but the penetration of the heart comes from suffering. It opens up the inner understanding in man.

Mohandas Karamchand (Mahatma) Gandhi

Suffering is the badge of the human race, not the sword.

Mohandas Karamchand (Mahatma) Gandhi

Suffering is the law of human beings, war is the law of the jungle. But suffering is infinitely more powerful than the law of the jungle for converting the opponent and opening his ears, which are otherwise shut to the voice of reason.

Mohandas Karamchand (Mahatma) Gandhi

We always have to choose between suffering our own pain or suffering other people's. We can't *not* suffer.

Graham Greene

We need to suffer that we may learn to pity.

Letitia Elizabeth Landon

Know how sublime a thing it is to suffer and be strong.

Henry Wadsworth Longfellow

It is a glorious thing to be indifferent to suffering, but only to one's own suffering.

Robert Lynd

We are healed of a suffering only by experiencing it to the full.

Marcel Proust

To love all mankind a cheerful state of being is required; but to see into mankind, into life, and still more into ourselves, suffering is requisite.

Jean Paul Richter

Suffering is the surest means of making us truthful to ourselves.

Jean Charles Léonard de Sismondi

Humanity either makes, or breeds, or tolerates all its afflictions, great or small.

Herbert George Wells

See also: ADVERSITY, GRIEF, MISERY, PAIN.

SUICIDE

There are some vile and contemptible men who, allowing themselves to be conquered by misfortune, seek a refuge in death.

Agathon

To die in order to avoid anything that is evil and disagreeable, is not the part of a brave man, but of a coward; for it is cowardice to shun the trials and crosses of life, not undergoing death because it is honorable, but to avoid evil.

Aristotle

Suicide sometimes proceeds from cowardice, but not always; for cowardice sometimes prevents it; since as many live because they are afraid to die, as die because they are afraid to live.

Charles Caleb Colton

The miserablest day we live there is many a better thing to do than die.

George Darley

The will to live is not irrational. It is also natural. Attachment to life is not a delusion. It is very real. Above all, life has a purpose. To seek to defeat that purpose is a sin. Therefore suicide is very rightly held to be a sin.

Mohandas Karamchand (Mahatma) Gandhi

O deaf to nature and to Heaven's command, Against thyself to lift the murdering hand! Oh, damned despair, to shun the living light, And plunge thy guilty soul in endless night!

Lucretius

When all the blandishments of life are gone the coward sneaks to death; the brave lives on.

Martial

He is not valiant that dares to die; but he that boldly bears calamity.

Philip Massinger

Men would not be so hasty to abandon the world either as monks or as suicides, did they but see the jewels of wisdom and faith which are scattered so plentifully along its paths; and lacking which no soul can come again from beyond the grave to gather.

William Mountford

Suicide is a crime the most revolting to the feelings; nor does any reason suggest itself to our understanding by which it can be justified. It certainly originates in that species of fear which we denominate poltroonery. For what claim can that man have to courage who trembles at the frowns of fortunes? True heroism consists in being superior to the ills of life in whatever shape they may challenge him to combat.

Napoleon I (Bonaparte)

Suicide is extraordinarly rare among Jews.

William Zebina Ripley

Suicides are weak-minded, and are overcome by external causes repugnant to their nature.

Baruch (Benedict) Spinoza

When we have lost everything, when we have no more hope, life is a disgrace, and death a duty.

Voltaire (François Marie Arouet)

See also: DEATH, DESPAIR, DEPRESSION, MENTAL HEALTH, MURDER.

SUMMER

Sumer is icumen in.
Lhude sing cuccu!
Groweth sed, and bloweth med,
And springeth the wude nu—
Sing cuccu!

Anonymous

All the live murmur of a summer's day.

Matthew Arnold

One swallow alone does not make the summer.

Miguel de Cervantes Saavedra

Where'er you walk cool gales shall fan the glade,
Trees where you sit shall crowd into a shade.
Where'er you tread the blushing flowers shall rise,
And all things flourish where you turn your eyes.

Alexander Pope

See also: AUTUMN, SPRING, WINTER.

SUN

The sun does not shine for a few trees and flowers but for the wide world's joy. So God sits, effulgent, in heaven, not for a favored few, but for the universe of life, and there is no creature so poor or low that he may not look up with childlike confidence, and say, "My father! thou art mine."

Henry Ward Beecher

Thou earliest minister of the Almighty, who chose thee for his shadow; thou chief star, centre of many stars, thou dost rise, and shine, and set in glory!

George Gordon Byron (Lord Byron)

In the warm shadow of her loveliness;
He kissed her with his beams.

Percy Bysshe Shelley

Fairest of all the lights above,
Thou sun, whose beams adorn the spheres,
And with unwearied swiftness move,
To form the circles of our years.

Isaac Watts

See also: DAY, LIGHT, SUNRISE, SUNSET.

SUNDAY: see SABBATH.

SUNRISE

Day!
Faster and more fast,
O'er night's brim, day boils at last;
Boils, pure gold, o'er the cloud-cup's brim
Where spurting and suppress'd it lay
For not a froth-flake touched the rim
Of yonder gap in the solid gray
Of the eastern cloud, and hour away;
But forth one wavelet, then another, curled,
Till the whole sunrise, not to be supprest,
Rose, reddened, and its seething breast
Flickered in bounds, grew gold, then
    overflowed the world.

Robert Browning

Wake! For the sun who scatter'd into flight
The stars before him from the field of night,
    Drives night along with them from heav'n,
    and strikes
The sultan's turret with a shaft of light.

Omar Khayyám

But yonder comes the powerful King of
    Day,
Rejoicing in the East.

James Thomson

See also: DAY, LIGHT, MORNING, SUN.

SUNSET

The death-bed of a day how beautiful!

Gamaliel Bailey

Behold him setting in his western skies,
The shadows lengthening as the vapours
    rise.

John Dryden

Sunsets in themselves are generally superior to sunrises; and with the sunset we appreciate images drawn from departed peace, and faded glory.

George Stillman Hillard

Softly the evening came. The sun from the
    western horizon
Like a magician extended his golden wand
    o'er the landscape;
Twinkling vapors arose; and sky and water
    and forest
Seemed all on fire at the touch, and melted
    and mingled together.

Henry Wadsworth Longfellow

See also: EVENING, NIGHT, SUN, TWILIGHT.

SUPERFLUITY

There are, while human miseries abound a thousand ways to waste superfluous wealth, without one fool or flatterer at your board, without one hour of sickness or disgust.

John Armstrong

Wherever desirable superfluities are imported, industry is excited, and thereby plenty is produced. Were only necessaries permitted to be purchased, men would work no more than was necessary for that purpose.

Benjamin Franklin

Manage as we may, misery and suffering will always cleave to the border of superfluity.

Friedrich Heinrich Jacobi

What man in his right senses, that has wherewithal to live free, would make himself a slave for superfluities? What does that man want who has enough? Or what is he the better for abundance that can never be satisfied?

Sir Roger L'Estrange

Were the superfluities of a nation valued, and made a perpetual tax or benevolence, there would be more almshouses than poor, more schools than scholars, and enough to spare for government beside.

William Penn

He who accustoms himself to buy superfluities, may be obliged, ere long, to sell his necessities.

Charles Simmons

Our superfluities should give way to our brother's conveniences, and our conveniences, to our brother's necessities; yea, even our necessities should give way to their extremity for the supplying of them.

Ralph Venning

The superfluous, a thing highly necessary.
Voltaire (François Marie Arouet)

See also: EXPENSE, EXTRAVAGANCE, LUXURY, RICH AND POOR, RICHES, WEALTH.

SUPERIORITY

Almost every man you meet feels himself superior to you in some way; and a sure way to his heart is to let him realize that you recognize his importance.

Dale Carnegie

It is difficult to be convinced of one's superiority unless one can make the inferior suffer in some obvious way.

Max Radin

It is a great art to be superior to others without letting them know it.
Henry Wheeler Shaw (Josh Billings)

See also: EXCELLENCE, PERFECTION.

SUPERSTITION

As it addeth deformity to an ape to be so like a man, so the similitude of superstition to religion makes it the more deformed.

Francis Bacon

The master of superstition is the people, and in all superstition wise men follow fools.

Francis Bacon

There is a superstition in avoiding superstition, when men think they do best if they go farthest from the superstition,—by which means they often take away the good as well as the bad.

Francis Bacon

Superstition is the religion of feeble minds.
Edmund Burke

Superstition is a senseless fear of God; religion the intelligent and pious worship of the deity.

Cicero

Superstitions are, for the most part, but the shadows of great truths.

Tryon Edwards

Superstition renders a man a fool, and scepticism makes him mad.

Henry Fielding

Superstition is the poetry of life. It is inherent in man's nature; and when we think it is wholly eradicated, it takes refuge in the strangest holes and corners, whence it peeps out all at once, as soon as it can do it with safety.

Johann Wolfgang von Goethe

We are all tattooed in our cradles with the beliefs of our tribe; the record may seem superficial, but it is indelible. You cannot educate a man wholly out of the superstitious fears which were implanted in his imagination, no matter how utterly his reason may reject them.

Oliver Wendell Holmes

That the corruption of the best thing produces the worst, is grown into a maxim, and is commonly proved, among other instances, by the pernicious effects of superstition and enthusiasm, the corruptions of true religion.

David Hume

Weakness, fear, melancholy, together with ignorance, are the true souces of superstition. Hope, pride, presumption, a warm indignation, together with ignorance, are the true sources of enthusiasm.

David Hume

Superstition is the only religion of which base souls are capable.

Joseph Joubert

Liberal minds are open to conviction. Liberal doctrines are capable of improvement. There are proselytes from atheism; but none from superstition.

Junius

Superstition always inspires bitterness; religion, grandeur of mind. The superstitious man raises beings inferior to himself to deities.

Johann Kaspar Lavater

I think we cannot too strongly attack superstition, which is the disturber of society; nor too highly respect genuine religion, which is the support of it.

Jean Jacques Rousseau

There is nothing people will not maintain when they are slaves to superstition; and candour and a sense of justice are, in such a case, the first things lost.

George Santayana

Religion worships God, while superstition profanes that worship.

Seneca

By superstitions I mean all hypocritical arts of appeasing God and procuring his favor without obeying his laws, or reforming our sins: infinite such superstitions have been invented by heathens, by Jews, by Christians themselves, especially by the Church of Rome, which abounds with them.

Thomas Sherlock

How blest would our age be if it could witness a religion freed from all the trammels of superstition!

Baruch (Benedict) Spinoza

Superstition is not, as has been defined, an excess of religious feeling, but a misdirection of it, an exhausting of it on vanities of man's devising.

Richard Whately

See also: CREDULITY, FEAR, IGNORANCE.

SUPREME COURT: *see* COURT.

SUSPENSE

Decision destroys suspense, and suspense is the charm of existence.

Benjamin Disraeli

The suspense—the fearful, acute suspense, of standing idly by while the life of one we dearly love is trembling in the balance; the racking thoughts that crowd upon the mind, and make the heart beat violently, and the breath come thick; the desperate anxiety "to be doing something" to relieve the pain or lessen the danger which we have no power to alleviate; and the sinking of soul which the sad sense of our helplessness produces, —what tortures can equal these, and what reflections or efforts can, in the full tide and fever of the time, allay them.

Charles John Huffam Dickens

But not long; for in the tedious minutes' exquisite interval I'm on the rack; for sure the greatest evil man can know bears no proportion to this dread suspense.

James Anthony Froude

Of all the conditions to which the heart is subject, suspense is one that most gnaws and cankers into the frame. One little month of suspense, when it involves death, we are told by an eye-witness, is sufficient to plough fixed lines and furrows in a convict of five-and-twenty,—sufficient to dash the brown hair with gray, and to bleach the gray to white.

Edward G. Bulwer-Lytton (Baron Lytton)

Uncertainty! fell demon of our fears! The human soul that can support despair, supports not thee.

David Mallet

It is a miserable thing to live in suspense: it is the life of a spider.

Jonathan Swift

See also: ANTICIPATION, EXPECTATION, FEAR, MYSTERY, UNCERTAINTY.

SUSPICION

Ignorance is the mother of suspicion.

William Rounseville Alger

Suspicion is the poison of true friendship.

Augustine of Hippo

Suspicions amongst thoughts are like the bats amongst birds, they ever fly by twilight: certainly they are to be repressed, or at least well guarded, for they cloud the mind, lose friends, check business, dispose kings to tyranny, husbands to jealousy, and wise men to irresolution and melancholy; they are defects, not in the heart, but in the brain.

Francis Bacon

There is nothing makes a man suspect much, more than to know little, and therefore men should remedy suspicion by procuring to know more, and not keep their suspicions in smother.

Francis Bacon

Don't seem to be on the lookout for crows, else you'll set other people watching.

George Eliot (Mary Ann Evans)

The cankers of suspicion cannot be cured by arguments or explanations.

Mohandas Karamchand (Mahatma) Gandhi

I believe in trusting. Trust begets trust. Suspicion is foiled and only stinks. He who trusts has never yet lost in the world. A suspicious man is lost to himself and the world. Let those who have made of nonviolence a creed beware of suspecting opponents. Suspicion is the brood of violence. Non-violence cannot but trust. I must, at any rate, refuse to believe anything against anybody, much less against my honoured fellow worker, unless I have absolute proof.

Mohandas Karamchand (Mahatma) Gandhi

The virtue of a coward is suspicion.

George Herbert

Undue suspicion is more abject baseness even than the guilt suspected.

Aaron Hill

Suspicion is no less an enemy to virtue than to happiness. He that is already corrupt is naturally suspicious, and he that becomes suspicious will quickly be corrupt.

Samuel Johnson

The less we know the more we suspect.

Henry Wheeler Shaw (Josh Billings)

Open suspecting of others comes of secretly condemning ourselves.

Sir Philip Sidney

Discreet and well-founded suspicion avoids a multitude of evils, which credulity brings upon itself. We ought always to be suspicious enough to avoid all improper and forbidden trust in man, or in our own hearts.

Charles Simmons

It is hardly possible to suspect another without having in one's self the seeds of the baseness the other is accused of.

Stanislaus I (Leszczyński)

There is no rule more invariable than that we are paid for our suspicions by finding what we suspect.

Henry David Thoreau

To be suspicious is to invite treachery.

Voltaire (François Marie Arouet)

He that lives in perpetual suspicion lives the life of a sentinel never relieved, whose business it is to look out for and expect an enemy, which is an evil not very far short of perishing by him.

Edward Young

See also: DISTRUST, DOUBT, UNCERTAINTY.

SYMPATHY

Sympathy wanting, all is wanting. Personal magnetism is the conductor of the sacred spark that puts us in human communion, and gives us to company, conversation, and ourselves.

Amos Bronson Alcott

Can I see another's woe,
And not be in sorrow too?
Can I see another's grief
And not seek for kind relief?

William Blake

Next to love, sympathy is the divinest passion of the human heart.

Edmund Burke

Public feeling now is apt to side with the persecuted, and our modern martyr is full as likely to be smothered with roses as with coals.

Edwin Hubbel Chapin

All sympathy not consistent with acknowledged virtue is but disguised selfishness.

Samuel Taylor Coleridge

He that sympathizes in all the happiness of others, perhaps himself enjoys the safest happiness; and he that is warned by the folly of others has perhaps attained the soundest wisdom.

Charles Caleb Colton

No radiant pearl, which crested fortune wears,
No gem, that twinkling hangs from beauty's ears;
Not the bright stars, which night's blue arch adorn;
Nor rising sun, that gilds the vernal morn;
Shine with such lustre as the tear that flows
Down virtue's manly cheek for other's woes.

Charles Robert Darwin

To rejoice in another's prosperity, is to give content to your own lot; to mitigate another's grief, is to alleviate or dispel your own.

Tryon Edwards

More helpful than all wisdom or counsel is one draught of simple human pity that will not forsake us.

George Eliot (Mary Ann Evans)

The only true knowledge of our fellowman is that which enables us to feel with him—which gives us a fine ear for the heart-pulses that are beating under the mere clothes of circumstance and opinion.

George Eliot (Mary Ann Evans)

Our sympathy is cold to the relation of distant misery.

Edward Gibbon

The capacity of sorrow belongs to our grandeur, and the loftiest of our race are those who have had the profoundest sympathies, because they have had the profoundest sorrows.

Henry Giles

It is certain my belief gains quite infinitely the very moment I can convince another mind thereof.

Baron Friedrich von Hardenberg (Novalis)

Shame on those hearts of stone, that cannot melt in soft adoption of another's sorrow!

Aaron Hill

A sympathizer is a fellow that's for you as long as it doesn't cost anything.

Frank McKinney (Kin) Hubbard

It is an eternal truth in the political as well as the mystical body, that "where one member suffers, all the members suffer with it."

Junius

One of the greatest of all mental pleasures is to have our thoughts often divined; ever entered into with sympathy.

Letitia Elizabeth Landon

Our sympathy is never very deep unless founded on our own feelings. We pity, but do not enter into the grief which we have never felt.

Letitia Elizabeth Landon

The more sympathies we gain or awaken for what is beautiful, by so much deeper will be our sympathy for that which is most beautiful, the human soul.

James Russell Lowell

It may, indeed, be said that sympathy exists in all minds, as Faraday has discovered that magnetism exists in all metals; but a certain temperature is required to develop the hidden property, whether in the metal or the mind.

Edward G. Bulwer-Lytton (Baron Lytton)

To commiserate is sometimes more than to give, for money is external to a man's self, but he who bestows compassion communicates his own soul.

William Mountford

Humanitarianism needs no apology. . . . Unless we . . . feel it toward all men without exception, we shall have lost the chief redeeming force in human history.

Ralph Barton Perry

It is a lively spark of nobleness to descend in most favor to one when he is lowest in affliction.

Sir Philip Sidney

There is a kind of sympathy in souls that fits them for each other; and we may be assured when we see two persons engaged in the warmths of a mutual affection, that there are certain qualities in both their minds which bear a resemblance to one another.

Sir Richard Steele

The world has no sympathy with any but positive griefs; it will pity you for what you lose, but never for what you lack.

Anne Sophie Swetchine

Sympathy is the first great lesson which man should learn. It will be ill for him if he proceeds no farther; if his emotions are but excited to roll back on his heart, and to be fostered in luxurious quiet. But unless he learns to feel for things in which he has no personal interest, he can achieve nothing generous or noble.

Sir Thomas Noon Talfourd

Every man rejoices twice when he has a partner of his joy; a friend shares my sorrow and makes it but a moiety, but he swells my joy and makes it double.

Jeremy Taylor

See also: COMPASSION, CONSOLATION, PITY.

T

TACT

Women and foxes, being weak, are distinguished by superior tact.

Ambrose Gwinnett Bierce

Tact consists in knowing how far we may go too far.

Jean Cocteau

Never join with your friend when he abuses his horse or his wife, unless the one is to be sold, and the other to be buried.

Charles Caleb Colton

Difficulties melt away under tact.

Benjamin Disraeli

A want of tact is worse than a want of virtue.

Benjamin Disraeli

A tact which surpassed the tact of her sex as much as the tact of her sex surpasses the tact of ours.

Thomas Babington Macaulay

It's not what you say, but how you say it that makes all the difference in human relationships.

Hughes Mearns

Some people mistake weakness for tact. If they are silent when they ought to speak and so feign an agreement they do not feel, they call it being tactful. Cowardice would be a much better name. Tact is an active quality that is not exercised by merely making a dash for cover. Be sure, when you think you are being extremely tactful, that you are not in reality running away from something you ought to face.

Sir Frank Medlicott

See also: DELICACY, DIPLOMACY, DISCRETION, MANNERS, SENSE, SENSIBILITY.

TALENT

Talent is like a faucet; while it is open, one must write. Inspiration is a farce that poets have invented to give themselves importance.

Jean Anouilh

The toughest thing about success is that you've got to keep on being a success. Talent is only a starting point in this business. You've got to keep on working that talent. Someday I'll reach for it and it won't be there.

Irving Berlin

Talent, lying in the understanding, is often inherited; genius, being the action of reason or imagination, rarely or never.

Samuel Taylor Coleridge

Talent for talent's sake is a bauble and a show. Talent working with joy in the cause of universal truth lifts the possessor to new power as a benefactor.

Ralph Waldo Emerson

Talent is the capacity of doing anything that depends on application and industry; it is a voluntary power, while genius is involuntary.

William Hazlitt

Talent is like money: you don't have to have some to talk about it.

Jules Renard

Talent is something, but tact is everything. Talent is serious, sober, grave, and respectable; tact is all that, and more too. It is not a seventh sense, but is the life of all the five. It is the open eye, the quick ear, the judging taste, the keen smell, and the lively touch; it is the interpreter of all riddles, the surmounter of all difficulties, the remover of all obstacles.

William Pitt Scargill

Here is how I define talent: a gift which God has presented to us secretly, and which we reveal without perceiving it.

Charles de Secondat (Baron de Montesquieu)

Talent is a cistern; genius a fountain.

Edwin Percy Whipple

If a man has a talent and cannot use it, he has failed. If he has a talent and uses only half of it, he has partly failed. If he has a talent and learns somehow to use the whole of it, he has gloriously succeeded, and won a satisfaction and a triumph few men ever know.

Thomas Clayton Wolfe

See also: ABILITY, EFFICIENCY, GENIUS.

TALKATIVENESS: *see* LOQUACITY.

TALKING

It has been said in praise of some men, that they could talk whole hours together upon anything; but it must be owned to the honor of the other sex, that there are many among them who can talk whole hours together upon nothing.

Joseph Addison

It has been well observed, that the tongue discovers the state of the mind no less than that of the body; but, in either case, before the philosopher or the physician can judge, the patient must open his mouth.

Charles Caleb Colton

I know a lady that loves talking so incessantly, she won't give an echo fair play; she has that everlasting rotation of tongue that an echo must wait till she dies, before it can catch her last words!

William Congreve

They think too little who talk too much.

John Dryden

If men who did things talked half as much as men who know how things ought to be done, life would not be worth living.

Edward VIII (Duke of Windsor)

A civil guest will no more talk all, than eat all the feast.

George Herbert

When I think of talking, it is of course with a woman. For talking at its best being an inspiration, it wants a corresponding divine quality of receptiveness, and where will you find this but in a woman?

Oliver Wendell Holmes

No man would listen to you talk if he didn't know it was his turn next.

Edgar Watson (Ed) Howe

Every time I read where some woman gave a short talk I wonder how she stopped.

Frank McKinney (Kin) Hubbard

The silent bear no witness against themselves.

Aldous Leonard Huxley

The man who talks everlastingly and promiscuously, and who seems to have an exhaustless magazine of sound, crowds so many words into his thoughts, that he always obscures, and very frequently conceals them.

Washington Irving

A man should be careful never to tell tales of himself to his own disadvantage; people may be amused, and laugh at the time, but they will be remembered, and brought up against him upon some subsequent occasion.

Samuel Johnson

The lover and physician are both popular from the same cause. We talk to them only of ourselves. That, I daresay, was the origin of confession—egotism under the name of religion.

Letitia Elizabeth Landon

We often say things because we can say them well, rather than because they are sound and reasonable.

Walter Savage Landor

As it is the characteristic of great wits to say much in few words, so it is of small wits to talk much and say nothing.

Duc François de La Rochefoucauld

Women can give you an exact and circumstantial account of some quite insignificant conversation with a friend years before; and what is worse, they do.

(William) Somerset Maugham

There is only one rule for being a good talker: learn to listen.

Christopher Darlington Morley

As empty vessels make the loudest sound, so they that have least wit are the greatest babblers.

Plato

The talkative listen to no one, for they are ever speaking. And the first evil that attends those who know not how to be silent, is, that they hear nothing.

Plutarch

Talkative people who wish to be loved are hated; when they desire to please, they bore; when they think they are admired, they are laughed at; they injure their friends, benefit their enemies, and ruin themselves.

Plutarch

One learns taciturnity best among those who have none, and loquacity among the taciturn.

Jean Paul Richter

I have always had a great respect for a Philippine proverb; "Into the closed mouth the fly does not get."

Theodore Roosevelt, Jr.

I am most fond of talking and thinking; that is to say, talking first and thinking afterward.

Sir Osbert Sitwell

There is the same difference between the tongues of some, as between the hour and the minute hand; one goes ten times as fast, and the other signifies ten times as much.

Sydney Smith

Such as thy words are, such will thy affections be esteemed; and such will thy deeds as thy affections, and such thy life as thy deeds.

Socrates

The tongue of a fool is the key of his counsel, which, in a wise man, wisdom hath in keeping.

Socrates

Cautiously avoid speaking of the domestic affairs either of yourself, or of other people. Yours are nothing to them but tedious gossip; and theirs are nothing to you.

Philip Dormer Stanhope (Lord Chesterfield)

Brisk talkers are usually slow thinkers. There is, indeed, no wild beast more to be dreaded than a communicative man having nothing to communicate. If you are civil to the

voluble they will abuse your patience; if brusque, your character.

Jonathan Swift

See also: ARGUMENT, BABBLE, CONTROVERSY, CONVERSATION, DISCUSSION, ELOQUENCE, GOSSIP, LANGUAGE, LOQUACITY, ORATORY, REPARTEE, RHETORIC, SPEECH, TATTLING, TONGUE.

TASTE

I think I may define taste to be that faculty of the soul which discerns the beauties of an author with pleasure, and the imperfections with dislike.

Joseph Addison

Good taste is better than bad taste, but bad taste is better than no taste.

(Enoch) Arnold Bennett

Bad taste is a species of bad morals.

Christian Nestell Bovee

It is for the most part in our skill in manners, and in the observances of time and place and of decency in general, that what is called taste consists; and which is in reality no other than a more refined judgment. The cause of a wrong taste is a defect of judgment.

Edmund Burke

People care more about being thought to have taste than about being thought either good, clever, or amiable.

Samuel Butler

Taste, if it mean anything but a paltry connoisseurship, must mean a general susceptibility to truth and nobleness, a sense to discern, and a heart to love and reverence all beauty, order, goodness, wheresoever, or in whatsoever forms and accompaniments, they are to be seen. This surely implies, as its chief condition, a finely-gifted mind, purified into harmony with itself, into keenness and justness of vision; above all, kindled into love and generous admiration.

Thomas Carlyle

A truly elegant taste is generally accompanied with excellency of heart.

Henry Fielding

A man who wants to control his animal passions easily does so if he controls his palate.

Mohandas Karamchand (Mahatma) Gandhi

One should eat not in order to please the palate, but just to keep the body going. When each organ of sense subserves the body and through the body the soul, its special relish disappears and then alone does it begin to function in the way nature intended it to do.

    Mohandas Karamchand (Mahatma) Gandhi

Passion in man is generally co-existent with a hankering after the pleasures of the palate.

    Mohandas Karamchand (Mahatma) Gandhi

May not taste be compared to that exquisite sense of the bee, which instantly discovers and extracts the quintessence of every flower, and disregards all the rest of it?

    Fulke Greville (First Baron Brooke)

Delicacy of taste is favorable to love and friendship, by confining our choice to few people, and making us indifferent to the company and conversation of the greater part of men.

    David Hume

Taste may change, our inclinations never change.

    Duc François de La Rochefoucauld

Talk what you will of taste, you will find two of a face as soon as two of a mind.

    Alexander Pope

An aptitude for discovering certain merits goes hand in hand with an inability to respond to certain others. Inequity is necessary in creative taste.

    Jean Rostand

Submission to good taste is often facilitated by an absence of personal taste.

    Jean Rostand

Taste is, so to speak, the microscope of the judgment.

    Jean Jacques Rousseau

A fastidious taste is like a squeamish appetite; the one has its origin in some disease of the mind, as the other has in some ailment of the stomach.

    Robert Southey

See also: APPRECIATION, ARTIST, CULTIVATION, DISCERNMENT, JUDGMENT, PERCEPTION, REFINEMENT, STYLE.

TATTLING

The tongue is the worst part of a bad servant.

    Juvenal

The excessive pleasure we feel in talking of ourselves, ought to make us apprehensive that we afford little to our hearers.

    Duc François de La Rochefoucauld

Timely blossom, infant fair,
Fondling of a happy pair,
Every morn, and every night,
Their solicitous delight,
Sleeping, waking, still at ease,
Pleasing without skill to please.
Little gossip, blithe and hale,
Tattling many a broken tale.

    Ambrose Philips

I have ever heard it said that spies and tale-bearers have done more mischief in this world than poisoned bowl or the assassin's dagger.

    Johann Christoph Friedrich von Schiller

See also: BABBLE, GOSSIP, TONGUE.

TAX

Neither will it be, that a people overlaid with taxes should ever become valiant and martial.

    Francis Bacon

Taxing is an easy business. Any projector can contrive new impositions; any bungler can add to the old; but is it altogether wise to have no other bounds to your impositions than the patience of those who are to bear them?

    Edmund Burke

There is one difference between a tax collector and a taxidermist—the taxidermist leaves the hide.

    Mortimer Maxwell Caplin

Taxes are the sinews of the state.

    Cicero

What a benefit would the government render to itself, and to every city, village, and hamlet in the States, if it would tax whiskey and rum almost to the point of prohibition! Was it Bonaparte who said that he found vices very good patriots? "He got five millions from the love of brandy, and he should be glad to know which of the virtues would pay him as much." Tobacco and opium have broad backs, and will cheerfully carry the load of armies, if you choose to make them pay high for such joy as they give, and such harm as they do.

Ralph Waldo Emerson

The taxes are indeed very heavy, and if those laid by the government were the only ones we had to pay, we might more easily discharge them; but we have many others, and much more grievous to some of us. We are taxed twice as much by our idleness, three times as much by our pride, and four times as much by our folly; and from these taxes the commissioners cannot ease or deliver us by allowing an abatement.

Benjamin Franklin

Anyone may so arrange his affairs that his taxes shall be as low as possible: he is not bound to choose that pattern which best pays the Treasury. Everyone does it, rich and poor alike, and all do right; for nobody owes any public duty to pay more than the law demands.

Learned Hand

Taxes are the price we pay for civilized society.

Oliver Wendell Holmes, Jr.

Thinking is one thing no one has ever been able to tax.

Charles Franklin Kettering

In levying taxes and in shearing sheep it is well to stop when you get down to the skin.

Austin O'Malley

Millions for defence; not a cent for tribute.

Charles Cotesworth Pinckney

Taxation under every form presents but a choice of evils.

David Ricardo

The income tax has made more liars out of the American people than gold has.

Will (William Penn Adair) Rogers

As the general rule in constitutional states liberty is a compensation for the heaviness of taxation, and in despotic states the equivalent for liberty is the lightness of taxation.

Charles de Secondat (Baron de Montesquieu)

The thing generally raised on city land is taxes.

Charles Dudley Warner

See also: GOVERNMENT, MONEY, WEALTH.

TEACHER

A teacher affects eternity; he can never tell where his influence stops.

Henry Brooks Adams

The best teachers are those who make the fewest pretensions.

Mortimer Jerome Adler

I am indebted to my father for living, but to my teacher for living well.

Alexander III of Macedonia

A teacher who is not dogmatic is simply a teacher who is not teaching.

Gilbert Keith Chesterton

Educators should be chosen not merely for their special qualifications, but more for their personality and their character, because we teach more by what we are than by what we teach.

Will (William James) Durant

All your scholarship, all your study of the scriptures will be in vain if you fail to translate their teachings into your daily life.

Mohandas Karamchand (Mahatma) Gandhi

I have always felt that the true text book for the pupil is his teacher.

Mohandas Karamchand (Mahatma) Gandhi

An imperfect teacher may be tolerable in mundane matters, but not in spiritual matters.

Mohandas Karamchand (Mahatma) Gandhi

It is for teachers to make attractive and intelligible what to the pupils may at first appear repulsive or uninteresting.

Mohandas Karamchand (Mahatma) Gandhi

During the Middle Ages Europe was far too much influenced by celibate men. Today much too big a part in public life is played by celibate women, and too little by mothers. I find no new ideas more genuinely disgusting than that held by many educated authorities that a woman ceases to be suitable as a teacher when she becomes a mother.

John Burdon Sanderson Haldane

Teachers should be held in the highest honor. They are the allies of legislators; they have agency in the prevention of crime; they aid in regulating the atmosphere, whose incessant action and pressure cause the life-blood to circulate, and to return pure and healthful to the heart of the nation.

Lydia Howard Sigourney

No one can be a genuine teacher unless he is himself actively sharing in the human attempt to understand men and their world.

Alexander Meiklejohn

One of the greatest failures of our contemporary training of teachers is that they become mere technicians. . . . They do not learn the beliefs and motives and values for the sake of which the classroom exists.

Alexander Meiklejohn

A tutor should not be continually thundering instruction into the ears of his pupil, as if he were pouring it through a funnel, but induce him to think, to distinguish, and to find out things for himself; sometimes opening the way, at other times leaving it for him to open; and so accommodate his precepts to the capacity of his pupil.

Michel Eyquem de Montaigne

The close observer soon discovers that the teacher's task is not to implant facts but to place the subject to be learned in front of the learner and, through sympathy, emotion, imagination, and patience, to awaken in the learner the restless drive for answers and insights which enlarge the personal life and give it meaning.

Nathan Marsh Pusey

See also: EDUCATION, STUDENT, TEACHING.

TEACHING

To know how to suggest is the art of teaching.

Henri Frédéric Amiel

The one exclusive sign of a thorough knowledge is the power of teaching.

Aristotle

Those who educate children well are more to be honored than even their parents, for these only give them life, those the art of living well.

Aristotle

Teaching is not a lost art, but the regard for it is a lost tradition.

Jacques Martin Barzun

If, in instructing a child, you are vexed with it for want of adroitness, try, if you have never tried before, to write with your left hand, and then remember that a child is all left hand.

John Frederick Boyes

Many earnest persons, who have found direct education for themselves fruitless and unprofitable, declare that they first began to learn when they began to teach, and that in the education of others they discovered the secret of their own.

Gamaliel Bradford

A man should first direct himself in the way he should go. Only then should he instruct others.

Buddha

The method of teaching which approaches most nearly to the method of investigation, is incomparably the best; since, not content with serving up a few barren and lifeless truths, it leads to the stock on which they grew.

Edmund Burke

A wisely chosen illustration is almost essential to fasten the truth upon the ordinary mind, and no teacher can afford to neglect this part of his preparation.

Howard Crosby

The most important method of education always has consisted of that in which the pupil was urged to actual performance.

Albert Einstein

In all our efforts for education—in providing adequate schools, research, and study—we must never lose sight of the very heart of education: good teaching itself. Good teachers do not just happen. They are the product of the highest personal motivation, encouraged and helped in their work by adequate salaries and the respect, support, good will of their neighbors. The quality of American teaching has never been better. But the rewards for too many teachers are not commensurate with their work and their role in American life. It is my earnest hope that along with progress in other aspects of education, the states and communities will give increasing attention to this tap-root of all education—good teachers, and hence good teaching.

Dwight David Eisenhower

When we teach a child to read, our primary aim is not to enable it to decipher a way-bill or receipt, but to kindle its imagination, enlarge its vision, and open for it the avenues of knowledge.

Charles William Eliot

A school free to concentrate on those services that only schools can give is in a position to do more effective teaching than one that must be all things to all children and to their parents, too.

John Henry Fischer

Let our teaching be full of ideas. Hitherto it has been stuffed only with facts.

Anatole France

The object of teaching a child is to enable him to get along without his teacher.

Elbert Green Hubbard

Other people can't make you see with their eyes. At best they can only encourage you to use your own.

Aldous Leonard Huxley

Modern cynics and skeptics . . . see no harm in paying those to whom they entrust the minds of their children a smaller wage than is paid to those to whom they entrust the care of their plumbing.

John Fitzgerald Kennedy

The right defence against false sentiments is to inculcate just sentiments. By starving the sensibility of our pupils we only make them easier prey to the propagandist when he comes. For famished nature will be avenged and a hard heart is no infallible protection against a soft head.

Clive Staples (C. S.) Lewis

I cannot think but that the world would be better and brighter if our teachers would dwell on the Duty of Happiness as well as the Happiness of Duty.

Sir John Lubbock

The best teacher is the one who suggests rather than dogmatizes, and inspires his listener with the wish to teach himself.

Edward G. Bulwer-Lytton (Baron Lytton)

The teacher who is attempting to teach without inspiring the pupil with a desire to learn is hammering on cold iron.

Horace Mann

Improvement depends far less upon length of tasks and hours of application than is supposed. Children can take in but a little each day; they are like vases with a narrow neck; you may pour little or pour much, but much will not enter at a time.

Jules Michelet

In the education of children there is nothing like alluring the interest and affection; otherwise you only make so many asses laden with books.

Michel Eyquem de Montaigne

Do not train boys to learning by force and harshness; but direct them to it by what amuses their minds, so that you may be the better able to discover with accuracy the peculiar bent of the genius of each.

Plato

The true aim of every one who aspires to be a teacher should be, not to impart his own opinions, but to kindle minds.

Frederick William Robertson

Instruction in things moral is most necessary to the making of the highest type of citizenship.

Theodore Roosevelt

The apparent facility of learning is the cause why children are ruined. People do not observe that this very facility is a proof that they learn nothing. Their smooth and polished brain reflects like a mirror the objects presented to it; but nothing remains, nothing penetrates. The child retains the words, the ideas are reflected; those who listen understand them; the child does not understand them at all.

Jean Jacques Rousseau

The time for acquiring knowledge is so short, it passes away so rapidly, there are so many matters necessary to be acquired, that it is folly to expect it should be sufficient to make a child learned. The question ought not to be to teach it the sciences, but to give it a taste for them, and methods to acquire them when the taste shall be better developed.

Jean Jacques Rousseau

Everybody who is incapable of learning has taken to teaching.

Oscar Wilde

See also: CITIZENSHIP, COUNSEL, EDUCATION, GUIDANCE, INSTRUCTION, PREACHING, PRECEPT, UNIVERSITY.

TEARS

Tears are Summer showers to the soul.

Alfred Austin

Jewish tears are the heaviest. They have the weight of many centuries.

Léon Bloy

Never a tear bedims the eye
That time and patience will not dry.

(Francis) Bret Harte

What poetry there is in human tears!

Heinrich Heine

God made both tears and laughter, and both for kind purposes; for as laughter enables mirth and surprise to breathe freely, so tears enable sorrow to vent itself patiently. Tears hinder sorrow from becoming despair and madness; and laughter is one of the very privileges of reason, being confined to the human species.

(James Henry) Leigh Hunt

There is a sacredness in tears. They are not the mark of weakness, but of power. They speak more eloquently than ten thousand tongues. They are the messengers of overwhelming grief, of deep contrition, and of unspeakable love.

Washington Irving

What would women do if they could not cry? What poor, defenceless creatures they would be.

Douglas William Jerrold

We often shed tears, which deceive ourselves after having deceived others.

Duc François de La Rochefoucauld

The most efficient water power in the world—woman's tears.

Wilson Mizner

When the big lip and wat'ry eye
Tell me the rising storm is nigh.

Matthew (Matt) Prior

When I consider life and its few years—
A wisp of fog between us and the sun;
A call to battle and the battle done
Ere the last echo dies within our ears,
I wonder at the idleness of tears.

Lizette Woodworth Reese

The young man who has not wept is a savage, and the old man who will not laugh is a fool.

George Santayana

Tears are a good alternative but a poor diet.

Henry Wheeler Shaw (Josh Billings)

Tears are the safety-valves of the heart when too much pressure is laid on it.

Albert Richard Smith

Tears, idle tears, I know not what they mean,
Tears from the depths of some divine despair.

Alfred, Lord Tennyson

Scorn the proud man that is ashamed to weep.

Edward Young

See also: GRIEF, SADNESS, SORROW.

TECHNOLOGY

As nuclear and other technological achievements continue to mount, the normal life span will continue to climb. The hourly productivity of the worker will increase. How is the increase in leisure time and the extension of life expectancy to be spent? Will it be for the achievement of man's better aspirations or his degradation to the level of a well-fed, well-kept slave of an all-powerful state? Indeed, merely to state that question sharply reminds us that in these days and in the years ahead the need for philosophers and theologians parallels the need for scientists and engineers.

Dwight David Eisenhower

The economic and technological triumphs of the past few years have not solved as many problems as we thought they would, and, in fact, have brought us new problems we did not foresee.

Henry Ford II

Electric circuitry has overthrown the regime of "time" and "space" and pours upon us instantly and continuously the concerns of all other men. It has reconstituted dialogue on a global scale. Its message is Total Change, ending psychic, social, economic, and political parochialism. The old civic, state, and national groupings have become unworkable. Nothing can be further from the spirit of the new technology than "a place for everything and everything in its place." You can't *go* home again.

(Herbert) Marshall McLuhan

The medium, or process, of our time—electric technology—is reshaping and restructuring patterns of social interdependence and every aspect of our personal life. It is forcing us to reconsider and reevaluate practically every thought, every action, and every institution formerly taken for granted. Everything is changing—you, your family, your neighborhood, your education, your job, your government, your relation to "the others." And they're changing dramatically.

(Herbert) Marshall McLuhan

Ever since men began to modify their lives by using technology they have found themselves in a series of technological traps (e.g. air pollution).

Roger Revelle

Technology was not of itself a juggernaut of destruction. Our machines did not whirl us down the road to perdition. They merely ran over us as we squatted by the roadside.

Henry Morton Robinson

Nothing you can't spell will ever work.

Will (William Penn Adair) Rogers

In military technology in particular, where the level of the United States and the U.S.S.R. is very much the same and where the investment of scientists and money is also similar, it would be astonishing if either society kept for long anything like a serious, much less a decisive, technical lead.

Sir Charles Percy Snow

Military objectives are nearly always more precise than benevolent ones: which is why military technology has been easier for ingenious men to think about.

Sir Charles Percy Snow

Technocracy is just communism with spats.

John Cyprian Stevens

What is more difficult, to think of an encampment on the moon or of Harlem rebuilt? Both are now within the reach of our resources. Both now depend upon human decision and human will. I pray that the imagination we unlock for defense and arms and outer space may be unlocked as well for grace and beauty in our daily lives. As an economy, we need it. As a society, we shall perish without it.

Adlai Ewing Stevenson

Technology is not the toy of the prosperous; it is, potentially, the servant of all societies trying to engineer an escape from their poverty.

George David Woods

See also: ASTRONAUT, COMMUNICATIONS MEDIA, COMPUTER, CYBERNETICS, SCIENCE, SPACE.

TEENAGER: *see* ADOLESCENCE.

TELEVISION

A television drama is one of the most perishable items known to man. . . . Television is a strange medium limited by a thousand technical problems, hemmed in by taboos and advertising policies, cheapened by the innumerable untalented and officious people you will always find in a billion-dollar industry. Nevertheless, for the writers there is still area for deep and unprobed work.

Paddy Chayefsky

A very bad thing happened to the advertising business 30 years ago, and that was the invention of radio—I say bad because the advertising people, both in companies and in agencies, then got into show business. They loved it. This was just what they had been waiting for. . . . Then along came television and this made it worse.

Fairfax Mastick Cone

Individuals, most notably the great television and radio commentators, make a profession of knowing and saying with elegance and unction what their audiences will find most acceptable.

John Kenneth Galbraith

Conversation in this country has fallen upon evil days. . . . It is drowned out in singing commercials by the world's most productive economy that has so little to say for itself it has to hum it. It is hushed and shushed in dimly lighted parlors by television audiences who used to read, argue, and even play bridge, an old-fashioned card game requiring speech.

Rufus Wilmot Griswold

As a practitioner, I know that television is the most potent advertising medium ever devised, and I make most of my living from it. But, as a private person, I would gladly pay for the privilege of watching it without commercial interruptions.

David MacKenzie Ogilvy

It was the funeral of President Kennedy that most strongly proved the power of television to invest an occasion with the character of corporate participation. It involves an entire population in a ritual process. (By comparison, press, movies, and radio are mere packaging devices for consumers.) In television, images are projected at you. You are the screen. The images wrap around you. You are the vanishing point. This creates a sort of inwardness, a sort of reverse perspective which has much in common with Oriental art.

(Herbert) Marshall McLuhan

The impact of television on our culture is just indescribable. There's a certain sense in which it is nearly as important as the invention of printing.

Carl Sandburg

It was through TV that the Kennedy profile, the sincere Kennedy tones, the Kennedy thoughts could get to the people. He did not have to run the risk of having his ideas and his words shortened and adulterated by a correspondent. This was the TV era, not only in campaigning, but in holding the presidency.

Hugh Sidey

I would think that television is the most important vehicle for the dissemination of art that has ever come to hand. I think it is just as important as the invention of printing was in the fifteenth century.

Francis Henry Taylor

There are days when any electrical appliance in the house, including the vacuum cleaner, seems to offer more entertainment possibilities than the TV set.

Harriet Van Horne

I hate television. I hate it as much as peanuts. But I can't stop eating peanuts.

Orson Welles

See also: COMMUNICATIONS MEDIA, SCIENCE.

TEMPER

Temper, if ungoverned, governs the whole man.

Anthony Ashley Cooper (Lord Shaftesbury)

Temperament is temper that is too old to spank.

Charlotte Greenwood

It is an unhappy, and yet I fear a true reflection, that they who have uncommon easiness and softness of temper have seldom very noble and nice sensations of soul.

Fulke Greville (First Baron Brooke)

Good temper, like a sunny day, sheds a brightness over everything; it is the sweetener of toil and the soother of disquietude.

Washington Irving

A tart temper never mellows with age; and a sharp tongue is the only edged tool that grows keener with constant use.

Washington Irving

Too many have no idea of the subjection of their temper to the influence of religion, and yet what is changed if the temper is not? If a man is as passionate, malicious, resentful, sullen, moody, or morose after his conversion as before it, what is he converted from or to?

John Angell James

The happiness and misery of men depend no less on temper than fortune.

Duc François de La Rochefoucauld

A man who cannot command his temper should not think of being a man of business.

Philip Dormer Stanhope (Lord Chesterfield)

See also: ANGER, DISPOSITION, EMOTION, GOOD NATURE, PASSION, RAGE, RASHNESS.

TEMPERANCE

Temperance gives nature her full play, and enables her to exert herself in all her force and vigor.

Joseph Addison

I dare not drink for my own sake, I ought not to drink for my neighbor's sake.

Theodore Ledyard Cuyler

Temperance is the control of all the functions of our bodies. The man who refuses liquor, goes in for apple pie and develops a paunch is no ethical leader for me.

John Erskine

Temperance puts wood on the fire, meal in the barrel, flour in the tub, money in the purse, credit in the country, contentment in the house, clothes on the children, vigor in the body, intelligence in the brain, and spirit in the whole constitution.

Benjamin Franklin

Temperance is the lawful gratification of a natural and healthy appetite.

John Bartholomew Gough

I have four good reasons for being an abstainer—my head is clearer, my health is better, my heart is lighter, and my purse is heavier.

Thomas Guthrie

Fools! not to know how health and temperance bless the rustic swain, while luxury destroys her pampered train.

Hesiod

If temperance prevails, then education can prevail; if temperance fails, then education must fail.

Horace Mann

Many a man has won glory for lifelong temperance through a queasy stomach.

Austin O'Malley

The receipts of cookery are swelled to a volume, but a good stomach excels them all; to which nothing contributes more than industry and temperance.

William Penn

Temperance and labor are the two best physicians; the one sharpens the appetite—the other prevents indulgence to excess.

Jean Jacques Rousseau

The only way you can fight booze is by ceasing to make life chronically painful for the masses.

George Bernard Shaw

The temperate are the most truly luxurious. By abstaining from most things, it is surprising how many things we enjoy.

William Gilmore Simms

See also: ABSTINENCE, MODERATION.

TEMPTATION

I see the devil's hook, and yet cannot help nibbling at his bait.

George William Bagby (Moses Adams)

Temptations without imply desires within; men ought not to say, "How powerfully the devil tempts," but "How strongly I am tempted."

Henry Ward Beecher

Temptations, when we meet them at first, are as the lion that roared upon Samson; but if we overcome them, the next time we see them we shall find a nest of honey within them.

John Bunyan

The temptation is not here, where you are reading about it or praying about it. It is down in your shop, among bales and boxes, ten-penny nails, and sand-paper.

Edwin Hubbel Chapin

Better shun the bait than struggle in the snare.

John Dryden

Most confidence has still most cause to doubt.

John Dryden

The last temptation is the greatest treason:
To do the right deed for the wrong reason.

Thomas Stearns Eliot

Temptations are a file which rub off much of the rust of our self-confidence.

François de Salignac de La Mothe-Fénelon

To realize God's presence is the one sovereign remedy against temptation.

François de Salignac de La Mothe-Fénelon

There are some actions from which an escape is a godsend, both for the man who escapes and for those about him. Man, as soon as he gets back his consciousness of right, is thankful to the Divine mercy for the escape. As we know that a man often succumbs to temptation however much he may resist it, we also know that Providence often intercedes and saves him in spite of himself. How all this happens,—how far a man is free and how far a creature of circumstances,—how far free-will comes into play and where fate enters on the scene—all this is a mystery and will remain mystery.

Mohandas Karamchand (Mahatma) Gandhi

I know there is not any memory with less satisfaction in it than the memory of some temptation we resisted.

James Branch Cabell

The absence of temptation is the absence of virtue.

Johann Wolfgang von Goethe

The difference between those whom the world esteems as good and those whom it condemns as bad, is in many cases little else than that the former have been better sheltered from temptation.

Augustus and Julius Hare

Why resist temptation—there will always be more.

Don Herold

That fortitude which has encountered no dangers, that prudence which has surmounted no difficulties, that integrity which has been attacked by no temptation, can at best be considered but as gold not yet brought to the test, of which, therefore, the true value cannot be assigned.

Samuel Johnson

A new variety of temptation is, as we grow older, unusual.

Edward Verrall Lucas

God chooses that men should be tried, but let a man beware of tempting his neighbor. God knows how and how much, and where and when. Man is his brother's keeper, and must keep him according to his knowledge.

George Macdonald

St. Augustine teaches that there is in each man a Serpent, an Eve, and an Adam. Our senses and natural propensities are the Serpent; the excitable desire is Eve; and the reason is the Adam. Our nature tempts us perpetually; criminal desire is often excited; but sin is not completed till reason consents.

Blaise Pascal

God is better served in resisting a temptation to evil than in many formal prayers.

William Penn

After listening to thousands of prayers for pardon to offenders, I can hardly recall a case where I did not feel that I might have fallen as my fellow-man has done, if I had been subjected to the same demoralizing influences and pressed by the same temptations.

Horatio Seymour

Some temptations come to the industrious, but all temptations attack the idle.

Charles Haddon Spurgeon

Every temptation is great or small according as the man is.

Jeremy Taylor

Temptation is a part of life. No one is immune—at any age. For temptation is present wherever there is a choice to be made, not only between good and evil, but also between a higher and lower good. For some, it may be a temptation to sensual gratification; for others a temptation to misuse their gifts, to seek a worthy aim by unworthy means, to lower their ideal to win favor with the electorate, or with their companions and associates.

Ernest Trice Thompson

Few men have virtue to withstand the highest bidder.

George Washington

No degree of temptation justifies any degree of sin.

Nathaniel Parker Willis

When a man resists sin on human motives only, he will not hold out long.

Daniel Wilson

See also: DESIRE, DEVIL, LUST, OPPORTUNITY, PASSION.

TENDERNESS

As for her sympathies and tender feelings,
She was so charitably solicitous
She used to weep if she but saw a mouse
Caught in a trap, if he were dead or bleeding.

Geoffrey Chaucer

When death, the great reconciler, has come, it is never our tenderness that we repent of, but our severity.

George Eliot (Mary Ann Evans)

Tenderness, without a capacity of relieving, only makes the man who feels it more wretched than the object which sues for assistance.

Oliver Goldsmith

Tenderness is the repose of passion.

Joseph Joubert

See also: AFFECTION, COMPASSION, GENTLENESS, KINDNESS, LOVE, SENSITIVENESS, SYMPATHY.

TERROR

Her lips were red, her looks were free,
Her locks were yellow as gold:
Her skin was white as leprosy,
The Night-mare LIFE-IN-DEATH was she,
Who thicks man's blood with cold.

Samuel Taylor Coleridge

Let us confess it, no longer is our world ruled by a balance of power, it is shocked into policies by a balance of terror.

Richard James Cushing

We have a big net that we can catch whales in, but the fine mesh net to catch the very deadly small fish of terrorism and assassination and kidnapping and so on is yet to be developed.

Henry Cabot Lodge

See also: ANXIETY, FEAR, SUPERSTITION.

THANKFULNESS

When I'm not thank'd at all, I'm thank'd enough,
I've done my duty, and I've done no more.

Henry Fielding

Best of all is it to preserve everything in a pure, still heart, and let there be for every pulse a thanksgiving, and for every breath a song.

Konrad von Gesner

When thankfulness o'erflows the swelling heart, and breathes in free and uncorrupted praise for benefits received, propitious Heaven takes such acknowledgment as fragrant incense, and doubles all its blessings.

George Lillo

The worship most acceptable to God, comes from a thankful and cheerful heart.

Plutarch

From too much love of living,
From hope and fear set free,
We thank with brief thanksgiving
Whatever gods may be,
That no life lives forever,
That dead men rise up never;
That even the weariest river
Winds somewhere safe to sea.

Algernon Charles Swinburne

God has two dwellings: one in heaven, and the other in a meek and thankful heart.

Izaak Walton

See also: APPRECIATION, GRATITUDE.

THEATER

The idea that the theatre is managed in accordance with pure morals is a vain imagination. Those who build and manage theatres do so with the view of a good investment and profitable employment. They know the taste of their customers. They must either conform to these tastes, or lose money by opposing them. A theatre conducted on such principles as would make it safe to the morals of youth would not pay its proprietor.

William Arnot

What I like about Hollywood is that one can get along quite well by knowing two words of English—swell and lousy.

Vicki Baum

A play should give you something to think about. When I see a play and understand it the first time, then I know it can't be much good.

Thomas Stearns Eliot

I got all the schooling any actress needs. That is, I learned to write well enough to sign contracts.

Hermione Gingold

It is instructive to recall that the modern theatre against which the churches so often have railed, originated in the bosom of the church.

Isaac Goldberg

Although it is said of plays that they teach morality, and of the stage that it is the mirror of human life, these assertions are mere declamations, and have no foundation in truth and experience.

Sir John Hawkins

It is remarkable how virtuous and generously disposed every one is at a play. We uniformly applaud what is right, and condemn what is wrong, when it costs us nothing but the sentiment.

William Hazlitt

There is that in theatrical representation which awakens whatever romance belongs to our character. The magic lights, the pomp of scene, the fair, false, exciting life that is detailed before us, crowding into some three short hours all our most busy ambition could desire—all these appeals to our senses are not made in vain. Our taste for castle building and visions deepens upon us, and we

chew a mental opium which stagnates the other faculties, but wakes that of the ideal.
Edward R. Bulwer Lytton (Owen Meredith)

In the theatre, a hero is one who believes that all women are ladies, a villain one who believes that all ladies are women.
George Jean Nathan

The playwright of today must dig at the roots of the sickness of today as he feels it— the death of the old God and the failure of science and materialism to give any satisfactory new one of the surviving primitive, religious instinct to find a meaning for life in, and to comfort its fears of death with.
Eugene Gladstone O'Neill

I'll match my flops with anybody's but I wouldn't have missed 'em. Flops are a part of life's menu and I've never been a girl to miss out on any of the courses.
Rosalind Russell

The writer for the theatre in America today has a special relation with his audience. It is the same relation that Marie Antoinette must have had with the crowds along the streets on the way to the . . . guillotine.
Irwin Shaw

The duty of dramatists is to express their times and guide the public through the perplexities of those times.
Robert Emmet Sherwood

We are a nation that has always gone in for the loud laugh, the wow, the belly laugh and the dozen other labels for the roll-'em-in-the-aisles gagerissimo. This is the kind of laugh that delights actors, directors, and producers, but dismays writers of comedy because it is the laugh that often dies in the lobby. The appreciative smile, the chuckle, the soundless mirth, so important to the success of comedy, cannot be understood unless one sits among the audience and feels the warmth created by the quality of laughter that the audience takes home with it.
James Grover Thurber

See *also*: ACTOR AND ACTRESS, AMUSEMENT, MOTION PICTURES, SHOWMANSHIP, TELEVISION, TRAGEDY.

THEOLOGY

Theology is but the science of mind applied to God. As schools change, theology must necessarily change. Truth is everlasting, but our ideas of truth are not. Theology is but our ideas of truth classified and arranged.
Henry Ward Beecher

The way to begin a Christian life is not to study theology. Piety before theology. Right living will produce right thinking. Theologies are well in their place, but repentance and love must come before all other experiences.
Henry Ward Beecher

A theology at war with the laws of physical nature would be a battle of no doubtful issue. The laws of our spiritual nature give still less chance of success to the system which would thwart or stay them.
William Ellery Channing

The moment a religion seeks support from philosophy, its ruin is inevitable. . . . Religion, like every other form of absolutism, should be above justification.
Heinrich Heine

The theological systems of men and schools are always determined by the character of their ideal of Christ, the great central fact of the Christian system.
Josiah Gilbert Holland

The divine test of a man's worth is not his theology but his life.
Morris Joseph

Reason, however sound, has little weight with ordinary theologians.
Baruch (Benedict) Spinoza

The best theology is rather a divine life than a divine knowledge.
Jeremy Taylor

We live in a time when theology has been able to attract so many virile minds that even those who have tried to ignore theology are beginning to find it difficult to maintain their pose.
David Elton Trueblood

As the grave grows nearer my theology is growing strangely simple, and it begins and ends with Christ as the only Saviour of the lost.
Henry Benjamin Whipple

Fortunately, religion depends as little upon theology as love upon phrenology.

Israel Zangwill

See also: AGNOSTICISM, BIBLE, CHRISTIANITY, CREED, DOCTRINE, GOD, MINISTER, PHILOSOPHY, PREACHING, RELIGION, SECT.

THEORY

To despise theory is to have the excessively vain pretension to do without knowing what one does, and to speak without knowing what one says.

Bernard Le Bovier de Fontenelle

A favorite theory is a possession for life.

William Hazlitt

Conjecture as to things useful, is good; but conjecture as to what it would be useless to know, is very idle.

Samuel Johnson

It is much easier to design than to perform. A man proposes his schemes of life in a state of abstraction and disengagement, exempt from the enticements of hope, the solicitations of affection, the importunities of appetite, or the depressions of fear, and is in the same state with him that teaches upon land the art of navigation, to whom the sea is always smooth, and the wind always prosperous.

Samuel Johnson

None of us can go a little way with a theory; when it once possesses us, we are no longer our own masters. It makes us speak its words, and do violence to our nature.

John Henry Newman

The theory that can absorb the greatest number of facts, and persist in doing so, generation after generation, through all changes of opinion and detail, is the one that must rule all observation.

John Weiss

See also: SPECULATION, THOUGHT.

THOUGHT

A man would do well to carry a pencil in his pocket, and write down the thoughts of the moment. Those that come unsought for are commonly the most valuable, and should be secured, because they seldom return.

Francis Bacon

Unless a man can link his written thoughts with the everlasting wants of men, so that they shall draw from them as from wells, there is no more immortality to the thoughts and feelings of the soul than to the muscles and the bones.

Henry Ward Beecher

Thinking is a strenuous art—few practice it: and then only at rare times.

David Ben-Gurion

The greatest events of an age are its best thoughts. Thought finds its way into action.

Christian Nestell Bovee

Thinking is not a heaven-born thing. . . . It is a gift men and women make for themselves. It is earned, and it is earned by effort. There is no effort, to my mind, that is comparable in its qualities, that is so taxing to the individual, as to think, to analyze fundamentally.

Louis Dembitz Brandeis

The maxim "Think for yourself," is basic; but the further maxim, "Think socially," must be added if philosophy is to do its whole duty.

Edgar Sheffield Brightman

All the problems of the world could be settled easily if men were only willing to think. The trouble is that men very often resort to all sorts of devices in order not to think, because thinking is such hard work.

Nicholas Murray Butler

A thinking man is the worst enemy the Prince of Darkness can have; every time such an one announces himself, I doubt not there runs a shudder through the nether empire; and new emissaries are trained with new tactics, to, if possible, entrap and hoodwink and handcuff him.

Thomas Carlyle

The principal joy of intellectual activity is involved in the attainment of a satisfactory conclusion, a moment in which the intellectual struggle gives way to a brief interval of serene comfort of the mind.

Clarence Cason

Those who have finished by making all others think with them, have usually been those who began by daring to think for themselves.

Charles Caleb Colton

Learning without thought is labor lost; thought without learning is perilous.

Confucius

It is the hardest thing in the world to be a good thinker without being a good self-examiner.

Anthony Ashley Cooper (Lord Shaftesbury)

The rich are too indolent, the poor too weak, to bear the insupportable fatigue of thinking.

William Cowper

A thinker who does not suffer his problem, who does not live his thought, is not a thinker; he is a mere elocutionist, repeating thoughts that have been thought by others.

Benedetto Croce

All day long the door of the sub-conscious remains just ajar; we slip through to the other side, and return again, as easily and secretly as a cat.

Walter John de la Mare

Mankind might be divided between the multitude who hate to be kept waiting because they get bored and the happy few who rather like it because it gives them time for thought.

Ernest Dimnet

Nurture your mind with great thoughts; to believe in the heroic makes heroes.

Benjamin Disraeli

Some people study all their life, and at their death they have learned everything except to think.

François Urbain Domergue

It is astonishing what an effort it seems to be for many people to put their brains definitely and systematically to work. They seem to insist on somebody else doing their thinking for them.

Thomas Alva Edison

Temples have their sacred images; and we see what influence they have always had over a great part of mankind; but, in truth, the ideas and images in men's minds are the invisible powers that constantly govern them; and to these they all pay universally a ready submission.

Jonathan Edwards

Great men are they who see that spiritual is stronger than any material force—that thoughts rule the world.

Ralph Waldo Emerson

The key to every man is his thought. Sturdy and defying though he look, he has a helm which he obeys, which is the idea after which all his facts are classified. He can only be reformed by showing him a new idea which commands his own.

Ralph Waldo Emerson

Thinking is the hardest work there is, which is the probable reason why so few engage in it.

Henry Ford

We tell our thoughts, like our children, to put on their hats and coats before they go out.

Henry Watson Fowler

Always aim at complete harmony of thought and word and deed. Always aim at purifying your thoughts and everything will be well. There is nothing more potent than thought. Deed follows word and word follows thought. The word is the result of a mighty thought, and where the thought is mighty and pure the result is always mighty and pure.

Mohandas Karamchand (Mahatma) Gandhi

Control over thought is a long, painful and laborious process. But I am convinced that, no time, no labour and no pain is too much for the glorious result to be reached.

Mohandas Karamchand (Mahatma) Gandhi

Hide not your thoughts. If it is shameful to reveal them, it is more shameful to think them.

Mohandas Karamchand (Mahatma) Gandhi

The purity of thought is possible only with a faith in God bordering on definite experience.

Mohandas Karamchand (Mahatma) Gandhi

All truly wise thoughts have been thought already thousands of times; but to make them truly ours, we must think them over again honestly, till they take root in our personal experience.

Johann Wolfgang von Goethe

In matters of conscience first thoughts are best; in matters of prudence last thoughts are best.

Robert Hall

We shall succeed only so far as we continue that most distasteful of all activity, the intolerable labor of thought.

Learned Hand

The men of action are, after all, only the unconscious instruments of the men of thought.

Heinrich Heine

Thought is invisible nature; nature, visible thought.

Heinrich Heine

The thought precedes the deed as the lightning the thunder.

Heinrich Heine

Wise men think out their thoughts; fools proclaim them.

Heinrich Heine

Ye fools, so closely to search my trunk! . . . My contraband goods I carry about in my head, not hid in my clothing.

Heinrich Heine

Life has taught me to think, but thinking has not taught me how to live.

Alexander Ivanovich Herzen

A thought is often original, though you have uttered it a hundred times. It has come to you over a new route, by a new and express train of association.

Oliver Wendell Holmes

A great many people think they are thinking when they are merely rearranging their prejudices.

William James

Mankind have a great aversion to intellectual labor; but even supposing knowledge to be easily attainable, more people would be content to be ignorant than would take even a little trouble to acquire it.

Samuel Johnson

The things a man believes most profoundly are rarely on the surface of his mind or on the tip of his tongue. Newly acquired notions, formulas learned by rote from books, decisions based on expediency, the fashionable ideas of the moment—these are right on top of the pile, ready to be sampled and displayed in bright after-dinner conversation. But the ideas that make up a man's philosophy of life are somewhere way down below.

Eric Allen Johnston

Fully to understand a grand and beautiful thought requires, perhaps, as much time as to conceive it.

Joseph Joubert

Where all think alike, no one thinks very much.

Walter Lippmann

Earnest men never think in vain though their thoughts may be errors.

Edward G. Bulwer-Lytton (Baron Lytton)

To many men and many governments the life of the human mind is a danger to be feared more than any other danger, and the word which cannot be purchased, cannot be falsified, and cannot be killed is the enemy most hunted for and most hated.

Archibald MacLeish

The great thinker is seldom a disputant. He answers other men's arguments by stating the truth as he sees it.

Daniel March

The happiness of your life depends upon the quality of your thoughts, therefore guard accordingly; and take care that you entertain no notions unsuitable to virtue and reasonable nature.

Marcus Aurelius

If you make people think they're thinking, they'll love you; but if you really make them think, they'll hate you.

Donald Robert Perry (Don) Marquis

It will be a shock to men when they realize that thoughts that were fast enough for today are not fast enough for tomorrow. But thinking tomorrow's thoughts today is one kind of future life.

Christopher Darlington Morley

People like to imagine that because all our mechanical equipment moves so much faster, that we are thinking faster too.

Christopher Darlington Morley

This is the most unselfish of eras because hardly anyone is egotist enough to wish to do his own thinking. There are always so many ready and eager to do it for us.

Christopher Darlington Morley

Human thought is ever advancing, ever grappling with and trying to understand the problems of Nature and the universe, and what I tell you today may be wholly insufficient and out-of-date tomorrow.

Jawaharlal Nehru

It is easy to admire the beauties of the universe and to live in a world of thought and imagination. But to try to escape in this way from the unhappiness of others, caring little what happens to them, is no sign of courage or fellow-feeling. Thought, in order to justify itself, must lead to action.

Jawaharlal Nehru

Man being made a reasonable, and so a thinking creature, there is nothing more worthy of his being, than the right direction and employment of his thoughts, since upon this depend both his usefulness to the public, and his own present and future benefit in all respects.

William Penn

Thinking is the talking of the soul with itself.

Plato

As soon as thoughts are ordered they begin to seem less sincere.

Jean Rostand

Thinking is like loving and dying. Each of us must do it for himself.

Josiah Royce

We may divide thinkers into those who think for themselves, and those who think through others. The latter are the rule, and the former the exception. The first are original thinkers in a double sense, and egotists in the noblest meaning of the word. It is from them only that the world learns wisdom. For only the light which we have kindled in ourselves can illuminate others.

Arthur Schopenhauer

Living truth is that alone which has its origin in thinking. Just as a tree bears year after year the same fruit and yet fruit which is each year new, so must all permanently valuable ideas be continually born again in thought.

Albert Schweitzer

I have asked several men what passes in their minds when they are thinking, and I could never find any man who could think for two minutes together. Everybody has seemed to admit that it was a perpetual deviation from a particular path, and a perpetual return to it; which, imperfect as the operation is, is the only method in which we can operate with our minds to carry on any process of thought.

Sydney Smith

Some people pass through life soberly and religiously enough, without knowing why, or reasoning about it, but, from force of habit merely, go to heaven like fools.

Laurence Sterne

Our thoughts are epochs in our lives; all else is but as a journal of the winds that blow while we are here.

Henry David Thoreau

The sober second thought of the people is seldom wrong.

Martin Van Buren

Every great originating mind produces in some way a change in society; every great originating mind, whose exercise is controlled by duty, effects a beneficial change. This effect may be immediate, may be remote. A nation may be in a tumult to-day for a thought which the timid Erasmus placidly penned in his study more than two centuries ago.

Edwin Percy Whipple

Thinking is the most unhealthy thing in the world, and people die of it just as they die of any other disease. Fortunately, in England at any rate, thought is not catching.

Oscar Wilde

Thoughts that do often lie too deep for tears.

William Wordsworth

See also: CONTEMPLATION, IDEA, LOGIC, MEDITATION, REASON, REFLECTION, SPECULATION, STUDY, THEORY.

THREAT

He fears not threats who fears not death.

Pierre Corneille

The man who threatens the world is always ridiculous; for the world can easily go on

without him, and, in a short time, will cease
to miss him.

Samuel Johnson

I consider it a mark of great prudence in a
man to abstain from threats or any contemptuous expressions, for neither of these weak-
en the enemy, but the one makes him more
cautious, and the other excites his hatred,
and a desire to revenge himself.

Niccolò Machiavelli

See also: BLUSTERING, CURSE, OATH, QUARREL.

THRIFT

Did wisely from expensive sins refrain,
And never broke the Sabbath, but for gain.

John Dryden

Penny saved is a penny got.

Henry Fielding

Thrift is the Philosopher's Stone.

Thomas Fuller

See also: BARGAIN, ECONOMY, FRUGALITY.

TIME

Nothing lies on our hands with such uneasiness as time. Wretched and thoughtless
creatures! In the only place where covetousness were a virtue we turn prodigals.

Joseph Addison

Time is so fleeting that if we do not remember God in our youth, age may find us incapable of thinking about him.

Hans Christian Andersen

He that will not apply new remedies must
expect new evils; for time is the greatest innovator.

Francis Bacon

A man that is young in years may be old in
hours, if he has lost no time.

Francis Bacon

To choose time is to save time.

Francis Bacon

Time flies and draws us with it. The moment in which I am speaking is already far
from me.

Nicolas Boileau-Despréaux

The grand Instructor, Time.

Edmund Burke

The silent touches of time.

Edmund Burke

Time was invented by Almighty God in order to give ideas a chance.

Nicholas Murray Butler

'Tis strange—but true; for truth is always
strange; Stranger than fiction.

George Gordon Byron (Lord Byron)

The difference between Orthodoxy or My-
doxy and Heterodoxy or Thy-doxy.

Thomas Carlyle

Much may be done in those little shreds and
patches of time, which every day produces,
and which most men throw away, but which
nevertheless will make at the end of it no
small deduction from the life of man.

Charles Caleb Colton

Time is the most undefinable yet paradoxical of things; the past is gone, the future has
not come, and the present becomes the past
even while we attempt to define it, and, like
the flash of the lightning, at once exists and
expires.

Charles Caleb Colton

Let us attend to the present, and as to the
future, we shall know how to manage when
the occasion arrives. Time is a great master;
he arranges things well.

Pierre Corneille

Time is childhood's leaden wings; it is age's
rushing, soundless river.

Walter John de la Mare

The man who anticipates his century is always persecuted when living, and is always
pilfered when dead.

Benjamin Disraeli

Time will teach more than all our thoughts.

Benjamin Disraeli

When you sit with a nice girl for two hours,
you think it's only a minute. But when you
sit on a hot stove for a minute, you think it's
two hours. That's relativity.

Albert Einstein

Time present and time past
Are both perhaps present in time future,
And time future contained in time past.

Thomas Stearns Eliot

All my possessions for a moment of time.
Elizabeth I

Time and tide wait for no man.
English Proverb

Time will discover everything to posterity; it is a babbler, and speaks even when no question is put.
Euripides

God, who is liberal in all his other gifts, shows us, by the wise economy of his providence, how circumspect we ought to be in the management of our time, for he never gives us two moments together.
François de Salignac de La Mothe-Fénelon

Time preserves nothing that you make without its help.
Anatole France

If time be of all things the most precious, wasting time must be the greatest prodigality, since lost time is never found again; and what we call time enough always proves little enough. Let us then be up and doing, and doing to the purpose; so by diligence shall we do more with less perplexity.
Benjamin Franklin

He lives long that lives well, and time misspent is not lived, but lost.
Thomas Fuller

Time is a merciless enemy, as it is also a merciless friend and healer.
Mohandas Karamchand (Mahatma) Gandhi

Our judgments about things vary according to the time left us to live—that we think is left us to live.
André Gide

It is better to be doing the most insignificant thing than to reckon even a half-hour insignificant.
Johann Wolfgang von Goethe

We always have time enough, if we will but use it aright.
Johann Wolfgang von Goethe

Time, you old gipsy man,
Will you not stay,
Put up your caravan
Just for one day?
Ralph Hodgson

Time will bring to light whatever is hidden; it will conceal and cover up what is now shining with the greatest splendor.
Horace

What a folly to dread the thought of throwing away life at once, and yet have no regard to throwing it away by parcels and piecemeal.
John Howe

You'll find as you grow older that you weren't born such a very great while ago after all. The time shortens up.
William Dean Howells

A man's time, when well husbanded, is like a cultivated field, of which a few acres produces more of what is useful to life, than extensive provinces, even of the richest soil, when overrun with weeds and brambles.
David Hume

Time, with all its celerity, moves slowly on to him whose whole employment is to watch its flight.
Samuel Johnson

The great rule of moral conduct is, next to God, to respect time.
Johann Kaspar Lavater

Time is money.
Edward G. Bulwer-Lytton (Baron Lytton)

The lifeless boughs of time.
Edgar Lee Masters

Time is a great legalizer, even in the field of morals.
Henry Louis Mencken

Our yesterdays follow us; they constitute our life, and they give character and force and meaning to our present deeds.
Joseph Parker

Time is what we want most, but what alas! we use worst.
William Penn

There is a time to be born, and a time to die, says Solomon, and it is the memento of a truly wise man; but there is an interval between these two times of infinite importance.
Legh Richmond

Time, like a flurry of wild rain, shall drift across the darkened plane.
Sir Charles George Douglas Roberts

All that time is lost which might be better employed.
Jean Jacques Rousseau

The greatest loss of time is delay and expectation, which depend upon the future. We let go the present, which we have in our power, and look forward to that which depends upon chance,—and so relinquish a certainty for an uncertainty.
Seneca

Pastime is a word that should never be used but in a bad sense; it is vile to say a thing is agreeable, because it helps to pass the time away.
William Shenstone

Measure, time and number are nothing but modes of thought or rather of imagination.
Baruch (Benedict) Spinoza

Know the true value of time; snatch, seize, and enjoy every moment of it. No idleness; no laziness; no procrastination;—never put off till to-morrow what you can do to-day.
Philip Dormer Stanhope (Lord Chesterfield)

What I most value next to eternity, is time.
Anne Sophie Swetchine

Let it be forgotten, as a flower is forgotten,
  Forgotten as a fire that once was singing gold,
Let it be forgotten for ever and ever,
  Time is a kind friend, he will make us old.
Sara Teasdale

Oh as I was young and easy in the mercy of his means,
Time held me green and dying
Though I sang in my chains like the sea.
Dylan Thomas

As if you could kill time without injuring eternity!
Henry David Thoreau

  Time is
Too Slow for those who Wait,
Too Swift for those who Fear,
Too Long for those who Grieve,
Too short for those who Rejoice,
  But for those who Love
    Time is not.
Henry van Dyke

There is no difference between time and any of the three dimensions of space except that our consciousness moves along it.
Herbert George Wells

See also: AGE, ANTIQUITY, DELAY, FUTURE, PAST, PRESENT, PROCRASTINATION.

TIMIDITY

Who fears to ask doth teach to be deny'd.
Robert Herrick

The man who makes no mistakes does not usually make anything.
Edward John Phelps

Willing to wound, and yet afraid to strike,
Just a hint a fault, and hesitate dislike.
Alexander Pope

He who begs timidly invites a refusal.
Seneca

See also: BASHFULNESS, BLUSH, DIFFIDENCE.

TITLE

A fool, indeed, has great need of a title, it teaches men to call him count, and duke, and to forget his proper name of fool.
John Crowne

The three highest titles that can be given a man are those of a martyr, hero, saint.
William Ewart Gladstone

Titles, instead of exalting, debase those who act not up to them.
Duc François de La Rochefoucauld

It is not titles that reflect honor on men, but men on their titles.
Niccolò Machiavelli

Virtue is the first title of nobility.
Molière (Jean Baptiste Poquelin)

See also: ARISTOCRACY, NOBILITY, RANK.

TOBACCO: see SMOKING.

TOLERANCE

History and one's own experience show that more tangible good comes of smiling tolerance than from fanatical zeal.
Ernest Boyd

We anticipate a time when the love of truth shall have come up to our love of liberty, and men shall be cordially tolerant and earnest believers both at once.
Phillips Brooks

Error tolerates, truth condemns.
Fernan Caballero

The danger of a broad view is that it is often a shallow view.
Sir Arthur Stanley Eddington

The responsibility of tolerance lies with those who have the wider vision.
George Eliot (Mary Ann Evans)

Toleration is a good thing in its place; but you cannot tolerate what will not tolerate you, and is trying to cut your throat.
James Anthony Froude

Tolerance comes with age; I see no fault committed that I myself could not have committed at some time or other.
Johann Wolfgang von Goethe

Tolerance is the only real test of civilization.
Sir Arthur Helps

Tolerance is the positive and cordial effort to understand another's beliefs, practices and habits, without necessarily sharing or accepting them.
Joshua Loth Liebman

It has been freshly demonstrated that tolerance is, to a degree we do not like to admit, a product of prosperity.
Halford Edward Luccock

Tolerance cannot afford to have anything to do with the fallacy that evil may convert itself to good.
Freya Madeleine Stark

The tolerance of all religions is a law of nature, stamped on the hearts of all men.
Voltaire (François Marie Arouet)

See also: BROADMINDEDNESS, LIBERAL, OPEN-
MINDEDNESS.

TOMORROW

Trust on and think Tomorrow will repay;
Tomorrow's falser than the former day;
Lies worse; and while it says, we shall be
    blest
With some new Joys, cuts off what we possest.
John Dryden

One today is worth two tomorrows.
Benjamin Franklin

Where art thou, beloved Tomorrow?
When young and old, and strong and weak,
Rich and poor, through joy and sorrow,
Thy sweet smiles we ever seek,—
In thy place—ah! well-a-day!
We find the thing we fled—
    Today!
Percy Bysshe Shelley

See also: DELAY, FUTURITY, PROCRASTINATION.

TONGUE

The tongue is, at the same time, the best part of man, and his worst: with good government, none is more useful; without it, none is more mischievous.
Anacharsis

Scholars are men of peace; they bear no arms; but their tongues are sharper than a razor; their pens carry further, and give a louder report than thunder. I had rather stand in the shock of a basilisk, than in the fury of a merciless pen.
Sir Thomas Browne

We cannot control the evil tongues of others; but a good life enables us to disregard them.
Cato the Younger

The Chinese have a saying, that an unlucky word dropped from the tongue, cannot be brought back again by a coach and six horses.
Oliver Goldsmith

A tart temper never mellows with age; and a sharp tongue is the only edged tool that grows keener and sharper with constant use.
Washington Irving

The tongue is but three inches long, yet it can kill a man six feet high.
Japanese Proverb

By examining the tongue, physicians find out the diseases of the body; and philosophers, the diseases of the mind and heart.
Justin

A wound from a tongue is worse than a wound from a sword; for the latter affects only the body, the former the spirit.
Pythagoras

It is observed in the course of wordly things, that men's fortunes are oftener made by their tongues than by their virtues; and more men's fortunes overthrown thereby than by their vices.

Sir Walter Raleigh

The tongue of a fool is the key of his counsel which, in a wise man, wisdom hath in keeping.

Socrates

Open your mouth and purse cautiously; and your stock of wealth and reputation shall, at least in repute, be great.

Johann Georg von Zimmermann

See also: LOQUACITY, TALKING.

TOTALITARIANISM

While we are focusing attention on Southeast Asia, we are really neglecting the situation here at home; and I believe it is in the United States that our greatest danger from totalitarianism, whether from the right or the left, lies.

George David Aiken

The great strength of the totalitarian state lies in its ability to force those who fear it to imitate it.

Adolf Hitler

See also: DESPOTISM, TYRANNY.

TRADE: *see* OCCUPATION.

TRADE UNION: *see* UNIONS.

TRADING

It takes two to make love and two partners to make trade agreements. Unrequited trade or unrequited exports pay no better than unrequited love.

Richard Austen Butler

There is nothing so useful to man in general, nor so beneficial to particular societies and individuals, as trade. This is that alma mater, at whose plentiful breast all mankind are nourished.

Henry Fielding

There is a Spanish proverb, that one who would grow rich must buy of those who go to be executed, as not caring how cheap they sell; and sell to those who go to be married, as not caring how dear they buy.

Thomas Fuller

The remarkable postwar expansion of international trade brought strength and growth

to the free world economy. It enriched the lives of people everywhere—and thus it served the cause of peace.

Lyndon Baines Johnson

See also: BUSINESS, COMMERCE, OCCUPATION.

TRADITION

Tradition is an important help to history, but its statements should be carefully scrutinized before we rely on them.

Joseph Addison

To a significant degree people express their traditions through their local organizations.

Saul David Alinsky

I am well satisfied that if you let in but one little finger of tradition, you will have in the whole monster—horns and tail and all.

Thomas Arnold

What an enormous magnifier is tradition! How a thing grows in the human memory and in the human imagination, when love, worship, and all that lies in the human heart, is there to encourage it.

Thomas Carlyle

Tradition does not mean that the living are dead but that the dead are alive.

Gilbert Keith Chesterton

I am no indiscriminate superstitious worshipper of all that goes under the name of ancient. I never hesitated to endeavour to demolish all that is evil or immoral, no matter how ancient it may be, but with that reservation I must confess to you that I am an adorer of ancient institutions, and it hurts me to think that people in their rush for everything modern despise all their ancient traditions and ignore them in their lives.

Mohandas Karamchand (Mahatma) Gandhi

It takes an endless amount of history to make even a little tradition.

Henry James

The tradition of all past generations weighs like an Alp upon the brain of the living.

Karl Marx

Tradition never needed saving: it somehow has a way of looking out for itself, and if it has not the seeds of perennial generation it had better die.

Henry Rankin Poore

Tradition, as held by the Romanists, is subordinate to Scripture and dependent on it, about as some parasite plants are on the tree that supports them. The former cling to the latter, and rest upon it; then gradually overspread it with their own foliage, till, by little and little, they weaken, and then smother it.

Richard Whately

See also: CUSTOM, HABIT, PRECEDENT.

TRAGEDY

All tragedies are finish'd by a death,
All comedies are ended by a marriage;
The future states of both are left to faith.

George Gordon Byron (Lord Byron)

Tragedy warms the soul, elevates the heart, and can and ought to create heroes. In this sense, perhaps, France owes a part of her great actions to Corneille.

Napoleon I (Bonaparte)

The tragedy is not that things are broken. The tragedy is that they are not mended again.

Alan Stewart Paton

The world is a comedy to those who think; a tragedy to those who feel.

Horace Walpole

See also: ADVERSITY, LITERATURE, THEATER.

TRANSITION

When our first parents were driven out of Paradise, Adam is believed to have remarked to Eve: "My dear, we live in an age of transition."

William Ralph Inge

It is, of course, a trite observation to say that we live "in a period of transition." Many people have said this at many times. Adam may well have made the remark to Eve on leaving the Garden of Eden.

Harold Macmillan

See also: CHANGE, NOVELTY, REVOLUTION.

TRANSPORTATION

The automobile has not merely taken over the street, it has dissolved the living tissue of the city. Its appetite for space is absolutely insatiable; moving and parked, it devours urban land, leaving the buildings as mere islands of habitable space in a sea of dangerous and ugly traffic. . . . Gas-filled, noisy and hazardous, our streets have become the most inhumane landscape in the world.

James Marston Fitch

The old piston-engined aircraft that used to batter the 15-or-16 hour way to Gander or Idlewild demanded a different sort of personality from the pilot. . . . In those days, a man still flew an aircraft as he might sail a boat or drive a racing car. It was a thing to be done with a certain style, even a certain recklessness, and the most famous of these pilots came to be known as the North Atlantic Barons. It was a title of which they were proud. Some wore beards. Some wore monacles. They had a conscious personal myth inherited from wartime flying. But the big jets have changed all this . . . its pilots no longer need flair and doggedness so much as absolute precision. The pilot as man of action is being succeeded by the pilot as technocrat.

John Pearson

The helicopter has become the most universal vehicle ever created and used by man. It approaches closer than any other to fulfillment of mankind's ancient dreams of the flying horse and the magic carpet.

Igor Ivanovitch Sikorsky

With progress in roads came more cars, more roads for the cars, and more cars for the roads that had been built to accommodate more cars.

Time

Railway travelling is not travelling at all; it is merely being sent to a place, and very little different from becoming a parcel.

John Ruskin

See also: AUTOMOBILE, AVIATION, TRAVEL.

TRAVEL

Men may change their climate, but they cannot change their nature. A man that goes out a fool cannot ride or sail himself into common sense.

Joseph Addison

There was once a twin brother named Bright
Who could travel much faster than light.
He departed on day, in a relative way,
And came home on the previous night.

Anonymous

The world is a great book, of which they who never stir from home read only a page.
Augustine of Hippo

Travel, in the younger sort, is a part of education; in the elder, a part of experience. He that travelleth into a country before he hath some entrance into the language, goeth to school, and not to travel.
Francis Bacon

The wise traveler, the self-indulgent and the happy one, is he who never looks at his time-table and hides his watch.
John Mason Brown

Peregrinations charm our senses with such unspeakable and sweet variety, that some count him unhappy that never travelled—a kind of prisoner, and pity his case; that, from his cradle to his old age, he beholds the same, and still the same.
Richard Eugene Burton

Those who visit foreign nations, but associate only with their own countrymen, change their climate, but not their customs. They see new meridians, but the same men; and with heads as empty as their pockets, return home with travelled bodies, but untravelled minds.
Charles Caleb Colton

Travel teaches toleration.
Benjamin Disraeli

Too often travel, instead of broadening the mind, merely lengthens the conversation.
Elizabeth Drew

If you travel you see people in variety. But if you stay home you see them in development.
Josef Washington Hall (Upton Close)

Methods of locomotion have improved greatly in recent years, but places to go remain about the same.
Don Herold

All travel has its advantages. If the traveller visits better countries, he may learn to improve his own; and if fortune carries him to worse, he may learn to enjoy his own.
Samuel Johnson

The use of travelling is to regulate imagination by reality, and, instead of thinking how things may be, to see them as they are.
Samuel Johnson

One telling Socrates that such an one was nothing improved by his travels, " I very well believe it," said he, "for he took himself along with him."
Michel Eyquem de Montaigne

A traveller without observation is a bird without wings.
Saadi (Muslih-ud-Din)

Usually speaking, the worst bred person in company is a young traveller just returned from abroad.
Jonathan Swift

Only that travelling is good which reveals to me the value of home, and enables me to enjoy it better.
Henry David Thoreau

See also: ADVENTURE, AUTOMOBILE, AVIATION, EXPERIENCE, OBSERVATION, TRANSPORTATION, WALKING.

TREASON

Is there not some chosen curse, some hidden thunder in the stores of heaven, red with uncommon wrath, to blast the man who owes his greatness to his country's ruin!
Joseph Addison

A traitor is good fruit to hang from the boughs of the tree of liberty.
Henry Ward Beecher

There is no traitor like him whose domestic treason plants the poniard within the breast that trusted to his truth.
George Gordon Byron (Lord Byron)

Treason pleases, but not the traitor.
Miguel de Cervantes Saavedra

Where trust is greatest, there treason is in its most horrid shape.
John Dryden

Treason doth never prosper; for if it prosper, none dare call it treason.
Sir John Harington

Caesar had his Brutus; Charles the First, his Cromwell; and George the Third—["Treason!" cried the Speaker]—*may profit by their example.* If *this* be treason, make the most of it.
Patrick Henry

There is something peculiarly sinister and insidious in even a charge of disloyalty. Such a charge all too frequently places a stain on the reputation of an individual which is indelible and lasting, regardless of the complete innocence later proved.

John Lord O'Brian

See also: CONSPIRACY, REBELLION.

TREATY

Treaties are like roses and young girls. They last while they last.

Charles André Joseph Marie de Gaulle

See also: ALLIANCE, AMBASSADOR, DIPLOMACY, UNITED NATIONS.

TREE

The groves were God's first temples. Ere man learned
To hew the shaft, and lay the architrave,
And spread the roof above them—ere he framed
The lofty vault, to gather and roll back
The sound of anthems; in the darkling wood,
Amidst the cool and silence, he knelt down
And offered to the Mightiest solemn thanks
And supplication.

William Cullen Bryant

I like trees because they seem more resigned to the way they have to live than other things do.

Willa Sibert Cather

Many a family tree needs trimming.

Frank McKinney (Kin) Hubbard

Those green-robed senators of the mighty woods,
Tall oaks, branch-charmed by the earnest stars
Dream, and so dream all night without a stir.

John Keats

The trees, like the longings of the earth, stand a-tiptoe to peep at the heaven.

Sir Rabindranath Tagore

See also: FLOWER, NATURE.

TRIAL

The hardest trial of the heart is, whether it can bear a rival's failure without triumph.

John Aikin

God had one Son on earth without sin, but never one without suffering.

Augustine of Hippo

We are always in the forge, or on the anvil; by trials God is shaping us for higher things.

Henry Ward Beecher

The surest way to know our gold is to look upon it and examine it in God's furnace, where He tries it that we may see what it is. If we have a mind to know whether a building stands strong or no, we must look upon it when the wind blows. If we would know whether a staff be strong, or a rotten, broken reed, we must observe it when it is leaned on and weight is borne upon it. If we would weigh ourselves justly we must weigh ourselves in God's scales that He makes us of to weigh us.

Jonathan Edwards

It was a beautiful and striking reply, given by one in affliction, who, when asked how it was that he bore it so well, replied, "It lightens the stroke, I find, to draw near to Him who handles the rod."

Tryon Edwards

Prosperity tries the fortunate, adversity the great.

Pliny the Younger

A truly virtuous person is like good metal,—the more he is fired, the more he is fined; the more he is opposed, the more he is approved. Wrongs may well try him and touch him, but they cannot imprint on him any false stamp.

Duc de Armand Jean du Plessis Richelieu

See also: ADVERSITY, AFFLICTION, TROUBLE.

TRIFLES

Sometimes when I considered what tremendous consequences come from little things—a chance word, a tap on the shoulder, or a penny dropped on a newsstand I am tempted to think . . . there are no little things.

Bruce Barton

There is nothing insignificant—nothing.

Samuel Taylor Coleridge

Little things affect little minds.

Benjamin Disraeli

It is in those acts which we call trivialities that the seeds of joy are forever wasted.

George Eliot (Mary Ann Evans)

The creation of a thousand forests is in one acorn.

Ralph Waldo Emerson

There is a kind of latent omniscience not only in every man, but in every particle.
Ralph Waldo Emerson

There is no real elevation of mind in a contempt of little things. It is, on the contrary, from too narrow views that we consider those things of little importance, which have, in fact, such extensive consequences.
François de Salignac de La Mothe-Fénelon

The smallest hair throws its shadow.
Johann Wolfgang von Goethe

Little things are great to little men.
Oliver Goldsmith

The greatest things ever done on earth have been done by little and little—little agents, little persons, little things, by every one doing his own work, filling his own sphere, holding his own post, and saying, "Lord, what wilt thou have me to do?"
Thomas Guthrie

Trivial circumstances, which show the manners of the age, are often more instructive as well as entertaining, than the great transactions of wars and negotiations, which are nearly similar in all periods, and in all countries of the world.
David Hume

He crossed words of which he knew nothing; and perhaps we all do as much every moment, over things of divinest meaning.
(James Henry) Leigh Hunt

Not for the mighty world, O Lord, tonight, nations and kingdoms in their fearful might. Let me be glad the kettle gently sings, let me be glad for little things.
Edna Jaques

There is nothing too little for so little a creature as man. It is by studying little things that we attain the great art of having as little misery and as much happiness as possible.
Samuel Johnson

The million little things that drop into our hands, the small opportunities each day brings He leaves us free to use or abuse and goes unchanging along His silent way.
Helen Adams Keller

Those who give too much attention to trifling things become generally incapable of great ones.
Duc François de La Rochefoucauld

He who esteems trifles for themselves is a trifler; he who esteems them for the conclusions to be drawn from them, or the advantage to which they can be put, is a philosopher.
Edward G. Bulwer-Lytton (Baron Lytton)

Trifles make perfection, but perfection itself is no trifle.
Michelangelo (Buonarroti)

Men are led by trifles.
Napoleon I (Bonaparte)

It is curious how sometimes a relatively minor event impresses one more than a major happening. Trivial words or gestures are apt to reveal an individual far more than his studied poses and utterances.
Jawaharlal Nehru

Little things make a difference psychologically.
Jawaharlal Nehru

If the nose of Cleopatra had been a little shorter it would have changed the history of the world.
Blaise Pascal

Do little things now; so shall big things come to thee by and by asking to be done.
Persian Proverb

Nothing is more unworthy of a wise man, or ought to trouble him more, than to have allowed more time for trifling, and useless things, than they deserved.
Plato

Think nothing too little; seek for the cross in the daily incidents of life, look for the cross in everything. Nothing is too little which relates to man's salvation, nor is there anything too little in which either to please God or to serve Satan.
Edward Bouverie Pusey

There is a care for trifles which proceeds from love of conscience, and is most holy; and a care for trifles which comes of idleness and frivolity, and is most base.
John Ruskin

A little and a little, collected together, become a great deal; the heap in the barn consists of single grains, and drop and drop make the inundation.
Saadi (Muslih-ud-Din)

It is the little bits of things that fret and worry us; we can dodge an elephant, but we can't a fly.

Henry Wheeler Shaw (Josh Billings)

Trifles discover a character more than actions of importance. In regard to the former, a person is off his guard, and thinks it not material to use disguise. It is no imperfect hint toward the discovery of a man's character to say he looks as though you might be certain of finding a pin upon his sleeve.

William Shenstone

The chains which cramp us most are those which weigh on us least.

Anne Sophie Swetchine

Small causes are sufficient to make a man uneasy when great ones are not in the way. For want of a block he will stumble at a straw.

Jonathan Swift

Delude not yourself with the notion that you may be untrue and uncertain in trifles and in important things the contrary. Trifles make up existence, and give the measure by which to try us; and the fearful power of habit, after a time, suffers not the best will to ripen into action.

Baron Karl Maria von Weber

He that has "a spirit of detail" will do better in life than many who figured beyond him in the university. Such an one is minute and particular. He adjusts trifles; and these trifles compose most of the business and happiness of life. Great events happen seldom, and affect few; trifles happen every moment to everybody; and though one occurrence of them adds little to the happiness or misery of life, yet the sum total of their continual repetition is of the highest consequence.

Daniel Webster

The power of duly appreciating little things belongs to a great mind; a narrow-minded man has it not, for to him they are great things.

Richard Whately

See also: GREATNESS, SIZE.

TRIVIA: see TRIFLES.

TROUBLE

Never trouble trouble till trouble troubles you.

American Proverb

Men are born to trouble at first, and are exercised in it all their days. There is a cry at the beginning of life and a groan at the end of it.

William Arnot

There are many troubles which you cannot cure by the Bible and the hymn book, but which you can cure by a good perspiration and a breath of fresh air.

Henry Ward Beecher

Adversity, if a man is set down to it by degrees, is more supportable with equanimity by most people than any great prosperity arrived at in a single lifetime.

Samuel Butler

We triumph without glory when we conquer without danger.

Pierre Corneille

He that seeks trouble always finds it.

English Proverb

Women like to sit down with trouble as if it were knitting.

Ellen Anderson Gholson Glasgow

Trouble creates a capacity to handle it.

Oliver Wendell Holmes, Jr.

When troubles comes from God, then naught behoves like patience; but for troubles wrought of men, patience is hard—I tell you it is hard.

Jean Ingelow

The true way of softening one's troubles is to solace those of others.

Marquise de Maintenon

There is nothing so consoling as to find that one's neighbor's troubles are at least as great as one's own.

George Moore

It is not the will of God to give us more troubles than will bring us to live by faith on Him; He loves us too well to give us a moment of uneasiness but for our good.

William Romaine

The wise man thinks about his troubles only when there is some purpose in doing so; at other times he thinks about other things.

Bertrand Arthur William Russell

There are people who always anticipate trouble, and in that way they manage to enjoy many sorrows that never really happen to them.

Henry Wheeler Shaw (Josh Billings)

If all men were to bring their miseries together in one place, most would be glad to take each his own home again rather than take a portion out of the common stock.

Solon

See also: ADVERSITY, TRAGEDY.

TRUISM

Half the noblest passages in poetry are truisms; but these truisms are the great truths of humanity; and he is the true poet who draws them from their fountains in elemental purity, and gives us to drink.

Letitia Elizabeth Landon

Never reason from what you do not know.

Andrew Michael Ramsay

Deny first-truths, and reasoning is void. If an opponent denies them, we can only add: "Be not as the horse and the mule, who have no understanding."

Charles Simmons

Fundamental truths should be both clear and familiar truths; self-evident truths are a solid foundation for reasoning.

Charles Simmons

See also: APOTHEGM, FACT.

TRUST

He who believes in nobody knows that he himself is not to be trusted.

Berthold Auerbach

A trustee is held to something stricter than the morals of the market place. Not honesty alone, but the punctilio of an honor the most sensitive, is then the standard of behavior.

Benjamin Nathan Cardozo

The man who trusts men will make fewer mistakes than he who distrusts them.

Conte Camillo Benso di Cavour

We must not let go manifest truths because we cannot answer all questions about them.

Jeremy Collier

Woe to the man whose heart has not learned while young to hope, to love—and to put its trust in life!

Joseph Conrad

You may be deceived if you trust too much, but you will live in torment if you do not trust enough.

Frank Crane

Trust everybody, but cut the cards.

Finley Peter Dunne

To trust God when we have securities in our iron chest is easy, but not thankworthy; but to depend on Him for what we cannot see, as it is more hard for man to do, so it is more acceptable to God.

Owen Felltham

To trust is a virtue. It is weakness that begets distrust.

Mohandas Karamchand (Mahatma) Gandhi

The trust which we put in ourselves causes us to feel trust in others.

Duc François de La Rochefoucauld

Trust him little who praises all, him less who censures all, and him least who is indifferent about all.

Johann Kaspar Lavater

Men are able to trust one another, knowing the exact degree of dishonesty they are entitled to expect.

Stephen Butler Leacock

To be trusted is a greater compliment than to be loved.

James Ramsay MacDonald

Trust God where you cannot trace Him. Do not try to penetrate the cloud He brings over you; rather look to the bow that is on it. The mystery is God's; the promise is yours.

John Ross Macduff

Trust in God does not supersede the employment of prudent means on our part. To expect God's protection while we do nothing is not to honor but to tempt providence.

Pasquier Quesnel

If thou be subject to any great vanity or ill, then therein trust no man; for every man's folly ought to be his greatest secret.

Sir Walter Raleigh

How calmly may we commit ourselves to the hands of Him who bears up the world.

Jean Paul Richter

As we know men at first only by their words, we must trust them till their deeds belie their words. We sometimes find that people whom we have suspected to be enemies are not in reality so; we are then very much ashamed of our mistake: it is sufficient to be prepared to hate when we have proper grounds for it.

Marquise de Sévigné

The soul and spirit that animates and keeps up society is mutual trust.

Robert South

The only way to make a man trustworthy is to trust him; and the surest way to make him untrustworthy is to distrust him and show him your distrust.

Henry Lewis Stimson

I think that we may safely trust a good deal more than we do. We may waive just so much care of ourselves as we honestly bestow elsewhere.

Henry David Thoreau

See also: BELIEF, CONFIDENCE, DUTY, EXPECTATION, FAITH, HOPE.

TRUTH

Truth does not consist in minute accuracy of detail, but in conveying a right impression; and there are vague ways of speaking that are truer than strict facts would be. When the Psalmist said, "Rivers of water run down mine eyes, because men keep not thy law," he did not state the fact, but he stated a truth deeper than fact, and truer.

Henry Alford

Truth is not only violated by falsehood; it may be equally outraged by silence.

Henri Frédéric Amiel

If it is the truth what does it matter who says it.

Anonymous

If the world goes against truth, then Athanasius goes against the world.

Athanasius the Great

There are three parts in truth: first, the inquiry, which is the wooing of it; secondly, the knowledge of it, which is the presence of it; and thirdly, the belief, which is the enjoyment of it.

Francis Bacon

I am not struck so much by the diversity of testimony as by the many-sidedness of truth.

Stanley Baldwin

First, let the Truth itself teach you that you should seek it in your neighbors before seeking it in its own nature. Later, you will see why you should seek it in yourself before seeking it in your neighbors.

Bernard of Clairvaux

Truth is only developed in the hour of need; time, and not man, discovers it.

Vicomte Louis Gabriel Ambroise de Bonald

Facts that are not frankly faced have a habit of stabbing us in the back.

Sir Harold Bowden

If a thousand old beliefs were ruined in our march to truth we must still march on.

Stopford Augustus Brooke

Some men love truth so much that they seem in continual fear lest she should catch cold on over-exposure.

Samuel Butler

It is strange but true; for truth is always strange, stranger than fiction.

George Gordon Byron (Lord Byron)

Statistics—I can prove anything by statistics —except the truth.

George Canning

I have always found that the honest truth of our own mind has a certain attraction for every other mind that loves truth honestly.

Thomas Carlyle

Truths turn into dogmas the moment they are disputed.

Gilbert Keith Chesterton

Men occasionally stumble over the truth, but most of them pick themselves up and hurry off as if nothing had happened.

Sir Winston Leonard Spencer Churchill

Most writers regard truth as their most valuable possession, and therefore are most economical in its use.

Samuel Langhorne Clemens (Mark Twain)

Truth is stranger than fiction, but it is because Fiction is obliged to stick to possibilities; Truth isn't.

    Samuel Langhorne Clemens (Mark Twain)

The interests of society often render it expedient not to utter the whole truth, the interests of science never: for in this field we have much more to fear from the deficiency of truth, than from its abundance.

    Charles Caleb Colton

What a man sees only in his best moments as truth is truth in all moments.

    Joseph Cook

Truth is the most powerful thing in the world, since even fiction itself must be governed by it, and can only please by its resemblance.

    Anthony Ashley Cooper (Lord Shaftesbury)

Truth and love are two of the most powerful things in the world; and when they both go together they cannot easily be withstood.

    Ralph Cudworth

Experience has taught me, when the versions of the same story given by two wire services differ materially, to prefer the less exciting.

    Elmer Holmes Davis

He that opposes his own judgment against the consent of the times ought to be backed with unanswerable truths; and he that has truth on his side is a fool, as well as a coward, if he is afraid to own it because of other men's opinions.

    Daniel Defoe

What we have in us of the image of God is the love of truth and justice.

    Demosthenes

A truth that one does not understand becomes an error.

    Adolphe Desbarolles

There is but one sure road of access to truth—the road of patient, cooperative inquiry operating by means of observation, experiment, record, and controlled reflection.

    John Dewey

Truth is as old as God,
His twin identity—
And will endure as long as He,

A co-eternity,
And perish on the day
That He is borne away
From mansion of the universe,
A lifeless Deity.

    Emily Dickinson

When you have eliminated the impossible, whatever remains, *however improbable,* must be the truth.

    Sir Arthur Conan Doyle

Ultimately, our troubles are due to dogma and deduction; we find no new truth because we take some venerable but questionable proposition as the indubitable starting point, and never think of putting this assumption itself to a test of observation or experiment.

    Will (William James) Durant

Evil thoughts, lusts, and malicious purposes cannot go forth, like wandering pollen, from one human mind to another, finding unsuspected lodgement, if virtue and truth build a strong defence.

    Mary Baker Eddy

If you are out to describe the truth, leave elegance to the tailor.

    Albert Einstein

The greatest homage we can pay to truth is to use it.

    Ralph Waldo Emerson

No truth so sublime but it may be seen to be trivial to-morrow in the light of new thoughts.

    Ralph Waldo Emerson

Truth comes home to the mind so naturally, that when we learn it for the first time, it seems as though we did no more than recall it to our memory.

    Bernard Le Bovier de Fontenelle

The proselyting spirit is inseparable from the love of truth, for it is only the effort to win others to our way of thinking.

    Georg Forster

The confusion and undesigned inaccuracy so often to be observed in conversation, especially in that of uneducated persons, proves that truth needs to be cultivated as a talent, as well as recommended as a virtue.

    Elizabeth Fry

All the religions, of the world, while they may differ in other respects, unitedly proclaim that nothing lives in this world but Truth.

Mohandas Karamchand (Mahatma) Gandhi

The seeker after truth should be humbler than the dust. The world crushes the dust under its feet, but the seeker after truth should be so humble himself that even the dust could crush him. Only then, and not till then, will we have a glimpse of Truth.

Mohandas Karamchand (Mahatma) Gandhi

Funny how people despise platitudes, when they are usually the truest thing going. A thing has to be pretty true before it gets to be a platitude.

Katharine Fullerton Gerould

To love the truth is to refuse to let oneself be saddened by it.

André Gide

It is easier to perceive error than to find truth, for the former lies on the surface and is easily seen, while the latter lies in the depth, where few are willing to search for it.

Johann Wolfgang von Goethe

A charitable untruth, an uncharitable truth, and an unwise management of truth or love, are all to be carefully avoided of him that would go with a right foot in the narrow way.

Joseph Hall

Follow not truth too near the heels, lest it dash out thy teeth.

George Herbert

The grand character of truth is its capability of enduring the test of universal experience, and coming unchanged out of every possible form of fair discussion.

Sir John Frederick William Herschel

Religious truth, touch what points of it you will, has always to do with the being and government of God, and is, of course, illimitable in its reach.

Roswell Dwight Hitchcock

Man approaches the unattainable truth through a succession of errors.

Aldous Leonard Huxley

The pursuit of truth is just a polite name for the intellectual's favorite pastime of sub-stituting simple and therefore false abstractions for the living complexities of reality.

Aldous Leonard Huxley

The path of truth is the path of progress.

Harold Le Claire Ickes

You can take a chess-board as black squares on a white ground, or as white squares on a black ground, and neither conception is a false one.

William James

Accustom your children to a strict attention to truth, even in the most minute particulars. If a thing happened at one window, and they, when relating it, say that it happened at another, do not let is pass, but instantly check them; you do not know where deviations from truth will end.

Samuel Johnson

Truth, like beauty, varies in its fashions, and is best recommended by different dresses to different minds; and he that recalls the attention of mankind to any part of learning which time has left behind it, may be truly said to advance the literature of his own age.

Samuel Johnson

One day Soshi was walking on the bank of a river with a friend. "How delightfully the fishes are enjoying themselves in the water!" exclaimed Soshi. His friend spake to him thus: "You are not a fish; how do you know that the fishes are enjoying themselves?" "You are not myself," returned Soshi; "how do you know that I do not know that the fishes are enjoying themselves?"

Okakura Kakuzo

Truth is not introduced into the individual from without, but was within him all the time.

Sören Aabye Kierkegaard

Stick to the old truths and the old paths, and learn their divineness by sick beds, and in every-day work, and do not darken your mind with intellectual puzzles, which may breed disbelief, but can never breed vital religion or practical usefulness.

Charles Kingsley

Truth does not do as much good in the world as its counterfeit does mischief.

Duc François de La Rochefoucauld

Receiving a new truth is adding a new sense.

Baron Justus von Liebig

Truth, whether in or out of fashion, is the measure of knowledge, and the business of the understanding; whatsoever is beside that, however authorized by consent, or recommended by rarity, is nothing but ignorance, or something worse.

John Locke

Truth is by its very nature intolerant, exclusive, for every truth is the denial of its opposing error.

Christoph Ernest Luthardt

Peace if possible, but truth at any rate.

Martin Luther

A truth that disheartens because it is true is of far more value than the most stimulating of falsehoods.

Count Maurice Maeterlinck

You need not tell all the truth, unless to those who have a right to know it all. But let all you tell be truth.

Horace Mann

Man with his burning soul has but an hour of breath to build a ship of truth in which his soul may sail—sail on the sea of death, for death takes toll of beauty, courage, youth, of all but truth.

John Masefield

The way of truth is like a great road. It is not difficult to know it. The evil is only that men will not seek it.

Mencius

It is hard to believe that a man is telling the truth when you know that you would lie if you were in his place.

Henry Louis Mencken

Ah, what a dusty answer gets the soul
When hot for certainties in this our life.

George Meredith

Truth is not a diet but a condiment.

Christopher Darlington Morley

There is an idiom in truth which falsehood never can imitate.

Sir Francis Napier

It is better to understand a part of truth and apply it to our lives, than to understand nothing at all and flounder helplessly in a vain attempt to pierce the mystery of existence.

Jawaharlal Nehru

A partial truth is sometimes more dangerous than falsehood, a truth that had had its day blinds one to the reality of the present.

Jawaharlal Nehru

Truth, as ultimate reality, if such there is, must be eternal, imperishable, unchanging. But that infinite, eternal and unchanging truth cannot be apprehended in its fulness by the finite mind of man which can only grasp, at most, some small aspect of it limited by time and space, and by the state of development of that mind and the prevailing ideology of the period.

Jawaharlal Nehru

The people have a right to the truth as they have a right to life, liberty and the pursuit of happiness.

Frank Norris

Still is the might of truth, as it has been:
Lodg'd in the few, obey'd, and yet unseen.
  Rear'd on lone heights, and rare,
  His saints their watch-flame bear,
And the mad world sees the wide-circling blaze,
Vain searching whence it streams, and how to quench its rays.

John Henry Newman

It is twice as hard to crush a half-truth as a whole lie.

Austin O'Malley

I have seldom known any one who deserted truth in trifles, that could be trusted in matters of importance.

William Paley

There are two peculiarities in the truths of religion: a divine beauty which renders them lovely, and a holy majesty which makes them venerable. And there are two peculiarities in errors: an impiety which renders them horrible, and an impertinence which renders them ridiculous.

Blaise Pascal

Of all duties, the love of truth, with faith and constancy in it, ranks first and highest. To love God and to love truth are one and the same.

Silvio Pellico

Seven years of silent inquiry are needful for a man to learn the truth, but fourteen in order to learn how to make it known to his fellowmen.

Plato

Truth is so great a perfection, that if God would render himself visible to men, he would choose light for his body and truth for his soul.

Pythagoras

The old faiths light their candles all about, but burly Truth comes by and blows them out.

Lizette Woodworth Reese

Great men tell the truth and are never believed. Lesser men are always believed, but seldom have the brains or the courage to tell the truth.

Kenneth Roberts

The deepest truths are the simplest and the most common.

Frederick William Robertson

Most of the change we think we see in life
Is due to truths being in and out of favour.

Edwin Arlington Robinson

I cannot get along either with those who shun the blunt truth or those who make their peace with it too easily.

Jean Rostand

I should hesitate to deprive any being of the illusion he lives by; but humanity as a whole interests me only insofar as it can stand up to truth.

Jean Rostand

It is after truth has been discovered that we become aware of the simpler approach by which we might have reached it.

Jean Rostand

One cannot bring a given set of truths to light without obscuring others. Every discovery covers up.

Jean Rostand

The only thing one cannot embellish without causing its death is truth.

Jean Rostand

Truth is always served by great minds, even if they fight it.

Jean Rostand

Philosophy should be piecemeal and provisional like science; final truth belongs to heaven, not to this world.

Bertrand Arthur William Russell

Truth is a jewel which should not be painted over; but it may be set to advantage and shown in a good light.

George Santayana

A truth that is merely acquired from others only clings to us as a limb added to the body, or as a false tooth, or a wax nose. A truth we have acquired by our own mental exertions, is like our natural limbs, which really belong to us. This is exactly the difference between an original thinker and the mere learned man.

Arthur Schopenhauer

One must never, when dealing with primitives, hold out hopes of recovery to the patient and his relatives, if the case is really hopeless. . . . One must tell the truth without reservation. They wish to know it and they can endure it, for death is to them something natural. They are not afraid of it, but face it calmly.

Albert Schweitzer

It is the special privilege of truth always to grow on candid minds.

Frederick Henry Scrivener

My way of joking is to tell the truth. It's the funniest joke in the world.

George Bernard Shaw

Men must love the truth before they thoroughly believe it.

Robert South

Perfect truth is possible only with knowledge, and in knowledge the whole essence of the thing operates on the soul and is joined essentially to it.

Baruch (Benedict) Spinoza

When a man has no design but to speak plain truth, he may say a great deal in a very narrow compass.

Sir Richard Steele

The most striking contradiction of our civilization is the fundamental reverence for truth which we profess and the thoroughgoing disregard for it which we practice.

Vilhjalmur Stefansson

But men do not seek the truth. It is truth that pursues men who run away and will not look around.

(Joseph) Lincoln Steffens

As Thales measured the pyramids from their shadows, so we may measure the height and antiquity of the truth, by the extent of its corruptions.

Edward Stillingfleet

When two truths seem directly opposed to each other, we must not question either, but remember there is a third—God—who reserves to himself the right to harmonize them.

Anne Sophie Swetchine

Some modern zealots appear to have no better knowledge of truth, nor better manner of judging it, than by counting noses.

Jonathan Swift

Fear is not in the habit of speaking truth; when perfect sincerity is expected, perfect freedom must be allowed; nor has any one who is apt to be angry when he hears the truth, any cause to wonder that he does not hear it.

Tacitus

Truth is established by investigation and delay; falsehood prospers by precipitancy.

Tacitus

To all appearances, fiction is the native dialect of mankind, and the truth an esoteric language as yet but imperfectly learned and little loved.

Carl Van Doren

He who seeks truth should be of no country.

Voltaire (François Marie Arouet)

Seize upon truth, wherever it is found, amongst your friends, amongst your foes, on Christian or on heathen ground; the flower's divine where'er it grows.

Isaac Watts

Truth is always congruous and agrees with itself; every truth in the universe agrees with all others.

Daniel Webster

Every one wishes to have truth on his side, but it is not every one that sincerely wishes to be on the side of truth.

Richard Whately

There are no whole truths; all truths are half-truths. It is trying to treat them as whole truths that plays the devil.

Alfred North Whitehead

See also: ACCURACY, AMBIGUITY, CONFESSION, FACT, HONESTY, INTEGRITY, KNOWLEDGE, REALISM, SCIENCE, SINCERITY, STATISTICS.

TWILIGHT

Parting day
Dies like the dolphin, whom each pang imbues
With a new colour as it gasps away,
The last till loveliest, till—'tis gone—and all is gray.

George Gordon Byron (Lord Byron)

From that high mount of God whence light and shade
Spring both, the face of brightest heaven had changed
To grateful twilight.

John Milton

When twilight dews are falling soft
Upon the rosy sea, love,
I watch the star, whose beam so oft
Has lighted me to thee, love.

Thomas Moore

Twilight, ascending slowly from the east,
Entwined in duskier wreaths her braided locks
O'er the fair front and radiant eyes of day;
Night followed, clad with stars.

Percy Bysshe Shelley

See also: EVENING, MOON, NIGHT, SUNSET.

TYRANNY

A king ruleth as he ought; a tyrant as he lists; a king to the profit of all, a tyrant only to please a few.

Aristotle

I can see why so many movements against injustice became such absolute tyrannies.

Samuel Nathaniel Behrman

Tyranny and anarchy are never far asunder.

Jeremy Bentham

Every wanton and causeless restraint of the will of the subject, whether practised by a monarch, a nobility, or a popular assembly, is a degree of tyranny.

Sir William Blackstone

Bad laws are the worst sort of tyranny.
Edmund Burke

Free governments have committed more flagrant acts of tyranny than the most perfectly despotic governments we have ever known.
Edmund Burke

A tyrant never tasteth of true friendship, nor of perfect liberty.
Diogenes

From behind the Iron Curtain, there are signs that tyranny is in trouble and reminders that its structure is as brittle as its surface is hard.
Dwight David Eisenhower

We should know by now that where weakness and dependence are not transformed into strength and self-reliance, we can expect only chaos, and then tyranny, to follow.
John Fitzgerald Kennedy

Tyranny is always weakness.
James Russell Lowell

Hateful is the power, and pitiable is the life, of those who wish to be feared rather than to be loved.
Cornelius Nepos

Where law ends, tyranny begins.
William Pitt (Lord Chatham)

It is worthy of observation that the most imperious masters over their own servants are at the same time the most abject slaves to the servants of other masters.
Seneca

The most tyrannical governments are those which make crimes of opinions, for everyone has an inalienable right to his thoughts.
Baruch (Benedict) Spinoza

The closed door and sealed lips are prerequisites to tyranny.
Frank Lebby Stanton

There is a natural and necessary progression, from the extreme of anarchy to the extreme of tyranny; and arbitrary power is most easily established on the ruins of liberty abused to licentiousness.
George Washington

See *also*: DESPOTISM, TOTALITARIANISM.

TYRANT

Degeneracy follows every autocratic system of violence, for violence inevitably attracts moral inferiors. Time has proved that illustrious tyrants are succeeded by scoundrels.
Albert Einstein

Of all the evils that infest a state, a tyrant is the greatest; his sole will commands the laws, and lords it over them.
Euripides

Rebellion to tyrants is obedience to God.
Benjamin Franklin

Tyrants forego all respect for humanity in proportion as they are sunk beneath it. Taught to believe themselves of a different species, they really become so, lose their participation with their kind, and in mimicking the god dwindle into the brute.
William Hazlitt

Necessity is the argument of tyrants; it is the creed of slaves.
William Pitt

Tyrants are seldom free; the cares and the instruments of their tyranny enslave them.
George Santayana

Tyrants have always some slight shade of virtue; they support the laws before destroying them.
Voltaire (François Marie Arouet)

See *also*: DESPOTISM, TYRANNY.

U

UGLINESS

I cannot tell by what logic we call a toad, a bear, or an elephant ugly; they being created in those outward shapes and figures which best express the actions of their inward forms; and having passed that general visitation of God, who saw that all that He had made was good.

Sir Thomas Browne

Ugliness is a point of view; an ulcer is wonderful to a pathologist.

Austin O'Malley

I doubt if there is anything in the world uglier than a midwestern city.

Frank Lloyd Wright

She is most splendidly, gallantly ugly.

William Wycherley

See also: BEAUTY, DEFORMITY, DEPRAVITY.

UNBELIEF

In all unbelief there are these two things: a good opinion of one's self, and a bad opinion of God.

Horatius Bonar

There is but one thing without honor, smitten with eternal barrenness, inability to do or to be, and that is unbelief. He who believes nothing, who believes only the shows of things, is not in relation with nature and fact at all.

Thomas Carlyle

Unbelief, in distinction from disbelief, is a confession of ignorance where honest inquiry might easily find that just so much light is necessary, and no more. Whatever is beyond, brings darkness and confusion.

Anthony Ashley Cooper (Lord Shaftesbury)

How deeply rooted must unbelief be in our hearts, when we are surprised to find our prayers answered, instead of feeling sure that they will be so, if they are only offered up in faith, and in accordance with the will of God!

Augustus and Julius Hare

Disbelief in futurity loosens in a great measure the ties of morality, and may be for that reason pernicious to the peace of civil society.

David Hume

Take my word for it, it is not prudent to trust yourself to any man who does not believe in a God or in a future after death.

Sir Robert Peel

I would rather dwell in the dim fog of superstition than in air rarified to nothing by the air-pump of unbelief, in which the panting breast expires, vainly and convulsively gasping for breath.

Jean Paul Richter

Charles II, hearing Vossius, a free-thinker, repeating some incredible stories of the Chinese, turned to those about him and said, "This learned divine is a very strange man; he believes everything but the Bible."

Samuel Smiles

See also: AGNOSTICISM, ATHEISM, CREDULITY, DISTRUST, DOUBT, INCREDULITY, SKEPTICISM, THEOLOGY.

UNDERSTANDING

It is by no means necessary to understand things to speak confidently about them.

Pierre Augustin Caron de Beaumarchais

Nine-tenths of the serious controversies which arise in life result from misunderstanding.

Louis Dembitz Brandeis

He who calls in the aid of an equal understanding, doubles his own; and he who profits by a superior understanding, raises his powers to a level with the height of the understanding he unites with.

Edmund Burke

Men know much which they do not understand, and they understand much which they do not have the moral sense or power to utilize profitably to themselves and their fellow men.

John Emmett Edgerton

There exists a passion for comprehension, just as there exists a passion for music. Without this passion there would be neither mathematics nor rational science.

Albert Einstein

What of us who have to catch up, always
To catch up with the high-powered car, or with
The unbalanced budget, to cope with competition,
To weather the sudden thunder of the uneasy
Frontier? We also loom with the earth
Over the waterways of space. Between
Our birth and death we may touch understanding
As a moth brushes a window with its wing.

Christopher Fry

I hold myself indebted to any one from whose enlightened understanding another ray of knowledge communicates to mine. Really to inform the mind is to correct and enlarge the heart.

Junius

There is a great difference between knowing a thing and understanding it. You can know a lot about something and not really understand it.

Charles Franklin Kettering

A man of understanding finds less difficulty in submitting to a wrong-headed fellow, than in attempting to set him right.

Duc François de La Rochefoucauld

The improvement of the understanding is for two ends; first, our own increase of knowledge; secondly, to enable us to deliver that knowledge to others.

John Locke

No one knows what strength of parts he has till he has tried them. And of the understanding one may most truly say, that its force is generally greater than it thinks till it is put to it. Therefore the proper remedy is, to set the mind to work, and apply the thoughts vigorously to the business, for it holds in the struggles of the mind, as in those of war, that to think we shall conquer is to conquer.

John Locke

Men are of three different capacities: one understands intuitively, another only understands so far as it is explained, and a third understands neither of himself nor by explanation: the first is excellent, the second commendable, and the third altogether useless.

Niccolò Machiavelli

The things that a man does not say often reveal the understanding and penetration of his mind even more than the things he says.

Robert Andrews Millikan

Understanding is a two-way street.

Anna Eleanor Roosevelt

Our dignity is not in what we do, but what we understand. The whole world is doing things.

George Santayana

It is difficult to get a man to understand something when his salary depends upon his not understanding it.

Upton Sinclair

I have learned not to mock, lament or execrate, but to understand human actions.

Baruch (Benedict) Spinoza

I know of no evil so great as the abuse of the understanding, and yet there is no one vice more common.

Sir Richard Steele

See also: INTELLIGENCE, WISDOM.

UNHAPPINESS

Man's unhappiness comes of his greatness; it is because there is an infinite in him, which, with all his cunning, he cannot quite bury under the finite.

Thomas Carlyle

A perverse temper, and a discontented, fretful disposition, wherever they prevail, render any state of life unhappy.

Cicero

We never enjoy perfect happiness; our most fortunate successes are mingled with sadness; some anxieties always perplex the reality of our satisfaction.

Pierre Corneille

It is better not to be than to be unhappy.

John Dryden

The most unhappy of all men is he who believes himself to be so.

David Hume

Men who are unhappy, like men who sleep badly, are always proud of the fact.

Bertrand Arthur William Russell

See *also*: AFFLICTION, DISCONTENTMENT, PAIN, SADNESS, SORROW, SUFFERING.

UNION OF SOVIET SOCIALIST REPUBLICS: *see* RUSSIA.

UNIONS

Union membership is a subject well able to rile the emotions. For many people, there is no objective view possible, no middle ground; you're either for unions or "agin 'em" and that's that . . .

Joseph Henry Foegen

Collective bargaining, when everything is said and done, is what unions are all about.

Herbert Lewis Marx, Jr.

The most startling and significant change during the 1960's in the American labor movement has been the new attitude of the individual union member towards his labor union. . . . Today, many, many union members, while still maintaining varying attitudes toward management, have come to look on the union as a third party, to be dealt with at arm's length.

Herbert Lewis Marx, Jr.

With a few notable exceptions, American labor unions generally stick close to routine business—the representation of their members, encounters with management, and maintenance of their own internal power structure.

Herbert Lewis Marx, Jr.

We are pooling our resources so we can take on the task of organizing the great mass of unorganized workers in America and build a greater industrial democracy. It is our belief that a united labor movement will be able to

devote the talent and strength of our trade unions to greater service to the people of the United States.

George Meany and Walter Reuther

The labor movement's basic purpose is to achieve a better life for its members. A union that fails in this purpose has failed utterly.

New York Times

The American labor movement as it has grown and evolved has been fashioned by the character, spirit, and aspirations common to the workers of the United States [Bureau of Labor Statistics].

United States Department of Labor

See *also*: BUSINESS, CAPITAL AND LABOR, OCCUPATION, WAGE, WOMAN AND WORK, WORK.

UNITED NATIONS

The new member states which we shall shortly have the pleasure of welcoming will bring the Assembly nearer in practice to what it ideally is—an assembly fully representative of the whole human race. If, to match this accession of strength, we can bring to our work a corresponding sense of community, as dwellers on this small and threatened planet, then indeed this Assembly may deserve a noble title—the assembly of humanity.

Frederick Henry Boland

Who is this rare bird, perched at the eerie dead center of the world's hurricane, whom all men delight to praise? A Machiavelli with a Boy Scout's exterior? A gross flatterer? . . . A monstrous appeaser? Clean is the word for Hammarskjold. A blond, tanned man, clean shaven, a man just out of a bath. "Central Casting," looking him over quickly for a feature part . . . would assign him without a second thought as the sympathetic brother of the grieving heroine; or the third Swiss guide in an Alpine rescue . . . The secret of his good nature, his interminable patience . . . is probably that he was born in a small country that must for survival measure with a steady hand the crushing weight of the giants who stand on either side.

(Alfred) Alistair Cooke

The United Nations was not set up to be a reformatory. It was assumed that you would be good before you got in and not that being in would make you good.

John Foster Dulles

The UN is not just a product of do-gooders. It is harshly real. The day will come when men will see the UN and what it means clearly. Everything will be all right—you know when? When people, just people, stop thinking of the United Nations as a weird Picasso abstraction, and see it as a drawing they made themselves.

Dag Hammarskjold

It is our earnest wish that the UN—in its structure and in its means—may become ever more equal to the magnitude and nobility of its tasks, and that the day may come when every human being will find therein an effective safeguard for the rights which derive directly from his dignity as a person.

John XXIII (Angelo Giuseppe Roncalli)

We are a nation of differences, and the values and principles that protect those differences are the sources of a unity far more lasting and stronger than any contrived harmony could be.

Lyndon Baines Johnson

We prefer world law, in the age of self-determination, to world war in the age of mass extermination.

John Fitzgerald Kennedy

This organization is created to prevent you from going to hell. It isn't created to take you to heaven.

Henry Cabot Lodge

The United Nations can't guarantee peace any more than a doctor can guarantee health. But would that be a good reason for doing away with doctors?

André Maurois

You can look at the UN through many eyes—the eye of faith, of hope, of charity, the eye of disillusion, the eye of mockery, the eye of fear or distaste, even the eye of poetry; but whatever your bias, vantage point or field of vision, you can hardly fail to recognize it as one of the supremely interesting sights of our time.

James Morris

The whole basis of the United Nations is the right of all nations—great or small—to have weight, to have a vote, to be attended to, to be a part of the twentieth century.

Adlai Ewing Stevenson

There is a disadvantage in being anywhere other than the seat of power. And every issue that comes to the UN has its antecedents before it gets here. The State Department has been involved in the negotiations, and now the situation has become insoluble, so it gets dumped onto us.

Adlai Ewing Stevenson

The Charter of the United Nations which you have just signed is a solid structure upon which we can build a better world. History will honor you for it. Between the victory in Europe and the final victory in Japan, in this most destructive of all wars, you have won a victory against war itself.

Harry S Truman

I speak not as the Secretary-General of the United Nations, not as an Asian, not as a Burmese, but as a human being, a member of that speices, *Homo sapiens,* whose continued existence is in the balance.

U Thant

My feeling is that in the Seventies, if there are Seventies, the world will witness four big powers—the United States of America, Europe, Russia and China.

U Thant

My feeling is that nobody should aspire to be Secretary General of the United Nations for more than one term. Knowing the functions of the office as I do, I think it is a very killing job, and from time to time it is a very frustrating job.

U Thant

See also: AMERICA, AUSTRALIA, CANADA, CHINA, CUBA, EGYPT, ENGLAND, FRANCE, GERMANY, GREECE, INDIA, IRELAND, ISRAEL, ITALY, JAPAN, KOREA, MEXICO, NETHERLANDS, POLAND, RUSSIA, SCOTLAND, VIETNAM.

UNITED STATES OF AMERICA:
see AMERICA.

UNITY

Men's hearts ought not to be set against one another, but set with one another, and all against evil only.

Thomas Carlyle

Unity to be real must stand the severest strain without breaking.

Mohandas Karamchand (Mahatma) Gandhi

What science calls the unity and uniformity of nature, truth calls the fidelity of God.

James Martineau

Unity is always better than disunity, but an enforced unity is a sham and dangerous affair, full of explosive possibilities. Unity must be of the mind and heart, a sense of belonging together and of facing together those who attack it.

Jawaharlal Nehru

The multitude which does not reduce itself to unity is confusion; the unity which does not depend upon the multitude, is tyranny.

Blaise Pascal

The number two hath, by the heathen, been accounted accurst, because it was the first departure from unity.

Joseph Trapp

We were two and had but one heart between us.

François Villon

See also: LOVE, MARRIAGE, PEACE, UNION.

UNIVERSE

The Universe is but one vast Symbol of God.

Thomas Carlyle

All this visible universe is only an imperceptible point in the vast bosom of nature. The mind of man cannot grasp it. It is in vain that we try to stretch our conceptions beyond all imaginable space; we bring before the mind's eye merely atoms in comparison with the reality of things. It is an infinite sphere, of which the centre is everywhere, the circumference nowhere. In short, the strongest proof of the almighty power of God is that our imagination loses itself in the conception.

Blaise Pascal

The universe is one of God's thoughts.

Johann Christoph Friedrich von Schiller

See also: CREATION, EARTH, WORLD.

UNIVERSITY

Today the great university in a metropolis must have a special and urgent concern for the future of the city and the future of those in our cities who lack full equality of opportunity.

McGeorge Bundy

The great universities of the world have been more often fields of battle than ivory towers of contemplation.

James Bryant Conant

A university should be a place of light, of liberty, and of learning.

Benjamin Disraeli

I suspect that when a university becomes very closely oriented to the current needs of government it takes on some of the atmosphere of a place of business while losing that of a place of learning.

James William Fulbright

The university is not engaged in making ideas safe for students. It is engaged in making students safe for ideas.

Clark Kerr

A university . . . by its very name professes to teach universal knowledge.

John Henry Newman

A university is, according to the usual designation, an *alma mater*, knowing her children one by one, not a foundry, or a mint, or a treadmill.

John Henry Newman

A university training is the great ordinary means to a great but ordinary end; it aims at raising the intellectual tone of society, at cultivating the public mind, at purifying the national taste, at supplying true principles to popular enthusiasm and fixed aims to popular aspirations, at giving enlargement and sobriety to the ideas of the age, at facilitating the exercise of political power, and refining the intercourse of private life.

John Henry Newman

The task of a university is the creation of the future, so far as rational thought and civilized modes of appreciation can affect the issue.

Alfred North Whitehead

See also: EDUCATION, KNOWLEDGE, STUDENT.

UNKINDNESS

He who has once stood beside the grave, to look back upon the companionship which has been forever closed, feeling how impotent there is a wild love, or the keen sorrow, to give one instant's pleasure to the pulseless heart, or atone in the lowest measure to the departed spirit for the hour of unkindness, will scarcely for the future incur that debt to the heart which can only be discharged to the dust.

John Ruskin

More hearts pine away in secret anguish for unkindness from those who should be their comforters, than for any other calamity in life.

Edward Young

See also: ABUSE, CRUELTY, INJURY, INSULT.

USEFULNESS

In the school of Pythagoras it was a point of discipline, that if among the probationers, there were any who grew weary of studying to be useful, and returned to an idle life, they were to regard them as dead; and, upon their departing, to perform their obsequies, and raise them tombs with inscriptions, to warn others of the like mortality, and quicken them to refine their souls above that wretched state.

Joseph Addison

Knowest thou not, thou canst not move a step on this earth without finding some duty to be done, and that every man is useful to his kind, by the very fact of his existence?

Thomas Carlyle

All the good things of this world are no further good than as they are of use; and whatever we may heap up to give to others, we enjoy only as much as we can make useful to ourselves and others, and no more.

Daniel Defoe

To be of service is a solid foundation for contentment in this world.

Charles William Eliot

The useful and the beautiful are never separated.

Periander

I believe that the rendering of useful service is the common duty of mankind and that only in the purifying fire of sacrifice is the dross of selfishness consumed and the greatness of the human soul set free.

John Davison Rockefeller, Jr.

See also: BENEFICENCE, EXPEDIENCY, WORTH.

USURER

A money-lender. He serves you in the present tense; he lends you in the conditional mood; keeps you in the subjunctive; and ruins you in the future!

Joseph Addison

Go not to a covetous old man, with any request, too soon in the morning, before he hath taken in that day's prey; for his covetousness is up before him, and he before thee, and he is in ill humor; but stay till the afternoon, till he be satiated upon some borrower.

Thomas Fuller

He was a man versed in the world, as pilot in his compass; the needle pointed ever to that interest which was his loadstar; and he spread his sails with vantage to the gale of others' passions.

Ben (Benjamin) Jonson

See also: AVARICE, BORROWING, CREDIT, DEBT, LENDING, MISER, MONEY.

V

VAGRANT

He that has a home, and a family, has given hostages to the community for good citizenship, but he that has no such connecting interests, is exposed to temptation, to idleness, and in danger of becoming useless, if not a burden and a nuisance in society.

Samuel Johnson

Beware of those who are homeless by choice! You have no hold on a human being whose affections are without a taproot!

Robert Southey

See also: RESTLESSNESS, SLOTH.

VAINGLORY: *see* VANITY.

VALENTINE'S DAY

Oft have I heard both youths and maidens say
Birds choose their mates and couple, too, this day:
But by their flight I never can divine
When I shall couple with my Valentine.

Robert Herrick

Hail to thy returning festival, old Bishop Valentine! Great is thy name in the rubric. . . . Like unto thee, assuredly, there is no other mitred father in the calendar.

Charles Lamb

The fourteenth of February is a day sacred to St. Valentine! It was a very odd notion, alluded to by Shakespeare, that on this day birds begin to couple; hence, perhaps, arose the custom of sending on this day letters containing professions of love and affection.

Noah Webster

See also: HOLIDAY, LOVE.

VALOR

Valor would cease to be a virtue if there were no injustice.

Agesilaus II

It is said of untrue valors, that some men's valors are in the eyes of them that look on.

Francis Bacon

It is a brave act of valor to contemn death; but where life is more terrible than death it is then the truest valor to dare to live.

Sir Thomas Browne

The mean of true valor lies between the extremes of cowardice and rashness.

Miguel de Cervantes Saavedra

Bravery is not a quality of the body, it is of the soul. I have seen cowards encased in tough muscle, and rare courage in the frailest body.

Mohandas Karamchand (Mahatma) Gandhi

He who perishes sword in hand is no doubt brave; but who faces death without fairing his little finger and without flinching is braver.

Mohandas Karamchand (Mahatma) Gandhi

If it is brave, as it is, to die to a man fighting against odds, it is braver still to refuse to fight and yet refuse to yield to the usurper.

Mohandas Karamchand (Mahatma) Gandhi

Let us all be brave enough to die the death of a martyr, but let no one lust for martyrdom.

Mohandas Karamchand (Mahatma) Gandhi

Fear to do base and unworthy things is valor; if they be done to us, to suffer them is also valor.

Ben (Benjamin) Jonson

No man can answer for his own valor or courage, till he has been in danger.

Duc François de La Rochefoucauld

True valor, on virtue founded strong, meets all events alike.

David Mallet

Valor is a gift. Those having it never know for sure whether they have it till the test comes. And those having it in one test never know for sure if they will have it when the next test comes.

Carl Sandburg

True valor is like honesty; it enters into all that a man sees and does.

Henry Wheeler Shaw (Josh Billings)

Dare to do your duty always; this is the height of true valor.

Charles Simmons

See also: BOLDNESS, BRAVERY, COURAGE, HERO-ISM, SOLDIER, WAR.

VALUE

Every book worth putting on the shelves of a library is either a value in itself or about values—value in this instance meaning a quality of living.

Henry Seidel Canby

Teach us that wealth is not elegance, that profusion is not magnificence, that splendor is not beauty.

Benjamin Disraeli

Some values are . . . like sugar on the doughnut, legitimate, desirable, but insufficient, apart from the doughnut itself. We need substance as well as frosting.

Ralph Tyler Flewelling

Friendship, love, philosopher's stone—
These three things men value along.

Heinrich Heine

Surely there comes a time when counting the cost and paying the price aren't things to think about any more. All that matters is value—the ultimate value of what one does.

James Hilton

Nothing can have value without being an object of utility.

Karl Marx

The terms *good* and *bad* indicate no positive quality in things regarded in themselves. . . . Thus one and the same thing can be at the same time good for the melancholy, bad for the mourner, and neither good nor bad for the deaf.

Baruch (Benedict) Spinoza

See also: MERIT, VIRTUE, WORTH.

VANITY

Vanity is the weakness of the ambitious man, which exposes him to the secret scorn and derision of those he converses with, and ruins the character he is so industrious to advance by it.

Joseph Addison

Vain-glorious men are the scorn of the wise, the admiration of fools, the idols of parasites, and the slaves of their own vaunts.

Francis Bacon

When a man has no longer any conception of excellence above his own, his voyage is done; he is dead; dead in the trespasses and sins of blear-eyed vanity.

Henry Ward Beecher

Vanity is a strong temptation to lying; it makes people magnify their merit, over-flourish their family, and tell strange stories of their interest and acquaintance.

Jeremy Collier

If you cannot inspire a woman with love of you, fill her above the brim with love of herself; all that runs over will be yours.

Charles Caleb Colton

Ladies of fashion starve their happiness to feed their vanity, and their love to feed their pride.

Charles Caleb Colton

Vanity plays lurid tricks with our memory.

Joseph Conrad

All my fame is due to myself alone.

Pierre Corneille

Feminine vanity, that divine gift which makes women charming.

Benjamin Disraeli

The vaniest woman is never thoroughly conscious of her beauty till she is loved by the man who sets her own passion vibrating in return.

George Eliot (Mary Ann Evans)

Vanity is as ill at ease under indifference, as tenderness is under the love which it cannot return.

George Eliot (Mary Ann Evans)

Of all our infirmities, vanity is the dearest to us; a man will starve his other vices to keep that alive.

Benjamin Franklin

A vain man can never be altogether rude. Desirous as he is of pleasing, he fashions his manners after those of others.

Johann Wolfgang von Goethe

Vanity is the poison of agreeableness; yet as poison, when properly applied, has a salutary effect in medicine, so has vanity in the commerce and society of the world.

Fulke Greville (First Baron Brooke)

In a vain man, the smallest spark may kindle into the greatest flame, because the materials are always prepared for it.

David Hume

Vanity indeed is a venial error; for it usually carries its own punishment with it.

Junius

A vain man finds it wise to speak good or ill of himself: a modest man does not talk of himself.

Jean de La Bruyère

It is our own vanity that makes the vanity of others intolerable to us.

Duc François de La Rochefoucauld

Vanity makes us do more things against inclination than reason.

Duc François de La Rochefoucauld

Virtue would not go far if vanity did not keep it company.

Duc François de La Rochefoucauld

She neglects her heart who studies her glass.

Johann Kaspar Lavater

When men will not be reasoned out of a vanity, they must be ridiculed out of it.

Sir Roger L'Estrange

Vanity, indeed, is the very antidote to conceit; for while the former makes us all nerve to the opinion of others, the latter is perfectly satisfied with its opinion of itself.

Edward G. Bulwer-Lytton (Baron Lytton)

Alas for human nature, that the wounds of vanity should smart and bleed so much longer than the wounds of affection!

Thomas Babington Macaulay

As soon as you begin to take yourself seriously and imagine that your virtures are important because they are yours, you become the prisoner of your own vanity and even your best works will blind and deceive you. Then, in order to defend yourself, you will begin to see sins and faults everywhere in the actions of other men. And the more unreasonable importance you attach to yourself and your own works, the more you will tend to build up your own idea of yourself by condemning other people. Some of the most virtuous men in the world are also the bitterest and most unhappy, because they have unconsciously come to believe that all their happiness depends on their being more virtuous than other men.

Thomas Merton

There is no arena in which vanity displays itself under such a variety of forms as in conversation.

Blaise Pascal

To be a man's own fool is bad enough, but the vain man is everybody's.

William Penn

Every man has just as much vanity as he wants understanding.

Alexander Pope

There is no folly of which a man who is not a fool cannot get rid except vanity; of this nothing cures a man except experience of its bad consequences, if indeed anything can cure it.

Jean Jacques Rousseau

Men are just starting to use cosmetics. And this part of the business should expand into untold millions in the next fifty years. Men are just as vain as women, and sometimes even more so.

Helena Rubinstein

Vanity is the quicksand of reason.

George Sand

Vanity is as advantageous to a government, as pride is dangerous.

Charles de Secondat (Baron de Montesquieu)

Take away from mankind their vanity and their ambition, and there would be but few claiming to be heroes or patriots.

Seneca

Every occasion will catch the senses of the vain man, and with that bridle and saddle you may ride him.

Sir Philip Sidney

Vanity is the foundation of the most ridiculous and contemptible vices—the vices of affectation and common lying.

Adam Smith

Vanity makes men ridiculous, pride odious, and ambition terrible.

Sir Richard Steele

The strongest passions allow us some rest, but vanity keeps us perpetually in motion. What a dust do I raise! says the fly upon a coach-wheel. And at what a rate do I drive! says the fly upon the horse's back.

Jonathan Swift

Vanity is so intimately associated with our spiritual identity that whatever hurts it, above all if it came from it, is more painful in the memory than serious sin.

William Butler Yeats

See also: BOASTING, CONCEIT, SELF-PRAISE.

VARIETY

Variety's the very spice of life,
That gives it all its flavour.

William Cowper

Variety is the mother of enjoyment.

Benjamin Disraeli

Not chaos-like together crushed and bruised,
But, as the world, harmoniously confused:
Where order in variety we see,
And where, though all things differ, all
    agree.

Alexander Pope

The most delightful pleasures cloy without variety.

Publilius Syrus

Variety of mere nothings gives more pleasure than uniformity of something.

Jean Paul Richter

I take it to be a principal rule of life, not to be too much addicted to any one thing.

Terence

See also: ADVENTURE, CHANGE, DEVIATION, IN-
    NOVATION, LIBERAL, NONCONFORM-
    ITY, NOVELTY, ORIGINALITY.

VEGETARIANISM

I do not regard flesh-food as necessary for us at any stage and under any clime in which it is possible for human beings ordinarily to live. I hold flesh-food to be unsuited to our species. We err in copying the lower animal world if we are superior to it. Experience teaches that animal food is unsuited to those who would curb their passions.

Mohandas Karamchand (Mahatma) Gandhi

Vegetarianism is one of the priceless gifts of Hinduism. It may not be lightly given up. It is necessary therefore to correct the error that vegetarianism has made us weak in mind or body or passive or inert in action. The greatest Hindu reformed have been most active in their generation and they have invariably been vegetarians.

Mohandas Karamchand (Mahatma) Gandhi

See also: DIET, HEALTH.

VENGEANCE

Deep vengeance is the daughter of deep silence.

Conte Vittorio Alfieri

Vengeance has no foresight.

Napoleon I (Bonaparte)

Is it to be thought unreasonable that the people, in atonement for the wrongs of a century, demanded the vengeance of a single day?

Maximilien François Marie de Robespierre

If you have committed iniquity, you must expect to suffer; for vengeance with its sacred light shines upon you.

Sophocles

See also: HATE, RESENTMENT, REVENGE.

VERBOSITY

Redundancy of language is never found with deep reflection. Verbiage may indicate observation, but not thinking. He who thinks much, says but little in proportion to his thoughts. He selects that language which will convey his ideas in the most explicit and direct manner. He tries to compress as much thought as possible into a few words. On the contrary, the man who talks everlastingly and promiscuously, who seems to have an exhaustless magazine of sound, crowds so many words into his thoughts that he always obscures, and very frequently conceals them.

Washington Irving

In general those who nothing have to say
Contrive to spend the longest time in doing it.

James Russell Lowell

See also: BABBLE, LOQUACITY, TONGUE.

VICE

The willing contemplation of vice is vice.
Arabian Proverb

Vice incapacitates a man from all public duty; it withers the powers of his understanding, and makes his mind paralytic.
Edmund Burke

Vice—that digs her own voluptuous tomb.
George Gordon Byron (Lord Byron)

This is the essential evil of vice, that it debases a man.
Edwin Hubbel Chapin

The vicious obey their passions as slaves do their masters.
Diogenes

Crime and vice generally require darkness for prowling. They disappear when light plays upon them.
Mohandas Karamchand (Mahatma) Gandhi

A man who broods on evil is as bad as a man who does evil if he is no worse.
Mohandas Karamchand (Mahatma) Gandhi

Vice pays a homage to virtue, and sometimes the way it chooses is to expect virtue, not to fall from its pedestal even whilst vice is rampant round about.
Mohandas Karamchand (Mahatma) Gandhi

Many a man's vices have at first been nothing worse than good qualities run wild.
Augustus and Julius Hare

One big vice in a man is apt to keep out a great many smaller ones.
(Francis) Bret Harte

Beware of the beginnings of vice. Do not delude yourself with the belief that it can be argued against in the presence of the exciting cause. Nothing but actual flight can save you.
Benjamin Robert Haydon

To attack vices in the abstract, without touching persons, may be safe fighting, but it is fighting with shadows.
Junius

The vices operate like age; bringing on disease before its time, and in the prime of youth they leave the character broken and exhausted.
Junius

No man ever arrived suddenly at the summit of vice.
Juvenal

When our vices have left us we flatter ourselves that we have left them.
Duc François de La Rochefoucauld

Every age and nation has certain characteristic vices, which prevail almost universally, which scarcely any person scruples to avow, and which even rigid moralists but faintly censure. Succeeding generations change the fashion of their morals with the fashion of their hats and their coaches; take some other kind of wickedness under their patronage and wonder at the depravity of their ancestors.
Thomas Babington Macaulay

There are vices which have no hold upon us, but in connection with others, and which, when you cut down the trunk, fall like the branches.
Blaise Pascal

But when to mischief mortals bend their will,
How soon they find fit instruments of ill!
Alexander Pope

Vice is a monster of so frightful mien,
As to be hated needs but to be seen;
Yet seen too oft, familiar with her face,
We first endure, then pity, then embrace.
Alexander Pope

Vices are often habits rather than passions.
Antoine Rivarol

Experience tells us that each man most keenly and unerringly detects in others the vice with which he is most familiar himself.
Frederick William Robertson

Vices are contagious, and there is no trusting the well and sick together.
Seneca

Why is there no man who confesses his vices? It is because he has not yet laid them aside. It is a waking man only who can tell his dreams.
Seneca

Vice always leads, however fair at first, to wilds of woe.

James Thomson

See also: BASENESS, CORRUPTION, CRIME, DE-PRAVITY, DISSIPATION, EVIL, LICENTIOUSNESS, SIN, VIRTUE AND VICE, WICKEDNESS.

VICTORY

Anybody can win, unless there happens to be a second entry.

George Ade

Victories that are easy are cheap. Those only are worth having which come as the result of hard fighting.

Henry Ward Beecher

To the victors belong the spoils.

William Learned Marcy

Who overcomes by force hath overcome but half his foe.

John Milton

Victory or Westminster Abbey.

Viscount Horatio Nelson

It is the contest that delights us, not the victory. We are pleased with the combat of animals, but not with the victor tearing the vanquished. What is sought for is the crisis of victory, and the instant it comes, it brings satiety.

Blaise Pascal

We have met the enemy and they are ours.

Oliver Hazard Perry

In victory the hero seeks the glory, not the prey.

Sir Philip Sidney

I do not think that winning is the most important thing. I think winning is the only thing.

William (Bill) Veeck

The smile of God is victory.

John Greenleaf Whittier

See also: PROSPERITY, SUCCESS, WEALTH.

VIETNAM

President Eisenhower further enhanced his popularity and secured an enviable place in history when he backed Gen. Matthew Ridgeway in his opposition to sending large numbers of U.S. troops into Vietnam in an effort to make secure that part of their colonial empire for the French.

George David Aiken

In the name of good sense, of the attachment we retain in Indo-China, of the two-century-old friendship we bear for America, we hold it necessary that she put an end to the ordeal by bringing her forces back to her soil.

Charles André Joseph Marie de Gaulle

If we were not in Vietnam, all that part of the world would be enjoying the obscurity it so richly deserves.

John Kenneth Galbraith

America is not fighting to win a war. We are fighting to give an application to an old Greek proverb, which is that the purpose of war is not to annihilate an enemy but to get him to mend his ways. And we are confident we can get the enemy to mend his ways.

Arthur J. Goldberg

Vietnam is thousands of miles away from the United States. The Vietnamese people have never done any harm to the United States. But contrary to the pledges made by its representatives at the 1954 Geneva conference, the United States Government has ceaselessly intervened in Vietnam; it has unleashed and intensified the war of aggression in South Vietnam with a view to prolonging the partition of Vietnam and turning South Vietnam into a neocolony and a military base of the United States.

Ho Chi Minh

In North Vietnam, thousands of United States aircraft have dropped hundreds of thousands of tons of bombs, destroying towns, villages, factories, roads, bridges, dikes, dams and even churches, pagodas, hospitals, schools.

Ho Chi Minh

The Vietnamese people deeply love independence, freedom and peace. But in the face of United States aggression they have risen up, united as one man. Fearless of sacrifices and hardships, they are determined to carry on their resistance until they have won genuine independence and freedom and true peace. Our just cause enjoys strong sympathy and support from the peoples of the whole world, including broad sections of the American people.

Ho Chi Minh

The war in Vietnam is fueled by those who believe that they somehow might be able to accomplish their ends by means of terror and violence. America's purpose there is to give peaceful change a real chance to succeed.

Lyndon Baines Johnson

We are not an Asian power. Our interests do not lie on the Asian mainland. We are a Pacific power with peripheral interests in Asia. The distinction is of immense importance to the future of this Nation.

Michael Mansfield

The South Vietnamese election is over, and the voting demonstrated the overwhelming unity of the South Vietnamese in assuring their nation the right of self-determination.

Spark Masayuki Matsunga

The primary purpose for which nations signed the [Charter of the United Nations] is to enforce the peace wherever the peace is threatened. In this instance this means enforcing the peace against the United States because in South Vietnam we happen to stand in open violation of the charter article after article.

Wayne Lyman Morse

It [Vietnam] poisons everything. It has disrupted the economy, envenomed our politics, hurt the alliance, divided our people, and now it is interfering with this critical question of the arms race.

James Barrett Reston

I just had the greatest brainwashing that anyone can get when you go over to Vietnam, not only from the generals, but also from the diplomatic corps over there.

George W. Romney

Draft card and flag burners, demonstrators, and pickets receive attention beyond their importance and are portrayed as legitimate protesters exercising their right to dissent. Under the guise of academic freedom, some of our college faculty members and students heap abuse and scorn upon their Government. Those who engage in these acts are a tiny minority of our total population. The vast majority of Americans, whether they agree or disagree with the administration and its policies, do support our Government and our men in Vietnam who are doing the fighting.

Richard L. Roudebush

[We are in Vietnam for the] defense, protection and salvation not only of our country but . . . of civilization itself. . . . It is an honorable and an heroic thing to fight for those ideals and principles we account worthy of preservation.

Francis Joseph Spellman

This war in Vietnam is, I believe, a war for civilization. Certainly it is not a war of our seeking. It is a war thrust upon us and we cannot yield to tyranny.

Francis Joseph Spellman

There is a consensus of opinion all over South Vietnam today, in all the military forces and also in the civilian setup, that if we don't eliminate this target limitation it isn't right to send these men out to risk their lives in an expensive airplane to bomb just an empty barracks or bus.

William Stuart Symington

I am afraid [if the present trend in Vietnam continues] that direct confrontation, first of all between Washington and Peking is inevitable.

U Thant

See also: ASIA, NATION, WAR.

VIGILANCE

Eternal vigilance is the price of liberty.

Thomas Jefferson

He is most free from danger, who, even when safe, is on his guard.

Publilius Syrus

It is the enemy who keeps the sentinel watchful.

Anne Sophie Swetchine

See also: CAUTION, WATCHFULNESS.

VILLAINY

Villainy that is vigilant will be an overmatch for virtue, if she slumber at her post.

Charles Caleb Colton

Villainy, when detected, never gives up, but boldly adds impudence to imposture.

Oliver Goldsmith

It is the masterpiece of villainy to smoothe the brow, and so outface suspicion.

John Howard

See also: BASENESS, CRIME, ROGUERY.

VIOLENCE

The nation recoils with horror over the second assassination in the Kennedy family. What an astounding commentary upon violence in the land.

Everett McKinley Dirksen

I am your anointed Queen. I will never be by violence constrained to do anything. I thank God I am endued with such qualities that if I were turned out of the Realm in my petticoat I were able to live in any place in Christome.

Elizabeth I

It is organized violence on top which creates individual violence at the bottom.

Emma Goldman

The violence done us by others is often less painful than that which we do to ourselves.

Duc François de La Rochefoucauld

Nothing good ever comes of violence.

Martin Luther

See also: GUN, RIOT, WAR.

VIRGINITY

Virginity is not honored simply because it is virginity, but because it is consecrated to God.

Augustine of Hippo

Where the virgins are soft as the roses they
     twine
And all save the spirit of man is divine?

George Gordon Byron (Lord Byron)

But a celestial brightness,—a more ethereal
     beauty—
Shone on her face and encircled her form
     when, after confession,
Homeward serenely she walked with God's
     benedictions upon her.
When she had passed, it seemed like the
     ceasing of exquisite music.

Henry Wadsworth Longfellow

Holy virginity and that perfect chastity which is consecrated to the service of God are indubitably the most precious treasures which the Founder of the Church has left in heritage to the society which He established.

Pius XII (Eugenio Pacelli)

Let the words of a virgin, though in a good cause, and to as good purpose, be neither violent, many, nor first, nor last. It is less shame for her to be lost in a blushing silence, than to be found in a bold eloquence.

Francis Quarles

See also: CELIBACY, CHASTITY.

VIRTUE

Every man is ready to give in a long catalogue of those virtues and good qualities he expects to find in the person of a friend; but very few of us are careful to cultivate them in ourselves.

Joseph Addison

Virtue is like a rich stone, best plain set.

Francis Bacon

Virtue alone is the unerring sign of a noble soul.

Nicolas Boileau-Despréaux

If you can be well without health, you may be happy without virtue.

Edmund Burke

No state of virtue is complete save as it is won by a conflict with evil, and fortified by the struggles of a resolute and even bitter experience.

Horace Bushnell

Virtue is not to be considered in the light of mere innocence, or abstaining from harm; but as the exertion of our faculties in doing good.

Joseph Butler

Virtue knows that it is impossible to get on without compromise, and tunes herself, as it were, a trifle sharp to allow for an inevitable fall in playing.

Samuel Butler

No virtue can be real that has not been tried. The gold in the crucible alone is perfect; the loadstone tests the steel, and the diamond is tried by the diamond, while metals gleam the brighter in the furnace.

Pedro de La Barca Calderón

By what causes has so inconsiderable a beginning, as that of the colonies of New England, under such formidable, and apparently almost insurmountable difficulties, resulted, in so brief a period, in such mighty consequences? They are to be found in the high moral and intellectual qualities of the pilgrims: their faith, piety, and confident trust in a superintending Providence; their stern virtues; their patriotic love of liberty and order; their devotion to learning; and their indomitable courage and perseverance. These are the causes which surmounted every obstacle, and which have led to such mighty results.

John Caldwell Calhoun

It is not virtue, but a deceptive copy and imitation of virtue, when we are led to the performance of duty by pleasure as its recompense.

Cicero

The advantage to be derived from virtue is so evident, that the wicked practise it from interested motives.

Luc de Clapiers (Marquis de Vauvenargues)

The first days of spring have less of beauty than the budding virtue of a young man.

Luc de Clapiers (Marquis de Vauvenargues)

No man can purchase his virtue too dear, for it is the only thing whose value must ever increase with the price it has cost us. Our integrity is never worth so much as when we have parted with our all to keep it.

Charles Caleb Colton

To be able under all circumstances to practise five things constitutes perfect virtue; these five are gravity, generosity of soul, sincerity, earnestness, and kindness.

Confucius

The most virtuous of all men, says Plato, is he that contents himself with being virtuous without seeking to appear so.

François de Salignac de La Mothe-Fénelon

We should cease to grow the moment we cease to discriminate between virtue and vice.

Mohandas Karamchand (Mahatma) Gandhi

The world, though not itself virtuous, pays an unconscious homage to virtue.

Mohandas Karamchand (Mahatma) Gandhi

When you enjoy loving your neighbor it ceases to be a virtue.

Kahlil Gibran

That virtue which requires to be ever guarded is scarce worth the sentinel.

Oliver Goldsmith

They who disbelieve in virtue because man has never been found perfect, might as reasonably deny the sun because it is not always noon.

Augustus and Julius Hare

Virtue has many preachers, but few martyrs.

Claude Adrien Helvetius

Beware of making your moral staples consist of the negative virtues. It is good to abstain, and to teach others to abstain, from all that is sinful or hurtful. But making a business of it leads to emaciation of character unless one feeds largely on the more nutritious diet of active benevolence.

Oliver Wendell Holmes

If he does really think there is no distinction between virtue and vice, why, sir, when he leaves our house let us count our spoons.

Samuel Johnson

Nothing is more unjust, however common, than to charge with hypocrisy him that expresses zeal for those virtues which he neglects to practise; since he may be sincerely convinced of the advantages of conquering his passions without having yet obtained the victory, as a man may be confident of the advantages of a voyage or a journey, without having courage or industry to undertake it, and may honestly recommend to others those attempts which he neglects himself.

Samuel Johnson

The great slight the men of wit who have nothing but wit; the men of wit despise the great who have nothing but greatness; the good man pities them both, if with greatness or wit, they have not virtue.

Jean de La Bruyère

Perfect virtue is to do unwitnessed what we should be capable of doing before all the world.

Duc François de La Rochefoucauld

Birth is nothing where virtue is not.

Molière (Jean Baptiste Poquelin)

It would not be easy, even for an unbeliever, to find a better translation of the rule of virtue from the abstract into the concrete, than to endeavor so to live that Christ would approve our life.

John Stuart Mill

To rest the reward of virtuous actions on the approbation of the world is an unsafe and unstable foundation, particularly in an age like this, which is so corrupt and ignorant: the good opinion of the vulgar is injurious.

Michel Eyquem de Montaigne

The person who talks most of his own virtues is often the least virtuous.

Jawaharlal Nehru

Virtue is its own reward, and brings with it the truest and highest pleasure; but if we cultivate it only for pleasure's sake, we are selfish, not religious, and will never gain the pleasure, because we can never have the virtue.

John Henry Newman

The virtue of a man ought to be measured not by his extraordinary exertions, but by his every-day conduct.

Blaise Pascal

To be innocent is to be not guilty; but to be virtuous is to overcome our evil feelings and intentions.

William Penn

Wealth is a weak anchor, and glory cannot support a man; this is the law of God, that virtue only is firm, and cannot be shaken by a tempest.

Pythagoras

Virtue is a state of war, and to live in it we have always to combat with ourselves.

Jean Jacques Rousseau

It is with virtue as with fire. It exists in the mind, as fire does in certain bodies, in a latent or quiescent state.

Benjamin Rush

Flogging on weekdays and sermons on Sundays do not constitute the ideal technique for the production of virtue.

Bertrand Arthur William Russell

Nine of the Ten Commandments are negative. If throughout life you abstain from murder, theft, fornication, perjury, blasphemy, and disrespect towards your parents, your Church, and your King, you are conventionally held to deserve moral admiration even if you have never done a single kind or generous or useful action. This very inadequate notion of virtue is an outcome of taboo morality, and has done untold harm.

Bertrand Arthur William Russell

Virtue I love, without austerity; pleasure, without effeminacy; and life, without fearing its end.

Seigneur de Saint-Évremond

Virtue is certainly the most noble and secure possession a man can have. Beauty is worn out by time or impaired by sickness—riches lead youth rather to destruction than welfare, and without prudence are soon lavished away; while virtue alone, the only good that is ever durable, always remains with the person that has once entertained her. She is preferable both to wealth and a noble extraction.

Richard Savage

It is the edge and temper of the blade that make a good sword, not the richness of the scabbard; and so it is not money or possessions that make man considerable, but his virtue.

Seneca

Virtue is that perfect good which is the complement of a happy life; the only immortal thing that belongs to mortality.

Seneca

Virtue consists, not in abstaining from vice, but in not desiring it.

George Bernard Shaw

Virtue is action in accord with the laws of one's own nature.

Baruch (Benedict) Spinoza

A great deal of virtue, at least the outward appearance of it, is not so much from any fixed principle, as the terror of what the world will say, and the liberty it will take upon the occasions we shall give.

Laurence Sterne

Philosophers and clergymen are always discussing why we should be good—as if anyone doubted that he ought to be.

George Macaulay Trevelyan

Virtue is everywhere the same, because it comes from God, while everything else is of man.

Voltaire (François Marie Arouet)

Good company and good discourse are the very sinews of virtue.

Izaak Walton

Always in times of stress it is the simple virtues that really count.

John Gilbert Winant

VIRTUE AND VICE

Certainly, virtue is like precious odors, most fragrant when they are incensed or crushed; for prosperity doth best discover vice, but adversity doth best discover virtue.

Francis Bacon

Virtue will catch as well as vice by contact; and the public stock of honest, manly principle will daily accumulate. We are not too nicely to scrutinize motives as long as action is irreproachable. It is enough to deal out its infamy to convicted guilt and declared apostasy.

Edmund Burke

He that is good will infallibly become better, and he that is bad will as certainly become worse; for vice, virtue, and time are three things that never stand still.

Charles Caleb Colton

The martyrs to vice far exceed the martyrs to virtue, both in endurance and in number. So blinded are we by our passions that we suffer more to be damned than to be saved.

Charles Caleb Colton

Vice stings us even in our pleasures, but virtue consoles us even in our pains.

Charles Caleb Colton

Every vice was once a virtue, and may become respectable again, just as hatred becomes respectable in wartime.

Will (William James) Durant

Misfortune does not always wait on vice, nor is success the constant guest of virtue.

Samuel Hazard

Vice can deceive under the shadow and guise of virtue.

Juvenal

Nature seems to have prescribed to every man at his birth the bounds of his virtues and vices.

Duc François de La Rochefoucauld

We do not despise all those who have vices, but we do despise all those who have not a single virtue.

Duc François de La Rochefoucauld

It has ever been my experience that folks who have no vices have very few virtues.

Abraham Lincoln

I prefer an accommodating vice to an obstinate virtue.

Molière (Jean Baptiste Poquelin)

A few vices are sufficient to darken many virtues.

Plutarch

As to the general design of providence, the two extremes of vice may serve to keep up the balance of things. When we speak against one capital vice, we ought to speak against its opposite; the middle betwixt both is the point for virtue.

Alexander Pope

We have only one story. All novels, all poetry, are built on the neverending contest in ourselves of good and evil. And it occurs to me that evil must constantly respawn, while good, while virtue, is immortal. Vice has always a new fresh young face, while virtue is venerable as nothing else in the world is.

John Ernst Steinbeck

VISION

Visions of glory, spare my aching sight!
Ye unborn ages, crowd not on my soul.

Thomas Gray

Do I sleep? do I dream?
  Do I wonder and doubt?
Are things what they seem?
  Or is visions about?

(Francis) Bret Harte

Was it a vision, or a waking dream?
Fled is that music:—do I wake or sleep?

John Keats

It is a dream, sweet child! a waking dream,
A blissful certainty, a vision bright,
Of that rare happiness, which even on earth
Heaven gives to those it loves.

Henry Wadsworth Longfellow

VISITORS

Visitors are insatiable devourers of time, and fit only for those who, if they did not visit, would do nothing.

William Cowper

Fish and visitors smell in three days.

Benjamin Franklin

See also: ACQUAINTANCE, GUEST, HOSPITALITY.

VIVACITY

The vivacity which augments with years is not far from folly.

Duc François de La Rochefoucauld

I do not dislike extreme vivacity in children; but would see enough of it to make an animated character, when the violence of animal spirits shall subside in time. It is easier to restrain excess than to quicken stupidity. Gravity in childhood may become stupidity in old age.

Lydia Howard Sigourney

See also: ACTION, CHEERFULNESS, ENERGY, ENTHUSIASM, LIFE, SPIRIT.

VIVISECTION

It is inexcusable for scientists to torture animals; let them make their experiments on journalists and politicians.

Henrik Ibsen

See also: ANIMAL, LIFE.

VOCATION

A good vocation is simply a firm and constant will whereby one is called to serve God in whatsoever manner and place Almighty God beckons him.

Francis of Sales

The most important thing in life is the choice of calling: it is left to chance.

Blaise Pascal

The test of a vocation is the love of the drudgery it involves.

Logan Pearsall Smith

See also: PROFESSION, SPECIALTY, TRADE.

VOICE

The devil hath not in all his quiver's choice
An arrow for the heart like a sweet voice.

George Gordon Byron (Lord Byron)

The tones of human voices are mightier than strings or brass to move the soul.

Friedrich Klopstock

The sweetest of all sounds is that of the voice of the woman we love.

Jean de La Bruyère

Thy voice is celestial melody.

Henry Wadsworth Longfellow

A voice so thrilling ne'er was heard
In spring-time from the cuckoo bird,
Breaking the silence of the seas
Among the farthest Hebrides.

Henry Wadsworth Longfellow

How sweetly sounds the voice of a good woman! When it speaks it ravishes all senses.

Philip Massinger

When those we have loved have long vanished from the earth, then will the beloved voice come back and bring with it all our old tears and the disconsolate heart that sheds them.

Jean Paul Richter

There is no index of character so sure as the voice.

Tancred

See also: SONG, SOUND, SPEECH.

VOLUPTUOUSNESS

The voluptuous and effeminate are never brave; they have no courage in time of danger.

François de Salignac de La Mothe-Fénelon

Voluptuousness, like justice, is blind; but that is the only resemblance between them.

Blaise Pascal

See also: INDULGENCE, LICENTIOUSNESS, LUST, LUXURY, SENSUALITY, VICE.

VOTING

A vote is not an object of art. It is the sacred and most important instrument of democracy and of freedom.

Abe Fortas

Bad officials are elected by good citizens who do not vote.

George Jean Nathan

A straw vote only shows which way the hot air blows.

William Sydney Porter (O. Henry)

See also: DEMOCRACY, POLITICIAN, POLITICS, PRESIDENT, STATESMANSHIP.

VOW

Lovers' vows seem sweet in every whispered word.

George Gordon Byron (Lord Byron)

The vows that woman makes to her fond lover are only fit to be written on air, or on the swiftly passing stream.

Catullus

Personally I hold that a man, who deliberately and intelligently takes a pledge and then breaks it, forfeits his manhood. And just as a copper coin treated with mercury not only becomes valueless when found out but also makes its owner liable to punishment, in the same way a man who lightly pledges his word and then breaks it becomes a man of straw and fits himself for punishment here as well as hereafter.

Mohandas Karamchand (Mahatma) Gandhi

A vow is fixed and unalterable determination to do a thing, when such a determination is related to something noble which can only uplift the man who makes the resolve. A vow is to all other indifferent resolves what a right angle is to all other angles. And just as a right angle gives an invisible and correct measure, so does a man of vows, rightly followed, gives of himself an unvariable and correct measure.

Mohandas Karamchand (Mahatma) Gandhi

Your capacity to keep your vow will depend on the purity of your life. A gambler or a drunkard, or a dissolute character can never keep a vow.

Mohandas Karamchand (Mahatma) Gandhi

Hasty resolutions are of the nature of vows, and to be equally avoided.

William Penn

See also: COURTSHIP, MARRIAGE, OATH, PROMISE, THREAT.

VULGARITY

There are no people who are quite so vulgar as the over-refined ones.

Samuel Langhorne Clemens (Mark Twain)

To endeavor to work upon the vulgar with fine sense is like attempting to hew blocks with a razor.

Alexander Pope

By vulgarity I mean that vice of civilization which makes man ashamed of himself and his next of kin, and pretend to be somebody else.

Solomon Schechter

Vulgarity is more obvious in satin than in homespun.

Nathaniel Parker Willis

See also: IMPURITY, INSENSIBILITY, MEDIOCRITY, MOB, POPULACE.

W

WAGE

Low wages are not cheap wages.
Louis Dembitz Brandeis

Nature has her laws, and this is one—a fair day's wage for a fair day's work.
Benjamin Disraeli

One of labor's long-range objectives is to achieve in every basic industry a guaranteed annual wage so that the consumers of this country can have a sustained income month in and month out, because only on that basis can we sustain an economy of full employment and full production and full distribution.
Walter Philip Reuther

There is nothing more demoralizing than a small but adequate income.
Edmund Wilson

See also: CAPITAL AND LABOR, CAPITALISM, INDUSTRY, MONEY, REWARD, UNIONS.

WAGER

Fools for arguments use wagers.
Samuel Butler

Most men, until by losing rendered sager,
Will back their opinions by a wager.
George Gordon Byron (Lord Byron)

See also: CARDS, CHANCE, DICE, GAMBLING.

WAITING

Everything comes to him who waits—among other things, death.
Francis Herbert Bradley

They also serve who only stand and wait.
John Milton

Real work lies in knowing how to wait.
Jean Rostand

It is the slowest pulsation which is the most vital. The hero will then know how to wait as well as to make haste. All good abides with him who waiteth wisely.
Henry David Thoreau

See also: DELAY, PATIENCE, PROCRASTINATION, SLOTH.

WALKING

The sum of the whole is this: walk and be happy; walk and be healthy. The best way to lengthen out our days is to walk steadily and with a purpose. The wandering man knows of certain ancients, far gone in years, who have staved off infirmities and dissolution by earnest walking—hale fellows, close upon ninety, but brisk as boys.
Charles John Huffam Dickens

If you are for a merry jaunt I will try for once who can foot it farthest.
John Dryden

It is good walking when one hath his horse in hand.
John Lyly

See also: EXERCISE, RECREATION, TRAVEL, VAGRANT.

WANT

If any one say that he has seen a just man in want of bread, I answer that it was in some place where there was no other just man.
Clement I (Clemens Romanus)

Want is a bitter and a hateful good,
Because its virtues are not understood;
Yet many things, impossible to thought,
Have been by need to full perfection brought;
The daring of the soul proceeds from thence,
Sharpness of wit and active diligence;
Prudence at once, and fortitude it gives;
And, if in patience taken, mends our lives.
John Dryden

It is not from nature, but from education and habits, that our wants are chiefly derived.

Henry Fielding

Of all the enemies of idleness, want is the most formidable. Want always struggles against idleness; but want herself is often overcome, and every hour shows some who had rather live in ease than in plenty.

Samuel Johnson

To men pressed by their wants all change is ever welcome.

Ben (Benjamin) Jonson

He can feel no little wants who is in pursuit of grandeur.

Johann Kaspar Lavater

Every one is poorer in proportion as he has more wants, and counts not what he has, but wishes only for what he has not.

Manilius

The fewer our wants, the nearer we resemble the gods.

Socrates

The stoical scheme of supplying our wants by lopping off our desires, is like cutting off our feet when we want shoes.

Jonathan Swift

Choose rather to want less, than to have more.

Thomas à Kempis

See also: ADVERSITY, DESIRE, NEED, NECESSITY, POVERTY, RICH AND POOR, WISH.

WAR

War is the science of destruction.

John Stevens Cabot Abbott

The one distinctive advance in civil society achieved by the Anglo-Saxon world is fairly betokened by the passing away of this notion of a peculiar possession in the way of honor which had to be guarded by arms.

Sir Norman Angell

Except for human slaughter and maiming and all that goes with them, inflation is the most destructive of all the consequences of the war.

Bernard Mannes Baruch

I recall what Bismarck said after 1871; that if he beat France again soon, it was Germany that would pay her an indemnity. It

took a genius like Bismarck to see that it was to the interest of the victor to help restore the vanquished.

Bernhard Berenson

Battle—a method of untying with the teeth a political knot that would not yield to the tongue.

Ambrose Gwinnett Bierce

It seems perfectly clear to me that we can never make any real progress toward permanent peace so long as we recognize the institution of war as legitimate and clothe it with glory.

William Edgar Borah

The tendency is to be broadminded about other people's security.

Aristide Briand

Those whom war has joined together, let no peace put asunder.

James Francis Byrnes

Let us pity and forgive those who urge increased armaments, for "they know not what they do."

Andrew Carnegie

I have seen so many wars and revolutions in the world. . . . Men do not know what they are, what they do. They do not know that we are human beings, brothers.

Pablo Casals

In war, whichever side may call itself the victor, there are no winners, but all are losers.

Neville Chamberlain

The human tragedy reaches its climax in the fact that after all the exertions and sacrifices of hundreds of millions of people and of the victories of the Righteous Cause, we have still not found Peace or Security, and that we lie in the grip of even worse perils than those we have surmounted.

Sir Winston Leonard Spencer Churchill

I would say to the House, as I have said to those who have joined this government: I have nothing to offer but blood, toil, tears and sweat. You ask what is our policy? I will say it is to wage war—by sea, land and air, with all our might and with all the strength that God can give us; to wage war against a monstrous tyranny never surpassed in the dark lamentable catalogue of human crimes. That is our policy.

Sir Winston Leonard Spencer Churchill

No one can guarantee success in war, but only deserve it.

Sir Winston Leonard Spencer Churchill

To quell the Japanese resistance man by man and conquer the country yard by yard might well require the loss of a million American lives and half that number of British. Now all this nightmare picture had vanished. In its place was the vision—fair and bright indeed it seemed—of the end of the whole war in one or two violent shocks.

Sir Winston Leonard Spencer Churchill

This [victory in Egypt] is not the end. It is not even the beginning of the end. But it is, perhaps, the end of the beginning.

Sir Winston Leonard Spencer Churchill

War is the desperate, vital problem of our time.

Thomas Alva Edison

The bomb has been made more effective . . . Unless another war is prevented it is likely to bring destruction on a scale never before held possible and even now hardly conceived, and . . . little civilization would survive it.

Albert Einstein

I do not believe that civilization will be wiped out in a war fought with the atomic bomb. Perhaps two-thirds of the people of the earth might be killed, but enough men capable of thinking, and enough books, would be left to start again, and civilization could be restored.

Albert Einstein

The man who enjoys marching in line and file to the strains of music falls below my contempt; he received his great brain by mistake—the spinal cord would have been amply sufficient.

Albert Einstein

War is low and despicable, and I had rather be smitten to shreds than participate in such doings.

Albert Einstein

As never before, the essence of war is fire, famine and pestilence. They contribute to its outbreak; they are among its weapons; they become its consequences.

Dwight David Eisenhower

As we look at the probable face of future warfare, if ever we must face that tragedy, we acknowledge that every hamlet and important city in the United States is likely to be in the front lines.

Dwight David Eisenhower

Every gun that is made, every warship launched, every rocket fired signifies, in the final sense, a theft from those who hunger and are not fed, those who are cold and not clothed. We pay for a single fighter plane with a half-millioin bushels of wheat. We pay for a single destroyer with new homes that could have housed more than eight thousand people.

Dwight David Eisenhower

When people speak to you about a preventive war, you tell them to go and fight it. After my experience, I have come to hate war. War settles nothing.

Dwight David Eisenhower

The essence of war is violence. Moderation in war is imbecility.

John Arbuthnot Fisher

My centre is giving way, my right is in retreat; situation excellent. I shall attack.

Ferdinand Foch

There never was a good war, or a bad peace.

Benjamin Franklin

When wars do come, they fall upon the many, the producing class, who are the sufferers.

Ulysses Simpson Grant

Only two great groups of animals, men and ants, indulge in highly organized mass warfare.

Charles Homer Haskins

Never think that war, no matter how necessary, nor how justified, is not a crime. Ask the infantry and ask the dead.

Ernest Hemingway

They wrote in the old days that it is sweet and fitting to die for one's country. But in modern war there is nothing sweet nor fitting in your dying. You will die like a dog and for no good reason.

Ernest Hemingway

Older men declare war. But it is youth that must fight and die. And it is youth who must inherit the tribulation, the sorrow, and the triumphs that are the aftermath of war.

Herbert Clark Hoover

War comes as the great failure of man, out of fear, lust for power, injustice, or misery left unrectified.

Cordell Hull

Nations which have adopted peacetime conscription have fought just as many wars as they fought before adopting it, and have suffered just as many defeats.

Aldous Leonard Huxley

From time immemorial wars have been, especially for noncombatants, the supremely thrilling excitement.

William James

War is an instrument entirely inefficient toward redressing wrong; and multiplies, instead of indemnifying losses.

Thomas Jefferson

Dress it as we may, feather it, daub it with gold, huzza it, and sing swaggering songs about it, what is war, nine times out of ten, but murder in uniform?

Douglas William Jerrold

For Americans who stayed at home—and for many who did not—the First World War had a certain unreality that has ever since made it seem more remote, and always less interesting, than the Civil War.

Alfred Kazin

Mankind must put an end to war or war will put an end to mankind.

John Fitzgerald Kennedy

I know that we do not want war and I know that you do not. If there must be a war, let's be on the same side.

Nikita Sergeevich Khrushchev

War as a destroying power will end by being self-destructive; ultimately, it will lose meaning and purpose, and nations will devote themselves to peaceful, constructive tasks.

Jacob Klatzkin

Modern warfare is an intricate business about which no one knows everything and few know very much.

William Franklin (Frank) Knox

I believe that wars, in particular civil wars, consist of only ten percent action and of ninety percent passive suffering.

Arthur Koestler

There is no such thing as an inevitable war. If war comes it will be from failure of human wisdom.

Andrew Bonar Law

O snap the fife and still the drums and show the monster as she is.

Richard Le Gallienne

The plain truth is that the war is imperialistic on both sides.

Nikolai Lenin

O God assist our side: at least, avoid assisting the enemy and leave the rest to me.

Leopold I, Prince of Anhalt-Dessau

Men know far more about the art of warmaking than about the art of peace-building.

Max Lerner

You are not going to get peace with millions of armed men. The chariot of peace cannot advance over a road littered with cannon.

David Lloyd George

I know war as few other men now living know it, and nothing to me is more revolting. I have long advocated its complete abolition, as its very destructiveness on both friend and foe has rendered it useless as a means of settling international disputes.

Douglas MacArthur

He who makes war his profession cannot be otherwise than vicious. War makes thieves, and peace brings them to the gallows.

Niccolò Machiavelli

Of all the evils to public liberty, war is perhaps the most to be dreaded, because it comprises and develops every other. War is the parent of armies; from these proceed debts and taxes. And armies, and debts, and taxes, are the known instruments for bringing the many under the dominion of the few. In war, too, the discretionary power of the executive is extended; its influence in dealing out offices, honors, and emoluments is multiplied; and all the means of seducing the minds are added to those of subduing the force of the people! No nation could preserve its freedom in the midst of continual warfare.

James Madison

And this I hate—not men, nor flag nor race, But only War with its wild, grinning face.

Joseph Dana Miller

War will disappear, like the dinosaur, when changes in world conditions have destroyed its survival value.

Robert Andrews Millikan

The old proverb that Beelzebub has to be driven out by Beelzebub is a dangerous one: the use of evil will create more evil, war more hostile feelings, and the use of force more need of force.

Fridtjof Nansen

Success in war, like charity in religion, covers a multitude of sins.

Sir Francis Napier

War, which society draws upon itself, is but organized barbarism, an inheritance of the savage state, however disguised or ornamented.

Napoleon III (Louis Napoleon)

The monk that invented gunpowder did as much to stop war as did all the sermons of his brethren.

Austin O'Malley

Men lack unity in their principles, in their ideas and in their view of life and of the world. As long as they are divided they will continue to be ignorant of one another, to hate and to fight against one another.

Paul VI (Giovanni Battista Montini)

The grim fact is that we prepare for war like precocious giants and for peace like retarded pygmies.

Lester Bowles Pearson

Hell, Heaven or Hoboken by Christmas.

John Joseph Pershing

The furnaces of war have historically been stoked by those who are driven by the ideology of hate and violence, by those that hold man and his innate dignity in total contempt. From Nuremburg to the concentration camps of Auschwitz into the holocaust of World War II were only short steps.

William Proxmire

It is only necessary to make war with five things: with the maladies of the body, the ignorances of the mind, with the passions of the body, with the seditions of the city, and the discords of families.

Pythagoras

War is a contagion, whether it be declared or undeclared. It can engulf states and peoples remote from the original scene of hostilities. We cannot have complete protection in a world of disorder in which confidence and security have broken down.

Franklin Delano Roosevelt

When an epidemic of physical disease starts to spread, the community approves and joins on a quarantine of the patient in order to protect the health of the community against the spread of the disease. War is a contagion whether it be declared or undeclared. It can engulf states and peoples remote from the original scene of hostility.

Franklin Delano Roosevelt

War comes today as the result of one of three causes: either actual or threatened wrong by one country to another, or suspicion by one country that another intends to do it wrong . . . or, from bitterness of feeling, dependent in no degree whatever upon substantial questions of difference. . . . The least of these three causes of war is actual injustice.

Elihu Root

If the intellectual has any function in society, it is to preserve a cool and unbiased judgment in the face of all solicitations to passion. . . . During the war, the ordinary virtues, such as thrift, industry, and public spirit, were used to swell the magnitude of the disaster by producing a greater energy in the work of mutual extermination.

Bertrand Arthur William Russell

There is only one virtue, pugnacity; only one vice, pacifism. That is an essential condition of war.

George Bernard Shaw

They made a speech, and played a trumpet and dressed me in a uniform and then they killed me.

Irwin Shaw

War is hell.

William Tecumseh Sherman

Lord Cherwell forecast that in 1943 bombing of built-up districts would deprive about one-third of the population of Germany of their homes, and that this might be decisive.

Sir Charles Percy Snow

Without any doubt the area-bombing offensive was an expensive failure. About 500,000

German men, women and children were killed, but in the whole bombing offensive 160,000 U.S. and British airmen, the best young men of both countries, were lost. German war production went on rising steadily until it reached its peak in August, 1944.

Sir Charles Percy Snow

There is nothing honorable about war as such—but it is an honorable and an heroic thing to fight for those ideals and principles we account worthy of preservation.

Francis Joseph Spellman

Heroic men can die upon the battlefield in vain, because of what occurs after a war, as well as because of what happens during a war.

Harold Edward Stassen

After we have won this war we shall have only one alternative to preparing for the next war. That is to prevent the next war.

Edward Reilley Stettinius

The human race *is* a family. Men *are* brothers. All wars are civil wars. All killing is fratricidal—as the poet Owen put it, "I am the enemy you killed, my friend."

Adlai Ewing Stevenson

Military power without a moral base is always intolerable.

Adlai Ewing Stevenson

We must all have learnt, even the tyrants, that in another total war—with or without unleashing all the demons locked in the atom—there can be no victors, only survivors.

Adlai Ewing Stevenson

It is a puzzling fact that international conduct is so often judged by far lower standards than are the acts of individuals. . . . Men who would not think of assaulting another to gain an end—who would indeed suffer great loss, and be proud to suffer it, rather than obtain their rights by such a method—feel that a nation should be ever ready to assert its claims by blows.

George Malcolm Stratton

The great force for forging a society into a solid mass has always been war.

William Graham Sumner

In the forum of reason and deliberation war never can be anything but a makeshift . . . A statesman who proposes war as an instru-

mentality admits his incompetency; a politician who makes use of war as a counter in the game of parties is a criminal.

William Graham Sumner

The difficulty about arguing is that when you get before an audience everybody is in favor of peace. . . . But when it comes to an election the issue as to international peace does not play any part at all.

William Howard Taft

Wars are not "acts of God." They are caused by man, by man-made institutions, by the way in which man has organized his society. What man has made, man can change.

Frederick Moore Vinson

To be prepared for war is one of the most effectual ways of preserving peace.

George Washington

The imponderables and the unforseen cannot be ignored in formulating foreign policy. That is why a preventive war should always be regarded as an act of criminal folly.

Sumner Welles

Militarism and warfare are childish things, if they are not more horrible than anything childish can be. They must become things of the past.

Herbert George Wells

There is no such thing as civilized warfare.

William Allen White

As long as war is regarded as wicked it will always have its fascinations. When it is looked upon as vulgar, it will cease to be popular.

Oscar Wilde

It is a fearful thing to lead this great peaceful people into war, into the most terrible and disastrous of all wars, civilization itself seeming to be in the balance. But the right is more precious than peace, and we shall fight for the things which we have always carried nearest our hearts—for democracy, for the right of those who submit to authority to have a voice in their own governments, for the rights and liberties of small nations, for a universal dominion of right by such a concert of free peoples as shall bring peace and safety to all nations and make the world itself at last free.

(Thomas) Woodrow Wilson

We Americans cannot conceive of a war without a moral background. . . . It may now be accepted as the principle that any weak saddle-colored nation that happens to be situated near us and also happens to possess a lot of mahogany or hemp or cocoanuts or gold mines had better look out. We have our moral eye on such people and are likely to introduce American morality at any moment.

William E. Woodward

See also: ARMY, CONTENTION, FORCE, NAVY, NUCLEAR WARFARE, REBELLION, REVOLUTION, SOLDIER, VIETNAM, VIOLENCE.

WASTE

It has always been more difficult for a man to keep than to get; for, in the one case, fortune aids, but in the other, sense is required. Therefore, we often see a person deficient in cleverness rise to wealth; and then, from want of sense, roll head over heels to the bottom.

Basil the Great

Wilful waste brings woeful want.

Thomas Fuller

Waste cannot be accurately told, though we are sensible how destructive it is. Economy, on the one hand, by which a certain income is made to maintain a man genteelly; and waste, on the other, by which on the same income another man lives shabbily, cannot be defined. It is a very nice thing; as one man wears his coat out much sooner than another, we cannot tell how.

Samuel Johnson

See also: EXTRAVAGANCE, PRODIGALITY.

WATCHFULNESS

We ought not to be careless and indifferent about the future. But as there are goods in life possible to be obtained, and evils capable of being avoided, so we should provide ourselves with proper means to obtain the one and escape the other. Watchfulness and industry are natural virtues, and recommended to us by the conduct even of brute creatures. If we neglect our own interest, we deserve the calamities which come upon us; and have no reason to hope for the compassion of others, when we take no care of ourselves.

John Conybeare

A soul without watchfulness is, like a city without walls, exposed to the inroads of all its enemies.

Thomas Secker

See also: ATTENTION, CAUTION, VIGILANCE.

WATER

Water, taken in moderation, cannot hurt anybody.

Samuel Langhorne Clemens (Mark Twain)

Deep waters noiseless are; and this we know,
That chiding streams betray small depth below.

Robert Herrick

Water is the only drink for a wise man.

Henry David Thoreau

See also: NATURE, RIVER, WATER POLLUTION.

WATER POLLUTION

There can be no doubt that National and State action is needed if our lakes and streams and the air we breathe are to be restored to their former purity, and I have supported measures aimed at accomplishing this goal. But Government cannot do the job alone; without the cooperation and assistance of the private sector, any program to reduce pollution will inevitably encounter difficulties and delays.

Birch Bayh

Among these treasures of our land is water—fast becoming our most valuable, most prized, most critical resource. A blessing where properly used—but it can bring devastation and ruin when left uncontrolled.

Dwight David Eisenhower

It should be clear by now that we are in a race with disaster. Either the world's water needs will be met, or the inevitable result will be mass starvation, mass epidemic and mass poverty greater than anything we know today.

Lyndon Baines Johnson

We in Government have begun to recognize the critical work which must be done at all levels—local, State and Federal—in ending the pollution of our waters.

Robert Francis Kennedy

See also: AIR POLLUTION, HEALTH, WATER.

WEAKNESS

The weakest soul, within itself unblest,
Leans for all pleasure on another's breast.
Oliver Goldsmith

In all our weaknesses we have one element
of strength if we recognize it. Here, as in
other things, knowledge of danger is often
the best means of safety.
Edward Payson Roe

Men are in general so tricky, so envious, and
so cruel, that when we find one who is only
weak, we are happy.
Voltaire (François Marie Arouet)

We all have weaknesses. But I have figured
that others have put up with mine so tolerably that I would be much less than fair not
to make a reasonable discount for theirs.
William Allen White

See also: COWARDICE, DEPENDENCE, FAILING.

WEALTH

People who are arrogant on account of their
wealth are about equal to the Laplanders,
who measure a man's worth by the number
of his reindeer.
Frederika Bremer

The wealth of man is the number of things
which he loves and blesses, which he is
loved and blessed by.
Thomas Carlyle

Surplus wealth is a sacred trust which its
possessor is bound to administer in his lifetime for the good of the community.
Andrew Carnegie

The gratification of wealth is not found in
mere possession or in lavish expenditure, but
in its wise application.
Miguel de Cervantes Saavedra

Prefer loss to the wealth of dishonest gain;
the former vexes you for a time; the latter
will bring you lasting remorse.
Chilon

He that will not permit his wealth to do any
good to others while he is living, prevents it
from doing any good to himself when he is
dead; and by an egotism that is suicidal and
has a double edge, cuts himself from the
truest pleasure here and the highest happiness hereafter.
Charles Caleb Colton

It is only when the rich are sick that they
fully feel the impotence of wealth.
Charles Caleb Colton

The real wealth, not only of America, but of
the world, is in the resources of the ground
we stand on, and in the resources of the human mind.
Norman Cousins

Abundance is a blessing to the wise;
The use of riches in discretion lies;
Learn this, ye men of wealth—a heavy purse
In a fool's pocket is a heavy curse.
Richard Cumberland

The concentration of wealth is made inevitable by the natural inequalityof men.
Will (William James) Durant

Wealth consists not in having great possessions, but in having few wants.
Epicurus

It is no longer a distinction to be rich. . . .
People do not care for money as they once
did. . . . What we accumulate by way of
useless surplus does us no honor.
Henry Ford

Wealth is not his that has it, but his that enjoys it.
Benjamin Franklin

When I caution you against becoming a miser, I do not therefore advise you to become
a prodigal or a spendthrift.
Horace

Wealth is nothing in itself; it is not useful
but when it departs from us; its value is
found only in that which it can purchase. As
to corporeal enjoyment, money can neither
open new avenues of pleasure, nor block up
the passages of anguish. Disease and infirmity still continue to torture and enfeeble, perhaps exasperated by luxury, or promoted by
softness. With respect to the mind, it has
rarely been observed that wealth contributes
much to quicken the discernment or elevate
the imagination, but may, by hiring flattery,
or laying diligence asleep, confirm error and
harden stupidity.
Samuel Johnson

Let us not envy some men their accumulated riches; their burden would be too heavy
for us; we could not sacrifice, as they do,
health, quiet, honor, and conscience, to ob-

tain them: it is to pay so dear for them that the bargain is a loss.

Jean de La Bruyère

The most brilliant fortunes are often not worth the littleness required to gain them.

Duc François de La Rochefoucauld

If you look up a dictionary of quotations you will find few reasons for a sensible man to desire to become wealthy.

Robert Lynd

Excess of wealth is cause of covetousness.

Christopher Marlowe

There's nothing so comfortable as a small bankroll. A big one is always in danger.

Wilson Mizner

When a man dies, the people ask, "what property has he left behind him?" But the angels, as they bend over his grave, inquire, "what good deeds hast thou sent on before thee?"

Mahomet (Mohammed)

Less coin, less care; to know how to dispense with wealth is to possess it.

Sir Joshua Reynolds

It requires a great deal of boldness and a great deal of caution to make a great fortune; and when you have got it, it requires ten times as much wit to keep it.

Meyer Amschel Rothschild

A great fortune is a great servitude.

Seneca

He is richest who is content with the least, for content is the wealth of nature.

Socrates

The advantages of wealth are greatly exaggerated.

(Amasa) Leland Stanford

See also: MONEY, RICH, SUCCESS.

WEATHER

Oh, what a blamed uncertain thing
  This pesky weather is;
It blew and snew and then it thew,
  And now, by jing, it's friz.

Philander Chase Johnson

Everybody talks about the weather but nobody does anything about it.

Charles Dudley Warner

See also: AUTUMN, NATURE, RAIN, SPRING, SUMMER, WINTER.

WELCOME

'Tis sweet to hear the watch-dog's honest bark
  Bay deep-mouth'd welcome as we draw near home;
'Tis sweet to know there is an eye will mark
  Our coming, and look brighter when we come.

George Gordon Byron (Lord Byron)

Welcome as kindly showers to the long parched earth.

John Dryden

Come in the evening, come in the morning,
Come when expected, come without warning;
Thousands of welcomes you'll find here before you,
And the oftener you come, the more we'll adore you.

Irish Rhyme

See also: GUEST, HOSPITALITY, VISITOR.

WELL-DOING

We do not choose our own parts in life, and have nothing to do with those parts. Our duty is confined to playing them well.

Epictetus

Thinking well is wise; planning well, wiser; doing well wisest and best of all.

Persian Proverb

Rest satisfied with doing well, and leave others to talk of you as they please.

Pythagoras

Whatever is worth doing at all, is worth doing well.

Philip Dormer Stanhope (Lord Chesterfield)

See also: BENEFICENCE, BENEVOLENCE, CHARITY, DEEDS, GENEROSITY, GOODNESS, HELP, KINDNESS, LIBERALITY, MAGNANIMITY, PHILANTHROPY.

WICKEDNESS

There is a method in man's wickedness; it grows up by degrees.

Francis Beaumont and John Fletcher

There is wickedness in the intention of wickedness, even though it be not perpetrated in the act.

Cicero

To see and listen to the wicked is already the beginning of wickedness.

Confucius

One may detest the wickedness of a brother without hating him.

Mohandas Karamchand (Mahatma) Gandhi

Combinations of wickedness would overwhelm the world, by the advantage which licentious principles afford, did not those who have long practised perfidy grow faithless to each other.

Samuel Johnson

No wickedness proceeds on any grounds of reason.

Livy

The wicked flee when no man pursueth, but they make better time when someone is after them.

Charles Henry Parkhurst

The happiness of the wicked passes away like a torrent.

Jean Baptiste Racine

It is a statistical fact that the wicked work harder to reach hell than the righteous do to enter heaven.

Henry Wheeler Shaw (Josh Billings)

The sure way to wickedness is always through wickedness.

Seneca

See also: BASENESS, CORRUPTION, CRIME, DEPRAVITY, DISHONESTY, FRAUD, INFAMY, MEANNESS, MISCHIEF, ROGUERY, SIN, VICE, VILLAINY, WRONG.

WIDOW AND WIDOWER

Drying a widow's tears is one of the most dangerous occupations known to man.

Elizabeth Gilmer (Dorothy Dix)

So far as is known, no widow ever eloped.

Edgar Watson Howe

The death of a man's wife is like cutting down an ancient oak that has long shaded the family mansion. Henceforth the glare of the world, with its cares and vicissitudes, falls upon the widower's heart, and there is nothing to break their force, or shield him from the full weight of misfortune. It is as if his right hand were withered; as if one wing of his angel was broken, and every move-

ment that he made brought him to the ground. His eyes are dimmed and glassy, and when the film of death falls over him, he misses those accustomed tones which might have smoothed his passage to the grave.

Alphonse de Lamartine

See also: DEATH, HUSBAND, HUSBAND AND WIFE, MARRIAGE, WIFE.

WIFE

Wives are young men's mistresses, companions for middle age, and old men's nurses.

Francis Bacon

The graveyards are full of women whose houses were so spotless you could eat off the floor. Remember the second wife always has a maid.

Heloise Cruse

Here lies my wife; here let her lie! Now she's at rest, and so am I.

John Dryden

There is one thing more exasperating than a wife who can cook and won't, and that's the wife who can't cook and will.

Robert Lee Frost

For a wife take the daughter of a good mother.

Thomas Fuller

Wife is not the husband's bondslave, but his companion and his helpmate, and an equal partner in all his joys and sorrows—as free as the husband to choose her own path.

Mohandas Karamchand (Mahatma) Gandhi

I chose my wife, as she did her wedding-gown, for qualities that would wear well.

Oliver Goldsmith

Back of every achievement is a proud wife and a surprised mother-in-law.

Brooks Hays

Of all the home remedies, a good wife is the best.

Frank McKinney (Kin) Hubbard

Heaven will not be heaven to me if I do not meet my wife there.

Andrew Jackson

A good wife is like the ivy which beautifies the building to which it clings, twining its tendrils more lovingly as time converts the ancient edifice into a ruin.

Samuel Johnson

The highest gift and favor of God is a pious, kind, godly, and domestic wife, with whom you can live peaceably, and to whom you can intrust all your possessions, indeed, your body and your life.

Martin Luther

The sum of all that makes a just man happy consists in the well choosing of his wife.

Philip Massinger

To be a man in a true sense is, in the first place and above all things to have a wife.

Jules Michelet

Who is the fool that does not wish his wife to be dumb? Would to God that mine were affected with that disease! I would beware of curing her.

Molière (Jean Baptiste Poquelin)

A wife is essential to great longevity; she is the receptacle of half a man's cares, and two-thirds of his ill-humor.

Charles Reade

Her pleasures are in the happiness of her family.

Jean Jacques Rousseau

My dear, my better half.

Sir Philip Sidney

Of earthly goods, the best is a good wife;
A bad, the bitterest curse of human life.

Simonides

Teacher, tender comrade, wife,
A fellow-farer true through life.

Robert Louis Stevenson

Try praising your wife, even if it does frighten her at first.

William Ashley (Billy) Sunday

An ideal wife is any woman who has an ideal husband.

Booth Tarkington

See also: LOVE, MARRIAGE, MOTHER, SEXES, WOMAN.

WILL

Then . . . is our will truly free, when it serves neither vice nor sin.

Augustine of Hippo

Great souls have wills; feeble ones have only wishes.

Chinese Proverb

The general of a large army may be defeated, but you cannot defeat the determined mind of a peasant.

Confucius

If we make God's will our law, then God's promise shall be our support and comfort, and we shall find every burden light, and every duty a joy.

Tryon Edwards

There is nothing good or evil save in the will.

Epictetus

To deny the freedom of the will is to make morality impossible.

James Anthony Froude

Do God's will as if it were thy will, and he will accomplish thy will as if it were his own.

Rabbi Gamaliel

If we develop the force of will, we shall find that we do not need the force of arms.

Mohandas Karamchand (Mahatma) Gandhi

Strength does not come from physical capacity. It comes from an indomitable will.

Mohandas Karamchand (Mahatma) Gandhi

He who has a firm will molds the world to himself.

Johann Wolfgang von Goethe

It is the will that makes the action good or bad.

Robert Herrick

People do not lack strength; they lack will.

Victor Marie Hugo

Will is character in action.

William McDougall

We cannot be held to what is beyond our strength and means; for at times the accomplishment and execution may not be in our power; and indeed there is nothing really in our own power except the will: on this are necessarily based and founded all the principles that regulate the duty of man.

Michel Eyquem de Montaigne

"My will, and not thine be done," turned paradise into a desert. "Not my will, but thine be done," turned the desert into paradise, and made Gethsemane the gate of heaven.

Edmond Dehaut de Pressensé

No action will be considered blameless, unless the will was so, for by the will the act was dictated.

Seneca

See also: AIM, DECISION, DESIRE, ENTHUSIASM, FIRMNESS, INTENTION, PURPOSE, RESOLUTION, SELF-WILL, WISH.

WILLS (TESTAMENT)

He that defers his charity until he is dead is, if a man weighs it rightly, rather liberal of another man's goods than his own.

Francis Bacon

Posthumous charities are the very essence of selfishness, when bequeathed by those who, when alive, would part with nothing.

Charles Caleb Colton

You give me nothing during your life, but you promise to provide for me at your death. If you are not a fool, you know what you make me wish for.

Martial

What you leave at your death let it be without controversy, else the lawyers will be your heirs.

Francis Osborne

See also: DEATH, INHERITANCE.

WIND

A breeze came wandering from the sky, Light as the whispers of a dream.

William Cullen Bryant

A wailing, rushing sound, which shook the walls as though a giant's hand were on them; then a hoarse roar, as if the sea had risen; then such a whirl and tumult that the air seemed mad; and then, with a lengthened howl, the waves of wind swept on.

Charles John Huffam Dickens

Perhaps the wind wails so in winter for the summer's dead; and all sad sounds are nature's funeral cries for what has been and is not.

George Eliot (Mary Ann Evans)

Take a straw and throw it up into the air, You may see by that which way the wind is.

John Selden

Sweet and low, sweet and low,
    Wind of the western sea,
Low, low, breathe and blow,
    Wind of the western sea!
Over the rolling waters go,
Come from the dying moon, and blow,
    Blow him again to me;
While my little one, while my pretty one, sleeps.

Alfred, Lord Tennyson

See also: CLOUD, NATURE, RAIN.

WINE

Polished brass is the mirror of the body and wine of the mind.

Aeschylus

A vine bears three grapes, the first of pleasure, the second of drunkenness, and the third of repentance.

Anacharsis

The conscious water saw its God, and blushed.

Richard Crashaw

Wine and youth are fire upon fire.

Henry Fielding

O for a draught of vintage, that hath been
    Cooled a long age in the deep-delvèd earth,
Tasting of Flora and the country green,
    Dance and Provençal song, and sunburnt mirth!
O for a beaker full of the warm South,
    Full of the true, the blushful Hippocrene,
      With beaded bubbles winking at the brim,
      And purple-stained mouth.

John Keats

There is a devil in every berry of the grape.

Koran

Wine is the most healthful and most hygienic of beverages.

Louis Pasteur

See also: ALCOHOL, CONVIVIALITY, DRINKING, DRUNKENNESS, INTEMPERANCE.

WINTER

Look! the massy trunks
Are cased in the pure crystal; each light
    spray,
Nodding and tinkling in the breath of heav-
    en,
Is studded with its trembling water-drops,
That glimmer with an amethystine light.
                William Cullen Bryant

On a lone winter evening, when the frost
Has wrought a silence.
                        John Keats

Full knee-deep lies the winter snow,
And the winter winds are wearily sighing.
                Alfred, Lord Tennyson

Stern winter loves a dirge-like sound.
                    William Wordsworth

See also: AUTUMN, SPRING, SUMMER.

WIRETAPPING

The dragnet character of wiretapping, the
injury done by it to the rights of the wholly
innocent as well as of the guilty, the absolute irresponsibility of tappers, who cannot
be detected and called to account for their
acts, all make it a peculiarly dangerous police technique.
                        Alan Barth

There is nothing fastidious about wiretapping. It provides a fertile source for blackmail; its utility for law enforcement is less
apparent.
                        Alan Barth

A wiretap is no respecter of citizenship or
loyalty.
                        Alan Barth

Writs of assistance and general warrants are
but puny instruments of tyranny and oppression when compared with wiretapping.
                Louis Dembitz Brandeis

There is not a syllable in the Constitution
that gives the Federal Government the right
to spy on civilians.
                        Samuel Ervin

It makes no sense whatever to deny law enforcement officers the right to tap the very
wires being used by organized criminals to
commit crime and carry out their conspira-
torial activities.
                    John L. McClellan

Wiretapping is being practiced primiscuous-
ly today. Private detectives are tapping
wires and are invading the privacy of homes
under existing law, and nothing is done
about it.
                    John L. McClellan

There is, however, one field in which, given
the conditions in the world today, wiretapping is very much in the public interest.
This nation is arming for national defense. It
is the duty of our people to take every single step to protect themselves. I have no
compunction in saying that wiretapping
should be used against those persons, not
citizens of the United States, and those few
citizens who are traitors to their country,
who today are engaged in espionage or sab-
otage against the United States.
                Franklin Delano Roosevelt

The use of wiretapping to aid law-
enforcement officers raises squarely the most
delicate problem in the field of democratic
statesmanship. It is more than desirable, it is
necessary that criminals be detected and
prosecuted as vigilantly as possible. It is
more necessary that the citizens of a democracy be protected in their rights of privacy
from unwarranted snooping. As an instrument for oppression of free citizens, I can
think of none worse than indiscriminate
wiretapping.
                Franklin Delano Roosevelt

See also: PRIVACY, SPYING.

WISDOM

When a man is made up wholly of the dove,
without the least grain of the serpent in his
composition, he becomes ridiculous in many
circumstances of life, and very often discredits his best actions.
                        Joseph Addison

A person should not shoot a bird resting on
his own head.
                    Bantu Tribe proverb

In seeking wisdom thou art wise; in imagining
that thou hast attained it thou art a fool.
                        Simon Ben Azzai

Pain is the father, and love the mother, of
wisdom.
                        Ludwig Börne

Wisdom prepares for the worst, but folly leaves the worst for the day when it comes.

Richard Cecil

It is better to speak wisdom foolishly like the saints than to speak folly wisely like the deans.

Gilbert Keith Chesterton

Our wisdom, whether expressed in public or private, belongs to the world, but our follies belong to those we love.

Gilbert Keith Chesterton

Common-sense in an uncommon degree is what the world calls wisdom.

Samuel Taylor Coleridge

The two powers which in my opinion constitute a wise man are those of bearing and forbearing.

Epictetus

Among mortals second thoughts are wisest.

Euripides

Some are weather-wise, some are otherwise.

Benjamin Franklin

It is unwise to be too sure of one's own wisdom. It is healthy to be reminded that the strongest might weaken and the wisest might err.

Mohandas Karamchand (Mahatma) Gandhi

Not mad rush, but unperturbed calmness brings wisdom. This maxim holds as true today as when it was first propounded ages ago.

Mohandas Karamchand (Mahatma) Gandhi

Wisdom is no monopoly of one continent or one race.

Mohandas Karamchand (Mahatma) Gandhi

The wisdom of the ignorant somewhat resembles the instinct of animals; it is diffused only in a very narrow sphere, but within the circle it acts with vigor, uniformity, and success.

Oliver Goldsmith

He is wise who knows the sources of knowledge—who knows who has written and where it is to be found.

Archibald Alexander Hodge

Every man is a damn fool for at least five minutes every day; wisdom consists in not exceeding the limit.

Elbert Green Hubbard

The wise man is he who knows the relative value of things.

William Ralph Inge

The art of being wise is the art of knowing what to overlook.

William James

Very few men are wise by their own counsel, or learned by their own teaching; for he that was only taught by himself had a fool to his master.

Ben (Benjamin) Jonson

Wisdom is knowing what to do next; virtue is doing it.

David Starr Jordan

The first point of wisdom is to discern that which is false; the second, to know that which is true.

Lactantius

It is more easy to be wise for others than for ourselves.

Duc François de La Rochefoucauld

Our wisdom is not less at the mercy of fortune than our goods.

Duc François de La Rochefoucauld

Wisdom is to the soul what health is to the body.

Duc François de La Rochefoucauld

One fool can ask more questions in a minute than twelve wise men can answer in an hour.

Nikolai Lenin

Great wisdom consists in not demanding too much of human nature, and yet not altogether spoiling it by indulgence.

Lin Yutang

The wise man has his foibles, as well as the fool. But the difference between them is, that the foibles of the one are known to himself and concealed from the world; and the foibles of the other are known to the world and concealed from himself.

John Mitchell Mason

To know that which before us lies in daily life is the prime wisdom.

John Milton

If we build with wisdom, and with courage, and with patience, those that come after us will be helped by our work.

Dwight Whitney Morrow

Speed is good when wisdom leads the way.

Edward Roscoe Murrow

The older I grow the more I feel the lack of wisdom in myself. Perhaps, it may be that that very feeling is a sign of having some wisdom.

Jawaharlal Nehru

If wise men were hairs, the world would need a wig.

Austin O'Malley

Wisdom consists in perceiving when human nature and this perverse world necessitate making exceptions to abstract truths.

Wendell Phillips

Perfect wisdom hath four parts, viz., wisdom, the principle of doing things aright; justice, the principle of doing things equally in public and private; fortitude, the principle of not flying danger, but meeting it; and temperance, the principle of subduing desires and living moderately.

Plato

What is it to be wise? 'Tis but to know how little can be known—to see all other's faults and feel our own.

Alexander Pope

Nine-tenths of wisdom consists in being wise in time.

Theodore Roosevelt

Life is full of perils, but the wise man ignores those that are inevitable.

Bertrand Arthur William Russell

He who learns the rules of wisdom without conforming to them in his life is like a man who ploughs in his field but does not sow.

Saadi (Muslid-ud-Din)

If wisdom were conferred with this proviso, that I must keep it to myself and not communicate it to others, I would have none of it.

Seneca

It's a wise man who profits by his own experience, but it's a good deal wiser one who lets the rattlesnake bite the other fellow.

Henry Wheeler Shaw (Josh Billings)

The Delphic oracle said I was the wisest of all the Greeks. It is because that I alone, of all the Greeks, know that I know nothing.

Socrates

Much wisdom often goes with fewest words.

Sophocles

Human wisdom is the aggregate of all human experience, constantly accumulating, selecting, and reorganizing its own materials.

Joseph Story

There is one person that is wiser than anybody, and that is everybody.

Alexandre de Talleyrand-Périgord

The dog has seldom been successful in pulling Man up to its level of sagacity, but Man has frequently dragged the dog down to his.

James Grover Thurber

It may be said, almost without qualification, that true wisdom consists in the ready and accurate perception of analogies. Without the former quality, knowledge of the past is uninstructive; without the latter, it is a deceptive.

Richard Whately

Wisdom is ofttimes nearer when we stoop than when we soar.

William Wordsworth

See also: COMMON SENSE, DISCERNMENT, INTELLIGENCE, JUDGMENT, KNOWLEDGE, LEARNING, PRUDENCE, SENSE, UNDERSTANDING, WIT.

WISH

Every wish is like a prayer with God.

Elizabeth Barrett Browning

A man will sometimes devote all his life to the development of one part of his body— the wishbone.

Robert Lee Frost

Happy the man who early learns the wide chasm that lies between his wishes and his powers!

Johann Wolfgang von Goethe

If wishes were horses beggars might ride.

English Proverb

Many of us spend half our time wishing for things we could have if we didn't spend half our time wishing.

Alexander Woollcott

See also: AMBITION, ASPIRATION, DESIRE, HOPE, WANT, WILL.

WIT

Wit is a treacherous dart. It is perhaps the only weapon with which it is possible to stab oneself in one's own back.

Geoffrey Bocca

A witty man is admired for his mental adroitness rather than for his mental hilarity.

Leonard Feeney

Wit should be used as a shield for defence rather than as a sword to wound others.

Thomas Fuller

Wit is a form of lightning calculation; humour the exploitation of disproportion.

Russell Green

Wit is the salt of conversation, not the food.

William Hazlitt

For wit and borrowers it is wholesome when they surprise us unannounced.

Heinrich Heine

He who has provoked the shaft of wit, cannot complain that he smarts from it.

Samuel Johnson

A man of wit would often be at a loss were it not for the company of fools.

Duc François de La Rochefoucauld

Wit consists in assembling, and putting together with quickness, ideas in which can be found resemblance and congruity, by which to make up pleasant pictures and agreeable visions in the fancy.

John Locke

Impropriety is the soul of wit.

(William) Somerset Maugham

The impromptu reply is precisely the touchstone of the man of wit.

Molière (Jean Baptiste Poquelin)

Wit is the only wall
Between us and the dark.

Mark Van Doren

See also: HUMOR, JESTING, LEVITY, RAILLERY, REPARTEE, RIDICULE, SARCASM, SATIRE, WISDOM.

WOMAN

Find a man anywhere who has saved any considerable amount of money and he is likely to tell you that some woman made him do it.

James Randolph Adams

Women wish to be loved without a why or wherefore—not because they are pretty or good, or well-bred, or graceful, or intelligent, but because they are themselves.

Henri Frédéric Amiel

There is nothing enduring in life for a woman except what she builds in a man's heart.

Dame Judith Anderson

Modern invention has banished the spinning wheel, and the same law of progress makes the woman of today a different woman from her grandmother.

Susan Brownell Anthony

Woman's love is writ in water,
Woman's faith is traced in sand.

William Edmonstoune Aytoun

The errors of women spring, almost always, from their faith in the good, or their confidence in the true.

Honoré de Balzac

To feel, to love, to suffer, to devote herself will always be the text of the life of a woman.

Honoré de Balzac

Woman—last at the cross, and earliest at the grave.

Eaton Stannard Barrett

You see, dear, it is not true that woman was made from man's rib; she was really made from his funny bone.

Sir James Matthew Barrie

The way to fight a woman is with your hat. Grab it and run.

John Barrymore

The future of society is in the hands of mothers; if the world was lost through woman she alone can save it.

Louis de Beaufort

Women do about all the reading and play-going that is done in America; at least they are responsible for most of the play-going, since men mostly "go along" under their influence. They keep up most of our music, they maintain most of our painting and sculpture, they are the mainstay of our churches, our educational, cultural, and social institutions, they are the arbiters of taste and style for both sexes and in all particulars.

Henry Augustine Beers

The status of American women is a tremendous cause of worry in that country. American women are ruling the American society. The United States is a matriarchy, and this is a very unhealthy thing because fundamentally women like strong men.

Joshua Bierer

I wish Adam had died with all his ribs in his body.

Dion Boucicault

A Frenchwoman, when double-crossed, will kill her rival; the Italian woman would rather kill her deceitful lover; the Englishwoman simply breaks off relations—but they all will console themselves with another man.

Charles Boyer

No home offers scope enough to-day for the trained energies of an intelligent modern woman.

Pearl Sydenstricker Buck

She is not made to be the admiration of all, but the happiness of one.

Edmund Burke

Alas! the love of women! it is known
To be a lovely and a fearful thing!
George Gordon Byron (Lord Byron)

In her first passion woman loves her lover,
   In all the others all she loves is love.
George Gordon Byron (Lord Byron)

It is reputed that quite a number of women have had consciences.

James Branch Cabell

Lost is our freedom,
When we submit to women so:
   Why do we need them,
When in their best they work our woe?
Thomas Campion

A capacity for self-pity is one of the last things that any woman surrenders.

Irvin Shrewsbury Cobb

There are three classes into which all old women are divided: first, that dear old soul; second, that old woman; and third, that old witch.

Samuel Taylor Coleridge

Being a woman is a terribly difficult task, since it consists principally in dealing with men.

Joseph Conrad

The deepest tenderness a woman can show to a man, is to help him to do his duty.
Dinah Maria Mulock Craik

I think housework is the reason most women go to the office.

Heloise Cruse

The test of civilization is the estimate of woman.

George William Curtis

The growing freedom of women can hardly have any other outcome than the production of more realistic and more human morals.

John Dewey

Each age has its own beauty, and the wise woman recognizes this, and does not attempt to make of the present age a poor imitation of the past one.

Maria Richards Dewing

A female friend, amiable, clever, and devoted, is a possession more valuable than parks and palaces; and without such a muse, few men can succeed in life, none can be content.

Benjamin Disraeli

All manner of chastisements failing, man finally gave up his attempts to dull the keen edge of that sharpest of all weapons—a woman's tongue.

Fairfax Davis Downey

Woman's honor is nice as ermine, will not bear a soil.

John Dryden

The emancipation of women, despite the biological problems which it entails, indicates a certain growing gentility in the once-murderous male.

Will (William James) Durant

A woman's lot is made for her by the love she accepts.

George Eliot (Mary Ann Evans)

It has been women who have breathed gentleness and care into the harsh progress of mankind.

Elizabeth II

Many of our girls feel that their bodily perfect'on exempts them from the necessity of developing their inner energies.

James Montgomery Flagg

Woman is often fickle; very foolish is he who trusts them.

Francis I

It is not education which makes women less domestic, but wealth.

Katharine Jeanne Gallagher

I believe in the proper education of women. But I do not believe that woman will not make her contribution to the world by mimicking or running a race with man. She can run the race but she will not rise to the great heights she is capable of by mimicking man. She has to be the complement of man.

Mohandas Karamchand (Mahatma) Gandhi

I have regarded woman as an incarnation of tolerance. A servant wrongly suspected may throw up his job, a son in the same case may leave his father's roof, and a friend may put an end to the friendship. The wife, if she suspects her husband, will keep quiet, but if the husband suspects her, she is ruined.

Mohandas Karamchand (Mahatma) Gandhi

Man has converted her into a domestic drudge and an instrument of his pleasure, instead of regarding her as his helpmate and better half. The result is a semi-paralysis of our society. Woman has rightly been called the mother of the race. We owe it to her and to ourselves to undo the great wrong that we have done her.

Mohandas Karamchand (Mahatma) Gandhi

Of all the evils for which man has made himself responsible, none is so degrading, so shocking or so brutal as his abuse of the better half of humanity, to me, the female sex, not the weaker sex.

Mohandas Karamchand (Mahatma) Gandhi

To call a woman a member of the weaker sex is a libel. In what way is woman the weaker sex, I do not know. If the implication is that she lacks the brute instinct of man, or does not possess it in the same measure as man, the charge may be admitted.

But then, woman becomes, as she is, the nobler sex. If she is weak in striking, she is strong in suffering.

Mohandas Karamchand (Mahatma) Gandhi

There is little in our analysis to support the widespread bel'ef that most educated women are trapped in situations which create frustration and disappointment and it is the rare woman indeed who is able to fulfill her potentiality. The opposite is much closer to the truth.

Eli Ginzberg

The society of women is the element of good manners.

Johann Wolfgang von Goethe

Somebody must be longsuffering and meek. With all their follies and vanities and limitations, it has been the women who have always practiced this negative but essential virtue.

Corra May White Harris

Women give us solace, but if it were not for women we should never need solace.

Don Herold

A beautiful and chaste woman is the perfect workmanship of God, the true glory of angels, the rare miracle of earth, and the sole wonder of the world.

Georg Hermes

The position of women has no fixed relation to the general level of culture. It has been higher in the remote past than in recent times, and amongst savages it is by no means uniformly low.

Leonard Trelawney Hobhouse

The woman who climbs to a high post and then wants everybody to know how important she is, is the worst enemy of her own sex.

Claire Giannini Hoffman

How many women are born too finely organized in sense and soul for the highway they must walk with feet unshod! Life is adjusted to the wants of the stronger sex. There are plenty of torrents to be crossed in its journey; but their stepping-stones are measured by the strides of men, and not of women.

Oliver Wendell Holmes

All women is up against it, and it's a dirty shame, too, because women ain't so bad. They ain't much use, maybe, but they ain't so bad.

Sidney Coe Howard

When I see the elaborate study and ingenuity displayed by women in the pursuit of trifles, I feel no doubt of their capacity for the most herculean undertakings.

Julia Ward Howe

I don't know of anything better than a woman if you want to spend money where it'll show.

Frank McKinney (Kin) Hubbard

Men are women's playthings; woman is the devil's.

Victor Marie Hugo

Men have sight; women insight.

Victor Marie Hugo

No one knows like a woman how to say things which are at once gentle and deep.

Victor Marie Hugo

There is no reason why we should not some day have a female chief of staff or even a commander in chief.

Lyndon Baines Johnson

Women for the most part do not love us. They do not choose a man because they love him, but because it pleases them to be loved by him. They love love of all things in the world, but there are very few men whom they love personally.

Alphonse Karr

A woman's guess is much more accurate than a man's certainty.

Rudyard Kipling

If a beautiful woman speaks favourably of the beauty of another woman, we may be sure that she possesses more of the kind of beauty she is praising. If a poet praises the verses of another poet, you may wager anything that they are stupid, and of no real value.

Jean de La Bruyère

Women are ever in extremes; they are either better or worse than men.

Jean de La Bruyère

There is a woman at the beginning of all great things.

Alphonse de Lamartine

Of all the rights of women, the greatest is to be a mother.

Lin Yutang

Earth has nothing more tender than a woman's heart when it is the abode of Piety.

Martin Luther

No woman objects to being called intelligent provided she is assured that it has done no harm to her looks.

Aubrey Clarence Menen

In all societies women have played a much more important role than their menfolk are generally ready to admit.

Ashley Montagu

As any psychologist will tell you, the worst thing you can possibly do to a woman is to deprive her of a grievance.

Beverly Nichols

The thing needed . . . to raise women (and to raise men too) is these friendships without love between men and women. And if between married men and married women, all the better.

Florence Nightingale

A beautiful young lady is an accident of nature. A beautiful old lady is a work of art.

Louis Nizer

A woman's greatest glory is to be little talked about by men, whether for good or ill.

Pericles

If men knew how women pass the time when they are alone, they'd never marry.

William Sydney Porter (O. Henry)

Any woman who has a career and a family automatically develops something in the way of two personalities, like two sides of a dollar bill, each different in design. But one can complement the other to make a valuable whole. Her problem is to keep one from draining the life from the other. She can achieve happiness only as long as she keeps the two in balance.

Ivy Baker Priest

Because the women in our society are increasingly called upon to fill dual roles as breadwinners and homemakers, it is vitally important they receive the vocational education and training they need to excel in these diverse areas.

Roman C. Pucinski

A woman's heart, like the moon, is always changing, but there is always a man in it.

Punch

Women were surely intended to be beautiful, and it is a low trick on the part of Creation to make some of them ravishing and to give Phi Beta keys to the rest of us as a sop.

Marjorie Rawlings

One of the lost souls in our modern technological society is our American woman.

Roger Revelle

Her dignity consists in being unknown to the world; her glory is in the esteem of her husband; her pleasures in the happiness of her family.

Jean Jacques Rousseau

A handsome woman is a jewel; a good woman is a treasure.

Saadi (Muslid-ud-Din)

Woman reduces us all to a common denominator.

George Bernard Shaw

Love, which is only an episode in the life of a man, is the entire history of woman's life.

Madame de Staël

All a woman has to do in this world is contained within the duties of a daughter, a sister, a wife, and a mother.

Sir Richard Steele

There can be no higher ambition for a Christian woman than to be a faithful wife and a happy and influential mother. It is the place which God has given woman, and she who fills it well, is as honorable and honored as the most illustrious man can be.

Charles Augustus Stoddard

There is something still more to be dreaded than a Jesuit and that is a Jesuitess.

Eugène Sue

O Woman, you are not merely the handiwork of God, but also of men; these are ever endowing you with beauty from their own hearts. . . . You are one-half woman and one-half dream.

Sir Rabindranath Tagore

Women have tongues of craft, and hearts of guile,
They will, they will not; fools that on them trust;
For in their speech is death, hell in their smile.

Torquato Tasso

With more and more women of our own day, there is an urge to creativeness which lies underneath and deeper, above and beyond the begetting of children. These women have a contract with life itself, which is not discharged by the mere procreation of their species. Men recognize and try to honour this contract in themselves as a matter of course. . . . They do not acknowledge and respect the same thing so readily in women.

Laurens Van der Post

All the reasonings of men are not worth one sentiment of women.

Voltaire (François Marie Arouet)

Woman is like the reed which bends to every breeze, but breaks not in the tempest.

Richard Whately

Women, after attaining maturity, educate themselves more frequently than men educate themselves. The self-education is the education that sticks.

William Allen White

There are only two kinds of women, the plain and the colored.

Oscar Wilde

There is no such thing as romance in our day, women have become too brilliant; nothing spoils a romance so much as a sense of humor in the woman.

Oscar Wilde

See also: DAUGHTER, SEXES, WIFE.

WOMAN AND WORK

No amount of preaching, exhortation, sympathy, benevolence, will render the condition of our working-women what it should be so long as the kitchen and the needle are substantially their only resources.

Horace Greeley

I have heard a lot of opinions about the life of Russian women and the way they are dressed. But the worst work for a woman is prostitution. . . . In Paris you cannot walk down the street without having a woman accost you in order to subsist. Here in Russia, if a woman works like a man, she is at least not in a degrading situation but honestly earns her living.

Nikita Sergeevich Khrushchev

The concept of the woman of the shipyards, of the mines, of heavy labor as it is exalted and practiced by some countries that would want to inspire progress is anything but a modern concept. It is, on the contrary, a sad return toward epochs that Christian civilization buried long ago.

Pius XII (Eugenio Pacelli)

See also: BUSINESS, WOMAN, WORK.

WONDER

It was through the feeling of wonder that men now and at first began to philosophize.

Aristotle

The man who cannot wonder, who does not habitually wonder and worship, is but a pair of spectacles behind which there is no eye.

Thomas Carlyle

He who can no longer pause to wonder and stand rapt in awe, is as good as dead; his eyes are closed.

Albert Einstein

All wonder is the effect of novelty on ignorance.

Samuel Johnson

As knowledge increases, wonder deepens.

Charles Morgan

See also: ADMIRATION, CURIOSITY, MIRACLES, MYSTERY, UNCERTAINTY.

WORD

It is with a word as with an arrow—once let it loose and it does not return.

Abd-el-Kader

Words are merely the vehicle on which thoughts ride; and when the vehicle creaks too loudly in the wheels it distracts attention from the cargo.

James Randolph Adams

Men suppose their reason has command over their words; still it happens that words in return exercise authority on reason.

Francis Bacon

There are words which sever hearts more than sharp swords; there are words the point of which sting the heart through the course of a whole life.

Frederika Bremer

Words are the clothes that thoughts wear—only the clothes.

Samuel Butler

Eating words has never given me indigestion.

Sir Winston Leonard Spencer Churchill

Short words are best and the old words when short are best of all.

Sir Winston Leonard Spencer Churchill

The difference between the right word and the almost right word is the difference between lightning and the lightning bug.

Samuel Langhorne Clemens (Mark Twain)

What you keep by you, you may change and mend; but words, once spoken, can never be recalled.

Wentworth Dillon (Earl of Roscommon)

With words we govern men.

Benjamin Disraeli

Although words exist for the most part for the transmission of ideas, there are some which produce such violent disturbance in our feelings that the role they play in transmission of ideas is lost in the background.

Albert Einstein

No man has a prosperity so high or firm, but that two or three words can dishearten it; and there is no calamity which right words will not begin to redress.

Ralph Waldo Emerson

The finest words in the world are only vain sounds, if you cannot comprehend them.

Anatole France

The pleasure and excitement of words is that they are living and generating things.

Christopher Fry

Words are the counters of wise men, and the money of fools.

Thomas Hobbes

Words are tools which automatically carve concepts out of experience.

Julian Sorrell Huxley

A thousand words will not leave so deep an impression as one deed.

Henrik Ibsen

"The last word" is the most dangerous of infernal machines; and husband and wife should no more fight to get it than they would struggle for the possession of a lighted bomb-shell.

Douglas William Jerrold

Words are not merely the vehicles in which thought is delivered; they are part of thinking.

Peter Brian Medawar

Such little, puny things are words in rhyme: poor feeble loops and strokes as frail as hairs.

Christopher Darlington Morley

Words are magic things often enough, but even the magic of words sometimes cannot convey the magic of the human spirit and of a nation's passion.

Jawaharlal Nehru

Words are tricky things always. In the final analysis the word is the biggest thing in the world. All the knowledge we have, everything we possess, is a collection of words which represents ideas, of course.

Jawaharlal Nehru

Words are like leaves; and where they most abound,
Much fruit of sense beneath is rarely found

Alexander Pope

Sticks and stones may break my bones,
But words can never harm me.

Old English Rhyme

Try not to let phrases discourage words.

Jean Rostand

Such as your words are, such will your affections be esteemed; and such will your deeds be as your affections; and such your life as your deeds.

Socrates

A good word is an easy obligation; but not to speak ill requires only our silence, which costs us nothing.

John Tillotson

One great use of words is to hide our thoughts.

Voltaire (François Marie Arouet)

The notion that thought can be perfectly or even adequately expressed in verbal symbols is idiotic.

Alfred North Whitehead

For of all sad words of tongue or pen,
The saddest are these: "It might have been!"

John Greenleaf Whittier

The knowledge of words is the gate of scholarship.

John Wilson

See also: LANGUAGE, LOQUACITY, NAME, NICK-NAME, RHETORIC, SLANG, SLOGAN, SPEECH, WRITING.

WORK

Nothing is really work unless you would rather be doing something else.

Sir James Matthew Barrie

Find your place and hold it: find your work and do it. And put everything you've got into it.

Edward William Bok

If you do your work with complete faithfulness, . . . you are making as genuine a contribution to the substance of the universal good as is the most brilliant worker whom the world contains.

Phillips Brooks

We have too many people who live without working, and we have altogether too many who work without living.

Charles Reynolds Brown

Few persons realize how much of their happiness is dependent upon their work, upon the fact that they are kept busy and not left to feed upon themselves. Happiness comes most to persons who seek her least, and think least about it. It is not an object to be sought; it is a state to be induced. It must follow and not lead. It must overtake you, and not you overtake it. How important is health to happiness, yet the best promoter of health is *something to do*.

Blessed is the man who has some congenial work, some occupation in which he can put his heart, and which affords a complete outlet to all the forces there are in him.

John Burroughs

Every man's work, whether it be literature or music or pictures or architecture or anything else, is always a portrait of himself, and the more he tries to conceal himself the more clearly will his character appear in spite of him.

Samuel Butler

Blessed is the man that has found his work. One monster there is in the world, the idle man.

Thomas Carlyle

Concentration is my motto—first honesty, then industry, then concentration.

Andrew Carnegie

For life to be large and full, it must contain the care of the past and of the future in every passing moment of the present. Our daily work must be done to the glory of the dead, and for the good of those who come after.

Joseph Conrad

A man is a worker. If he is not that he is nothing.

Joseph Conrad

All growth depends upon activity. There is no development physically or intellectually without effort, and effort means work. Work is not a curse; it is the prerogative of intelligence, the only means to manhood, and the measure of civilization.

(John) Calvin Coolidge

There are at all times in America about a million men who are without work because they are not able to work, unwilling to take the work offered them or don't want to work. They go to an office or factory seeking work, but secretly hoping and praying that they will not be able to get it.

James John Davis

Work is work if you're paid to do it, and it's pleasure if you pay to be allowed to do it.

Finley Peter Dunne

As a cure for worrying, work is better than whiskey.

Thomas Alva Edison

I never did anything worth doing by accident, nor did any of my inventions come by accident.

Thomas Alva Edison

Work is the meat of life, pleasure the dessert.

Bertie Charles Forbes

He who would really benefit mankind must reach them through their work.

Henry Ford

The difference between a voluntary worker and a hireling lies in the fact that whereas a hireling gives his service to whosoever pays his price, a national voluntary worker gives his service only to the nation for the cause he believes in and he serves it even though he might have to starve.

Mohandas Karamchand (Mahatma) Gandhi

The society which scorns excellence in plumbing because plumbing is a humble activity, and tolerates shoddiness in philosophy because philosophy is an exalted activity, will have neither good plumbing nor good philosophy. Neither its pipes nor its theories will hold water.

John W. Gardner

Work is love made visible. And if you cannot work with love but only with distaste, it is better that you should leave your work and sit at the gate of the temple and take alms of those who work with joy.

Kahlil Gibran

Man must work. That is certain as the sun. But he may work grudgingly or he may work gratefully; he may work as a man, or he may work as a machine. There is no work so rude, that he may exalt it; no work so impassive, that he may not breathe a soul into it; no work so dull that he may not enliven it.

Henry Giles

Folks who never do any more than they get paid for, never get paid for any more than they do.

Elbert Green Hubbard

I believe in work, hard work and long hours of work. Men do not break down from overwork, but from worry and dissipation.

Charles Evans Hughes

I like work; it fascinates me. I can sit and look at it for hours.

Jerome Klapka Jerome

Work and status must be guaranteed to every child on earth because that lack of status and of security and the presence of joblessness and hunger can become the percussion cap on the atomic bombs of earth's destruction.

Joshua Loth Liebman

Men seldom die of hard work; activity is God's medicine. The highest genius is willingness and ability to do hard work. Any other conception of genius makes it a doubtful, if not a dangerous possession.

Robert Stuart MacArthur

A nation's welfare depends on its ability to master the world; that on its power of work; and that on its power of thought.

Theodore Parker

Work expands so as to fill the time available for its completion. . . . The thing to be done swells in importance and complexity in a direct ratio with the time to be spent.

Cyril Northcote Parkinson

The force, the mass of character, mind, heart or soul that a man can put into any work, is the most important factor in that work.

Andrew Preston Peabody

It violates right order whenever capital so employs the working or wage-earning classes as to divert business and economic activity entirely to its own arbitrary will and advantage without any regard to the human dignity of the workers, the social character of economic life, social justice, and the common good.

Pius XI (Achille Ambrogio Damiano Ratti)

Labor is not merely the fatigue of body without sense or value; nor is it merely a humiliating servitude. It is a service of God, a gift of God, the vigor and fullness of human life, the gage of eternal rest.

Pius XII (Eugenio Pacelli)

I only know one truth: work alone makes you happy. And this sole truth of which I am certain, I am always forgetting.

Jules Renard

Of this alone I become more and more aware: everything depends on work. We owe it everything; it regulates our lives.

Jules Renard

Happiness lies not in the mere possession of money; it lies in the joy of achievement, in the thrill of creative effort. The joy and moral stimulation of work no longer must be forgotten in the mad chase of evanescent profits.

Franklin Delano Roosevelt

I believe in the inherent right of every citizen to employment at a living wage and I pledge my support to whatever measures I may deem necessary for inaugurating self-liquidating public works . . . to provide employment for all surplus labor at all times.

Franklin Delano Roosevelt

I don't pity any man who does hard work worth doing. I admire him. I pity the creature who doesn't work, at whichever end of the social scale he may regard himself as being.

Theodore Roosevelt

A man can be freed from the necessity of work only by the fact that he or his fathers before him have worked to a good purpose.

Theodore Roosevelt

Work is of two kinds: first, altering the position of matter at or near the earth's surface relatively to other such matter; second, telling other people to do so. The first kind is unpleasant and ill paid; the second is pleasant and highly paid.

Bertrand Arthur William Russell

Certain moralists, without meaning to be satirical, often say that the sovereign cure for unhappiness is work. Unhappily, the work they recommend is better fitted to dull pain than to remove its cause.

George Santayana

The man who does not work for the love of work but only for money is not likely to make money nor to find much fun in life.

Charles M. Schwab

A day's work is a day's work, neither more nor less, and the man who does it needs a day's sustenance, a night's repose, and due leisure, whether he be painter or ploughman.

George Bernard Shaw

A man should inure himself to voluntary labor, and not give up to indulgence and pleasure, as they beget no good constitution of body nor knowledge of mind.

Socrates

There will be little drudgery in this better ordered world. Natural power harnessed in machines will be the general drudge. What drudgery is inevitable will be done as a service and duty for a few years or months out of each life; it will not consume nor degrade the whole life of anyone.

Herbert George Wells

Job discrimination because of age still threatens any worker who must change employment status, even people in their thirties and forties. This problem persists largely because misinformation nourishes old-fashioned attitudes about the capabilities of so-called older workers.

Harrison Arlington Williams, Jr.

Work is something you want to get done; play is something you just like to be doing.

Harry Leon Wilson

See also: BUSINESS, CAPITALISM, CAPITAL AND LABOR, DILIGENCE, EFFORT, EMPLOYMENT, EXERTION, INDUSTRY, LABOR, OCCUPATION, PERSEVERANCE.

WORLD

The world is God's workshop for making men.

Henry Ward Beecher

The world will, in the end, follow only those who have despised as well as served it.

Samuel Butler

Contact with the world either breaks or hardens the heart.

Sébastien Roch Nicolas Chamfort

There are many that despise half the world; but if there be any that despise the whole of it, it is because the other half despises them.

Charles Caleb Colton

What is meant by a "knowledge of the world" is simply an acquaintance with the infirmities of men.

Charles John Huffam Dickens

"The world," is a conventional phrase, which being interpreted, signifies all the rascality in it.

Charles John Huffam Dickens

All the world's ends, arrangements, changes, disappointments, hopes, and fears, are without meaning, if not seen and estimated by eternity!

Tryon Edwards

This is the way the world ends
Not with a bang but with a whimper.

Thomas Stearns Eliot

I would rather live in a world where my life is surrounded by mystery than live in a world so small that my mind could comprehend it.

Harry Emerson Fosdick

We all, whether we know it or not, are fighting to make the kind of a world that we should like.

Oliver Wendell Holmes, Jr.

The world gets better every day—then worse again in the evening.

Frank McKinney (Kin) Hubbard

The world is neither wise nor just, but it makes up for all its folly and injustice by being damnably sentimental.

Thomas Henry Huxley

The world is to each man according to each man.

Robert Green Ingersoll

He who imagines he can do without the world deceives himself much; but he who fancies the world cannot do without him is still more mistaken.

Duc François de La Rochefoucauld

The only fence against the world is a thorough knowledge of it.

John Locke

That one vast thought of God which we call the world.

Edward G. Bulwer-Lytton (Baron Lytton)

Worldism, as a cultural stage, will be reached when the dominant activities of mankind take place on a world scale.

Scott Nearing

The universe, broad and deep and high, is a handful of dust which God enchants. His is the mysterious magic which possesses—not protoplasm, merely but—the world.

Theodore Parker

The world is God's epistle to mankind—his thoughts are flashing upon us from every direction.

Plato

The world was not created once and for all for each of us. In the course of life things that we never imagined are added to it.

Marcel Proust

The world is a kind of spiritual kindergarten where bewildered infants are trying to spell God with the wrong blocks.

Edward Arlington Robinson

There can be no secure peace now but a common peace of the whole world; no prosperity but a general prosperity.

James Harvey Robinson

A man's feet should be planted in his country, but his eyes should survey the world.

George Santayana

This world is a dream within a dream; and as we grow older, each step is an awakening. The youth awakes, as he thinks, from childhood; the fullgrown man despises the pursuits of youth as visionary; and the old man looks on manhood as a feverish dream. Death the last sleep? No! it is the last and final awakening!

Sir Walter Scott

A good man and a wise man may at times be angry with the world, at times grieved for it; but be sure no man was ever discontented with the world who did his duty in it.

Robert Southey

The only true method of action in this world is to be in it, but not of it.

Anne Sophie Swetchine

We may be pretty certain that persons whom all the world treats ill deserve the treatment they get. The world is a looking-glass, and gives back to every man the reflection of his own face. Frown at it, and it will in turn look sourly upon you; laugh at it and with it, and it is a jolly, kind companion; and so let all young persons take their choice.

William Makepeace Thackeray

The world is a comedy to those who think, a tragedy to those who feel.

Horace Walpole

We may despise the world, but we cannot do without it.

Ignaz Heinrich Karl Wessenburg

See also: EARTH, HUMANITY, LIFE, MAN, NATURE, SOCIETY, UNIVERSE.

WORLDLINESS

It is not this earth, nor the men who inhabit it, nor the sphere of our legitimate activity, that we may not love; but the way in which the love is given, which constitutes worldliness.

Frederick William Robertson

A seeming ignorance is often a most necessary part of worldly knowledge.

Philip Dormer Stanhope (Lord Chesterfield)

See also: FASHION, MATERIALISM, SENSUALITY, WORLD.

WORRY

Don't tell me that worry doesn't do any good. I know better. The things I worry about don't happen.

Anonymous

There are two days about which nobody should ever worry, and these are yesterday and tomorrow.

Robert Jones Burdette

Anxiety destroys our figure.

Benjamin Disraeli

Care is a god, invisible but omnipotent. It steals the bloom from the cheek and lightness from the pulse; it takes away the appetite, and turns the hair grey.

Benjamin Disraeli

It's a funny thing that when a man hasn't got anything on earth to worry about, he goes off and gets married.

Robert Lee Frost

The reason why worry kills more people than work is that more people worry than work.

Robert Lee Frost

There is nothing that wastes the body like worry, and one who has any faith in God should be ashamed to worry about anything whatsoever. It is a difficult rule no doubt for the simple reason that faith in God with the majority of mankind is either an intellectual belief or a blind belief, a kind of superstitious fear of something indefinable. But to ensure absolute freedom from worry requires a living utter faith which is a plant of slow, almost unperceived, growth and requires to be constantly watered by tears that accompany genuine prayer. They are the tears of a lover who cannot brook a moment's separation from the loved one, or of the penitent who knows that it is some trace of impurity in him that keeps him away from the loved one.

Mohandas Karamchand (Mahatma) Gandhi

Why worry one's head over a thing that is inevitable? Why die before one's death?

Mohandas Karamchand (Mahatma) Gandhi

I have never yet met a healthy person who worried very much about his health, or a really good person who worried much about his own soul.

John Burdon Sanderson Haldane

Worry is interest paid on trouble before it becomes due.

William Ralph Inge

I have lost everything, and I am so poor now that I really cannot afford to let anything worry me.

Joseph Jefferson

It is better to try to bear the ills we have, than anticipate those which may befall us.

Duc François de La Rochefoucauld

Worry affects the circulation—the heart, the glands, the whole nervous system. I have never known a man who died from over-work, but many who died from doubt.

Charles Horace Mayo

It ain't no use putting up your umbrella till it rains.

Alice Caldwell Rice

Worry is a thin stream of fear trickling through the mind. If encouraged, it cuts a channel into which all other thoughts are drained.

Arthur Somers Roche

See also: ANXIETY, CARE, FEAR, TROUBLE.

WORSHIP

Come now, little man! flee for a while from your tasks, hide yourself for a little space from the turmoil of your thoughts. For a little while give your time to God, and rest in him for a little.

Anselm

Man is a religious being; the heart instinctively seeks for a God. Whether he worships on the banks of the Ganges, prays with his face upturned to the sun, kneels toward Mecca or, regarding all space as a temple, communes with the Heavenly Father according to the Christian creed, man is essentially devout.

William Jennings Bryan

What greater calamity can fall upon a nation than the loss of worship.

Thomas Carlyle

Worship is transcendent wonder.

Thomas Carlyle

Ritual will always mean throwing away something; *destroying* our corn or wine upon the altar of our gods.

Gilbert Keith Chesterton

We should worship as though the Deity were present. If my mind is not engaged in my worship, it is as though I worshipped not.

Confucius

It is only when men begin to worship that they begin to grow.

(John) Calvin Coolidge

As the skull of a man grows broader,
  So do his creeds.
And his gods they are shaped in his image
  And mirror his needs.
And he clothes them with thunders and beauty,
  He clothes them with music and fire,
Seeing not, as he bows by their altars,
  That he worships his own desire.

Donald Robert Perry (Don) Marquis

A church-going people are apt to be a law-abiding people.

Edwards Amasa Park

It is an axiom of the Christian faith that the mode of worship must correspond to the essence of God, which is spiritual; and the feeling of the worshipper must correspond to the character of God, which is paternal.

Joseph Parrish Thompson

See also: ADMIRATION, ADORATION, CHRISTI-ANITY, CHURCH, CLERGY, ESTEEM, HOLINESS, MINISTER, PIETY, PRAISE, PRAYER, RELIGION, REVERENCE, SECT.

WORTH

I am not sure that God always knows who are His great men; He is so very careless of what happens to them while they live.

Mary Hunter Austin

For anything worth having one must pay the price; and the price is always work, patience, love, self-sacrifice.

John Burroughs

Worth begets in base minds, envy; in great souls, emulation.

Henry Fielding

Where quality is the thing sought after, the thing of supreme quality is cheap, whatever the price one has to pay for it.

William James

One of the most important truths in the world is that there is worth enough in any rascal to cost the spilling of the Precious Blood.

Austin O'Malley

See also: EXCELLENCE, EXPENSE, GOODNESS, MERIT, PERFECTION, VIRTUE.

WRITING

After being turned down by numerous publishers, he decided to write for posterity.

George Ade

The mighty have no theory of technique,
But leave it to
Second-story men of letters and small critics.

Leonard Bacon

Art [literature] is not a branch of pedagogy.

James Branch Cabell

Persons who set themselves up as writers and word dealers have a special responsibility in the power age. If they cannot be trusted to talk honestly, who can be trusted? If they can be sold out to the highest bidder like hogs on the hoof, where is an interdependent culture going to land?

Stuart Chase

Writing a book is an adventure; to begin with it is a toy and an amusement, then it becomes a master, and then it becomes a tyrant; and the last phase is just as you are about to be reconciled to your servitude—you kill the monster and fling it . . . to the public.

Sir Winston Leonard Spencer Churchill

The artist [in literature] appeals to that part of our being which is not dependent on wisdom; to that in us which is a gift and not an acquisition—and, therefore, more permanently enduring. He speaks to our capacity for delight and wonder, to the sense of mystery surrounding our lives; to our sense of pity, and beauty, and pain.

Joseph Conrad

My task which I am trying to achieve is, by the power of the written word, to make you hear, to make you feel—it is, before all, to make you *see*. That, and no more, and it is everything.

Joseph Conrad

A man who teaches about writing should certainly, I think, write two or three books in his life to show that he has at least tried to practice the craft he discourses upon.

Bonamy Dobrée

It has taken me years of struggle, hard work and research to learn to make one simple gesture, and I know enough about the art of writing to realize that it would take as many years of concentrated effort to write one simple, beautiful sentence.

Isadora Duncan

Clarity is the supreme politeness of him who wields a pen.

Jean Henri Fabre

All good writing is *swimming under water* and holding your breath.

Francis Scott Key Fitzgerald

You don't write because you want to say something; you write because you've got something to say.

Francis Scott Key Fitzgerald

You become a good writer just as you become a good joiner: by planing down your sentences.

Anatole France

A writer's problem does not change. He himself changes and the world he lives in changes but his problem remains the same. It is always how to write truly and, having found what is true, to project it in such a way that it becomes a part of the experience of the person who reads it.

Ernest Hemingway

Any man who will look into his heart and honestly write what he sees there, will find plenty of readers.

Edgar Watson Howe

Writers seldom write the things they think. They simply write the things they think others folks think they think.

Elbert Green Hubbard

Everything which I have created as a poet has had its origin in a frame of mind and a situation in life; I never wrote because I had, as they say, found a good subject.

Henrik Ibsen

For myself I live, live intensely and am fed by life, and my value, whatever it be, is in my own kind of expression of that.

Henry James

The historian, essentially, wants more documents than he can really use; the dramatist only wants more liberties than he can really take.

Henry James

Welcome, O life! I go to encounter for the millionth time the reality of experience and to forge in the smithy of my soul the uncreated conscience of my race.

James Joyce

A good many young writers make the mistake of enclosing a stamped, self-addressed envelope, big enough for the manuscript to come back in. This is too much of a temptation to the editor.

Ringgold Wilmer (Ring) Lardner

A poem or story, though published in the biggest United States magazine of the newsstand type is not published at all; the fight has to begin all over again if it is to win any place as a "classic," even for a year!

(Nicolas) Vachel Lindsay

Writing is like religion. Every man who feels the call must work out his own salvation.

George Horace Lorimer

To produce a mighty book, you must choose a mighty theme. No great and enduring volume can ever be written on the flea, though many there be that have tried it.

Herman Melville

The impulse to create beauty is rather rare in literary men . . . Far ahead of it comes the yearning to make money. And after the yearning to make money comes the yearning to make a noise.

Henry Louis Mencken

Every prima-donna has to write her memoirs. It's part of the tradition. It is also a very human wish-fulfillment.

Grace Moore

Of all that is written, I love only what a person hath written with his blood.

Friedrich Wilhelm Nietzsche

There seems to be no physical handicap or chance of environment that can hold a real writer down, and there is no luck, no influence, no money that will keep a writer going when she is written out.

Kathleen Norris

The psychologist knows that what makes for supreme greatness in writing fiction is not intelligence nearly so much as half a dozen other traits.

Walter Boughton Pitkin

The obscurity of a writer is generally in proportion to his incapacity.

Quintilian

In Hollywood the woods are full of people that learned to write, but evidently can't read. If they could read their stuff, they'd stop writing.

Will (William Penn Adair) Rogers

A great writer is a man who knows how to surprise by telling us what we have always known.

Jean Rostand

There is time for writing, and time for becoming the man who will write.

Jean Rostand

Whatever may be our natural talents, the art of writing is not acquired all at once.

Jean Jacques Rousseau

The worst thing that ever happened to writing is that it became a business.

Dagobert David Runes

I write fast because I have not the brains to write slow.

Georges Simenon

The writer does the most who gives his reader the most knowledge, and takes from him the least time.

Sydney Smith

Writing isn't hard; no harder than ditch-digging.

Edward Everett Tanner (Patrick Dennis)

A writer is dear and necessary for us only in the measure in which he reveals to us the inner working of his soul.

Count Lev (Leo) Nikolaevich Tolstoi

I have come to the conclusion that there is no such thing as normality. That is what makes story-telling such an absorbing task, the attempt to reduce to order the anarchic raw materials of life.

Evelyn Arthur St. John Waugh

The writer must be willing, above everything else, to take chances, to risk making a fool of himself—or even to risk revealing the fact that he *is* a fool.

Jessamyn West

See also: ALLEGORY, AUTHORSHIP, BALLAD, BIOGRAPHY, BOOK, FABLE, FICTION, HISTORY, JOURNALISM, LETTER, LIBRARY, LITERATURE, NOVEL, PEN, POETRY, PRESS, RHETORIC, ROMANCE, STYLE, TRAGEDY, WORD.

WRONG

The essence of immorality is the tendency to make an exception of one's self.

Jane Addams

It is better to suffer wrong than to do it, and happier to be sometimes cheated than not to trust.

Samuel Johnson

Wrong is but falsehood put in practice.

Walter Savage Landor

There are few people who are more often in the wrong than those who cannot endure to be so.

Duc François de La Rochefoucauld

There is a moral element in us that makes us like to know that we are doing wrong when we are doing it.

Robert Staughton Lynd

It is vain to trust in wrong; as much of evil, so much of loss, is the formula of human history.

Theodore Parker

A man should never be ashamed to own he has been in the wrong, which is but saying in other words that he is wiser to-day than he was yesterday.

Alexander Pope

The remedy for wrongs is to forget them.

Publilius Syrus

See also: BASENESS, CORRUPTION, CRIME, CRUELTY, DEPRAVITY, DISHONESTY, ERROR, EVIL, FRAUD, ILLS, INJUSTICE, MEANNESS, MISCHIEF, MISTAKE, SIN, VICE, VILLAINY, WICKEDNESS.

Y

YESTERDAY

There are two days in the week about which and upon which I never worry. Two carefree days, kept sacredly free from fear and apprehension. One of these days is Yesterday.... And the other ... is Tomorrow.

Robert Jones Burdette

But where are the snows of yesteryear?

François Villon

Whose yesterdays look backward with a smile.

Edward Young

See also: ANTIQUITY, FUTURE, PAST, PRESENT.

YIDDISH

Our hope for the future would be much stronger, if we did not rob our sons and daughters of our tongue. . . . One word, one expression, taken from the speech of the people, is more effective than ten abstract ideas.

Achad Haam (Asher Ginzberg)

With this cosmopolitan jargon, made of the rages of every language, he Morris Rosenfeld created a music like that of a lamenting harp.

Léon Bloy

Yiddish, the language which will ever bear witness to the violence and murder inflicted on us, bear the marks of our expulsions from land to land, the language which absorbed the wails of the fathers, the laments of the generations, the poison and bitterness of history, the language whose precious jewels are the undried, uncongealed Jewish tears.

Isaac Loeb Peretz

See also: ISRAEL, JEW, JUDAISM.

YOM KIPPUR

Except for Yom Kippur, the Sabbath of Sabbaths, Jews were required to eat on the Sabbath even when a fast day fell on it. Its music had a special sweetness; its prayers had a flavor of their own.

Philip Sidney Bernstein

The Jewish new year begins in the early fall. Its observances are far removed in spirit from the celebrations surrounding January 1, for it ushers in a ten-day period of penitence culminating in the fast of Yom Kippur.

Philip Sidney Bernstein

The religious content of the day became so profound, and the synagogue ritual became so rich, that Yom Kippur has remained till this very day the greatest day in the Jewish year.

Hayyim Schauss

Yom Kippur did not assume its importance as the greatest fast day of the year and the great day for all Jews all at once; it went through a long period of evolution. Nor is its ritual uniform; it is made up of various customs and ceremonies, some very ancient and some that were added in later years.

Hayyim Schauss

Yom Kippur never actually became entirely a day of sorrow, a day which casts shadow on all. Despite the fast, the confession, and the wailing, it remains a festival with an undercurrent of joy. One must not eat, but still, one wears festive clothes.

Hayyim Schauss

See also: HANUKKAH, JUDAISM, PASSOVER.

YOUTH

All lovely things will have an ending,
All lovely things will fade and die,
And youth, that's now so bravely spending,
Will beg a penny by and by.

Conrad Potter Aiken

Young men are fitter to invent than to judge, fitter for execution than for counsel, and fitter for new projects than for settled business.

Francis Bacon

Frustrations and denials which seem to youth cruel and unfair often are important equipment for life.

Bruce Barton

Youth is the first victim of war; the first fruit of peace. It takes 20 years or more of peace to make a man; it takes only 20 seconds of war to destroy him.

Baudouin I

It is the glory of the present age that in it one can be young.

Randolph Silliman Bourne

The red sweet wine of youth.

Rupert Brooke

The world's tragedy is that it must be grown up; in other words, that it must be run by men who, though they know much, have forgotten what they were in their youth.

John Mason Brown

Tell me what are the prevailing sentiments that occupy the minds of your young men, and I will tell you what is to be the character of the next generation.

Edmund Burke

Youth is to all the glad season of life, but often only by what it hopes, not by what it attains or escapes.

Thomas Carlyle

The egotism and turbulence of youth—is it not too often merely the need of a worthy cause to absorb the first violence of a responsible will?

Joyce Cary

It is a truth but too well known, that rashness attends youth, as prudence does old age.

Cicero

I remember my youth and the feeling that will never come back any more—the feeling that I could last forever, outlast the sea, the earth, and all men.

Joseph Conrad

Almost everything that is great has been done by youth.

Benjamin Disraeli

The two greatest stimulants in the world are youth and debt.

Benjamin Disraeli

The Youth of a Nation are the trustees of Posterity.

Benjamin Disraeli

Innocent youth is a priceless possession not to be squandered away for the sake of a momentary excitement, miscalled pleasure.

Mohandas Karamchand (Mahatma) Gandhi

The destiny of any nation, at any given time, depends on the opinions of its young men under five-twenty.

Johann Wolfgang von Goethe

Girls we love for what they are; young men for what they promise to be.

Johann Wolfgang von Goethe

Nobody can be so amusingly arrogant as a young man who has just discovered an old idea and thinks it is his own.

Sydney Justin Harris

Over the trackless past, somewhere, lie the lost days of our tropic youth.

(Francis) Bret Harte

I love the acquaintance of young people; because, in the first place, I do not like to think myself growing old. In the next place, young acquaintances must last longest, if they do last; and then young men have more virtue than old men; they have more generous sentiments in every respect.

Samuel Johnson

I, for one, hope that youth will again revolt and again demoralize the dead weight of conformity that now lies upon us.

Howard Mumford Jones

It is not possible for civilization to flow backwards while there is youth in the world.

Helen Adams Keller

Youth has steadily gained on the enemy . . . through it alone shall salvation come.

Helen Adams Keller

Youth had been a habit of hers so long that she could not part with it.

Rudyard Kipling

Youth is a continual intoxication; it is the fever of reason.

Duc François de La Rochefoucauld

When we are out of sympathy with the young, then I think our work in this world is over.

George Macdonald

Two things youth desires beyond all others, freedom from ridicule, and intensity of sensation.

Louis Wardlaw Miles

Reckless youth makes rueful age.

Thomas Moore

Youth is the opportunity to do something and to become somebody.

Theodore Thornton Munger

There is as close a connection between youth and faith as between age and compromise.

Austin O'Malley

The heart of youth is reached through the senses; the senses of age are reached through the heart.

Nicholas Edme Restif de la Bretonne

The youth of the soul is everlasting, and eternity is youth.

Jean Paul Richter

Consider what heavy responsibility lies upon you in your youth, to determine, among realities, by what you will be delighted, and, among imaginations, by whose you will be led.

John Ruskin

Keep true to the dreams of thy youth.

Johann Christoph Friedrich von Schiller

Nothing is more disturbing than the defection of so many of the young from the purposes and institutions of a society which they claim to find stifling and absurd and which unquestionably gives them a profound feeling of impotence and meaninglessness. While much of the rhetoric of contemporary youth seems to me overwrought and even hysterical, those over 30 would be foolish not to see in it symptoms of deep and alarming disquietude.

Arthur Meier Schlesinger

Youth, when thought is speech and speech is truth.

Sir Walter Scott

Youth is a wonderful thing; what a crime to waste it on children.

George Bernard Shaw

In youth we run into difficulties, in old age difficulties run into us.

Henry Wheeler Shaw (Josh Billings)

Youth ever thinks that good whose goodness or evil he sees not.

Sir Philip Sidney

Don't laugh at youth for his affectations; he is only trying on one face after another to find his own.

Logan Pearsall Smith

What is more enchanting than the voices of young people, when you can't hear what they say?

Logan Pearsall Smith

Young men are as apt to think themselves wise enough, as drunken men are to think themselves sober enough. They look upon spirit to be a much better thing than experience, which they call coldness. They are but half mistaken; for though spirit without experience is dangerous, experience without spirit is languid and ineffective.

Philip Dormer Stanhope (Lord Chesterfield)

For God's sake give me the young man who has brains enough to make a fool of himself.

Robert Louis Balfour Stevenson

Youth today must be strong, unafraid, and a better taxpayer than its father.

Harry Vincent Wade

What could be more charming than a boy before he has begun to cultivate his intellect? He is beautiful to look at; he gives himself no airs; he understands the meaning of art and literature instinctively; he goes about enjoying his life and making other people enjoy theirs.

Virginia Woolf

See also: AGE, AGE AND YOUTH, AGES OF MAN, AMBITION, ASPIRATION, CHILDREN, ENERGY, HOPE, IDEAL, INFANCY, INNOCENCE, LOVE, MAIDENHOOD, ROMANCE.

Z

ZEAL

Whether zeal or moderation be the point we aim at, let us keep fire out of the one, and frost out of the other.

Joseph Addison

Nothing hath wrought more prejudice to religion, or brought more disparagement upon truth, than boisterous and unseasonable zeal.

Washington Barrow

When we see an eager assailant of wrongs, a special reformer, we feel like asking him, What right have you, sir, to your one virtue? Is virtue piecemeal?

Ralph Waldo Emerson

Zealots have an idol, to which they consecrate themselves high-priests, and deem it holy work to offer sacrifices of whatever is most precious.

Nathaniel Hawthorne

People give the name of zeal to their propensity to mischief and violence, though it is not the cause, but their interest that inflames them.

Michel Eyquem de Montaigne

Zeal without knowledge is like expedition to a man in the dark.

John Newton

To be furious in religion is to be irreligiously religious.

William Penn

For virtue's self may too much zeal be had;
The worst of madness is a saint run mad.

Alexander Pope

Zeal for the public good is the characteristic of a man of honor and a gentleman, and must take place of pleasures, profits, and all other private gratifications. Whoever wants this motive, is an open enemy, or an inglorious neuter to mankind, in proportion to the misapplied advantages with which nature and fortune have blessed him.

Sir Richard Steele

Violent zeal even for truth has a hundred to one odds to be either petulancy, ambition, or pride.

Jonathan Swift

All true zeal for God is a zeal also for love, mercy, and goodness.

Robert Ellis Thompson

See also: AMBITION, BIGOTRY, EARNESTNESS, ENTHUSIASM, FANATICISM, INTOLERANCE, PREJUDICE.

Thoughts
from the
Bible

All scripture is given by inspiration of God, and is profitable

for doctrine, for reproof, for correction, for instruction

in righteousness: That the man of God may be

perfect, throughly furnished unto all

good works.

2 Timothy 3:16-17

A

ABILITY

If so be the Lord will be with me, then I shall be able to drive them out.

Joshua 14:12

If ye have faith as a grain of mustard seed . . . nothing shall be impossible unto you.

Matthew 17:20

All things are possible to him that believeth.

Mark 9:23

God is faithful, who will not suffer you to be tempted above that ye are able; but will with the temptation also make a way to escape, that ye may be able to bear it.

1 Corinthians 10:13

I can do all things through Christ which strengtheneth me.

Philippians 4:13

See also: POWER, STRENGTH.

ABSENCE

The Lord watch between me and thee, when we are absent one from another.

Genesis 31:49

Absent in body, but present in spirit.

1 Corinthians 5:3

As ye have always obeyed, not as in my presence only, but now much more in my absence, work out your own salvation with fear and trembling.

Philippians 2:12

See also: OMNIPRESENCE.

ABSTINENCE

Wine is a mocker, strong drink is raging: and whosoever is deceived thereby is not wise.

Proverbs 20:1

Look not thou upon the wine when it is red, when it giveth his colour in the cup, when it moveth itself aright. At the last it biteth like a serpent, and stingeth like an adder.

Proverbs 23:31, 32

Moreover when ye fast, be not, as the hypocrites, of a sad countenance: for they disfigure their faces, that they may appear unto men to fast.

Matthew 6:16

Be not drunk with wine, wherein is excess.

Ephesians 5:18

Touch not; taste not; handle not.

Colossians 2:21

See also: RENUNCIATION, TEMPERANCE.

ACCOMPLISHMENT

The desire accomplished is sweet to the soul.

Proverbs 13:19

The Lord will do great things.

Joel 2:21

My meat is to do the will of him that sent me, and to finish his work.

John 4:34

I have not run in vain, neither laboured in vain.

Philippians 2:16

See also: ACTION, WORKS.

ACCUSATION

Thou shalt not raise a false report: put not thine hand with the wicked to be an unrighteous witness.

Exodus 23:1

Blessed are ye, when men shall revile you, and persecute you, and shall say all manner of evil against you falsely, for my sake.

Matthew 5:11

See also: JUDGMENT.

ADULTERY

Thou shalt not commit adultery.

Exodus 20:14

Can a man take fire in his bosom, and his clothes not be burned? Can one go upon hot coals, and his feet not be burned? So he that goeth in to his neighbour's wife: whosoever toucheth her shall not be innocent.

Proverbs 6:27–29

Whoso committeth adultery with a woman lacketh understanding: he that doeth it destroyeth his own soul.

Proverbs 6:32

Whosoever looketh on a woman to lust after her hath committed adultery with her already in his heart.

Matthew 5:28

The works of the flesh are manifest, which are these; Adultery, fornication, uncleanness, lasciviousness.

Galatians 5:19

See also: ABSTINENCE, COVETOUSNESS, SIN.

ADVERSITY

A friend loveth at all times, and a brother is born for adversity.

Proverbs 17:17

If thou faint in the day of adversity thy strength is small.

Proverbs 24:10

And though the Lord give you the bread of adversity, and the water of affliction, yet shall not thy teachers be removed into a corner any more, but thine eyes shall see thy teachers.

Isaiah 30:20

See also: AFFLICTION, TROUBLE.

AFFLICTION

Thou shalt eat no leavened bread with it; seven days shalt thou eat unleavened bread therewith, even the bread of affliction; for thou camest forth out of the land of Egypt in haste: that thou mayest remember the day when thou camest forth out of the land of Egypt all the days of thy life.

Deuteronomy 16:3

Although affliction cometh not forth of the dust, neither doth trouble spring out of the ground; yet man is born unto trouble, as the sparks fly upward.

Job 5:6,7

Many are the afflictions of the righteous: but the Lord delivereth him out of them all.

Psalms 34:19

Before I was afflicted I went astray; but now I have kept thy word.

Psalms 119:67

He was afflicted, yet he opened not his mouth: he is brought as a lamb to the slaughter, and as a sheep before her shearers is dumb, so he openeth not his mouth.

Isaiah 53:7

See also: SORROW, SUFFERING, TROUBLE.

AGE

Thou shalt rise up before the hoary head, and honour the face of the old man.

Leviticus 19:32

With the ancient is wisdom; and in length of days understanding.

Job 12:2

The fear of the Lord prolongeth days.

Proverbs 10:27

The hoary head is a crown of glory, if it be found in the way of righteousness.

Proverbs 16:31

Rebuke not an elder, but intreat him as a father.

1 Timothy 5:1

Aged men be sober, grave, temperate, sound in faith, in charity, in patience.

Titus 2:2

See also: YOUTH.

ALMS

If thou hast abundance, give alms accordingly; If thou have but little, be not afraid to give according to that little.

Tobit 4:8

Water will quench a flaming fire; and alms maketh an atonement for sins.

Ecclesiasticus 3:30

Take heed that ye do not your alms before men, to be seen of them. . . . But when thou doest alms, let not thy left hand know what thy right hand doeth.

Matthew 6:1–3

Sell that ye have, and give alms.

Luke 12:33

See also: GIFT; GIVING; WORKS, GOOD.

AMBITION

The Lord preserveth the faithful, and plentifully rewardeth the proud doer.

Psalms 31:23

He that is greedy of gain troubleth his own house.

Proverbs 15:27

All things are full of labour; man cannot utter it: the eye is not satisfied with seeing, nor the ear filled with hearing.

Ecclesiastes 1:8

He that is greatest among you shall be your servant. And whosoever shall exalt himself shall be abased; and he that shall humble himself shall be exalted.

Matthew 23:11, 12

If any man desire to be first, the same shall be last of all, and servant of all.

Mark 9:35

Set your affection on things above, not on things on the earth.

Colossians 3:2

See also: BOASTING, PRIDE.

ANGEL

And he [the angel] said, Let me go, for the day breaketh. And he [Jacob] said, I will not let Thee go, except thou bless me.

Genesis 32:26

Be not forgetful to entertain strangers: for thereby some have entertained angels unawares.

Hebrews 13:2

God spared not the angels that sinned, but cast them down to hell, and delivered them into chains of darkness.

2 Peter 2:4

See also: DEVIL.

ANGER

Wrath killeth the foolish man and envy slayeth the silly one.

Job 5:2

He that is slow to anger is better than the mighty; and he that ruleth his spirit than he that taketh a city.

Proverbs 16:32

Make no friendship with an angry man, and with a furious man thou shalt not go: Lest thou learn his ways, and get a snare to thy soul.

Proverbs 22:24, 25

Be ye angry, and sin not: let not the sun go down upon your wrath.

Ephesians 4:6

Let every man be swift to hear, slow to speak, slow to wrath: For the wrath of man worketh not the righteousness of God.

James 1:19, 20

See also: VENGEANCE, WRATH.

ANTICHRIST

Even now there are many antichrists.

1 John 2:18

He is antichrist, that denieth Father and son.

1 John 2:22

See also: DEVIL, EVIL.

ANXIETY

Yea, though I walk through the valley of the shadow of death, I will fear no evil: for thou art with me; thy rod and thy staff they comfort me.

Psalms 23:4

The Lord shall give thee rest from thy sorrow, and from thy fear.

Isaiah 14:3

Take no thought for your life, what ye shall eat, or what ye shall drink; nor yet for your body, what ye shall put on. Is not the life more than meat, and the body than raiment?

Matthew 6:25

Let not your heart be troubled: ye believe in God, believe also in me.

John 14:1

In nothing be anxious.

Philippians 4:6

God hath not given us the spirit of fear; but of power, and of love, and of a sound mind.

2 Timothy 1:7

See also: CARE, COURAGE.

APPEARANCE

Man looketh on the outward appearance, but the Lord looketh on the heart.

1 Samuel 16:7

Judge not according to the appearance.

John 7:24

See also: DECEIT, HYPOCRISY.

ATONEMENT

On the tenth day of this seventh month there shall be a day of atonement: it shall be an holy convocation unto you; and ye shall afflict your souls, and offer an offering made by fire unto the Lord.

Leviticus 23:27

For if, when we were enemies, we were reconciled to God by the death of his Son, much more, being reconciled, we shall be saved by his life. And not only so, but we also joy in God through our Lord Jesus Christ, by whom we have now received the atonement.

Romans 5:10, 11

The blood of Jesus Christ his Son cleanseth us from all sin.

1 John 1:7

See also: RECONCILIATION, REDEMPTION.

AVARICE: *see* COVETOUSNESS.

B

BAPTISM

Go ye therefore, and teach all nations, baptizing them in the name of the Father, and of the Son and of the Holy Spirit.

Matthew 28:19

Repent, and be baptized everyone of you in the name of Jesus Christ for the remission of sins, and ye shall receive the gift of the Holy Spirit.

Acts 2:38

One Lord, one Faith, one Baptism.

Ephesians 4:5

See also: CONVERSION, REGENERATION.

BEAUTY

He will beautify the meek with salvation.

Psalms 149:4

He hath made every thing beautiful in his time.

Ecclesiastes 3:11

Beauty is a fading flower.

Isaiah 28:1

How beautiful upon the mountains are the feet of him that bringeth good tidings.

Isaiah 52:7

Think of the flowers growing in the fields; They never have to work or spin; yet I assure you that not even Solomon in all his regalia was robed like one of these.

Matthew 6:28, 29

How beautiful are the feet of them that preach the gospel of peace, and bring glad tidings of good things.

Romans 10:15

See also: GOODNESS, NATURE.

BELIEF

Whosoever shall offend one of these little ones that believe in me, it is better for him that a millstone were hanged about his neck and he were cast into the sea.

Mark 9:42

He that believeth not shall be damned

Mark 16:16

Jesus saith unto him, Thomas, because thou hast seen me, thou hast believed: blessed are they that have not seen, and yet have believed.

John 20:29

Charity . . . believeth all things.

1 Corinthians 13:7

I know whom I have believed.

2 Timothy 1:12

See also: FAITH, HOPE, TRUST.

BIBLE

Thy word is a lamp unto my feet, and a light unto my path.

Psalms 119:105

Search the scriptures; for in them ye think ye have eternal life: and they are they which testify of me.

John 5:39

The scripture cannot be broken.

John 10:35

These are written, that ye might believe that Jesus is the Christ, the Son of God; and that believing ye might have life through his name.

John 20:31

Wot ye not what the scripture saith?

Romans 11:2

Whatsoever things were written aforetime were written for our learning, that we through patience and comfort of the scriptures might have hope.

Romans 15:4

All scripture is given by inspiration of God, and is profitable for doctrine, for reproof, for correction, for instruction in righteousness: That the man of God may be perfect, throughly furnished unto all good works.

2 Timothy 3:16, 17

But the word of the Lord endureth for ever.

1 Peter 1:25

No prophecy of the scripture is of any private interpretation. For the prophecy came not in old time by the will of man: but holy men of God spake as they were moved by the Holy Ghost.

2 Peter 1:20, 21

Be mindful of the words which were spoken before by the holy prophets, and of the commandment of us the apostles of the Lord and Saviour.

2 Peter 3:2

See also: LAW.

BIGOTRY

The Egyptians might not eat bread with the Hebrews; for that is an abomination unto the Egyptians.

Genesis 43:32

Seest thou a man wise in his own conceit? there is more hope of a fool than of him.

Proverbs 26:12

How is it that he eateth and drinketh with publicans and sinners?

Mark 2:16

The Jews have no dealings with the Samaritans.

John 4:9

See also: HYPROCRISY, SELF-RIGHTEOUSNESS.

BLESSING

He whom thou blessest is blessed, and he whom thou cursest is cursed. . . . Blessed is he that blesseth thee, and cursed is he that curseth thee.

Numbers 22:6; 24:9

Bless the Lord, O my soul; and all that is within me, bless his holy name.

Psalms 103:1

The blessing of the Lord, it maketh rich, and he addeth no sorrow with it.

Proverbs 10:22

Blessed be the Father of our Lord Jesus Christ, who hath blessed us with all spiritual blessings.

Ephesians 1:3

Out of the same mouth proceedeth blessing and cursing.

James 3:10

Grace be with you, mercy, and peace, from God the Father, and from the Lord Jesus Christ, the Son of the Father, in truth and love.

2 John 1:3

Mercy unto you, and peace, and love, be multiplied.

Jude 1:2

See also: GIFT, GLORY, PRAISE.

BOASTING

Talk no more so exceeding proudly; let not arrogancy come out of your mouth: for the Lord is a God of knowledge, and by him actions are weighed.

1 Samuel 2:3

Let another man praise thee, and not thine own mouth; a stranger, and not thine own lips.

Proverbs 27:2

See also: CONCEIT, PRIDE.

BODY

Take no thought of your life, what ye shall eat, or what ye shall drink; nor yet for your body, what ye shall put on. Is not the life more than meat, and the body than raiment?

Matthew 6:25

Know ye not that your bodies are the members of Christ?

1 Corinthians 6:15

Know ye not that your body is the temple of the Holy Ghost which is in you, which ye have of God, and ye are not your own?

1 Corinthians 6:19

Now ye are the body of Christ.

1 Corinthians 12:27

Christ shall be magnified in my body, whether it be by life, or by death.

Philippians 1:20

The body without the spirit is dead.

James 2:26

See also: SOUL, SPIRIT.

BORROWING

If thou lend money to any of my people that is poor by thee, thou shalt not be to him as an usurer,. neither shalt thou lay upon him usury.

Exodus 22:25

A good man sheweth favour, and lendeth: he will guide his affairs with discretion.

Psalms 112:5

Give to him that asketh thee, and from him that would borrow of thee turn not thou away.

Matthew 5:42

If ye lend to them of whom ye hope to receive, what thank have ye?

Luke 6:34

See also: MONEY.

BRIBERY

Thou shalt take no gift: for the gift blindeth the wise, and perverteth the words of the righteous.

Exodus 23:8

Gather not my soul with sinners, nor my life with bloody men: In whose hands is mischief, and their right hand is full of bribes.

Psalms 26:9, 10

See also: DECEIT, MONEY.

BROTHERHOOD

Am I my brother's keeper.?

Genesis 4:9

Behold, how good and how pleasant it is for brethren to dwell together in unity!

Psalms 133:1

A brother offended is harder to be won than a strong city.

Proverbs 18:19

Whosoever is angry with his brother without a cause shall be in danger of the judgment.

Matthew 5:22

Be kindly affectioned one to another with brotherly love: in honor preferring one another.

Romans 12:10

Let brotherly love continue.

Hebrews 13:1

If a man say, I love God, and hateth his brother, he is a liar.

1 John 4:20

See also: FRIENDSHIP, LOVE.

BURDEN

Cast thy burden upon the Lord, and he shall sustain thee: he shall never suffer the righteous to be moved.

Psalms 55:22

For my yoke is easy, and my burden is light.

Matthew 11:30

[We] have borne the burden and heat of the day.

Matthew 20:12

Bear ye one another's burdens.

Galatians 6:2

Every man shall bear his own burden.

Galatians 6:5

See also: AFFLICTION, SUFFERING.

BUSINESS

Seest thou a man diligent in his business? He shall stand before kings.

Proverbs 22:29

He is a merchant, the balances of deceit are in his hand.

Hosea 12:7

He that had received the five talents went and traded with the same, and made them other five talents.

Matthew 25:16

Make not my Father's house an house of merchandise.

John 2:16

See also: MONEY, RICHES, WEALTH.

C

CALLING

The Lord hath anointed me to preach good tidings.

Isaiah 61:1

Follow me, and I will make you fishers of men.

Matthew 4:19

The harvest truly is great, but the labourers are few: pray ye therefore the Lord of the harvest, that he would send forth labourers into his harvest.

Luke 10:2

Walk worthy of the vocation wherewith ye are called.

Ephesians 4:1

See also: MINISTRY, ORDINATION.

CELIBACY

There are some eunuchs, which were so born from their mother's womb: and there are some eunuchs which were made eunuches of men: and there be eunuchs, which have made themselves eunuches for the kingdom of heaven's sake.

Matthew 19:12

He that is unmarried careth for the things that belong to the Lord, how he may please the Lord: But he that is married careth for the things that are of the world, how he may please his wife.

1 Corinthians 7:32, 33

He that standeth stedfast in his heart, having no necessity, but hath power over his own will, and hath so decreed in his heart that he will keep his virgin, doeth well.

1 Corinthians 7:37

See also: ADULTERY, CHASTITY, PURITY.

CHARITY

Though I speak with the tongues of men and of angels, and have not charity, I am become as sounding brass, or a tinkling cymbal. And though I have the gift of prophecy, and understand all mysteries, and all knowledge; and though I have all faith, so that I could remove mountains, and have not charity, I am nothing. And though I bestow all my goods to feed the poor, and though I give my body to be burned, and have not charity, it profiteth me nothing.

1 Corinthians 13:1–3

Charity never faileth.

1 Corinthians 13:8

Now abideth faith, hope, charity, these three; but the greatest of these is charity.

1 Corinthians 13:13

Put on charity, which is the bond of perfectness.

Colossians 3:14

Charity shall cover the multitude of sins.

1 Peter 4:8

See also: GIVING, LOVE, MERCY, SERVICE.

CHASTITY

Lust not after her beauty in thine heart; neither let her take thee with her eyelids.

Proverbs 6:25

It is good for man not to touch a woman. Nevertheless, to avoid fornication, let every man have his own wife, and let every woman have her own husband.

1 Corinthians 7:1, 2

It is better to marry than to burn.

1 Corinthians 7:9

See also: ADULTERY, PURITY.

CHEERFULNESS

A merry heart maketh a cheerful countenance.
Proverbs 15:13

Be of good cheer; it is I; be not afraid.
Matthew 14:27

See also: CONTENTMENT, JOY.

CHILDREN

Lo, children are an heritage of the Lord: and the fruit of the womb is his reward.
Psalms 127:3

As arrows are in the hand of a mighty man; so are children of the youth. Happy is the man that hath his quiver full of them.
Psalms 127:4, 5

Train up a child in the way he should go: and when he is old, he will not depart from it.
Proverbs 22:6

Except ye be converted, and become as little children, ye shall not enter into the kingdom of heaven.
Matthew 18:3

Suffer little children, and forbid them not, to come unto me: for of such is the kingdom of heaven.
Matthew 19:14

Out of the mouth of babes and sucklings thou hast perfected praise.
Matthew 21:16

See also: PARENT.

CHOICE

I have set before you life and death, blessing and cursing: therefore choose life, that both thou and thy seed may live.
Deuteronomy 30:19

Choose you this day whom ye will serve.
Joshua 24:15

Let us choose to us judgment: let us know among ourselves what is good.
Job 34:4

Ye have not chosen me, but I have chosen you, and ordained you, that ye should go and bring forth fruit.
John 15:16

See also: CONVERSION, FREEDOM, GOD, RECONCILIATION.

CHRIST

The foxes have holes, and the birds of the air have nests; but the Son of man hath not where to lay his head.
Matthew 8:20

For God so loved the world, that he gave his only begotten Son, that whosoever believeth in him should not perish, but have everlasting life.
John 3:16

But we preach Christ crucified, unto the Jews a stumblingblock, and unto the Greeks foolishness.
1 Corinthians 1:23

Thanks be unto God for his unspeakable gift.
2 Corinthians 9:15

And are built upon the foundation of the apostles and prophets, Jesus Christ himself being the chief corner stone.
Ephesians 2:20

Christ is all, and in all.
Colossians 3:11

Jesus . . . was made a little lower than the angels.
Hebrews 2:9

Jesus Christ the same yesterday, and to day, and for ever.
Hebrews 13:8

See also: BROTHERHOOD, REDEMPTION.

CHRISTIAN

And the disciples were called Christians first in Antioch.
Acts 11:26

Then Agrippa said unto Paul, Almost thou persuadest me to be a Christian.
Acts 26:28

See also: CHRIST, CHURCH.

CHURCH

How amiable are thy tabernacles, O Lord of hosts! Blessed are they that dwell in thy house. I had rather be a doorkeeper in the house of my God, than to dwell in the tents of wickedness.
Psalms 84:1,4,10

I was glad when they said unto me,
Let us go into the house of the Lord.

Psalms 122:1

And I say also unto thee, That thou art Peter, and upon this rock I will build my church; and the gates of hell shall not prevail against it.

Matthew 16:18

Feed the church of God, which he hath purchased with his own blood.

Acts 20:28

Other foundation can no man lay than that is laid, which is Jesus Christ.

1 Corinthians 3:11

Christ . . . loved the church, and gave himself for it; That he might sanctify and cleanse it with the washing of water by the word, That he might present it to himself a glorious church, not having spot, or wrinkle, or any such thing; but that it should be holy and without blemish.

Ephesians 5:25b–27

See also: CHRISTIAN, KINGDOM OF GOD.

COMFORT

Sing, O heavens; and be joyful, O earth; and break forth into singing, O mountains: for the Lord hath comforted his people, and will have mercy upon his afflicted.

Isaiah 49:13

As one whom his mother comforteth, so will I comfort you.

Isaiah 66:13

Blessed are they that mourn: for they shall be comforted.

Matthew 5:4

Come unto me, all ye that labour and are heavy laden, and I will give you rest.

Matthew 11:28

Whatsoever things were written aforetime were written for our learning, that we through patience and comfort of the Scriptures might have hope.

Romans 15:4

See also: COURAGE, STRENGTH.

COMPLAINT

Wherefore doth a living man complain, a man for the punishment of his sins?

Lamentations 3:39

Murmur not among yourselves.

John 6:43

Who are thou that repliest against God? Shall the thing formed say to him that formed it, Why hast thou made me thus?

Romans 9:20

See also: AFFLICTION, DESPAIR, SUFFERING.

CONCEIT

Answer a fool according to his folly, lest he be wise in his own conceit.

Proverbs 26:5

The sluggard is wiser in his own conceit than seven men that can render a reason.

Proverbs 26:16

The rich man is wise in his own conceit; but the poor that hath understanding searcheth him out.

Proverbs 28:11

Mind not high things, but condescend to men of low estate. Be not wise in your own conceit.

Romans 12:16

See also: BOASTING, PRIDE.

CONFESSION

They shall confess their sin which they have done.

Numbers 5:7

I said, I will confess my transgression unto the Lord; and thou forgavest the iniquity of my sin.

Psalms 32:5

He that covereth his sins shall not prosper: but whoso confesseth and forsaketh them shall have mercy.

Proverbs 28:13

God be merciful to me a sinner.

Luke 18:13

See also: CONVERSION, REPENTANCE.

CONSCIENCE

The wicked flee when no man pursueth: the righteous are bold as a lion.

Proverbs 28:1

Herein do I exercise myself, to have always a conscience void of offence toward God, and toward men.

Acts 24:16

When ye sin so against the brethren, and
wound their weak conscience, ye sin against
Christ.

1 Corinthians 8:12

The end of the commandment is charity out
of a pure heart, and of a good conscience,
and of faith unfeigned.

1 Timothy 1:5

See also: FEAR, HEART.

CONTENTION

Only by pride cometh contention: but with
the well advised is wisdom.

Proverbs 13:10

A fools lips enter into contention, and his
mouth calleth for strokes.

Proverbs 18:6

Whosoever shall smite thee on thy right
cheek, turn to him the other also.

Matthew 5:39

Where envying and strife is, there is confusion and every evil work.

James 3:16

See also: ANGER, HATE, WAR.

CONTENTMENT

My cup runneth over.

Psalms 23:5

I have learned, in whatsoever state I am,
therewith to be content.

Philippians 4:11

Be content with such things as ye have.

Hebrews 13:5

See also: HAPPINESS, JOY.

CONVERSION

If the wicked will turn from all his sins that
he hath committed, and keep all my statutes,
and do that which is lawful and right, he
shall surely live, he shall not die.

Ezekiel 18:21

It is time to seek the Lord, till he come and
rain righteousness upon you.

Hosea 10:12

Except ye be converted, and become as little
children, ye shall not enter into the kingdom
of heaven.

Matthew 18:3

When thou art converted, strengthen thy
brethren.

Luke 22:32

Repent ye therefore, and be converted, that
your sins may be blotted out.

Acts 3:19

He which converteth the sinner from the error
of his way shall save a soul from death, and
shall hide a multitude of sins.

James 5:20

See also: CONFESSION, REPENTANCE.

COUNSEL

A wise man will hear, and will increase learning; and a man of understanding shall attain
unto wise counsels.

Proverbs 1:5

Where no counsel is, the people fall: but in
the multitude of counsellors there is safety.

Proverbs 11:14

The way of a fool is right in his own eyes:
but he that hearkeneth unto counsel is wise.

Proverbs 12:15

Hear counsel, and receive instruction; that
thou mayest be wise in thy latter end.

Proverbs 19:20

See also: INSTRUCTION, KNOWLEDGE.

COURAGE

Be of good courage, and he shall strengthen
your heart, all ye that hope in the Lord.

Psalms 31:24

Strengthen ye the weak hands, and confirm
the feeble knees.

Isaiah 35:3

I can do all things through Christ that
strengtheneth me.

Philippians 4:13

The Lord is my helper, and I will not fear
what man shall do unto me.

Hebrews 13:6

See also: ANXIETY, STRENGTH.

COVETOUSNESS

Thou shall not covet thy neighbour's house,
thou shalt not covet thy neighbour's wife,
nor his manservant, nor his maidservant, nor

his ox, nor his ass, nor any thing that is thy neighbour's.

Exodus 20:17

The wicked boasteth of his heart's desire, and blesseth the covetous, whom the Lord abhorreth.

Psalms 10:3

Incline my heart unto thy testimonies, and not to covetousness.

Psalms 119:36

Take heed, and beware of covetousness: for a man's life consisteth not in the abundance of the things which he possesseth.

Luke 12:15

They that will be rich fall into temptation and a snare, and into many foolish and hurtful lusts, which drown men in destruction and perdition.

1 Timothy 6:9

See also: DESIRE, LUST.

CREATION

In the beginning God created the heaven and the earth.

Genesis 1:1

God created man in his own image, in the image of God created he him.

Genesis 1:27

God saw every thing that he had made, and, behold, it was very good.

Genesis 1:31

I form the light, and create darkness: I make peace, and create evil: I the Lord do all these things.

Isaiah 45:7

The heavens declare the glory of God; and the firmament sheweth his handywork.

Psalms 19:1

He hath made every thing beautiful in his time.

Ecclesiastes 3:11

We are his workmanship.

Ephesians 2:10

See also: ETERNITY, GOD.

CROSS

He that taketh not his cross, and followeth after me, is not worthy of me.

Matthew 10:38

Whosoever will come after me, let him deny himself, and take up his cross, and follow me.

Mark 8:34

But God forbid that I should glory, save in the cross of our Lord Jesus Christ.

Galatians 6:14

See also: REDEMPTION, SALVATION.

CURSE

As he loved cursing, so let it come unto him: as he delighted not in blessing, so let it be far from him.

Psalms 109:17

Bless them that curse you.

Matthew 5:44

There shall be no more curse.

Revelation 22:3

See also: EVIL, HATE.

D

DEATH

For dust thou art, and unto dust shalt thou return.

Genesis 3:19

The righteous hath hope in his death.

Proverbs 14:32

The sorrows of death compassed me.

Psalms 18:4

I have said, Ye are gods; . . . But ye shall die like men.

Psalms 82:6, 7

We have made a covenant with death.

Isaiah 28:15

Passed from death unto life.

John 5:24

The last enemy that shall be destroyed is death.

1 Corinthians 15:26

O death, where is thy sting. O grave, where is thy victory.

1 Corinthians 15:55

He that is dead is freed from sin.

Romans 6:7

Who shall deliver me from the body of this death?

Romans 7:24

To be carnally minded is death.

Romans 8:6

And I looked, and behold a pale horse: and his name that sat on him was Death.

Revelation 6:8

Blessed are the dead which die in the Lord from henceforth: Yea, saith the Spirit, that they may rest from their labours; and their works do follow them.

Revelation 14:13

See also: IMMORTALITY, LIFE.

DECEIT

He that worketh deceit shall not dwell within my house: he that telleth lies shall not tarry in my sight.

Psalms 101:7

As a mad man who casteth firebrands, arrows, and death, So is the man that deceiveth his neighbour, and saith, Am I not in sport?

Proverbs 26:18, 19

A double minded man is unstable in all his ways.

James 1:8

See also: FALSEHOOD, HYPOCRISY.

DESIRE

My soul thirsteth for thee, my flesh longeth for thee in a dry and thirsty land, where no water is.

Psalms 63:1

The desire accomplished is sweet to the soul.

Proverbs 13:19

With my soul have I desired thee in the night; yea, with my spirit within me will I seek thee early.

Isaiah 26:9

Desire spiritual gifts.

1 Corinthians 14:1

See also: COVETOUSNESS, HOPE, LUST.

DESPAIR

A merry heart doeth good like a medicine: but a broken spirit drieth the bones.

Proverbs 17:22

The harvest is past, the summer is ended, and we are not saved.

Jeremiah 8:20

Men ought always to pray, and not to faint.

Luke 18:1

We are perplexed, but not in despair.

2 Corinthians 4:8

See also: HOPE, SUFFERING.

DEVIL

How art thou fallen from heaven, O Lucifer, son of the morning!

Isaiah 14:12

Get thee behind me, Satan.

Mark 8:33

Resist the devil, and he will flee from you.

James 4:7

Be sober, be vigilant; because your adversary the devil, as a roaring lion, walketh about, seeking whom he may devour.

1 Peter 5:8

See also: ANGEL, EVIL, SIN.

DISCIPLE

The disciple is not above his master, nor the servant above his lord.

Matthew 10:24

If any man come to me, and hate not his father, and mother, and wife, and children, and brethren, and sisters, yea, and his own life also, he cannot be my disciple.

Luke 14:26

See also: EXAMPLE, FAITHFULNESS.

DISCONTENTMENT

All things are full of labour; man cannot utter it: the eye is not satisfied with seeing, nor the ear filled with hearing.

Ecclesiastes 1:8

Let us not be desirous of vain glory, provoking one another, envying one another.

Galatians 5:26

Ye lust, and have not; ye kill, and desire to have, and cannot obtain.

James 4:2

See also: COMPLAINT, ENVY.

DISHONOR

Thou hast known my reproach, and my shame, and my dishonour.

Psalms 69:19

He that is of a perverse heart shall be despised.

Proverbs 12:8

Hath not the potter power over the clay, of the same lump to make one vessel unto honour, and another unto dishonour?

Romans 9:21

See also: IRREVERENCE.

DOUBT

O thou of little faith, wherefore didst thou doubt?

Matthew 14:31

And he that doubteth is damned if he eat.

Romans 14:23

See also: INFIDELITY, UNBELIEF.

DRUNKENNESS

Wine is a mocker, strong drink is raging: and whosoever is deceived thereby is not wise.

Proverbs 20:1

The drunkard and the glutton shall come to poverty.

Proverbs 23:21

Whoredom and wine and new wine take away the heart.

Hosea 4:11

Be not drunk with wine, wherein is excess.

Ephesians 5:18

They that be drunken are drunken in the night. But let us, who are of the day, be sober.

1 Thessalonians 5:7

See also: ABSTINENCE, TEMPERANCE.

DUTY

Withhold not good from them to whom it is due, when it is in the power of thine hand to do it.

Proverbs 3:27

Fear God, and keep his commandments: for this is the whole duty of man.

Ecclesiastes 12:13

We have done that which was our duty to do.

Luke 17:10

Render therefore unto Caesar the things which be Caesar's, and unto God the things which be God's.

Luke 20:25

Render therefore to all their dues: tribute to whom tribute is due; custom to whom custom; fear to whom fear; honour to whom honour.

Romans 13:7

See also: RESPONSIBILITY, WORSHIP.

E

ENVY

Wrath killeth the foolish man, and envy slayeth the silly one.

Job 5:2

Envy thou not the oppressor, and choose none of his ways.

Proverbs 3:31

Charity envieth not.

1 Corinthians 13:4

Where envying and strife is, there is confusion and every evil work.

James 3:16

See also: COVETOUSNESS, HATE.

ETERNITY

The counsel of the Lord standeth for ever, the thoughts of his heart to all generations.

Psalms 33:11

Before the mountains were brought forth, or ever thou hadst formed the earth and the world, even from everlasting to everlasting, thou art God.

Psalms 90:2

His righteousness remaineth for ever.

2 Corinthians 9:9

See also: GOD, IMMORTALITY.

EVIL

The imagination of man's heart is evil from his youth.

Genesis 8:21

And unto man he said, Behold, the fear of the Lord, that is wisdom; and to depart from evil is understanding.

Job 28:28

Fret not thyself because of evildoers, neither be thou envious against the workers of iniquity. For they shall soon be cut down like the grass, and wither as the green herb.

Psalms 37:1–2

The fear of the Lord is to hate evil.

Proverbs 8:13

Sufficient unto the day is the evil thereof.

Matthew 6:34

A good man out of the good treasure of the heart bringeth forth good things: and an evil man out of the evil treasure bringeth forth evil things.

Matthew 12:35

For that which I do I allow not: for what I would, that do I not: but what I hate, that do I . . . For the good that I would I do not, but the evil which I would not, that I do.

Romans 7:15, 19

Recompense to no man evil for evil.

Romans 12:17

Evil communications corrupt good manners.

1 Corinthians 15:33

Abstain from all appearance of evil.

1 Thessalonians 5:22

See also: GOOD AND EVIL, GOODNESS, SIN.

EXAMPLE

Like people, like priest.

Hosea 4:9

I have given you an example, that ye should do as I have done to you.

John 13:15

Be thou an example of the believers, in word, in conversation, in charity, in spirit, in faith, in purity.

1 Timothy 4:12

Take, my brethren, the prophets, who have spoken in the name of the Lord, for an example of suffering affliction, and of patience.

James 5:10

For even hereunto were ye called: because Christ also suffered for us, leaving us an example, that ye should follow his steps.

1 Peter 2:21

See also: DISCIPLE.

EXPECTATION

Those that wait upon the Lord, they shall inherit the earth.

Psalms 37:9

Our eyes wait upon the Lord our God, until that he have mercy upon us.

Psalms 123:2

Blessed are all they that wait for him.

Isaiah 30:18

Blessed are those servants, whom the Lord when he cometh shall find watching.

Luke 12:37

The earnest expectation of the creature waiteth for the manifestation of the sons of God.

Romans 8:19

See also: HAPPINESS, HEAVEN, HOPE, KINGDOM OF GOD.

F

FAITH

In the fear of the Lord is strong confidence: and his children shall have a place of refuge.

Proverbs 14:26

I know that my redeemer liveth.

Job 19:25

If ye have faith as a grain of mustard seed, ye shall say unto this mountain, Remove hence to yonder place; and it shall remove; and nothing shall be impossible unto you.

Matthew 17:20

Blessed are they that have not seen, and have believed.

John 20:29

The just shall live by faith.

Romans 1:17

We walk by faith, not by sight.

2 Corinthians 5:7

I have fought a good fight, I have finished my course, I have kept the faith.

2 Timothy 4:7

Faith is the substance of things hoped for, the evidence of things not seen.

Hebrews 11:1

For as the body without the spirit is dead, so faith without works is dead also.

James 2:26

Shew me thy faith without thy works, and I will shew thee my faith by my works.

James 2:18

I . . . exhort you that ye should earnestly contend for the faith which was once delivered unto the saints.

Jude 1:3

See also: BELIEF, HOPE, TRUST.

FAITHFULNESS

The Lord preserveth the faithful.

Psalms 31:23

Faithful are the wounds of a friend.

Proverbs 27:6

Thou hast been faithful over a few things, I will make thee ruler over many things.

Matthew 25:23

He that is faithful in that which is least is faithful also in much: and he that is unjust in the least is unjust also in much.

Luke 16:10

See also: FRIENDSHIP, LOVE.

FALSEHOOD

Thou shalt not bear false witness against thy neighbour.

Exodus 20:16

Ye shall not steal, neither deal falsely, neither lie one to another.

Leviticus 19:11

A false witness shall not be unpunished, and he that speaketh lies shall not escape.

Proverbs 19:5

A poor man is better than a liar.

Proverbs 19:22

A lying tongue hateth those that are afflicted by it.

Proverbs 26:28

See also: DECEIT, HYPOCRISY.

FAMILY

The son dishonoureth the father, the daughter riseth up against her mother, the daughter in law against her mother in law; a man's enemies are the men of his own house.

Micah 7:6

See also: CHILDREN, MARRIAGE, PARENTS.

FASTING: *see* ABSTINENCE.

FEAR

The fear of the Lord is the beginning of wisdom.

Psalms 111:10

Happy is the man that feareth always; but he that hardeneth his heart shall fall into mischief.

Proverbs 28:14

Let us hear the conclusion of the whole matter: fear God, and keep his commandments: for this is the whole duty of man.

Ecclesiastes 12:13

He that fleeth from the fear shall fall into the pit; and he that getteth up out of the pit shall be taken in the snare.

Jeremiah 48:44

Fear God. Honour the king.

1 Peter 2:17

See also: ANXIETY, COURAGE.

FLATTERY

A man that flattereth his neighbour spreadeth a net for his feet.

Proverbs 29:5

Woe unto you, when all men shall speak of you! for so did their fathers to the false prophets.

Luke 6:26

See also: DECEIT, HYPOCRISY.

FOOL

He that is slow to wrath is of great understanding: but he that is hasty of spirit exalteth folly.

Proverbs 14:29

As a dog returneth to his vomit, so a fool returneth to his folly.

Proverbs 26:11

A fool uttereth all his mind: but a wise man keepeth it in till afterwards.

Proverbs 29:11

Dead flies cause the ointment of the apothecary to send forth a stinking savour: so doth a little folly him that is in reputation for wisdom and honour.

Ecclesiastes 10:1

The words of a wise man's mouth are gracious; but the lips of a fool will swallow up himself.

Ecclesiastes 10:12

Every one that heareth these sayings of mine, and doeth them not, shall be likened unto a foolish man, which built his house upon the sand.

Matthew 7:26

Professing themselves to be wise, they became fools.

Romans 1:22

God hath chosen the foolish things of the world to confound the wise.

1 Corinthians 1:27

If any man among you seemeth to be wise in this world, let him become a fool, that he may be wise.

1 Corinthians 3:18

See also: IGNORANCE.

FORGIVENESS

Thou hast forgiven the iniquity of thy people, thou has covered all their sin.

Psalms 85:2

The discretion of a man deferreth his anger; and it is his glory to pass over a transgression.

Proverbs 19:11

Though your sins be as scarlet, they shall be as white as snow; though they be red like crimson, they shall be as wool.

Isaiah 1:18

Thine iniquity is taken away, and thy sin purged.

Isaiah 6:7

Let the wicked forsake his way, and the unrighteous man his thoughts: and let him return unto the Lord, and he will have mercy upon him; and to our God, for he will abundantly pardon.

Isaiah 55:7

To the Lord our God belong mercies and forgiveness.

Daniel 9:9

Resist not evil: but whosoever shall smite thee on thy right cheek, turn to him the other also.

Matthew 5:39

Forgive us our debts, as we forgive our debtors.

Matthew 6:12

If ye forgive not men their trespasses, neither will your Father forgive your trespasses.

Matthew 6:15

The Son of man hath power on earth to forgive sins.

Matthew 9:8

Judge not, and ye shall not be judged: condemn not, and ye shall not be condemned: forgive, and ye shall be forgiven.

Luke 6:37

If thy brother trespass against thee, rebuke him; and if he repent, forgive him.

Luke 17:3

Father, forgive them; for they know not what they do.

Luke 23:34

Behold the Lamb of God, which taketh away the sin of the world.

John 1:29

Be ye kind one to another, tenderhearted, forgiving one another, even as God for Christ's sake hath forgiven you.

Ephesians 4:32

Even as Christ forgave you, so also do ye.

Colossians 3:13

If we confess our sins, he is faithful and just to forgive us our sins, and to cleanse us from all unrighteousness.

1 John 1:9

See also: LOVE, MERCY.

FREEDOM

Ye shall know the truth, and the truth shall make you free.

John 8:32

If the Son therefore shall make you free, ye shall be free indeed.

John 8:36

There is neither Jew nor Greek, there is neither bond nor free, there is neither male nor female: for ye are all one in Christ Jesus.

Galatians 3:28

Stand fast therefore in the liberty wherewith Christ hath made us free, and be not entangled again with the yoke of bondage.

Galatians 5:1

As free, and not using your liberty for a cloke of maliciousness, but as the servants of God.

1 Peter 2:16

See also: LIBERTY.

FRIENDSHIP

He that repeateth a matter separateth very friends.

Proverbs 17:9

A man that hath friends must shew himself friendly: and there is a friend that sticketh closer than a brother.

Proverbs 18:24

Make no friendship with an angry man; and with a furious man thou shalt not go: Lest thou learn his ways, and get a snare to thy soul.

Proverbs 22:24, 25

Faithful are the wounds of a friend; but the kisses of an enemy are deceitful.

Proverbs 27:6

A Faithful friend is a strong defense: and he that hath found such an one hath found a treasure.

Ecclesiasticus 6:14

Forsake not an old friend, for the new is not comparable unto him.

Ecclesiasticus 9:10

I was wounded in the house of my friends.

Zechariah 13:6

Make to yourself friends.

Luke 16:9

Greater love hath no man than this, that a man lay down his life for his friends.

John 15:13

See also: BROTHERHOOD, FAITHFULNESS, LOVE.

G

GIFT

Thou shalt take no gift: for the gift blindeth the wise, and perverteth the words of the righteous.

Exodus 23:8

Every man is a friend to him that giveth gifts.

Proverbs 19:6

A gift destroyeth the heart.

Ecclesiastes 7:7

Every good gift and every perfect gift is from above, and cometh down from the Father of lights.

James 1:17

See also: GIVING, HELP, KINDNESS.

GIVING

The liberal soul shall be made fat: and he that watereth shall be watered also himself.

Proverbs 11:25

If thine enemy be hungry, give him bread to eat; and if he be thirsty, give him water to drink.

Proverbs 25:21

He that giveth unto the poor shall not lack.

Proverbs 28:27

Cast thy bread upon the waters: for thou shalt find it after many days.

Ecclesiastes 11:1

Give to him that asketh thee, and from him that would borrow of thee turn not thou away.
Matthew 5:42

Freely ye have received; freely give.
Matthew 10:8

Whosoever hath, to him shall be given, and he shall have more abundance: but whosoever hath not, from him shall be taken away even that he hath.
Matthew 13:12

Whosoever shall give you a cup of water to drink in my name . . . shall not lose his reward.
Mark 9:41

Give, and it shall be given unto you; good measure, pressed down, and shaken together, and running over.
Luke 6:38

Silver and gold have I none; but such as I have give I thee.
Acts 3:6

It is more blessed to give than to receive.
Acts 20:35

He that giveth, let him do it with simplicity.
Romans 12:8

God loveth a cheerful giver.
2 Corinthians 9:7

See also: GIFT, LOVE, SACRIFICE.

GLORY

Thine, O Lord, is the greatness, and the power, and the glory.
1 Chronicles 29:11

The heavens declare the glory of God.
Psalms 19:1

Who is this King of glory? The Lord of hosts, he is the King of glory.
Psalms 24:10

The hoary head is a crown of glory, if it be found in the way of righteousness.
Proverbs 16:31

For men to search their own glory is not glory.
Proverbs 25:27

Holy, holy, holy, is the Lord of hosts: the whole earth is full of his glory.
Isaiah 6:3

Glory to God in the highest.
Luke 2:14

Glorify God in your body, and in your spirit, which are God's.
1 Corinthians 6:20

Whether therefore ye eat, or drink, or whatever ye do, do all to the glory of God.
1 Corinthians 10:31

There is one glory of the sun, and another glory of the moon, and another glory of the stars: for one star differeth from another star in glory.
1 Corinthians 15:41

Pray for us, that the word of the Lord may have free course, and be glorified.
2 Thessalonians 3:1

The spirit of glory and of God resteth upon you.
1 Peter 4:14

See also: BOASTING, HEAVEN, PRAISE.

GOD

Shall not the Judge of all the earth do right?
Genesis 18:25

God said unto Moses, I am that I am.
Exodus 3:14

The Lord God, merciful and gracious, long-suffering, and abundant in goodness and truth.
Exodus 34:6

Know therefore that the Lord thy God, he is God, the faithful God, which keepeth covenant and mercy with them that love him and keep his commandments to a thousand generations.
Deuteronomy 7:9

The Lord your God is a God of gods, a Lord of lords, a great God, a mighty, and a terrible.
Deuteronomy 10:17

The eternal God is thy refuge, and underneath are the everlasting arms.
Deuteronomy 33:27

Canst thou by searching find out God?
Job 11:7

The fool hath said in his heart, There is no God.

Psalms 14:1

For the Lord is a great God, and a great King above all gods.

Psalms 95:3

Give thanks unto him, and bless his name. For Jehovah is good; his lovingkindness endureth for ever, And his faithfulness unto all generations.

Psalms 100:4, 5

Who coverest thyself with light as with a garment: who stretchest out the heavens like a curtain: Who layeth the beams of his chambers in the waters: who maketh the clouds his chariot: who walketh upon the wings of the wind: Who maketh his angels spirits; his ministers a flaming fire.

Psalms 104:2–4

Though the Lord be high, yet hath he respect unto the lowly.

Psalms 138:6

Trust ye in the Lord for ever: for in the Lord Jehovah is everlasting strength.

Isaiah 26:4

I am God, and there is none else.

Isaiah 45:22

Our Father which art in heaven.

Matthew 6:9

There is one God; and there is none other than he.

Mark 12:32

No man hath seen God at any time.

John 1:18

Behold the Lamb of God, which taketh away the sin of the world.

John 1:29

The Father is in me, and I in him.

John 10:38

If this counsel or this work be of men, it will come to nought: But if it be of God, ye cannot overthrow it.

Acts 5:38, 39

God is no respecter of persons.

Acts 10:34

For in him we live, and move, and have our being: as certain also of your own poets have said, For we are also his offspring.

Acts 17:28

Let God be true, but every man a liar.

Romans 3:4

We know that all things work together for good to them that love God.

Romans 8:28

If God be for us, who can be against us?

Romans 8:31

Eye hath not seen, nor ear heard, neither have entered into the heart of man, the things which God hath prepared for them that love him.

1 Corinthians 2:9

I have planted, Apollos watered; but God gave the increase.

1 Corinthians 3:6

Be not deceived; God is not mocked.

Galatians 6:7

Our God is a consuming fire.

Hebrews 12:29

It is a fearful thing to fall into the hands of the living God.

Hebrews 10:31

I am Alpha and Omega, the beginning and the end, the first and the last.

Revelation 22:13

See also: CHRIST, CREATION, ETERNITY, OMNIPOTENCE, OMNIPRESENCE, OMNISCIENCE, PROVIDENCE.

GOLDEN RULE

All things whatsoever ye would that men should do to you, do ye even so to them: for this is the law and the prophets.

Matthew 7:12

As ye would that men should do to you, do ye also to them likewise.

Luke 6:31

See also: CHARITY, LOVE, MERCY.

GOOD AND EVIL

Your eyes shall be opened, and ye shall be as gods, knowing good and evil.

Genesis 3:5

Woe unto them that call evil good, and good evil.

Isaiah 5:20

Out of the mouth of the most High proceedeth not evil and good?

Lamentations 3:38

For the good that I would I do not; but the evil which I would not, that I do.

Romans 7:19

Abhor that which is evil; cleave to that which is good.

Romans 12:9

Be not overcome of evil, but overcome evil with good.

Romans 12:21

I would have you wise unto that which is good, and simple concerning evil.

Romans 16:19

See also: GOODNESS; EVIL; SIN; WORKS, GOOD.

GOODNESS

I will make all my goodness pass before thee.

Exodus 33:19

There is none that doeth good, no, not one.

Psalms 14:3

Surely goodness and mercy shall follow me all the days of my life.

Psalms 23:6

Thou crownest the year with thy goodness.

Psalms 65:11

Withhold not good from them to whom it is due, when it is in the power of thine hand to do it.

Proverbs 3:27

A good man out of the good treasure of his heart bringeth forth that which is good.

Luke 6:45

All things work together for good to them that love God.

Romans 8:28

Prove all things; hold fast that which is good.

1 Thessalonians 5:21

See also: EVIL, GOOD AND EVIL.

GOSSIP

The words of a talebearer are as wounds, and they go down into the innermost parts of the belly.

Proverbs 18:8

Where no wood is, there the fire goeth out: so where there is no talebearer, the strife ceaseth.

Proverbs 26:20

Refuse profane and old wives' fables.

1 Timothy 4:7

Let none of you suffer as . . . a busybody in other men's matters.

1 Peter 4:15

See also: MALICE, SLANDER.

GRACE

He giveth grace unto the lowly.

Proverbs 3:34

Where sin abounded, grace did much more abound.

Romans 5:20

Shall we continue in sin, that grace may abound? God forbid.

Romans 6:1, 2

If by grace, then it is no more of works; otherwise grace is no more grace. But if it be of works, then it is no more grace: otherwise work is no more work.

Romans 11:6

Ye are fallen from grace.

Galatians 5:4

By grace are ye saved through faith—and that not of yourselves—It is the gift of God, not of works, lest any man should boast.

Ephesians 2:8, 9

Unto every one of us is given grace according to the measure of the gift of Christ.

Ephesians 4:7

God is able to make all grace abound toward you.

2 Corinthians 9:8

My grace is sufficient for thee: for my strength is made perfect in weakness.

2 Corinthians 12:9

The grace of the Lord Jesus Christ, and the love of God, and the communion of the Holy Ghost, be with you all.

2 Corinthians 13:14

See also: CHRIST, GIVING, LOVE.

GREATNESS

Thine, O Lord, is the greatness and the power, and the glory, and the victory, and the majesty: for all that is in the heaven and in the earth is thine; thine is the kingdom, O Lord, and thou art exalted as head above all.

1 Chronicles 29:11

And seekest thou great things for thyself? seek them not.

Jeremiah 45:5

He that is least among you all, the same shall be great.

Luke 9:48

Whosoever will be chief among you, let him be your servent.

Matthew 20:27

See also: HUMILITY, PRIDE.

H

HAPPINESS

Happy is the man whom God correcteth: therefore despise not thou the chastening of the Almighty.

Job 5:17

The hope of the righteous shall be gladness.

Proverbs 10:28

He that keepeth the law, happy is he.

Proverbs 29:18

Wherefore are all they happy that deal very treacherously?

Jeremiah 12:1

See also: CHEERFULNESS, CONTENTMENT, JOY.

HATE

Thou shalt not hate thy brother in thine heart.

Leviticus 19:17

Hatred stirreth up strifes: but love covereth all sins.

Proverbs 10:12

He that hateth me hateth my Father also.

John 15:23

He that saith he is in the light, and hateth his brother, is in darkness.

1 John 2:9

He that hateth his brother is in darkness, and walketh in darkness, and knoweth not whither he goeth, because that darkness hath blinded his eyes.

1 John 2:11

If a man say, I love God, and hateth his brother, he is a liar: for he that loveth not his brother whom he hath seen, how can he love God whom he hath not seen?

1 John 4:20

See also: ANGER, CURSE, MALICE.

HEALING

O Lord, my God, I cried unto thee, and thou hast healed me.

Psalms 30:2

Who forgiveth all thine iniquities; who healeth all thy diseases.

Psalms 103:3

He healeth the broken in heart, and bindeth up their wounds.

Psalms 147:3

Honour a physician with the honour due unto him for the uses which ye may have of him: for the Lord hath created him. For of the most High cometh healing, and he shall receive honour of the king. The skill of the physician shall lift up his head: and in the sight of great men he shall be in admiration.

Ecclesiasticus 38:1–3

With his stripes are we healed.

Isaiah 53:5

For I will restore health unto thee, and I will heal thee of thy wounds, saith the Lord.

Jeremiah 30:17

But unto you that fear my name shall the Sun of righteousness arise with healing in his wings.

Malachi 4:2

Thy faith hath made thee whole.

Matthew 9:22

Physician, heal thyself.

Luke 4:23

He hath faith to be healed.

Acts 14:9

Thy prayer of faith shall save the sick, and the Lord shall raise him up.

James 5:15

And the leaves of the tree were for the healing of the nations.

Revelation 22:2

See also: COMFORT, GRACE, INFIRMITY.

HEART

Thou, even thou only, knowest the hearts of all the children of men.

1 Kings 8:39

The Lord searcheth all hearts and understandeth all the imaginations of the thoughts.

1 Chronicles 28:9

Create in me a clean heart, O God; and renew a right spirit within me.

Psalms 51:10

Keep thy heart with all diligence; for out of it are the issues of life.

Proverbs 4:23

He that is of a merry heart hath a continual feast.

Proverbs 15:15

Out of the abundance of the heart the mouth speaketh.

Matthew 12:34

Those things which proceed out of the mouth come forth from the heart; and they defile the man.

Matthew 15:18

Where your treasure is, there will your heart be also.

Luke 12:34

See also: LOVE, MIND, SOUL, SPIRIT.

HEAVEN

The Lord is in his holy temple, the Lord's throne is in heaven.

Psalms 11:4

In thy presence is fulness of joy; at thy right hand there are pleasures for evermore.

Psalms 16:11

I will dwell in the house of the Lord for ever.

Psalms 23:6

The habitation of thy holiness and of thy glory.

Isaiah 63:15

Rejoice, and be exceeding glad: for great is your reward in heaven: for so persecuted they the prophets which were before you.

Matthew 5:12

Lay up for yourselves treasures in heaven, where neither moth nor rust doth corrupt, and where thieves do not break through nor steal.

Matthew 6:20

Not every one that saith unto me, Lord, Lord, shall enter into the kingdom of heaven; but he that doeth the will of my Father which is in heaven.

Matthew 7:21

We know that if our earthly house of this tabernacle were dissolved, we have a building of God, an house not made with hands, eternal in the heavens.

2 Corinthians 5:1

Ye have in heaven a better and an enduring substance.

Hebrews 10:34

An inheritance incorruptible, and undefiled, and that fadeth not away, reserved in heaven for you.

1 Peter 1:4

We, according to his promise, look for new heavens and a new earth, wherein dwelleth righteousness.

2 Peter 3:13

See also: HAPPINESS, IMMORTALITY, LIFE.

HELL

But he knoweth not that the dead are there; and that her guests are in the depths of hell.

Proverbs 9:18

Hell from beneath is moved for thee to meet thee at thy coming.

Isaiah 14:9

Wide is the gate, and broad is the way, that leadeth to destruction, and many there be which go in thereat: Because strait is the gate, and narrow is the way, which leadeth unto life, and few there be that find it.

Matthew 7:13, 14

Into hell, into the fire that never shall be quenched: Where their worm dieth not.

Mark 9:43, 44

See also: DEATH, EVIL, SIN.

HELP

Give us help from trouble: for vain is the help of man.

Psalms 60:11

Strengthen ye the weak hands, and confirm the feeble knees.

Isaiah 35:3

We then that are strong ought to bear the infirmities of the weak, and not to please ourselves.

Romans 15:1

See also: GIVING, LOVE, SERVICE.

HERESY

In vain they do worship me, teaching for doctrines the commandments of men.

Matthew 15:9

Beware lest any man spoil you through philosophy and vain deceit, after the tradition of men, after the rudiments of the world, and not after Christ.

Colossians 2:8

A man that is a heretic after the first and second admonition reject.

Titus 3:10

Be not carried about with divers and strange doctrines.

Hebrews 13:9

Whosoever transgresseth, and abideth not in the doctrine of Christ, hath not God.

2 John 1:9

See also: DECEIT, FALSEHOOD.

HOLINESS

Holy, holy, holy, is the Lord of hosts: the whole earth is full of his glory.

Isaiah 6:3

Give not that which is wholly unto the dogs, neither cast ye your pearls before swine, lest they trample them under their feet, and turn again and rend you.

Matthew 7:6

See also: GOODNESS, RIGHTEOUSNESS.

HOLY GHOST

Whosoever speaketh against the Holy Ghost, it shall not be forgiven him, neither in this world, neither in the world to come.

Matthew 12:32

But when the Comforter is come, whom I will send unto you from the Father, even the Spirit of truth, which proceedeth from the Father, he shall testify of me: And ye also shall bear witness, because ye have been with me from the beginning.

John 15:26, 27

He said unto them, Have ye received the Holy Ghost since ye believed? And they said unto him, We have not so much as heard whether there be any Holy Ghost.

Acts 19:2

See also: GOD, GOODNESS, LOVE.

HOPE

My days are swifter than a weaver's shuttle, and are spent without hope.

Job 7:6

Be of good courage, and he shall strengthen your heart, all ye that hope in the Lord.

Psalms 31:24

Why art thou cast down, O my soul? and why art thou disquieted within me? hope in God.

Psalms 43:5

I will hope continually, and will yet praise thee more and more.

Psalms 71:14

Hope deferred maketh the heart sick: but when the desire cometh, it is a tree of life.

Proverbs 13:12

The righteous hath hope in his death.

Proverbs 14:32

Blessed is the man that trusteth in the Lord, and whose hope the Lord is.

Jeremiah 17:7

Thou art my hope in the day of evil.
Jeremiah 17:17

The Lord is my portion, saith my soul; therefore will I hope in him.
Lamentations 3:24

Prisoners of hope.
Zechariah 9:12

Who against hope believed in hope.
Romans 4:18

Tribulation worketh patience; and patience, experience; and experience, hope.
Romans 5:3, 4

Now the God of hope fill you with all joy and peace in believing, that ye may abound in hope, through the power of the Holy Ghost.
Romans 15:13

Now abideth faith, hope, charity.
1 Corinthians 13:13

We have such hope, we use great plainness of speech.
2 Corinthians 3:12

The hope which is laid up for you in heaven.
Colossians 1:5

Christ in you, the hope of glory.
Colossians 1:27

Lay hold upon the hope set before us: which hope we have as an anchor of the soul, both sure and stedfast.
Hebrews 6:18b, 19

Faith is the substance of things hoped for, the evidence of things not seen.
Hebrews 11:1

Putting on the breastplate of faith and love; and for an helmet, the hope of salvation.
1 Thessalonians 5:8

Our Lord Jesus Christ himself, and God, even our Father, which hath loved us, and hath given us everlasting consolation and good hope through grace.
2 Thessalonians 2:16

Hope to the end.
1 Peter 1:13

See also: CHARITY, FAITH, LOVE, TRUST.

HOSPITALITY

The stranger that dwelleth with you shall be unto you as one born among you, and thou shalt love him as thyself.
Leviticus 19:34

Ye shall have one manner of law, as well for the stranger, as for one of your own country.
Leviticus 24:22

Receive ye one another, as Christ also received us to the glory of God.
Romans 15:7

See also: HELP, KINDNESS, LOVE.

HUMILITY

Lord, thou hast heard the desire of the humble: thou wilt prepare their heart, thou wilt cause thine ear to hear.
Psalms 10:17

Before honour is humility.
Proverbs 15:33

Better is it to be of an humble spirit with the lowly than to divide the spoil with the proud.
Proverbs 16:19

By humility, and the fear of the Lord are riches, and honour, and life.
Proverbs 22:4

I dwell in the high and holy place, with him also that is of a contrite and humble spirit, to revive the spirit of the humble, and to revive the heart of the contrite ones.
Isaiah 57:15

Blessed are the poor in spirit: for theirs is the kingdom of heaven.
Matthew 5:3

Whosoever therefore shall humble himself as this little child, the same is greatest in the kingdom of heaven.
Matthew 18:4

Whosoever will be great among you, let him be your minister; And whosoever will be chief among you, let him be your servant.
Matthew 20:26, 27

Whosoever shall exalt himself shall be abased; and he that humbleth himself shall be exalted.
Matthew 23:12

God resisteth the proud, but giveth grace unto the humble.

James 4:6

Humble yourselves in the sight of the Lord, and he shall lift you up.

James 4:10

See also: MEEKNESS, PRIDE.

HYPOCRISY

The hypocrite's hope shall perish.

Job 8:13

What is the hope of the hypocrite, though he hath gained, when God taketh away his soul?

Job 27:8

An hypocrite with his mouth destroyeth his neighbour.

Proverbs 11:9

Thou hypocrite, first cast out the beam out of thine own eye; and then shalt thou see clearly to cast out the mote out of thy brother's eye.

Matthew 7:5

See also: BIGOTRY, FALSEHOOD, FLATTERY.

I

IDOL

Thou shalt not make unto thee any graven image, or any likeness of anything that is in heaven above, or that is in the earth beneath, or that is in the water under the earth.

Exodus 20:4

For rebellion is as the sin of witchcraft, and stubbornness is as iniquity and idolatry.

1 Samuel 15:23

See also: EVIL, WORSHIP.

IGNORANCE

That the soul be without knowledge, it is not good.

Proverbs 19:2

If any man think that he knoweth anything, he knoweth nothing yet as he ought to know.

1 Corinthians 8:2

With well doing ye may put to silence the ignorance of foolish men.

1 Peter 2:15

See also: FOOL.

IMMORTALITY

For I know that my redeemer liveth, and that he shall stand at the latter day upon the earth: And though after my skin worms destroy this body, yet in my flesh shall I see God.

Job 19:25, 26

As for me, I will behold thy face in righteousness: I shall be satisfied, when I awake, with thy likeness.

Psalms 17:15

I am the resurrection, and the life: He that believeth in me, though he were dead, yet shall he live.

John 11:25

He that raised up Christ from the dead shall also quicken your mortal bodies by his Spirit that dwelleth in you.

Romans 8:11

They do it to obtain a corruptible crown; but we an incorruptible.

1 Corinthians 9:25

Our Saviour Jesus Christ, who hath abolished death, and hath brought life and immortality to light through the gospel.

2 Timothy 1:10

This is the promise that He hath promised us, even eternal life.

1 John 2:25

See also: DEATH, ETERNITY, HEAVEN.

IMPARTIALITY

Thou shalt not respect the person of the poor, nor honour the person of the mighty: but in righteousness shalt thou judge thy neighbour.

Leviticus 19:5

Ye shall hear the small as well as the great.

Deuteronomy 1:17

He maketh his sun to rise on the evil and on the good, and sendeth rain on the just and on the unjust.

Matthew 5:45

God is no respecter of persons.

Acts 10:34

Whatsoever good thing any man doeth, the same shall he receive of the Lord, whether he be bond or free.

Ephesians 6:8

See also: JUSTICE.

INDUSTRIOUSNESS

In all labour there is profit.

Proverbs 14:23

My heart rejoiced in all my labour: and this was my portion of all my labour.

Ecclesiastes 2:10

The labourer is worthy of his hire.

Luke 10:7

Not slothful in business; fervent in spirit; serving the Lord.

Romans 12:11

See also: SERVICE, WORK.

INFIDELITY

Woe unto them that seek deep to hide their counsel from the Lord, and their works are in the dark, and they say, Who seeth us? and who knoweth us?

Isaiah 29:15

Lo, they have rejected the word of the Lord; and what wisdom is in them?

Jeremiah 8:9

He that is not with me is against me; and he that gathereth not with me scattereth.

Luke 11:23

What part hath he that believeth with an infidel?

2 Corinthians 6:15

See also: UNBELIEF.

INFIRMITY

The spirit of a man will sustain his infirmity.

Proverbs 18:14

We then that are strong ought to bear the infirmities of the weak.

Romans 15:1

I take pleasure in infirmities . . . for Christ's sake: for when I am weak, then am I strong.

2 Corinthians 12:10

See also: INSTABILITY.

INJUSTICE

The unjust knoweth no shame.

Zephaniah 3:5

He that is unjust in the least is unjust also in much.

Luke 16:10

See also: EVIL, JUSTICE, SIN.

INSTABILITY

Meddle not with them that are given to change.

Proverbs 24:21

Why gaddest thou about so much to change thy way?

Jeremiah 2:36

No man can serve two masters: for either he will hate the one, and love the other; or else he will hold to the one, and despise the other. Ye cannot serve God and mammon.

Matthew 6:24

Be no more children, tossed to and fro, and carried about with every wind of doctrine, by the sleight of men, and cunning craftiness, whereby they lie in wait to deceive.

Ephesians 4:14

A double minded man is unstable in all his ways.

James 1:8

See also: INFIRMITY.

INSTRUCTION

Come, ye children, hearken unto me: I will teach you the fear of the Lord.

Psalms 34:11

Take fast hold of instruction; let her not go: keep her; for she is thy life.

Proverbs 4:13

The father to the children shall make known thy truth.

Isaiah 38:19

Provoke not your children to wrath: but bring them up in the nurture and admonition of the Lord.

Ephesians 6:4

See also: COUNSEL.

INTEGRITY

If I have walked with vanity, or if my foot hath hasted to deceit; Let me be weighed in an even balance, that God may know mine integrity.

Job 31:5, 6

Judge me, O Lord; according to my righteousness, and according to mine integrity that
is in me.

Psalms 7:8

The integrity of the upright shall guide them.

Proverbs 11:3

Provide things honest in the sight of all men.

Romans 12:17

Walk honestly.

1 Thessalonians 4:12

See also: FAITHFULNESS, RIGHTEOUSNESS.

J

JOY

The joy of the Lord is your strength.

Nehemiah 8:10

God giveth to a man that is good in his sight
wisdom, and knowledge, and joy.

Ecclesiastes 2:26

My servants shall sing for joy of heart.

Isaiah 65:14

These things have I spoken unto you, that my
joy might remain in you, and that your joy
might be full.

John 15:11

Now the God of hope fill you with all joy
and peace in believing, that ye may abound
in hope.

Romans 15:13

The fruit of the Spirit is love, joy, peace.

Galatians 5:22

See also: CHEERFULNESS, REJOICING.

JUDGMENT

The judgments of the Lord are true and
righteous altogether. More to be desired are
they than gold, yea than much fine gold:
sweeter also than honey and the honeycomb.

Psalms 19:9, 10

Thou are weighed in the balances, and art
found wanting.

Daniel 5:27

And why beholdest thou the mote that is in
thy brother's eye, but considereth not the
beam that is in thine own eye? Or how wilt
thou say to thy brother, Let me pull out the
mote out of thine eye; and, behold, a beam
is in thine own eye? Thou hypocrite, first cast
out the beam out of thine own eye; and then
shalt thou see clearly to cast out the mote of
thy brother's eye.

Matthew 7:3–5

Judge not, and ye shall not be judged: condemn not, and ye shall not be condemned:
forgive, and ye shall be forgiven.

Luke 6:37

Out of thine own mouth will I judge thee.

Luke 19:22

See also: JUSTICE, PRUDENCE, RETRIBUTION.

JUSTICE

He that ruleth over men must be just.

2 Samuel 23:3

Defend the poor and fatherless; do justice to
the afflicted and needy.

Psalms 82:3

The path of the just is as the shining light,
that shineth more and more unto the perfect
day.

Proverbs 4:18

None calleth for justice, nor any pleadeth for
truth: they trust in vanity, and speak lies;
they conceive mischief, and bring forth
iniquity.

Isaiah 59:4

What doth the Lord require of thee, but to
do justly, and to love mercy, and to walk
humbly with thy God?

Micah 6:8

Masters, give unto your servants that which
is just and equal.

Colossians 4:1

See also: IMPARTIALITY, INJUSTICE.

JUSTIFICATION

By his knowledge shall my righteous servant
justify many; for he shall bear their iniquities.

Isaiah 53:11

By him all that believe are justified from all
things.

Acts 13:39

Not the hearers of the law are just before God, but the doers of the law shall be justified.

Romans 2:13

A man is justified by faith without the deeds of the law.

Romans 3:28

Being justified by faith, we have peace with God through our Lord Jesus Christ.

Romans 5:1

Being justified by his grace, we should be made heirs according to the hope of eternal life.

Titus 3:7

See also: FAITH, RECONCILIATION.

K

KINDNESS

According to the kindness that I have done unto thee, thou shalt do unto me.

Genesis 21:23

With everlasting kindness will I have mercy on thee.

Isaiah 54:8

Be kindly affectioned one to another with brotherly love; in honour preferring one another.

Romans 12:10

Put on . . . bowels of mercies, kindness, humbleness of mind, meekness, longsuffering.

Colossians 3:12

Add to . . . godliness brotherly kindness; and to brotherly kindness charity.

2 Peter 3:8

See also: CHARITY, GIVING, SERVICE.

KINGDOM OF GOD

It is easier for a camel to go through the eye of a needle, than for a rich man to enter into the kingdom of God.

Matthew 19:24

Suffer the little children to come unto me, and forbid them not: for of such is the kingdom of God.

Mark 10:14

Blessed be ye poor: for yours is the kingdom of God.

Luke 6:20

See also: CHRISTIAN, CHURCH, HEAVEN.

KNOWLEDGE

The fear of the Lord is the beginning of knowledge.

Proverbs 1:7

In much wisdom is much grief: and he that increaseth knowledge increaseth sorrow.

Ecclesiastes 1:18

They are wise to do evil, but to do good they have no knowledge.

Jeremiah 4:22

My people are destroyed for lack of knowledge: because thou hast rejected knowledge, I will also reject thee.

Hosea 4:6

Knowledge puffeth up, but charity edifieth.

1 Corinthians 8:1

Be filled with the knowledge of his will in all wisdom and spiritual understanding.

Colossians 1:9

See also: UNDERSTANDING, WISDOM.

L

LAW

The law of the Lord is perfect, converting the soul: the testimony of the Lord is sure, making wise the simple.

Psalms 19:7

He that keepeth the law, happy is he.

Proverbs 29:18

Think not that I am come to destroy the law, or the prophets: I am not come to destroy, but to fulfil.

Matthew 5:17

It is easier for heaven and earth to pass, than one tittle of the law to fail.

Luke 16:17

The law was given by Moses, but grace and truth came by Jesus Christ.

John 1:17

Not the hearers of the law are just before God, but the doers of the law shall be justified.

Romans 2:13

A man is justified by faith without the deeds of the law.

Romans 3:28

He that loveth another hath fulfilled the law.

Romans 13:8

This is the love of God, that we keep his commandments.

1 Timothy 1:8

See also: JUSTICE, LOVE, OBEDIENCE.

LENDING: *see* BORROWING.

LIBERTY

Proclaim liberty throughout all the land unto all the inhabitants thereof.

Leviticus 25:10

I will walk at liberty: for I seek thy precepts.

Psalms 119:45

The creature itself also shall be delivered from the bondage of corruption into the glorious liberty of the children of God.

Romans 8:21

See also: FREEDOM.

LIFE

I would not live alway: let me alone; for my days are vanity.

Job 7:16

Lord, make me to know mine end, and the measure of my days, what it is; that I may know how frail I am.

Psalms 39:4

Strait is the gate, and narrow is the way, which leadeth unto life.

Matthew 7:14

He that findeth his life shall lose it: and he that loseth his life for my sake shall find it.

Matthew 10:39

In him was life; and the life was the light of men.

John 1:4

I am the bread of life.

John 6:35

I am come that they might have life, and that they might have it more abundantly.

John 10:10

I am the way, the truth, and the life: no man cometh unto the Father, but by me.

John 14:6

The gift of God is eternal life.

Romans 6:23

To live is Christ, and to die is gain.

Philippians 1:21

What is your life? It is even a vapour, that appeareth for a little time, and then vanisheth away.

James 4:14

Be thou faithful unto death, and I will give thee a crown of life.

Revelation 2:10

See also: DEATH, IMMORTALITY.

LIGHT

The commandment is a lamp: and the law is light.

Proverbs 6:23

The Lord is my light and my salvation.

Psalms 27:1

I am the light of the world: he that followeth me shall not walk in darkness, but shall have the light of life.

John 8:12

Ye are the light of the world.

Matthew 5:14

If we walk in the light, as he is in the light, we have fellowship one with another, and the blood of Jesus Christ his Son cleanseth us from all sin.

1 John 1:7

See also: CHRIST, GOODNESS, TRUTH.

LOVE

Thou shalt love thy neighbour as thyself.

Leviticus 19:18

The stranger that dwelleth with you shall be unto you as one born among you, and thou shalt love him as thyself.

Leviticus 19:34

Thy love to me was wonderful, passing the love of women.

2 Samuel 1:26

Love your enemies.

Matthew 5:44

A new commandment I give unto you, That ye love one another; as I have loved you, that ye also love one another.

John 13:34

Love is the fulfilling of the law.

Romans 13:10

All the law is fulfilled in one word, even in this; Thou shalt love thy neighbour as thyself.

Galatians 5:14

Whom the Lord loveth he chasteneth.

Hebrews 12:6

Beloved, let us love one another; for love is of God; and every one that loveth is born of God, and knoweth God. He that loveth not knoweth not God; for God is love.

1 John 4:7

He that loveth not knoweth not God; for God is love.

1 John 4:8

If we love one another, God dwelleth in us, and his love is perfected in us.

1 John 4:12

This is the love of God, that we keep his commandments.

1 John 5:3

Love covereth a multitude of sins.

1 Peter 4:8

See also: CHARITY, FRIENDSHIP, KINDNESS.

LUST

Lust not after her beauty in thine heart; neither let her take thee with her eyelids.

Proverbs 6:25

The cares of this world, and the deceitfulness of riches, and the lusts of other things entering in, choke the word, and it becometh unfruitful.

Mark 4:19

When lust hath conceived, it bringeth forth sin: and sin, when it is finished, bringeth forth death.

James 1:15

All that is in the world, the lust of the flesh, and the lust of the eyes, and the pride of life, is not of the Father, but is of the world.

1 John 2:16

See also: ADULTERY, DESIRE.

LYING: *see* FALSEHOOD.

M

MALICE

Workers of iniquity, which speak peace to their neighbours, but mischief is in their hearts.

Psalms 28:3

He that seeketh mischief, it shall come unto him.

Proverbs 11:27

A righteous man regardeth the life of his beast: but the tender mercies of the wicked are cruel.

Proverbs 12:10

Let all bitterness, and wrath, and anger, and clamour, and evil speaking, be put away from you, with all malice.

Ephesians 4:31

See also: ANGER, HATE, INJUSTICE.

MAN

So God created man in his own image, in the image of God created he him; male and female created he them.

Genesis 1:27

The Lord God formed man of the dust of the ground, and breathed into his nostrils the breath of life; and man became a living soul.

Genesis 2:7

Man doth not live by bread only.

Deuteronomy 8:3

Shall a man be more pure than his maker?

Job 4:17

Man that is born of a woman is of few days, and full of trouble. He cometh forth like a flower, and is cut down: he fleeth also as a shadow and continueth not.

Job 14:1, 2

What is man, that thou art mindful of him? Thou hast made him a little lower than the angels.

Psalms 8:4, 5

As for man, his days are as grass: as a flower of the field, so he flourisheth.

Psalms 103:15

I am fearfully and wonderfully made.

Psalms 139:14

We are the clay, and thou [Lord] our potter.

Isaiah 64:8

Thus saith the Lord; Cursed be the man that trusteth in man.

Jeremiah 17:5

The first man is of the earth, earthy.

1 Corinthians 15:47

See also: BROTHERHOOD, CREATION.

MARRIAGE

It is not good that the man should be alone.

Genesis 2:18

What therefore God hath joined together, let not man put asunder.

Matthew 19:6

When they shall rise from the dead, they neither marry, nor are given in marriage; but are as the angels which are in heaven.

Mark 12:25

It is better to marry than to burn.

1 Corinthians 7:9

He that is married careth for the things that are of the world, how he may please his wife. She that is married careth for the things of the world, how she may please her husband.

1 Corinthians 7:33, 34

For this cause shall a man leave his father and mother, and shall be joined unto his wife, and they two shall be one flesh.

Ephesians 5:31

See also: ADULTERY, CELIBACY, WOMAN.

MEDITATION

His delight is in the law of the Lord, and in his law doth he meditate day and night.

Psalms 1:2

I will meditate also of all thy work, and talk of thy doings.

Psalms 77:12

Whatsoever things are true, whatsoever things are honest, whatsoever things are just, whatsoever things are pure, whatsoever things are lovely, whatsoever things are of good report; if there be any virtue, and if there be any praise, think on these things.

Philippians 4:8

See also: PRAYER.

MEEKNESS

Blessed are the meek: for they shall inherit the earth.

Matthew 5:5

Take my yoke upon you, and learn of me; for I am meek and lowly in heart: and ye shall find rest unto your souls.

Matthew 11:29

The fruit of the Spirit is love, joy, peace, longsuffering, gentleness, goodness, faith, Meekness, temperance.

Galatians 5:22, 23

Walk worthy of the vocation wherewith ye are called, With all lowliness and meekness, with longsuffering, forbearing one another in love.

Ephesians 4:1, 2

Follow after righteousness, godliness, faith, love, patience, meekness.

1 Timothy 6:11

See also: HUMILITY, RESIGNATION.

MERCY

The wicked borroweth, and prayeth not again: but the righteous sheweth mercy, and giveth.

Psalms 37:21

Let not mercy and truth forsake thee: bind them about thy neck; write them upon the table of thine heart.

Proverbs 3:3

The merciful man doeth good to his own soul.

Proverbs 11:17

He that hath mercy on the poor, happy is he.

Proverbs 14:21

What doth the Lord require of thee, but to do justly, and to love mercy, and to walk humbly with thy God?

Micah 6:8

Blessed are the merciful: for they shall obtain mercy.

Matthew 5:7

See also: FORGIVENESS, LOVE.

MIND

I delight in the law of God after the inward man: But I see another law in my members, warring against the law of my mind, and bringing me into captivity to the law of sin.

Romans 7:22, 23

Let every man be fully persuaded in his own mind.

Romans 14:5

For God hath not given us the spirit of fear; but of power, and of love, and of a sound mind.

2 Timothy 1:7

See also: KNOWLEDGE, UNDERSTANDING.

MINISTRY

Let thy priests be clothed with righteousness.

Psalms 132:9

Behold, I send you forth as sheep in the midst of wolves: be ye therefore wise as serpents, and harmless as doves.

Matthew 10:16

Go, stand and speak in the temple to the people all the words of this life.

Acts 5:20

How beautiful are the feet of them that preach the gospel of peace, and bring glad tidings of good things!

Romans 10:15

He gave some, apostles; and some, prophets; and some, evangelists; and some, pastors and teachers.

Ephesians 4:11

If a man desire the office of a bishop, he desireth a good work. A bishop then must be blameless, the husband of one wife, vigilant, sober, of good behaviour, given to hospitality, apt to teach; Not given to wine, no striker, not greedy of filthy lucre; but patient, not a brawler, not covetous; One

that ruleth well his own house, having his children in subjection with gravity; (For if a man know not how to rule his own house, how shall he take care of the church of God?) Not a novice, lest being lifted up with pride he fall into the condemnation of the devil. Moreover he must have a good report of them which are without; lest he fall into reproach and the snare of the devil.

1 Timothy 3:1–7

A bishop must be blameless, as the steward of God; not selfwilled, not soon angry, not given to wine, no striker, not given to filthy lucre; But a lover of hospitality, a lover of good men, sober, just, holy, temperate; Holding fast the faithful word as he hath been taught, that he may be able by sound doctrine both to exhort and to convince the gainsayers.

Titus 1:7–9

As every man hath received the gift, even so minister the same one to another, as good stewards of the manifold grace of God. If any man minister, let him do it as of the ability which God giveth.

1 Peter 4:10, 11

See also: ORDINATION, SERVICE.

MONEY

The love of money is the root of all evil.

1 Timothy 6:10

Teaching things which they ought not, for filthy lucre's sake.

Titus 1:11

See also: GIVING, POVERTY, RICHES.

MORTALITY

We must needs die, and are as water spilt on the ground, which cannot be gathered up again.

2 Samuel 14:14

Man that is born of a woman is of few days, and full of trouble. He cometh forth like a flower, and is cut down: he fleeth also as a shadow, and continueth not.

Job 14:1, 2

The living know that they shall die.

Ecclesiastes 9:5

All flesh is grass, and all the goodliness thereof is as the flower of the field: The grass withereth, the flower fadeth.

Isaiah 40:6, 7

See also: DEATH, LIFE.

MOTHER

And Adam called his wife's name Eve; because she was the mother of all living.
Genesis 3:20

Despise not thy mother when she is old.
Proverbs 23:22

Her children arise up, and call her blessed.
Proverbs 31:28

As is the mother, so is her daughter.
Ezekiel 16:44

See also: PARENT.

N

NATURE

The heavens declare the glory of God; and
the firmament sheweth his handywork.
Psalms 19:1

Doth not even nature itself teach you.
1 Corinthians 11:14

That was not first which is spiritual, but that
which is natural; and afterward that which
is spiritual.
1 Corinthians 15:46

See also: CREATION.

NEIGHBOR

Withdraw thy foot from thy neighbour's
house; lest he be weary of thee, and so hate
thee.
Proverbs 25:17

Better is a neighbour that is near than a
brother far off.
Proverbs 27:10

Hast thou heard a word against thy neighbor?
Let it die within thee, trusting that it will
not burst thee.
Ecclesiasticus 19:10

Love thy neighbour as thyself.
Matthew 19:19

See also: BROTHERHOOD, CHARITY, LOVE.

O

OBEDIENCE

All that the Lord hath said will we do, and
be obedient.
Exodus 24:7

When thou art in tribulation, and all these
things are come upon thee, even in the latter
days, if thou turn to the Lord thy God, and
shalt be obedient unto his voice; (For the
Lord thy God is a merciful God;) he will not
forsake thee, neither destroy thee, nor forget
the covenant of thy fathers which he sware
unto them.
Deuteronomy 4:30, 31

We ought to obey God rather than men.
Acts 5:29

Ye have purified your souls in obeying the
truth.
1 Peter 1:22

See also: LAW, LOVE, WORSHIP.

OMNIPOTENCE

I know that thou canst do every thing.
Job 42:2

With God all things are possible.
Matthew 19:26

The Lord God omnipotent reigneth.
Revelation 19:6

See also: GOD, POWER.

OMNIPRESENCE

Will God indeed dwell on the earth? behold,
the heaven and the heaven of heavens cannot
contain thee.
1 Kings 8:27

Whither shall I go from thy spirit? or whither
shall I flee from thy presence?
Psalms 139:7

The eyes of the Lord are in every place, beholding the evil and the good.
Proverbs 15:3

Can any hide himself in secret places that I shall not see him? saith the Lord. Do I not fill heaven and earth? saith the Lord.

Jeremiah 23:24

See also: GOD.

OMNISCIENCE

I know thy abode, and thy going out, and thy coming in.

2 Kings 19:27

The Lord searcheth all hearts, and understandeth all the imaginations of the thoughts.

1 Chronicles 28:9

Great is our Lord, and of great power: his understanding is infinite.

Psalms 147:5

The very hairs of your head are all numbered.

Matthew 10:29

Known unto God are all his works from the beginning of the world.

Acts 15:18

See also: GOD, KNOWLEDGE, WISDOM.

OPPRESSION

Thou shalt neither vex a stranger, nor oppress him: for ye were strangers in the land of Egypt.

Exodus 22:21

Ye shall not oppress one another.

Leviticus 25:14

He delivereth the poor in his affliction, and openeth their ears in oppression.

Job 36:15

The Lord also will be a refuge for the oppressed, a refuge in times of trouble.

Psalms 9:9

Surely oppression maketh a wise man mad.

Ecclesiastes 7:7

Is not this the fast that I have chosen? to loose the bands of wickedness, to undo the heavy burdens, and to let the oppressed go free.

Isaiah 58:6

See also: PERSECUTION, SUFFERING.

ORDINATION

The Lord hath anointed me to preach good tidings.

Isaiah 61:1

I ordained thee a prophet unto the nations.

Jeremiah 1:5

Ye have not chosen me, but I have chosen you, and ordained you, that ye should go and bring forth fruit, and that your fruit should remain.

John 15:16

See also: CHURCH, MINISTRY, SERVICE.

P

PARENT

Honour thy father and thy mother.

Exodus 10:12

My son, hear the instruction of thy father, and forsake not the law of thy mother.

Proverbs 1:8

He that wasteth his father, and chaseth away his mother, is a son that causeth shame, and bringeth reproach.

Proverbs 19:26

Hearken unto thy father that begat thee, and despise not thy mother when she is old.

Proverbs 23:22

He that loveth father or mother more than me is not worthy of me.

Matthew 10:37

Children, obey your parents in the Lord: for this is right. Honour thy father and mother; which is the first commandment with promise.

Ephesians 6:1, 2

Fathers, provoke not your children to anger, lest they be discouraged.

Colossians 3:21

See also: CHILDREN, INSTRUCTION, MOTHER.

PATIENCE

Rest in the Lord, and wait patiently for him.

Psalms 37:7

In your patience possess ye your souls.
Luke 21:19

By patient continuance in well doing seek for glory and honour and immortality.
Romans 2:7

Tribulation worketh patience; And patience, experience; and experience, hope.
Romans 5:3, 4

Rejoicing in hope; patient in tribulation.
Romans 12:12

Be patient toward all men.
1 Thessalonians 5:14

The Lord direct your hearts into the love of God, and into the patient waiting for Christ.
2 Thessalonians 3:5

The servant of the Lord must not strive; but be gentle unto all men, apt to teach, patient.
2 Timothy 2:24

What glory is it, if, when ye be buffeted for your faults, ye shall take it patiently? but if, when ye do well, and suffer for it, ye take it patiently, this is acceptable with God.
1 Peter 2:20

See also: MEEKNESS, SUFFERING.

PATRIOTISM

Righteousness exalteth a nation.
Proverbs 14:34

Blessed is the nation whose God is the Lord.
Psalms 33:12

Render therefore unto Caesar the things that are Caesar's, and unto God the things that are God's.
Mark 12:17

See also: FIDELITY.

PEACE

The Lord will bless his people with peace.
Psalms 29:11

Mark the perfect man, and behold the upright: for the end of that man is peace.
Psalms 37:37

Great peace have they which love thy law: and nothing shall offend them.
Psalms 119:165

Peace be within thy walls, and prosperity within thy palaces.
Psalms 122:7

When a man's ways please the Lord, he maketh even his enemies to be at peace with him.
Proverbs 16:7

His name shall be called . . . The Prince of Peace.
Isaiah 9:6

Thou wilt keep him in perfect peace, whose mind is stayed on thee: because he trusteth in thee.
Isaiah 26:3

They have healed also the hurt of the daughter of my people slightly, saying, Peace, peace, when there is no peace.
Jeremiah 6:14

Blessed are the peacemakers: for they shall be called children of God.
Matthew 5:9

Think not that I am come to send peace on earth: I came not to send peace, but a sword.
Matthew 10:34

Glory to God in the highest, and on earth peace, good will toward men.
Luke 2:14

Peace be to this house.
Luke 10:5

Peace I leave with you, my peace I give unto you.
John 14:27

If it be possible, as much as lieth in you, live peaceably with all men.
Romans 12:18

The peace of God, which passeth all understanding.
Philippians 4:7

To be spiritually minded is life and peace.
Romans 8:6

See also: BROTHERHOOD, LOVE, WAR.

PERFECTION

Thou shalt be perfect with the Lord thy God.
Deuteronomy 18:13

Be ye therefore perfect, even as your Father which is in heaven is perfect.

Matthew 5:48

We preach, warning every man, and teaching every man in all wisdom; that we may present every man perfect in Jesus Christ.

Colossians 1:28

Let us go on unto perfection.

Hebrews 6:1

Whoso keepeth his word, in him verily is the love of God perfected.

1 John 2:5

If we love one another, God dwelleth in us, and his love is perfected in us.

1 John 4:12

See also: CHARITY, HOLINESS.

PERSECUTION

The wicked watcheth the righteous, and seeketh to slay him.

Psalms 37:32

Blessed are they which are persecuted for righteousness' sake: for theirs is the kingdom of heaven. Blessed are ye, when men shall revile you, and persecute you, and shall say all manner of evil against you falsely, for my sake. Rejoice, and be exceedingly glad: for great is your reward in heaven: for so persecuted they the prophets which were before you.

Matthew 5:10–12

I take pleasure in infirmities, in reproaches, in necessities, in persecutions, in distresses for Christ's sake: for when I am weak, then am I strong.

2 Corinthians 12:10

See also: OPPRESSION, SUFFERING.

PIETY

Blessed is the man that feareth the Lord, that delighteth greatly in his commandments.

Psalms 112:1

Blessed is every one that feareth the Lord; that walketh in his ways.

Psalms 128:1

Learn first to shew piety at home.

1 Timothy 5:4

See also: RIGHTEOUSNESS, WORSHIP.

PITY

It is of the Lord's mercies that we are not consumed, because his compassions fail not.

Lamentations 3:22

Be ye all of one mind, having compassion one of another.

1 Peter 3:8

See also: MERCY, SYMPATHY.

PLEASURE

He that loveth pleasure shall be a poor man: he that loveth wine and oil shall not be rich.

Proverbs 21:17

I said in mine heart, Go to now, I will prove thee with mirth, therefore enjoy pleasure: and, behold, this also is vanity.

Ecclesiastes 2:1

That which fell among thorns are they, which, when they have heard, go forth, and are choked with cares and riches and pleasures of this life, and bring no fruit to perfection.

Luke 8:14

She that liveth in pleasure is dead while she liveth.

1 Timothy 5:6

See also: CONTENTMENT, JOY.

PLENTY

He that tilleth his land shall have plenty of bread.

Proverbs 28:19

The harvest truly is plenteous, but the labourers are few.

Matthew 9:37

My God shall supply all your need according to his riches in glory by Christ Jesus.

Philippians 4:19

See also: RICHES.

POSSESSIONS

The upright shall have good things in possession.

Proverbs 28:10

He that putteth his trust in me shall possess the land, and shall inherit my holy mountain.

Isaiah 57:13

Unto every one that hath shall be given, and he shall have abundance: but from him that hath not shall be taken away even that which he hath.

Matthew 25:29

As poor, yet making many rich; as having nothing, yet possessing all things.

2 Corinthians 6:10

See also: COVETOUSNESS, RICHES.

POVERTY

If thy brother be waxen poor, and fallen in decay with thee; then shalt thou relieve him.

Leviticus 25:35

The needy shall not always be forgotten: the expectation of the poor shall not perish for ever.

Psalms 9:18

Blessed is he that considereth the poor: the Lord will deliver him in time of trouble.

Psalms 41:1

Defend the poor and fatherless: do justice to the afflicted and needy.

Psalms 82:3

The destruction of the poor is their poverty.

Proverbs 10:15

There is that maketh himself rich, yet hath nothing: there is that maketh himself poor, yet hath great riches.

Proverbs 13:7

Whoso mocketh the poor reproacheth his Maker.

Proverbs 17:5

The rich and the poor meet together: the Lord is the maker of them all.

Proverbs 22:2

Better is a poor and a wise child than an old and foolish king, who will no more be admonished.

Ecclesiastes 4:13

What mean ye that ye beat my people to pieces, and grind the faces of the poor? saith the Lord God of Hosts.

Isaiah 3:15

Blessed are the poor in spirit: for theirs is the kingdom of heaven.

Matthew 5:3

The poor always ye have with you.

John 12:8

We should remember the poor.

Galatians 2:10

See also: ALMS, CHARITY, GIVING, RICHES.

POWER

All power is given unto me in heaven and in earth.

Matthew 28:18

The powers that be are ordained of God.

Romans 13:1

But we have this treasure in earthen vessels, that the excellency of the power may be of God, and not of us.

2 Corinthians 4:7

Now unto him that is able to do exceeding abundantly above all that we ask or think, according to the power that worketh in us. Unto him be glory in the church by Christ Jesus.

Ephesians 3:20, 21

See also: ABILITY, STRENGTH.

PRAISE

I will call on the Lord, who is worthy to be praised.

2 Samuel 22:4

I will praise thee, O Lord my God, with all my heart: and I will glorify thy name for evermore.

Psalms 86:12

Praise the Lord, call upon his name, declare his doings among all the people, make mention that his name is exalted.

Isaiah 12:4

Let us offer the sacrifice of praise to God continually.

Hebrews 13:15

See also: GLORY, THANKSGIVING.

PRAYER

When thou prayest, thou shalt not be as the hypocrites are: for they love to pray standing in the synagogues and in the corners of the streets, that they may be seen of men. . . . But thou, when thou prayest, enter into thy closet, and when thou hast shut thy door, pray to thy Father which is in secret; and thy

Father which seeth in secret shall reward thee openly.

Matthew 6:5, 6

Your Father knoweth what things ye have need of, before ye ask him.

Matthew 6:8

Ask, and it shall be given you; seek, and ye shall find; knock, and it shall be opened unto you.

Matthew 7:7

What things soever ye desire, when ye pray, believe that ye receive them, and ye shall receive them.

Mark 11:24

Lord, teach us to pray.

Luke 11:1

Men ought always to pray, and not to faint.

Luke 18:1

Pray without ceasing.

1 Thessalonians 5:17

Pray for us.

2 Thessalonians 3:1

The prayer of faith shall save the sick, and the Lord shall raise him up; and if he have committed sins, they shall be forgiven. Confess your faults one to another, and pray one for another, that ye may be healed. The effectual fervent prayer of a righteous man availeth much.

James 5:15, 16

See also: MEDITATION, WORSHIP.

PREACHING

It pleased God by the foolishness of preaching to save them that believe.

1 Corinthians 1:21

For we preach not ourselves, but Christ Jesus the Lord.

2 Corinthians 4:5

Preach the word; be instant in season, out of season; reprove, rebuke, exhort with all long-suffering and doctrine.

2 Timothy 4:2

See also: BIBLE, MINISTRY.

PREPARATION

Prepare your hearts unto the Lord, and serve him only.

1 Samuel 7:3

Go to the ant, thou sluggard; consider her ways, and be wise: Which having no guide, overseer, or ruler, Provideth her meat in summer, and gathereth her food in the harvest.

Proverbs 6:6-8

Prepare ye the way of the Lord, make straight in the desert a highway for our God.

Isaiah 40:3

Be ye also ready: for in such an hour as ye think not the Son of man cometh.

Matthew 24:44

See also: HEAVEN, IMMORTALITY.

PRIDE

When pride cometh, then cometh shame: but with the lowly is wisdom.

Proverbs 11:2

Only by pride cometh contention.

Proverbs 13:10

The Lord will destroy the house of the proud.

Proverbs 15:25

Pride goeth before destruction, and an haughty spirit before a fall.

Proverbs 16:18

A man's pride shall bring him low: but honour shall uphold the humble in spirit.

Proverbs 29:23

Pride is hateful before God and man.

Ecclesiasticus 10:7

Pride is the beginning of sin.

Ecclesiasticus 10:13

Whosoever shall exalt himself shall be abased; and he that shall humble himself shall be exalted.

Matthew 23:12

He that is greatest among you, let him be as the younger; and he that is chief, as he that doth serve.

Luke 22:26

God resisteth the proud, and giveth grace to the humble.

1 Peter 5:5

See also: BOASTING, CONCEIT.

PROPHET

If the prophet be deceived when he hath spoken a thing, I the Lord have deceived that prophet, and I will stretch out my hand upon him, and will destroy him.

Ezekiel 14:9

Your sons and your daughters shall prophesy, your old men shall dream dreams, your young men shall see visions.

Joel 2:28

Beware of false prophets, which come to you in sheep's clothing, but inwardly they are ravening wolves.

Matthew 7:15

A prophet is not without honour, but in his own country, and among his own kin, and in his own house.

Mark 6:4

We know in part, and we prophesy in part.

1 Corinthians 13:9

See also: MINISTRY, ORDINATION, SERVICE.

PROTECTION

He shall give his angels charge over thee, to keep thee in all thy ways.

Psalms 91:11

My God is the rock of my refuge.

Psalms 94:22

Who is he that will harm you, if ye be followers of that which is good?

1 Peter 3:13

See also: PROVIDENCE.

PROVIDENCE

God will provide.

Genesis 22:8

The lot is cast into thy lap; but the whole disposing thereof is of the Lord.

Proverbs 16:33

He maketh his sun to rise on the evil and on the good, and sendeth rain on the just and on the unjust.

Matthew 5:45

Take no thought of your life, what ye shall eat.

Luke 12:22

See also: GOD, PROTECTION.

PRUDENCE

A fool's wrath is presently known: but a prudent man covereth shame.

Proverbs 12:16

A prudent man concealeth knowledge: but the heart of fools proclaimeth foolishness.

Proverbs 12:23

The simple believeth every word: but the prudent man looketh well to his going.

Proverbs 14:15

A prudent man foreseeth the evil, and hideth himself: but the simple pass on, and are punished.

Proverbs 22:3

Who is wise, and he shall understand these things? prudent, and he shall know them? for the ways of the Lord are right, and the just shall walk in them: but the transgressors shall fall therein.

Hosea 14:9

See also: COUNSEL, WISDOM.

PURITY

With the pure thou wilt show thyself pure.

2 Samuel 22:27

Shall a man be more pure than his maker?

Job 4:17

Blessed are the pure in heart: for they shall see God.

Matthew 5:8

Whatsoever things are pure . . . think on these things.

Philippians 4:8

Unto the pure all things are pure.

Titus 1:15

And every man that hath this hope in him purifieth himself, even as he is pure.

1 John 3:3

See also: RIGHTEOUSNESS.

R

RECONCILIATION

If when we were enemies, we were reconciled to God by the death of his Son; much more, being reconciled, we shall be saved by his life.

Romans 5:10

God was in Christ, reconciling the world unto himself, not imputing their trespasses unto them; and hath committed unto us the word of reconciliation.

2 Corinthians 5:19

In all things it behoved him to be made like unto his brethren, that he might be a merciful and faithful high priest in things pertaining to God, to make reconciliation for the sins of the people.

Hebrews 2:17

See also: REDEMPTION, SALVATION.

REDEMPTION

Surely he hath borne our griefs, and carried our sorrows: yet we did esteem him stricken, smitten of God, and afflicted. But he was wounded for our transgressions, he was bruised for our iniquities: the chastisement of our peace was upon him; and with his stripes we are healed.

Isaiah 53:4, 5

The Son of man came not to be ministered unto, but to minister, and to give his life a ransom for many.

Matthew 20:28

I am the good shepherd: the good shepherd giveth his life for the sheep.

John 10:10

Of him are ye in Christ Jesus, who of God is made unto us wisdom, and righteousness, and sanctification, and redemption.

1 Corinthians 1:30

God sent forth his Son, made of a woman, made under the law, To redeem them that were under the law, that we might receive the adoption of sons.

Galatians 4:4, 5

In whom we have redemption through his blood, the forgiveness of sins, according to the riches of his grace.

Ephesians 1:7

In whom we have redemption through his blood, even the forgiveness of sins.

Colossians 1:14

Who gave himself for us, that he might redeem us from all iniquity, and purify unto himself a peculiar people, zealous of good works.

Titus 2:14

Neither by the blood of goats and calves, but by his own blood he entered in once into the holy place, having obtained eternal redemption for us.

Hebrews 9:12

Ye were not redeemed with corruptible things, as silver and gold, from your vain conversation received by tradition from your fathers; But with the precious blood of Christ, as of a lamb without blemish and without spot.

1 Peter 1:18, 19

See also: RECONCILIATION, SALVATION.

REGENERATION

A new heart also will I give you, and a new spirit will I put within you: and I will take away the stony heart out of your flesh, and I will give you an heart of flesh.

Ezekiel 36:26

The wind bloweth where it listeth, and thou hearest the sound thereof, but canst not tell whence it cometh, and whither it goeth: so is every one that is born of the Spirit.

John 3:8

Every one that doeth righteousness is born of him.

1 John 2:29

We know that we have passed from death unto life, because we love the brethren.

1 John 3:14

Whosoever believeth that Jesus is the Christ is born of God.

1 John 5:1

According to his mercy he saved us, by the washing of regeneration, and renewing of the Holy Ghost.

Titus 3:5

See also: BAPTISM, CONVERSION.

REJOICING

Make a joyful noise unto the Lord, all ye lands.

Psalms 100:1

I will greatly rejoice in the Lord, my soul shall be joyful in my God; for he hath clothed me with the garments of salvation, he hath covered me with the robe of righteousness.

Isaiah 61:10

Rejoice in the Lord alway: and again I say, Rejoice.

Philippians 4:4

Rejoice, inasmuch as ye are partakers of Christ's sufferings; that, when his glory shall be revealed, ye may be glad also with exceeding joy.

1 Peter 4:13

See also: CHEERFULNESS, HAPPINESS, JOY.

RELIGION

Fear God, and keep his commandments: for this is the whole duty of man.

Ecclesiastes 12:13

If any man among you seem to be religious, and bridleth not his tongue, but deceiveth his own heart, this man's religion is vain. Pure religion and undefiled before God and the Father is this: To visit the fatherless and widows in their affliction, and to keep himself unspotted from the world.

James 1:26, 27

See also: DUTY, PIETY, WORSHIP.

RENUNCIATION

Whosoever will come after me let him deny himself, and take up his cross, and follow me.

Mark 8:34

There is no man that hath left house, or parents, or brethren, or wife, or children, for the kingdom of God's sake, Who shall not receive manifold more in this present time, and in the world to come life everlasting.

Luke 18:29, 30

He must increase, but I must decrease.

John 3:30

They that are Christ's have crucified the flesh with the affections and lusts.

Galatians 5:24

See also: ABSTINENCE, TEMPERANCE.

REPENTANCE

Let the wicked forsake his way, and the unrighteous man his thoughts; and let him return unto the Lord, and he will have mercy upon him; and to our God, for he will abundantly pardon.

Isaiah 55:7

Repent ye: for the kingdom of heaven is at hand.

Matthew 3:2

I came not to call the righteous, but sinners to repentance.

Mark 2:17

Except ye repent, ye shall all likewise perish.

Luke 13:3

Joy shall be in heaven over one sinner that repenteth, more than over ninety and nine just persons, which need no repentance.

Luke 15:7

Repent ye, therefore, and be converted that your sins may be blotted out.

Acts 3:19

Godly sorrow worketh repentance to salvation not to be repented of.

2 Corinthians 7:10

See also: CONFESSION, CONVERSION.

REPROOF

Let the righteous smite me; it shall be a kindness: and let him reprove me; it shall be an excellent oil, which shall not break my head.

Psalms 141:5

Reprove not a scorner, lest he hate thee: rebuke a wise man, and he will love thee.

Proverbs 9:8

All things that are reproved are made manifest by the light: for whatsoever doth make manifest is light.

Ephesians 5:13

Preach the word; be instant in season, out of season; reprove, rebuke, exhort with all long-suffering and doctrine.

2 Timothy 4:2

See also: GOOD AND EVIL, JUDGMENT.

RESIGNATION

Naked came I out of my mother's womb, naked shall I return thither: the Lord gave, and the Lord hath taken away; blessed be the name of the Lord.

Job 1:21

It is good for me that I have been afflicted; that I might learn thy statutes.

Psalms 119:7

If it be possible, let this cup pass from me: nevertheless not as I will, but as thou wilt.

Matthew 26:39

I have learned, in whatsoever state I am, therewith to be content.

Philippians 4:11

Be content with such things as ye have.

Hebrews 13:5

See also: MEEKNESS, PATIENCE.

RESPONSIBILITY

Every man shall be put to death for his own sin.

Deuteronomy 24:16

If ye were blind, ye should have no sin: but now ye say, We see; therefore your sin remaineth.

John 9:41

Every one of us shall give account of himself to God.

Romans 4:12

Work out your own salvation with fear and trembling.

Philippians 2:12

See also: DUTY.

RESURRECTION

Many of them that sleep in the dust of the earth shall awake, some to everlasting life, and some to shame and everlasting contempt.

Daniel 12:2

The hour is coming, in the which all that are in the graves shall hear his voice, and shall come forth; they that have done good, unto the resurrection of life; and they that have done evil, unto the resurrection of damnation.

John 5:28, 29

My flesh shall rest in hope.

Acts 2:26

Why should it be thought a thing incredible with you, that God should raise the dead?

Acts 26:8

For since by man came death, by man came also the resurrection of the dead. For as in Adam all die, even so in Christ shall all be made alive.

1 Corinthians 15:21, 22

See also: HEAVEN, IMMORTALITY, LIFE.

RETRIBUTION

Thus saith the Lord God, I will even deal with thee as thou hast done.

Ezekiel 16:59

He that keepeth the commandment keepeth his own soul; but he that despiseth his ways shall die.

Proverbs 19:16

According to their deeds, accordingly he will repay, fury to his adversaries, recompense to his enemies.

Isaiah 59:18

Whosoever will save his life shall lose it: but whosoever will lose his life for my sake, the same shall save it.

Luke 9:24

If ye live after the flesh, ye shall die: but if ye through the Spirit do mortify the deeds of the body, ye shall live.

Romans 8:13

Whatsoever a man soweth, that shall he also reap.

Galatians 6:7

He that doeth wrong shall receive for the wrong which he hath done: and there is no respect of persons.

Colossians 3:25

See also: JUSTICE, REWARD.

REVERENCE

Ye shall keep my sabbaths, and reverence my sanctuary: I am the Lord.

Leviticus 19:30

God is greatly to be feared in the assembly of the saints, and to be had in reverence of all them that are about him.

Psalms 89:7

Holy and reverend is his name.

Psalms 111:9

At the name of Jesus every knee should bow.

Philippians 2:10

Let us have grace, whereby we may serve God acceptably with reverence and godly fear.

Hebrews 12:28

See also: WORSHIP.

REWARD

The Lord knoweth the days of the upright: and their inheritance shall be for ever.

Psalms 37:18

According to their deeds, accordingly he will repay.

Isaiah 59:18

He shall reward every man according to his works.

Matthew 16:27

Love ye your enemies, and do good, and lend, hoping for nothing again; and your reward shall be great.

Luke 6:35

Cast not away therefore your confidence, which hath great recompense of reward.

Hebrews 10:35

See also: HEAVEN, RETRIBUTION.

RICHES

The Lord maketh poor, and maketh rich: he bringeth low, and lifteth up.

1 Samuel 2:7

He heapeth up riches, and knoweth not who shall gather them.

Psalms 39:6

Be not thou afraid when one is made rich, when the glory of his house is increased; For when he dieth he shall carry nothing away: his glory shall not descend after him.

Psalms 49:16, 17

The rich man is wise in his own conceit; but the poor that hath understanding searcheth him out.

Proverbs 28:11

A faithful man shall abound with blessings: but he that maketh haste to be rich shall not be innocent.

Proverbs 28:20

The sleep of a labouring man is sweet, whether he eat little or much: but the abundance of the rich will not suffer him to sleep.

Ecclesiastes 5:12

It is easier for a camel to go through the eye of a needle, than for a rich man to enter into the kingdom of God.

Matthew 19:24

Woe unto you that are rich! for ye have received your consolation. Woe unto you that are full! for ye shall hunger.

Luke 6:24

See also: BLESSING, GIFT, POVERTY.

RIGHTEOUSNESS

Mercy and truth are met together; righteousness and peace have kissed each other.

Psalms 85:10

The desire of the righteous is only good.

Proverbs 11:23

The wicked flee when no man pursueth: but the righteous are bold as a lion.

Proverbs 28:1

The work of righteousness shall be peace; and the effect of righteousness quietness and assurance for ever.

Isaiah 32:17

Be not righteous over much; neither make thyself over wise.

Ecclesiastes 7:16

Blessed are they which do hunger and thirst after righteousness: for they shall be filled.

Matthew 5:6

Put on the new man, which after God is created in righteousness and true holiness.

Ephesians 4:24

The fruit of righteousness is sown in peace of them that make peace.

James 3:18

See also: GOODNESS, INTEGRITY.

S

SABBATH

God blessed the seventh day, and sanctified it: because that in it he had rested from all his work which God created and made.

Genesis 2:3

Remember the sabbath day, to keep it holy. Six days shalt thou labour, and do all thy work: but the seventh day is the sabbath of the Lord thy God.

Exodus 20:8-10

Six years thou shalt sow thy field, and six years thou shalt prune thy vineyard, and gather in the fruit thereof; but in the seventh year shall be a sabbath of rest unto the land, a sabbath for the Lord: thou shalt neither sow thy field, nor prune thy vineyard.

Leviticus 25:3, 4

See also: WORSHIP.

SACRIFICE

To obey is better than sacrifice, and to hearken than the fat of rams.

1 Samuel 15:22

Neither will I offer burnt offerings unto the Lord my God of that which doth cost me nothing.

2 Samuel 24:24

Offer the sacrifices of righteousness.

Psalms 4:5

Go ye and learn what that meaneth, I will have mercy and not sacrifice.

Matthew 9:13

Greater love hath no man than this, that a man lay down his life for his friends.

John 15:13

I am crucified with Christ.

Galatians 2:20

Sacrifice and offering thou wouldest not, but a body hast thou prepared me.

Hebrews 10:5

Offer up spiritual sacrifices.

1 Peter 2:5

See also: REDEMPTION, WORKS, GOOD.

SADNESS: *see* SORROW.

SAINT

The Lord . . . forsaketh not his saints.

Psalms 37:28

Precious in the sight of the Lord is the death of his saints.

Psalms 116:15

See also: GOODNESS, RIGHTEOUSNESS.

SALVATION

The Lord is my strength and song, and he is become my salvation.

Exodus 15:2

The Lord is my light and my salvation; whom shall I fear? the Lord is the strength of my life; of whom shall I be afraid?

Psalms 27:1

Keep ye judgment, and do justice: for my salvation is near to come, and my righteousness to be revealed.

Isaiah 56:1

She shall bring forth a son, and thou shalt call his name Jesus: for he shall save his people from their sins.

Matthew 1:21

All flesh shall see the salvation of God.

Luke 3:6

Salvation is of the Jews.

John 4:22

I am the door: by me if any man enter in, he shall be saved.

John 10:9

Neither is there salvation in any other: for there is none other name under heaven given among men, whereby we must be saved.

Acts 4:12

If thou shalt confess with thy mouth the Lord Jesus, and shalt believe in thine heart that God hath raised him from the dead, thou shalt be saved.

Romans 10:9

Whosoever shall call upon the name of the Lord shall be saved.

Romans 10:13

The preaching of the cross is to them that perish, foolishness; but unto us which are saved, it is the power of God.

1 Corinthians 1:18

Behold, now is the accepted time; behold, now is the day of salvation.

2 Corinthians 6:2

By grace are ye saved through faith; and that not of yourselves; it is the gift of God.

Ephesians 2:8

Work out your own salvation with fear and trembling.

Philippians 2:12

The grace of God that bringeth salvation hath appeared to all men.

Titus 2:11

Being made perfect, he became the author of eternal salvation unto all them that obey him.

Hebrews 5:9

Lay apart all filthiness and superfluity of naughtiness, and receive with meekness the engrafted word, which is able to save your souls.

James 1:21

See also: CHRIST, RECONCILIATION, REDEMPTION, SOUL.

SCRIPTURE: *see* BIBLE.

SELF-DENIAL

If any man will come after me, let him deny himself, and take up his cross, and follow me.

Matthew 16:24

Greater love hath no man than this, that a man lay down his life for his friends.

John 15:13

Present your bodies a living sacrifice, holy, acceptable unto God.

Romans 12:1

See also: RENUNCIATION.

SELFISHNESS

If ye do good to them which do good to you, what thank have ye?

Luke 6:33

Let no man seek his own.

1 Corinthians 10:24

Look not every man on his own things, but every man also on the things of others.

Philippians 2:4

Whoso hath the world's good, and seeth his brothers hath need, and shutteth up his bowels of compassion from him, how dwelleth the love of God in him?

1 John 3:17

See also: AVARICE, RICHES.

SELF-RIGHTEOUSNESS

If I justify myself, mine own mouth shall condemn me.

Job 9:20

All the ways of a man are clean in his own eyes; but the Lord weigheth the spirits.

Proverbs 16:2

Woe unto them that are wise in their own eyes, and prudent in their own sight!

Isaiah 5:21

Which say, Stand by thyself, come not near to me; for I am holier than thou. These are a smoke in my nose, a fire that burneth all the day.

Isaiah 65:5

Ye are they which justify yourselves before men; but God knoweth your hearts.

Luke 16:15

They being ignorant of God's righteousness, and going about to establish their own righteousness, have not submitted themselves unto the righteousness of God.

Romans 10:3

Let him that thinketh he standeth take heed lest he fall.

1 Corinthians 10:12

See also: BIGOTRY, CONCEIT, HYPROCRISY.

SERVICE

Serve the Lord with fear, and rejoice with trembling.

Psalms 2:11

Here am I; send me.

Isaiah 6:8

Come, ye blessed of my Father, inherit the kingdom prepared for you from the foundation of the world: For I was an hungred, and ye gave me meat: I was thirsty, and ye gave me drink: I was a stranger, and ye took me in: Naked, and ye clothed me: I was sick, and ye visited me: I was in prison, and ye came unto me.

Matthew 25:34-36

We are unprofitable servants: we have done that which was our duty to do.

Luke 17:10

Present your bodies a living sacrifice, holy, acceptable unto God, which is your reasonable service.

Romans 12:1

Be kindly affectioned one to another with brotherly love; in honour preferring one another; Not slothful in business; fervent in spirit; serving the Lord.

Romans 12:10, 11

By love serve one another.

Galatians 5:13

As the servants of Christ, doing the will of God from the heart; With good will doing service, as to the Lord, and not to men: Knowing that whatsoever good thing any man doeth, the same shall he receive of the Lord.

Ephesians 6:6-8

Whatsoever ye do, do it heartily, as to the Lord, and not unto men; Knowing that of the Lord ye shall receive the reward of the inheritance: for ye serve the Lord Christ.

Colossians 3:23, 24

God is not unrighteous to forget your work and labour of love, which ye have shewed toward his name, in that ye have ministered to the saints, and do minister.

Hebrews 6:10

If a brother or sister be naked, and destitute of daily food, and one of you say unto them, Depart in peace, be ye warmed and filled; notwithstanding ye give them not those things which are needful to the body; what doth it profit?

James 2:15, 16

See also: GIVING; HELP; WORKS, GOOD.

SIN

If thou, Lord, shouldest mark iniquities, O Lord, who shall stand?

Psalms 130:3

One sinner destroyeth much good.

Ecclesiastes 9:18

The way of sinners is made plain with stones but at the end thereof is the pit of hell.

Ecclesiasticus 21:10

Though your sins be as scarlet, they shall be white as snow.

Isaiah 1:18

He that is without sin among you, let him first cast a stone.

John 8:7

Wherefore, as by one man sin entered into the world, and death by sin; and so death passed upon all men, for that all have sinned.

Romans 5:12

The wages of sin is death.

Romans 6:23

There is nothing unclean of itself: but to him that esteemeth any thing to be unclean, to him it is unclean.

Romans 14:14

When lust hath conceived, it bringeth forth sin: and sin, when it is finished, bringeth forth death.

James 1:15

To him that knoweth to do good, and doeth it not, to him it is sin.

James 4:17

If we say that we have no sin, we deceive ourselves, and the truth is not in us.

1 John 1:8

He that committeth sin is of the devil.

1 John 3:8

See also: EVIL, FORGIVENESS, MALICE.

SINCERITY

Fear the Lord, and serve him in sincerity and in truth.

Joshua 24:14

Grace be with all them that love our Lord Jesus Christ in sincerity.

Ephesians 6:24

This I pray . . . That ye may approve things that are excellent; that ye may be sincere and without offence till the day of Christ.

Philippians 1:9, 10

Laying aside all malice, and all guile, and hypocrisies, and envies, and all evil speakings, As newborn babes, desire the sincere milk of the word, that ye may grow thereby.

1 Peter 2:1, 2

See also: INTEGRITY, RIGHTEOUSNESS.

SLANDER

Thou shalt not raise a false report: put not thine hand with the wicked to be an unrighteous witness.

Exodus 23:1

Whoso privily slandereth his neighbour, him will I cut off.

Psalms 101:5

He that hideth hatred with lying lips, and he that uttereth a slander, is a fool.

Proverbs 10:18

Blessed are ye, when men shall revile you, and persecute you, and shall say all manner of evil against you falsely, for my sake.

Matthew 5:11

Do violence to no man, neither accuse any falsely.

Luke 3:14

He that speaketh evil of his brother, and judgeth his brother, speaketh evil of the law, and judgeth the law.

James 4:11

See also: FALSEHOOD.

SLOTH

By much slothfulness the building decayeth; and through idleness of the hands the house droppeth through.

Ecclesiastes 10:18

Not slothful in business; fervent in spirit; serving the Lord.

Romans 12:11

Be not slothful, but followers of them who through faith and patience inherit the promises.

Hebrews 6:12

See also: RETRIBUTION, SERVICE.

SOBRIETY

Aged men be sober, grave, temperate, sound in faith, in charity, in temperance.

Titus 2:2

Teach the young women to be sober.

Titus 2:4

The end of all things is at hand: be ye therefore sober, and watch unto prayer.

1 Peter 4:7

See also: ABSTINENCE, TEMPERANCE.

SORROW

Sorrow is better than laughter: for by the sadness of the countenance the heart is made better.

Ecclesiastes 7:3

Surely he hath borne our griefs, and carried our sorrows.

Isaiah 53:4

Is it nothing to you, all ye that pass by? behold, and see if there be any sorrow like unto my sorrow.

Lamentations 1:12

Ye shall weep and lament, but the world will rejoice; and ye shall be sorrowful, but your sorrow shall be turned into joy.

John 16:20

Godly sorrow worketh repentance to salvation not to be repented of.

2 Corinthians 7:10

See also: SUFFERING.

SOUL

And the Lord God formed man of the dust of the ground, and breathed into his nostrils the breath of life; and man became a living soul.

Genesis 2:7

My soul is continually in my hand.

Psalms 119:109

I shall go softly all my years in the bitterness of my soul.

Isaiah 38:15

Fear not them which kill the body, but are not able to kill the soul.

Matthew 10:28

For what is a man profited, if he shall gain
the whole world, and lose his own soul? or
what shall a man give in exchange for his
soul?

Matthew 16:26

My soul doth magnify the Lord.

Luke 1:46

Thou fool, this night thy soul shall be required of thee.

Luke 12:20

In your patience possess ye your souls.

Luke 21:19

Abstain from fleshly lusts, which war against
the soul.

1 Peter 2:11

See *also*: LIFE, SPIRIT.

SPIRIT

The spirit of a man will sustain his infirmity
but a wounded spirit who can bear?

Proverbs 18:14

Then shall the dust return to the earth as it
was: and the spirit shall return unto God who
gave it.

Ecclesiastes 12:7

With my soul have I desired thee in the
night; yea, with my spirit within me will I
seek thee early.

Isaiah 29:9

A new heart also will I give you, and a new
spirit will I put within you.

Ezekiel 36:26

The spirit indeed is willing, but the flesh is
weak.

Matthew 26:41

Into thy hands I commend my spirit.

Luke 23:46

It is the spirit that quickeneth.

John 6:63

The first Adam was made a living soul; the
last Adam was made a quickening spirit.

1 Corinthians 15:45

Not of the letter, but of the spirit: for the
letter killeth, but the spirit giveth life.

2 Corinthians 3:6

See *also*: DESIRE, LIFE, SOUL.

STAR

Let there be lights in the firmament of the
heaven to divide the day from the night.

Genesis 1:14

When the morning stars sang together, and
all the sons of God shouted for joy.

Job 38:7

Canst thou bind the sweet influences of
Pleiades, or the loose bands of Orion?

Job 38:31

I am the root and offspring of David, and the
bright and morning star.

Revelation 22:16

See *also*: CREATION, HEAVEN.

STRENGTH

God is our refuge and our strength, a **very**
present help in trouble.

Psalms 46:1

A wise man is strong; yea, a man of knowledge increaseth strength.

Proverbs 24:5

They that wait on the Lord shall renew their
strength; they shall mount up with wings as
eagles; they shall run, and not be weary;
and they shall walk, and not faint.

Isaiah 40:31

My grace is sufficient for thee: for my
strength is made perfect in weakness.

2 Corinthians 12:9

Be strong in the Lord, and in the power of
his might.

Ephesians 6:10

I can do all things through Christ which
strengtheneth me.

Philippians 4:13

See *also*: OMNIPOTENCE, POWER.

SUFFERING

Like as a woman with child, that draweth
near the time of her delivery, is in pain, and
crieth out in her pangs; so have we been in
thy sight, O Lord.

Isaiah 26:17

He was wounded for our transgressions, he
was bruised for our iniquities.

Isaiah 53:5

I reckon that the sufferings of this present time are not worthy to be compared with the glory which shall be revealed in us.

Romans 8:18

Christ also suffered for us, leaving us an example, that ye should follow his steps.

1 Peter 2:21

Rejoice, inasmuch as ye are partakers of Christ's sufferings; that, when his glory shall be revealed, ye may be glad also with exceeding joy.

1 Peter 4:13

See also: AFFLICTION, PERSECUTION, SORROW.

SYMPATHY

Rejoice with them that do rejoice, and weep with them that weep.

Romans 12:15

See also: COMFORT, MERCY.

T

TEMPERANCE

The drunkard and glutton shall come to poverty.

Proverbs 23:21

Every man that striveth for the mastery is temperate in all things.

1 Corinthians 9:25

Be not drunk with wine, wherein is excess.

Ephesians 5:18

Add to your faith virtue; and to virtue knowledge; And to knowledge temperance.

2 Peter 1:5, 6

See also: ABSTINENCE, RENUNCIATION.

TEMPTATION

A violent man enticeth his neighbour, and leadeth him into the way that is not good.

Proverbs 16:29

Lead us not into temptation, but deliver us from evil.

Matthew 6:13

God is faithful, who will not suffer you to be tempted above that ye are able; but will

with the temptation also make a way to escape, that ye may be able to bear it.

1 Corinthians 10:13

In that he himself hath suffered being tempted, he is able to succour them that are tempted.

Hebrews 2:18

Blessed is the man that endureth temptation: for when he is tried, he shall receive the crown of life, which the Lord hath promised to them that love him.

James 1:12

Be vigilant; because your adversary the devil, as a roaring lion, walketh about, seeking whom he may devour.

1 Peter 5:8

Because thou hast kept the word of my patience, I also will keep thee from the hour of temptation.

Revelation 3:10

See also: CHASTITY, DEVIL, EVIL, SIN.

THANKSGIVING

We thy people and sheep of thy pasture will give thee thanks for ever: we will shew forth thy praises to all generations.

Psalms 79:13

It is a good thing to give thanks unto the Lord.

Psalms 92:1

In every thing by prayer and supplication with thanksgiving let your requests be made known unto God.

Philippians 4:6

Whatsoever ye do in word or deed, do all in the name of the Lord Jesus, giving thanks to God and the Father by him.

Colossians 3:17

In every thing give thanks.

1 Thessalonians 5:18

Every creature of God is good, and nothing to be refused, if it be received with thanksgiving.

1 Timothy 4:4

Let us offer the sacrifice of praise to God continually, that is, the fruit of our lips giving thanks to his name.

Hebrews 13:5

See also: PRAISE.

TIME

A thousand years in thy sight are but as yesterday when it is past, and as a watch in the night.

Psalms 90:4

To every thing there is a season, and a time to every purpose under the heaven.

Ecclesiastes 3:1

There is . . . a time to be born, and a time to die; a time to plant, and a time to pluck up that which is planted; A time to kill, and a time to heal; a time to break down, and a time to build up; A time to weep, and a time to laugh; a time to mourn, and a time to dance. . . . A time to love, and a time to hate.

Ecclesiastes 3:1–8

Our time is a very shadow that passeth away.

Wisdom 2:5

Can ye not discern the signs of the times?

Matthew 16:3

See also: ETERNITY, IMMORTALITY.

TRINITY

There are three that bear record in heaven, the Father, the Word, and the Holy Ghost: and these three are one.

1 John 5:7

See also: GOD, HOLY GHOST.

TROUBLE

Man is born unto trouble, as the sparks fly upward.

Job 5:7

Man that is born of a woman is of few days, and full of trouble.

Job 14:1

Call upon me in the day of trouble: I will deliver thee, and thou shalt glorify me.

Psalms 50:15

Let not your heart be troubled: ye believe in God, believe also in me.

John 14:1

See also: AFFLICTION, SORROW, SUFFERING.

TRUST

Though he slay me, yet will I trust in him.

Job 13:15

In God have I put my trust: I will not be afraid what man can do unto me.

Psalms 56:11

Put not your trust in princes.

Psalms 146:3

Trust . . . in the living God.

1 Timothy 6:17

See also: FAITH, HOPE.

TRUTH

Mercy and truth are met together; righteousness and peace have kissed each other.

Psalms 85:10

Buy the truth, and sell it not.

Proverbs 23:23

Grace and truth came by Jesus Christ.

John 1:17

If ye continue in my word, then are ye my disciples indeed; And ye shall know the truth, and the truth shall make you free.

John 8:31, 32

I am the way, the truth, and the life.

John 14:6

When he, the Spirit of truth, is come, he will guide you into all truth.

John 16:13

Every one that is of the truth heareth my voice.

John 18:37

Wherefore putting away lying, speak every man truth with his neighbour.

Ephesians 4:25

See also: FALSEHOOD, SINCERITY.

U

UNBELIEF

The fool hath said in his heart, There is no God.

Psalms 14:1

If ye will not believe, surely ye shall not be established.

Isaiah 7:9

Lord, I believe: help thou mine unbelief.

Mark 9:24

He that believeth and is baptized shall be saved; but he that believeth not shall be damned.

Mark 16:16

He that believeth on the Son hath everlasting life: and he that believeth not the Son shall not see life; but the wrath of God abideth on him.

John 3:36

Except ye see signs and wonders, ye will not believe.

John 4:48

If I do not the works of my Father, believe me not. But if I do, though ye believe not me, believe the works: that ye may know, and believe, that the Father is in me, and I in him.

John 10:37

How then shall they call on him in whom they have not believed? and how shall they believe in him of whom they have not heard?

Romans 10:14

I obtained mercy, because I did it ignorantly in unbelief.

1 Timothy 1:13

Take heed, brethren, lest there be in any of you an evil heart of unbelief, in departing from the living God.

Hebrews 3:12

See also: FAITH, INFIDELITY.

UNDERSTANDING

O that they were wise, that they understood this, that they would consider their latter end!

Deuteronomy 32:29

I have given thee a wise and understanding heart.

1 Kings 3:12

I have more understanding than all my teachers: for thy testimonies are my meditation.

Psalms 119:99

Wisdom is the principal thing; therefore get wisdom: and with all thy getting get understanding.

Proverbs 4:7

I will pray with the spirit, and I will pray with the understanding also: and I will sing with the spirit, and I will sing with the understanding also.

1 Corinthians 14:15

Be not children in understanding: howbeit in malice be ye children, but in understanding be men.

1 Corinthians 14:20

See also: KNOWLEDGE, WISDOM.

V

VENGEANCE

To me belongeth vengeance, and recompence.

Deuteronomy 32:35

Jealousy is the rage of a man: therefore he will not spare in the day of vengeance.

Proverbs 6:34

Avenge not yourselves, but rather give place unto wrath: for it is written, Vengeance is mine; I will repay, saith the Lord.

Romans 12:19

If thine enemy hunger, feed him; if he thirst, give him drink: for in so doing thou shalt heap coals of fire on his head.

Romans 12:20

Not rendering evil for evil, or railing for railing: but contrariwise blessing.

1 Peter 3:9

See also: HATE, RETRIBUTION, WRATH.

VIGILANCE

I watch, and am as a sparrow alone upon the house top.

Psalms 102:7

If the goodman of the house had known in what watch the thief would come, he would have watched, and would not have suffered his house to be broken up.

Matthew 24:43

Take ye heed, watch and pray: for ye know not when the time is.

Mark 13:33

Blessed are those servants, whom the Lord when he cometh shall find watching.

Luke 12:37

Watch ye, stand fast in the faith, quit you like men, be strong.

1 Corinthians 16:13

Continue in prayer, and watch in the same with thanksgiving.

Colossians 4:2

Let us not sleep, as do others; but let us watch and be sober.

1 Thessalonians 5:6

Blessed is he that watcheth.

Revelation 16:15

See also: DEATH, RIGHTEOUSNESS.

VIRGIN BIRTH

Now all this was done, that it might be fulfilled which was spoken of the Lord by the prophet, saying, Behold, a virgin shall be with child, and shall bring forth a son, and they shall call his name Emmanuel, which being interpreted is, God with us.

Matthew 1:22, 23

See also: CHRIST.

VISION

Where there is no vision, the people perish.

Proverbs 29:18

I have multiplied visions, and used similitudes.

Hosea 12:10

And it shall come to pass afterward, that I will pour out my spirit upon all flesh; and your sons and your daughters shall prophesy, your old men shall dream dreams, your young men shall see visions.

Joel 2:28

Write the vision, and make it plain upon tables, that he may run that readeth it.

Habakkuk 2:2

Whereupon, O King Agrippa, I was not disobedient unto the heavenly vision.

Acts 26:19

See also: HEAVEN, PROPHET.

VOW

When thou shalt vow a vow unto the Lord thy God, thou shalt not slack to pay it: for the Lord thy God will surely require it of thee.

Deuteronomy 23:21

Pay thy vows unto the most High.

Psalms 50:14

When thou vowest a vow unto God, defer not to pay it.

Ecclesiastes 5:4

Thou shalt not forswear thyself, but shalt perform unto the Lord thine oaths.

Matthew 5:33

Swear not, neither by heaven, neither by the earth, neither by any other oath: but let your yea be yea; and your nay, nay.

James 5:12

See also: BAPTISM, DUTY, MARRIAGE.

W

WAR

I am for peace: but when I speak, they are for war.

Psalms 120:7

He shall judge among the nations, and shall rebuke many people; and they shall beat their swords into plowshares, and their spears into pruninghooks: nation shall not lift up sword against nation, neither shall they learn war any more.

Isaiah 2:4

Thou art my battle axe and weapons of war: for with these will I break in pieces the nations.

Jeremiah 51:20

Love your enemies.

Luke 6:27

No man that warreth entangleth himself with the affairs of this life; that he may please him who hath chosen him to be a soldier.

2 Timothy 2:4

Ye fight and war, yet ye have not, because ye ask not.

James 4:2

See also: CONTENTION.

WEALTH: *see* RICHES.

WISDOM

The price of wisdom is above rubies.
Job 28:18

Great men are not always wise.
Job 32:9

So teach us to number our days, that we may apply our hearts unto wisdom.
Psalms 90:12

In much wisdom is much grief.
Ecclesiastes 1:18

Be ye therefore wise as serpents, and harmless as doves.
Matthew 10:16

The wisdom of this world is foolishness with God.
1 Corinthians 3:19

See also: KNOWLEDGE, PRUDENCE.

WOMAN

And the rib, which the Lord God had taken from man, made he a woman and brought her unto the man. And Adam said, This is now bone of my bones, and flesh of my flesh: she shall be called Woman, because she was taken out of Man.
Genesis 2:22

It is better to dwell in a corner of the housetop, than with a brawling woman in a wide house.
Proverbs 21:9

See also: MAN, MARRIAGE.

WONDER

Declare his glory among the heathen, his wonders among all people.
Psalms 96:3

His name shall be called Wonderful.
Isaiah 9:6

How great are his signs! and how mighty are his wonders!
Daniel 4:3

Jesus of Nazareth, a man approved of God among you by miracles and wonders and

signs, which God did by him in the midst of you, as ye yourselves also know.
Acts 2:22

See also: CREATION, HEAVEN.

WORK

In the sweat of thy face shalt thou eat bread.
Genesis 3:19

Six days shalt thou work, but on the seventh day thou shalt rest.
Exodus 34:21

All things are full of labour; man cannot utter it: the eye is not satisfied with seeing, nor the ear filled with hearing.
Ecclesiastes 1:8

I must work the works of him that sent me, while it is day: the night cometh, when no man can work.
John 9:4

The labourer is worthy of his hire.
Luke 10:7

See also: INDUSTRIOUSNESS; WORKS, GOOD.

WORKS, GOOD

Let your light so shine before men, that they may see your good works, and glorify your Father which is in heaven.
Matthew 5:16

Do good to them that hate you.
Matthew 5:44

Do works meet for repentance.
Acts 26:20

As we have therefore opportunity, let us do good unto all men.
Galatians 6:10

Be not weary in well doing.
2 Thessalonians 3:13

Rich in good works.
1 Timothy 6:18

Be ye doers of the word, and not hearers only.
James 1:22

Faith, if it hath not works, is dead.
James 2:17

Shew me thy faith without thy works, and I will shew thee my faith by my works.

James 2:18

As the body without the spirit is dead, so faith without works is dead also.

James 2:20

By works a man is justified, and not by faith only.

James 2:24

Let us not love in word, neither in tongue; but in deed. .

1 John 3:18

See also: CHARITY, GIVING, SACRIFICE.

WORLD

Know ye not that the friendship of the world is emnity with God? whosoever therefore will be a friend of the world, is the enemy of God.

James 4:4

For all that is in the world, the lust of the flesh, and the lust of the eyes, and the pride of life, is not of the Father, but is of the world.

1 John 2:16

See also: LUST.

WORRY

Why art thou cast down, O my soul? and why art thou disquieted within me? hope in God.

Psalms 43:5

Fear thou not; for I am with thee.

Isaiah 41:10

Which of you by taking thought can add one cubit unto his stature?

Matthew 6:27

Take therefore no thought for the morrow: for the morrow shall take thought for the things of itself. Sufficient unto the day is the evil thereof.

Matthew 6:34

Thou art . . . troubled about many things: but one thing is needful.

Luke 10:41, 42

See also: ANXIETY, CARE, COURAGE.

WORSHIP

Worship the Lord in the beauty of holiness.

1 Chronicles 16:29

All the earth shall worship thee, and shall sing unto thee; they shall sing to thy name.

Psalms 66:4

O come, let us worship and bow down: let us kneel before the Lord our maker. For he is our God; and we are the people of his pasture, and the sheep of his hand.

Psalms 95:6, 7

I was glad when they said unto me, Let us go into the house of the Lord.

Psalms 122:1

I will worship toward thy holy temple, and praise thy name for thy lovingkindness and for thy. truth: for thou hast magnified thy word above all thy name.

Psalms 138:2

For where two or three are gathered together in my name, there am I in the midst of them.

Matthew 18:20

Thou shalt worship the Lord thy God, and him only shalt thou serve.

Luke 4:8

God is a Spirit: and they that worship him must worship him in spirit and in truth.

John 4:24

I bow my knees unto the Father of our Lord Jesus Christ

Ephesians 3:14

At the name of Jesus every knee should bow, of things in heaven, and things in earth, and things under the earth; and that every tongue should confess that Jesus Christ is Lord, to the glory of God the Father.

Philippians 2:10, 11

All nations shall come and worship before thee.

Revelation 15:4

See also: DUTY, GOD, IDOL, SERVICE.

WRATH

Wrath killeth the foolish man.

Job 5:2

A soft answer turneth away wrath.

Proverbs 15:1

Let not the sun go down upon your wrath.

Ephesians 4:26

See also: ANGER.

Y

YOUTH

Thou shalt rise up before the hoary head, and honour the face of the old man, and fear thy God: I am the Lord.

Leviticus 19:32

My son, hear the instruction of thy father, and forsake not the law of thy mother.

Proverbs 1:8

Rejoice, O young man, in thy youth; and let thy heart cheer thee in the days of thy youth, and walk in the ways of thine heart, and in the sight of thine eyes: but know thou, that for all these things God will bring thee into judgment.

Ecclesiastes 11:9

Remember now thy Creator in the days of thy youth, while the evil days come not, nor the years draw nigh, when thou shalt say, I have no pleasure in them.

Ecclesiastes 12:1

It is good for a man that he bear the yoke in his youth.

Lamentations 3:27

Let no man despise thy youth.

1 Timothy 4:12

Young men likewise exhort to be sober minded.

Titus 2:6

Likewise, ye younger, submit yourselves unto the elder. Yea, all of you be subject one to another, and be clothed with humility: for God resisteth the proud, and giveth grace to the humble.

1 Peter 5:5

See also: AGE.

Z

ZEAL

Come with me, and see my zeal for the Lord.

2 Kings 10:16

A zeal of God, but not according to knowledge.

Romans 10:2

Forasmuch as ye are zealous of spiritual gifts, seek that ye may excel to the edifying of the church.

1 Corinthians 14:12

It is good to be zealously affected always in a good thing.

Galatians 4:18

See also: CHURCH, LOVE, SERVICE.

Thoughts
from
Shakespeare

My words fly up, my thoughts remain below:

Words without thoughts, never to heaven go.

Hamlet. Act III. Sc. 3

A

ABHORRENCE

Shall they hoist me up,
And show me to the shouting varletry
Of censuring Rome? Rather a ditch in Egypt
Be gentle grave unto me, rather on Nilus'
mud
Lay me stark naked, and let the water-flies
Blow me into abhorring!
Antony and Cleopatra. Act V. Sc. 2

Therefore I say again,
I utterly abhor, yea from my soul,
Refuse you for my judge; whom yet once
more,
I hold my most malicious foe, and think not
At all a friend to truth.
Henry VIII. Act II. Sc. 4

Whilst I was big in clamour, came there in a
man,
Who having seen me in my worst estate,
Shunn'd my abhorr'd society.
King Lear. Act V. Sc. 3

He will come to her in yellow stockings, and
'tis a colour she abhors; and cross gartered,
a fashion she detests.
Twelfth Night. Act II. Sc. 5

See also: ENEMY, HATE.

ABILITY

Whose skill was almost as great as his honesty; had it stretched so far, would have made nature immortal, and death should have play for lack of work.
All's Well That Ends Well. Act I. Sc. 1

Sure, he that made us with such large discourse,
Looking before and after, gave us not
That capability and godlike reason
To fust in us unused.
Hamlet. Act IV. Sc. 2

That which ordinary men are fit for, I am
qualified in; and the best of me is diligence.
King Lear Act I. Sc. 4

Out of my lean and low ability I'll lend you
something.
Twelfth Night. Act III. Sc. 4

See also: POWER, STRENGTH.

ABSENCE

I dote on his very absence, and I wish them
a fair departure.
Merchant of Venice. Act I. Sc. 2

All days are nights to see till I see thee,
And nights bright days when dreams do show
thee me.
Sonnet XLIII

How like a winter hath my absence been
From thee, the pleasure of the fleeting year!
What freezings have I felt, what dark days
seen!
What old December's bareness everywhere.
Sonnet XCVII

See also: MEETING, MEMORY, PARTING.

ACCIDENT

I have shot mine arrow o'er the house
And hurt my brother.
Hamlet. Act V. Sc. 2

Wherein I spake of most disastrous chances,
Of moving accidents by flood and field.
Othello. Act I. Sc. 3

As the unthought-on accident is guilty
Of what we wildly do, so we profess
Ourselves to be the slaves of chance, and
flies
Of every wind that blows.
Winter's Tale. Act IV. Sc. 3

See also: CHANCE, FORTUNE.

ACTION

In such business
Action is eloquence, and the eyes of the ignorant
More learned than the ears.

Coriolanus. Act III. Sc. 2

Suit the action to the word, the word to the action.

Hamlet. Act III. Sc. 2

The blood more stirs
To rouse a lion, than to start a hare.

Henry IV. Pt. I. Act I. Sc. 3

We must not stint
Our necessary actions, in the fear
To cope malicious censurers.

Henry VIII. Act I. Sc. 2

Things done well,
And with a care, exempt themselves from fear;
Things done without example, in their issue
Are to be fear'd.

Henry VIII. Act I. Sc. 2

If it were done, when 'tis done, then 'twere well
It were done quickly.

Macbeth. Act I. Sc. 7

So smile the Heavens upon this holy act
That after-hours with sorrow chide us not!

Romeo and Juliet. Act II. Sc. 6

We may not think the justness of each act
Such and no other then event doth form it.

Troilus and Cressida. Act II. Sc. 2

How my achievements mock me!
I will go meet them.

Troilus and Cressida. Act IV. Sc. 2

See also: DEED, LABOR, WORK.

ACTOR AND ACTRESS

Like a dull actor now,
I have forgotten my part, and I am out,
Even to a full disgrace.

Coriolanus. Act V. Sc. 3

Good, my lord, will you see the players well bestowed? Do you hear, let them be well used; for they are the abstracts, and brief chronicles of the time. After your death you were better have a bad epitaph, than their ill report while you lived.

Hamlet. Act II. Sc. 2

Speak the speech, I pray you, as I pronounced it to you, trippingly on the tongue; but if you mouth it, as many of your players do, I had as lief the town-crier spoke my lines. Nor do not saw the air too much with your hands thus; but use all gently; for in the very torrent, tempest, (and as I may say) the whirlwind of passion, you must acquire and beget a temperance that may give it smoothness.

Hamlet. Act III. Sc. 2

O, there be players that I have seen play,— and heard others praise, and that highly— not to speak it profanely, that neither, having the accent of Christians, nor the gait of Christian, pagan, nor man, have so strutted and bellowed, that I have thought some of nature's journeymen had made men, and not made them well, they imitated humanity so abominably.

Hamlet. Act III. Sc. 2

See also: THEATER.

ADMIRATION

Season your admiration for a while.

Hamlet. Act I. Sc. 2

Nor shall this peace sleep with her; but as when
The bird of wonder dies, the maiden phoenix,
Her ashes new-create another heir
As great in admiration as herself.

Henry VIII. Act III. Sc. 2

What you do
Still betters what is done. When you speak, sweet,
I'd have you do it ever.

Winter's Tale. Act IV. Sc. 3

See also: APPLAUSE, FAME, PRAISE.

ADVERSITY

Sweet are the uses of adversity;
Which, like the toad, ugly and venomous,
Wears yet a precious jewel in his head.

As You Like It. Act II. Sc. 1

They can be meek that have no other cause,
A wretched soul, bruis'd with adversity,
We bid be quiet, when we hear it cry.

Comedy of Errors. Act II. Sc. 1

Bold adversity
Cries out for noble York and Somerset,
To beat assailing death from his weak legions.
And whiles the honourable captain there

Drops bloody sweat from his war wearied
   limbs.
Henry VI. Pt. I. Act IV. Sc. 4

His overthrow heap'd happiness upon him;
For then, and not till then, he felt himself,
And found the blessedness of being little.
Henry VIII. Act IV. Sc. 2

Then know, that I have little wealth to lose;
A man I am cross'd with adversity.
Two Gentlemen of Verona. Act IV. Sc. 1

See also: AFFLICTION, GRIEF, LOSS, MISERY.

ADVICE

When a wise man gives thee better counsel,
give me mine again.
King Lear. Act II. Sc. 4

Here comes a man of comfort, whose advice
Hath often still'd my brawling discontent.
Measure for Measure. Act IV. Sc. 1

I pray thee cease thy counsel,
Which falls into mine ears as profitless
As water in a sieve.
Much Ado About Nothing. Act V. Sc. 1

Direct not him, whose way himself will
   choose;
'Tis breath thou lack'st, and that breath wilt
   thou lose.
Richard II. Act II. Sc. 1

See also: EDUCATION, EXPERIENCE.

AFFECTION

        So loving to my mother,
That he might not beteem the winds of
   heaven
Visit her face too roughly.
Hamlet. Act I. Sc. 2

Then let thy love be younger than thyself,
Or thy affection cannot hold the bent.
Twelfth Night. Act II. Sc. 4

Affection is a coal that must be cool'd;
Else suffer'd it will set the heart on fire.
Venus and Adonis

See also: FRIEND, LOVE, WOOING.

AFFLICTION

    Henceforth I'll bear
Affliction till it do cry out itself,
Enough, enough, and die.
King Lear. Act IV. Sc. 6

Thou art a soul in bliss; but I am bound
Upon a wheel of fire; that mine own tears
Do scald like molten lead.
King Lear. Act IV. Sc. 7

Affliction is enamour'd of thy parts,
And thou art wedded to calamity.
Romeo and Juliet. Act III. Sc. 3

See also: ADVERSITY, MISFORTUNE.

AGE, OLD

For we are old, and on our quick'st decrees
The inaudible and noiseless foot of time
Steals ere we can effect them.
All's Well that Ends Well. Act V. Sc. 3

Though I look old, yet I am strong and lusty;
For in my youth I never did apply
Hot and rebellious liquors in my blood;
Nor did not with unbashful forehead woo
The means of weakness and debility;
Therefore my age is as a lusty winter,
Frosty, but kindly.
As You Like It. Act II. Sc. 3

And his big manly voice,
Turning again towards childish treble, pipes
And whistles in his sound.
As You Like It. Act II. Sc. 7

Though now this grained face of mine be hid
In sap-consuming winter's drizzle snow,
And all the conduits of my blood froze up,
Yet hath my night of life some memory.
Comedy of Errors. Act V. Sc. 1

      What should we speak of
When we are old as you? When we shall hear
The rain and wind beat dark December.
Cymbeline. Act III. Sc. 3

An old man is twice a child.
Hamlet. Act II. Sc. 2

        At your age,
The hey-day in the blood is tame, it's humble,
And waits upon the judgment.
Hamlet. Act III. Sc. 4

Some smack of age in you, some relish of the
saltness of time.
Henry IV. Pt. II. Act I. Sc. 2

Begin to patch up thine old body for heaven.
Henry IV. Pt. II. Act II. Sc. 4

Minutes, hours, days, weeks, months, and
   years.
Pass'd over to the end they were created,
Would bring white hairs unto a quiet grave.
Ah, what a life were this!
Henry VI. Pt. III. Act II. Sc. 5

         O father Abbot,
An old man, broken with the storms of State,
Is come to lay his weary bones among ye;
Give him a little earth for charity.
Henry VIII. Act IV. Sc. 2

      His silver hairs
Will purchase us a good opinion,
And buy men's voices to commend our deeds.
Julius Caesar. Act II. Sc. 1

As you are old and reverend, should be wise.
King Lear. Act I. Sc. 4

        O, heavens,
If you do love old men, if your sweet sway
Allow obedience, if you yourselves are old,
Make it your cause.
King Lear. Act II. Sc. 4

       You are old;
Nature in you stands on the very verge
Of her confine.
King Lear. Act II. Sc. 4

You see me here, you gods, a poor old man,
As full of grief as age; wretched in both.
King Lear. Act II. Sc. 4

Pray, do not mock me:
I am a very foolish fond old man,
Fourscore and upward; and, to deal plainly,
I fear I am not in my perfect mind.
King Lear. Act IV. Sc. 7

      My way of life
Is fallen into the sear, the yellow leaf:
And that which should accompany old age,
As honor, love, obedience, troops of friends,
I must not look to have; but, in their stead,
Curses not loud, but deep, mouth-honor,
   breath,
Which the poor heart would fain deny, and
   dare not.
Macbeth. Act V. Sc. 3

Superfluity comes sooner by white hairs, but
competency lives longer.
Merchant of Venice. Act I. Sc. 2

When the age is in, the wit is out.
Much Ado About Nothing. Act III. Sc. 5

The wrinkles which thy glass will truly show,
   Of mouthed graves will give thee memory,
Thou by thy dial's shady stealth maiest know,
   Time's thievish progress to eternity.
Sonnet LXXII.

Men shut their doors against a setting sun.
Timon of Athens. Act I. Sc. 2

Give me a staff of honor for mine age,
But not a sceptre to control the world.
Titus Andronicus. Act I. Sc. 2

See also: CHILDREN, PAST, TIME, YOUTH.

AGONY

Mirth cannot move a soul in agony.
Love's Labour's Lost. Act V. Sc. 2

See also: AFFLICTION, MISERY, TRIAL.

AGRICULTURE

The strawberry grows underneath the nettle,
And wholesome berries thrive and ripen best
Neighbor'd by fruit of baser quality.
Henry V. Act I. Sc. 1

Methinks, I have a great desire to a bottle of
hay: good hay, sweet hay, hath no fellow.
Midsummer Night's Dream. Act IV. Sc. 1

Fruits that blossom first will first be ripe.
Othello. Act II. Sc. 3

The ripest fruit first falls.
Richard II. Act II. Sc. 1

      Superfluous branches
We lop away, that bearing bough may live.
Richard II. Act III. Sc. 4

You sunburn'd sickle men, of August weary,
Come hither from the furrow, and be merry.
Tempest. Act IV. Sc. 1

See also: GARDEN, TREE.

ALCHEMY

       The glorious sun
Stays in his course, and plays the alchymist;
Turning, with splendour of his precious eye,
The meager cloddy earth to glittering gold.
King John. Act III. Sc. 1

You are an alchymist; make gold of that.
Timon of Athens. Act V. Sc. 1

See also: GOLD.

AMBITION

It were all one
That I should love a bright particular star,
And think to wed it, he is so above me.
All's Well That Ends Well. Act I. Sc. 1

The very substance of the ambitious is merely
the shadow of a dream.
Hamlet. Act II. Sc. 2

Ill-weav'd ambition, how much art thou
shrunk!
When that this body did contain a spirit,
A kingdom for it was too small a bound;
But now, two paces of the vilest earth
Is room enough.
Henry IV. Pt. I. Act V. Sc. 4

I am not covetous for gold;
Nor care I who doth feed upon my cost;
It yearns me not if men my garments wear;
Such outward things dwell not in my desires:
But if it be a sin to covet honor
I am the most offending soul alive.
Henry V. Act IV. Sc. 3

Virtue is chok'd with foul ambition.
Henry VI. Pt. II. Act III. Sc. 1

Mark but my fall, and that that ruin'd me.
Cromwell, I charge thee, fling away ambition,
By that sin, fell the angels; how can man
then,
The image of his Maker, hope to win by it?
Love thyself last; cherish those hearts that
hate thee;
Corruption wins not more than honesty.
Henry VIII. Act III. Sc. 2

There is, betwixt that smile we would aspire
to,
That sweet aspect of princes, and their ruin,
More pangs and fears than war or women
have.
Henry VIII. Act III. Sc. 2

'Tis a common proof,
That lowliness is young ambition's ladder,
Whereto the climber upward turns his face;
But when he once attains the upmost round,
He then unto the ladder turns his back,
Looks in the clouds, scorning the base degrees
By which he did ascend.
Julius Caesar. Act II. Sc. 1

Ambition's debt is paid.
Julius Caesar. Act III. Sc. 1

The noble Brutus
Hath told you Caesar was ambitious:
If it were so, it was a grievous fault;
And grievously hath Caesar answered it.
Julius Caesar. Act III. Sc. 2

I have no spur
To prick the sides of my intent, but only
Vaulting ambition; which o'erleaps itself,
And falls on the other—
Macbeth. Act I. Sc. 7

See also: FAME, REPUTATION, SUCCESS.

ANGEL

And flights of angels sing thee to thy rest.
Hamlet. Act V. Sc. 2

Angels are bright still, though the brightest
fell.
Macbeth. Act IV. Sc. 3

See also: DEVIL, GOD, HEAVEN, HELL.

ANGER

If I had a thunderbolt in mine eye,
I can tell who should down.
As You Like It. Act I. Sc. 2

Being once chaf'd, he cannot
Be rein'd again to temperance; then he speaks
What's in his heart.
Coriolanus. Act III. Sc. 3

Put him to choler straight; He hath been us'd
Ever to conquer, and to have his worth
Of contradiction.
Coriolanus. Act III. Sc. 3

Anger's my meat; I sup upon myself,
And so shall starve with feeding.
Coriolanus. Act IV. Sc. 2

What, drunk with choler?
Henry IV. Pt. I. Act I. Sc. 3

Anger is like
A full-hot horse; who being allow'd his way,
Self-mettle tires him.
Henry VIII. Act I. Sc. 1

Touch me with noble anger!
And let not women's weapon, water drops
Stain my man's cheeks.
King Lear. Act II. Sc. 4

That in the captain's but a choleric word,
Which in the soldier is flat blasphemy.
Measure for Measure. Act II. Sc. 2

Alas why gnaw you so your nether lip?
Some bloody passion shakes your very frame;
These are portents; but yet I hope, I hope,
They do not point on me.
                    Othello. Act V. Sc. 2

In rage deaf as the sea, hasty as fire.
                    Richard II. Act I. Sc. 1

Come not within the measure of my wrath.
          Two Gentlemen of Verona. Act V. Sc. 4

See also: HATE, PASSION, REVENGE.

ANGLING: *see* FISHING.

ANIMAL

The mouse ne'er shunn'd the cat, as they did
          budge
From rascals worse than they.
                    Coriolanus. Act I. Sc. 6

Steed threatens steed, in high and boastful
          neighs,
Piercing the night's dull ear.
                    Henry V. Chorus to Act IV.

                    The little dogs and all,
Tray, Blanche, and Sweet-heart, see, they
          bark at me.
                    King Lear. Act III. Sc. 6

                    Mine enemy's dog,
Though he had bit me, should have stood
          that night
Against my fire.
                    King Lear. Act IV. Sc. 7

Thou hast seen a farmer's dog bark at a
beggar?
                    King Lear. Act IV. Sc. 6

Give me another horse, bind up my wounds.
                    Richard III. Act V. Sc. 3

A horse, a horse! my kingdom for a horse!
                    Richard III. Act V. Sc. 4

The Elephant hath joints, but none for courtesy; his legs are legs for necessity, not for
flexure.
                    Troilus and Cressida. Act II. Sc. 3

See also: BAT, BIRD, COCK, CROW, DOVE,
          EAGLE, FALCON, INSECT, LARK, OWL,
          RAVEN, SWAN.

APPAREL

The soul of this man is his clothes.
          All's Well That Ends Well. Act II. Sc. 5

                    So tedious is this day,
As in the night before some festival
To an impatient child, that hath new robes,
And may not wear them.
                    Romeo and Juliet. Act III. Sc. 2

With silken coats, and caps, and golden
          rings,
With ruffs, and cuffs, and farthingales, and
          things;
With scarfs, and fans, and double change of
          bravery,
With amber bracelets, beads, and all this
          knavery.
                    Taming of the Shrew. Act IV. Sc. 3

See also: FASHION, VANITY.

APPETITE

                    Epicurean cooks
Sharpen with cloyless sauce his appetite.
                    Antony and Cleopatra. Act II. Sc. 1

                    Read o'er this;
And after, this; and then to breakfast, with
What appetite you have.
                    Henry VIII. Act III. Sc. 2

Now good digestion wait on appetite,
And health on both!
                    Macbeth. Act III. Sc. 4

Doth not the appetite alter? A man loves the
meat in his youth, that he cannot endure in
his age.
          Much Ado About Nothing. Act II. Sc. 3

Who can cloy the hungry edge of appetite?
                    Richard II. Act I. Sc. 3

See also: COOKING, DESIRE, DRINK, EATING,
          HUNGER.

APPLAUSE

                    They threw their caps
As they would hang them on the horns o'
          the moon,
Shouting their emulation.
                    Coriolanus. Act I. Sc. 1

I would applaud thee to the very echo,
That should applaud again.
                    Macbeth. Act V. Sc. 3

I love the people,
But do not like to stage me to their eyes;
Though it do well, I do not relish well
Their loud applause, and *aves* vehement;
Nor do I think the man of safe discretion,
That does affect it.
> *Measure for Measure*. Act I. Sc. 1

See also: ADMIRATION, COMPLIMENT, FAME, FLATTERY, HONOR, PRAISE.

ARCHITECTURE

'Fore God, you have here a goodly dwelling, and a rich,
> *Henry IV*. Pt. II. Act V. Sc. 3

He that hath a house to put his head in, has a good head piece.
> *King Lear*. Act III. Sc. 2

See also: ART, CARPENTER, HOME.

ARGUMENT

If reasons were as plenty as blackberries, I would give no man a reason upon compulsion.
> *Henry IV*. Pt. I. Act II. Sc. 4

And sheath'd their swords for lack of argument.
> *Henry V*. Act III. Sc. 1

There is occasions and causes why and wherefore in all things.
> *Henry V*. Act V. Sc. 1

Romans, countrymen, and lovers! hear me for my cause; and be silent, that you may hear.
> *Julius Caesar*. Act III. Sc. 2

Strong reasons make strong actions.
> *King John*. Act III. Sc. 4

They are yet but ear-kissing argument.
> *King Lear*. Act II. Sc. 1

She hath prosperous art
When she will play with reason and discourse,
And well she can persuade.
> *Measure for Measure*. Act I. Sc. 3

His reasons are two grains of wheat hid in two bushels of chaff; you shall seek all day ere you find them; and, when you have them, they are not worth the search.
> *Merchant of Venice*. Act I. Sc. 1

Leave this keen encounter of our wits,
And fall somewhat into a slower method.
> *Richard III*. Act I. Sc. 2

I have no other but a woman's reason;
I think him so, because I think him so.
> *Two Gentlemen of Verona*. Act I. Sc. 2

See also: DISSENSION, ELOQUENCE, ORATORY, REASON, SPEECH, TALK, WIT, WORD.

ART

To gild refined gold, to paint the lily,
To throw a perfume on the violet,
To smooth the ice, or add another hue
Unto the rainbow, or with taper-light.
> *King John*. Act IV. Sc. 2

His art with nature's workmanship at strife,
As if the dead the living should exceed.
> *Venus and Adonis*. Line 292

See also: ARCHITECTURE, AUTHORSHIP, DANCE, MUSIC, POETRY, SONG.

ASTRONOMY

My lord, they say five moons were seen tonight:
Four fixed; and the fifth did whirl about
The other four in wondrous motion.
> *King John*. Act IV. Sc. 2

Those earthly god-fathers of heaven's lights,
That give a name to every fixed star.
> *Love's Labour's Lost*. Act I. Sc. 1

And teach me how
To name the bigger light, and how the less,
That burn by day and night.
> *Tempest*. Act I. Sc. 2

See also: HEAVEN, MOON, NIGHT, STAR.

AURORA: *see* DAWN.

AUTHORITY

There is no fettering of authority.
> *All's Well that Ends Well*. Act II. Sc. 4

Thou hast seen a farmer's dog bark at a beggar.
And the creature run from the cur: There,
There, thou might'st behold the great image of authority;
A dog's obey'd in office.
> *King Lear*. Act IV. Sc. 6

Those he commands, move only in command,
Nothing in love: now does he feel the title
Hang loose about him, like a giant's robe
Upon a dwarfish thief.
> *Macbeth*. Act V. Sc. 2

Thus can the demi-god, Authority
Make us pay down for our offense by weight.
Measure for Measure. Act I. Sc. 3

And though authority be a stubborn bear, yet
he is oft led by the nose with gold.
Winter's Tale. Act IV. Sc. 4

See also: GOVERNMENT, POWER, TYRANNY.

AUTHORSHIP

Devise, wit; write, pen; for I am for whole
volumes in folio.
Love's Labour's Lost. Act I. Sc. 2

Let there be gall enough in thy ink; though
thou write with a goose pen, no matter.
Twelfth Night. Act III. Sc. 2

Write till your ink be dry; and with your tears
Moist it again; and frame some feeling line,
That may discover such integrity.
Two Gentlemen of Verona. Act III. Sc. 2

See also: BOOK, LIBRARY, READING.

AVARICE

Decrepit miser; base, ignoble wretch;
I am descended of a gentler blood.
Henry VI. Pt. I. Act V. Sc. 4

There grows,
In my most ill-compos'd affection, such
A stanchless avarice, that, were I king,
I should cut off the nobles for their lands.
Macbeth. Act IV. Sc. 3

This avarice
Strikes deeper, grows with more pernicious
root.
Macbeth. Act IV. Sc. 3

There is thy gold; worse poison to men's
souls.
Romeo and Juliet. Act V. Sc. 1

See also: GOLD, MONEY, WEALTH.

B

BALLAD

I had rather be a kitten, and cry mew!
Than one of these same meter ballad-mongers.
Henry IV. Pt. I. Act 11. Sc. 1

I love a ballad but even too well; if it be
doleful matter, merrily set down, or a very
pleasant thing indeed, and sung lamentably.
Winter's Tale. Act IV. Sc. 3

See also: MUSIC, SINGER, SONG.

BARBER

Our courteous Antony,
Being barber'd ten times o'er, goes to the feast.
Antony and Cleopatra. Act III. Sc. 2

Whose beard they have sing'd off with brands
of fire;
And, ever as it blaz'd, they threw on him
Great pails of puddled mire to quench the
hair:
My master preaches patience to him, and the
while
His man with scissors nicks him for a fool.
Comedy of Errors. Act V. Sc. 1

And his chin, new reap'd,
Show'd like a stubble land at harvest home.
Henry IV. Pt. I. Act I. Sc. 3

This ancient ruffian, sir, whose life I have
spar'd,
At suit of his grey beard.
King Lear. Act II. Sc. 2

What a beard hast thou got! thou hast got
more hair on thy chin, than Dobbin my thill-
horse has on his tail.
Merchant of Venice. Act II. Sc. 2

I must to the barber's; for, methinks, I am
marvelous hairy about the face.
Midsummer Night's Dream. Act IV. Sc. 1

He that hath a beard is more than a youth;
and he that hath no beard is less than a man.
Much Ado About Nothing. Act II. Sc. 1

The barber's man hath been seen with him;
and the old ornament of his cheek hath already stuffed tennis-balls.
Much Ado About Nothing. Act III. Sc. 2

My fleece of woolly hair, that now uncurls.
Titus Andronicus. Act II. Sc. 3

See also: BEAUTY, HAIR, PERFUME.

BAT

Ere the bat hath flown
His cloister'd flight.
Macbeth. Act III. Sc. 2

See also: ANIMAL, BIRD.

BEAUTY

For her own person,
It beggar'd all description.
Antony and Cleopatra. Act II. Sc. 2

Beauty provoketh thieves sooner than gold.
As You Like It. Act I. Sc. 3

Of Nature's gifts thou may'st with lilies boast,
And with the half-blown rose.
King John. Act III. Sc. 1

Beauty is bought by judgment of the eye,
Not utter'd by base sale of chapmen's
    tongues.
Love's Labour's Lost. Act II. Sc. 1

Beauty doth varnish age.
Love's Labour's Lost. Act IV. Sc. 3

Beauty is a witch,
Against whose charms faith melteth into
blood.
Much Ado About Nothing. Act II. Sc. 1

I'll not shed her blood;
Nor scar that whiter skin of hers than snow,
And smooth as monumental alabaster.
Othello. Act V. Sc. 2

Beauty is but a vain and doubtful good;
A shining gloss that vadeth suddenly;
A flower that dies when first it 'gins to bud;
A brittle glass that's broken presently;
    A doubtful good, a gloss, a glass, a
        flower,
    Lost, vaded, broken, dead within an
        hour.

And as goods lost are seld or never found,
As vaded gloss no rubbing will refresh,
As flowers dead lie wither'd on the ground,
As broken glass no cement can redress,
    So beauty blemish'd once's forever lost,
    In spite of physic, painting, pain, and
        cost.
The Passionate Pilgrim. St. 13

See where she comes, apparell'd like the
    Spring.
Pericles. Act I. Sc. 1

O, she doth teach the torches to burn bright!
Her beauty hangs upon the cheek of night,
As a rich jewel in an Ethiop's ear:
Beauty too rich for use, for earth too dear!
Romeo and Juliet. Act I. Sc. 5

Beauty's ensign yet
Is crimson in thy lips, and in thy cheeks,
And death's pale flag is not advanced there.
Romeo and Juliet. Act V. Sc. 3

Her beauty makes
This vault a feasting presence full of light.
Romeo and Juliet. Act V. Sc. 3

Say that she frown; I'll say she looks as clear
As morning roses newly wash'd with dew.
Taming of the Shrew. Act II. Sc. 1

There's nothing ill can dwell in such a temple:
If the ill spirit have so fair a house,
Good things will strive to dwell with't.
Tempest. Act I. Sc. 2

'Tis beauty truly blent, whose red and white,
Nature's own sweet and cunning hand laid on.
Twelfth Night. Act I. Sc. 5

See also: ART, FACE, NATURE, WOMAN.

BEGGING

Beggar that I am, I am even poor in thanks.
Hamlet. Act II. Sc. 2

Well, whiles I am a beggar, I will rail,
And say,—there is no sin but to be rich;
And being rich, my virtue then shall be,
To say,—there is no vice but beggary.
King John. Act II. Sc. 2

I see, Sir, you are liberal in offers:
You taught me first to beg; and now, me-
    thinks,
You teach me how a beggar should be an-
    swer'd.
Merchant of Venice. Act IV. Sc. 1

Speak with me, pity me, open the door,
A beggar begs that never begg'd before.
Richard II. Act V. Sc. 3

See also: BORROWING, CHARITY, POVERTY.

BELIEF

I always thought,
It was both impious and unnatural,
That such immanity and bloody strife
Should reign among professors of one faith.
Henry VI. Pt. I. Act V. Sc. 1

To add greater honours to his age
Than man could give him, he died fearing
    God.
Henry VIII. Act IV. Sc. 2

Stands not within the prospect of belief.
Macbeth. Act I. Sc. 3

See also: FAITH, GOD, RELIGION, TRUST.

BELL

Sweet bells jangled, out of time and harsh.
Hamlet. Act III. Sc. 1

Then get thee gone; and dig my grave thy-
self;
And bid the merry bells ring to thine ear,
That thou art crowned, not that I am dead.
Henry IV. Pt. II. Act IV. Sc. 4

See also: MUSIC, SONG.

BIRD

All furnished, all in arms;
All plum'd, like estridges that wing the wind
Bated, like eagles having lately bath'd;
Glittering in golden coats, like images;
As full of spirit as the month of May,
And gorgeous as the sun at midsummer;
Wanton as the youthful goats, wild as young
bulls.
Henry IV. Pt. I. Act IV. Sc. 1

Who finds the partridge in the puttock's nest,
But may imagine how the bird was dead,
Although the kite soar with unblooded beak?
Henry VI. Pt. II. Act III. Sc. 2

I am the cygnet to this pale faint swan,
Who chants a doleful hymn to his own death;
And, from the organ-pipe of frailty, sings
His soul and body to their lasting rest.
King John. Act V. Sc. 7

The hedge-sparrow fed the cuckoo so long,
That it had its head bit off by its young.
King Lear. Act I. Sc. 4

The Cuckoo then on every tree,
Mocks married men, for thus sings he,
Cuckoo!
Cuckoo! Cuckoo! O word of fear,
Unpleasing to married ear.
Love's Labour's Lost. Act V. Sc. 2

This guest of Summer,
The temple-haunting martlet, does approve,
By his lov'd mansionry, that the heaven's
breath
Smells wooingly here; no jutty, frieze,
Buttress, nor coigne of vantage, but this bird
Hath made its pendent bed, and procreant
cradle:

Where they most breed and haunt, I have
observ'd,
The air is delicate.
Macbeth. Act I. Sc. 6

The poor wren,
The most diminutive of birds, will fight,
Her young ones in her nest, against the owl.
Macbeth. Act IV. Sc. 2

The martlet
Builds in the weather on the outward wall,
Even in the force and road of casualty.
Merchant of Venice. Act II. Sc. 9

The throstle with his note so true,
The wren with little quill.
Midsummer Night's Dream. Act II. Sc. 1

As wild geese that the creeping fowler eye,
Or russet-pated choughs, many in sort,
Rising and cawing at the gun's report,
Sever themselves, and madly sweep the sky.
Midsummer Night's Dream. Act III. Sc. 2

For look where Beatrice, like a lapwing, runs
Close by the ground, to hear our conference.
Much Ado About Nothing. Act III. Sc. 1

Dost thou love hawking? thou hast hawks
will soar
Above the morning lark.
Taming of the Shrew. Induction. Sc. 2

What, is the jay more precious than the lark,
Because his feathers are more beautiful?
Taming of the Shrew. Act IV. Sc. 3

See also: DOVE, EAGLE, FALCON, LARK, NIGHT-
INGALE, OWL, RAVEN, SWAN.

BLACKSMITH

I saw a smith stand with his hammer thus,
The whilst his iron did on his anvil cool.
King John. Act IV. Sc. 2

He doth nothing but talk of his horse; and
he makes it a great appropriation to his own
good parts that he can shoe him himself.
Merchant of Venice. Act I. Sc. 2

See also: OCCUPATION.

BLESSING

The benediction of these covering heavens
Fall on their heads like dew.
Cymbeline. Act V. Sc. 5

Jove bless thee, master parson.
> *Twelfth Night.* Act IV. Sc. 2

See also: GIFT, GOD, GRACE, HELP.

BLINDNESS

He that is stricken blind, cannot forget
The precious treasure of his eyesight lost.
> *Romeo and Juliet.* Act I. Sc. 1

See also: DARKNESS, EYE, NIGHT.

BLUSH

I will go wash;
And when my face is fair, you shall perceive
Whether I blush or no.
> *Coriolanus.* Act I. Sc. 9

Prolixious blushes that banish what they sue for.
> *Measure for Measure.* Act II. Sc. 4

I have mark'd
A thousand blushing apparitions start
Into her face; a thousand innocent shames,
In angel whiteness bear away those blushes.
> *Much Ado About Nothing.* Act IV. Sc. 1

Yet will she blush, here be it said,
To hear her secrets so betrayed.
> *The Passionate Pilgrim.* Pt. XIX. Line 53

I have no one to blush with me,
To cross their arms and hang their heads with mine.
> *The Rape of Lucrece.* Line 792

Two red fires in both their faces blazed;
She thought he blush'd, . . .
And blushing with him, wistly on him gazed.
> *The Rape of Lucrece.* Line 1354

And bid the cheek be ready with a blush
Modest as morning when she coldly eyes
The youthful Phoebus.
> *Troilus and Cressida.* Act I. Sc. 3

Come, quench your blushes; and present yourself
That which you are, mistress o' the feast.
> *Winter's Tale.* Act IV. Sc. 3

See also: BEAUTY, MODESTY, SHAME.

BOAT

The oars were silver:
Which to the tune of flutes kept stroke.
> *Antony and Cleopatra.* Act II. Sc. 2

Behold the threaden sails,
Borne with the invisible and creeping wind,
Draw the huge bottoms through the furrow'd sea,
Breasting the lofty surge.
> *Henry V.* Act III. Chorus

See also: OCEAN, RIVER.

BOOK

O, sir, we quarrel in print, by the book;
as you have books for good manners.
> *As You Like It.* Act V. Sc. 4

Keep thy pen from lender's books, and defy the foul fiend.
> *King Lear.* Act III. Sc. 4

Sir, he hath never fed of the dainties that are bred in a book.
> *Love's Labour's Lost.* Act IV. Sc. 2

We turn'd o'er many books together.
> *Merchant of Venice.* Act IV. Sc. 1

I had rather than forty shillings,
I had my book.
> *The Merry Wives of Windsor.* Act I. Sc. 1

That book, in many's eyes doth show the glory,
That in gold clasps, locks in the golden story.
> *Romeo and Juliet.* Act I. Sc. 3

O, let my books be then the eloquence
And dumb presager of my speaking breast;
Who plead for love, and look for recompense,
More than that tongue that more hath more express'd.
> *Sonnet XXIII*

Knowing I lov'd my books, he furnished me with volumes that I prize above my dukedom.
> *The Tempest.* Act I. Sc. 2

Deeper than did ever plummet sound,
I'll drown my book.
> *The Tempest.* Act V. Sc. 1

See also: AUTHORSHIP, EDUCATION, LIBRARY, PLAGIARISM, READING.

BORROWING

Neither a borrower, nor a lender be:
For loan oft loses both itself and friend;
And borrowing dulls the edge of husbandry.
> *Hamlet.* Act I. Sc. 3

See also: BEGGING, PLAGIARISM.

BRAVERY

He did not look far
Into the service of the time, and was
Discipled of the bravest; he hasted long,
But on us both did haggish age steal on,
And wore us out of act.
All's Well That Ends Well. Act I. Sc. 2

Think you a little din can daunt mine ears?
Have I not in my time heard lions roar?
Taming of the Shrew. Act I. Sc. 2

See also: COURAGE, VALOR.

BUSINESS

To things of sale a seller's praise belongs.
Love's Labour's Lost. Act IV. Sc. 3

Losses,
That have of late so huddled on his back,
Enough to press a royal merchant down,
And pluck commiseration of his state
From brassy bosoms, and rough hearts of
flint.
Merchant of Venice. Act IV. Sc. 1

A merchant of great traffic through the world.
Taming of the Shrew. Act I. Sc. 1

I have bills for money by exchange
From Florence, and must here deliver them.
Taming of the Shrew. Act IV. Sc. 2

Traffic's thy god, and thy god confound thee!
Timon of Athens. Act I. Sc. 1

See also: GOLD, MONEY.

BUTCHER

Who finds the heifer dead, and bleeding fresh,
And sees fast by a butcher with an axe,
But will suspect 'twas he that made the
slaughter?
Henry VI. Pt. II. Act III. Sc. 2

Why, that's spoken like an honest drover; so
they sell bullocks.
Much Ado About Nothing. Act II. Sc. 1

See also: OCCUPATION.

C

CALUMNY

Virtue itself 'scapes not calumnious strokes.
Hamlet. Act I. Sc. 3

Be thou as chaste as ice, as pure as snow,
thou shalt not escape calumny.
Hamlet. Act III. Sc. 1

No might nor greatness in mortality
Can censure 'scape; back-wounding calumny
The whitest virtue strikes.
Measure for Measure. Act III. Sc. 2

Calumny will sear
Virtue itself;—these shrugs, these hums, and
ha's.
Winter's Tale. Act II. Sc. 1

See also: GOSSIP, REPUTATION, SLANDER.

CARE

Some must watch, while some must sleep;
So runs the world away.
Hamlet. Act III. Sc. 2

He cannot long hold out these pangs;
The incessant care and labour of his mind
Hath wrought the mure, that should confine
it in,
So thin, that life looks through and will
break out.
Henry IV. Pt. II. Act IV. Sc. 4

O polished perturbation! golden care!
That keep'st the ports of slumber open wide
To many a watchful night.
Henry IV. Pt. II. Act IV. Sc. 4

Care is no care, but rather a corrosive,
For things that are not to be remedied.
Henry VI. Pt. I. Act III. Sc. 3

Care keeps his watch in every old man's eye,
And where care lodges, sleep will never lie;
But where unbruised youth with unstuff'd
brain
Doth couch his limbs, there golden sleep
doth reign.
Romeo and Juliet. Act II. Sc. 3

I am sure, care's an enemy to life.
Twelfth Night. Act I. Sc. 3

See also: CAUTION, DISCRETION.

CARPENTER

When on my three-foot stool I sit.
Cymbeline. Act III. Sc. 3

He talks of wood: it is some carpenter.
Henry VI. Pt. I. Act V. Sc. 1

FLAVIUS:
Speak, what trade art thou?
FIRST CITZEN:
Why, sir, a carpenter.
MARULLUS:
Where is thy leather apron, and thy rul?e
What dost thou with they best apparel on?
Julius Caesar. Act I. Sc. 1

See also: OCCUPATION.

CAUSE

Your cause doth strike my heart.
Cymbeline. Act I. Sc. 7

Find out the cause of this effect:
Or, rather say, the cause of this defect;
For this effect defective, comes by cause.
Hamlet. Act II. Sc. 2

God befriend us, as our cause is just.
Henry IV. Pt. I. Act V. Sc. 1

Mine's not an idle cause.
Othello. Act I. Sc. 2

See also: REASON.

CAUTION

Love all, trust a few,
Do wrong to none: be able for thine enemy
Rather in power, than use; and keep thy
friend
Under thy own life's key: be check'd for
silence,
But never tax'd for speech.
All's Well that Ends Well. Act I. Sc. 1

All these you may avoid, but the Lie direct;
and you may avoid that too, with an If. I
knew when seven justices could not take up
a quarrel; but when the parties were met
themselves, one of them thought but of an If,
as, If you said so, then I said so; and they
shook hands, and swore brothers. Your If is
the only peace-maker; much virtue in If.
As You Like It. Act V. Sc. 4

But that I am forbid
To tell the secrets of my prison-house,
I could a tale unfold, whose lightest word
Would harrow up thy soul.
Hamlet Act I. Sc. 5

When me mean to build,
We first survey the plot, then draw the model,
And, then we see the figure of the house,
Then must we rate the cost of the erection
Which if we find outweighs ability,

What do we then, but draw anew the model
In fewer offices, or, at least desist
To build at all?
Henry IV. Pt. II. Act I. Sc. 3

We may outrun,
By violent swiftness, that which we run at,
And lose by overrunning.
Henry VIII. Act I. Sc. 1

Know you not,
The fire that mounts the liquor till it run
o'er
In seeming to augment it, wastes it? Be
advis'd.
Henry VIII. Act I. Sc. 1

Think him as a serpent's egg,
Which, hatch'd, would, as his kind, grow
mischievous;
And kill him in the shell.
Julius Caesar. Act II. Sc. 1

Lock up my doors; and when you hear the
drum,
And the vile squealing of the wry-neck'd
fife,
Clamber not you up to the casements then.
Merchant of Venice. Act II. Sc. 5

Let every eye negotiate for itself. And trust
no agent.
Much Ado About Nothing. Act II. Sc. 1

It engenders choler, planteth anger;
And better 'twere that both of us did fast,
Since, of ourselves, ourselves are choleric,
Than feed it with such over-roasted flesh.
Taming of the Shrew. Act IV. Sc. 1

See also: CARE, PRUDENCE.

CEREMONY

What infinite heart's ease must kings neglect
That private men enjoy?
And what have kings that privates have not
too,
Save ceremony, save general ceremony?
Henry V. Act IV. Sc. 1

O ceremony, show me but thy worth!
What is thy soul of adoration?
Art thou aught else but place, degree, and
form,
Creating awe and fear in other men?
Henry V. Act IV. Sc. 1

What art thou, thou idol ceremony?
What kind of god art thou, that suffer'st more
Of mortal griefs than do thy worshippers.
                    Henry V. Act IV. Sc. 1

When love begins to sicken and decay,
It useth an enforced ceremony;
There are no tricks in plain and simple faith.
                    Julius Caesar. Act IV. Sc. 2

                    To feed, were best at home;
From thence, the sauce to meat is ceremony;
Meeting were bare without it.
                    Macbeth. Act III. Sc. 4

Ceremony was but devis'd at first
To set a gloss on faint deeds, hollow welcomes,
Recanting goodness, sorry ere 'tis shown.
                    Timon of Athens. Act I. Sc. 2

See also: WORSHIP.

CHANCE

I shall show the cinders of my spirits
Through the ashes of my chance.
                    Antony and Cleopatra. Act V. Sc. 2

Against ill chances, men are ever merry;
But heaviness foreruns the good event.
                    Henry IV. Pt. II. Act IV. Sc. 2

See also: CIRCUMSTANCE, DESTINY, FATE, FORTUNE, PROVIDENCE.

CHANGE

This world is not for aye; nor 'tis not strange
That even our loves should with our fortunes change.
                    Hamlet. Act III. Sc. 2

                    That we would do,
We should do when we would; for this *"would"* changes,
And hath abatements and delays as many,
As there are tongues, are hands, are accidents;
And then this *"should"* is like a spendthrift's sigh,
That hurts by easing.
                    Hamlet Act IV. Sc. 7

This is the state of man; To-day he puts forth
The tender leaves of hope, to-morrow blossoms,
And bears his blushing honours thick upon him.
                    Henry VIII. Act III. Sc. 2

                    Thou hast describ'd
A hot friend cooling: Ever note, Lucilius,
When love begins to sicken and decay,
It useth an enforced ceremony.
                    Julius Caesar. Act IV. Sc. 2

When we were happy, we had other names.
                    King John. Act V. Sc. 4

The love of wicked friends converts to fear;
That fear, to hate; and hate turns one or both,
To worthy danger, and deserved death.
                    Richard II. Act V. Sc. 1

All things that we ordained festival,
Turn from their office to black funeral:
Our instruments, to melancholy bells:
Our wedding cheer, to a sad burial feast;
Our solemn hymns to sullen dirges change;
Our bridal flowers serve for a buried corse,
And all things change them to the contrary.
                    Romeo and Juliet. Act IV. Sc. 5

                    I am not so nice,
To change true rules for odd inventions.
                    Taming of the Shrew. Act III. Sc. 1

Full fathom five thy father lies;
Of his bones are coral made;
Those are pearls that were his eyes:
Nothing of him that doth fade,
But doth suffer a sea-change
Into something rich and strange.
                    Tempest. Act I. Sc. 2

Our revels now are ended: these our actors,
As I foretold you, were all spirits, and
Are melted into air, into thin air;
And, like the baseless fabric of this vision,
The cloud-capp'd towers, the gorgeous palaces,
The solemn temples, the great globe itself,
Yea, all which it inherit, shall dissolve;
And, like this insubstantial pageant faded,
Leave not a rack behind.
                    Tempest. Act IV. Sc. 1

See also: CHOICE, INCONSTANCY, VARIETY.

CHAOS

                    Nay, had I power, I should
Pour the sweet milk of concord into hell,
Uproar the universal peace, confound
All unity on earth.
                    Macbeth. Act IV. Sc. 3

See also: DISSENSION, STORM, WAR.

CHARACTER

I know him a notorious liar,
Think him a great way fool, solely a coward;
Yet these fix'd evils sit so fit in him,
That they take place, when virtue's steely
    bones
Look bleak in the cold wind.
All's Well That Ends Well. Act I. Sc. 1

Long is it since I saw him,
But time hath nothing blur'd those lines of
    favour
Which he wore.
Cymbeline. Act IV. Sc. 2

But I have that within which passeth show;
These, but the trappings and the suits of
    woe.
Hamlet. Act I. Sc. 2

Be thou familiar, but by no means vulgar.
Hamlet. Act I. Sc. 3

Though I am not splenetive and rash,
Yet have I something in me dangerous.
Hamlet. Act V. Sc. 1

Look, as I blow this feather from my face,
And as the air blows it to me again,
Obeying with my wind when I do blow,
And yielding to another when it blows,
Commanded always by the greater gust;
Such is the lightness of you common men.
Henry VI. Pt. III. Act III. Sc. 1

Men's evil manners live in brass; their virtues
we write in water.
Henry VIII. Act IV. Sc. 2

O, he sits high in all the people's hearts:
And that which would appear offence in us.
His countenance, like richest alchymy,
Will change to virtue and to worthiness.
Iulius Caesar. Act I. Sc. 3

Thou art, most rich, being poor;
Most choice, forsaken; and most lov'd,
    despis'd.
Thee and thy virtues here I seize upon.
King Lear. Act I. Sc. 1

I do profess to be no less than I seem; to
serve him truly, that will put me in trust; to
love him that is honest; to converse with him
that is wise, and says little; to fear judgment;
to fight, when I cannot choose; and to eat
no fish.
King Lear. Act I. Sc. 4

What thou would'st highly,
That would'st thou holily; would'st not play
    false,
And yet would'st wrongly win.
Macbeth. Act I. Sc. 5

But I remember now
I am in this earthly world; where, to do
    harm,
Is often laudable; to do good, sometime,
Accounted dangerous folly.
Macbeth. Act IV. Sc. 2

Be absolute for death; either death, or life,
shall thereby be the sweeter.
Measure for Measure. Act III. Sc. 1

They say, best men are moulded out of faults.
And, for the most, become much more the
    better,
For being a little bad.
Measure for Measure. Act V. Sc. 1

Nature hath fram'd strange fellows in her
    time:
Some that will evermore peep through their
    eyes,
And laugh, like parrots, at a bagpiper:
And other of such vinegar aspect,
That they'll not show their teeth in way of
    smile,
Though Nestor swear the jest be laughable.
Merchant of Venice. Act I. Sc. 1

Good name in man and woman, dear my
    lord,
Is the immediate jewel of their souls:
Who steals my purse steals trash; 'tis some-
    thing, nothing;
    .   .   .
But he that filches from me my good name,
Robs me of that which not enriches him,
And makes me poor indeed.
Othello. Act III. Sc. 3

Why, now I see there's mettle in thee; and
even, from this instant, do build on thee a
better opinion than ever before.
Othello. Act IV. Sc. 2

He hath a daily beauty in his life
That makes me ugly.
Othello. Act V. Sc. 1

Look, what thy soul holds dear, imagine it
To lie that way thou go'st, not whence thou
    com'st;
Suppose the singing birds, musicians;

The grass whereon thou tread'st, the presence
strew'd;
The flowers, fair ladies; and thy steps, no
more
Than a delightful measure, or a dance.
Richard II. Act I. Sc. 3

Now do I play the touch,
To try if thou be current gold indeed.
Richard III. Act IV. Sc. 2

My nature is subdued
To what it works in.
Sonnet CXI

Unknit that threat'ning unkind brow;
And dart not scornful glances from those
eyes,
To wound thy lord, thy king, thy governor;
It blots thy beauty, as frosts do bite the
meads;
Confounds thy fame, as whirlwinds shake
fair buds.
Taming of the Shrew. Act V. Sc. 2

How this grace
Speaks his own standing! what a mental
power
This eye shoots forth! How big imagination
Moves in this lip! to the dumbness of the
gesture
One might interpret.
Timon of Athens. Act I. Sc. 1

Now the melancholy god protect thee: and
the tailor make thy doublet of changeable
taffata, for thy mind is a very opal.
Twelfth Night. Act II. Sc. 4

He wants wit that wants resolved will.
Two Gentlemen of Verona. Act II. Sc. 6

His words are bonds, his oaths are oracles;
His love sincere, his thoughts immaculate;
.   .   .
His heart as far from fraud as heaven from
earth.
Two Gentlemen of Verona. Act II. Sc. 7

See also: ABILITY, DIGNITY, HONESTY, REPUTA-
TION, SINCERITY, WORTH.

CHARITY

For his bounty
There was no winter in't; an autumn 'twas
That grew the more by reaping. His delights
Were dolphin like.
Antony and Cleopatra. Act V. Sc. 2

For this relief, much thanks; 'tis bitter cold,
And I am sick at heart.
Hamlet. Act I. Sc. 1

An old man, broken with the storms of state,
Is come to lay his weary bones among ye;
Give him a little earth for charity!
Henry VIII. Act IV. Sc. 2

So may he rest; his faults lie gently on him!
Henry VIII. Act IV. Sc. 2

Charity,
Which renders good for bad, blessings for
curses.
Richard III. Act I. Sc. 2

We are born to do benefits. . . . O, what a
precious comfort 'tis to have so many, like
brothers, commanding one another's fortunes!
Timon of Athens. Act I. Sc. 2

See also: BEGGING, FRIENDSHIP, GIFT, KIND-
NESS, LOVE, MERCY.

CHASTITY

My chastity's the jewel of our house,
Bequeathed down from my ancestors.
All's Well That Ends Well. Act IV. Sc. 2

The very ice of chastity is in them.
As You Like It. Act III. Sc. 4

Chaste as the icicle,
That's curded by the frost from purest snow,
And hangs on Dian's temple.
Coriolanus. Act V. Sc. 3

As chaste as unsunn'd snow.
Cymbeline. Act II. Sc. 5

Whiter than new snow on a raven's back.
Romeo and Juliet. Act III. Sc. 2

See also: INNOCENCE, MODESTY, VIRTUE.

CHEERFULNESS

Had she been light, like you,
Of such a merry, nimble, stirring spirit,
She might have been a grandam ere she died;
And so may you; for a light heart lives long.
Love's Labour's Lost. Act V. Sc. 2

Look cheerfully upon me.
Here, love; thou see'st how diligent I am.
Taming of the Shrew. Act IV. Sc. 3

Pluck up thy spirits, look cheerfully upon
me.
Taming of the Shrew. Act IV. Sc. 3

He makes a July's day short as December;
And, with his varying childness, cures in me
Thoughts that would thick my blood.
A Winter's Tale. Act I. Sc. 2

A merry heart goes all the day,
Your sad tires in a mile-a.
Winter's Tale. Act IV. Sc. 2

See also: CONTENTMENT, HAPPINESS, JOY.

CHILDREN

O lord! my boy, my Arthur, my fair son!
My life, my joy, my food, my all the world!
My widow-comfort, and my sorrow's cure.
King John. Act III. Sc. 4

We have no such daughter, nor shall ever
see
That face of her's again; therefore begone
Without our grace, our love, our benizon.
King Lear. Act I. Sc. 1

Your children were vexation to your youth,
But mine shall be a comfort to your age.
Richard III. Act IV. Sc. 4

I am all the daughters of my father's house,
And all the brothers too.
Twelfth Night. Act II. Sc. 4

See also: MOTHER, YOUTH.

CHOICE

Which of them shall I take?
Both? one? or neither? Neither can be en-
joy'd,
If both remain alive.
King Lear. Act V. Sc. 1

I will not choose what many men desire,
Because I will not jump with common spirits,
And rank me with the barbarous multitudes.
Merchant of Venice. Act II. Sc. 9

Preferment goes by letter, and affection.
Othello. Act I. Sc. 1

There's a small choice in rotten apples.
Taming of the Shrew. Act I. Sc. 1

See also: CHANGE, OPPORTUNITY, VARIETY.

CHRIST

In those holy fields
Over whose acres walk'd those blessed feet,
Which fourteen hundred years ago, were
nail'd
For our advantage on the bitter cross.
Henry IV. Pt. I. Act I. Sc. 1

See also: GOD, RELIGION.

CHRISTMAS

At Christmas I no more desire a rose,
Than wish a snow in May's new-fangled
shows.
Love's Labour's Lost. Act I. Sc. 1

See also: HOLIDAY.

CIRCUMSTANCE

My circumstances
Being so near the truth as I will make them,
Must first induce you to believe.
Cymbeline. Act II. Sc. 4

If circumstances lead me, I will find
Where truth is hid.
Hamlet. Act II. Sc. 2

What means this passionate discourse,
This peroration with such circumstance.
Henry VI. Pt. II. Act I. Sc. 1

Leave frivolous circumstances.
Taming of the Shrew. Act V. Sc. 1

See also: CHANCE, DESTINY, FATE, FORTUNE,
LIFE, OPPORTUNITY.

CLOUD

Yon towers, whose wanton tops do buss the
clouds.
Troilus and Cressida. Act IV. Sc. 5

See also: RAIN, SKY, STORM, SUN.

COCK

The cock, that is the trumpet to the morn,
Doth with his lofty and shrill-sounding
throat
Awake the God of day.
Hamlet. Act I. Sc. 1

The morning cock crew loud;
And at the sound it shrunk in haste away,
And vanish'd from our sight.
Hamlet. Act I. Sc. 2

The early village cock
Hath twice done salutation to the morn.
Richard III. Act V. Sc. 3

See also: ANIMAL, BIRD.

COMPARISON

Comparisons are odorous.
Much Ado About Nothing. Act III. Sc. 5

What, is the jay more precious than the lark,
Because his feathers are more beautiful?
Or is the adder better than the eel,
Because his painted skin contents the eye?
                    Taming of the Shrew. Act IV. Sc. 3

See also: CONTRAST, JUDGMENT, WORTH.

COMPLIMENT

                    'Twas never merry world
Since lowly feigning was call'd compliment.
                    Twelfth Night. Act III. Sc. 1

See also: APPLAUSE, FLATTERY, PRAISE.

CONCEIT

Conceit in weakest bodies strongest works.
                    Hamlet. Act III. Sc. 4

I am not in the roll of common men.
                    Henry IV. Pt. I. Act III. Sc. 1

See also: PRIDE, SELF-LOVE, VANITY.

CONFESSION

                    Confess yourself to heaven;
Repent what's past; avoid what is to come.
                    Hamlet. Act III. Sc. 4

Confess thee freely of thy sin;
For to deny each article with oath
Cannot remove, or choke, the strong concep-
    tion
That I do groan withal.
                    Othello. Act V. Sc. 2

See also: REPENTANCE.

CONFIDENCE

I renounce all confidence.
                    Henry VI. Pt. I. Act I. Sc. 2

Trust not him that hath once broken faith.
                    Henry VI. Pt. III. Act IV. Sc. 4

Your wisdom is consum'd in confidence
Do not go forth to-day.
                    Julius Caesar. Act II. Sc. 2

I would have some confidence with you that
decerns you nearly.
                    Much Ado About Nothing. Act III. Sc. 5

Be as just and gracious unto me,
As I am confident and kind to thee.
                    Titus Andronicus. Act I. Sc. 1

See also: BELIEF, DECISION, FAITH, TRUST.

CONSCIENCE

Thus conscience does make cowards of us
    all;
And thus the native hue of resolution
Is sicklied o'er with the pale cast of thought.
                    Hamlet. Act III. Sc. 1

Every subject's duty is the king's; but every
subject's soul is his own.
                    Henry V. Act IV. Sc. 1

Ah, what a sign it is of evil life,
Where death's approach is seen so terrible!
                    Henry VI. Pt. II. Act. III. Sc. 3

I know myself now; and I feel within me
A peace above all earthly dignities;
A still and quiet conscience.
                    Henry VIII. Act III. Sc. 2

Now, if you can blush, and cry guilty, car-
    dinal,
You'll show a little honesty.
                    Henry VIII. Act III. Sc. 2

                    Better be with the dead,
Whom we, to gain our peace, have sent to
    peace,
Than on the torture of the mind to lie
In restless ecstacy.
                    Macbeth. Act III. Sc. 2

I hate the murderer, love him murdered.
The guilt of conscience take thou for thy
    labour,
But neither my good word, nor princely
    favour;
With Cain go wander through the shade of
    night,
And never show thy head by day, nor light.
                    Richard II. Act V. Sc. 6

The worm of conscience still be-gnaw thy
    soul!
Thy friends suspect for traitors whilst thou
    liv'st,
And take deep traitors for thy dearest friends!
                    Richard III. Act I. Sc. 3

Conscience is a blushing shame-faced spirit
That mutinies in a man's bosom; it fills
One full of obstacles.
                    Richard III. Act I. Sc. 4

Conscience is a word that cowards use,
Devised at first to keep the strong in awe.
                    Richard III. Act V. Sc. 3

Soft, I did but dream.
O coward conscience, how dost thou afflict
  me!
Richard III. Act V. Sc. 3

My conscience had a thousand several
  tongues,
And every tongue brings in a several tale,
And every tale condemns me for a villain.
Richard III. Act V. Sc. 3

I know thou art religious,
And hast a thing within thee called con-
  science;
With twenty popish tricks and ceremonies,
Which I have seen thee careful to observe.
Titus Andronicus. Act V. Sc. 1

See also: GUILT, MIND, REPENTANCE, SELF-
  EXAMINATION.

CONSIDERATION

Consideration like an angel came,
And whipp'd the offending Adam out of him;
Leaving his body as a paradise,
To envelope and contain celestial spirits.
Henry V. Act I. Sc. 1

What you have said,
I will consider; what you have to say,
I will with patience hear; and find a time
Both meet to hear and answer.
Julius Caesar. Act I. Sc. 2

A stirring dwarf we do allowance give
Before a sleeping giant.
Troilus and Cressida. Act II. Sc. 3

See also: CARE, KINDNESS, THOUGHT.

CONSOLATION

I will be gone;
That pitiful rumour may report my flight,
To consolate thine ear.
All's Well That Ends Well. Act III. Sc. 2

Grief is crowned with consolation.
Antony and Cleopatra Act I. Sc. 2

Shall we now
Contaminate our fingers with base bribes?
Julius Caesar. Act IV Sc. 3

See also: GRIEF, KINDNESS, PITY, SYMPATHY,
  TEARS.

CONSPIRACY

O conspiracy!
Sham'st thou to show thy dang'rous brow by
  night,
When evils are most free?
Julius Caesar. Act II. Sc. 1

Take no care
Who chafes, who frets, and where conspirers
  are:
Macbeth shall never vanquish'd be.
Macbeth. Act IV. Sc. 1

Open-eye Conspiracy
His time doth take.
Tempest. Act II. Sc. 1. Song

I had forgot that foul conspiracy
Of the beast Caliban, and his confederates,
Against my life.
Tempest. Act IV. Sc. 1

See also: SECRECY, TREASON.

CONSTANCY

Now from head to foot
I am marble-constant: now the fleeting moon
No planet is of mine.
Antony and Cleopatra. Act V. Sc. 2

O constancy, be strong upon my side!
Set a huge mountain 'tween my heart and
  tongue!
I have a man's mind, but a woman's might.
Julius Caesar. Act II. Sc. 4

I could be well nerv'd if I were as you;
If I could pray to move, prayers would move
  me;
But I am constant as the northern star
Of whose true fix'd and resting quality
There is no fellow in the firmament.
Julius Caesar. Act III. Sc. 1

He that parts us, shall bring a brand from
  heaven,
And fire us hence, like foxes.
King Lear. Act V. Sc. 3

Thou dost conspire against thy friend, Iago,
If thou but think'st him wrong'd and mak'st
  his ear
As stranger to thy thoughts.
Othello. Act III. Sc. 3

If ever thou shalt love,
In the sweet pangs of it remember me;
For such as I am all true lovers are:
Unstaid and skittish in all motions else,
Save in the constant image of the creature
That is belov'd.
Twelfth Night. Act II. Sc. 4

I would have men of such constancy put to
sea, that their business might be everything,
and their intent everywhere; for that's it that
always makes a good voyage of nothing.
Twelfth Night. Act. II. Sc. 4

O heaven! were man
But constant, he were perfect; that one error
Fills him with faults; makes him run through
all th' sins.
Inconstancy falls off ere it begins.
Two Gentlemen of Verona. Act V. Sc. 4

See also: FIDELITY, FRIENDSHIP, TRUTH.

CONTAMINATION

Shall we now
Contaminate our fingers with base bribes?
Julius Caesar. Act IV. Sc. 3

They that touch pitch will be defiled.
Much Ado About Nothing. Act III. Sc. 3

See also: GUILT, SIN, VICE.

CONTEMPLATION

When holy and devout religious men
Are at their beads, 'tis hard to draw them
thence;
So sweet is zealous contemplation.
Richard III. Act III. Sc. 7

Contemplation makes a rare turkey-cock of
him! how he jets
Under his advanced plumes!
Twelfth Night. Act II. Sc. 5

See also: MEDITATION, PRAYER, THOUGHT.

CONTEMPT

Call me what instrument you will, though
you can fret me, you cannot play upon me.
Hamlet. Act III. Sc. 2

Becomes it thee to taunt this valiant age,
And twit with cowardice a man half dead?
Henry VI. Pt. I. Act III. Sc. 2

I had rather chop this hand off at a blow,
And with the other fling it at thy face,
Than bear so low a sail to strike to thee.
Henry VI. Pt. III. Act V. Sc. 1

I had rather be a dog, and bay the moon;
Than such a Roman.
Julius Caesar. Act IV. Sc. 3

He talks to me that never had a son.
King John. Act III. Sc. 4

Get thee glass eyes;
And, and like a scurvy politician, seem
To see the things thou dost not.
King Lear. Act IV. Sc. 6

But, (alas!) to make me
A fixed figure, for the hand of Scorn
To point his slow unmoving finger at.
Othello. Act IV. Sc. 2

O what a deal of scorn looks beautiful
In the contempt and anger of his lip!
Twelfth Night. Act III. Sc. 1

See also: CRITICISM, DISGRACE, HATE.

CONTENTION

The Retort Courteous; the Quip Modest; the
Reply Churlish; the Reproof Valiant; the
Counter check Quarrelsome; the Lie with
Circumstance; the Lie Direct.
As You Like It. Act. V. Sc. 4

Greatly to find quarrel in a straw,
When honour's at the stake.
Hamlet. Act IV. Sc. 4

Por. A quarrel, ho, already! what's the matter?
Gra. About a hoop of gold, a paltry ring.
Merchant of Venice. Act V. Sc. 1

In a false quarrel there is no true valour.
Much Ado About Nothing. Act V. Sc. 1

Thou! why thou wilt quarrel with a man that
hath a hair more, or a hair less, in his beard
than thou hast. Thou wilt quarrel with a man
for cracking nuts, having no other reason, but
because thou hast hazel eyes.
Romeo and Juliet. Act III. Sc. 1

Thy head is as full of quarrels as an egg is
full of meat.
Romeo and Juliet. Act III. Sc. 1

See also: ARGUMENT, DISSENSION, WAR.

CONTENTMENT

I earn that I eat, get that I wear; owe no man
hate; envy no man's happiness; glad of other
men's good, content with my harm.
As You Like It. Act III. Sc. 2

I'm glad of't with all my heart;
I had rather be a kitten and cry mew,
Than one of these same metre ballad-mon-
     gers.
               Henry IV. Pt. I. Act III. Sc. 1

For mine own part, I could be well content
To entertain the lag-end of my life
With quiet hours.
               Henry IV. Pt. I. Act V. Sc. 1

          The shepherd's homely curds,
His cold thin drink out of his leathern bottle,
His wonted sleep under a fresh tree's shade,
All which secure and sweetly he enjoys,
Is far beyond a prince's delicates,
His viands sparkling in a golden cup,
His body couched in a curious bed,
When care, mistrust, and treason wait on
     him.
               Henry VI. Pt. III. Act II. Sc. 5

My crown is in my heart, not on my head,
Not deck'd with diamonds and Indian stones,
Nor to be seen: my crown is called content;
A crown it is that seldom kings enjoy.
               Henry VI. Pt. III. Act III. Sc. 1

          Our content
Is our best having.
               Henry VIII. Act II. Sc. 3

'Tis better to be lowly born,
And range with humble livers in content,
Than to be perk'd up in a glittering grief,
And wear a golden sorrow.
               Henry VIII. Act II. Sc. 3

          Shut up
In measureless content.
               Macbeth. Act II. Sc. 1

My more-having, would be as a sauce
To make me hunger more.
               Macbeth. Act IV. Sc. 3

He is well paid that is well satisfied.
               Merchant of Venice. Act IV. Sc. 1

If it were now to die,
'Twere to be most happy; for, I fear
My soul hath her content so absolute,
That not another comfort like to this
Succeeds in unknown fate.
               Othello. Act II. Sc. 1

'Tis not so deep as a well, nor so wide as a
church door, but 'tis enough, 'twill serve.
               Romeo and Juliet. Act III. Sc. 1

See also: HAPPINESS, JOY, PEACE.

CONTRAST

Those that are good manners at the court
are as ridiculous in the country, as the behaviour of the country is most mockable at
the court.
               As You Like It. Act III. Sc. 2

Nature hath meal and bran, contempt and
grace.
               Cymbeline. Act IV. Sc. 2

See also: COMPARISON, VARIETY.

COOKING

          Epicurean cooks
Sharpen with cloyless sauce his appetite.
               Antony and Cleopatra. Act II. Sc. 1

Will you go with me? We'll mend our dinner
here.
               Comedy of Errors. Act IV. Sc. 3

Would the cook were of my mind!
               Much Ado About Nothing. Act I. Sc. 3

Get me twenty cunning cooks.
               Romeo and Juliet. Act IV. Sc. 2

CAPULET:
What's there?
FIRST SERVANT:
Things for the cook, sir: but I know not
what.
               Romeo and Juliet. Act IV. Sc. 4

          'Tis burnt; and so is all the meat:
What dogs are these? Where is the rascal
     cook?
How durst you, villains, bring it from the
     dresser,
And serve it thus to me that love it not?
               Taming of the Shrew. Act IV. Sc. 1

Where's the cook? is supper ready, the house
trimmed, rushes strewed, cobwebs swept?
               Taming of the Shrew. Act IV. Sc. 1

PANDARUS:
He that will have a cake out of the wheat
must needs tarry the grinding.
TROILUS:
Have I not tarried?
PANDARUS:
Ay, the grinding: but you must tarry the
bolting.
TROILUS:
Have I not tarried?
PANDARUS:
Ay, the bolting: but you must tarry the
leavening.

TROILUS:
Still have I tarried.

PANDARUS:
Ay, to the leavening: but here's yet in the word hereafter, the kneading, the making of the cake, the heating of the oven, and the baking: nay, you must stay the cooling too, or you may chance to burn your lips.
Troilus and Cressida. Act I. Sc. I

See also: APPETITE, EATING, HUNGER.

COURAGE

In that day's feats

.   .   .   .

He prov'd the best man i' the field; and for his meed
Was brow-bound with the oak.
Coriolanus. Act II. Sc. 2

To be, or not to be, that is the question:—
Whether 'tis nobler in the mind, to suffer
The slings and arrows of outrageous fortune;
Or, to take arms against a sea of troubles,
And, by opposing, end them?
Hamlet. Act III. Sc. 1

The blood more stirs
To rouse a lion than to start a hare.
Henry IV. Pt. I. Act I. Sc. 3

Come let us take a muster speedily:
Doomsday is near; die all, die merrily.
Henry IV. Pt. I. Act IV. Sc. 1

Fearless minds climb soonest unto crowns.
Henry VI. Pt. III. Act IV. Sc. 7

Why, courage, then! what cannot be avoided,
'Twere childish weakness to lament, or fear.
Henry VI. Pt. III. Act V. Sc. 4

But how much unexpected, by so much, We must awake endeavor for defense; For courage mounteth with occasion.
King John. Act II. Sc. 1

I dare do all that may become a man:
Who dares do more, is none.
Macbeth. Act 1. Sc. 7

We fail!
But screw your courage to the sticking-place,
And we'll not fail.
Macbeth. Act I. Sc. 7

'Tis much he dares;
And, to that dauntless temper of his mind,
He hath a wisdom that doth guide his valour
To act in safety,
Macbeth. Act III. Sc. 1

What man dare, I dare:
Approach thou like the rugged Russian bear,
The arm'd rhinoceros, or the Hyrcan tiger,
Take any shape but that, and my firm nerves
Shall never tremble.
Macbeth. Act III. Sc. 4

He hath borne himself beyond the promise of his age; doing in the figure of a lamb, the feats of a lion.
Much Ado About Nothing. Act I. Sc. 1

Wise men ne'er wail their present woes,
But presently prevent the ways to wail.
Richard II. Act III. Sc. 2

I have set my life upon a cast,
And I will stand the hazard of the die.
Richard III. Act V. Sc. 4

Think you, a little din can daunt mine ears?
Have I not in my time heard lions roar?

.   .   .   .

Have I not heard great ordnance in the field,
And heaven's artillery thunder in the skies?

.   .   .   .

And do you tell me of a woman's tongue,
That gives not half so great a blow to hear,
As will a chestnut in a farmer's fire?
Taming of the Shrew. Act I. Sc. 2

He's truly valiant that can wisely suffer
The worst that man can breathe.
Timon of Athens. Act III. Sc. 5

The thing of courage,
As rous'd with rage, with rage doth sympathise,
And, with an accent tun'd in self-same key,
Returns to chiding fortune.
Troilus and Cressida. Act I. Sc. 3

See also: BRAVERY, VALOR, VIRTUE.

COURTESY

The thorny point
Of bare distress hath ta'en from me the show
Of smooth Civility.
As You Like It. Act II. Sc. 7

I am the very pink of courtesy.
Romeo and Juliet. Act II. Sc. 4

See also: GENTLEMAN, GENTLENESS, MANNERS.

COURTSHIP: *see* WOOING.

COWARDICE

> Who knows himself a braggart,
> Let him fear this; for it will come to pass,
> That every braggart shall be found an ass.
> *All's Well That Ends Well*. Act IV. Sc. 3

> You souls of geese,
> That bear the shapes of men, how have you
> run
> From slaves that apes would beat!
> *Coriolanus*. Act I. Sc. 4

> It was great pity, so it was,
> That villainous saltpetre should be digg'd
> Out of the bowels of the harmless earth,
> Which many a good tall fellow had destroyed
> So cowardly; and but for these vile guns
> He would himself have been a soldier.
> *Henry IV*. Pt. I. Act I. Sc. 3

> What a slave art thou, to hack thy sword as
> thou hast done; and then say, it was in fight.
> *Henry IV*. Pt. I. Act II. Sc. 4

> I may speak it to my shame,
> I have a truant been to chivalry.
> *Henry IV*. Pt. I. Act V. Sc. 1

> I would give all my fame for a pot of ale, and
> safety.
> *Henry V*. Act III. Sc. 2

> So bees with smoke, and doves with noisome
> stench,
> Are from their hives, and houses, driven
> away.
> They call'd us, for our fierceness, English
> dogs;
> Now, like whelps, we crying run away.
> *Henry VI*. Pt. I. Act I. Sc. 5

> So cowards fight when they can fly no
> further;
> So doves do peck the falcon's piercing talons;
> So desperate thieves, all hopeless of their
> lives,
> Breathe out invectives 'gainst the officers.
> *Henry VI*. Pt. III. Act I. Sc. 4

> I hold it cowardice,
> To rest mistrustful where a noble heart
> Hath pawn'd an open hand in sign of love.
> *Henry VI*. Pt. III. Act IV. Sc. 2

> Cowards die many times before their deaths;
> The valiant never taste of death but once.
> Of all the wonders that I yet have heard,
> It seems to me most strange that men should
> fear;
> Seeing that death, a necessary end,
> Will come, when it will come.
> *Julius Caesar*. Act II. Sc. 2

> Dost thou now fall over to my foes?
> Thou wear a lion's hide! doff it for shame,
> And hang a calf's skin on those recreant
> limbs.
> *King John*. Act III. Sc. 1

> Would'st thou have that
> Which thou esteem'st the ornament of life,
> And live a coward in thine own esteem;
> Letting I dare not wait upon I would,
> Like the poor cat i' the adage?
> *Macbeth*. Act I. Sc. 7

> How many cowards, whose hearts are all as
> false
> As stairs of sand, wear yet upon their chins
> The beards of Hercules, and frowning Mars;
> Who, inward search'd, have livers white as
> milk?
> *Merchant of Venice*. Act III. Sc. 2

> By this good light, this is a very shallow
> monster:—I afear'd of him?—a very weak
> monster:—The man i' the moon?—a most
> poor credulous monster:—Well drawn, mon-
> ster, in good sooth.
> *Tempest*. Act II. Sc. 2

> Plague on't; an I thought he had been
> valiant, and so cunning in fence, I'd have
> seen him damned ere I'd have challenged
> him.
> *Twelfth Night*. Act III. Sc. 4

See also: FEAR, FOOL.

COWSLIP

> The even mead, that erst brought sweetly
> forth
> The freckled cowslip, burnet, and green
> clover.
> *Henry V*. Act V. Sc. 2

> The cowslips tall her pensioners be;
> In their gold coats spots you see:
> Those be rubies, fairy favours;
> In those freckles live their savours.
> *Midsummer Night's Dream*. Act II. Sc. 1

See also: FLOWER.

CRIME

Foul deeds will rise,
Though all the earth o'erwhelm them, to
men's eyes.
Hamlet. Act I. Sc. 2

If little faults, proceeding on distemper,
Shall not be wink'd at, how shall we stretch
our eye
When capital crimes, chew'd swallow'd, and
digested,
Appear before us?
Henry V. Act II. Sc. 2

Beyond the infinite and boundless reach
Of mercy, if thou didst this deed of death,
Art thou damn'd, Hubert.
King John. Act IV. Sc. 3

Tremble thou wretch,
That has within thee undivulged crimes,
Unwhipp'd of justice.
King Lear. Act III. Sc. 2

There shall be done a deed of dreadful note.
Macbeth. Act III. Sc. 2

The times have been
That, when the brains were out, the man
would die,
And there an end; but now they rise again,
With twenty mortal murders on their crowns,
And push us from our stools.
Macbeth. Act III. Sc. 4

Unnatural deeds
Do breed unnatural troubles: Infected minds
To their deaf pillows will discharge their
secrets.
Macbeth. Act V. Sc. 1

The villainy you teach me, I will execute;
and it shall go hard but I will better the instruction.
Merchant of Venice. Act III. Sc. 1

If you bethink yourself of any crime
Unreconcil'd as yet to heaven and grace,
Solicit for it straight.
Othello. Act V. Sc. 2

O, would the deed were good!
For now the devil, that told me—I did well.
Says, that this deed is chronicled in hell.
Richard II. Act V. Sc. 5

See also: EVIL, GUILT, PRISON, PUNISHMENT,
SIN, TREASON, VICE.

CRITICISM

In such a time as this it is not meet
That every nice offence should bear its com-
ment.
Julius Caesar. Act IV. Sc. 3

'Tis a physic
That's bitter to sweet end.
Measure for Measure. Act IV. Sc. 6

For I am nothing if not critical.
Othello. Act II. Sc. 1

See also: ARGUMENT, DISSENSION, REPROOF.

CROW

Light thickens; and the crow
Makes wing to the rooky wood.
Macbeth. Act III. Sc. 2

The crow doth sing as sweetly as the lark.
Merchant of Venice. Act V. Sc. 1

See also: ANIMAL, BIRD.

CRUELTY

I must be cruel, only to be kind.
Hamlet. Act III. Sc. 4

As flies to wanton boys are we to the gods;
They kill us for their sport.
King Lear. Act IV. Sc. 1

You are the cruell'st she alive,
If you will lead these graces to the grave,
And leave the world no copy.
Twelfth Night. Act I. Sc. 5

If ever, henceforth, thou
These rural latches to his entrance open,
Or hoop his body more with thy embraces,
I will devise a death as cruel for thee
As thou art tender to't.
Winter's Tale. Act IV. Sc. 3

See also: AFFLICTION, PUNISHMENT, REVENGE,
WAR, WOUND.

CURIOSITY

I have perceived a most faint neglect of late;
which I have rather blamed as mine own
jealous curiosity, than as a very pretence and
purpose of unkindness.
King Lear. Act I. Sc. 4

They mocked thee for too much curiosity.
Timon of Athens. Act IV. Sc. 3

See also: EDUCATION, KNOWLEDGE.

CUSTOM

Custom calls me to 't:—
What custom wills, in all things should we
   do 't?
The dust on antique time would lie unswept,
And mountainous error be too highly heap'd
For truth to overpeer.

Coriolanus. Act II. Sc. 3

And to my mind, though I am a native here,
And to the manner born, it is custom
More honor'd in the breach than the observ-
   ance.

Hamlet. Act I. Sc. 4

That monster, custom, . . . is angel yet
   in this,
That to the use of actions fair and good
He likewise gives a frock, or livery,
That aptly is put on.

Hamlet. Act III. Sc. 4

Use can almost change the stamp of nature.

Hamlet. Act III. Sc. 4

New customs,
Though they be never so ridiculous,
Nay, let 'em be unmanly, yet are followed.

Henry VIII. Act I. Sc. 3

The tyrant custom, most grave senators,
Hath made the flinty and steel couch of war
My thrice driven bed of down.

Othello. Act I. Sc. 3

How use doth breed a habit in a man!
This shadowy desert, unfrequented woods,
I better brook than flourishing peopled
   towns.

Two Gentlemen of Verona. Act V. Sc. 4

See also: FASHION, HABIT.

D

DANCE

They have measured many a mile,
To tread a measure with you on this grass.

Love's Labour's Lost. Act V. Sc. 2

When you do dance, I wish you
A wave o' th' sea, that you might ever do
Nothing but that.

Winter's Tale. Act IV. Sc. 3

See also: ART, GRACE, MUSIC.

DARKNESS

I charge thee, Satan, hous'd within this man,
To yield possession to my holy prayers,
And to thy state of darkness hie thee straight;
I conjure thee by all the saints in heaven.

Comedy of Errors. Act IV. Sc. 4

Brief as the lightning in the collied night,
That, in a spleen, unfolds both heaven and
   earth,
And ere a man had power to say—Behold!
The jaws of darkness do devour it up.

Midsummer Night's Dream. Act I. Sc. 1

The charm dissolves apace;
And as the morning steals upon the night,
Melting the darkness, so their rising senses
Begin to chase the ignorant fumes that
   mantle
Their clearer reason.

Tempest. Act V. Sc. 1

See also: BLINDNESS, EVIL, NIGHT, SHADOW.

DAWN

Hark! hark! the lark at heaven's gate sings.
   And Phoebus 'gins arise,
His steeds to water at those springs
   On chalic'd flowers that lies;
And winking Mary-buds begin
   To ope their golden eyes;
With every thing that pretty bin:
   My lady sweet, arise;
      Arise, arise.

Cymbeline. Act II. Sc. 3 *Song*

For night's swift dragons cut the clouds full
   fast,
And yonder shines Aurora's harbinger;
At whose approach, ghosts, wandering here
   and there,
Troop home to churchyards:

Midsummer Night's Dream. Act III. Sc. 2

The wolves have prey'd: and look, the gentle
   day,
Before the wheels of Phoebus, round about,
Dapples the drowsy east with spots of gray.

Much Ado About Nothing. Act V. Sc. 3

See also: DAY, MORNING, SUNRISE.

DAY

O, such a day,
So fought, so follow'd and so fairly won.

Henry IV. Pt. II. Act I. Sc. 1

What hath this day deserv'd? what hath it
   done;
That it in golden letters should be set,
Among the high tides in the kalendar?
> *King John.* Act III. Sc. 1

The sun is in the heaven, and the proud day,
Attended with the pleasures of the world,
Is all too wanton.
> *King John.* Act III. Sc. 3

See also: DAWN, LIGHT, MORNING, SUNRISE.

DEATH

Where art thou death?
> *Antony and Cleopatra.* Act V. Sc. 2

Golden lads and girls all must,
As chimney-sweepers, come to dust.
> *Cymbeline.* Act IV. Sc. 2 *Song*

The graves stood tenantless, and the sheeted
   dead
Did squeak and gibber in the Roman streets.
> *Hamlet.* Act I. Sc. 1

Thou know'st 'tis common; all that live must
   die,
Passing through nature to eternity.
> *Hamlet.* Act I. Sc. 2

I do not set my life at a pin's fee;
And, for my soul, what can it do to that,
Being a thing immortal?
> *Hamlet.* Act I. Sc. 4

Cut off even in the blossoms of my sin,
Unhous'd, disappointed, unanel'd;
No reckoning made, but sent to my account
With all my imperfections on my head.
> *Hamlet.* Act I. Sc. 5

In that sleep of death what dreams may come.
> *Hamlet.* Act III. Sc. 1

To die,—to sleep,
No more; and, by a sleep, to say we end
The heart-ache, and the thousand natural
   shocks
That flesh is heir to,—'tis a consummation
Devoutly to be wished.
> *Hamlet.* Act III. Sc. 1

We shall profane the service of the dead,
To sing sage requiem, and such rest to her,
As to peace-parted souls.
> *Hamlet.* Act V. Sc. 1

O proud death!
What feast is toward in thine eternal cell,
That thou so many princes, at a shoot,
So bloodily hast struck?
> *Hamlet.* Act V. Sc. 2

And we shall feed like oxen at a stall,
The better cherish'd still the nearer death.
> *Henry IV.* Pt. I. Act V. Sc. 2

A man can die but once;—we owe God a
death.
> *Henry IV.* Pt. II. Act III. Sc. 2

Death, as the Psalmist saith, is certain to all;
all shall die.
> *Henry IV.* Pt. II. Act III. Sc. 2

FALSTAFF:
What! is the old king dead?
PISTOL:
As nail in door.
> *Henry IV.* Pt. II. Act V. Sc. 3

'A made a finer end and went away, an it
had been any christom child; 'a parted even
just between twelve and one, e'en at the
turning o' th' tide: for after I saw him fum-
ble with the sheets, and play with the flowers,
and smile upon his fingers' ends, I knew
there was but one way; for his nose was as
sharp as a pen, and 'a babbled of green
fields. How now, sir John? quoth I: what,
man! be of good cheer. So 'a cried out—
God, God, God! three or four times; now I,
to comfort him, bid him 'a should not think
of God; I hoped there was no need to trouble
himself with any such thoughts yet.
> *Henry V.* Act II. Sc. 3

He dies, and makes no sign.
> *Henry VI.* Pt. II. Act III. Sc. 3

My sick heart shows,
That I must yield my body to the earth,
And, by my fall, the conquest to my foe.
Thus yields the cedar to the axe's edge,
Whose arms gave shelter to the princely
   eagle;
Under whose shade the ramping lion slept;
Whose top-branch overpeer'd Jove's spread-
   ing tree,
And kept low shrubs from winter's powerful
   wind.
> *Henry VI.* Pt. III. Act V. Sc. 2

Why, what is pomp, rule, reign, but earth
   and dust?
And, live we how we can, yet die we must.
> *Henry VI.* Pt. III. Act V. Sc. 2

Death! my lord
Their clothes are after such a pagan cut too.
Henry VIII. Act I. Sc. 3

He gave his honours to the world again,
His blessed part to Heaven, and slept in
   peace.
Henry VIII. Act IV. Sc. 2

When beggars die, there are no comets seen;
The heavens themselves blaze forth the death
   of princes.
Julius Caesar. Act II. Sc. 2

Death, a necessary end,
Will come when it will come.
Julius Caesar. Act II. Sc. 2

That we shall die we know; 'tis but the time,
And drawing days out, that men stand upon.
Julius Caesar. Act III. Sc. 1

He that cuts off twenty years of life
Cuts off so many years of fearing death.
Julius Caesar. Act III. Sc. 1

We must die, Messala:
With meditating that she must die once,
I have the patience to endure it now.
Julius Caesar. Act IV. Sc. 3

Death, death! oh, amiable, lovely death,

   .   .   .   .

Come grin on me, and I will think thou
   smil'st.
King John. Act III. Sc. 4

We cannot hold mortalitie's strong hand.
King John. Act IV. Sc. 2

Have I not hideous death within my view,
Retaining but a quantity of life
Which bleeds away, even as a form of wax
Resolveth from its figure 'gainst the fire?
King John. Act V. Sc. 4

O, our lives' sweetness!
That we the pain of death would hourly die,
Rather than die at once!
King Lear. Act V. Sc. 3

Nothing in his life
Became him like the leaving it.
Macbeth. Act I. Sc. 4

After life's fitful fever, he sleeps well;
Treason has done his worst: nor steel, nor
   poison,
Malice domestic, foreign levy, nothing,
Can touch him further.
Macbeth. Act III. Sc. 2

Safe in a ditch he bides,
With twenty trenched gashes on his head;
The least a death to nature.
Macbeth. Act III. Sc. 4

The weariest and most loathed worldly life,
That age, ache, penury, and imprisonment
Can lay on nature, is a paradise
To what we fear of death.
Measure for Measure. Act III. Sc. 1

If I must die,
I will encounter darkness as a bride,
And hug it in mine arms.
Measure for Measure. Act III. Sc. 1

To be imprison'd in the viewless winds,
And blown with restless violence round-
   about
The pendent world; or to be worse than
   worst
Of those, that lawless and incertain thoughts
Imagine howlings!—'tis too horrible!
Measure for Measure. Act III. Sc. 1

Dar'st thou die?
The sense of death is most in apprehension;
And the poor beetle that we tread upon,
In corporal sufferance feels a pang as great
As when a giant dies.
Measure for Measure. Act III. Sc. 1

What's yet in this,
That bears the name of life? Yet in this life
Lie hid more thousand deaths: yet death we
   fear,
That makes these odds all even.
Measure for Measure. Act III. Sc. 1

Here is my journey's end, here is my butt,
And very sea-mark of my utmost sail.
Othello. Act V. Sc. 2

Nothing can we call our own but death;
And that small model of the barren earth,
Which serves as paste and cover to our bones.
Richard II. Act III. Sc. 2

Let's choose executors, and talk of wills:
And yet not so,—for what can we bequeath,
Save our deposed bodies to the ground?
Richard II. Act III. Sc. 2

Within the hollow crown,
That rounds the mortal temples of a king,
Keeps death his court; and there the antic
   sits,
Scoffing his state, and grinning at his pomp.
Richard II. Act III. Sc. 2

And there, at Venice, gave
His body to that pleasant country's earth,
And his pure soul unto his captain Christ,
Under whose colours he had fought so long.
Richard II. Act IV. Sc. 1

Go thou, and fill another room in hell.
That hand shall burn in never-quenching
   fire,
That staggers thus my person.—Exton, thy
   fierce hand
Hath, with thy king's blood, stain'd the
   king's own land.
Mount, mount my soul! thy seat is up on
   high;
Whilst my gross flesh sinks downward, here
   to die.
Richard II. Act V. Sc. 5

I pass'd, methought, the melancholy flood
With that sour ferryman which poets write
   of,
Unto the kingdom of perpetual night.
Richard III. Act I. Sc. 4

'Tis a vile thing to die, my gracious lord,
When men are unprepared, and look not for
   it.
Richard III. Act III. Sc. 2

Woe, destruction, ruin, loss, decay;
The worst is—death, and death will have his
   day.
Richard III. Act III. Sc. 2

Death lies on her, like an untimely frost
Upon the sweetest flower of all the field.
Romeo and Juliet. Act IV. Sc. 5

Death, that hath suck'd the honey of thy
   breath,
Hath had no power yet upon thy beauty:
Thou art not conquer'd; beauty's ensign yet
Is crimson in thy lips, and in thy cheeks,
And death's pale flag is not advanced there.
Romeo and Juliet. Act V. Sc. 3

Eyes, look your last!
Arms, take your last embrace! and lips, O
   you,
The doors of breath, seal with a righteous
   kiss
A dateless bargain to engrossing death.
Romeo and Juliet. Act V. Sc. 3

How oft, when men are at the point of death,
Have they been merry! which their keepers
   call
A lightning before death.
Romeo and Juliet. Act V. Sc. 3

The wills above be done! but I would fain
die a dry death.
Tempest. Act I. Sc. 1

He that dies, pays all debts.
Tempest. Act III. Sc. 2

See also: EPITAPH, GRAVE, MORTALITY, MUR-
DER, SUICIDE.

DECAY

The ripest fruit first falls, and so doth he;
His time is spent.
Richard II. Act II. Sc. 1

In the sweetest bud
The eating canker dwells.
Two Gentlemen of Verona. Act I. Sc. 1

See also: DEATH, GRAVE.

DECEIT

Here we wander in illusions;
Some blessed power deliver us from hence.
Comedy of Errors. Act IV. Sc. 3

With one auspicious, and one dropping eye;
With mirth in funeral, and with dirge in
   marriage,
In equal scale weighing delight and dole.
Hamlet. Act I. Sc. 2

They fool me to the top of my bent. I will
   come by and by.
Hamlet. Act III. Sc. 2

There's neither honesty, manhood, nor good
fellowship in thee.
Henry IV. Pt. II. Act I. Sc. 2

All is confounded, all!
Reproach and everlasting shame
Sits mocking in our plumes.
Henry V. Act IV. Sc. 5

Beguiles him, as the mournful crocodile
With sorrow snares relenting passengers;
Or as the snake, roll'd in a flowering bank,
With shining checker'd slough, doth sting a
   child,
That, for the beauty, thinks it excellent.
Henry VI. Pt. II. Act III. Sc. 2

Why, I can smile, and murther whiles I
   smile;
And cry, content to that which grieves my
   heart;
And wet my cheeks with artificial tears,
And frame my face to all occasions.
Henry VI. Pt. III. Act III. Sc. 2

A quicksand of deceit.
> *Henry VI. Pt. III. Act V. Sc. 4*

His promises were, as he then was, mighty;
But his performance, as he is now, nothing.
> *Henry VIII. Act IV. Sc. 2*

Led so grossly by this meddling priest,
Dreading the curse that money may buy out.
> *King John. Act III. Sc. 1*

The instruments of darkness tell us truths;
Win us with honest trifles, to betray us
In deepest consequence.
> *Macbeth. Act I. Sc. 3*

An evil soul, producing holy witness,
Is like a villain with a smiling cheek;
A goodly apple rotten at the heart:
O, what a goodly outside falsehood hath!
> *Merchant of Venice. Act I. Sc. 3*

All that glisters is not gold.
> *Merchant of Venice. Act II. Sc. 7*

The world is still deceiv'd with ornament.
In law, what plea so tainted and corrupt,
But, being season'd with a gracious voice,
Obscures the show of evil? In religion,
What damned error, but some sober brow
Will bless it, and approve it with a text,
Hiding the grossness with fair ornament?
> *Merchant of Venice. Act III. Sc. 2*

Make the Moor thank me, love me, and reward me,
For making him egregiously an ass.
> *Othello. Act II. Sc. 1*

Ah, that deceit should steal such gentle
shapes,
And with a virtuous visor hide deep vice.
> *Richard III. Act II. Sc. 2*

O, that deceit should dwell
In such a gorgeous palace!
> *Romeo and Juliet. Act III. Sc. 2*

Thus much of this, will make
Black, white; foul, fair; wrong, right;
Base, noble; old, young; coward, valiant.
Ha, you gods! why this?
> *Timon of Athens. Act IV. Sc. 3*

See also: FALSEHOOD, HYPOCRISY, TREASON.

DECISION

Pleasure and revenge,
Have ears more deaf than adders to the voice
Of any true decision.
> *Troilus and Cressida. Act II. Sc. 2*

See also: ACTION, DEED, RESOLUTION.

DEED

From lowest place when virtuous things pro-
ceed,
The place is dignified by the doer's deed:
Where great additions swell, and virtue
none,
It is a dropsied honour; good alone
Is good without a name.
> *All's Well That Ends Well. Act II. Sc. 3*

He covets less
Than misery itself would give; rewards
His deeds with doing them; and is content
To spend the time, to end it.
> *Coriolanus. Act II. Sc. 2*

I never saw
Such noble fury in so poor a thing;
Such precious deeds in one that promis'd
nought
But beggary and poor looks.
> *Cymbeline. Act V. Sc. 5*

The flighty purpose never is o'ertook,
Unless the deed go with it.
> *Macbeth. Act IV. Sc. 1*

A deed without a name.
> *Macbeth. Act IV. Sc. 1*

They look into the beauty of thy mind,
And that, in guess, they measure by thy
deeds.
> *Sonnet LXIX*

I give thee thanks in part of thy deserts,
And will with deeds requite thy gentleness.
> *Titus Andronicus. Act I. Sc. 2*

Go in, and cheer the town; we'll forth, and
fight;
Do deeds worth praise, and tell you them at
night.
> *Troilus and Cressida. Act V. Sc. 3*

See also: ACTION, CHARITY, LABOR, WORK.

DELIGHT

Man delights not me, no, nor woman neither,
though, by your smiling, you seem to say so.
> *Hamlet. Act II. Sc. 2*

Why, all delights are vain; and that most
    vain,
Which, with pain purchas'd, doth inherit
    pain.
        Love's Labour's Lost. Act I. Sc. 1

These violent delights have violent ends,
And in their triumph die; like fire and pow-
    der,
Which, as they kiss, consume.
        Romeo and Juliet. Act II. Sc. 6

See also: CONTENMENT, HAPPINESS, PLEAS-
    URE, WELCOME.

DESIRE

                I have
Immortal longings in me.
        Antony and Cleopatra. Act V. Sc. 2

Can one desire too much of a good thing?
        As You Like It. Act IV. Sc. 1

Thy wish was father, Harry, to that thought:
I stay too long by thee, I weary thee.
        Henry IV. Pt. II. Act IV. Sc. 4

Where nothing wants, that want itself doth
    seek.
        Love's Labour's Lost. Act IV. Sc. 3

See also: APPETITE, HOPE, LOVE, PASSION.

DESOLATION

My desolation does begin to make
A better life.
        Antony and Cleopatra. **Act V. Sc. 2**

There is no creature loves me;
And if I die no soul shall pity me.
        Richard III. Act V. Sc. 3

See also: DESPAIR, MISERY, POVERTY, SADNESS.

DESPAIR

O! that this too too solid flesh would melt,
Thaw, and resolve itself into a dew.
        Hamlet. Act I. Sc. 2

Would I were dead! if God's good will were
    so:
For what is in this world, but grief and woe?
        Henry VI. Pt. III. Act II. Sc. 5

I would, that I were low laid in my grave;
I am not worth this coil that's made for me.
        King John. Act II. Sc. 1

So weary with disasters, tugg'd with fortune,
That I would set my life on any chance
To mend it, or be rid on't.
        Macbeth. Act III. Sc. 1

You take my house, when you do take the
    prop
That doth sustain my house; you take my
    life,
When you do take the means whereby I live.
        Merchant of Venice. Act IV. Sc. 1

I am a tainted wether of the flock,
Meetest for death; the weakest kind of fruit
Drops earliest to the ground, and so let me.
        Merchant of Venice. Act IV. Sc. 1

For nothing canst thou to damnation add,
Greater than that.
        Othello. Act III. Sc. 3

            Of comfort no man speak;
Let's talk of graves, of worms, and epitaphs.
        Richard II. Act III. Sc. 2

            Discomfort guides my tongue,
And bids me speak of nothing but despair.
        Richard II. Act III. Sc. 2

I shall despair.—There is no creature loves
    me;
And, if I die, no soul shall pity me:—
Nay, wherefore should they? since that I
    myself
Find in myself no pity to myself.
        Richard III. Act V. Sc. 3

O break, my heart!—poor bankrout, break at
    once!
To prison, eyes! ne'er look on liberty!
Vile earth, to earth resign; end motion here;
And thou, and Romeo, press one heavy bier!
        Romeo and Juliet. Act III. Sc. 2

                    Let me have
A dram of poison; such soon-speeding gear,
As will disperse itself through all the veins,
That the life-weary taker may fall dead;
And that the trunk may be discharg'd of
    breath
As violently, as hasty powder fir'd
Doth hurry from the fatal cannon's womb.
        Romeo and Juliet. Act V. Sc. 1

For he being dead, with him is beauty slain,
And, beauty dead, black chaos comes again.
        Venus and Adonis. St. 170

Thou tyrant!
Do not repent these things, for they are
    heavier
Than all thy woes can stir: therefore, betake
    thee
To nothing but despair.
                    Winter's Tale. Act III. Sc. 2

See also: AFFLICTION, GRIEF, HOPE, MELAN-
    CHOLY, MISERY.

DESTINY

A man may fish with the worm that hath
eat of a king; and eat of the fish that hath
fed of that worm.
                    Hamlet. Act IV. Sc. 3

We shall be winnow'd with so rough a wind,
That even our corn shall seem as light as
    chaff,
And good from bad find no partition.
                    Henry IV. Pt. II. Act IV. Sc. 1

Here burns my candle out, ay, here it dies,
Which, whiles it lasted, gave king Henry
    light.
                    Henry VI. Pt. III. Act II. Sc. 6

I have touch'd the highest point of all my
    greatness:
And, from that full meridian of my glory,
I haste now to my setting.
                    Henry VIII. Act III. Sc. 2

Think you I bear the shears of destiny?
Have I commandment on the pulse of life?
                    King John. Act IV. Sc. 2

For it is a knell
That summons thee to heaven, or to hell.
                    Macbeth. Act II. Sc. 1

See also: CHANCE, FATE, FORTUNE, LUCK.

DEVIL

Nay, then let the devil wear black, for I'll
have a suit of sables.
                    Hamlet. Act III. Sc. 2

The prince of darkness is a gentleman.
                    King Lear. Act III. Sc. 4

Let me say amen betimes, lest the devil cross
my prayers.
                    Merchant of Venice. Act III. Sc. 1

The lunatic, the lover and the poet,
Are of imagination all compact:
One sees more devils than vast hell can hold.
                    Midsummer Night's Dream. Act V. Sc. 1

What, man! defy the devil: consider, he's
an enemy to mankind.
                    Twelfth Night. Act III. Sc. 4

See also: ANGEL, HELL, SIN, TEMPTATION.

DEW

I must go seek some dew-drops here,
And hang a pearl in every cowslip's ear.
                    Midsummer Night's Dream. Act II. Sc. 1

See also: DAWN, MORNING, NIGHT, SUNRISE.

DIGNITY

Clay and clay differs in dignity,
Whose dust is both alike.
                    Cymbeline. Act IV. Sc. 2

Let none presume
To wear an undeserved dignity.
                    Merchant of Venice. Act II. Sc. 9

See also: CHARACTER, GREATNESS, HONOR.

DISAPPOINTMENT

A friend should bear his friend's infirmities,
But Brutus makes mine greater than they are.
                    Julius Caesar. Act IV. Sc. 3

All is but toys; renown, and grace, is dead;
The wine of life is drawn, and the mere lees
Is left this vault to brag of.
                    Macbeth. Act II. Sc. 3

But earthly happier is the rose distill'd,
Than that, which, with'ring on the virgin
    thorn,
Grows, lives, and dies, in single blessedness.
                    Midsummer Night's Dream. Act I. Sc. 1

See also: DISCONTENTMENT, REGRET, SORROW.

DISCONTENTMENT

O how wretched
Is that poor man that hangs on princes'
    favors!
There is, betwixt that smile we would aspire
    to,
That sweet aspect of princes, and their ruin,
More pangs and fears than wars or woman
    have;
And when he falls, he falls like Lucifer,
Never to hope again.
                    Henry VIII. Act III. Sc. 2

See also: DISAPPOINTMENT, ENVY, SADNESS,
    SORROW.

DISCRETION

Let your own discretion be your tutor: suit the action to the word, the word to the action.
Hamlet. Act III. Sc. 2

The better part of valor is discretion; in the which better part I have saved my life.
Henry IV. Pt. I. Act V. Sc. 4

Covering discretion with a coat of folly.
Henry V. Act II. Sc. 4

I have seen the day of wrong through the little hole of discretion.
Love's Labour's Lost. Act V. Sc. 2

For 'tis not good that children should know any wickedness: old folks, you know, have discretion, as they say, and know the world.
Merry Wives of Windsor. Act II. Sc. 2

Let's teach ourselves that honourable stop, Not to out-sport discretion.
Othello. Act II. Sc. 3

See also: CARE, JUDGMENT, REFLECTION.

DISEASE

O, he's a limb, that has but a disease; Mortal, to cut it off; to cure it easy.
Coriolanus. Act III. Sc. 1

This sickness doth infect
The very life-blood of our enterprise.
Henry IV. Pt. I. Act IV. Sc. 1

This apoplexy is, as I take it, a kind of lethargy, an't please your lordship; a kind of sleeping in the blood, a whoreson tingling.
Henry IV. Pt. II. Act I. Sc. 2

I'll forbear;
And am fallen out with my more headier will,
To take the indispos'd and sickly fit
For the sound man.
King Lear. Act II. Sc. 4

Therefore, the moon, the governess of floods, Pale in her anger, washes all the air, That rheumatic diseases do abound.
Midsummer Night's Dream. Act II. Sc. 2

See also: HEALTH, QUACKERY, SICKNESS.

DISGRACE

And wilt thou still be hammering treachery, To tumble down thy husband and thyself, From top of honour to disgrace's feet?
Henry VI. Pt. II. Act I. Sc. 2

See also: CONSCIENCE, GUILT, SHAME.

DISSENSION

Believe me, lords, my tender years can tell, Civil dissension is a viperous worm, That gnaws the bowels of the commonwealth.
Henry VI. Pt. I. Act III. Sc. 1

If they perceive dissension in our looks, And that within ourselves we disagree, How will their grudging stomachs be provoked
To wilful disobedience and rebel?
Henry VI. Pt. I. Act IV. Sc. 1

Now join your hands, and with your hands your hearts,
That no dissension hinder government.
Henry VI. Pt. III. Act IV. Sc. 6

See also: ARGUMENT, REBELLION.

DOUBT

Our doubts are traitors,
And make us lose the good we oft might win, By fearing to attempt.
Measure for Measure. Act I. Sc. 5

To be once in doubt,
Is once to be resolv'd.
Othello. Act III. Sc. 3

No hinge, nor loop,
To hang a doubt on; or woe upon thy life!
Othello. Act III. Sc. 3

Modest doubt is call'd
The beacon of the wise.
Troilus and Cressida. Act II. Sc. 2

See also: FAITH, SUSPICION.

DOVE

The dove and very blessed spirit of peace.
Henry IV. Pt. II. Act IV. Sc. 1

So shows a snowy dove trooping with crows.
Romeo and Juliet. Act I. Sc. 5

See also: ANIMAL, BIRD.

DREAM

Thou hast beat me out
Twelve several times, and I have nightly
    since
Dreamt of encounters 'twixt thyself and me.
Coriolanus. Act IV. Sc. 5

There is some ill a-brewing toward my rest,
For I did dream of money bags to-night.
Merchant of Venice. Act II. Sc. 5

I have had a most rare vision. I have had a
dream,—past the wit of man to say what
dream it was.
Midsummer Night's Dream. Act IV. Sc. 1

This is the rarest dream that e'er dull sleep
Did mock sad fools withal.
Pericles. Act V. Sc. 1

Oh! I have pass'd a miserable night,
So full of fearful dreams, of ugly sights,
That, as I am a Christian faithful man,
I would not spend another such a night,
Though 'twere to buy a world of happy days.
Richard III. Act I. Sc. 4

Never yet one hour in his bed
Did I enjoy the golden dew of sleep,
But with his timorous dreams was still
    awak'd.
Richard III. Act IV. Sc. 1

Sometimes she driveth o'er a soldier's neck,
And then dreams he of cutting foreign
    throats,
Of breaches, ambuscadoes, Spanish blades,
Of healths five fathom deep.
Romeo and Juliet. Act I. Sc. 4

I talk of dreams,
Which are the children of an idle brain,
Begot of nothing but vain fantasy;
Which is as thin of substance as the air;
And more inconstant than the wind.
Romeo and Juliet. Act I. Sc. 4

If I may trust the flattering truth of sleep,
My dreams presage some joyful news at
    hand:
My bosom's lord sits lightly in his throne;
And, all this day, an unaccustom'd spirit
Lifts me above the ground with cheerful
    thoughts.
Romeo and Juliet. Act V. Sc. 1

We are such stuff
As dreams are made on; and our little life
Is rounded with a sleep.
Tempest. Act IV. Sc. 1

See also: FAIRY, FANCY, IMAGINATION, MER-
MAID, SLEEP, THOUGHT.

DRINK

Drink down all unkindness.
Merry Wives of Windsor. Act I. Sc. 1

See also: INTEMPERANCE, TOAST, WINE.

DUTY

Blow wind! come wrack!
At least we'll die with the harness on our
    back.
Macbeth. Act V. Sc. 5

I do perceive here a divided duty.
Othello. Act I. Sc. 3

Such duty as the subject owes the prince,
Even such a woman oweth to her husband.
Taming of the Shrew. Act V. Sc. 2

I thought the remnant of mine age
Should have been cherish'd by her childlike
    duty.
Two Gentlemen of Verona. Act III. Sc. 1

See also: ACTION, CHARACTER, TRUST.

E

EAGLE

I saw Jove's bird, the Roman eagle, wing'd
From the spungy south to this part of the
    west,
There vanish'd in the sunbeams.
Cymbeline. Act IV. Sc. 2

All furnish'd, all in arms;
All plum'd, like estridges that with the wind
Bated,—like eagles having lately bath'd;
Glittering in golden coats, like images.
Henry IV. Pt. I. Act IV. Sc. 1

But flies an eagle flight, bold, and forth. on,
Leaving no tract behind.
Timon of Athens. Act I. Sc. 1

The eagle suffers little birds to sing,
And is not careful what they mean thereby.
Titus Andronicus. Act IV. Sc. 4

See also: ANIMAL, BIRD.

EATING

Perhaps, some merchant hath invited him,
And from the marts he's somewhere gone to
  dinner.
Good sister let us dine and never fret.
  Comedy of Errors. Act II. Sc. 1

Unquiet meals make ill digestions.
  Comedy of Errors. Act V. Sc. 1

He hath eaten me out of house and home.
  Henry IV. Pt. II. Act II. Sc. 1

Let me not stay a jot for dinner; go, get
it ready.
  King Lear. Act I. Sc. 4

And men sit down to that nourishment which
is called supper.
  Love's Labour's Lost. Act I. Sc. 1

          To feed, were best at home;
From thence, the sauce to meat is ceremony,
Meeting were bare without it.
  Macbeth. Act III. Sc. 4

          At dinner-time
I pray you have in mind where we must
  meet.
  Merchant of Venice. Act I. Sc. 1

They are as sick, that surfeit with too much,
as they that starve with nothing.
  Merchant of Venice. Act I. Sc. 2

I wished your venison better; it was ill kill'd.
  Merry Wives of Windsor. Act I. Sc. 1

Come, we have a hot venison pasty to dinner; come, gentlemen, I hope we shall drink
down all unkindness.
  Merry Wives of Windsor. Act I. Sc. 1

I will make an end of my dinner; there's
pippins and cheese to come.
  Merry Wives of Windsor. Act I. Sc. 2

          A surfeit of the sweetest things
The deepest loathing to the stomach brings.
  Midsummer Night's Dream. Act II. Sc. 3

What say you to a piece of beef and mustard?
  Taming of the Shrew. Act IV. Sc. 3

I fear, it is too choleric a meat:
How say you to a fat tripe, finely broil'd?
  Taming of the Shrew. Act IV. Sc. 3

See also: APPETITE, COOKING, HUNGER.

ECHO

The babbling echo mocks the hounds
Replying shrilly to the well-tun'd horns,
As if a double hunt were heard at once.
  Titus Andronicus. Act II. Sc. 3

See also: VOICE.

EDUCATION

SMITH:
He can write and read, and cast contempt.
JACK CADE:
O monstrous!
SMITH:
We took him setting of boy's copies.
JACK CADE:
Here's a villain.
  Henry VI. Pt. II. Act IV. Sc. 2

God hath blessed you with a good name:
to be a well-favored man is the gift of fortune; but to write and read comes by nature.
  Much Ado About Nothing. Act III. Sc. 3

See also: BOOK, KNOWLEDGE, LEARNING, STU-
  DENT, STUDY.

ELOQUENCE

To try thy eloquence, now 'tis time.
  Antony and Cleopatra. Act III. Sc. 10

Action is eloquence.
  Coriolanus. Act III. Sc. 2

That aged ears play truant at his tales,
And younger hearings are quite ravished;
So sweet and voluble is his discourse.
  Love's Labour's Lost. Act II. Sc. 1

          Every tongue, that speaks
But Romeo's name, speaks heavenly elo-
  quence.
  Romeo and Juliet. Act III. Sc. 2

Say, she be mute, and will not speak a word;
Then I'll commend her volubility,
And say she uttereth piercing eloquence.
  Taming of the Shrew. Act II. Sc. 1

See also: ORATORY, SPEECH, WIT.

ENEMY

They are our outward consciences.
  Henry V. Act IV. Sc. 1

Heat not a furnace for your foe so hot
That it do singe yourself.
Henry VIII. Act I. Sc. 1

You have many enemies, that know not
Why they are so, but, like to village curs,
Bark when their fellows do.
Henry VIII. Act II. Sc. 4

I do believe,
Induced by potent circumstances, that
You are mine enemy; and make my challenge.
You shall not be my judge.
Henry VIII. Act II. Sc. 4

O cunning enemy, that, to catch a saint,
With saints dost bait thy hook!
Measure for Measure. Act II. Sc. 2

See also: DISSENSION, FRIENDSHIP, HATE, RE-
VENGE, WAR.

ENGLAND

Your isle, which stands
As Neptune's park, ribbed and paled in
With rocks unscaleable, and roaring waters.
Cymbeline. Act III. Sc. 1

Britain is
A world by itself; and we will nothing pay
For wearing our own noses.
Cymbeline. Act III. Sc. 1

O England!—model to thy inward greatness,
Like little body with a mighty heart,—
What might'st thou do, that honour would
thee do,
Were all thy children kind and natural!
But see thy fault!
Henry V. Act II. Chorus

This royal throne of kings, this scepter'd isle,
This earth of majesty, this seat of Mars,
This other Eden, demi-paradise;
This fortress built by nature for herself,
Against infection and the hand of war;
This happy breed of men, this little world;
This precious stone set in the silver sea.
Richard II. Act II. Sc. 1

See also: LOYALTY, PATRIOTISM.

ENJOYMENT

Fast asleep! It is no matter;
Enjoy the honey-heavy dew of slumber:
Thou hast no figures, nor no fantasies,
Which busy care draws in the brains of men.
Julius Caesar. Act II. Sc. 1

See also: HAPPINESS, JOY, PLEASURE.

ENTHUSIASM

His rash fierce blaze of riot cannot last;
For violent fires soon burn out themselves;
Small showers last long, but sudden storms
are short.
Richard II. Act II. Sc. 1

See also: AMBITION, STRENGTH, YOUTH.

ENVY

In seeking tales and informations
Against this man, (whose honesty the devil
And his disciples only envy at,)
Ye blew the fire that burns ye.
Henry VIII. Act V. Sc. 2

Such men as he be never at heart's ease,
Whiles they behold a greater than them-
selves:
And therefore are they very dangerous.
Julius Caesar. Act I. Sc. 2

See, what a rent the envious Casca made.
Julius Caesar. Act III. Sc. 2

No metal can,
No, not the hangman's axe, bear half the
keenness
Of thy sharp envy.
Merchant of Venice. Act IV. Sc. 1

Arise, fair sun, and kill the envious moon,
Who is already sick and pale with grief,
That thou her maid art far more fair than
she.
Be not her maid, since she is envious.
Romeo and Juliet. Act II. Sc. 2

We make ourselves fools to disport our-
selves;
And spend our flatteries, to drink those men,
Upon whose age we void it up again,
With poisonous spite and envy.
Timon of Athens. Act I. Sc. 2

The general's disdain'd
By him one step below; he, by the next;
That next, by him beneath; so every step,
Exampled by the first pace that is sick
Of his superior, grows to an envious fever
Of pale and bloodless emulation.
Troilus and Cressida. Act I. Sc. 3

See also: JEALOUSY.

EPITAPH

After your death you were better have a bad
epitaph, than their ill report while you lived.
Hamlet. Act II. Sc. 2

Either our history shall, with full mouth
Speak freely of our acts, or else our grave,
Like Turkish mute, shall have a tongueless
  mouth,
Not worshipp'd with a waxen epitaph.
                    Henry V. Act I. Sc. 2

You cannot better be employ'd Bassanio,
Than to live still, and write mine epitaph.
          Merchant of Venice. Act IV. Sc. 1

On your family's old monument
Hang mournful epitaphs.
      Much Ado About Nothing. Act IV. Sc. 1

          And, if your love
Can labour aught in sad invention,
Hang her an epitaph upon her tomb,
And sing it to her bones: sing it to-night.
      Much Ado About Nothing. Act V. Sc. 1

          Of comfort no man speak:
Let's talk of graves, of worms, and epitaphs.
              Richard II. Act III. Sc. 2

See also: DEATH, GRAVE.

EQUALITY

Equality of two domestic powers
Breeds scrupulous faction.
          Antony and Cleopatra. Act I. Sc. 3

          Mean and mighty, rotting
Together, have our dust.
                Cymbeline. Act IV. Sc. 2

Heralds, from off our towers we might behold,
From first to last, the onset and retire
Of both your armies; whose equality
By our best eyes cannot be censured:
Blood hath bought blood, and blows have
  answer'd blows;
Strength match'd with strength, and power
  confronted power;
Both are alike, and both alike we like.
              King John. Act I. Sc. 2

          She in beauty, education, blood,
Holds hand with any princess of the world.
              King John. Act II. Sc. 2

See also: FREEDOM, JUSTICE, LIBERTY.

ERROR

          Purposes mistook
Fall'n on the inventor's heads.
                Hamlet. Act V. Sc. 2

How far your eyes may pierce, I cannot
  tell;
Striving to better, oft we mar what's well.
              King Lear. Act I. Sc. 4

It may be right; but you are in the wrong
To speak before your time.
          Measure for Measure. Act V. Sc. 1

Omission to do what is necessary
Seals a commission to a blank of danger.
        Troilus and Cressida. Act III. Sc. 3

The error of our eye directs our mind.
What error leads must err.
         Troilus and Cressida. Act V. Sc. 2

See also: EVIL, FALSEHOOD, FAULT, FOOL, SIN,
  TRUTH, VICE.

EVIL

The evil that men do lives after them;
The good is oft interred with their bones.
              Julius Caesar. Act III. Sc. 2

          The world is grown so bad
That wrens make prey where eagles dare not
  perch.
              Richard III. Act I. Sc. 3

But then I sigh, and, with a piece of Scripture,
Tell them, that God bids us do good for evil.
              Richard III. Act I. Sc. 3

See also: ADVERSITY, ERROR, HATE, MISCHIEF,
  REVENGE, SIN.

EXAMPLE

Thieves for their robbery have authority,
When judges steal themselves.
          Measure for Measure. Act II. Sc. 2

See also: EXPERIENCE, INFLUENCE, LEARNING.

EXPECTATION

Oft expectation fails, and most oft there
Where most it promises; and oft it hits
Where hope is coldest, and despair most fits.
        All's Well That Ends Well. Act II. Sc. 1

          There have sat
The livelong day, with patient expectation,
To see great Pompey pass the streets of Rome.
              Julius Caesar. Act I. Sc. 1

When clouds are seen, wise men put on their
  cloaks;
When great leaves fall, then winter is at hand;

When the sun sets, who doth not look for
night?
Untimely storms make men expect a dearth.
Richard III. Act II. Sc. 3

Promising is the very air o' the time;
It opens the eyes of expectation:
Performance is ever the duller for his act;
And, but in the plainer and simpler kind of
people,
The deed of saying is quite out of use.
Timon of Athens. Act V. Sc. 1

Expectation whirls me round.
The imaginary relish is so sweet
That it enchants my sense.
Troilus and Cressida. Act III. Sc. 2

See also: AMBITION, DESIRE, HOPE, TRUST.

EXPERIENCE

Unless experience be a jewel; that I have
purchased at an infinite rate.
Merry Wives of Windsor. Act II. Sc. 2

What we have we prize not to the worth,
Whiles we enjoy it; but being lack'd and lost,
Why then we rack the value; then we find
The virtue, that possession would not show us
While it was ours.
Much Ado About Nothing. Act IV. Sc. 1

Men
Can counsel, and speak comfort to that grief
Which they themselves not feel; but tasting
it,
Their counsel turns to passion, which before
Would give preceptial medicine to rage,
Fetter strong madness in a silken thread,
Charm ache with air, and agony with words.
Much Ado About Nothing. Act V. Sc. 1

My grief lies onward, and my joy behind.
Sonnet L

See also: EXAMPLE, KNOWLEDGE, LEARNING.

EXTREMES

Like to the time o' the year between the
extremes
Of hot and cold: he was nor sad nor merry.
Antony and Cleopatra. Act I. Sc. 1

Not fearing death, nor shrinking for dis-
tress,
But always resolute in most extremes.
Henry VI. Pt. I. Act IV. Sc. 1

Who can be patient in such extremes?
Henry VI. Pt. III. Act I. Sc. 1

Where two raging fires meet together,
They do consume the thing that feeds their
fury:
Though little fire grows great with little
wind,
Yet extreme gusts will blow out fire and all.
Taming of the Shrew. Act II. Sc. 1

See also: INTEMPERANCE, MODERATION.

EYE

Thou tell'st me, there is murder in mine eye;
'Tis pretty sure, and very probable,
That eyes, that are the frail'st and softest
things,
Who shut their coward gates on atomies,
Should be call'd tyrants, butchers, murderers!
As You Like It. Act III. Sc. 5

Faster than his tongue
Did make offence, his eye did heal it up.
As You Like It. Act III. Sc. 5

An eye like Mars, to threaten or command.
Hamlet. Act III. Sc. 4

The image of a wicked heinous fault
Lives in his eye: that close aspect of his
Does show the mood of a much-troubled
breast.
King John. Act IV. Sc. 2

You have seen
Sunshine and rain at once. . . . Those happy
smilets,
That play'd on her ripe lip, seem'd not to
know
What guests were in her eyes; which parted
thence,
As pearls from diamonds dropp'd.
King Lear. Act IV. Sc. 3

Where is any author in the world,
Teaches such beauty as a woman's eye?
Love's Labour's Lost. Act IV. Sc. 3

From women's eyes this doctrine I derive;
They sparkle still the right Promethean fire;
They are the books, the arts, the academies,
That show, contain, and nourish all the world;
Else, none at all in aught proves excellent.
Love's Labour's Lost. Act Iv. Sc. 3

A lover's eyes will gaze an eagle blind.
Love's Labour's Lost. Act IV. Sc. 3

From her eyes
I did receive fair speechless messages.
Merchant of Venice. Act I. Sc. 1

I see how thine eye would emulate the diamond: Thou hast the right arched bent of the brow.
Merry Wives of Windsor. Act III. Sc. 3

I have a good eye, uncle; I can see a church by daylight.
Much Ado About Nothing. Act II. Sc. 1

Disdain and scorn ride sparkling in her eyes.
Much Ado About Nothing. Act III. Sc. 1

Her eyes like marigolds, had sheath'd their light;
And, canopied in darkness, sweetly lay,
Till they might open to adorn the day.
Rape of Lucrece. Line 397

Her eye in heaven
Would through the airy region stream so bright,
That birds would sing and think it were not night.
Romeo and Juliet. Act II. Sc. 2

Alack! there lies more peril in thine eye,
Than twenty of their swords.
Romeo and Juliet. Act II. Sc. 2

Thy eyes' windows fall,
Like death, when he shuts up the day of life.
Romeo and Juliet. Act IV. Sc. 1

The fringed curtains of thine eyes advance,
And say, what thou seest yond.
Tempest. Act I. Sc. 2

Her two blue windows faintly she up-heaveth,
Like the fair sun, when in his fresh array
He cheers the morn, and all the earth relieveth;
And as the bright sun glorifies the sky,
So is her face illumin'd with her eye.
Venus and Adonis. Line 482

See also: BLINDNESS, DARKNESS, FACE, LIGHT.

F

FACE

All men's faces are true, whatso'er their hands are.
Antony and Cleopatra. Act II. Sc. 6

A countenance more in sorrow than in anger.
Hamlet. Act I. Sc. 2

In thy face
I see thy fury: if I longer stay
We shall begin our ancient bickerings.
Henry VI. Pt. II. Act I. Sc. 1

There is a fellow somewhat near the door, he should be a brasier by his face.
Henry VIII. Act V. Sc. 3

I have seen better faces in my time,
Than stands on any shoulder that I see.
King Lear. Act II. Sc. 2

There's no art
To find the mind's construction in the face.
Macbeth. Act I. Sc. 4

Your face, my thane, is a book, where men
May read strange matters: To beguile the time,
Look like the time.
Macbeth. Act I. Sc. 5

You have such a February face,
So full of frost, of storm, and cloudiness.
Much Ado About Nothing. Act V. Sc. 4

Compare her face with some that I shall show,
And I will make thee think thy swan a crow.
Romeo and Juliet. Act I. Sc. 2

His cheek the map of days outworn.
Sonnet LXVIII

Black brows they say
Become some women best, in a semicircle
Or a half-moon, made with a pen.
Winter's Tale. Act II. Sc. 1

See also: BEAUTY, EYE.

FAIRY

This is the fairy land:—O, spite of spites,
We talk with goblins, owls, and elvish sprites.
Comedy of Errors. Act II. Sc. 2

They are fairies, he that speaks to them shall die:
I'll wink and couch: no man their works must eye.
Merry Wives of Windsor. Act V. Sc. 5

Fairies, black, gray, green, and white,
You moonshine revellers, and shades of night.
Merry Wives of Windsor. Act V. Sc. 5

Set your heart at rest,
The fairy-land buys not the child of me.
Midsummer Night's Dream. Act II. Sc. 2

The honey-bags steal from the humble-bees,
And, for night-tapers, crop their waxen thighs,
And light them at the fiery glow-worm's eyes.
Midsummer Night's Dream. Act III. Sc. 1

In silence sad,
Trip we after the night's shade:
We the globe can compass soon,
Swifter than the wand'ring moon.
Midsummer Night's Dream. Act IV. Sc. 1

O, then, I see Queen Mab hath been with
you.
She is the fairie's midwife; and she comes
In shape no bigger than an agate-stone
On the forefinger of an alderman.
Romeo and Juliet. Act I. Sc. 4

Where the bee sucks, there suck I;
In a cowslip's bell I lie;
There I couch when owls do cry.
On the bat's back I do fly.
Tempest. Act V. Sc. 1. *Song*

See also: DREAM, FANCY, IMAGINATION, MER-
MAID, SLEEP.

FAITH

Thou almost mak'st me waver in my faith,
To hold opinion with Pythagoras,
That souls of animals infuse themselves
Into the trunks of men,
Merchant of Venice. Act IV. Sc. 1

See also: BELIEF, CONFIDENCE, FIDELITY, GOD,
RELIGION, TRUST.

FALCON

A falcon tow'ring in her pride of place,
Was by a mousing owl hawk'd at and kill'd.
Macbeth. Act II. Sc. 4

My falcon now is sharp, and passing empty;
And, till she stoop, she must not be full-
gorg'd,
For then she never looks upon her lure.
Taming of the Shrew. Act IV. Sc. 1

See also: ANIMAL, BIRD.

FALSEHOOD

He will lie, sir, with such volubility, that you
would think truth were a fool.
All Well That Ends Well. Act IV. Sc. 3

To lapse in fulness
Is sorer than to lie for need; and falsehood
Is worse in kings than beggars.
Cymbeline. Act III. Sc. 6

Your bait of falsehood takes this carp of
truth.
Hamlet. Act II. Sc. 1

'Tis as easy as lying.
Hamlet. Act III. Sc. 2

These lies are like the father that begets
them; gross as a mountain, open, palpable.
Henry IV. Pt. I. Act II. Sc. 4

Lord, Lord, how the world is given to lying!
I grant you I was down, and out of breath;
and so was he: but we rose both at an instant, and fought a long hour by Shrewsbury
clock.
Henry IV. Pt. I. Act V. Sc. 4

For my part, if a lie may do thee grace,
I'll gild it with the happiest terms I have.
Henry IV. Pt. I. Act V. Sc. 4

Lord, Lord, how subject we old men are to
this vice of lying!
Henry IV. Pt. II. Act III. Sc. 2

Whose tongue soe'er speaks false,
Not truly speaks; who speaks not truly, lies.
King John. Act IV. Sc. 3

Oh, what a goodly outside falsehood hath!
Merchant of Venice. Act I. Sc. 3

Thou liest in thy throat; that is not the matter I challenge thee for.
Twelfth Night. Act III. Sc. 4

See also: DECEIT, HYPOCRISY, SLANDER.

FAME

Better leave undone, than by our deeds ac-
quire
Too high a fame, when he we serve's away.
Antony and Cleopatra. Act III. Sc. 1

Let fame, that all hunt after in their lives,
Live register'd upon our brazen tombs.
Love's Labour's Lost. Act I. Sc. 1

Death makes no conquest of this conqueror:
For now he lives in fame, though not in life.
Richard I. Act III. Sc. 1

He lives in fame, that died in virtue's cause.
Titus Andronicus. Act I. Sc. 2

See also: APPLAUSE, HONOR, REPUTATION.

FANCY

Pacing through the forest,
Chewing the food of sweet and bitter fancy.
As You Like It. Act IV. Sc. 3

Tell me, where is fancy bred;
Or in the heart, or in the head?
How begot, how nourished?
Reply, Reply,
It is engender'd in the eyes
With gazing fed; and fancy dies
In the cradle where it lies.
Merchant of Venice. Act III. Sc. 2

So full of shapes is fancy,
That it alone is high fantastical.
Twelfth Night. Act I. Sc. 1

Let fancy still my sense in Lethe steep;
If it be thus to dream still let me sleep!
Twelfth Night. Act IV. Sc. 1

See also: DREAM, IMAGINATION.

FAREWELL

Farewell and stand fast.
Henry IV. Pt. I. Act II. Sc. 2

Farewell the plumed troops, and the big
wars,
That make ambition virtue! O, farewell!
Farewell the neighing steed, and the shrill
trump,
The spirit-stirring drum, the ear-piercing fife.
Othello. Act III. Sc. 3

Here's my hand.
And mine, with my heart in't. And now
farewell,
Till half an hour hence.
Tempest. Act III. Sc. 1

See also: ABSENCE, PARTING.

FASHION

The glass of fashion, and the mould of form,
The observ'd of all observers.
Hamlet. Act III. Sc. 1

Their clothes are after such a pagan cut, too,
That, sure, they have worn out Christendom.
Henry VIII. Act I. Sc. 3

New customs,
Though they be never so ridiculous,
Nay, let them be unmanly, yet are follow'd.
Henry VIII. Act I. Sc. 3

You, Sir, I entertain for one of my hundred;
only, I do not like the fashion of your garments.
King Lear. Act III. Sc. 6

I see; . . . that the fashion wears out more
apparel than the man.
Much Ado About Nothing. Act III. Sc. 3

I'll be at charge for a looking-glass;
And entertain a score or two of tailors,
To study fashions to adorn my body.
Since I am crept in favour with myself,
I will maintain it with some little cost.
Richard III. Act I. Sc. 2

See also: APPAREL, CUSTOM, VANITY.

FATE

My fate cries out,
And makes each petty artery in this body
As hardy as the Nemean lion's nerve.
Hamlet. Act I. Sc. 4

Some must watch, while some must sleep;
So runs the world away.
Hamlet. Act III. Sc. 2

Our wills, and fates, do so contrary run,
That our devices still are overthrown;
Our thoughts are ours, their ends none of our
own.
Hamlet. Act III. Sc. 2

Let Hercules himself do what he may,
The cat will mew, and dog will have his day.
Hamlet. Act V. Sc. 1

Imperial Caesar, dead and turn'd to clay,
Might stop a hole to keep the wind away:
O, that that earth, which kept the world in
awe,
Should patch a wall, to expel the winter's
flaw!
Hamlet. Act V. Sc. 1

O heavens! that one might read the book of
fate;
And see the revolutions of the times
Make mountains level, and the continent
(Weary of solid firmness,) melt itself
Into the sea!
Henry IV. Pt. II. Act III. Sc. 1

What fates impose, that men must needs
abide,
It boots not to resist both wind and tide.
Henry VI. Pt. III. Act IV. Sc. 3

Farewell, a long farewell, to all my greatness!
This is the state of man; to-day he puts forth
The tender leaves of hope; to-morrow
    blossoms,
And bears his blushing honours thick upon
    him:
The third day comes a frost, a killing frost;
And, when he thinks, good easy man, full
    surely
His greatness is a ripening,—nips his root,
And then he falls, as I do.
                    Henry VIII. Act III. Sc. 2

If thou read this, O Caesar, thou may'st live;
If not, the Fates with traitors do contrive.
                    Julius Caesar. Act II. Sc. 3

O mighty Caesar! Dost thou lie so low?
Are all thy conquests, glories, triumphs,
    spoils,
Shrunk to this little measure?
                    Julius Caesar. Act III. Sc. 1

Fates! we will know your pleasures:—
That we shall die we know; 'tis but the time,
And drawing days out, that men stand upon.
                    Julius Caesar. Act III. Sc. 1

But yesterday, the word of Caesar might
Have stood against the world; now lies he
    there,
And none so poor to do him reverence.
                    Julius Caesar. Act III. Sc. 2

            The worst is not worst
So long as we can say, This is the worst,
                    King Lear. Act IV. Sc. 1

                    Men must endure
Their going hence, even as their coming
    hither.
                    King Lear. Act V. Sc. 2

            What should be spoken here,
Where, our fate, hid within an auger-hole,
May rush, and seize us?
                    Macbeth. Act II. Sc. 3

But yet I'll make assurance doubly sure,
And take a bond of fate: thou shalt not live.
                    Macbeth. Act IV. Sc. 1

What's done, cannot be undone.
                    Macbeth. Act V. Sc. 1

If he had been as you, and you as he,
You would have slipp'd like him.
                    Measure for Measure. Act II. Sc. 2

There is divinity in odd numbers,
Either in nativity, chance or death.
                    Merry Wives of Windsor. Act V. Sc. 1

        But, O vain boast
Who can control his fate?
                    Othello. Act V. Sc. 2

A man whom both the waters and the wind,
In that vast tennis-court, hath made the ball
For them to play upon.
                    Pericles. Act II. Sc. 1

They that stand high have many blasts to
    shake them;
And if they fall they dash themselves to
    pieces.
                    Richard III. Act I. Sc. 3

What is done cannot be now amended.
                    Richard III. Act IV. Sc. 4

        You fools! I and my fellows
Are ministers of fate; the elements
Of whom your swords are temper'd, may as
    well
Wound the loud winds, or with bemock'd-at
    stabs
Kill the still-closing waters, as diminish
One dowle that's in my plume.
                    Tempest. Act III. Sc. 3

Fate, show thy force; ourselves we do not
    owe;
What is decreed must be; and be this so.
                    Twelfth Night. Act I. Sc. 5

As the unthought-on accident is guilty
To what we wildly do, so we profess
Ourselves to be the slaves of chance, and flies
Of every wind that blows.
                    Winter's Tale. Act IV. Sc. 3

See also: CHANCE, DESTINY, FORTUNE, GOD,
    LIFE, LUCK, PROVIDENCE.

FAULT

Every one fault seeming monstrous, till his
fellow fault came to match it.
                    As You Like It. Act III. Sc. 2

        Patches set upon a little breath,
Discredit more in hiding for the fault,
Than did the fault before.
                    King John. Act IV. Sc. 2

            Excusing of a fault
Doth make the fault the worse by the excuse.
                    King John. Act IV. Sc. 2

Go to your bosom;
Knock there; and ask your heart what it
    doth know
That's like my brother's fault.
                Measure for Measure. Act II. Sc. 2

Condemn the fault, and not the actor of it!
Why every fault's condemn'd, ere it bè done:
Mine were the very cipher of a function,
To fine the faults, whose fine stands in
    record,
And let go by the actor.
                Measure for Measure. Act III. Sc. 2

They say, best men are moulded out of
    faults;
And, for the most, become much more the
    better
For being a little bad: so may my husband.
                Measure for Measure. Act V. Sc. 1

Her only fault (and that is fault enough)
Is,—that she is intolerable curst,
And shrewd, and forward: so beyond all
    measure,
That, were my state far worser than it is,
I would not wed her for a mine of gold.
                Taming of the Shrew. Act I. Sc. 2

Faults that are rich, are fair.
                Timon of Athens. Act I. Sc. 2

See also: ERROR, GUILT, SIN, VICE.

FAVOR

Which of you, shall we say, doth love us
    most?
That we our largest bounty may extend
Where nature doth with merit challenge.
                King Lear. Act I. Sc. 1

Sickness is catching; O, were favour so,
(Your words I catch,) fair Hermia, ere I go.
                Midsummer Night's Dream. Act I. Sc. 1

See also: GIFT, GRACE, KINDNESS.

FEAR

I could a tale unfold, whose lightest word
Would harrow up thy soul; freeze thy young
    blood;
Make thy two eyes, like stars, start from
    their spheres;
Thy knotted and combined locks to part,
And each particular hair to stand on end,
Like quills upon the fretful porcupine.
                Hamlet. Act I. Sc. 5

There is not such a word
Spoke of in Scotland, as the term of fear.
                Henry IV. Pt. I. Act IV. Sc. 1

Thou tremblest and the whiteness in thy
    cheek
Is apter than thy tongue to tell thy errand.
                Henry IV. Pt. II. Act I. Sc. 1

Things done well,
And with a care, exempt themselves from
    fear;
Things done without example, in their issue
Are to be feared.
                Henry VIII. Act I. Sc. 2

I am sick and capable of fears;
Opress'd with wrongs, and therefore full of
    fears;
A widow, husbandless, subject to fears;
A woman, naturally born to fears.
                King John. Act III. Sc. 1

And make my seated heart knock at my ribs.
                Macbeth. Act I. Sc. 3

Present fears
Are less than horrible imaginings.
                Macbeth. Act I. Sc. 3

Is this a dagger which I see before me,
The handle toward my hand?
                Macbeth. Act II. Sc. 1

A dagger of the mind; a false creation,
Proceeding from the heat-oppressed brain.
                Macbeth. Act II. Sc. 1

We eat our meal in fear, and sleep
In the affliction of those terrible dreams,
That shake us nightly.
                Macbeth. Act III. Sc. 2

Take any shape but that, and my firm nerves
Shall never tremble.
                Macbeth. Act III. Sc. 4

Thou can'st not say I did it; never shake
Thy gory locks at me.
                Macbeth. Act III. Sc. 4

You can behold such sights,
And keep the natural ruby of your cheeks,
When mine is blanch'd with fear.
                Macbeth. Act III. Sc. 4

His flight was madness: When our actions do
    not,
Our fears do make us traitors.
                Macbeth. Act IV. Sc. 2

Or in the night, imagining some fear,
How easy is a bush suppos'd a bear?
Midsummer Night's Dream. Act V. Sc. 1

'Tis time to fear, when tyrants seem to kiss.
Pericles. Act I. Sc. 2

To fear the foe, since fear oppresseth strength,
Gives, in your weakness, strength unto your
foe.
Richard II. Act III. Sc. 2

Truly, the hearts of men are full of fear:
You cannot reason almost with a man
That looks not heavily, and full of dread.
Richard III. Act II. Sc. 3

They spake not a word;
But, like dumb statues or breathing stones,
Star'd each on other, and look'd deadly pale.
Richard III. Act III. Sc. 7

And, being thus frighted, swears a prayer or
two,
And sleeps again.
Romeo and Juliet. Act I. Sc. 4

A faint cold fear thrills through my veins,
That almost freezes up the heart of life.
Romeo and Juliet. Act IV. Sc. 3

If ever fearful
To do a thing, when I the issue doubted,
Whereof the execution did cry out
Against the non-performance; 'twas a fear
Which oft infects the wisest.
Winter's Tale. Act I. Sc. 2

See also: COWARDICE, DESPAIR, DOUBT.

FEASTING

But, first—
Or last, your fine Egyptian cookery
Shall have the fame. I have heard that Ju-
lius Caesar
Grew fat with feasting there.
Antony and Cleopatra. Act II. Sc. 6

Who rises from a feast
With that keen appetite that he sits down?
Merchant of Venice. Act II. Sc. 6

This night I hold an old accustom'd feast,
Whereto I have invited many a guest,
Such as I love; and you among the store,
One more, most welcome, makes my number
more.
Romeo and Juliet. Act I. Sc. 2

My cake is dough: But I'll in among the rest;
Out of hope of all,—but my share of the feast.
Taming of the Shrew. Act V. Sc. 1

Each man to his stool, with that spur as
he would to the lip of his mistress; your
diet shall be in all places alike. Make not a
city feast of it, to let the meat cool ere we
can agree upon the first place.
Timon of Athens. Act III. Sc. 6

Our feasts
In every mess have folly, and the feeders
Digest with it a custom, I should blush
To see you so attir'd.
Winter's Tale. Act IV. Sc. 3

See also: DRINK, EATING, WINE.

FICKLENESS

Was ever feather so lightly blown to and fro,
as this multitude?
Henry VI. Pt. II. Act IV. Sc. 8

Sigh no more, ladies, sigh no more,
Men were deceivers ever;
One foot in sea, and one on shore;
To one thing constant never.
Much Ado About Nothing. Act II. Sc. 3

See also: CHANGE, INCONSTANCY.

FIDELITY

You draw me, you hard-hearted adamant;
But yet you draw not iron, for my heart
Is true as steel.
Midsummer Night's Dream. Act II. Sc. 2

See also: CONSTANCY, FAITH, FRIENDSHIP, LOY-
ALTY, TRUST.

FIRE

A little fire is quickly trodden out; which,
being suffer'd, rivers cannot quench.
Henry VI. Pt. III. Act IV. Sc. 8

The fire i' the flint
Shows not till it be struck.
Timon of Athens. Act I. Sc. 1

Fire that's closest kept burns most of all.
Two Gentlemen of Verona. Act I. Sc. 2

See also: COOKING, LIGHT, NIGHT.

FISHING

Give me mine angle, we'll to the river; there,
My music playing far off, I will betray

Tawney-finn'd fishes; my bended hook shall
pierce
Their slimy jaws.
Antony and Cleopatra. Act II. Sc. 5

Trail'st thou the puissant pike?
Henry V. Act IV. Sc. 1

The pleas'nt angling is to see the fish
Cut with her golden oars the silver stream,
And greedily devour the treacherous bait.
Much Ado About Nothing. Act III. Sc. 1

THIRD FISHERMAN:
Master I marvel how the fishes live in the sea.
FIRST FISHERMAN:
Why, as men do a-land: the great ones eat
up the little ones.
Pericles. Act II. Sc. 1

See also: ANIMAL, ENJOYMENT.

FLAG

This token serveth for a flag of truce
Betwixt ourselves and all our followers.
Henry VI. Pt. I. Act III. Sc. 1

A garish flag,
To be the aim of every dangerous shot.
Richard III. Act IV. Sc. 4

See also: ENGLAND, PATRIOTISM, WAR.

FLATTERY

'Faith, there have been many great men that
have flattered the people, who ne'er loved
them; and there be many that they have
loved, they know not wherefore: so that, if
they love they know not why, they hate upon
no better ground.
Coriolanus. Act II. Sc. 2

Mine eyes
Were not in fault, for she was beautiful:
Mine ears, that heard her flattery; nor mine
heart,
That thought her like her seeming; it had
been vicious
To have mistrusted her.
Cymbeline. Act V. Sc. 5

Should the poor be flatter'd?
No, let the candied tongue lick absurd
pomp;
And crook the pregnant hinges of the knee,
Where thrift may follow fawning.
Hamlet. Act III. Sc. 2

Lay not that flattering unction to your soul.
Hamlet. Act III. Sc. 4

By heaven, I cannot flatter; I defy
The tongues of soothers; but a braver place
In my heart's love, hath no man than yourself:
Nay, task me to my word; approve me, lord.
Henry IV. Pt. I. Act IV. Sc. 1

What drink'st thou oft, instead of homage
sweet,
But poison'd flattery?
Henry V. Act IV. Sc. 1

But when I tell him he hates flatterers,
He says he does; being then most flattered.
Julius Caesar. Act II. Sc. 1

They do abuse the king that flatter him,
For flattery is the bellows blows up sin.
Pericles. Act I. Sc. 2

O, that men's ears should be
To counsel deaf, but not to flattery!
Timon of Athens. Act I. Sc. 2

Take no repulse, whatever she doth say;
For, "get you gone," she doth not mean,
"away."
Flatter and praise, commend, extol their
graces;
Though ne'er so black, say they have angels'
faces.
That man that hath a tongue I say is no man,
If with his tongue he cannot win a woman:
Two Gentlemen of Verona. Act III. Sc. 1

See also: APPLAUSE, COMPLIMENT, VANITY.

FLOWER

The violets, cowslips, and the primroses,
Bear to my closet:—
Cymbeline. Act I. Sc. 6

Flowers are like the pleasures of the world.
Cymbeline. Act IV. Sc. 2

Thou shalt not lack
The flower that's like thy face, pale prim-
rose, nor
The azur'd harebell, like thy veins.
Cymbeline. Act IV. Sc. 2

There's rosemary, that's for remembrance;
And there's pansies, that's for thought.
Hamlet. Act IV. Sc. 5

Nothing teems,
But hateful docks, rough thistles, kecksies,
burs,
Losing both beauty and utility.
Henry V. Act V. Sc. 2

Like the lily,
That once was mistress of the field, and
    flourish'd,
I'll hang my head, and perish.
Henry VIII. Act III. Sc. 1

In emerald tufts, flowers purple, blue, and
    white;
Like sapphire, pearl, and rich embroidery.
Merry Wives of Windsor. Act V. Sc. 5

Over-canopied with lush woodbine,
With sweet musk-roses with eglantine.
Midsummer Night's Dream. Act II. Sc. 2

I know a bank where the wild thyme blows.
Midsummer Night's Dream. Act II. Sc. 2

Strew thy green with flowers; the yellows,
    blues,
The purple violets, and marigolds.
Pericles. Act IV. Sc. 1

Sweet flowers are slow and weeds make haste.
Richard III. Act II. Sc. 4

Within the infant rind of this small flower
Poison hath residence, and med'cine power:
For this, being smelt, with that part cheers
    each part:
Being tasted, slays all senses with the heart.
Romeo and Juliet. Act II. Sc. 3

The summer's flower is to the summer sweet,
Though to itself it only live and die;
But if that flower with base infection meet,
The basest weed outbraves his dignity;
    For sweetest things turn sourest by their
        deeds,
    Lilies that fester smell far worse than
        weeds.
Sonnet XCIV.

              Daffodils,
That come before the swallow dares, and take
The winds of March with beauty; violets dim,
But sweeter than the lids of Juno's eyes,
Or Cytherea's breath; pale primroses,
That die unmarried ere they can behold
Bright Phoebus in his strength, a malady
Most incident to maids; bold oxlips and
The crown-imperial; lilies of all kinds,
The flower-de-luce being one!
Winter's Tale. Act IV. Sc. 3

      The fairest flowers o' th' season
Are our carnations, and streak'd gillyflowers.
Winter's Tale. Act IV. Sc. 3

      The fairest flowers o' the season
Are our carnations, and streak'd gillyvors,
Which some call natur's bastards:

.   .   .   .

Then make your garden rich in gillyvors,
And do not call them bastards.
Winter's Tale. Act IV. Sc. 3

See also: HONEYSUCKLE,   MARIGOLD,   PANSY,
ROSE, VIOLET.

FOLLY: *see* FOOL.

FOOL

Sir, for a *quart d'ecu* he will sell the fee-
simple of his salvation, the inheritance of it;
and cut the entail from all remainders.
All's Well That Ends Well. Act IV. Sc. 3

And rail'd on lady Fortune in good terms.
As You Like It. Act II. Sc. 7

A fool! I met a fool i' the forest,
A motley fool; a miserable world:
As I do live by food, I met a fool;
Who laid him down, and bask'd him in the
    sun.
As You Like It. Act II. Sc. 7

          O noble fool!
A worthy fool! Motley's the only wear.
As You Like It. Act II. Sc. 7

I had rather have a fool to make me merry,
than experience to make me sad; and to
travel for it too.
As You Like It. Act IV. Sc. 1

The fool doth think he is wise, but the wise
man knows himself to be a fool.
As You Like It. Act V. Sc. 1

I am an ass, indeed; you may prove it by
my long ears. I have served him from the
hour of my nativity to this instant, and
have nothing at his hands for my service but
blows; when I am cold, he heats me with
beating.
Comedy of Errors. Act IV. Sc. 4

Fools are not mad folks.
Cymbeline. Act II. Sc. 3

Let the doors be shut upon him; that he
may play the fool nowhere but in's own
house.
Hamlet. Act III. Sc. 1

Well, thus we play the fools with the time;
and the spirits of the wise sit in the clouds,
and mock us.
Henry IV. Pt. II. Act II. Sc. 2

A fool's bolt is soon shot.
Henry V. Act III. Sc. 7

To gild refined gold, to paint the lily,
To throw a perfume on the violet,
To smooth the ice, or add another hue
Unto the rainbow, or with taper-light
To seek the beauteous eye of heaven to gar-
nish,
Is wasteful, and ridiculous excess.
King John. Act IV. Sc. 2

The fool hath planted in his memory
An army of good words; and I do know
A many fools, that stand in better place,
Garnish'd like him, that for a trickey word
Defy the matter.
Merchant of Venice. Act III. Sc. 5

Like a fair house, built upon another man's
ground; so that I have lost my edifice by
mistaking the place where I erected it.
Merry Wives of Windsor. Act II. Sc. 2

What say you to young Master Fenton? he
capers, he dances, he has eyes of youth, he
writes verses,
Merry Wives of Windsor. Act III. Sc. 2

O murderous coxcomb! what should such a
fool
Do with so good a wife?
Othello. Act V. Sc. 2

To wisdom he's a fool that will not yield.
Pericles. Act II. Sc. 4

He capers nimbly in a lady's chamber,
To the lascivious pleasing of a lute.
Richard III. Act I. Sc. 1

This fellow's wise enough to play the fool;
And to do that well craves a kind of wit.
Twelfth Night. Act III. Sc. 1

Marry, sir; they praise me, and make an
Ass of me; now my foes tell me plainly I am
an ass; so that, by my foes, Sir, I profit in
the knowledge of myself.
Twelfth Night. Act V. Sc. 1

I hold him but a fool, that will endanger
His body for a girl that loves him not.
Two Gentlemen of Verona. Act V. Sc. 4

See also: IGNORANCE, VANITY, WISDOM.

FOOT

So light a foot
Will ne'er wear out the everlasting flint.
Romeo and Juliet. Act II. Sc. 6

See also: FOOTSTEP.

FOOTSTEP

Nay, her foot speaks.
Troilus and Cressida. Act IV. Sc. 5

The grass stoops not, she treads on it so light.
Venus and Adonis. Line 1028.

See also: FOOT.

FORGIVENESS

I pardon him, as heaven shall pardon me.
Richard II. Act V. Sc. 3

See also: CHARITY, MERCY, PITY.

FORTUNE

Fortune knows,
We scorn her most, when most she offers
blows.
Antony and Cleopatra. Act III. Sc. 9

Happy is your grace,
That can translate the stubbornness of for-
tune
Into so quiet and so sweet a style.
As You Like It. Act II. Sc. 1

All other doubts, by time let them be clear'd:
Fortune brings in some boats, that are not
steer'd.
Cymbeline. Act IV. Sc. 3

They are a pipe for Fortune's finger
To sound what stop she please. Give me that
man
That is not passion's slave, and I will wear
him
In my heart's core, aye, in my heart of heart,
As I do thee.
Hamlet. Act III. Sc. 2

Will fortune never come with both hands
full,
But write her fair words still in foulest
letters?
She either gives a stomach, and no food—
Such as are the poor, in health; or else a
feast,
And takes away the stomach—such are the
rich,
That have abundance, and enjoy it not.
Henry IV. Pt. II. Act IV. Sc. 4

Ye gods, it doth amaze me,
A man of such feeble temper should
So get the start of the majestic world,
And bear the palm alone.
Julius Caesar. Pt. II. Act I. Sc. 2

Fortune is merry,
And in this mood will give us any thing.
Julius Caesar. Act III. Sc. 2

When fortune means to men most good,
She looks upon them with a threatening eye.
King John. Act III. Sc. 4

A good man's fortune may grow out at heels.
King Lear. Act II. Sc. 2

Fortune, ne'er turns the key to the poor.
King Lear. Act II. Sc. 4

Well, heaven forgive him and forgive us all!
Some rise by sin, and some by virtue fall:
Some run from brakes of vice, and answer
  none,
And some condemned for a fault alone.
Measure for Measure. Act II. Sc. 1

O fortune, fortune! all men call thee fickle.
Romeo and Juliet. Act III. Sc. 5

I find my zenith, doth depend upon
A most auspicious star; whose influence
If now I court not, but omit, my fortunes
Will ever after droop.
Tempest. Act I. Sc. 2

How some men creep in skittish Fortune's
  hall,
While others play the idiots in her eyes!
Troilus and Cressida. Act III. Sc. 3

See also: CHANCE, FATE, LUCK.

FRAILTY

Frailty, thy name is woman!
Hamlet. Act I. Sc. 2

I thank thee, who hast taught
My frail mortality to know itself.
Pericles. Act I. Sc. 1

Sometimes we are devils to ourselves,
When we will tempt the frailty of our powers,
Presuming on their changeful potency.
Troilus and Cressida. Act IV. Sc. 4

Alas! our frailty is the cause, not we;
For, such as we are made of, such we be.
Twelfth Night. Act II. Sc. 2

See also: COWARDICE, WOMAN.

FRAUD

His heart as far from fraud as heaven from
  earth.
Two Gentlemen of Verona. Act II. Sc. 7

See also: DECEIT, FALSEHOOD, HYPOCRISY.

FREEDOM

Come, there's no more tribute to be paid.
Our kingdom is stronger than it was at that
time; and, as I said, there is no more such
Caesars other of them may have crooked
noses; but, to owe such straight arms, none.
Cymbeline. Act III. Sc. 1

When the mind's free,
The body's delicate.
King Lear. Act III. Sc. 4

See also: EQUALITY, JUSTICE, LIBERTY.

FRIENDSHIP

Keep thy friend
Under thy own life's key.
All's Well That Ends Well. Act I. Sc. 1

Thy father and myself in friendship,
First tried our soldiership! He did look far
Into the service of the time, and was
Discipled of the bravest.
All's Well That Ends Well. Act I. Sc. 2

We still have slept together,
Rose at an instant, learn'd, play'd, eat to-
  gether;
And whereso'er we went, like Juno's swans,
Still we went coupled, and inseparable.
As You Like It. Act I. Sc. 3

Most friendship is feigning.
As You Like It. Act II. Sc. 7 *Song*

We came into this world like brother and
  brother;
And now let's go hand in hand, not one before another.
Comedy of Errors. Act V. Sc. 1

This hath been
Your faithful servant; I dare lay mine honour,
He will remain so.
Cymbeline. Act I. Sc. 2

Give thy thoughts no tongue,
Nor any unproportion'd thought his act.
Be thou familiar, but by no means vulgar.
The friends thou hast, and their adoption
  tried,
Grapple them to thy soul with hooks of steel;

But do not dull thy palm with entertainment
Of each new-hatch'd, unfledg'd comrade.
Hamlet Act I. Sc. 3

Who not needs shall never lack a friend;
And who in want a hollow friend doth try,
Directly seasons him his enemy.
Hamlet. Act III. Sc. 2

Call you that backing of your friends? A
plague upon such backing! give me them
that will face me.
Henry IV. Pt. I. Act II. Sc. 4

May he live
Longer than I have time to tell his years!
Ever beloved and loving, may his rule be!
And, when old time shall lead him to his
end,
Goodness and he fill up one monument!
Henry VIII. Act II. Sc. 1

Where you are liberal of your loves and
counsels,
Be sure you be not loose; for those you make
friends
And give your hearts to, when they once
perceive
The least rub in your fortunes, fall away
Like water from ye, never found again
But where they mean to sink ye.
Henry VIII. Act II. Sc. 1

A friend should bear his friend's infirmities,
But Brutus makes mine greater than they
are.
Julius Caesar. Act IV. Sc. 3

And, father cardinal, I have heard you say,
That we shall see and know our friends in
heaven,
If that be true, I shall see my boy again;
For, since the birth of Cain, the first male
child,
To him that did but yesterday suspire,
There was not such a gracious creature
born.
King John. Act III. Sc. 4

To wail friends lost,
Is not by much so wholesome, profitable,
As to rejoice at friends but newly found.
Love's Labour's Lost. Act V. Sc. 2

I would be friends with you, and have your
love.
Merchant of Venice. Act I. Sc. 3

When did friendship take
A breed for barren metal of his friend?
Merchant of Venice. Act I. Sc. 3

For in companions
That do converse and waste the time to-
gether,
Whose souls do bear an equal yoke of love,
There must be needs a like proportion
Of lineaments, of manners, and of spirit.
Merchant of Venice. Act III. Sc. 4

Two lovely berries moulded on one stem:
So, with two seeming bodies, but one heart.
Midsummer Night's Dream. Act III. Sc. 2

Friendship is constant in all other things,
Save in the office and affairs of love:
Therefore, all hearts in love use their own
tongues;
Let every eye negociate for itself,
And trust no agent.
Much Ado About Nothing. Act II. Sc. 1

If you read this line, remember not
The hand that writ it; for I love you so,
That I in your sweet thoughts would be
forgot,
If thinking on me then should make you woe.
Sonnet LXXI

I had rather crack my sinews, break my back,
Than you should such dishonour undergo.
Tempest. Act III. Sc. 1

I am not of that feather, to shake off
My friend when he must need me. I do
know him
A gentleman, that well deserves a help,
Which he shall have: I pay the debt, and
free him.
Timon of Athens. Act I. Sc. 1

Friendship's full of dregs.
Timon of Athens. Act I. Sc. 2

Ceremony was but devis'd at first
To set a gloss on faint deeds, hollow wel-
comes,
Recanting goodness, sorry ere 'tis shown;
But where there is true friendship, there
needs none.
Timon of Athens. Act I. Sc. 2

My heart is ever at your service.
Timon of Athens. Act I. Sc. 2

For by these
Shall I try my friends. You shall perceive,
how you
Mistake my fortunes; I am wealthy in my
friends.
Timon of Athens. Act II. Sc. 2

The amity that wisdom knits not, folly may
easily untie.
Troilus and Cressida. Act II. Sc. 3

See also: AFFECTION, LOVE, SYMPATHY.

FUTURE

Who would fardels bear,
To grunt and sweat under a weary life;
But that the dread of something after death,
The undiscover'd country, from whose bourn
No traveller returns, puzzles the will;
And makes us rather bear those ills we have,
Than fly to others, that we know not of?
Hamlet. Act III. Sc. 1

Ay, but to die and go we know not where;
To lie in cold obstruction, and to rot.
Measure for Measure. Act III. Sc. 1

God (if Thy will be so),
Enrich the time to come with smooth-faced
peace,
With smiling plenty, and fair prosperous
days!
Richard III. Act V. Sc. 4

See also: FATE, TIME, TOMORROW.

G

GAIN

Share the advice betwixt you; if both gain
all,
The gift doth stretch itself as't is receiv'd,
And is enough for both.
All's Well That Ends Well. Act II. Sc. 1

Men, that hazard all,
Do it in hope of fair advantages:
A golden mind stoops not to shows of dross.
Merchant of Venice. Act II. Sc. 7

No profit grows, where is no pleasure ta'en;—
In brief, sir, study what you most affect.
Taming of the Shrew. Act I. Sc. 1

See also: AVARICE, WEALTH.

GARDEN

Now 'tis the spring, and weeds are shallow
rooted;
Suffer them now, and they'll o'ergrow the
garden,
And choke the herbs for want of husbandry.
Henry VI. Act III. Sc. 1

See also: AGRICULTURE, FLOWER, NATURE.

GENIUS

There is none but he
Whose being I do fear: and under him
My genius is rebuk'd; as, it is said,
Mark Antony's was by Caesar.
Macbeth. Act III. Sc. 1

See also: ABILITY, GREATNESS, MIND.

GENTLEMAN

My master hath been an honourable gentleman; tricks he hath had in him which
gentlemen have.
All's Well That Ends Well. Act V. Sc. 3

I freely told you, all the wealth I had
Ran in my veins,—I was a gentleman.
Merchant of Venice. Act III. Sc. 2

An affable and courteous gentleman.
Taming of the Shrew. Act I. Sc. 2

"I am a gentleman"—I'll be sworn thou art;
Thy tongue, thy face, thy limbs, actions and
spirit,
Do give thee five-fold blazon.
Twelfth Night. Act. I. Sc. 5

See also: COURTESY, MANNERS.

GENTLENESS

If ever you have look'd on better days;
If ever been where bells have knoll'd to
church;
If ever sat at any good man's feast;
If ever from your eyelids wip'd a tear,
And know what 'tis to pity and be pitied:
Let gentleness my strong enforcement be.
As You Like It. Act II. Sc. 7

They are as gentle
As zephyrs, blowing below the violet.
Cymbeline. Act V. Sc. 2

Those that do teach young babes,
Do it with gentle means and easy tasks:
He might have chid me so; for, in good faith,
I am a child to chiding.
Othello. Act IV. Sc. 2

See also: KINDNESS, LOVE, MANNERS.

GIFT

CELIA:
Let us sit, and mock the good housewife,
Fortune, from her wheel, that her gifts may
henceforth be bestowed equally.
ROSALIND:
I would we could do so; for her benefits are

mightly misplaced: and the bountiful blind woman doth most mistake in her gifts to women.
>> *As You Like It.* Act I. Sc. 2

Rich gifts wax poor, when givers prove unkind.
>> *Hamlet.* Act III. Sc. 1

If the boy have not a woman's gift,
To rain a shower of commanded tears,
An onion will do well for such a shift.
>> *Taming of the Shrew.* Induction

Win her with gifts, if she respect not words;
Dumb jewels often, in their silent kind,
More than quick words, do move a woman's mind.
>> *Two Gentlemen of Verona.* Act III. Sc. 1

See also: CHARITY, FAVOR, KINDNESS.

GLORY

Glory is like a circle in the water,
Which never ceaseth to enlarge itself,
Till, by broad spreading, it disperse to naught.
>> *Henry VI.* Pt. I. Act I. Sc. 2

>> I have ventur'd,
Like little wanton boys that swim on bladders,
This many summers in a sea of glory;
But far beyond my depth: my high-blown pride
At length broke under me.
>> *Henry VIII.* Act III. Sc. 2

Like madness is the glory of this life.
>> *Timon of Athens.* Act I. Sc. 2

Who'd be so mock'd with glory? or to live
But in a dream of friendship?
To have his pomp, and all what state compounds,
But only painted, like his varnish'd friends?
>> *Timon of Athens.* Act IV. Sc. 2

See also: AMBITION, FAME, HONOR, PRAISE.

GOD

God is our fortress; in whose conquering name
Let us resolve to scale their flinty bulwarks.
>> *Henry VI.* Pt. I. Act II. Sc. 1

God shall be my hope,
My stay, my guide, and lantern to my feet.
>> *Henry VI.* Pt. II. Act II. Sc. 3

Heaven is above all yet; there sits a Judge
That no king can corrupt.
>> *Henry VIII.* Act III. Sc. 1

See also: CHRIST, FAITH, HEAVEN, PRAYER, PROVIDENCE, RELIGION, WORSHIP.

GOLD

There is gold for you; sell me your good report.
>> *Cymbeline.* Act II. Sc. 3

>> 'Tis gold
Which buys admittance; oft it doth; yea, and makes
Diana's rangers false themselves, yield up
Their deer to the stand o' the stealer: and 'tis gold
Which makes the true man kill'd, and saves the thief;
Nay, sometime, hangs both thief and true man.
>> *Cymbeline.* Act III. Sc. 3

A mere hoard of gold, kept by a devil; till sack commences it, and sets it in act and use.
>> *Henry IV.* Pt. II. Act IV. Sc. 3

How quickly nature falls into revolt,
When gold becomes her object!
For this the foolish over-careful fathers
Have broke their sleep with thoughts, their brains with care.
Their bones with industry;
For this they have engrossed and pil'd up
The canker'd heaps of strange-achieved gold;
For this they have been thoughtful to invest
Their sons with arts and martial exercises.
>> *Henry IV.* Pt. II. Act IV. Sc. 4

Thou that so stoutly hast resisted me,
Give me thy gold, if thou hast any gold,
For I have bought it with an hundred blows.
>> *Henry VI.* Pt. III. Act II. Sc. 5

There is thy gold; worse poison to men's souls,
Doing more murther in this loathsome world,
Than these poor compounds that thou mayst not sell:
I sell thee poison, thou hast sold me none.
>> *Romeo and Juliet.* Act V. Sc. 1

See also: ALCHEMY, MONEY, WEALTH.

GOODNESS

There lives within the very flame of love
A kind of wick, or snuff, that will abate it;
And nothing is at a like goodness still;
For goodness, growing to a pleurisy,
Dies in its own too-much.
Hamlet. Act IV. Sc. 7

There is some soul of goodness in things evil,
Would men observingly distil it out.
Henry V. Act IV. Sc. 1

My meaning in saying he is a good man is, to have you understand me that he is sufficient.
Merchant of Venice. Act I. Sc. 3

How far that little candle throws his beams!
So shines a good deed in a naughty world.
Merchant of Venice. Act V. Sc. 1

One good deed dying tongueless
Slaughters a thousand, waiting upon that,
Our praises are our wages.
Winter's Tale. Act I. Sc. 2

See also: CHARACTER, CHARITY, VIRTUE.

GOSSIP

The nature of bad news infects the teller.
Antony and Cleopatra. Act I. Sc. 2

Foul whisperings are abroad.
Macbeth. Act V. Sc. 1

If my gossip report, be an honest woman of her word.
Merchant of Venice. Act III. Sc. 1

See also: RUMOR, SLANDER, TALK, TONGUE.

GOVERNMENT

A man busied about decrees;
Condemning some to death, and some to exile;
Ransoming him, or pitying, threat'ning the other.
Coriolanus. Act I. Sc. 6

For government, through high, and low, and lower,
Put into parts, doth keep in one consent;
Congreeing in a full and natural close,
Like music.
Henry V. Act I. Sc. 2

Why this it is, when men are rul'd by women.
Richard III. Act I. Sc. 1

See also: AUTHORITY, PATRIOTISM, POLITICS.

GRACE

God give him grace to groan.
Love's Labour's Lost. Act IV. Sc. 3

O then, what graces in my love do dwell,
That he hath turn'd a heaven unto a hell!
Midsummer Night's Dream. Act I. Sc. 1

Hail to thee, lady! and the grace of heaven,
Before, behind thee, and on every hand,
Enwheel thee round!
Othello. Act II. Sc. 1

O, mickle is the powerful grace that lies
In plants, herbs, stones, and their true qualities.
Romeo and Juliet. Act II. Sc. 3

For several virtues
Have I lik'd several women, never any
With so full soul, but some defect in her
Did quarrel with the noblest grace she ow'd,
And put it to the foil.
Tempest. Act III. Sc. 1

See also: COURTESY, GENTLENESS, GOD, HOLINESS, MANNERS.

GRATITUDE

"I thank you for your voices,—thank you,—
Your most sweet voices."
Coriolanus. Act II. Sc. 3

Now the good gods forbid,
That our renowned Rome, whose gratitude
Towards her deserved children is enroll'd
In Jove's own book, like an unnatural dam
Should now eat up her own.
Coriolanus. Act III. Sc. 1

Let but the commons hear this testament,
(Which, pardon me, I do not mean to read,)
And they would go and kiss dead Caesar's wounds,
And dip their napkins in his sacred blood;
Yea, beg a hair of him for memory,
And, dying, mention it within their wills,
Bequeathing it, as a rich legacy,
Unto their issue.
Julius Caesar. Act III. Sc. 2

I can no other answer make, but thanks,
And thanks: and ever oft good turns
Are shuffled off with such uncurrent pay.
Twelfth Night. Act III. Sc. 3

See also: INGRATITUDE, THANKFULNESS.

GRAVE

Bea from hence his body,
And mourn you for him: let him be regarded
As the most noble corse that ever herald
Did follow to his urn.
Coriolanus. Act V. Sc. 6

The sepulchre,
Wherein we saw thee quietly inurn'd,
Hath op'd ponderous and marble jaws.
Hamlet. Act I. Sc. 4

They bore him barefac'd on the bier;
.   .   .   .   .
And on his grave rains many a tear.
Hamlet. Act IV. Sc. 5

Lay her i' the earth;
And from her fair and unpolluted flesh,
May violets spring!
Hamlet. Act V. Sc. 1

Within their chiefest temple I'll erect
A tomb, wherein his corpse shall be interr'd.
Henry VI. Pt. I. Act II. Sc. 2

Gilded tombs do worms infold.
Merchant of Venice. Act II. Sc. 7

Let's choose executors, and talk of wills;
And yet not so,—for what can we bequeath,
Save our deposed bodies to the ground?
Richard II. Act III. Sc. 2

Taking the measure of an unmade grave.
Romeo and Juliet. Act III. Sc. 3

See also: DEATH, EPITAPH, HEAVEN, HELL.

GREATNESS

Greatness knows itself.
Henry IV. Pt. I. Act IV. Sc. 3

Why, man, he doth bestride the narrow
world,
Like a Colossus; and we petty men
Walk under his huge legs, and peep about
To find ourselves dishonorable graves.
Julius Caesar. Act I. Sc. 2

Now, in the name of all the gods at once,
Upon what meat doth this, our Caesar feed,
That he has grown so great?
Julius Caesar. Act I. Sc. 2

Are yet two Romans living, such as these?—
The last of all the Romans, fare thee well!
Julius Caesar. Act V. Sc. 3

But thou art fair; and at thy birth, dear boy,
Nature and fortune join'd to make thee
great.
King John. Act III. Sc. 1

The mightier man, the mightier is the thing
That makes him honour'd, or begets him
hate:
For greatest scandal waits on greatest state.
Lucrece. Line 1006

Your name is great
In mouths of wisest censure.
Othello. Act II. Sc. 3

They that stand high have many blasts to
shake them;
And if they fall they dash themselves to
pieces.
Richard III. Act I. Sc. 3

Some are born great, some achieve greatness,
And some have greatness thrust upon them.
Twelfth Night. Act II. Sc. 5

See also: DIGNITY, FAME, HONOR, REPUTATION,
VIRTUE.

GRIEF

If thou engrossest all the griefs as thine,
Thou robb'st me of a moiety.
All's Well That Ends Well. Act III. Sc. 2

O! grief hath chang'd me, since you saw me
last;
And careful hours, with Time's deformed
hand
Have written strange departures in my face.
Comedy of Errors. Act V. Sc. 1

That we two are asunder, let that grieve him,—
(Some griefs are med'cinable.)
Cymbeline. Act III. Sc. 2

Great griefs, I see, medicine the less.
Cymbeline. Act IV. Sc. 2

'Tis sweet and commendable in your nature,
Hamlet,
To give these mourning duties to your
father;
But, you must know, your father lost a
father;
That father lost, lost his; and the survivor
bound
In filial obligation, for some term
To do obsequious sorrow: But to persevere
In obstinate condolement, is a course
Of impious stubbornness.
Hamlet. Act I. Sc. 2

But I have that within which passeth show;
These, but the trappings and the suits of
    woe.
            Hamlet. Act I. Sc. 2

We must be patient: but I cannot choose
but weep, to think they should lay him i' the
cold ground.
            Hamlet. Act IV. Sc. 5

         What is he, whose grief
Bears such an emphasis? whose phrase of
    sorrow
Conjures the wand'ring stars, and makes
    them stand
Like wonder-wounded hearers?
            Hamlet. Act V. Sc. 1

My heart is drown'd with grief,
   .   .   .   .
My body round engirt with misery;
For what's more miserable than discontent?
      Henry VI. Pt. II. Act III. Sc. 1

    Grief softens the mind,
And makes it fearful and degenerate.
      Henry VI. Pt. II. Act IV. Sc. 4

I cannot weep; for all my body's moisture
Scarce serves to quench my furnace-burning
    heart.
      Henry VI. Pt. III. Act II. Sc. 1

What private griefs they have, alas! I know
    not,
That made them do it.
        Julius Caesar. Act III. Sc. 2

Grief is proud, and makes his owner stoop.
          King John. Act III. Sc. 1

I am not mad;—I would to heaven, I were!
For then, 'tis like I should forget myself:
O, if I could, what grief should I forget!
          King John. Act III. Sc. 4

Grief fills the room up of my absent child;
Lies in his bed, walks up and down with me,
Puts on his pretty looks, repeats his words,
Remembers me of all his gracious parts,
Stuffs out his vacant garments with his form;
Then have I reason to be fond of grief.
          King John. Act III. Sc. 4

The mind much sufferance doth o'er-skip,
When grief hath mates.
        King Lear. Act III. Sc. 6

        Grief that does not speak,
Whispers the o'er-fraught heart, and bids it
    break.
        Macbeth. Act IV. Sc. 3

Every one can master a grief, but he that has
    it.
    Much Ado About Nothing. Act III. Sc. 2

               Men
Can counsel, and speak comfort to that grief
Which they themselves not feel; but tasting it
Their counsel turns to passion, which before
Would give preceptial medicine to rage,
Fetter strong madness with silken thread,
Charm ache with air, and agony with words.
    Much Ado About Nothing. Act V. Sc. 1

        Nor doth the general care
Take hold on me; for my particular grief
Is of so flood-gate and o'erbearing nature,
That it engluts and swallows other sorrows,
And it is still itself.
          Othello. Act I. Sc. 3

Each substance of a grief hath twenty
    shadows,
Which show like grief itself, but are not so:
For sorrow's eye, glazed with blinding tears,
Divides one thing entire to many objects.
        Richard II. Act II. Sc. 2

      My grief lies all within;
And these external manners of laments
Are merely shadows to the unseen grief,
That swells with silence in the tortur'd soul.
        Richard II. Act IV. Sc. 1

You may my glories and my state depose,
But not my griefs; still am I king of those.
        Richard II. Act IV. Sc. 1

Griefs of mine own lie heavy in my breast;
Which thou wilt propagate, to have it press'd
With more of thine.
      Romeo and Juliet. Act I. Sc. 1

    Some grief shows much of love,
But much of grief shows still some want of
    wit.
      Romeo and Juliet. Act III. Sc. 5

Alas, poor man! grief has so wrought on him,
He takes false shadows for true substances.
      Titus Andronicus. Act III. Sc. 2

She looks upon his lips, and they are pale;
She takes him by the hand, and that is cold;
She whispers in his ears a heavy tale,
As if they heard the woful words she told;
 She lifts the coffer-lids that close his eyes,
 Where, lo! two lamps, burnt out, in darkness lies.
   Venus and Adonis. Line 1123

      But I have
That honourable grief lodg'd here, which burns
Worse than tears drown.
   Winter's Tale. Act II. Sc. 1

See also: AFFLICTION, DEATH, MISERY, SADNESS, SORROW, TEARS.

GROWTH

Gardener, for telling me this news of woe,
I would the plants thou graft'st may never grow.
   Richard II. Act III. Sc. 4

   "Ay," quoth my uncle Gloster,
"Small herbs have grace, great weeds do grow apace:"
And since, methinks, I would not grow so fast,
Because sweet flowers are slow, and weeds make haste.
   Richard III. Act II. Sc. 4

      O, my lord,
You said that idle weeds are fast in growth;
The prince my brother hath outgrown me far.
   Richard III. Act III. Sc. 1

See also: CHILDREN, GARDEN, YOUTH.

GUEST

 Do not dull thy palm with entertainment
Of each new-hatch'd, unfledg'd comrade.
   Hamlet. Act I. Sc. 3

   Unbidden guests
Are often welcomest when they are gone.
   Henry VI. Pt. I. Act II. Sc. 2

MACBETH:
Here's our chief guest.
LADY MACBETH:
If he had been forgotten
It had been as a gap in our great feast.
   Macbeth. Act III. Sc. 1

Be bright and jovial among your guests tonight.
   Macbeth. Act III. Sc. 2

   See, your guests approach:
Address yourself to entertain them sprightly,
And let's be red with mirth.
   Winter's Tale. Act IV. Sc. 3

Methinks, a father
Is, at the nuptial of his son, a guest
That best becomes the table.
   Winter's Tale. Act IV. Sc. 3

See also: FAREWELL, HOSPITALITY, WELCOME.

GUILT

And then it started like a guilty thing
Upon a fearful summons.
   Hamlet. Act I. Sc. 1

See also: CONSCIENCE, CRIME, EVIL, MURDER, PUNISHMENT, SIN.

H

HABIT

For use almost can change the stamp of nature,
And master the devil, or throw him out
With wondrous potency.
   Hamlet. Act III. Sc. 4

Use doth breed a habit in a man!
   Two Gentlemen of Verona. Act V. Sc. 4

See also: CUSTOM, MANNERS.

HAIR

ROSALIND:
His hair is of good colour.
CELIA:
An excellent colour; your chestnut was ever the only colour.
   As You Like It. Act III. Sc. 4

How ill white hairs become a fool and jester!
   Henry IV. Pt. II. Act V. Sc. 5

Comb down his hair; look! look! it stands upright.
   Henry VI. Pt. II. Act III. Sc. 3

Bind up those tresses: O, what love I note
In the fair multitude of those her hairs!
Where but by chance a sliver drop hath fallen,
Even to that drop ten thousand wiry friends
Do glew themselves in sociable grief;

Like true, inseparable, faithful loves,
Sticking together in calamity.

King John. Act III. Sc. 4

Her sunny locks

Hang on her temples like a golden fleece.

Merchant of Venice. Act I. Sc. 1

Her hair is auburn, mine is perfect yellow:
If that be all the difference in his love,
I'll get me such a colour'd periwig.

Two Gentlemen of Verona. Act IV. Sc. 4

See also: BARBER, BEAUTY, PERFUME, WOMAN.

HAND

All the perfumes in Arabia will not sweeten
this little hand.

Macbeth. Act V. Sc. 1

What accursed hand

Hath made thee handless?

Titus Andronicus. Act III. Sc. 1

O, that her hand,

In whose comparison all whites are ink,
Writing their own reproach; to whose soft
 seizure
The cygnet's down is harsh, and spirit of
 sense
Hard as the palm of ploughman.

Troilus and Cressida. Act I. Sc. 1

See also: FACE, FOOT, HELP, WOMAN.

HAPPINESS

How bitter a thing it is to look into happiness
through another man's eyes!

As You Like It. Act V. Sc. 2

Our day of marriage shall be yours;

One feast, one house, one mutual happiness.

Two Gentlemen of Verona. Act V. Sc. 4

See also: CHEERFULNESS, CONTENTMENT, JOY,
  PLEASURE.

HASTE

Swift, swift, you dragons of the night, that
 dawning
May bare the raven's eye!

Cymbeline. Act II. Sc. 2

Nay, but make haste; the better foot before.

King John. Act IV. Sc. 2

Stand not upon the order of your going,
But go at once.

Macbeth. Act III. Sc. 4

He tires betimes, that spurs too fast betimes;
With eager feeding, food doth choke the
 feeder:
Light vanity insatiate cormonant,
Consuming means, soon preys upon itself.

Richard II. Act II. Sc. 1

Too rash, too unadvis'd, too sudden;
Too like the lightning, which doth cease to
 be,
Ere one can say—It lightens.

Romeo and Juliet. Act II. Sc. 2

Wisely, and slow; They stumble, that run
 fast.

Romeo and Juliet. Act II. Sc. 3

See also: IMPATIENCE.

HATE

'Tis greater skill

In a true hate, to pray they have their will.

Cymbeline. Act II. Sc. 5

How like a fawning publican he looks!
I hate him, for he is a Christian:
But more, for that, in low simplicity,
He lends out money gratis, and brings down
The rate of usance here with us in Venice.

The Merchant of Venice. Act I. Sc. 3

I do hate him as I do hell pains.

Othello. Act I. Sc. 1

See also: ANGER, ENEMY, ENVY.

HEALTH

Maybe he is not well:

Infirmity doth still neglect all office,
Whereto our health is bound.

King Lear. Act II. Sc. 4

Now, good digestion wait on appetite,
And health on both!

Macbeth. Act III. Sc. 4

Testy sick men, when their deaths be near,
No news but health from their physicians
 know.

Sonnet CXL

See also: DISEASE, LIFE, MEDICINE, SICKNESS.

HEART

At this sight

My heart is turn'd to stone: and while 'tis
 mine.
It shall be stony.

Henry VI. Pt. II. Act V. Sc. 2

The very firstlings of my heart shall be
The firstlings of my hand.
Macbeth. Act IV. Sc. 1

See also: LOVE, PASSION.

HEAVEN

It is not so with Him that all things knows,
As't is with us that square our guess by
shows,
But most it is presumption in us, when
The help of Heaven we count the act of men.
All's Well That Ends Well. Act II. Sc. 1

The treasury of everylasting joy!
Henry VI. Pt. II. Act II. Sc. 1

Father cardinal, I have heard you say,
That we shall see and know our friends in
heaven:
If that be true, I shall see my boy again;
For, since the birth of Cain, the first male
child,
To him that did but yesterday suspire,
There was not such a gracious creature born.

. . . .

And so he'll die; and, rising so again,
When I shall meet him in the court of heaven
I shall not know him.
King John. Act III. Sc. 4

There's husbandry in heaven,
Their candles are all out.
Macbeth. Act II. Sc. 1

Heaven's above all; and there be souls must
be saved, and there be souls must not be
saved.
Othello. Act II. Sc. 3

All places that the eye of heaven visits,
Are to a wise man ports and happy havens.
Richard II. Act 1. Sc. 3

The self-same heaven
That frowns on me looks sadly upon him.
Richard III. Act V. Sc. 3

See also: FUTURE, GOOD, HAPPINESS, HELL,
IMMORTALITY, SKY, SOUL.

HELL

Black is the badge of hell,
The hue of dungeons, and the scowl of night.
Love's Labour's Lost. Act IV. Sc. 3

I think the devil will not have me damned,
lest the oil that is in me should set hell on fire.
Merry Wives of Windsor. Act V. Sc. 5

Hell is empty
And all the devils are here.
Tempest. Act I. Sc. 2

See also: DEVIL, HEAVEN, PUNISHMENT.

HELP

Now, ye familiar spirits, that are cull'd,
Out of the powerful regions under earth,
Help me this once.
Henry VI. Pt. I. Act V. Sc. 3

Now, God be prais'd! that to believing souls
Gives light in darkness, comfort in despair!
Henry VI. Pt. II. Act II. Sc. 1

That comfort comes too late;
'Tis like a pardon after execution;
That gentle physic, given in time, had cur'd
me;
But now I am past all comforts here, but
prayers.
Henry VIII. Act IV. Sc. 2

Help me, Cassius, or I sink!
Julius Caesar. Act I. Sc. 2

'Tis not enough to help the feeble up,
But to support him after.
Timon of Athens. Act I. Sc. 1

See also: KINDNESS, SYMPATHY.

HOLIDAY

Now I am in a holiday humour.
As You Like It. Act IV. Sc. 1

If all the year were playing holidays,
To sport would be as tedious as to work.
Henry IV. Pt. I. Act I. Sc. 2

Being holiday, the beggar's shop is shut.
Romeo and Juliet. Act V. Sc. 1

See also: CEREMONY, CHRISTMAS, VALENTINE'S
DAY.

HOLINESS

All his mind is bent to holiness,
To number Ave-Marias on his beads:
His champions are the prophets and apostles;
His weapons, holy saws of sacred writ;
His study is his tilt-yard, and his loves
Are brazen images of canonis'd saints.
Henry VI. Pt. II. Act I. Sc. 3

He who the sword of heaven will bear
Should be as holy as severe;
Pattern in himself, to know,

Grace to stand, and virtue go;
More nor less to others paying,
Than by self offences weighing.
Shame to him, whose cruel striking
Kills for faults of his own liking!
> *Measure for Measure.* Act III. Sc. 2

Our holy lives must win a new world's crown.
> *Richard II.* Act V. Sc. 2

See also: GOD, GOODNESS, GRACE, VIRTUE.

HOME

At night we'll feast together:
Most welcome home!
> *Hamlet.* Act II. Sc. 2

I'll still stay, to have thee still forget,
Forgetting any other home but this.
> *Romeo and Juliet.* Act II. Sc. 2

This is my home of love.
> *Sonnet CIX*

While I play the good husband at home, my
son and my servant spend all at the university.
> *Taming of the Shrew.* Act V. Sc. 1

See also: FAREWELL, TRAVEL, WELCOME.

HONESTY

HAMLET:
What's the news
ROSENCRANTZ:
None, my lord; but that the world's grown
honest.
HAMLET:
Then is dooms-day near.
> *Hamlet.* Act II. Sc. 2

Ay, sir; to be honest, as this world goes, is to
be one man picked out of two thousand.
> *Hamlet.* Act II. Sc. 2

There is no terror, Cassius, in your threats;
For I am arm'd so strong in honesty,
That they pass by me, as the idle wind,
Which I respect not.
> *Julius Caesar.* Act IV. Sc. 3

An honest tale speeds best, being plainly
told.
> *Richard III.* Act IV. Sc. 4

At many times I brought in my accounts;
Laid them before you; you would throw them
off,

And say, you found them in mine honesty.
> *Timon of Athens.* Act II. Sc. 2

See also: HONOR, SINCERITY, TRUTH.

HONEYSUCKLE

Thou shalt not lack
The flower that's like thy face, pale prim-
rose, nor
The azur'd harebell, like thy veins.
> *Cymbeline.* Act IV. Sc. 2

Bid her steal into the pleached bower,
Where honeysuckles, ripen'd by the sun,
Forbid the sun to enter;—like favorites,
Made proud by princes, that advance their
pride
Against that power that bred it.
> *Much Ado About Nothing.* Act III. Sc. 1

See also: FLOWER.

HONOR

See, that you come
Not to woo honour, but to wed it; when
The bravest questant shrinks, find what you
seek,
That fame may cry you loud.
> *All's Well That Ends Well.* Act II. Sc. 1

Honours thrive,
When rather from our acts we them derive
Than our foregoers.
> *All's Well That Ends Well.* Act II. Sc. 3

A scar nobly got, or a noble scar, is a good
livery of honour.
> *All's Well That Ends Well.* Act IV. Sc. 5

If I lose mine honour,
I lose myself; better I were not yours,
Than yours so branchless.
> *Antony and Cleopatra.* Act III. Sc. 4

He's honourable,
And, doubling that, most holy.
> *Cymbeline.* Act III. Sc. 4

And pluck up drowned honour by the locks.
> *Henry IV.* Pt. I. Act I. Sc. 3

Methinks, it were an easy leap
To pluck bright honour from the pale-fac'd
moon.
> *Henry IV.* Pt. I Act I. Sc. 3

Honour pricks me on.
> *Henry IV.* Pt. I. Act V. Sc. 1

Can honour set to a leg? No. Or an arm?
No. Or take away the grief of a wound?
No. Honour hath no skill in surgery, then?
No. What is honour? A word. What is that
word honour?
Henry IV. Pt. I. Act V. Sc. 1

But if it be a sin to covet honour,
I am the most offending soul alive.
Henry V. Act IV. Sc. 3

For Brutus is an honourable man;
So are they all, all honourable men.
Julius Caesar. Act III. Sc. 2

By heaven, I had rather coin my heart,
And drop my blood by drachmas, than to
wring
From the hard hands of peasants their vile
trash,
By any indirection!
Julius Caesar. Act IV. Sc. 3

Thou art a fellow of a good respect;
Thy life hath had some smatch of honour in it.
Julius Caesar. Act V. Sc. 5

And if his name be George, I'll call him
Peter;
For new-made honour doth forget men's
names.
King John. Act I. Sc. 1

Let none presume
To wear an undeserv'd dignity.
O, that estates, degrees, and offices,
Were not deriv'd corruptly! and that clear
honour
Were purchas'd by the merit of the wearer!
Merchant of Venice. Act II. Sc. 9

Mine honour let me try;
In that I live, and for that will I die.
Richard II. Act I. Sc. 1

He was not born to shame:
Upon his brow shame is asham'd to sit;
For 'tis a throne where honour may be
crown'd
Sole monarch of the universal earth.
Romeo and Juliet. Act III. Sc. 2

Tedious it were to tell, and harsh to hear;
Sufficeth, I am come to keep my word.
Taming of the Shrew. Act III. Sc. 2

'Tis the mind that makes the body rich;
And as the sun breaks through the darkest
clouds,

So honour peereth in the meanest habit.
Taming of the Shrew. Act IV. Sc. 3

Honour travels in a strait so narrow,
Where one but goes abreast.
Troilus and Cressida. Act III. Sc. 3

See also: DIGNITY, GREATNESS, HONESTY, SOL-
DIER, VALOR.

HOPE

Farewell
The hopes of court! my hopes in heaven do
dwell.
Henry VIII. Act III. Sc. 2

The miserable have no other medicine,
But only hope:
I have hope to live, and am prepar'd to die.
Measure for Measure. Act III. Sc. 1

True hope is swift, and flies with swallow's
wings,
Kings it makes gods, and meaner creatures
kings.
Richard III. Act V. Sc. 2

I died for hope, ere I could lend thee aid:
But cheer thy heart, and be thou not dis-
may'd.
Richard III. Act V. Sc. 3

Hope is a lover's staff; walk hence with that
And manage it against despairing thoughts.
Two Gentlemen of Verona. Act III. Sc. 1

See also: BELIEF, DESIRE, FAITH, TRUST.

HOSPITALITY

My master is of churlish disposition,
And little recks to find the way to heaven
By doing deeds of hospitality.
As You Like It. Act II. Sc. 4

I am your host;
With robbers' hands, my hospitable favours
You should not ruffle thus.
King Lear. Act III. Sc. 7

See also: FRIENDSHIP, GUEST, WELCOME.
HUMILITY

Love and meekness, my lord,
Become a churchman better than ambition;
Win straying souls with modesty again,
Cast none away.
Henry VIII. Act V. Sc. 2

It is the witness still of excellency,
To put a strange face on his own perfection.
Much Ado About Nothing. Act II. Sc. 3

See also: MODESTY, SHAME, VIRTUE.

HUMOR

Now I perceive the devil understands Welsh;
And 'tis no marvel, he's so humorous.
Henry IV. Pt. I. Act III. Sc. 1

See also: JESTING, LAUGHTER, SATIRE, WIT.

HUNGER

They said they were an-hungry; sigh'd forth
  proverbs;
That, hunger broke stone walls; that, dogs
  must eat;
That meat was made for mouths; that, the
  gods sent not
Corn for the rich men only:—With these
  shreds
They vented their complainings.
Coriolanus. Act I. Sc. 1

Cassius has a lean and hungry look.
Julius Caesar. Act I. Sc. 2

See also: APPETITE, COOKING, DESIRE, EATING.

HUSBAND

No worse a husband than the best of men.
Antony and Cleopatra. Act II. Sc. 2

I will attend my husband, be his nurse,
Diet his sickness, for it is my office.
Comedy of Errors. Act V. Sc. 1

That lord whose hand must take my plight
  shall carry
Half my love with him, half my care, and
  duty.
King Lear. Act I. Sc. 1

If I should marry him I should marry twenty
  husbands.
Merchant of Venice. Act I. Sc. 2

Thy husband is thy lord, thy life, thy keeper,
Thy head, thy sovereign; one that cares for
  thee,
And for thy maintenance.
Taming of the Shrew. Act V. Sc. 2

See also: LOVE, MATRIMONY, WIFE.

HYPOCRISY

My tables, my tables,—meet it is I set it
  down,
That one may smile, and smile, and be a
  villain;
At least, I'm sure it may be so in Denmark.
Hamlet. Act I. Sc. 5

With devotion's visage,
And pious action, we do sugar o'er
The devil himself.
Hamlet. Act III. Sc. 1

God hath given you one face, and you
Make yourselves another.
Hamlet. Act III. Sc. 1

I will speak daggers to her, but use none;
My tongue and soul in this be hypocrites.
Hamlet. Act III. Sc. 2

Thinking, by this face,
To fasten in our thoughts that they have
  courage;
But 'tis not so.
Julius Caesar. Act V. Sc. 1

Away, and mock the time with fairest show:
False face must hide what the false heart doth
  know.
Macbeth. Act I. Sc. 7

O, what may man within him hide,
Though angel on the outward side!
Measure for Measure. Act III. Sc. 2

So smooth he daub'd his vice with show of
  virtue,
  .   .   .   .
He liv'd from all attainder of suspects.
Richard III. Act III. Sc. 5

O serpent heart, hid with a flow'ring face!
Did ever a dragon keep so fair a cave?
Romeo and Juliet. Act III. Sc. 2

See also: DECEIT, FALSEHOOD, FRAUD.

I

IDLENESS

I rather would entreat thy company,
To see the wonders of the world abroad,
Than, living dully sluggardis'd at home,
Wear out thy youth with shapeless idleness.
Two Gentlemen of Verona. Act I. Sc. 1

See also: NEGLECT, SLEEP.

IGNORANCE

Ignorance is the curse of God,
Knowledge the wing wherewith we fly to
  heaven.
Henry VI. Pt. II. Act IV. Sc. 7

That unlettered, small-knowing soul.
> *Love's Labour's Lost.* Act I. Sc. 1

O thou monster ignorance, how deformed
dost thou look!
> *Love's Labour's Lost.* Act IV. Sc. 2

Well, for your favour, sir, why, give God
thanks, and make no boast of it; and for
your writing and reading, let that appear
when there is no need of such vanity.
> *Much Ado About Nothing.* Act III. Sc. 3

There is no darkness but ignorance.
> *Twelfth Night.* Act IV. Sc. 2

Madam, thou errest: I say, there is no darkness, but ignorance; in which thou art more
puzzled, than the Egyptians in their fog.
> *Twelfth Night.* Act IV. Sc. 2

See also: FOOL, KNOWLEDGE, WISDOM.

IMAGINATION

In my minds eye, Horatio.
> *Hamlet.* Act I. Sc. 2

This is the very coinage of your brain,
This bodiless creation ecstasy.
> *Hamlet.* Act III. Sc. 4

This is a gift that I have, simple, simple;
a foolish extravagant spirit, full of forms,
figures, shapes, objects, apprehensions, motions, revolutions. These are begot in the
ventricle of memory, nourished in the womb
of *pia mater,* and delivered upon the mellow-
ing of occasion.
> *Love's Labour's Lost.* Act IV. Sc. 2

Present fears
Are less than horrible imaginings.
> *Macbeth.* Act I. Sc. 3

The lunatic, the lover and the poet
Are of imagination all compact.
> *Midsummer Night's Dream.* Act V. Sc. 1

And, as imagination bodies forth
The forms of things unknown, the poet's pen
Turns them to shapes, and gives to airy
nothing
A local habitation and a name.
> *Midsummer Night's Dream.* Act V. Sc. 1

A wild dedication of yourselves
To unpath'd waters, undream'd shores.
> *Winter's Tale.* Act IV. Sc. 3

See also: DREAM, FANCY, THOUGHT.

IMMORTALITY

Look, here's the warrant, Claudio, for thy
death:
'Tis now dead midnight, and by eight
tomorrow
Thou must be made immortal.
> *Measure for Measure.* Act IV. Sc. 2

I held it ever,
Virtue and cunning were endowments
greater
Than nobleness and riches: careless heirs
May the two latter darken and expend;
But immortality attends the former,
Making a man a god.
> *Pericles.* Act III. Sc. 2

See also: DEATH, FUTURE, GOD, HEAVEN, HELL,
MORTALITY, SOUL, SPIRIT.

IMPATIENCE

I am on fire,
To hear this rich reprisal is so nigh,
And yet not ours.
> *Henry IV.* Pt. I. Act IV. Sc. 1

See also: DISCONTENTMENT, HASTE, TIME.

IMPOSSIBILITY

It is as hard to come as for a camel
To thread the postern of a needle's eye.
> *Richard II.* Act V. Sc. 5

See also: ABILITY, POWER, TRIAL.

INCONSTANCY

They are not constant; but are changing still.
> *Cymbeline.* Act II. Sc. 5

O, swear not by the moon, the inconstant
moon,
That monthly changes in her circled orb,
Lest that thy love prove likewise variable.
> *Romeo and Juliet.* Act II. Sc. 2

Love is not love
Which alters when it alteration finds,
Or bends with the remover to remove;
O, no! it is an ever-fixed mark,
That looks on tempests and is never
shaken;
It is the star to every wandering bark,
Whose worth's unknown, although his
height be taken.
> *Sonnet CXVI*

As one nail by strength drives out another,
So the remembrance of my former love
Is by a newer object quite forgotten.
> *Two Gentlemen of Verona.* Act II. Sc. 4

See also: CHANGE, CONSTANCY, FICKLENESS.

INDEPENDENCE

I'll never
Be such a gosling to obey instinct; but stand,
As if a man were author of himself,
And knew no other kin.
Coriolanus. Act V. Sc. 3

Speak then to me, who neither beg, nor fear;
Your favours, nor your hate.
Macbeth. Act I. Sc. 3

Be lion-mettled, proud; and take no care
Who chafes, who frets, or where conspirers
are.
Macbeth. Act IV. Sc. 1

See also: FREEDOM, LIBERTY, REBELLION.

INDIFFERENCE

Away, you trifler!—Love?—I love thee not,
I care not for thee, Kate; this is no world
To play with mammets and to tilt with lips;
We must have bloody noses, and crack'd
crowns,
And pass them current too. Gods me, my
horse!
Henry IV Pt. I. Act II. Sc. 3

You care not who sees your back: Call you
that backing of your friends? A plague upon
such backing!
Henry IV. Part I. Act II. Sc. 4

Set honour in one eye, and death i' the other,
And I will look on both indifferently.
Julius Caesar. Act I. Sc. 2

See also: CARE, CHANCE, LUCK.

INFLUENCE

He was, indeed, the glass
Wherein the noble youth did dress them-
selves.
Henry IV. Pt. II. Act II. Sc. 3

See also: POWER, SYMPATHY, TEACHER, VICE,
VIRTUE.

INGRATITUDE

Blow, blow, thou winter wind,
Thou art not so unkind
As man's ingratitude;
Thy tooth is not so keen,
Because thou art not seen,
Although thy breath be rude.

.   .   .   .

Freeze, freeze, thou bitter sky,

That dost not bite so nigh
As benefits forgot:
Though thou the waters warp,
Thy sting is not so sharp
As friends remember'd not.
As You Like It. Act II. Sc. 7. *Song*

Ingratitude is monstrous; and for the multitude to be ingrateful, were to make a
monster of the multitude.
Coriolanus. Act II. Sc. 3

He hath eaten me out of house and home.
Henry IV. Pt. II. Act II. Sc. 1

That man, that sits within a monarch's heart,
And ripens in the sunshine of his favour,
Would he abuse the countenance of the king,
Alack, what mischiefs might he set abroach,
In shadow of such greatness!
Henry IV. Pt. II. Act IV. Sc. 2

This was the most unkindest cut of all;
For when the noble Caesar saw him stab,
Ingratitude, more strong than traitor's arms,
Quite vanquish'd him: then burst his mighty
heart;
And, in his mantle muffling up his face,
Even at the base of Pompey's statue,
Which all the while ran blood, great Caesar
fell.
Julius Caesar. Act III. Sc. 2

Sharper than a serpent's tooth it is
To have a thankless child.
King Lear. Act I. Sc. 4

Ingratitude! thou marble-hearted fiend,
More hideous when thou show'st thee in a
child,
Than the sea-monster!
King Lear. Act I. Sc. 4

All the stor'd vengeances of heaven fall
On her ungrateful top.
King Lear. Act II. Sc. 4

What! would'st thou have a serpent sting thee
twice?
Merchant of Venice. Act IV. Sc. 1

Comfort, dear mother; God is much
displeas'd
That you take with unthankfulness his doing:
In common worldly things 'tis called un-
grateful,
With dull unwillingness to repay a debt,
Which with a bounteous hand was kindly
lent;
Much more to be thus opposite with Heaven;
For it requires the royal debt it lent you.
Richard III. Act II. Sc. 2

I hate ingratitude more in a man,
Than lying, vainness, babbling, drunkenness,
Or any taint of vice.
Twelfth Night. Act III. Sc. 4

See also: DECEIT, GRATITUDE, THANKFULNESS.

INNKEEPER

Shall I not take mine ease in mine inn?
Henry IV. Pt. I. Act III. Sc. 3

Now spurs the lated traveller apace,
To gain the timely inn.
Macbeth. Act III. Sc. 3

See also: OCCUPATION.

INNOCENCE

O, take the sense, sweet, of my innocence;
Love takes the meaning of love's conference.
Midsummer Night's Dream. Act II. Sc. 3

Hence, bashful cunning!
And prompt me, plain and holy innocence!
Tempest. Act III. Sc. 1

We were twinn'd lambs, that did frisk i' the
sun.
And bleat the one at the other. What we
chang'd
Was innocence for innocence; we knew not
The doctrine of ill-doing, nor dream'd
That any did.
Winter's Tale. Act I. Sc. 2

Innocence shall make
False accusation blush, and tyranny
Tremble at patience.
Winter's Tale. Act III. Sc. 2

See also: BLUSH, CHASTITY, CHILDREN, MOD-
ESTY, VIRTUE.

INSANITY

Though this be madness, yet there is method
in it.
Hamlet. Act II. Sc. 2

Madam, I swear, I use no art at all.
That he is mad, 'tis true; 'tis true 'tis pity;
And pity 'tis 'tis true.
Hamlet. Act II. Sc. 2

It shall be so;
Madness in great ones must not unwatch'd
go.
Hamlet. Act III. Sc. 1

I am not mad;—I would to heaven, I were!
For then, 'tis like I should forget myself.
King John. Act III. Sc. 4

We are not ourselves,
When nature, being oppress'd, commands
the mind
To suffer with the body.
King Lear. Act II. Sc. 4

Were such things here as we do speak about?
Or have we eaten of the insane root
That takes the reason prisoner?
Macbeth. Act I. Sc. 3

Fetter strong madness in a silken thread,
Charm ache with air, and agony with words.
Much Ado About Nothing. Act V. Sc. 1

See also: FOOL, MELANCHOLY, MIND, THOUGHT.

INSECT

Often, to our comfort, shall we find
The sharded beetle in a safer hold
Than is the full-winged Eagle.
Cymbeline. Act III. Sc. 3

Why rather, sleep, liest thou in smoky cribs,
Upon uneasy pallets stretching thee,
And hushed with buzzing night-flies to thy
slumber,
Than in the perfum'd chambers of the great,
Under the canopies of costly state
And lull'd with sounds of sweetest melody?
Henry IV. Pt. II. Act III. Sc. 1

So work the honey-bees;
Creatures, that, by a rule in nature, teach
The act of order to a peopled kingdom.
They have a king, and officers of sorts:
Where some like magistrates, correct at
home;
Others, like merchants, venture trade abroad;
Others, like soldiers, armed in their stings,
Make boot upon the summer's velvet buds;
Which pillage they with merry march bring
home
To the tent-royal of their emperor:
Who, busied in his majesties, surveys
The singing masons building roofs of gold;
The civil citizens kneading up the honey;
The poor mechanic porters crowding in
Their heavy burthens at his narrow gate;
The sad-ey'd justice, with his surly hum,
Delivering o'er to executors pale
The lazy yawning drone.
Henry V. Act I. Sc. 2

Your words, they rob the Hybla bees,
And leave them honeyless.
Julius Caesar. Act V. Sc. 1

The crows, and choughs, that wing the mid-
way air,
Show scarce so gross as beetles.
King Lear. Act IV. Sc. 6

The poor beetle, that we tread upon,
In corporal sufferance finds a pang as great
As when a giant dies.
Measure for Measure. Act III. Sc. 1

See also: ANIMAL, FLOWER.

INSTINCT

Instinct is a great matter; I was a coward
on instinct. I shall think the better of myself, and thee, during my life; I for a valiant
lion, and thou for a true prince.
Henry IV. Pt. I. Act II. Sc. 4

See also: ABILITY, ANIMAL, MIND, THOUGHT.

INTEMPERANCE

O monstrous! but one halfpenny-worth of
bread to this intolerable deal of sack!
Henry IV. Pt. I. Act II. Sc. 4

Now in madness,
Being full of supper and distempering
draughts,
Upon malicious bravery, dost thou come
To start my quiet.
Othello. Act I. Sc. 1

Every inordinate cup is unblessed, and the
ingredient is a devil.
Othello. Act II. Sc. 2

O that men should put an enemy in their
mouths to steal away their brains! that we
should, with joy, pleasance, revel, and applause, transform ourselves into beasts!
Othello. Act II. Sc. 3

I have drunk but one cup to-night, . . . and,
behold, what innovation it makes here; I am
unfortunate in the infirmity, and dare not
task my weakness with any more.
Othello. Act II. Sc. 3

I have very poor and unhappy brains for
drinking: I could wish courtesy would invent
some other custom of entertainment.
Othello. Act II. Sc. 3

I will ask him for my place again; he shall
tell me, I am a drunkard! Had I as many
mouths as Hydra, such an answer would
stop them all. To be now a sensible man, by
and by a fool, and presently a beast!
Othello. Act II. Sc. 3

I told you, Sir, they were red hot with drink-
ing;
So full of valour that they smote the air
For breathing in their faces; beat the ground
For kissing of their feet.
Tempest. Act IV. Sc. 1

OLIVIA:
What's a drunken man like, fool?
CLOWN:
Like a drowned man, a fool and madman;
one draught above heat makes him a fool;
the second mads him; and a third drowns
him.
Twelfth Night. Act I. Sc. 5

See also: DRINK, EATING, WINE.

INVENTION

This is a man's invention, and his hand.
As You Like It. Act IV. Sc. 3

See also: GENIUS, KNOWLEDGE.

ISLAND

The isle is full of noises,
Sounds, and sweet airs, that give delight and
hurt not.
Tempest. Act III. Sc. 2

See also: ENGLAND.

J

JEALOUSY

So full of artless jealousy is guilt,
It spills itself in fearing to be spilt!
Hamlet. Act IV. Sc. 5

Trifles, light as air
Are to the jealous confirmations strong
As proofs of holy writ.
Othello. Act III. Sc. 3

O, beware, my lord of jealousy;
It is the green-eyed monster, which doth
mock
The meat it feeds on. That cuckold lives in
bliss,
Who, certain of his fate, loves not his
wronger;
But, O, what damned minutes tells he o'er,
Who dotes, yet doubts; suspects, yet strongly
loves!
Othello. Act III. Sc. 3

I perchance, am vicious in my guess
As, I confess, it is my nature's plague
To spy into abuses; and oft, my jealousy
Shapes faults that are not.

Othello. Act III. Sc. 3

Jealous souls will not be answer'd so;
They are not ever jealous for the cause,
But jealous for they're jealous.

Othello. Act III. Sc. 4

Andronicus, would thou wert shipp'd to hell,
Rather than rob me of the people's hearts.

Titus Andronicus. Act I. Sc. 2

If I shall be condemn'd
Upon surmises; all proofs sleeping else,
But what your jealousies awake; I tell you,
'Tis rigour, and not law.

Winter's Tale. Act III. Sc. 2

See also: ENVY, HATE, SUSPICION.

JESTING

How ill white hairs become a fool and jester;
I have long dream'd of such a kind of man,
So surfeit-swell'd, so old, and so profane.

Henry IV. Pt. II. Act V. Sc. 5

Jesters do often prove prophets.

King Lear. Act V. Sc. 3

A jest's prosperity lies in the ear
Of him that hears it, never in the tongue
Of him that makes it.

Love's Labour's Lost. Act V. Sc. 2

I do not like this fooling.

Troilus and Cressida. Act V. Sc. 2

See also: HUMOR, LAUGHTER, SATIRE, SMILE,
WIT.

JEW

I am a Jew: Hath not a Jew eyes? hath not
a Jew hands, organs, dimensions, senses, affections, passions? fed with the same food,
hurt with the same weapons, subject to the
same diseases, healed by the same means,
warmed and cooled by the same winter and
summer, as a Christian is?

Merchant of Venice. Act III. Sc. 1

See also: BUSINESS, RELIGION.

JEWEL

The jewel best enamelled
Will lose his beauty; and though gold 'bides
still,

That others touch, yet often touching will
Wear gold.

Comedy of Errors. Act II. Sc. 1

Give me the ring of mine you had at dinner,
Or, for my diamond, the chain you promis'd.

Comedy of Errors. Act IV. Sc. 3

'Tis plate of rare device: and jewels,
Of rich and exquisite form; their value's great;
And I am something curious, being strange,
To have them in safe stowage.

Cymbeline. Act I. Sc. 7

Your ring first;
And here the bracelet of the truest princess,
That ever swore her faith.

Cymbeline. Act V. Sc. 5

Our chains and our jewels.
Your broaches, pearls, and owches.

Henry IV. Pt. II. Act II. Sc. 4

Ever out of frame;
And never going aright, being a watch,
But being watch'd that it may still go right!

Love's Labour's Lost. Act III. Sc. 1

Jewels; two stones, two rich and precious
stones,
Stol'n by my daughter!

Merchant of Venice. Act II. Sc. 8

A quarrel, . . .
About a hoop of gold, a paltry ring.

Merchant of Venice. Act V. Sc. 1

I'll give my jewels, for a set of beads.

Richard II. Act III. Sc. 3

JEWELLER:
I have a jewel here.
MERCHANT:
O, pray let's see't.

Timon of Athens. Act I. Sc. 1

The clock upbraids me with the waste of
time.

Twelfth Night. Act III. Sc. 1

See also: GOLD, WOMAN.

JOURNALISM: *see* NEWS.

JOY

My plenteous joys,
Wanton in fullness, seek to hide themselves
In drops of sorrow.

Macbeth. Act I. Sc. 4

I wish you all the joy that you can wish.
Merchant of Venice. Act III. Sc. 2

See also: DELIGHT, HAPPINESS, PLEASURE.

JUDGE

Between two hawks, which flies the higher
  pitch,
Between two dogs, which hath the deeper
  mouth,
Between two blades, which bears the better
  temper,
Between two horses, which doth bear him
  best,
Between two girls, which hath the merriest
  eye,
I have, perhaps, some shallow spirit of judg-
  ment:
But in these nice sharp quillets of the law,
Good faith, I am no wiser than a daw.
Henry VI. Pt. I. Act II. Sc. 4

Heaven is above all yet; there sits a Judge,
That no King can corrupt.
Henry VIII. Act III. Sc. 1

He who the sword of heaven will bear
Should be as holy as severe;
Pattern in himself, to know,
Grace to stand, and virtue go;
More nor less to others paying,
Than by self offenses weighing.
Shame to him, whose cruel striking
Kills for faults of his own liking!
Measure for Measure. Act III. Sc. 2

To offend and judge, are distinct offices,
And of opposed natures.
Merchant of Venice. Act II. Sc. 9

You are a worthy judge;
You know the law; your exposition
Hath been most sound.
Merchant of Venice. Act IV. Sc. 1

            What is my offence?
Where is the evidence that doth accuse me?
What lawful quest have given their verdict
  up
Unto the frowning judge?
Richard III. Act I. Sc. 4

See also: JUDGMENT, JUSTICE, LAW.

JUDGMENT

He that of greatest works is finisher
Oft does them by the weakest minister:
So holy writ in babes hath judgment shown
When judges have been babes.
All's Well That Ends Well. Act II. Sc. 1

            I see, men's judgments are
A parcel of their fortunes; and things out-
  ward
Do draw the inward quality after them,
To suffer all alike.
Antony and Cleopatra. Act III. Sc. 11

Give every man thine ear, but few thy
  voice;
Take each man's censure, but reserve thy
  judgment.
Hamlet. Act I. Sc. 3

No reckoning made, but sent to my account
With all my imperfections on my head.
Hamlet. Act I. Sc. 5

Forbear to judge for we are sinners all.
Henry VI. Pt. II. Act III. Sc. 3

            What we oft do best,
By sick interpreters, once, weak ones, is
Not ours, or not allow'd; what worst, as oft,
Hitting a grosser quality, is cried up
For our best act.
Henry VIII. Act I. Sc. 2

O judgment, thou art fled to bruitish beasts,
And men have lost their reason!
Julius Caesar. Act III. Sc. 2

The jury passing on the prisoner's life,
May, in the sworn twelve, have a thief or two
Guiltier than him they try.
Measure for Measure. Act II. Sc. 1

            How would you be,
If He, which is the top of judgment, should
But judge you as you are?
Measure for Measure. Act II. Sc. 2

I stand for judgment: answer: shall I have
  it?
Merchant of Venice. Act IV. Sc. 1

            I charge you by the law,
Whereof you are a well deserving pillar,
Proceed to judgment.
Merchant of Venice. Act IV. Sc. 1

A Daniel come to judgment! yea, a Daniel.
Merchant of Venice. Act IV. Sc. 1

The urging of that word, judgment, hath
bred a kind of remorse in me.
Richard III. Act I. Sc. 4

See also: CRIME, CRUELTY, DECISION, DISCRE-
  TION, EVIL, GUILT, JUDGE, MERCY,
  OPINION, PRISON, PUNISHMENT,

JUSTICE

There is more owing her than is paid; and
more shall be paid her than she'll demand.
All's Well That Ends Well. Act I. Sc. 3

Use every man after his desert, and who
  should
'Scape whipping!
Hamlet. Act I. Sc. 2

He will give the devil his due.
Henry IV. Pt. I. Act I. Sc. 2

What stronger breast-plate than a heart un-
  tainted?
Thrice is he arm'd that hath his quarrel just;
And he but naked, though lock'd up in steel,
Whose conscience with injustice is corrupted.
Henry VI. Pt. II. Act III. Sc. 2

And not ever
The justice and the truth o' the question car-
  ries
The due o' the verdict with it: At what ease
Might corrupt minds procure knaves as cor-
  rupt
To swear against you? such things have been
  done.
Henry VIII. Act V. Sc. 1

This shows you are above,
Your justicers; that these our nether crimes
So speedily can venge!
King Lear. Act IV. Sc. 2

The Gods are just, and of our pleasant vices
Make instruments to scourge us.
King Lear. Act V. Sc. 3

This even-handed justice
Commends the ingredients of our poison'd
  chalice
To our own lips.—He's here in double trust:
First, as I am his kinsman and his subject,
Strong both against the deed; then, as his
  host,
Who should against his murderer shut the
  door,
Not bear the knife myself.
Macbeth. Act I. Sc. 7

What's open made
To justice, that justice seizes. What know
  the laws,
That thieves do pass on thieves? 'Tis very
  pregnant,
The jewel that we find we stoop and take it,

Because we see it; but what we do not see
We tread upon and never think of it.
Measure for Measure. Act II. Sc. 1

I show it most of all, when I show justice;
For then I pity those I do not know,
Which a dismiss'd offence would after gall;
And do him right, that, answering one foul
  wrong,
Lives not to act another.
Measure for Measure. Act II. Sc. 2

How would you be,
If He, which is the top of judgment, should
But judge you as you are? O, think on that;
And mercy then will breathe within your
  lips,
Like man new made.
Measure for Measure. Act II. Sc. 2

Thyself shalt see the act:
For, as thou urgest justice, be assur'd
Thou shalt have justice, more than thou de-
  sir'st.
Merchant of Venice. Act IV. Sc. 1

This bond is forfeit;
And lawfully by this the Jew may claim
A pound of flesh.
Merchant of Venice. Act IV. Sc. 1

He shall have merely justice, and his bond.
Merchant of Venice. Act IV. Sc. 1

O, I were damn'd beyond all depth in hell,
But that I did proceed upon just grounds
To this extremity.
Othello. Act V. Sc. 2

I have done the state some service, and they
  know it;
No more of that; I pray you, in your letters,
When you shall these unlucky deeds relate,
Speak of me as I am; nothing extenuate,
Nor set down aught in malice.
Othello. Act V. Sc. 2

Impartial are your eyes, and ears;
Were he my brother, nay, my kingdom's heir,
Now by my sceptre's awe I make a vow,
Such neighbour nearness to our sacred blood
Should nothing privilege him, nor partialize
The unstopping firmness of my upright soul.
Richard II. Act I. Sc. 1

See also: EQUALITY, FREEDOM, LIBERTY.

K

KINDNESS

When your head did but ache,
I knit my handkerchief about your brows,
(The best I had, a princess wrought it me,)
And I did never ask it you again:
And with my hand at midnight held your
    head,
And, like the watchful minutes to the hour,
Still and anon cheer'd up the heavy time;
Saying,—"What lack you?"—and,—"Where lies
    your grief?"
King John. Act IV. Sc. 1

See also: CHARITY, GOODNESS, SYMPATHY.

KISS

Strangers and foes do sunder, and not kiss.
All's Well That Ends Well. Act II. Sc. 5

We have kiss'd away
Kingdoms and provinces.
Antony and Cleopatra. Act III. Sc. 8

And his kissing is as full of sanctity as the
touch of holy bread.
As You Like It. Act III. Sc. 4

O, a kiss
Long as my exile, sweet as my revenge!
Now, by the jealous queen of heaven, that
    kiss
I carried from thee, dear.
Coriolanus. Act V. Sc. 3

Ere I could
Give him that parting kiss, which I had set
Betwixt two charming words, comes in my
    father,
And, like the tyrannous breathing of the
    north,
Shakes all our buds from growing.
Cymbeline. Act I. Sc. 4

I understand thy kisses, and thou mine,
And that's a feeling disputation.
Henry IV. Part I. Act III. Sc. 1

Truly; I have thee with a most constant heart.
Henry IV. Pt. II. Act II. Sc. 4

It is not a fashion for the maids in France
to kiss before they are married.
Henry V. Act V. Sc. 2

I can express no kinder sign of love,
Than this kind kiss.
Henry VI. Pt. II. Act I. Sc. 1

The hearts of princes kiss obedience,
So much they love it.
Henry VIII. Act III. Sc. 1

With this kiss take my blessing: God protect
    thee,
Into whose hand I give thy life.
Henry VIII. Act V. Sc. 4

Upon thy cheek lay I this zealous kiss,
As seal to this indenture of my love.
King John. Act II. Sc. 1

Take, O take those lips away,
    That so sweetly were foresworn;
And those eyes, the break of day,
    Lights that do mislead the morn;
But my kisses bring again,
    Seals of love, but sealed in vain.
Measure for Measure. Act IV. Sc. 1. *Song*

Very good; well kissed! an excellent courtesy.
Othello. Act II. Sc. 1

Thou know'st this,
'Tis time to fear, when tyrants seem to kiss.
Pericles. Act I. Sc. 2

Teach not thy lip such scorn; for it was made
For kissing, lady, not for such contempt.
Richard III. Act I. Sc. 2

Their lips were four red roses on a stalk,
And, in their summer beauty, kiss'd each
    other.
Richard III. Act IV. Sc. 3

They may seize
On the white wonder of dear Juliet's hand
And steal immortal blessing from her lips;
Who, even in pure and vestal modesty
Still blush, as thinking their own kisses sin.
Romeo and Juliet. Act III. Sc. 3

This done, he took the bride about the neck,
And kiss'd her lips with such a clamorous
    smack,
That, at the parting, all the church did echo.
Taming of the Shrew. Act III. Sc. 2

I'll take that winter from your lips.
>> *Troilus and Cressida.* Act IV. Sc. 5

Why, then we'll make exchange; here, take
    you this,
And seal the bargain with a holy kiss.
>> *Two Gentlemen of Verona.* Act II. Sc. 2

Kissing with inside lip? stopping the career
of laughter with a sigh?
>> *Winter's Tale.* Act I. Sc. 2

                 You may ride us,
With one soft kiss, a thousand furlongs, ere
With spur we heat an acre.
>> *Winter's Tale.* Act I. Sc. 2

See also: AFFECTION, LOVE, WOMAN, WOOING.

KNOWLEDGE

I know a hawk from a handsaw.
>> *Hamlet.* Act II. Sc. 2

Ignorance is the curse of God,
Knowledge the wing wherewith we fly to
    heaven.
>> *Henry VI.* Pt. II. Act IV. Sc. 7

Too much to know, is, to know naught but
    fame.
>> *Love's Labour's Lost.* Act I. Sc. 1

BIRON:
What is the end of study?
KING:
Why, that to know, which else we should
not know.
BIRON:
Things hid and barr'd, you mean, from com-
mon sense?
KING:
Ay, that is study's god-like recompense.
>> *Love's Labour's Lost.* Act I. Sc. 1

If you can look into the seeds of time,
And say, which grain will grow, and which
    will not,
Speak then to me.
>> *Macbeth.* Act I. Sc. 3

An unlesson'd girl, unschool'd, unpractis'd;
Happy in this, she is not yet so old
    But she may learn.
>> *Merchant of Venice.* Act III. Sc. 2

See also: EDUCATION, LEARNING, MIND, STU-
    DENT, STUDY, TEACHER.

L

LABOR

Why such impress of shipwrights whose sore
    task
Does not divide the Sunday from the week.
>> *Hamlet.* Act I. Sc. 1

The labour we delight in, physics pain.
>> *Macbeth.* Act II. Sc. 3

Now the hungry lion roars,
    And the wolf behowls the moon;
Whilst the heavy ploughman snores,
    All with weary task fore-done.
>> *Midsummer Night's Dream.* Act V. Sc. 2

I have had my labour for my travel.
>> *Troilus and Cressida.* Act I. Sc. 1

See also: ACTION, DEED, WORK.

LANGUAGE

He has strangled
His language in his tears.
>> *Henry VIII.* Act V. Sc. 1

O, but they say, the tongues of dying men
Enforce attention like deep harmony:
Where words are scarce, they're seldom spent
    in vain:
For they breathe truth, that breathe their
    words in pain.
He, that no more may say, is listn'd more.
>> *Richard II.* Act II. Sc. 1

There was speech in their dumbness, language in their very gesture.
>> *Winter's Tale.* Act II. Sc. 2

See also: LINGUIST, ORATORY, SPEECH, TALK,
    TONGUE, WIT, WORD.

LARK

Then my dial goes not true; I took the lark
    for a bunting.
>> *All's Well That Ends Well.* Act II. Sc. 5

Hark! hark! the lark at heaven's gate sings,
    And Phoebus 'gins arise,
His steeds to water at those springs
    On chalic'd flowers that lies.
>> *Cymbeline.* Act II. Sc. 3. *Song*

Some say, that ever 'gainst that season comes
Wherein our Saviour's birth is celebrated,
The bird of dawning singeth all night long:
And then, they say, no spirit can walk abroad;
The nights are wholesome; then no planets strike,
No fairy takes, nor witch hath power to charm,
So hallow'd and so gracious is the time.
Hamlet. Act I. Sc. 1

It was the lark, the herald of the morn.
Romeo and Juliet. Act III. Sc. 5

It is the lark that sings so out of tune,
Straining harsh discords and unpleasing sharps.
Romeo and Juliet. Act III. Sc. 5

Lo! here the gentle lark, weary of rest,
From his moist cabinet mounts up on high,
And wakes the morning, from whose silver breast
The sun ariseth in his majesty.
Venus and Adonis. Line 853

See also: ANIMAL, BIRD.

LATIN: *see* LINGUIST.

LAUGHTER

With his eyes in flood with laughter.
Cymbeline. Act I. Sc. 7

O, you shall see him laugh till his face be like a wet cloak ill laid up.
Henry IV. Pt. II. Act V. Sc. 1

The brain of this foolish-compounded clay, man, is not able to invent anything that tends to laughter, more than I invent, or is invented on me.
Henry IV. Pt. II. Act I. Sc. 2

O, I am stabb'd with laughter.
Love's Labour's Lost. Act V. Sc. 2

They laugh that win.
Othello. Act IV. Sc. 1

See also: JESTING, JOY, MERRIMENT, SMILE.

LAW

You wear out a good wholesome forenoon in hearing a cause between an orange-wife and a fosset-seller; and then rejourn the contro-

versy of threepence to a second day of audience.
Coriolanus. Act II. Sc. 1

He hath resisted law,
And therefore law shall scorn him further trial
Than the severity of the public power.
Coriolanus. Act III. Sc. 1

In the corrupted currents of the world,
Offence's gilded hand may shove by justice;
And oft 'tis seen, the wicked prize itself
Buys out the law: But 'tis not so above.
There is no shuffling, there the action lies
In his true nature; and we ourselves compell'd,
Even to the teeth and forehead of our faults,
To give in evidence.
Hamlet. Act III. Sc. 3

SECOND CLOWN:
But is this "law."
FIRST CLOWN:
Ay, marry is't; crowner's-quest law.
Hamlet. Act V. Sc. 1

But, I prithee, sweet wag, shall there be gallows standing in England when thou art king?—and resolution thus fobbed as it is with the rusty curb of old father antick the law.
Henry IV. Pt. I. Act I. Sc. 2

Faith, I have been a turant in the law;
And never yet could frame my will to it;
And, therefore, frame the law unto my will.
Henry VI. Pt. I. Act II. Sc. 4

The first thing we do, lets kill all the lawyers.
Henry VI. Pt. II. Act IV. Sc. 2

Press not a falling man too far; 'tis virtue:
His faults lie open to the laws; let them,
Not you, correct him.
Henry VIII. Act III. Sc. 2

When law can do no right,
Let it be lawful, that law bar no wrong.
King John. Act III. Sc. 1

'Tis like the breath of an unfee'd lawyer; you gave me nothing for't.
King Lear. Act I. Sc. 4

Bold of your worthiness, we single you
As our best-moving fair solicitor.
Love's Labour's Lost. Act II. Sc. 1

We must not make a scare-crow of the law,
Setting it up to fear the birds of prey,
And let it keep one shape, till custom make it
Their perch, and not their terror.
> *Measure for Measure. Act II. Sc. 1*

To offend and judge, are distinct offices, and
of opposed nature.
> *Merchant of Venice. Act II. Sc. 9*

In law, what plea so tainted and corrupt,
But, being season'd with a gracious voice,
Obscures the show of evil?
> *Merchant of Venice. Act III. Sc. 2*

He's a justice of peace in his country, simple
  though I stand here.
> *Merry Wives of Windsor. Act I. Sc. 1*

> The bloody book of law
You shall yourself read in the bitter letter,
After your own sense.
> *Othello. Act I. Sc. 3*

> I am a subject
And challenge law: attorneys are denied me;
And therefore personally I lay my claim
To my inheritance.
> *Richard II. Act II. Sc. 3*

Before I be convict by course of law,
To threaten me with death is most unlawful.
> *Richard III. Act I. Sc. 4*

Do as adversaries do in law,—
Strive mightily, but eat and drink as friends.
> *Taming of the Shrew. Act I. Sc. 2*

We are for law; he dies.
> *Timon of Athens. Act III. Sc. 5*

It pleases time and fortune, to lie heavy
Upon a friend of mine, who, in hot blood,
Hath stepp'd into the law; which is past
  depth
To those that, without head, plunge into't.
> *Timon of Athens. Act III. Sc. 5*

They have been grand jury-men since before
Noah was a sailor.
> *Twelfth Night. Act III. Sc. 2*

Still you keep o' the windy side of the law.
> *Twelfth Night. Act III. Sc . 4*

See also: CRIME, GOVERNMENT, JUDGE, JUS-
  TICE, PUNISHMENT.

LEARNING

Learning is but an adjunct to ourself,
And where we are, our learning likewise is.
> *Love's Labour's Lost. Act IV. Sc. 3*

O this learning! what a thing it is.
> *Taming of the Shrew. Act I. Sc. 2*

See also: EDUCATION, KNOWLEDGE, STUDY.

LETTER

> My letters
Before did satisfy you.
> *Antony and Cleopatra. Act II. Sc. 2*

The letter is too long by half a mile.
> *Love's Labour's Lost. Act V. Sc. 2*

Here are a few of the unpleasant'st words
That ever blotted paper.
> *Merchant of Venice. Act III. Sc. 2*

What! have I 'scaped love-letters in the holy-
day time of my beauty, and am I now a subject for them?
> *Merry Wives of Windsor. Act II. Sc. 1*

> I have a letter from her
Of such contents as you will wonder at;
The mirth whereof so larded with my matter,
That neither, singly, can be manifested,
Without the show of both.
> *Merry Wives of Windsor. Act IV. Sc. 6*

Jove, and my stars, be praised!—Here is yet
a postscript.
> *Twelfth Night. Act II. Sc. 5*

If this letter move him not, his legs cannot.
I'll give 't him.
> *Twelfth Night. Act III. Sc. 4*

Let me hear from thee by letters.
> *Two Gentlemen of Verona. Act I. Sc. 1*

See also: ABSENCE, MEMORY, NEWS.

LIBERTY

> I must have liberty
Withal, as large a charter as the wind,
To blow on whom I please.
> *As You Like It. Act II. Sc. 7*

Why, headstrong liberty is lash'd with woe,
There's nothing, situate under heaven's eye,
But hath his bound, in earth, in sea, in sky.
> *Comedy of Errors. Act II. Sc.1*

Every bondman in his own land bears
The power to cancel his captivity.
Julius Caesar. Act I. Sc. 3

Boundless intemperance
In nature is a tyranny, it hath been
Th' untimely emptying of the happy throne,
And fall of many kings.
Macbeth. Act IV. Sc. 3

See also: EQUALITY, FREEDOM, SLAVERY.

LIBRARY

He furnish'd me,
From my own library, with volumes that
I prize above my dukedom.
Tempest. Act I. Sc. 2

Come, and take choice of all my library,
And so beguile thy sorrow.
Titus Andronicus. Act IV. Sc. 1

See also: BOOK, READING.

LIFE

The web of our life is of a mingled yarn,
good and ill together.
All's Well That Ends Well. Act IV. Sc. 3

O excellent! I love long life better than figs.
Antony and Cleopatra. Act I. Sc. 2

And this our life, exempt from public haunt,
Finds tongues in trees, books in the running
brooks,
Sermons in stones, and good in every thing.
As You Like It. Act II. Sc. 1

And so from hour to hour, we ripe and ripe,
And then from hour to hour, we rot and rot.
And thereby hangs a tale.
As You Like It. Act II. Sc. 7

Why, what should be the fear?
I do not set my life at a pin's fee.
Hamlet. Act I. Sc. 4

A man's life's no more than to say, One.
Hamlet. Act V. Sc. 2

O gentlemen, the time of life is short;
To spend that shortness basely were too long,
If life did ride upon a dial's point,
Still ending at the arrival of an hour.
Henry IV. Pt. I. Act V. Sc. 2

Winding up days with toil, and nights with
sleep.
Henry V. Act IV. Sc. 1

Let life be short; else shame will be too long.
Henry V. Act IV. Sc. 5

The sands are number'd that make up my life;
Here must I stay, and here my life must end.
Henry VI. Pt. III. Act I. Sc. 4

This is the state of man: To-day he puts
forth
The tender leaves of hope; to-morrow blos-
soms,
And bears his blushing honours thick upon
him:
The third day comes a frost, a killing frost;
And,—when he thinks, good easy man, full
surely
His greatness is a ripening,—nips his root,
And then he falls, as I do.
Henry VIII. Act III. Sc. 2

I cannot tell, what you and other men
Think of this life; but, for my single self,
I had as lief not be, as live to be
In awe of such a thing as I myself.
Julius Caesar. Act I. Sc. 2

Nor stony tower, nor walls of beaten brass,
Nor airless dungeon, nor strong links of iron,
Can be retentive to the strength of spirit;
But life, being weary of these worldly bars,
Never lacks power to dismiss itself.
Julius Caesar. Act I. Sc. 3

This day I breathed first: time is come round;
And where I did begin there shall I end;
My life is run his compass.
Julius Caesar. Act V. Sc. 3

Life is as tedious as a twice-told tale,
Vexing the dull ear of a drowsy man.
King John. Act III. Sc. 4

When we are born, we cry, that we are come
To this great stage of fools.
King Lear. Act IV. Sc. 6

Thy life's a miracle.
King Lear. Act IV. Sc. 6

That but this blow
Might be the be-all and the end-all here,
But here, upon this bank and shoal of time,—
We'd jump the life to come.
Macbeth. Act I. Sc. 7

Had I but died an hour before this chance,
I had liv'd a blessed time; for from this in-
stant,
There's nothing serious in mortality:

All is but toys; renown, and grace is dead;
The wine of life is drawn, and the mere lees
Is left this vault to brag of.
                              Macbeth. Act II. Sc. 3

Out, out, brief candle!
Life's but a walking shadow.
                              Macbeth. Act V. Sc. 5

I bear a charmed life.
                              Macbeth. Act V. Sc. 7

Some rise by sin, and some by virtue fall;
Some run from brakes of vice, and answer
        none;
And some condemned for a fault alone.
                Measure for Measure. Act II. Sc. 1

Thou hast nor youth, nor age;
But, as it were an after-dinner's sleep,
Dreaming on both; for all thy blessed youth
Becomes as aged, and doth beg the alms
Of palsied eld; and when thou art old and
        rich,
Thou hast neither heat, affection, limb, nor
        beauty,
To make thy riches pleasant.
                Measure for Measure. Act III. Sc. 1

Reason thus with life,—
If I do lose thee, I do lose a thing
That none but fools would keep.
                Measure for Measure. Act III. Sc. 1

Life is a shuttle.
        Merry Wives of Windsor. Act V. Sc. 1

It is silliness to live, when to live is a torment;
and then we have a prescription to die, when
death is our physician.
                              Othello. Act I. Sc. 3

Her father lov'd me; oft invited me;
Still question'd me the story of my life,
From year to year; the battles, seiges, for-
        tunes,
That I have pass'd.
                              Othello. Act I. Sc. 3

See also: DEATH, DESTINY, FATE, IMMORTAL-
        ITY, MAN, SOUL, TIME.

LIGHT

Light, seeking light, doth light of light be-
        guile:
So, ere you find where light in darkness lies,
Your light grows dark by losing of your eyes.
                Love's Labour's Lost. Act I. Sc. 1

See also: DAY, EYE, MORNING, SUN, SUNRISE,
        SUNSET, TWILIGHT.

LINGUIST

This is your devoted friend, sir, the manifold linguist.
        All's Well That Ends Well. Act IV. Sc. 3

Away with him, away with him; he speaks
Latin.
                Henry VI. Pt. II. Act IV. Sc. 7

O! good, my lord, no Latin;
I'm not such a truant since my coming
As not to know the language I have liv'd in.
                Henry VIII. Act III. Sc. 1

You taught me language, and my profit on't
Is, I know how to curse; the red plague rid
        you,
For learning me your language!
                              Tempest. Act I. Sc. 2

Speaks three or four languages word for word
without book.
                Twelfth Night. Act I. Sc. 3

By your own report
A linguist.
        Two Gentlemen of Verona. Act IV. Sc. 1

See also: LANGUAGE.

LISTENING

This cuff was but to knock at your ear, and
beseech listening.
                Taming of the Shrew. Act IV. Sc. 1

See also: SPEECH, TONGUE, VOICE.

LOSS

Wise men ne'er sit and wail their loss,
But cheerly seek how to redress their harms.
                Henry VI. Pt. III. Act V. Sc. 4

See also: ADVERSITY, GAIN.

LOVE

The brains of my Cupid's knock'd out; and I
begin to love, as an old man loves money,
with no stomach.
        All's Well That Ends Well. Act III. Sc. 2

There's beggary in the love that can be
reckoned.
                Antony and Cleopatra. Act I. Sc. 1

If thou remember'st not the slightest folly
That ever love did make thee run into,
Thou hast not lov'd.
                As You Like It. Act II. Sc. 4

We, that are true lovers, run into strange
capers; but as all is mortal in nature, so is all
nature in love mortal in folly.
As You Like It. Act II. Sc. 4

It is as easy to count atomies, as to resolve
the propositions of a lover.
As You Like It. Act III. Sc. 2

Love is merely a madness; and, I tell you,
deserves as well a dark house and whip, as
madmen do: and the reason why they are
not so punished and cured, is, that the
lunacy is so ordinary, that the whippers are
in love too.
As You Like It. Act III. Sc. 2

Good shepherd, tell this youth what 'tis to
love.
It is to be all made of sighs and tears;—
.   .   .   .
It is to be all made of faith and service;—
.   .   .
It is to be all made of fantasy.
As You Like It. Act V. Sc. 2

Let me twine
Mine arms about that body, where against
My grained ash an hundred times hath
broke,
And scarr'd the moon with splinters!
Coriolanus. Act IV. Sc. 5

Here I clip
The anvil of my sword; and do contest
As hotly and as nobly with thy love,
As ever in ambitious strength I did
Contend against thy valour.
Coriolanus. Act IV. Sc. 5

Lovers,
And men in dangerous bonds, pray not alike.
Cymbeline. Act III. Sc. 2

I know not why
I love this youth; and I have heard you say,
Love's reason's without reason.
Cymbeline. Act IV. Sc. 2

This is the very ecstacy of love;
Whose violent property foregoes itself,
And leads the will to desperate undertakings.
Hamlet. Act II. Sc. 1

He is far gone, far gone: and truly in my
youth I suffered much extremity for love;
very near this.
Hamlet. Act II. Sc. 2

Forty thousand brothers
Could not, with all their quantity of love,
Make up my sum.
Hamlet. Act V. Sc. 1

Though last, not least in love!
Julius Caesar. Act III. Sc. 1

Have you not love enough to bear with me,
When that rash humour which my mother
gave me
Makes me forgetful?
Julius Caesar. Act IV. Sc. 3

Love's not love,
When it is mingled with regards that stand
Aloof from the entire point.
King Lear. Act I. Sc. 1

I am sure my love's
More ponderous than my tongue.
King Lear. Act I. Sc. 1

When love speaks the voice of all the gods
Makes heaven drowsy with the harmony.
Love's Labour's Lost. Act IV. Sc. 3

So sweet a kiss the golden sun gives not
To those fresh morning drops upon the rose,
As thy eye-beams, when their fresh rays have
smot
The night of dew that on my cheeks down
flows:
Nor shines the silver moon one-half so bright
Through the transparent bosom of the deep,
As doth thy face through tears of mine give
light.
Love's Labour's Lost. Act IV. Sc. 3

Love is blind, and lovers cannot see
The pretty follies that themselves commit.
Merchant of Venice. Act II. Sc. 6

I have not seen
So likely an ambassador of love;
A day in April never came so sweet,
To show how costly summer was at hand,
As this fore-spurrer comes before his lord.
Merchant of Venice. Act II. Sc. 9

Swearing till my very roof was dry
With oaths of Love.
Merchant of Venice. Act III. Sc. 2

Love like a shadow flies, when substance
love pursues;
Pursuing that that flies, and flying what
pursues.
Merry Wives of Windsor. Act II. Sc. 2

Your eyes are load-stars; and your tongue's
 sweet air
More tuneable than lark to shepherd's ear.
 Midsummer Night's Dream. Act I. Sc. 1

Love looks not with the eyes, but with the
 mind;
And therefore is winged Cupid painted
 blind.
 Midsummer Night's Dream. Act I. Sc. 1

Do I not in plainest truth
Tell you—I do not, nor I cannot, love you?
 Midsummer Night's Dream. Act II. Sc. 2

I look'd upon her with a soldier's eye,
That lik'd but had a rougher task in hand
Than to drive liking to the name of love:
But now I am return'd, and that war-
 thoughts
Have left their places vacant, in their rooms
Come thronging soft and delicate desires.
 Much Ado About Nothing. Act I. Sc. 1

Friendship is constant in all other things,
Save in the office and affairs of love:
Therefore, all hearts in love use their own
 tongues;
Let every eye negotiate for itself,
And trust no agent.
 Much Ado About Nothing. Act II. Sc. 1

Speak low if you speak love.
 Much Ado About Nothing. Act II. Sc. 1

I will not be sworn but love may transform
me to an oyster; but I'll take my oath on it,
till he have made an oyster of me, he shall
never make me such a fool.
 Much Ado About Nothing. Act II. Sc. 3

Some Cupid kills with arrows, some with
 traps.
 Much Ado About Nothing. Act III. Sc. 1

Upon this hint I spake;
She lov'd me for the dangers I had pass'd;
And I lov'd her, that she did pity them.
This only is the witchcraft I have us'd;
Here comes the lady, let her witness it.
 Othello. Act I. Sc. 3

Perdition catch my soul,
But I do love thee! and when I love thee not,
Chaos is come again.
 Othello. Act III. Sc. 3

What! keep a week away? seven days and
 nights?

Eight-score eight hours? and lovers' absent
 hours,
More tedious than the dial eight-score times?
Oh, weary reckoning!
 Othello. Act III. Sc. 4

If Heaven would make me such another
 world
Of one entire and perfect chrysolite,
I'd not have sold her for it.
 Othello. Act V. Sc. 2

Love is a smoke rais'd with the fume of
 sighs;
Being purg'd, a fire sparkling in a lovers'
 eyes;
Being vex'd, a sea nourish'd with lovers'
 tears;
What is it else? a madness most discreet,
A choking gall, and a preserving sweet.
 Romet and Juliet. Act I. Sc. 1

It is my soul, that calls upon my name;
How silver-sweet sound lovers' tongues by
 night,
Like softest music to attending ears.
 Romeo and Juliet. Act II. Sc. 2

See, how she leans her cheek upon her hand!
O, that I were a glove upon that hand,
That I might touch that cheek!
 Romeo and Juliet. Act II. Sc. 2

Sleep dwell upon thine eyes, peace in they
 breast!
Would I were sleep and peace, so sweet to
 rest!
 Romeo and Juliet. Act II. Sc. 2

Stony limits cannot hold love out;
And what love can do, that dares love at-
 tempt.
 Romeo and Juliet. Act II. Sc. 2

This bud of love, by Summer's ripening
 breath,
May prove a beauteous flower when next we
 meet.
Good night, good night! as sweet repose and
 rest
Come to thy heart, as that within my breast!
 Romeo and Juliet. Act II. Sc. 2

'Tis almost morning, I would have thee gone:
And yet no further than a wanton's bird;
Who lets it hop a little from her hand,
Like a poor prisoner in his twisted gyves,
And with a silk thread plucks it back again,
So loving jealous of his liberty.
 Romeo and Juliet. Act II. Sc. 2

Love's heralds should be thoughts
Which ten times faster glide than the sun's
 beams
Driving back shadows over low'ring hills;
Therefore do nimble-pinion'd doves draw
 love;
And therefore hath the wind-swift Cupid
 wings.
    Romeo and Juliet. Act II. Sc. 5

Love moderately; long love doth so;
Too swift arrives as tardy as too slow.
    Romeo and Juliet. Act II. Sc. 6

Give me my Romeo: and, when he shall die,
Take him, and cut him out in little stars,
And he will make the face of heaven so fine,
That all the world will be in love with night,
And pay no worship to the garish sun.
    Romeo and Juliet. Act III. Sc. 2

   Love knows, it is a greater grief
To bear love's wrong, than hate's known injury.
      Sonnet XL

Love alters not with his brief hours and
 weeks,
But bears it out even to the edge of doom.
      Sonnet CXVI

     To be wise, and love,
Exceeds man's might; that dwells with gods
 above.
    Troilus and Cressida. Act III. Sc. 2

They say, all lovers swear more performance than they are able, and yet reserve an
ability that they never perform.
    Troilus and Cressida. Act III. Sc. 2

O spirit of love, how quick and fresh art
 thou!
That, notwithstanding thy capacity
Receiveth as the sea, nought enters there,
Of what validity and pitch soe'er,
But falls into abatement and low price,
Even in a minute.
    Twelfth Night. Act I. Sc. 1

  Let thy love be younger than thyself
Or thy affection cannot hold the bent:
For women are as roses; whose fair flower,
Being once display'd, doth fall that very
 hour.
    Twelfth Night. Act II. Sc. 4

Reason thus with reason fetter;
Love sought is good, but given unsought, is
 better.
    Twelfth Night. Act III. Sc. 1

He was more than over shoes in love.
    Two Gentlemen of Verona. Act I. Sc. 1

Love is your master, for he masters you;
And he that is so yoked by a fool,
Methinks should not be chronicled for wise.
    Two Gentlemen of Verona. Act I. Sc. 1

To be in love, where scorn is bought with
 groans;
Coy looks with heart-sore sighs; one fading
 moment's mirth
With twenty watchful, weary, tedious nights;
If haply won, perhaps a hapless gain;
If lost, why then a grievous labour won.
    Two Gentlemen of Verona. Act I. Sc. 1

  Writers say, As the most forward bud
Is eaten by the canker ere it blow,
Even so by love the young and tender wit
Is turn'd to folly; blasting in the bud,
Losing his verdure even in the prime.
    Two Gentlemen of Verona. Act I. Sc. 1

How wayward is this foolish love,
That, like a testy babe, will scratch the nurse,
And presently, all humbled, kiss the rod.
    Two Gentlemen of Verona. Act I. Sc. 2

I do not seek to quench your love's hot fire;
But qualify the fire's extreme rage,
Lest it should burn above the bounds of
 reason.
    Two Gentlemen of Verona. Act II. Sc. 7

Except I be by Sylvia in the night,
There is no music in the nightingale.
    Two Gentlemen of Verona. Act III. Sc. 1

     You know that love
Will creep in service where it cannot go.
    Two Gentlemen of Verona. Act IV. Sc. 2

The strongest, love will instantly make
 weak:
Strike the wise dumb; and teach the fool to
 speak.
    Venus and Adonis. Line 145

What 'tis to love? how want of love tor-
 menteth?
    Venus and Adonis. Line 202

     Why, that was when
Three crabbed months had sour'd themselves
 to death,
Ere I could make thee open thy white hand,

And clap thyself my love; then didst thou utter,
"I am yours for ever."
A Winter's Tale. Act I. Sc. 2

See also: AFFECTION, CHILDREN, HUSBAND, KISS, MATRIMONY, MOTHER, PASSION, PATRIOTISM, WOMAN, WOOING.

LOYALTY

Master, go on, and I will follow thee,
To the last gasp, with truth and loyalty.
As You Like It. Act II. Sc. 3

To thine own-self be true;
And it must follow, as the night the day.
Thou can'st not then be false to any man.
Hamlet. Act I. Sc. 3

Where is loyalty?
If it be banish'd from the frosty head,
Where shall it find harbour in the Earth?
Henry VI. Pt. II. Act V. Sc. 1

Had I but serv'd my God with half the zeal
I serv'd my king, he would not in my age
Have left me naked to mine enemies.
Henry VIII. Act III. Sc. 2

Not that I loved Caesar less, but that
I loved Rome more.
Julius Caesar. Act III. Sc. 2

Look thou be true; do not give dalliance
Too much the rein; the strongest oaths are straw
To th' fire i' th' blood.
Tempest. Act IV. Sc. 1

The swallow follows not summer more
Willingly than we your lordship.
Timon of Athens. Act III. Sc. 6

See also: FIDELITY, FRIENDSHIP, PATRIOTISM.

LUCK

By the luckiest stars.
All's Well That Ends Well. Act I. Sc. 3

Mine hours were nice and lucky.
Antony and Cleopatra. Act III. Sc. 2

And good luck go with thee.
Henry V. Act IV. Sc. 3

Tidings do I bring, and lucky joys,
And golden times.
Henry VI. Pt. II. Act V. Sc. 3

All planets of good luck, I mean.
Henry VIII. Act V. Sc. 1

What, what, what? ill luck?
Merchant of Venice. Act III. Sc. 1

As good luck would have it.
Merry Wives of Windsor. Act III. Sc. 5

Good luck lies in odd numbers . . . they say,
there is divinity in odd numbers, either in
nativity, chance or death.
Merry Wives of Windsor. Act V. Sc. 1

Pray thou for us,
And good luck grant thee thy Demetrius.
Midsummer Night's Dream. Act I. Sc. 1

Not from the stars do I my judgment pluck;
And yet methinks I have astronomy,
But not to tell of good or evil luck,
Of plagues, of dearths, or seasons' quality.
Sonnet XIV

'Tis a lucky day, boy.
Winter's Tale. Act III. Sc. 2

See also: CHANCE, FORTUNE.

LUXURY

Rings put upon his fingers,
A most delicious bouquet by his bed,
And brave attendants near him when he wakes,
Would not the beggar then forget himself?
Taming of the Shrew. Induction

See also: GOLD, MONEY, VANITY, WEALTH.

M

MAN

Men have died from time to time, and worms
have eaten them, but not for love,
As You Like It. Act IV. Sc. 1

He was a man, take him for all in all,
I shall not look upon his like again.
Hamlet. Act I. Sc. 2

What a piece of work is a man! How noble in
reason! how infinite in faculty, in form, and
moving, how express and admirable! in
action, how like an angel! in apprehension,
how like a god! the beauty of the world! the

paragon of animals! And yet, to me, what is this quintessence of dust? man delights not me, no nor women neither, though by your smiling, you seem to say so.
Hamlet. Act II. Sc. 2

I have thought some of Nature's journeymen had made men, and not made them well, they imitated humanity so abominably.
Hamlet. Act III. Sc. 2

Give me that man
That is not passion's slave, and I will wear him
In my heart's core, ay, in my heart of heart,
As I do thee.
Hamlet. Act III. Sc. 2

A combination, and a form, indeed,
Where every god did seem to set his seal,
To give the world assurance of a man.
Hamlet. Act III. Sc. 4

What is a man
If his chief good, and market of his time,
Be but to sleep and feed?
Hamlet. Act IV. Sc. 4

Men that make
Envy, and crooked malice, nourishment,
Dare bite the best.
Henry VIII. Act V. Sc. 2

Men at some time are masters of their fates,
The fault, dear Brutus, is not in our stars,
But in ourselves, that we are underlings.
Julius Caesar. Act I. Sc. 2

The foremost man of all this world.
Julius Caesar. Act IV. Sc. 3

His life was gentle; and the elements
So mix'd in him, that Nature might stand up,
And say to all the world. This was a man!
Julius Caesar. Act V. Sc. 5

FIRST MURDERER:
We are men, my liege.
MACBETH:
Ay, in the catalogue ye go for men.
Macbeth. Act III. Sc. 1

God made him, and therefore let him pass for a man.
Merchant of Venice. Act I. Sc. 1

A proper man as one shall see in a summer's day.
Midsummer Night's Dream. Act I. Sc. 2

Are you good men and true?
Much Ado About Nothing. Act III. Sc. 3

Now hath Time made me his numbering clock:
My thoughts are minutes; and, with sighs, they jar
Their watches on into mine eyes, the outward watch,
Where to my finger, like a dial's point,
Is pointing still, in cleansing them from tears.
The sounds that tell what hour it is.
Are clamorous groans, that strike upon my heart,
Which is the bell.
Richard II. Act V. Sc. 5

Why, he's a man of wax.
Romeo and Juliet. Act I. Sc. 3

I wonder men dare trust themselves with men.
Timon of Athens. Act I. Sc. 2

Men, like butterflies,
Show not their mealy wings but to the summer.
Troilus and Cressida. Act III. Sc. 3

O heavens! were man
But constant, he were perfect; that one error
Fills him with faults.
Two Gentlemen of Verona. Act V. Sc. 4

See also: CHARACTER, LIFE, LOVE, WOMAN.

MANNERS

But I,—that am not shap'd for sportive tricks,
Nor made to court an amorous looking-glass.
Richard III. Act I. Sc. 1

See also: COURTESY, GENTLEMAN.

MARIGOLD

Winking Marybuds begin to ope their golden eyes.
Cymbeline. Act II. Sc. 3

Here's flowers for you;
Hot lavender, mints, savory, marjoram;
The marigold, that goes to bed with th' sun,
And with him rises weeping.
Winter's Tale, Act IV, Sc. 3

See also: FLOWER, TREE.

MARRIAGE

If you shall marry,
You give away this hand, and that is mine;
You give away Heaven's vows, and those are
    mine;
You give away myself, which is known mine.
All's Well That Ends Well. Act V. Sc. 3

Men are April when they woo, December
when they wed; maids are May when they
are maids, but the sky changes when they
are wives.
As You Like it. Act IV. Sc. 1

I will fasten on this sleeve of thine:
Thou art an elm, my husband, I, a vine.
Comedy of Errors. Act II. Sc. 2

Men's vows are women's traitors! All good
    seeming,
By thy revolt, O husband, shall be thought
Put on for villany; not born, where 't grows;
But worn, a bait for ladies.
Cymbeline. Act III. Sc. 4

Ere yet the salt of most unrighteous tears
Had left the flushing in her galled eyes,
She married.
Hamlet. Act I. Sc. 2

The instances that second marriage move,
Are base respects of thrift, but none of love.
Hamlet. Act III. Sc. 2

God, the best maker of all marriages,
Combine your hearts in one.
Henry V. Act V. Sc. 2

Marriage is a matter of more worth
Than to be dealt in by attorneyship;

   .   .   .   .

For what is wedlock forced but a hell,
An age of discord and continual strife?
Whereas the contrary bringeth bliss,
And is a pattern of celestial peace.
Whom should we watch with Henry being a
    king,
But Margaret, that is daughter to a king?
Henry VI. Pt. I. Act V. Sc. 5

He counsels a divorce: a loss of her,
That, like a jewel, has hung twenty years
About his neck, yet never lost her lustre;
Of her, that loves him with that excellence
That angels love good men with; even of her
That when the greatest stroke of fortune falls,
Will bless the king.
Henry VIII. Act II. Sc. 2

O ye gods,
Render me worthy of this noble wife!
Julius Caesar. Act II. Sc. 1

O Cassius, you are yoked with a lamb
That carries anger as the flint bears fire;
Who, much enforced, shows a hasty spark,
And straight is cold again.
Julius Caesar. Act IV. Sc. 3

He is the half part of a blessed man,
Left to be finished by such as she;
And she a fair divided excellence,
Whose fulness of perfection lies in him.
King John. Act II. Sc. 2

A world-without-end bargain.
Love's Labour's Lost. Act V. Sc. 2

Happy in this, she is not yet so old
But she may learn; happier than this,
She is not bred so dull but she can learn;
Happiest of all, is, that her gentle spirit
Commits itself to yours to be directed,
As from her lord, her governor, her king.
Merchant of Venice. Act III. Sc. 2

As are those dulcet sounds in break of day,
That creep into the dreaming bridegroom's
    ear,
And summon him to marriage.
Merchant of Venice. Act III. Sc. 2

I will marry her, sir, at your request; but if
there be no great love in the beginning, yet
Heaven may decrease it upon better acquaintance. I hope, upon familiarity will grow more
content; I will marry her, that I am freely
dissolved, and dissolutely.
Merry Wives of Windsor. Act I. Sc. 1

An' thou wilt needs thrust thy neck into a
yoke, wear the print of it, and sigh away
Sundays.
Much Ado About Nothing. Act I. Sc. 1

I would not marry her, though she were endowed with all that Adam had left him before he transgressed; she would have made
Hercules have turned spit: yea and have
cleft his club to make the fire too. . . .
I would to God some scholar would conjure
her; for certainly while she is here, a man
may live as quiet in hell, as in a sanctuary.
Much Ado About Nothing. Act II. Sc. 1

No: the world must be peopled. When I said,
I would die a bachelor. I did not think I
should live till I were married.
Much Ado About Nothing. Act II. Sc. 3

Most potent, grave, and reverend signiors,
My very noble and approv'd good masters,
That I have ta'en away this old man's daugh-
ter,
It is most true; true, I have married her;
The very head and front of my offending
Hath this extent, no more.
Othello. Act I. Sc. 3

          Let husbands know,
Their wives have sense like them: they see,
    and smell,
And have their palates both for sweet and
    sour,
As husbands have.
Othello. Act IV. Sc. 3

She's not well married that lives married
    long
But she's best married that dies married
    young.
Romeo and Juliet. Act IV. Sc. 5

If she deny to wed, I'll crave the day
When I shall ask the banns, and when be
    married.
Taming of the Shrew. Act II. Sc. 1

         What mockery will it be,
To want the bridegroom, when the priest at-
    tends
To speak the ceremonial rites of marriage.
Taming of the Shrew. Act III. Sc. 2

         She shall watch all night;
And, if she chance to nod, I'll rail and
    bawl,
And with the clamour keep her still awake.
This is the way to kill a wife with kindness.
Taming of the Shrew. Act IV. Sc. 1

O, monstrous arrogance! thou liest, thou
    thread,
Thou thimble,
Thou yard, three-quarters, half-yard, quarter,
    nail,
Thou flea, thou nit, thou winter cricket thou:
Brav'd in mine own house with a skein of
    thread!
Away, thou rag, thou quantity, thou rem-
    nant;
Or I shall so be-mete thee with thy yard,
As thou shalt think on prating whilst thou
    liv'st!
I tell thee, I, that thou hast marr'd her
    gown.
Taming of the Shrew. Act IV. Sc. 3

Thy husband commits his body
To painful labour, both by sea and land;

    .   .   .   .

And craves no other tribute at thy hands,
But love, fair looks, and true obedience,—
Too little payment for so great a debt.
Taming of the Shrew. Act V. Sc. 2

         Let still the woman take
An elder than herself; so wears she to him,
So sways she level in her husband's heart.
For boy, however we do praise ourselves,
Our fancies are more giddy and unfirm,
More longing, wavering, sooner lost and won,
Than woman's are.
Twelfth Night. Act II. Sc. 4

Now go with me, and with this holy man,
Into the chantry by:
And underneath that consecrated roof
Plight me the full assurance of your faith.
Twelfth Night. Act IV. Sc. 3

         She is mine own;
And I as rich in having such a jewel
As twenty seas, if all their sand were pearl,
The water nectar, and the rocks pure gold.
Two Gentlemen of Verona. Act II. Sc. 4

See also: CHILDREN, HUSBAND, LOVE, WIFE,
    WOMAN, WOOING.

MASON

The elder of them, being put to nurse,
And, ignorant of his birth and parentage,
Became a bricklayer when he came to age.
Henry VI. Pt. II. Act IV. Sc. 2

Sir, he made a chimney in my father's house,
and the bricks are alive at this day to testify
it.
Henry VI. Pt. II. Act IV. Sc. 2

See also: OCCUPATION.

MEDICINE

By medicine life may be prolonged, yet death
Will seize the doctor too.
Cymbeline. Act V. Sc. 2

         Diseases, desperate grown,
By desperate appliances are reliev'd
Or not at all.
Hamlet. Act IV. Sc. 2

         No cataplasm so rare,
Collected from all simples that have virtue
Under the moon, can save the thing from
    death.
Hamlet. Act IV. Sc. 7

In poison there is physic; and these news,
Having been well, that would have made me
    sick;
Being sick, have in some measure made me
    well.
                    Henry IV. Pt. II. Act I. Sc. 1

'Tis time to give them physic, their diseases
Are grown so catching.
                    Henry VIII. Act I. Sc. 3

                        In this point
All his tricks founder; and he brings his
    physic
After his patient's death.
                    Henry VIII. Act III. Sc. 2

Before the curing of a strong disease,
Even in the instant of repair and health,
The fit is strongest; evils that take leave,
On their departure most of all show evil.
                    King John. Act III. Sc. 4

                    Take physic, pomp;
Expose thyself to feel what wretches feel.
                    King Lear. Act III. Sc. 4

MACBETH:
How does you patient doctor?
DOCTOR:
Not so sick, my lord,
As she is troubled with thick-coming fancies.
                    Macbeth. Act V. Sc. 3

MACBETH:
Canst thou not minister to a mind diseas'd;
Pluck from the memory a rooted sorrow:
Raze out the written trouble of the brain;
And, with some sweet oblivious antidote,
Cleanse the stuff'd bosom of that perilous stuff,
Which weighs upon the heart?
DOCTOR:
Therein the patient
Must minister to himself.
MACBETH:
Throw physic to the dogs; I'll none of it.
                    Macbeth. Act V. Sc. 3

                If thou couldst, doctor, cast
The water of my land, find her disease,
And purge it to a sound and pristine health.
I would applaud thee to the very echo,
That should applaud again.
                    Macbeth. Act V. Sc. 3

                    In such a night,
Medea gather'd the enchanted herbs
That did renew old Aeson.
                    Merchant of Venice. Act V. Sc. 1

Methinks you prescribe to yourself very pre-
    posterously.
                    Merry Wives of Windsor. Act II. Sc. 2

I do remember an apothecary,—
And hereabouts he dwells,—whom late I
    noted
In tatter'd weeds, with overwhelming brows,
Culling of simples; meagre were his looks,
Sharp misery had worn him to the bones:
And in his needy shop a tortoise hung,
An alligator stuff'd, and other skins
Of ill-shap'd fishes; and about his shelves
A beggarly account of empty boxes,
Green earthen pots, bladders and musty
    seeds,
Remnants of packthread, and old cakes of
    roses,
Were thinly scatter'd to make up a show.
                    Romeo and Juliet. Act V. Sc. 1

                    You rub the sore
When you should bring the plaster.
                    Tempest. Act II. Sc. 1

                Trust not the physician;
His antidotes are poison, and he slays
More than you rob.
                    Timon of Athens. Act IV. Sc. 3

When I was sick you gave me bitter pills.
                    Two Gentlemen of Verona. Act II. Sc. 4

See also: DISEASE, HEALTH, QUACKERY, SICK-
    NESS, WOUND.

MEDITATION

In maiden meditation, fancy-free.
                    Midsummer Night's Dream. Act II. Sc. 2

He is divinely bent to meditation;
And in no worldly suits would he be mov'd,
To draw him from his holy exercise.
                    Richard III. Act III. Sc. 7

See also: PRAYER, SELF-EXAMINATION.

MEETING

When shall we three meet again
In thunder, lightning or in rain?
                    Macbeth. Act I. Sc. 1

See also: ABSENCE, HOSPITALITY, WELCOME.

MELANCHOLY

I can suck melancholy out of a song.
                    As You Like It. Act II. Sc. 5

O, melancholy!
Who ever yet could sound thy bottom? find
The ooze, to show what coast thy sluggish
     crare
Might easiliest harbour in?
                    Cymbeline. Act IV. Sc. 2

Tell me, sweet lord, what is't that takes from
     thee
Thy stomach, pleasure, and thy golden sleep?
Why dost thou bend thy eyes upon the earth;
And start so often when thou sitt'st alone?
Why hast thou lost the fresh blood in thy
     cheeks;
And given my treasures, and my rights of
     thee,
To thick-ey'd musing and curs'd melancholy?
                    Henry IV. Pt. I. Act II. Sc. 3

The greatest note of it is his melancholy.
     Much Ado About Nothing. Act III. Sc. 2

Melancholy is the nurse of frenzy.
          Taming of the Shrew. Induction. Sc. 2

See also: INSANITY, SADNESS, SORROW.

MEMORY

Remember thee?
Yea, from the table of my memory
I'll wipe away all trivial fond records.
                    Hamlet. Act I. Sc. 5

Die two months ago, and not forgotten yet?
Then there's hope a great man's memory may
outlive his life half a year.
                    Hamlet. Act III. Sc. 2

Briefly thyself remember.
                    King Lear. Act IV. Sc. 6

Memory, the warder of the brain,
Shall be a fume.
                    Macbeth. Act I. Sc. 7

I cannot but remember such things were,
That were most precious to me.
                    Macbeth. Act IV. Sc. 3

I should not see the sandy hour-glass run,
But I should think of shallows and of flats;
And see my wealthy Andrew dock'd in sand,
Vailing her high-top lower than her ribs,
To kiss her burial.
          Merchant of Venice. Act I. Sc. 1

If a man do not erect in this age his own
tomb ere he dies, he shall live no longer in
monument, than the bell rings, and the
widow weeps. . . . An hour in clamour,
and a quarter in rheum.
          Much Ado About Nothing. Act V. Sc. 2

I remember a mass of things, but nothing
distinctly; a quarrel, but nothing wherefore.
                    Othello. Act II. Sc. 3

I count myself in nothing else so happy,
As in a soul rememb'ring my good friends;
And, as my fortune ripens with thy love,
It shall be still thy true love's recompense.
                    Richard II. Act. II. Sc. 2

How sharp the point of this remembrance is!
                    Tempest. Act V. Sc. 1

O thou that dost inhabit in my breast,
Leave not the mansion so long tenantless;
Lest, growing ruinous, the building fall,
And leave no memory of what it was.
     Two Gentlemen of Verona. Act V. Sc. 4

Looking on the lines
Of my boy's face, my thoughts I did recoil
Twenty-three years; and saw myself un-
     breech'd,
In my green velvet coat; my dagger muzzled,
Lest it should bite its master, and so prove,
As ornaments oft do, too dangerous.
                    Winter's Tale. Act I. Sc. 2

See also: PAST, REFLECTION, THOUGHT.

MERCHANT: *see* BUSINESS.

MERCY

Pent to linger
But with a grain a day, I would not buy
Their mercy at the price of one fair word.
                    Coriolanus. Act III. Sc. 3

Whereto serves mercy,
But to confront the visage of offence?
                    Hamlet. Act III. Sc. 3

You must not dare, for shame, to talk of
     mercy;
For your own reasons turn into your bosoms,
As dogs upon their masters, worrying you.
                    Henry V. Act II. Sc. 2

Open the gate of mercy, gracious God!
My soul flies through these wounds to seek
     out thee.
                    Henry VI. Pt. III. Act I. Sc. 4

Close pent-up guilts,
Rive your concealing continents, and cry
These dreadful summoners grace.
King Lear. Act III. Sc. 2

Mercy is not itself, that oft looks so;
Pardon is still the nurse of second woe.
Measure for Measure. Act II. Sc. 1

How would you be,
If He, who is the top of Judgment, should
But judge you as you are? O think on that;
And mercy then will breathe within your
lips,
Like man new made.
Measure for Measure. Act II. Sc. 2

Well believe this,
No ceremony that to great ones 'longs,
Not the king's crown, nor the deputed sword,
The marshal's truncheon, nor the judge's
robe,
Become them with one half so good a grace,
As mercy does.
Measure for Measure. Act II. Sc. 2

Lawful mercy
Is nothing kin to foul redemption.
Measure for Measure. Act II. Sc. 4

Though justice be thy plea, consider this—
That in the course of justice, none of us
Should see salvation; we do pray for mercy;
And that same prayer doth teach us all to
render
The deeds of mercy.
Merchant of Venice. Act IV. Sc. 1

The quality of mercy is not strain'd;
It droppeth, as the gentle rain from heaven
Upon the place beneath: it is twice bless'd;
It blesseth him that gives, and him that
takes;
'Tis mightiest in the mightiest; it becomes
The throned monarch better than his crown;
His sceptre shows the force of temporal
power,
The attribute to awe and majesty,
Wherein doth sit the dread and fear of kings.
But mercy is above this sceptred sway,
It is enthroned in the heart of kings,
It is an attribute to God Himself:
And earthly power doth then show likest
God's,
When mercy seasons justice.
Merchant of Venice. Act IV. Sc. 1

Mercy but murders, pardoning those that
kill.
Romeo and Juliet. Act III. Sc. 1

Straight in her heart did mercy come.
Sonnet CXLV

Wilt thou draw near the nature of the gods?
Draw near them then in being merciful;
Sweet mercy is nobility's true badge.
Titus Andronicus. Act I. Sc. 2

See also: CHARITY, JUDGMENT, LOVE, PITY.

MERIT

O, that estates, degrees, and offices,
Were not deriv'd corruptly! and that clear
honour
Were purchas'd by the merit of the wearer.
Merchant of Venice. Act II. Sc. 9

See also: ABILITY, SUCCESS, WORTH.

MERMAID

O, train me not, sweet mermaid, with thy
note,
To drown me in thy sister flood of tears.
Comedy of Errors. Act III. Sc. 2

Once I sat upon a promontory,
And heard a mermaid, on a dolphin's back,
Uttering such dulcet and harmonious breath,
That the rude sea grew evil at her song;
And certain stars shot madly from their
spheres,
To hear the sea-maid's music.
Midsummer Night's Dream. Act II. Sc. 2

See also: FAIRY, IMAGINATION.

MERRIMENT

What should a man do, but be merry?
Hamlet. Act III. Sc. 2

And if you can be merry then, I'll say
A man may weep upon his wedding day.
Henry VIII. Prologue

Hostess, clap to the doors; watch to-night,
pray to-morrow,—Gallants, lads, boys, hearts
of gold, all the titles of good fellowship
come to you! What, shall we be merry?
Shall we have a play extempore?
Henry IV. Pt. I. Act II. Sc. 4

'Tis ever common,
That men are merriest when they are from
home.
Henry V. Act I. Sc. 2

A merrier man,
Within the limit of becoming mirth,
I never spent an hour's talk withal.
Love's Labour's Lost. Act II. Sc. 1

Be large in mirth; anon, we'll drink a measure
The table round.
                        Macbeth. Act III. Sc. 4

With mirth and laughter let old wrinkles
    come;
And let my liver rather heat with wine,
Than my heart cool with mortifying groans.
                Merchant of Venice. Act I. Sc. 1

Where is our usual manager of mirth?
What revels are in hand? Is there no play,
To ease the torturing hour?
            Midsummer Night's Dream. Act V. Sc. 1

As merry as the day is long.
        Much Ado About Nothing. Act II. Sc. 1

From the crown of his head to the sole of
his foot, he is all mirth; he hath twice or
thrice cut Cupid's bow string, and the little
hangman dare not shoot at him; he hath a
heart as sound as a bell, and his tongue is
the clapper; for what his heart thinks, his
tongue speaks.
        Much Ado About Nothing. Act III. Sc. 2

Frame your mind to mirth and merriment,
Which bars a thousand harms, and lengthens
life.
        Taming of the Shrew. Induction, Sc. 2

Merrily, merrily, shall I live now,
Under the blossom that hangs on the bough.
                        Tempest. Act V. Sc. 1

                        Every room
Hath blaz'd with lights, and brayed with
    minstrelsy.
                Timon of Athens. Act II. Sc. 2

Jog on, jog on the foot-path way
    And merrily hent the stile-a:
A merry heart goes all the day,
    Your sad tires in a mile-a.
                Winter's Tale. Act IV. Sc. 3

And let's be red with mirth.
                Winter's Tale. Act IV. Sc. 3

See also: HAPPINESS, JOY, LAUGHTER.

MIND

                        Not Hercules
Could have knock'd out his brains, for he had
    none.
                Cymbeline. Act IV. Sc. 2

O, what a noble mind is here o'erthrown!
The courier's, soldier's, scholar's, eye, tongue,
    sword!
                        Hamlet. Act III. Sc. 1

When the mind is quicken'd, out of doubt,
The organs, though defunct and dead before,
Break up their drowsy grave, and newly
    move
With casted slough and fresh legerity.
                Henry V. Act IV. Sc. 1

'Tis but a base, ignoble mind
That mounts no higher than a bird can soar.
            Henry VI. Pt. II. Act II. Sc. 1

                        There's no art
To find the mind's construction in the face.
                Macbeth. Act I. Sc. 4

Spirits are not finely touched
But to fine issues.
            Measure for Measure. Act I. Sc. 1

Your mind is tossing on the ocean;
There, where your argosies with portly sail,
Like signiors and rich burghers on the flood,
    .   .   .   .   .
Do overpeer the petty traffickers,
That curt'sy to them.
                Merchant of Venice. Act I. Sc. 1

'Tis the mind that makes the body rich.
                Taming of the Shrew. Act IV. Sc. 3

See also: KNOWLEDGE, SOUL, THOUGHT.

MIRACLE

                        Great floods have flown
From simple sources; and great seas have
    dried,
When miracles have by the greatest been
    denied.
            All's Well That Ends Well. Act II. Sc. 1

It must be so: for miracles are ceas'd;
And therefore we must needs admit the
    means
How things are perfected.
                        Henry V. Act I. Sc. 1

See also: FAITH, RELIGION.

MISCHIEF

There's mischief in this man.
                        Henry VIII. Act I. Sc. 2

Now let it work: mischief thou art afoot,
Take thou what course thou wilt.
                Julius Caesar. Act III. Sc. 2

To mourn a mischief that is past and gone,
Is the next way to draw new mischief on.
Othello. Act I. Sc. 3

O mischief! thou art swift
To enter in the thoughts of desperate men!
Romeo and Juliet. Act V. Sc. 1

See also: CRIME, DECEIT, FOOL.

MISERY

Then being there alone,
Left and abandon'd of his velvet friends,
" 'Tis right," quoth he; "thus misery doth part
The flux of company."
As You Like It. Act II. Sc. 1

One woe doth tread upon another's heel,
So fast they follow.
Hamlet. Act IV. Sc. 7

Misery makes sport to mock itself.
Richard II. Act II. Sc. 1

Meagre his looks,
Sharp misery had worn him to the bones.
Romeo and Juliet. Act V. Sc. 1

Famine is in thy cheeks,
Need and oppression starveth in thy eyes,
Contempt and beggary hang upon thy back,
The world is not thy friend, nor the world's law.
Romeo and Juliet. Act V. Sc. 1

Misery acquaints a man with strange bed-fellows.
Tempest. Act II. Sc. 2

See also: AFFLICTION, DESPAIR, MISFORTUNE, PAIN, REMORSE, SORROW.

MISFORTUNE

Cold news for me;
Thus are my blossoms blasted in the bud,
And caterpillars eat my leaves away.
Henry VI. Pt. II. Act III. Sc. 1

Is not this a lamentable thing, that of the skin of an innocent lamb should be made parchment? that parchment, being scribbled o'er, should undo a man?
Henry VI. Pt. II. Act IV. Sc. 2

Lo, now my glory smear'd in dust and blood!
My parks, my walks, my manors that I had,
Even now forsake me; and, of all my lands,

Is nothing left me, but my body's length!
Why, what is pomp, rule, reign, but earth and dust?
And, live we how we can, yet die we must.
Henry VI. Pt. III. Act V. Sc. 2

The worst is not
So long as we can say, "This is the worst."
King Lear. Act IV. Sc. 1

O give me thy hand,
One writ with me in sour misfortune's book.
Romeo and Juliet. Act V. Sc. 3

We have seen better days.
Timon of Athens. Act IV. Sc. 2

See also: ADVERSITY, EVIL, MISERY, TROUBLE.

MODERATION

PANDARUS:
Be moderate, be moderate.
CRESSIDA:
Why tell you me of moderation?
The grief is fine, full, perfect, that I taste,
And no less in a sense as strong as that
Which causeth it: How can I moderate it?
Troilus and Cressida. Act IV. Sc. 4

See also: CONTENTMENT, EXTREME, TEMPER-ANCE.

MODESTY

I never in my life
Did hear a challenge urg'd more modestly,
Unless a brother should a brother dare
To gentle exercise and proof of arms.
Henry IV. Pt. I. Act V. Sc. 2

Can it be,
That modesty may more betray our sense
Than woman's lightness? Having waste ground enough,
Shall we desire to raise the sanctuary,
And pitch our evils there?
Measure for Measure. Act II. Sc. 2

Not stepping o'er the bounds of modesty.
Romeo and Juliet. Act IV. Sc. 2

See also: BLUSH, INNOCENCE, VIRTUE.

MONEY

But, by the Lord, lads, I am glad you have the money.
Henry IV. Pt. I. Act II. Sc. 4

Money is a good soldier sir, and will on.
> *Merry Wives of Windsor.* Act II. Sc. 2

Put but money in thy purse. . . . Fill thy
purse with money.
> *Othello.* Act I. Sc. 3

Importune him for moneys; be not ceas'd
With slight denial; nor then silenc'd, when—
"Commend me to your master"—and the cap
Plays in the right hand thus;—but tell him
My uses cry me.
> *Timon of Athens.* Act II. Sc. 1

See also: AVARICE, BUSINESS, GOLD, POVERTY,
WEALTH.

MONTH

Well apparell'd April on the heel
Of limping winter treads.
> *Romeo and Juliet.* Act I. Sc. 2

Rough winds do shake the darling buds of
May.
> *Sonnet XVIII*

When proud-pied April, dress'd in all his trim,
Hath put a spirit of youth in everything.
> *Sonnet XCVIII*

See also: DAY, FUTURE, PAST, TIME.

MONUMENT

This grave shall have a living monument.
> *Hamlet.* Act V. Sc. 1

She sat, like patience on a monument,
Smiling at grief.
> *Twelfth Night.* Act II. Sc. 4

See also: DEATH, EPITAPH, GRAVE.

MOON

The moon of Rome; chaste as the icicle,
That's curded by the frost from purest snow
> *Coriolanus.* Act V. Sc. 3

How sweet the moonlight sleeps upon this
bank.
> *Merchant of Venice.* Act V. Sc. 2

The moon, the governess of floods,
Pale in her anger, washes all the air,
That rheumatic diseases do abound:
And, through this distemperature we see
The seasons alter.
> *Midsummer Night's Dream.* Act II. Sc. 2

It is the very error of the moon;
She comes more nearer earth than she was
wont,
And makes men mad.
> *Othello.* Act V. Sc. 2

See also: CLOUD, NIGHT, SKY, STAR.

MORNING

But, look, the morn in russet mantle clad,
Walks o'er the dew of yon high eastern hill.
> *Hamlet.* Act I. Sc. 1

The day begins to break, and night is fled,
Whose pitchy mantle over-veil'd the earth.
> *Henry VI.* Pt. I. Act II. Sc. 2

See how the morning opes her golden gates,
And takes her farewell of the glorious sun!
How well resembles it the prime of youth,
Trimm'd like a yonker prancing to his love.
> *Henry VI.* Pt. III. Act II. Sc. 1

An hour before the worshipp'd sun
Peer'd forth the golden window of the east.
> *Romeo and Juliet.* Act I. Sc. 1

The grey-ey'd morn smiles on the frowning
night,
Chequering the eastern clouds with streaks
of light.
> *Romeo and Juliet.* Act II. Sc. 3

Night's candles are burnt out, and jocund day
Stands tiptoe on the misty mountain tops.
> *Romeo and Juliet.* Act III. Sc. 5

The golden sun salutes the morn,
And, having gilt the ocean with his beams,
Gallops the zodiac in his glistening coach.
> *Titus Andronicus.* Act II. Sc. 1

The hunt is up, the morn is bright and gray;
The fields are fragrant, and the woods are
green;
Uncouple here, and let us make a bay.
> *Titus Andronicus.* Act II. Sc. 2

The busy day,
Wak'd by the lark, hath rous'd the ribald
crows,
And dreaming night will hide our joys no
longer.
> *Troilus and Cressida.* Act IV. Sc. 2

See also: DAWN, DAY, LIGHT, SUNRISE.

MORTALITY

Had I but died an hour before this chance,
I had liv'd a blessed time: for, from this in-
stant,
There's nothing serious in mortality.
Macbeth. Act II. Sc. 3

See also: DEATH, GRAVE, IMMORTALITY, LIFE,
     SOUL.

MOTHER

And all my mother came into mine eyes,
And gave me up to tears.
Henry V. Act IV. Sc. 6

See also: CHILDREN, HUSBAND, WIFE.

MURDER

Murder most foul, as in the best it is;
But this most foul, strange, and unnatural.
Hamlet. Act I. Sc. 5

Murder, though it have no tongue, will speak
With most miraculous organ.
Hamlet. Act II. Sc. 2

He took my father grossly, full of bread;
With all his crimes broad blown, as fresh as
     May;
And, how his audit stands, who knows, save
     heaven?
Hamlet. Act III. Sc. 3

Butchers and villains, bloody cannibals!
How sweet a plant have you untimely
     cropp'd!
You have no children, butchers! if you had,
The thought of them would have stirr'd up
     remorse.
Henry VI. Pt. III. Act V. Sc. 5

O, pardon me, thou piece of bleeding earth,
That I am meek and gentle with these
     butchers!
Thou art the ruins of the noblest man,
That ever lived in the tide of times.
Woe to the hand that shed this costly blood!
Over thy wounds now do I prophecy.
Julius Caesar. Act III. Sc. 1

Will all great Neptune's ocean wash this
     blood
Clean from my hand? No; this my hand will
     rather
The multitudinous seas incarnadine,
Making the green one red.
Macbeth. Act II. Sc. 2

Blood hath been shed ere now, i' the golden
     time
Ere human statute purg'd the general weal;
Ay, and since too, murders have been per-
     form'd
Too terrible for the ear: the times have been,
That, when the brains were out, the man
     would die,
And there an end: but now, they rise again,
With twenty mortal murders on their crowns,
And push us from our stools. This is more
     strange
Than such a murder is.
Macbeth. Act III. Sc. 4

Is not the causer of these timeless deaths
As blameful as the executioners?
Richard III. Act I. Sc. 2

The great King of kings
Hath in the table of his law commanded,
That thou shalt do no murder: Wilt thou then
Spurn at his edict, and fulfill a man's?
Take heed; for he holds vengeance in his
     hand,
To hurl upon their heads that break his law.
Richard III. Act I. Sc. 4

To kill, I grant, is sin's extremest gust,
But, in defence, by mercy, tis most just.
Timon of Athens. Act III. Sc. 5

See also: DEATH, GRAVE, SUICIDE.

MUSIC

Give me some music; music, moody food
Of us that trade in love.
Antony and Cleopatra. Act II. Sc. 5

I am advised to give her music o' mornings;
they say it will penetrate.
Cymbeline. Act II. Sc. 3

It will discourse most excellent music.
Hamlet. Act III. Sc. 2

Let there be no noise made, my gentle friends;
Unless some dull and favourable hand
Will whisper music to my weary spirit.
Henry IV. Pt. II. Act IV. Sc. 4

How irksome is this music to my heart!
When such strings jar, what hope of harmony?
Henry VI. Pt. II. Act II. Sc. 1

Everything that heard him play,
Even the billows of the sea,
Hung their heads, and then lay by;
In sweet music is such art:

Killing care and grief of heart
Fall asleep, or, hearing, die.
Henry VIII. Act III. Sc. 1

Orpheus with his lute made trees,
And the mountain-tops that freeze,
  Bow themselves, when he did sing:
To his music, plants and flowers
Ever sprung; as sun and showers,
  There had made a lasting spring.
Henry VIII. Act III. Sc. 1

                    The choir,
With all the choicest music of the kingdom,
Together sung *Te Deum.*
Henry VIII. Act IV. Sc. 1

                  Play me that sad note
I nam'd my knell, whilst I sit meditating
On that celestial harmony I go to.
Henry VIII. Act IV. Sc. 2

One who the music of his own vain tongue,
Doth ravish, like enchanting harmony.
Love's Labour's Lost. Act I. Sc. 1

            Music oft hath such a charm,
To make bad good, and good provoke to
  harm.
Measure for Measure. Act IV. Sc. 1

Let music sound while he doth make his
  choice;
Then, if he lose, he makes a swan-like end,
Fading in music.
Merchant of Venice. Act III. Sc. 2

Come, ho, and wake Diana with a hymn;
With surest touches pierce your mistress' ear,
And draw her home with music.
Merchant of Venice. Act V. Sc. 1

How sweet the moonlight sleeps upon this
  bank!
Here will we sit, and let the sounds of music
Creep in our ears; soft stillness, and the night,
Become the touches of sweet harmony.
Merchant of Venice. Act V. Sc. 1

I am never merry when I hear sweet music.
Merchant of Venice. Act V. Sc. 1

The man that hath no music in himself,
And is not moved with concord of sweet
  sounds,
Is fit for treasons, stratagems, and spoils.
Merchant of Venice. Act V. Sc. 1

The Music of the spheres! list my Marina.
Pericles. Act V. Sc. 1

                  Music do I hear?
Ha! ha! keep time. How sour sweet music is,
When time is broke, and no proportion kept!
Richard II. Act V. Sc. 5

Wilt thou have music? hark! Apollo plays,
And twenty caged nightingales do sing.
Taming of the Shrew. Induction. Sc. 2

Preposterous ass! that never read so far
To know the cause why music was ordain'd!
Was it not to refresh the mind of man,
After his studies or his usual pain?
Taming of the Shrew. Act III. Sc. 1

Music crept by me upon the waters;
Allaying both their fury and my passion,
With its sweet air.
Tempest. Act I. Sc. 2

Take but degree away, untune that string,
And, hark, what discord follows!
Troilus and Cressida. Act I. Sc. 3

If music be the food of love, play on,
Give me excess of it; that, surfeiting,
The appetite may sicken, and so die.
That strain again,—it had a dying fall:
O, it came o'er my ear like the sweet sound
That breathes upon a bank of violets,
Stealing, and giving odour.
Twelfth Night. Act I. Sc. 1

See also: BALLAD, SINGER, SONG.

N

NAME

              The one so like the other,
As could not be distinguish'd but by names.
Comedy of Errors. Act I. Sc. 1

              Then shall our names,
Familiar in their mouths as household
  words—

    .   .   .   .

Be in their flowing cups freshly remember'd.
Henry V. Act IV. Sc. 3

I cannot tell what the dickens his name is.
Merry Wives of Windsor. Act III. Sc. 2

What's in a name? that which we call a rose,
By any other name would smell as sweet.
Romeo and Juliet. Act II. Sc. 2

I do beseech you,
(Chiefly, that I might set it in my prayers,)
What is your name?
Tempest. Act III. Sc. 1

See also: CHARACTER, HONOR, REPUTATION.

NATURE

In nature's infinite book of secrecy
A little I can read.
Antony and Cleopatra. Act I. Sc. 2

How hard it is to hide the sparks of nature!
Cymbeline. Act III. Sc. 3

To hold, as 'twere, the mirror up to nature;
to shew virtue her own feature, scorn her
own image, and the very age and body of the
time his form and pressure.
Hamlet. Act III. Sc. 2

Diseased nature oftentimes breaks forth
In strange eruptions.
Henry IV. Pt. I. Act III. Sc. 1

Nature does require
Her times of preservation, which, perforce,
I her frail son, amongst my brethren mortal,
Must give my tendance to.
Henry VIII. Act III. Sc. 2

One touch of nature makes the whole world
kin,—
That all, with one consent, praise new-born
gawds,
Though they are made and moulded of things
past;
And give to dust, that is a little gilt,
More laud than gift o'er dusted.
Troilus and Cressida. Act III. Sc. 3

How sometimes nature will betray its folly,
Its tenderness, and make itself a pastime
To harder bosoms!
Winter's Tale Act I. Sc. 2

Nature is made better by no mean,
But nature makes that mean: so, o'er that
art,
Which, you say, adds to nature, is an art
That nature makes.
Winter's Tale. Act IV. Sc. 3

See also: ANIMAL, BIRD, GARDEN, RIVER, SEA-
SON.

NECESSITY

He must needs go that the Devil drives.
All's Well That Ends Well. Act I. Sc. 3

Now sit we close about the taper here,
And call in question our necessities.
Julius Caesar. Act IV. Sc. 3

Necessity's sharp pinch!
King Lear. Act II. Sc. 4

Teach thy necessity to reason thus;
There is not virtue like necessity.
Richard II. Act I. Sc. 3

To make a virtue of necessity.
Two Gentlemen of Verona. Act IV. Sc. 1

See also: DESIRE, DUTY, OBEDIENCE.

NEGLECT

Self-love, my liege, is not so vile a sin
As self-neglecting.
Henry V. Act II. Sc. 4

See also: LOSS, RESPONSIBILITY.

NEWS

Though it be honest, it is never good
To bring bad news; give to a gracious mes-
sage
An host of tongues; but let ill tidings tell
Themselves, when they be felt.
Antony and Cleopatra. Act II. Sc. 5

Ram thou thy fruitful tidings in mine ears,
That long time have been barren.
Antony and Cleopatra. Act II. Sc. 5

Pr'ythee, friend,
Pour out the pack of matter to mine ear,
The good and bad together.
Antony and Cleopatra. Act II. Sc. 5

CELIA:
Here comes Monsieur le Beau,
ROSALIND:
With his mouth full of news.
CELIA:
Which he will put on us as pigeons feed
their young.
ROSALIND:
Then shall we be news-crammed.
As You Like It. Act I. Sc. 2

Prythee, take the cork out of thy mouth,
that
I may drink thy tidings.
As You Like It. Act III. Sc. 2

If it be summer news,
Smile to 't before: if winterly, thou need'st
But keep that countenance still.
Cymbeline. Act III. Sc. 3

Report me and my cause aright
To the unsatisfied.
Hamlet. Act V. Sc. 2

There's villainous news abroad
Henry IV. Pt. I. Act II. Sc. 4

The first bringer of unwelcome news
Hath but a losing office, and his tongue
Sounds ever after as a sullen bell,
Remember'd knolling a departed friend.
Henry IV. Pt. II. Act I. Sc. 1

What news, lord Bardolph? every minute
now
Should be the father of some stratagem;
The times are wild.
Henry IV. Pt. II. Act I. Sc. 1

I drown'd these news in tears.
Henry VI. Pt. III. Act II. Sc. 1

News fitting to the night
Black, fearful, comfortless, and horrible.
King John. Act V. Sc. 6

My heart hath one poor string to stay it by,
Which holds but till thy news be uttered.
King John. Act V. Sc. 7

Bring me no more reports.
Macbeth. Act V. Sc. 3

Tell him, there's a post come from my master,
with his horn full of news.
Merchant of Venice. Act V. Sc. 1

O God, defend me! how am I beset—
What kind of catechising call you this?
Much Ado About Nothing. Act IV. Sc. 1

Master, master! news, old news, and such
news as you never heard of.
Taming of the Shrew. Act III. Sc. 3

Pr'ythee, say on:
The setting of thine eye and cheek, proclaim
A matter from thee; and a birth, indeed,
Which throes thee much to yield.
Tempest. Act II. Sc. 1

How goes it now, Sir? this news, which is
called true, is so like an old tale, that the
verity of it is in strong suspicion.
Winter's Tale. Act V. Sc. 2

See also: GOSSIP, LETTER, RUMOR.

NIGHT

In the dead waste and middle of the night.
Hamlet. Act I. Sc. 2

Making night hideous.
Hamlet. Act I. Sc. 4

'Tis now the witching time of night;
When churchyards yawn, and hell itself
breathes out
Contagion to this world.
Hamlet. Act III. Sc. 2

Hung be the heavens with black, yield day
to night!
Comets, importing change of times and states,
Brandish your crystal tresses in the sky;
And with them scourge the bad revolting
stars,
That have consented unto Henry's death.
Henry VI. Pt. I. Act I. Sc. 1

Night is fled,
Whose pitchy mantle overveil'd the earth.
Henry VI. Pt. I. Act II. Sc. 2

The gaudy, blabbing, and remorseful day
Is crept into the bosom of the sea.
Henry VI. Pt. II. Act IV. Sc. 1

Pry'thee, nuncle, be contented; 'tis a naughty
night to swim in.
King Lear. Act III. Sc. 4

I must become a borrower of the night,
For a dark hour, or twain.
Macbeth. Act III. Sc. 1

Come, seeling night,
Skarf up the tender eye of pitiful day;
And, with thy bloody and invisible hand,
Cancel, and tear to pieces, that great bond
Which keeps me pale!
Macbeth. Act III. Sc. 2

Light thickens; and the crow
Makes wings to the rooky wood;
Good things of day begin to droop an
drowse;
Whiles night's black agents to their prey do
rouse.
Macbeth. Act III. Sc. 2

The night is long that never finds the day.
Macbeth. Act IV. Sc. 3

This night, methinks, is but the daylight
sick;
It looks a little paler; 'tis a day;
Such as the day is when the sun is hid.
Merchant of Venice. Act V. Sc. 1

The moon shines bright:—In such a night as
this,
When the sweet wind did gently kiss the
trees,
And they did make no noise.
Merchant of Venice. Act V. Sc. 1

How sweet the moonlight sleeps upon this
bank:
Here will we sit, and let the sounds of music
Creep in our ears; soft stillness, and the
night,
Become the touches of sweet harmony.
Merchant of Venice. Act V. Sc. 1

Brief as the lightning in the collied night,
That, in a spleen, unfolds both heaven and
earth,
And ere a man hath power to say,—"Be-
hold!"
The jaws of darkness do devour it up.
Midsummer Night's Dream. Act I. Sc. 1

Dark night, that from the eye his function
takes,
The ear more quick of apprehension makes;
Wherein it doth impair the seeing sense,
It pays the hearing double recompense.
Midsummer Night's Dream. Act III. Sc. 2

The iron tongue of midnight hath tol'd
twelve.—
Lovers to bed.
Midsummer Night's Dream. Act V. Sc. 1

This in the night
That either makes me, or fordoes me quite.
Othello. Act V. Sc. 1

Come, gentle night; come, loving, black-
brow'd night.
Romeo and Juliet, Act III. Sc. 2

See also: DARKNESS, EVENING, TWILIGHT.

NIGHTINGALE

The nightingale, if she should sing by day,
When every goose is cackling, would be
thought

No better a musician than the wren.
How many things by season season'd are
To their right praise, and true perfection!
Merchant of Venice. Act V. Sc. 1

Wilt thou be gone? it is not yet near day:
It was the nightingale, and not the lark,
That pierc'd the fearful hollow of thine ear;
Nightly she sings on yon pomegranate tree:
Believe me, love, it was the nightingale.
Romeo and Juliet. Act III. Sc. 5

See also: ANIMAL, BIRD.

NOBILITY

His nature is too noble for the world:
He would not flatter Neptune for his trident
Or Jove for his power to thunder.
Coriolanus. Act III. Sc. 1

This was the noblest Roman of them all;
All the conspirators, save only he,
Did that they did in envy of great Caesar;
He only, in a general honest thought,
And common good to all, made one of them.
His life was gentle; and the elements
So mix'd in him, that Nature might stand up
And say to all the world: This was a man!
Julius Caesar. Act V. Sc. 5

See also: CHARACTER, ROYALTY, WORTH.

O

OATH

'Tis not the many oaths that make the truth;
But the plain single vow, that is vow'd true.
All's Well That Ends Well. Act IV. Sc. 2

But if you swear by that that is not, you are
not forsworn: no more was this knight, swearing by his honour, for he never had any.
As You Like It. Act I. Sc. 2

And then a whoreson jackanapes must take
me up for swearing; as if I borrowed mine
oaths of him, and might not spend them at
my pleasure.
Cymbeline. Act II. Sc. 1

When a gentleman is disposed to swear, it is
not for any standers-by to curtail his oaths.
Cymbeline. Act II. Sc. 1

And fall a cursing, like a very drab.
Hamlet. Act II. Sc. 2

That suck'd the honey of his music vows.
                    Hamlet. Act III. Sc. 1

It is a great sin, to swear unto a sin;
But greater sin, to keep a sinful oath.
                    Henry VI. Pt. II. Act V. Sc. 1

Or having sworn too hard-a-keeping oath,
Study to break it, and not break my troth.
                    Love's Labour's Lost. Act I. Sc. 1

What fool is not so wise,
To lose an oath to win a paradise.
                    Love's Labour's Lost. Act IV. Sc. 3

An oath, an oath, I have an oath in heaven:
Shall I lay perjury upon my soul?
No, not for Venice.
                    Merchant of Venice. Act IV. Sc. 1

I'll take thy word for faith, not ask thine oath;
Who shuns not to break one will sure crack both.
                    Pericles. Act I. Sc. 2

            Do not swear at all;
Or, if thou wilt, swear by thy gracious self,
Which is the god of my idolatry,
And I'll believe thee.
                    Romeo and Juliet. Act II. Sc. 2

It is the purpose that makes strong the vow;
But vows to every purpose must not hold.
                    Troilus and Cressida. Act V. Sc. 3

For it comes to pass oft, that a terrible oath,
with a swaggering accent sharply twanged
off, gives manhood more approbation than
ever proof itself would have earned him.
                    Twelfth Night. Act III. Sc. 4

Unheedful vows may heedfully be broken;
                    Two Gentlemen of Verona. Act II. Sc. 6

See also: DECISION, DUTY, LOYALTY, PATRIOTISM, PROMISE.

OBEDIENCE

And thy commandment all alone shall live
Within the book and volume of my brain.
                    Hamlet. Act I. Sc. 5

Obey thy parents; keep thy word justly;
swear not; commit not with man's sworn
spouse; set not thy sweet heart on proud
array.
                    King Lear. Act III. Sc. 4

It fits thee not to ask the reason why,
Because we bid it.
                    Pericles. Act I. Sc. 1

Obey, and be attentive.
                    Tempest. Act I. Sc. 2

See also: AUTHORITY, GOVERNMENT, LAW.

OBLIVION

What's past, and what's to come, is strew'd
    with husks
And formless ruin of oblivion.
                    Troilus and Cressida. Act IV. Sc. 5

See also: MEMORY.

OCCUPATION

To business that we love we rise betime,
And go to it with delight.
                    Antony and Cleopatra. Act IV. Sc. 4

The hand of little employment hath the
daintier sense.
                    Hamlet. Act V. Sc. 1

I'll give thrice so much land to any well
    deserving friend;
But in the way of bargain, mark ye me,
I'll cavil on the ninth part of a hair.
                    Henry IV. Pt. I. Act III. Sc. 1

See also: ACTOR AND ACTRESS, AGRICULTURE,
    ARCHITECTURE, ART, AUTHORSHIP,
    BARBER, BLACKSMITH, BUTCHER,
    CARPENTER, COOKING, DANCE, FISH-
    ING, INNKEEPER, LAW, LINGUIST,
    MASON, MUSIC, PAINTING, POET, POL-
    ITICS, PREACHING, SHOE, SINGER,
    STUDENT, TAILOR, TEACHER.

OCEAN

The always-wind-obeying deep.
                    Comedy of Errors. Act I. Sc. 1

The Sea's a thief.
                    Timon of Athens. Act IV. Sc. 3

See also: RIVER, SEA.

OLD AGE: *see* AGE, OLD.

OPINION

We will proceed no further in this business.
He hath honour'd me of late; and I have
    bought
Golden opinions from all sorts of people,
Which would be worn now in their newest
    gloss,
Not cast aside so soon.
                    Macbeth. Act I. Sc. 7

Opinion's but a fool, that makes us scan,
The outward habit by the inward man.
Pericles. Act II. Sc. 2

See also: ARGUMENT, BELIEF, JUDGMENT.

OPPORTUNITY

There's place, and means, for every man
alive.
All's Well That Ends Well. Act IV. Sc. 3

Who seeks, and will not take, when once 'tis
offer'd,
Shall never find it more.
Antony and Cleopatra. Act II. Sc. 7

That man, that sits within a monarch's heart,
.   .   .   .
Would he abuse the countenance of the king,
Alack, what mischiefs might be set abroach.
Henry IV. Pt. II. Act IV. Sc. 2

A staff is quickly found to beat a dog.
Henry VI. Pt. II. Act III. Sc. 1

There is a tide in the affairs of men,
Which, taken at the flood, leads on to fortune,
Omitted, all the voyage of their life
Is bound in shallows and in miseries.
Julius Caesar. Act IV. Sc. 3

Urge them, while their souls
Are capable of this ambition;
Lest zeal, now melted, by the windy breath
Of soft petitions, pity and remorse,
Cool and congeal again to what it was.
King John. Act II. Sc. 2

See also: ACCIDENT, CHANCE, CIRCUMSTANCE.

ORATORY

Be not thy tongue thy own shame's orator.
Comedy of Errors. Act III. Sc. 2

List his discourse of war, and you shall hear
A fearful battle render'd you in music.
Henry V. Act I. Sc. 1

I come not, friends, to steal away your hearts;
I am no orator, as Brutus is;
.   .   .   .
I only speak right on.
Julius Caesar. Act III. Sc. 2

Doubt not, my lord; I'll play the orator,
As if the golden fee, for which I plead,
Were for myself.
Richard III. Act III. Sc. 5

Bid me discourse, I will enchant thine ear,
Or, like a fairy, trip upon the green.
Venus and Adonis. St. 25. Line 145

See also: ACTOR AND ACTRESS, ELOQUENCE.

ORDER

Not a mouse
Shall disturb this hallow'd house:
I am sent, with broom, before,
To sweep the dust behind the door.
Midsummer Night's Dream. Act V. Sc. 2

The heavens themselves, the planets, and this
centre,
Observe degree, priority, and place,
Insisture, course, proportion, season, form,
Office, and custom, in all line of order.
Troilus and Cressida. Act I. Sc. 3

See also: AUTHORITY, GOVERNMENT, LAW.

OWL

Nightly sings the staring owl, To-who;
Tu-whit to-who, a merry note.
Love's Labour's Lost. Act V. Sc. 2. Song

It was the owl that shriek'd the fatal bellman,
Which gives the stern'st good night.
Macbeth. Act II. Sc. 2

The clamorous owl, that nightly hoots and
wonders
At our quaint spirits.
Midsummer Night's Dream. Act II. Sc. 3

See also: ANIMAL, BIRD.

P

PAINTING

Look here, upon this picture, and on this.
Hamlet. Act III. Sc. 4

What demi-god
Hath come so near creation?
Merchant of Venice. Act III. Sc. 2

Dost thou love pictures?
Taming of the Shrew. Induction, Sc. 2

TIMON:
Wrought he not well that painted it?
APEMANTUS:
He wrought better that made the painter;
and yet he's but a filthy piece of work.
Timon of Athens. Act I. Sc. 1

I'll say of it
It tutors nature: artificial strife
Lives in these touches, livelier than life.
                    Timon of Athens. Act I. Sc. 1

The painting is almost the natural man:
For since dishonour traffics with man's na-
    ture,
He is but outside; pencill'd figures are
Ev'n such as they give out.
                    Timon of Athens. Act I. Sc. 1

Come, draw this curtain, and let's see your
    picture.
                    Troilus and Cressida. Act III. Sc. 2

See also: ART, OCCUPATION.

PANSY

Pray you, love, remember: And there is
pansies, that's for thoughts.
                    Hamlet. Act IV. Sc. 5

        The bolt of Cupid fell
... Upon a little western flower,—
Before, milk-white, now purple with love's
    wound,
And maidens call it love-in-idleness.
            Midsummer Night's Dream. Act II. Sc. 2

See also: FLOWER, GARDEN, TREE.

PARDON: *see* FORGIVENESS.

PARTING

Hereafter, in a better world than this,
I shall desire more love and knowledge of
    you.
                    As You Like It. Act I. Sc. 2

If we do meet again, why, we shall smile;
If not, why then this parting was well made.
                    Julius Caesar. Act V. Sc. 1

            At once, good night:—
Stand not upon the order of your going,
But go at once.
                    Macbeth. Act III. Sc. 4

They say he parted well, and paid his score;
And so, God be with him.
                    Macbeth. Act V. Sc. 7

Good night, good night! parting is such sweet
    sorrow,
That I shall say—good-night, till it be to-mor-
    row.
                    Romeo and Juliet. Act II. Sc. 2

See also: ABSENCE, FAREWELL, DEATH.

PASSION

A little fire is quickly trodden out;
Which, being suffer'd, rivers cannot quench.
                    Henry VI. Pt. III. Act IV. Sc. 8

                His flaw'd heart,
    .   .   .   .
Twixt two extremes of passion, joy and grief.
                    King Lear. Act V. Sc. 3

See also: ABHORRENCE, ANGER, DESIRE, HATE,
    LOVE, REVENGE.

PAST

What's past is prologue.
                    Tempest. Act II. Sc. 1

See also: FUTURE, TIME, YOUTH.

PATIENCE

Patience, unmov'd, no marvel though she
    pause;
They can be meek that have no other cause.
A wretched soul, bruis'd with adversity,
We bid be quiet when we hear it cry;
But were we burthen'd with like weight of
    pain,
As much, or more, we should ourselves com-
    plain.
                    Comedy of Errors. Act II. Sc. 1

And makes us rather bear those ills we have,
Than fly to others that we know not of?
                    Hamlet. Act III. Sc. 1

Cudgel thy brains no more about it, for your
dull ass will not mend his pace with beating.
                    Hamlet. Act V. Sc. 1

I will with patience hear: and find a time
Both meet to hear and answer such high
    things
Till then, my noble friend, chew upon this.
                    Julius Caesar. Act I. Sc. 2

A high hope for a low heaven: God grant us
    patience!
                    Love's Labour's Lost. Act I. Sc. 1

Sufferance is the badge of all our tribe.
                    Merchant of Venice. Act I. Sc. 3

                I do oppose
My patience to his fury, and am arm'd
To suffer, with a quietness of spirit,
The very tyranny and rage of his.
                    Merchant of Venice. Act IV. Sc. 1

'Tis all men's office to speak patience
To those that wring under the load of sorrow,
But no man's virtue, nor sufficiency,
To be so moral when he shall endure
The like himself.
Much Ado About Nothing. Act V. Sc. 1

How poor are they, that have not patience!—
What wound did ever heal but by degrees?
Othello. Act II. Sc. 3

Had it pleas'd Heaven
To try me with affliction

.   .   .   .

I should have found, in some part of my soul,
A drop of patience.
Othello. Act IV. Sc. 2

Like Patience, gazing on kings' graves, and
smiling
Extremity out of act.
Pericles. Act V. Sc. 1

That which in mean men we entitle patience,
Is pale cold cawardice in noble breasts.
Richard II. Act I. Sc. 2

Since you will buckle fortune on my back,
To bear her burden, whe'r I will, or no,
I must have patience to endure the load.
Richard III. Act III. Sc. 7

He that will have a cake out of the wheat
Must needs tarry the grinding.
Troilus and Cressida. Act I. Sc. 1

She never told her love,
But let concealment, like a worm i' the bud,
Feed on her damask cheek; she pin'd in
thought;
And, with a green and yellow melancholy,
She sat like patience on a monument,
Smiling at grief.
Twelfth Night. Act II. Sc. 4

There's some ill planet reigns;
I must be patient, till the heaven's look
With an aspect more favourable.
A Winter's Tale. Act II. Sc. 1

See also: IMPATIENCE, PERSEVERANCE, RESIGNATION.

PATRIOTISM

Had I a dozen sons,—each in my love alike,

.   .   .   .

I had rather have eleven die nobly for their
country, than one voluptously surfeit out of
action.
Coriolanus. Act I. Sc. 3

I do love
My country's good, with a respect more tender,
More holy, and profound, than mine own
life.
Coriolanus. Act III. Sc. 3

Be just, and fear not:
Let all the ends, thou aim'st at, be thy country's,
Thy God's, and truth's; then if thou fall'st,
O Cromwell,
Thou fall'st a blessed martyr.
Henry VIII. Act III. Sc. 2

See also: ENGLAND, FLAG, LOYALTY.

PEACE

A peace is of the nature of a conquest;
For then both parties nobly are subdued,
And neither party loser.
Henry IV. Pt. II. Act IV. Sc. 2

In peace, there's nothing so becomes a man
As modest stillness and humility.
Henry V. Act III. Sc. 1

Peace,
Dear muse of arts, plenties, and joyful births.
Henry V. Act V. Sc. 2

Blessed are the peace-makers on earth.
Henry VI. Pt. II. Act II. Sc. 1

Still in thy right hand carry gentle peace,
To silence envious tongues.
Henry VIII. Act III. Sc. 2

See also: CONTENTMENT, REPOSE, REST.

PERFECTION

Whose beauty did astonish the survey
Of richest eyes; whose words all ears took
captive;
Whose dear perfection, hearts that scorn'd to
serve.
Humble call'd mistress.
All's Well That Ends Well. Act V. Sc. 3

By Jupiter, an angel! or, if not,
An earthly paragon!
Cymbeline. Act III. Sc. 6

How many things by season season'd are
To their right praise, and true perfection.
Merchant of Venice. Act V. Sc. 1

See also: BEAUTY, ORDER, SUCCESS.

PERFUME

So perfumed that
The winds were lovesick.
Antony and Cleopatra. Act II. Sc. 2

From the barge
A strange invisible perfume hits the sense
Of the adjacent wharfs.
Antony and Cleopatra. Act II. Sc. 2

Hast thou not learn'd me how
To make perfumes? distil? preserve? yea, so
That our great king himself doth woo me oft
For my confections?
Cymbeline. Act I. Sc. 6

All the perfumes of Arabia will not sweeten
this little hand.
Macbeth. Act V. Sc. 1

The perfumed tincture of the roses.
Sonnet LIV

Your papers,
Let me have them very well perfumed,
For she is sweeter than perfume itself
To whom they go.
Taming of the Shrew. Act I. Sc. 2

Perfume for a lady's chamber.
Winter's Tale. Act IV. Sc. 3

See also: BEAUTY, WOMAN.

PERSEVERANCE

Such a nature,
Sickled with good success, disdains the sha-
dow
Which he treads on at noon.
Coriolanus. Act I. Sc. 1

Perseverance
Keeps honour bright: To have done, is to
hang
Quite out of fashion, like a rusty mail
In monumental mockery.
Troilus and Cressida. Act III. Sc. 3

See also: ABILITY, PATIENCE, SUCCESS.

PERSUASION

Persuade me not; I will make a Star-chamber
matter of it.
Merry Wives of Windsor. Act I. Sc. 1

See also: INFLUENCE, TEACHER.

PHILOSOPHY

There are more things in heaven and earth,
Horatio,
Than are dreamt of in your philosophy.
Hamlet. Act I. Sc. 5

Adversity's sweet milk, philosophy.
Romeo and Juliet. Act III. Sc. 3

See also: ARGUMENT, LIFE, MIND, REASON.

PICTURE: *see* PAINTING.

PITY

My pity hath been balm to heal their wounds,
My mildness hath allay'd their swelling griefs.
Henry VI. Pt. III. Act IV. Sc. 8

Which, of you, if you were a prince's son,
Being pent from liberty, as I am now,—
If two such murderers as yourself came to
you,—
Would not entreat for life?
My friend, I spy some pity in thy looks;
O, if thine eye be not a flatterer,
Come thou on my side, and entreat for me,
As you would beg, were you in my distress.
A begging prince what beggar pities not?
Richard III. Act I. Sc. 4

Tear-falling pity dwells not in this eye.
Richard III. Act IV. Sc. 2

Is there no pity sitting in the clouds,
That sees into the bottom of my grief?
Romeo and Juliet. Act III. Sc. 5

But, I perceive,
Men must learn now with pity to dispense;
For policy sits above conscience.
Timon of Athens. Act III. Sc. 2

Pity is the virtue of the law,
And none but tyrants use it cruelly.
Timon of Athens. Act III. Sc. 5

O heavens! can you hear a good man groan,
And not relent, or not compassion him?
Titus Andronicus. Act IV. Sc. 1

VIOLA:
I pity you.
OLIVIA:
That's a degree of love.
Twelfth Night. Act III. Sc. 1

See also: CHARITY, MERCY, SYMPATHY.

PLAGIARISM

When he speaks,
The air, . . . is still,
And the mute wonder lurketh in men's ears,
To steal his sweet and honey'd sentences.
Henry V. Act I. Sc. 1

See also: AUTHORSHIP, BOOK, BORROWING,
NEWS, QUOTATION.

PLEASURE

Boys mature in knowledge,
Pawn their experience to their present
pleasure.
Antony and Cleopatra. Act I. Sc. 4

See also: CONTENTMENT, HAPPINESS, JOY.

POET

Never durst poet touch a pen to write,
Until his ink were temper'd with Love's sighs.
Love's Labour's Lost. Act IV. Sc. 3

The poet's eye, in a fine frenzy rolling,
Doth glance from heaven to earth, from earth
to heaven,
And as imagination bodies forth
The forms of things unknown, the poet's pen
Turns them to shapes, and gives to airy
nothing
A local habitation and a name.
Midsummer Night's Dream. Act V. Sc. 1

Such a deal of wonder is broken out in within
this hour, that the ballad makers cannot be
able to express it.
Winter's Tale. Act V. Sc. 2

See also: POETRY.

POETRY

I would the gods had made thee poetical.
As You Like It. Act III. Sc. 3

O for a muse of fire, that would ascend
The brightest heaven of invention!
Henry V. Chorus

The elegancy, facility, and golden cadence of
poesy.
Love's Labour's Lost. Act IV. Sc. 2

See also: ART, IMAGINATION, POET, WORD.

POLITICS

Something is rotten in the state of Denmark.
Hamlet. Act I. Sc. 4

Turn him to any cause of policy,
The Gordian knot of it he will unloose,
Familiar as his garter: that, when he speak,
The air, a charter'd libertine, is still.
Henry V. Act I. Sc. 1

O, that estates, degrees, and offices,
Were not deriv'd corruptly! and that clear
honour
Were purchased by the merit of the wearer!
Merchant of Venice. Act II. Sc. 9

See also: GOVERNMENT, LAW, PATRIOTISM.

POPULARITY

I have seen the dumb men throng to see him,
And the blind to hear him speak:
Matrons flung gloves,
Ladies and maids their scarfs and handker-
chiefs,
Upon him he passed; the nobles bended,
As to Jove's statue; and the commons made
A shower and thunder with their caps and
shouts.
Coriolanus. Act II. Sc. 1

The ladies call him sweet;
The stairs, as he treads on them, kiss his feet.
Love's Labour's Lost. Act V. Sc. 2

See also: APPLAUSE, FAME, REPUTATION.

POST: *see* LETTER.

POVERTY

No, Madam, 'tis not so well that I am poor;
though many of the rich are damned.
All's Well That Ends Well. Act I. Sc. 3

He that wants money, means and content, is
without three good friends.
As You Like It. Act III. Sc. 2

I am as poor as Job, my lord; but not so
patient.
Henry IV. Pt. II. Act I. Sc. 2

There shall be, in England, seven half-penny
loaves sold for a penny: the three hooped
pot shall have ten hoops; and I will make it
felony to drink small beer.
Henry IV. Pt. II. Act IV. Sc. 2

It is still her use,
To let the wretched man outlive his wealth,
To view with hollow eye, and wrinkled brow,
An age of poverty.
Merchant of Venice. Act IV. Sc. 1

Poor, and content, is rich, and rich enough;
But riches, fineless, is as poor as winter,
To him that ever fears he shall be poor.
                    Othello. Act III. Sc. 3

Steep'd me in poverty to the very lips.
                    Othello. Act IV. Sc. 2

Poverty, but not my will, consents.
                    Romeo and Juliet. Act V. Sc. 1

What will this come to?
He commands us to provide and give great
    gifts,
And all out of an empty coffer.
                    Timon of Athens. Act I. Sc. 2

No matter what; he's poor, and that's revenge
    enough.
                    Timon of Athens. Act II. Sc. 4

See also: BEGGING, HUNGER, WEALTH.

POWER

                    The Devil hath power
To assume a pleasing shape.
                    Hamlet. Act II. Sc. 2

See also: AUTHORITY, STRENGTH, TYRANNY.

PRAISE

    Praising what is lost,
Makes the remembrance dear.
            All's Well That Ends Well. Act V. Sc. 3

All tongues speak of him, and the bleared
    sights
Are spectacled to see him.
                    Coriolanus. Act II. Sc. 1

            In his commendations I am fed;
It is a banquet to me.
                    Macbeth. Act I. Sc. 4

Thou wilt say anon he is some kin to thee,
Thou spend'st such high-day wit in praising
    him.
            Merchant of Venice. Act II. Sc. 9

Speak me fair in death.
            Merchant of Venice. Act IV. Sc. 1

Now, God be prais'd; that to believing souls
Gives light in darkness, comfort in despair.
            Henry VI. Pt. II. Act II. Sc. 1

Our praises are our wages.
            Winter's Tale. Act I. Sc. 2

See also: ADMIRATION, APPLAUSE, FLATTERY,
    GLORY, POPULARITY, WORSHIP.

PRAYER

We, ignorant of ourselves,
Beg often our own harms, which the wise
    powers
Deny us for our good: so we find we profit,
By losing of our prayers.
            Antony and Cleopatra. Act II. Sc. 1

Bow, stubborn knees! and heart with strings
    of steel,
Be soft as sinews of the new-born babe.
                    Hamlet. Act III. Sc. 3

All his mind is bent to holiness,
To number Ave-Maries on his beads:
                    Henry VI. Pt. II. Act I. Sc. 3

Let never day nor night unhallow'd pass,
But still remember what the Lord hath done.
                    Henry VI. Pt. II. Act II. Sc. 1

                    Rather let my head
Stoop to the block than these knees bow to
    any,
Save to the God of heaven and to my king.
                    Henry VI. Pt. II. Act IV. Sc. 1

Go with me, like good angels, to my end;
And, as the long divorce of steel falls on me,
Make of your prayers one sweet sacrifice,
And lift my soul to heaven.
                    Henry VIII. Act II. Sc. 1

                    My prayers
Are not words duly hallow'd, nor my wishes
More worth than empty vanities; yet prayers
    and wishes,
Are all I can return.
                    Henry VIII. Act II. Sc. 3

Now I am past all comfort here, but prayers.
                    Henry VIII. Act IV. Sc. 2

                    True prayers,
That shall be up at heaven, and enter there,
Ere sun-rise.
                    Measure for Measure. Act II. Sc. 2

When I would pray and think, I think and
    pray
To several subjects: Heaven hath my empty
    words.
                    Measure for Measure. Act II. Sc. 4

His worst fault is, that he is given to prayer;
he is something peevish that way: but nobody but has his fault,—but let that pass.
                    Merry Wives of Windsor. Act I. Sc. 4

Well, if my mind were but long enough to
say my prayers, I would repent.
> *Merry Wives of Windsor.* Act IV. Sc. 5

If you bethink yourself of any crime
Unreconcil'd as yet to heaven and grace,
Solicit for it straight.
> *Othello.* Act V. Sc. 2

To thee I do commend my watchful soul,
Ere I let fall the windows of mine eyes;
Sleeping, and waking, O defend me still.
> *Richard III.* Act V. Sc. 3

Get him to say his prayers, Good Sir Toby,
get him to pray.
> *Twelfth Night.* Act III. Sc. 4

See also: MEDITATION, RELIGION, WORSHIP.

PREACHING

Sermons in stones and good in everything.
> *As You Like It.* Act II. Sc. 1

Do not, as some ungracious pastors do,
Show me the steep and thorny way to
  Heaven,
Whilst, like a puff'd and reckless libertine,
Himself the primrose path of dalliance
  treads,
And recks not his own read.
> *Hamlet.* Act I. Sc. 3

Who should be pitiful, if you be not?
Or who should study to prefer a peace,
If holy churchmen take delight in broils?
> *Henry VI.* Pt. I. Act III. Sc. 1

He who the sword of heaven will bear
Should be as holy as severe;
Pattern in himself, to know,
Grace to stand, and virtue go.
> *Measure for Measure.* Act III. Sc. 2

It is a good divine that follows his own instructions; I can easier teach twenty what
were good to be done, than to be one of the
twenty to follow mine own teachings.
> *Merchant of Venice.* Act I. Sc. 2

MAYOR OF LONDON:
See, where his grace stands 'tween two
clergymen!
DUKE OF BUCKINGHAM:
And, see, a book of prayer in his hand;
True ornaments to know a holy man.
> *Richard III.* Act III. Sc. 7

Indeed, left nothing fitting for your purpose
Untouch'd, slightly handled, in discourse.
> *Richard III.* Act III. Sc. 7

See also: ELOQUENCE, GOD, ORATORY, RELIG-
  ION, WORSHIP.

PRESUMPTION

He will steal himself into a man's favour, and,
for a week, escape a great deal of discoveries;
but when you find him out, you have him
ever after.
> *All's Well That Ends Well.* Act III. Sc. 6

How dare the plants look up to heaven, from
  whence
They have their nourishment?
> *Pericles.* Act I. Sc. 2

See also: KINDNESS, PROVIDENCE.

PRIDE

Who cries out on pride,
That can therein tax any private party?
Doth it not flow as hugely as the sea.
> *As You Like It.* Act II. Sc. 7

Such a nature,
Tickled with good success, disdains the
  shadow
Which he treads on at noon.
> *Coriolanus.* Act I. Sc. 1

Prouder than rustling in unpaid-for silk.
> *Cymbeline.* Act III. Sc. 3

She bears a duke's revenues on her back,
And in her heart she scorns our poverty.
> *Henry VI.* Pt. II. Act I. Sc. 3

I have ventur'd,
Like little wanton boys that swim on bladders,
This many summers in a sea of glory;
But far beyond my depth: my high-blown
  pride
At length broke under me.
> *Henry VIII.* Act III. Sc. 2

But man, proud man!
Drest in a little brief authority;
Most ignorant of what he's most assur'd,
His glassy essence,—like an angry ape,
Plays such fantastic tricks before high
  Heaven,
As make the angels weep.
> *Measure for Measure.* Act II. Sc. 2

He is so plaguy proud, that the death tokens
  of it
Cry—*No recovery*.
> *Troilus and Cressida.* Act II. Sc. 3

He that is proud, eats up himself; pride is
his own glass, his own trumpet, his own

chronicle; and whatever praises itself but in the deed, devours the deed in the praise.
Troilus and Cressida. Act II. Sc. 3

I do hate a proud man, as I hate the engendering of toads.
Troilus and Cressida. Act II. Sc. 3

Pride hath no other glass
To show itself, but pride; for supple knees
Feed arrogance, and are the proud man's fees
Troilus and Cressida. Act III. Sc. 3

O world, how apt the poor are to be proud!
Twelfth Night. Act III. Sc. 1

See also: CONCEIT, SELF-LOVE, VANITY.

PRINTING

Thou hast most traitorously corrupted the youth of the realm in erecting a grammar school: and whereas, before, our forefathers had no other books but the score and the tally, thou hast caused printing to be used; and, contrary to the King, his crown, and dignity, thou hast built a paper-mill.
Henry VI. Pt. II. Act IV. Sc. 7

See also: BOOK, NEWS, OCCUPATION.

PRISON

I have been studying how I may compare
This prison, where I live, unto the world:
And, for because the world is populous,
And here is not a creature but myself,
I cannot do it;—yet I'll hammer it out.
Richard II. Act V. Sc. 5

See also: CRIME, PUNISHMENT.

PROMISE

Thy promises are like Adonis' gardens,
That one day bloomed, and fruitful were the next.
Henry VI. Part I. Act I. Sc. 6

His promises were, as he then was, mighty;
But his performance, as he now is, nothing.
Henry VIII. Act IV. Sc. 2

That keep the word of promise to our ear,
And break it to our hope.
Macbeth. Act V. Sc. 7

He promised to meet me two hours since;
and he was ever precise in promise-keeping.
Measure for Measure. Act I. Sc. 2

Verily!
You put me off with limber vows: But I,
Though you would seek to unsphere the stars with oaths,
Should yet say, Sir, no going. Verily,
You shall not go; a lady's verily is
As potent as a lord's.
Winter's Tale. Act I. Sc. 1

See also: HOPE, OATH, WORD.

PROPHET

In nature's infinite book of secrecy,
A little I can read.
Antony and Cleopatra. Act I. Sc. 2

See also: FUTURE, TOMORROW.

PROVIDENCE

He that of greatest works is finisher,
Oft does them by the weakest minister;
So holy writ in babes hath judgment shown,
When judges have been babes.
All's Well That Ends Well. Act II. Sc. 1

He that doth the ravens feed,
Yea, providently caters for the sparrow,
Be comfort to mine age!
As You Like It. Act II. Sc. 3

We defy augury: there is a special providence in the fall of a sparrow. If it be now, 'tis not to come; if it be not to come, it will be now; if it be not now, yet it will come; the readiness is all.
Hamlet. Act V. Sc. 2

There is a divinity that shapes our ends,
Rough-hew them how we will.
Hamlet. Act V. Sc. 2

O God! thy arm was here,
And not to us, but to thy arm alone,
Ascribe we all.—When without stratagem,
But in plain shock, and even play of battle,
Was ever known so great and little loss
On one part and on th' other?—Take it, God,
For it is only thine!
Henry V. Act IV. Sc. 8

Merciful heaven!
Thou rather, with thy sharp and sulphurous bolt,
Split'st the unwedgeable and gnarled oak,
Than the soft myrtle.
Measure for Measure. Act II. Sc. 2

For nought so vile that on the earth doth live,
But to the earth some special good doth give.
>> *Romeo and Juliet*. Act II. Sc. 3

See also: CHANCE, DESTINY, FATE, GOD.

PUNISHMENT

Thou shalt be whipp'd with wire, and stew'd
   in brine,
Smarting in ling'ring pickle.
>> *Antony and Cleopatra*. Act II. Sc. 5

Some of us will smart for it.
>> *Much Ado About Nothing*. Act V. Sc. 1

O, Heaven, that such companions thou'dst
   unfold;
And put in every honest hand a whip,
To lash the rascal naked through the world.
>> *Othello*. Act IV. Sc. 2

See also: JUDGMENT, JUSTICE, LAW, PRISON.

Q

QUACKERY

I bought an unction of a mountebank,
So mortal, that but dip a knife in it,
Where it draws blood, no cataplasm so rare,
Collected from all simples that have virtue
Under the moon, can save the thing from
   death,
That is but scratch'd withal.
>> *Hamlet*. Act IV. Sc. 7

See also: DISEASE, HEALTH, MEDICINE.

QUALITY

Come, give us a taste of your quality.
>> *Hamlet*. Act II. Sc. 2

The best of this kind are but shadows; and
the worst are no worse, if imagination amend
them.
>> *Midsummer Night's Dream*. Act V. Sc. 1

See also: CHARACTER, NOBILITY, WORTH.

QUIET

       I pray you, bear me hence
From forth the noise and rumour of the
   field;
Where I may think the remnant of my
   thoughts

In peace, and part this body and my soul
With contemplation and devout desires.
>> *King John*. Act V. Sc. 4

See also: PEACE, SILENCE.

QUOTATION

       To your audit comes
Their distract parcels in combined sums.
>> *A Lover's Complaint*. Line 230

They have been at a great feast of languages
and stolen the scraps.
>> *Love's Labour's Lost*. Act V. Sc. 1

The Devil can cite Scripture for his purpose.
>> *Merchant of Venice*. Act I. Sc. 3

See also: AUTHORSHIP, BOOK, PLAGIARISM.

R

RAIN

O Earth, I will befriend thee more with rain,
  .   .   .   .
Than youthful April shall with all his
   showers:
In summer's drought I'll drop upon thee still.
>> *Titus Andronicus*. Act III. Sc. 1

For the rain it raineth every day.
>> *Twelfth Night*. Act V. Sc. 1. *Song*

See also: CLOUD, SKY, STORM, SUN.

RAVEN

The croaking raven doth bellow for revenge.
>> *Hamlet*. Act III. Sc. 2

       The raven himself is hoarse
That croaks the fatal entrance of Duncan
Under my battlements.
>> *Macbeth*. Act I. Sc. 5

       O, it comes o'er my memory,
As doth the raven o'er the infectious house,
Boding to all.
>> *Othello*. Act IV. Sc. 1

Did ever raven sing so like a lark,
That gives sweet tidings of the sun's uprise?
>> *Titus Andronicus*. Act III. Sc. 1

See also: ANIMAL, BIRD.

READING

He hath never fed of the dainties that are bred in a book; he hath not eat paper, as it were; he hath not drunk ink: his intellect is not replenished; he is only an animal, only sensible in the duller parts.

Love's Labour's Lost. Act IV. Sc. 2

We burn daylight;—here, read, read.

Merry Wives of Windsor. Act II. Sc. 1

See also: AUTHORSHIP, BOOK, LEARNING.

REASON

Find out the cause of this effect:
Or, rather say, the cause of this defect;
For this effect defective, comes by cause.

Hamlet. Act II. Sc. 2

Give you a reason on compulsion! if reasons were as plenty as blackberries, I would give no man a reason upon compulsion.

Henry IV. Pt. I. Act II. Sc. 4

But, since the affairs of men rest still uncertain.
Let's reason with the worst that may befall.

Julius Caesar. Act V. Sc. 1

See also: ARGUMENT, MIND, PHILOSOPHY.

REBELLION

In soothing them, we nourish 'gainst our senate
The cockle of rebellion, insolence, sedition,
Which we ourselves have plough'd for, sow'd and scatter'd
By mingling them with us, the honour'd number.

Coriolanus. Act III. Sc. 1

Sure, He that made us with such large discourse,
Looking before and after, gave us not
That capability and god-like reason,
To fust in us unus'd.

Hamlet. Act IV. Sc. 4

Good reasons must, of force, give place to better.

Julius Caesar. Act IV. Sc. 3

Unthread the rude eye of rebellion.

King John. Act V. Sc. 4

See also: DISSENSION, TREASON, WAR.

RECKLESSNESS

I am one, my liege,
Whom the vile blows and buffets of the world
Have so incens'd, that I am reckless what
I do to spite the world.

Macbeth. Act III. Sc. 1

See also: CRUELTY, FOOL, VILLAINY.

RECOMPENSE

Thou art so far before,
That swiftest wing of recompense is slow
To overtake thee.

Macbeth. Act I. Sc. 4

See also: MERIT, REWARD, WORTH.

RECREATION

Where is our usual manager of mirth?
What revels are in hand? Is there no play,
To ease the anguish of a torturing hour?

Midsummer Night's Dream. Act V. Sc. 1

See also: ENJOYMENT, PLEASURE.

REDEMPTION

Why, all the souls that were, were forfeit once;
And He that might the vantage best have took,
Found out the remedy.

Measure for Measure. Act II. Sc. 2

See also: CHRIST.

REFLECTION

Think on thy sins.

Othello. Act V. Sc. 2

See also: MEDITATION, PRAYER, THOUGHT.

REFORM

My desolation does begin to make
A better life.

Antony and Cleopatra. Act V. Sc. 2

Like bright metal on a sullen ground,
My reformation, glittering o'er my fault,
Shall show more goodly, and attract more eyes,
Than that which hath no foil to set it off.

Henry IV. Pt. I. Act I. Sc. 2

See also: CHANGE, REPENTANCE, SIN.

REGRET

I could have better spar'd a better man.

Henry IV. Pt. I. Act V. Sc. 4

See also: GRIEF, REPENTANCE, SADNESS.

RELIGION

In religion,
What damned error, but some sober brow
Will bless it, and approve it with a text.
Merchant of Venice. Act III. Sc. 2

See also: BELIEF, CHRIST, FAITH, GOD, HEAVEN,
HELL, PRAYER, SOUL, WORSHIP.

REMORSE

Unnatural deeds
Do breed unnatural troubles: Infected minds
To their deaf pillows will discharge their
secrets,
More needs she the divine than the physician.
Macbeth. Act V. Sc. 1

Abandon all remorse;
On horror's head horrors accumulate.
Othello. Act III. Sc. 3

See also: CONSCIENCE, REPENTANCE, SORROW.

REPARATION

What if this cursed hand
Were thicker than itself with brother's blood?
Is there not rain enough in the sweet heavens,
To wash it white as snow?
Hamlet. Act III. Sc. 3

See also: REFORMATION, REMORSE, SIN.

REPENTANCE

Well, I'll repent and that suddenly, while I
am in some liking; I shall be out of heart
shortly, and then I shall have no strength
to repent. An' I have not forgotten what the
inside of a church is made of, I am a pepper-
corn, a brewer's horse: the inside of a church!
Company, villainous company, hath been the
spoil of me.
Henry IV. Pt. I. Act III. Sc. 3

Under your good correction, I have seen,
When, after execution, judgment hath
Repented o'er his doom.
Measure for Measure. Act II. Sc. 2

And wet his grave with my repentant tears.
Richard III. Act I. Sc. 2

See also: CONSCIENCE, REFORM, SIN.

REPOSE

Our foster-nurse of nature is repose,
The which he lacks; that to provoke in him,

Are many simples operative, whose power
Will close the eye of anguish.
King Lear. Act IV. Sc. 4

See also: PEACE, REST, SLEEP.

REPROOF

I will chide no breather in the world, but
myself; against whom I know most faults.
As You Like It. Act III. Sc. 2

Chide him for faults, and do it reverently,
When you perceive his blood inclined to
mirth.
Henry IV. Pt. II. Act IV. Sc. 4

Better a little chiding than a great deal of
heartbreak.
Merry Wives of Windsor. Act V. Sc. 5

See also: JUDGMENT.

REPUTATION

I have offended reputation:
A most unnoble swerving.
Antony and Cleopatra. Act III. Sc. 9

I would to God thou and I knew where a
commodity of good names were to be bought.
Henry IV. Pt. I. Act I. Sc. 2

Men's evil manners live in brass; their virtues
We write in water.
Henry VIII. Act IV. Sc. 2

Reputation, reputation, reputation! O, I have
lost my reputation! I have lost the immortal
part, sir, of myself.
Othello. Act II. Sc. 3

Reputation is an idle and most false imposi-
tion; oft got without merit, and lost without
deserving.
Othello. Act II. Sc. 3

The purest treasure mortal times afford,
Is spotless reputation; that away,
Men are but gilded loam or painted clay.
Richard II. Act I. Sc. 1

Thy death-bed is no lesser than the land
Wherein thou liest in reputation sick.
Richard II. Act II. Sc. 1

I see, my reputation at stake:
My fame is shrewdly gor'd.
Troilus and Cressida. Act III. Sc. 3

See also: FAME, GOSSIP, NAME, SLANDER.

RESIGNATION

What's gone, and what's past help,
Should be past grief.
Winter's Tale. Act III. Sc. 2

See also: HUMILITY, PATIENCE, RELIGION.

RESOLUTION

Eat, speak, and move, under the
Influence of the most received star;
And though the devil lead the measure
Such are to be followed.
All's Well That Ends Well. Act II. Sc. 1

Determine on some course,
More than a wild exposure to each chance
That starts i' the way before thee.
Coriolanus. Act IV. Sc. 1

Bell, book, and candle, shall not drive me
back,
When gold and silver becks me to come on.
King John. Act III. Sc. 3

Be stirring as the time; be fire with fire;
Threaten the threat'ner, and outface the brow
Of bragging horror: so shall inferior eyes,
That borrow their behaviours from the great;
Grow great by your example, and put on
The dauntless spirit of resolution.
King John. Act V. Sc. 1

From this moment,
The very firstlings of my heart shall be
The firstlings of my hand. And even now,
To crown my thoughts with acts, be it
thought and done.
Macbeth. Act IV. Sc. 1

I'll fight, till from my bones my flesh be
hack'd
Give me my armour.
Macbeth. Act V. Sc. 3

I have a sword, and it shall bite upon my
necessity.
Merry Wives of Windsor. Act II. Sc. 1

I'll not be made a soft and dull-eyed fool,
To shake the head, relent, and sigh, and
yield
To Christian intercessors.
Merchant of Venice. Act III. Sc. 3

I'll have my bond; I will not hear thee speak;
I'll have my bond; and therefore speak no
more.
Merchant of Venice. Act III. Sc. 3

For what I will, I will, and there an end.
Two Gentlemen of Verona. Act I. Sc. 3

See also: ACTION, DECISION, STRENGTH.

RESPONSIBILITY

It is meat and drink to me to see a clown;
By my troth, we that have good wits have
much to answer for.
As You Like It. Act V. Sc. 1

See also: CONSCIENCE, DUTY.

REST

Weariness
Can snore upon the flint, when restive sloth
Finds the down pillow hard.
Cymbeline. Act III. Sc. 6

Who, with a body filled, and vacant mind,
Gets him to rest, cramm'd with distressful
bread.
Henry V. Act IV. Sc. 1

See also: PEACE, REPOSE, SLEEP.

RESULT

Great floods have flown
From simple sources.
All's Well That Ends Well. Act II. Sc. 1

Things bad begun make strong themselves
by ill.
Macbeth. Act III. Sc. 2

O most lame and impotent conclusion!
Othello. Act II. Sc. 1

These violent delights have violent ends,
And in their triumph die, like fire and
powder.
Romeo and Juliet. Act II. Sc. 6

See also: CAUSE, CIRCUMSTANCE.

RETRIBUTION

If thou speak'st false,
Upon the next tree shalt thou hang alive,
Till famine cling thee: If thy speech be sooth,
I care not if thou dost for me as much.
Macbeth. Act V. Sc. 5

Eating the bitter bread of banishment.
Richard II. Act III. Sc. 1

See also: CRIME, PUNISHMENT, REVENGE.

REVENGE

I will kill thee a hurdred ard fifty ways.
                                As You Like It. Act V. Sc. 1

It warms the very sickness in my heart,
That I shall live and tell him to his teeth,
Thus diddest thou.
                                Hamlet. Act IV. Sc. 7

            Priest, beware your beard:
I'mean to tug it, and to cuff you soundly:
Under my feet I stamp thy cardinal's hat;
In spite of pope, or dignities of church,
Here by the cheeks I drag thee up and down.
                                Henry VI. Pt. I. Act I. Sc. 3

Be ready, gods, with your thunderbolts,
Dash him to pieces!
                                Julius Caesar. Act IV. Sc. 3

If I can catch him once upon the hip,
I will feed fat the ancient grudge I bear him.
                                Merchant of Venice. Act I. Sc. 3

If it will feed nothing else it will feed my
revenge.
                                Merchant of Venice. Act III. Sc. 1

If a Jew wrong a Christian, what is his humility? revenge. If a Christian wrong a Jew,
what should his sufferance be by Christian
example? why, revenge.
                                Merchant of Venice. Act III. Sc. 1

Now infidel, I have thee on the hip.
                                Merchant of Venice. Act IV. Sc. 1

You'll ask me, why I rather choose to have
A weight of carrion flesh, than to receive
Three thousand ducats: I'll not answer that:
But, say, it is my humour; Is it answer'd?
                                Merchant of Venice. Act IV. Sc. 1

To have him suddenly convey'd from
    hence:—
Cancel his bond of life, dear God, I pray,
That I may live to say, The dog is dead!
                                Richard III. Act IV. Sc. 4

Bring me within the level of your frown,
But shoot not at me in your waken'd halls.
                                Sonnet CXVII

Vengeance is in my heart, death in my hand,
Blood and revenge are hammering in my
    head.
                                Titus Andronicus. Act II. Sc. 3

See also: ANGER, HATE, PASSION, PUNISHMENT,
    RETRIBUTION,

REVERENCE

            Rather let my head
Stoop to the block, than these knees bow to
    any,
Save to the God of heaven, and to my king.
                                Henry VI. Pt. II. Act IV. Sc. 1

See also: HONOR, WORSHIP.

RIVER

            The higher Nilus swells,
The more it promises; as it ebbs, the seeds-
    man
Upon the slime and ooze scatters his grain,
And shortly comes to harvest
                                Antony and Cleopatra. Act II. Sc. 7

    Affrighted with their bloody looks,
Ran fearfully among the trembling reeds,
And hid his crisp head in the hollow bank.
                                Henry IV. Pt. I. Act I. Sc. 3

    Thrice from the banks of Wye,
And sandy-bottom'd Severn, have I sent him,
Bootless home, and weather-beaten back.
                                Henry IV. Pt. I. Act III. Sc. 1

Draw them to Tiber banks, and weep your
    tears
Into the channel, till the lowest stream
Do kiss the most exaulted shores of all.
                                Julius Caesar. Act I. Sc. 1

See also: BOAT, OCEAN, TRAVEL.

ROSE

From off this brier pluck a white rose with
    me.
                                Henry VI. Pt. I. Act II. Sc. 4

Then will I raise aloft the milk-white rose,
With whose sweet smell the air shall be per-
    fumed.
                                Henry VI. Pt. II. Act I. Sc. 1

There will we make our peds of roses,
And a thousand fragrant posies.
                                Merry Wives of Windsor. Act III. Sc. 1

            Hoary-headed frosts
Fall in the fresh lap of the crimson rose.
                                Midsummer Night's Dream. Act II. Sc. 2

The red rose on triumphant brier.
                                Midsummer Night's Dream. Act III. Sc. 1

Gloves as sweet as damask roses.
                                Winter's Tale. Act IV. Sc. 3. Song

See also: FLOWER,

ROYALTY

His legs bestrid the ocean; his rear'd arm
Crested the world: his voice was propertied
As all the tuned spheres, and that to friends;
But when he meant to quail and shake the
  orb,
He was as rattling thunder. For his bounty,
There was no winter in 't.
Antony and Cleopatra. Act V. Sc. 2

        The gates of Monarchs
Are arch'd so high that giants may get
  through
And keep their impious turbans on.
Cymbeline. Act III. Sc. 3

        Frame them
To royalty unlearned; honour untaught;
Civility not seen from other.
Cymbeline. Act IV. Sc. 2

So excellent a king; that was, to this,
Hyperion to a Satyr.
Hamlet. Act I. Sc. 2

The head is not more native to the heart,
The hand more instrumental to the mouth
Than is the throne of Denmark to my father.
Hamlet. Act I. Sc. 2

There's such divinity doth hedge a king,
That treason can but peep to what it would.
Hamlet. Act IV. Sc. 5

Uneasy lies the head that wears a crown.
Henry IV. Pt. II. Act III. Sc. 1

        Heaven knows, my son,
By what by-paths and indirect crook'd ways,
I met this crown; and I myself know well,
How troublesome it sat upon my head.
Henry IV. Pt. II. Act IV. Sc. 4

Every subject's duty is the king's; but every
  subject's soul is his own.
Henry V. Act IV. Sc. 1

Since I may say, now lie I like a king.
Henry V. Act IV. Sc. 1

She had all the royal makings of a queen;
As holy oil, Edward Confessor's crown,
The rod, and bird of peace, and all such
  emblems,
Laid nobly on her.
Henry VIII. Act IV. Sc. 1

There was a Brutus once, that would have
  brook'd
The eternal devil to keep his state in Rome,
As easily as a king.
Julius Caesar. Act I. Sc. 2

The colour of the king doth come and go
Between his purpose and his conscience.
King John. Act IV. Sc. 2

       The gallant monarch is in arms;
And like an eagle o'er his aery towers,
To souse annoyance that comes near his nest.
King John. Act V. Sc. 2

Ay, every inch a king.
King Lear. Act IV. Sc. 6

Upon my head they placed a fruitless crown.
Macbeth. Act III. Sc. 1

       The king-becoming graces,
As justice, verity, temperance, stableness,
Bounty, perseverence, mercy, loveliness,
Devotion, patience, courage, fortitude,
I have no relish of them.
Macbeth. Act IV. Sc. 3

A substitute shines brightly as a king,
Until a king be by; and then his state
Empties itself, as doth the inland brook
Into the main of waters.
Merchant of Venice. Act V. Sc. 1

        Heaven forbid,
That kings should let their ears hear their
  faults hid.
Pericles. Act I. Sc. 2

We are enforc'd to farm our royal realm,
The revenue whereof shall furnish us
For our affairs in hand.
Richard II. Act I. Sc. 4

Let us sit upon the ground,
And tell sad stories of the death of kings:—
How some have been depos'd, some slain in
  war,
Some haunted by the ghosts they have
  depos'd,
Some poison'd by their wives, some sleeping
  kill'd,
All murder'd.
Richard II. Act III. Sc. 2

Yet looks he like a king; behold his eye,
As bright as is the eagle's, lightens forth
Controlling majesty.
Richard II. Act III. Sc. 3

See also: NOBILITY, POWER, TYRANNY.

RUMOR

> Rumour is a pipe
> Blown by surmises, jealousies, conjectures;
> And of so easy and so plain a stop,
> That the blunt monster with uncounted
>   heads,
> The still-discordant wavering multitude,
> Can play upon it.
> > *Henry IV*. Pt. II. Act I. Induction

See also: CALUMNY, GOSSIP, NEWS, SLANDER.

S

SADNESS

> Be sad, good brothers
> Sorrow so royally in you appears,
> That I will deeply put the fashion on.
> > *Henry IV*. Pt. II Act V. Sc. 2

See also: DISCONTENTMENT, SORROW, TEAR.

SATIRE

> The tongues of mocking wenches are as keen
>   As is the razor's edge invisible,
> Cutting a smaller hair than may be seen,
>   Above the sense of sense; so sensible
> Seemeth their conference, their conceits have
>   wings,
> Fleeter than arrows, bullets, wind, thought,
>   swifter things.
> > *Love's Labour's Lost*. Act V. Sc. 2

See also: CRITICISM, HUMOR, WIT.

SEASON

> Here feel we not the penalty of Adam.
> The season's difference,—as the icy fang,
> And churlish chiding of the winter's wind,
> Which when it bites and blows upon my body,
> Even till I shrink with cold, I smile, and say
> This is no flattery.
> > *As You Like It*. Act II. Sc. 1

> Winter's not gone yet, if the wild geese fly
>   that way.
> > *King Lear*. Act II. Sc. 4

> When daisies pied, and violets blue,
> And lady-smocks all silver white,
> And cuckoo-buds of yellow hue,
> Do paint the meadows with delight.
> > *Love's Labour's Lost*. Act V. Sc. 1

> The spring, the summer,
> The chilling autumn, angry winter, change
> Their wonted liveries.
> > *Midsummer Night's Dream*. Act II. Sc. 2

> Thy eternal summer shall not fade.
> > *Sonnet XVIII*

See also: NATURE, RAIN, SUN.

SECRECY

> And whatsoever else shall hap to-night,
> Give it an understanding, but no tongue.
> > *Hamlet*. Act I. Sc. 2

> If you have hitherto conceal'd this sight,
> Let it be tenable in your silence still.
> > *Hamlet*. Act I. Sc. 2

> Within the bond of marriage, tell me, Brutus,
> Is it excepted, I should know no secrets
> That appertain to you?
> > *Julius Caesar*. Act II. Sc. 1

> Two may keep counsel, putting one away.
> > *Romeo and Juliet*. Act II. Sc. 4

> Two may keep counsel when the third's
>   away.
> > *Titus Andronicus*. Act IV. Sc. 2

See also: CURIOSITY.

SELF-EXAMINATION

> Speak no more:
> Thou turn'st mine eyes into my very soul;
> And there I see such black and grained spots,
> As will not leave their tint.
> > *Hamlet*. Act III. Sc. 4

> Go to your bosom;
> Knock there; and ask your heart, what it
>   doth know.
> > *Measure for Measure*. Act II. Sc. 6

See also: CONSCIENCE, REFLECTION.

SELF-LOVE

> O villanous! I have looked upon the world
> for four times seven years! and since I could
> distinguish between a benefit and an injury,
> I never found a man that knew how to love
> himself.
> > *Othello*. Act I. Sc. 3

> I to myself am dearer than a friend.
> > *Two Gentlemen of Verona*. Act II. Sc. 6

See also: CONCEIT, PRIDE, VANITY.

SHADOW

Come like shadows, so depart.
Macbeth. Act IV. Sc. 1

Some there be that shadows kiss;
Such have but a shadow's bliss.
Merchant of Venice. Act II. Sc. 9

Shadows to-night
Have struck more terror to the soul of
Richard,
Than can the substance of ten thousand
soldiers,
Armed in proof, and led by shallow Rich-
mond.
Richard III. Act V. Sc. 3

Checker'd shadow.
Titus Andronicus. Act II. Sc. 3

See also: CLOUD, DARKNESS, NIGHT.

SHAME

I have some wounds upon me, and they
smart
To hear themselves remembered.
Coriolanus. Act I. Sc. 9

O, shame! Where is thy blush?
Hamlet. Act III. Sc. 4

See also: BLUSH, CONSCIENCE, DISGRACE, GUILT,
HUMILITY, MODESTY.

SHIP

The barge she sat in, like a burnish'd throne,
Burn'd on the water: the poop was beaten
gold;
Purple the sails, and so perfumed, that
The winds were love-sick with them: the
oars were silver;
Which to the tune of flutes kept stroke, and
made
The water, which they beat, to follow faster,
As amorous of their strokes.
Antony and Cleopatra. Act II. Sc. 2

See also: BOAT, OCEAN, RIVER, TRAVEL.

SHOE

FLAVIUS:
Thou art a cobbler, art thou?
SECOND CITIZEN:
Truly, sir, all that I live by is with the awl:
. . . I am, indeed, sir, a surgeon to old shoes.
Julius Caesar. Act I. Sc. 1

What trade are you?
Truly, sir, in respect of a fine workman, I
am but, as you would say, a cobbler.
Julius Caesar. Act I. Sc. 1

MARULLUS:
What trade art thou? answer me directly.
SECOND CITIZEN:
A trade, sir, that I hope I may use with a safe
conscience; which is indeed, sir, a mender of
bad soles.
Julius Caesar. Act I. Sc. 1

FLAVIUS:
Wherefore art not in the shop today?
Why dost thou lead these men about the
streets?
SECOND CITIZEN:
Truly sir, to ear out their shoes, to get my-
self into more work.
Julius Caesar. Act I. Sc. 1

See also: APPAREL, OCCUPATION.

SICKNESS

He had a fever when he was in Spain,
And, when the fit was on him, I did mark
How he did shake; 'tis true, this god did
shake:
His coward lips did from their colour fly;
And that same eye, whose bend doth awe the
world,
Did lose his lustre.
Julius Caesar. Act I. Sc. 2

What, is Brutus sick;
And will he steal out of his wholesome bed,
To dare the vile Contagion of the night?
Julius Caesar. Act II. Sc. 1

My long sickness
Of health, and living, now begins to mend,
And nothing brings me all things.
Timon of Athens. Act V. Sc. 2

See also: DISEASE, HEALTH, MEDICINE.

SIGN

Sometimes we see a cloud that's dragonish,
A vapour, sometime like a bear, or lion,
A tower'd citadel, a pendent rock,
A forked mountain, or blue promontory
With trees upon't that nod unto the world,
And mock our eyes with air: thou hast seen
these signs;
They are the black vesper's pageants.
Antony and Cleopatra. Act IV. Sc. 12

If he be not in love with some woman, there
is no believing old signs: He brushes his hat
o' mornings; What should that bode?
Much Ado About Nothing. Act II. Sc. 2

See also: ACTION, DEED, EXAMPLE.

SILENCE

Be check'd for silence,
But never tax'd for speech.
All's Well That Ends Well. Act I. Sc.1

You shall not say I yield, being silent, I
would not speak.
Cymbeline. Act III. Sc. 3

I'll speak to thee in silence.
Cymbeline. Act V. Sc. 4

It is not, nor it cannot come to good;
But break, my heart; for I must hold my
tongue.
Hamlet. Act I. Sc. 2

The rest is silence.
Hamlet. Act V. Sc. 2

Silence is only commendable
In a neat's tongue dried, and a maid not
vendible.
Merchant of Venice. Act I. Sc. 1

Silence is the perfectest herald of joy:
I were but little happy if I could say how
much.
Much Ado About Nothing. Act II. Sc. 1

Silence that dreadful bell.
Othello. Act II. Sc. 2

Say, she be mute, and will not speak a word;
Then I'll commend her volubility,
And say she uttereth piercing eloquence.
Taming of the Shrew. Act II. Sc. 1

What! gone without a word?
Ay, so true love should do: it cannot speak;
For truth hath better deeds than words to
grace it.
Two Gentlemen of Verona. Act II. Sc. 2

See also: PEACE, REPOSE, REST, QUIET.

SIN

What then? what rests?
Try what repentance can: What can it not?
Yet what can it; when one can not repent?
O wretched state! O bosom, black as death!

O limed soul, that, struggling to be free
Art more engag'd.
Hamlet. Act III. Sc. 3

Commit
The oldest sins the newest kind of ways.
Henry IV. Pt. II. Act IV. Sc. 4

It is a great sin, to swear unto a sin;
But greater sin, to keep a sinful oath.
Henry VI. Pt. II. Act V. Sc. 1

Some sins do bear their privilege on earth.
King John. Act I. Sc. 1

Robes and furr'd gowns hide all. Plate sin
with gold.
And the strong lance of justice hurtless
breaks;
Arm it in rags, a pigmy's straw doth pierce it.
King Lear. Act IV. Sc. 6

O fie, fie, fie!
Thy sin's not accidental, but a trade.
Measure for Measure. Act III. Sc. 1

I'll not be made a soft and dull-ey'd fool,
To shake the head, relent, and sigh, and
yield
To Christian intercessors.
Merchant of Venice. Act III. Sc. 3

O, what authority and show of truth
Can cunning sin cover itself withal!
Much Ado About Nothing. Act IV. Sc. 1

Few love to hear the sins they love to act.
Pericles. Act I. Sc. 1

Though some of you, with Pilate, wash your
hands,
Showing an outward pity; yet you Pilates
Have here deliver'd me to my sour cross,
And water cannot wash away your sin.
Richard II. Act IV. Sc. 1

The world is grown so bad
That wrens make prey where eagles dare not
perch.
Richard III. Act I. Sc. 3

See also: CRIME, FORGIVENESS, GUILT, VICE.

SINCERITY

I do not shame
To tell you what I was, since my conversion
So sweetly tastes, being the thing I am.
As You Like It. Act IV. Sc. 3

He hath a heart as sound as a bell, and his tongue is the clapper; for what his heart thinks his tongue speaks.
Much Ado About Nothing. Act III. Sc. 2

But I will wear my heart upon my sleeve
For daws to peck at; I am not what I am.
Othello. Act I. Sc. 1

Men should be what they seem;
Or, those that be not, would they might seem none!
Othello. Act III. Sc. 3

Speak of me as I am; nothing extenuate,
Nor set down aught in malice; then must thou speak
Of one that loved not wisely, but too well.
Othello. Act V. Sc. 2

Oh! how much more doth Beauty beauteous seem,
By that sweet ornament which truth doth give!
Sonnet LIV

See also: FIDELITY, HONESTY, TRUTH.

SINGER

Every night he comes,
With music of all sorts, and songs compos'd
To her unworthiness: It nothing steads us
To chide him from our eaves; for he persists;
As if his life lay on't.
All's Well That Ends Well. Act III. Sc. 7

Thou hast by moonlight at her window sung,
With feigning voice, verses of feigning love.
Midsummer Night's Dream. Act I. Sc. 1

O, she will sing the savageness out of a bear.
Othello. Act IV. Sc. 1

His tongue is now a stringless instrument.
Richard II. Act II. Sc. 1

The lark, at break of day arising
From sullen earth, sings hymns at Heaven's gate.
Sonnet XXIX

Nay, now you are too flat,
And mar the concord with too harsh a descant.
Two Gentlemen of Verona. Act I. Sc. 2

But one Puritan amongst them, and he sings psalms to hornpipes.
Winter's Tale. Act IV. Sc. 2

See also: BALLAD, MUSIC, SONG.

SKY

This majestical roof, fretted with golden fire.
Hamlet. Act II. Sc. 2

See also: CLOUD, HEAVEN, MOON, SUNRISE, SUNSET, THUNDER, TWILIGHT.

SLANDER

For slander lives upon succession;
For-ever housed, where it gets possession.
Comedy of Errors. Act III. Sc. 1

'Tis slander;
Whose edge is sharper than the sword whose tongue
Outvenoms all the worms of Nile; whose breath
Rides on posting winds, and doth belie
All corners of the world; kings, queens, and states,
Maids, matrons, nay the secrets of the grave
This viperous slander enters.
Cymbeline. Act III. Sc. 4

'Tis slander,—whose breath
Rides on the posting winds, and doth belie
All corners of the world.
Cymbeline. Act III. Sc. 4

Be thou as chaste as ice, as pure as snow, thou shalt not escape calumny.
Hamlet. Act III. Sc. 1

So, haply, slander,—
Whose whisper o'er the world's diameter,
As level as the cannon to his blank,
Transports his poison'd shot—may miss our name,
And hit the woundless air.
Hamlet. Act IV. Sc. 1

No might nor greatness in mortality
Can censure 'scape; back-wounding calumny
The whitest virtue strikes: What king so strong,
Can tie the gall up in the slanderous tongue.
Measure for Measure. Act III. Sc. 2

Slander'd to death by villains;
That dare as well answer a man, indeed,
As I dare take a serpent by the tongue:
Boys, apes, braggarts, jacks, milksops.
Much Ado About Nothing. Act V. Sc. 1

Done to death by slanderous tongues
Was the Hero that here lies.
Much Ado About Nothing. Act V. Sc. 3

Who steals my purse, steals trash; 'tis some-
thing, nothing;
'Twas mine, 'tis his, and has been slave to
thousands;
But he, that filches from me my good name,
Robs me of that which not enriches him,
And makes me poor indeed.
Othello. Act III. Sc. 3

I will be hang'd, if some eternal villain,
Some busy and insinuating rogue,
Some cogging, cozening slave, to get some
office,
Have not devis'd this slander.
Othello. Act IV. Sc. 2

That thou art blamed, shall not be thy
defect;
For slander's mark was ever yet the fair;

    .   .   .   .

So thou be good, slander doth but approve
Thy worth the greater.
Sonnet LXX

            If I can do it,
By aught that I can speak in his dispraise,
She shall not long continue to love him.
Two Gentlemen of Verona. Act III. Sc. 2

See also: CALUMNY, GOSSIP, RUMOR.

SLAVERY

Base is the slave that pays.
Henry V. Act II. Sc. 1

"You have among you many a purchas'd
slave,
Which like your asses, and your dogs, and
mules,
You use in abject and in slavish parts,
Because you bought them."
Merchant of Venice. Act IV. Sc. 1

See also: FREEDOM, LIBERTY.

SLEEP

O sleep, thou ape of death, lie dull upon
her;
And be her sense but as a monument.
Cymbeline. Act II. Sc. 2

He that sleeps feels not the toothache.
Cymbeline. Act V. Sc. 4

Sleeping within mine orchard,
My custom always of the afternoon.
Hamlet. Act I. Sc. 5

To sleep! perchance to dream; ay, there's
the rub;
For in that sleep of death what dreams may
come,
When we have shuffled off this mortal coil,
Must give us pause.
Hamlet. Act III. Sc. 1

On your eyelids crown the god of sleep,
Charming your blood with pleasing heaviness;
Making such difference betwixt wake and
sleep
As is the difference betwixt day and night,
The hour before the heavenly harness'd team
Begins his golden progress in the east.
Henry IV. Pt. I. Act III. Sc. 1

How many thousand of my poorest subjects
Are at this hour fast asleep! O sleep, O gentle
sleep,
Nature's soft nurse, how have I frighted
thee,
That thou no more wilt weigh my eyelids
down,
And steep my senses in forgetfulness?
Henry IV. Pt. II. Act III. Sc. 1

Canst thou, O partial sleep! give thy repose
To the wet sea-boy in an hour so rude;
And, in the calmest and most stillest night,
With all appliances and means to boot,
Deny it to a king?
Henry IV. Pt. II. Act III. Sc. 1

This sleep is sound, indeed this is a sleep
That from this golden rigol hath divorc'd
So many English kings.
Henry IV. Pt. II. Act IV. Sc. 4

O polish'd perturbation! golden care!
That keep'st the ports of slumber open wide
To many a watchful night! sleep with it now!
Yet not so sound, and half so deeply sweet
As he, whose brow, with homely biggen
bound,
Snores out the watch of night.
Henry IV. Pt. II. Act IV. Sc. 4

    Fast asleep? It is no matter;
Enjoy thy honey-heavy dew of slumber;
Thou hast no figures, nor no fantasies,
Which busy care draws in the brains of
men;
Therefore thou sleep'st so sound.
Julius Caesar. Act II. Sc. 1

    Bid them come forth and hear me,
Or at their chamber-door I'll beat the drum,
Till it cry—Sleep to death.
King Lear. Act II. Sc. 4

Sleep shall, neither night nor day,
Hang upon his penthouse lid.
Macbeth. Act I. Sc. 3

Methought I heard a voice cry, Sleep no
more!
Macbeth does murder sleep, the innocent
sleep.
Macbeth. Act II. Sc. 2

Sleep that knits up the ravell'd sleave of
care,
The death of each day's life, sore labour's
bath,
Balm of hurt minds, great nature's second
course,
Chief nourisher in life's feast.
Macbeth. Act II. Sc. 2

Shake off this downy sleep, death's counter-
feit,
And look on death itself!—
Macbeth. Act II. Sc. 3

Thy best of rest is sleep,
And that thou oft provok'st; yet grossly
fear'st
Thy death, which is no more.
Measure for Measure. Act III. Sc. 1

He sleeps by day
More than the wild cat: drones hive not with
me,
Therefore I part with him.
Merchant of Venice. Act II. Sc. 5

Sleep that sometimes shuts up sorrow's eye,
Steal me awhile from mine own company.
Midsummer Night's Dream. Act III. Sc. 2

Thou lead them thus,
Till o'er their brows death-counterfeiting
sleep,
With leaden legs and batty wings doth creep.
Midsummer Night's Dream. Act III. Sc. 2

And I pray you let none of your people stir
me: I have an exposition of sleep come
upon me.
Midsummer Night's Dream. Act IV. Sc. 1

Not poppy, nor mandragora,
Nor all the drowsy syrups of the world,
Shall ever medicine thee to that sweet sleep
Which thou ow'dst yesterday.
Othello. Act III. Sc. 3

Never yet one hour in his bed
Did I enjoy the golden dew of sleep,
But with his timorous dreams was still
awak'd.
Richard III. Act IV. Sc. 1

I let fall the windows of mine eyes.
Richard III. Act V. Sc. 3

Sleep dwell upon thine eyes, peace in thy
breast!
Would I were sleep and peace, so sweet to
rest!
Romeo and Juliet. Act II. Sc. 2

Thy eyes' windows fall,
Like death, when he shuts up the day of
life;
Each part, depriv'd of supple government,
Shall, stiff, and stark, and cold, appear like
death.
Romeo and Juliet. Act IV. Sc. 1

See also: DREAM, NIGHT, REPOSE, REST.

SMILE

Nobly he yokes
A smiling with a sigh: as if the sigh
Was that it was, for not being such a smile;
The smile, mocking the sigh, that it would
fly
From so divine a temple, to commix
With winds, that sailors rail at.
Cymbeline. Act IV. Sc. 2

One may smile, and smile, and be a villain.
Hamlet. Act I. Sc. 5

Seldom he smiles; and smiles in such a sort,
As if he mock'd himself, and scorn'd his
spirit
That could be mov'd to smile at anything.
Julius Caesar. Act I. Sc. 2

Those happy smilets
That play'd on her ripe lip, seem'd not to
know
What guests were in her eyes; which parted
thence,
As pearls from diamonds dropp'd.
King Lear. Act IV. Sc. 3

See also: HAPPINESS, JOY, LAUGHTER.

SOCIETY

Society is no comfort to one not sociable.
Cymbeline. Act IV. Sc. 2

To make society
The sweeter welcome, we will keep ourself
Till supper-time alone.
Macbeth. Act III. Sc. 1

See also: FASHION, LIFE, MAN, MANNERS.

SOLDIER

Worthy fellows; and like to prove most sinewy swordsmen.
All's Well That Ends Well. Act II. Sc. 1

Then a soldier;
Full of strange oaths and bearded like the pard,
Jealous in honour, sudden and quick in quarrel,
Seeking the bubble reputation
Even in the cannon's mouth.
As You Like It. Act II. Sc. 7

Give them great meals of beef, and iron and steel, they will eat like wolves, and fight like devils.
Henry V. Act III. Sc. 7

A braver soldier never couched lance,
A gentler heart did never sway in court.
Henry VI. Pt. I. Act III. Sc. 2

I am a soldier; and unapt to weep,
Or to exclaim on fortune's fickleness.
Henry VI. Pt. I. Act V. Sc. 3

Drummer, strike up, and let us march away.
Henry VI. Pt. III. Act IV. Sc. 7

I said an elder soldier, not a better.
Did I say a better?
Julius Caesar. Act IV. Sc. 3

Fie, my lord, fie! a soldier and afear'd?
Macbeth. Act V. Sc. 1

God's soldier be he!
Had I as many sons as I have hairs,
I would not wish them to a fairer death:
And so his knell is knoll'd.
Macbeth. Act V. Sc. 7

You may relish him more in the soldier, than in the scholar.
Othello. Act II. Sc. 1

He is a soldier fit to stand by Caesar,
And give direction.
Othello. Act II. Sc. 3

'Tis the soldier's life
To have their balmy slumbers wak'd with strife.
Othello. Act II. Sc. 3

The painful warrior, famoused for fight,
After a thousand victories once foiled,
Is from the books of honor razed quite,
And all the rest forgot for which he toiled.
Sonnet XXV

May that soldier a mere recreant prove,
That means not, hath not, or is not in love!
Troilus and Cressida. Act I. Sc. 3

See also: BRAVERY, COURAGE, VALOR, WAR.

SONG

Now, good Cesario, but that piece of song,
That old and antique song we heard last night;
Methought it did relieve my passion much,
More than light airs and recollected terms,
Of these most brisk and giddy-paced times:
Come; but one verse.
Twelfth Night. Act II. Sc. 4

See also: BALLAD, MUSIC, SINGER.

SORROW

Wherever sorrow is, relief would be:
If you do sorrow at my grief in love,
By giving love, your sorrow and my grief
Were both extermin'd.
As You Like It. Act III. Sc. 5

Peace; sit you down,
And let me wring your heart; for so I shall,
If it be made of penetrable stuff.
Hamlet. Act III. Sc. 4

When sorrows come, they come not single spies,
But in battalions!
Hamlet. Act IV. Sc. 5

A plague of sighing and grief.
Henry IV. Pt. I. Act II. Sc. 4

O, if this were seen,
The happiest youth, viewing his progress through,
What perils past, what crosses to ensue,
Would shut the book, and sit him down and die.
Henry IV. Pt. I. Act III. Sc. 1

'Tis better to be lowly born,
And range with humble livers in content,
Than to be perk'd up in a glistering grief,
And wear a golden sorrow.
Henry VIII. Act II. Sc. 3

I will instruct my sorrow to be proud.
King John. Act III. Sc. 1

Here I and sorrow sit:
Here is my throne, bid kings come bow to it.
King John. Act III. Sc. 1

Down, thou climbing sorrow.
King Lear. Act II. Sc. 4

The tempest in my mind
Doth from my senses take all feelings else,
Save what beats there.
King Lear. Act III. Sc. 4

Bad is the trade that must play fool to
sorrow.
King Lear. Act IV. Sc. 1

Give sorrow words; the grief that does not
speak
Whispers the o'erfraught heart and bids it
break.
Macbeth. Act IV. Sc. 3

Each new moon,
New widows howl, new orphans cry; new
sorrows
Strike heaven on the face, that it resound
As if it felt with Scotland, and yell'd out
Like syllable of dolour.
Macbeth. Act IV. Sc. 3

Your cause of sorrow
Must not be measur'd by his worth, for then
It hath no end.
Macbeth. Act V. Sc. 7

I am not merry, but I do beguile
The thing I am by seeming otherwise.
Othello. Act II. Sc. 1

This sorrow's heavenly,
It strikes where it doth love.
Othello. Act V. Sc. 2

One sorrow never comes but brings an heir,
That may succeed as his inheritor.
Pericles. Act I. Sc. 4

Sorrow ends not when it seemeth done.
Richard II. Act I. Sc. 2

Joy being altogether wanting,
It doth remember me the more of sorrow.
Richard II. Act III. Sc. 4

Sorrow breaks seasons and reposing hours;
Makes the night morning, and the noontide
night.
Richard III. Act I. Sc. 4

Eighty odd years of sorrow have I seen,
And each hour's joy wracked with a week of
teen.
Richard III. Act IV. Sc. 1

If sorrow can admit society,
Tell o'er your woes again by viewing mine.
Richard III. Act IV. Sc. 4

Sorrow conceal'd, like an oven stopp'd,
Doth burn the heart to cinders.
Titus Andronicus. Act II. Sc. 5

To weep with them that weep doth ease
some deal,
But sorrow flouted at is double death.
Titus Andronicus. Act III. Sc. 1

I have (as when the sun doth light a storm)
Buried this sigh in wrinkle of a smile:
But sorrow, that is couch'd in seeming glad-
ness,
Is like that mirth fate turns to sudden sad-
ness.
Troilus and Cressida. Act I. Sc. 1

Forgive me, Valentine if hearty sorrow
Be a sufficient ransom for offence,
I tender 't here; I do as truly suffer,
As e'er I did commit.
Two Gentlemen of Verona. Act V. Sc. 4

See also: AFFLICTION, DISCONTENT, SADNESS.

SOUL

Whether in sea or fire, in earth or air,
The extravagant and erring spirit hies
To his confine.
Hamlet. Act I. Sc. 1

Within this wall of flesh
There is a soul, counts thee her creditor.
King John. Act III. Sc. 3

Thy soul's flight,
If it find Heaven, must find it out to-night.
Macbeth. Act III. Sc. 1

Think'st thou, I'll endanger my soul gratis?
Merry Wives of Windsor. Act II. Sc. 2

And her immortal part with angels lives.
Romeo and Juliet. Act V. Sc. 1

See also: HEART, IMMORTALITY, LIFE, MIND,
SPIRIT.

SPEECH

Before we proceed any further, hear me
speak.
Coriolanus. Act I. Sc. 1

Under which king, Bezonian? speak or die.
Henry IV. Pt. II. Act V. Sc. 3

Hear me, for I will speak.
Julius Caesar. Act IV. Sc. 3

I had a thing to say,—
But I will fit it, with some better time.
King John. Act III. Sc. 3

She speaks poignards, and every word stabs.
Much Ado About Nothing. Act II. Sc. 1

Rude am I in my speech,
And little bless'd with the set phrase of peace;
For since these arms of mine had seven years'
pith,
Till now some nine moons wasted, they have
us'd
Their dearest action in the tented field;
And little of this great world can I speak,
More than pertains to feats of broil and
battle;
And therefore little shall I grace my cause,
In speaking for myself.
Othello. Act I. Sc. 3

Our fair discourse hath been as sugar
Making the hard way sweet and delectable.
Richard II. Act II. Sc. 3

I would be loath to cast away my speech;
for, besides that it is excellently well penn'd,
I have taken great pains to con it.
Twelfth Night. Act I. Sc. 5

See also: ELOQUENCE, LANGUAGE, ORATORY,
TALK, TONGUE, VOICE, WORD.

SPIRIT

There needs no ghost, my lord, come from
the grave
To tell us this.
Hamlet. Act I. Sc. 5

I can call spirits from the vasty deep,
Why, so can I; or so can any man
But will they come, when you do call for
them?
Henry IV. Pt. I. Act III. Sc. 1

What are these,
So wither'd, and so wild in their attire;
That look not like the inhabitants o' th'
earth,
And yet are on 't?
Macbeth. Act I. Sc. 3

Now it is the time of night,
That the graves, all gaping wide,
Every one lets forth his sprite,
In the church-way paths to glide.
Midsummer Night's Dream. Act V. Sc. 1

See also: SOUL.

SPIRITS, ALCOHOLIC: *see* WINE.

SPRING: *see* SEASON.

STAR

Our jovial Star reign'd at his birth.
Cymbeline. Act V. Sc. 4

Two stars keep not their motion in one
sphere.
Henry IV. Pt. I. Act V. Sc. 4

The skies are painted with unnumber'd
sparks,
They are all fire, and every one doth shine;
But there's but one in all doth hold his place
Julius Caesar. Act III. Sc. 1

The stars above govern our condition.
King Lear. Act IV. Sc. 3

The unfolding star calls up the shepherd.
Measure for Measure. Act IV. Sc. 2

These blessed candles of the night.
Merchant of Venice. Act V. Sc. 1

Look, how the floor of heaven
Is thick inlaid with patines of bright gold.
There's not the smallest orb which thou be-
hold'st,
But in his motion like an angel sings,
Still quiring to the young-ey'd cherubins:
Such harmony is in immortal souls;
But whilst this muddy vesture of decay
Doth grossly close it in, we cannot hear it.
Merchant of Venice. Act V. Sc. 1

Witness yon even-burning lights above!
> *Othello.* Act III. Sc. 3

Those gold candles fix'd in heaven's air.
> *Sonnet XXI*

See also: MOON, SKY.

STOICISM

I have felt so many quirks of joy, and grief,
That the first face of neither, on the start,
Can woman me unto 't.
> *All's Well That Ends Well.* Act III. Sc. 2

See also: PATIENCE, PHILOSOPHY, RESIGNA-
TION.

STORM

As far as I could ken thy chalky cliffs,
When from thy shore the tempest beat us
  back,
I stood upon the hatches in the storm.
> *Henry VI.* Pt. II. Act III. Sc. 2

I have seen tempests, when the scolding
  winds
Have riv'd the knotty oaks; and I have seen
The ambitious ocean swell, and rage, and
  foam,
To be exaulted with the threat'ning clouds
But never till to-night, never till now,
Did I go through a tempest dropping fire.
> *Julius Caesar.* Act I. Sc. 3

Blow, wind: swell, billow; and swim, bark!
The storm is up, and all is on the hazard.
> *Julius Caesar.* Act V. Sc. 1

Blow, winds, and crack your cheeks! rage,
  blow!
You cataracts and hurricanoes spout
Till you have drench'd our steeples.
> *King Lear.* Act III. Sc. 2

Merciful heaven!
Thou rather, with thy sharp and sulphurous
  bolt,
Splitt'st the unwedgable and gnarled oak,
Than the soft myrtle.
> *Measure for Measure.* Act II. Sc. 2

See also: CLOUD, RAIN, SKY.

STRENGTH

O, it is excellent
To have a giant's strength, but it is tyran-
nous
To use it like a giant.
> *Measure for Measure.* Act II. Sc. 2

The king's name is a tower of strength,
Which they upon the adverse faction want.
> *Richard III.* Act V. Sc. 3

See also: ABILITY, POWER, RESOLUTION.

STUDENT

Then the whining school-boy, with his
  satchel,
And shining morning face, creeping like
  snail
Unwillingly to school.
> *As You Like It.* Act II. Sc. 7

He was a scholar, and a ripe and good one;
Exceeding wise, fair-spoken, and persuading;
Lofty and sour to them that lov'd him not;
But, to those men that sought him, sweet as
  summer.
> *Henry VIII.* Act IV. Sc. 2

See also: EDUCATION, STUDY.

STUDY

I'll talk a word with this same learned
  Theban:
What is your study?
> *King Lear.* Act III. Sc. 4

So study evermore is overshot;
While it doth study to have what it would,
It doth forget to do the thing it should.
And when it hath the thing it hunteth most,
'Tis won, as towns with fire; so won, so lost.
> *Love's Labour's Lost.* Act I. Sc. 1

Study is like the heaven's glorious sun,
That will not be deep-search'd with saucy
  looks;
Small have continual plodders ever won,
Save base authority from other's books.
> *Love's Labour's Lost.* Act I. Sc. 1

See also: BOOK, EDUCATION, LEARNING, STU-
DENT, TEACHER.

SUBMISSION

Alas! what need you be so boist'rous-rough?
I will not struggle, I will stand stone-still.
> *King John.* Act IV. Sc. 1

Thus ready for the way of life or death.
I wait the sharpest blow.
> *Pericles.* Act I. Sc. 1

See also: HUMILITY.

SUCCESS

Didst thou never hear
That things ill got had ever bad success?
Henry VI. Pt. III. Act II. Sc. 2

To climb steep hills
Requires slow pace at first.
Henry VIII. Act I. Sc. 1

Now is the winter of our discontent
Made glorious summer by this sun of York;
And all the clouds, that lower'd upon our
house,
In the deep bosom of the ocean buried.
Richard III. Act I. Sc. 1

They that stand high, have many blasts to
shake them;
And, if they fall, they dash themselves to
pieces.
Richard III. Act I. Sc. 3

See also: FAME, FORTUNE, HAPPINESS, HONOR,
LUCK, VICTORY, WEALTH.

SUICIDE

Bravest at the last:
She levell'd at our purposes, and, being
royal,
Took her own way.
Antony and Cleopatra. Act V. Sc. 2

Against self-slaughter
There is a prohibition so divine
That cravens my weak hand.
Cymbeline. Act III. Sc. 4

The more pity, that great folk should have
countenance in this world to drown or hang
themselves, more than their even Christian.
Hamlet. Act V. Sc. 1

He that cuts off twenty years of life
Cuts off so many years of fearing death.
Julius Caesar. Act III. Sc. 1

You ever gentle gods, take my breath from
me;
Let not my worser spirit tempt me again
To die before you please.
King Lear. Act IV. Sc. 6

See also: CRIME, DEATH, LIFE, MURDER.

SUMMER: *see* SEASON.

SUN

O sun,
Burn the great sphere thou mov'st in! darkling stand

The varying shore o' the world!
Antony and Cleopatra. Act IV. Sc. 13

The heavenly-harness'd team
Begins his golden progress in the east
Henry IV. Pt. I. Act III. Sc. 1

The glorious sun
Stays in his course, and plays the alchymist:
Turning, with splendour in his precious eye,
The meagre cloddy earth to glittering gold.
King John. Act III. Sc. 1

I 'gin to be a-weary of the sun,
And wish th' estate o' the world were now
undone.
Macbeth. Act V. Sc. 5

Shine out, fair sun, till I have bought a glass,
That I may see my shadow as I pass.
Richard III. Act I. Sc. 2

Lo, in the orient when the gracious light
Lifts up his burning head, each under eye
Doth homage to his new-appearing sight,
Serving with looks his sacred majesty;
And having climb'd the steep-up heavenly
hill,
Resembling strong youth in his middle age,
Yet mortal looks adore his beauty still,
Attending on his golden pilgrimage;
But when from highmost pitch, with weary
car,
Like feeble age, he reeleth from the day,
The eyes, 'fore duteous, now converted are
From his low tract, and look another way.
Sonnet VII

That orbed continent, the fire
That severs day from night.
Twelfth Night. Act V. Sc. 1

The self-same sun that shines upon his court,
Hides not his visage from our cottage, but
Looks on alike.
Winter's Tale. Act IV. Sc. 3

See also: DAY, LIGHT, SKY, SUNRISE, SUNSET.

SUNRISE

He fires the proud tops of the eastern pines,
And darts his light through every guilty
hole.
Richard II. Act III. Sc. 2

The golden sun salutes the morn,
And, having gilt the ocean with his beams,
Gallops the zodiac in his glistering coach,
And overlooks the highest peering hills.
Titus Andronicus. Act II. Sc. 1

See also: DAWN, MORNING, SUN.

SUNSET

The setting sun, and music at the close,
As the last taste of sweets, is sweetest last.
Richard II. Act II. Sc. 1

When the sun sets, who doth not look for night?
Richard III. Act II. Sc. 3

See also: EVENING, NIGHT, SUN.

SUSPICION

All is not well;
I doubt some foul play.
Hamlet. Act I. Sc. 2

Suspicion always haunts the guilty mind;
The thief doth fear each bush an officer.
Henry VI. Pt. III. Act V. Sc. 6

Would he were fatter:—But I fear him not:
Yet if my name were liable to fear,
I do not know the man I should avoid
So soon as that spare Cassius.
Julius Caesar. Act I. Sc. 2

There is some ill a brewing towards my rest,
For I did dream of money-bags to-night
Merchant of Venice. Act II. Sc. 5

See also: DOUBT, JEALOUSY.

SWAN

The swan's down feather,
That stands upon the swell at full of tide,
And neither way inclines.
Antony and Cleopatra. Act III. Sc. 2

I have seen a swan
With bootless labour swim against the tide,
And spend her strength with over-matching waves.
Henry VI. Pt. III. Act I. Sc. 4

All the water in the ocean,
Can never turn a swan's black legs to white,
Although she lave them hourly in the flood.
Titus Andronicus. Act IV. Sc. 2

See also: ANIMAL, BIRD.

SYMBOL: *see* SIGN.

SYMPATHY

A tear for pity, and a hand
Open as day for melting charity.
Henry IV. Pt. II. Act IV. Sc. 4

A sympathy in choice.
Midsummer Night's Dream. Act I. Sc. 1

See also: FRIENDSHIP, PITY, MERCY.

T

TAILOR

Thou villain base,
Know'st not me by my clothes?
GUIDERIUS:
No, nor thy tailor, rascal,
Who is thy grandfather? he made those clothes,
Which, as it seems, make thee.
Cymbeline. Act IV. Sc. 2

Costly thy habit as thy purse can buy,
But not express'd in fancy; rich, not gaudy!
For the apparel oft proclaims the man.
Hamlet. Act I. Sc. 3

DUKE OF CORNWALL:
Thou art a strange fellow: a tailor make a man?
EARL OF KENT:
A tailor, sir; a stone-cutter, or a painter, could not have made him so ill, though they had been but two hours at the trade.
King Lear. Act II. Sc. 2

I'll be at charges for a looking glass;
And entertain a score or two of tailors
To study fashions to adorn my body.
Richard III. Act I. Sc. 2

Thy gown? why, ay;—Come, tailor, let us see't.
O mercy, God! what masking stuff is here?
What's this? a sleeve? 'tis like a demicannon:
What! up and down, carv'd like an apple-tart?
Here's snip, and nip, and cut, and slish, and slash,
Like to a censer in a barber's shop:—
Why, what, o' devil's name, tailor, call'st thou this?
Taming of the Shrew. Act IV. Sc. 3

See also: APPAREL, OCCUPATION.

TALKING

Many a man's tongue shakes out his master's undoing.
All's Well That Ends Well. Act II. Sc. 4

Let me have audience for a word or two.
As You Like It. Act V. Sc. 2

I profess not talking; Only this—
Let each man do his best.
Henry IV. Pt. I. Act V. Sc. 2

The red wine first must rise
In their cheeks: then we shall have them
Talk to us in silence.
Henry VIII. Act I. Sc. 4

If I chance to talk a little while, forgive me,
I had it from my father.
Henry VIII. Act I. Sc. 4

A man in all the world's new fashion planted.
That hath a mint of phrases in his brain.
Love's Labour's Lost. Act. I. Sc. 1

Pray thee, let it serve for table talk;
Then, howsoe'er thou speak'st, 'mong other things
I shall digest it.
Merchant of Venice. Act III. Sc. 5

One doth not know
How much an ill word way empoison liking.
Much Ado About Nothing. Act III. Sc. 1

My load shall never rest.
I'll watch him, tame and talk him out of patience;
His bed shall seem a school, his board a shrift.
Othello. Act III. Sc. 3

Talkers are no good doers; be assur'd,
We go to use our hands, and not our tongues.
Richard III. Act I. Sc. 3

A gentleman, nurse, that loves to hear himself talk; and will speak more in a minute, than he will stand to in a month.
Romeo and Juliet. Act II. Sc. 4

What a spendthrift is he of his tongue!
Tempest. Act II. Sc. 1

The heart hath treble wrong,
When it is barr'd the aidance of the tongue.
Venus and Adonis. Line 329

See also: GOSSIP, SPEECH, TONGUE.

TEACHER

When I am forgotten, as I shall be,
And sleep in dull cold marble,

.   .   .   .

Say, I taught thee.
Henry VIII. Act III. Sc. 2

We'll set thee to school to an ant, to teach thee there's no labouring in the winter.
King Lear. Act II. Sc. 4

Schoolmasters will I keep within my house,
Fit to instruct her youth. . . . To cunning men
I will be very kind; and liberal
To mine own children, in good bringing up.
Taming of the Shrew. Act I. Sc. 1

I do present you with a man of mine
Cunning in music and the mathematics,
To instruct her fully in those sciences.
Taming of the Shrew. Act II. Sc. 1

See also: EDUCATION, LEARNING, STUDENT.

TEARS

'Tis the best brine a maiden can season her praise in.
All's Well That Ends Well. Act I. Sc. 1

What's the matter,
That this distempered messenger of wet,
The many-colour'd Iris, rounds thine eye?
All's Well That Ends Well. Act I. Sc. 3

The tears live in an onion that should water this sorrow.
Antony and Cleopatra. Act. I. Sc. 2

The big round tears
Coursed one another down his innocent nose
In piteous chase
As You Like It. Act II. Sc. 1

I had not so much of man in me,
And all my mother came into mine eyes,
And gave me up to tears.
Henry V. Act IV. Sc. 6

Sad unhelpful tears; and with dimm'd eyes
Look after him, and cannot do him good.
Henry VI. Pt. II. Act III. Sc. 1

See, see, what showers arise,
Blown with the windy tempest of my heart.
Henry VI. Pt. III. Act II. Sc. 5

What I should say
My tears gainsay; for every word I speak,
Ye see, I drink the waters of mine eyes.
Henry VI. Pt. III. Act V. Sc. 4

I am about to weep; but, thinking that
We are a queen, (or long have dream'd so)
   certain
The daughter of a king, my drops of tears
I'll turn to sparks of fire.
Henry VIII. Act II. Sc. 4

I did not think to shed a tear
In all my miseries; but thou hast forc'd me
Out of my honest truth to play the woman.
Henry VIII. Act III. Sc. 2

He has strangled
His language in his tears.
Henry VIII. Act. V. Sc. 1

Thy heart is big; get thee apart and weep,
Passion, I see, is catching; for mine eyes,
Seeing those beads of sorrow stand in thine,
Begin to water.
Julius Caesar. Act III. Sc. 1

If you have tears, prepare to shed them now.
Julius Ceasar. Act. III. Sc. 2

Let not women's weapons, water-drops,
Stain my man's cheek!
King Lear. Act II. Sc. 4

No, I'll not weep:—
I have full cause of weeping; but this heart
Shall break into a hundred thousand flaws,
Or ere I'll weep.
King Lear. Act II. Sc. 4

There she shook
The holy water from her heavenly eyes,
And clamour moisten'd.
King Lear. Act IV. Sc. 3

Trust not those cunning waters of his eyes,
For villainy is not without such rheum;
And he, long traded in it, makes it seem
Like rivers of remorse and innocency.
King John. Act IV. Sc. 3

That instant, shut
My woeful self up in a mourning house,
Raining the tears of lamentation.
Love's Labour's Lost. Act V. Sc. 2

My plenteous joys,
Wanton in fulness, seek to hide themselves
In drops of sorrow.
Macbeth. Act I. Sc. 4

And he, a marble to her tears, is washed with
   them but relents not.
Measure for Measure. Act III. Sc. 1

LEONATO:
Did he break into tears?
MESSENGER:
In great measure.
LEONATO:
A kind overflow of kindness: There are no
faces truer than those that are so washed.
Much Ado About Nothing. Act I. Sc. 1

If that the earth could teem with woman's
   tears,
Each drop she falls would prove a crocodile.
Othello. Act IV. Sc. 1

One, whose subdu'd eyes,
Albeit unused to the melting mood,
Drop tears as fast as the Arabian trees
Their medicinal gum.
Othello. Act V. Sc. 2

Venus smiles not in a house of tears.
Romeo and Juliet. Act IV. Sc. 1

Those eyes of thine, from mine have drawn
   salt tears,
Sham'd their aspects with store of childish
   drops.
Richard III. Act I. Sc. 2

The liquid drops of tears that you have shed
Shall come again, transform'd to orient pearl;
Advantaging their loan, with interest
Of ten-times double gain of happiness.
Richard III. Act IV. Sc. 4

Then fresh tears
Stood on her cheeks, as doth the honey-dew
Upon a gather'd lily almost wither'd.
Titus Andronicus. Act III. Sc. 1

Eye-offending brine.
Twelfth Night. Act I. Sc. 1.

Why, man, if the river were dry, I am able
to fill it with my tears: if the wind were
down, I could drive the boat with my sighs.
Two Gentlemen of Verona. Act II. Sc. 3

I so lively acted with my tears,
That my poor mistress, moved therewithal,
Wept bitterly.
Two Gentlemen of Verona. Act IV. Sc. 4

Once a day I'll visit
The chapel where they lie; and tears, shed there,
Shall be my recreation. So long as Nature
Will bear up with this exercise,
So long I daily vow to use it.
Winter's Tale. Act III. Sc. 2

See also: GRIEF, SADNESS, SORROW.

TEMPER

The brain may devise laws for the blood; but a hot temper leaps o'er a cold decree; such a hare is madness, the youth, to skip o'er the meshes of good counsel, the cripple.
Merchant of Venice. Act I. Sc. 2

See also: ANGER, HATE, PASSION.

TEMPERANCE

Make less thy body, hence, and more thy grace;
Leave gormandizing.
Henry IV. Pt. II. Act V. Sc. 5.

Ask God for temperance, that's the appliance only
Which your disease requires.
Henry VIII. Act I. Sc. 1

See also: DRINK, EATING, MODERATION, WINE.

TEMPTATION

How quickly nature falls into revolt
When gold becomes her object.
Henry IV. Pt. II. Act IV. Sc. 4

Bell, book and candle, shall not drive me back,
When gold and silver becks me to come on.
King John. Act III. Sc. 3

How oft the sight of means to do ill deeds
Makes ill deed done!
King John. Act IV. Sc. 2

Devils soonest tempt, resumbling spirits of light.
Love's Labour's Lost. Act IV. Sc. 3

Most dangerous
Is that temptation, that doth goad us on
To sin in loving virtue.
Measure for Measure. Act II. Sc. 2

I am that way going to temptation,
Where prayers cross.
Measure for Measure. Act II. Sc. 2

To beguile many, and be beguil'd by one.
Othello. Act IV. Sc. 1

Know'st thou not any whom corrupting gold
Would tempt unto a close exploit of death?
Richard III. Act IV. Sc. 2

Sometimes we are devils to ourselves,
When we will tempt the frailty of our powers,
Presuming on their changeful potency.
Troilus and Cressida. Act IV. Sc. 4

See also: DEVIL, GUILT, HELL, SIN, VICE.

THANKFULNESS

Thou thought'st to help me; and such thanks I give
As one near death to those that wish him live.
All's Well That Ends Well. Act II. Sc. 1

To this great fairy I'll commend thy acts,
Make her thanks bless thee.
Antony and Cleopatra. Act IV. Sc. 8

Let never day nor night unhallow'd pass,
But still remember what the Lord hath done.
Henry VI. Pt. II. Act II. Sc. 1

See also: GIFT, GRATITUDE, INGRATITUDE.

THEATER

If it be true, that "good wine needs no bush,"
'tis true that a good play needs no epilogue.
As You Like It. Epilogue.

What's Hecuba to him, or he to Hecuba,
That he shall weep for her? What would he do,
Had he the motive and the cue for passion,
That I have? He would drown the stage with tears.
Hamlet. Act II. Sc. 2

The play's the thing.
Wherein I'll catch the conscience of the king.
Hamlet. Act II. Sc. 2

Is it not monstrous, that this player here,
But in a fiction, in a dream of passion,
Could force his soul so to his whole conceit,
That, from her working, all his visage wann'd.
Hamlet. Act II. Sc. 2

I have heard, that guilty creatures, sitting at a play,
Have by the very cunning of the scene
Been struck so to the soul, that presently
They have porcelain'd their malefactions.
Hamlet. Act II. Sc. 2

Come, sit down, every mother's son, and re-
hearse your parts.
Midsummer Night's Dream. Act III. Sc. 1

Is there no play,
To ease the anguish of a torturing hour?
Midsummer Night's Dream. Act V. Sc. 1

A play there is, my lord, some ten words
long.
Which is as brief as I have known a play;
But by ten words, my lord, it is too long,
Which makes it tedious.
Midsummer Night's Dream. Act V. Sc. 1

In a theatre, the eyes of men,
After a well grac'd actor leaves the stage,
Are idly bent on him that enters next,
Thinking his prattle to be tedious.
Richard II. Act V. Sc. 2

I can counterfeit the deep tragedian;
Speak, and look back, and pry on every side,
Tremble and start at wagging of a straw,
Intending deep suspicion.
Richard III. Act III. Sc. 5

A beggarly account of empty boxes.
Romeo and Juliet. Act V. Sc. 1

See also: ACTOR AND ACTRESS, OCCUPATION.

THIEF

A cut-purse of the empire and the rule;
That from a shelf the precious diadem stole,
And put it in his pocket.
Hamlet. Act III. Sc. 4

A plague upon't when thieves cannot be true
one to another.
Henry IV. Pt. I. Act II. Sc. 2

Let me tell you, Cassius, you yourself
Are much condemn'd to have an itching palm.
Julius Caesar. Act IV. Sc. 3

Thieves for their robbery have authority,
When judges steal themselves.
Measure for Measure. Act II. Sc. 2

The robb'd that smiles, steals something
from the thief:
He robs himself that spends a bootless grief.
Othello. Act I. Sc. 3

The sun's a thief, and with his great attrac-
tion
Robs the vast sea; the moon's an arrant thief,
And her pale fire she snatches from sun:

The sea's a thief, whose liquid surge resolves
The moon into salt tears; the earth's a thief,
That feeds and breeds by a composture stolen
From general excrement: each thing's a thief.
The laws, your curb and whip, in their rough
power
Have uncheck'd theft.
Timon of Athens. Act IV. Sc. 3

There's boundless theft in limited professions.
Timon of Athens. Act IV. Sc. 3

See also: CRIME, PRISON, PUNISHMENT, VICE.

THOUGHT

There is nothing either good or bad, but
thinking makes it so: to me it is a prison.
Hamlet. Act II. Sc. 2

The incessant care and labour of his mind
Hath wrought the mure, that should confine
it in,
So thin, that life looks through, and will
break out
Henry IV. Pt. II. Act IV. Sc. 4

Now behold,
In the quick forge and working-house of
thought,
How London doth pour out her citizens!
Henry V. Act V. Chorus

My thoughts are whirled like a potter's wheel.
Henry VI. Pt. I. Act I. Sc. 5

Why do you keep alone,
Of sorriest fancies your companions making?
Using those thoughts, which should indeed
have died
With them they think on? Things without
all remedy,
Should be without regard.
Macbeth. Act III. Sc. 2

A maiden hath no tongue but thought.
Merchant of Venice. Act III. Sc. 2

I pray thee, speak to me as to thy thinkings,
As thou dost ruminate; and give thy worst of
thoughts
The worst of words.
Othello. Act III. Sc. 3

See also: MEDITATION, MEMORY, MIND, REA-
SON, WISDOM.

THUNDER

To stand against the deep dread-bolted
 thunder,
In the most terrible and nimble stroke
Of quick, cross lightning.
    King Lear. Act IV. Sc. **7**

Are there no stones in heaven,
But what serve for the thunder?
    Othello. Act V. Sc. **2**

       The thunder,
That deep and dreadful organ-pipe, pro-
 nounc'd
The name of Prosper; it did bass my trespass.
    Tempest. Act III. Sc. **3**

See also: CLOUD, RAIN, SKY, STORM.

TIME

Let's take the instant, by the forward top;
For we are old, and on our quick'st decrees
The inaudible and noiseless foot of time,
Steals, ere we can effect them.
   All's Well That Ends Well. Act V. Sc. **3**

And, looking on it, with lack-lustre eye,
Says, very wisely, It is ten o'clock;
Thus we may see, quoth he, how the world
 wags.
    As You Like It. Act II. Sc. **7**

Time travels in divers paces with divers
people.
    As You Like It. Act III. Sc. **2**

Well, Time is the old justice that examines
all such offenders, and let Time try.
    As You Like It. Act IV. Sc. **1**

There's a time for all things.
    Comedy of Errors. Act II. Sc. **2**

The time is out of joint.
    Hamlet. Act I. Sc. **5**

Time, that takes survey of all the world,
Must have a stop.
    Henry IV. Pt. I. Act V. Sc. **4**

   See the minutes how they run
How many make the hour full complete,
How many hours bring about the day,
How many days will finish up the year,
How many years a mortal man may live.
   Henry VI. Pt. III. Act II. Sc. **5**

So many hours must I take my rest;
So many hours must I contemplate.
    Henry VI. Pt. III. Act II. Sc. **5**

   We trifle time away; I long
To have this young one made a Christian.
    Henry VIII. Act V. Sc. **2**

    How many ages hence,
Shall this our lofty scene be acted over,
In states unborn, and accents yet unknown?
    Julius Caesar. Act III. Sc. **1**

 The ides of March are come.
SOOTHSAYER:
Ay, Caesar; but not gone.
    Julius Caesar. Act III. Sc. **I**

Time shall unfold what plighted cunning
 hides;
Who covers faults at last with shame derides.
    King Lear. Act I. Sc. **1**

    Come, what come may,
Time and the hour runs through the roughest
 day.
    Macbeth. Act I. Sc. **3**

 'Gainst the tooth of time,
And razure of oblivion.
    Measure for Measure. Act V. Sc. **1**

 We should hold day with the Antipodes,
If you would walk in absence of the sun.
    Merchant of Venice. Act V. Sc. **1**

Time goes on crutches till love have all his
 rites.
   Much Ado About Nothing. Act II. Sc. **1**

    Time's the king of men;
He's both their parent, and he is their grave,
And gives them what he will, not what they
 crave.
    Pericles. Act II. Sc. **3**

Time's glory is to calm contending kings,
To unmask falsehood and bring truth **to**
 light,
To stamp the seal of time in aged things,
To wake the morn and sentinel the night,
To wrong the wronger till he render right,
 To ruinate proud buildings with thy hours,
 And smear with dust their glittering golden
  towers.
    Rape of Lucrece. Line **939**

O, call back yesterday, bid time return.
> *Richard II*. Act III. Sc. 2

Devouring Time, blunt thou the lion's paws,
And make the earth devour her own sweet
brood;
Pluck the keen teeth from the fierce tiger's
jaws,
And burn the long-lived phoenix in her
blood;
Make glad and sorry seasons, as thou fleet'st,
And do whate'er thou wilt, swift-footed Time,
To the wide world, and all her fading sweets;
But I forbid thee one most heinous crime;
O, carve not with thy hours my love's fair
brow,
Nor draw no lines there with thy antique
pen;
Him in thy course untainted do allow
For beauty's pattern to succeeding men.
Yet, do thy worst, old Time; despite thy
wrong,
My love shall in my verse ever live young.
> *Sonnet XIX*

Time doth transfix the flourish set on youth,
And delves the parallels in beauty's brow.
> *Sonnet LX*

When I have seen by Time's fell hand de-
faced
The rich-proud cost of outworn buried age;
When sometime lofty towers I see down-
razéd,
And brass eternal, slave to mortal rage;
When I have seen the hungry ocean gain
Advantage on the kingdom of the shore,
And the firm soil win of the watery main,
Increasing store with loss, and loss with
store;
When I have seen such interchange of state,
Or state itself confounded to decay;
Ruin hath taught me thus to ruminate,—
That Time will come and take my love away.
This thought is as a death, which cannot
choose
But weep to have that which it fears to lose.
> *Sonnet LXIV*

O, how shall summer's honey breath hold out
Against the wreckful siege of battering days,
When rocks impregnable are not so stout,
Nor gates of steel so strong, but Time decays?
O fearful meditation! where, alack,
Shall Time's best jewel from Time's chest lie
hid?
Or what strong hand can hold his swift foot
back?
Or who his spoil of beauty can forbid?
> *Sonnet LXV*

Time is like a fashionable host,
That slightly shakes his parting guest by the
hand;
And with his arms outstretch'd, as he would
fly,
Grasps-in the comer: Welcome ever smiles.
> *Troilus and Cressida*. Act III. Sc. 3

Time hath, my lord, a wallet at his back,
Wherein he puts alms for oblivion
A great-sized monster of ingratitudes;
Those scraps are good deeds past, which are
devour'd
As fast as they are made, forgot as soon
As they are done.
> *Troilus and Cressida*. Act III. Sc. 3

Beauty, wit,
High birth, vigour of bone, desert in service,
Love, friendship, charity, are subjects all
To envious and calumniating time.
> *Troilus and Cressida*. Act III. Sc. 3

The end crowns all,
And that old common arbitrator, Time,
Will one day end it.
> *Troilus and Cressida*. Act IV. Sc. 5

The whirligig of time brings in his revenges.
> *Twelfth Night*. Act V. Sc. 1

Time is the nurse and breeder of all good.
> *Two Gentlemen of Verona*. Act III. Sc. 1

The same I am, ere ancient order was,
Or what is now receiv'd. I witness to
The times that brought them in; so shall I do
To the freshest things now reigning, and
make stale
The glistering of this present.
> *Winter's Tale*. Act IV. Chorus

See also: FUTURE, PAST, TOMORROW.

TOAST

The cannons to the heavens, the heavens to
earth:
Now the king drinks to Hamlet.
> *Hamlet*. Act V. Sc. 2

See also: DRINK, FEASTING, WINE.

TOMORROW

To-morrow and to-morrow, and to-morrow,
Creeps in this petty pace from day to day,
To the last syllable of recorded time;
And all our yesterdays have lighted fools
The way to dusty death.
> *Macbeth*. Act V. Sc. 5

See also: FUTURE, PAST, TIME.

TONGUE

Tongues I'll hang on every tree,
That shall evil sayings show.
As You Like It. Act III. Sc. 2

My tongue, though not my heart, shall have
his will.
Comedy of Errors. Act IV. Sc. 2

On the tip of his subduing tongue
All kind of arguments and question deep,
All replication prompt and reason strong,
For his advantage still did wake and sleep;
To make the weeper laugh, the laugher weep,
He had the dialect and different skill,
Catching all passions in his craft of will.
Lover's Complaint. Line 122

My tongue's use is to me no more,
Than an unstringed viol, or a harp.
Richard II. Act I. Sc. 3

See also: GOSSIP, SPEECH, TALK.

TOOTHACHE

For there was never yet philosopher
That could endure the tooth-ach patiently.
Much Ado About Nothing. Act V. Sc. 1

See also: HEALTH, MEDICINE, SICKNESS.

TRANSPORTATION

Our chariot and our horsemen be in readiness.
Cymbeline. Act III. Sc. 5

Come, my coach! Good-night, ladies.
Hamlet. Act IV. Sc. 5

Many carriages he hath dispatched.
King John. Act V. Sc. 7

My coach, which stays for us
At the park gate.
Merchant of Venice. Act III. Sc. 4

See also: BOAT, SHIP, TRAVEL.

TRAVEL

When I was at home, I was in a better place;
but travelers must be content.
As You Like It. Act II. Sc. 4

Farewell, Monsieur traveller. Look you lisp
and wear strange suits; disable all the benefits
of your own country.
As You Like It. Act IV. Sc. 1

Travell'd gallants
That fill the court with quarrels, talk and
tailors.
Henry VIII. Act I. Sc. 3

I'll put a girdle round about the earth
In forty minutes.
Midsummer Night's Dream. Act II. Sc. 2

I spoke of most disastr'us chances;

Of being taken by the insolent foe
And sold to slavery; of my redemption
thence,
And portance. In my traveller's history,
Wherein of antres vast, and deserts idle,
(Rough quarries, rocks, and hills whose heads
touch heaven,
It was my hint to speak,) such was my process;—
And of the Cannibals that each other eat.
Othello. Act I. Sc. 3

See also: BOAT, SHIP, TRANSPORTATION.

TREASON

Thus do all traitors;
If their purgation did consist in words,
They are as innocent as grace itself.
As You Like It. Act I. Sc. 3

The man was noble,
But with his last attempt he wiped it out;
Destroy'd his country; and his name remains
To the ensuing age abhorr'd.
Coriolanus. Act V. Sc. 3

Though those that are betray'd
Do feel the treason sharply, yet the traitor
Stands in worse case of woe.
Cymbeline. Act III. Sc. 4

There's such divinity doth hedge a King,
That treason can but peep to what it would,
Acts little of his will.
Hamlet. Act IV. Sc. 5

I did pluck allegiance from men's hearts,
Loud shouts and salutations from their
mouths,
Even in the presence of the crowned king.
Henry IV. Pt. I. Act III. Sc. 2

Treason is but trusted like the fox;
Who, ne'er so tame, so cherish'd, and locked
up,
Will have a wild trick of his ancestors.
Henry IV. Part I. Act V. Sc. 2

Rebellion in this land shall lose his sway,
Meeting the check of such another day.
Henry IV. Part I. Act. V. Sc. 5

Some guard these traitors to the block of
death;
Treason's true bed, and yielder up of death.
Henry IV. Part II. Act IV. Sc. 2

Treason, and murder, ever kept together,
As two yoke-devils sworn to either's purpose,
Working so grossly in a natural cause,
That admiration did not whoop at them.
Henry V. Act II. Sc. 2

To say the truth, so Judas kiss'd his master;
And cried—all hail! whereas he meant—all
harm.
Henry VI. Pt. III. Act V. Sc. 7

Et tu Brute?—Then fall, Caesar.
Julius Caesar. Act III. Sc. 1

Know, my name is lost;
By treason's tooth bare gnawn, and canker-
bit.
King Lear. Act V. Sc. 3

Some of you, with Pilate, wash your hands,
Showing an outward pity; yet you Pilates
Have here deliver'd me to my sour cross,
And water cannot wash away your sin.
Richard II. Act IV. Sc. 1

Talk'st thou to me of ifs?—Thou art a traitor:
—Off with his head.
Richard III. Act III. Sc. 4

I am sorry I must never trust thee more,
But count the world a stranger for thy sake,
The private wound is deepest.
Two Gentlemen of Verona. Act V. Sc. 4

See also: CRIME, GOVERNMENT, PATRIOTISM,
    REBELLION, TYRANNY.

TREE

Hath not old custom made this life more
sweet
Than that of painted pomp? are not these
woods
More free from peril than the envious court?
As You Like It. Act II. Sc. 1

Under the greenwood tree
Who loves to lie with me,
And tune his merry note
Unto the sweet bird's throat,
Come hither, come hither, come hither:
Here shall he see no enemy,
But winter and rough weather.
As You Like It. Act II. Sc. 5

Gives not the hawthorn bush a sweeter shade
To shepherds, looking on their silly sheep,
Than doth a rich embroider'd canopy
To kings, that fear their subjects' treachery?
Henry VI. Pt. III. Act II. Sc. 5

Thus yields the cedar to the axe's edge,
Whose arms gave shelter to the princely
eagle.
Henry VI. Pt. III. Act V. Sc. 2

Slips of yew,
Silver'd in the moon's eclipse.
Macbeth. Act IV. Sc. 1

Will these moss'd trees,
That have out-liv'd the eagle, page thy heels,
And skip when thou point'st out?
Timon of Athens. Act IV. Sc. 3

I have a tree, which grows here in my close,
That mine own use invites me to cut down,
And shortly must I fell it.
Timon of Athens. Act V. Sc. 2

A barren, detested vale, you see, it is;
The trees, though summer, yet forlorn and
lean,
O'ercome with moss and baleful mistletoe.
Titus Andronicus. Act II. Sc. 3

See also: FLOWER, GARDEN, NATURE.

TRIAL

A grievous burden was thy birth to me;
Tetchy and wayward was thy infancy.
Richard III. Act IV. Sc. 4

See also: AFFLICTION, SORROW.

TRIFLES

Trifles, light as air.
Othello. Act III. Sc. 3

Come gentlemen, we sit too long on trifles,
And waste the time, which looks for other
revels.
Pericles. Act II. Sc. 3

A snapper up of unconsidered trifles.
>> *A Winter's Tale*. Act IV. Sc. 2

See also: DEED, LIFE.

TRUST

>> I will believe
Thou wilt not utter what thou dost not know;
And so far will I trust thee.
>> *Henry IV*. Pt. I. Act II. Sc. 3

My life upon her faith.
>> *Othello*. Act I. Sc. 3

To thee I do commend my watchful soul,
Ere I let fall the windows of mine eyes;
Sleeping, and waking, O, defend me still!
>> *Richard III*. Act V. Sc. 3

My man's as true as steel.
>> *Romeo and Juliet*. Act II. Sc. 4

See also: BELIEF, CONFIDENCE, FAITH, HOPE.

TRUTH

'Tis not the many oaths that make the truth;
But the plain single vow, that is vow'd true.
>> *All's Well That Ends Well*. Act IV. Sc. 2

That truth should be silent, I had almost forgot.
>> *Antony and Cleopatra*. Act II. Sc. 2

>> To thine own self be true;
And it must follow, as the night the day,
Thou canst not then be false to any man.
>> *Hamlet*. Act I. Sc. 3

If circumstances lead me, I will find
Where truth is hid, though it were hid indeed
Within the centre.
>> *Hamlet*. Act II. Sc. 2

Mark now, how plain a tale shall put you down.
>> *Henry IV*. Pt. I. Act II. Sc. 4

>> Tell truth, and shame the devil.
If thou have power to raise him, bring him hither.
And I'll be sworn, I have power to shame him hence.
O, while you live, tell truth: and shame the devil.
>> *Henry IV*. Pt. I. Act III. Sc. 1

What, can the devil speak true?
>> *Macbeth*. Act I. Sc. 3

>> But 'tis strange:
And oftentimes, to win us to our harm,
The instruments of darkness tell us truths;
Win us with honest trifles, to betray us
In deepest consequence.
>> *Macbeth*. Act I. Sc. 3

>> Truth is truth
To th' end of reckoning.
>> *Measure for Measure*. Act V. Sc 1

Truth makes all things plain.
>> *Midsummer Night's Dream*. Act V. Sc. 1

I cannot hide what I am: I must be sad when
I have a cause, and smile at no man's jests;
eat when I have stomach, and wait for no
man's leisure; sleep when I am drowsy, and
tend on no man's business; laugh when I am
merry, and claw no man in his humour.
>> *Much Ado About Nothing*. Act I. Sc. 3

They breathe truth, that breathe their words in pain.
>> *Richard II*. Act II. Sc. 1

Methinks, the truth should live from age to age,
As 'twere retail'd to all posterity,
Even to the general all-ending day.
>> *Richard III*. Act III. Sc. 1

See also: BELIEF, CONSTANCY, ERROR, FIDEL-
ITY, SINCERITY, THOUGHT, WISDOM.

TWILIGHT

The glow-worm shows the Matin to be near,
And 'gins to pale his uneffectual fire.
>> *Hamlet*. Act I. Sc. 5

The hour before the heavenly-harness'd team
Begins his golden progress in the east.
>> *Henry IV*. Pt. I. Act III. Sc. 1

The west yet glimmers with some streaks of day:
Now spurs the lated traveller apace,
To gain the timely inn.
>> *Macbeth*. Act III. Sc. 3

The weary sun hath made a golden set,
And, by the bright track of his fiery car
Gives token of a goodly day to-morrow.
>> *Richard III*. Act V. Sc. 3

Gilding pale streams with heavenly alchemy.
>> *Sonnet XXXIII*

See also: NIGHT, SKY, STAR, SUNSET.

TYRANNY

How can tyrants safely govern home,
Unless abroad they purchase great alliance?

Henry VI. Pt. III. Act III. Sc. 3

This tyrant whose sole name blisters our
 tongues,
Was once thought honest.

Macbeth. Act IV. Sc. 3

O nation miserable,

With an untitled tyrant bloody scepter'd,
When shalt thou see thy wholesome days
 again?

Macbeth. Act IV. Sc. 3

I grant him bloody,

Luxurious, avaricious, false, deceitful,
Sudden, malicious, smacking of every sin
That has a name.

Macbeth. Act IV. Sc. 3

Bleed, bleed, poor country!
Great tyranny, lay thou thy basis sure,
For goodness dares not check thee!

Macbeth. Act IV. Sc. 3

O, it is excellent

To have a giant's strength; but it is tyrannous
To use it like a giant.

Measure for Measure. Act II. Sc. 2

Sith 'twas my fault to give the people scope,
'Twould be my tyranny to strike and gall
 them
For what I bid them do.

Measure for Measure. Act IV. Sc. 1

I knew him tyrannous, and tyrants' fears
Decrease not, but grow faster than the years.

Pericles. Act I. Sc. 2

He hath no friends but what are friends for
 fear;
Which in his dearest need, will fly from him.

Richard III. Act V. Sc. 2

For what is he they follow? truly gentlemen,
A bloody tyrant, and a homicide;
One rais'd in blood, and one in blood estab-
 lish'd;
One that made means to come by what he
 hath,
And slaughter'd those that were the means to
 help him;
A base foul stone, made precious by the foil

Of England's chair, where he is falsely set;
One that hath ever been God's enemy.

Richard III. Act V. Sc. 3

See also: GOVERNMENT, POLITICS, REBELLION.

U

UNBELIEF

More strange than true. I never may believe
These antique fables, nor these fairy toys.

Midsummer Night's Dream. Act V. Sc. 1

See also: BELIEF, DOUBT.

UNDERTAKER

The houses that he makes last till doomsday.

Hamlet. Act V. Sc. 1

What is he, that builds stronger than either
the mason, the shipwright, or the carpenter?

Hamlet. Act V. Sc. 1

HAMLET:
Hath this fellow no feeling of his business,
that he sings at gravemaking?
HORATIO:
Custom hath made it in him a property of
easiness.

Hamlet. Act V. Sc. 1

See also: DEATH, GRAVE, OCCUPATION.

UNITY

So we grew together,

Like to a double cherry, seeming parted,
But yet a union in partition;
Two lovely berries moulded on one stem:
So, with two seeming bodies, but one heart;
Two of the first, like coats in heraldry,
Due but to one, and crowned with one crest.

Midsummer Night's Dream. Act III. Sc. 2

See also: FRIENDSHIP, MARRIAGE, ORDER.

UNKINDNESS

Rich gifts wax poor when givers prove unkind.

Hamlet. Act III. Sc. 1

She hath tied

Sharp-tooth'd unkindness, like a vulture here.

King Lear. Act II. Sc. 4

Unkindness may do much;
And his unkindness may defeat my life,
But never taint my love.
Othello. Act IV. Sc. 2

In nature there's no blemish but the mind;
None can be call'd deform'd, but the unkind.
Twelfth Night. Act III. Sc. 4

See also: CRUELTY, KINDNESS, NEGLECT.

V

VALENTINE'S DAY

To-morrow is Saint Valentine's day
   All in the morning betime,
And I a maid at your window,
   To be your Valentine.
Hamlet. Act IV. Sc. 5

            Saint Valentine is past;
Begin these wood-birds but to couple now?
Midsummer Night's Dream. Act IV. Sc. 1

See also: HOLIDAY.

VALOR

      When valour preys on reason,
It eats the sword it fights with.
Antony and Cleopatra. Act III. Sc. 2

         What's brave, what's noble,
Let's do it after the high Roman fashion,
And make death proud to take us.
Antony and Cleopatra. Act IV. Sc. 13

Methought, he bore him in the thickest troop
As doth a lion in a herd of neat:
Or as a bear, encompass'd round with dogs;
Who, having pinch'd a few, and make them
   cry,
The rest stand all aloof, and bark at him.
Henry VI. Pt. III. Act II. Sc. 1

Muster your wits: stand in your defence;
Or hide your heads like cowards, and fly
   hence.
Love's Labour's Lost. Act V. Sc. 2

He's truly valiant, that can wisely suffer
The worst that man can breathe; and make
   his wrongs
His outsides; wear them like his raiment,
   carelessly:

And ne'er prefer his injuries to his heart,
To bring it into danger.
Timon of Athens. Act III. Sc. 5

See also: BRAVERY, COURAGE, SOLDIER.

VANITY

Light vanity, insatiate cormorant,
Consuming means, soon preys upon itself.
Richard II. Act II. Sc. 1

Where doth the world thrust forth a vanity
That is not quickly buzz'd into his ears?
Richard II. Act II. Sc. 1

See also: CONCEIT, PRIDE, SELF-LOVE.

VARIETY

Age cannot wither her, nor custom stale
Her infinite variety.
Antony and Cleopatra. Act II. Sc. 2

See also: CHANGE, CHOICE, FASHION.

VEGETATION

If aught possess thee from me, it is dross,
Usurping ivy, briar, or idle moss;
Who, all for want of pruning, with intrusion
Infect thy sap, and live on thy confusion.
Comedy of Errors. Act II. Sc. 2

               I will go root away
The noisome weeds, that without profit suck
The soil's fertility from wholesome flowers.
Richard II. Act III. Sc. 4

How lush and lusty the grass looks! how
green!
Tempest. Act II. Sc. 1

A barren detested vale, you see it is;
The trees, though summer, yet forlorn and
   lean,
O'ercome with moss and baleful misseltoe.
Titus Andronicus. Act II. Sc. 3

See also: FLOWER, GARDEN, TREE.

VICE

            O, dishonest wretch!
Wilt thou be made a man out of my vice?
Measure for Measure. Act III. Sc. 1

There is no vice so simple, but assumes
Some mark of virtue on his outward parts.
Merchant of Venice. Act III. Sc. 2

Vice repeated is like the wand'ring wind,
Blows dust in others' eyes, to spread itself.
Pericles. Act I. Sc. 1

See also: CRIME, EVIL, GUILT, SIN.

VICTORY

With the losers let it sympathize;
For nothing can seem foul to those that win.
Henry IV. Pt. I. Act V. Sc. 1

I came, saw, and overcame.
Henry IV. Pt. II. Act IV. Sc. 3

To whom God will, there be the victory.
Henry VI. Pt. III. Act II. Sc. 5

Thus far our fortune keeps an upward course,
And we are grac'd with wreaths of victory.
Henry VI. Pt. III. Act V. Sc. 3

A victory is twice itself when the achiever
brings home full numbers.
Much Ado About Nothing. Act I. Sc. 1

See also: GLORY, SOLDIER, SUCCESS, WAR.

VILLAINY

O villainy!—How? Let the door be lock'd;
Treachery! seek it out.
Hamlet. Act V. Sc. 2

And thus I clothe my naked villainy
With odd old ends, stol'n forth of holy writ
And seem a saint when most I play the devil
Richard III. Act I. Sc. 3

Villain and he be many miles away.
Romeo and Juliet. Act III. Sc. 5

The learned pate
Ducks to the golden fool: All is oblique;
There's nothing level in our cursed natures,
But direct villainy.
Timon of Athens. Act IV. Sc. 3

See also: CRIME, EVIL, REBELLION.

VIOLET

Who are the violets now
That strew the green lap of the new-come
Spring.
Richard II. Act V. Sc. 2

The sweet south
That breathes upon a bank of violets,
Stealing, and giving odour.
Twelfth Night. Act I. Sc. 1

Violets dim,
But sweeter than the lids of Juno's eyes.
Winter's Tale. Act IV. Sc. 3

See also: FLOWER.

VIRTUE

To show virtue her own feature, scorn her
own image, and the very age and body of
the time, his form and presence.
Hamlet. Act III. Sc. 2

For in the fatness of these pursy times,
Virtue itself of vice must pardon beg.
Hamlet. Act III. Sc. 4

Assume a virtue, if you have it not.
That monster, custom, who all sense doth eat
Of habit's evil, is angel yet in this;
That to the use of actions fair and good
He likewise gives a frock, or livery,
That aptly is put on.
Hamlet. Act III. Sc. 4

Virtue is chok'd with foul ambition.
Henry VI. Pt. II. Act III. Sc. 1

If I am
Traduc'd by ignorant tongues, which neither
know
My faculties, nor person, yet will be
The chronicles of my doing!—let me say
'Tis but the fate of place, and the rough
brake
That virtue must go through.
Henry VIII. Act I. Sc. 2

My robe
And my integrity to heaven, is all
I dare now call mine own.
Henry VIII. Act III. Sc. 2

My heart laments that virture cannot live
Out of the teeth of emulation.
Julius Caesar. Act II. Sc. 3

According to his virture let us use him.
With all respect and rites of burial.
Within my tent his bones to-night shall lie,
Most like a soldier, order'd honourably.
Julius Caesar. Act V. Sc. 5

His virtues
Will plead like angels, trumpet-tongued,
against
The deep damnation of his taking-off.
Macbeth. Act I. Sc. 7

Thyself and thy belongings
Are not thine own so proper, as to waste
Thyself upon thy virtues, they on thee,
Heaven doth with us as we with lighted
    torches do,
Not light them, for themselves; for if our
    virtues
Did not go forth of us 'twere all alike
As if we had them not.
Measure for Measure. Act. I. Sc. 1

Never could the strumpet,
With all her double vigour, art, and nature
Once stir my temper; but this virtuous maid
Subdues me quite!—Ever till now,
When men were fond, I smil'd, and wonder'd,
    how.
Measure for Measure. Act II. Sc. 2

Most dangerous
Is that temptation, that doth goad us on
To sin in loving virtue.
Measure for Measure. Act II. Sc. 2

Virtue is bold, and goodness never fearful.
Measure for Measure. Act III. Sc. 1

Can virtue hide itself? Go to, mum, you are
he; graces will appear, and there's an end.
Much Ado About Nothing. Act II. Sc. 1

The trumpet of his own virtues.
Much Ado About Nothing. Act V. Sc. 2

I held it ever,
Virtue and cunning were endowments greater
Than nobleness and riches: carless heirs
May the two latter darken and expend;
But immortality attends the former,
Making a man a god.
Pericles. Act III. Sc. 2

Virtue itself turns vice, being misapplied;
And vice sometime's by action dignified.
Romeo and Juliet. Act II. Sc. 3

Virtue, that transgresses, is but patched with
sin; and sin that amends, is but patched with
virtue.
Twelfth Night. Act I. Sc. 3

See also: GOODNESS, INNOCENCE, TRUTH, WIS-
    DOM, WORTH.

VOICE

Her voice was ever soft,
Gentle, and low; an excellent thing in woman.
King Lear. Act V. Sc. 3

See also: LANGUAGE, ORATORY, SINGER, SONG,
    SPEECH, TALK, TONGUE, WORD.

W

WAR

War is no strife
To the dark house, and the detested wife.
All's Well That Ends Well. Act II. Sc. 3

All the god's go with you! Upon your sword
Sit laurel victory, and smooth success
Be strew'd before your feet!
Antony and Cleopatra. Act I. Sc. 3

Had we no other quarrel else to Rome, but
    that
Thou art thence banish'd, we would muster
    all
From twelve to seventy; and, pouring war
Into the bowels of ungrateful Rome,
Like a bold flood o'erbeat.
Coriolanus. Act IV. Sc. 5

Thou know'st, great son,
The end of war's uncertain.
Coriolanus. Act V. Sc. 3

The toil of the war,
A pain that only seems to seek out danger
I' the name of fame and honour; which dies
    i' the search.
Cymbeline. Act III. Sc. 3

All was lost,
But that the heavens fought.
Cymbeline. Act V. Sc. 3

Give me the cups;
And let the kettle to the trumpet speak,
The trumpet to the cannonier without,
The cannons to the heavens, the heavens to
    the earth.
Hamlet. Act V. Sc. 2

We must have bloody noses—and crack'd
    crowns,
And pass them current too.—Gods me, my
    horse!
Henry IV. Pt. I. Act II. Sc. 3

The fire-eyed maid of smoky war,
All hot and bleeding will we offer them.
Henry IV. Pt. I. Act IV. Sc. 1

Tut, tut; good enough to toss; food for powder, food for powder; they'll fill a pit as well as better.
Henry IV. Pt. I. Act IV. Sc. 2

The arms are fair
When the intent for bearing them is just.
Henry IV. Pt. I. Act V. Sc. 2

His valour shown upon our crests to-day,
Hath taught us how to cherish such high deeds,
Even in the bosom of our adversaries.
Henry IV. Pt. I. Act V. Sc. 5

Our battle is more full of names than yours;
Our men more perfect in the use of arms,
Our armour all as strong, our cause the best;
Then reason wills our hearts should be as good.
Henry IV. Pt. II. Act IV. Sc. 1

Let's march without the noise of threat'ning drum.
Henry IV. Pt. II. Act IV. Sc. 4

O my poor kingdom, sick with civil blows!
When that my care could not withhold thy riots,
What wilt thou do when riot is thy care?
Henry IV. Pt. II. Act IV. Sc. 4

It is most meet we arm us 'gainst the foe;
For peace itself should not so dull a kingdom,
 . . . .
But that defences, musters, preparations,
Should be maintain'd, assembled, and collected,
As were a war in expectation.
Henry V. Act II. Sc. 4

    The nimble gunner
With lynstock now the devilish cannon touches,
And down goes all before him.
Henry V. Act III. Chorus

In peace, there's nothing so becomes a man
As modest stillness, and humility:
But when the blast of war blows in our ears,
Then imitate the action of the tiger.
Stiffen the sinews, summon up the blood.
Henry V. Act III. Sc. 1

Once more unto the breach, dear friends, once more
Or close the wall up with our English dead.
Henry V. Act III. Sc. 1

The gates of mercy shall be all shut up;
And the flesh'd soldier, rough and hard of heart,
In liberty of bloody hand, shall range
With conscience wide as hell; mowing like grass
Your fresh-fair virgins and your flowering infants.
Henry V. Act III. Sc. 3

The armourers, accomplishing the knights,
With busy hammers, closing rivets up,
Give dreadful note of preparation.
Henry V. Act IV. Chorus

From camp to camp, through the foul womb of night,
The hum of either army stilly sounds.
Henry V. Act IV. Chorus

There are few die well that die in a battle.
Henry V. Act IV. Sc. 1

He which hath no stomach to this fight
Let him depart; his passport shall be made.
Henry V. Act IV. Sc. 3

Whilst my trump did sound, or drum struck up,
His sword did ne'er leave striking in the field.
Henry VI. Pt. I. Act I. Sc. 4

    O war! thou son of hell,
Whom angry heavens do make their minister,
Throw in the frozen bosoms of our part
Hot coals of vengeance!—Let no soldier fly:
He that is truly dedicate to war
Hath no self-love; nor he that loves himself
Hath not essentially, but by circumstance,
The name of valour.
Henry VI. Pt. II. Act V. Sc. 2

Shall we go throw away our coats of steel,
And wrap our bodies in black mourning gowns,
Numbering our Ave-Marias with our beads?
Or shall we on the helmets of our foes
Tell our devotion with revengeful arms?
Henry VI. Pt. III. Act II. Sc. 1

Sound trumpets!—let our bloody colours wave!—
And either victory, or else a grave.
Henry VI. Pt. III. Act II. Sc. 2

So underneath the belly of their steeds,
That stain'd their fetlocks in his smoking blood,
The noble gentleman gave up the ghost.
Henry VI. Pt. III. Act II. Sc. 3

They shall have wars and pay for their presumption.
> *Henry VI*. Pt. III. Act IV. Sc. 1

Caesar's spirit, ranging for revenge,
With Até by his side, come hot from hell,
Shall in these confines, with a monarch's
    voice,
Cry "Havock," and let slip the dogs of war.
> *Julius Caesar*. Act III. Sc. 1

Be thou as lightning in the eyes of France;
For ere thou canst report I will be there,
The thunder of my cannon shall be heard.
> *King John*. Act I. Sc. 1

The cannons have their bowels full of wrath,
And ready mounted are they, to spit forth
Their iron indignation 'gainst your walls.
> *King John*. Act II. Sc. 1

Now, for the bare-pick'd bone of majesty
Doth dogged war bristle his angry crest,
And snarleth in the gentle eyes of peace.
> *King John*. Act IV. Sc. 3

Your breath first kindled the dead coals of
    war
And brought in matter that should feed this
    fire;
And now 'tis far too huge to be blown out
With that same weak wind which enkindled
    it.
> *King John*. Act V. Sc. 2

I drew this gallant head of war,
And cull'd these fiery spirits from the world,
To outlook conquest, and to win renown
Even in the jaws of danger and of death.
> *King John*. Act V. Sc. 2

Blow, wind! come wrack!
At least we'll die with harness on our back.
> *Macbeth*. Act V. Sc. 5

Hang out our banners on the outward walls;
The cry is still, "They come."
> *Macbeth*. Act V. Sc. 5

Lay on, Macduff;
And damn'd be him that first cries, "Hold,
    enough."
> *Macbeth*. Act V. Sc. 7

O, farewell!
Farewell the neighing steed and the shrill
    trump,
The spirit-stirring drum, the ear-piercing fife,

The royal banner; and all quality,
Pride, pomp, and circumstance of glorious
    war!

.   .   .   .

Farewell! Othello's occupation's gone!
> *Othello*. Act III. Sc. 3

He is come to ope
The purple testament of bleeding war.
> *Richard II*. Act III. Sc. 3

The bay-trees in our country all are wither'd,
And meteors fright the fixed stars of heaven;
The pale-fac'd moon looks bloody on the
    earth,
And lean-look'd prophets whisper fearful
    change;
Rich men look sad, and ruffians dance and
    leap,—
The one, in fear to lose what they enjoy,
The other, to enjoy by rage and war.
> *Richard II*. Act II. Sc. 4

Grim-visag'd war hath smoothed his wrinkled
    front.
> *Richard III*. Act I. Sc. 1

Thus far into the bowels of the land
Have we march'd without impediment.
> *Richard III*. Act V. Sc. 2

Fight, gentlemen of England! fight boldly,
    yeomen!
Draw, archers, draw your arrows to the head!
Spur your proud horses hard, and ride in
    blood;
Amaze the welkin with your broken staves!
> *Richard III*. Act V. Sc. 3

Put in their hands thy bruising irons of wrath,
That they may crush down, with heavy fall
The usurping helmets of our adversaries.
> *Richard III*. Act V. Sc. 3

Such civil war is in my love and hate,
That I an accessary needs must be
To that sweet thief which sourly robs from
    me.
> *Sonnet XXXV*

The noon-tide sun, call'd forth the mutinous
    winds
And 'twixt the green sea and the azur'd vault
Set roaring war.
> *Tempest*. Act V. Sc. 1

Follow thy drum;
With man's blood paint the ground, gules,
gules;
Religious canons, civil laws, are cruel;
Then what should war be?
Timon of Athens. Act IV. Sc. 3

For I must talk of murders, rapes, and
massacres,
Acts of black night, abominable deeds,
Complots of mischief, treason, villainies
Ruthful to hear, yet piteously perform'd.
Titus Andronicus. Act V. Sc. 1

See also: DISSENSION, PEACE, SOLDIER.

WATER

Honest water, which ne'er left man i' the
mire.
Timon of Athens. Act I. Sc. 2

More water glideth by the mill
Than wots the miller of.
Titus Andronicus. Act II. Sc. 1

See also: CLOUD, OCEAN, RAIN, RIVER.

WEALTH

All gold and silver rather turn to dirt!
As 'tis no better reckon'd, but of those
Who worship dirty gods.
Cymbeline. Act III. Sc. 6

Well, whiles I am a beggar, I will rail,
And say,—there is no sin, but to be rich;
And being rich, my virtue then shall be,
To say,—there is no vice, but beggary.
King John. Act II. Sc. 2

If thou art rich, thou art poor;
For, like an ass whose back with ingots bows,
Thou bear'st thy heavy riches but a journey,
And death unloads thee.
Measure for Measure. Act III. Sc. 1

For they say, if money go before, all ways
do lie open.
Merry Wives of Windsor. Act II. Sc. 2

O, what a world of vile ill-favour'd faults
Looks handsome in three hundred pounds a
year!
Merry Wives of Windsor. Act III. Sc. 4

Why, give him gold enough and marry him
to a puppet, or an aglet-baby; or an old trot
with ne'er a tooth in her head, though she

have as many diseases as two-and-fifty-horses!
why, nothing comes amiss, so money comes
withal.
Taming of the Shrew. Act I. Sc. 2

See also: AVARICE, GOLD, MONEY.

WELCOME

Bid that welcome
Which comes to punish us, and we punish it,
Seeming to bear it lightly.
Antony and Cleopatra. Act IV. Sc. 12

Bid him welcome; This is the motley-minded
gentleman.
As You Like It. Act V. Sc. 4

A table-full of welcome makes scarce one
dainty dish.
Comedy of Errors. Act III. Sc. 1

I hold your dainties cheap, sir, and your welcome dear.
Comedy of Errors. Act III. Sc. 1

Small cheer, and great welcome, makes a
merry feast.
Comedy of Errors. Act III. Sc. 1

A hundred thousand welcomes: I could weep,
And I could laugh; I am light and heavy:
Welcome.
Coriolanus. Act II. Sc. 1

Sir, you are very welcome to our house:
It must appear in other ways than words,
Therefore, I scant this breathing courtesy.
Merchant of Venice. Act V. Sc. 1

Trust me, sweet,
Out of this silence, yet, I pick'd a welcome.
Midsummer Night's Dream. Act V. Sc. 1

Welcome ever smiles,
And farewell goes out sighing.
Trolius and Cressida. Act III. Sc. 3

His worth is warrant for his welcome.
Two Gentlemen of Verona. Act II. Sc. 4

I reckon this always,—that a man is never
undone till he be hanged; nor never welcome
to a place till some certain shot be paid and,
the hostess say, welcome.
Two Gentlemen of Verona. Act II. Sc. 5

See also: GUEST, HOSPITALITY, KINDNESS.

WIFE

As for my wife,
I would you had her spirit in such another;
The third o' the world is yours; which, with
a snaffle
You may pace easy, but not such a wife.
Antony and Cleopatra. Act II. Sc. 2

I will attend my husband, be his nurse,
Diet his sickness, for it is my office,
And will have no attorney but myself;
And therefore let me have him home with me.
Comedy of Errors. Act V. Sc. 1

You are my true and honourable wife;
As dear to me as are the ruddy drops
That visit my sad heart.
Julius Caesar. Act II. Sc. 1

Happy in this, she is not yet so old
But she may learn; happier than this,
She is not bred so dull but she can learn;
Happiest of all, is, that her gentle spirit
Commits itself to yours to be directed.
Merchant of Venice. Act III. Sc. 2

A light wife doth make a heavy husband.
Merchant of Venice. Act V. Sc. 1

I will be master of what is mine own;
She is my goods, my chattels; she is my house,
My household stuff, my field, my barn,
My horse, my ox, my ass, my anything;
And here she stands, touch her whoever dare.
Taming of the Shrew. Act III. Sc. 2

Why, man, she is mine own;
And I as rich in having such a jewel,
As twenty seas, if all their sands were pearl,
The water nectar, and the rocks pure gold.
Two Gentlemen of Verona. Act II. Sc. 4

Should all despair
That have revolted wives, the tenth of man-
kind
Would hang themselves.
Winter's Tale. Act I. Sc. 2

See also: CHILDREN, HOME, HUSBAND, LOVE,
MARRIAGE, MOTHER, WOMEN.

WILL

Will is deaf, and hears no needful friends.
Lucrece. Line 495

My will enkindled by mine eyes and ears,
Two traded pilots 'twixt the dangerous shores
Of will and judgment.
Troilus and Cressida. Act II. Sc. 2

That what he will, he does; and does so much,
That proof is call'd impossibility.
Troilus and Cressida. Act V. Sc. 5

See also: DECISION, DEED, RESOLUTION.

WIND

Blow, blow, thou winter wind!
Thou art not so unkind
As man's ingratitude;
Thy tooth is not so keen,
Because thou art not seen,
Although thy breath be rude.
As You Like It. Act II. Sc. 7

The southern wind
Doth play the trumpet to his purposes;
And, by his hollow whistling in the leaves,
Foretells a tempest and a blustering day.
Henry IV. Pt. I. Act V. Sc. 1

FALSTAFF:
What wind blew you hither, Pistol?
PISTOL:
Not the ill wind which blows no man to good.
Henry IV. Pt. II. Act V. Sc. 3

Now sits the wind fair, and we will aboard.
Henry V. Act II. Sc. 2

Ill blows the wind that profits nobody.
Henry VI. Pt. III. Act II. Sc. 5

The sweet wind did gently kiss the trees,
And they did make no noise.
Merchant of Venice. Act V. Sc. 1

Is't possible? Sits the wind in that corner?
Much Ado About Nothing. Act II. Sc. 3

A fuller blast ne'er shook our battlements:
If it hath ruffian'd so upon the sea,
What ribs of oak, when mountains melt on
them
Can hold the mortise?
Othello. Act II. Sc. 1

The wind, who woos
Even now the frozen bosom of the north.
And, being anger'd, puffs away from thence,
Turning his face to the dew-dropping south.
Romeo and Juliet. Act I. Sc. 4

See also: STORM, ZEPHYR.

WINE

Give me a bowl of wine—
In this I bury all unkindness.
Julius Caesar. Act IV. Sc. 3

Come, come; good wine is a good familiar
creature, if it be well used; exclaim no more
against it.

Othello. Act II. Sc. 3

O thou invisible spirit of wine! If thou hast
no name to be known by, let us call thee devil.

Othello. Act II. Sc. 3

Give me a bowl of wine:
I have not that alacrity of spirit,
Nor cheer of mind, that I was wont to have.

Richard III. Act V. Sc. 3

He calls for wine:—A health, quoth he, as if
He'd been aboard, carousing to his mates
After a storm.

Taming of the Shrew. Act III. Sc. 2

See also: DRINK, TEMPERANCE, TOAST.

WINTER: *see* SEASON.

WISDOM

Full oft we see
Cold wisdom waiting on superfluous folly.

All's Well That Ends Well. Act I. Sc. 1

Wisdom and fortune combating together,
If that the former dare but what it can,
No chance may shake it.

Antony and Cleopatra. Act III. Sc. 11

Wise men ne'er sit and bewail their loss,
But cheerly seek how to redress their harms.

Henry VI. Pt. III. Act V. Sc. 4

Thou shouldst not have been old till thou
hadst been wise.

King Lear. Act I. Sc. 5

To that dauntless temper of his mind,
He hath a wisdom that doth guide his valour
To act in safety.

Macbeth. Act III. Sc. 1

You are wise,
Or else you love not; For to be wise and love,
Exceeds man's might.

Troilus and Cressida. Act III. Sc. 2

Well, God give them wisdom that have it;
and those that are fools, let them use their
talents.

Twelfth Night. Act I. Sc. 5

See also: KNOWLEDGE, LEARNING, TRUTH.

WIT

Make the doors upon a woman's wit, and it
will out at the casement; shut that, and twill
out at the key-hole; stop that, 'twill fly with
the smoke out at the chimney.

As You Like It. Act IV. Sc. 1

They have a plentiful lack of wit.

Hamlet. Act II. Sc. 2

Since brevity is the soul of wit,
And tediousness the limbs and outward
flourishes,
I will be brief.

Hamlet. Act II. Sc. 2

I am not only witty in myself, but the cause
that wit is in other men.

Henry IV. Pt. II. Act I. Sc. 2

His eye begets occasion for his wit;
For every object that the one doth catch,
The other turns to a mirth-moving jest.

Love's Labour's Lost. Act II. Sc. 1

Great men may jest with saints; 'tis wit in
them;
But, in the less, foul profanation.

Measure for Measure. Act II. Sc. 2

He doth, indeed, show some sparks that are
like wit.

Much Ado About Nothing. Act II. Sc. 3

A good old man, sir; he will be talking; as
they say, When the age is in, the wit is out.

Much Ado About Nothing. Act III. Sc. 5

Sir, your wit ambles well; it goes easily.

Much Ado About Nothing. Act V. Sc. 1

Thy wit is as quick as the greyhound's mouth
—it catches.

Much Ado About Nothing. Act V. Sc. 2

Look, he's winding up the watch of his wit;
By and by it will strike.

Tempest. Act II. Sc. 1

Upon her wit doth earthly honour wait,
And virtue stoops and trembles at her frown.

Titus Andronicus. Act II. Sc. 1

Those wits that think they have thee, do
very oft prove fools; and I, that am sure I
lack thee, may pass for a wise man: for what
says Quinapalus? Better a witty fool, than a
foolish wit.

Twelfth Night. Act I. Sc. 5

See also: EPITAPH, HUMOR, SATIRE.

WOMAN

Age cannot wither her, nor custom stale
Her infinite variety.
Antony and Cleopatra. Act III. Sc. 6

Long ere she did appear: the trees by the
way
Should have borne men; and expectation
fainted.
Antony and Cleopatra. Act III. Sc. 6

If ladies be but young, and fair,
They have the gift to know it.
As You Like It. Act II. Sc. 7

Run, run, Orlando: carve on every tree
The fair, the chaste, and unexpressive she.
As You Like It. Act III. Sc. 2

O most delicate fiend!
Who is't can read a woman?
Cymbeline. Act V. Sc. 5

Frailty, thy name is Woman!—
A little month: or ere those shoes were old,
With which she follow'd my poor father's
body
Like Niobe, all tears; why she even she . . .
married with my uncle.
Hamlet. Act I. Sc. 2

One that was a woman, sir; but, rest her
soul, she's dead.
Hamlet. Act V. Sc. 1

She's beautiful; and therefore to be woo'd:
She is a woman; therefore to be won.
Henry IV. Pt. I. Act V. Sc. 3

'Tis beauty that doth oft make women proud;
    .   .   .
'Tis virtue that doth make them most admir'd;
    .   .   .
'Tis government that makes them seem divine.
Henry VI. Pt. III. Act I. Sc. 4

Her sighs will make a battery in his breast;
Her tears will pierce into a marble heart;
The tiger will be mild, while she doth mourn;
And Nero will be tainted with remorse,
To hear, and see, her plaints.
Henry VI. Pt. III. Act III. Sc. 1

Two women plac'd together makes cold
weather.
Henry VIII. Act I. Sc. 4

I grant, I am a woman; but, withal,
A woman that lord Brutus took to wife:
I grant, I am a woman; but, withal,
A woman well-reputed Cato's daughter.
Julius Caesar. Act II. Sc. 1

        Ah me! how weak a thing
The heart of woman is!
Julius Caesar. Act II. Sc. 4

There was never yet fair woman but she
made mouths in a glass.
King Lear. Act III. Sc. 2

A child of our grandmother Eve, a female;
or, for thy more sweet understanding, a
woman.
Love's Labour's Lost. Act I. Sc. 1

Fair ladies, mask'd, are roses in their bud:
Dismask'd, their damask sweet commixture
shown,
Are angels vailing clouds, or roses blown.
Love's Labour's Lost. Act V. Sc. 2

ANGELO:
Nay, women are frail too.
ISABELLA:
Ay, as the glasses where they view themsel-
ves:
Which are as easy broke as they make forms.
Measure for Measure. Act II. Sc. 4

She speaks poignards, and every word stabs:
if her breath were as terrible as her termina-
tions, there were no living near her; she
would infect the north star.
Much Ado About Nothing. Act II. Sc. 1

Would it not grieve a woman to be over-
master'd with a piece of valiant dust? to
make an account of her life to a clod of wayward marl?
Much Ado About Nothing. Act II. Sc. 1

          I never yet saw man,
    .   .   .   .
But she would spell him backward; if fair-
fac'd
She would swear the gentleman should be
her sister;
If black, why nature, drawing of an antic,
Made a foul blot.
Much Ado About Nothing. Act III. Sc. 1

One woman is fair; yet I am well: another is
wise; yet I am well: another virtuous; yet I
am well: But till all graces be in one woman,
one woman shall not come in my grace.
Much Ado About Nothing. Act III. Sc. 3

A maid
That paragons description, and wild fame;
One that excels the quirks of blazoning pens,
And in the essential vesture of creation,
Does bear all excellency.
Othello. Act II. Sc. 1

You are pictures out of doors;
Bells in your parlours; wild-cats in your kitchens;
Saints in your injuries; devils being offended;
Players in your housewifery, and housewives in your beds.
Othello. Act. II. Sc. 1

Have you not heard it said full oft,
A woman's nay doth stand for naught?
Passionate Pilgrim. Pt. XIX

Have I not in a pitched battle heard
Loud 'larums, neighing steeds, and trumpets clang?
And do you tell me of a woman's tongue?
Taming of the Shrew. Act I. Sc. 2

Why, then thou canst not break her to the lute?
Why, no; for she hath brake the lute to me.
Taming of the Shrew. Act II. Sc. 1

Say, that she rail, why, then I'll tell her plain
She sings as sweetly as a nightingale;
Say, that she frown; I'll say, she looks as clear
As morning roses newly wash'd with dew;
Say, she be mute, and will not speak a word;
Then I'll commend her volubility,
And say she uttereth piercing eloquence.
Taming of the Shrew. Act II. Sc. 1

Why are our bodies soft, and weak, and smooth,
Unapt to toil, and trouble in the world,
But that our soft conditions, and our hearts,
Should well agree with our external parts?
Taming of the Shrew. Act V. Sc. 2

A woman mov'd is like a fountain troubled,
Muddy, ill-seeming, thick, bereft of beauty.
Taming of the Shrew. Act V. Sc. 2

I am asham'd, that women are so simple
To offer war, where they should kneel for peace;
Or seek for rule, supremacy and sway,
When they are bound to serve, love, and obey.
Taming of the Shrew. Act V. Sc. 2

She is a pearl
Whose price has launch'd above a thousand ships,
And turn'd crown'd kings to merchants.
Troilus and Cressida. Act II. Sc. 2

A woman impudent and mannish grown
Is not more loath'd than an effeminate man.
Trolius and Cressida. Act III. Sc. 3

Fie, fie upon her!
There's language in her eye, her cheek, her lip,
Nay, her foot speaks; her wanton spirits look out
At every joint and motion of her body.
Troilus and Cressida. Act IV. Sc. 5

Then let thy love be younger than thy self,
Or thy affection cannot hold the bent:
For women are as roses, whose fair flower,
Being once display'd, doth fall that very hour.
Twelfth Night. Act II. Sc. 4

Muse not that I thus suddenly proceed;
For what I will, I will, and there an end.
Two Gentlemen of Verona. Act I. Sc. 3

Never give her o'er;
For scorn at first, makes after-love the more.
If she do frown, 'tis not in hate of you,
But rather to beget more love in you;
If she do chide, 'tis not to have you gone,
For why, the fools are mad if left alone.
Two Gentlemen of Verona. Act III. Sc. 1

To be slow in words is a woman's only virtue.
Two Gentlemen of Verona. Act III. Sc. 1

If, one by one, you wedded all the world,
Or, from the all that are took something good,
To make a perfect woman, she, you kill'd,
Would be unparallel'd.
Winter's Tale. Act V. Sc. 1

Women will love her, that she is a woman,
More worth than any man; men, that she is
The rarest of all women.
Winter's Tale. Act V. Sc. 1

See also: BEAUTY, HUSBAND, KISS, LOVE, MATRI-
MONY, MOTHER, WIFE, WOOING.

WOOING

A heaven on earth I have won, by wooing thee.
All's Well That Ends Well. Act. IV. Sc. 2

Never will I trust to speeches penn'd,
Nor to the motion of a school-boy's tongue;

. . . .

Nor woo in rhyme, like a blind harper's song.
Love's Labour's Lost. Act V. Sc. 2

Be merry; and employ your chiefest thoughts
To courtship, and such fair ostents of love
As shall conveniently become you there.
Merchant of Venice. Act II. Sc. 8

Thou hast by moonlight by her window sung,
With feigning voice, verses of feigning love;
And stol'n the impression of fantasy
With bracelets of thy hair, rings, gawds,
conceits,
Knacks, trifles, nosegays, sweetmeats; mes-
sengers
Of strong prevailment in unharden'd youth.
Midsummer Night's Dream. Act I. Sc. 1

We cannot fight for love, as men may do;
We should be woo'd, and were not made to
woo.
Midsummer Night's Dream. Act II. Sc. 2

The pleasantest angling is to see the fish
Cut with her golden oars the silver stream
And greedily devour the treacherous bait;
So angle we for Beatrice.
Much Ado About Nothing. Act III. Sc. 1

I was not born under a rhyming planet, nor
I cannot woo in festival terms.
Much Ado About Nothing. Act V. Sc. 2

She wish'd she had not heard it; yet she
wish'd
That heaven had made her such a man: She
thank'd me;
And bade me, if I had a friend that lov'd her,
I should but teach him how to tell my story,
And that would woo her.
Othello. Act I. Sc. 3

Was ever woman in this humour woo'd?
Was ever woman in this humour won?
Richard III. Act I. Sc. 2

O, gentle Romeo,
If thou dost love, pronounce it faithfully:
Or if thou think'st I am too quickly won,
I'll frown, and be perverse, and say thee nay,
So thou wilt woo; but, else, not for the world.
Romeo and Juliet. Act II. Sc. 2

Women are angels, wooing:
Things won are done, joy's soul lies in the
doing:
That she belov'd knows nought, that knows
not this,—
Men prize the thing ungain'd more than it is.
Troilus and Cressida. Act I. Sc. 2

But, though I lov'd you well, I woo'd you
not:
And yet, good faith, I wish'd myself a man;
Or that we women had men's privilege
Of speaking first.
Troilus and Cressida. Act III. Sc. 2

Take no repulse, whatever she doth say:
For "get you gone," she doth not mean
"away."
Two Gentlemen of Verona. Act III. Sc. 1

That man that hath a tongue, I say is no
man,
If with his tongue he cannot win a woman.
Two Gentlemen of Verona. Act III. Sc. 1

Win her with gifts, if she respect not words;
Dumb jewels often, in their silent kind,
More quick than words, do move a woman's
mind.
Two Gentlemen of Verona. Act III. Sc. 1

See also: LOVE, MARRIAGE, WIFE, WOMAN.

WORD

Ill deeds are doubled with an evil word.
Comedy of Errors. Act III. Sc. 2

Unpack my heart with words,
And fall a cursing, like a very drab.
Hamlet. Act II. Sc. 2

POLONIUS:
What do you read, my Lord?
HAMLET:
Words, words, words!
Hamlet. Act II. Sc. 2

My words fly up, my thoughts remain below:
Words without thoughts, never to heaven go.
Hamlet. Act III. Sc. 3

Familiar in his mouth as household words.
Henry V. Act IV. Sc. 3

'Tis well said again;
And 'tis a kind of good deed, to say well:
And yet words are no deeds.
Henry VIII. Act III. Sc. 2

Good words are better than bad strokes.
Julius Caesar. Act V. Sc. 1

Zounds! I was never so bethump'd with words;
Since I first call'd my brother's father, dad.
King John. Act II. Sc. 2

He draweth out the thread of his verbosity finer than the staple of his argument.
Love's Labour's Lost. Act V. Sc. 1

Madam, you have bereft me of all words,
Only my blood speaks to you in my veins.
Merchant of Venice. Act III. Sc. 2

But words are words; I never yet did hear
That the bruis'd heart was pierced through the ear.
Othello. Act I. Sc. 3

I know thou'rt full of love and honesty,
And weigh'st thy words before thou giv'st them breath.
Othello. Act III. Sc. 3

How long a time lies in one little word?
Four lagging winters, and four wanton springs,
End in a word: Such is the breath of kings.
Richard II. Act I. Sc. 3

The tongues of dying men
Enforce attention, like deep harmony:
Where words are scarce, they are seldom spent in vain;
For they breathe truth, that breathe their words in pain.
Richard II. Act II. Sc. 1

These words are razors to my wounded heart.
Titus Andronicus. Act I. Sc. 2

Words, words, mere words, no matter from the heart.
Troilus and Cressida. Act V. Sc. 3

Words are grown so false, I am loath to prove reason with them.
Twelfth Night. Act III. Sc. 1

A fine volley of words, gentlemen, and quickly shot off.
Two Gentlemen of Verona. Act II. Sc. 4

See also: GOSSIP, SPEECH, TALK, TONGUE.

WORK

Why, Hal, 'tis my vocation, Hal: 'tis no sin for a man to labour in his vocation.
Henry IV. Pt. I. Act I. Sc. 2

Why, universal plodding prisons up
The nimble spirits in the arteries;
As motion, and long-during action, tires
The sinewy vigour of the traveller.
Love's Labour's Lost. Act IV. Sc. 3

Excellently done, if God did all.
Twelfth Night. Act I. Sc. 5

See also: ACTION, LABOR, OCCUPATION.

WORLD

This wide and universal theatre
Presents more woeful pageants than the scene
Wherein we play in.
As You Like It. Act II. Sc. 7

How weary, stale, flat, and unprofitable
Seems to me all the uses of this world.
Hamlet. Act I. Sc. 2

This earth, that bears thee dead,
Bears not alive so stout a gentleman.
Henry IV. Pt. I. Act V. Sc. 4

World, world, O world!
But that thy strange mutations makes us hate thee,
Life would not yield to age.
King Lear. Act IV. Sc. 1

The earth hath bubbles, as the water has,
And these are of them.
Macbeth. Act I. Sc. 3

Why, then the world's mine oyster,
Which I with sword will open.
Merry Wives of Windsor. Act II. Sc. 2

The world is grown so bad
That wrens may prey where eagles dare not perch.
Richard III. Act I. Sc. 3

See also: GOD, NATURE, SOCIETY.

WORSHIP

Stoop, boys: this gate
Instructs you how to adore the heavens; and bows you
To morning's holy office: The gates of monarchs
Are arch'd so high, that giants may get through

And keep their impious turbans on, without
Good morrow to the sun.
Cymbeline. Act III. Sc. 3

Get a prayer-book in your hand,
And stand between two churchmen.
Richard III. Act III. Sc. 7

See also: PRAYER, PREACHING, RELIGION.

WORTH

O, how thy worth with manners may I sing'
When thou art all the better part of me?
What can mine own praise to mine own self
bring?
And what is 't but mine own when I praise
thee?
Sonnet XXXIX

What's aught but as 'tis valued?
Troilus and Cressida. Act II. Sc. 2

See also: JUDGMENT, MERIT, SUCCESS.

WOUND

Show you sweet Caesar's wounds, poor, poor,
dumb mouths,
And bid them speak for me.
Julius Caesar. Act III. Sc. 2

What wound did ever heal, but by degrees?
Othello. Act II. Sc. 3

He in peace is wounded, not in war.
The Rape of Lucrece. Line 831

Mine honour be the knife's that makes my
wound.
The Rape of Lucrece. Line 1201

Her contrite sighs unto the clouds be-
queathed
Her winged spright, and through her wounds
doth fly,
Life's lasting date from cancell'd destiny.
The Rape of Lucrece. Line 1727

He jests at scars, that never felt a wound.
Romeo and Juliet. Act II. Sc. 2

The wound of peace is surety,
Surety secure.
Troilus and Cressida. Act II. Sc. 2

The private wound is deepest: O time most
accurs'd!
'Mongst all foes, that a friend should be the
worst.
Two Gentlemen of Verona. Act V. Sc. 4

See also: AFFLICTION, CRUELTY, SOLDIER, WAR.

Y

YOUTH

He wears the roses of youth upon him.
Antony and Cleopatra. Act III. Sc. 2

The spirit of youth,
That means to be of note, begins betimes.
Antony and Cleopatra. Act IV. Sc. 4

Crabbed age and youth cannot live together,
Youth is full of pleasance, age is full of care;
Youth like summer morn, age like winter
weather,
Youth like summer brave, age like winter
bare.
Youth is full of sport, age's breath is short,
Youth is nimble, age is lame;
Youth is hot and bold, age is weak and cold.
Youth is wild and age is tame.
Age, I do abhor thee, youth, I do adore thee.
The Passionate Pilgrim. St. 12

So wise, so young, they say, do ne'er live
long.
Richard III. Act III. Sc. 1

Behold, my lords,
Although the print be little, the whole matter
And copy of the father: eye, nose, lip,
The trick of his frown, his forehead; nay,
the valley,
The pretty dimples of his chin and cheek;
his smiles;
The very mould and frame of hand, nail,
finger.
Winter's Tale. Act II. Sc. 3

See also: AGE, OLD; CHILDREN; HOPE.

Z

ZEPHYR

They are as gentle
As zephyrs, blowing below the violet.
Cymbeline. Act IV. Sc. 2

See also: NATURE, STORM, WIND.

Source Indexes

Author Index

A

384, 397, 414, 434, 462, 500, 525, 543, 555, 559, 622, 699, 710, 739, 780

Armour, Jonathan Ogden (1863–1927), American industrialist; son of founder of Armour & Company, meat packers, 1

Armour, Thomas D. (*nickname:* Tommy) (1898–1968), American golfer and author, born in Scotland, 330

Armstrong, (Grace) April Oursler (1926–), American author, 277

Armstrong, John (1709–1779), Scottish physician and poet, 700

Arnold, Sir Edwin (1832–1904), English poet and journalist, 501, 557

Arnold, Matthew (1822–1888), English poet and critic, 3, 5, 19, 156, 181, 186, 218, 225, 253, 300, 303, 305, 315, 326, 383, 554, 555, 560, 590, 613, 655, 659, 678, 688, 699

Arnold, Thomas (1795–1842), English educator; father of Matthew Arnold, 21, 131, 399, 727

Arnold, Thurman Wesley (1891–), American lawyer, 146

Arnot, William (1808–1875), Scottish Presbyterian clergyman, 229, 717, 732

Arnott, Neil (1788–1874), Scottish physician, 157

Aron, Raymond (1905–), French educator, historian and journalist, 533

Arouet, François Marie. *See* **Voltaire.**

Arrom, Cecilia Francisca Josefa de. *See* **Caballero, Fernán.**

Arrowsmith, William (1924–), American author and editor, 240

Ascham, Roger (1515–1568), English writer and scholar, 270

Ascoli, Max (1898–), American author and editor, born in Italy; naturalized (1939), 139, 305, 350, 391, 564

Ashbrook, John Milan (1928–), American politician, 174

Ashmore, Harry Scott (1916–), American author, journalist and editor, 428

Astor, Viscountess Nancy Langhorne, (1879–1964), first woman member of British Parliament, born in the United States, 516

Athanasius, Saint (*called:* Athanasius the Great)

(293?–373), Greek father of the Church, 734

Atkinson, Brooks (*given names:* Justin Brooks) (1894–), American critic, 50

Atkinson, Edward (1827–1905), American textile manufacturer and writer, 633

Atlee, Clement Richard, 1st Earl (1883–1967), English politician; prime minister (1945–1951), 678

Atterbury, Francis (1662–1732), English Anglican bishop, 78

Attwood, William (1919–), American author, journalist and diplomat, 179

Auchincloss, Louis (1917–), American author, 515

Auden, Wystan Hugh (1907–), English poet, 240, 331, 335, 441, 462, 488, 498, 560

Auerbach, Berthold (1812–1882), German novelist and story writer, 286, 504, 655, 733

Auerbach, Jacob (1810–1887), German Jewish biblical scholar and editor, 412

Aughey, John Hill (1828–1911), American Presbyterian clergyman and educator, 378

Augustine, Saint (*Latin name:* Aurelius Augustinus) (354–430), church father and philospher; bishop of Hippo, 2, 85, 87, 157, 159, 231, 265, 273, 277, 285, 315, 348, 350, 370, 451, 470, 482, 552, 595, 622, 623, 702, 729, 730, 754, 770

Aurel. *See* **Mortier, Aurélie de Faucamberge.**

Aurelius, Marcus. *See* **Marcus Aurelius.**

Ausonius, Decimus Magnus (310–395), Roman scholar, 73, 300, 396

Austen, Jane (1775–1817), English novelist, 25

Austin, Alfred (1835–1913), English journalist, editor, and poet, 712

Austin, Mary Hunter (1868–1934), American novelist and playwright, 576, 786

Avebury, 1st Baron. *See* **Lubbock Sir John.**

Avon, Earl of. *See* **Eden, (Robert) Anthony.**

Aytoun, William Edmondstoune (1813–1865), Scottish poet and parodist, 70, 775

Ayub Khan, Mohammad (1907–), president of Pakistan, 495

Azarias, Father (*real name:* Patrick Francis Mullany) (1847–1893), American Roman Catholic educator; belonged to Brothers of the Christian Schools, 133

B

Babbitt, Irving (1865–1933), American scholar and educator, 428

Babcock, Maltbie Davenport (1858–1901), American Presbyterian clergyman, 98, 696

Bacon, Francis (1561–1626), English philosopher and author, 4, 5, 11, 15, 20, 21, 41, 44, 46, 47, 50, 59, 69, 71, 78, 89, 90, 91, 101, 117, 124, 125, 131, 132, 142, 151, 172, 173, 174, 176, 186, 188, 192, 219,

land (1872–1903), 564

Blount, Sir Thomas Pope (1649–1697), English author, 228, 433

Bloy, Léon (1846–1917), French author, 132, 472, 712, 790

Bluestone, Ed (contemporary), American writer, editor, 19

Boardman, George Dana (1828–1903), American Baptist clergyman and author, 118, 184, 348, 511, 578

Boas, Franz (1858–1942), American anthropologist and ethnologist, born in Germany, 224, 519, 600

Bocca, Geoffrey (1923–), English author and journalist, 775

Boerne, Ludwig. *See* Börne, Ludwig.

Boethius, Anicius Manlius Severinus (480?–?524), Roman philosopher, 301, 490

Bogan, Louise (1897–), American poet, 560

Bohn, Henry George (1796–1884), English publisher and translator, of German parentage, 476

Boileau-Despréaux, Nicolas (1636–1711), French critic and poet, 89, 288, 296, 350, 462, 511, 550, 560, 723, 754

Boiste, Pierre Claude Victoire (1765–1824), French author, 138

Bok, Edward William (1863–1930), American editor, born in Netherlands, 781

Boland, Frederick Henry (1904–), Irish diplomat, 743

Bolingbroke, 1st Viscount (*full name:* **Henry St. John**) (1678–1751), English statesman and orator, 187, 219, 376, 584, 693, 696

Bolitho, William (*full name:* **William Bolitho Ryall**) (1891–1930), British journalist and author, 11

Bolton, Robert (1697–1763), English Anglican clergyman and author; dean of Carlisle, 170

Bonald, Vicomte Louis Gabriel Ambroise de (1754–1840), French publicist and philosopher, 95, 734

Bonaparte, Joseph (1768–1785), king of Naples and Spain; brother of Napoleon I, 306

Bonaparte, Napoleon. *See* Napoleon I.

Bonar, Horatius (1808–1889), Scottish clergyman and hymn writer, 192, 741

Bonaventura (*or:* **Bonaventure**), **Saint** (*real name:* **Giovanni di Fidanza**) (1221–1274), Italian scholastic philosopher, 613

Bonhoeffer, Dietrich (1906–1945), German theologian, 135

Bonnard, Chevalier Bernard de (1744–1784), French poet, 666

Bonnell, James (1653–1699), English statesman, 634

Bonstetten, Charles Victor de (*or:* **Karl Viktor von**) (1745–1832), Swiss author, 21

Boorstin, Daniel (1914–), American author and educator, 380

Boothe, Clare. *See* Luce, Clare Boothe.

Borah, William Edgar (1865–1940), American lawyer and statesman, 540, 761

Borden, Mary (1886–), English novelist, 468

Börne, Ludwig (*original name:* **Löb Baruch**) (1786–1837), German political author and satirist, of Jewish descent, 114, 288, 302, 528, 543, 628, 642, 772

Borsodi, Ralph (1888–), American author, 101, 235, 240, 361, 441

Bossidy, John Collins (1860–1928), American oculist; supposed author of quatrain: "And this is good old Boston, The home of the bean and the cod . . .", 33, 96

Bossuet, Jacques Bénigne (1627–1704), French Roman Catholic prelate, 122, 192, 356, 366, 525, 559

Boucicault, Dion (*original name:* **Dionysius Lardner Boursiquot**) (1820?–1890), Irish actor and playwright, 776

Boufflers, Catherine Stanislas Jean de (1738–1815), French poet and courtier, 380, 409, 483, 569

Bouhours, Dominique (1628–1702), French Roman Catholic clergyman, 495, 666

Bourdillon, Francis William (1852–1921), English poet, 451

Bourgeois, Jeanne Marie. *See* Mistinguette.

Bourne, Randolph Silliman (1886–1918), American historian and author, 30, 33, 168, 219, 220, 311, 583, 791

Bovee, Christian Nestell (1820–1904), American author, 5, 71, 91, 111, 124, 125, 146, 159, 166, 175, 178, 181, 186, 188, 196, 200, 205, 215, 219, 224, 229, 256, 276, 280, 311, 315, 318, 324, 382, 383, 387, 412, 417, 419, 426, 451, 468, 470, 478, 484, 491, 493, 497, 504, 538, 540, 553, 564, 570, 579, 586, 634, 641, 646, 661, 663, 666, 675, 707, 719

Bowden, Sir Harold, 2d Baronet (1880–1960), English manufacturer, 734

Bowen, Catherine Drinker (1897–), American author, 60

Bowen, Charles Synge Christopher, Baron Bowen (1835–1894), English jurist, 483

Bowen, Francis (1811–1890), American philosopher and educator; professor, Harvard University (1853–1890), 159, 355

Bowring, Sir John (1792–1872), English statesman and linguist, 282

Boyd, Andrew Kennedy (1825–1899), Scottish Presbyterian clergyman and author, 235, 477

Boyd, Ernest (1887–1946), Irish critic and essayist, 725

Boyer, Charles (1899–), French actor, 776

Boyes, John Frederick (1811–1879), English author, 38, 237, 595, 710

Boyle, Robert (1627–1691), British physicist and chemist, born in Ireland, 48, 204

Boyle, Roger, 1st Earl Orrery (1621–1679), Irish soldier and playwright, 414

Bradford, Gamaliel (1863–1932), American biographer, 28, 710

Bradley, Francis Herbert (1846–1924), English philosopher, 43, 263, 585, 760

Bradley, Omar Nelson (1893–), American general, 152

Brady, Nicholas (1659–1726), Irish Anglican clergyman; collaborated with Nahum Tate in metrical version of Psalms, *New Version of the Psalms of David*, 621

Braine, John (1922–), English novelist, 61

Braley, Berton (1882–1966), American poet and novelist, 677

Bramah, Ernest (*real name: Ernest Bramah Smith*) (1869?–1942), English author of detective fiction, 8, 155, 165

Brandeis, Louis Dembitz (1856–1941), American jurist, 5, 30, 48, 101, 137, 146, 200, 232, 256, 271, 292, 306, 310, 335, 382, 386, 410, 424, 429, 432, 441, 532, 553, 573, 606, 627, 637, 681, 719, 741, 760, 772

Brandt, Karl (1899–), American agricultural economist, born in Germany; came to U.S. (1933), 139

Brandt, Willy (1913–), West German politician, 323

Brann, William Cowper (1855–1898), American journalist, 96, 544

Breasted, James Henry (1865–1935), American Orientalist, archaeologist and historian, 139

Bremer, Fredrika (1801-1865), Swedish novelist, born in Finland, 767, 780

Brennan, William Joseph, Jr. (1906–), American jurist; associate justice, U. S. Supreme Court (1956–), 526, 637

Breton, Nicholas (*or: Britton or Brittaine*) (1545?–?1626), English poet, 252

Bretonne, Nicholas Edme Retif de la. *See* Restif de la Bretonne, Nicholas Edme.

Breysig, Kurt (1866–1940), German historian, 412

Brezhnev, Leonid Il'ich (1906–), Russian politician, 144

Briand, Aristide (1862–1932), French statesman, 761

Bridges, Charles (1794–1869), English Anglican clergyman, 195

Bridges, Robert Seymour (1844–1930), English poet; poet laureate (1913–1930), 367

Bridges, William, (1606–1670), English clergyman, 277

Briffault, Robert Stephen (1876–1948), English surgeon and novelist, 44

Bright, John (1811–1889), English orator and statesman, 253, 298

Brightman, Edgar Sheffield (1884–1953), American philosopher, 614, 719

Brillat-Savarin, Anthelme (1755–1836), French politician and author; member of the National Assembly, 46, 595

Brinkley, David (1920–), American news commentator, 564

Brisbane, Arthur (1864–1936), American journalist, 377, 495, 531, 570

Brissot, Jacques Pierre (*surnamed: de Warville*) (1754–1793), French journalist and ardent Revolutionary leader, 673

Bristed, Charles Astor (1820–1874), American author, 424

Britt, Steuart Henderson (1907–), American author of books about advertising, 13

Broadhurst, Henry (1840–1911), English politician, 575

Brodbeck, May (1917–), American author, 377

Brodie, James Fairbairn (1854–1910), American Congregational clergyman, 179

Bromfield, Louis (1896–1956), American author, 25, 148, 162, 277, 377

Bronstein, Leib Davydovich. *See* Trotsky, Leon.

Brontë, Charlotte (1816–1855), English novelist, 38, 188, 462, 479

Brontë, Emily (1818–1848), English novelist and poet, 277

Brooke, 1st Baron. *See* Greville, Sir Fulke.

Brooke, Rupert (1887–1915), English poet, 250, 791

Brooke, Stopford Augustus (1832–1916), Irish clergyman and author; Anglican clergyman (1857–1876); Unitarian minister (1876–1895), 734

Brooks, Phillips (1835–1893), American Episcopal bishop, 18, 76, 129, 130, 236, 339, 342, 403, 441, 614, 682, 725, 781

Brooks, Richard Edwin (1865–1919), American sculptor, 503

Brooks, Thomas (1608–1680), English Puritan clergyman, 212, 339, 576, 659

Brooks, Van Wyck (1886-1963), American essayist, critic and translator, 342, 354, 361, 369, 383

Brougham, Henry Peter, 1st Baron Brougham and Vaux (1778–1868), Scottish jurist and political leader; co-founder of *Edinburgh Review*, 342, 603, 673

Broun, (Matthew) Heywood Campbell (1888–1939), American journalist and author, 74, 123, 226, 317, 458, 621

Brower, Charles D. (1863–1945), American explorer, 376

Brown, Brendan Francis (1898–), 391

Brown, Charles Reynolds (1862–1950), American Congregational clergyman and educator, 781

Brown, Derby (1883–), American advertising executive, 13

Brown, George Spencer (contemporary), English writer, 296

Brown, H. Rap (*full name: Hubert Gerold Brown*) (1943–), American political activist and author, 678

Brown, Hugh B. (1883–), American Mormon clergyman and educator, 99

Brown, John (of Haddington) (1722–1787), Scottish biblical commentator and author, 78, 147, 394

Brown, John Mason (1900–), American literary critic, 21, 90, 539, 564, 729, 791

Brown, Thomas Edward (1830–1897), British poet, 318

Brown, William Adams (1865–1943), American Presbyterian theologian; professor, Union Theological Seminary (1898–1936), 614

Browne, Charles Farrar (*original surname:*

Brown; *pseudonym:* Artemus Ward)
(1834–1867), American humorist, 689

Browne, Sir Thomas (1605–1682), English physician and author, 19, 192, 277, 420, 525, 529, 550, 552, 575, 668, 674, 726, 741, 747

Browning, Elizabeth Barrett (1806–1861), English poet, 125, 295, 350, 623, 674, 774

Browning, Robert (1812–1889), English poet, 8, 19, 47, 56, 116, 188, 258, 317, 353, 408, 578, 586, 664, 700

Bruce, Michael (1746–1767), Scottish poet and schoolmaster, 84

Brush, Katharine (*née:* Ingham) (1902–1952), American novelist, 153

Bruyere, Jean de La. *See* La Bruyere, Jean de.

Bryan, William Jennings (1860-1925), American lawyer and politician, 209, 259, 329, 564, 786

Bryant, William Cullen (1794–1878), American poet and editor, 21, 63, 84, 346, 450, 582, 730, 771, 772

Bryce, James, 1st Viscount (1838–1922), British jurist, historian, and diplomat; born in Ireland, of a Scottish family, 476

Brydges, Sir Samuel Egerton (1762–1837), English author, 189, 232, 518

Bryson, Lyman Lloyd (1888–1959), American educator, 82, 117, 139, 220, 270, 369

Buchan, John, 1st Baron Tweedsmuir (1875–1940), Scottish author; governor general of Canada (1935–1940), 30, 139, 241, 361, 370

Buchanan, Robert Williams (1841–1901), British poet and novelist, 676

Buchanan, Scott Milross (1895–   ), American educator and foundation consultant, 474, 647

Buck, Charles (1771–1815), English Independent clergyman, 82, 261, 326

Buck, Pearl Sydenstricker (1892–   ), American novelist, 139, 218, 451, 485, 584, 776

Buckingham, George Villiers. *See* Villiers, George.

Buckley, William Frank, Jr. (1925–   ), American magazine editor and author, 241

Buckstone, John Baldwin (1802–1879), English comedian and playwright, 114

Buddha. *See* Gautama Buddha.

Buffon, Comte Georges Louis Leclerc de (1707–1788), French naturalist, 61, 319, 485, 543, 693

Bullett, Gerald (1893–1958), English author, 50

Bulwer-Lytton. *See* Lytton.

Bunche, Ralph Johnson (1904–   ), American political scientist and diplomat, 376

Bundy, McGeorge (1919–   ), American educator and government official, 745.

Bunsen, Baron Christian Karl Josias Von (1791–1860), Prussian diplomat, lay theologian and scholar, 78, 402

Bunting, Earl (1893–   ), American business management consultant, 101

Bunyan, John (1628–1688), English preacher and author, 82, 192, 207, 302, 318, 374, 396, 491, 576, 668, 674, 715

Buonarroti, Michelangelo. *See* Michelangelo.

Burbank, Luther (1849–1926), American horticulturist, 71, 257, 376, 511, 661

Burckhardt, Jakob (1818–1897), Swiss historian of art and culture, 210

Burdette, Robert Jones (1844–1914), American Baptist clergyman, humorist, and author, 442, 785, 790

Burgess, Frank Gelett (1866–1951), American humorist and illustrator, 90, 117, 176, 458, 470, 675

Burgh, James (1714–1775), Scottish author, 559, 589, 629

Burke, Edmund (1729–1979), British statesman and orator, 9, 11, 15, 37, 41, 42, 43, 50, 71, 113, 117, 124, 129, 135, 136, 152, 157, 172, 179, 181, 187, 188, 199, 200, 208, 214, 241, 248, 249, 264, 265, 267, 275, 283, 288, 294, 306, 314, 335, 348, 350, 366, 369, 383, 386, 388, 394, 399, 413, 414, 429, 437, 462, 468, 470, 485, 506, 507, 514, 515, 521, 527, 532, 533, 534, 541, 543, 553, 560, 586, 592, 603, 614, 631, 641, 663, 665, 668, 673, 681, 689, 695, 696, 701, 703, 707, 708, 710, 723, 740, 742, 751, 754, 757, 776, 791

Burleigh, William Henry (1812–1871), American journalist and poet, 417

Burnham, William (1684–1750), American author, 288

Burns, Hendry Stuart Mackenzie (1900–   ), Scottish petroleum executive, 268

Burns, Robert (1759–1796), Scottish poet, 152, 185, 293, 315, 419, 484, 588, 602, 651

Burr, Aaron (1756–1836), American Revolutionary officer and politician; son of Aaron Burr (1717–1757), 585

Burrell, David James (1844–1926), American Presbyterian clergyman, 498

Burritt, Elihu (1810–1879), American linguist and advocate of international peace, 504

Burroughs, John (1837–1921), American naturalist, 781, 786

Burton, Richard Eugene (1861–1940), American poet; professor of literature at Rollins College (1933–1940), 18, 66, 84, 159, 165, 220, 224, 257, 311, 378, 489, 529, 635, 729

Burton, Robert (*pseudonym:* Democritus Junior) (1577–1640), English Anglican clergyman and author; vicar, St. Thomas' Oxford (1616–1640), 70, 171, 268, 552, 558, 676

Bushnell, Horace (1802–1876), American Congregational clergyman, 18, 43, 130, 282, 346, 394, 442, 543, 610, 614, 754

Bussy, Comte de (*full name:* Roger de Rabutin; *known also as:* Comte Roger de Bussy-Rabutin) (1618–1693), French soldier and author, 626

Butler, Joseph (1692–1752), English Anglican theologian, 91, 159, 529, 754

Butler, Nicholas Murray (1862–1947), American educator, 21, 156, 200, 271, 719, 723

Butler, Ralph Starr (1882–   ), American advertising executive, 13

Butler, Richard Austen (1902–　　　), British Conservative politician, born in India, 727

Butler, Samuel (1612–1680), English satirical poet, 25, 429, 452, 495, 525, 529, 578, 598, 646, 760

Butler, Samuel (1835–1902), English satirist, 35, 36, 98, 271, 319, 342, 442, 452, 458, 633, 647, 661, 694, 707, 732, 734, 754, 780, 782, 784

Buttrick, George Arthur (1892–　　　), American Presbyterian clergyman and editor, born in England, 74, 384

Buxton, Charles (1823–1871), English author, 90, 125, 155, 159, 181, 182, 246, 274, 531, 559, 585, 586

Buxton, Sir Thomas Fowell (1786–1845), English philanthropist, 185, 238, 299, 401

Byrd, Richard Evelyn (1888–1957), American polar explorer, 442

Byrnes, James Francis, (1879–　　　), American jurist, 299, 311, 531, 761

Byron, George Gordon, 6th Baron (1788–1824), English poet, 2, 10, 11, 28, 56, 58, 66, 71, 83, 95, 104, 113, 130, 137, 152, 159, 187, 191, 192, 199, 200, 206, 211, 232, 265, 276, 283, 295, 311, 316, 325, 332, 345, 346, 349, 350, 354, 355, 356, 364, 388, 398, 399, 408, 414, 419, 432, 452, 462, 470, 472, 473, 478, 479, 518, 550, 559, 602, 609, 630, 636, 642, 646, 651, 676, 677, 681, 688, 691, 700, 723, 728, 729, 734, 739, 751, 754, 758, 760, 768, 776

C

Caballero, Fernán (pseudonym of: Cecilia Francisca Josefa de Arrom; née: Böhl von Faber) (1797?–1877), Spanish novelist, 147, 726

Cabell, James Branch (1879–1958), American novelist and essayist, 544, 554, 716, 776, 787

Cabot, Richard Clarke (1868–1939), American physician, 377

Cain, Arthur Homer (1913–　　　), American psychologist, 676

Calderón de la Barca, Pedro (1600–1681), Spanish playwright and poet, 5, 500, 652, 754

Calhoun, John Caldwell (1782–1850), American lawyer, 67, 388, 755

Califano, Joseph Anthony, Jr. (1931–　　　), American lawyer and government official, 335

Calisch. See also Kalisch.

Calisch, Edward N. (1865–1945), American rabbi, 410

Calvert, George Henry (1803–1889), American verse writer, 322

Calvert, Robert, Jr. (1922–　　　), American career information specialist and author, 549

Calverton, Victor Francis (1900–1940), American author and lecturer, 129

Calvin, John (1509–1564), French theologian and reformer; founder of Calvinism, 78, 159, 385, 592

Camara, Helder Pessoa (1908–　　　), Archbishop of Olinda and Recife, Brazil, 130, 132

Cameron, Simon (1799–1889), American financier and politician, 99

Campbell, Charles Macfie (1876–1943), American physician, born in Scotland; naturalized (1918), 481

Campbell, George (1719–1796), Scottish theologian, 220

Campbell, Thomas (1777–1844), British poet, born in Scotland, 223, 265, 342, 513, 543

Campion, Thomas (1567–1620), English poet and musician, 776

Campistron, Jean Galbert de (1656–1723), French playwright, 356

Camus, Albert (1913–1960), French author; awarded Nobel prize in literature (1957), 50

Canby, Henry Seidel (1878–1961), American author and editor, 33, 405, 748

Canfield, Dorothy. See Fisher, Dorothy Canfield.

Canham, Erwin D. (1904–　　　), American author and editor of Christian Science Monitor, 582

Canning, George (1770–1827), British statesman, 109, 734

Cannon, James J. (nickname: Jimmy) 1909–　　　), American columnist, 68, 96

Caplin, Alfred Gerald. See Capp, Al.

Caplin, Mortimer Maxwell (1916–　　　), American lawyer; U.S. commissioner of internal revenue (1961–1965), 708

Capp, Al (real name: Alfred Gerald Caplin) (1909–　　　), American cartoonist and author, 50

Caraccioli, Francesco (1752–1799), Neapolitan revolutionist and admiral, 653

Cardozo, Benjamin Nathan (1870–1938), American jurist; associate justice, U.S. Supreme Court (1932–1938), 213, 270, 415, 437, 614, 689, 733

Carleton, William (1794–1869), Irish novelist, 168, 290, 357

Carlson, Anton Julius (1875–1956), American physiologist, 647

Carlson, Henry Clifford (*nickname:* Doc) (1894–), American coach and author, 69

Carlyle, Thomas (1795–1881), Scottish essayist and historian, 5, 9, 26, 36, 40, 41, 45, 46, 74, 76, 78, 83, 91, 109, 117, 124, 139, 143, 168, 188, 197, 199, 200, 232, 238, 280, 287, 303, 334, 342, 348, 353, 355, 361, 366, 367, 372, 378, 386, 394, 400, 420, 424, 427, 440, 442, 448, 458, 463, 488, 505, 511, 531, 534, 543, 553, 568, 586, 591, 594, 609, 611, 614, 622, 626, 627, 637, 646, 666, 668, 688, 707, 719, 723, 734, 741, 742, 744, 745, 746, 767, 780, 782, 786, 791

Carmichael, Stokely (1941–), American Negro leader, 87

Carnap, Rudolph (1891–), American philosopher, born in Germany, 483

Carnegie, Andrew (1835–1919), American industrialist and philanthropist, born in Scotland, 118, 350, 517, 603, 635, 658, 696, 761, 767, 782

Carnegie, Dale (1888–1955), American author and lecturer, 182, 294, 311, 376, 442, 551, 701

Carnot, Lazare Hippolyte (1801–1888), French politician and journalist, 689

Carper, Jean Elinor (1932–), American editor and author, 228

Carr, Albert (1856–?), American author, 137, 544

Carr, John Dickson (*pseudonym:* Carter Dickson) (1905–), American novelist, 153

Carrell, Alexis (1873–1944), French surgeon and biologist, 576

Carroll, Lewis. See Dodgson, Charles Lutwidge.

Carson, Rachel Louise (1907–1964), American author, 647

Carter, John Franklin (*pseudonym:* Jay Franklin) (1897–), American commentator and author, 205

Cary, Alice (1820–1871), American poet, 300

Cary, Joyce (*full name:* Arthur Joyce Lunel Cary) (1888–1957), British novelist, 791

Cary, Lucius (2d Viscount Falkland) (1610?–1643), English author, 255

Casals, Pablo (1876–), Spanish cellist, conductor, and composer, 761

Case, Elizabeth York (1840–1911), American verse writer, 74

Case, Frank (1870–1946), American author and hotel keeper, 21, 116, 153, 583

Cason, Clarence (*full name:* Clarence Elmore Cason) (1896–1935), American author and editor, 505, 719

Castle, William Richards (1878–1963), American author, 515

Castro, Fidel (1927–), Cuban revolutionary and political leader; prime minister of Cuba (1959–), 185, 631

Castro, Josue de (1908–), Brazilian physician and educator, 25, 373

Cather, Willa Sibert (1873–1947), American novelist, 205, 377, 389, 730

Catherwood, Mary (*née:* Hartwell) (1847–1901), American novelist, 671

Catledge, Turner (1901–), American author, 240

Cato, Marcus Porcius (*known as:* Cato the Censor *and* Cato the Elder) (234–149 B.C.), Roman statesman, 19, 38, 106, 252, 332, 564, 570, 595, 621, 666, 675

Cato, Marcus Porcius (*surnamed:* Uticensis; *known as:* Cato the Younger) (95–46 B.C.), Roman Stoic philosopher, 726

Catt, Carrie Chapman (*née:* Lane) 1859–1947), American suffragist and lecturer, 350

Catton, (Charles) Bruce (1899–), American journalist and historian, 34

Catullus, Gaius Valerius (84?–54 B.C.), Roman lyric poet, 759

Caussin, Nicolas (1583–1651), French Roman Catholic clergyman and author, 212, 280

Cavour, Conte Camillo Benso di (1810–1861), Italian statesman, 215, 733

Cawein, Madison Julius (1865–1914), American poet, 570

Cecil, Richard (1748–1810), English clergyman, 18, 71, 160, 232, 241, 248, 272, 299, 374, 381, 394, 420, 483, 555, 578, 591, 595, 614, 623, 653, 681, 773

Cecil, Robert (*given names:* Edgar Algernon Robert) (1st Viscount Cecil of Chelwood) (1864–1958), English statesman, 49

Cervantes Saavedra, Miguel de (1547–1616), Spanish novelist, 7, 10, 44, 61, 71, 89, 197, 274, 389, 391, 409, 461, 481, 488, 561, 591, 609, 674, 675, 682, 699, 729, 747, 767

Cesare Bonesana. See Beccaria, Marchese di.

Cézanne, Paul (1839–1906), French painter; a leader of post-impressionism, 537

Chadwick, Sir Edwin (1800–1890), English social reformer, 241, 402

Chagall, Marc (1887–), Russian painter, 537

Chamberlain, Joseph (1836–1914), British statesman, 509

Chamberlain, Neville (*full name:* Arthur Neville Chamberlain) (1869–1940), British statesman, 546, 761

Chambers, Talbot Wilson (1819–1896), American Reformed Protestant Dutch clergyman, 91

Chamfort, Sébastien Roch Nicolas (1741–1794), French author and wit, 106, 116, 125, 144, 247, 284, 427, 495, 552, 555, 642, 678, 784

Chandler, Harry (1864–1944), American newspaper publisher, 517

Channing, William Ellery (1780–1842), American Unitarian clergyman, 17, 71, 78, 83, 91, 186, 220, 232, 235, 241, 282, 291, 306,

311, 342, 395, 403, 437, 463, 534, 603, 614, 627, 656, 663, 673, 684, 718

Chapin, Edwin Hubbel (1814–1880), American clergyman, 5, 18, 38, 42, 45, 82, 98, 131, 138, 163, 165, 219, 232, 251, 270, 280, 283, 284, 315, 332, 370, 376, 391, 442, 472, 481, 498, 501, 511, 515, 531, 535, 671, 690, 703, 715, 751

Chaplin, Charles Spencer (*nickname:* **Charlie**) (1889–   ), English motion-picture actor, 427

Chapman, George (1559?–1634), English poet and playwright, 15, 37, 178, 257, 272, 504, 655

Charles I (1600–1649), king of Great Britain (1625–1649), 40, 611

Charron, Pierre (1541–1603), French Roman Catholic theologian and philosopher, 84, 168, 187, 207, 259, 340, 403, 506, 526

Chase, Edna Woolman (1877–1957), American editor of *Vogue*, 284

Chase, Ilka (1905–   ), American author, 276, 402

Chase, Mary Ellen (1887–   ), American educator and author, 48, 698

Chase, Stuart (1888–   ), American author, 13, 101, 317, 787

Chasles, Philarète (1798–1873), French scholar and author, 531

Chateaubriand, Vicomte François René de (1768–1848), French author and statesman, 49, 63, 325, 361, 415, 420, 505, 682

Chatfield, Paul. See **Smith, Horatio.**

Chatham, Lord. See **Pitt, William.**

Chaucer, Geoffrey (1340?–1400), English poet, 47, 67, 485, 579, 716

Chayefsky, Paddy (1923–   ), American playwright, 713

Cheever, George Barrell (1807–1890), American clergyman and author; Congregationalist (1833–1838); Presbyterian (1838–1844); Church of Puritans, New York City (1846–1867), 59, 315, 372, 611, 614

Chenevix, Richard (1774–1830), Irish playwright and scientist, 275

Chénier, Marie Joseph de (1764–1811), French politician and poet, 607

Cherbuliez, Victor (*pseudonym:* **G. Valbert**) (1829–1899), French novelist and critic, born in Switzerland; naturalized (1880), 475

Cherington, Paul Terry (1876–1944), American marketing expert and author, 241

Chesterfield, Lord (*full name:* **Philip Dormer Stanhope, 4th Earl of Chesterfield**) (1694–1773), English statesman and man of letters, 16, 26, 60, 65, 116, 151, 153, 170, 196, 212, 215, 222, 229, 275, 293, 301, 314, 330, 354, 357, 360, 379, 392, 410, 422, 428, 434, 436, 469, 482, 487, 542, 563, 589, 637, 647, 652, 667, 687, 694, 707, 714, 725, 768, 785, 792

Chesterton, Gilbert Keith (1874–1936), English journalist and author, 13, 48, 50, 112, 132, 139, 143, 200, 253, 259, 404, 411, 429,

448, 452, 470, 570, 589, 606, 614, 626, 633, 709, 727, 734, 773, 786

Chevalier, Maurice (1888–   ), French actor and singer, 22

Child, Lydia Maria Francis (1802–1880), American abolitionist and author, 124, 295, 478

Childs, George William (1829–1894), American publisher, 264

Chilon (*or:* **Cheilon** *or* **Chilo**) (560 *or* 556 B.C.), Spartan ephor; ranked as one of the Seven Sages, or Seven Wise Men of Greece, 312, 767

Choate, Rufus (1799–1859), American lawyer and senator, 78, 485

Christie, Agatha Mary Clarissa (*née:* **Miller**) (1891–   ), English author of mystery and detective fiction, 373

Christlieb, Theodor (1833–1889), German theologian, 326

Christophe, Georges (1912–1944), French Roman Catholic clergyman; died in German concentration camp, 684

Chrysostom, Saint John (345?–407), a father of the Greek Church, 37, 73, 236, 257, 285, 353, 370, 479, 629

Churchill, Charles (1731–1764), English poet and satirist, 228, 248, 257, 353, 393, 646

Churchill, Sir Winston Leonard Spencer (1874–1965), British statesman and author; prime minister (1940–1945; 1951–1955), 13, 27, 43, 61, 64, 66, 88, 139, 149, 153, 173, 182, 213, 253, 283, 292, 342, 359, 378, 458, 513, 537, 544, 546, 553, 586, 648, 734, 761, 762, 780, 787

Cibber, Colley (1671–1757), English actor and playwright; poet laureate (1730–1757), 429, 528

Cicero, Marcus Tullius (106–43 B.C.), Roman orator and philosopher, 5, 20, 22, 28, 46, 58, 64, 75, 89, 98, 126, 177, 186, 191, 197, 205, 218, 232, 238, 248, 292, 297, 312, 316, 325, 326, 332, 339, 345, 346, 362, 368, 369, 380, 384, 386, 387, 392, 399, 400, 401, 415, 429, 434, 448, 468, 479, 480, 485, 491, 493, 511, 529, 533, 535, 541, 555, 575, 582, 589, 603, 607, 614, 643, 659, 663, 684, 692, 701, 708, 742, 755, 768, 791

Cierva, Juan de la (1896–1936), Spanish aeronautical engineer; inventor of the autogiro, 65

Clapiers, Luc de. See **Vauvenargues, Marquis de.**

Clapper, Raymond (1892–1944), American author, journalist and radio commentator, 35, 148, 213, 246, 565, 574, 686

Clarendon, 1st Earl (*full name:* **Edward Hyde**) (1609–1674), English statesman and historian, 93, 173, 257, 290, 388, 430, 583

Clark, Alexander (1834–1879), American clergyman, 73

Clark, John Maurice (1884–1963), American economist and historian, 437

Clark, Nathan George (1825–1896), American author, 146

D

Davison, Henry Pomeroy (1867–1922), American financier, 696

Davy, Sir Humphry (1778–1829), English chemist, 615

Dawes, Charles Gates (1865–1951), American lawyer, financier, and politician, 217

Dawson, George (1821–1876), English preacher, lecturer, and politician, 440

Day, Clarence Shepard, Jr. (1874–1935), American author, 92, 498, 511

Day, Jeremiah (1773–1867), American educator, 591

Debs, Eugene Victor (1855–1926), American socialist, 310

Decanio, Steve (contemporary), American radical, 360

Decker, Thomas. See Dekker, Thomas.

de Clapiers, Luc. See Vauvenargues, Marquis de.

Defoe, Daniel (1660–1731), English journalist and novelist, 64, 145, 583, 735, 746

de Gaulle, Charles André Joseph Marie (1890–), French general; interim president of France (1945–1946); president of the Fifth Republic (1959–1969), 34, 108, 303, 511, 564, 730, 752

de Gérando (or: Dégerando). See Gérando, Baron Joseph Marie de.

Dekker (or: Decker), Thomas (1572?–1632), English playwright, 38, 176, 329, 349

de Laharpe, Jean François. See Laharpe, Jean François de.

de la Mare, Walter John (1873–1956), English poet and novelist, 228, 442, 443, 485, 663, 674, 720, 723

de la Motte-Guyon, Jeanne. See Guyon, Madame.

Deland, Margaret (in full: Margaretta Wade Deland; née: Campbell) (1857–1945), American novelist, 498

Delany, Patrick (1685?–1768), Irish clergyman, 195, 686

Deloraine, Lord. See Scott, Henry, Earl of Deloraine.

Delsarte, François Alexandre Nicolas Chéri (1811–1874), French inventor of a system of calisthenics, 51

Deluzy, Madame Dorothée (1747–1830), French actress, 171, 178, 179, 300, 553

Demades (380–319 B.C.), Athenian orator and politician, 493

De Maistre, Joseph Marie. See Maistre, Joseph Marie, comte de.

Dement, William Charles (1928–), American psychiatrist, 228

Demiashkevich, Michael John (1891–1938), American educator, born in Russia, 226

De Mille, Agnes George (1909–), American dancer and choreographer, 191

De Mille, Cecil Blount (1881–1959), American motion picture producer, 177

Democritus (5th and 4th centuries B.C.), Greek philosopher, 366, 386, 397

Democritus Junior. See Burton, Robert.

Demosthenes (385?–322 B.C.), Athenian orator and statesman, 74, 115, 343, 417, 489, 574, 656, 686, 696, 735

Denham, Sir John (1615–1669), English poet, 28

Dennis, Patrick. See Tanner, Edward Everett.

De Quincey, Thomas (1785–1859), English author, 448, 625

de Rougement, Denis. See Rougement, Denis de.

De Roussy de Sales, Raoul Jean Jacques François (1896–1942), French journalist, 140, 457, 606

De Sales, Francis. See Francis of Sales.

De Sales, Raoul. See De Roussy de Sales, Raoul Jean Jacques François.

Desbarolles, Adolphe (1801–1886), French painter, 735

Descartes, René (1596–1650), French scientist and philosopher, 165, 269, 528

de Staël, Madame. See Staël, Madame de.

De Thou, François Auguste. See Thou, François Auguste de.

Deutsch, Albert (1905–), American journalist and social historian, 481

de Vere, Aubrey Thomas (1814–1902), Irish poet, 232, 579

Devereux, Robert. See Essex, 2d Earl.

De Voto, Bernard Augustine (1897–1955), American author, 149, 201, 403, 449, 485

De Vries, Peter (1910–), American author, 125, 157

Dewar, Thomas Robert, 1st Baron Dewar of Homestall (1864–1930), British distiller, sportsman and raconteur, born in Scotland, 529, 696

Dewey, John (1859–1952), American philosopher and educator, 51, 126, 140, 168, 201, 241, 242, 257, 271, 276, 277, 306, 332, 350, 380, 460, 498, 555, 584, 596, 607, 615, 627, 648, 671, 677, 735, 776

Dewey, Thomas Edmund (1902–), American lawyer, 102

Dewing, Maria Richards (née: Oakey) (1845–1927), American painter, 776

De Witt, Jan (1625–1672), Dutch statesman, 227

De Wolf, Lotan Harold (1905–), American educator; ordained Methodist minister; professor of theology (1944–), 74

Dexter, Henry Martyn (1821–1890), American Congregational clergyman and author, 119

Dick, Thomas (1774–1857), Scottish philosopher, 205

Dickens, Charles John Huffam (1812–1870), English novelist, 17, 88, 98, 126, 154, 189, 221, 235, 300, 356, 364, 369, 376, 379, 384, 470, 492, 501, 511, 644, 661, 760, 771, 784

Dickey, John Sloan (1907–), American historian, 242

Dickinson, Emily Elizabeth (1830–1886), American poet, 71, 281, 358, 696, 735

Dickinson, Goldsworthy Lowes (1862–1932), English essayist, 49, 264

Dickson, Carter. See Carr, John Dickson.

Diderot, Denis (nickname: Pantophile Diderot) (1713–1784), French encyclopedist and

Dubnov, Semen Markovich (1860–1941), American Jewish historian, born in Russia; killed by Nazis (1941), 256

Du Bois, William Edward Burghardt (1868–1963), American educator, editor, and author, 201

Duclos, Charles Pinot (1704–?1772), French author of fiction, essays, and history, 624

Dudevant, Aurore. *See* Sand, George.

Dufor, 1st Earl of. *See* Lloyd George, David.

Duganne, Augustine Joseph Hickey (1823–1884), American poet, 559

Dulles, John Foster (1888–1959), American lawyer and statesman; U.S. secretary of state (1953–1959), 149, 198, 213, 216, 277, 298, 438, 540, 743

DuLorens, Jacques (1580?–1655), French author, 374

Dumas, Alexandre (*known as:* Dumas père) (1802–1870), French novelist and playwright, 75, 87, 189, 362, 672, 696

Duncan, Isadora (1878–1927), American dancer, 787

Duncan, William (1717–1760), Scottish author, 318

Dunn, Elizabeth Clarke (1903–   ), American author, 117

Dunne, Finley Peter (1867–1936), American humorist, 174, 204, 458, 534, 733, 782

Dunsany, Lord (*full name:* Edward John Moreton Drax Plunkett; 18th Baron Dunsany) (1878–1957), Irish poet and playwright, 588

Dupuy, Alexis (1774–1849), French veterinary, 470

Durant, Will (*full name:* William James Durant) (1885–   ), American editor and author, 39, 71, 140, 247, 263, 354, 403, 420, 429, 438, 443, 463, 615, 648, 709, 735, 757, 767, 776

Durivage, Francis Alexander (1814–1881), American author, 71, 479

Du Vergier de Hauranne, Jean (*known as:* Abbé de Saint-Cryan) (1581–1643), French Jansenist theologian, 583

Dwight, John Sullivan (1813–1893), American music critic; supplied various Unitarian pulpits (1836–1841), 79, 126, 212, 628

Dykes, John Bacchus (1823–1876), English clergyman and composer of hymn tunes, 198

Dylan, Bob (*real name:* Robert Allen Zimmerman) (1941–   ), American singer, composer, and author, 443

Dzhugashvili, Iosif Vissarionovich. *See* Stalin, Joseph.

E

Earle, John (1601–1665), English Anglican clergyman and author; bishop of Salisbury, 250

Eastman, Max Forrester (1883–1969), American editor and author, 615, 621

Eban, Abba Solomon (1915–   ), Israeli government official; used forename "Aubrey" until Israel became a state, then reverted to real name, 406

Eban, Aubrey. *See* Eban, Abba.

Ebner-Eschenbach, Baroness Marie von (*née:* Countess Dubsky) (1830–1916), Austrian novelist and poet, 20

Eddington, Sir Arthur Stanley (1882–1944), English astronomer, 726

Eddy, Mary Morse (*née:* Baker) (1821–1910), American founder of the Christian Science Church, 498, 735

Eden, (Robert) Anthony (Earl of Avon) (1897–   ), English statesman; prime minister (1955–1957), 154

Edgerton, John Emmett (1879–1938), American author, 742

Edgeworth, Maria (1767–1849), English novelist, 158, 610, 665

Edison, Thomas Alva (1847–1931), American inventor, 218, 319, 628, 720, 762, 782

Edman, Irwin (1896–1954), American philosopher and educator; taught at Columbia (1920–1954), 427

Edson, Charles Leroy (1881–   ), American newspaper editor and poet, 372, 565

Edward VIII (*full name:* Edward Albert Christian George Andrew Patrick David; *after abdication known as:* Duke of Windsor) (1894–   ), king of Great Britain and Ireland (January 20–December 11, 1936), 539, 706

Edwards, Jonathan (1703–1758), American Congregational clergyman and theologian, 339, 436, 438, 483, 511, 587, 662, 687, 720, 730

Edwards, Robert Chambers (*nickname:* Bob) (1864–1922), Canadian journalist, born in Scotland, 45, 276, 332, 366, 420, 456

Edwards, Tryon (1809–1894), American Congregational clergyman and author; compiler of the *New Dictionary of Thoughts,* 3, 4, 19, 22, 26, 38, 39, 43, 48, 58, 64, 95, 98, 115, 126, 129, 147, 153, 154, 160, 163, 167, 170, 178, 192, 198, 199, 205, 209, 211, 225, 227, 233, 267, 274, 275, 277, 286, 291, 341, 358, 370, 440, 450, 474, 479, 485, 489, 507, 511, 517, 529, 556, 557, 576, 578, 583, 595, 615, 633, 644, 656, 669, 670, 672, 690, 701, 703, 730, 770, 784

Eggleston, Edward (1837–1902), American author, 552

F

G

Glass, Carter (1858–1946), American statesman, 437

Glenn, John Herschel (1921–), American astronaut, 34, 58

Glueck, Nelson (1900–), American rabbi, 137

Goddard, James Lee (1923–), American physician, 230

Godfrey, Arthur (1903–), American radio and television entertainer, 586

Godwin, Parke (1816–1904), American journalist and author, 124, 625

Goebbels, Joseph Paul (1897–1945), German politician, 29, 589

Goethals, George Washington (1858–1928), American army officer and engineer; chief engineer on Panama Canal Commission after two civilian engineers resigned, 1, 420

Goethe, Johann Wolfgang von (1749–1832), German poet, 7, 16, 22, 42, 51, 61, 73, 79, 114, 119, 126, 153, 167, 171, 175, 186, 214, 227, 233, 251, 253, 278, 282, 286, 307, 320, 325, 336, 343, 348, 349, 350, 354, 359, 362, 365, 367, 383, 384, 388, 389, 395, 397, 404, 413, 415, 420, 426, 427, 436, 443, 448, 453, 457, 464, 468, 482, 483, 505, 509, 512, 527, 529, 534, 543, 565, 568, 574, 581, 587, 590, 593, 604, 607, 616, 626, 627, 628, 630, 635, 645, 655, 660, 661, 687, 694, 701, 716, 720, 724, 726, 731, 736, 749, 770, 774, 777, 791

Gogh, Vincent van (1853–1890), Dutch painter, etcher, and lithographer; associated with postimpressionist school, 327

Golas Thaddeus (contemporary), American author, 307, 403

Goldberg, Arthur J. (1908–), American Supreme Court justice and United States ambassador to the United Nations, 216, 547, 752

Goldberg, Isaac (1887–1938), American author, 117, 296, 378, 717

Goldbogen, Avrom Hirsch. See Todd, Mike.

Goldman, Emma (1869–1940), American anarchist and author, born in Russia, 754

Goldoni, Carlo (1707–1793), Italian playwright, 89, 450

Goldsmith, Oliver (1728–1774), British poet, playwright and novelist, 2, 8, 19, 42, 115, 124, 138, 153, 226, 229, 258, 267, 275, 297, 302, 314, 318, 325, 332, 346, 351, 387, 388, 392, 415, 427, 429, 430, 450, 485, 491, 493, 516, 520, 563, 571, 595, 604, 622, 658, 692, 716, 726, 731, 753, 755, 767, 769, 773

Goldwyn, Samuel (original surname: Goldfish) (1882–), American motion picture producer, born in Poland; naturalized (1902), 503

Gollomb, Joseph (1881–1951), American author and journalist, 571

Gompers, Samuel (1850–1924), American labor leader, 243

Gondi, Jean François Paul de. See Retz, Cardinal de.

Goodman, Godfrey (1583–1656), English Anglican clergyman and author; bishop of Gloucester, 331

Goodrich, Samuel Griswold (pseudonym: Peter Parley) (1793–1860), American author, 539

Goodspeed, Edgar Johnson (1871–1962), American Greek scholar and educator, 79

Gordon, Walter (1907–), American educator and architect, 108

Gore, Sir David Ormsby. See Harlech, Lord.

Göring, Hermann (1893–1946), German politician, 347

Gough, George Woolley (1869–), English author, 149

Gough, John Bartholomew (1817–1886), American temperance lecturer and author, 230, 249, 715

Gould, Bruce (full name: Charles Bruce Gould) (1898–), American editor, 374

Graham, Gordon. See Cunninghame, Graham, Robert Bontine.

Graham, Philip L. (1915–1963), American publisher and journalist, 411

Graham, William Franklin (nickname: Billy) (1918–), American evangelist, 129, 327

Grant, Cary (real name: Archibald Alexander Leach) (1904–), American movie actor, born in England; naturalized (1942), 419

Grant, Ulysses Simpson (1822–1885), American general and eighteenth president of the United States, 79, 424, 632, 762

Grasset, Bernard (1881–1955), French publisher, 351

Grattan, Henry (1746–1820), Irish orator and statesman, 24

Graves, Richard (1715–1804), English poet and novelist, 153

Graves, Robert Ranke (1895–), Irish poet, critic, and miscellaneous writer, 560

Gray, Asa (1810–1888), American botanist, 278

Gray, Thomas (1716–1771), English poet, 265, 287, 292, 500, 561, 757

Grayson, David. See Baker, Ray Stannard.

Greeley, Horace (1811–1872), American journalist and political leader, 61, 79, 82, 204, 307, 345, 392, 526, 581, 594, 779

Green, Russell (1893–), English author, 775

Green, William (1873–1952), American labor leader; president, American Federation of Labor (1924–1952), 505

Greene, Graham (1904–), English author, 61, 173, 664, 698

Greene, Mary Anne Everett (née: Wood) (1818–1895), English historian, 516

Greenwood, Charlotte (1893–), American actress, 714

Greer, David H. (1844–1919), Episcopalian bishop of New York, 411

Gregg, Alan (1890–1957), American physician, 590, 665

Gregory I, Saint, (*called:* Gregory the Great) (540?–604), pope (590–604), 39, 79, 89, 99

Grenfell, Sir Wilfred Thomason (1865–1940), English physician and missionary, 116, 420, 554, 665

Grenville, George, Baron Lansdowne (1667–1735), English poet and playwright, 409

Greville, Sir Fulke (1st Baron Brooke) (1554–1628), English poet and statesman, 72, 155, 156, 199, 207, 224, 227, 312, 318, 383, 427, 464, 490, 505, 515, 528, 551, 554, 563, 568, 580, 656, 679, 690, 708, 714, 749

Grey, Lady Jane (1537–1554), English noblewoman; great-granddaughter of Henry VII, 79

Grieg, Edvard (1843–1907), Norwegian composer, 312

Grigg, Edward William Macleay. *See* Altrincham, 1st Baron.

Grimm, Baron Friedrich Melchior von (1723–1807), French journalist and critic, born in Germany; naturalized French citizen, driven out of France by Revolution; lived in Russia (1792–1795); Russian minister to Hamburg (1796–1807), 283, 325, 569

Griswold, Alfred Whitney (1906–1963), American historian and educator; president of Yale University (1950–1963), 376, 402, 433, 662

Griswold, Rufus Wilmot (1815–1857), American critic and anthologist, 182, 713

Groot, Huig de. *See* Grotius, Hugo.

Groppi, Ugo (contemporary), Italian Roman Catholic clergyman and author, 133

Gross, Calvin Edward (1919–), American educator, 243

Grossman, Moses Henry (1873–1942), American jurist, 430

Grotius, Hugo (*Dutch name:* Huig de Groot) (1583–1645), Dutch jurist and statesman, 673

Grout, Henry Whittemore (1858–), English essayist, 92

Groves, Leslie Richard (1896–), American army officer; military head of atomic bomb project (from 1942), 523

Grundy, Joseph Ridgway (1863–1961), American politician, 102

Guedalla, Philip (1889–1944), English author, 3, 62, 226, 343, 697

Guérard, Albert Léon (1880–1959), American educator and author, born in Poland, 129

Guérin, Eugénie de (1805–1848), French author, 622

Guest, Edgar Albert (1881–1959), American journalist and author, born in England, 697

Guicciardini, Francesco (1483–1540), Italian historian and statesman, 28, 196, 292, 383, 547, 590, 656, 670

Guillaume, Alfred (1888–), English theologian, 494

Guiney, Louise Imogen (1861–1920), American poet and essayist; resident, Oxford, England (1901–1920), 243

Guiterman, Arthur (1871–1943), American poet; born in Vienna of American parentage, 642

Guizot, Élisabeth Charlotte Pauline (*née:* de Meulan) (1773–1827), French author, 371, 491, 627, 652

Guizot, François Pierre Guillaume (1787–1874), French historian and statesman, 49, 90, 153, 494

Gundersen, Gunnar (1897–), American physician, 476

Gunther, John (1901–), American journalist, 74

Gurney, Joseph John (1788–1847), English Quaker philanthropist, 119

Guthrie, Thomas (1803–1873), Scottish clergyman and philanthropist; helped found the Free Church of Scotland (1843), 18, 230, 715, 731

Guyon, Madame (*full name:* Jeanne Marie de la Motte-Guyon) (1648–1717), French mystic, 18

H

Habington, William (1605–1654), English poet, 193

Haig, Douglas, 1st Earl (1861–1928), British soldier, 135

Haile Selassie (*real name:* Ras Taffari) (1891–), emperor of Ethiopia, 140

Hailsham, Lord (*full name:* Quintin McGarel Hogg, 2d Viscount Hailsham) (1907–), English author, 49

Haldane, John Burdon Sanderson (1892–1964), British scientist, 114, 243, 395, 471, 565, 580, 697, 709, 786

Hale, Edward Everett (1822–1909), American Unitarian clergyman, 146

Hausner, Gideon Maks (1915–), Israeli lawyer, born in Poland; migrated to Palestine (1927), 321

Havard, William (1710–1778), English actor and playwright, 178, 289, 307, 346, 398, 545

Havemann, Ernest (1912–), American journalist, 453

Haweis, Hugh Reginald (1838–1901), English Anglican clergyman and author, 394

Hawes, Elizabeth (1903–), American author, 14

Hawes, Joel (1789–1867), American Congregational clergyman and author, 26, 197, 224, 232, 509, 627

Hawkins (or: Hawkyns), Sir John (1532–1595), English naval commander and slave trader, 717

Hawthorne, Nathaniel (1804–1864), American novelist, 70, 98, 160, 196, 275, 278, 315, 341, 360, 374, 400, 427, 464, 495, 497, 666, 793

Haydon, Benjamin Robert (1786–1846), English historical painter, 751

Hayes, Helen (1900–), American actress, 453

Hayes, Rutherford Birchard (1822–1893), nineteenth president of the United States, 107, 540

Hays, (Lawrence) Brooks (1898–), American lawyer and politician, 68, 769

Hazard, Samuel (1784–1870), American historian, 757

Hazlitt, William (1778–1830), English essayist and critic, 6, 8, 12, 47, 84, 109, 115, 155, 168, 172, 177, 183, 197, 199, 214, 222, 247, 248, 249, 281, 282, 291, 294, 297, 317, 340, 374, 413, 461, 497, 559, 571, 580, 604, 624, 652, 655, 668, 677, 705, 717, 719, 740, 775

Heard, Gerald (in full: Henry Fitz Gerald Heard) (1889–), English author, 650

Hearn, Lafcadio (full name: Patricio Lafcadio Tessima Carlos Hearn) (1850–1904), Japanese author, born in Greece of British parents; became Japanese citizen under name of Yakumo Koizumi, 611

Heath, Edward (full name: Edward Richard George Heath) (1916–), English politician; Lord Privy Seal (1960–), 362

Heath, James (1629–1664), English historian and engraver; illustrated Scott and Shakespeare, 317

Heatter, Gabriel (1890–), American journalist, 4, 661

Heavysege, Charles (1816–1876), Canadian author, 126

Heber, Reginald (1783–1826), English prelate and hymn writer; bishop of Calcutta (1822–1826), 206, 262

Hecht, Ben (1894–1964), American author, 138, 327, 453

Hecker, Isaac Thomas (1819–1888), American Roman Catholic priest, 616

Hegesippus (4th century B.C.), Athenian orator, 528

Heifetz, Jascha (1901–), American composer and violinist, born in Russia, 505

Heine, Heinrich (originally: Harry) (1797–1856), German lyric poet and literary critic, 6, 8, 20, 30, 51, 133, 137, 143, 146, 149, 169, 184, 191, 193, 207, 221, 227, 228, 254, 259, 271, 286, 289, 290, 304, 320, 323, 325, 373, 377, 382, 400, 402, 411, 448, 449, 490, 505, 507, 511, 517, 529, 537, 538, 539, 542, 552, 558, 559, 562, 590, 641, 642, 654, 688, 712, 718, 721, 748, 775

Heller, Walter E. (contemporary), American economist; chairman of President John F. Kennedy's Council of Economic Advisers, 237

Helps, Sir Arthur (1813–1875), English historian, 324, 471, 726

Helvetius, Claude Adrien (1715–1771), French philosopher, 206, 320, 755

Hemans, Felicia Dorothea (née: Browne) (1793–1835), English poet, 18, 193, 228, 300, 501, 692

Hemingway, Ernest (1899–1961), American author, 177, 247, 464, 495, 499, 762, 787

Hemminger, Graham Lee (1896–1949), American author, 676

Hendrick, Ellwood (1861–1930), American chemist, 616

Henri, Robert (1865–1929), American painter, 126

Henry, Matthew (1662–1714), English nonconformist clergyman, 18, 83, 131, 135, 153, 332, 343, 458, 547, 616, 635

Henry, O. See Porter, William Sydney.

Henry, Patrick (1736–1799), American Revolutionary leader and orator, 79, 146, 292, 418, 438, 729

Henry, Philip (1631–1696), English nonconformist clergyman, 364, 404, 477, 648, 669

Henshaw, John Prentis Kewley (1792–1852), American Protestant Episcopalian clergyman; bishop of Rhode Island, 131

Heraclitus (6th–5th century B.C.), Greek philosopher, 278

Herbert, Edward, 1st Baron Herbert of Cherbury (1583–1648), English philosopher and diplomat, 59, 301, 464

Herbert, George (1593–1633), English Roman Catholic clergyman and poet; brother of Edward, 1st Baron Herbert of Cherbury, 49, 73, 211, 238, 292, 293, 301, 317, 318, 324, 358, 359, 415, 421, 453, 458, 559, 592, 595, 629, 635, 651, 657, 658, 664, 703, 706, 736

Herder, Johann Gottfried von (1744–1803), German philosopher and author, 632

Herford, Oliver (1863–1935), English author and illustrator, 112, 287, 443

Hergesheimer, Joseph (1880–1954), American novelist, 22

Hoffman, Claire Giannini (1904–), American bank director, 777

Hofmannsthal, Hugo von (1874–1929), Austrian poet and playwright, 146

Hofstadter, Samuel H. (1894–), American legal historian, 27

Hogarth, William (1697–1764), English painter and engraver, 112

Hogg, Quintin McGarel. See Hailsham, Lord.

Holland, Josiah Gilbert (1819–1881), American editor and author, 51, 119, 120, 198, 221, 365, 378, 430, 510, 544, 553, 627, 658, 718

Hollis, Christopher (1902–), English journalist, 215

Holmes, John Haynes (1879–1964), American clergyman; ordained in Unitarian ministry; later became independent, 499, 755

Holmes, Oliver Wendell (1809–1894), American poet and author, 4, 22, 44, 82, 92, 107, 120, 141, 163, 212, 227, 232, 259, 265, 284, 357, 359, 377, 400, 401, 411, 421, 426, 443, 453, 458, 490, 495, 529, 551, 558, 561, 627, 648, 652, 656, 660, 663, 688, 691, 701, 706, 721, 755, 777

Holmes, Oliver Wendell (1841–1935), American jurist; son of Oliver Wendell Holmes (1809–1894); associate justice, U. S. Supreme Court (1902–1932), 58, 116, 164, 412, 421, 430, 443, 464, 587, 607, 709, 732, 784

Home, Henry (Lord Kames) (1696–1782), Scottish jurist and philosopher, 42, 116, 122, 126, 313, 318, 325, 397, 402, 458, 461, 575, 624, 625, 656, 670

Homer (850?–?800 B.C.), traditional Greek epic poet, 19, 209, 359, 369, 500, 628

Hood, Edwin Paxton (1820–1885), English Congregational clergyman and author, 92, 478

Hood, Thomas (1799–1845), English poet and humorist, 8, 83, 92

Hooker, Herman (1802–1865), American Episcopal clergyman and author, 193, 487

Hooker, Richard (1554?–1600), English theologian, 478

Hoole, John (1727–1803), English translator and playwright, 164

Hooper, Sir Frederic, 1st Baronet (1892–1963), English business executive, 14

Hoover, Glenn E. (contemporary), American economist, 574

Hoover, Herbert Clark (1874–1964), thirty-first president of the United States, 30, 31, 368, 378, 391, 430, 438, 531, 571, 762

Hoover, John Edgar (1895–), American lawyer and criminologist; director, Federal Bureau of Investigation (1924–), 179

Hope, Anthony. See Hawkins, Sir Anthony Hope.

Hope, Bob (full name: Leslie Townes Hope) (1904–), American radio, film and television comedian, born in England, 427, 428

Hopfner, Johann Georg Christian (1765–1827),

German classical scholar and theologian, 131

Hopkins, Ezekiel (1644–1690), English Calvinist bishop and author, 22

Hopkins, Frank Snowden (1908–), American diplomat, 133, 499

Hopkins, Gerard Manley (1844–1889), English Jesuit and poet, 236, 327

Hopkins, Mark (1802–1887), American educator and author; professor at Williams College (1830–1887), president (1836–1872), 243, 637, 656

Horace (full name: Quintus Horatius Flaccus) (65–8 B.C.), Roman lyric poet and satirist, 12, 29, 37, 57, 67, 98, 107, 124, 143, 166, 206, 257, 268, 272, 292, 318, 387, 398, 399, 404, 448, 475, 477, 495, 515, 528, 538, 568, 580, 630, 636, 651, 656, 692, 724, 767

Horn, Alfred Aloysius (real name: Alfred Aloysius Smith; known as: Trader Horn) (d. 1931), British author, 243

Horne, George (1730–1792), English Anglican clergyman and author; bishop of Norwich, 250, 278, 332, 477, 517, 611, 616, 634

Hornsby, Rogers (1896–1963), American baseball player, 69

Houdar de La Motte, Antoine. See Lamotte-Houdar.

Houghton, 1st Baron. See Milnes, Richard Monckton.

Housman, Alfred Edward (1859–1936), English classical scholar and poet, 40, 421, 443, 561

Houssaye, Arsène (originally: Arsène Housset) (1815–1896), French author, 479

Howard, John (1726?–1790), English prison reformer, 753

Howard, Sidney Coe (1891–1939), American playwright, 778

Howe, Edgar Watson (nickname: Ed) (1853–1937), American editor and author, 4, 16, 68, 155, 178, 252, 611, 638, 690, 706, 769, 787

Howe, John (1630–1705), English Puritan clergyman, 222, 616, 634, 724

Howe, Julia (née: Ward) (1819–1910), American leader in woman-suffrage movement, 778

Howe, Nathaniel (1764–1837), American Congregational clergyman, 379, 473, 552

Howell, Jeremiah Brown (1772–1822), American lawyer and politician, 223, 362, 652

Howells, William Dean (1837–1920), American author, 76, 169, 374, 501, 724

Howitt, Mary Botham (1799–1888), English author, 127, 199, 461

Howson, John Saul (1816–1885), English Anglican clergyman and author, 109

Hubbard, Alice (née: Moore) (1861–1915), American author, 102

Hubbard, Elbert Green (1856–1915), American author, editor and printer, 1, 43, 102, 120, 141, 163, 193, 320, 377, 444, 453, 460,

I

J

K

Kafka, Franz (1883–1924), Austrian poet and author of psychological and philosophical fiction, 364

Kahn, Otto Hermann (1867–1934), American banker and opera patron, born in Germany of naturalized Americans, 51, 697

Kakuzo, Okakura. See Okakura Kakuzo.

Kallen, Horace Meyer (1882–), American educator, born in Germany, 51, 52, 152, 307, 380, 400

Kaltenborn, H. V. (in full: Hans von Kaltenborn) (1878–1965), American editor and radio commentator, 310, 517

Kames, Lord. See Home, Henry.

Kant, Immanuel, (1724–1804), German philosopher, 26, 76, 122, 267, 278, 395, 568, 670, 672

Karr, Alphonse (full name: Jean Baptiste Alphonse Karr) (1808–1890), French journalist and novelist, 110, 778

Katzenbach, Nicholas de Belleville (1922–), American lawyer and government official, 180

Kaufman, Moses Ralph (1900–), American psychiatrist and educator, 593

Kavanagh, Julia (1824–1877), Irish novelist, 401

Kazantzakis, Nikos (1885–1957), Greek author and playwright, 130

Kazin, Alfred (1915–), American author and critic, 53, 214, 763

Keating, Stephen Flaherty (1918–), American corporation executive, 675

Keats, John (1795–1821), English poet, 27, 64, 72, 156, 266, 276, 505, 689, 730, 757

Keats, John (Cresswell) (1920–), American author, 228, 771, 772

Keith, Alexander (1791–1880), Scottish Presbyterian clergyman and author, 261

Keith, Sir Arthur (1866–1955), British anthropologist, born in Scotland, 80, 617

Kelland, Clarence Budington (1881–1964), American author, 686

Keller, Helen Adams (1880–1968), American author and lecturer; lost both sight and hearing by illness at age of 19 months, 18, 56, 80, 88, 93, 125, 177, 444, 453, 653, 683, 697, 731, 791

Kelley, James Byron (1889–1960), American engineer, 521

Kelly, George A. (1905–), American psychologist, 210

Kelly, Hugh (1739–1777), Irish playwright and author, 317

Kelsey, George Dennis Sale (1910–), American Baptist theologian and educator, 600

Kelty, Mary Ann (1789–1873), English author, 175

Kemmerer, Walter William, Jr. (1931–), American physician; chief, Biomedical Specialties Branch, National Aeronautics and Space Administration (1966–), 444, 497

Kempis, Thomas à. See Thomas à Kempis.

Kennan, George Frost (1904–), American historian and diplomat, 530

Kennedy, Edward Moore (nickname: Ted) (1932–), American politician, 264, 378

Kennedy, Gerald Hamilton (1907–), American Methodist bishop and author, 117, 484

Kennedy, John Fitzgerald (1917–1963), thirty-fifth president of the United States, 31, 54, 77, 110, 116, 137, 138, 150, 162, 174, 202, 228, 243, 244, 298, 307, 308, 336, 393, 405, 415, 432, 438, 465, 486, 510, 514, 545, 547, 561, 572, 574, 580, 581, 587, 627, 638, 639, 649, 654, 666, 685, 711, 740, 744, 763

Kennedy, Margaret (1896–), English novelist, 357

Kennedy, Robert Francis (1925–1968), American lawyer and government official; attorney general (1961–1965); senator (1965–1968), 150, 209, 282, 368, 587, 634, 766

Kent, James (1763–1847), American jurist, 80

Kerr, Alexander (1828–1919), American educator, born in Scotland, 390

Kerr, Clark (1911–), American educator and labor economist, 745

Kett, Henry (1761–1825), English Anglican clergyman and miscellaneous writer, 101, 281

Kettering, Charles Franklin (1876–1958), American electrical engineer and manufacturer, 14, 118, 146, 315, 403, 625, 649, 709, 742

Keynes, John Maynard (1883–1946), English economist, 237

Khan, Mohammad Ayub. See Ayub Khan, Mohammad.

Khrushchev, Nikita Sergeevich (1894–), Russian political leader; premier of Soviet Union (1958–1964), 31, 61, 77, 110, 137, 145, 150, 496, 523, 528, 564, 582, 643, 763, 780

Kieffer, Jean Daniel (1767–1833), French orientalist, 74

Kierkegaard, Sören Aabye (1813–1855), Danish philosopher and theologian, 736

L

Lindner, Robert Mitchell (1914–1956), American psychologist and author, 8, 158

Lindsay, John Vliet (1921–   ), American politician, 180, 515

Lindsay, (Nicholas) Vachel (1879–1931), American poet, 190, 545, 788

Ling, Nicholas (fl. 1600), English author, 381

Link, Henry Charles (1889–1952), American psychologist, 289, 417

Lin Yutang (originally: Lin Yut'ang) (1895–   ), Chinese author and philosopher, 93, 166, 605, 649, 773, 778

Lippmann, Walter (1889–   ), American editor and author, 32, 160, 163, 292, 299, 336, 404, 405, 421, 439, 547, 566, 594, 596, 617, 639, 659, 679, 685, 690, 721

Litvinov, Maksim Maksimovich (1876–1951), Russian Communist leader and statesman, 547

Livingstone, David (1813–1873), Scottish missionary and explorer, 80

Livy (Latin: Titus Livius) (59 B.C.–17 A.D.), Roman historian, 258, 265, 425, 493, 665, 769

Lloyd, Henry Demarest (1847–1903), American author, 118

Lloyd, William (1627–1717), English prelate; bishop of St. Asaph (1680); bishop of Lichfield and Coventry (1692); bishop of Worcester (1700), 410, 519

Lloyd George, David (1st Earl of Dufor) (1863–1945), British statesman; born in Manchester of Welsh parents, 276, 439, 566, 763

Locher, Ralph Sidney (1915–   ), American lawyer and politician, born in Romania of American parents; mayor of Cleveland (1966–1967), 634

Locke, John (1632–1704), English philosopher, 6, 17, 45, 49, 80, 127, 152, 169, 186, 187, 188, 199, 208, 244, 284, 296, 302, 322, 330, 348, 387, 417, 421, 433, 449, 488, 499, 527, 539, 580, 595, 608, 610, 622, 631, 633, 639, 655, 673, 679, 693, 737, 742, 775, 784

Lockhart, John Gibson (1794–1854), Scottish editor, novelist and biographer; magnum opus: 7 volume Life of Sir Walter Scott (whose daughter was his wife), 478

Lockwood, Lee (contemporary), American photographer and journalist, 185

Lodge, Henry Cabot (1850–1924), American legislator and author, 32, 35

Lodge, Henry Cabot (1902–   ), American politician and diplomat; grandson of Henry Cabot Lodge (1850–1924), 327, 717, 744

Lodge, Sir Oliver Joseph (1851–1940), English physicist and author, 193

Logan, John (1748–1788), Scottish clergyman and poet; published the poems of Michael Bruce and claimed to himself authorship of Ode to the Cuckoo, thought to be Bruce's work, 64

Logan, Joshua (1908–   ), American playwright, director and producer, 506

Lombardi, Vince (1913–1970), American football coach, 451, 687

Lombroso, Cesare (1836–1909), Italian physician and criminologist, 381

London, Jack (1876–1916), American author, 122, 444, 587

London, Meyer (1871–1926), American socialist and labor leader, born in Poland, 514

Long, Edward Vaughan (1908–   ), American lawyer and politician, 585

Long, Russell Billiu (1918–   ), U.S. senator (La.), 99

Longfellow, Henry Wadsworth (1807–1882), American poet, 3, 29, 75, 83, 84, 97, 111, 127, 155, 162, 172, 182, 183, 193, 207, 252, 281, 283, 293, 320, 345, 356, 358, 393, 413, 415, 441, 454, 478, 480, 482, 502, 518, 553, 560, 581, 582, 584, 597, 602, 628, 630, 644, 645, 668, 674, 684, 689, 698, 700, 754, 757, 758

Longinus, Dionysius Cassius (213?–?273), Greek platonic philosopher, 26, 695

Lorimer, George Horace (1868–1937), American editor; editor Saturday Evening Post (1899–1936), 492, 496, 584, 586, 788

Louis XI (1423–1483), king of France (1461–1483), 584

Louis XIV (called: the Sun King) (1638–1715), king of France (1643–1715), 430

Love, Christopher (1618–1651), English Anglican theologian, 145

Lover, Samuel (1797–1868), Irish novelist, 137

Low, David (1891–   ), British cartoonist and caricaturist, born in New Zealand, 258

Lowell, Abbott Lawrence (1856–1943), American political scientist and educator; professor, Harvard (1900–1909); president of Harvard (1909–1933), 244

Lowell, James Russell (1819–1891), American poet, essayist, and diplomat, 26, 32, 43, 60, 69, 127, 155, 271, 284, 285, 303, 320, 337, 382, 388, 402, 405, 447, 484, 491, 560, 644, 664, 691, 704, 740, 750

Lubbock, Sir John (1st Baron Avebury) (1834–1913), English naturalist and author, 125, 711

Lucan (full Latin name: Marcus Annaeus Lucanus) (39–65 A.D.), Roman poet, 37, 193, 199, 554, 590

Lucas, Edward Verrall (1868–1938), English publisher and author, 716

Lucas, Samuel (1818–1868), English journalist and author, 364

Luccock, Halford Edward (1885–1961), American Methodist clergyman, 484, 617, 726

Luce, Clare Boothe (1903–   ), American author and diplomat, 204

Lucretius Carus, Titus (99?–?55 B.C.), Roman poet, 12, 553, 699

Ludwig, Emil (1881–1948), German biographer, 49

Luks, George Benjamin (1867–1933), American painter, 19

M

Medici, Giovanni de. *See* Leo X.

Medlicott, Sir Frank (1903–   ), English solicitor, 705

Meerloo, Joost Abraham Maurits (1903–   ), American psychiatrist and author, born in Holland, 403

Mehta, Ved Parkash (1934–   ), Indian author, 390

Meiklejohn, Alexander (1872–1964), American educator, born in England, 141, 366, 465, 710

Melanchthon *or* Melanthon (*Grecized surname of:* Philipp Schwarzert) (1497–1560), German scholar and religious reformer; collaborated with Martin Luther in the Protestant Reformation, 90, 577

Melmoth, William (*pseudonym:* Sir Thomas Fitzosborne) (1710–1799), English author, 169, 253

Melville, Herman (1819–1891), American novelist, 94, 194, 286, 392, 444, 788

Menander of Athens (343?–?291 B.C.), Greek comic playwright and poet, 57, 89, 100, 107, 160, 173, 191, 194, 215, 387, 422, 506, 660

Mencius (*Chinese:* Meng-tzu *or* Meng-tse) (372?–?298 B.C.), Chinese philosopher, 197, 313, 737

Mencken, Henry Louis (1880–1956), American editor and satirist, 23, 66, 67, 161, 175, 177, 302, 351, 367, 377, 444, 501, 520, 556, 593, 649, 724, 737, 788

Mendès-France, Pierre (1907–   ), French politician and author, 691

Menen, Aubrey Clarence (1912–   ), British author, 778

Meng-tzu. *See* Mencius.

Menninger, Karl Augustus (1893–   ), American psychiatrist, 180, 368, 593

Menninger, William Claire (1899–   ), American psychiatrist and author; with brother Karl directs Menninger Foundation, 14

Menzies, Sir Robert Gordon (1894–   ), Australian statesman, 202

Mercier, Charles Alfred (1816–1894), American author; wrote in French, 479

Méré, Georges Brossin, chevalier de (*real name:* Antoine Gombaud, chevalier de Méré) (1610–1684), French moralist, 72

Meredith, George (1828–1909), English novelist and poet, 41, 116, 737

Meredith, Owen. *See* Lytton, Edward Robert Bulwer.

Merle d'Aubigné, Jean Henri (1794–1872), Swiss Protestant theologian and historian, 343, 377, 399

Merton, Thomas (1915–1968), American author and Trappist monk, 207, 371, 749

Metastasio (*originally:* Pietro Antonio Domenico Bonaventura Trapassi) (1698–1782), Italian poet and playwright, 5, 207, 345

Metternich, Prince Klemens Wenzel Nepomuk Lothar von (1773–1859), Austrian states-

man, 363, 632

Michelangelo (*or:* Michael Angelo; *full name:* Michelangelo Buonarroti) (1475–1564), Italian sculptor, painter, architect, and poet of the High Renaissance, 52, 194, 731

Michelet, Jules (1798–1874), French historian, 502, 711, 770

Michelson, Albert Abraham (1852–1931), American physicist, born in Germany, 116

Michener, James Albert (1907–   ), American author, 456

Mickiewicz, Adam (1798–1855), Polish poet, 562

Middleton, Conyers (1683–1750), English clergyman, 122, 123, 469

Middleton, Thomas (1570?–1627), English playwright, 330

Mikes, George (1912–   ), English historian and journalist, born in Hungary, 372

Mikoyan, Anastas Ivanovich (1895–   ), Russian politician, 14

Miles, Louis Wardlaw (1873–1944), American author, 792

Mill, John Stuart (1806–1873), English philosopher and economist, 75, 189, 220, 223, 237, 266, 308, 392, 580, 628, 649, 678, 689, 755

Millay, Edna St. Vincent (1892–1950), American author, 94, 154, 194, 454, 482, 618, 684

Miller, Arthur (1915–   ), American playwright, 11, 517

Miller, Cincinnatus Hiner *or* Heine (*pen name:* Joaquin Miller) (1839–1913), American poet, 466, 659

Miller, Harlan (contemporary), American journalist, 127

Miller, Hugh (1802–1856), Scottish geologist and man of letters, 334

Miller, Joaquin. *See* Miller, Cincinnatus Hiner.

Miller, Joseph Dana (1864–1939), American poet and editor, 763

Millikan, Robert Andrews (1868–1953), American physicist, 136, 234, 422, 618, 679, 742, 764

Milnes, Richard Monckton (1st Baron Houghton) (1809–1885), English poet, 553

Milton, John (1608–1674), English poet, 8, 11, 38, 42, 75, 80, 88, 94, 125, 135, 158, 165, 167, 194, 199, 212, 266, 292, 298, 326, 333, 353, 359, 373, 374, 409, 431, 433, 439, 447, 454, 457, 484, 492, 512, 513, 516, 528, 544, 548, 550, 551, 591, 605, 612, 622, 630, 653, 657, 669, 687, 695, 739, 752, 760, 774

Mirabeau, Comte de (*full name:* Honoré Gabriel Victor Riqueti) (1749–1791), French orator and revolutionist, 208, 366, 386

Mistinguette (*real name:* Jeanne Marie Bourgeois) (1874–1956), French dancer and actress, 422

Mitchel, Ormsby MacKnight (1809–1862), American astronomer, 80

Mitchell, Donald Grant (*pseudonym:* Ik Marvel) (1822–1908), American author, 29, 253

N

O

O'Brian, John Lord (1874–   ), American lawyer, 730

O'Brien, John Anthony (1893–   ), American Roman Catholic clergyman and author, 151, 328

O'Casey, Sean (1880–1964), Irish playwright, 582

O'Connell, Daniel (1775–1847), Irish politician, 82, 686

O'Donoghue, Michael (contemporary), American editor, 445

Oehlenschläger, Adam Gottlob (1779–1850), Danish poet and playwright, 127

O'Flaherty, Liam (1896–   ), Irish novelist, 651

Ogilvy, David Mackenzie (1911–   ), American advertising executive and author, born in England, 14, 15, 62, 103, 177, 268, 496, 714

Okakura, Kakuzo (1862–1913), Japanese art historian, 445, 736

Oldham, John Houldsworth (1874–   ), English author and editor, 601

Oliver, Frederick Scott (1864–1934), English historian, 566

O'Malley, Austin (1858–1932), American physician and author, 120, 127, 144, 231, 245, 313, 316, 352, 422, 448, 471, 578, 608, 612, 618, 649, 667, 681, 683, 690, 709, 715, 737, 741, 764, 774, 787, 792

Omar Khayyám (died about 1123), Persian poet and astronomer, 286, 358, 368, 681, 700

O'Neill, Eugene Gladstone (1888–1953), American playwright, 68, 166, 445, 572, 718

Opatoshu, Joseph (1886–1954), Yiddish author.

Oppenheim, James (1882–1932), American poet and author, 352

Oppenheimer (or: Oppenheim), Franz (1864–1943), German economist and sociologist.

O'Reilly, John Boyle (1844–1890), American poet and editor, born in Ireland; naturalized; associated with Boston *Pilot* (1870–1890), 227

O'Rell, Max. See Blouet, Paul.

Orford, Earl of. See Walpole, Sir Robert.

Origen (*Latin:* Origenes, *surnamed:* Adamantius) (185?–?254), Greek author, teacher, and church father, 209

Ormont, Jules (contemporary), American anthologist, 156, 279

Ormsby-Gore, Sir David. See Harlech, Lord.

Orr, Louis (1879–1966), American painter, 649

Orrery, Lord. See Boyle, Roger.

Ortega y Gasset, José (1883–1955), Spanish philosopher, author, and statesman; professor, University of Madrid (1911–1955), 363, 445, 484

Orwell, George (*pseudonym of:* Eric Arthur Blair) (1903–1950), English novelist and essayist, 41

Osborne, Francis (1593–1659), English miscellaneous author, 552, 559, 692, 771

Osgood, Samuel (1812–1880), American Congregational clergyman and critic, 577

O'Shea, William James (1864–1939), American educator, 245

Osler, Sir William (1849–1919), Canadian physician, 94, 194, 225, 261, 271, 371, 445

Ossoli, Marchioness. See Fuller, (Sarah) Margaret.

Otis, James (1725–1783), American Revolutionary statesman, 431

Otway, Thomas (1652–1685), English playwright, 388, 454, 506, 601

Ouida. See Ramée, Marie Louise de la.

Oursler, Fulton (*full name:* Charles Fulton Oursler) (1893–1952), American author, 418

Ouspensky, P. D. See Uspenskiĭ, Petr Dem'ianovich.

Overbury, Sir Thomas (1581–1613), English author, 37

Overstreet, Harry Allen (1875–   ), American educator and author, 245, 486, 517

Ovid (*full Latin name:* Publius Ovidius Naso) (43 B.C.–?17 A.D.), Roman poet, 75, 117, 125, 176, 215, 237, 325, 333, 400, 450, 471, 519, 590, 628, 635, 675

Owen, John Jason (1803–1869), American Presbyterian clergyman and author, 163

Owen, Robert (1771–1858), Welsh socialist and philanthropist, 519

Oxnam, Garfield Bromley (1891–1963), American Methodist bishop, author, and educator, 619

P

Q

R

Raphaelson, Samson (1896–   ), American playwright, 20, 357

Ras Taffari. *See* Haile Selassie.

Rascoe, Arthur Burton (1892–1957), American editor, anthologist, and author, 337, 412

Ratti, Achille Ambrogio Damiano. *See* Pius XI.

Ravel, Maurice Joseph (1875–1937), French composer, 506

Rawlings, Marjorie (*née:* Kinnan) (1896–1953), American novelist, 779

Ray (*before 1670:* Wray), John (1627?–1705), English naturalist and author, 44

Rayburn, Sam (1882–1961), American lawyer and politician, 204

Raynal, Guillaume Thomas François (1713–1796), French historian and philosopher; educated for the priesthood, 337, 566

Read, Sir Herbert (1893–1968), English editor, critic, poet, and museum curator, 52

Reade, Charles (1814–1884), English novelist and playwright, 2, 344, 559, 770

Reagan, Ronald (1911–   ), American actor and politician, 328, 338, 678

Reed, Eugene Clifton (1901–   ), American geologist, 203

Reed, Thomas Brackett (1839–1902), American lawyer and legislator, 530, 594

Reese, Lizette Woodworth (1856–1935), American author, 619, 712, 738

Reich, Charles Alan (1928–   ), American law professor and author, 266, 632

Reid, Thomas (1710–1796), Scottish philosopher, 671

Reinach, Salomon (1858–1932), French archaeologist, 619

Reischauer, Edwin Oldfather (1910–   ), American historian and diplomat, 55, 129, 151

Reitzel, Hans (1918–   ), Danish publisher, 114

Remarque, Erich Maria (1898–   ), American novelist, born in Germany, 46

Rembrandt (*full name:* Rembrandt Hermanszoon van Rijn) (1606–1669), Dutch painter and etcher, 234

Renan, Joseph Ernest (1823–1892), French philologist and historian, 130, 134, 188, 363, 538

Renard, Jules (1864–1910), French author, 144, 308, 445, 705, 783

Repplier, Agnes (1855–1950), American essayist, 32, 128, 431, 551, 670, 683

Restif de la Bretonne, Nicholas Edme (1734–1806), French author, 792

Reston, James Barrett (1909–   ), American author and journalist, 516, 572, 753

Retz, Cardinal de (*real name:* Jean François Paul de Gondi) (1614–1679), French ecclesiastic and politician; created Cardinal (1651); archbishop of Paris (1654–1662), 492, 690

Reuther, Walter Philip (1907–   ), American labor leader, 743, 760

Revelle, Roger (1909–   ), American educator, 713, 779

Reves, Emery (1904–   ), English author, 431

Reynolds, Sir Joshua (1723–1792), English portrait painter, 128, 249, 320, 392, 405, 425, 486, 538, 612, 768

Rhoades, Winfred (*full name:* Winfred Chesney Rhoades) (1872–   ), American author, 593, 596, 661

Rhyne, Charles Sylvanus (1912–   ), American lawyer, 432

Ricardo, David (1772–1823), English economist, 709

Riccoboni, Marie Jeanne (*née:* Laboras de Mézières) (1714–1792), French novelist and actress, 303

Rice, Alice Caldwell (*née:* Hegan) (1870–1942), American author, 786

Richard, Paul (1874–   ), American author, 36

Richelieu, Duc de Armand Jean du Plessis (*known as:* Eminence Rouge) (1585–1642), French statesman and cardinal, 730

Richmond, Legh (1772–1827), English clergyman and author of popular evangelical tracts, 724

Richter, Jean Paul (*full German name:* Johann Paul Friedrich Richter) (1763–1825), German novelist and humorist, 23, 38, 62, 77, 111, 121, 123, 128, 174, 176, 191, 194, 198, 209, 229, 249, 251, 283, 295, 301, 313, 316, 392, 395, 405, 418, 445, 461, 480, 490, 496, 502, 507, 518, 532, 538, 539, 541, 563, 581, 621, 631, 675, 683, 699, 707, 734, 741, 750, 758, 792

Rickenbacker, Edward Vernon (*nickname:* Eddie) (1890–   ), American aviator, 697

Rickover, Hyman George (1900–   ), American admiral, 245

Riddell, George Allardice, 1st Baron (1865–1934), English newspaper publisher, 412

Riesenberg, Felix (1879–1939), American engineer and author, 103

Riesser, Gabriel (1806–1863), German-Jewish author, 323

Riis, Jacob August (1849–1914), American journalist and author, born in Denmark, 372

Riley, James Whitcomb (1849–1916), American poet, 365

Rilke, Rainer Maria (1875–1926), German lyric poet and author, 161, 214, 455

Rinehart, Mary (*née:* Roberts) (1876–1958), American fiction writer and playwright, 445

Ripley, William Zebina (1867–1941), American economist, 699

Riqueti, Honoré. *See* Mirabeau, Comte de.

Rivarol, Antoine (1753–1801), French satirist, 329, 445, 494, 507, 526, 538, 631, 682, 751

R.L.S. *See* Stevenson, Robert Louis Balfour.

Robbins, Leonard Harman (1877–1947), American author, 566

313, 344, 357, 360, 379, 383, 385, 393, 402, 416, 436, 439, 446, 469, 487, 512, 544, 557, 589, 596, 605, 606, 608, 619, 621, 684, 692, 702, 708, 711, 715, 725, 749, 756, 770, 779, 788

Rowe, Nicholas (1674–1718), English poet and playwright, 2, 29, 123, 301, 344, 457, 472, 478, 480, 602, 612

Royce, Josiah (1855–1916), American philosopher, 456, 722

Rubel, Maximilien (1905–   ), French author, born in Austria, 473

Rubinstein, Artur (1886–   ), American concert pianist, born in Poland, 352, 506

Rubinstein, Helena (1870?–1965), American cosmetologist, born in Poland, 749

Rudin, Stanley Arthur (1929–   ), American psychologist, 230

Ruffini, Giovanni (1807–1881), Italian author in England, 173, 502, 602

Rufus, Quintus Curtius. *See* **Curtius Rufus, Quintus.**

Rumbold, Richard (1622?–1685), English conspirator, 49, 533

Rumford, Count. *See* **Thompson, Benjamin.**

Runbeck, Margaret Lee (1905–1956), American author, 352

Runes, Dagobert David (1902–   ), American author and editor, 23, 161, 788

Runyon, (Alfred) Damon (1880–1956), American journalist and author, 318

Rush, Benjamin (1745?–1813), American physician and political leader, 756

Rush, Richard (1780–1859), American sculptor in wood, 476

Rusk, David Dean (1909–   ), American statesman; U. S. secretary of state (1961–1969), 216, 300, 489

Ruskin, John (1819–1900), English art critic and author, 7, 9, 37, 48, 52, 54, 81, 99, 123, 125, 156, 187, 234, 239, 288, 291, 320, 341, 342, 344, 371, 386, 400, 425, 466, 519, 541, 544, 588, 619, 630, 641, 659, 728, 731, 746, 792

Russell, Bertrand Arthur William, 3rd Earl (1872–1970), English mathematician and philosopher, 128, 129, 174, 181, 203, 245, 263, 266, 268, 271, 286, 289, 352, 402, 431, 469, 474, 575, 608, 649, 733, 738, 743, 756, 764, 774, 783

Russell, George William (*pseudonym:* Æ) (1867–1935), Irish man of letters, 412, 608, 650

Russell, Lord John (1792–1878), English statesman, 26

Russell, Rosalind (1911–   ), American actress, 718

Russell, Thomas (1762–1788), English poet, 279

Rutherford, Mark. *See* **White, William Hale.**

Rutherford, Samuel (1600–1661), Scottish theologian, 145, 184, 645

Rutledge, John (1739–1800), American statesman, 496

Rutter, Joseph (*fl.* 1635), English poet, 388

Ryan, Abram Joseph (1838–1886), American Roman Catholic priest and poet, 184, 645

Ryan, John Augustine (1869–1945), American Roman Catholic theologian, 499, 619

Ryan, William F. (1922–   ), American politician, 476

S

Saadi (*or:* **Sadi**; *assumed name of:* **Muslih-ud-Din**) (1184?–1291), Persian poet, 87, 114, 123, 167, 209, 253, 280, 303, 325, 326, 328, 371, 381, 396, 434, 455, 457, 525, 667, 675, 729, 731, 774, 779

Saarinen, Eero (1910–1961), American architect, 53

Saavedra, Miguel de Cervantes. *See* **Cervantes Saavedra, Miguel de.**

Sadi. *See* **Saadi.**

Sadler, Lena Kellogg (1875–1939), American physician and author, 279

Sadler, Sir Michael Ernest (1861–1943), English educator, 245

Saint-Cyran, Abbé de. *See* **Du Vergier de Haur-anne, Jean.**

Saint-Evremond, Seigneur de (*full name:* **Charles de Marguetel de Saint-Denis**) (1613?–1703), French courtier, wit, and littérateur, 115, 272, 389, 625, 697, 756

Saint-Exupéry, Antoine de (1900–1944), French aviator and author, 151, 194, 249, 455, 662, 686

St. John, Bayle (1822–1859), English author, 487

St. John, Henry. *See* **Bolingbroke, 1st Viscount.**

St. John-Stevas, Norman Antony Francis (1929–   ), English author, barrister and journalist, 264

Saint-Just, Louis Antoine Léon de (1767–1794), French revolutionary leader, 40

Saint-Pierre. *See* **Bernardin de Saint-Pierre, Jacques Henri.**

Saintsbury, George Edward Bateman (1845–1933), English critic, journalist, and educator, 437

Sala, George Augustus Henry (1828–1895), English author; journalist and author of books of travel, social satire, novels, and autobiography, 170, 204, 680

Salk, Jonas Edward (1914–   ), American physician and educator; discoverer of antipolio vaccine (Salk vaccine); Commonwealth Professor of Experimental Medicine, University of Pittsburgh, School of Medicine, 4

Shenstone, William (1714–1763), English poet, 8, 198, 229, 287, 288, 301, 436, 490, 545, 551, 584, 687, 694, 725, 732

Sheridan, Richard Brinsley (1751–1816), Irish playwright and parliamentary orator, 23, 198, 317, 335, 558, 611, 647, 697

Sherlock, Thomas (1678–1761), English Anglican bishop, 194, 507, 702

Sherman, William Tecumseh (1820–1891), American army commander, 764

Sherwood, Robert Emmet (1896–1955), American playwright; awarded Pulitzer prize (1938), 181, 718

Shipley, William Davies (1745–1826), English Anglican clergyman; dean of St. Asaph, 75

Shipton, Martha (known as: Mother Shipton) (1488–1561), reputed witch and prophetess of Yorkshire, England, 63

Shirer, William Lawrence (1904–   ), American journalist and commentator, 363

Shirley, James (1596–1666), English playwright, 7, 38, 281, 341, 620

Shoemaker, Samuel Moor (nickname: Sam) (1893–1963), American Episcopalian clergyman, 148

Shorthouse, Joseph Henry (1834–1903), English novelist, 41

Shotwell, James Thomson (1874–   ), American historian, born in Canada, 234, 309, 439

Shuttleworth, Philip Nicholas (1782–1842), English Anglican bishop, 446

Sibbes (or: Sibbs or: Sibs), Richard (1577–1635), English Puritan clergyman, 396

Sibelius, Jean (1865–1957), Finnish composer, 184

Sidey, Hugh Swanson (1927–   ), American journalist and author, 714

Sidgwick, Henry (1838–1900), English philosopher, 608

Sidney, Algernon (1622–1683), English republican leader and martyr, 208

Sidney, Sir Philip (1554–1586), English poet, statesman, and soldier, 29, 57, 69, 85, 89, 124, 145, 174, 175, 178, 288, 313, 314, 344, 356, 422, 437, 462, 487, 530, 573, 605, 609, 627, 652, 703, 704, 749, 752, 770, 792

Sigourney, Lydia Howard (1791–1865), American author, 434, 455, 502, 710, 758

Sikorsky, Igor Ivanovitch (1889–   ), American aeronautical engineer, born in Russia, 728

Silone, Ignazio (1900–   ), Italian author, 209, 446

Silurist. See Vaughan, Henry.

Simenon, Georges (pseudonym of: Georges Sim) (1903–   ), Belgian novelist, 788

Simmons, Charles (1798–1856), American Congregational clergyman and author, 4, 36, 45, 249, 268, 269, 290, 291, 300, 305, 323, 341, 357, 385, 387, 388, 392, 393, 397, 400, 419, 440, 441, 472, 477, 484, 487, 488, 496, 501, 502, 589, 594, 602, 603, 631, 637, 639, 654, 677, 678, 695, 700, 703, 733, 748

Simms, William Gilmore (1806–1870), American author, 36, 117, 123, 158, 183, 513, 530, 588, 596, 630, 652, 682, 691, 715

Simon, Carlton (1871–1951), American physician and editor, 608

Simon, Seymour F. (1915–   ), American lawyer and politician, 223

Simonides of Ceos (6th–5th century B.C.), Greek poet, 538, 770

Simonson, Lee (1888–   ), American scenic designer and author, 446

Simpson, Sir John Roughton (1899–   ), English administration expert, 103

Sinclair, Sir John (1754–1835), Scottish writer on finance and agriculture, 224, 231

Sinclair, Upton Beall (1878–1968), American author and politician, 742

Singer, Isidore (1859–1939), American journalist, born in Austria, 620

Sismondi, Jean Charles Léonard Simonde de (1773–1842), Swiss historian and economist, 699

Sitwell, Dame Edith (1887–1964), English poet, critic and novelist, 285

Sitwell, Sir Osbert (1892–   ), English poet, playwright, and novelist, 707

Skelton, Philip (1707–1787), Irish Anglican clergyman, 236, 363, 585

Skinner, Cornelia Otis (1901–   ), American actress and monologist, 446

Skobelev, Mikhail Dmitrievich (1843–1882), Russian general, 38

Slick, Sam. See Haliburton, Thomas Chandler.

Smiles, Samuel (1812–1904), Scottish biographer, 84, 121, 246, 322, 393, 418, 492, 527, 533, 563, 741

Smith, Adam (1723–1790), Scottish economist, 77, 467, 625, 750

Smith, Albert Richard (1816–1860), English lecturer and humorist, 144, 712

Smith, Alexander (1830–1867), Scottish poet, 275, 279, 374, 419, 641

Smith, Alfred Emanuel (1873–1944), American political leader, 35, 170, 203, 461, 606

Smith, Elizabeth Oakes (1806–1893), American author; wife of Seba Smith (pseudonym: Major Jack Downing), American satirist, 227

Smith, Ernest Bramah. See Bramah, Ernest.

Smith, Gerrit (1797–1874), American philanthropist, 500

Smith, Gipsy Rodney (1860–1947), English evangelist, 97

Smith, Horatio (always known as: Horace Smith; pseudonym: Paul Chatfield) (1779–1849), English humorous poet and author, 237, 296, 534, 647

Smith, Logan Pearsall (1865–1946), American essayist, 17, 20, 83, 94, 352, 370, 396, 446, 496, 560, 636, 697, 758, 792

Smith, Sydney (1771–1845), English Anglican clergyman, essayist, and wit; canon of St. Paul's, London (1831–1845), 84, 98, 99,

165, 174, 249, 255, 256, 273, 314, 345, 352, 381, 390, 403, 418, 422, 431, 472, 512, 563, 573, 578, 580, 611, 623, 637, 682, 707, 722, 788

Smith, Thomas Vernor (1890–), American political philosopher, 100

Smith, Walter Bedell (1895–1961), American army officer, 299

Smith, Walter Wellesley (*known as:* **Red Smith**) (1905–), American sportswriter, 69

Smollett, Tobias George (1721–1771), British author, born in Scotland, 90, 629

Snow, Carmel (1887?–1961), American author and editor, *Harper's Bazaar* (1932–1955), 248

Snow, Sir Charles Percy (1905–), English novelist and scientist, 636, 650, 713, 764, 765

Sockman, Ralph Washington (1889–), American Methodist clergyman and author, 40, 328

Socrates (470?–399 B.C.), Greek philosopher, 46, 72, 121, 156, 161, 166, 194, 272, 281, 314, 366, 379, 385, 395, 397, 413, 416, 446, 450, 491, 530, 576, 625, 636, 670, 674, 707, 727, 761, 768, 774, 781, 783

Solon (638?–?559 B.C.), Athenian lawgiver, one of the Seven Wise Men of Greece, 88, 338, 624, 636, 733

Somerville, Thomas (1741–1830), Scottish Anglican clergyman and author, 528

Sophocles (496?–406 B.C.), Greek tragic playwright, 7, 36, 161, 333, 425, 590, 750, 774

Sousa, John Philip (1854–1932), American bandmaster and composer, 409

South, Robert (1634–1716), English court preacher, 23, 103, 158, 176, 197, 207, 211, 262, 275, 289, 296, 298, 314, 319, 333, 344, 346, 388, 396, 399, 487, 488, 496, 521, 570, 620, 625, 669, 694, 734, 738

Southerne, Thomas (1660–1746), British playwright, 29, 399, 681

Southey, Robert (1774–1843), English poet laureate (1813–1843), 46, 56, 58, 66, 99, 123, 218, 255, 309, 316, 365, 385, 401, 414, 455, 534, 554, 605, 708, 747, 785

Spaeth, Sigmund (1885–1965), American musician, lecturer, and author, 506

Spargo, John (1876–1966), American author, born in England, 338

Speier, Hans (1905–), American author and educator, born in Germany, 191

Spellman, Francis Joseph (1889–1967), American cardinal and archbishop of New York, 548, 577, 753, 765

Spencer, Herbert (1820–1903), English philosopher, 64, 121, 266, 267, 352, 605, 650

Spengler, Oswald (1880–1936), German philosopher, 142, 323, 620

Spenser, Edmund (1552?–1599), English poet,

89, 135, 166, 200, 218, 422, 482, 487, 548

Sperry, Willard Learoyd (1882–1954), American Congregational clergyman and author, 620

Spike, Robert Warren (? –?1966), American Congregational clergyman and author, 435

Spilhaus, Athelstan Frederick (1911–), American meteorologist, Oceanographer, and educator, born in South Africa; naturalized (1946), 139

Spinoza, Baruch (*or:* **Benedict**) (1632–1677), Dutch philosopher, 1, 64, 113, 116, 123, 143, 159, 195, 198, 203, 206, 266, 268, 281, 290, 291, 295, 305, 338, 353, 367, 385, 512, 514, 526, 597, 608, 609, 653, 674, 680, 695, 699, 702, 718, 725, 738, 740, 742, 748, 756

Spock, Benjamin McLane (1903–), American physician and author, 539

Sprague, Charles (1791–1875), American banker and poet, 188, 482

Sprat, Thomas (1635–1713), English prelate and author; dean of Westminster (1683–1713), 176, 355, 541

Spring, Gardiner (1785–1873), American Presbyterian clergyman, 591, 639

Spurgeon, Charles Haddon (1834–1892), English Baptist clergyman, 12, 81, 128, 131, 136, 196, 239, 250, 298, 319, 334, 392, 583, 716

Spurzheim, Johann Kaspar (1776–1832), German physician, co-founder [with Franz Gall] of phrenology, 563

Staël, Madame de (*full name:* **Anne Louise Germaine, Baronne de Staël-Holstein**) (1766–1817), French author, 23, 48, 109, 161, 195, 256, 301, 316, 580, 588, 620, 779

Staggers, Harley O. (1907–), American politician, 481

Stalin, Joseph (*real name:* **Iosif Vissarionovich Dzhugashvili**) (1879–1953), Russian political leader, 111, 246, 549, 678

Stamp, Josiah Charles (1st Baron Stamp) (1880–1941), British economist and banker, 540

Stanford, Charles (1823–1886), English Baptist clergyman, 192, 358

Stanford, (Amasa) Leland (1824–1893), American capitalist and politician, 496, 768

Stanhope, Philip Dormer. See **Chesterfield, Lord.**

Stanislas I (*Polish:* **Stanislaw**) **Leszczyński** (1677–1766), king of Poland (1704–1709), 23, 107, 161, 281, 293, 446, 550, 602, 625, 703

Stanley, Arthur Penrhyn (1815–1881), English Anglican clergyman, dean of Westminster, 56, 81, 121, 142, 472, 605

Stanley, Edward John (2nd Baron Stanley of Alderley) (1802–1869), English statesman, 570

Stanton, Frank Lebby (1857–1927), American journalist and poet, 740

Stark, Freya Madeleine (1893–), English historian, 164, 726

Sumner, Charles (1811–1874), American statesman, 154, 281, 674
Sumner, William Graham (1840–1910), American economist and sociologist, 226, 228,
503, 527, 589, 689, 765
Sunday, William Ashley (known as: Billy Sunday) (1862–1935), American evangelist
and Presbyterian clergyman, 136, 358,
770
Sutherland, George (1862–1942), American politician, born in England; to United States
as a boy, 680
Sutton, Horace Ashley (1919–   ), American
author and editor, 34
Swedenborg, Emanuel (1688–1772), Swedish
scientist and religious author, 7, 403
Swetchine, Anne Sophie (1782–1857), Russian-
French author, 24, 36, 118, 123, 156,
207, 341, 382, 626, 692, 693, 704, 725,
732, 739, 753, 785
Swift, Jonathan (1667–1745), English satirist,
poet, and Anglican clergyman; born in

Ireland; dean of St. Patrick's, Dublin, 16,
24, 26, 29, 45, 49, 88, 96, 103, 115, 170,
172, 206, 213, 220, 295, 303, 321, 334,
375, 389, 394, 396, 405, 419, 441, 469,
472, 496, 527, 530, 534, 540, 541, 560,
569, 570, 609, 633, 634, 646, 666, 672,
682, 692, 694, 702, 707, 729, 732, 739,
750, 761, 793
Swinburne, Algernon Charles (1837–1909), English poet, 66, 152, 184, 717
Swing, David (1830–1894), American Presbyterian theologian, 449
Swing, Raymond Gram (1887–1968), American
journalist and radio news commentator,
191, 549
Swinnerton, Frank Arthur (1884–   ), English
novelist and critic, 4
Symington, (William) Stuart (1901–   ),
American industrialist and politician, 753
Szilard, Leo (1898–1964), American physicist,
born in Hungary, 522

T

Tabb, John Banister (1845–1909), American
Roman Catholic priest and poet, 67, 88
Tacitus, Cornelius (55?–?120), Roman orator,
politician, and historian, 43, 104, 107,
143, 249, 268, 295, 355, 363, 409, 431,
533, 575, 590, 612, 659, 739
Taft, William Howard (1857–1930), twenty-
seventh president of the United States, 43,
567, 765
Tagore, Sir Rabindranath (written also: Ravin-
dranatha Thakura) (1861–1941), Hindu
poet, 8, 10, 11, 16, 17, 20, 40, 45, 46,
50, 53, 54, 56, 72, 87, 88, 98, 105, 116,
124, 128, 156, 166, 171, 174, 176, 179,
184, 189, 195, 198, 224, 225, 232, 248,
254, 269, 293, 295, 314, 368, 369, 500,
549, 730, 779
Taine, Hippolyte Adolphe (1828–1893), French
philosopher, critic, and author, 494, 680,
685
Talbot, Walter Le Mar (contemporary), American insurance executive, 663
Talfourd, Sir Thomas Noon (1795–1854), English jurist and author, 145, 664, 704
Talley, Alfred Joseph (1877–1952), American
jurist, 33
Talleyrand-Périgord, Alexandre Angelique de
(1736–1821), French cardinal (1817)
and archbishop of Paris, 217, 446, 461,
484, 625, 686, 697, 774
Talleyrand-Périgord, Charles Maurice de (Prince

de Bénévent) (1754–1838), French states-
man, 73, 251, 519
Talmage, Thomas de Witt (1832–1902), Ameri-
can clergyman in the Dutch Reformed
Church; editor, Christian Herald (1890–
1902), 518
Tancred (1078?–1112), Norman leader in First
Crusade, 272, 544, 758
Tanner, Edward Everett (pseudonym: Patrick
Dennis) (1921–   ), American author,
788
Tarkington, Booth (in full: Newton Booth Tark-
ington) (1869–1946), American novelist,
583, 770
Tasso, Torquato (1544–1595), Italian poet, 121,
425, 779
Tate, Allen (in full: John Orley Allen Tate)
(1899–   ), American poet, critic, and
biographer, 680
Tate, Nahum (1652–1715), British poet and
playwright, born in Ireland; poet laureate
(1692–1715); collaborated with Nicholas
Brady in metrical version of Psalms, New
Version of the Psalms of David, 621
Taussig, Frank William (1859–1940), American economist and educator, 698
Taylor, Bayard (sometimes called: James Bayard
Taylor) (1825–1878), American author,
550
Taylor, Charles (1935–   ), Canadian journalist, 129

U

V

W

X

Y

Z

Index of Other Sources

Albanian Proverb, 346

American Civil Liberties Union: an organization founded in 1920 to champion the "rights of man set forth in the Declaration of Independence," 688

American Medical Association: an organization founded in 1847 offering membership and professional services to physicians of good standing and representing these to the government and public, 21

American Proverb, 113, 732

Antarctica Pact: a treaty ratified on December 1, 1959, by the twelve nations of the International Geophysical Year and intended to dedicate Antarctica for peaceful purposes only and to restrict its use for military purposes, 546

Arabian Proverb, 15, 109, 296, 355, 589, 622, 751

Baltimore Beacon: American periodical, 480

Bantu Tribe Proverb, 772

Berliner Illustrirte: a West German periodical, 306

Buffalo Evening News: Buffalo, New York, newspaper published daily except Sunday, 672

Central Hanover Bank and Trust Company of New York, 481

Chinese New Year Motto, 436

Chinese Proverb, 18, 38, 168, 221, 267, 287, 332, 350, 364, 429, 543, 770

Commission on Civil Disorder, 1968. See National Advisory Commission on Civil Disorder.

Congressional Conference Report on Equal Opportunity in Housing (September 20, 1967), 324

Congressional Report on Housing, 1967. See Congressional Conference Report on Equal Opportunity in Housing, September 20, 1967.

Constitution of the United States, Amendment V, 662

County Grand Jury, Nashville, Tennessee, 347

Dhammapada: Buddhist canonical book, 354

East and West German Protestant Leaders: April 1967 statement, 306

Ebony: American Negro monthly pictorial news and variety magazine, 324

Economist: a British weekly magazine reporting domestic and foreign economies, 108

English Proverb, 171, 179, 379, 410, 427, 724, 732, 774

Esquire: American monthly magazine of men's interests and fashions, 297, 330

French Proverb, 20, 179, 417

German Motto, 451

German Proverb, 57, 183, 686

Hague Convention: international conventions aimed at regulating warfare drawn up by nations attending the Hague Conferences (1899 and 1907), 65

Hibernicus: a philosophical miscellany written by several Irishmen and published in 1734 in London, 629

Hindu Maxim, 76

Hindu Proverb, 100, 327

Hungarian Proverb, 669

International Treaty on the Peaceful Uses of Outer Space: an international treaty banning weapons in outer space and providing for mutual site inspection of space outposts (January 27, 1967), 685

Irish Rhyme, 768

Italian Proverb, 93, 252

Bible and Shakespeare

Reference Indexes

The following two indexes contain references for all Bible and Shakespeare selections. The books of the Bible and the works of Shakespeare are arranged alphabetically. In the Bible Reference Index, italics are used for the chapter and verse of each passage; in the Shakespeare Reference Index, italics are used for the acts and scenes of each play.

Bible Reference Index

Old Testament

New Testament

Shakespeare Reference Index

Plays

Poems

Subject Index

Bold-faced type indicates topic-headings and the page numbers on which they appear. In each entry care has been taken to be as brief as possible, capturing a general idea within a quotation. The reader should not, therefore, expect to find in the text the exact phraseology used in the index.

A

abandonment, 452
Abel, 96, 193
abhorrence, 855
ability, 1, 186, 514, **797, 855**
  accepting advice and, 16
  cowardice, lack of, 177
  executive, 103
  freedom to develop, 391
  intelligence increases physi-
    cal, 403
  merit and, 482
  and ministry, 828
  necessity and, 353
  want of, 482
abnormality, 242
abortion, 1–2
Abraham, 257
absence, 2, 797, 855
  pangs of, 478
absolution, 2
absolutism, 56
abstinence, 2, 85, 285, **797**
abstraction, 169
absurdity, 2–3, 116, 372
  reason underlies some seem-
    ing, 188
abundance:
  and alms, 798
  Marxist hope, economy of,
    150
abuse, 3
accent, 3
acceptance, 3
  of misfortune, 491
accident, 3–4, 63, 302, 362,
    387, **855**
  fame, an, 280
accomplishment, 797
  blessedness consists in, 87
accountancy, government as,
    335
accuracy, 4
  of woman's guess, 345
accusation, 797
achievement, 4, 268
  democracy, never a final, 201
  of destiny, 209
  patience and, 544
acquaintance, 4, 313
  cools desire, 200
  friendship and depth of, 314

acquirement, 5
action, 5, 37, 162, 209, 267,
    771, **856**
  danger and avoiding, 641
  eloquence, 888
  faith, tendency toward, 277
  good, 47
  and good will, 625
  happiness and, 351
  judgment of our, 160
  knowledge and virtuous, 422
  man, like angel in, 930
  principle of, 206
  principles, springs of, 585
  remedy for fear, 288
  self-knowledge learned by,
    660
  speed of, 197
  thought and, 402, 719, 721,
    722
  true method of, 785
  vice dignified by, 984
  with vigor, 197
  weighed by God, 801
  and will, 770
  word without, 378
activity:
  ennui, desire of, 255
  God's medicine, 783
  life, 441
  of mind, 168
  noble, 5
actor and actress, 7–8, 856
  God and nature, 235
Adam, 192, 193, 309, 442, 534,
    776, 960
Adam and Eve, 8, 502, 728, 849
  in each man, 716
  home, 365
  and mother of living, 829
adaptability, 8, 32
  of Christianity, 133
  to nature, 511
adaptation, 257
addiction, 597
  drug, 324
  (*See also* **drugs**)
Addison, Joseph, 92
adjustment, 8–9, 158
  genius of America, 31

  to present conditions, 623
  social, 391
administration, 9, 338
  government, 335
admiration 9, 290, **856**
  foundation of philosophy, **556**
  imitation and, 251
  versus criticism, 182
admonition, 819
adolescence, 9–10, 263
  fourteen, 270
adoration, 10
adulation, 294
adult, 10
  twenty-one, 270
adultery, 10, 62, **798**
  flirtation and, 295
advancement, 10–11
adventure, 11, 65, 193, 445
  writing a book, an, 61
adventurers, 611
adversary, 11
adversity, 11–12, 696, **798, 856–
    857**
  appear prosperous in, 493
  discipline and, 217
  friendship and, 312
  guilt and, 346
  hunger, most degrading, 373
  literature solaces, 448
  memory mitigates, 479
  and philosophy, 949
  remorse felt in, 621
  and trial, 730
advertising, 12–15
  art and, 13
  free press and, 310
  man and cynicism, 190
  on radio and TV, 519
advice, 15–17, 857
  common cold and, 144
  government not, 338
  of scholar, 611
aeronautics, 65
Aeschines, 15
Aeson, 934
aestheticism, God-proofing, 395
affectation, 17, 583
  children without, 339–340
  of wisdom, 388

arms, 50
foundation of state, 337
race, 522, 573
army, 50, 64
arrogance, 50
modesty and, 494
out of mouth, 801
in prosperity, 589
riches and, 634
supple knees feed, 953
arrow, 48
children as, 804
word like, 780
arsonist, 179
art, 8, 50–53, 861
and artist, 53, 54, 504
babblative and scribblative, 66
beauty in, 72
conscience and, 161
conversation as, 168
cookery as, 171
criticism as, 183
democracy as, 202
in democratic society, 53
fashion and, 284
fiction as, 291
and France, 303
in free society, 53
good humor, 372
impulse of, 188
of life, 445
limited to handicraft, 460
man's style in, 694
medicine, healing, 476
meeting point with science, 649
and nature, 942
old lady, work of, 778
peace, muse of, 948
not branch of pedagogy, 787
philosophy, of living, 556
politics, of government, 567
revelation of man, 630
to rule, 642
science and, 512
science, religion, and 615
soul of civilization, 142
in Soviet Communism, 149
television and dissemination of, 714
artichokes, 443
artist, 53–54, 182, 186
appeal of, 787
facts and, 382
not born, 293
poetry and, 561
and scientist, 650
arts, the, 55, 56
in France, 303
learning to enjoy, 243

Aryan, 228
ascension of Christ, 130
asceticism, 54
Asia, 54–56, 580, 753
communists and, 149
India, 390
military superiority of, 141
struggles in, 299
aspiration, 56
emulation, devil-shadow of, 251
good, opposite of ambition, 29
for life, 35
of people, 164
aspirin, 30
ass, 56, 329
assassination, 56–57, 717
of King, Martin Luther, 601
of president, 581
assertion, 57
argument and, 167
insult and, 401
unsupported, 182
associate, 57, 343
association, 58
astrology, 58
astronaut, 58
astronomy, 58, 861
atheism, 59, 142, 178, 701
anarchy, of divine authority, 36
Christianity and, 132
existentialism and, 269
atheist, 374
Catholics love, 454
pantheist, ashamed, 538
pious man and, 619
Russians, 643
and study of anatomy, 464
(*See also* atheism)
Athens, 30, 345, 527
Atlantic, 108
Atlas, 237
atom:
bomb, 191, 306, 522, 523, 524, 762
disintegration of, 522
energy of, 522
(*See also* nuclear energy, and nuclear warfare)
atomic age, 55, 523
atonement, 800
attention, 60
curiosity, parent of, 188
directed to the excellent, 181
genius, continued, 320

parent of memory, 188
secret of good memory, **479**
wearied by length, 578
attitude:
character and, 120
of critic, 184
philosophic, 555
auctioneer, 53
audacity, 553
success, child of, 696
(*See also* **boldness**)
audience, 60
addressing an, 578
August, 86
Augustine of Hippo, 157
aurora, 879
Auschwitz, 321, 764
Australia, 60
writer in, 61
authenticity, biblical, 80
author:
appreciation of, 182
successful, 534
(*See also* **authorship**)
authority, 60, 861–862
anarchy, hatred of human, 36
central government, 336
with children, 128
and democracy, 203
destruction of, 573
government is, 338
natural disobedience to, 221
proud man drest in brief, 952
result of, in religion, 68
authorship, 60–62, 92, 862
individuality of, 182
journalist and, 411
(*See also* author, **writing**)
autobiography, 62
of biographer, 83
our body, our, 90
automation, 63
automobile, 63, 364, 728
automobile racing, 63
autumn, 63–64
avarice, 64, 862
enemy of peace, 548
ennui and, 255
eyes and, 273
gambling, child of, 317, 318
(*See also* **covetousness**)
average, 64
aversion, 122
aviation, 64–65
(*See also* airplane)
awakening, final, 194
awkwardness, 65
Aziz Ezzet, 248

B

C

commonwealth, 282
  British, 359
  and dissension, 886
communication and manners, 810
communications media, 148
communism, 148–151, 171, 613
  business and, 102
  ignorance of, 380
  in Korea, 423
communist, 323
community, 679
  self-discipline of, 202
  unity with business, 101
companionship, 151–152
  accident counts for much, 3
  good humor and, 331
company, 292
comparison, 152, 871–872
compassion, 152, 417
  communicates the soul, 704
  hero and, 359
compensation, 152
competence, 352
competition, 152
  America and Russia, 144
  cooperation and, 171
  free, 103, 305
  freedom of choice and, 308
competitive system, 237
compilers, 558
complacency, 153
complaint, 152–153, 805
  firmness and, 293
  stirs to effort, 153
compliment, 153, 872
  deference and, 198
  dispensing with ceremony, 116
composer, 504, 505
composition, critics and, 183
compromise, 146, 153–154
  Church of England as, 41
  in eternal principles, no, 585
  ideal and possible, 608
  and virtue, 754
  world of pure reason, 608
computer, 154
  redemption and, 63
concealment, 154–155
  confidence and, 158
conceit, 155–156, 805, 872
  in offering advice, 16
concentration, 156
  as motto, 782
concord, 32
condemnation, 156
  of absurdity, 3
condescension, 190
conduct, 156–157
  character and, 118, 198
  depend not on fortune but, 303
  fickle course of, 291
  rules of, 469

superior man, earnest in, 235, 493
confession, 157, 805, 872
  egotism, 706
  excuses are, 268
  means half absolved, 2
  no defeat in, of error, 261
  prayer, 576
confessor, 197, 472
confidence, 117, 151, 157–158, 872
  conceit and, 156
  esteem and, 262
  in fear of Lord is, 810
  in friends, 287
  in people and politics, 565
  and reward, 839
  success produces, 697
  versus apprehension, 113
conflict:
  civilization solves, 139
  faith springs from, 227
  (See also contention)
conformity, 158
  holiness, to God, 364
  nonconformity and, 519
  in Soviet Communism, 149
cogestion in subway, 184
conglomeration, 140
congratulations, 153
congress, 159, 169, 180
  conscription and, 228
  inefficiency of, 201
  Supreme Court and, 175
Congressional Record, 159
conquest, 159
  endurance and, 251
conscience, 75, 159–162, 246, 285, 328, 401, 627, 628, 805–806, 872–873
  American, 601, 639
  baseness of character sears, 69
  cash register and, 495
  citizenship and, 137
  corrupted with injustice, 920
  courage and, 173
  doctrine rectifies, 226
  enlightened, 388
  and first thoughts, 721
  gallantry and, 317
  God in, 326
  and God's existence, 328
  good life, good for, 333
  integrity and, 402
  of king and theatre, 974
  law of majority, 461
  leadership and, 432
  makes man noble, 37
  memory, registry of, 478
  of nation, 24
  only reward, good, 545
  outward, 888
  policy sits above, 949
  propaganda and, 589

and Protestantism, 590
  prudence and freedom of, 592
  Quakers and, 598
  reason and, 609
  reputation and, 334
  shame, nature's, 665
  slogans, opiates for, 675
  substitute for, 190
  universal and individual, 394
  way to glory, 325
  and woman, 776
consciousness, 486
conscription, 228
  (See also draft)
consequence, 6, 38, 162
  of crime, 346
  history and, 362
  logical, 449
conservatism, 162–163
  age and, 20
  negative, 611
  radical and, 272
conservative (See conservatism)
consideration, 873
  effects of, 417
  for others, 186
  (See also attention)
consistency, 163
consolation, 163–164, 873
  Christ and everlasting, 820
conspiracy, 164, 873
  U. S. disorders of 1967, 640
constancy, 164, 873
  without knowledge, 117
Constantinople, 134
constitution, 164, 430
  British, 697
  Congress and, 159
  courage and, 173
  dissent, guaranteed by, 223
  government by, 337
  to protect Americans, 638
  of Russia, 56
  second class citizen and, 260
  separation of powers, 336
  Supreme Court interprets, 429
consumer, 14, 463
  the American, 62
  depression and, 430
  producer and, 430
contamination, 874
contemplation, 164–165, 603, 874
  of created things, 512
  of creature and Creator, 195
  of Deity, 456
  of God's works, 342
  self-knowledge and, 660
  of universe, 80
contemporaries, 482
contempt, 165, 874
  caused by vice, 23

D

E

experiment, 271
  economic, 162
expert, 271
explanation, 28
exploitation, free enterprise and, 305
expression:
  of belief, 74
  of man's delight in God's

work, 52
extermination, 162
extortion, blackmail and, 222
extravagance, 271–272
  generosity and, 268
  world does not admire, 238
extremes, 31, 272, 891
  senses cannot grasp, 268
  wealth and poverty, 633

eye, 38, 272–273, 891–892
  of artist, 53
  man's, should survey world, 785
  negotiate for itself, 928
  night and the, 944
  not satisfied with seeing, 799
  reproof, upbraiding of, 623
eyelids, 826

F

fable, 274
  history as, 363
face, 17, 67, 112, 184, 274–275,
    450, 892
  -flatterer and backbiter, 67
  mind's construction in, 937
  name, kind of, 509
  of old man, 798
fact, 45, 275, 606
  education and, 240
  ideal, not good as, 377
  suppression of every-day, 114
faction, 275
failing, 275–276
  difficult to fight, 11
  friends forgive, 313
failure, 26, 276–277, 644
  in business, 103
  China's, 129
  due to heredity, 697
  learn wisdom from, 492
  self-distrust, cause of, 224
  success and, 697
fairy, 892–893
faith, 131, 193, 246, 277–280,
    339, 467, 810–811, 841,
    893
  and aged men, 798
  atheist's, 59
  and beauty, 863
  charity and, 123
  and confidence, 872
  credit and, 177
  dance, act of, 191
  democratic, 200
  doubt and, 227
  fanatic, 283
  fear and, 289
  fruit of spirit, 827
  in God, 43, 785
  by grace saved through, 841
  great doers in history, men of, 671
  and healing, 818
  hope, love and, 207

in human experience, 614
in immortality, 384
in Jesus, 500
justified by, 824
in leader, 1
life upon, 980
and love, 927
makes Christian, 131
in man in America, 32
men sing with, 505
as might, 637
as mustard seed, 797
mystery and, 507
one, 800
parents and children, 394
prayer of, 834
reason and, 608
in reason and weapons, 607
saved through, 841
test of religious, 618
thou of little, 809
transmuted into character, 135
triumph of heart, 608
valor and, 598
woman's, traced in sand, 775
and works, 850
and youth, 792
faithful, Lord preserves, 799
faithfulness, 811
  unto all generations, 815
  sacred excellence, 292
falcon, 893
fall (See autumn)
falsehood, 167, 178, 197, 262,
    280, 811, 893
  has goodly outside, 883
  partial truth more dangerous
    than, 737
  and time, 976
  wrong as, 789
fame, 158, 280–282, 893
  and reputation, 956
  sacrifice for, 224
  seeking rest, 628

through thought and deed, 38
vapor, 526
familiarity, 282
family, 238, 282–283, 364, 539,
    811
  in agriculture, 25
  breakup in ghetto, 571
  corner-stone of America, 471
family planning, 85
fanaticism, 283, 533
fancy, 283, 894
Far East, 390
Faraday, Michael, 704
farewell, 283, 894
  goes out sighing, 987
  kiss, 419
farm, world is great, 155
farmer, 26
farming (See agriculture)
fascism, 283–284
  ignorance of, 380
fashion, 51, 284–285, 894
  custom and, 189
  literary, 448
fastidiousness, 285
fasting, 285, 797
  best medicine, 476
  brings us to God, 122
  (See also abstinence)
fat, 163
  (See also fatness)
fatalism, 285
fate, 286, 894–895
  fortunes called, 209
  we cannot conquer, 513
father, 61, 127, 128, 286, 539
  antichrist denies, 799
  and child's character, 120
  Christianity and, 134
  of crime, 180
  daughter and aging, 191
  education and, 240
  hear instruction of, 851
  in heaven, 815
  home and, 365

G

H

examine thy, 657
excited by greatness, 58
faith, triumph of, 608
false faith and false, 913
faults of, 287
fickle, 291
forms honor, 366
furnace-burning, 907
gift destroys, 813
give friend, 324
God rules men's, 327
God strengthens, 819
government must have, 336
of guile, women have, 779
half a, 235
hard, 578, 598
head and, 355, 959
home without, 364
honesty, love and justice in, 118
hope deferred and, 819
imagination of man's, 810
kind, and coronets, 334
of life, 897
light, lives long, 870
Lord looks on, 800
Lord searches all, 830
man's, and woman, 775
merry, goes all day, 871, 937
mirth and laughter, 937
new, 844
of a people, 186
and persuasion, 152
perverse, shall be despised, 809
phrase of human, 209
practical duty enriches, 234
prayer and, 576
purity of 72, 596
rejoiced in labor, 822
Scripture penetrates, 78
seat of pride, 583
service from, 842
set on fire, 857
slays all senses with, 899
tears, safety-valves of, 712
trial of, 730
troubled not, 846
true as steel, 897
two bodies, one, 902
of unbelief, 847
unpack with words, 992
upon my sleeve, 963
and valor, 982
vengeance in my, 958
wanting in resolution, 626
whoredom and wine take away, 809
and will, 978
win one's, 417
of woman, 990
woman's, like moon, 779
woman's, nothing more tender, 778
word which stings, 780

words, razors to, 993
write mercy on, 827
and writing, 787
of youth through senses, 792
heart disease, 357
heart-leaf, 199
heathenism, 133
heaven, 11, 29, 188, 194, 203, 218, 316, 333, 357–358, 446, 613, 818, 910, 967
children and kingdom of, 806
declares glory of God, 807
eternal wisdom of, 205
forgiveness, bridge to, 301
glimpses of, 56
of gospel, 334
grave, way to, 341
heals sorrow, 683
hell and, 359
humble to, 212
integrity to, 983
love comes from, 451
and old age, 857
reaching to, 184
and thunder, 976
and wife, 769
and wooing, 992
Hebraism and Hellenism, 358
Hebrew, 358
Hecuba, 974
helicopter, 728
hell, 61, 188, 194, 358–359, 818–819, 842, 910
alone, 449
and angels, 799
deed chronicled in, 878
despair and, 207
of gospel, 334
jealousy, injured lover's, 409
mistaken celibacy, 114
patriotism, religion of, 544
sin and, 842
in woman's smile, 779
for writers, 61
help, 7, 100, 359, 819, 910
of God, 197
mutual, 100
obstacles and, 214
the poor, 572
service and, 204
hemp, 766
hen, 162
Henry, Patrick, 169
heraldry, 175
Hercules, 877, 894
hereafter, 385, 658
(See also future state, immortality)
heredity, 359
environment and, 257
failure and success, 697
heresy, 75, 819
biologists sensitive to, 650
warning against, 822
heretic, 75

heritage, 363, 612
American, 243
children, Lord's, 804
hero, 64, 70, 344, 359–360, 424, 464, 544
defeat and, 198
enthusiasm begets, 256
seeks glory, 752
and women, 718
Herod, 52
heroin, 230
heroism, 158
hideousness, 166
hierarchy, 111
hierophants, 400
Himmler, 321
Hindu, 112, 141, 304
Hinduism, 177, 360
hint, 282
"hip," 361
hippie, 360–361
Hipporene, 771
hireling, 782
Hiroshima, 306, 523, 524
historian, 788
history, 47, 56, 361–363, 419
American, 30, 31
biography and, 83, 84
changes in, 118
Christ and, 130
Christianity and, 134
and Cleopatra's nose, 72
comes to life in library, 440
in countenance, 274
dictators and, 213
efforts to freeze, 208
Egypt's ancient, 247
as epitaph, 890
Europe as center of, 55
evil and, 789
false and incomplete, 55
fiction more instructive than, 291
freedom in, 309
God in, 326
of human opinion, 531
irresistible tides of, 209
Jewish religion, 412
journalism and, 411
of life, 441
literary, 448
Mohammed's sacred, 494
newspaper, one day's, 517
of pains and aches, 170
permanent tendency in, 203
of political thought, 574
in popular songs, 506
records success, 696
redemption and Bible, 610
short story and American, 33
and tradition, 727
truth and progress in, 587
unpleasant, 466

and "the last word," 781
husbandman, 555
husbandry, 865
  in heaven, 910
Hydra, 917
hydrogen bomb, 523
  (*See also* nuclear warfare)

hygiene, 481
hymn:
  at funeral, 194
  Methodist, 484
hyperbole, 267
hypocrisy, 247, 287, 355, 374–375, 821, 913

of actors, 8
equivocation and, 261
in Hollywood, 502–503
organized, 163
ostentation, signal of, 535
hypocrite, 193
hysteria, 538

I

I.Q. (intelligence quotient), 593
"*Ich bin ein Berliner,*" 77
idea, 376–377
  American, 200
  art and, 52
  civilization, ruling by, 141
  common, 148
  and event, 81
  experiment of, 162
  new, 114
  student with clear, 402
  universality of, 140
  and university, 745
  words and transmissions of, 780
  young man and old, 791
ideal, 6, 377–378
  art and, 52
  ascetic life, social, 54
  common, 148
  failure and, 276
idealism, American, 30, 35
ideology of Soviet Communism, 150
idioms, Hebrew, 358
idiot, 348
idleness, 378–379, 628, 913
  children hate, 127
  professional men and, 104
  want, enemy of, 761
Idlewild, 728
idol, 821
idolatry, 379–380
  flag, 293
  new, 82
Ignatius, Saint, 40
ignorance, 9, 48, 155, 182, 188, 380–381, 389, 821, 913–914
  cruelty and, 185
  discovered by study, 693
  education of facts, 240
  end of philosophy, 556
  impudence, effect of, 387
  knowledge and, 420
  mother of suspicion, 702
  mystery as, 507

of one's body, 90
painless evil, 216
part of worldly knowledge, 785
and prejudice, 579, 580
proud of learning, 434
of public, 53
and success, 696
and wonder, 780
illness (*See* sickness)
ills, 381–382
illusion, 45, 51, 63, 382, 738
imagination, 36, 382–383, 611, 623, 914
  and advance in science, 648
  boundless world of, 606
  children and, 127
  English have no, 254
  exploration of, 214
  life and, 444
  and lunatic, lover and poet, 885
  of man's heart, evil, 810
  memory, cabinet of, 478
  and poet, 950
  poetry and, 561
  reality and, 606
  short story and American, 33
  time, mode of, 725
imitation, 267, 383
  admiration and, 251
  flattery, 294
  and progress, 587
immaturity, 486
immigrant, 242, 383–384
  American, descendent of, 37
  in slums, 572
immorality, 142
  of arms sales, 50
  in arts, 53
  of birth control, 85
  (*See also* morality)
immortality, 23, 316, 326, 377, 384–385, 629, 821, 914
  attends virtue, 914
  beauty as, 72
  book, foretaste of, 92

idealism, defense of, 377
  life, childhood of, 443
  literature, of speech, 449
  result of beauty and wisdom, 71
  seek for, 831
  of soul, 684
  spirit of, 56
impartiality, 821–822
impatience, 385–386, 914
imperfection, 386
  most perfect have, 166
  perfection found in, 552
imperialism, 299
impertinence, 386
importance:
  hurting man's sense of, 181
  our own, 66
impossibility, 386, 914
impression, 386–387
impropriety, soul of wit, 775
improvement, 267, 387
  life devoted to, 4
  mental, 168
  (*See also* self-improvement)
improvidence, 388
impudence, 387
impulse, 387
  of America, 209
  of art, 188
inaccuracy, lying and, 458
inaction, 512
inactivity, 387–388
incentive of heaven, 29
inclination, 41, 188, 305, 388
  never change, 708
  and opinion, 529
  reason and, 606
income, 495, 496
  borrowing and, 96
  pay debt by raising, 238
  rich and poor, 634
incompatibility, 187
incongruity in life, 445
inconsistency, 388
inconstancy, 388, 914–915
incredulity, 388–389

J

envy withers another's, 258
follows sorrow, 845
fruit of spirit, 827
greater, he who conceals, 155
and grief, 167, 345
heavens rejoice, 844
laughter and, 427
lost, 18
and love, 76
of middle age, 21
mother of, 112
of newborn child, 394
in reading God's word, 79
and repentence, 837
and sacrifice, 645
amid sorrow, 843
soul of, 992
treasury of everlasting, 910
and trivialities, 730
of work, 783
in God's presence, 818
Jubilee, 192
Judaism, 133, **412**
Christianity as, 132
Passover of, 542
and the Reformation, 612
Judas, 84

Judea, 130
judge, 412–413, 919
and Constitution, 164
enemies, 183
neutrality of impartial, 515
judgment, 22, 45, 167, 194, 250,
413–414, **823, 919**
accurate, 4
and brotherhood, 802
common sense and, 147
education and, 240
and holy writ, 953
Last, 265
liberty of, 222
and luck, 930
military or political, 216
self-love impairs, 173
standard of, 182
taste, microscope of, 708
and time, 724
July, 86
June, 86, 106
jury, 414
ignorance of, 64
impartially selected, 28
just, the:
evil and, 821

sweet remembrance of, 621
(*See also* **righteousness**)
justice, 27, 268, 329, **414–416,**
823, 920, 959, 962
under communism, 149
conscience, best minister of,
161
criminal and, 639
eternal, 32
fidelity, sister of, 292
and glory, 152
of God, 160
Isaiah's religion of, 134
in leader, 1
mercy and, 482
mercy seasons, 936
and order, 514
pillar of government, 335
political, 27
recompense injury with, 609
religion and, 616
religious, 27
time, old, 976
voice of majority, 461
and voluptuousness, 758
justification, 51, **823–824**
Justinian, 520

K

Kaiser, Henry, 460
Kansas, 299
Kennedy, John F., 57, 581
Peace Corps and, 550
and television, 714
Kennedy, Robert F., 31, 264,
378
key, golden, 194
Khrushchev Colic, 476
killing, 809
kindergarten, world as, 784
kindness, 417–418, 433, **824,**
921
foe and, 252
gathers love, 331
kill wife with, 933
post-mortem, 264
recompense unkindness with,
609
king, 337, **418,** 919
and ceremony, 867
and death, 881
eternal heaven's, 135
and falsehood, 893
and flattery, 898

of glory, 814
honor the, 811
mercy in heart of, 936
theater and conscience of,
974
and tyrant, 739
King James, 313
King Lear, 263
King, Martin Luther, 68, 307,
601
kingdom, 860
kingdom of God, 419, 613, **824**
and renunciation, 837
and rich man, 839
(*See also* **church, heaven**)
kiss, 419, 921–922
kitchen, 326, 779
kites, 256
Klondike, 253
kneeling, 130
knees, 819, 850
"know thyself," 659–660
knowledge, 44, 203, 376, 389,
419–423, 433, **824,** 845,
922
action and, 5

advancing in, 60
appetite for, in children, 188
of Bible, 81
Bible as mine of, 78
boys mature in, 950
collection of words, 781
common sense and, 147
education, use of self, 240
excess of, 268
fly to heaven by, 913
foundations of State in, 241
of God and own soul, 326
growth of man of, 514
information and, 396
inspiration from, 400
investment in, 243
least, 75
literature of, 448
Lord, God of, 801
memory, receptacle of, 479
of myself, 900
philosophy, knowledge of,
556
prudent man conceals, 835
reading, foundation of, 604

L

M

N

O

P

pink elephant, 27
pitcher, baseball, 69
pitchmen, 146
pity, 290, **557**, 703, **832**, **949**,
 971
 for conceited, 155
 degree of love, 949
 social equality and, 260
 suffering and, 698
 woman's love and, 451
place, 557–558
plagiarism, 558, **950**
plague, crime like, 181
plainness, 820
planet, salvation of, 547
platitudes, political, 32
Plato, 60, 78, 79, 80, 112, 134,
 234, 358, 500, 583
Platonic essences, 333
play:
 children's, 127
 gambling, form of, 317
playwright (*See* theater)
pleasing, 559
pleasure, 89, 412, 655, **832**, **950**
 of art, 52
 attendant upon sacrifice, 645
 babe, well-spring of, 66
 bashfulness excludes, 69
 begets no knowledge, 783
 cares, mother of 112
 creates no happiness, 353
 of deceiving deceiver, 196
 and decision, 883
 dessert of life, 782
 exercise of, 240
 fatigued by, 646
 flowers, 898
 friendship and, 89
 and gain, 903
 happiness and, 351
 and heaven, 818
 and humility, 913
 indolence and, 392
 and innocent youth, 791
 of knowing, 421
 life and, 443
 means of art, 8
 novelty, parent of, 521
 occupation and love of, 527
 pain and, 537
 and persecution, 832
 poetry and, 562
 in possessions, 570
 refusal of, 54
 of rest, 167
 study as, 693
 toil and, 425
 and true religion, 613
 and variety, 750
 virtue brings, 756
 woman, instrument of, 777
 of woman, 779
 of words, 780
 and work, 782

plebeian, 240
plebiscite, 159
plenty, 832
pliability, 268
ploughman, 265
pluck, 456
Plutarch, 252, 619
poet, 182, 419, **560**, **950**
 beginner, 61
 God, world's, 329
 inspiration and, 400
 mediocrity in, 477
 talks against business, 61
 and verses of another, 778
 writes for money, 61
poetry, 47, 119, 182, 443, **560–
 562**, **950**
 English, 106
 Grecian history, 361
 history presents, 363
 in human tears, 712
 of Lord Byron, 263
 mediocrity in, 477
 painting, silent, 538
 and punning, 596
 speaking picture, 538
 truisms in, 733
point of view, 562
poison, 43, 207
poker, 576
Poland, 562
pole-star, 160
police, 14, 292, **562**
 brutality, 562
 and ghetto, 323
 racism and, 562
 weapons for, 179
policy, 562–563
politeness, 563–564
 clarity, supreme, 787
politician, 26, 277, 338, **564**,
 613
 bribery and, 99
 freedom and, 308
 "No Comment" of, 334
politics, 179, 182, **564–567**, **950**
 age of virtuous, 544
 and ceremony, 115
 generosity, expediency and,
 319
 people and, 565
 and pulpit, 136
 revolution in, 631
 self-knowledge, 660
poltroonery, 699
Polyphemus, 219
pools, 634
poor, the, 36, 612, 644
 defend the, 823, 833
 expectation of, 833
 and flattery, 898
 and fortune, 901
 giving and 813
 luxury and, 458
 mercy on, 827

 oppression and, 830
 poverty, destruction of, 833
 rich depend on, 204
 suffer from riot, 640
 (*See also* **poverty, rich and
 poor**)
Poor Richard, 45
poorhouse, 571
pope, 160, 199, 239, 386, **567**
Pope, Alexander, 92
poplar, 602
populace, 567–568
popular support, 9
popularity, 568, **950**
 accident, 526
 of book, 95
 greatness and, 344
population, 138, 568–569
 power, 513
 versus productivity, 25
pornography, 569
portrait, 537
 ballads, vocal, 67
 (*See also* **painting**)
position, 569
positiveness, 569
possessions, 569–570, 696, **832–
 833**
possibility, 570
 extraordinary, in ordinary
 people, 201
 philosophy and, 277
post (*See* **letter**)
posterity, 570
 contemporaries and, 482
 politics and, 566
 and writing, 787
 youth, trustees of, 791
potter, 809
pounds, 238
poverty, 142, 237, 303, 307,
 833, **950–951**
 cause of, 111
 debt-habit, twin of, 196
 deprives of spirit and virtue,
 195
 drunkard and glutton, 809
 ends monarchies, 624
 friends and, 311
 hears not reason, 607
 labor rids of, 425
 mother of crime, 180
 power to abolish, 639
 praise of, 54
 and pride, 952
 whites escaped from, 384
power, 60, 163, **573–575**, 814,
 833, **951**
 ambition and, 28
 in America, gift of, 31
 American, 34, 87
 appetite for, 213
 and atheism, 59
 atomic, 522
 of Bible, 81

Q

R

S

of divine perfection in art, 52
and light, 167
love flies like, 927
reputation like, 625
Shakespeare, William, 92, 119,
  167, 179, 448, 599
Jews and, 410
plagiarism and, 558
shame, 665, 961
  comes with pride, 834
  not born to, 912
  prudent man covers, 835
  sense of, in young girl, 199
  you have known my, 809
sheep, 461, 845
sheriff, Southern Negro and, 601
ship, 961
shoe, 961
shopkeeper, 253
short story, 33
shower, 602
showmanship, 666
shrewdness, 366
shrine of German classicism,
  ghetto, 323
shroud, 314
shuttle, 819
Shylock, 410
shyness, 494
Siberia, 235
Sibyl, 302
sickness, 666, 961
  national concern, 510
sight, 2, 663
sign, 52, 961–962
  Jesus approved by, 849
  how great, his, 849
  (See also miracle)
silence, 28, 182, 197, 433, 666–
  667, 821, 960, 962
  checked for, 867
  clamor of, 184
  conversation with English-
    man, 254
  golden and divine, 686
  music and, 505
  and to speak ill, 781
  truth outraged by, 734
  vengeance, daughter of, 750
  well doing silences, 821
  and winter, 772
silk, 543
simile:
  in argument, 49
  in Scripture, 578
simplicity, 186, 668
  and belief, 178
  eloquence, vehement, 248
  give with, 814
  of heart, 366
  of manner, 469
  and passions persuade, 534
sin, 40, 252, 622, 644, 668–670,
  962
  alms, atonement for, 798

birth control, 85–86
blood of Christ cleanses, 800
blush, nature's alarm of, 89
bonds of, 2
captivity to law of, 828
charity covers, 803
confess freely of, 872
confession of, 157, 805
conscience and, 162
consequences of one, 159
of constancy, 164
and conversion, 806
to covet honor, 912
covetousness and, 176
deadly, of cynicism, 190
depression and hidden, 157
distraction from real, 160
drunkenness, 231
flattery blows up, 898
and forgiveness, 812
and grace, 816
infidelity, root of, 394
laws discover, 431
Lord forgives iniquity of, 805
love covers all, 817
lying and, 458
novels instruct to, 520
and oath, 945
original, 402
pain, outcome of, 537
of philosopher, 555
pride, beginning of, 834
racial pride, 601
reconciliation for, 836
and reflection, 955
remission of, 800
repentance of, 622, 623, 837
to be rich, 987
scarlet, but books read, 603
self, root of, 654
suicide, 699
and temptation, 716
too large or too small, 498
and treason, 979
and virtue, 984
want salvation from, 610
and will, 770
sincerity, 51, 514, 670, 842–843,
  962–963
  merit of originality, 534
  and truth, 739
singer, 963
singularity, 237, 670
sinner, 578
sister, 779
sit-in, 222
situation, 137
sixteenth century, 612
size, 670–671
skeleton in every house, 651
skepticism, 671
skill, 41, 65
  in art, 54
  in criticism, 181

technological, 30
  (See also ability)
skirt, 468
sky, 30, 56, 184, 265, 963
skylark, 265
skyscraper, 47
slander, 120, 671–672, 843, 963–
  964
slang, 672–673
slap, 419
slavery, 309, 673–674, 964
  to ambitious man, 29
  evil and, 265
  Germans, 323
  money, form of, 496
  no reasoning in, 607
Slavs, 132
sleep, 112, 164, 246, 674–675,
  928, 964–965
  children disturb, 128
  exercise, patience and, 213
  health and, 356
  life rounded with, 887
slight, 401
slogan, 675
  principle and, 585
  success, 661
sloth, 675, 843
  labor and, 424
slum, 465, 572, 675
  immigrants to city, 572
  produces crime, 562
smile, 372, 675–676, 965
  in America, 33
  charity, 122
  hell in woman's, 779
  kind heart and, 357
  and reproach, 623
  and yesterday, 790
smog (See air pollution)
smoking, 676
  dangers in marijuana, 230
  room, in university, 244
snake, 289, 676
sneer, 677
  face life with, 446
snob, 677
snow, 296
soap, 241
sobriety, 843
  employment gives, 250
sociability, 677
"social adjustment," 391
social questions, 565
social welfare (See socialism)
social worker, 679
socialism, 142, 677–678
  Cuban Revolution and, 185
  Marx and scientific, 473
Socialist, 149, 393
society, 7, 57, 263, 678–680,
  965–966
  in America, 32
  America, voluntary, 31

American, ruled by women, 776
Black Power and American, 87
built on trust, 158, 734
character and, 121
Christianity and, 134
conflict of truth and needs in, 735
conforming to, 263
creating universal, 466
custom in, 189
disbelief pernicious to, 741
education and, 240, 245
education in democratic, 241
elements of, 278
English, 636
and excellence in work, 782
external advantages in civilized, 229
family as, 282
family, center of perfect, 226
founded on law and order, 181
free, 306, 309
genius and, 321
gentleness, love in, 323
ghetto and white, 324
guerilla war against, 180
for individual freedom, 307
innovators and, 431
lack of self-confidence in, 114
law and order, 431
life of man, 681
majority of, 203
man perfected by, 462
against manhood, 164
ordering of, 32
perfection of, 134
the poor and, 123
poverty and affluent, 572
poverty and free, 573
privacy of individual in, 585
and punishment of crime, 179
religion and, 616, 617
religion, basis of, 614
to safeguard freedom, 465
to safeguard human dignity, 465
and solitude, 681, 682
Sunday and noblest, 644
tax and civilized, 709
technological, and women, 779
thought and change in, 722
and traditions, 163
and war, 765
of women and good manners, 777
women's role in, 778
sociologists, 570
sociology, 432, 516
Socrates, 194, 358, 440
Christ and, 80
ideas of, 376

soil's cultivation, 25
solace and women, 777
solar system, 370
soldier, 250, 286, 680–681, 966
adoring God and, 10
good breeding and brute, 330
solitude, 65, 681–682
effect of riches, 636
imagination needs, 382
love and, 455
stranger and, 138
Sunday and noblest, 644
Solomon, 178, 800
Solon, 527
solvency, 496
son:
and daughter, 191
father and, 286
Son shall make you free, 813
song, 682
in Bible, 80
creed expressed in, 484
wine, women and, 217
sophistry, 27, 459, 682
sorrow, 18, 42, 69, 84, 300, 682–683, 843, 856, 966–967
adjunct of repentance, 622
age and, 315
and blessing of Lord, 801
content and golden, 875
countenance more in, 892
with courage, 261
of death, 807
dies with time, 111
employment, antidote against, 250
of failing to reach love, 56
guilt, nerve of, 346
he carried our, 836
joy and, 412
joys hide in drops, 918
linked with gladness, 167
Lord gives rest from, 799
mirth and, 488
and patience, 948
relativity of, 613
repentance, 622, 837
and resentment, 625
shows truth, 698
sympathy and, 703
and tears, 712
and trust in God, 18
soul, 71, 654, 684, 838, 843–844, 928, 910, 914, 959, 967–968
absolution of, 2
and adultery, 798
in agony, 858
and angry man, 799
atheism, disease of, 59
and avarice, 862
bravery, quality of, 747
and breath of God, 826
clothes, 860
confession and, 157

corroding, 514
criticism and, 183
curiosity, thirst of, 187
and death, 880
depravity of, 205
desire, sweet to, 797
evil, like villain, 883
eye, pulse of, 272
and flattering, 898
flies through wounds, 935
force of, work, 783
gather not with sinners, 802
gold, poison to, 904
and good name, 869
grace in, 339
head, palace of, 355
hell of living, 159
holiness, symmetry of, 364
human, 51
incapable of sadness, 645
intuition of, 164–165
joyful in God, 837
of language, 3
liberal, shall be fat, 813
love, motion of, 176
and merciful man, 827
metaphysics, anatomy of, 483
narrow and forgiveness, 301
obedience and purifying your, 829
and patience, 948
in patience possess your, 831
of a people, 186
praying exercises, 213
pulses of, 206
and quiet, 954
religion, science of, 616
rest for your, 827
science and immortal, 385
second nature in, 612
sensuality, grave of, 663
sighs after God, 326
subject's, 872
and tears, 712
and thinking, 722
thirsts for future life, 316
and tragedy, 728
uplifting the, 51
virtue, sign of, 754
washing the, 504
watchful, 952
without watchfulness, 766
why cast down, 819
will of, 770
wings of, 622
and wisdom, 773
woman, a lost, 779
and worm of conscience, 872
worry about, 785
and writer, 788
for writing, 61
youth of, 792
soul and body, 684
sound, 684
echo, shadow of, 237

T

U

V

W

611, 663, 772–774, 841, 849, 989
advice and, 16
affectation of, 388
age and, 20
and amity, 903
with the ancient, 798
cheerfulness and, 124
child's mistakes and, 125
conceit impairs, 155
consumed in confidence, 872
and contention, 806
cunning and, 187
cunning, dwarf of, 695
delay gives, 199
determination, truest, 253
economic, 237
fear of Lord as, 810
folly and, 387
fool to, 900
of God, 159
God's joy and, 823
good guess, 345
gravity, bark of, 341
growth of, 579
guides valor, 876
Heaven's eternal, 205
irony, joy of, 406
justice without, 415
keeping secret, 652
and law of God, 824
learned from failure, 492
from leisure, 611
liberty and, 437
loving heart, 356
with the lowly, 834
measured by sorrows, 683
meditation of life, 195
memory, not, 480
moderation and, 493
nature and, 512
nurtured by solitude, 165
in old age, 24
in our eyes, 841
philosopher and, 555
in piety, 557
portable, 44
proverbial, 591
repose of minds, 623
teaching in all, 832
terrified by fanaticism, 283
and the unfaithful, 822
virtue governs with, 344
war, failure of, 763
wise, the, 666
fool and, 386
hope animates, 367
instructed by reason, 607
make opportunities, 531
wise man, 4, 48, 165, 186, 188, 190, 209, 318
judges actions, 156
reads books and life, 93
takes counsel, 173
wish, 774–775

wishbone, 696
wit, 186, 250, 372, 410, **775,** 989
in conversation, 170
dinner and, 215
insanity destroys not, 399
memory, friend of, 479
much grief shows want of, 907
old age and, 858
reason chastely expressed, 606
repartee, highest order of, 621
resolved will and, 870
time and, 977
touchstone of, 621
troublesome fools with, 297
and virtue, 755
witch, 22, 776
witchcraft, 821
witness, 819
conscience as, 161
false, 811
of heaven, 180
against self, 662
unrighteous, 797
wits, 49
woes, 206
wolf, 128, 461, 267
woman, 20, 45, 665, 712, **775–779,** 843, 844, 849, **990–991**
adultery with, 798
bachelors know more about, 66
beauty of, 71
behavior of, 74
born to fears, 896
career of, 20
with child, 844
counsel of virtuous, 15
duty to husband, 887
education of, 244
English and French, 494
familiarity with, 282
frailty, name of, 901
gallantry to, 317
hair, ornament of, 349
honor of, 366
insignificant conversation of, 706
keenest sense in, 188
keeping secrets, 652
knowledge and, 420
losing faith in, 279
love of, 452
love of God better than, 826
makes home, 364
man and, 480
manners and, 468
and marriage, 933
money and, 68
old, 22
revenge, sweet to, 630

rose, 929
Russian, and living, 779–780
sensibility, power of, 663
smiles of, 675
songs, wine and, 217
superior to man, 665
tact of, 705
talking with, 706
as teacher, 709
tears of, 712
and useless speech, 686
vanity and, 748
voice of, 758, 984
vows of, 759
wit of, 989
woman and work, 779–780
womanhood, 627
wonder, 10, 419, 780, 847, **849**
belief and, 847
worship as, 786
Wonderful, 849
wooing, 991–992
wool, 812
word, 99, 114, 169, **780–781,** 992–993
without action, 378
actions more eloquent than, 5
and affliction, 798
bruise child, 127
in charity and meekness, 477–478
charm agony with, 916
of Christ, 81
commonplace, 169
deeds and, 198
enjoyment and, 255
example in, 810
faith in divine, 277
fewest, and wisdom, 774
of God, 77–82
heaven has my empty, 951
idea and, 376
lamp unto my feet, 801
of Lord endures, 801
orator and, 534
represents us, 5
result of thought, 720
spoken and written, 594
suit action to, 856
superior man, slow in, 235, 493
woman, slow in, 991
Wordsworth, William, 119
work, 19, 45, 781–784, 849, 993
ability of youth, 1
beginning, half the, 73
efficient, 246
envy, strife, and evil, 809
faith without, 277
of God, 52, 81
life as, 443
manual, 424
principle and, 209
reason and, 209
and waiting, 760

Y

Z